EVALUATION STUDIES REVIEW ANNUAL
Volume 4

Evaluation Studies

EDITORIAL ADVISORY BOARD

Review Annual

Evaluation Studies
Review Annual
Volume 4   1979

Edited by

Lee Sechrest
Stephen G. West
Melinda A. Phillips
Robin Redner
William Yeaton

SAGE PUBLICATIONS / BEVERLY HILLS / LONDON

DEDICATION

*To Susan F. Elliott, without whom all this would scarcely have been possible—
our thanks, admiration, and deep affection.*

For information address:

SAGE PUBLICATIONS, INC.
275 South Beverly Drive
Beverly Hills, California 90212

SAGE PUBLICATIONS LTD
28 Banner Street
London EC1Y 8QE, England

BT 4764-80   1/18/80

Printed in the United States of America

International Standard Book Number 0-8039-1329-X

International Standard Series Number 0364-7390

Library of Congress Catalog Card No. 76-15865

FIRST PRINTING

CONTENTS

PART IV: EVALUATION STUDIES

About the Editors

Lee Sechrest is Professor of Psychology at Florida State University, where he teaches courses in research methodology and program evaluation. Previously he was at Northwestern University, where he was involved in the development of their training program in evaluation research. He has written nearly 100 articles and is co-author of six books, the best known of which is *Unobtrusive Measures.* He is on the editorial boards of a number of journals, including *Journal of Community Health, Journal of Abnormal Psychology*, and *Health Policy Quarterly.* He is Chairman of the Panel of Editors for the *Journal Supplements Abstract Service.* Sechrest is a consultant to a number of government and private agencies involved in development and evaluation of social interactions.

Stephen G. West is Associate Professor of Psychology at Florida State University, where he teaches courses in social psychology, personality, and psychology and health behavior. He has taught at Duke University, the University of Texas at Austin, and the University of Wisconsin at Madison. He has published more than 20 articles in various journals and is coauthor of *A Primer of Social Psychological Theories* (forthcoming). He is an associate editor for the *Journal of Personality,* and a consulting editor of the *Journal of Personality and Social Psychology.* He has done evaluation research in the areas of health and energy.

Melinda A. Phillips is a doctoral student in clinical psychology at Florida State University. She received her B.A. in psychology from Indiana University (Indiana) and her M.S. in clinical psychology from Florida State University. She has done evaluation research in the area of community mental health. At present her research interests are in the areas of health behavior and program evaluation. She has published in the *Journal of Experimental Psychology: General,* and in the monograph series *New Directions in Research Methodology.* She has given two papers on program evaluation in community mental health.

Robin Redner is a doctoral candidate in social psychology at Florida State University. She received her B.A. from Northwestern University in psychology, and her M.S. in social psychology from Florida State University. She is currently working as a research assistant for the National Academy of Sciences Panel on Research on Rehabilitation of Criminal Offenders, and is interested in evaluation of rehabilitation programs. Her other recent interests include esthetic perception of the natural environment and behavior change strategies in relation to the environment. Her publications include a paper with Lee Sechrest on "Strength and Integrity of Treatments in Evaluation Studies."

William Yeaton has recently completed his Ph.D. in school psychology at Florida State University. His research interests include behavioral community psychology, empirical validation of procedures for diffusion of effective treatment, estimation of magnitudes of experimental effects, comparison of visual and statistical analyses of data, and program evaluation. He received his B.A. from the University of New Hampshire.

Preface

The editors of any volume confront difficult decisions, but that difficulty is magnified enormously when the field under review is as diverse and ill-defined as evaluation research. The task is further complicated by the exponential expansion of the field in a multitude of directions, many of which can be only dimly perceived at present. Consequently, for Volume 4 of the *Evaluation Studies Review Annual*, we made an important initial decision: The volume would concern methodological and technological issues rather than contributions representing evaluations of different types of programs. This led to the simple decision rule that articles should be included when there is an important lesson to be learned from them. That rule led to the inclusion of some articles that do not deal with evaluation in the purest sense, but which are nonetheless instructive or illustrative of the field. While we have tried in the selection of papers to represent the entire breadth touched by the evaluation enterprise, this breadth now virtually defies representation in a single volume.

The application of this rule led to a curious paradox in considering the essays which were instructive, yet otherwise seriously flawed. While contemplating our own and other's mistakes is one of the best methods of understanding a problem, those lessons are sometimes lost without strong criticism and commentary. Since at least some of the inadequate articles we encountered were not far from characteristic of their areas, we did not wish to single out individual authors for such public criticism. On the other hand, we also encountered some excellent reports on successful, but uneventful program evaluations. These evaluations, while exemplary in many respects, were unfortunately not particularly instructive for other evaluators, and hence were not included in the volume.

Evaluation research appears to be maturing; evidence of that is the number of thoughtful and insightful studies now appearing on the philosophy and strategies of program evaluation. Some of the early enthusiasm is now being tempered, but many of the critical assumptions underlying evaluation are being formalized, and the concepts involved are being sharpened. Those occurrences cannot but help the field in the long run. Any limitations implied by the newer, developing perspectives will be more than compensated by the improved prospects for definitive and useful answers to the critical questions facing not only researchers, but those who must make the difficult decisions about implementing their recommendations.

Our aims as editors of the *Annual* were to produce a volume that would interest a wide audience, and that would be both informative and pleasurable to read. We did exclude some papers, reluctantly, on grounds that they were perhaps overly technical to be of interest and value to a diverse audience. And we tended to be a bit biased toward papers less likely otherwise to come to the attention of the evaluation community; the tradeoff was between mainstream papers that most everyone would know about anyway, and papers less obviously relevant, but less likely to be known. We have some of both.

There is a limit, imposed by costs, on the number of papers included in the *Annual*. We had more good papers than we could include in every category of interest, and we could not include as much of the good unpublished material as we wished. We trust all those unpublished papers we had to exclude will soon be published elsewhere. We do want to call attention to the papers that are being printed for the first time in this volume (Chapters 1, 9, 10, 27, 32, 34, 35, and 41).

We want finally to acknowledge the excellent help we received from a number of the contributing editors to the *Annual*, all of whose names appear in the front matter. We also want to acknowledge the typing and general secretarial assistance of Susan Slatham and the tireless efforts of Sharon Campbell, who ran so many library errands and did much xeroxing.

We have acknowledged one other special person by dedicating this volume to her.

Lee Sechrest
Tallahassee, Fla.
April 1979

Introduction

Lee Sechrest, Stephen G. West, Melinda A. Phillips,
Robin Redner, William Yeaton

SOME NEGLECTED PROBLEMS IN
EVALUATION RESEARCH:
STRENGTH AND INTEGRITY OF TREATMENTS

Since the inception of evaluation as a field, its researchers have strongly emphasized methodology. This emphasis, most clearly articulated by Campbell and his associates (Campbell and Stanley, 1966; Cook and Campbell, 1975, 1979), has concerned the problems of designing investigations. Campbell and his associates have carefully analyzed a wide variety of research designs, and have clearly identified the major threats to validity posed by each. These analyses provide an understanding of problems that may arise in designing research, and have greatly enhanced the ability of researchers to rule out plausible alternative hypotheses through the use of appropriate designs. Thus, researchers are now less likely to reject the null hypothesis as a result of a design artifact. Instead, researchers are becoming more conservative: they are more willing tentatively to accept a conclusion that the treatment had no effect until the major threats to the internal and external validity of the investigation could be conclusively ruled out.

These design considerations are slowly leading to improvements of basic research, in which treatments are often highly standardized and in which there is an emphasis on refining the technique and procedure until the predicted effect can in fact be demonstrated. However, the improved knowledge of design and the possible threats to the validity of the research may have more complex effects in evaluation research, owing to some peculiar facts that are associated with the context of evaluation research. First, treatments as they are delivered in real settings are rarely standardized as they are in the best laboratory experiments. Real treatments are often complex, are sometimes delivered by poorly trained or unmotivated people, and can be totally disrupted by events in the real world. Thus, in many cases, the failure of the actual treatment to produce any significant effect may tell us nothing about the potential effect had the treatment been correctly implemented. The writings of Campbell and his associates have generally assumed that the treatment was intact and highly standardized, an assumption that may often be untenable in evaluation research.

A second problem in conducting evaluation research is that treatment programs take place within a political context. Unlike the basic researcher who can continue to refine his treatment until the predicted effect can be reliably achieved, the failure of a treatment program to produce immediate positive results in the real world will often lead to strong monetary and political pressure for termination of the program. In some cases, programs of considerable potential merit that are poorly implemented on their first attempt will be killed because of their failure to produce a significant measurable effect on the participants (e.g., see Patton in this volume). Unlike basic research, one failure to demonstrate the effect of a treatment program may have considerable potential impact, to the detriment of the recipients of a potentially successful, but inadequately tested program.

These concerns lead to a new interest in the role of the treatment in evaluation research. Consequently, this introduction will examine two critical issues in the evaluation of treatments. The first is the planned strength of treatment—the intensity with which the researcher intends that the treatment be delivered. The second is the integrity of treatment, which refers to the fidelity with which the treatment is actually delivered. As will be seen, these issues have important implications for the construct validity of evaluation research. It is our opinion that internal validity may have received disproportionate attention in evaluation research, to the detriment of the more basic construct validity of the treatments. We will contend that it is important to test programs first in their strongest form to assess the potential impact of the treatment, and then later to establish the minimal treatment in terms of cost, training of treatment personnel, and so forth, that will be effective in producing the desired outcome. Related to this issue, some guidelines and methods will be offered to assess the strength and the integrity of the treatments.

The reader may notice that two basic but related themes run throughout this introduction. The first is complexity. We have attempted herein to recognize that actual treatments as delivered in naturalistic settings are multifaceted and that these treatments may have effects on many different kinds of outcome measures. This theme is not surprising; the world is not simple. The second theme, in contrast, may be surprising to some readers. In contrast to the primarily methodological emphasis of most previous writings on evaluation research, we will insist that theories also have a critically important role in evaluation research. Along with careful design, careful conceptual analysis is an important foundation of good evaluation research. To cite but a few instances, only when the conceptual basis of a treatment is considered, can its strength and integrity be evaluated. Only when the factors that may mediate treatment effects are considered, can the likely effects and side effects of treatment be identified and traced through a network of outcome variables. Only when investigators consider the specific threats to the validity of their design (see, for example, the Mazur-Hart and Berman article in this volume), can they rule out some of these threats and reach a plausible, limited interpretation of their results. It is critical that evaluators be able to specify the theoretical links between the intervention planned and the outcome expected. And only when investigators carefully conceptualize their treatment and its effects can they have insight into the reasons for either the success or the failure of a treatment program. It is our belief that the integration of theory, conceptual analysis, and methodology provide the strongest possible foundation for evaluation research.

Finally, the reader should be forewarned that our examples will not be drawn equally from all of the content areas within evaluation research. Although we do believe that the general principles that we will propose are applicable to any area, we also believe that they can best be exemplified by illustration with clear studies from our special areas of expertise. For this reason, many of our examples will be gleaned from medicine and criminal justice, although we have attempted to include some examples from most areas of current interest.

With these explanations and caveats behind us, let us now consider our primary topic: the strength and integrity of treatments as problems in construct validity.

THE STRENGTH AND INTEGRITY OF TREATMENTS AS PROBLEMS IN CONSTRUCT VALIDITY

Construct Validity

The essence of construct validity (Cook and Campbell, 1975) is that one has a good understanding of the true or conceptual meaning of the treatment; it refers to our interpretation of treatments, not to the treatments themselves. For example, imagine comparing the effects of two types of therapy. Suppose it turned out that one of the therapies had been developed only recently, and hence its practitioners were youthful and inexperienced as opposed to the practitioners of the other, more established therapy. In this case, the truly effective part of the treatment might well be the experience of the therapists. As a result, type of therapy would not have construct validity as an explanation of any improvements observed in the clients of the two groups of therapists. Although Cook and Campbell (1975) have described four types of validity involved in experiments, more attention has been paid to internal validity. We believe that in program evaluation, construct validity should be equally often a concern—a belief generally overlooked. In fact, to a very substantial degree it has been ignored as a problem.

More generally, problems in construct validity lead to misinterpretation of the results by the original experimenter or subsequent investigators because the experimental treatment is assumed to be something it is not. Some of the major reasons a treatment may be minsunderstood include: (1) confounding of the intended independent variable with an associated variable, as in our therapy example above; (2) nonspecific treatment effects such as expectancy or placebo effects, which may be mistaken for experimental treatment effects; (3) inadequate description of the experimental or comparison treatment, which may determine whether the nature of the treatment is well understood; (4) inadequate theoretical formulation of the treatment, which may determine whether generalizations of the treatment are well founded and (5) inadequacy of the planned strength of treatment and the integrity with which it is delivered. The result of each of these problems is that the explanation or label attached to the treatment will be incorrect and, hence, conclusions based on the study will be in error. We will consider the final problem in some detail, since its importance has often been overlooked in evaluation research.

Strength of Treatment

Perhaps the area of evaluation research that has shown the greatest concern for issues of strength of its treatments is medicine. Based on their knowledge of the actions of a drug, a specific type of surgery, or a physical rehabilitation program, physicians will ordinarily plan to the best of their capability to deliver the "right" amount of treatment over the appropriate amount of time (see the Canadian Cooperative Study in this volume). Too high or too low a dosage of the drug, too short or too long a period over which it is given, or too frequent or infrequent delivery of the drug may all lead to a treatment program of less than optimal strength. This concern for the strength of the treatment may be extended to treatment programs in other areas. For example, the strength of a counseling intervention might be reflected in such variables as the number and length of sessions, their frequency, and the period over which they are given. The strength of an income maintenance program might be expressed by the amount of support offered, the length of time over which it is extended, and the formula for reduction of support as outside wages increase. In medicine, it is supposed that weak treatments lead to weak or nonexistent results and that they are to be avoided. Yet the same assumption is rarely even considered in designing treatment programs in other areas.

But medical researchers take this concern one step further. Treatment plans in medicine normally adjust the strength of treatment, based on the nature and the seriousness of the problem and the characteristics of the patient. A longer course of antibiotics will be prescribed for serious conditions than for less serious ones, and the dosage levels will be adjusted for such factors as drug sensitivities and body weight. Medical researchers typically attempt to keep treatments at an optimal level for each patient rather than simply planning the strongest treatment possible for the patient group. In medicine, treatments stronger than necessary are not only needlessly expensive but often dangerous.

We recognize that medical researchers are blessed with an unusually high degree of uniformity of response by patients to their treatments relative to treatment programs in other areas. A large portion of this uniformity is attributable to the substantial homogeneity of the patients in terms of anatomy and physiological processes. This is not to say that all patients with the same problem respond in the same way to a given treatment; but out of 100 patients with a typical medical problem, most will respond the same way to any treatment chosen. However, we would insist that the uniformity of patients' responses is not entirely an undeserved blessing, but rather derives in large part from the insistence of medical researchers on specifying the strength of their treatments. Considerable empirical work has been conducted on quantifying treatment strength to provide a basis for determining an optimal or strong treatment. If a physician wants to give a strong dose of tetracycline to a patient, he or she has a good idea of what would be considered a strong dose for a given patient and what the likely response should be. Moreover, such specific knowledge of the strength of treatment and of its expected effects allows the physician to detect unusual variations in response. This, in turn, often permits the physician to adjust the treatment to make things right through such techniques as lengthening the course of treatment or changing the dosage of the drug. Thus, knowledge of the strength of treatment tends both to reduce response variability and to enhance the practitioner's ability to detect unusual responses and to adjust the treatment appropriately.

Unlike medicine, other areas of evaluation research have shown little interest in strength of treatment. For example, what is a "strong" dosage of group counseling for a first conviction felon charged with robbery? What is the best level of financial support for a released ex-burglar that will make it possible for him to avoid going back to crime and still make it worthwhile to try to find a job? To be fair to criminal justice researchers, uniformity of response of criminal offenders to treatments is probably less likely than in the medical area. But only part of this problem arises from the complex determinants of criminal behavior—the remainder arises from the failure of many researchers to attempt to standardize their treatments, let alone to estimate their strength. Interventions that are grouped under the same label (e.g., group counseling) even within the same study may differ so radically that it is nearly impossible to detect any effects.

Obviously not all evaluation research has ignored issues of strength of treatment. The planners of the New Jersey Negative Income Tax Experiment devoted considerable thought to the particular values of the income guarantee and the marginal tax rates that were to be studied (Rossi and Lyall, 1976). Probably everyone associated with the project realized that the most favorable treatments to be tested were far from maximum strength for the hypotheses to be tested, but the investigators believed that the variations tested should lie within a "policy space" representing the combinations that might be politically acceptable. Within that policy space, however, one of the tested variations was thought to be close to the maximum intervention that would be acceptable.

There is no body of empirical research that investigators could use to classify strength of treatment, and that practitioners could use to plan rehabilitation. Although the above examples are taken from criminal justice and welfare, researchers in most other areas can hardly feel sanguine about the understanding of treatment strength in their own field. Ways of assessing strengths of treatments, both before and after they are delivered, are sorely needed in evaluation research.

Strength of treatment is an issue in construct validity because it is so easy when evaluating the results of a treatment to assume that something has happened that has not. If a decision about the effectiveness of a drug were made without knowing whether it was delivered in a strong enough dose, the scientific medical community would raise vociferous objections. A case in point is the UGPD clinical trial of an oral hypoglycemic in the treatment of diabetes (Klimt et al., 1970; see also Knatterud et al. in this volume). When the study directors concluded that the oral agents were ineffective and probably even dangerous, there was an immediate objection that every patient had been given the same dose (Seltzer, 1972), a seemingly reasonable scientific procedure, but one potentially objectionable on clinical grounds since dosages ordinarily would be adjusted according to patient characteristics. Yet when it has been concluded that some form of treatment does not work for the rehabilitation of criminal offenders, or that an educational program has not led to appreciable gains in pupil skills, few objections have been raised that the treatment may not have been strong enough. Any conclusions about whether a treatment is effective can be reached only in full knowledge of how strong the treatment was.

Integrity of Treatment

We make a conceptual distinction between the strength and integrity of treatment although after the fact they often amount to the same thing. Returning once again to the medical area of drug treatment, we may think of the strength of the treatment as it is planned and prescribed. Thus, eight tablets per day of tetracycline for six days is a strong treatment for urinary tract infection in the case of an adult. Half that dosage would be considered weak on a priori grounds. Integrity of treatment refers to the fidelity with which the treatment plan is carried out. Thus, unwitting substitution of a drug of lower strength, use of an adulterated or impure drug, or failure of the patient to take all the medication would all threaten the integrity of what would otherwise have been a good treatment plan. Similarly, there might be some reason to suppose that for a certain subset of prisoners, two individual counseling sessions per week for one year would be a fairly strong treatment. However, if the therapists available were untrained or did not believe in the treatment, if the sessions were never held, or if during the course of treatment the mode of therapy were switched, the integrity of what might have been a good plan would have been destroyed.

Strength of treatment is planned and may be assessed at any time; integrity can be fully assessed only after the treatment has been completed. Integrity of a treatment usually requires both a specific set of mechanisms to accomplish the task, and a provision for continuous monitoring. To maximize the integrity of treatment, the treatment must be well defined so that specific standards of judgment can be applied. Further, at any sign of deviation from those standards, there must be specific provision for a corrective action. When treatment is completed, it should be possible to estimate the degree to which the planned intervention was carried out. Results obtained in a test of the intervention must then be interpreted in light of the achieved integrity of treatment.

Assuring integrity of treatment is by no means simple, although the problems involved in doing so may be greater for some interventions and some circumstances than others.

A good illustration of some measures that may be taken to assure integrity of treatment is provided by the Kansas City Preventive Patrol Experiment (Kelling et al., 1974). One condition of the experiment required the officers to respond to calls for service within their beats but otherwise to stay out of them (reactive patrol). Instead they were to patrol in adjacent beats, thus producing a more intensive patrol in those beats. Obviously the integrity of the treatments would have been reduced to the extent that officers did in fact patrol within what were to be reactive beats, for not only would they be introducing preventive patrol into those beats but they would be reducing intensity of patrol in others. Concern for integrity was high because of obvious biases of the police toward preventive patrol. Since the study relied heavily on observers actually riding in patrol cars, it was possible to have reasonably good information concerning the officers' compliance to their prescribed assignments. The data did reveal that there were some restrictions violated on patrolling reactive beats, but the investigators concluded that, on balance, integrity of treatment was maintained at a high level. Readers interested in pursuing the issue of treatment integrity might wish to see the critique of the Kansas City experiment by Larson (1976).

A much more subtle but still instructive example is provided by another police patrol experiment. A study comparing one versus two officer staffing of patrol cars was carried out in San Diego (Boydstun et al., 1978). One would think that integrity of treatment would be straightforward and virtually assured. The study guidelines dictated assignments of officers to either one or two officer units, and limitations on manpower and cars would assure compliance. But at another level, questions about the treatment might be raised because the study clearly had as one of its premises that there would be no differences between types of units in assignment of calls, e.g., no tendency to assign more dangerous calls to two officer units. Although a difference in assignments could be regarded as an outcome within the San Diego study, that difference would jeopardize treatment integrity for purposes of generalizing findings to other cities. Although the data showed some biases in assignment of calls by dispatchers, the actual differences were minor, and were judged inconsequential for interpretation of the findings.

In contrast, the Alum Rock Educational Voucher Demonstration (see Wortman et al. in this volume) provides a good example of a treatment seriously compromised by issues of integrity. The initial concept of an educational voucher system involved the notion that all the schools in a locality or system would develop and market their own innovative programs, that parents would shop for the best schools for their children, that their choice of schools would be unconstrained by finances (since the tuition would be paid by voucher), and that schools would prosper or go under depending on their ability to provide attractive programs at a reasonable cost. However, as Wortman and St. Pierre (1977) noted, the defining features of a voucher system were compromised from the very first. Not all schools in the Alum Rock system were willing to participate, parents were not well informed about the program, most parents chose to send their children to the school nearest their home, financial support for individual schools was never decentralized and only a little of the voucher money was actually available for program innovations, and, for reasons of assuring job security, teachers were assured continuing support even if they were in schools with income deficits. There was in fact no voucher system to be tested. But once unleashed, the forces of change are inexorable, and at Alum Rock the evaluation went on, even if the program did not.

SOME GUIDELINES FOR ASSESSING THE STRENGTH AND INTEGRITY OF TREATMENTS

Given that issues of strength and integrity of treatment may be impeding progress in evaluation research, is there any way that the conscientious researcher may assess the strength and integrity of treatments?

The traditional approach to this problem evaluated the strength of treatment only by its outcome. If the effects were large, then the treatment was by definition a strong one; if the effects were small or nonexistent, the treatment was considered to be weak. However, weak outcomes may occur for any of three reasons: (1) some treatments are inherently weak and will do little for any condition (e.g., a single aspirin tablet); (2) some treatments are potentially strong, but are inappropriate for the specific condition (e.g., antibiotics used in treatment of viral diseases); and (3) some treatments are potentially strong but are given in only a weak form (e.g., a small dose of penicillin to treat an infection). This final case may result either from an initial plan that incorporated a weak form of the treatment, or from a plan that began with a strong form that went awry. To avoid the error of abandoning a potentially strong treatment that has not been adequately tested, it is necessary to make some a priori determination of treatment strength so that one can discriminate between poor outcomes attributable to the three reasons given above—reason 1 recommends abandoning the treatment, while reasons 2 and 3 recommend further exploration. Is it possible to make an a priori determination of the strength of a treatment? And if so, how? Although there are no simple answers, we offer some suggestions that we hope will guide evaluation researchers in their thinking.

A Priori Assessment of Strength of Treatment

Theoretical premises. These writers would suggest that evaluating strength of treatments begins by assessing the treatment's theoretical premises. Unfortunately, based on our review of the evaluation literature, the treatment able to specify a clear rationale and a mechanism of operation is certainly an endangered, if not extinct, species. Most theorizing, if it is present at all, is implicit, while in many cases it seems as if theory is lacking altogether, with interventions being tried for no better reason than they seemed like good ideas at the time.

To illustrate this point, consider the well-known study by Kassebaum et al. (1971) on counseling criminal offenders (see also the discussion of this study by Quay in this volume). On what a priori theoretical basis could these researchers have expected that an hour or two a week of counseling by poorly trained correctional officers would have any detectable effect on the response of the offenders to parole over a period of three years? The report gives us few clues since the closest thing to a theoretical hypothesis in the Kassebaum et al. study is a statement that counseling should weaken the commitment of prisoners to the criminal value system. How was this to be achieved? No specific link was proposed between the counseling and the weakening of that commitment and subsequent adjustment upon parole. The remaining hypotheses were empirically derived expectations about effects of counseling that specified no mechanisms to produce the effects.

Thus, as a first step in evaluating the strength of treatment, one can determine whether the treatment is well grounded in a theory that provides links between the type of intervention which is proposed, the specific type of population to which it is to be applied, and the outcomes that are anticipated. Those interventions not based on a careful conceptual analysis, or based on vague, general notions such as doing what seems beneficial for some disadvantaged group will eventually have some good effects (e.g., providing dental treatment for delinquents), should normally be viewed as weak treatments at best. Strong treatments are likely to have a clear and acceptable theoretical rationale that specifies not only a plan for treatment, but the mechanisms or processes that are expected to produce the desired change.

Expert Judgments

A second approach might be to have the treatment plan examined by experts who would then rate the treatment on the likelihood of its producing important changes, or who would estimate the amount of change likely from implementing the treatment. For example, experts in early childhood educational interventions might read a description of a program such as that reported by McKay et al. (1978) and either estimate the amount of change that might be expected from the intervention or make a direct judgment about the strength of the treatment. In their study of an early childhood compensatory educational intervention, some children received as much as three years (4000 hours) of preschool training, surely about as much as could ever be expected, and much more than in most studies (e.g., Headstart).

One possibility for obtaining useful judgments might be magnitude estimation, with the high end of the scale being defined as the strongest possible treatment imaginable, given our present state of knowledge. We are not experts, but we would judge the treatment in the McKay et al. study to have been rather strong, and in the case of the children who received three years of treatment probably very strong. It would not be easy to specify what else might have been done. As another example, an intervention designed to reduce a child's anxiety about hospitalization could be assessed by those experienced in caring for hospitalized children and perhaps by experts in child psychology. If, in general, all agreed that the treatment were a strong one, a test of it would be reasonable. If, on the other hand, experts judged the treatment to be weak, the wisdom of mounting a full-scale test would be questionable. In studies of varying levels of parole supervision, one might even have offenders estimate the consequences for their behavior of the different levels of supervision. If the strength of an intervention is to be estimated by an expert, it is important that the intervention be described as specifically as possible.

Two of the authors, Sechrest and Yeaton, have conducted a preliminary investigation of this idea. Twelve experts on the design of interventions to control cigarette smoking estimated the percentage of treated subjects who would cease smoking in response to fifty different experimental interventions reported in the literature. The average correlation between the judges' estimates and the actual percentage of those who ceased smoking was .47. Some of the judges achieved correlations up into the .70s. We believe that carefully selected judges could make good estimates of the strengths of various treatments in a variety of areas by the change likely to be produced. Even if such estimates were not totally accurate, they would almost certainly be better than no estimates at all, which is the current state of affairs.

Norms

A third approach to a priori assessment of strength of treatment would be to develop normative data representing the standard treatment. This is a common practice in medicine where treatment norms are routinely established for drug dosages and other medical treatments. This practice could easily be extended to other areas. For example, if it were known that the typical counseling program in prisons involved one hour per week for sixteen weeks, that the typical counselor had a college degree and one course in counseling, and that the typical counselee was a volunteer in the last six months of his sentence, any proposed counseling program to be tested could be compared with that standard. A program which offered only eight sessions would appear a priori to be weak and probably not worth testing unless a special case for it could be made. Similarly, norms could be established for Headstart programs, or for such aspects of parole as case load size, frequency of encounters, level of training, and any other variable that a careful analysis suggested would be important.

Parametric Study of Treatment Strength

A fourth method would establish a set of parameters for comparison, along with guidelines for assessing treatments with respect to these parameters. Experts might be used to establish weightings of the parameters so that they could be combined into a smaller set of indices or even into a single index of treatment strength. Although development of such an index may seem at first glance a nearly impossible task, recent advances in modeling judgment, through such techniques as policy capturing (Slovic et al., 1977; Slovic and Lichtenstein, 1971), and information integration (Anderson, 1974) suggest a solution. Specifically, experts could make judgments concerning the likely effectiveness of a series of descriptions of different treatment programs representing the full range of each of the parameters under consideration. Based on these judgments, algebraic models could then be developed that specified the weight of each parameter and the manner they were combined to form an overall judgment. To the extent that the expert's judgment models reflect the actual weighting and method of combination of the parameters, these models can assist in providing accurate estimates of the strength of treatment programs.

Alternatively, standardized reporting of the values of a set of treatment parameters would set the stage for a strength of treatment meta-analysis (cf. Cooper, 1979; Glass, 1976). The values of these parameters for the treatments in each study in a well-researched area could be entered into a regression equation and used to predict the magnitude of the outcome. This technique has the potential of providing data-based estimates of the weight that should be given to each parameter (and their interactions) in estimating the strength of treatment. While this is the preferred technique of developing a parametric estimation of treatment strength, it has the disadvantage of requiring a degree of standardization and conscientiousness that is not often found in researchers. Still, some areas such as medicine have made preliminary steps toward collecting data that would permit such an analysis.

Suggested Parameters for Study

Thus far we have proceeded as if the specific parameters of treatments were known, but this is unfortunately not true. Listing possible parameters for consideration in any area is not difficult, but any list would be arbitrary and would need to be revised in light of a careful conceptual analysis and the opinions of experts in the field. Despite the arbitrariness of any list, the following appear to the writers to be some of the aspects of human services treatments that are worth considering.

(1) *Qualifications of staff* The investigators could assess the extent to which the staff met the qualifications that are established by their field. In those cases where clear standards do not exist, experts could, for example, rate the staff on a five-point scale ranging from "not at all qualified" to "highly qualified."

(2) *Intensity of contact* This parameter refers to the amount of treatment per unit time, per week, for example, with vocational, educational, or counseling programs. Again, at present it might be impossible to do much more than rate some treatments on a simple scale ranging from low to high intensity treatment. The degree of probable involvement of staff and clients in the treatment process should also be assessed.

(3) *Length* The span over which treatment is carried out is another important parameter; its standards would obviously differ from one treatment to another. Ordinarily, treatments extended over time would be considered stronger than briefer treatments, but there could be a point of maximum benefit.

(4) *Focus of treatment* Generally speaking, a treatment would be considered stronger if it treats one or a few problems or outcomes, than if it is diffuse. For example, twenty-four counseling sessions devoted to problems of alcoholics may be stronger than twenty-four counseling sessions devoted to a wide variety of problems. Six months of training on a milling machine may be a stronger treatment than six months of general machine shop work.

(5) *Clarity of treatment plan* A treatment that had a well developed protocol to back it up would be considered stronger than one lacking such a protocol.

(6) *Differential assignment* A treatment plan that assessed the suitability of different candidates and which assigned them according to suitability would be considered a stronger treatment.

Again, there is no good basis for rigorous quantification of strength of treatment on the parameters listed, but even to begin would be a notable step. Empirical work might help to delineate the specific features of each parameter and the most useful ways of scaling them. Further work, as noted above, could produce weights or rankings of the parameters according to their importance for different types of treatment. Qualifications of staff might be of limited importance for some treatments because of near standardization of personnel, or because of limited staff input; the importance of staff qualifications could be very important for other treatments. If agreement on weights could be reached, the result of the strength of treatment assessment could be a single index permitting useful and revealing comparisons across different evaluations, settings, and programs—an index, moreover, that could be related to treatment outcomes.

Ideal Treatment

A final method for a priori assessment of treatment strength would be to describe an optimal or ideal form of treatment against which proposed treatments might be judged and ultimately standardized. In medicine, for example, analgesics are assessed by the standard provided by morphine, which has a value of 1.00. Except for recently tested combinations, all analgesics studied have values less than 1.00. Thus, morphine is the ideal standard, and if one wanted to employ an analgesic of moderate strength in conjunction with a behavioral intervention for low back pain, it would be possible to select one with a reasonably well known strength.

At present an ideal cannot be described for many behavioral and social interventions. But we think the goal is worth pursuing. If the strength of a treatment can be assessed on some absolute scale, it will clearly facilitate reaching a correct conclusion about the potential worth of the treatment. Potentially useful treatments may be abandoned if tested in a weak form, and improvable treatments may not be further developed if there is no recognition that they are not ideal. Assessing the strength of treatments may in the long run provide the best and most useful information, but that method is also to be the most elusive; its unavailability should not preclude the use of one or more of the alternatives we have suggested.

A Posteriori Evaluations of Strength of Treatment

Treatment strength must often be evaluated after the fact, e.g., when reading a research report on the evaluation of a treatment. The ideas sketched above for evaluating treatments a priori are, of course, applicable to a posteriori also. However, researchers could improve estimates of treatment strength by planning to collect data at the end of the treatment, thereby indicating its strength. A fairly strong tradition in laboratory social psychology uses *manipulation checks* (Aronson and Carlsmith, 1968) to determine whether the experimental manipulation was successful and had its intended effect. Similarly, it might be possible to build into some treatment evaluations data collection procedures which would indicate something about the strength of the treatment. For example, Kassebaum et al. (1971) administered questionnaires to inmates after a period of counseling. The inmates' responses suggested that counseling may not have been an especially strong treatment since inmates tended to deprecate the motives of counselees and to doubt the value of the counseling.

In instances where treatment outcomes are expected to be mediated by some intervening processes, posttreatment measures might help to determine whether those processes ever occurred. Thus, if treatment is expected to improve self esteem, which is in turn expected to improve resistance to peer pressures, a post-treatment self esteem measure might indicate whether the treatment was sufficient to produce the expected charge in the mediating variable. For example, Kassebaum et al. (1971) thought that favorable outcomes from counseling would be mediated by changes in the inmates' commitments to criminal value systems; but at least some questionnaire evidence indicated that change in commitment never was achieved.

Greater efforts should be required of investigators to establish strengths of treatments, and posttreatment questionnaires, if judiciously employed, could be a valuable aid in accomplishing that task. The investigator should keep in mind, however, the possibility that the participants' and surveyors' bias may affect their responses on such questionnaires (see for example the Scheier article in this volume).

A Priori Assessment of the Likely Integrity of Treatment

As we noted above, integrity of treatment refers to the fidelity in carrying out the planned treatment. Thus, the researcher can assess the actual integrity of treatment only after it has been delivered. However, it should be possible to make some assessment of the *likely* integrity achievable at some point prior to delivery of treatment. Essentially, that assessment involves examining the nature of the treatment and the plans devised to assure its delivery according to protocol. The conceptual distinction between strength and integrity of treatment is revealed by noting that it is possible to have a weak treatment delivered exactly according to plan; in fact, as will be suggested later, weaker treatments are likely to have a higher integrity of delivery.

The Treatment Plan

The first element to be examined is the treatment plan itself. As Quay (in this volume) notes, a conceptually sound and clear treatment plan is more likely to be delivered with integrity than a vague or poorly described plan—or at least so it would seem. It is possible that the failure to delineate the treatment which is to be delivered is more a failure of description—of communication—than of concept and protocol. Certainly there could be a very well conceived and sharply defined treatment concealed by dense, imprecise, or careless verbiage. Nonetheless, when a treatment plan is not clearly spelled out, evaluators of the project should be on guard (see also Cook and Gruder, in this volume).

The conceptual basis for a treatment should clarify the assumptions about target behavior on which the treatment is predicated and the links by which the processes involved in treatment are expected to result in behavior change. For example, if as stated by Kassebaum et al. (1971) the effects of group counseling on recidivism are mediated by weakening the commitment of inmates to a criminal value system, the mechanisms or processes in counseling that produce that weakening should be spelled out; and the way in which weakening of commitment to the value system is to reduce criminality at rather remote times in the future should also be specified. Further, to enhance the interpretability of the findings, specific methods of assessing whether the mediating processes are successfully established should be included. Or if reduced parole officer case loads lead to more intensive surveillance of clients and hence to reduced opportunities for criminal behavior, that chain of actions and consequences should be made explicit. To the extent that the reasoning is not made explicit, the attention of the parole officers is likely to be diverted to other concerns, such as organizational planning and administration, which would seriously undermine the treatment plan.

There are many elements which might be listed in an adequate treatment plan; just which elements should be listed would differ depending on the type of treatment. Still, it is possible to specify some that should almost always be present in human services delivery. These would include: (a) the methods used to select persons for treatment(s) and how any matching of persons to treatment occurs; (b) the frequency, length, and circumstances of any intervention with individuals or groups; (c) a description of the total services to be delivered, including the elapsed time in treatment; and (d) the identities, experiences, and training of the staff who are to deliver treatment, including vendors. These four listed items would be merely a minimal set, but even they are not described in many reports (see Wright and Dixon, 1977).

Staff Commitment

For most treatment interventions the commitment of the staff to the treatment program is vital. As some investigators have found (e.g., Jesness et al., 1975; Kassebaum et al., 1971), if staff are not committed to a treatment program, it is unlikely to be well implemented and delivered. It is difficult enough to deliver many treatments even with a completely committed staff; a half-hearted commitment, let alone outright resistance, is likely seriously to impair the treatment program. Ideally, the description of the program should include information pertaining to staff commitment. Such evidence might come in the form of questionnaire responses, interview data, or even unsolicited testimonials.

Supervisory Plan

Despite the best of plans and intentions, programs can fail for want of adequate supervision. A satisfactory proposal for evaluating a treatment should include a specific plan to supervise delivery of treatment to ensure that the delivery conforms to plan. For example, the supervisory plan should provide for monitoring the training of personnel, for checking on adherence to treatment protocols, for verification of staff activities, and the like (see Kelling, in this volume). To some extent an adequate program of supervision may seem to cast doubt on the qualifications and dedication of staff, but with a well-motivated and committed staff, supervision is a valuable method of verification and accountability, rather than an intrusion. Without a good plan for supervision, a project is always open to a charge of inferior treatment, especially if the treatment proves to have minimal or equivocal effects.

Documentation of Service Delivery

Related to the plan for supervising treatment staff is the plan to document that treatment as described did, in fact, take place. Every research proposal should include a specific plan by which it can be documented that services were delivered according to the plan described in the proposal. The plan should include mechanisms for establishing such basic preconditions of treatment as that treatment sessions took place, that those to be treated attended, that the treatment protocols were adhered to, and that the total amount of treatment can be estimated with confidence. Proposals to evaluate treatments should include such basic information as forms to record dates and places of sessions (along with the names of those in attendance), provisions for tape or video recording of sessions to be analyzed later for conformance to the requirements of treatment, spot-checking of treatment sessions by supervisors, interviews or questionnaires with subjects of treatment, and so on. Reputable survey research firms regularly do checks to determine that their interviewers perform according to instructions, that interviews actually take place, and so forth, and it does not seem less important that such quality control mechanisms should be applied in evaluations of treatments.

Complexity and Difficulty of Treatment

Generally speaking, we can expect that the more complicated or difficult a treatment is to administer, the greater the likelihood that its integrity will suffer. Where it is possible on a priori grounds to surmise that a treatment will be complex and difficult, concern for integrity of treatment should be sharpened. Unfortunately, the more complex the treatment, the more difficult it is to establish its integrity. When a treatment is as apparently simple as delivering a monetary subsidy to parolees for a period of time, it should not be difficult to document that the treatment was carried out as planned; although even with such a simple treatment it is reasonable to ask how parolees will be kept in contact with staff, how there can be assurance that parolees receiving the subsidy are in fact unemployed, and so on. Where the treatment is more complex, as in vocational training or counseling, for example, there are many more possibilities for shortcoming, and anticipations of problems in maintaining treatment integrity will be greater. When programs are very complex, e.g., requiring the delivery of a wide variety of services by diverse agencies, apprehensions should become even stronger.

Some treatments may also raise doubts about probable integrity because of the likelihood of resistance among professionals or from those in the community at large, or because of infeasibility growing out of excessive resources required to implement the program. To cite one example, Patton in this volume discusses an evaluation of a program designed to teach welfare recipients the rudiments of managing a household and being a parent. This evaluation showed that the program failed to produce any appreciable effect on these skills in the target population. Later investigation, however, revealed that the program had become so embroiled in political controversy that it was never implemented in the first place. Thus, complex, difficult, or politically controversial programs need to be carefully scrutinized for treatment integrity.

The fact that complex or otherwise difficult programs are suspect from the beginning may be an unfair indictment of treatments before they have been tried. But the history of treatment efforts in many fields justifies greater doubts for more difficult innovations. Investigators who propose to test the efficacy of unusually complex interventions should propose correspondingly careful and thorough devices to ensure that departures from the treatment plan are minimized, and that when departures occur they are detected and assessed. The more complex the treatment, the more detailed the plan for protecting treatment integrity should be in terms of appropriate treatment protocols, supervision, monitoring, and staff motivation.

A Posteriori Assessment of Treatment Integrity

As yet, the very notion of treatment integrity has so little currency that a priori assessment is rarely done. Unfortunately, a posteriori assessments are rarely conducted by either the investigators or their consultants (see the article by Cook and Gruder in this volume). Although it might be hoped that meta-evaluators could assess the strength and integrity of treatments from research reports, the necessary information is rarely provided. Worse still, such information may not be available at all since the investigators have failed to assess or even monitor their treatments.

Better documentation of treatments in many areas of evaluation research is imperative. For example, a recent review of criminal justice by Sechrest and Redner revealed that of twenty-nine reports surveyed, only six papers met even *minimum* standards for adequacy of description of the treatment. In a similar review, Wright and Dixon (1977) also lament the widespread failure of research reports to even describe, let alone document, treatments. One of the canons of science—and presumably evaluation research aspires to the status of science—is replicability. The results of many treatment programs absolutely *could not be replicated* because we would have little notion of how to begin. It is of little value that a research design is specified clearly and outcomes measures carefully described if the description of the treatment is so sketchy that a reader—or in some cases, the investigators themselves—cannot tell what intervention was really done.

In those currently rare cases when it is possible to assess treatment integrity after the fact (usually from a final report on a project), the facts to be considered are much the same as for a priori assessment. One wants to know whether there was a treatment protocol to be followed and, if so, how sensible and detailed it was. One wants to know what provisions were made for supervision of treatment delivery, and one wants documentation of delivery of services along with indicators of their quality. Data should be provided on intensity and length of treatment, attendance at sessions, and many other relevant variables.

TWO FINAL ISSUES

From their experience of reviewing the evaluation literature for 1978, the editors would like to make a strong plea for testing treatments strongly. This plea is based on two considerations: the prevalence and implications of no-effect results in evaluation research (but see the note by Blumstein in this volume), and the difficulty of making generalizations about the strength of complex treatment programs.

The Case for Strong Treatments

In testing the effects of any treatment there are several risks to be considered. One risk is the possibility that results will occasionally appear positive simply by chance. That risk is quantifiable by adapting a given level of significance, *alpha*, for use in statistical tests. Another risk is the possibility that a result will be negligible by chance alone. This second type of risk is difficult to quantify because there is no single convention such as setting p at .05 to operate as a guide, and because setting any level for *beta*, which determines the probability of detecting a real effect if it exists, requires a decision about the size of an effect one wishes to detect. We are rarely in a position in applied research settings to specify in advance just what would be considered an effect worth detecting. Cohen (1977) proposed some rules of thumb for what would be considered small, medium, and large effects in research in the behavioral sciences but his guidelines bear no relationship to needs required for decision making in the real world (see Sechrest and Yeaton, 1978).

But apart from statistical considerations, in applied research settings a powerful factor determining the probabilities of Type II errors is likely to be the strength of the treatment tested. Once a treatment has been tested and found wanting, there is an impetus for abandoning it without further consideration, particularly if it is at all expensive. Thus, if a family support program appears to have no effect, further efforts to explore the usefulness of such programs may cease without anyone ever inquiring whether the program was anywhere near optimal in its design and implementation. To minimize the probability that Type II errors will be made, these authors urge that in initial tests the strongest possible treatment be devised and tested. If even the strongest treatment has little effect, perhaps one may be justified in abandoning it. If the strongest treatment does have an effect, then an appropriate strategy might "decompose" the treatment to determine whether it might be effective in a weaker or less expensive form.

An argument that is sometimes raised against testing the strongest forms of treatments is that they are like the proverbial million dollar cure for cancer, a solution simply not affordable no matter how effective. These authors' response to that argument is twofold. First, it is usually important to know whether *in principle* some goal can be accomplished. If we then choose not to try to accomplish it because of the expense, we at least know why we are not pursuing it, and do not delude ourselves with the mistaken, however comforting, excuse that "nothing can be done." Knowing that a goal is attainable in principle can be very important in establishing priorities. The second response to the million dollar cure argument is that if we knew a way, however expensive, of dramatically improving work skill of disadvantaged youth, of decreasing the incidence of child abuse, or of rehabilitating criminal offenders, we would have a very useful guide to further research. When originally developed, the artificial kidney fell in the category of the million dollar cure, but further research and technological development have decreased the price of dialysis. If we knew what to do about poor school performance or other major social problems, even if it involved a very strong and expensive treatment, we would know something of great value.

Another argument in favor of testing treatments in their strongest form grows out of the very substantial difficulties in evaluation research of planning and successfully carrying out true experiments—the methodological achievement which provides the strongest basis for causal inferences linking treatments to outcomes. In general, the larger the effect one produces, the more robust is that effect against various hypotheses rival to the one that the effect can be attributed to the treatment. When there are lapses in methodology, whether at the point of planning or actually carrying out an experiment, those lapses admit as more or less plausible rival hypotheses a variety of explanations for the findings, e.g., that results may be attributed to maturation, to initial differences between noncomparable experimental and control groups, to extraneous and unanticipated events coincident with treatment, and so on (for an extended discussion see Campbell and Stanley, 1966; and Cook and Campbell, 1975, 1979). Most rival hypotheses are plausible in inverse proportion to the magnitude of the obtained effects.

When there is a really sizeable effect associated with a treated group, it is often implausible that it was caused by something other than the treatment (for examples see the McSweeney and Eisenberg et al. articles in this volume). Unfortunately, in many areas of evaluation research the effects likely to be achieved will be modest at best, and therefore vulnerable to a variety of alternative explanations when methodology is deficient. Weak treatments exacerbate the case considerably.

Critics of our position might point out that in those instances where treatments have positive effects, arguments from weak treatments would be especially persuasive; i.e., the results could be taken to imply that if stronger treatments were used, even more positive outcomes would be obtained. We concur. At the same time, we would point out that the relationship between treatment strength and outcome is not likely to be linear, and in some cases will not be even monotonic (i.e., some treatments may be stronger than optimal and consequently produce less favorable outcomes than weaker ones). In psychotherapy, for example, individual therapy would usually be considered a stronger treatment than group therapy, and a probing, insightful treatment would usually be considered a stronger treatment than a more rational, problem solving or supportive therapy. There is evidence, however, that with some kinds of patients, especially those considered borderline in adjustment or those likely to be labeled schizophrenic, group and less intensive treatments have better outcomes (Gottesfeld, 1977). Another example of an intervention which may have an optimum value is intensity of parole supervision, which, beyond some optimum value, may result in less favorable outcomes. It is also sometimes true that treatments are suspect because they are so weak that they seem scarcely able to produce the results attributed to them. For example, a widely known study showing the extensive effects of brief psychotherapeutic intervention on the use of health services (Cummings and Follette, 1976) is suspect precisely because the results seem to indicate that a *single* interview could be shown to have had an effect still detectable after *eight years*! Thus, using the results of weak treatments to estimate the likely effects of strong treatments is a risky procedure at best. Given the high risk that ineffective treatments will be abandoned quickly without further investigation, the authors maintain that each treatment should be tested in its strongest possible form to maximize the likelihood that it is given an adequate test.

Are Really Strong Treatments Realistic?

The question might be raised whether the strong treatments encouraged in this paper can be realistically implemented. Is it realistic to suppose that work release programs could be developed in which prisoners would be released for substantial periods into meaningful and good paying jobs where they might continue postrelease? Is it realistic to think of counseling programs with expert staff, individualized counseling programs, and intensive treatment over considerable periods? Could a vocational training program be developed with highly qualified instructors, high quality training materials, carefully selected occupational specialties, good placement programs, and all the other desirable characteristics? Perhaps not; these writers are not in a position to say. However, in the absence of strong treatments, care should be taken in drawing a pessimistic conclusion about treatments that supposedly do not work.

Implementing stronger treatments might be possible if strength of treatment were made more salient as an issue, and if greater pressures were put on those responsible for developing programs to plan stronger treatments. Not all increments in strength of treatment necessarily depend upon the availability of greater resources. For example, to the extent that a clear and thoughtful treatment protocol results in a stronger treatment, then all that is required is clearer thinking and more thoughtful people to develop those protocols.

In any case, it should be made clear whether particular treatments are studied because no better ones can be imagined or whether they are studied because current administrative arrangements would not permit better ones, or because some part of society is unwilling to provide the resources for better ones.

REFERENCES

ANDERSON, N. H. (1974) "Information integration therapy: a brief survey," in D. H. Krantz, R. C. Atkinson, and R. D. Luce (eds.) Contemporary Developments in Mathematical Psychology. San Francisco: W. H. Freeman.

ARONSON, E. and J. M. CARLSMITH (1968) "Experimentation in social psychology," pp. 1-79 in G. Lindzey and E. Aronson (eds.) Handbook of Social Psychology, vol. 2 (2nd ed.) Reading, MA: Addison-Wesley.

BOYDSTUN, J. E., M. E. SHERRY, and N. P. MOELTER (1978) Patrol Staffing in San Diego: One- or Two-Officer Units. Washington, DC: Police Foundation.

CAMPBELL, D. T. and J. C. STANLEY (1966) Experimental and Quasi-Experimental Designs for Research. Chicago: Rand McNally.

COHEN, J. (1977) Statistical Power Analysis for the Behavioral Sciences. New York: Academic Press.

COOK, T. D. and D. T. CAMPBELL (1979) The Design and Analysis of Quasi-Experiments for Field Settings. Chicago: Rand McNally.

——— (1975) "The design and conduct of quasi-experiments and true experiments in field settings," pp. 223-325 in M. D. Dunette and J. P. Campbell (eds.) Handbook of Industrial and Organizational Research. Chicago: Rand McNally.

COOPER, H. M. (1979) "Statistically combining independent studies: a meta-analysis of sex differences in conformity research." J. of Personality and Social Psychology 37, 131-146. 146.

CUMMINGS, N. A. and W. T. FOLLETE (1976) "Brief psychotherapy and medical utilization: an eight year follow-up," in H. Dorken and associates (eds.) The Professional Psychologist Today: New Developments in Law, Health Insurance, and Health Practice. San Francisco: Jossey-Bass.

GLASS, G. V (1976) "Primary, secondary, and meta-analysis research." Educ. Researcher 5(10): 3-8.

GOTTESFELD, H. (1977) Alternatives to Psychiatric Hospitilization. New York: Gardner Press.

JESNESS, C., T. ALLISON, P. McCORMICK, R. WEDGE, and M. YOUNG (1975) Cooperative Behavior Demonstration Project. Sacramento, CA: California Youth Authority.

KASSEBAUM, G., D. A. WARD, and D. M. WILNER (1971) Prison Treatment and Parole Survival. New York: John Wiley.

KLIMT, C., G. KNATTERUD, C. MEINART, and T. PROUT (1970) "A study of the effects of hypoglycemic agents on vascular complications in patients with adult-onset diabetes: I. design, methods, and base-line results, UGDP." Diabetes 19 (Supplement 2): 747-783.

KELLING, G. L., T. PATE, D. DIEKMAN, and C. E. BROWN (1974) The Kansas City Preventive Patrol Experiment: A Technical Report. Washington, DC: The Police Foundation.

LARSON, R. C. (1976) "What happened to patrol operations in Kansas City?" Evaluation 3, 117-123.

McKAY, H., L. SINESTERRA, A. McKAY, H. GOMEZ, and P. LLOREDA (1978) "Improving cognitive ability in chronically deprived children." Science 200, 270-278.

ROSSI, P. H. and K. C. LYALL (1976) Reforming Public Welfare: A Critique of the Negative Income Tax Experiment. New York: Russell Sage Foundation.

SECHREST, L. B. and W. YEATON (1978) "Estimating magnitudes of experimental effects." Florida State University. (unpublished).

SELTZER, H. S. (1972) "A summary of the criticisms of the findings and conclusions of the University Group Diabetes Program (UGPD)." Diabetes 19 (Supplement 2): 976-979.

SLOVIC, P., B. FISCHHOFF, and S. LICHTENSTEIN (1977) "Behavioral decision theory." Annual Rev. of Psychology 28, 1-39.

SLOVIC, P., and S. LICHTENSTEIN (1971) "Comparison of Bayesian and regression approaches to the study of judgement." Organizational Behavior and Human Performance 6, 649-744.

WRIGHT, W. E. and M. C. DIXON (1977) "Community prevention and treatment of juvenile delinquency." J. of Research in Crime and Delinquency 14, 35-67.

WORTMAN, P. M. and ST. PIERRE (1977) "The educational voucher demonstration: a secondary analysis." Education and Urban Society 9 (August): 471-492.

I

THE THEORY AND PHILOSOPHY OF
EVALUATION

The field of evaluation research is expanding rapidly, both in breadth of the activities to which it is being applied and in the depth of analysis and penetration within any one type of activity. Since evaluation has stemmed mainly from ideas about effectiveness and accountability of social interventions, it seems only reasonable that as evaluation research enlarges its scope, its potential influence should also increase. With the potential increase in influence comes an increase in the possibility to do either harm or good—or both. As the field of evaluation research matures, as we believe is happening, more thought is being given to the theoretical and philosophical underpinnings of evaluation and evaluation activities, and that thought is appearing in the form of more and increasingly sophisticated articles that expose both the strengths and the weaknesses of current beliefs and approaches. In the first section of this annual we include a set of papers which are provocative and constructive. Perhaps they raise more questions than they answer—that seems to be the norm for thoughtful papers—but they do point to directions for further thought and empirical exploration that we think, in the long run, should prove productive of further maturing in what is now a clearly established social science specialty.

The first two works in this volume may well arouse pangs of envy, perhaps tinged by outright resentment, in the hearts of many evaluation researchers. They were chosen for this volume and are presented first because they represent ideals about what evaluation research should be like. We recognize that there are few situations in which most program evaluators could come close to matching the circumstances that are portrayed in these two chapters, and they may seem to many too good to be true. Yet, we would insist that neither is a fantasy; although representing an ideal, each of them is real. We believe that there are important things to be learned from each.

Roland Tharp and Ronald Gallimore present not so much an evaluation as a model for the iterative development and testing of a program. It has been noted elsewhere (Sechrest, White, and Brown, 1979*) that one of the most needed methodologies is one that would evaluate a developing and changing program. Tharp and Gallimore contribute substantially to our understanding of what that methodology might be like. Their work may be seminal in its consequences for evaluation research.

We recognize that the conditions under which Tharp and Gallimore worked were remarkable and that they may not be easily achieved again; they may not even be achievable in some fields. Still it is likely that their model can be variously approximated, and familiarity with it may greatly enhance the prospects for attempting the task.

*SECHREST, L., S. O. WHITE, and E. BROWN (1979) "Rehabilitation of criminal offenders: problems and prospects." National Research Council.

1

The Ecology of Program Research and Evaluation
A Model of Evaluation Succession

Roland G. Tharp and Ronald Gallimore

This article proposes a model for research and development programs for social action. "Research and development" implies several features: (a) a complex social problem; (b) for which the solution is unknown; the development or invention of a solution which will require; (c) some time; in which; (d) some errors and corrections are anticipated; and in which; (e) the process and epistemology of science governs the outcome. These features are implicit in the term "research and development"; other features are also present, and this paper proposes to elucidate them, to examine the implications for evaluation processes, and to propose a model, drawn by analogy from ecology, which will order and clarify the complex research and development enterprise.

In the most general sense, all of science and technology may be seen as research and development. Ideas and data from one laboratory are adopted by another,

Authors' Note: This research was supported by the Kamehameha Early Education Program, of the Kamehameha Schools/Bishop Estate, Honolulu. Assistance was also provided by the Socio-behavioral Research Group, Mental Retardation Research Center, University of California, Los Angeles. The authors express deep appreciation for critical readings of the manuscript to Lee J. Cronbach, Donald T. Campbell, Terry Wade, Chet Hull, George Tarjan and Tom Weisner. Copies of KEEP Technical Reports may be obtained from Editor, KEEP, 1850 Makuakane Street, Honolulu 96817.

From Roland G. Tharp and Ronald Gallimore, "The Ecology of Program Research and Evaluation: A Model of Evaluation Succession." Unpublished manuscript, 1978.

research operations adapted and social programs evaluated. Outcomes in Oregon influence decisions in Liberia. If, however, the international social science and technology complex is a research and development program, it is a poor one. Local issues preclude generalization. Fedback from data is halting and slow; conditions giving rise to an outcome change more rapidly than old solutions can even be attempted. For these reasons, we are restricting our discussion to self-contained research and development programs which are particular encompassed enterprises, with precise boundaries of responsibility, and for which evaluation and experimental data, if not the generation of ideas, are specific to each.

RESEARCH AND DEVELOPMENT:
THE MORE GENERAL EVALUATION CASE

All self-contained research and development programs include evaluation. But not all program evaluations include a self-conscious research and development phase; in some cases development costs are reduced by adoption in toto of a packaged program which may then be subjected to *summative evaluation* if the user so elects.

In other cases, a self-conscious development phase of some length and magnitude is undertaken. Applications of evaluation to a development phase have been termed formative as opposed to summative evaluation by Scriven (1967), following Cronbach's earlier distinction between *outcome* and *process* evaluation (Cronbach, 1964). Others have also recognized that different standards are needed for the developing program as opposed to the completed one, e.g., the performance-feedback loops proposed by Walker (1972).

However, most "program evaluations" do summative evaluation of fixed programs. Most discussions in the literature are concerned with summative issues. Yet for every fixed program, there is a history *and a developmental process*—which may or may not have been internal to the existing program team, and which may or may not have been subjected to formative evaluation. The necessity of a development phase in all applied social science programs makes it possible to argue that *research and development is the more general case* for which *summative evaluation* of a fixed program is a limited (though indispensable) procedure applied to the end point of the research-and-development sequence, and during which *formative evaluation* (as it is usually conducted) is one of several possible procedures that may be applied before the end point. The model we present subsumes both formative and summative processes as well as the several methods of evaluation or ways of knowing which the full research and development process requires.

Our discussion here, by attending to the pure (albeit rare) form of self-contained research and development, can suggest explanations for the frequent failure of many social action programs, which truncate their initial stages and thereby lose the benefits of the full research and development process.

How often a full blown, self-contained research and development process should be employed in relation to truncated forms of evaluation, we do not know. Our experience suggests it should be more often than is now the case to break the cycle of enthusiastic beginnings and dismal endings that seem to characterize so many social and educational innovations.

Only by our involvement in the research and development program which serves as the example in this paper, have we been able to see reasons for the built-in futility of our previous efforts at program implementation. As the model presented here will suggest, self-contained research and development is a long, arduous, and expensive enterprise; it requires time, error, feedback, and correction; it cannot be a routine practice, nor is it to be always preferred to truncated derivatives. But even for those cases in which a full research and development process is proper and desirable, the necessary political and economic conditions are rarely available. We suggest that identification of these paradigmatic conditions is necessary if social scientists are to responsibly advise agencies and funding sources. If we must operate under conditions which predict failure or limited benefits, both they and we should know it.

THE EPISTEMOLOGY OF EVALUATION

Any consideration of evaluation issues (whether formative or summative) of fixed program effects, or the processes of research and development, must somehow deal with recently identified problems which lie on the border between social science and epistemology. If the basic question to be answered by evaluation is whether or not a program and which of its components are beneficial (Wortman, 1975), then the basic concern of evaluators must be with the *ways of knowing* whether or not benefit is present. There have appeared recently a number of foundational texts which make it clear that the *ways of knowing*, accepted and codified for conventional theoretical-experimental psychology, need reformation and a new understanding to guide social action. These texts include, but are not limited to, Bogdan and Taylor (1975); Campbell (in press); Campbell and Stanley (1963); Cook and Campbell (1975); Cronbach (1975), Johnson (1975); Scriven (1967); Walker (1972) and Wortman (1975). Drawing selectively from these and other sources, we suggest the following recapitulation.

While the true experiment, with random assignment of subjects to treated and untreated conditions, remains the ideal effectiveness test, such a design is often impossible to achieve, and various quasi-experimental designs have been created as alternatives, each of which introduces threats to the validity of the derived inferences (Campbell and Stanley, 1963; Cook and Campbell, 1975). Further, the true experiment, in and of itself, cannot guarantee each of the validities (internal, external, construct, and statistical) which we wish to presume in the creation of full understanding. Thus evaluation data are often like tessarae, individually flawed and irregular, which become satisfying only in the completed mosaic. Of foundational concern is the awareness that conventional fixed-condition experiments (with the ATI model as exemplar) are very likely incapable of extracting interaction conclusions of a high enough order to represent reality. This is because the multitude of factors which operate in field programs would require either (a) an impossible number of groups; or (b) an impossible degree of control across those groups. We are thus constrained toward particularized, localized, contextual conclusions, in which a coupling of experiment with "intensive local observation" becomes our available way of knowing (Cronbach, 1975).

It is no accident that there is a growing legitimization of inquiry into non-experimental data bases, the "qualitative knowing" discussed by Campbell (in press), radically advocated in Hamilton (1978), and urged early on by Cronbach (1964). It is also clear to us that a simple division of ways of knowing into qualitative and quantitative is inadequate to the actual processes of research, development, and evaluation. One of the purposes of the model presented here is to discover the several ways by which we acquire knowledge during research and development, and the proper places for use of each.

AN ECOLOGICAL MODEL OF RESEARCH AND DEVELOPMENT (R & D)

The model we propose here has predecessors. Notable among them is Wortman's elegant diagram of "an exhaustive set of evaluative or feedback processes," which poses a sequence of program development, with each stage attached to an appropriate validity concern, and attendant evaluation implication (1975: 565). Wortman notes that his proposed hierarchy does not correspond to either the theoretician's or the applied researcher's hierarchies as described by Cook and Campbell (1975). Wortman suggests that his model follows logically from the attempt to establish a cause-effect relationship. Our own model differs somewhat from all three, and the differences probably derive from two sources. First, while determining causal relationships is indispensible in all the sciences, there is an additional press in research and development, and that is for the *viability* of a developed program. Second, the solution to a complex program is almost certain to involve *multiple components*. It is the selecting, testing, and interrelating of the multiple program components on which research and development stands or falls. It is these two issues, viability and multiple components, for which an ecological model is particularly appropriate.

The purpose of this paper, then, is to propose a model for the idealized research and development enterprise, as it moves from accepting the challenge of a complex social problem all the way through to a stable, "climax" condition of program operation; to describe the conditions for its existence; its stages; the succession of steps in its evaluation; the ways of knowing appropriate to it; and to exemplify it with details from a multidisciplinary research and development project.

THE CLIMAX PROGRAM

The concept of *climax* is borrowed from ecology. A climax community is the final or stable community in a successional series (Odum, 1959: 266). The community may be conceptualized at various levels. It is ordinarily biotic, but may be usefully employed for less inclusive units, for example, the climax forest is an association of trees and plants which has come to occupy a given area, over a long period of time, and which, barring catastrophic changes in conditions, will not be replaced by another vegetation type. The concept of climax-program is proposed as a metaphor, which involves specifically these attributes: the living, organic nature of a complex association, nevertheless in dynamic equilibrium with its supporting environment, which, over a long period of time, has come to contain elements which will not be replaced by other element types, so long as the supporting environment remains unchanged.

The concept of climax is used as metaphor and not as full analogy, because the climax community, as understood in ecology, presumes a prior and regular sequence of stages, each of which may be recognized and from which the future climax may be predicted. So few social programs have come to climax that we cannot yet test the analogy, but it is certainly possible to see social programs existing in ecosystems, and we will in this paper propose certain stagelike progressions. Remaining within the metaphor, however, our own program had the advantage of what is known in ecology as *primary succession*, that is, of beginning on an area which had not been previously occupied: a new lava flow, or newly exposed sand. *Secondary succession*, in which a new program would come to occupy a burned-out or plowed-under area, is the more typical case, and programs grow differently from the ashes of old ones. Thus we will describe here the foundational, though not necessarily typical type: the primary-succession climax program.

Some biotic communities do reach climax; others of the same composition and direction do not, being arrested by geologic, climatic, or human interference. Biotic climax is not always desirable in human values, and is frequently prevented, in favor of farming, for example, or soft-wood forest harvesting. In the terms used here, the climax program refers to the direction and intention toward climax, as well as to the realization of the final stage, which may well remain an ideal.

This ideal stage, the climax condition of an evaluated program, may be described as follows: an association of program elements, organized for and producing a defined social benefit, which will continue to exist, and in which there will not be replacement by other element types, so long as social values, goals and supporting resources remain relatively constant. The climax condition does *not* suppose a constancy of individual elements, but presumes birth and death cycles of individual elements within the same type. The climax condition does not involve fixity, but supposes constant readjustment to environmental perturbations. It does not involve a completion of evaluation, but acknowledges constant evaluation pressure in the dynamics of element survival. It subjects each element to a test, based on various ways of knowing, but it admits that final program evaluation can never be of the trees, but only of the forest.

KEEP: AN EXAMPLE OF THE R & D CLIMAX PROGRAM

Before turning to a detailed discussion of the ecological model for research and development, it is necessary to provide a brief orientation to the research and development program which we will use as our major illustration.

The Kamehameha Early Education Project, or KEEP (Gallimore and Tharp, 1976; Jordan, et al., 1977; Tharp, et al., 1977; Tharp and Gallimore, 1975 and 1975) was funded by the estate of Princess Bernice Pauahi Bishop (sole surviving heir of King Kamehameha I) who dedicated in perpetuity the revenue from her lands to the education of Hawaiian (Polynesian) children. KEEP was organized to discover solutions for the problems of many Hawaiian-American children who do poorly in public schools. A second major goal was to discover and implement various training, consultation, and communication strategies for transmitting project findings to the public schools of Hawaii. Though studies have been conducted in cooperating public schools, the principal focus of activity is an especially constructed research and demonstration school. Each year a group of 30 five-year olds, at risk for academic failure, are blindly sampled from families living in a specific area of urban Honolulu. The children are enrolled in the KEEP kindergarten, remaining until they have completed third grade. The majority of the approximately 110 kindergarten through third graders at KEEP are from families receiving public assistance; three-fourths are Hawaiian, and the remainder are from the many ethnic groups of Hawaii (Filipino, Samoan, and so forth); the majority score below average on measures of school readiness at kindergarten entry.

A full school program is operated, following in large degree the practices of nearby public elementary schools. This was a deliberate strategy: We began with a "good" public school program and sought the "least changes" necessary to achieve average or better educational achievement. The research, development, and evaluation of those "least changes" followed the model presented here. The research took many forms with investigators from psychology, anthropology, education, and linguistics. This multidisciplinary approach was made necessary by the level of knowledge at the time we started in 1970: While there was agreement that Hawaiian children did poorly in public schools, there was great debate about why, and how to solve the problem. We elected a multidisciplinary, multiple-lines-of-investigation strategy, with particular focus on reading, language and dialect (the children speak Hawaiian Creole English), student industriousness, teacher training and consultation, and family and cultural studies. After seven years of full operation, significant progress has been made in several areas, with effective programs in student motivation, teacher training, and reading instruction now in use.

With this background, we can now turn to a discussion of several topics concerning the ecological model. First, what are the conditions necessary for a research and development program to achieve a climax condition?

NECESSARY CONDITIONS FOR THE CLIMAX PROGRAM

It is unlikely that climax can be reached in the absence of certain external conditions. In our own examples, four have been discernable.

(1) *Longevity.* The climax condition cannot be reached quickly. In our own case, nine years have brought the program to partial, though by no means total, climax conditions. Longevity itself is only the result of other stable conditions.

(2) *Stability of values and goals.* If a program is developed to meet a value which itself is unstable, little maturity can be anticipated. In our own case, the stable value has been to foster the educational success of native Hawaiian children. This value appears in prospect to be a highly stable one, unlikely to change until their educational success is at parity with majority culture children.

Longevity also requires a stable perception of an authentic relationship between the value and the goals which are presumed to foster it. At KEEP, decision makers believe that academic skill-learning in the early grades, particularly in reading, will foster success in the later years of education. Therefore, the first goal of the project was to develop and maintain a kindergarten through third grade school program which would teach Hawaiian children to be effective readers. Because our second goal was to export this model to the public schools of Hawaii, constraints were placed on our vision of the completed program, all relating to its acceptability to public school educators. For example, the program had to be not drastically more expensive than conventional ones, thus precluding expensive gadgetry, architecture, or pupil-teacher ratios. Because classrooms of Hawaii are culturally polyglot, the program could not be so culturally specific in its effectiveness that other children would be penalized. A program was needed that would look, cost, and act much like conventional reading instruction, but which would at least double other programs' effectiveness for Hawaiian children if our goal of reaching national norms was to be achieved.

The relationship of these goals to the basic value would be challenged by data showing a lack of correlation between early reading-academic success and later school success. While we will certainly examine those relationships, as the data become available, our funders and our community are confident enough of the connection to provide stability of values and goals.

(3) *Stability of funding.* Stability of funds may seem unnecessary to discuss: no more obvious need could be listed, and yet the lack of funding stability blasts most research and development projects on the vine. Because we were reliably funded for a period of ten years, it was possible to choose strategies on the basis of their intellectual merit and their long-term prospects. We did not have to produce immediate dramatic results in order to secure year-by-year renewal of operating funds. Many colleagues in similar programs must envision a program in full detail, install it, evaluate it, and pray, because subsequent years' operations are all staked on that first spin of the wheel. Only with long-range funding can research and development proceed rationally; for example, careful analysis of our unsuccessful years provided the evidence needed to reshape ourselves into an ultimately successful design. All strategy for research and development in a climax program depends on consideration of long-term effects, profiting from analysis of its own errors, and availing itself of the various methods of knowing which, in combination, gradually yield a little knowledge.

Sufficient funding stability is regrettably rare in research and development, let alone in more truncated program implementation. This need not be so. Programs must be given a time period appropriate to the complexity of the problem. During this period, accountability and the continuation of funds should not be on the basis of summative evaluation data, but based on assessment of the project's merit in scientific process, judgment, energy, and the like.

(4) *The power of the evaluator.* Nonevaluated programs can develop to climax; the public school apparatus of the United States is an example. In a research and development program, evaluation data become a major selection pressure by which some program elements wither and others fructify. The social scientist is tempted to argue that evaluation pressure should be the only pressure, and to long for absolute power. Given the frailty of our data bases and of our human natures this position is not persuasive. The argument is moot, in any event, because absolute evaluator authority never exists.

Even in the case of KEEP, where the authority of the writers was extremely high, evaluation was only one of many selection pressures. We had hire-and-fire authority over all personnel, including teachers; trained our own staff; selected curricula, materials, and pupils. Yet other forces limited our own: availability of personnel; funding constraints; the climate of opinion in the public schools; the political realities in the host institution and in the client community; and the authority of the estate administrators with whom we worked, and to whom we were fiscally accountable. The fact that in nine years not one imposed decision contravened our evaluation-based ones was not due to our direct authority. Cronbach points out that it takes some doing for an evaluator to maintain influence over a professional staff and community, and it takes negotiation rather than the exercise of power. He said, "I actually had 'evaluator power' once when I was both developer and evaluator for the Navy. But if I hadn't had rapport with the Navy instructors I'd have been out on my ear any day they chose to express discontent through their chain of command" (Cronbach, 1978).

The methods of rapport and influence building are beyond the scope of this article. We must here be content to observe that in research and development, evaluation data are properly the major selection pressure; that this pressure can never be maintained solely through power, nor should it be; and that under these difficult circumstances, maintaining evaluation pressure is the major task of administrators to insure the integrity of research and development. As programs mature, dedication to evaluation pressure begins to flag at all levels of the organization. Performance anxiety is debilitating to line staff; policy makers weary of the evaluation budget. The administration of the R & D program which survives must somehow rally the organization again and again, to the ethic and ideal of evaluation pressure.

THE WAYS OF KNOWING THE DEVELOPING PROGRAM

We will argue that the evaluated climax program employs all the ways of knowing, but that the different ways are employed differentially in the progression from *primary succession* to *climax*. Before these stages can be discussed, it is necessary to describe or classify what we mean by ways of knowing. They will be familiar to all students of the evaluation and methodology literature, though they may stand in unfamiliar guises and groups. Our classification does correspond to distinct processes in our own research, and may unite suggestions for methods made by prior writers.

We offer a fourfold classification: *experimentation*; *qualitative/personal knowing*; *data guidance*; and *program evaluation*.

Experimentation

This label includes both true experiments and quasi-experiments applied to program elements one at a time. Included are fixed-condition ANOVA designs; multivariate analyses of time-series data; simple correlational studies; and N of 1 time-series studies. Such knowledge can generate program elements, and can test in a hypothetical way, their probable value. Experiments done on isolated elements do not necessarily predict outcomes of these same elements when they are combined with others. For this reason, experiments can only gives us estimates of the value of a potential element to an overall program.

Program Evaluation

By this term we mean *only* that operation which compares *total program* effects to other-than-program effects. Because the climax program is composed of an association of elements, only the effects of the *association* may be known by this method. The acceptable design for this evaluation is the fixed effect, random assignment of subjects, treated versus nontreated conditions design.

This form of knowledge *presumes* fixed effects; therefore it is appropriate only when program elements are stable and replicable.

Data Guidance

This is appropriate to program elements which are not yet stable enough to allow experimentation or program evaluation. It involves very frequent or continuous monitoring of the effects of describable operations on the performance of specified objectives, the feedback of those data to the operators, and the modification of the operations in order to optimize performance. It is much like Lewin's "action research"; has been advocated by Walker; is much like the TOTE system in information theory (Miller, et al., 1960); is the basis of the instructional objectives method in education; and is the "ideal" method for clinical service delivery, according to the behavior therapies.

This widely advocated procedure is not appropriate to, nor a substitute for, program evaluation. It is, however, invaluable in certain developmental stages, as will be discussed below.

Qualitative Methods and Personal Knowing

It is this enormous category which allows us to suggest that the fourfold scheme is exhaustive. It includes personal memories, opinions, and judgments, both idiosyncratic and culturally shared; it includes disciplined, fine-grained observation, participant observation, ethnography, textual analysis, and other qualitative methods. In its highest form it is wisdom, in its lowest, delusion.

Personal knowledge may range from totally unsystematic intuitions to highly systematic ethnographies. Intuition and ethnography are certainly drastically different from each other, but they share common features. Both not only allow, but rely on the individuality of the observer; and both methods accept the unique, unmanipulated event as a datum.

Personal knowing is absolutely indispensible at two points in program development; it is *not* a substitute for program evaluation. Our experience leads us to value it somewhat more highly than does Campbell (in press), somewhat less than do Gadlin and Ingle (1975), and about the same as Erickson (1977) if we read these authors aright.

This four fold typology has allowed us to understand and improve our own program as it develops toward climax condition, because the emergence of various elements appear to follow clear sequences and these sequences rest differently on the forms of knowing.

THE SERAL STAGES TOWARD CLIMAX PROGRAM

In an ecosystem, the "sere" refers to all the sequenced association of elements which develop in a given situation. The *seral stages* are the relatively transitory associations of elements which precede the climax conditions. In KEEP, for example, an early seral stage was composed of thrée academic elements (reading, arithmetic, and social studies) plus a motivational element. (A program "element" is any unit which can be isolated by evaluation selection pressures.)

Only the motivational element survived throughout the sere. A major feature of the motivational element is training teachers through modeling and performance feedback (Sloat, et al., 1977; Speidel and Tharp, 1978) to use relatively high rates of praise and low rates of negative comments (Tharp and Gallimore, 1976). This praise-oriented behavior management composed the first program element at KEEP to survive sere to climax.

Two other elements have by now survived throughout the sere: the reading program (Crowell, 1976-77; O'Neal and Bogert, 1977; Au, 1976; Tharp, et al., 1977) and an oral language program, which includes many features described in Minicourse 2 of the Far West Laboratory (Speidel, 1978). Two additional elements, math and art, are presently in transition through the sere; at this point we do not know in what form, if any, they will appear in the climax program. Two other elements will be included in the climax program without succession through the sere: Hawaiian culture studies and physical education. This exclusion from evaluation pressure selection was arbitrary; the elements have established social and educational value.

In the second half of this report, various seral stages will be described. First, however, we must consider the ways of knowing, and their uses at different stages of the evaluation succession.

SERAL STAGES AND THE WAYS OF KNOWING: THE EVALUATION SUCCESSION

Table 1 illustrates the successive processes of knowing through which each infant program element moves in its cycle toward maturity. *Qualitative/personal knowing*, *experimentation*, *data guidance*, and *program evaluation* may be seen as the conditions which create and foster growth; they also constitute major selection pressures, a familiar observe in all living systems.

Column three of Table 1 presents the ways of knowing, in the order of their use, in a primary succession sere. Column four lists the selection pressure for each, and column one suggests general stages into which this process may be analyzed. Column two lists the succession of steps in evaluation, from the origination of a program element to its inclusion in program operations.

Before launching a more abstract discussion of these processes and stages, we will use the diagram to discuss an example of the development of a specific element. This element is the major one of our program and one of the few which have survived all selection pressures to date: the reading program element.

At Step 1, personal knowledge of our own staff, other experienced teachers, and expert consultants, led us to select as our initial curriculum, a middle-of-the-road, phonics-based program based on the Ginn 360 series. No known reading program had been successful with our population of concern, but the initial program seemed "sensible" to everyone.

TABLE 1
An Evaluation Succession for Program Research and Development

Stages	Stages in Program Element Development	Ways of Knowing	Validity Concerns	Selection Pressures
	Step 1. Initial selection: Values, theories, goals and objectives	Qualitative/personal	Construct & External	Does the idea have potential?
1–	Step 2. Treatment, independent variable formation	Experimentation: True or Quasi	External-internal or Internal-external	Are the relationships of enough magnitude?
2–	Step 3. Decision point: review, evaluate, translate; proceed, recycle	Qualitative/personal	Construct & External	Can treatments/independent variables be translated into stable, program element(s)?
3–	Step 4. Program element formation	Experimentation: True or Quasi	External-internal	Does it work in setting employed?
	Step 5. Decision point: review, evaluate; proceed, recycle	Qualitative/personal	Constructive & External	Is it worth further work?
	Step 6. Program element implementation	Data Guidance	External-internal	Can it be improved with tinkering?
	Step 7. Decision point review, evaluate; proceed	Qualitative/personal	Construct & External	When and if, in or out of the program?
	Step 8. Full scale program element operation	Program Evaluation	Internal & Conclusion, Statistical	Does the program element, with other elements in association bring benefit?

At Step 2, a quasi-experimental investigation revealed a robust correlation between the number of objectives achieved in the curriculum with measures of reading achievement. A small N true experiment produced greater number-of-letters-learned in group than in individual instruction. A series of such experiments contributed a pool of knowledge which was then considered by the staff.

The staff, using "experience," personal knowledge, and common sense, translated this experimentally-derived knowledge into a fixed program (Step 3).

Stage Two then began with a second experimental phase (Step 4), in which the program was fixed for one year, and an external group served as comparison. Data from this experiment demonstrated very low achievement as measured by achievement tests, and no difference from comparison groups.

The program was not continued (Step 5).

Another entire line of development had been conducted simultaneously and had proceeded through Stage One well enough that we could translate the knowledge into an alternative program element: a comprehension-based reading curriculum.

A one-semester experiment on that curriculum was conducted, using a true-experiment control-group design. The results were favorable, yielding a 25% increase in achievement over the phonics-based program and a substantial superiority over the control group.

In the opinion of the staff who had engaged in Cronbach's (1975) "intensive local observation" of this program, it could be improved and solidified, this proceeded by the good sense and best judgement of the most knowledgable staff members (Step 5).

A data guidance semester was then scheduled for the next class (Step 6). Careful observation of student behavior, teacher behavior, and performance data were employed. The program was altered throughout that semester, along many different lines. End of semester achievement test data were startlingly high—well above the fiftieth percentile on national norms.

Again the personal knowing of the staff provided the information needed to make the decision (Step 7). The comprehension-based curriculum was moved to formal program inclusion, which meant that it was maintained in a reasonably stable state during the next semester, when evaluation was undertaken.

Step 8, program evaluation, using true-experiment random assignment design, with controls receiving none of the KEEP program, was undertaken during the next semester. The evaluation data strongly supported the benefits attributable to the program.

The comprehension-based program was continued and expanded into all grades. However, experimentation on program facets, and the techniques of data guidance are continuing *on this program element*. That is, Stage 3 includes the ways of knowing on which Stages 1 and 2 rely, but it also employs Program Evaluation.

THE WAYS OF KNOWING:
USES AND LIMITATIONS

Experimentation

We have defined Experimentation to exclude the Program Evaluation method of testing overall, interacting-assemblage-of-elements effectiveness. In considering the uses and limitations of the experimentation, which investigates elements one at a time, we must remember that the fixed condition experiment can yield estimates of the magnitude of the effects of individual elements and estimates only. It is not logically possible to verify, in advance, the contribution of a potential element to the mature assembly of elements.

Two examples may be adduced. In the first, personal knowledge and logical analysis led us to investigate the possible contribution of phonological confusions to the reading programs of Hawaiian children (Smith et al., n.d.). Our subjects speak Hawaiian Creole as their first code, and five problematic contrasts with Standard English phonology were identified. (For example, the "th" sound does not appear in Hawaiian Creole, so that "three" and "tree" are heard with the same initial phoneme.) A Phone Discrimination test was developed, based on these five problematic contrasts, and was administered yearly to our pupils in the first grade and beyond. First grade correlations with reading achievements were high and negative, and with IQ partialled out, remained on the order of -.60. This led us to toy with designing a phoneme training program. However, after three years of data, it became apparent that the existing program corrected the specific phonological problems: entering second grade phone test scores and ending second grade reading achievement scores correlated not at all. However, entering first grade phone test scores continued to correlate with end-of-second-grade reading achievement. Thus a more general linguistic facility, of which phonological competence is a part, seems implicated.

The point to be made here is that the quasi-experimental data allowed us to estimate the magnitude of a specific phonological training element as rather low. We responded to these data by moving the teaching of the graphemes for the problem phonemes to last place on the list of phoneme and grapheme relationships, but did not go further with a specific phonological training element. The experiment eliminated an hypothesis.

A different outcome resulted from a fixed condition true experiment on our kindergarten children, testing the benefits of a general language training program —in this case the Far West Laboratory curriculum (Speidel, 1978; Speidel and Tharp, 1978). Selected for its emphasis on those linguistic issues identified as important by our correlation experiments, the Far West program, in only one semester, raised significantly the verbal ability scores of treated children over those of nontreated children, with other elements of our program held constant. Currently, we are engaged in a year of data guidance "tinkering" with that Far West element, and we expect that it will be adopted as a program element in our approaching climax condition. Incidently, a similar experiment using the Peabody Language Program yielded no difference in verbal ability or other relevant measures, and it was eliminated from consideration.

It is important to emphasize, however, that these *experiments* do not estimate the *independent* contribution of the Far West program to the overall educational benefit. They only speak to estimates of the effectiveness of the Far West as an element in a particular association of elements.

Would it be possible for fixed condition experimentation, with many factors, to isolate the sole contribution of the Far West program? Perhaps. Apparently Cronbach (1975) and certainly we, do not believe so. It is the purpose of this discussion to point out that, for the Climax program, it is not necessary or even appropriate to make that attempt.

Qualitative/Personal Knowing

As stated earlier, *qualitative knowing* may be precise or not, systematic or less so. In our experience, it always provides the filter and translation between the various stages of the other ways of knowing. Qualitative knowing provides initial hunches and then translates promising variables into classroom operations. Later, it estimates the probable worth of an element as it would exist in a potential assembly of elements. During a data guidance phase, the actual correlations chosen to bring an element nearer to performance standards are most often determined by "intense local observation." Deciding whether to let the element stand into the climax condition is invariably made on the basis of probability estimates which summarize a bank of personal knowledge. And during the climax program, it is again personal knowledge which detects and challenges weaker, dispensable, or improvable elements.

There have been substantial contributions to our program by ethnographic analyses, both of the Hawaiian community and family (Gallimore and Howard, 1968; Gallimore et al., 1974; Howard, 1974) and of our own classrooms (Jordan, 1976, 1977; Jordan et al., 1977). These systematic, disciplined, intense observations have contributed both hypotheses and survival pressure at every stage of our sere. The same is true to a lesser degree of more unsystematic knowing; knowing of the sort which would lead our experienced teachers to say: "If that is the goal, try this." Or, "It's not working. Not this way."

While we suggest that qualitative/personal knowing must continue into the climax condition, we do insist that it is not a substitute for program evaluation: in this regard we agree with Campbell (in press). We do want to admit personal knowing and qualitative methods as valuable and inescapable survival pressures even into the climax condition.

Data Guidance

When an element has survived the initial pressures of personal knowledge and some experimentation, it will become refined and stable enough to observe systematically, but not yet mature enough to warrant "official" inclusion in the program. At this point, a period of data guidance is appropriate.

In this way of obtaining knowledge, frequent measurements are compared with standards, and changes are made until the performance is acceptable. As an example, our reading program is based on a "comprehension" approach (teaching toward understanding a text), with less emphasis on phonics. During a data-guided semester, time-sampled teacher observations were analyzed weekly, and a criterion of "66% time-spent on comprehension" was adopted. Feedback was provided to each teacher; those who did not self-correct were offered consultation, training, and so forth, until the two-thirds comprehension criterion was achieved regularly. The corrections necessary for each teacher varied from simple feedback to complex interventions. These prescriptions came from many sources—many qualitative and personal.

More than the other ways of knowing, data guidance maintains an intimacy with empirical observations, but it does not itself provide any prescriptions. This is the limiting factor of data guidance; it is a way of knowing the disparity between performance and standard, but it is not itself a way of knowing the best correctives.

Data guidance continues into the climax condition. For example, our reading program element is now mature and has been evaluated-as-program for three years. Nevertheless, we continue data guidance procedures as a quality control. Proportion of teacher-time spent on various objectives is still measured weekly. While it rarely deviates from standard, we do occasionally tinker with one or another procedure to bring it back to criterion.

When is enough tinkering enough? When personal, careful judgement determines it to be so. When should an element, so judged, enter the program and Program Evaluation? When the element can be performed as described, for the period whose effects are to be evaluated.

Program Evaluation

The final survival challenge is to the assembly of elements—that dynamic, interactive, organic unit which is constituted of all those program operations surviving together in a homeostatic relationship.

Only their joint efforts can be evaluated, even when employing the ideal method for program evaluation: random assignment of subjects to program-treated and non program-treated conditions.

Thus our "reading" element is only one of many elements in our overall program. Although we believe its contributions to reading success to be some 80% of the total program contribution, it exists only in association with at least 10 other substantial elements. Some of those others are in younger stages of development, and are being changed regularly in response to emerging knowledge. Others, like our physical education element, were adopted arbitrarily and will probably not receive any scientific attention. But the reading component can be evaluated only as it exists in interaction with the full assemblage of elements. Only under the ultimate and stately arch of total program evaluation can the elements of the climax community come into a balanced relationship with research and development goals.

The Actual Versus the Ideal

The model proposed here is an ideal. It is not a biography of our own work. The model grew from reflections on mistakes as well as successes, though we are convinced that mistakes have lessened as the model has clarified. Recently, the model has served as a template for our decision-making, but even so, we have not been able always to follow our own prescriptions.

As an example, we have shared the common frustration of evaluators in achieving true random assignment of subjects to experimental and control groups for total program evaluation. Our school is a private one; students cannot be "assigned" to it. Therefore, we have not escaped the contamination of volunteerism: parents may well volunteer their children into the program for different reasons than they volunteer them into control groups.

Furthermore, the Hawaii State Department of Social Services (DSS) has rightly insisted on their clients' anonymity. Thus we have had to rely on a blindly mailed solicitation; we discover parents' identities only when they return a postcard, which leads to a personal contact. In an economically and socially disadvantaged population, it is not surprising that the rate of postcard return is less than 50%; it is frustrating to randomization because the better organized families may be those whose children finally arrive at our school, or become control group members.

Thus our results may generalize only to volunteering families. During the year of this writing, we have installed the program in two classes of a nearby public school. True randomization was apparently achieved, and preliminary results are comparable to the experimental control differences among children from our own volunteering families. This is evidence of the plausibility of the program effects; but the point here is that we must resort to assembling plausibility evidence, because of the failure to achieve true randomization in our original sample. Next year we are instituting new selection procedures which will allow generalization into a more clearly defined universe of children. It looks now as though we will move very close to randomization. But given the history of such efforts, it is premature even to discuss it.

It is the presence of the ideal model which pushes towards improvement. We could illustrate less-than-perfect fit to the model for any of the ways of knowing, and we could report the same condition: exigencies of local situations may preclude achievement of certain prescriptions; some programs may always have to depend on quasi-experimental designs, as described by Campbell and Stanley (1963). That does not lessen the value of a model, which is to serve as a guide, ideal, prod, and conscience.

VALIDITIES AND THE DEVELOPING PROGRAM

Cook and Campbell (1975) have taught that internal validity has general, though not absolute primacy: "random" assignment to experimental and control groups constitutes the design assurance that the program in the experimental school is in fact superior to conventional programs in the public schools. However, considerations of external validity are equivalent in priority; after all, if external validity is absent, no amount of internal validity can make research worth doing. In our instance, elegant designs for paired associate learning which are not valid for phoneme-grapheme teaching would be a waste of resources. External validity has often taken precedence over internal, construct, and statistical validity in our own work.

For example, we had reason to believe that KEEP children, being highly peer-oriented, might profit from doing desk work in "cubicles" that blocked seeing or touching one another, as opposed to work tables seating several (Chun et al., 1975). Although we had the resources to do so, we did not conduct this study in experimental rooms which would have allowed for a pure form investigation of degrees of isolation; rather, to meet the threat described by Campbell and Cook (1975: 235) as *Interaction of Setting and Treatment*, the study was conducted in a functioning classroom during arithmetic desk-work time. Our concern was with classroom cubicles versus classroom work tables, not the construct "degree of isolation."

In fact, a serious flaw in internal validity developed in this study, of the type Cook and Campbell label Compensatory Rivalry (228-229). During the first three days of data collection, the cubicle children outperformed the table children drastically, in both quantity and accuracy of problems completed. The teacher, instructed to supervise both groups simultaneously in her usual way became so irritated with the dawdling table children that she gave them a one-time, heavy dose of the behavior management procedures in which our teachers are well-versed: firm limit setting, followed by a rich diet of contingent social reinforcement. The table children immediately got to work and met the high rates of their cubicle peers.

This violation of internal validity ("ruining" the study), in fact produced a windfall discovery: however much the children may be peer-oriented, any effects of the orientation can be instantly washed out by a teacher competent in classroom management. Because we had previously developed a reliable control system, we folded the cubicles away.

When operating, then, in the mode of experimentation, our priorities were generally external validity, internal validity, construct validity, and statistical inference validity.

In assessing the overall effectiveness of the program (Program Evaluation), the priorities are altered to internal, statistical, construct, and external validity. This enterprise, though, presumes external validity in the program design.

And to further complicate matters, there is another mode of operation in which construct validity issues are of first priority: that mode which seeks to explain *why* the program is effective. In designing the reading program, we have taken from experimental results, quasi-experimental analyses, qualitative and ethnographic data, social science theory, the personal knowing of a large experienced staff, and happy accidents. In all respects which the designers considered crucial, these sources of knowledge converged on common recommendations; thus we have a program endorsed by our psychologists, educators, linguists, and anthropologists, but there is no agreement concerning its effectiveness; that is to say, disagreement exists regarding the potent and crucial elements of the program and to the way these elements articulate with larger theory. It is possible that this inquiry pursued will bring about a more muscular, more cost effective program. During this mode, construct validity has primacy.

SERE AND CLIMAX: CONCLUSION

The last of the seral stages is the climax. But a series is a sere only when resources and selection pressure remain the same. A climax condition exists only when resources and pressures continue stably; and it can be identified only by its own stability.

In the example of KEEP, we do not yet know whether we are in climax condition. Continuing program evaluation over the last three years has produced replications of high reading scores in five or six classes. The personal evaluations of our staff appear to be increasingly positive. Data guidance pressure requires steadily fewer performance adjustments. The signs of approaching climax increase. Yet we cannot be certain, and it is in the nature of the primary succession that climax condition can be identified only after the fact: *a program can be known to be in climax only when evaluation and selection pressure continues, and program elements remain, in general, the same.*

In research and development work, other characteristics of the ecosystem—goals or resources—may change so rapidly that a climax condition is never reached. In fact, conditions can be imagined in which subtle changes in the ecosystem could be detected only by the inaccessibility of the climax goal.

But presuming the climax condition, how long should summative program evaluation be continued? We have argued that the pressures of experimentation, data guidance, and personal knowledge are a continuing condition of research and development. If these pressures result in reaffirmations of the stable program, and if monitoring demonstrates that the program is being performed as it is described, then is there a time when summative evaluation can be stopped? Is there ever enough? In our own example, KEEP has three continuous years of data demonstrating program superiority to nonprogram (Gallimore et al., 1972-1978). Would it not be reasonable, and even ethically superior, to devote evaluation to further program implementation, rather than to (putatively) redundant summative evaluation?

Much merit attaches to that argument. In our own case continued annual summative evaluation begins to seem an ornate ritual to the ideal of evaluation pressure. Evaluation resources could be immediately diverted into export activities. On the other hand, the ecological metaphor offers a clear warning: the climax condition exists only in relation to a stable ecosystem, and few social problems-in-context are of certain stability. In our case, the ecosystem is a volatile one. The condition of the Hawaiian people is changing rapidly, in self-concept, in aspirations, in prosperity, and political power. The patterns of population distribution are changing, with more apparent urban-to-rural migration. Our own efforts to influence public education, if successful, will change comparison groups and perhaps the nature of the educational problems themselves. Thus a stable program may have its effects destabilized by changing social conditions, and these changes, vital to understand, can only be known by continued program evaluation. Perhaps once every other year is enough. Or every third year? Only "intensive local observation" can guide that decision, the personal knowing of a staff committed to evaluation pressure.

In conclusion, we must emphasize that a climax condition cannot be designed in advance. Were enough programs and their ecosystems described, predictions of the research and development sere might be made from a knowledge of the environment of values, resources, and selection pressures. We are far from such ability to predict. At the present time, program developers cannot determine in advance which association of elements will survive the selection pressures of the succession of evaluation steps. To specify this association in advance is to bank on impossible odds of luck in guessing and yet this is what the typical, short-term, fixed-program, summative-evaluated educational intervention must do. If there is one fact which the sere-and-climax metaphor can illuminate, it is this: The basic model for research and development is to maintain the selection pressure from all ways of knowing, in their appropriate places and intensities. If this is done, the climax association of elements will reveal itself. It will be that which stands.

REFERENCES

AU, K. (1976) KEEP Reading Research: 1972-75. Kamehameha Early Education Project Technical Report 57.
BOGDAN, R. and S. J. TAYLOR (1975) "Participant observation," in R. Bogdan and S. J. Taylor (eds.) Introduction to Qualitative Methodology. New York: John Wiley.
CAMPBELL, D. T. "Quantitative knowing in action research." J. of Social Issues. In press.
———— and J. C. STANLEY (1963) Experimental and Quasi-Experimental Designs for Research. Chicago: Rand McNally.
CHUN, S., G. SPEIDEL, and R. THARP (1975) Learning Center and Study Carrels: A Comparative Study. Kamehameha Early Education Project Technical Report 18.
COOK, T. D. and D. T. CAMPBELL (1975) "The design and conduct of quasi-experiments and true experiments in field settings," in M. D. Dunnette and J. P. Campbell (eds.) Handbook of Industrial and Organizational Research. Chicago: Rand McNally.
CRONBACH, L. J. (1978) Personal communication.
———— (1975) "Beyond the two disciplines of scientific psychology." Amer. Psychologist 30, 116-134.
———— (1964) "Evaluation for course improvement," pp. 231-248 in R. W. Heath (ed.) New Curricula. New York: Harper & Row.
CROWELL, D. (1977) Description of the KEEP Reading Program for Grades 1, 2, and 3: 1976-77. Kamehameha Early Education Project Technical Report 79.
ERICKSON, F. (1977) "Some approaches to inquiry in school-community ethnography." Anthropology and Education Q. 8, 58-69.

GADLIN, H. and G. INGLE (1975) "Through the one-way mirror: the limits of experimental self-reflection." Amer. Psychologist 30, 1003-1009.

GALLIMORE, R. and A. HOWARD [eds.] (1968) Studies in a Hawaiian Community: Na Makamaka O Nanakuli. Pacific Anthropological Records, No. 1. Honolulu: B. P. Bishop Museum, Department of Anthropology.

GALLIMORE, R. and R. THARP (1976) An Overview of Research Strategies and Findings 1971-1975 of the Kamehameha Early Education Program. Kamehameha Early Education Project Technical Report 66.

——— and K. SLOAT (n.d.) Analysis of Reading Achievement Tests Results for the Kamehameha Early Education Project: 1972-1978.

GALLIMORE, R., J. BOGGS, and C. JORDAN (1974) Culture, Behavior, and Education: A Study of Hawaiian-Americans. Beverly Hills, CA: Sage.

HAMILTON, D. [ed.] (1978) Beyond the Numbers Game: A Reader in Educational Evaluation. Berkeley, CA: McCutchan.

HOWARD, A. (1974) Ain't No Big Thing: Coping Strategies in a Hawaiian-American Community. Honolulu: Univ. Press of Hawaii.

JOHNSON, J. M. (1975) Doing Field Research. Honolulu: Univ. Press of Hawaii.

JORDAN, C. (1977) Learning-Teaching Interactions among Polynesian-Hawaiian Children in a School Context: Rationale, Method, and Preliminary Results. Kamehameha Early Education Project Technical Report 67.

——— et al. (1977) A Multi-Disciplinary Approach to Research in Education: the Kamehameha Early Education Program (KEEP). Kamehameha Early Education Project Technical Report 81.

——— (1976) Teaching Modes and School Adaptation. Kamehameha Early Education Project Technical Report 61.

MILLER, G. A., E. GALANTER, and K. H. PRIBAM (1960) Plans and the Structure of Behavior. New York: Holt, Rinehart, & Winston.

O'NEAL, K. and K. BOGERT (1977) Classroom Organization for the Language Arts Teacher: A System for Meeting Learner Needs Through the Use of Work Areas and Small Group Instruction. Kamehameha Early Education Project Technical Report 78.

ODUM, E. P. (1959) Fundamentals of Ecology. Philadelphia: W. B. Saunders.

SCRIVEN, M. (1967) "The Methodology of Evaluation," pp. 39-83 in R. W. Tyler, R. M. Gagne, and M. Scriven (eds.) Perspectives of Curriculum Evaluation, AERA Monograph Series on Curriculum Evaluation, No. 1. Chicago: Rand McNally.

SLOAT, K.S.M., R. G. THARP, and R. GALLIMORE (1977) "The incremental effectiveness of classroom-based teacher training techniques." Behavior Therapy 8, 810-818.

SMITH, F. et al. (n.d.) KEEP Phoneme Discrimination Test. Kamehameha Early Education Project Technical Report 64.

SPEIDEL, G. E. (1978) Developing Children's Oral Language: A Study of the Effectiveness of Mini-Course Instruction with Hawaiian Creole-Speaking Children. Kamehameha Early Education Project Technical Report 85.

——— and R. G. THARP (1978) The Effectiveness of Art and Language Instruction on the Intelligence and Achievement Scores of Disadvantaged Dialect Speaking Kindergarten Children. Kamehameha Early Education Project Technical Report 84.

——— (1978) "Training teachers in the use of positive feedback." Behavior Therapy. In press.

THARP, R. and R. GALLIMORE (1976) The Uses and Limits of Social Reinforcement and Industriousness for Learning to Read. Kamehameha Early Education Technical Report 60.

——— (1975) A Proposal to Build an Education and Research Program: A Kamehameha Early Education Project Proposal. Kamehameha Early Education Technical Report.

——— (1975a) The Mutual Problems of Hawaiian-American Students and Public Schools. Kamehameha Early Education Project Technical Report 1.

THARP, R. et al. (1977) Teaching Reading to the Educationally at Risk: A Multidisciplinary Research and Development Program. Kamehameha Early Education Technical Report 82.

WALKER, R. A. (1972) "The ninth panacea: program evaluation." Evaluation 1, 45-53.

WORTMAN, P. M. (1975) "Evaluation research: a psychological perspective." Amer. Psychologist 30, 562-575.

The randomized clinical trial in medicine is not different in principle from the evaluation of a program. We believe that the elegance of the well-conducted clinical trial provides a model of sorts for the evaluation of admittedly more complex interventions implemented in more complex circumstances. If we could do our program evaluations in the way portrayed by the Canadian Co-operative Study Group, that is surely the way we would do them.

We would like to call attention to several important features of the clinical trial of aspirin as an intervention to prevent strokes. To begin with, the problem permitted a simple, but elegant design, and it stemmed from a theory providing at least a reasonable link between the treatments employed and the outcomes studied. Yet the state of knowledge or clinical opinion at the beginning of the study did not rule out either randomization to treatment or a placebo. It was possible in the study to obtain data on integrity of the treatment, including integrity of the double-blind arrangement. The sample size was large, which was fortunate, because although the effect produced by the aspirin seems substantial on examination (e.g., in decreasing risk of stroke by 19%) and because of the relative infrequency of that outcome, even in the stroke-prone population studied, the results were significant at only the .05 level.

2

A Randomized Trial of Aspirin and Sulfinpyrazone in Threatened Stroke

Canadian Cooperative Study Group

Abstract Five hundred and eighty-five patients with threatened stroke were followed in a randomized clinical trial for an average of 26 months to determine whether aspirin or sulfinpyrazone, singly or in combination, influence the subsequent occurrence of continuing transient ischemic attacks, stroke or death.

Eighty-five subjects went on to stroke, and 42 died. Aspirin reduced the risk of continuing ischemic attacks, stroke or death by 19 per cent (P<0.05) and also reduced risk for the "harder," more important events of stroke or death by 31 per cent (P<0.05), but this ef-fect was sex-dependent: among men, the risk reduction for stroke or death was 48 per cent (P<0.005), whereas no significant trend was observed among women. For sulfinpyrazone, no risk reduction of ischemic attacks was observed, and the 10 per cent risk reduction of stroke or death was not statistically significant. No overall synergism or antagonism was observed between the two drugs. We conclude that aspirin is an efficacious drug for men with threatened stroke. (N Engl J Med 299:53-59, 1978)

D ISABLING or lethal thromboembolic stroke is frequently preceded by less devastating ischemic events.[1,2] These earlier episodes, whether transient or with residua and occurring in either the carotid or vertebrobasilar territories, indicate a poor prognosis; approximately 5 per cent of cases per year will go on to stroke, and an equal proportion of patients will die, usually from a vascular cause.[3-6]

Decreased cerebral blood flow due to hemodynamic factors or emboli of cardiac origin are responsible for a portion of these preceding episodes.[7] However, emboli arising from atheromatous lesions in the major arteries to the brain also produce a substantial proportion of these episodes in the form of transient ischemic attacks.[1,2] These emboli are composed of platelets with fibrin or of debris from atheromatous lesions. Since the debris can cause platelet-induced thrombosis in the target arteries,[8] platelet reactivity may be involved in both varieties of artery-to-artery emboli.

By 1970, it was apparent that the prevention of stroke by anticoagulants was less than ideal, and this method was not universally adopted as "standard therapy."[9] Surgery's role in preventing stroke was still unsettled despite a major collaborative randomized study.[10] However, certain drugs were available that were known to have an inhibitory effect on platelet function[11,12] and had had promising preliminary results among patients with cerebrovascular disease.[13,14] The assessment and discussion of this evidence by a group of Canadian neurologists, experimental pathologists, hematologists and methodologists led to the design and execution of a clinical trial, among patients with threatened stroke, of two drugs that alter platelet function. This report summarizes the methods and the principal clinical results of that trial.

Address reprint requests to Dr. H. J. M. Barnett at the Department of Neurological Sciences, University Hospital, London, ON N6A 5A5, Canada.

Supported by a grant (MA-4535) from the Medical Research Council of Canada.

The Canadian Cooperative Study Group consists of the following:

Neurologic Center: University of Western Ontario, H. J. M. Barnett, principal investigator.*

Methods Center: McMaster University, M. Gent, co-principal investigator*; D. L. Sackett, co-principal investigator*; and D. W. Taylor, chief statistician.*

Hematology: Co-ordinators: J. A. Blakely (Toronto)*; J. Hirsh (McMaster)*; J. F. Mustard (McMaster)*; and R. K. Stuart (University of Western Ontario).*

Participating Centers: Newfoundland: St. John's, W. Pryse-Phillips. Nova Scotia: Halifax, T. J. Murray. Quebec: Montreal, D. W. Baxter and J. Meloche. Quebec City, M. Drolet and D. Simard.* Ontario: Ottawa, E. Atack, R. F. Nelson and D. Preston. Kingston, H. B. Dinsdale.* Toronto, R. D. G. Blair, J. Edmeads, R. Gladstone, M. Hill, O. Kofman, B. Stewart and R. Wilson. London, H. J. M. Barnett,* C. Bolton, J. Brown, N. Jaatoul, A. Kertesz, J. D. Spence and S. Stewart. Alberta: Calgary, F. Leblanc,* R. Lee, F. W. Ramsay and T. Seland. British Columbia: Vancouver, V. Sweeney and J. Wong. Victoria, C. A. Simpson. New Westminster, R. D. Grosch and M. Knazan.

Research Staff: University of Western Ontario, P. Doucette, F. Geoghegan and S. Mann. McMaster University, J. Sicurella and G. Smith.

*Members of Executive Committee and Editorial Committee.

PATIENTS AND METHODS

The study was a multicenter, double-blind, factorial, randomized clinical trial.

Eligibility

Patients were eligible if they had experienced at least one cerebral or retinal ischemic attack in the three months before entry (during the first year of the trial only patients with multiple attacks were admitted, and the protocol was then revised to include patients with single attacks). Definitions for symptoms of transient ischemic attacks were developed and agreed upon by all participants. Certain symptoms were sufficient for entry when they constituted the only manifestation of an attack, whereas others had to occur in predefined combinations. Patients with residual symptoms beyond the 24-hour limit were eligible only if the symptoms were both stable and capable of subsequent observable further deterioration.

Exclusions

Neurologically stable patients were nonetheless excluded if they had coexisting morbid conditions that could explain their symptoms, if they were likely to die from other illness within 12 months, or if they were unable to take the test drugs. Participating centers were asked to submit information on all patients excluded from the trial.

Base-line Studies

The neurologic assessment at entry included an extensive documentation of the transient ischemic attacks (number of attacks in the prior one, three, six and 12 months, dates of first and most recent ischemic episodes, occurrence of residua and presence or absence of appropriate symptoms) and a detailed neurologic examination. Cerebral angiography (followed by a repeat neurologic assessment) was encouraged but optional. This entry evaluation also determined smoking habits, drug use within the prior month and any past history of diabetes mellitus, cardiomegaly, heart failure, angina pectoris, myocardial infarction, intermittent claudication, hypertension or cardiovascular operations. A detailed cardiovascular examination was carried out, as was an electrocardiography, chest x-ray study and a series of hematologic determinations and blood chemical tests. Mandatory tests of platelet function consisted of template bleeding times, platelet aggregation and glass-bead retention. Optional studies included ^{51}Cr-labeled platelet survival and tests for circulating platelet aggregates.

Allocation

When base-line studies had been completed, contact was made with the methods center at McMaster University, which was staffed 24 hours a day. Patients were stratified according to the presumed site of ischemia and the presence or absence of a residual deficit, and entered into a previously established randomization schedule (a separate randomization schedule, balanced every four patients, had been constructed for each stratum within each participating center). The trial medications were immediately started.

Regimens

Patients were randomized to one of four regimens throughout the study.* Each regimen was taken four times daily and consisted of: a 200-mg tablet of sulfinpyrazone plus a placebo capsule; a placebo tablet plus a 325-mg capsule of acetylsalicylic acid; both active drugs; or both placebos. Each active drug and its corresponding placebo were identical in size, shape, weight and color and were shipped to the participating centers in identical bottles of 130, labeled with four-digit random numbers. Neither the patients nor their physicians were told which regimen had been assigned, but both were given a 24-hour telephone number for emergency code-breaking. To prevent participating neurologists from inadvertently breaking the code by discovering the hypouricemia that sulfinpyrazone produces, uric acid values were deleted from local laboratory reports and sent directly to the methods center. At the end of the trial (but before the code was broken), the neurologists were asked to predict both the overall study results and the regimens for each of their patients.

Compliance and Contamination

Patients were asked to return unused medication at each follow-up visit, and pills were counted to estimate medication compliance.

*Supplies of active and placebo medication were prepared and supplied to the methods center by Ciba–Geigy, Ltd., of Canada.

Additional compliance information was contained in changes in serum uric acid, determinations of sulfinpyrazone blood levels and platelet aggregation in the presence of epinephrine (the latter measure also used to assess contamination with aspirin). The results of all these tests remained unavailable to the treating neurologist during the course of the study. Because of the ubiquity of aspirin-containing compounds all patients were urged to avoid cold remedies and other over-the-counter nostrums, and acetaminophen was recommended when an analgesic was needed. Finally, because many psychoactive drugs also affect platelet function, clinicians were advised to restrict their choice of tranquilizers to diazepam or chlordiazepoxide.

Follow-up Data

Patients were re-evaluated at one and three months and every three months thereafter. At each follow-up visit, the interim neurologic history was obtained, and the detailed neurologic and cardiovascular examinations were repeated. Smoking status, compliance and contamination were reassessed, and a brief, standardized search was made for side effects and toxicity. Hematologic, blood chemical and selected platelet-function studies were repeated at each follow-up visit, and electrocardiograms and chest x-ray films were obtained annually (or more frequently if clinically indicated). Finally, the methods center was approached by telephone, and a new supply of study drugs was identified.

Withdrawals

It was recognized at the outset that many patients might be withdrawn from the trial because of the discontinuation of study drugs, the initiation of contaminating medications, submission to operation or moving away from any center. Furthermore, both study drugs were thought capable of producing side effects that would demand their discontinuation. Accordingly, it was decided that such patients would constitute withdrawals but that their follow-up observation would continue despite cessation of the study drugs.

Events

Follow-up data were examined for the three events of transient ischemic attacks, stroke and death.

Transient ischemic attacks. Data from each follow-up examination were reviewed for the presence and number of attacks over each period of follow-up. The occurrence of any ischemic attack during a follow-up period constituted an event. Since patients who go on to stroke may not, and patients who die cannot, have further ischemic attacks, the last two events were included in this analysis of continuing attacks. Among subjects with multiple events, the date of the first relevant event was used for the analysis.

Stroke. Two groups of possible strokes were identified from follow-up data and submitted for adjudication. The first group consisted of patients in whom neurologists reported a stroke in a follow-up narrative summary; the second group had complained of one or more ischemic events with a residual neurologic deficit lasting for more than 24 hours at a follow-up visit. The records of both groups (purged of any information about their study drugs) were reviewed independently by two senior neurologists, and disagreements were resolved by discussion in the presence of one of the directors of the methods center who was also blind to the patient's therapy. These judges also ruled whether the stroke was minor (no impairment in activities of daily living), moderate (impairment in activities of daily living but residing at home and out of bed for all or part of the day) or severe (bedfast or institutionalized for reasons of disability). Since dead patients cannot proceed to stroke, death was included in these analyses.

Death. Finally, each death was documented and classified by its underlying cause (cerebrovascular, coronary, other vascular or nonvascular).

Eligibility of events. Because it was believed that sulfinpyrazone took one week to produce a biologically appreciable effect,[15] it was decided to exclude any events occuring in the first week of therapy with any of the four regimens. Furthermore, since the withdrawal of patients from the trial might be precipitated by a deterioration in their neurologic status (and thus their exclusion from subsequent analyses might bias the results in favor of their study regimen), any events occurring within the first six months after withdrawal were charged against the corresponding study regimen even if the patient stopped taking the study medication at the time of withdrawal. Any bias resulting from this maneuver should be against showing a benefit of treatment.

Statistical Analysis

Appropriate parametric and nonparametric tests were used to analyze base-line differences among study groups, associated hematologic investigations and compliance. Outcome analyses were carried out with the log-rank life-table method suggested by Peto et al.[16]

The primary analysis related to the overall assessment of benefit of aspirin and sulfinpyrazone. However, it was also judged important to examine the relative efficacy of these drugs among clinically sensible subgroups. The findings from these secondary analyses must be interpreted with some caution since the true significance levels are affected by the repeated challenging of the data.

Estimation of the number of patients required was based on the assumption that the annual incidence of stroke was 7 per cent and the annual death rate 4 per cent, and that one or other of the two drugs would reduce these rates by 50 per cent. The Type 1 error, α, was chosen to be 0.05, and the Type 2 error, β, 0.20. Allowing for dropouts, we estimated that some 600 patients would be required if they were entered uniformly over a five-year period, followed for at least one year and possibly up to six years.

Withdrawals were monitored to detect possible drug toxicity. The first examination of the data for efficacy occurred in April, 1976, when 569 patients had been entered into the study. At that time there was a trend favoring aspirin that was not statistically significant. It was decided to continue admitting patients until June 30, 1976, by which time it was expected to reach the target of 600 patients, and to follow them for a further 12 months; the data were then to be analyzed and reported.

RESULTS

Enrollment

Twenty-four centers entered patients into the trial between November 1, 1971, and June 30, 1976, and follow-up observation on the study drugs was concluded on June 30, 1977. During this time 649 patients were entered, of whom 64 were later found to be ineligible according to protocol entry requirements, resulting in a study population of 585. There was some imbalance among the ineligible subjects across the four treatment groups in that 25 were on placebo, 17 on sulfinpyrazone, 12 on aspirin and 10 on the combination therapy.

Six hundred and ninety-two patients were reported as exclusions, and these subjects, plus the 64 ineligibles, raised the total number of known exclusions to 756. Of these patients, 174 had coexisting morbid conditions that could explain their symptoms, 43 were considered likely to die from other illness within 12 months, 160 were unable to take the test drugs, and 72 had operations. Of the remaining 307 exclusions, 141 refused randomization, 53 had single attacks (excluded in the first year of the trial), 30 were misdiagnosed, 73 had a completed stroke before entry, and seven had a stroke and three had continuing ischemic episodes within the first seven days of therapy.

Characteristics at Entry

Definitions of symptoms of transient ischemic attacks were developed and applied consistently throughout this trial. The four treatment groups were found to be comparable in the distribution of various ischemic events before entry, to the neurologic signs at entry and to coexisting cardiovascular morbidity and risk factors at entry.* Tables 1 and 2 summarize the study patients in terms of the frequency of ischemic events before admission and their distribution according to site, sex and the presence of residua.

Stratification and randomization produced reasonably comparable treatment groups. Single-attack cases (admitted from the second year onward) constituted one fifth of entrants, and the number of attacks occurring in the three months before entry were evenly distributed among the four treatment groups. Roughly 65 per cent of entrants had ischemic-event symptoms referable to the carotid circulation, 25 per cent to the vertebrobasilar and 10 per cent to both. For each site, more than half the patients were free of residua. Again, the distribution of sites and residua was well balanced among the four treatments, as were neurologic symptoms and signs, coexisting cardiovascular morbidity and risk factors and other laboratory results. Four hundred and thirty-four patients (74 per cent) underwent cerebral angiography before admission to the trial; when symptoms in the carotid territory had led to admission, the angiography rate was 77 per cent.

Maintenance of Blindness

The treatment code was broken for only one patient during the course of the trial, and blindness appeared to have been well maintained. Neurologists were incorrect in their written predictions of the relative efficacy of the trial drugs and correctly predicted which of the four regimens individual patients had been assigned in only 18 per cent of cases (as compared with a chance value of 25 per cent).

Compliance

Pill counts were performed at each follow-up visit. For the final follow-up visit the compliance rate was 92 per cent across all treatment groups. Compliance appeared to be remarkably high, clearly exceeding that observed for most other long-term medications.[17]

Follow-up Observation, Side Effects and Withdrawals

Follow-up study from the seventh day to death, June 30, 1977, or six months after withdrawal (events during this period were included in the primary

*See NAPS document no. 03284 for 4 tables of symptoms that define transient ischemic attacks, symptoms of such attacks before entry, neurologic signs at entry and coexisting cardiovascular morbidity and risk factors at entry. Order from ASIS/ NAPS, c/o Microfiche Publications, P.O. Box 3513, Grand Central Station, New York, N.Y. 10017. Remit, in advance, for each NAPS accession number. Institutions & organizations may use purchase orders when ordering (however, there is a billing charge for this service). Make checks payable to Microfiche Publications. Photocopies are $5. Microfiche are $3 each. Outside the United States and Canada, postage is $1.

Table 1. Number of Transient Ischemic Events Occurring in the Three Months before Entry.

No. of Events	Sulfinpyrazone	Aspirin	Both	Neither	Totals
1	29 (19%)	29 (20%)	40 (27%)	31 (23%)	129 (22%)
2–4	68 (45%)	62 (43%)	57 (39%)	59 (43%)	246 (43%)
5–9	23 (15%)	31 (22%)	19 (13%)	19 (14%)	92 (16%)
10–29	21 (14%)	12 (8%)	18 (12%)	18 (13%)	69 (12%)
30+	11 (7%)	9 (6%)	12 (8%)	10 (7%)	42 (7%)
Subtotals	152 (100%)	143 (100%)	146 (100%)	137 (100%)	578 (100%)
"Several" (not further specified)	4	1	0	2	7
Totals	156	144	146	139	585
Mean duration (mo) between 1st ischemic event & entry	10.0	12.1	12.8	14.5	12.4

analyses) was achieved for 99 per cent of study patients. The duration of follow-up observation averaged 26 months and did not differ among the four treatment groups; 92 per cent of this period was spent on the study drugs.

Among side effects reported at the three-month follow-up visit, pain in the upper abdomen ($P<0.001$) and heartburn ($P<0.05$) were more common among patients allocated to aspirin-containing regimens. A total of 12 patients experienced sufficient gastrointestinal bleeding to produce hematemesis or melena during the trial; six were in the combination-therapy group; four were receiving sulfinpyrazone, two placebo, and none aspirin alone.

Forty-one per cent of study subjects stopped taking the trial medication before the close of the study. Of these 15 per cent had suffered strokes. 42 per cent had experienced further transient ischemic attacks only, and 43 per cent were free of either of these events. Although total withdrawals were evenly distributed across treatment groups, there were some interesting differences. Among withdrawals due to drug side effects (24 per cent of all withdrawals), 72 per cent of patients were receiving aspirin ($P<0.005$). There were also statistically significant differences ($P<0.01$)

across treatment groups among patients whose trial drugs were stopped by their physician (28 per cent of all withdrawals), placebo (41 per cent), sulfinpyrazone (26 per cent), aspirin (20 per cent) and the combination treatment (14 per cent). No differences among treatment groups were observed for the other reasons for withdrawal, including trial drugs stopped by patient (28 per cent), anticoagulants added (14 per cent), patient referred for operation (4 per cent) and patient moved away (3 per cent).

Events

The overall results for all study patients (from the seventh day to death, June 30, 1977, or six months after withdrawal) are summarized in Tables 3 and 4, which compare the observed and expected numbers of events (the latter number generated from the log-rank life-table method of Peto et al.[16] on the assumption that all four regimens are equally efficacious).

No statistically significant interaction (either synergy or antagonism) was found between aspirin and sulfinpyrazone. It was valid and efficient therefore to assess the benefit of aspirin and sulfinpyrazone singly by comparing the respective marginal totals. Aspirin produced a risk reduction of 19 per cent

Table 2. Distribution of Pre-entry Episodes According to Site, Sex and the Presence of Residua.

Site & Residuum	Sulfinpyrazone		Aspirin		Both		Neither		Totals
	MEN	WOMEN	MEN	WOMEN	MEN	WOMEN	MEN	WOMEN	
Carotid, with no residua	41 (35%)	16 (38%)	37 (37%)	25 (56%)	41 (41%)	23 (52%)	31 (34%)	18 (38%)	232 (40%)
Carotid, with residua	31 (27%)	8 (19%)	29 (29%)	8 (16%)	28 (28%)	9 (20%)	27 (30%)	13 (28%)	153 (26%)
Vertebrobasilar, with no residua	17 (15%)	6 (14%)	18 (19%)	4 (9%)	18 (17%)	4 (9%)	12 (13%)	7 (15%)	86 (15%)
Vertebrobasilar, with residua	11 (10%)	3 (10%)	6 (6%)	7 (16%)	8 (8%)	4 (9%)	7 (7%)	3 (4%)	49 (8%)
Both, with no residua	5 (4%)	6 (14%)	5 (5%)	2 (4%)	3 (3%)	3 (7%)	12 (13%)	4 (9%)	40 (7%)
Both, with residua	10 (9%)	2 (5%)	3 (3%)	0 (0%)	4 (4%)	1 (2%)	2 (2%)	3 (6%)	25 (4%)
Totals	115 (100%)	41 (100%)	98 (100%)	46 (100%)	102 (100%)	44 (100%)	91 (100%)	48 (100%)	585 (100%)

(χ^2 = 3.88; P<0.05) for continuing ischemic episodes, stroke or death, whereas patients receiving sulfinpyrazone experienced no risk reduction for these events.

For the "harder" and clinically more important events of stroke or death shown in Table 4, aspirin produced an observed risk reduction of 31 per cent (χ^2 = 3.95; P<0.05), whereas the 10 per cent reduction for sulfinpyrazone was not statistically significant (χ^2 = 0.309; P>0.5).

A summary of the stroke and death status of patients at the conclusion of the study is shown in Table 5. Of the 585 patients participating in the trial 114 suffered stroke or death (or both) from the seventh day of therapy to the end of the study or to six months after withdrawal. These patients were counted as treatment failures at the time of their first event.

Table 3. Effect of Sulfinpyrazone and Aspirin on the Occurrence of Continuing Transient Ischemic Attacks, Stroke or Death among All Patients in the Trial.

TRIAL DRUG	ASPIRIN	NO ASPIRIN	TOTAL ON SULFINPYRAZONE
Sulfinpyrazone	87/92.6* (0.94)†	101/95.5 (1.06)	188/188.2 (1.00)
No sulfinpyrazone	83/96.2 (0.86)	93/79.6 (1.17)	176/175.8 (1.00)
Total on aspirin	170/188.8 (0.90)	194/175.2 (1.11)	
Risk reduction with aspirin	$1 - \frac{0.90}{1.11} = 19\%$ (χ^2 = 3.88; P<0.05)		
Risk reduction with sulfinpyrazone	$1 - \frac{1.00}{1.00} = 0\%$ (χ^2 = 0.00; P>0.90)		

*Ratio of observed/expected no. of events.   †Ratio expressed in decimal form.

Another 23 patients experienced events that were not counted in the efficacy analysis. These included seven strokes that occurred during the first seven days of therapy and four strokes and 12 deaths that occurred more than six months after withdrawal from the study regimen.

The decision to exclude these 23 events did not produce a bias in favor of aspirin; on the contrary it produced a more conservative result. If the seven strokes occurring in the first seven days of therapy were included in the analysis the statistical significance of the aspirin effect would increase (χ^2 = 4.86; P<0.03), and would also increase if the 16 events occurring more than six months after withdrawal were included (χ^2 = 5.09; P<0.03).

Formal analysis showed that the benefit of aspirin was consistent from center to center. Of 24 centers, 14 (contributing 75 per cent of the study patients) exhibited trends in the occurrence of stroke or death that favored aspirin, five (contributing 10 per cent of study patients) exhibited no trend and the remaining five (contributing 15 per cent of study patients) exhibited a reverse trend.

Table 4. Effect of Sulfinpyrazone and Aspirin on the Occurrence of Stroke or Death among All Patients in the Trial.

TRIAL DRUG	ASPIRIN	NO ASPIRIN	TOTAL ON SULFINPYRAZONE
Sulfinpyrazone	20/29.3* (0.68)†	38/31.4 (1.21)	58/61.0 (0.95)
No sulfinpyrazone	26/27.2 (0.96)	30/26.1 (1.15)	56/53.0 (1.06)
Total on aspirin	46/56.6 (0.81)	68/57.4 (1.19)	
Risk reduction with aspirin	$1 - \frac{0.81}{1.19} = 31\%$ (χ^2 = 3.95; P<0.05)		
Risk reduction with sulfinpyrazone	$1 - \frac{0.95}{1.06} = 10\%$ (χ^2 = 0.31; P>0.50)		

*Ratio of observed/expected no. of events.   †Ratio expressed in decimal form.

The original design called for an examination of potential interactions between clinically cogent subgroups of patients and the trial drugs. No statistically significant differences were observed in therapeutic responses to either drug: for the different vascular sites of the transient ischemic attacks, for the presence or absence of residua or for single or multiple attacks before entry. In addition, there was no statistically significant difference in drug response for the presence or absence of amaurosis fugax, with age at entry, or for the presence or absence of demonstrated hypertension, hypercholesterolemia, cigarette smoking or obesity.

However, as suggested in Table 5, formal analysis revealed a statistically significant difference in the response to aspirin between male and female subjects (χ^2 = 9.11; P<0.003). Aspirin was of no benefit in reducing stroke or death among women. There was an observed increase in risk of 42 per cent, but it was not statistically significant (P = 0.35). However, as shown in Figure 1, aspirin markedly reduced the risk of stroke or death among men (risk reduction = 48 per cent; P<0.005).

Statistically significant differences were also found in the response to aspirin with the presence or absence of diabetes (P<0.02) and prior myocardial infarction (P<0.04) at entry; the benefit of aspirin was restricted to patients with negative histories for these conditions. When the life-table analyses were repeated, with simultaneous adjustment for sex, diabetes and prior myocardial infarction, the risk reduction for stroke or death was 35 per cent for aspirin (χ^2 = 5.11; P<0.03) and 15 per cent for sulfinpyrazone (χ^2 = 0.77; P>0.38).

The adjusted life-table analysis also revealed that the lack of benefit with aspirin for diabetic patients was restricted to women. For men, the risk reduction with aspirin was 51 per cent for those with diabetes and 47 per cent for those without diabetes. Thus, the greatest response was found among the 331 men who entered the trial without a prior myocardial infarction. Within this subgroup the observed benefit of aspirin was a risk reduction of 62 per cent for stroke or death (χ^2 = 12.38; P<0.001).

Table 5. Summary of First Events — Stroke or Death.

	MEN				WOMEN			
	SULFINPYRAZONE	ASPIRIN	BOTH	NEITHER	SULFINPYRAZONE	ASPIRIN	BOTH	NEITHER
No. of subjects	115	98	102	91	41	46	44	48
Cases with eligible events								
Death without prior stroke:								
Vascular cause	6	3	4	5	0	1	0	3
Nonvascular cause	3	0	2	2	0	0	0	0
Stroke (death* later in study†):								
Minor	1	1	0	0	0	0	0	0
Moderate	1	0	1	0	0	0	0	0
Major	1	3	0	2	0	1	1	1
Stroke (patient alive at end of study†):								
Minor	10	3	3*	4	1	4	2	2
Moderate	7	5	1	6	3	1	3	2
Major	5	2	1	3	0	2	2	0
Total with eligible events	34	17	12	22	4	9	8	8
Cases with ineligible events								
Events in 1st 7 days	1	2	0	2	2	0	0	0
Events >6 mo after withdrawal	5	3	2	2	2	2	0	0
Total with ineligible events	6	5	2	4	4	2	0	0

*All were vascular deaths.

Table 5 shows that, among men, the fewest events occurred in the group receiving the combination therapy. However, from the life-table analysis, there was no real evidence of any synergism between the two drugs ($\chi^2 = 1.98$; $P = 0.16$).

DISCUSSION

The results of this clinical trial, analyzed according to its design and methodologic decisions made before the analysis, show that patients randomized to aspirin (aspirin alone and aspirin plus sulfinpyrazone) had statistically significantly fewer occurrences of stroke or death than patients not randomized to aspirin (placebo and sulfinpyrazone alone). No such benefit was observed for sulfinpyrazone.

An additional finding in this trial was the different response to aspirin for men and women: only men benefited. This result is compatible with observations from other experiments in both man and other animals. Harris et al. have recently observed that only men showed a beneficial response to aspirin in the prevention of thromboembolism after total hip replacement,[18] and Kaegi et al. found that sulfinpyrazone had a greater effect in reducing thrombosis in arteriovenous shunts among men than among women.[15] Johnson et al. demonstrated statistically significant sex differences in human platelet sensitivity to aggregating stimuli,[19] and Uzunova, in collaboration with the same group of investigators, found that aspirin reduced both the thrombus weight and the mortality rate of testosterone-treated rats with indwelling abdominal aortic cannulas.[20]

Further analysis among men and women combined revealed a statistically significant difference in the response to aspirin between diabetic and nondiabetic subjects and between patients with and without a previous myocardial infarction, in whom the benefit of aspirin was confined to patients without these coexisting morbid conditions. Adjusted life-table analyses showed that the observed sex difference in response to aspirin could not be explained by differences in the distribution of diabetes and prior myocardial infarction between the sexes and also showed that, for men, the benefit of aspirin was not reduced

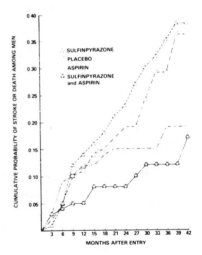

Figure 1. Cumulative Probability of Stroke or Death among Men in the Trial.

by the presence of diabetes. The greatest response to aspirin was observed among men who entered the trial without a previous myocardial infarction.

Since repeated statistical analyses may produce spurious findings one must interpret the outcomes of analyses for specific subgroups with caution. However, the observed highly significant benefit of aspirin in males ($P<0.005$), together with the supporting evidence on sex differences in other studies, leaves little doubt that aspirin is truly efficacious in men.

The results of this randomized trial extend the findings of a somewhat similar trial recently terminated in the United States.[21] In that trial, which involved a smaller number of patients and was restricted to aspirin, a trend toward decreased stroke or death was observed among aspirin takers, but the findings were not statistically significant. However, the United States trial did demonstrate a statistically significant benefit from aspirin for the occurrence of "favorable outcomes" (a composite of reduced transient ischemic attacks, stroke and death). Our trial has extended these findings to the "harder" outcomes of stroke or death and provides an experimentally validated basis for the treatment of a major form of cerebrovascular disease.

It would be reasonable, on the basis of these two studies, to recommend that men with transient cerebral ischemia or minor strokes who are able to tolerate it be treated with aspirin. It must be emphasized that patients suffering from peptic ulcers were excluded from our trial, and we therefore cannot extend our results to these patients nor anticipate the value of enteric-coated aspirin.

The failure of sulfinpyrazone to reduce stroke or death significantly in the present study is in sharp contrast to the recent investigation reporting that sulfinpyrazone was effective in reducing cardiac death in patients with a history of recent myocardial infarction.[22] The reason for this discrepancy is unclear. The most obvious possibility is that aspirin and sulfinpyrazone exert their antithrombotic effect through different mechanisms and that the pathophysiologic processes responsible for cardiac death in patients with myocardial infarction differ from the processes responsible for stroke in patients with a history of transient cerebral ischemia.

Although a life-table analysis did not show a statistically significant interaction between aspirin and sulfinpyrazone, a trend favoring the combination therapy was observed among men. This finding raises the possibility that the combination of aspirin and sulfinpyrazone is the treatment of choice in men, but

such a conclusion would have to be tested by a formal study comparing aspirin with the combination of aspirin and sulfinpyrazone.

REFERENCES

1. Fisher CM: Observations of the fundus oculi in transient monocular blindness. Neurology (Minneap) 9:333-347, 1959
2. Barnett HJM: Transient cerebral ischemia: pathogenesis, prognosis and management. Ann R Coll Physicians Surg Can 7:153-173, 1974
3. Drake WE Jr, Drake MA: Clinical and angiographic correlates of cerebrovascular insufficiency. Am J Med 45:253-270, 1968
4. Friedman GD, Wilson WS, Mosier JM: Transient ischemic attacks in a community. JAMA 210:1428-1434, 1969
5. Millikan CH: Treatment of occlusive cerebrovascular disease, Cerebrovascular Survey Report for Joint Council Subcommittee on Cerebrovascular Disease, National Institute of Neurological and Communicative Disorders and Stroke and National Heart and Lung Institute. (Revised Edition) Edited by RG Siekert. Rochester, Minnesota, Whiting, 1976, pp 141-171
6. Whisnant JP, Matsumoto N, Elveback LR: Transient cerebral ischemic attacks in a community Rochester, Minnesota, 1955 through 1969. Mayo Clin Proc 48:194-198, 1973
7. Barnett HJM: Pathogenesis of transient ischemic attacks, Cerebrovascular Diseases. Edited by P Scheinberg. New York, Raven Press, 1976, pp 1-21
8. Warren BA, Vales O: Electron microscopy of the sequence of events in the atheroembolic occlusion of cerebral arteries in an animal model. Br J Exp Pathol 56:205-215, 1975
9. Pearce JMS, Gubbay SS, Walton JN: Long-term anticoagulant therapy in transient cerebral ischemic attacks. Lancet 1:6-9, 1965
10. Bauer RB, Meyer JS, Fields WS, et al: Joint study of extracranial arterial occlusion. III. Progress report of controlled study of long-term survival in patients with and without operation. JAMA 208:509-518, 1969
11. Smythe HA, Orygzlo MA, Murphy EA, et al: The effect of sulfinpyrazone (Anturan) on platelet economy and blood coagulation in man Can Med Assoc J 92:818-821, 1965
12. Weiss HJ, Aledort LM: Impaired platelet/connective-tissue reaction in man after aspirin ingestion. Lancet 2:495-497, 1967
13. Evans G: Effect of drugs that suppress platelet surface interaction on incidence of amaurosis fugax and transient cerebral ischemia. Surg Forum 23:239-241, 1972
14. Blakely JA, Gent M: Platelets, drugs and longevity in a geriatric population, Platelets, Drugs and Thrombosis. Edited by J Hirsh, JF Cade, AS Gallus et al. Basel, S Karger 1975, pp 284-291
15. Kaegi A, Pineo GF, Shimizu A, et al: The role of sulfinpyrazone in the prevention of arterio-venous shunt thrombosis. Circulation 52:497-499, 1975
16. Peto R, Pike MC, Armitage P, et al: Design and analysis of randomized clinical trials requiring prolonged observation of each patient. II. Analysis and examples. Br J Cancer 35:1-39, 1977
17. Sackett DL: The magnitude of compliance and noncompliance, Compliance with Therapeutic Regimens. Edited by DL Sackett, RB Haynes. Baltimore, Johns Hopkins University Press, 1976, pp 16-19
18. Harris WH, Salzman EW, Athanasoulis CA, et al: Aspirin prophylaxis of venous thromboembolism after total hip replacement. N Engl J Med 297:1246-1249, 1977
19. Johnson M, Ramey E, Ramwell PW: Sex and age differences in human platelet aggregation. Nature 253:355-357, 1975
20. Uzunova AD, Ramey ER, Ramwell PW: Gonadal hormones and pathogenesis of occlusive arterial thrombosis. Am J Physiol 234:H454-H459, 1978
21. Fields WS, Lemak NA, Frankowski RF, et al: Controlled trial of aspirin in cerebral ischemia. Stroke 8:301-316, 1977
22. Anturane Reinfarction Trial Research Group: Sulfinpyrazone in the prevention of cardiac death after myocardial infarction: the Anturane Reinfarction Trial. N Engl J Med 298:289-295, 1978

Rossi observes that few evaluations of the delivery of human services are able to demonstrate any positive outcomes. Rossi asks why that should be and then identifies many major problems that stem from the nature of treatments that have been employed and even more directly from the ways they have been implemented. Rossi's work is especially relevant to issues of integrity of treatment which were raised in the introductory chapter of this volume. He provides many telling examples of various types of failures of integrity of treatment that should be sufficient cause for skepticism when considering reports of still more failed social interventions. Rossi's work provides a useful context for the chapters by Quay and Gottfredson.

3

Issues in the Evaluation of
Human Services Delivery

Peter H. Rossi

There is general agreement that human services (i.e., services that depena on airect inter-personal contact between a deliverer and a client) are difficult to evaluate. This article points out some of the sources of this difficulty: first of all, the theories lying behind the delivery systems are often deficient. Second, delivery of such services is highly operator-dependent and hence often radically transformed in delivery, in ways that tend to negate the intended treatment effects. A strategy for the evaluation of human services delivery is proposed consisting of several steps, in which the underlying theory is first tested, next the ability of any system to deliver the services in question, and finally whether given delivery systems can deliver a relatively pure version of the service.

$\mathcal{T}$he main message of this article is that evaluations of human services delivery systems are difficult to accomplish to the satisfaction of either evaluators or the professionals and administrators responsible for the design and operation of the systems, a theme that can hardly be news to the reader. Going beyond merely the reporting of troubles, this article elaborates this issue in two ways: first, we attempt to provide an understanding of why human services are so hard to evaluate satisfactorily, reviewing in the process both the nature of human services delivery systems and characteristic evaluation approaches. Second, we propose an evaluation strategy that is especially appropriate for human services and which attempts to make possible more satisfactory evaluations.

AUTHOR'S NOTE: *The preparation of this article was aided by a grant from the Russell Sage Foundation, "Measuring the Delivery of Public Services," whose assistance is gratefully acknowledged. The comments of several colleagues, Wayne Alves, Richard Berk, and Huey Chen, on an earlier draft were most helpful in sharpening the article at several points. An earlier version of this article was delivered at a conference on Issues in Service Delivery in Human Service Organizations, held at Wingspread under a grant from the Wood Johnson Foundation and the Silberman Foundation, June 1977.*

From Peter H. Rossi, "Issues in the Evaluation of Human Services Delivery," 2(4) *Evaluation Quarterly* 573-599 (1978). Copyright 1978 by Sage Publications, Inc.

There are many activities that go under the name of evaluation, ranging from offhand opinions, through news reporters' haphazard investigations, to social science research efforts as rigorous as the current state of the art in basic social science permits. For the purposes of this article, I want to restrict the term evaluation to the application of current, state-of-the-art social science research methods to the assessment of whether given social policies can achieve or are achieving their intended aims. This restriction excludes those evaluating activities that do not pretend to be social science and those that pretend but do not succeed. Admittedly, such characterizations are judgment calls, but ones upon which I am sure we would mainly all agree. Also excluded are researches that do not attempt to assess whether programs are fulfilling their goals, and hence are purely descriptive accounts. Policy analyses are also ignored on the grounds that they do not involve primary research activities.[1]

As we shall see in a later section of this article, this definition of evaluation research does cover a very wide range of activities, including research that attempts to discern what are the goals of a program, monitoring activities that seek to ascertain how a program is operating, process or formative evaluative activities, as well as impact assessments and field experiments (see Rossi and Wright, 1977).

If there is any empirical law that is emerging from the past decade of widespread evaluation research activities, it is that the expected value for any measured effect of a social program is zero. In short, most programs, when properly evaluated, turn out to be ineffective or at best marginally accomplishing their set aims. There are enough exceptions to prevent this empirical generalization from being phrased as the "Iron Law of Social Program Evaluation," but the tendency is strong enough to warrant placing bets on negative evaluation outcomes in the expectation of making a steady but modest side income.

The disappointments that have arisen from the results of program evaluations have led, on the one hand, to a reconsideration of programs and, on the other hand, to a reconsideration of evaluation research as an activity. Neither reassessments has led to much progress up to this point. It is apparently the case that evaluation research does not lead immediately to radical improvements in social programs. Nor does the failure of evaluation research to find positive effects of programs lead to its being discarded as an approach. Indeed, one can make the case that nothing succeeds like failure, a paradox whose resolution rests on the understanding that it is composed of half truths. Thus, some believe that evaluation results reflect reality while there is nothing wrong with evaluation research methods. Others believe the exact opposite. Each camp partially neutralizes the other with the result that there is widespread skepticism both about social programs and about evaluation research. Yet so far we cannot do without either.

ON THE NATURE OF HUMAN SERVICES DELIVERY SYSTEMS

The tertiary sector of our economy has been growing at a faster pace than any of the other sectors. Our affluent society apparently has mastered the problems involved in primary extraction and in the manufacture of finished products and has turned of late to putting the finishing touches on the "quality of life." This fine tuning of our social machinery involves the extension of existing human services and the invention of new forms of such services. Through government agencies and private entrepreneurs we now channel a considerable portion of our GNP into providing services that depend essentially on the delivery outside market mechanisms of some sort of "product" to clients through the use of more or less trained intermediaries. The essential aspect of human services is that the mode and content of the delivery itself is the product that is being delivered. Thus education is the interaction between students and the schools, the primary aspect of which is the activity of the classroom. Similarly, job counseling is the contact between a counselor and a client and the product is the content of these encounters. Of course, there is more to human services than human interaction in face-to-face encounters: schools consist of physical structures in which the schooling takes place, textbooks, writing implements, audio-visual aids, and the like. Similarly, job counseling may involve the use of aptitude tests, pamphlets, audio-visual displays, and so on.

The essential premise of human services systems is that there are pockets of deficiencies in our social structure that can be corrected through such encounters, or that naturally occurring processes accompanying human development can be speeded up or made more efficient with the use of human services delivery. We know that without formal schooling children will grow into adults and acquire some degree of verbal language skills. We also know that some families alone could rear children who are literate and have basic mathematical and other skills. But, the family as an institution is not very good at imparting such skills: without the public educational system, the disparities among families in these respects would tend to exacerbate inequalities in skills and knowledge while at the same time lowering the average levels of skills and knowledge below those seemingly required by our need for a relatively literate and knowledgeable labor force. Public education is simply more efficient than the family in aiding young children to develop the necessary skills and knowledge.

What is apparently very clear with respect to education, is not as clear in the cases of other types of human services. Thus, we do not have any institutions that are universally found in all societies that are concerned with the detection of crime or with the rehabilitation of prisoners that are released to freedom. Nor do we expect that unemployed persons will have on hand all the skills that would make it easy for them to get other jobs or that their families and friends will have all the information on hand that will make the transition back into the labor force as easy as possible.

Furthermore we recognize that there are gross inequalities among individuals and households in their abilities to deal successfully with the world about them. Although money cannot buy everything, the rich and the powerfully connected can buy many things on the open market that make life easier. The poor, those disadvantaged in some respect, or those whose skills and aptitudes are deficiently below normal all apparently need help or they will sink further down to new lows in depravity. Obviously, here is where human services come to the rescue.

It should be noted that there are two aspects to these problems of deficiencies in individuals and households. On the one hand, a deficient human being or household lacks or is deprived of experiences and/or resources that are essential to adequate functioning. Thus, according to this view everyone should have a chance at a reasonable job, or a reasonable chance to recover from an illness or injury. In short, we hold to concepts of *social minima* for units of our society. On the other hand, a society with deficient individuals and households suffers some disabilities because of those pockets of deficiency. An unrehabilitated released felon will commit additional crimes. An unemployed man is not contributing to the GNP. There is an underlying concept of a *societal minimum*, a minimum level of functioning for the society.

Corresponding to these two aspects of the problem of deficiencies in individuals and households, there is a duality that, on the one hand, expresses concern for individual suffering under deprivations, and, on the other hand, concern with social control. Thus an unrehabilitated prisoner is deemed to be a potentially unhappy person and also someone who is a menace to social order. In this conception of deficiencies, both society and the deficient individual or household have at least parallel if not identical interests: an unemployed person wants a job and the society wants to have a low level of unemployment or underemployment. Fix one and you fix the other. It should be noted that there are some areas where the parallelism is not so obvious. Certainly, society may want a low crime rate but some professional criminals might have little interest in being rehabilitated to follow occupations that are less interesting and remunerative. This duality becomes expressed with particular force in some human services delivery systems where the interests of clients and the interests of society diverge sharply.[2] We will return to this theme again in this article.

The establishment of a human services delivery system rests upon a number of critical assumptions, as follows.

(1) There are deficient individuals, households, or institutional arrangements. These deficiencies prevent optimal functioning of some individuals and households. Furthermore, the presence of these individual and/or institutional deficiencies in the society presents problems to the society.

(2) If the deficiencies can be corrected or compensated for, functioning can be changed so that individuals and households can function "normally" through the use of some sort of human service "treatment."

(3) The human services "treatment" can be delivered uniformly and widely through the training of delivery personnel and through the placement of them in an organization.

(4) There are no serious conflicts of interests between the social control goals of human services and the goals of clients.

The evaluation of human services delivery systems ordinarily takes place around points two and three. There is little doubt in conventional establishmentarian views that there are deficient institutions, individuals, and households in our society.

There is also agreement that it is possible to compensate for or correct these deficiencies by the provision of some sort of services. Thus schools can be viewed as supplementing family units in the provision of socialization, police as providing social control services that neighborhoods cannot otherwise provide. Transfer payments make up for deficiencies in household income, training programs for deficiencies in skills. Rehabilitation programs attempt to remedy the defects of previous socialization, and so on.

The conventional establishment viewpoint does not go unchallenged, however, by alternative models. Conservatives may recognize the deficiencies but deny that human services can provide effective remedies, or assert that the remedies create more problems than they cure. From the left come diagnoses that assert that deficiencies are inherent in the main structures of our society and can only be remedied by radical restructuring of the society itself. In between are viewpoints that stress institutional deficiencies and those that stress individual or household deficiencies. The extreme conservative and the extreme radical viewpoints, however, do not find their way into evaluative activities since they are based on models that contradict the policies that lead to the provision of services.

Little or no attention has been paid to designing or carrying through evaluations that question the fourth assumption on the above list. The utilitarian heritage of our liberal social philosophy equates—at least in the long run—the utility for an individual with social utility. However, in the case of some social programs this identity of interests is not clear. For some persons of low levels of educational attainment and correspondingly low repertories of job skills, getting a job may not be better than remaining on welfare, as many of the welfare mothers enrolled in the WIN program have learned. The WIN program that attempted to move welfare mothers into the labor force assumed that a low-paying job would appear more attractive to mothers of young children than remaining on the welfare rolls.

The main thrusts of evaluation center around assumptions two and three. It is assumed that there is some way in which these deficiencies in institutions, individuals, and households can be corrected (or compensated for) through treatments and that such treatments can be delivered effectively to clients with reasonable cost-to-benefit ratios. While few evaluations center around the fourth assumption, it can be shown that this assumption when violated in fact plays an important role in the failure of human services delivery systems.

THE FAILURE OF TREATMENT

Assuming that pockets of deficiency exist, then whether a treatment can be devised that will reduce the size of such pockets depends clearly on whether or not the conditions generating the deficiencies are properly understood. In short, treatment depends on the existence of a valid model of how the deficiency is produced and/or maintained. Thus, if a model of black unemployment differentials sees the high unemployment rate among blacks as due to a lack of skills that match current labor market demand, then•a reasonable treatment to apply is vocational training. Obviously, if the model is not valid, then vocational training will fail as a treatment. Or, if the model underlying the design of a prison is that criminals are members of a deviant subculture, then the design might minimize contact among prisoners and emphasize lofty sermons on the straight life. Clearly such a treatment is likely to fail.

An infinity of models may be devised to explain such deficiencies as poverty, crime, unemployment, illiteracy, and the corresponding treatments may also be infinite in number. Indeed, the same model may lead to quite different treatments depending on whether one emphasizes one or another part of the model. Thus a production-function model for public education might lead one to emphasize school inputs to learning or emphasize family inputs, the first treatment leading to heavier investment in teachers, schools, or teaching methods, while the second leading possibly to childrearing instruction for parents.

Furthermore, every treatment can be shown to "work" in the sense that, after experiencing the treatment, some of the deficient persons or households will improve. Our society is highly stochastic, with individuals and households moving from state to state with probabilities that are significantly large. Thus, poor individuals and households are quite likely to cross the poverty line if left untreated and some portion of those who are treated will also cross the line and appear to have been affected by the treatment. While the old are not going to get young over time, the opposite process appears to make young adult criminals into more law-abiding older adults. Men and women who never finished high school on time often manage to get their diplomas later in life. Some persons who have received vocational training will have higher wage rates after training, but so will their counterparts who have not taken training but who are just a few months older. In short, "spontaneous remission" is characteristic of these deficiencies.

Finally, it is difficult to separate the treatment from the manner of delivery. Human services treatments that are given by exceptionally devoted persons are as likely to be efficacious because of the devotion expressed in the delivery as because of the treatment. Individual tutoring of children seems always to work for the rich who have been able to hire skilled and devoted teachers. The results of any brand of therapy wielded by a devoted psychotherapist is probably as good as any other. However, the same treatment administered by the indifferent and unskilled may fail to have any impact. The *delivery* of human services treatments is critically important to their effectiveness, a theme that is treated at length in the next section of this paper. Before proceeding, however, it is important to point out that treatments can fail in the first place because they are inappropriate to the problem, because they have been generated by an invalid model of the phenomenon in question. They can also fail because the treatment itself has been poorly specified and is in fact indistinguishable from its mode of delivery.

THE FAILURE OF DELIVERY SYSTEMS

Assuming for the moment that an efficacious and theoretically valid treatment has been devised, then the next question is whether it can be delivered on a large scale. A related problem is whether the delivery system devised for the treatment either negates the treatment or transform it into something else. The delivery system is of special importance in human services because the ultimate delivery point is a human being whose needs may be such that they work at cross purposes to appropriate delivery.

A few examples of how delivery systems can fail may be appropriate at this point.

(1) The problem of the nonprogram. This is the case where a delivery system has been set up or an existing system has been designated as a deliverer, but no treatments are delivered. Lest the reader believe that these are rare instances, it turns out that there are many examples, as follows.

A network of advisors was set up to provide advice to new M.D.'s sent out to rural areas to help the doctors become accustomed to their new (and presumably strange) environments. Evaluators sent out after a year or so of the program discovered that the advisors rarely contacted the doctors after the first visit. Apparently, advisors (who kept on receiving their stipends) discovered, as did the doctors, that no advice was needed or wanted or appropriate.[3]

The Office of Education's attempt to find out exactly what new educational services were delivered to children in schools in poor neighborhoods under Title I of ESEA have been repeatedly frustrated by the inability of local educational authorities to describe their Title I activities in any detail (McLaughlin, 1975).

Attempts to decriminalize alcoholism and to use the police to bring alcoholics into treatment centers in Washington, D.C. and Minneapolis have found that when the police stopped arresting people for public drunkenness they did not necessarily scoop them up and bring them to treatment centers. Police get credits for arrests but not for ambulance service.

(2) The problem of creaming. Although the world is stochastic, it is also lawful. Hence a delivery system can simulate success by delivering treatments to individuals who are most likely to recover or to households that are most likely to rise spontaneously out of their deficient state. Some examples follow.

In the first years of the Job Corps, the screening methods used to test for "poverty" eliminated those whose families were too affluent, and for "potential," eliminated those who seemed "unlikely to benefit from the treatment."

FHA guarantees for mortgages, originally proposed as a means of helping the poor to purchase homes, became a subsidy for the middle class as FHA administrators took care to guarantee loans only for those who had good credit ratings.

Fellowships for graduate study, proposed as a move to bring more talent into particular fields of national importance, are given out competitively, assuring that those are subsidized who would go into such fields anyhow because of interest and aptitude (Davis, 1962).

A Planned Parenthood Clinic set up in the early 1950s on the South Side of Chicago ostensibly to provide contraceptive services to black ghetto residents found itself so swamped with student clients from the University of Chicago that it made few efforts to reach the blacks of the South Side.

(3) The problem of delivery negating treatment. The modes of delivery may operate in ways that negate the treatments. Some examples follow.

Case workers in a state public welfare system were found to have developed a classification of "good" clients and "bad" clients, the former to whom they offered all the options for payments allowable under regulations and the latter to whom they gave payment options only when asked for specifically. "Good" clients were those who presented themselves as suppliants and expressed gratitude easily for help proferred while "bad" clients were those who demanded payments as a matter of right.[4]

A negative income tax experiment, sparked in part by a desire to test a system that did not have a demeaning means test, developed a system of monthly family income reports that kept closer track of participating family earnings than could any public welfare system (Rossi and Lyall, 1976).

An experiment that was to test the effectiveness of group counseling in prison used prison guards as group leaders (Kassebaum et al., 1971).

There is some evidence that the contract learning experiments were sabotaged by the school systems into which they were conducted, with the consequence that the treatment was delivered in only a subset of the thirteen schools originally contracted for (Gramlich and Koshel, 1975).

(4) The problem of uncontrolled treatment variation. Discretion on program implementation left to the front line delivery system may be so great that treatments vary in significant ways from site to site. Such intersite variation may exist especially when treatments are forms of delivery with the content of services to be delivered left to local delivery systems to determine. Some of the best examples can be found in the early programs of the Office of Economic Opportunity, as follows.

The Community Action Program left considerable discretion to local communities to engage in a variety of actions, constrained only by the requirement that there be "maximum feasible participation" on the part of poor citizens. As a consequence, it is almost impossible to document what the CAP programs in fact did.

A similar lack of content definition also characterized the Model Cities Program.

Project Head Start gave money to local communities to set up preschool teaching projects for underprivileged children. Programs started up had a variety of sponsoring agencies, differing coverages, varying content, and the like. To evaluate Head Start is to evaluate a program that is so heterogeneous in essential respects that it cannot be called *a* program at all.

(5) The problem of ritual compliance. Lack of commitment to a program on the part of a front line delivery system can have the result that minimal delivery of the program occurs. The treatment in not negated, it simply is watered down almost to the point of nonexistence.

In an effort to assure more contact between professors and their students, a state legislature mandated semester reports from each professor with detailed counts of "contact hours" to be entered. A considerable professorial effort went into stretching every potential contact opportunity into a contact hour. Thus, there were more advisees reported than there were students to be advised.

To comply with affirmative action directives, university departments often place ads in national professional publications for positions already informally filled, announcing the selection officially only when replies to ads have been received and the resulting applications rejected.

(6) The problem of overly sophisticated treatments. Some treatments that might work well in the hands of highly trained and highly motivated deliverers may be given to a mass delivery system whose levels of training and motivation are considerably less and hence the treatment fails. In short, there is a considerable difference between pilot and production runs of sophisticated treatments.

Thus, although many educators have come forth with teaching methods that have worked well within their experimental classrooms and schools, the adoption of such teaching methods in ordinary school systems have not proved very successful. (In part this is a problem of the delivery being part of the treatment.) Computer-assisted learning, individualized instruction, and so on, are examples of techniques that seem to do less well when applied outside of the centers where they were developed.

(7) The problem of client heterogeneity. A treatment that works well with one type of client may not work well with another. This problem is especially acute if the pilot tests of a treatment are done with a special population and then applied in a production run with a quite different client population.

In the New Jersey-Pennsylvania Income Maintenance Experiment, ethnicity turned out to be one of the characteristics distinguishing subgroups with different work effort responses: black households increased their work effort under a guaranteed income plan; whites decreased; and Puerto Ricans showed no significant work effort effect (all compared with controls who were not on payment plans) [Rossi and Lyall, 1976].

The early somewhat spectacular finding that preschool children could be taught very effectively using electric typewriters, did not hold up in repeated studies. Apparently middle-class preschool children were aided by the method, especially in the skilled hands of its originator, while lower-class children were unable to benefit similarly from the treatment.

(8) The problem of client rejection of treatment. This problem stems from rejection of the treatment by potential clients with the result that the treatment cannot be delivered to the extent desired.

The Housing Allowance Experiments currently underway have experienced participation rates considerably below (30%-40%) full coverage of eligible population groups (Carlson and Heinberg, 1977) despite apparently obvious advantages to potential participants.

Community Mental Health Centers designs to provide outpatient treatment to clients in need find that it is difficult to get potential clients to come to the centers. Even patients conditionally discharged from state mental hospitals who have been assigned to centers as a condition of their discharge often do not appear at centers for their treatments.

WHY TREATMENTS FAIL

The litany of delivery problems outlined above has its roots in the fact that human services delivery cannot be made operator-free. Rules for deliverers can be developed that seemingly take discretion out of the hands of operators, but the proliferation of rules itself can be seen as one of the sources of operator discretion. Thus the manuals governing (in principle) the activities of a caseworker in the Massachusetts Public Welfare Department are nearly a foot thick, more than anyone can be expected to know intimately. Hence, there is considerable variation from caseworker to caseworker, from local office to local office, and from season to season as to which rules are enforced and which provisions of the manual are in fact used.

Another way of putting this problem is that many human services treatments are insufficiently robust and are unable to survive mishandling on the part of delivery systems. Even seemingly robust treatments in the form of transfer payments can become transformed in the course of being administered by a delivery system.

Often insufficient attention is paid to the problem of motivating human services operators to deliver treatments as specified. Thus, in the case of the Washington, D.C. and Minneapolis decriminalization of public drunkenness, no thought was given to motivating the police on the beat to escort drunks to the alcoholism treatment centers. Similarly, the contract learning experiments made not attempts to reassure the regular teachers who feared that their jobs were threatened by the private contractors who competed with their regular classes.

Another source of difficulty may lie in the professionalization of some of the deliverers of human services. It is of the essence of a professional occupation that incumbents function with minimal supervision, the assumption being that professionals need little supervision because their training fits them to make appropriate discretionary decisions about the content, pacing, and outcome of their work. When to professionalization is added immunity from market and price effects, than a delivery system may be particularly difficult to affect by administrative directives mandating changes in delivery practices. Thus, my colleagues and I found in a comparative study of fifteen major metropolitan areas that police practices and public welfare agency practices were more subject to variation from place to place than were the practices of educators (Rossi et al., 1974). Indeed, it was possible to predict more closely how police behaved toward black residents (as reported by blacks themselves) on the basis of policies professed by police chiefs and mayors than it was to predict how teachers behaved toward their pupils on the basis of pronouncements of mayors and school superintendents. The behavior of the caseworkers in public welfare agencies fell in between but resembled more the case of the police than the case of public education.

The current issues surrounding the cost of medical care and its quality also illustrates how difficult it is to establish some modicum of control over a highly professionalized delivery system. Despite the proliferation of hospital planning councils, hospitals still tend to build more beds than they need and to install expensive equipment the use of which frequently fails to justify the investment. Serious abuses exist in the overuse of surgery and in the wholesale prescribing of tranquilizing drugs and antibiotics in cases where such treatments are clearly not indicated. A peer review system functions only when the abuses are flagrantly obvious.

These observations suggest that we need an engineering counterpart to the "pure" social sciences. An academic mechanical physicist can design a bridge according to a new concept, but it takes an engineer to select the materials, prepare sites, and work out details of how the new design should be implemented. Insufficient attention has been paid to the development side of "research and development" activities in the social sciences.[5] We need to devise ways in which we can test out various production forms of a treatment in which the characteristics of delivery system are taken into account and to develop treatments robust enough to survive considerable mishandling.

A STRATEGY FOR EVALUATING HUMAN
SERVICES DELIVERY SYSTEMS

In this section we propose a strategy for evaluating human services delivery systems that takes into account the characteristics of such systems as described in previous sections. Before doing so, however, it is important to point out that only those human services delivery systems (or any social program, for that matter) can be evaluated whose intended aims are delimitable, measurable, and not inherently contradictory. For example, a program that is designed to increase the quality of life in America cannot be evaluated until specific content is given to the phrase "quality of life," a difficult, if not impossible task. Incompatible goals are also a contradiction of evaluability: thus a preschool educational program that is designed to serve all segments of the class structure and at the same time decrease the gap in learning between classes is most likely contradictory in aims and hence cannot be evaluated.[6]

Assuming human services programs that have definite, noncontradictory, and measurable goals, then there are three points at which the treatment involved can be and should be evaluated.

(1) The question may be raised whether the treatment *is effective* in achieving its goals, given the most favorable delivery method.

(2) There is the question whether the treatment *can be delivered* by a delivery system that can reach the appropriate target population at reasonable cost levels while maintaining the integrity of the treatment.

(3) There is the issue of whether a given delivery system that, in principle, can deliver a treatment *in fact will do so* at a level of quantity and quality necessary to assure a reasonable level of effectiveness and will be accepted by the target population.

Note that as far as evaluation outcomes are concerned, these three questions are interlocking ones. A treatment that has been found to be ineffective on the first level cannot be evaluated as successful on the second and third levels. Similarly, a treatment that is judged effective on some pilot basis may fail to be effective in practice because it cannot be delivered either by the best of all possible delivery systems or by the usual mass delivery system that an enacted program would use.

This nested quality of the three evaluation questions strongly suggests that an effective evaluation strategy ought to be based on a progression of evaluative activities proceeding from an attempt to answer positively the first question, and so on through all three.

(1) Is a treatment effective? A treatment in principle is effective to the extent that the treatment flows from a model of the phenomenon in question that is a valid reflection of the process involved. Thus a treatment for juvenile delinquency that is based on a model of delinquency in which brain injury is the causative agent is likely to fail because the underlying model is faulty.[7] An effective treatment should be effective, at minimum, under delivery circumstances that are most favorable to effectiveness and, at maximum, be effective no matter what the form of delivery.

These considerations lead to a first step in an effective strategy of evaluation, that is, one concerned with testing the effectiveness of a treatment under maximum favorable conditions or under a varying set of conditions that is sufficiently diverse to make possible the separation of effectiveness of a treatment from its mode of delivery. Indeed, the evaluative activity that is variously called "process evaluation" or "formative evaluation" is often most appropriate to this task.

It also makes sense that treatment evaluations at this stage should be small scale, "pilot" studies that maximize internal validity—in this case, the ability to make strong statements about the effectiveness of the treatment. Carefully designed randomized experiments would be particularly appropriate, assuming that the treatments lend themselves to laboratory or field experimentation, an issue to which we will turn later. If the treatment is one that can vary in amount of intensity and can be delivered by a number of techniques that appear a priori to be roughly equally appropriate, then a pilot experiment could be designed that would vary level of treatment and delivery technique simultaneously. The end result of such an elaborate pilot phase would be more useful knowledge about the more appropriate levels of treatment and the most effective modality of delivery.

A good example of the type of design suggested above can be found in the Kassebaum et al. (1971) study of group counseling with prison inmates in which several levels of treatment and technique were integrated into a randomized design. One may reasonably raise the question concerning this study of whether the treatments varied enough in levels from one experimental condition to another and whether there was sufficient variation in the techniques of delivery,[8] but the general outline of the design remains a good one and particularly appropriate to the issue addressed in this section.

It should be noted that randomized controlled experiments in human services delivery are relatively rare. The major field experiments in social programs of the past decade typically center around the delivery of transfer payments as treatments rather than human services as typically defined. The five negative income tax experiments involve payments to poor and near-poor families that are conditioned upon their earnings. The current experiments on housing allowances for poor and near-poor families also use transfer payments as treatments, in some experimental groups being conditional upon improvements in their housing. The health insurance experiment currently under way also involves federal subsidies on a sliding scale for full coverage medical and hospital insurance. Finally the Department of Labor financed experiment providing unemployment compensation payments to felons released from state prisons is another example of the use of money as a treatment.

Of course, it is an oversimplification to regard the payments in such experiments as fully comparing the treatments: In fact, the treatments consist not only of the payments but of all the contacts between the paying organizations and families in the experimental groups. In the negative income tax experiments monthly reports of earnings were required as a condition of eligibility and some discretionary powers were given to persons who computed payments.

Nevertheless, it is fair to say that the reason transfer payments are at the core of the treatments studied in the major field experiments is because payments appear to be robust treatments that can be standardized and delivered in relatively fixed ways compared to such treatments as parole supervision, job counseling, and the like. Such experiments are easier to interpret since one can be more certain that the treatments were delivered—checks can be traced, amounts can be ascertained. In contrast, whether parole supervision of any sort actually took place is problematic and parole supervision can range in intensity from brief superficial contacts between a parole officer and a parolee to more intensive encounters. It is instructive to note that the one negative income tax experiment in Gary, Indiana, that tried to introduce social services as an additional treatment in one of the experimental conditions failed to implement that treatment. It was simply too difficult to standardize sufficiently the social services rendered, to deliver the services in a systematic way, and to get client acceptance of such services.

This suggests that designing human services delivery experiments according to classical randomized design will be very difficult, a task that is sure to tax the ingenuity of experimental design experts and social service professionals. For, unless the treatment can be made more or less standard and delivered in a standard way, then the interpretation of experimental results will be difficult, if not impossible.

(2) Can the treatment be delivered? A treatment that survives the tests suggested above using a randomized design next has to be considered from the point of view of an appropriate delivery system. If the delivery techniques have been varied in the pilot experimental phase, some knowledge about effective delivery has also resulted from this phase. Such results, however, are not to be trusted entirely. A treatment that works well within an experimental context with personnel specially trained by an advocate of the treatment may fail in the field when an attempt is made to use personnel and organizations that cannot match the dedication and skill of the group that has run the randomized experiment. In short, the next task is to test the external validity of a treatment, its ability to be transferred into the "real" world of existing organizations.

There are a few precedents for such delivery system testing that can be cited. The Follow Through Planned Variation evaluations of the Office of Education (Cline, 1975) were intended to perform this function for a variety of compensatory learning techniques, but the execution was flawed. The idea behind the evaluation was to get several school systems each to choose one of several teaching methods, to implement those innovations within the school systems, making provision for reasonable controls within schools. Since there were to be several school systems testing each method, it was hoped that information would be generated on the relative effectiveness of the different teaching methods and on the relative effectiveness of variations in the delivery systems. The failure of the evaluation occurred because treatments were varied in unsystematic ways when implemented.

A second example is the so-called "Administrative Experiment" designed to test the ability of local authorities to administer a housing allowance program (Carlson and Heinberg, 1977). Local communities were asked to bid for designation as a demonstration for a housing allowance program in their cities. Eight successful bidders were chosen from among competing cities. Agencies within the cities varied from place to place—in some cities the program was administered by separately established agencies, in other cities by an already established housing authority or planning department. Cities were chosen to represent a spread in size and region, although none of the very large metropoli were among the group. Unfortunately, the administrative demonstrations were not monitored carefully enough and with sufficient attention to problems of valid inferences about relative effectiveness so that at the present time it is not possible to make statements about how effective the delivery systems were.[9]

A third example is the Transitional Aid Research Project of the Department of Labor. In a pilot randomized experiment in Baltimore, the U.S. Department of Labor (1977) found that in providing payments resembling unemployment compensation payments to prisoners released from the Maryland state prisons, those who received payments were less often arrested for property crimes in the year following their release. The pilot experiment was run by a dedicated researcher, Dr. Kenneth Lenihan, who recruited a staff of counselors, payment clerks, and so on. Currently the Department of Labor is funding two additional large scale randomized experiments in the states of Georgia and Texas, in which state agencies administer the payment plans and collect data on released felons. Up to the date of writing, the experimental design appears to have been implemented correctly and payment systems are operating well. The purpose of the larger scale experiment was both to replicate the Baltimore experiences of Lenihan and also to test whether or not existing state agencies can administer such payments in a way that would retain their effectiveness. The administration of the plan and the collection of research data on the released felons are being monitored carefully by the Department of Labor and a set of subcontractors.

This Project provides an excellent example of research designed to test whether existing delivery systems can function effectively in delivering a treatment that is known to be effective. One might have wanted a few more replications, possibly ones administered by different state agencies and covering some of the largest metropolitan areas, but the appetites of researchers are well known to be insatiable.

(3) Is a treatment being delivered? Assuming that a treatment passes with flying colors the tests described in 1 and 2 above, there is still the question whether, when implemented as a statutory program with widespread coverage, treatments are in fact being delivered in appropriate ways. To answer this question requires the setting up of monitoring systems that measure and assess treatment delivery.

To the extent that the human services treatment delivered is some interpersonal transaction between a deliverer and a client, the measurement of delivery is rendered extremely difficult and expensive. To the extent that there is some observable, relatively objective outcome of the delivery, then the task of monitoring becomes that much easier and less expensive. For example, it is possible to obtain fairly accurate counts of how many clients have been served by a family planning agency and how many intrauterine devices or other types of contraceptive methods have been prescribed. Similarly, AFDC client loads can be counted, authorized payments summed and averaged, and other quantitative indices defined and computed. What is difficult to measure is the style and content of contraceptive advice given in client visits or whatever counseling takes place in the caseworkers' contacts with AFDC applicants. Were clients treated with due regard for their human dignity? Was the advice appropriate to the client? Did the counseling given resemble closely enough what the program designers had intended to be given? These essentially qualitative aspects of client-deliverer contacts are difficult to measure at an acceptable level of cost.

The remarks made above are not to be taken as meaning that quantitative measures of client-deliverer contacts are not important. Indeed, one can learn a great deal about how human services are being delivered by considering such relatively simple indices as client loads, socioeconomic composition of client populations, counts of specific service delivered, and so on. For example, in the routine monitoring of hospitalizations in a New England state, it was discovered that in one of the hospitals an extraordinary number of appendectomies were being conducted. Further investigation brought to light the fact that one surgeon was contributing almost all of the surplus appendectomies. The inquiry led to the setting up of a hospital peer review committee that subsequently disciplined the offending doctor. Or, a comparison across states in the per capita state prison populations brings to light some startling interstate differences in criminal justice systems, some states moving prisoners quickly through their systems and others retaining prisoners for longer terms. Such "epidemiological" studies of the functioning of delivery systems can be very valuable for understanding the gross features of the delivery system, for pinpointing problems in functioning, and, in some cases, for laying the basis for an evaluation of effectiveness.[10]

An accounting system that is run by the delivery system itself is clearly the least expensive way of monitoring, although subject to the possibility of generating self-servicing statistics. A reporting system that is useful both to the delivery system and to outside monitors is obviously desirable since such a system tends to motivate the deliverers to maintain high quality. Thus, in the juvenile court system of Connecticut a reporting system was devised that served both as the data base for monitoring operation and as the case file on each juvenile brought through the system. The forms used were developed through extensive consultation between a central research and evaluation staff, caseworkers, and the juvenile courts. As a consequence, the quality of the resulting data appears to be high.

Monitoring the more qualitative aspects of human services delivery is a more difficult and expensive task. Yet there are some good examples: Reiss (1971) placed observers in police patrol cars who filled out systematic reports of each encounter between the police and citizens in a sample of duty tours. In a now classic study of a state employment service, Blau (1955) sat in as an observer as clients were interviewed as they registered in the agency.

"Windshield" surveys have been devised to measure the cleanliness of streets in various neighborhoods as a measure of the effectiveness of street cleaning and garbage removal crews. In some of the studies, streets were compared against "standardized" photographs indicating extremely, moderately, and poorly cleaned streets and the streets rated according to their resemblances to the standard photographs.

Considerable effort has gone into the measurement of human services delivery systems through interviews with clients (or potential clients). Thus, my colleagues and I analyzed interviews with samples of black residents in fifteen major metropolitan areas that asked about instances of police brutality either experienced directly or known about, as well as satisfaction with the services of neighborhood stores, schools, and public welfare offices (Rossi et al., 1974). In the New Jersey-Pennsylvania Income Maintenance Experiment, participants were asked about their knowledge of the payment plans they had experienced in an effort to discern whether correct knowledge about the plans experienced affected their labor force responses (Rossi and Lyall, 1976).

Direct observation of deliverer-client contacts are obviously expensive and in addition unwieldly as a research operation. It is also not clear the extent to which the presence of observers affects the ways in which human services are delivered. Reiss (1971) informs the readers of his monograph that the police in the patrol cars soon became accustomed to having observers around, but this observation can only be an impression.

Client interviews are cheaper and are potentially quite useful. It is important that such interviews not rely simply on global assessments of delivery system behavior (e.g., how satisfied are you with your case-worker?), but also provide quite specific information on the content and utility of contacts. For example, it probably is more useful to know whether the deliverers address clients by their first or last name than it is to know the clients' assessment of how politely they have been handled. Similarly, it is more important to know whether a policeman stopped and frisked an arrestee than it is to know whether he thinks the police "are doing a good job."

This article has devoted so much space to the topic of monitoring ongoing programs out of the conviction that such activities are extremely important in the assessment of the effectiveness of human services delivery. A treatment that is not being delivered or is being delivered in a defective way obviously cannot be effective, although correct delivery is not any guarantee of effectiveness. The same ingenuity that has brought social science research to its present state of competence in other areas, if focused on the problem of program monitoring, should result in effective and informative monitoring operations. A monitoring system is useful not only for evaluation but also for correcting administrative faults. A human services systems administrator who does not know whether his program is operating as designed is obviously an inefficient administrator who has to operate largely in the dark.

(4) Is the production run of a program effective? The final question is
whether a treatment that has been proven effective in a tightly designed
pilot experiment, and has been shown to be delivered correctly and
efficiently by a delivery system, is in fact having its intended effects
when implemented as a matter of social policy. Presumably, a treatment
that has survived the previous hurdles should be effective, but not
necessarily so. There are many intervening events that can lead to
ineffectiveness as an enacted social policy. Specification error (or
erroneous models) in the original experiment may have misled the
investigator into mistaking a correlated effect for a real one. Historical
shifts may have made an appropriate model into an inappropriate one;
for example, the unemployed in times of high unemployment may
contain a different mix of population types than does the unemployed
in times of low unemployment. Or women seeking birth control information in a period of high fertility may be quite different with different
needs for treatment than women who come to birth control clinics in
a period of low fertility. It is also possible that the pilot experiment
inadvertently creamed the target population of clients.

An ongoing social program that is already in place and functioning
at its intended coverage and funding cannot be evaluated through the
use of the more powerful research designs. In particular, randomized
experiments ordinarily cannot be used since the construction of a
control group through randomization will mean depriving some individuals or households of treatments to which they would otherwise be
entitled by law or ethics. Hence, such programs usually can only be
evaluated by quasi-experimental methods. It should be pointed out
that the success of quasi-experimental methods depends very heavily
for their utility on a valid understanding of the causal processes underlying the phenomenon in question. Thus, if we want to evaluate the
effectiveness of family planning programs in reducing fertility rates, we
clearly have to know something about what effects fertility in order to
hold constant in our statistical models those factors that affect fertility
in the absence of a family planning program.

There are essentially two broad types of quasi-experimental designs
that are appropriate to the evaluation of ongoing programs.

(1) Correlational designs based on cross-site program variation. Our
nested forms of government provide a useful source of variation in
program delivery. Thus, we can anticipate that in some states and in
some local communities a program will have excellent coverage and in
other places be so slight as to be almost nonexistent (and sometimes, in

fact, nonexistent because of the failure of states and local governments to opt for the program). At the present time our public welfare system is hardly uniform across states and sometimes within states. Some public welfare programs are extremely generous (e.g., New York and Massachusetts) and others are penurious beyond belief (e.g., Alabama and Mississippi). Coverage may vary from state to state, with the more generous states in this respect covering not only families whose heads are unemployable but also heads that are employable. In some places, efforts are made to publicize the welfare program eligibility requirements in order to obtain as large a coverage as possible of the eligible population. In other states, public welfare eligibility requirements are held almost as state secrets.

This variation from place to place in the intensity and coverage of treatments provides a means for evaluating effectiveness. Simply put, treatment levels that are heavy and broadcast widely among eligible populations should produce more effects than do treatment levels with the opposite characteristics, ceteris paribus. Thus, Cutright and Jaffe (1977), in their analysis of the effectiveness of the family planning program, essentially examined the fertility rates of groups of counties that had programs with wide coverage with the fertility rates of groups of counties with opposite program characteristics, holding constant county characteristics known to be related to fertility (e.g., age composition, socioeconomic level, and the like).

The phrase ceteris paribus is, of course, the obstacle to be overcome. Hence the stress on a priori understanding of the phenomenon in question.[11] It is previous knowledge about what cause inter-area variation in fertility that made it possible for Cutright and Jaffe (1977) to make other things equal statistically. It is the questioning of that knowledge in the Coleman report that produced the controversies surrounding its interpretation, with the economists claiming that Coleman had misspecified his model of how individuals varied naturally in their educational achievement levels.

(2) Time series designs based on variation over time. The second approach to the evaluation of ongoing programs rests on the existence of variations over time in the extent and intensity of treatments. Thus, changes in the level of treatment obviously occur at the start of a program, the change going from zero to an initial delivery level, and subsequent changes in policy produce variations in the amount and coverage of treatments over time.

A change in one or both respects should produce a change in a desired effect, ceteris paribus, if the treatment is effective. In a time series analysis of the effect of the 1974 Massachusetts gun control law, Deutscher and Alt (1977) found that crimes in which firearms were used declined significantly after the gun control law went into effect. His analysis took into account the long-range trends in such crimes in Massachusetts by constructing a model that fit such trends and extrapolating that model to cover the period after the gun control law went into effect. Similar analyses have been made of the effect of changes in our national labor relations laws on the incidence of strikes, and of the changes in speed limits on traffic deaths.

The ability to undertake time series analyses depends, obviously, on the existence of accurate measurements of intended program effects taken over a relatively long period of time. Thus deaths from traffic accidents, reports of crimes committed and known to the police, the incidence of industrial strikes, and fertility measures are all examples of measures for which relatively long and reliable time series exist. For other types of intended effects for which time series are not available, longitudinal analyses cannot be taken.

The technical issues surrounding the use of cross-sectional and time series designs have been dealt with at length in other publications (Hibbs, 1976). One need only summarize in the context of this paper: a variety of statistical models are available that, when appropriately employed in connection with valid substantive models, can produce firm evaluations of ongoing programs.

CONCLUSIONS

This article has attempted to provide a generalized characterization of human services and a detailed account of some of the difficulties in evaluating the effectiveness of such services. We pointed out that the critical feature of human services is that they are highly operator-dependent and difficult to standardize. Hence, it is alway problematic whether a treatment is being delivered as designed, whether the mode of delivery is adding some unintended treatment to the basic one, and finally whether a treatment can be delivered in a reasonable way at all by the typical human services organizations.

The paper also sets forth a strategy for the evaluation of human services treatments. A progressive series of tests are suggested starting with a tight experimental design for the evaluation of the effectiveness of a treatment under the best possible mode of delivery, through a final evaluation by means of correlational designs that test the effectiveness of a human services program that has been enacted into social policy.

Although the article stresses the boobytraps and pitfalls that lie in the way of someone wishing to do evaluations of human services treatments, it is not intended to advocate an avoidance of this area of social science research. Rather, by pointing out some of the difficulties, it is hoped that the article has presented a challenge to some of the more ingenious research designers to try their hand at this rather difficult game.

NOTES

1. Policy analysis may be viewed as the application of social science theory along with the results of social science research to the examination of policy alternatives. Properly undertaken, policy analyses assume that alternative policies have been evaluated and that their effectiveness values are known.

2. This duality is closely related to that involved in the provision of public goods. It makes little sense for any individual to pay taxes unless paying taxes is made compulsory for all since the marginal utility for any individual of the majority of public services is very small.

3. The author cannot cite a public reference for this example, since knowledge of it stems from a consulting relationship with the organization that contracted to deliver the services.

4. These generalizations stem from observations made of caseworker/client transactions in four Massachusetts public welfare offices during the summer of 1976.

5. The R&D centers funded by the Office of Education, although not very successful as a group either in research or in development, were in principle a step in the right direction. They were intended as centers in which effective educational treatments would be developed and then tested out in cooperation with school systems until an effective diffusable system could be worked out. Some of the reasons for the poor performance of the R&D centers are given in Rossi (1976).

6. There are two types of contradiction possible: first, some goals are logically incompatible in the sense that the achievement of one goal makes it logically impossible to achieve another goal (e.g., reducing payments to unemployed persons, ceteris paribus, and maintaining the purchasing power of the unemployed). Second, some goals are empirically incompatible in the sense that achieving one goal empirically implies diminishing the ability to achieve another. The example given in the text is that of empirical incompatibility.

7. If the treatment is frontal lobotomy, the treatment is likely to be successful in the sense that it cures delinquent behavior, but also "cures" (or eliminates) other types of behavior as well, including much of the behavior forms that allow the individual to

function normally in the society. A treatment that is effective must not only eliminate the condition in question but also not impose other deficiencies upon the individual. Untoward side effects must also be avoided, a point that may often be overlooked.

8. The question whether an experiment of this sort tested a sufficiently wide range of the treatment is one that can always be raised post facto when results are found that indicate that treatments had no discernible effect. The question is whether the advocates of the treatment and its potential users agree a priori that the range of treatment covers what they consider to be a reasonable test of the treatments' effectiveness. As a matter of strategy, I suggest that such treatments exceed the range of reasonable treatment levels, anticipating the criticism that the trial of the treatment was unfair in the range of treatments tested.

9. It should be borne in mind that one of the motivations of the Department of Housing and Urban Development in funding the administrative "experiment" was to buy political support and time while two very well designed randomized experiments were being run: a demand experiment is testing the effectiveness of the treatments in bringing about an increase in the quality of housing occupied by families under allowance payment plans. A supply experiment would test the responses of local housing markets to the existence of payment plans, hopefully by increasing the supply of acceptable low-cost housing, as opposed to raising prices on existing housing.

10. Two outstanding examples of the use of existing records in extremely creative ways ought to be cited here: first, Cutright and Jaffe (1977) used counts of clients served in family planning clinics in groups of counties throughout the country to evaluate clinic effectiveness by relating such counts to subsequent birthrates. Second, the Vera Institute traced a large sample of felony arrests through to the final dispositions of each case, providing excellent accounts of the circumstances under which plea bargaining is used and the kinds of cases that are brought finally to trial. The Vera Institute researchers also conducted intensive studies of subsamples of cases, interviewing the states' attorneys and defense attorneys in these cases in order to obtain an understanding of the decision processes used.

11. The issues involved in specification errors have been thoroughly reviewed in Cain (1975).

REFERENCES

BLAU, P. M. (1955) Dynamics of Bureaucracy. Chicago: Univ. of Chicago Press.
CAIN, G. G. (1975) "Regression and selection models to improve non-experimental comparisons," pp. 297-317 in C.A. Bennett and A.A. Lumsdaine (eds.) Evaluation and Experiment. New York: Academic.
CARLSON, D. B. and J. D. HEINBERG (1977) How Housing Allowances Work. Washington, DC: Urban Institute.
CLINE, M. G. (1975) Education as Experimentation: Evaluation of the Follow Through Planned Variation Model. Cambridge: Abt Associates.
CUTRIGHT, P. and F. S. JAFFE (1977) Impact of Family Planning Programs on Fertility: The U.S. Experience. New York: Praeger.

DAVIS, J. A. (1962) Stipends and Spouses. Chicago: Univ. of Chicago Press.

DEUTSCHER, J. and F. B. Alt (1977) "The effect of Massachusetts' gun control law on gun-related crimes in the city of Boston." Evaluation Q. 1: (November): 543-567.

GRAMLICH, E. M. and P. P. KOSHEL (1975) Educational Performance Contracting. Washington, DC: Brookings Institution.

HIBBS, D. A., Jr. (1976) "On analyzing the effects of policy interventions: Box-Jenkins and Box-Tiao vs. structural equation models," in D. L. Heise (ed.) Sociological Methodology, 1975. San Francisco: Jossey-Bass.

KASSEBAUM, G., D. WARD, and D. WILNER (1971) Prison Treatment and Parole Survival. New York: John Wiley.

McLAUGHLIN, M. W. (1975) Evaluation and Reform: The Elementary and Secondary Education Act of 1965/Title I. Cambridge: Ballinger.

REISS, A. J. (1971) The Police and the Public. New Haven: Yale Univ. Press.

ROSSI, P. H. (1976) "Assessing organizational capacity for educational R&D in academic institutions." Educational Researcher 5.

———— and K. LYALL (1976) Reforming Public Welfare. New York: Russell Sage Foundation.

ROSSI, P. H. and S. R. WRIGHT (1977) "Evaluation research: an assessment of theory, practice and politics." Evaluation Q. 1: 5-52.

ROSSI, P. H., R. A. BERK, and B. K. EIDSON (1974) The Roots of Urban Discontent. New York: Wiley-Interscience.

U.S. Department of Labor (1977) Unlocking the Second Gate: R&D Monograph No. 45. Washington, DC: Government Printing Office.

Peter H. Rossi is Professor of Sociology and Director of the Social and Demographic Research Institute at the University of Massachusetts, Amherst. He is Editor of Social Science Research and President-Elect of the Evaluation Research Society. He is also coauthor (with Walter Williams) of Evaluating Social Programs (Academic Press, 1972).

Issues of methodology have virtually preoccupied evaluation researchers, but Quay illustrates graphically the importance of the issues we have referred to earlier as strength and integrity of treatment. As Quay makes clear, if treatments are weak to begin with, or are poorly implemented, issues of methodological adequacy become academic since there may be nothing to evaluate anyway. Although Quay's work concerns the treatment of criminal offenders, we believe the issues he raises are pertinent to any field in which interventions may be devised and tested.

4

The Three Faces of Evaluation
What Can Be Expected To Work

Herbert C. Quay

Evaluations of intervention programs have concentrated on the adequacy of research design and the specification of outcome, while tending to ignore the integrity of the programs being evaluated. This third face of evaluation, assessing program integrity, involves information as to the adequacy of the conceptualization of the treatment, the duration and intensity of the program, the quality and quantity of personnel, and the match of treatment, treater and treated. The study by Kassebaum, Ward, and Wilner (1971), which utilizes an exemplary research design and provides considerable information on program integrity, is analyzed in detail to demonstrate that the almost complete lack of program integrity rendered the drawing of conclusions about the efficacy of group counseling in the correctional setting impossible from the results reported in this research. Continued lack of attention to the question of program integrity can only lead to further, and generally unproductive, debate about "what works." It is suggested that techniques be developed for the objective assessment of the elements of program integrity for commonly used treatment strategies in corrections.

While the adequacy of the research design and the measurement of outcome are clearly related to the confidence with which the results of any intervention study can be interpreted, experimental design and outcome specification are necessary but not sufficient conditions for the evaluation of any treatment

Author's Note: *This paper was first delivered at the National Conference on Criminal Justice Evaluation, Washington, DC, February 22-24, 1977. Reprints available from the author, P.O. Box 248074, University of Miami, Coral Gables, FL, 33124.*

program. The dangers of overemphasis on design, data analysis, and outcome measures to the exclusion of other criteria of adequacy are, unfortunately, manifest in the widely cited review of correctional treatment by Martinson (1974).

This review has had considerable impact on correctional administrators, although its conclusions have been questioned in a recently published critique (Palmer, 1975). What has been obscured in the controversy over "what works" are the dangers of overreliance on restricted notions of what constitutes "good evaluation." It is unfortunate that both Martinson and his critics have failed to consider the studies reviewed on dimensions other than experimental design.

Before we can legitimately conclude that a method of correctional treatment has been shown not to work, there is a great deal we need to know beyond experimental design and outcome criteria. This third face of evaluation involves the assessment of the integrity of the treatment program itself. We need to be as equally concerned with the "what" of evaluation as with the "how."

Assessing the integrity of any intervention is a multidimensional matter, and we do not pretend to have identified all of the possible elements. We do, however, suggest that there are four areas related to intervention integrity and that each area has identifiable subaspects.

TREATMENT CHARACTERISTICS AND EMPIRICAL BASES

Specificity with which the intervention can be conceptualized

Crucial to the integrity with which an intervention can be carried out is the clarity of its conceptual basis. Addressing this issue is basically asking, What, exactly, *is* the treatment? Put another way, how accurately can we describe (and perhaps measure) the independent variable? The more specific the conceptualization, the greater the ease, all else being equal, of the implementation, and , perhaps more importantly, the greater the likelihood that others can replicate the treatment procedures.

The empirical basis of the intervention

Assuming that the intervention can be reasonably well specified, how well it is grounded in empirical research becomes the next point of concern. Are its operations and techniques based on research findings or is the empirical base for its procedures lacking? While the validation of procedures in the laboratory does not guarantee their successful translation into the natural setting, the firmer the empirical base, the more likely is a successful transition to the "real world."

The proven utility of the intervention in less "complex" settings

The correctional setting is a complex one, with frequently conflicting demands on its staff (custody versus treatment) and its clients (institutional adjustment versus behavior change). Before a treatment is imported into such an inhospitable matrix of forces, it ought to have demonstrated its utility in more benign climates. An intervention which already carries with it evidence for its utility in the consulting room, clinic, or classroom would seem a better bet for the correctional setting than one which did not. This is not to say that one can not conceptualize treatment approaches which may be uniquely suited to the correctional setting. The fact of the matter is, however, that rarely, if ever, are treatment approaches created de novo, in corrections.

THE SERVICE DELIVERED

A second group of factors involved in program integrity has to do with the service actually delivered to clients: Does what actually happens meet the specifications of treatment?[1]

Monitoring program elements

Of crucial importance to program integrity is the answer to the question, What actually happened? One cannot take programs at face value, and some accounting of what actually went on is clearly necessary. If counseling is the treatment, one needs to know if counseling sessions were actually held, how well were they attended, and whether or not what went on in the sessions constituted counseling as specified by the particular model of counseling utilized. These are critical questions, because without generally affirmative answers, there really is no intervention to evaluate.

Duration of the service

Some intervention may specify duration, at least in general terms, a priori. Others, particularly those based on operant conditioning, make duration a function of continuously or periodically measured results. However the recommended duration is arrived at, the extent to which this criterion is met must be considered in assessing program integrity.

Intensity of the service

The prescribed length of a single counseling session, or of an academic class, or a Synanon game, may be in many ways arbitrary, and more a function of opinion than of fact, but some limits must be respected. Ten minutes per day of remedial reading is not likely to increase reading skills very much, let alone reduce recidivism.

PERSONNEL

A third aspect of program integrity has to do with those who are delivering the service. Since most treatment techniques are dependent upon who is doing the treatment, questions related to personnel may well be the most important in evaluating program integrity. There are at least three identifiable subareas related to personnel.

Degree of expertise

It is probably best if the personnel implementing the treatment program know what they are supposed to be doing before beginning the intervention; this applies equally to planners, administrators, service deliverers, and researchers. While personnel qualifications are sometimes difficult to specify, one would not generally expect accountants to build bridges. Prior education, reflected usually by academic degrees, may not provide ironclad guarantees of expertise, but such credentials are better than no evidence for competence at all.

Amount of training provided

Many correctional interventions simply cannot be implemented if all personnel are required to have a high degree of prior expertise. In cases where personnel have few skills present at the outset, the nature and amount of training becomes critical. Intelligent and motivated correctional officers can become reasonably good at personal counseling, but not as a result of three one-hour lectures, only two of which they attended. Again, performance may be more important than training, but most people would rather, if absolutely necessary, be operated on by a nurse than an orderly.

Degree of supervision

Almost all human service providers receive some degree of help and guidance in their efforts, if only informally through meetings and discussions with peers. When the service is to be provided by those with relatively little experience, training and supervision become most important. How often, how intense, how utilized; the more information we have about each of the above, the better.

THE MATCH OF TREATER, TREATMENT, AND TREATED

There is a great deal of evidence for the proposition that neither juvenile nor adult offenders are homogeneous with respect to characteristics related to responsiveness to differing kinds of interventions. In no other areas of human services are all clients expected to react equally well to all treatment approaches, and the case of corrections is certainly no different. The extent to which the intervention is appropriate to the needs of its clients should be addressed; blanket applications of almost any treatment without regard for client characteristics are doomed to failure at the outset.

PROGRAM INTEGRITY AND THE EVALUATION OF CORRECTIONAL TREATMENT

It is unfortunate but nevertheless true that many of the treatment studies in corrections have provided little information relative to program integrity. A notable exception is the detailed report on a large-scale study of the efficacy of group counseling by Kassebaum et al. (1971).

This project is referred to twice in the Martinson (1974) article.[2] Under the heading "Group Counseling" we find: "Two [studies] (Kassebaum, 1971; Harrison, 1964) report no long-lasting effects" (p. 31). Under "Transforming the Institutional Environment," Martinson states: "Another study by Kassebaum, Ward and Wilner (1971) dealt with a program which had been able to effect an exceptionally extensive and experimentally rigorous transformation of the institutional environment. This sophisticated study had a follow-up period of 36 months, and it found that the program had no significant effect on parole failure or success rates" (p. 33).[3]

It is unquestionably true that no effects of the treatment were demonstrated and that the research design was adequate. Yet a reading of the report reveals much about *why,* in this particular instance, group counseling did not work. An examination of this excellent report from the point of view of what it says about many of the elements of program integrity proposed above is revealing.

With respect to the conceptualization of the treatment, in discussing what group counseling is, Kassebaum et al. (1971) report:

> Nonetheless, Fenton's description of the interactional processes of the sessions (what goes on between group members and the leader) is couched in very general terms, and the theoretical bases on which group counseling is built are not clearly spelled out. The aims of group counseling are not easily operationalized, nor is it described it terms that lend themselves to the precise analysis of group structure or process [p. 59].

The utility of the process, as judged by those actually involved in it in the California Department of Corrections, is revealed in data provided in Table 3.1 on page 64. Here it is reported that only 40% of group counselors agreed that "group counseling induces personality change," and only 30% agreed that "inmates from group counseling violate parole less." This latter finding means that less than one-third of practicing group counselors felt that the treatment would effect the major dependent variable of the study (recidivism) and the *only* dependent variable subsequently of interest to Martinson (1974).

Despite these problems in conceptualizing the treatment and the expressed doubts about its efficacy as practiced by the California Department of Corrections, it was nevertheless possible to study its effects. As stated by the investigators: "The limitation in conceptual precision, however, does not prevent us from studying the effects of group counseling participation when an appropriate research design is employed" (Kassebaum et al., 1971, p. 59).

What can be learned about the service actually delivered to the clients and the personnel involved in that delivery? According to Kassebaum et al.

> Operationally, group counseling means that ten or twelve inmates meet one or two hours per week under the guidance of a lay group leader. Some leaders are administrative personnel,

caseworkers, teachers, guards, or clerical and technical staff workers; others are therapeutic specialists (physicians, social workers, and psychologists). Nonprofessional personnel in group leader roles, to some extent, are trained and supervised by the group counseling supervisor in each prison. In most cases, these supervisors hold B.A. degrees and have received graduate training in social work [p. 59].

We do not intend to convey the impression that professionals cannot do group therapy, but if such is the case, training, initial and continued, is crucial. Kassebaum et al. (1971) address the issue of training in some detail. Initially they report that "although one community living unit and the mandatory group counseling programs had begun, the supplemental training for group leaders was not yet in operation" (p. 84).

This is a rather important point, and the authors go on to discuss training in considerable detail in Chapter IV. Some reasonable judgments can be made about the quality of training from the following quotations:

Two training programs for group counselors were conducted at Men's Colony—East. During the first year and one half of the institution's operation the in-service training of group counselors was provided through a series of one-hour monthly lectures by the supervisor of group counseling. In addition, sessions were scheduled in which group leaders raised specific questions that arose from problems in conducting their groups. These meetings were poorly attended, and it was our impression that many of the men who did come seemed to be apathetic and disinterested [p. 86].

During the study period the counseling coordinator was seldom consulted by the new group leaders. Although a small library of books on counseling and therapy was housed in the co-ordinator's office, it was little used at the time of the study. No list of available titles had been distributed to group leaders [p. 87].

It was our view that at the time the study began the instruction given to correctional personnel in counseling techniques was limited and was generally not regarded as very helpful to the leaders. It should be kept in mind that CMCE had just opened, and many of its staff were men entirely new to corrections. In-service training time was in short supply and heavily committed to the more immediate tasks of operating a new prison [p. 87].

Reacting to this situation, the research project itself decided to offer supplementary training. Measures were taken to combat the indifference and absenteeism characterizing the counselor's response to the regular in-service counselor training. This training focused more on the personalities of the counselors than on the technical aspects of counseling, and the researchers seemed to feel that something was gained.

The project staff's attempts to monitor the services delivered by direct observation were limited but revealing. In discussing the small groups, the researchers observe:

Our observations and discussions with staff and inmates led us to conclude that the small groups were frequently beset with the following problems:

(1) A tendency for superficiality, a lack of emotional involvement, and evidence of insincerity.

(2) A tendency for talkative members to monopolize the discussion to the exclusion and boredom of others.

(3) A feeling of frustration and a lack of confidence in leaders' or members' ability to "do the job" without professional supervision.

(4) A tendency to focus on stories and personal accounts that were not further analyzed or used for discussion but were used to provide competition for another inmate's account of his preprison experiences or exploits.

(5) A tendency for staff members to permit periods of silence up to the length of the entire session because of their misinterpretation of "nondirective counseling" or their own inability to elicit discussion instead of personal narratives and storytelling. In some cases this may reflect inadequate training, in other cases it reflects inadequate counselors.

However, as in the case of Group No. 3, some groups exhibited behavior which was, in the opinion of the observers, similar to therapy groups in noncorrectional settings where the leader is unobstrusive [sic] but in command of the situation, and his manner suggests relaxed self-confidence. The members spoke critically and spontaneously and gave evidence of trusting the leader and one another. Based on feedback from inmate interviews (which we consider later in this chapter), conversations with staff members, and the reports of the on-site research staff, there were some, but not many, groups (like No. 3) in which the conduct of the sessions approximated the goals of counseling set forth in the departmental training manual [p. 123].

Since group stability had previously been suggested to relate to success, the researchers undertook to locate stable groups. They reported:

We believed that Harrison's findings about the superior performance of stable groups remained open to further empirical examination, since no control groups were used, but we found that we could not identify any groups as CMCE that met his criteria of stability. (The CMCE group counseling coordinator in regard to this issue glumly remarked, "We have a stable group if there's less than one leader change during a month.") Men moved in and out of groups frequently as their jobs or institutional activities required, as they stopped attending counseling sessions, as the leaders changed, and the like. No group had the same leader for an entire year because of changes in work shifts, job assignments, vacation and other absences, meetings, etc. [p. 247].[4]

On the basis of the information provided, one is hard pressed to conclude other than that the service actually delivered by minimally trained and inexpert personnel was inadequate to the task—a view already expressed by other counselors in the system.

Now we may turn to the target population, the inmates—their nature, the perceptions of the process, and the methods whereby they were selected.

Chapter V begins:

At the time our study was set for full operation at Men's Colony—East, 76 counseling groups had been established in the three quads under study. Twenty-three of the groups involved mandatory participation in small groups and 53 involved groups made up of voluntary participants. In addition, there were three community living groups made up of 50 men each, in which participation was mandatory [p. 118].

One can conclude that most participation was frankly involuntary. The reasons for attendance by inmates are reported:

Of particular interest to us was the finding that was based on the interviews conducted with men in prison and on parole, that the most consistently expressed view of group counseling was that its value was chiefly in satisfying the Adult Authority at parole hearings. Like class attendance in some universities, inmates felt that a participation in group counseling might not be a major factor in getting paroled, but a lack of participation was likely to be regarded negatively by the Adult Authority [pp. 31-32].

As to the nature of the participants, we find:

The composition of the inmate groups also varied. A few included inmates with several years experience at doing time together at San Quentin or some other prison; other groups were composed entirely of men who were strangers to each other and who were serving their first term in prison. Most groups were mixtures of these extremes [p. 118].

Clearly, there was no attempt by the program managers to select, or even identify, those most likely to have benefited from the treatment, nor was there an attempt to compose the counseling groups in any systematic way.

What of the clients' perceptions of the treatment? On the basis of interviews with inmate the authors reported:

Interviews conveyed the strong impression that relatively few inmates entered group counseling with the conviction that they were participating in a meaningful treatment program. The usual advice new inmates received from others was to the effect that counseling was not adequately nor honestly run, but that participation looked good to the Adult Authority, and, in fact, counseling was one of the measurable items of an inmate's experience in prison (like school attendance, trade training, and disciplinary reports) that could be considered. Although participation may not help inmates to make parole, its absence, generally noticed by the Adult Authority, is often interpreted as a lack of interest in helping oneself and getting involved in the treatment program. For the Adult Authority, the record of length of participation in group counseling is a useful index of prisoner experience because it joins that relatively small list of activities that can be quantified and used in plus-or-minus fashion in determining parole eligibility [p. 131].

Survey data obtained revealed such findings as: "Two-thirds agreed that correctional officers were not competent to run groups" (p. 136). Further, "There was agreement that men did not talk frankly (four out of five), and one-half of the respondents agreed that if too much was revealed it would be used against them" (p. 136).

It is obvious that group therapy as a "group setting necessary for clients to feel free to discuss with security their own and each other's feelings and attitudes toward the situation in which they find themselves" (p. 59) was never accomplished.

Given the overall quality of the intervention, made abundantly clear by Kassebaum et al. (1971) but totally ignored by both Martinson (1974) and Lipton et al. (1975), what reasonable person could have expected recidivism, or anything else, to have been reduced, especially among, as we have seen, those with prior experience in California prison group therapy? Finally, one wonders how this treatment could possibly be described as one "which had been able to effect an exceptionally intensive and experimentally rigorous *transformation* [italics ours] of the institutional environment" (Martinson, 1974, p. 33).

It is unlikely that any other research report available for review contained the wealth of information on program integrity provided by Kassebaum et al. However, such does not negate the fact that conclusions about the effects of group counseling and milieu intervention should have been tempered by a consideration of the extent to which program integrity was seriously lacking in this program effort.

We do not wish to beg the question of outcome, even when narrowly defined in terms of recidivism—itself a term not always meaning the same thing in different studies. But to continue to ignore all aspects of the integrity of the treatment in arriving at conclusions about what does and doesn't work will be a major error—one, unfortunately, with serious policy and practical consequences for corrections beyond those already suffered.

ASSESSING PROGRAM INTEGRITY

The development of techniques for the assessment of program integrity must have as high a priority as the development and routinizing (see Glaser, 1974) of evaluation. For purposes of evaluating the impact of treatment training on line correctional staff, Johnson (1975) has developed a schedule to assess the integrity of the positive-reinforcement programming type of correctional intervention. This schedule provides a quantitative estimate, through ratings of various program dimensions, of the integrity of an intervention based on the particular model. Field tests have suggested that the scale can be used reliably, and further research with it is underway.

We urge the development of technique for the assessment of the integrity of programs based on other models. Without attention to this third face of evaluation, valid conclusions as to the efficacy of various rehabilitative strategies will continue to elude us.

NOTES

1. Suchman (1967, p. 31) seems to recognize the need to evaluate program integrity when he indicates that "description and standardization of the activity is a component of evaluation." He does not subsequently expand on this point, however.

2. In the entire article, one finds very little concern for the nature of the service delivered as possibly affecting the outcome. The problems in implementation and staff attitudes reported by Zivan (in Martinson, 1974) are reported and represent the only reference, in any detail, to program integrity problems in the entire review. Some greater attention is given to the nature of the target population in terms of amenability of the entire target group or some subgroup thereof (e.g., Adams, p. 29; Goldberg & Adams, p. 33; the Warren Studies, all in Martinson, 1974). Yet amenability effects are, on the whole, disregarded in arriving at his conclusions (see also Palmer, 1975).

3. In the subsequently published and much less widely cited book (Lipton et al., 1975), this research is referred to under a number of headings [e.g., Group Counseling (p. 224, pp. 236-237); Milieu Therapy (pp. 242-243, pp. 252-253, pp. 259-261)]. None of these citations contains details of the project beyond a brief description of its design and results.

4. Despite the failure to find groups meeting the criteria of stability, the authors analyzed outcomes of what could be called "more" and "less" stable groups. No differences emerged.

REFERENCES

Glaser, D. *Routinizing evaluation: getting feedback on effectiveness of crime and delinquency programs.* Rockville, MD: National Institute of Mental Health, Center for Studies of Crime and Delinquency, 1974.

Johnson, V. S. The positive reinforcement programming congruence scales. Unpublished manuscript, 1975.

Kassebaum, G., Ward, D., & Wilner, D. *Prison treatment and parole survival: an empirical assessment.* New York: John Wiley, 1971.

Lipton, D., Martinson, R., & Wilks, J. *The effectiveness of correctional treatment.* New York: Praeger, 1975.

Martinson, R. What works? Questions and answers about prison reform. *The Public Interest,* 1974, 35, 22-54.

Palmer, T. Martinson revisited. *Journal of Research in Crime and Delinquency,* July 1975, 133-152.

Suchman, E. A. *Evaluative research.* New York: Russell Sage Foundation, 1967.

Herbert C. Quay is Director of the Program in Applied Social Sciences and Professor of Psychology and Pediatrics at the University of Miami. He received the Ph.D. in Psychology from the University of Illinois in 1958. He has been involved with problems of delinquency and criminology with particular reference to offender classification for over 25 years.

The idea that "nothing works" to rehabilitate criminals has become a truism in the research on treatment of criminal offenders. This is in spite of the fact that the originator of the phrase considers it a misinterpretation (Martinson et al., 1976). With sardonic style, Gottfredson's article elucidates the strategies used by critics of rehabilitation research to destroy the importance of positive findings. Some may say that the strategies are, in fact, valid for examining research, but Gottfredson's work is critical not of the techniques per se, but of an attitude of defeatism and reluctance to give credit where it may be due. The implication of the work for rehabilitation research is not that positive findings should be accepted uncritically, but that it may be time to stop attacking rehabilitative treatments, and instead follow up on those studies that show positive findings or, at the very least, attempt experimentally to resolve the issues raised by the criticisms. Note, however, that the points made by Gottfredson can stand as challenges to critics of research in nearly any other area of social amelioration.

*MARTINSON, R., T. PALMER, and S. ADAMS (1976) Rehabilitation, Recidivism, and Research. Hackensack, NJ: National Council on Crime and Delinquency.

5

Treatment Destruction Techniques

Michael R. Gottfredson

The conventional wisdom in criminology is that treatment programs have been found to be ineffective. This paper outlines several methods that may be used to defend this wisdom: (1) contaminate the treatment, (2) stress the criterion problem, (3) appeal to common sense, (4) demonstrate that rehabilitation is premised on faulty theory, and (5) seek universals. In addition, methods for uncovering the tyranny inherent in all treatment programs are discussed briefly.

The conventional wisdom in criminology is that rehabilitation has been found to be ineffective. In fact, the lack of demonstrated effectiveness is agreed upon by criminologists of nearly every persuasion and theoretical orientation:

> True successes in rehabilitation have been virtually nonexistent. (Doleschal and Klapmuts, 1973:610)

> Rehabilitative treatment has not been shown to be effective in reducing recidivism: the recidivism rates of those treated in different programs by different methods do not differ from the rates of those not treated at all, whether in the U.S. or elsewhere. (van den Haag, 1975:188)

> In the last few years . . . the weight of informed opinion in the United States about correctional rehabilitation has shifted to the negative. Rehabilitation, while still recognized as a meritorious goal, is no longer seen as a practical possibility within our correctional structure by the empirical observer. (Conrad, 1973:208)

Even a panel from the National Research Council of the National Academy of Sciences, in a report on deterrence and incapacitation, argues that rehabilitation is ineffective:

> The available research on the impact of various treatment strategies both in and out of prison seems to indicate that, after controlling for initial selection differences, there are generally *no statistically significant* differences between the subsequent recidivism of offenders, regardless of the form of "treatment." (National Research Council, 1978:66; emphasis added)

Reprinted with permission of the National Council on Crime and Delinquency, from Michael R. Gottfredson, "Treatment Destruction Techniques," *Journal of Research in Crime and Delinquency,* January 1979, pp. 39-54.

Confronted with this unanimity, there are still those who persist in their attempts to reopen the case for treatment and to argue the facts with claims of a scientific point of view (see, e.g., Palmer, 1975, and Adams, 1977). These revisionists suggest that if traditional standards of scientific proof are applied to much of the treatment research literature—for example, standards relating to the control of extraneous variance, sampling, and the reliability and validity of instrumentation—many of the better studies in the field provide us with knowledge about effective treatment. Some defenders of conventional wisdom dismiss this revisionism simply by questioning the motives and objectivity of those who suggest that there are convincing indications that some treatment programs are effective and that further research is desirable. But motives can only be inferred, making them inherently disputable and, hence, inconclusive evidence in rebuttals. Fortunately, there is a variety of general principles (or, more accurately, pseudoscientific criteria) that may be invoked to fend off any attack on our conventional wisdom regarding the effectiveness of treatment.

In fact, there are at least five distinguishable methods that may be used to demonstrate the ineffectiveness of any and all treatment modalities in the criminal justice system. Individually (but, most effectively, in combination), these methods are capable of destroying any positive results that might appear in the literature. Perhaps more important, each can be used to show that continuing research in the area would be a mistake. Because of the power inherent in these methods, it may well be useful to describe and catalog them carefully; many of them are already an integral part of the working vocabulary of many criminologists. Because no study or research proposal can withstand an assault from a carefully chosen arsenal of these destruction techniques, their value is obvious; they will be defined briefly below and examples of their use will be provided.[1]

CONTAMINATE THE TREATMENT

To contaminate the treatment, simply raise plausible alternative interpretations for the reported effect. Not plausible interpretations that suggest there was *no* effect; on the contrary, suggest that the effect reported in the study was due to some treatment *other than that suggested by the authors of the study.* Obviously, if there is ambiguity about precisely *what* caused an effect, it is absurd to claim effectiveness. The method is universally applicable, and capable of use against the best studies, the most rigorous designs.

As with all the treatment destruction techniques discussed here, the style

1. These methods should not be confused with standard methodological criteria that have been established for the conduct of behavioral research (such as sampling principles, reliability of instrumentation, and principles of experimental design). The distinction is that, to be applicable, standard methodological critiques depend on what the treatment researchers have done, whereas the destruction techniques discussed here do not. The methods described here can always be invoked (for instance, regardless of the rigor of the sampling design) and therefore are probably more useful.

with which this method is invoked is critical. Rarely is the concern in eval-uations of treatment studies with the specific study per se. We are interested in a bigger issue—the effectiveness of rehabilitation in the criminal justice system. To that end, the critique of individual studies should have a psychological impact that is lasting and generalizable. And that is a matter of *style*.

Clues to effective style for contaminating the treatment are available in the literature. Timing appears to be essential. For maximum impact, the technique should be invoked only after a review of the study has appeared to show a substantial treatment effect. Let the reader grasp this ray of light in an otherwise darkened room of negative findings. Suddenly, snap the windowshade shut by contaminating the treatment. When properly done, the method has such power that the reader is likely to generalize, if only to avoid the appearance of seeing light. Some examples will demonstrate the power of the technique:

> There is a third study that does report an overall positive finding as op-posed to a partial one. Truax (1966) found that girls subjected to group psychotherapy and then released were likely to spend less time rein-carcerated in the future. But what is most interesting about this improve-ment is the very special and important circumstance under which it oc-curred. The therapists chosen for this program did not merely have to have the proper analytic training; they were specially chosen for their "em-pathy" and "non-possessive warmth." In other words, it may well have been the therapists' special personal gifts rather than the fact of treatment itself which produced the favorable result. (Martinson, 1974:32)

Note how adroitly the glimmer of hope is first raised, and then is followed by a rapid shot of contamination. (When applying this method, it is of utmost importance that the critic not spawn further treatment research by attempting to resolve the rival hypotheses.)

Multiple contamination is usually more effective than a single rival hypothesis:

> Five of these studies have dealt with youthful probationers from 13 to 18 who were assigned to probation officers with small caseloads or provided with other ways of receiving more intensive supervision. . . . These studies report that, by and large, intensive supervision does work—that the special-ly treated youngsters do better according to some measure of recidivism. Yet these studies left some important questions unanswered. For instance, was this improved performance a function merely of the number of con-tacts a youngster had with his probation officer? Did it also depend on the length of time in treatment? Or was it the quality of supervision that was making the difference rather than the quantity? (Martinson, 1974:42)

Some scientific-minded observers will note that contaminating the treatment is pure scientific method; when applied to experimental research generally, it sets the stage for future research because a significant effect, even if there is uncertainty about what caused it, can be studied further by designing another experiment to separate out various competing factors. Such reasoning, however, should not deter those employing the contaminate-the-treatment destruction technique. To accept this general approach would require an admission that research in treatment, as in all science, is a cumulative process. Acceptance of such principles implies that treatment research should continue, a conclusion that is inconsistent with the demands of conventional wisdom, as will be shown below. In any event, when embedded in a review of what is known about treatment, this technique can always prove that nothing is known with *certainty*.

STRESS THE CRITERION PROBLEM

Many treatment strategies in criminal justice have as their aim the reduction of the probability of future law violations on the part of those treated. They therefore require as a criterion measure some indicator of illegal behavior. But because, as everyone knows, it is impossible to measure illegal conduct accurately, every study is vulnerable to attack on the basis of the criterion problem. Not all parole violators are criminal; not all those engaged in illegal conduct are caught (or better yet, discovered); not all those arrested are guilty; not all those arrested are convicted. So, regardless of the care given to refinement of outcome measures, the criterion is vulnerable. If the investigators use arrest, point out it was not conviction. If they use conviction, ask about those not caught. If they use self-reported measures, wonder aloud about the veracity of criminals.[2] It is a perfectly general technique—no study is immune. Simply raising the aura of the criterion problem is usually sufficient to question the effectiveness of treatment.[3]

Stressing the criterion problem has two applications. First, it can be used to destroy an individual study, by questioning the specific criterion chosen by the authors. Second, it can be used to show generally that every study ever undertaken—or, more important, that ever will be undertaken—is suspect.

Some crusty philosophers of science will undoubtedly argue that the criterion problem is universal in science. Accuracy in measurement, they will point out, is always a matter of degree, and progress in science is largely attributed to refining the tools by which we observe nature. Thus, there are no perfectly reliable and valid criteria, only goals toward which we strive. What is important, they will argue, is that the criterion used have *some* validity (the

2. Disregard the generally high consistency among these measures for serious illegal behavior. If the investigators are presumptuous enough to use criteria other than measures of illegal conduct (e.g., changes in attitudes, work habits, or self-concept), simply point out that the main concern of the criminal justice system is crime and not self-actualization. Either way you've got them.

3. There is absolutely no obligation to attempt to ferret out the potential impact of the criterion problem on the size of the effect reported or even to be specific about how the experimental/control differences could result from a particular criterion problem.

more the better, admittedly) and that the association between the treatment and the criterion rest on this true variance.

Treatment researchers are likely to argue that major improvements have been made in recent years regarding measurement of the criterion. Thus, they will argue, multiple-outcome measures are now fairly common, and some research even attempts to scale the criterion along a seriousness dimension. Some might even note that many effectiveness claims are supported regardless of the criterion used. The main points they are likely to make is that the criterion problem should be recognized, serious efforts should be made to deal with it in research, and results should be interpreted in light of the potential bias associated with the criterion.

Those familiar with recent advances in criminology will perceive the fatal defect in these arguments. Rehabilitation in criminal justice is concerned with changing the behavior of those treated, but the "behavior" of those treated is dependent on the behavior of agents of social control. Criminals are those whom agents of social control choose to define as criminal; thus, any criterion of criminality may be as much a measure of the behavior of social control agents as a measure of the behavior of the persons in the sample. The first hypothesis that must be advanced upon the discovery of an "effective" treatment, therefore, is that it was the behavior of the agents of social control that was altered, not the behavior of the sample.[4] In its extreme, this technique effectively negates the claim that the criterion in treatment research has *any* true variance, thus refuting the notion that rehabilitation ever could work since it attempts to change something that does not exist.

Perhaps the most effective example of the use of "stressing the criterion problem" is provided in a recent critique of the California Community Treatment Program (CTP) (Lerman, 1975). Using parole revocation rates as a measure of recidivism, the treatment researchers claimed effectiveness (Palmer, 1971). However, Lerman shows that the rate of parole *suspensions* for alleged violations—which he terms "youth behavior"—is greater for the experimental group than for the control group. But, because the experimental group had lower rates of *revocation* than the controls, Lerman concludes:

> In actuality, CTP can only demonstrate that rates of official decision making changed. The program influenced the labeling and social control process, and not the rates of behavioral input that presumably triggers the discretionary reactions to youth. (Lerman, 1975:61)

His argument is that the farther into the criminal justice process one penetrates (in this case from parole suspensions to parole revocations), the less likely one is to obtain criteria that are valid.

---

4. Only the cynic will argue that it doesn't matter and that if criminality is largely socially constructed, then effecting treatment by altering the definitional propensity of agents of social control is a successful treatment.

Of course it would be possible to make the argument the other way around (i.e., to argue that these criteria demonstrate effectiveness). The experimental group was much more closely supervised and therefore at greater risk of being *suspended* by parole agents, and the treatment program for some experimentals included brief suspensions for acts probably not *typically* resulting in a suspension.[5] Therefore, it might be preferable to use as a criterion some measure that involves a relatively independent assessment of the legitimacy of the charges (e.g., by a parole board at a *revocation* hearing) and the seriousness of the infractions. Some might argue that this would be reimprisonment, the criterion used by CTP.[6] But Lerman (1975:50) rebuts this logic: "The further we proceed in the discretionary labeling process in order to obtain violational data, the greater is the likelihood that we shall be measuring *official* behavior rather than youth behavior." Thus, according to Lerman, investigations are more valid than arrests, arrests more valid than charges, and charges more valid than convictions as criteria for treatment studies. The fact that others may suggest, and frequently have suggested, exactly the opposite is the outstanding feature of this destruction technique.

Although there are numerous ways that the criterion problem may be stressed, the general argument always should be that because no criminality criterion is *completely* valid, it is impossible to know anything. One particularly destructive technique is to point out that the *absence* of recidivism might be more indicative of the failure of treatment than is the presence of recidivism:

> Recidivism should not be confused with social maladjustment, nor should the absence of recidivism be equated with rehabilitation. Because an offender does not again become involved with the criminal justice system, one cannot assume that he is socially adjusted or rehabilitated. He may, in fact, be a more effective criminal, or he may not engage in criminal activity but may be deviant in a variety of other ways—for example, he may be unemployed or he may be mentally ill. (Lipton, Martinson, and Wilks, 1975:608)

---

5. It is fairly easy to cull from the data support for the "differential at-risk" hypothesis. The suspension rate for the experimental group for status offenses and technical violations was three times as great as was the suspension rate for the control group for these offenses. It would seem logical that at least part of this difference can be attributed to the much closer supervision by parole officers in the experimental group because the treatment plan called for intensive supervision. By extension, this closer supervision probably also accounts for some of the suspensions for more serious charges in the experimental group as well.

6. Considerable support for the use of this criterion is provided in additional follow-up data reported by Palmer (1974). It should be noted that revocation was not the sole criterion reported by the CTP staff, but rather they reported a large array of criterion measures (see, e.g., Palmer, 1974).

Stressing the criterion problem essentially involves demonstrating the lack of a one-to-one relationship between the study's measure of recidivism and actual illegal conduct. Since this technique invokes a standard that is unattainable in behavioral research, and despite the fact that such a standard is unnecessary for scientific confidence, it is extremely effective and totally general. It might be noted that this destruction technique could be used in reverse (i.e., to point out that a claim of ineffectiveness cannot be made with certainty). But this use of the method is of limited interest and will not be discussed here in detail.

SHOW THAT MASSIVE EFFORTS HAVE FAILED
(APPEAL TO COMMON SENSE)

The treatment ideology has dominated our thinking about crime for decades. On the basis of this ideology, massive investments have been made in programs and personnel. After all this effort, it is time we learned to recognize failure when we see it. If this plethora of resources has failed to produce unambiguous demonstrations of effectiveness, why continue the search?

The choice of the unit of analysis for demonstrating that massive efforts have failed is critical. It can be either money or time; it should not be the number of rigorous, independent experimental studies that have been undertaken. Nor should the focus be placed on the extent of careful program development with sound implementation of theoretically useful treatments. That is, if the number of scientifically acceptable studies in conjunction with quality treatment programs are used to judge the amount of effort expended thus far, the treatment proponents' cry that "it has never been tried" might appear credible.

Bailey's oft-cited survey of the literature published during the twenty-year period between 1940 and 1960 uncovered only 22 studies with "some form of control group design." Seventeen of these (77 percent) were reported to have positive results. Robison and Smith (1971), another frequently cited review, discussed only 10 studies, clearly not chosen to be representative of the literature, most of which did not involve experimental designs. Wright and Dixon (1977) searched the juvenile delinquency literature for studies conducted between 1965 and 1974, finding only 9 that used "random assignment of subjects, inferential analyses of their data, an outcome measure of delinquent behavior (self-reported, police records, court records), and at least six months' follow-up after the subjects had left the project." Of these, 6 (67 percent) reported positive results. Logan (1967) reviewed 100 studies, published between about 1940 and 1970, 18 of which had both some form of control group (loosely defined) and some follow-up in the community. Ten of these (56 percent) were evaluated by Logan to have positive results.

If these reviews of the treatment literature do not appear to rebut the treatment researcher's harp that "it hasn't been tried yet," the massive review of

Lipton, Martinson, and Wilks (1975) must. These authors reviewed 231 treatment studies in corrections, published between 1945 and 1967. However, those researchers claiming that "it hasn't been tried" are not likely to be satisfied with this 231 figure. They are likely to point out that, of these 231, only 138 used some measure of recidivism as a criterion. Of these, only 65 used a design that met the minimum standards for scientific confidence; that is, a design in which (1) "the researcher can effectively control the selection of subjects, the administration of treatment, the measurement of variables and physically control or restrict the interference of unwanted outside factors" (Lipton et al., 1975:16); and (2) there is either a matched or a random allocation control group. Of these 65, the treatment advocates are likely to stress that 32 (49 percent) reported positive results. If the field of studies is further restricted according to the quality ratings given by Lipton et al. (1975) to only "A" studies ("acceptable for the survey with no more than minimal research shortcomings")[7] then the number falls to 40. Of these, 19 (48 percent) reported positive results.[8] Those who claim that "it hasn't been tried" will undoubtedly argue that the large number of *potential* studies, given the vast array of types of offenses, types of offenders, and types of treatment—when coupled with the strong indicators of success reported to date—suggests that 40 studies hardly scratch the surface. These studies might best be viewed, they may argue, as the foundation for further research.

Therefore, when invoking the critique that massive efforts have failed to uncover substantial treatment effects, it is clear that it is the efforts of the reviewers rather than the efforts of the researchers that should be alluded to. The *reviewers* have searched through decades of literature and scrutinized hundreds of studies to reach the conclusion of ineffectiveness, whereas the *researchers* have undertaken only about three dozen control group studies with random allocation. Clearly, it is preferable to stress that the ideology of the criminal justice system has been geared toward rehabilitation for *decades*, rather than to note that the average number of scientifically acceptable studies during 1940–65 *soared* to one per year.[9]

7. "B" studies were "acceptable for the survey with research shortcomings that place reservations on interpretation of findings" (Lipton et al., 1974:6). The authors do not specify the criteria used to classify the studies into "A" or "B."

8. The restrictions used to arrive at the 40 studies are those required for a study to receive a "1A" or "2A" rating by Lipton et al. All of the "1A" studies (five) reported statistically significant results in the direction favorable to the treatment hypothesis.

9. See, for example, Lerman's statement that "Robison and Smith (1971), reviewing over a decade of innovative correctional research, reached a similar conclusion regarding ineffectiveness" (1975:95). This is more compatible with the "massive efforts" technique than a report that "Robison and Smith (1971), reviewing ten studies, some of which were capable of providing evidence on the question, reached a similar conclusion regarding ineffectiveness."

DEMONSTRATE THAT TREATMENT STRATEGIES
ARE PREMISED ON FAULTY THEORY

If it can be demonstrated that the assumptions upon which rehabilitative programs are built are false, then, as a consequence, the empirical claims of all treatment programs must also be false. This method is not only a useful mechanism by which entire classes of studies can be destroyed, but it can also effectively deny the utility of further research into the question. Obviously, there is little need to ascertain the empirical validity of theoretically impossible relationships.

There are several routes that may be taken in disproving the theory of rehabilitation, but since they all ultimately arrive at the same point, there is little practical benefit in choosing one over the other. They all destroy the need for future research. The most common method is what may be referred to as the "medical delusion." Because it is the most widely agreed-upon means of showing that all rehabilitation is premised upon faulty theory, a brief discussion of how it works is warranted.

That all rehabilitative programs rest on the "medical delusion" and, as a consequence, are doomed to empirical failure is easy to prove. This probably accounts for the technique's widespread adoption:

> Our present treatment programs are based on a theory of crime as a "disease"—that is to say, as something foreign and abnormal in the individual which can presumably be cured. (Martinson, 1974:49)

> Only diseases can be cured by treatment. Few offenders are sick. (van den Haag, 1975:188)

> The treatment approach assumes that the causes of crime, which inhere somewhere in the person of the offender or in his social situation and must be remedied, are *pathological*. By this is meant that offenders are *abnormal* in a way which makes them socially *unhealthy*. (Weiler, 1974:124)

The "rehabilitationists" must necessarily view delinquency or criminality as symptomatic of pathology. In order to eradicate the symptom, the theory goes, it is necessary to cure the pathology. To support this idea, the "rehabilitationists" must construct a faulty world view, consisting of the dichotomous classification of the criminal (sick) on the one hand and the law abider (healthy) on the other. The destruction technique, therefore, simply consists of noting the theoretical implausibility of this medical delusion. Obviously, we are all capable of committing crimes. If necessary it is even possible to point to data showing that everyone does bad things sometimes.

Some treatment researchers are likely to resent this portrait of their theories as being a naive caricature. When pressed, they are likely to agree with Schur (1973:29) that "the treatment reaction is grounded in the *assumption of basic* differentness," but they would typically refer to these as individual differences. Many of them would disagree, however, that they ever said, or meant to imply, that criminality is an all-or-nothing affair. Rather, what most behavioral scientists mean by the phrase "individual differences" is a *continuum* of behavioral differences (see Hirschi, 1975). There are a few saints, a few sinners, and a lot of folks somewhere in between. Such a notion is consistent with, and usually demanded by, every positivistic theory of etiology, be it psychological, sociological, or economic. It is even consistent with the data showing that everyone does bad things sometimes—and the same data that show that a few people do bad things much more than others (see Hirschi, 1975). Depending on the theory, most "rehabilitationists" would argue that these differences (variations) arise from differences (variations) in the ways that parents, siblings, friends, teachers, school systems, and the economic order are experienced by people as they move through life. Some say what is important is the way these factors produce criminality; others, the way that they inhibit it. Few would claim that these factors produce two altogether different kinds of people. The treatment task is to identify which of these producing or inhibiting factors are capable of being decreased or enhanced. They would argue that emphasizing the statement of *some* rehabilitationists, who clearly do ascribe to the medical model (e.g., Menninger, 1968), as being a logically required premise for *all* rehabilitation programs is unfair. Thus, they might argue that whether or not some forms of vocational education programs reduce recidivism for some offenders is a question that can be answered apart from an assumption that job skills cure the disease of unemployment.

These arguments are no impediment to the use of the "medical delusion" technique. "Correction," "diagnostic center," and "treatment"—the very terms used by rehabilitationists—demand a medical analogy. The theory of crime as pathology, which is the least common denominator of all rehabilitation programs, confuses a moral judgment with a medical judgment.

Continuing their rebuttal, many who cling to the rehabilitative ideal will argue that not only is it false to claim that all rehabilitation programs are based on the single faulty theory of pathology, but also that most programs have never been based on *any* theory. At that point they should be attacked for engaging in atheoretical research.

SEEK UNIVERSALS

This is perhaps the most widely known of the various destruction techniques (see, e.g., Palmer, 1975). In seeking universals, it is only necessary to show either (1) that although the treatment method has been found to work with some offenders, it is ineffective with others, or, more simply, (2) that it has not even been tried on everyone.

Palmer (1975:140), although clearly critical of the method, demonstrates its utility and generality. Using the example of group counseling, he points out:

> if, out of ten studies, three or four were associated with negative outcomes, then the findings for *group counseling as a whole* would be considered conflicting or contradictory, even though all remaining studies may have produced clear positive results. Whether or not any specific patterns of success had been observed—e.g., in connection with older adolescent girls (say that every study of this offender group, four in all, yielded positive results)—it would still be the case that the method of group counseling, when viewed as a totality, would have failed to satisfy the criterion in question. . . . (Palmer, 1975:140)

Martinson (1974) demonstrates application of the method to community treatment. He asks whether "the way to rehabilitate offenders is to deal with them outside an institutional setting" (Martinson, 1974:38), and then proceeds to review studies of community treatment ranging from Outward Bound programs, individual psychotherapy in the community, and group psychotherapy in the community, to intensive supervision and parole. Some dealt with adolescents, others with adults; some with individuals, others with gangs. Despite the fact that at some levels of disaggregation (e.g., individual counseling with adolescents)[10] there are notable and consistent positive results, *taken as a whole,* the results of community treatment are mixed. Thus, invoking the technique of "seeking universals," Martinson (1974:47) concludes the review of the section by saying, "In sum, even in the case of treatment programs administered outside penal institutions, we simply cannot say that this treatment in itself has an appreciable effect on offender behavior."

As Palmer (1975) has noted, the relative size of the offender subgroup for which the treatment is shown to be effective does not appear to be an impediment to the use of this destruction technique. Something either works for everyone or it does not.

In case the generality inherent in the method is not apparent, it should be stressed that the only thing required to make it work is to increase the level of aggregation. Thus, if some types of individual psychotherapy work with young institutionalized males, as apparently they do (Lipton, Martinson, and Wilks, 1975:211), but not with institutionalized young females, aggregate the two subgroups and conclude that individual counseling fails (see, e.g., Martinson, 1974:31).

---

10. For example, in Lipton, Martinson, and Wilks (1975:213), the parent study serving as a basis for Martinson's review, the authors conclude, "While clearly definitive information is not yet available, it appears that individual psychotherapy administered to young offenders in the community can be effective in reducing recidivism when it is focused on immediate, day-to-day problems rather than being psychodynamically oriented."

SOME SELECTED SUMMARY TECHNIQUES

A truly effective treatment destruction effort does not cease with the demonstration that the results of a particular study, or group of studies, cannot be interpreted unambiguously. Embedded within every treatment study worthy of destruction are the seeds of policy analysis, waiting only for the critic to bring them to fruition.

Perhaps the most powerful argument against rehabilitation (and, by extension, against research in the área) is that it offends our sense of moral decency. The ultimate criterion for a rehabilitative strategy is that it works to prevent crime. There is nothing *inherent* in the theory that places any limit on the amount of punishment that can be invoked in the name of treatment:

> These treatments have on occasion become, and have the potential for becoming, so draconian as to offend the moral order of a democratic society. (Martinson, 1974:46)

Rehabilitationists will be hard pressed to dispute the fact that things have been done in the past in the name of rehabilitation that are offensive, regardless of whether or not they "worked." And, on a purely philosophical basis, there are no restraints on the severity of punishment permissible under the treatment rationale. Thus, the treatment philosophy has permitted the castration of sex offenders and lobotomies of the "incurably" violent.

Those who cling to the rehabilitative ideal will undoubtedly argue that every punishment philosophy—whether based on utilitarian aims or not—has trouble with the notion of limits. Thus, there is nothing *inherent* in the general deterrence doctrine that prohibits whipping parking violators, provided that it would effectively deter. Similarly with incapacitation; hanging pickpockets (or, less severely, cutting off their hands) is a sure method of precluding their opportunity to offend. As for retribution, the rehabilitationists might argue that getting even is seldom regarded as enough.

Those who cling to rehabilitation might even argue that, as with rehabilitation, the alternative punishment rationales have in fact gotten out of hand in the past. Pickpockets actually have been hanged to prevent the picking of pockets by others, and blood feuds inspired by retribution have tended to get bloody. They might even point to modern incapacitation-based preventive detention laws that allow punishment even in the absence of a finding of guilt.[11] They are likely to argue that setting limits on punishments is a complex issue, usually contingent on several punishment rationales as well as the offense under consideration (see O'Leary, Gottfredson, and Gelman, 1975).

---

11. Rehabilitationists might also point out that many of the most onerous punishments—such as castration and lobotomies—that have been attributed to a rehabilitative rationale actually were based on an incapacitative intent.

Of course, these arguments need not be addressed. The task is to destroy treatment, not to defend the alternatives.

A derivative postulate of the notion that immorality is inherent in treatment is the now firmly established truth that benevolence is actually tyranny in disguise. In criminal justice, the overwhelming evidence indicates that well-intentioned reforms have evil consequences.[12] The link that needs to be established is that rehabilitation researchers essentially are trying to do good for the offender. Most researchers in the area would probably not dispute this (although most might argue that they also are seeking programs that do good for society as well). They probably believe that being hanged, incarcerated, or otherwise penalized is typically not in the best interests of most people. Thus, these researchers are likely to suggest that if they can somehow get people to stop doing things that have the potential of getting them hanged, incarcerated, or otherwise penalized, this might be beneficial for the offender. Most would argue, however, that there are some things that could be done to offenders to keep them out of jail that would not, ultimately, be in the offenders' best interests; that is, treatment researchers would probably claim that they could distinguish between vocational education and prefrontal lobotomies.

The destruction technique requires noting only that the *motives* underlying treatment research have led to evil consequences. Because all treatment strategies are ultimately motivated by the "best interests of the client" and because it can be shown that such motives in the past have produced results contrary to the best interests of the client, every program is suspect. Hence, the issue of effectiveness need not be raised.

Occasionally, a treatment research program comes along that, on its face, appears to be an exception to the law that beneficient motives produce tyrannical results. Ignoring the lessons of the past, the researchers might claim boldly that it is possible both to reduce recidivism effectively and to do so within the boundaries of common decency. Initially, this appeared to be the case with the famous Community Treatment Project (CTP). However, behind the facade of the "community treatment" perspective lay a punitive result, as Lerman (1975) has shown. Because the methods of proof used by Lerman appear capable of generalization, a discussion of them might be useful in the event that similar research programs are proposed in the future.

Briefly, the CTP research initially set out to accomplish three goals[13]: (1) to test the feasibility of releasing some California Youth Authority (CYA) wards directly to a treatment program in the community, (2) to determine the effectiveness of this community-based treatment, and (3) to develop hypotheses about differential treatment plans. The design appeared straightforward.

12. Curiously, most contemporary reformers use this fact as a basis for urging that their reforms would be beneficial.

13. This description is adapted from Lerman (1975:20–22).

Eligible cases were to be assigned randomly to experimental and control groups. The control cases went the traditional CYA route and experimentals into a three-staged program: Stage A was an intensive period of treatment lasting about eight months; Stage B was a transition period; and Stage C was a minimum supervision period. The differential treatment strategy was to be based on the theory of interpersonal maturity.

The tyranny latent in the program eventually was uncovered by Lerman. He demonstrated that the experimental group was, in fact, subject to more social control than treatment; the average amount of time in detention for the experimentals was about ten times the average amount of time spent in "treatment," according to Lerman's calculations. Thus, he concludes, the program for the experimentals was far more punitive than it was beneficial.

Lerman was being generous by his calculations. He only defined *detentions* as "social control." After all, the experimentals were under some form of state control *twenty-four hours a day,* either in detention or under parole supervision. Using this broader concept of social control, the ratio of social control to treatment increases from 10 to 1 to about 60 to 1.

The genius of the method, of course, rests on the selection of the basis for comparison. The treatment researchers might argue that the proper comparison should be between the ratio of treatment to social control in the experimental group and the same ratio in the control group. A comparison of these ratios, they might argue, would indicate that the experimentals received a greater dose of treatment relative to social control than did the persons in the traditional CYA program. That is, they might argue that the basis for comparison should be the cases regularly processed, rather than a standard of no social control at all. Pointing to Lerman's (1975:53) figures for noncriminal violators, they might argue that the experimental group averaged 18 days in detention compared to the average of 240 days experienced by the control group during the first 8 months of the social control period (a ratio of about 13 to 1 in favor of the experimentals). Or, being fair, they might include the detention periods for the entire project, since the data subsequent to the initial phase are somewhat more supportive of the benevolence-turned-tyranny doctrine. This would produce an average of 258 detention days for the controls and 24 for the experimentals (and the ratio plummets to about 11 to 1). Thus, they might argue that, when compared to the control group, the experimental group experienced far less social control.

The destruction technique can withstand this logic. The program staff promised *treatment,* and even using Lerman's conservative figures, they delivered more social control than treatment. Because anything compared with nothing will always be greater than nothing, it will always be possible to prove that all treatment programs in criminal justice involve more social control than does absolute freedom.

CONCLUSION

Although implausible, in the event that a combination of these destruction techniques does not convincingly destroy a positive research report, it is possible to borrow the ultimate destruction technique from Bailey (1966:156):

> When one recalls that these results, in terms of success or failure of the treatment used, *are based upon the conclusions of the authors of the reports, themselves,* then the implications . . . regarding the effectiveness of correctional treatment become rather discouraging. (Emphasis added)

Because it is inconceivable that anyone other than the author of the research will be the one to report the findings, and because such self-reports are inherently suspect, our conventional wisdom is unlikely to be upset.

REFERENCES

ADAMS, S.
1977   "Evaluating Correctional Treatments." *Criminal Justice and Behavior* 4 (4): 323–339.

BAILEY, W.
1966   "Correctional Outcome: An Evaluation of 100 Reports." *Journal of Criminal Law, Criminology and Police Science* 57(2): 153–160.

CONRAD, J.
1973   "Corrections and Simple Justice." *Journal of Criminal Law, Criminology and Police Science* 64(2): 208–217.

DOLESCHAL, E., and KLAPMUTS, N.
1973   "Toward a New Criminology." *Crime and Delinquency Literature* 5 (4): 607--627.

HIRSCHI, T.
1973   "Labelling Theory and Juvenile Delinquency: An Assessment of the Evidence." In *The Labelling of Deviance,* W. Gove, ed. Beverly Hills: Sage.

LERMAN, P.
1975   *Community Treatment and Social Control.* Chicago: University of Chicago Press.

LIPTON, D., MARTINSON, R., and WILKS, J.
1975   *The Effectiveness of Correctional Treatment.* New York: Praeger.

LOGAN, C.
1967   "Evaluation Research in Crime and Delinquency: A Reappraisal." *Journal of Criminal Law, Criminology and Police Science* 63 (3): 378–387.

MARTINSON, R.
1974 "What Works?—Questions and Answers about Prison Reform." *The Public Interest* (Spring): 22–54.

MENNINGER, K.
1968 *The Crime of Punishment.* New York: Viking.

NATIONAL RESEARCH COUNCIL
1978 *Deterrence and Incapacitation: Estimating the Effects of Criminal Sanctions on the Crime Rate.* Washington, D.C.: National Academy of Sciences.

O'LEARY, V., GOTTFREDSON, M., and GELMAN, A.
1975 "Contemporary Sentencing Proposals." *Criminal Law Bulletin* 11 (5): 555–586.

PALMER, T.
1971 "California's Community Treatment Program for Delinquent Adolescents." *Journal of Research in Crime and Delinquency* 8 (1): 74–92.

1974 "The Youth Authority's Community Treatment Project." *Federal Probation* (March): 3–14.

1975 "Martinson Revisited." *Journal of Research in Crime and Delinquency* 12 (2): 133–152.

ROBISON, J., and SMITH, G.
1971 "The Effectiveness of Correctional Programs." *Crime and Delinquency* 17 (1): 67–80.

SCHUR, E.
1973 *Radical Non-Intervention: Rethinking the Delinquency Problem.* Englewood Cliffs, N.J.: Prentice-Hall.

VAN DEN HAAG, E.
1975 *Punishing Criminals.* New York: Basic Books.

WEILER, P.
1974 "The Reform of Punishment." In *Studies on Sentencing,* Law Reform Commission of Canada. Ottawa, Canada: Information Canada.

WRIGHT, W., and DIXON, M.
1977 "Community Treatment of Juvenile Delinquency: A Review of Evaluation Studies." *Journal of Research in Crime and Delinquency* 14 (1): 35–67.

The loss of power resulting from field approximation of laboratory research is a concept familiar to researchers in psychology. Boruch and Gomez go beyond the acknowledgement of this decrease in sensitivity by providing tentative statistical models to estimate the magnitude of this power decay. For the evaluation researcher, there are also a wealth of suggestions for measuring factors associated with loss of power in the field, and invaluable hints for rectifying this power decay. Implementation of these suggestions would add credence to evaluatory conclusions of no difference.

Issues of strength and integrity of treatment found elsewhere in this volume are also cogently analyzed here. Boruch and Gomez's concern for the reliability and validity of measures chosen are basic perspectives from which they develop many plausible shortcomings of current evaluation practice using examples from multiple fields of study. Replete with practical advice, the work is unique in its accompanying theoretical approach to impact evaluations.

6

Sensitivity, Bias, and Theory
in Impact Evaluation

Robert F. Boruch and Hernando Gomez

Ordinary design of experiment technology invites underpowered (insensitive) experiments because the measurement facts of life go unrecognized. The purpose of this article is to identify these measurement lapses, and contribute to the development of more rigorous and socially beneficial program evaluations. Measurement should concern itself not only with reliability of the dependent variable but, more importantly, with validity of measurement and with measurement (systematic observation) of the treatment variable. Orthodox measurement theory should be augmented by input from program managers, developers, and the substantive theorist. A technical appendix outlines a theory of measurement in field evaluation.

This article's aim is simply to present some theory and technique that will improve our ability to understand the effects of a new social program. Our special interest lies in the measurement of treatment and response, so that we may anticipate the power of an evaluation design, enhance that power, and understand the evaluation results. By *impact evaluation*, we mean estimating in the least equivocal and least biased way the relative effect of a program on its target group. The estimate may be made with respect to a control group, a competing treatment group, or to some other standard. Goal-free evaluation and other approaches with different aims fall outside the scope of this article. One of the motives for exploring the topic is frustration. Evaluations often yield "no significant differences," and that finding is often a matter of weak evaluation design. Poor design is partly a function of measurement. Another motive is developing a more informative theory of statistical power for evaluations. In orthodox form, the theory is arid and underutilized. We believe it should be embellished to reflect better the realities of social experimentation and so we present an outline for augmenting the theory.

THIS RESEARCH WAS SUPPORTED *by National Institute of Education Contract NIE-C-74-0115. Some useful comments on an earlier draft were kindly provided by David Rindskopf and John McSweeny.*
REQUESTS FOR REPRINTS *should be sent to Robert F. Boruch, Department of Psychology, Northwestern University, Evanston, Illinois 60201.*

The first section illustrates very briefly the problems of ensuring power in evaluation design, links the problem to measurement issues, then offers a modest guide to its reconnaissance. A second section discusses the response variable in evaluations, and the third section presents the treatment program. The illustrations come from a variety of social sciences because the problems addressed here are general.

The Problem of Ensuring Power

Consider the following scenario. A theorist invents a novel compensatory education program, tests it fairly in a laboratory experiment, and finds that the effect on children's achievement is notable. The effect size is a half standard deviation difference between the experimental group's mean and some standard. A foundation decides that the program is promising, supports a half dozen field versions of the program, and submits each to evaluation. These field experiments show no evidence of a notable effect, that is, treated and untreated groups exhibit no major difference.

Our interest lies in the reasons for the failure to detect effects in the field. We assume, as will sometimes be the case, that the standard tactics for ensuring the power of experimental tests, such as blocking, have been used (Cohen, 1969). We make the more tenuous assumption that for evaluations based on quasi-experimental designs, newer tactics for avoiding statistical biases have been used (Campbell & Boruch, 1975).

Our small theory posits that partial irrelevance of the response variable and degradation of the treatment variable in the field can be major causes of the failure to detect effects. To carry this idea beyond simpleminded speculation, consider the same example made more concrete. With a program effect of a half standard deviation in the laboratory, a sample of size 40, and a conventional significance level such as .01, the power of the laboratory test will be about .92, that is, the chances are 9 out of 10 that an effect will be detected in such laboratory tests.

The algebraic version of our small theory shows that this power cannot be reasonably expected in the field. In particular, the response variables chosen by evaluation contractors are often only partly relevant to the program content. A standardized achievement test chosen for convenience in the field, for instance, may only be 75% relevant to the program content. And because of natural random variation in quality of measurement, the test's reliability may dip to .80. Further, it will usually be the case that the treatment delivered in the laboratory will not be the treatment delivered in the field. Simple indifference among field staff may reduce the treatment's fidelity to 75% of its design value, and natural random variation in staff delivery and in student receipt will reduce the uniformity of treatment as well. It is easy to show that under all these conditions, the power drops to about .30. That is, the chances of discovering the effect in the field are small.

This, we believe, is a dreadful but realistic state of affairs. The phenomenon is roughly analogous to voltage drops in the transmission of electrical power from a utility station to a customer. The precipitous drop in statistical power is due to the fact that invalidity of response and infidelity of treatment have a multiplicative rather than an additive, effect. The following remarks present the theory and evidence in a bit more detail.

AUGMENTING STANDARD THEORY

The appendix summarizes the theory in words and, to avoid violating minority group sensibilities, in algebra as well. We first posit a treatment variable as ideal or theorized and a response variable as ideal or theorized; each is potentially measurable. We suppose that in the laboratory test, both the response and treatment variables are ideal. *Treatment variable* here means *both* novel program and normal conditions (i.e., both treatment and control or both of two competing treatments). The normal theoretical assumption is that the response and treatment variables are functionally related. The simplest form of the assumption is that the response is an additive function of treatment effect and some unknowable random variables, as described in the appendix. This little model, of course, underlies any orthodox analysis of variance. We regard the model as adequate in the laboratory and less adequate in the field.

Consider first how the notion of response variable might be augmented to better reflect reality. The example on compensatory education implies that problems of measurement must be divided into two categories. The first concerns the choice or construction of a measurement device that under good conditions, is valid with respect to the treatment variable. That is, elements of response are nicely linked in theory to elements of treatment. The second issue involves degradation of this nice measure in field settings. To represent generic validity of the response variable, we rely on a simple model which shows that observable response is an imperfect function of response as theorized; reliable but irrelevant variation in response accounts for the imperfection. To recognize the fact that the generically good response measure is further degraded randomly in the field, we add to the model some random error, called *unreliability*.

Consider next the variable labeled *treatment*. It is reasonable to propose, based on the evidence at hand, that classical statistical conceptions of treatment be augmented in two ways. First, admit that gross structural differences between the treatment as theorized and the treatment as actually imposed in the field will appear. The simplest way to represent this idea is to posit an index of structural integrity or fidelity of treatment that, like a proportion, varies between 0 and 1. In the simplest case, this might be the percentage of overlap between the staff behaviors prescribed for inducing client change in an experimental program and the staff behaviors actually exhibited in the field. Second, recognize that in social programs, the actual level of treatment imposition and reception will vary on a continuum for each client. Even if that variation cannot be measured, it does affect sensitivity and so ought to be recognized in design. The idea of a macrolevel bias, induced by structural infidelity of treatment, and a microlevel variation at the recipient level can be simplified by using a regression model. That is, describe treatment in the field as a function of its structural integrity and as a function of individual variation in imposition and receipt.

The response and treatment variables in the field are represented here then by simple regression models that recognize variation in fidelity. By augmenting the usual analysis of variance model with these and computing the power for both the simple and the augmented models, it is easy to show the drop in power (see the appendix).

The Response Variable

Ensuring that the response variables adequately reflect treatment effects is a cyclical dilemma in exploratory research. We don't know if the variable is relevant until we detect effects, but to detect effects, we need to know if the variable is relevant. Any arguments about relevance in this instance are primarily theoretical. For confirmatory field research, and especially for policy-related evaluations, however, we believe there ought to be both sound theory and data to support the contention that the response variable proposed is indeed relevant to the treatment variable. The distinction between exploratory and confirmatory research is consistent with Kempthorne's (1975) use of the terms. That is the case considered here.

Relevance of the Response Measure

Our aim is to identify a measure of the response variable that is relevant to treatment, relevance being determined by some clear criteria. Having said this ever so piously, it is difficult to say more because the criteria for determining relevance are not often simple. They include substantive theory, prior data, and pilot tests. And they include models for understanding how the response variable is related to the actual status of the individual and to the program content.

SUBSTANTIVE THEORY

Few substantive theories of human behavior specify how relevance of a response variable with respect to a treatment program ought to be established. More important for field evaluations, the theoretical linkages between response and treatment ought to be laid out beforehand, but rarely are. At least one group of evaluators, Wholey, Nay, Scanlon, and Schmidt (1975), have built a notable reputation partly by trying to specify such linkages in ongoing programs.

Their general approach focuses on determining the extent to which a program can be evaluated. Their strategy is to lay out the *assumed* linkages between program activity and program objectives in a rhetorical program model. This literally describes, for example, how components of a community mental health center program are expected to affect inappropriate use of state mental hospitals, maintenance of economically viable community programs, quality of service, and so on. By eliminating untestable assumptions about linkage between program elements and objectives and by eliminating unmeasurable objectives, the analysts produce an evaluatable program model. The product is a rudimentary theory of why treatment and response variables may be related. It is a simple strategy in the sense that it seeks only to establish plausible and testable linkages. It is sophisticated in the sense that it can help an individual avoid choosing gratuitous response variables for an evaluation, that is, it helps to eliminate naive reliance on those variables as indicators of program quality.

To be concrete about what appears to be good practice for *new* theory-based programs, we cite both good and bad examples and confess our inability to do much more with substantive theory. George Fairweather and others built community mental health programs whose content, activity, and target group are dedicated in theory to patients' social adjustment, so their use of multiple indicators of social adjustment, behavioral and otherwise, makes sense. In education, the Heber, Garber, Harrington, Hoffman, and Falender (Note 1) work was designed on the basis of a theory that links infant IQ to stimulation in early infancy, so their use of standard measures of IQ as a response variable has a special place in their program evaluation. Waldo and Chiricos (1977) justified their use of recidivism as a response variable in evaluations of work release programs on the basis of five different theories of the way such programs affect the ex-offender's behavior. At the level of individual interaction in the classroom, Brophy (Note 2) and his colleagues rationalized the linkage between microlevel student behaviors and microlevel teacher behaviors toward the student.

These examples illustrate the painstaking effort that is sometimes required to establish a linkage, and sometimes they are dead wrong. They do stand as a bit of an embarrassment to the less careful researcher. The latter category includes researchers who believe a program developer's contention that a program objective is "social adjustment," only to find out later that the staff who have direct contact with the clients not only reject the idea but can't agree on specific objectives themselves. It includes the researcher who, with touching optimism and slender rationalization, measures children's IQs after 3 months of a busing program to discover that busing has no effect on IQ. And so on.

Relying on weak substantive theory appears to be more risky than relying on available data, and so we consider evidence next.

PRIOR DATA

The data available prior to an evaluation can be used to argue that a particular response measure is indeed sensitive to the program and so should be measured in the field test. The data can be used to help decide *which* measures of an attribute are most likely to reflect differences in the field, some measures being more robust against deliberate or accidental corruption than others. And the data can be used to guess the likely size of the program's effect under formal evaluation, that is, to establish the power of the experimental design. This last function represents a higher consciousness level, so it is the main focus of the following remarks.

The nature of the available data varies enormously, of course. Most often the evidence on a response measure will be complicated to interpret, if simple to collect. Multiple regression of a response variable on treatment-related variables can be informative *provided* we recognize the shortcomings of estimated regression coefficients. The little brutes can be inflated *or* deflated by measurement error in the variates (Cochran, 1968). And if the substantive theory, and therefore the regression equation, fails to include some variables that nature says are important, then the bias in estimates of the coefficients may be unknowable (Campbell & Boruch, 1975). Perhaps more commonly the evidence is very difficult to interpret, being based on simple correlations or cross-tabulations that are unencumbered by any information about reliability of measures, the nature of the sample on which the statistic is based, or the sampling process. It is at this point that weak theory and weak data force more active approaches to establishing the relevance of response measures, notably pilot studies, which we consider later.

Regardless of the data's nature, access to the information is growing. Such archives as the DOPE (Databank of Program Evaluations) file at the University of California, Los Angeles, MEDLARS (Medical Literature Analysis and Retrieval System) in medical research, ERIC (Educational Resources Information Center) in education, though imperfect in many respects, can be helpful in building dossiers on response variable use in evaluation. At the very least, they report whether a given response variable was affected by a treatment program. And at most, they provide information on the variable's reliability or validity with respect to other standards.

They beg for better exploitation. These resources are being augmented sporadically by the release of raw data from completed program evaluations. The secondary analyses of these data can yield better understanding of the size of program effect under various conditions and some feeling for the degree to which a response variable is relevant to the program. Finally, metaevaluations of the sort constructed by Glass (1976) are also useful in this enterprise. At their best, they consolidate information about the size of effect of roughly similar programs from field studies, which information should be used to estimate the size of effect for the response variable and program at hand.

The crude statistics on reliability and validity that are usually published for standardized measures are also pertinent here. These constitute indirect evidence because measures may be internally consistent, quite reliable in conventional test–retest settings, and valid with respect to the standards chosen by the publisher of the inventory. But they may still be unrelated in theory or in practice to the program under evaluation. This does suggest that reviews published by Buros, ERIC, and similar services ought to include references to experiments in which the measure has been used as a response measure. The absence of statistics on the sensitivity of a measure with respect to a treatment variable makes these reviews much less useful than they could be.

ADOPTION, ADAPTION, AND CONSTRUCTION

The problem of deciding whether to adopt a standardized measure of response rather than to build one from scratch is not new. But it has become a bit more crucial, since the quality of program evaluations depends partly on the decision. The argument for the adoption of a standardized measure in a program evaluation is usually based on the measure's convenience and properties. That is, the measure is readily available and it is known to discriminate reliably among individuals in a standardization sample. Two important problems are implicit in the practice, however. First, the measure's relevance to the social program's target group is often unclear. Despite its reliability and validity with respect to a standardization sample, it may not be a valid indicator of the pertinent attribute in the idiosyncratic sample at hand. The second, more unique, problem concerns the measure's relevance to the program at hand.

In health services research, for instance, health status indicators that weight mortality heavily have been standard. Yet they are not particularly good indicators of the health status of many groups to which health services are targeted, notably economically deprived families (*International Journal*, 1976). And they are insensitive to many of the health program's activities (e.g. venereal disease control). In criminal justice research, recidivism is a standard indicator of the impact of new rehabilitation programs. It too is imperfect because many programs, recognizing a natural ceiling on what can be accomplished, direct their attention to reducing the severity of the recidivist's crime and to introducing lower cost or more equitable restitution to the victim.

Bianchini's (in press) research on the problem in evaluating compensatory education programs is among the most informative. He has examined California Achievement Test data within grade groups for both standardization samples and schools eligible for Emergency School Assistance Act (ESAA) funds.

Although he found that the achievement test had good properties in the standardization sample, it was notably less valid an indicator of ability in the ESAA sample. In particular, the test floor for the latter sample puts 10%-25% of the students (depending on grade) at or below chance level scores, in contrast to a 3%-7% rate in the standardization sample. And though the range of scores was the same for the two samples, the pileup at the lower extreme of the test for the ESAA sample raised the mean difficulty level of the test for that sample and lowered the measure's validity as an indicator of ability. This in turn made it a less valid gauge of the program's effects, if indeed the program was effective. To establish crudely how relevant the standard tests are to curriculum, he simply counted vocabulary common to tests and instruction. Doing so for the Stanford Reading Test, used in response to state legislative requirements for standardized testing, he found students performing well below national norms; but overlap in vocabulary content was only 20%. The Cooperative Reading Tests, used more recently by the state, placed California students closer to the national average; but test–curriculum content overlap was closer to 60%. Bianchini has suggested that the discrepancy in test results was due to the unique characteristics of the standardization samples and the differences in curriculum content associated with each.

The point is that standard measures may be used to place people validly on a broad continuum of health or ability, but their quality in this respect implies virtually nothing about their validity in the extreme ranges. Even when valid there, the indicator may be only partly relevant to program objectives—the overlap in indicator content and program content may be low. As Bianchini (in press) pointed out, the first problem is the ordinary one of ensuring that the test has good properties in the sample at hand.

The construction of new response measures presents no less difficult a problem. In principle, it is possible to develop indicators of ability, say, that do not depend for their validity on the standardization sample and that can be used to estimate ability accurately in extreme ranges. Item parameters need to be independent of the standardization sample to avoid ceiling and floor effects, for instance. In practice, this is supposed to be one of the benefits of using such models as those suggested in Bock (1975) by Rasch, Samejima, and Bock to scale items in a test or inventory. The use of the models in major education and nutrition experiments and elsewhere has been promising (Gomez, Note 3). Without the technical support and large samples that these methods demand, however, some less effective tactics are justified.

Strategies for the construction of response variables that suit the setting vary considerably. They are based on common sense or what passes for common sense occasionally embellished by good statistical sense. For Tyler (in press), the problem has been to avoid naive adoption of standardized achievement tests for assessing novel education programs. He has focused instead on the construction of tests that are obviously relevant to the program content. In particular, he espouses the notion that test items ought to be constructed and compiled on the basis of what teachers are teaching. For Fairweather and Tornatsky (1977) in mental health and for Katz and Akpom (1976) in health services research, the problem was similarly framed: Examine the content of a program and build instruments that overlap in an obvious way with program content. In each case, the effort was coupled with side study to ensure that the responses were reliable in the simplest sense and valid with respect to one standard — program objectives or content.

For Brickell (1976), merely having established a linkage between content of a test and content of a program was insufficient. He found, in evaluating career education programs, that response variables constructed on the basis of program objectives, content, and teacher behaviors do not differentiate between program participants and nonparticipants. He regarded this failure to detect program effects as contrary to the impressionistic opinions of his classroom observers. So, in a new cycle of test construction, Brickell and company developed a test based on children's behavior in the career education classroom, especially those behaviors and skills that are likely to differentiate such children from nonparticipants. The tactic isn't unreasonable; its mathematical analogue, a discriminant analysis, is over 50 years old. And it does yield results — participants and nonparticipants do differ notably on the response variable. Unfortunately, Brickell's entertaining story line was not supported by any information about the properties of resulting tests, nor with any analysis of the way participants and nonparticipants differ prior to the program evaluation. The tactic is promising and open to debate and investigation.

The arguments over adoption versus construction of new response variables are not likely to go away in the near future. We see no option when novel programs are tested on small and idiosyncratic target populations but to tailor the measures. We see no option but to adopt or adapt standard measures for global programs run over longer periods if the program under evaluation is directed to populations used as a basis for developing the standardized measure. The use of both tailored and standard measures seems natural for research falling between the two extremes and for tests of novel programs. In the latter case, the use of both new and standard indicators is warranted to establish relations between the two.

SIDE THEORIES

Most social theories fail to attend at all to the idea that validity of the response variable will be degraded in field evaluations of theory-based programs. That disability is being corrected in a few quarters. Total survey design theory, for example, is a formal effort to couple classical sampling theory to more realistic assumptions about how people respond — fallibly (Reeder, 1976). Credibility approaches to marketing research involve theory to recognize that some people will not do what they say they'll do (Brown, 1969). Still other theories are auxiliary, tied more closely to the use of evaluative data.

In broadening his theory of social experimentation, for example, Campbell (1975) exposured a side theory on corruption of social indicators. The idea is that as soon as it becomes well known that a measure is being used in making policy decisions, notably in program evaluations, the measure will be corrupted in some degree. To get beyond the statement, one must identify the main influences on corruption. For Knightly (1975), in what must stand as a model on crude theory in war reporting, this meant tracing the quality of battle statistics as a function of incompetent journalists, self-interested generals, self-serving politicians, and the minority, the virtuous members of each camp. For program evaluations, the magnitude of corruption ought to be anticipated at least approximately. The task is less formidable, given methodological studies on how response bias depends on the training and attitudes of interviewers, level of threat to the respondent, and so on (Reeder, 1976; Sudman & Bradburn 1974). The task of controlling corruption has become less formidable with the advent of specialized methods for eliciting sensitive information in surveys. So-called randomized response techniques and other methods are effective alternatives to pious assurances of confidentiality (Boruch & Cecil, in press).

The more general theories of validity of the response variable depend on changes in the target population and social system, as well as on the use of the indicator. Mortality satistics are a less informative indicator of health status than they once were, at least in the United States, partly because age-specific mortality is now so low for many age categories. And so they are not especially relevant to many health services programs (Elinson, in press). Unemployment statistics are today a less informative indicator of economic hardship than they were when the unemployment statistics program started because income transfer payments and other factors dilute the economic hardship dimension of those data notably (Levitan & Taggart, 1976). Self-reported victimization rates may supplement ordinary crime statistics partly because the latter's relevance can be affected by changes in the social definition of *reportable crimes* and the political and institutional influences on the accuracy of crime statistics.

All of this points up the fact that the special theory of response can be constructed to guide the understanding of validity of response. For evaluations, the theory is crucial: The failure to anticipate the degraded quality of response will degrade the quality of an evaluation. The simple model used in the appendix, adapted from Cleary, Linn, and Walster (1970), illustrates the point. It is possible to anticipate the degradation in power and perhaps even to control it, provided that validity of the response variable with respect to treatment can be guessed.

PILOT FEASIBILITY TESTS AND SIDE STUDIES

Mark Twain, according to Mark Twain, was not terribly bright. But even he had the wit to collect test–retest reliabilities and validity data on phrenologists' readings of his bumps and palmists' readings of his paw. (The most reliable palmister vouchsafed that Twain had no sense of humor [Clemens, 1917/1959].) Some researchers exhibit a sturdier indifference to common sense.

Projects without a trace of concern for the matter include the Federal Reserve Board's evaluation of the Philadelphia School District, the Federal Aviation Administration's evaluation of the Concorde's impact on communities in the airport's vicinity, and most of the recent studies of the impact of desegregation. For these and other cases, establishing the validity of a response measure in the field is essential for obtaining decent estimates of program effect. Regardless of these cases, it is reasonable to argue that the theoretical relevance of a proposed measure of response to treatment is not a sufficient guarantee of the variable's relevance for the program under field conditions.

To make matters concrete, we reiterate two recommendations that often fall on deaf ears. First, mount pilot feasibility tests prior to the main evaluation to establish properties of response measures and to determine the feasibility of evaluation design. Second, mount side studies during the main evaluation to ensure that the properties of measures are knowable and to ensure that when they warrant adjustment they can be adjusted. The idea is to anticipate problems using a pilot, understand and control problems using side study, and use data obtained in both at the analysis stage of the evaluation.

Pilot feasibility study here means a small-scale evaluation mounted *primarily* to troubleshoot the evaluation design and measurement system. The approach is especially feasible in multisite evaluations: Sins committed at pilot sites are transformed to virtues at later sites. Examples here include the Diet–Heart Feasibility Study (1968), the Negative Income Tax Experiment, and others. At a minimum, the pilots provide estimates of variance in response, reliability, and validity. Those statistics can be used to modify the design of subsequent evaluations, when statistical power is crucial, and in a pinch may be used to adjust bias in estimates of program effect produced by the design or by the measurement system.

The purpose of side studies adjoined to main evaluations is observation and control of variations in validity of response. Simple changes in reliability, for example, can often be expected in repeated measures designs for evaluating educational programs, complex clinical programs in mental health and health services, and elsewhere. The failure even to recognize changes in reliability means biased estimates of effect at worst and complicated analytic problems at best (Campbell & Boruch, 1975). Failing to estimate the magnitude of change in reliability means no postfacto correction is possible even if the algebra for correction can be developed. Side studies can be cheap, with subsamples of people and subsamples of their behavior. Mounting side studies as an afterthought is tempting partly because there is no formal theory on the topic. That formal theory needs to be developed.

Finally, we do not mean to imply here that these efforts are primarily qualitative or ad hoc in character. There is absolutely no reason to ignore the participant–observer, informant, and other tactics in monitoring and controlling response measurement. In fact, any quantitative effort must begin with the qualitative idea that the observation is fallible. There have been only a few interesting efforts to combine the two traditions better in evaluative research (Fisher & Berliner, Note 4).

The Treatment Variable

Classical theory in experimental design assumes that the prescribed level of treatment is either present or absent. Our contention is that this assumption needs to be augmented routinely for field experimentation; otherwise, it may hinder the development of better theory of evaluation. Classical measurement theory is no less parochial. Its traditional focus on individual attributes, such as achievement level, extroversion, and so on, is crucial; the imperfection lies in not expanding theory to constructs like treatment. The management sciences speak to neither group, though program dimensions and degree of program implementation seem to fit neatly in their territory as well. There are exceptions, to be sure, and they are discussed below. The focus is on infidelity of treatment and its implications for measurement and power of evaluations.

STEREOTYPICAL PROBLEMS

For simplicity's sake, we begin with three stereotypical problems in identifying and measuring treatment in field studies: (a) policy packaged as program, (b) the structurally incomplete program, and (c) incomplete program reception or delivery at the individual level. The message is simple. In the social and behavioral sciences and in education, the treatment labels may be meaningless or misleading, or they may be accurate but imprecise. To the extent that these issues are ignored, evaluations will be less informative and evaluation designs will be less powerful than they ought to be.

Policy Packaged as Program

Social policy at any level of governance is often labeled as program and tested as such, when in fact the operational features of the policy are unknown and perhaps unknowable. A formal test of the impact of the policy under this condition is an empty exercise.

Desegregation is a case in point. It is interpreted as a program by some researchers, but its nature goes unexplored, its existence goes unverified, except in the grossest possible sense. For example, the Riverside California desegregation study (Moskowitz & Wortman, Note 5) reported no operational indicators of desegregation more sophisticated than a monochromatic body count. What makes the matter more invidious is that the program in this instance is not clear with respect to commonsense concepts of integration — physical busing is not racial integration. Nor can it be assumed that at smaller levels of social enterprise, policy of Type A can be distinguished from policy of Type B. Blind expert ratings of recorded therapy sessions sometimes show no differences between therapy types that are advertised as being different.

More commonly, the policy of program plan is specified so vaguely that almost any novel activity could be labeled as consistent with the program and the translation of the plan into action could be quite variable. The poor specification implies that we cannot know whether the program put into the field is actually the one implied by the plan. For example, the Executive

High School Internship Program is a national project dedicated, under its written policy, to encouraging leadership training by experience among bright high school students. There is good evidence that despite the national headquarters' emphasis, the programs generated at the local level are career education programs and are not particularly well tied to leadership. So an evaluaton design that attempts to estimate the program's impact on leadership is more likely to be a test of its headquarters' pronouncements than a test of its actual effects. Similarly, an evaluation design based on the presumption that all community mental health centers supported by the state of Illinois are dedicated to improving personal adjustment, as they are advertised to do, is also bound to be specious. For under their mandate, the organization, operation, and clients of the centers vary greatly, and their local policies may deviate considerably from state policy.

Structural Imperfections in Program Implementation

That a new social program will be implemented imperfectly is obvious once said. It is even more reasonable to expect the level of program implementation to influence the size of the program's effect on its target population. Yet the problem of identifying imperfection and of measuring it has not received much formal attention from the behavioral or social scientists in academe. Especially in evaluation studies, this buck gets passed to the program manager. There is, however, a developing fund of knowledge that can be used for more sophisticated work. It ranges from case studies on the one hand to efforts to quantify the observations on the other.

The acuteness of the problem and the evolutionary character of the solutions are most evident from the case studies, post mortems really. For instance, Weikart and Banet's (1975) attempts to introduce Piagetian ideas into regular classroom teaching led, in the early stages, to confusion and some loss of confidence among teachers (i.e., program implementors). The later efforts involved not only far more specific instruction and actual choice of curriculum materials, as well as a more collaborative style of research, but the development of tactics to accommodate scheduling difficulties engendered by the open classrooms and to alleviate the pressures exercised by excluded colleagues and unenthusiastic supervisors on the participating teachers. Gramlich and Koshel's (1975) surprisingly candid study of the performance contracting experiments put greater emphasis on the mismatch between the contractors' claims about their personnel, flexibility, and speed and the contractor's actual abilities. Both studies recognized that despite teachers' initial enthusiasm and agreement to participate, their adherence to an unfamiliar regimen cannot be taken for granted. That analogous problems occur in other sectors is also clear, judging by Fairweather and Tornatsky's study (1977) in mental health, Williams' (1976) in poverty research, McLaughlin's (1975) in compensatory education, and others. As case studies, these are precious but insufficient reading. They help us speculate about the factors that may produce incomplete programs, and so may help to explain the evaluator's finding that the program had only a small effect. But they are not especially helpful in understanding how to systematize observation of the problem and how to tie the observation to formal analysis.

To be sure, there are fragments of methodology that may be helpful here. For the program manager, it is reasonable to develop checklists (measurement of a crude sort) to reflect the gross administrative state of a program. The U.S. Agency for International Development's (1974) inventory for monitoring programs typifies the genre. Mead's (Note 6) work is a considerable elaboration of the same theme but under the rubric of institutional analysis. He focused on administrative, political, and economic factors that affect program implementation and provided some guides, but he presented no concrete methodology for their measurement. Although useful for crude control, these techniques are not often well tied to response variables, except rhetorically, and are not linked at all to experimental or quasi-experimental design technology or to measurement theory.

Examples of the next step along the measurement-control continuum are not hard to find. In field testing innovative teacher training programs, Crawford, Gage, and Stallings (Note 7) capitalized on structured classroom observations, measuring rates, and consistency of teacher behaviors to determine the extent to which the prescribed teaching strategy was met. They designed their system of observation to establish whether teachers in control conditions have adopted the novel program also, to establish the presence of John Henry effects, and the like. That work runs parallel to Fairweather and Tornatsky's (1977) efforts in mental health to ensure, through systematic observation, that adoption level matches plans. It is reflected in research by Walberg (1974) and Brophy (Note 2) in education, by Sloane, Staples, Cristol, Yorkston, and Shipple (1975) in therapy evaluation, and others. That is, one builds inventories to systematically assay the level of major program elements and the level of competing elements in the program.

The final cluster of pertinent activities involves settings in which control is impossible but partially relevant data plentiful. Factor analysts and most users of structural equations try to find surrogate measures of treatment, for instance, in measuring amount of "schooling" by grade level, measuring quality of schooling by the number of books in a library, and so on. The more thoughtful efforts are illustrated by Orlinsky and Howard (1975), who factor analyzed process variables in therapeutic settings to better understand what that is about. Activities like these evolve naturally from the use of treatment-related variables in more mundane regression analyses. In the latter cases, however, measures of the treatment variables are usually devoid of validity estimates, so we may find, as Jencks (1972) did in reanalyzing the survey of equality of educational opportunity (Coleman et al., 1966 that the information on treatment process is of doubtful worth if it comes from poorly informed informants.

Although methodological developments here are fragmentary, substantive theory is in far worse condition. It is nearly impossible, for example, to find a social or behavioral science theory that specifies the probable ceiling on implementation of the theory-based program. Nor do substantive theories often specify which components of the program need to be adopted in the field for the program to be effective. That failure means the analyst cannot determine whether the program is in place, much less whether the intensity is sufficient to say that the program exists. Theories that specify the target population well are few, and those that specify how to contact members of the target group are fewer still. Yet the process of identification and selection of program participants does seem to be a natural part of the theory-based program and of the theory itself.

Variation in Program Reception at the Individual Level

This topic, like the preceding one, is not new, but it is understated in the design, measurement, and analysis literature. Some examples may help to illustrate its character.

The Kaiser-Permanente studies (Cutler et al., 1973) of the impact of free multiphasic screening on health status was designed as a randomized test with very large samples. The regimen for the treatment group, annual multiphasic screening, was *not* followed by the majority of individuals during the first year. In response to wholesale deviations detected by the simplest of measurement systems, body counts, telephone operators were employed to regularly remind individuals of their checkups, which brought cooperation rates to 65%. Exactly the same problems occur in drug studies, diet studies, and other investigations in which the members of the target group have some discretion in adhering to treatment. Similar feedback and encouragement strategies were adopted in the experimental tests of the impact of television show Sesame Street, in which encouragement constitutes a major treatment component. The absence of early warning systems of this sort has led to the termination of tests on parent effectiveness training (Weaver, Note 8), on judicial procedures for assignment of offenders to special treatment programs (Conner, 1977), and others. The problem requires not only construction of real time monitoring and feedback systems but designs which recognize that natural variation in simple adherence to treatment will degrade power of an experiment.

The more interesting and relevant problem involves the idea that the imposition of treatment, its receipt by the individual, or both, can be regarded as a continuum. That is, underlying the labeled fixed treatment is a continuum of treatment imposition that is potentially measurable but normally goes unobserved. The clinician trying out a new approach does vary in using it with each patient; the patient's reception may vary as a consequence or independently. Tutors hired under grants to teach young children do not spend the same time with each, nor are they uniformly enthusiastic, energetic, and perceptive with each child. The level and nature of activity in work release programs, prison contracts, and the like, in prison rehabilitation vary greatly, for the labeled treatment is only shorthand for a variety of activities.

Intuition suggests that latent variation in the reception of a program should affect the sensitivity of an evaluation. And indeed a 30-year-old paper by Berkson verifies the intuition algebraically (Berkson, 1950; Boruch, 1975). To capitalize on the notion, though, requires a good deal more work, notably systematically observing the variation even if one can't control it.

That is where a major gap in the literature of psychometrics seems to lie. Principles (of reliability and validity) are there, to be sure, but there is no coherent theory or practice for dealing with the idea. Instead, there are fragments. In the randomized tests of Sesame Street, Ball and Bogatz (1973) measured the children's viewing hours, which made *viewing* more than just a label, and a notable part of both primary and secondary analysis (Cook, Appleton, Conner, Schaffer, Tamkin, & Weber, 1975). In some tests of compensatory education programs, personnel training programs, and the like, absence from class is a crude indicator of reception at the individual level. In some medical research, fixed dosage is divided by weight of the subject to get at the latent reception. Beyond these simple tactics, we have virtually nothing in the way of cheap but effective measurement schemes. Although the problem is second in importance to structural imperfection in treatments, it too warrants investigation.

The Problem in Other Disciplines

The problem of measuring the treatment variable is not confined to the social sciences, of course. The controversy appears in the physical sciences, where, for example, allegations of 20% margins on reliability of measurement and control of variables in nuclear reactor cooling systems have been a grave concern (Primack & von Hippel, 1974). Bureaucracies have simply forgotten to implement program plans for pesticide control (U.S. General Accounting Office, 1968). They have denied the existence of treatments and mislabeled them: Recall U.S. Defense Department denial of the use of poison gasses at the Dugway Proving Grounds. Confirmatory tests of polio vaccine were disrupted briefly by vaccine that induced poliomyelitis rather than preventing it, a problem of quality control over batch production that affects any test of a new pharmaceutical.

These are extreme cases to be sure, but the less extreme are just as easy to identify. We mention them for the sake of context. The problems of identifying and measuring the treatment are severe enough in the social sciences to produce the idea that the social researcher couldn't find the way to the bathroom without help. The fact of the matter is that if this orientation difficulty is true, we have lots of company.

PILOT FEASIBILITY TESTS

Pilot tests or side studies, mounted prior to a full-scale evaluation, seem well justified here. Neither social theory nor available data are usually sufficient to specify how one ought to measure dimensions of treatment, much less what the likely degree of program implementation is. Pilot tests, even demonstration projects, can provide early information on probable level of program implementation or adoption in the larger field tests. They may also be used to try out new methods for gauging variations in reception of treatment by members of the target sample and variation in delivery by members of the program staff.

Some large-scale efforts to adhere to this strategy have already been mentioned. The 1962 Diet-Heart Feasibility Studies (National Heart Institute, 1969) were mounted to see if diet regimens could be imposed and to assay the level of adherence to the diet by volunteers, *rather* than to test the diet's effects. As the first of several sites in the Negative Income Tax Experiments, the New Jersey program disclosed some embarrassing and unexpected difficulties in income transfer arrangements, problems avoided at later sites, (Riecken et al., 1974). In education, the strategy undertaken by Crawford et al. (Note 7) was similar: Their prior research on training teachers for novel programs provided a good deal of advance information on how to ensure adherence to the prescribed teaching regimen and how to observe adherence rate economically. Other examples are given in Riecken et al. (1974).

The product of pilot tests ought not to be simply the identification of treatment-related variables and the statistics that reflect the quality of their measurement. We know so little about how long it takes to mount social programs in complex bureaucratic settings that time itself becomes a measure of interest. In this instance, the pilot may provide better evidence for scheduling outcome measures in the actual field trial, thereby anticipating the chronic complaint of the program manager: You measured too soon, we weren't ready, the program's not operational yet, and so on.

STATISTICAL MODELS FOR ANALYSIS

To predict the influence of problems like these on the power of an evaluation design and to gauge the impact of prophylactic action, the problem must be characterized algebraically as well as literally. That is, we need to model the problem to understand its influence. In fact, some work on the topic has been done, though far less than is necessary.

In his early work in biomedical research, Berkson (1950) posited a model in which mean level of treatment was fixed and delivered as advertised, but there is some latent variability about that mean. Estimates of treatment effect from randomized experiments under this condition are unbiased, but power is lower than it would otherwise be. In elaborations on the theme, Fedorov (1974) derived the consequence of latent variation for factorial experiments and for cases in which the latent variation is systematic (e.g., cyclic) rather than random. The same idea can be generalized in simpler form by measuring at least some of the latent variability within treatment and control conditions. That is, in addition to observing who is a member of the nominal treatment and nominal control groups, we measure observable variation in intensity of treatment and of the control group's incidental access to similar or identical treatment. The regression of response on the fixed (dummy) treatment variable consititutes a conventional between-groups regression (i.e., an analysis of variance) and provides an unbiased estimate of effect in a randomized test. The simultaneous regression of response on both the dummy variables and the measured latent variables gives us some additional information about the within-groups regression (i.e., how self-selection and variation within treatment predict variation in response). The model and estimation process is simple (Boruch, 1975), but testing hypotheses can be statistically complicated (Proctor, 1976).

A parallel but not independent schema for understanding sources of variation in observations of the treatment variable can be based on analysis of variance components. The generalizability theory presented by Cronbach, Gleser, Nanda, and Rajaratnam (1972), for example, is a framework for doing so. The components may include temporal variation (e.g., test–retest reliability) and interrater variation, as well as variation of more direct interest, such as adherence to the treatment regimen. The approach has been tried in educational research to untangle complex teaching processes

(Cronbach et al., 1972, chapt. 7), in therapy research (Howard, Orlinsky, & Perilstein, 1976), in research on the quality of census surveys, and elsewhere.

The model for treatment specified in Appendix A is simple but differs from those described. It says that in the field, treatment deviates from structural plan or laboratory program and that the discrepancy can be recognized by describing actual treatment as a simple linear function of planned treatment and latent random variation. This model is only an approximation, but it's better than nothing, which is what we had at the start of this article. There are more realistic alternatives, but they are very complicated and must wait for another time.

Conclusion

We have tried to deliver three messages here. The first is that orthodox experimental design and the quasi-experimental approaches need to be augmented for evaluating social programs. The reader may already have guessed that. The embellishments we suggested are not all original and certainly not simple. But they can enhance the sensitivity of field tests of social programs and give us a better understanding of why notable effects fail to turn up when they're supposed to.

The second message is an exhortation to be catholic. There is little excuse (aside from time, money, and our own parochial reading habits) for failing to recognize that these problems cut across all the social and behavioral sciences, including our jaded sister, economics. They are not even unique there, for we can find similar dilemmas in the early history of agricultural statistics and medical research.

This applies also to specialties within the discipline. That is, the program manager with intuition about "degree of program implementation" ought to be accommodated by the evaluation designer responsible for predicting the power of the field experiment. Both will have something valuable to say to the measurement specialist, who must determine the extent to which degree of program implementation is measurable and who must choose or construct response variables that are relevant to treatment. And finally, the academic theorist or the theorist in mufti (i.e., the program developer) must be brought into the circle at the evaluation design level if at no other. For if he or she cannot provide literal guidance, none of the others will be able to manage their responsibilities terribly well.

REFERENCE NOTES

1. Heber, R., Garber, H., Harrington, S., Hoffman, C., & Falender, C., *Rehabilitation of families at risk for mental retardation*. Madison: University of Wisconsin,

Rehabilitation Research and Training Center, 1972.
2. Brophy, J. *Training teachers in experiments.* Paper presented at the meeting of the American Educational Research Association, New York, February 1977.
3. Gomez, H. *Applications of the Rasch model for estimating abilities in the Cali experiments on nutrition and education.* (Methodology and Evaluation Research Report NIE-O1G). Evanston, Ill.: Northwestern University, 1977.
4. Fisher, C. W., & Berliner, D. C. *Quasi-clinical inquiry in research on classroom teaching and learning.* Paper presented at the annual meeting of the American Educational Research Association, New York, April 1977.
5. Moskowitz, J., & Wortman, P. M. *Reanalysis of the Riverside California desegregation study.* Manuscript in preparation, 1977.
6. Mead, L. M. Institutional analysis: A preliminary methodology (Working Paper 0797-03). Washington, D.C.: The Urban Institute, 1977.
7. Crawford, J., Gage, N. L., & Stallings, J. A. *Methods for maximizing the validity of experiments on teaching.* Paper presented at the annual meeting of the American Educational Research Association, New York, April 1977.
8. Weaver, R. *Failure of the parent effectiveness training (P.E.T.) evaluation.* Unpublished manuscript, Northwestern University, 1975.

REFERENCES

Ball, S., & Bogatz, G. A. *Reading with television: An evaluation of the "Electric Company"* (Vols. 1 & 2). Princeton, N.J.: Educational Testing Service, 1973.
Berkson, J. Are there two regressions? *Journal of the American Statistical Association,* 1950, *45*, 164–180.
Bianchini, J. Achievement tests and differential norms. In M. Wargo & R. Green (Eds.), *Minority group testing.* New York: McGraw-Hill, in press.
Bock, R. D. *Multivariate statistical methods in behavioral research.* New York: McGraw-Hill, 1975.
Boruch, R. F. Coupling randomized experiments and approximations to experiments in social program evaluation. *Sociological Methods and Research,* 1975, *4*, 31–53.
Boruch, R. F., & Cecil, J. S. *Assuring confidentiality and privacy in social research.* Boston: Cambridge University Press (Rose Series), in press.
Brickell, H. M. Needed: Instruments as good as our eyes. *Journal of Career Education.* 1976, *2*(3), 56–66.
Brown, R. V. *Research and the credibility of estimates.* Boston: Harvard University Press, 1969.
Campbell, D. T. Assessing the impact of planned social change. In G. M. Lyons (Ed.), *Social research and public policies.* Hanover, N.H.: Dartmouth, 1975.
Campbell, D. T., & Boruch, R. F. Making the case for randomized experiments: Six ways in which quasi-experimental evaluations in compensatory education tend to underestimate effects. In A. Lumsdaine & C. Bennett (Eds.), *Evaluation and measurement.* New York: Academic Press, 1975.
Cleary, T. A., Linn, R. L., & Walster, G. W. The effect of reliability and validity on power of statistical tests. In E. F. Gorgotta & G. W. Bornstedt (Eds.), *Sociological*

methodology. San Francisco: Jossey-Bass, 1970.

Clemens, S. L. *The autobiography of Mark Twain* (C. Neider, Ed.). Harper, 1959. (Originally published, 1917).

Cochran, W. G. Errors of measurement in statistics. *Technometrics*, 1968, *10*, 637–666.

Cohen, J. *Statistical power analysis for the behavioral sciences.* New York: Academic Press, 1969.

Coleman, J. S., Campbell, E. Q., Hobson, C. J., McPartland, J., Mood, A. M., Weinfield, F. D., & York, R. L. *Equality of educational opportunity* (Vol. 1 & 2). Washington, D.C.: U.S. Government Printing Office, 1966.

Conner, R. F. Selecting a control group: An analysis of the randomization process in twelve social reform programs. *Evaluation Quarterly*, 1977, *1*, 195–244.

Cook, T. D., Appleton, H., Conner, R., Schaffer, A., Tamkin, G., & Weber, S. J. *Sesame Street revisited.* New York: Russell Sage Foundation, 1975.

Cronbach, L. J., Gleser, G. C., Nanda, H., & Rajaratnam, N. *The dependability of behavioral measurements: The theory of generalizability for scores and profiles.* New York: Wiley, 1972.

Cutler, J. L., Ramcharan, S., Feldman, R., Siegelaub, A. B., Campbell, B., Friedman, G. D., Dales, L. G., & Collen, M. F. Multiphasic checkup evaluation study: I. Methods and population. *Preventive Medicine*, 1973, *2*, 197–206.

Diet–Heart Feasibility Study Group. The diet-heart feasibility study. *Circulation*, 1968, **37**(3, Supplement 1), 1–428.

Elinson, J. Insensitive health statistics and the dilemma of the HSA's. *American Journal of Public Health,* in press.

Fairweather, G., & Tornatsky, L. *Experimental methods for social policy research.* New York: Pergamon Press, 1977.

Fedorov, V. V. Regression problems with controllable variables subject to error. *Biometrika*, 1974, *61*, 49–56.

Glass, G. V. Primary, secondary, and meta-analysis of research. *Educational Researcher*, 1976, *5*(10), 3–8.

Gramlich, E. M., & Koshel, P. P. Is real world experimentation possible? The case of educational performance contracting. *Policy Analysis*, 1975, *1*(3), 511–530.

Howard, K. I., Orlinsky, D. E., & Perilstein, J. Contribution of therapists to patients' experiences in psychotherapy: A components of variance model for analyzing process data. *Journal of Consulting and Clinical Psychology*, 1976, *44*, 520–526.

International Journal of Health Services Research, 1976, *6*(3).

Jencks, C. S. The quality of the data collected by the Equality of Opportunity Survey. In F. Mosteller & D. P. Moynihan (Eds.), *On equality of educational opportunity.* New York: Vintage Books, 1972.

Katz, S., & Akpom, C. A. A measure of primary sociobiological functions. *International Journal of Health Services*, 1976, *6*, 493–508.

Kempthorne, O. Inference from experiments and randomization. In J. N. Srivistava (Ed.), *A survey of statistical design and linear models.* Amsterdam: North-Holland, 1975.

Knightly, P. *The first casualty.* New York: Harcourt Brace Jovanovich, 1975.

Levitan, S. A., & Taggart, R. Do our statistics measure the real labor market hardships? In, *Proceedings of the American Statistical Association: Social Statistics Section.* Washington, D.C.: American Statistical Association, 1976.

McLaughlin, M. M. W. *Evaluation and reform: The Elementary and Secondary Education Act of 1965/Title I.* Cambridge, Mass.: Ballinger, 1975.

National Heart Institute, Diet-Heart Review Panel. Mass field trials of the diet-heart question. *American Heart Association Monograph* (No. 38). New York: American Heart Association, 1969.

Orlinsky, D. E., & Howard, K. I. *Varieties of psycho-therapeutic experience.* New York: Columbia Teachers College Press, 1975.

Primack, J., & von Hippel, F. *Advice and dissent: Scientists in the political arena.* New York: Basic Books, 1974.

Proctor, C. H. Testing for contextual effect. In, *Proceedings of the American Statistical Association: Social Statistics Section Part II.* Washington, D.C.: American Statistical Association, 1976.

Reeder, L. G. (Ed.). *Advances in health survey research methods.* Rockville, Md.: National Center for Health Services Research, 1976.

Riecken, H. W., Boruch, R. F., Campbell, D. T., Glennan, T. K., Pratt, J., Rees, A., & Williams, W. *Social experimentation: A method for planning and evaluating social programs.* New York: Academic Press, 1974.

Sloane, R. B., Staples, F. R., Cristol, A. H., Yorkston, N. J., & Shipple, K. Short-term analytically oriented psychotherapy versus behavior therapy. *American Journal of Psychiatry,* 1975, *132,* 373-377.

Sudman, S., & Bradburn, N. M. *Response effects in surveys: A review and synthesis.* Chicago: Aldine, 1974.

Tyler, R. Achievement test selection for program evaluation: Comments on Hoepfner's paper. In M. Wargo & R. Green (Eds.), *Minority group testing.* New York: McGraw-Hill, in press.

U.S. Agency for International Development, Office of Development, Program Review, and Evaluation. *Project evaluation guidelines* (3rd ed.). Washington, D. C.: U.S. Government Printing Office, 1974.

U.S. General Accounting Office. *Need to improve regulatory enforcement procedures involving pesticides (B-133192).* Washington, D.C.: U.S. Government Printing Office, September 10, 1968.

Walberg, H. J. (Ed.). *Evaluating educational performance: A source book of methods, instruments, and examples.* Berkeley, Calif.: McCutchan, 1974.

Waldo, G. P., & Chiricos, T. G. Work release and recidivism. *Evaluation Quarterly,* 1977, *1*(1), 87-108.

Wargo, M., & Green, R. (Eds.). *Minority group testing.* New York: McGraw-Hill, in press.

Weikart, D. P., & Banet, D. P. Planned variation from the perspective of a model sponsor. *Policy Analysis,* 1975, 1(3), 485-510.

Wholey, J. S., Nay, J. N., Scanlon, J. W., & Schmidt, R. E. Evaluation: When is it really needed? *Evaluation Magazine,* 1975, 2(2), 89-93.

Appendix on next page

Appendix: Small Theory of Measurement in Field Evaluation in Symbols and in Words

A. The Linkage

$\eta = \tau + e$

$e \sim (0, \sigma^2)$

Response, η, is a simple additive function of treatment, τ, and of unspecified, possibly unknowable, influences, e.

B. The Response

$Y = K\eta + \phi$

$\phi \sim (0, \sigma_\phi^2)$

$Y' = K\eta + \phi + \xi$

$\xi \sim (0, \sigma_\xi^2)$

The response variable, Y, is only a partially valid indicator of response to treatment, $0 < K < 1$.

The response variable Y' is not only partially valid, but is subject to random errors in measurement, ξ.

C. The Treatment

$T = \gamma\tau$

$T' = \gamma\tau + \delta$

$\delta \sim (0, \sigma_\delta^2)$

The treatment τ is imposed incompletely, $0 < K < 1$.

Not only is treatment structurally incomplete but it varies along a continuum for each individual.

D. In the laboratory or low-noise setting, we have $\eta = \tau + e$ with noncentrality parameter $\lambda_\eta = (N\Sigma\tau^2/\sigma^2)$. In the field, we have

$Y' = K\gamma\tau + K\delta + Ke + \phi + \xi$

$$\lambda'_\eta = \frac{NK^2\gamma^2\Sigma\tau^2}{K^2\sigma^2 + K^2\sigma_\delta^2 + \sigma_\phi^2 + \sigma_\xi^2}$$

Table 1A: Noncentrality Parameters and Probability of Type II Errors

A. Linkage

$$\lambda = \frac{N\Sigma\tau^2}{\sigma^2}$$

Let $N = 40$, $\tau = .5$, $\sigma^2 = 1$, $\sigma_\eta^2 = 1.25$, $df_1 = 1$, and $df_2 = 39$.

$$\lambda_\eta = 10 \Rightarrow p(\text{II}) = .08$$

B. Response Variable

$$\lambda_y = \frac{K^2 N\Sigma\tau^2}{K^2\sigma^2 + \sigma_\phi^2}$$

Let $K = 3/4 = $ validity of Y, so $\sigma_\phi^2 = 35/64$.

$$\lambda_y = 5.07 \Rightarrow p(\text{II}) \doteq$$

$$\lambda'_y = \frac{K^2 N\Sigma\tau^2}{K^2\sigma^2 + \sigma_\phi^2 + \sigma_\xi^2}$$

Let reliability of $Y' = .80$, so $\sigma_\xi^2 = 10/32$.

$$= 3.96 \Rightarrow p(\text{II}) = .46$$

C. Integrity of Treatment

$$\lambda'_T = \frac{NK^2\gamma^2\Sigma\tau^2}{K^2\gamma_\delta^2 + K^2\sigma^2 + \sigma_\phi^2 + \sigma_\xi^2}$$

Let $\gamma = 3/4$, $\sigma_\xi^2 = (\sigma_\tau^2/4) = 1/16$.

$$\lambda'_T = 2.17 \Rightarrow p(\text{II}) \doteq .72$$

Note. $p(\text{II})$ is the probability of a Type II error; λ is the noncentrality parameter

Received June 1, 1977

The federal government is currently spending about two billion dollars per year to produce knowledge about social problems, and there is evidence that reliance on the social science community to produce dependable and useful information is increasing. However, there are many signs of dissatisfaction with the performance of the social science research community, and demands for accountability, for evidence of usefulness, are also increasing.

Surprisingly little is known about the overall pattern of federal expenditures, and there clearly is no overall strategy guiding the distribution of federal funds and no criteria by which it can be said whether the right amount of money is being spent. The National Research Council was invited to undertake a study of federal expenditures on knowledge about social problems. The following is a chapter from their report and it details the distribution of federal expenditures. The data provide some interesting insights into patterns of funding, and the conclusions, although not startling, are nonetheless not entirely obvious. They provide some useful hints about the ways in which funding of program evaluations is likely to come about.

7

Federal Spending for Social Knowledge Production and Application

National Research Council

Federal expenditures for social R&D have grown rapidly over the past decade, particularly with the advent of the new social programs. The Office of Management and Budget (OMB) and the staff of the science and technology adviser to the President have tracked these expenditures as part of the special analysis of R&D items in the federal budget. But a great deal more can be learned about the recent pattern of federal support for social knowledge production and application by classifying these expenditures in several new ways.

Our survey examined some 180 agencies[1] in 44 organizational entities that support identifiable amounts of knowledge production and application in 12 social policy areas. We identified the distinct programs of funding for social knowledge production and application within each of these agencies and then classified these programs in ways that reflected our analytical objectives. This method required extensive interviewing within the departments and agencies in addition to inspecting budget data.

We developed four classifications. The first is by type of activity, as defined in Chapter 1; the second is by policy area; the third is by type and organizational location of the funding agency; and the fourth is by the objective or audience of the activity being supported. This chapter

[1]The term "agency" refers to any organizational unit of a cabinet-level department (including bureaus, divisions, offices, and services) or any independent organizational unit, other than a cabinet-level department, whose principal officer reports directly to the President.

Reproduced from *The Federal Investment in Knowledge of Social Problems* (1978), pages 16-34, with permission of the National Academy of Sciences, Washington, DC.

examines the data by applying these classifications singly and in combination.[2]

FUNDING PATTERNS BY TYPE OF ACTIVITY

The level of federal funding for fiscal 1976 for each type of social knowledge production and application activity is presented in Table 1. It is noteworthy that two-thirds of all obligations in that year were for knowledge production and one-third for application. The largest category of spending was research, including basic, applied, and policy research, which accounted for more than one-third of all obligations. However, the substantial obligations for policy formulation demonstrations, for program evaluations, and for general purpose statistics suggest the importance of other means by which the federal government invests in the production of knowledge of social problems.

Table 1 also reveals that the two categories of demonstration projects accounted for almost one-fifth of all obligations for social knowledge production and application. The support of demonstrations as a means of gaining new knowledge, as well as of applying knowledge, has received far too little attention. The figures show that federal obligations for demonstrations were divided roughly evenly between projects that sought new information (demonstrations for policy formulation) and projects that promoted the adoption of a program (demonstrations for policy implementation). These figures exclude a third type of spending, for operating programs masquerading as "demonstrations," where the objective is neither to gain nor to disseminate knowledge.[3]

Table 1 shows that almost $600 million was obligated by the federal government to knowledge application activities in fiscal 1976. Except

[2]Further details of the definitions and methods of our survey of budget obligations appear in the Appendix, and detailed breakdowns by individual agency appear in Abramson (1978). In one respect, however, our analytical quarry remained out of range. Although a great deal can be found out by classifying funding programs, each of these programs includes a number of individually funded projects, which may differ from one another in terms that bear on our principles of classification. We sought wherever possible to reflect this variety by apportioning a program among two or more categories, but refining these judgments by extending our survey to many thousands of individual projects would have swamped our resources. We note where our findings might be modified if they were rooted in data on individual projects.

[3]For a detailed discussion of demonstrations, see Cheryl D. Hayes, "Toward a Conceptualization of the Function of Demonstrations," hereafter cited as Hayes, "Demonstrations," *in* Glennan (1978).

TABLE 1 Funding Patterns: Social Knowledge Production and Application Activities (fiscal 1976 obligations, $ millions)

Activity	$	%
Knowledge production		
Research	655	36
Demonstrations for policy formulation	204	11
Program evaluation	62	3
General purpose statistics	294	16
Total	1,215	67
Knowledge application		
Demonstrations for policy implementation	183	10
Development of materials	121	7
Dissemination	294	16
Total	598	33
TOTAL	1,813	100

Numbers may not total due to rounding.
NOTE: Caution should be used when making comparisons between the data above and the data on "research and development" collected by the National Science Foundation and the Office of Management and Budget. As noted in Chapter 1, several of the above categories fall outside the definition of R&D used by the federal government. Thus, the $1.8 billion total should not be interpreted as being part of total federal obligations for research and development. A fuller discussion of these data and definitions appears in the Appendix.

for the development of materials, our categories of knowledge application have traditionally been excluded from figures on R&D. This is true of the largest of our categories, the activities we group under "dissemination." This figure is almost certainly on the low side, since it includes only separately identifiable projects for dissemination. Nonetheless, this and the other figures in these categories indicate the general magnitude of recent explicit federal investment in the application of knowledge to social problems.

FUNDING PATTERNS BY POLICY AREA

In addition to providing estimates of the amounts spent for social knowledge production and application, our survey sought to provide a basis for analyzing the allocation of funding by subject. Working with a classification of policy areas similar to those proposed by the General Accounting Office and the House Budget Committee, we identified twelve areas, grouped in four broad categories: human resources, community resources, natural resources, and science and technology. The human resources category includes health, education, employment and training, and social services and income security. The community services category includes economic growth, transportation, housing and community development, law enforcement and justice, and international affairs. The natural resources category includes natural resources and the environment and energy development and conservation. Finally, the science and technology category includes a set of programs designed to strengthen the nation's science and technology base.

Table 2 presents the distribution of support for social knowledge production and application among the twelve policy areas. Human resources claim about 60 percent of the total, with community resources, including economic growth, accounting for another 28 percent. The table discloses interesting variations in funding for knowledge production and for knowledge application among policy areas. For example:

• In education, there is a high proportion of funding for knowledge application (60 percent) as opposed to knowledge production. This is because most of this work is supported by the practitioner-dominated Office of Education; emphasis has been placed on policy implementation demonstrations and the development of materials rather than on research.

• In health, in contrast, the proportions are almost exactly the opposite. Much of this spending for knowledge production can be traced to the National Institutes of Health, which have placed much greater emphasis on basic research and the creation of new knowledge than on the application of existing knowledge. This emphasis has influenced the activities of many agencies that are concerned with social problems related to health.

• In social services and income security, there is little funding for knowledge application, largely because policy makers who use such research are federal officials, and so dissemination can be informal.

Table 3 shows how the relative allocation of social knowledge production and application obligations among the policy areas compares with the relative allocation of the total federal budget authority (including knowledge production and application, operating programs, administrative expenses, etc.) among comparable policy areas.

Two observations can be made from these figures. The first is that the federal investment in social knowledge production and application

TABLE 2   Funding Patterns: Social Knowledge Production and Application by Policy Area (fiscal 1976 obligations, $ millions)

Policy Area	Knowledge Production		Knowledge Application		Total	
	$	%	$	%	$	%
Human resources						
Health	265	61	171	39	436 (24)[a]	100
Education	156	40	237	60	394 (22)	100
Employment and training	118	85	21	15	139 (8)	100
Social services and income security	92	82	21	18	112 (6)	100
Total	631		450		1,081 (60)	
Community resources						
Economic growth	178	86	29	14	206 (11)	100
Transportation	84	74	29	26	114 (6)	100
Housing and community development	62	58	45	42	106 (6)	100
Law enforcement and justice	47	72	18	28	65 (4)	100
International affairs	17	73	6	27	23 (1)	100
Total	388		127		514 (28)	
Natural resources						
Natural resources and environment	111	97	4	3	114 (6)	100
Energy development and conservation	28	95	2	5	30 (2)	100
Total	139		6		144 (8)	
Science and technology base	58	78	16	22	74 (4)	100
TOTAL	1,215		598		1,813 (100)	

Numbers may not total due to rounding.
[a]Numbers in parentheses are column percentages.

TABLE 3   Comparison of Funding Patterns for Social Knowledge Production and Application with Total Federal Civilian Budget by Policy Area (fiscal 1976 obligations, $ millions)

Policy Area	Funding for Knowledge Production and Application		Total Civilian Budget[a]		Funding for Knowledge Production and Application (Col. 1)/ Total Civilian Budget (Col. 3)
	$	%	$	%	
Human resources					
Health	436	24	32,339	11	0.013
Education	394	22	7,889	3	0.050
Employment and training	139	8	7,910	3	0.018
Social services and income security	112	6	144,281	48	0.001
Total	1,081	60	192,419	64	0.006
Community resources					
Economic growth	(206)[b]	(11)[b]	No comparable OMB function		
Transportation	114	6	9,906	3	0.012
Housing and community development[c]	106	6	14,332	5	0.007
Law enforcement and justice	65	4	3,264	1	0.020
International affairs	23	1	6,450	2	0.004
Total	308	17	33,952	11	0.009
Natural resources					
Natural resources and environment	114	6	15,667	5	0.007
Energy development and conservation	30	2	3,522	1	0.009
Total	144	8	19,189	6	0.008
Science and technology base	74	4	1,145	*	0.065
Other civilian functions[d]			56,132	19	
TOTAL	1,813	100	302,837[e]	100	0.006

Numbers may not total due to rounding.
[a]Source: *The Budget of the United States Government*, Fiscal 1977, Part 8, Tables 2 and 14.
[b]Excluded from subtotal.
[c]Includes OMB function of revenue sharing in addition to community and regional development.
[d]Includes agriculture, commerce, veterans' benefits, general government, interest, allowances, and undistributed offsetting receipts.
[e]National defense and space research and technology are excluded from budget total.
*Less than 0.5 percent.

represents a small though varied fraction of total program costs. For all policy areas, this fraction averages only six-tenths of one percent (0.006). In the special case of science and technology, where R&D outlays (mainly nonsocial) account for most of the total, the fraction invested in social knowledge production and application is still only seven percent. Of the substantive policy areas, only in education, where program costs are primarily met from nonfederal sources, is the investment in social knowledge production and application more than two percent of total program costs.

The second observation is that there is a rough equivalence between the fraction that a policy category claims of the whole federal budget, on the one hand, and of the federal investment in social knowledge production and application, on the other. These two fractions tend to vary together in the totals for the four policy categories of human resources, community resources, natural resources, and science and technology. At this level of aggregation, support for social knowledge production and application does appear to "follow the budget." But the variation at the level of policy area is considerable and shows, for example, how relatively slight is the investment in the creation and use of knowledge on social services and income security.

FUNDING PATTERNS BY AGENCY

The most revealing findings to emerge from our survey of spending for social knowledge production and application have to do with the organizational location of the programs of support. Table 4 presents data on levels of fiscal 1976 federal support for knowledge production and application at the level of the department or independent agency. These data show how much of the spending is accounted for by a few departments and agencies. Of the 44 organizational entities summarized in the table, the Department of Health, Education, and Welfare is the largest supporter of social knowledge production and application, accounting for nearly 40 percent of the total—almost $730 million. Four other departments spent over $100 million on social knowledge production and application in fiscal 1976, and a total of 23 agencies spent more than $5 million.

There is further evidence on this point in Table 5, which lists the 20 agencies with the largest budgets for social knowledge production and application; they account for 71.6 percent of the $1.8 billion total. Significantly, these agencies represent a wide spectrum of types of mission and activity. The largest agency, the Office of Education (OE), comprises primarily operating programs. Although research is not a major priority, OE has seen education innovation as a program goal for at least the past 15 years and obligates a substantial portion of its funds to demonstration activities. Three of the 20 agencies—the National Science Foundation, the National Institutes of Health, and the National Institute of Education—specialize primarily in research; two— the Bureau of the Census and the Bureau of Labor Statistics—are statistical agencies that also have the support of knowledge production and application activities as a primary mission.[4] As might be expected, given HEW's share of total social knowledge production and application spending, 9 of the 20 are HEW agencies.

But the evidence on organizational location should not be misread: 180 distinct federal agencies are involved in funding social knowledge production and application activities, and many of the agencies on the top-20 list are aggregates of a number of smaller and fairly autonomous funding programs. Indeed, the decentralization of the funding effort is striking.

Decentralization has been the natural consequence of the way authorization has been given for programs of support of social research and development. The prevailing approach is clearly reflected in authorizing legislation. A recent compilation of R&D statutes by the Congressional Research Service for the House Committee on Science and Technology found that ". . . most Federal R&D laws appear to relate to 'mission oriented' research and development and to be administered by agencies directly involved with specific missions and responsibilities" (U.S. Congress, House 1976b, p. 3). The major exceptions are the statutes dealing with the National Science Foundation and the Smithsonian Institution, agencies whose legislation provides a clear mandate to broad areas of basic research.

This evidence led David ("Two Transformations," *in* Stokes 1978), in analyzing the emerging federal role in social research and development, to conclude that the commitment of federal funds has largely been shaped by policy and program legislation that only incidentally contained provisions authorizing or directing the conduct of mission-related R&D. In other words, the legal and political basis for R&D activities within an agency has followed, rather than preceded, the policy and program commitments that specify the agency's purpose and responsibilities—its mission. This pattern accounts for the location of most R&D programs within the operating federal departments rather

---

[4]For more information on the role of the primary and secondary statistical agencies of the federal government, see President's Commission on Federal Statistics (1971).

TABLE 4 Funding Patterns: Social Knowledge Production and Application Activities by Department or Agency (fiscal 1976 obligations, $ millions)

Department or Agency	Knowledge Production Activities					Knowledge Application Activities				TOTAL
	Research	Policy Formulation Demonstrations	Program Evaluation	General Purpose Statistics	Total	Policy Implementation Demonstrations	Development of Materials	Dissemination	Total	
Department of Agriculture	62	*	3	41	106	–	1	176	177	282
Department of Commerce	22	4	2	77	106	1	*	7	8	114
Department of Defense	40	2	*	2	45	–	13	1	14	58
Department of Health, Education, and Welfare[a]										
Health Related[b]	139	34	9	31	212	37	6	33	76	287
Education[c]	46	81	17	4	149	79	54	23	156	305
Income Security[d]	20	21	2	–	43	2	–	1	3	46
Human Development[e]	38	19	10	2	70	12	2	7	21	91
Total—Department of Health, Education, and Welfare	243	155	38	37	474	130	62	64	256	729
Department of Housing and Urban Development	10	19	4	11	44	7	3	5	14	58
Department of the Interior	9	–	1	2	12	*	1	1	1	13
Department of Justice	28	*	5	13	47	12	–	6	18	65
Department of Labor	19	3	2	68	92	2	6	7	15	107
Department of State	14	1	2	–	17	1	*	6	7	24
Department of Transportation	43	9	1	21	74	10	8	10	27	101
Department of the Treasury	11	–	–	15	25	–	–	–	–	25
Appalachian Regional Commission	1	4	1	–	5	8	–	–	8	13

161

Agency										
Civil Service Commission	2	–	*	*	2	2	1	–	3	6
Commission on Civil Rights	5	–	–	–	5	–	–	2	2	7
Community Services Administration	2	1	–	–	3	5	–	–	5	8
Energy Research and Development Administration	12	–	–	–	12	–	–	–	–	12
Environmental Protection Agency	12	–	1	–	13	–	–	–	–	13
Executive Office of the President[f]	4	–	*	–	4	–	–	1	1	6
Federal Reserve System	6	–	–	3	9	–	–	–	–;	9
National Foundation on the Arts and the Humanities	1	–	*	–	1	–	14	3	18	18
National Science Foundation	76	2	1	1	80	3	13	*	17	97
Smithsonian Institution	8	–	*	–	8	–	*	1	1	10
Veterans Administration	2	2	*	1	5	2	–	–	2	7
Independent agencies[g]	15	–	–	–	15	–	–	1	1	16
Other agencies[h]	8	1	2	1	12	1	–	3	4	15
TOTAL	655	204	62	294	1,215	183	121	293	598	1,813

Numbers may not total due to rounding.

[a] The activities of the Assistant Secretary for Planning and Evaluation have been included throughout the four policy areas.

[b] Alcohol, Drug Abuse, and Mental Health Administration; Center for Disease Control; Food and Drug Administration; Health Resources Administration; Health Services Administration; National Institutes of Health; and Assistant Secretary for Health.

[c] National Institute of Education; Office of Education; Assistant Secretary for Education.

[d] Social and Rehabilitation Service; Social Security Administration.

[e] Office of Human Development.

[f] Council of Economic Advisors; Council on Environmental Quality; Office of Telecommunications; Council on Wage and Price Stability.

[g] Civil Aeronautics Board; Consumer Product Safety Commission; Federal Communications Commission; Federal Home Loan Bank Board; Federal Power Commission; International Trade Commission; Interstate Commerce Commission; Nuclear Regulatory Commission; Securities and Exchange Commission; Federal Trade Commission.

[h] ACTION; Federal Mediation and Conciliation Service; General Services Administration; Small Business Administration; United States Information Agency; Arms Control and Disarmament Agency; National Center for Productivity and Quality of Working Life; Advisory Commission on Intergovernmental Relations; Federal Energy Administration; Equal Employment Opportunity Commission; Tennessee Valley Authority.

* Less than $0.5 million.

TABLE 5 Twenty Agencies with Largest Budgets for Social Knowledge
Production and Application (fiscal 1976 obligations, $ millions)

Agency	Department	Knowledge Production	Knowledge Application	Total
1. Office of Education	HEW	89	124	213
2. Extension Service	USDA	2	166	168
3. National Science Foundation		80	17	97
4. Alcohol, Drug Abuse, and Mental Health Administration	HEW	78	7	85
5. Office of Human Development	HEW	55	21	76
6. National Institute of Education	HEW	46	28	74
7. Health Resources Administration	HEW	55	13	68
8. Bureau of the Census	Commerce	65	1	67
9. National Institutes of Health	HEW	42	22	64
10. Bureau of Labor Statistics	Labor	56	–	56
11. Policy Development and Research	HUD	50	5	55
12. Law Enforcement Assistance Administration	Justice	41	18	58
13. Health Services Administration	HEW	21	31	52
14. Assistant Secretary for Planning and Evaluation	HEW	34	–	34
15. Statistical Reporting Service	USDA	31	–	31
16. Economic Research Service	USDA	25	6	31
17. National Highway Traffic Safety Administration	DOT	17	10	27
18. Social Security Administration	HEW	25	1	26
19. Cooperative State Research Service	USDA	25	–	25
20. Office of the Secretary	DOT	20	4	24
TOTAL		857	473	1,330

Numbers may not total due to rounding.

than in independent R&D agencies. It also accounts for the decentralization of R&D programs to several mission agencies within major departments.

The mission-related character of much of the federal support of the production and application of knowledge of social problems can be summarized by classifying the organizations in which the programs are located. For this purpose, we developed a fourfold categorization of supporting agencies:

Associated with operating programs. Offices that have programmatic responsibility to administer federal programs: for example, Food and Nutrition Service (Agriculture); Economic Development Administration (Commerce); Office of Education (HEW); National Park Service (Interior); and the Federal Highway Administration (Transportation).

Associated with policy-making offices. Offices that do not directly administer programs and that frequently have oversight responsibility for a number of federal programs or have staff advisory responsibility for nonprogrammatic federal policies: for example, the Office of the Assistant Secretary for Planning and Evaluation (HEW); the Office of Planning, Budgeting, and Evaluation (Office of Education/HEW); Advisory Commission on Intergovernmental Relations; U.S. Commission on Civil Rights; and the Council of Economic Advisers.

Associated with agencies whose primary mission is R&D funding. For example: the National Institute of Education (HEW); the Agricultural Research Service (Agriculture); the National Center for Health Services Research (HEW); and the National Science Foundation.

Associated with agencies whose primary mission is the collection or analysis of statistics. For example: Statistical Reporting Service (Agriculture); Bureau of the Census (Commerce); National Center for Education Statistics (HEW); and the National Criminal Justice Information and Statistical Service (Law Enforcement Assistance Administration/Justice).

Table 6 presents data on the allocation of federal support for knowledge production and application in fiscal 1976 by this classification. Although some agencies were difficult to categorize, the data show the extent to which program operations influence social knowledge production and application. More than 50 percent of total social knowledge production and application obligations—more than 75 percent of

TABLE 6 Funding Patterns: Type of Supporting Agency by Social Knowledge Production and Application Activities (fiscal 1976 obligations, $ millions)

| | Type of Supporting Agency | | | | | | | | | |
| | Operating Programs | | Policy-Making Offices | | R&D Funding Agencies | | Statistical Agencies | | Total | |
Activity	$	%	$	%	$	%	$	%	$	%
Knowledge production										
Research	258 (28)[a]	39	70 (40)	11	311 (63)	48	16 (8)	3	655 (36)	100
Policy formulation demonstrations	109 (12)	53	37 (21)	18	59 (12)	29	–	–	204 (11)	100
Program evaluation	28 (3)	46	25 (14)	40	9 (2)	14	* (*)	*	62 (3)	100
General purpose statistics	73 (8)	25	21 (12)	7	3 (1)	1	197 (91)	67	294 (16)	100
Total	468 (50)	39	152 (87)	13	382 (78)	31	213 (99)	18	1,215 (67)	100
Knowledge application										
Policy implementation demonstrations	166 (18)	91	7 (4)	4	10 (2)	6	–	–	183 (10)	100
Development of materials	72 (8)	59	3 (2)	2	46 (9)	38	–	–	121 (7)	100
Dissemination	224 (24)	76	12 (7)	4	55 (11)	19	3 (1)	1	294 (16)	100
Total	462 (50)	77	22 (13)	4	111 (23)	19	3 (1)	*	598 (33)	100
TOTAL	930 (100)	51	174 (100)	10	493 (100)	27	216 (100)	12	1,813 (100)	100

Numbers may not total due to rounding.   [a]Numbers in parentheses are column percentages.   *Less than $0.5 million or 0.5 percent.

the support for knowledge application activities—is associated with operating programs. In contrast, only 27 percent of total social knowledge production and application support is channeled through R&D agencies, although these are the agencies most usually associated with federal support of social knowledge production and application in the minds of investigators and the public. Furthermore, despite the increased emphasis on research to support policy making in recent years, less than 10 percent of federally supported social knowledge production and application is directly associated with offices primarily performing policy-making functions.[5]

Further findings emerge from the data in Table 6. R&D agencies support 47 percent of all research, while agencies associated with operating programs support another 40 percent. Approximately 70 percent of support for the production of social statistics is centered in a relatively small number of agencies and programs that specialize in statistical activities. The bulk of the relatively small amount of support for program evaluations, 86 percent, is administered by agencies associated with operating programs and policy-making offices.

A general conclusion that emerges from the data in Table 6 is the diversity of knowledge production and application activities supported by all except the statistical agencies. Every category of social knowledge production and application is carried out at a multimillion dollar level by agencies associated with operating programs, agencies associated with policy-making functions, and R&D agencies. For example, although more than half of policy-formulation demonstrations are associated with operating programs, significant support for such demonstrations comes from other types of agencies as well. Similarly, all types of agencies are involved in producing general purpose statistics.

FUNDING PATTERNS BY GOAL AND AUDIENCE

It would be easy to conclude from the prominence of operating program agencies among the supporters of social knowledge production and application that these activities are intended primarily to serve users in the federal government. But such an inference would miss a critical aspect of the intent of those activities, an aspect by no means obvious when we began our study. To describe the goal and audience

[5]We do not by this mean to exclude the possibility that some of the activities supported by mission agencies are directed to policy questions. Plainly they are, in some cases in response to the wishes of departmental policy offices.

of social knowledge production and application, we devised a fivefold classification of the objectives of the funding agencies:

• the improvement of federal programs;
• the improvement of federal policies;
• the creation and provision of knowledge and developed programs or materials for nonfederal audiences—knowledge for third parties;
• the general advancement of knowledge concerning individual and social behavior without specific concern for application; and
• the collection and analysis of statistics.

This categorization proved to be substantially more difficult and judgmental than the categorization according to organizational location and function. For example, the National Institute of Mental Health (NIMH) supports considerable basic disciplinary research as well as research centered on a variety of social and mental health problems. It also supports a significant amount of research that is intended to be useful to practitioners in community mental health centers, social service agencies, and third parties generally. Although the political rhetoric surrounding the program emphasizes the latter activity, we concluded the predominant function of NIMH to be the advancement of knowledge and classified the agency accordingly.[6]

As shown in Table 7, important findings emerge from the data on total spending by major goal and audience. First, third-party interests dominate federal interests: more than 50 percent of all federal support is by agencies whose primary function is the production and application of knowledge for nonfederal audiences. The combined federal social knowledge production and application obligations by agencies whose primary goal is the improvement of federal programs and the improvement of federal policies are less than 25 percent of the total. Thus, spending on behalf of third-party (nonfederal) audiences is apparently greater than spending for first-party (federal) audiences by a ratio of more than two to one.

Second, only about 10 percent of all federal spending for social knowledge production and application is for the advancement of knowledge without specific concern for application. The bulk of support for the production and application of knowledge related to social problems, more than 75 percent, is administered by agencies whose primary goal is the improvement or formulation of programs and policies.

[6]Clearly, we would have gained added information on goals and audience by carrying the analysis to the level of individual projects if this had been feasible.

TABLE 7 Funding Patterns: Goal or Audience by Social Knowledge Production and Application Activities (fiscal 1976 obligations, $ millions)

| | Goal or Audience | | | | | | | | | | | |
| | Improvement of Federal Programs | | Improvement of Federal Policy | | Knowledge for Third Parties | | Advancement of Knowledge | | Statistical Collection | | Total | |
Activity	$	%	$	%	$	%	$	%	$	.%	$	%
Knowledge production	206	17	170	14	443	37	167	14	230	19	1,215	100
	(82)ᵃ		(90)		(47)		(86)		(99)		(67)	
Knowledge application	44	7	18	3	506	85	27	5	3	*	598	100
	(18)		(10)		(53)		(14)		(1)		(33)	
TOTAL	250	14	188	10	948	52	194	11	232	3	1,813	100
	(100)		(100)		(100)		(100)		(100)		(100)	

Number may not total due to rounding.
ᵃNumbers in parentheses are column percentages.
*Less than 0.5 percent.

Table 8 presents a cross-classification of total social knowledge production and application obligations by organizational location and function and by major goal and audience. It is significant to note that of the total federal support associated with operating programs and policy-making offices, more than 72 percent was intended for use by third-party audiences; only 26 percent was intended for the use of federal officials in the improvement of federal programs. Thus, nonfederal audiences have a major stake in the policies and practices governing federal support for knowledge production and application.

A much smaller portion of the funds for social knowledge production and application is spent by agencies (or their subdivisions) that have as a primary mission the improvement of federal programs or policies. More than half of the total for social knowledge production and application is spent by offices that have as a primary audience nonfederal decision makers, with most of the remainder spent by offices that have as a primary goal the advancement of knowledge without specific concern for application.

CONCLUSIONS

Several conclusions about the system of federal support for social knowledge production and application emerge from the patterns of funding examined in this chapter.

First, the types of activity are far more varied than the term "social R&D" suggests. They include a wide range of activities concerned with the production and use of knowledge of social problems. Indeed, research, as it would generally be understood by the research community, claimed no more than 36 percent of the total obligations of $1.8 billion in fiscal 1976. More than one-third of these obligations was for applications of knowledge of social problems.

Second, the policy areas to which this spending is directed also cover a broad range. Approximately 60 percent of the total is concerned with human resources, and community resources accounts for 28 percent. There is wide variation among policy areas in the division of support between knowledge-producing and knowledge-applying activities. In every policy area, the federal government invests part of its total spending for the production and use of social knowledge, but this fraction is an exceedingly small part of total program costs in every area and averages only six-tenths of one percent for all policy areas.

Third, the organizational location of funding programs shows a strong pattern of decentralization. Because the federal investment has

TABLE 8 Funding Patterns: Organizational Location by Goal or Audience (fiscal 1976 obligations, $ millions)

| Goal or Audience | Organizational Location | | | | | | | | Total | |
| | Associated with Operating Programs | | Associated with Policy-Making Offices | | Associated with R&D Funding Agencies | | Associated with Statistical Agencies | | | |
	$	%	$	%	$	%	$	%	$	%
Improvement of federal programs	243 (26)ᵃ	97	–	–	7 (1)	3	–	–	250 (14)	100
Improvement of federal policies	13 (1)	7	144 (82)	77	31 (6)	17	–	–	188 (10)	100
Knowledge for third parties	670 (72)	71	18 (10)	2	260 (53)	27	–	–	948 (52)	100
Advancement of knowledge	–	–	–	–	194 (39)	100	–	–	194 (11)	100
Statistical collection	4 (*)	2	13 (7)	5	–	–	216 (100)	93	232 (13)	100
TOTAL	930 (100)	51	174 (100)	10	493 (100)	27	216 (100)	12	1,183 (100)	100

Numbers may not total due to rounding.
ᵃNumbers in parentheses are column percentages.
*Less than 0.5 percent.

been a corollary of the creation and assignment of social programs to mission agencies, more than half of federal support of social knowledge production and application is associated with mission agencies, with much smaller amounts associated with departmental policy offices, independent R&D agencies, and specialized statistical agencies. This pattern means that the departments and agencies with the heaviest responsibilities for social programs also tend to have the largest aggregate budgets for social knowledge production and application. Indeed, the combined obligations within the Department of Health, Education, and Welfare account for roughly 40 percent of the total for the entire executive branch. Of the 180 agencies that support social knowledge production and application, the 20 with the largest budgets account for more than 70 percent of the total expenditures.

Fourth, the audiences of social knowledge production and application activities lie to a remarkable degree outside the federal government. Spending on behalf of third-party users exceeds spending for federal users by a ratio of more than two to one. This ratio is even higher if one considers only the support for social knowledge production and application that is associated with the mission agencies. Only 10 percent of the total is spent by agencies primarily concerned with the advancement of knowledge.

For many years it has been the common and preferred practice to award research grants on the basis of competitive proposals. The following editorial raises some troublesome questions about the procedures by which grant proposals are prepared, reviewed, and finally awarded; the questions cast doubt on the reasonableness of the whole enterprise. Yet the alternatives do not seem to offer improvement—reminding one of Winston Churchill's assertion that democracy is the worst form of government except for all the alternatives. The editorialist ends by asking for consideration of less burdensome ways of distributing research funds than what now exist. Perhaps the evaluation research community might both share the concern and contribute worthwhile ideas.

8

The Burden of Competitive Grants

A. Carl Leopold

In 1960, when U.S. science was beginning to depend heavily on grants and contracts for research support, Leo Szilard wrote a fanciful story.* In it he suggested that if some person or some group should ever want to bring research progress to a standstill, they could do so by establishing a competitive grants system under which all researchers would be required to prepare written proposals describing what they wished to work on. The commitment of time by the research community in writing, reviewing, and supervising such a universal grant system would effectively halt research progress. It may be that now, in the late 1970's, we should ask ourselves whether the load of the competitive grant and contract system is becoming excessive and whether it is time to seek alternatives.

The numbers of research proposals submitted to the principal federal granting agencies in 1978 were as follows: 28,000 to the National Science Foundation, 13,000 to the National Institutes of Health, 3,500 to the Department of Energy, 1,000 to the Environmental Protection Agency, and 2,000 to the Department of Agriculture. This makes a rough total of 47,500 proposals in 1 year.

Calculating the amount of time it takes to write a proposal is not easy, but 3 weeks would be a conservative estimate for the average time invested in each proposal. Thus last year, on the order of 2700 man-years were invested in proposal writing. This is probably a low estimate, since it often takes 3 months to write a proposal, and proposals by groups can take as much as 3 man-years.

Any estimate of the time investment must include those involved in the reviewing process. Allowing 3 man-days for review adds another 575 man-years, making a total estimated investment by the research community of approximately 3300 man-years during 1978. Since most research scientists

From A. Carl Leopold, "The Burden of Competitive Grants," 203 *Science* 607 (February 16, 1979).

are in the academic community, where perhaps half their time is available for research, the figure of 3300 man-years of research time may, in fact, represent the entire research time of 6600 academic persons during 1978.

The preparation and even the review of research proposals does have an educational effect. An essential part of the preparation of the research proposal is the examination of the literature and consideration of research directions that might be most profitable. But the cost in time to the research community is nevertheless a very heavy burden.

The problem is exacerbated by the fact that in every competitive program the majority of the proposals are rejected. The rejection rate can vary from 60 percent in some programs to 95 percent in others, but in general, it ranges between 70 percent and 85 percent. Thus roughly three of every four proposals fail to obtain funding for the researchers.

In the early days of federal support of research, when support was increasing year by year, distribution of grants on the basis of competition was an effective means of getting money to competent and productive persons. In the late 1960's, however, the amount of money (corrected for inflation) available for the support of research began to level off, and the growth period has now ended. Competition has become increasingly-keen and the proportion of proposals that can be funded has declined. The investment of research time in the proposal system, however, may continue to increase.

With the investment of an estimated 6600 persons' research time in writing and reviewing proposals, perhaps it is now appropriate to ask whether Szilard's fanciful story is turning into a serious matter. Should consideration be given to ways of providing research support without adding to the heavy burden of our present grants and contracts system?—A. CARL LEOPOLD, *Boyce Thompson Institute for Plant Research, Ithaca, New York 14853*

---

*L. Szilard, *The Voice of the Dolphins, and Other Stories* (Simon & Schuster, New York, 1961), p. 100.

II

ALTERNATIVE METHODOLOGIES
AND STRATEGIES

There is no question that under ideal circumstances a true experiment, involving randomization of cases to treatment conditions would be the preferred research design for evaluating almost all programs. However, in the less than ideal circumstances under which evaluation researchers regularly work, it is inevitable that evaluations are going to have to be made on the basis of methodologically less than optimal, but in fact at least doable, research designs and strategies. We, ourselves, prefer to insist on a true experiment, and settle for less only when it is clear that less is all that is attainable. Hence, arguments in favor of true experiments with randomization are important ammunition. One frequent charge against randomization is that it will prove unacceptable or that it is unethical. The first two articles in this section present information which is potentially quite useful in arguing for randomization. The remaining articles exemplify some of the strongest alternative strategies when true experiments simply cannot be done. We believe that they are worth careful study since they display both the strengths of the methods they espouse or employ and the problems in analysis and interpretation that remain. Although authors of individual papers do not always themselves spell out either the strengths or weaknesses of their work to which we refer, we believe that the points we make in our introductions are reasonable and do not do injustice to the original authors.

Evaluation research has characteristically suffered under a peculiar handicap: Although random assignment of subjects to treatments is necessary to evaluate the effects of a treatment with any degree of certainty, many have objected to that form of assignment on ethical grounds. The objection often stems from a feeling that random assignment may deny beneficial treatment (or resources) to those most in need, although objections are occasionally raised on other grounds; e.g., withholding resources from those most deserving or the very fact that random assignment is such a gamble.

That objection has been examined empirically in the following chapter and has been found to be less important to persons involved in the receipt of a limited resource than others have supposed. In fact, random assignment was judged to be more fair than various other forms of assignment. Obviously one study cannot eliminate ethical concerns, but it does lend support to the principle of random assignment and does present a model for the further examination of this ethical question. On the other hand, consideration of the details of the study does raise questions about the probable generality of the findings since the resource to be distributed was probably of little relative importance when compared to many social interventions. Future research, guided by the excellent model provided here, should involve the study of more important, critical interventions, both positive and negative in value.

9

Random Assignment
The Fairest of Them All

Camille B. Wortman and Vita C. Rabinowitz

Potential participants in a special educational program were led to believe that selection for the program would be governed by a merit, need, first come-first served, or random principle. Within each principle, self-interest was manipulated by giving respondents false feedback regarding their standing on the criterion to be employed. Random assignment was judged fairer and more satisfying than the other criteria. Moreover, there was no evidence that self-interest affected fairness ratings of selection by random assignment, while it clearly affected the perceived fairness of all other criteria. These findings indicate that some of our pessimism regarding the feasibility of randomized field tests may be unwarranted.

There seems to be general agreement that, as a society, we should evaluate the effectiveness of our ameliorative social programs (1, 2, 3, 4). It also seems clear (1, 2, 3) that the best way to determine the effectiveness of a social program is to conduct a field experiment in which participants are randomly assigned to treatment and control conditions. The notion of random assignment has met with some criticism, however (1, 4, 5, 6).

It has been argued that participants will regard randomization as a less fair way of allocating desirable or scarce resources than more traditional methods like merit, need, or a first come-first served approach. For example, a recent editorial in Science (6) has characterized random assignment as "not only a denial of rationality [but] also a denial of man's humanity." Despite these claims, few investigators have experimentally probed participants' reactions to random assignment (7), and virtually none have compared reactions to randomization with reactions to alternative methods of selection.

Ours was a field experiment in which participants were informed that they would be assigned to an innovative educational program on the basis of one of four selection criteria: merit, need, first come-first served, or random assign-

From Camille B. Wortman and Vita C. Rabinowitz, "Random Assignment: The Fairest of Them All." Unpublished manuscript, 1978.

ment. We were interested in determining how fair participants would view the selection by these various criteria. A second purpose of the study was to examine whether participants' self-interest would affect their reaction to the selection criteria employed. Do people judge the appropriateness of a particular selection criterion on absolute grounds, or are their judgments likely to be swayed by considering how their own interests can best be served? Is a respondent who believes he or she is meritorious, for example, likely to be biased in favor of a merit system?

The study employed a 4 x 4 factorial design with selection procedure (merit, need, first come-first served, random assignment) and expectation of being selected into the desirable treatment via that procedure (low, medium, high, or no information on self-interest) as independent variables. Respondents were 259 males and females enrolled in an introductory psychology course at Northwestern University. Cell sizes ranged from 12 to 17 and averaged about 16.

Near the beginning of the term, the respondents were told of an innovative educational program (8) for which they might be eligible. They were told that a series of "minicourse" seminars would be offered by skilled leaders on topics of great interest to undergraduates but not typically offered in the curriculum (i.e., meditation, biofeedback, child abuse). Students interested in enrolling in the seminars were asked to fill out a "special topics test" on the areas to be covered in the minicourses. The test contained fifty multiple choice questions, and was allegedly designed "to assess how much the students already knew about the minicourse topics." Students were urged to complete the tests at home, taking as much time as necessary to answer the questions as well as they could. They were told to hand in their completed test at the instructor's office before the next class session, and were warned to get it in as early as possible. Care was taken to ensure that it would be difficult for the students to know how they had done on the test, or how early they had returned their test relative to others.

One week later, every student who had completed a test received a personalized set of materials about the seminars, stating that "unfortunately, there are about twice as many students who want to take the seminars as there are minicourse spaces available." As a solution to the problem of which students would be admitted to the seminars, one quarter of the students were told that top priority would be given to those who scored highest on the special topics test (merit principle), one quarter to those who scored lowest on the test (need principle), one quarter to those who handed in the special topics test first (first come-first served principle), and the final quarter to those whose randomly assigned number was selected (random principle).

Self-interest was manipulated by giving the subjects within each selection procedure false feedback about their standing on the criteria employed, and hence, on their chances of getting into the program. Subjects in the high self-interest condition were led to believe that their chances of getting into the seminars were very good. For subjects assigned to a merit system, this was accomplished by informing them that they had scored well (i.e., in the top third) on the special topics test. Subjects in the need system were told that their chances were very good because they had scored poorly (i.e., in the bottom third) on the special topics test. First come-first served subjects in the high self-interest condition were led to believe that they were among the first third of the subjects to turn in their special topics test, and random assignment subjects in this condition were informed that they had received a random number in the top third of those assigned.

Subjects in the moderate self-interest condition were told that their chances of getting into the seminars were difficult to specify at this time because their test score was about average (merit and need), because they had been among the middle third to hand in their special topics test (first come-first served), or because the random number assigned to them was in the middle third of the distribution (random assignment). Subjects in the low self-interest condition were informed that their chances of getting into the seminars were not very good, either because their score was low (merit), their score was high (need), they had been among the last third of students to hand in their test (first come-first served), or their random number was in the bottom third of the distribution (random assignment). The remaining subjects in each condition received no information relevant to their self-interest; merit and need subjects were not told their score on the test; first come-first served subjects were not told how soon they had turned in their test relative to others, and random assignment subjects were not told their random number.

To lend credence to this spiel, all subjects except those in the no information condition received specific information designed to bear on their standing: merit and need subjects received a bogus test score and bogus class means; first come-first served subjects received a bogus number indicating the order in which they handed in their test; and random assignment subjects received a bogus random number.

Although sixteen different versions of the account were distributed, it was unlikely that students noticed that the accounts differed. Students had taken a short quiz prior to receiving their materials, and were sitting at least one seat apart from their nearest neighbors. After they had finished reading their accounts, each student was asked to answer a few questions about selection into the program "in case participation must be limited again next year." The first question asked for an overall rating of satisfaction with the selection procedure that was supposedly being used. The next four questions, appearing in a different random order for every respondent, asked them to rate how fair they considered each of the selection procedures. One of these was the one that had ostensibly been chosen for that year, and the remaining three were the other procedures manipulated in the experiment, procedures that we allegedly "considered before choosing the one that we did." In order to check on the effectiveness of the manipulations, subjects were asked how likely it was that they would be admitted to the seminars, how well they did on the test, and how early they had turned in their tests relative to others. Finally, subjects were asked two questions designed to assess whether the proposed program was regarded as attractive and worthwhile: they were asked how interested they were in gaining admission into the program, and how willing they would be to participate in "time consuming interviews" at the end of the term to assess the impact of the program, whether or not they had been admitted. Each question was accompanied by a bipolar scale with 1 and 15 at the poles. After completing the questions, all subjects were debriefed, and all who wished to enroll in the seminars were permitted to do so.

Unless otherwise noted, the dependent variables were analyzed by a 4 by 4 multivariate analysis of variance with procedure and self-interest as the two factors. Analyses of the manipulation check items suggest that test score feedback and information about when students returned their tests were accurately perceived. Across all selection procedures, perceived likelihood of admission varied directly with self-interest ($F(3,242) = 107.371$, $p < .001$). However, even participants who answered "don't know" to manipulation check items, as well as the nine who answered them incorrectly, were included in the analyses, thus effecting a slight conservative bias. Fortunately, there was no evidence that perceived likelihood of admission varied with the procedure assigned, or that self-interest interacted with procedure. These analyses also revealed that the subjects regarded the potential program as quite desirable ($X = 14.254$). Furthermore, they viewed the innovation as important enough to agree to a lengthy interview that would assess its effectiveness ($X = 13.020$). Assessments of the attractiveness and importance of the innovation were not affected by assignment procedure or self-interest.

In general, our major analyses were designed to answer two questions: First, is there an overall preference in the population for some of the selection procedures over others? Next, does self-interest on a particular selection criterion affect the assessment of that criteria or is the evaluation of some criteria more affected by self-interest than others?

Data from two sources were used to address our first question. First, an overall comparison of the perceived fairness of each of the four selection procedures was made. When we pooled the data from all students, regardless of the criterion to which they were assigned or their standing on the self-interest variable, we found that the criteria did in fact differ in how they were regarded ($F(3,242) = 53.87$, $p < .001$). To isolate the specific source of this effect, post hoc multiple comparisons were conducted (9). A Newman Keuls test revealed that the students, taken together, regarded the random assignment procedure ($X = 10.480$) as reliably more fair than the need procedure ($X = 7.748$), the first come-first served procedure ($X = 6.477$) or the merit procedure ($X = 5.82$) (all p's $< .01$).

An alternative way of addressing our first question is to examine whether students selected for a given procedure rated it as more fair or more satisfactory than students selected for other procedures. The analysis of variance for the fairness question again revealed a significant effect for procedure ($F(3,242) = 67,831$, $p < .001$) and a Newman Keuls test again revealed that subjects in the

TABLE 1

Cell and Marginal Mean Ratings of Satisfaction with the
Selection Procedure Assigned

| | Selection Procedure Assigned | | | | |
Expectancy Level	Merit	Need	First come-First served	Random Assignment	Marginal Mean
None	5.588	7.385	5.500	9.611	7.04
Low	3.471	5.250	4.059	8.20	5.154
Medium	6.533	9.765	5.471	8.063	7.44
High	9.529	10.176	9.882	11.647	10.29
Marginal Mean	6.30	8.252	6.24	9.42	7.54

NOTE: All ratings were made on a 15 point bipolar scale where a rating of one meant not at all satisfied and 15 meant extremely satisfied.

random assignment condition (X = 11.413) regarded their selection criteria as more fair (p < .05) than subjects in the need (X = 8.890), merit (X = 6.552) or first come-first served conditions (X = 6.360). As can be seen by an inspection of Tables 1 and 2, ratings of satisfaction with the procedure were quite consistent with ratings of fairness. Satisfaction was found to vary with the procedure employed (F(3,242) = 10.049, p < .001). Again, random assignment received the highest ratings, and the Newman Keuls test revealed that the random assignment (X = 9.420) procedure was rated reliably higher than the merit (X = 6.300) and first come-first served (X = 6.240) procedures (p's < .05), and marginally higher than need (X = 8.252).

Our next analysis was designed to determine whether judgments of the fairness of some of the selection criteria were more affected by self-interest than others. Indeed, the subjects' ratings of the fairness of the procedure to which they were assigned were found to interact with the self-interest variable (F(9.242) = 6.980, p < .01). Newman Keuls tests were performed to indicate how self-interest on each criteria affected the judgment of fairness of that criteria. Within the merit condition, subjects in the high self-interest cell (X = 9.529) rated a merit system as fairer than those in all other levels, and those in the medium (X = 6.000) and no information conditions (X = 6.235) rated merit as fairer than those in the low self-interest condition (X = 4.471) (all p's < .01). For subjects in the need condition, those with high (X = 9.882) and medium (X = 11.176) levels of self-interest rated these criteria as fairer than those with low expectancies (X = 6.188) or no information (X = 7.846) (all p's < .01). Similarly, first come-first served subjects in the high self-interest condition (X = 10.412) rated this selection procedure as fairer than those in the medium (X = 5.824), low (X = 4.059) and no information (X = 5.063) on self-interest conditions (all p's < .01).

In contrast, there were no significant differences in perceived fairness of the selection criteria among random assignment subjects in the different self-interest conditions. These subjects' assessment of the fairness of their selection pro-

TABLE 2

Cell and Marginal Mean Ratings of Fairness of Each of Four
Selection Procedures: Merit, Inverse Merit, First Come-
First Served, and Random Assignment

Expectancy Level	Perceived Fairness of	Selection Procedure Assigned				
		Merit	Need	First come-First served	Random Assignment	Marginal Means
None	M	6.235	6.692	5.750	3.333	5.389
	N	8.118	7.846	7.875	4.556	7.01
	F	4.588	7.154	5.063	5.167	5.380
	R	10.313	9.917	10.875	11.412	10.689
Low	M	4.471	8.000	5.292	4.933	5.662
	N	7.941	6.188	6.529	6.467	6.793
	F	7.882	6.563	4.059	7.076	6.370
	R	9.765	12.062	1.882	11.267	11.231
Medium	M	6.00	7.118	3.706	4.250	5.299
	N	9.059	11.176	8.471	6.688	9.01
	F	7.118	6.647	5.824	6.438	6.500
	R	9.588	10.529	10.588	11.667	10.561
High	M	9.529	7.294	5.706	5.00	6.910
	N	6.824	9.882	8.706	7.824	8.316
	F	4.824	7.357	10.412	8.412	7.740
	R	8.941	8.706	9.529	11.312	9.596
Marginal Means	M	6.552	7.310	5.105	4.356	5.820
	N	7.98	8.890	6.030	6.350	7.748
	F	6.126	6.920	6.360	6.750	6.477
	R	9.642	10.310	10.716	11.413	10.480

NOTE: All ratings were made on a 15 point bipolar scale where a rating of one meant not at all satisfied and 15 meant extremely satisfied.

cedure was uniformly high regardless of their particular level of self-interest (X's = 11.412, 11.267, 11.667 and 11.312) for the no information, low, medium, and high self-interest levels. As can be seen in Table 1, a similar pattern emerged when subjects' judgments of satisfaction were examined, although the procedure x self-interest interaction fell short of statistical significance.

Taken as a whole, the data suggest that some of the initial pessimism regarding the use of random assignment may be unwarranted. Subjects rated randomization as fairer than the other criteria regardless of the criterion to which they had been assigned or their level of self-interest in that criterion. Furthermore, those assigned via randomization rated their procedure as fairer than those assigned to other procedures rated them. Ratings of the other selection criteria were found to increase with self-interest to a greater extent than ratings of random assignment, which was regarded as a very fair procedure regardless of self-interest level.

Viewing the data from other perspectives provides further evidence that randomization may be more attractive to research participants than originally imagined. In field settings, most participants are likely to lack specific information about how they stand on various selection criteria in comparison to other participants. Do these subjects, considered alone, prefer randomization to the other, more rational criteria? Our results suggest that they do. Scheffe post hoc multiple comparison tests revealed that within the no information condition, subjects as a whole preferred randomization to any of the other techniques ($F(3,50) = 20.81$, $p < .001$). Furthermore, no information subjects actually assigned via random assignment regarded their selection procedure as significantly fairer ($F(3.62) = 32.691$, $p < .001$) and more satisfactory ($F(3.62) = 7.097$, $p < .01$) than subjects assigned to the other procedures regarded theirs to be. Thus, the respondents in our study, most typical of those in evaluation settings, showed a clear preference for random assignment.

In a program evaluation setting, the subjects most likely to be opposed to random assignment would seem to be those who have strong self-interest in an alternative procedure. Using Scheffe tests which compare these subjects' fairness ratings of the random assignment procedure with their ratings of their assigned procedure and with the other two criteria taken together, the data suggest that even these subjects give random assignment relatively high ratings, and rate it higher than the other two criteria: Thus, subjects who felt that they were meritorious, and hence, likely to be assigned to the treatment since merit was the criterion being used, rated random assignment ($X = 8.941$) no less fair than the merit system ($X = 9.529$) and significantly fairer than the need ($X = 6.824$) and the first come-first served approach ($X = 4.824$) ($F(3,62) = 12.092$, $p < .01$). Those who strongly expected to be admitted into the minicourses via the first come-first served procedure regarded random assignment ($X = 9.529$) as no less fair than the first come-first served procedure ($X = 10.412$), and as more fair than the need ($X = 8.706$) and merit conditions ($X = 5.706$) ($F(3,63) = 3.91$, $p < .05$). Finally, subjects in need condition who had high self-interest also failed to rate their assigned procedures ($X = 9.882$) as fairer than the random assignment procedure ($X = 8.706$). However, they rated random assignment as fairer than merit ($X = 7.294$), or a first come-first served procedure ($X = 7.357$) ($F(3,59) = 6.91$, $p < .01$).

The data are quite consistent in suggesting that in the absence of strong self-interest, randomization is the preferred mode of allocating a scarce and desirable treatment. Even subjects who have a strong self-interest in a particular selection criterion rated random assignment almost as high as this criterion, and higher than any other approach. Of course, the results should be replicated in other settings with other participants. Nonetheless, that our findings were attained in a competitive college atmosphere is highly encouraging. This suggests that even in settings where a particular principle (merit) usually operates, and even among populations which typically benefit from the application of that principle, selection by random assignment may be a viable, indeed preferred, alternative. Our data indicate that some of the objections to random assignment that administrators expect from participants may never materialize, and that among the majority of participants, random assignment is likely to be judged as the fairest of them all.

REFERENCES

1. Boruch, R. G. (1974) "On common contentions about randomized field experiments." In R. F. Boruch and H. W. Wiechen (eds.) Experimental Testing of Public Policy. Boulder, CO: Westview.
2. Campbell, D. T. (1969) "Reforms as experiments." Amer. Psychologist 24, 262-272.
3. Campbell, D. T. (in press) "Methods for the experimenting society." Amer. Psychologist.
4. Guttentag, M. (1973) "Evaluation of social intervention programs." Annals of the New York Academy of Sciences 218, 3-15.
5. Feinberg, S. E. (1971) "Randomization and social affairs." Science 22 (January): 255-261.
6. Wolfe, D. (1970) "Chance, or human judgment?" Science 167, 1201.
7. Hillis, J. W. and C. B. Wortman (1976) "Some determinants of public acceptance of randomized control group experimental designs." Sociometry, 39, 2, 91-96.
8. Wortman, C. B. and J. W. Hillis (1975) "Some 'thrilling' short articles for use in an introductory psychology class." Teaching of Psychology, 2, 3, 134-135.
9. Keppel, G. (1973) Design and Analysis. Englewood Cliffs, NJ: Prentice-Hall.
10. Wortman, C. B., M. Hendricks and J. W. Hillis "Factors affecting participant reactions to random assignment in ameliorative social programs." J. of Personality and Social Psychology 33, 3, 256-266.

There is widespread agreement that when it is possible the true experiment provides the strongest basis for a causal inference linking the intervention to the outcome. The sine qua non of the true experiment is random assignment of subjects or cases to treatment conditions. Yet, the very process of randomization often meets with objections on the grounds that it is arbitrary in necessitating the withholding of treatment from individuals who might otherwise receive it.

The following reports on a novel alternative to ordinary randomization which at least seemed fairer and was more acceptable in a criminal justice setting. Interesting questions may be raised: Is the result really random, or does the potential for some subtle bias remain? Is the procedure useable in other types of settings such as health care? Are there possible variants other than temporal assignment that might be exploited, e.g., spatial or order of appearance?

10

Random Time Quota Selection
An Alternative to Random Selection in Experimental Evaluation

Sally Hillsman Baker and Orlando Rodriguez

Researchers conducting control group experiments in field settings where the "treatment" involves client services often encounter opposition from clients and practitioners when clients must be assigned randomly to experimental and control groups. This paper describes an alternative selection procedure used in the evaluation of a criminal court diversion program. Experimentals and controls were selected under a quota system (that is, nonrandomly), but the quotas were assigned under randomly chosen variable-length time periods. The resulting experimental and control were compared on socioeconomic and criminal background and characteristics of their court case, and found to be similar. Some guidelines are suggested for the use of this technique, and its comparative advantages in relation to other alternatives to random selection are discussed.

No procedure is more important and problematic for experimental evaluation than equal probability or random selection—the assignment of subjects to experimental and control groups on a random basis.

In program evaluation, when researchers are attempting to implement an experimental design in a field, rather than laboratory setting, resistance to random selection is often encountered from one or another of the actors involved. Prospective clients may object to being chosen randomly. If they consent to the procedure they may later object if they have been placed in the control

Authors' Note: An earlier version of this paper was presented at the Annual Meeting of the American Sociological Association, San Francisco, September 1978. The paper was prepared under Grants 76-NI-99-0040 and 77-NI-99-0075 from the National Institute of Law Enforcement and Criminal Justice, Law Enforcement Assitance Administration, U.S. Department of Justice. Points of view or opinions stated in this document are those of the authors and do not necessarily represent the official position or policies of the U.S. Department of Justice or Vera Institute of Justice.

From Sally Hillsman Baker and Orlando Rodriguez, "Random Time Quota Selection: An Alternative to Random Selection in Experimental Evaluation." Unpublished manuscript, 1978.

group. Program personnel may object to random selection because they foresee administrative problems arising from the procedure (for example, bad publicity or unruly clients). Personnel may also object out of a sense of ethics, that is, the duty of offering services to all who need them.

Other actors may object as well. For example, many programs are subject to monitoring by agencies or groups—the community, a funding agency, or a government agency. Any and all of these actors may react adversely to the idea of denying services through the selection of prospective clients into a control group for the purpose of evaluating a program. This is especially the case in legal settings, where random selection is entwined with the notion of due process and equal protection. For example, assigning a defendant to a control group might be seen by his or her defense attorney as an arbitrary denial of a favorable disposition that the client is entitled to.

This argument might be countered by the researcher with the statement that the aim of evaluation is to establish precisely whether or not a service is actually being given. Does treatment actually work? Is the client's life being improved by the program? By comparing program outcomes with outcomes for controls, this question can be answered (see Boruch, 1976: 187). However, this argument does not seem too weighty to a practitioner confronted with the problem of performing a service for the client. The client needs a service, therefore service should not be denied. To the practitioner, the question whether service actually makes a difference seems too removed and academic for real individuals with problems needing immediate attention.

In the face of these practical problems, researchers have devised alternative methods of selecting subjects for control groups (see especially Campbell and Stanley, 1966). One alternative is the use of comparison groups. Clients are selected for treatment in the usual manner. All clients then constitute the experimental group. The group's pre- and posttest measures are compared with those of a group that has not been considered for selection into the program. The comparison group are people similar to the clients in treatment-related characteristics but not eligible for treatment. For example, they might be people outside the program's catchment area, or people who received alternative or no services prior to the program's existence.

The drawbacks of this alternative are obvious. Much must be known about the comparison group before one could be sure that it is comparable to the experimental group. Even if many characteristics of the comparison group are known, one is never sure that an important comparison characteristic is missing. Moreover one is missing the essential datum of readiness or eligibility to participate in the program. How, in the comparison group, can we distinguish those who would not have wanted the program from those who would have been rejected by the program? For these reasons, the use of comparison groups is a risky procedure. It is not impossible, but it requires a great deal of preevaluation research to ensure that experimentals and the comparison group are basically similar. In addition, the research must artificially duplicate the program's selection process in order to weed out those the program would have been likely to reject and those who would have been likely to reject the program.

Another alternative to random selection is delayed treatment for controls. Under this procedure, treatment for controls is delayed until the period of experimentals' treatment is completed. This answers the practitioner's objection that services are being denied, and, at the same time, gives the researcher a control group. However, not all settings allow this procedure to be used. Where delays in service are impossible, or where the decision to give treatment must be immediate, this alternative is not practicable. It is noteworthy that it is in legal settings where the above condition of immediate decision-making (for example, having to dispose of a case) is often found.

Methodologically, the delayed treatment control group alternative suffers from possible contamination of measures through controls' expectations about future services. Thus, individuals in a delayed control group may be likely to alter their behavior in a positive (or negative) direction in the expectation that they will receive treatment at a later date.

In brief, when experimental conditions prohibit the use of the traditional random selection procedure, other, less desirable, alternatives are possible. This paper presents a third alternative to random selection: random time quota selection. Under this procedure, experimentals and controls are selected under a quota system, that is, nonrandomly, but the quotas are assigned under a randomly chosen variable-length time period.[1] After using this procedure in an ongoing evaluation of the Court Employment Program, a New York City court diversion program, we have concluded that this is a feasible alternative in experimental situations where random selection is not permissible. In the pages below, the procedure is described in detail and its results are evaluated.

THE SELECTION PROCEDURE

The Court Employment Program (CEP) diverts defendants pretrial from traditional court processing and offers them employment, educational counseling, and referrals. While these services are being offered, the defendant's criminal case is postponed pending completion of the program. Defendants are offered (but not guaranteed) dismissal of charges as long as they fulfill their responsibilities within the program.

To carry out the research, the design of the procedures for selecting defendants for the research population had to rely heavily on close cooperation between the Vera and CEP research screening staff. To establish adequate experimental and control groups, the assignment of defendants to the research population had to take place as late as possible in the CEP eligibility screening process, and after the prosecutor (a key decision maker in the diversion process) had agreed to diversion. CEP obtained clients by both actively soliciting cases prearraignment and by evaluating the eligibility of cases referred to it postarraignment by judges or defense counsel. The research wanted to consider assigning to the research group only defendants who had passed through the full CEP screening process successfully and who had been approved for diversion by the prosecutor (an Assistant District Attorney designated as the CEP-liaison). Judicial review of the diversion decision was the only step in the diversion process that could not be taken *before* the case was assigned by the research.[2]

To implement this research intake procedure, it was necessary to obtain the cooperation of the Legal Aid Society, whose attorneys represented many of the eligible defendants, and that of the District Attorneys of three separate New York City counties. The District Attorneys readily agreed to the research intake procedures and to the research's original proposal to use a traditional equal probability (random) selection method for determining which defendants would be assigned by the research to the experimental (diverted) and control (non-diverted) groups (see Goldman, 1977). The Legal Aid Society and LEAA's Legal Counsel, however, were concerned that the research intake procedures would deny some defendants diversion services to create a control group. They were also afraid that an equal probability selection procedure would be "arbitrary" and thus deny defendants equal protection and due process.

As a consequence, the final procedures implemented by the research were designed so that no defendant was denied diversion services solely because of the need for a control group. In addition, the specific assignment device developed; while approximating an equal probability method, it did not subject individual defendants directly to a randomizing procedure. This was achieved by securing CEP's agreement to generate an excess of defendants eligible and approved for diversion. Since CEP could provide services only to a limited number of defendants (given its level of funding), a pool of defendants existed in the Criminal Courts who were eligible for diversion but who were not being screened by the program. Therefore, during the ten months needed to complete research intake, CEP screeners worked to identify more eligible defendants than the program could realistically divert and to secure the prosecutor's approval for their diversion. CEP diverted only some of these approved defendants; these are in the research experimental group. The remainder, not diverted, constitute an "overflow" and are the research control group.

ASSIGNMENT METHOD

The mechanism for determining which of these eligible defendants were diverted (experimentals) and which were "overflow" (controls) was developed and administered entirely by the research. It was designed to approximate an equal probability assignment by assuring concurrent intake into the two groups and by preventing either CEP or research staff from influencing individual decisions. Its major characteristics are the construction of a CEP quota and the use of variable length time periods.

Because CEP secured approval to divert more defendants than it could reasonably give services, it was appropriate to develop a quota system in order to select those cases CEP would divert during a given period (e.g., a month, week, or day). When added over the long run, these quotas should equal the number of cases CEP had funds to divert. Once a quota was filled, the remaining cases screened and approved during any period would constitute an overflow of eligible defendants to be processed normally by the court. These cases could then be assigned to a control group for purposes of research.

The research staff controlled the mechanism for establishing the CEP quota and thus determined the assignment decisions. That screening staff would have known immediately after the assignment of the day's first approved case that all the remaining defendants screened that day would be either part of CEP's quota or the overflow. This knowledge undoubtedly would have altered their behavior in selecting cases. Variable length periods also meant the size of the CEP quota was never the same (i.e., a long period would have a larger quota than a short period). Since no one but the researchers monitoring the selection knew the length of the time period or the size of the quota, CEP screening staff could not predict when a case was assigned to their quota (or the overflow), whether it would be the only one that day, or whether several would be assigned before their quota was filled (or a new quota begun).[3]

The periods used in the research assignment were determined as follows. First, the total number of work days in six months of research intake was multiplied by eight, the number of hours worked per day by CEP screeners.[4] The figure that resulted was the total number of screening hours the research had to divide into variable length assignment periods. The length of each time period was selected on logical grounds. If the periods were too short, the assignment procedure would soon approximate a toss of a coin model and could be challenged as "arbitrary"; if they were too long, the selection of experimental controls would not be current. Consequently, time periods varying in length from 11 to 21 hours were chosen. Under this system, new assignment periods would begin approximately every one to three days and the shift would occur at different times during the 9 A.M. to 5 P.M. screening day. The total number of screening hours during the first six months of intake was divided, therefore, into an equal number of 11, 13, 15, 17, 19, and 21 hour periods. The *order* in which these periods were used was randomly determined before the start of the research.

To establish the size of *CEP's quota* for each period, the research estimated the number of cases for which CEP was likely to secure approval during the next period (e.g., the next 13 hours). This estimate was based on the average number of cases approved during all preceding periods (calculated as the mean number per hour). If this figure was, for example, 0.3 cases per hour, the expected number of cases during the next 13 hour assignment period would be 4 ($0.3 \times 13 = 3.9$). It was originally assumed that CEP would be able to generate approximately twice the cases it could divert. The CEP quota, therefore, was set at 50 percent of the expected number of cases approved during any period (or 2 in the example begun above.)

Because CEP's quota was always filled first and because its screening performance was highly irregular,[5] it was necessary to build an adjustment factor into the CEP quota to assure CEP diverted approximately 50 percent of the cases over the long run. In each time period this factor was based on the proportion of all previous cases that had been assigned to the experimental group. If this figure was 50 percent of the total cases assigned, then half the expected number of cases in the next assignment period was assigned to CEP's quota. If the figure was less than 50 percent, the proportion in the experimental group was lagging, and CEP's quota was increased in the next period to bring the proportions closer to 50-50. If the figure was above 50 percent, the CEP quota was reduced.[6]

These procedures for identifying and assigning defendants to the research population were carried out without major alteration. During the ten-month intake period, 666 defendants were assigned by the research. However, two adjustments in the original design were made in response to CEP's organizational needs. The first involved the percent of cases in CEP's quota and the second the assignment of codefendants.

It must be recalled that the entire research intake design rested upon the CEP screeners' ability to identify and secure approval for more eligible cases than CEP had resources to service. There had to be, in fact, an "overflow." Only then, given the constraints of the research, was a CEP quota appropriate. Within three months after research intake began, CEP became concerned that it was not screening a sufficient number of cases to fill its service requirement and to generate an overflow of *equal* size. As a result, the research agreed to increase CEP's quota to 65 percent (rather than 50%) of all expected cases; the overflow, therefore, would be 35 percent. These new assignment percentages remained during the second three months of the research intake period, after which time CEP agreed to return to 50 percent. The major consequence of this deviation from the original design is that the size of the experimental and control groups are not equal; 410 defendants (61% of the total assigned) are in the experimental group and 256 (38%) in the control group.[7]

The second adjustment involved the assignment of codefendants. Eligible defendants who were also codefendants were always given the same research assignment: Both were either part of CEP's quota or the overflow. The reason for this was practical: CEP could not get the prosecutor's approval to divert a defendant if his codefendant was not also diverted. The prosecution was concerned that a successfully diverted defendant would return to court after receiving a dismissal and testify in the case of the codefendant that he and not the codefendant was responsible for the offense. However, even if random selection had been allowed, the research would have had to compromise on the question of codefendants.

EXCEPTIONS TO THE RESEARCH ASSIGNMENT

Another problem faced by experimental research in field (or natural) settings is the demand that exceptions be made to the selection procedures. Vera researchers had hoped the random time quota selection procedures would limit this problem (in comparison to a truly random procedure) if not eliminate it completely. While CEP and the researchers were quite successful explaining the overflow and quota selection situation to individual defendants, defense attorneys, and judges, exceptions to the research assignment did occur. These fell into three categories. The two most important to the controlled design are defendants assigned as part of CEP's quota who were subsequently not diverted and defendants assigned as overflows (controls) who were diverted. In addition, some defendants were diverted to CEP but were not called into the Vera Monitor for assignment to the research. The explanation of those exceptions follows.

Whereas the research assignment was made as close to the end of the screening process as possible, there was no way to avoid having judicial review of the diversion decision occur after defendants had been assigned. Even if the prosecutor approved diversion and the defendant was assigned as part of CEP's quota, the defendant still had to appear before a judge (at arraignment or subsequent appearance) where the ADA, defense counsel, and CEP screener would jointly request a four-month adjournment for the defendant to be diverted to CEP. Judges in New York City generally assert the prerogative of judicial review and would occasionally refuse to divert the case. Less frequently, a defendant assigned to the control group was diverted to CEP. It is important to note that CEP encouraged judges to support the agency's decision about whom to divert. Screeners and their supervisors resisted attempts to divert cases they had rejected (for whatever reason). However, the agency operates on the basis of informal agreements with the court, and maintaining a good relationship with judges is essential to its continued operations.[8] Therefore, in some cases when a judge insisted a case be diverted despite its overflow status, CEP would feel obliged to take the case. Twelve percent of all assigned defendants (15% of experimentals and 6% of controls) were the subject of judicial reverses of their assignment status.

Finally, some defendants screened and diverted from Manhattan and Brooklyn are also not included in the research design. These cases were excepted from the research assignment for one of two reasons: Either a judge diverted the case to CEP without the agency having screened it or a judge demanded that a defendant be diverted and CEP's director of court operations or the program director believed rejection of the case as an overflow would jeopardize the agency's informal relations with the court. These sixty-six defendants (one out of ten defendants screened in these two boroughs) are not included in the research.

While not desirable from the point of view of experimentation, the exceptions to research assignment encountered in this evaluation are not an unusual occurrence in evaluations. The last two types of exceptions to the research assignment decision would have also occurred under random time quota method. Exceptions to the assignment procedure occurred because program screeners felt that countering these exceptions would jeopardize the credibility of the program. If anything, random selection would probably have increased the program's perception that its credibility was in jeopardy and would have led to even more exceptions for the assignment decision.

EVALUATION OF THE SELECTION PROCEDURE

To assess the adequacy of the selection procedure, the experimental and control groups were compared on variables related to characteristics of the arrest case, defendants' prior criminal background, demographic characteristics, employment and educational experience, and uses and needs for social services (see Table 1). All these variables are relevant to the selection of defendants for diversion and to the hypothesized outcomes of the diversion process. That is, the program and others involved in the diversion decision take many of these characteristics into account when considering whether to divert a defendant and they determine the kinds of services the defendant will receive while in the program. The data indicate that the experimental and control groups are essentially similar in important demographic characteristics, criminal, employment and educational background.[9]

A note on presentation of the data. To assess the extent of bias in the assignment procedures, members of the research population must be compared according to whether the research *assigned* them to the experimental or the control group, rather than according to whether they were actually diverted or not at arraignment. Defendants diverted to the program without being subject to the research assignment are of course excluded from this analysis.

Experimentals and controls were compared on over forty characteristics relating to their court case, prior criminal involvement, personal background, employment, education, and use of, and need for, social services. In all of these characteristics, differences between experimentals and controls were found to be statistically insignificant between the .01 and .001 levels. Table 1 shows some of the differences between the two groups on a selected number of these characteristics. Looking at the table, it may be seen that there is little difference between experimentals and controls on the type of offense for which they were arrested, their prior arrest record, the number of illegal activities they were engaging in, their ages and ethnic background, and their employment and educational background. Thus, the two groups are basically similar and comparable with respect to measurement of program impact on future employment, education, and illegal behavior.

TABLE 1
Selected Characteristics of the Research Population
by Research Assignment Status

	Experimental	Control	Total
Type of Arrest Charge			
Theft	75%	75%	75%
Robbery	7	9	8
Assault without robbery	11	7	9
Other	8	9	8
Total (=100%)[a]	(350)	(220)	(570)
$\chi_3^2 = 1.96$[b]			
Official Prior Adult Conviction Record	12%	10%	11%
Total (N=100%)[a]	(341)	(223)	(564)
$\chi^2 < 1$[a]			
Official Prior Adult Arrest	42%	36%	39%
Total (N=100%)[a]	(355)	(229)	(584)
$\chi^2 = 2.02$[a]			
Age mean	20.3	20.0	20.2
N =[a]	(385)	(233)	(618)
T = .672[b]			
Ethnicity			
Black	51%	50%	51%
White	9	18	12
Hispanic	40	32	37
Total (=100%)[a]	(401)	(239)	(640)
$\chi_2^2 = 12.17; p < .005$[c]			
Enrolled in School	35%	40%	37%
N =[a]	(379)	(222)	(601)
$\chi^2 = 1.10$[b]			

a. Missing data or no answers excluded from tables.
b. Not statistically significant.
c. Statistically significant.

SOME IMPORTANT CONSIDERATIONS IN THE USE OF RANDOM TIME QUOTA SELECTION

In the discussion of implementing the random time quota selection procedure in our research, we mentioned various features of the procedure and discussed problems that arose from their use. For the sake of future implementations in other research, it would be useful to highlight these features, so that they may be kept in mind when planning the procedure.

Establishment of a quota

It is necessary to estimate how many clients the program is likely to serve during the evaluation period, and then double that number to ensure that there will be an overflow (that is, control) group. The researcher must have a reasonable expectation that there will, in fact, be an overflow—that is, an excess of demand in relation to the supply of services. If this condition is not likely to be met, the researcher can expect serious strains to develop in carrying out the selection procedure. Program personnel will perceive a credibility problem with other actors in the setting, and may become increasingly reluctant to carry out the selection procedure.

Who sets the quotas?

The researcher must control the criteria for determining when a quota has been met. Therefore, the researcher has to convince all actors in the evaluation setting that the quotas will be carried out impartially, regardless of which parties may lose out in the procedure. In our research, we were able to show that the control group was consistently underrepresented throughout the research assignment period. Prior to implementation, the logic of the procedure was carefully explained to the program's administrators, so that they would be able to anticipate what problems were likely to arise during the course of the evaluation period.

Quota time periods

The minimum and maximum length of the quota periods must be a compromise between what makes sense methodologically and what will be acceptable to program personnel and other actors. The shorter the time periods, the more closely the procedure approximates random selection, but the more likely the objections to it as being arbitrary. A good compromise seems to be periods ranging in length from less than a work day to two or three workdays.

The quota adjustment factor

This procedure must have a built-in adjustment mechanism to even out the percentages assigned to the experimental and control groups. The adjustment mechanism works best when the numbers selected are close to the number expected, that is, the base for establishing the quota. If the expected number was overestimated, the procedure tends to underrepresent controls, as was the case in our research. This is due to the fact that the adjustment mechanism works slowly, that is, only in the long run does it equalize the two groups. If the expected number has been overestimated, the opposite effect takes place, that is, the experimental group will be underrepresented in relation to the control group. In either case, the quota system works to the benefit of the program in that experimentals are always assigned first.

COMPARATIVE ADVANTAGES OF RANDOM QUOTA SELECTION IN RELATION TO OTHER PROCEDURES

It is difficult to establish abstractly what the advantages of one procedure are in relation to others. The researcher has to weigh the known disadvantages and advantages of using each procedure in a given experimental situation.

It should be an obvious point that the best approach would be to convince all actors in an experimental setting of the advantages of random selection; for example, the fact that all subjects have an equal probability of being chosen into the experimental groups. It may therefore be the most truly "equal" form of due process. It should be kept in mind, however, that random selection does not solve all problems. For example, in our research, random selection would not have solved, and could have exacerbated, the problem of exceptions to the research assignment.

If random selection is not feasible, delayed treatment is the second best methodological alternative. As we have pointed out, however, this is not always acceptable in experimental settings. If none of the actors involved mind delayed treatment *and* if the research can ensure that controls' expectations about future services from the program will not bias pretest measures, delayed treatment is the best alternative.

In a choice between random time quota selection and comparison groups, random time quotas seem to us a better alternative. One stands a better chance of approximating the ideal of a control group under random time quota selection, because the control group simultaneously comes from the same research population. With the comparison group procedure, the comparison group must be chosen so that it approximates the characteristics of the research population. As we indicated before, it is always difficult to know beforehand all the relevant comparison characteristics of a research population.

NOTES

1. The development of these selection procedures was based on the ideas of Lucy Friedman, John Feinblatt, formerly of the Vera Institute, and Eric A. Seiff, formerly of the New York City Legal Aid Society.

2. The court's consent to a four-month adjournment was required for formal diversion to CEP to take place.

3. The experimental literature does not mention the possibility of randomly selecting the lengths of periods during an assignment procedure. A very likely reason for this is that experimenters have never been confronted with the problem this evaluation presented. One finds references to random selection of experimental situations (Brunswik, 1949: 37), but this problem is tangential to our concern.

4. To secure a sufficient number of cases, research intake was continued for an additional four months. At the end of the first six months, the research continued to generate time periods using the method described above.

5. Given the erratic flow of cases through the criminal courts, CEP might get many cases approved one day and none the next.

6. In practice, therefore, CEP's quota equalled the percent of cases previously assigned to the overflow (e.g., if the experimental group had 45% of the cases, the overflow had 55%, CEP's next quota would be 55% of the expected number of cases).

7. Another factor affecting the unequal size of the two groups was the necessity to always assign cases to the experimental group *first*. When intake was slow for a long duration (several assignment periods), the number assigned to the experimental group increased faster than those assigned to the control group. Because the number of cases involved was so small (2-4 each period), the adjustment factor used could not fully correct the balance.

8. As in many jurisdictions, diversion in New York City is not mandated by a court rule or state law. CEP is an independent organization funded by the city but having no official relationship to criminal justice agencies. As such, it diverts on the basis of prosecutorial discretion, but judges may assert judicial discretion in sentencing and refuse to approve the continuance for diversion. CEP therefore, must have good relations with the court and prosecutors as well as defense counsel.

9. One exception is ethnicity. Whites were more likely to be in the control group than experimentals. Given the fact that this is the only selection variable on which the two groups differed, it's importance may be discounted.

REFERENCES

BORUCH, R. F. (1976) "On common contentions about randomized field experiments," in M. Guttentag and S. Saar (eds.) Evaluation Studies Review Annual 1. Beverly Hills, CA: Sage.

BRUNSWIK, E. (1947) Systemic and Representative Designs of Psychological Experiments. Berkeley: Univ. of California Press.

CAMPBELL, D. T. and J. STANLEY (1966) Experimental and Quasi-Experimental Designs for Research. Chicago: Rand McNally.

GOLDMAN, J. (1977) "A randomization procedure for trickle process evaluations." Evaluation Q. 1 (August): 3.

Large sums are being spent across the United States to staff emergency and rescue units with paramedics trained in techniques of advanced life support. There has been very little evidence of the effectiveness of paramedics when compared with emergency medical technicians with much less training. The task of getting the evidence is by no means easy. The political repercussions of an experiment in which paramedics would be sent randomly to calls would be enormous. Eisenberg et al. took advantage of a quasi-experimental situation that came about because adjacent areas of Kings County, Washington, had different staffing patterns for rescue units—one area had paramedics, the other did not. The two were similar in most respects, including the pattern of heart arrests requiring intervention to save lives. The following two chapters show that paramedics do save more lives than emergency medical technicians and that there is a small but measurable effect on community mortality rates for heart attacks. The study involves a fairly weak design in an absolute sense, but it is saved by two features: (1) cardiac arrests and their consequences are probably relatively invariant from community to community unless there is a difference in interventions; and (2) the magnitude of the effect is relatively large and difficult to explain away by various rival hypotheses. With respect to the latter point, consider how problematic the findings would have been had the differences between areas been small.

One final note: a randomized trial of paramedic services has been done in England.

11

Paramedic Programs and Out-of-Hospital Cardiac Arrest
I. Factors Associated with Successful Resuscitation

Mickey Eisenberg, Lawrence Bergner, and Alfred Hallstrom

Abstract: As part of an evaluation of whether the addition of paramedic services can reduce mortality from out-of-hospital cardiac arrest compared to previously existing emergency medical technician (EMT) services, factors associated with successful resuscitation were studied. A surveillance system was established to identify cardiac arrest patients receiving emergency care and to collect pertinent information associated with the resuscitation. Outcomes (death, admission, and discharge) were compared in two areas with different types of prehospital emergency care (basic emergency medical technician services vs. paramedic services).

During the period April 1976 through August 1977, 604 patients with out-of-hospital cardiac arrest received emergency resuscitation. Eighty-one per cent of these episodes were attributed to primary heart disease. Considered separately, four factors were found to have a significant association with higher admission and discharge rates: 1) paramedic service, 2) rapid time to initiation of cardiopulmonary resuscitation (CPR), 3) rapid time to definitive care, and 4) bystander-initiated CPR. Using multivariate analysis, rapid time to initiation of CPR and rapid time to definitive care were most predictive of admission and discharge. Age was also weakly predictive of discharge. These findings suggest that if reduction in mortality is to be maximized, cardiac arrest patients must have CPR initiated within four minutes and definitive care provided within ten minutes. (Am. J. Public Health 69:30–38, 1979.)

Introduction

The goal of paramedic programs* is to reduce mortality from medical emergencies. Few studies have attempted to evaluate the attainment of this goal. Rather than studying the outcome, namely a reduction in mortality, most studies have focused on structure or process.[1-4] The few studies considering outcome have been uncontrolled case series[5-8] or uncontrolled community studies.[9, 10] While it is indisputable that paramedics can save lives, particularly patients in cardiac arrest due to ventricular fibrillation, the quantitation of this on a community basis has not been demonstrated. Furthermore, the identification of factors associated with successful resuscitation has not been well documented.

The purpose of this paper is to identify factors associated with successful resuscitation from out-of-hospital cardiac arrest. The results are from the initial period of a three-year outcome evaluation of paramedic services in King County, Washington.

Methodology

The overall study, known locally as Product Restart and reported in detail elsewhere[11] is designed to evaluate whether the addition of a paramedic program can reduce mortality from sudden cardiac arrest when compared to the previously existing emergency medical technician (EMT) services. The study, located in suburban King County, Washington, began in April 1976. King County is the largest metropolitan community in the state of Washington and includes the city of Seattle. The study area (1976 population 598,000) is comprised of the more densely populated suburban ring surrounding Seattle. It does not include Seattle, which has paramedic services provided by the Seattle Fire Department. During the initial period of the study, part of the area received EMT services and the remainder received paramedic services (see Figure 1). The two areas are very similar in demographic characteristics such as proportion of population over age 65 and male to female ratio. The population is over 98 per cent Caucasian. Both areas are predominately middle to upper middle class with the paramedic area having slightly higher socioeconomic characteristics. Information was obtained on every cardiac arrest incident meeting the

From the Robert Wood Johnson Clinical Scholars Program, University of Washington, King County Department of Public Health, and the Department of Biostatistics, University of Washington. Address reprint requests to Dr. Mickey Eisenberg, Emergency Medical Services Division, King County Department of Public Health, 5th Floor, Smith Tower, Seattle, WA 98104. This paper, submitted to the Journal February 8, 1978, was revised and accepted for publication June 24, 1978.

*A paramedic program is defined as an emergency service whereby individuals trained in advanced life support (defibrillation, intubation, cardiac medications) can respond to out-of-hospital emergencies. Paramedics receive up to 1,500 hours of training. In many communities paramedic programs offer a variety of emergency services but most are characterized by treatment of patients with suspected myocardial infarction and cardiac arrest. The terminology for these programs is not uniform. They are also known as mobile intensive care, mobile coronary care, or advanced emergency medical technician programs. In contrast to paramedics, emergency medical technicians (EMTs) receive only 80 hours of training and are able to provide only basic life support such as cardiopulmonary resuscitation (CPR).

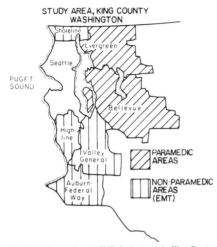

FIGURE 1—Paramedic and EMT Study Areas in King County, Washington*

case definition which occurred in the study area in suburban King County.** Only out-of-hospital events were considered and all ages were included. Trauma (accidents, gunshot wounds, etc.) was specifically excluded because of previous unsuccessful efforts to define and demonstrate adequately a valid tool to assess emergency intervention.[12]

A questionnaire was completed by all 34 emergency agencies (27 fire departments, two paramedic programs, four ambulance companies, and King County Police) in the two study areas following each cardiac arrest in which CPR was performed. In addition, back-up surveillance systems (review of hospital logs and County Division of Emergency Medical Service Incident Report forms) were maintained to identify incidents not directly reported. Approximately 5 per cent of the cases were identified by the back-up surveillance systems. For each cardiac arrest the following information was obtained:

1) Patient identifying information
2) Type of prehospital care (EMT or paramedic)
3) Time from collapse to initiation of CPR
4) Time from collapse to definitive care (defined as advanced emergency procedures such as defibrillation, intubation, and emergency medications)

5) Duration of CPR
6) Response time of the emergency agency
7) The person or agency initiating CPR
8) Whether the collapse was witnessed
9) Weight of the patient
10) ECG rhythm (the busiest EMT departments were provided with lightweight portable ECG machines to record the cardiac rhythm. We obtained ECG rhythm strips in 25 per cent of EMT cases and a tracing or a report of the rhythm in virtually 100 per cent of those treated by paramedics)
11) Outcome: Death or admission to an intensive care or coronary care unit was used as a measurable outcome rather than "admission" to the emergency room, since frequently CPR is continued after arrival in the emergency room, thus making it difficult to decide where death occurs for unsuccessful resuscitation.

Times were determined through fire department or ambulance company dispatch logs, run reports, and phone interviews with bystanders. Times were rounded to the closest half-minute. Times were considered unknown in those instances (22 per cent) when a time of collapse could not be determined, for example in unwitnessed cardiac arrest. In addition, each incident was classified by etiology. Clinical information was obtained from the hospital, and autopsy and death certificate information was reviewed. Primary heart disease was defined as death certificate or hospital discharge diagnosis of acute or chronic ischemic heart disease (ICDA codes 410–414).[†] Admitted patients were followed to determine if discharge occurred and were followed after discharge to determine long-term survival.

Statistical Analysis

Associations between individual variables and resulting outcomes were computed using Chi Square. In order to determine which variables were the best predictors of outcome, logistic regression analysis was used. Logistic regression analysis is an attempt to regress a discrete outcome variable, in this case death, admission, or discharge against both discrete (for example, sex) and continuous (such as response time) variables. Maximum likelihood techniques applied to the logistic model were used to relate the probability of a favorable outcome for an individual to his/her values on a number of variables such as age, sex, time to initiation of CPR, time to definitive care, type of service, etc.

Results

During the period of April 1976, through August 1977, 604 incidents of out-of-hospital cardiac arrest in which CPR was initiated occurred in the study area. The annual incidence (7.1/10,000) was similar in paramedic and EMT areas. The vast majority, 487 (81 per cent), of these events were ascribed to a primary heart disease etiology. Other conditions associated with cardiac arrest in the community were

---

*Seattle, not included in this study, has paramedic services provided by the Seattle Fire Department.

**A case was defined as a patient with cardiac arrest with a pulseless condition (confirmed by an EMT or paramedic) for whom CPR was initiated.

---

†Acute and chronic heart disease were not separated in analysis because we do not believe local physicians adequately distinguish between them on death certificates.

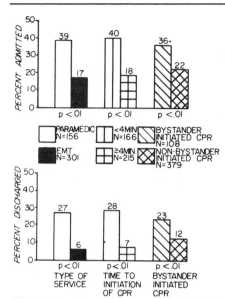

FIGURE 2—Type of Service, Time to Initiation of CPR, Bystander-Initiated CPR and Outcome of Cardiac Arrests Due to Primary Heart Disease, April 1976-August 1977, King County, Washington

cancer (4 per cent), neurologic disease (3 per cent), respiratory disease (3 per cent), drowning (2 per cent), sudden infant death (2 per cent), suicide and non-suicide drug overdoses (2 per cent); all other etiologies comprised 3 per cent. Although the study did not collect information on CPR performed on trauma patients, through empirical observation and from information provided by the King County Medical Examiner such cases represented less than 5 per cent of the total CPR incidents in the community.

Type of service (paramedic), a short time to initiation of CPR, bystander initiated CPR, and a short time to definitive care were each significantly associated with successful outcome (Figures 2 and 3).‡‡ A striking association was found between the type of service and outcome. For primary heart disease patients experiencing cardiac arrest in paramedic areas, 39 per cent were admitted to hospital, compared to 17 per cent in non-paramedic areas (p < .01). In paramedic areas 27 per cent were discharged alive compared to 6 per cent in non-paramedic areas (p < .01). If CPR was initiated within four minutes of collapse, 40 per cent of patients were admitted and if CPR took four or more minutes to initiate, 18

‡‡In considering this and all subsequent relationships, only the 487 CPR incidents due to primary heart disease are considered.

per cent were admitted (p < .01); 28 per cent and 7 per cent respectively were discharged (p < .01).* If a citizen-bystander initiated CPR, 36 per cent of patients were admitted compared to 22 per cent for emergency personnel-initiated CPR (p < .01). For discharge these rates were 23 per cent and 12 per cent respectively (p < .01) (Figure 2).

As seen in Figure 3, an approximately linear relationship existed between time from collapse to definitive care and outcome. If, for example, time to definitive care was less than six minutes, 67 per cent of patients were admitted and 52 per cent discharged. On the other hand if time to definitive care was greater than 12 minutes, 16 per cent were admitted and 6 per cent discharged. The average time to definitive care in the paramedic area was nine minutes and in the EMT area it was 28 minutes.

The above relationships between outcome and certain variables pertain to all patients with cardiac arrest due to primary heart disease regardless of cardiac rhythm at the time of the arrest. Cardiac rhythms were determined at the scene in 50 per cent of the cardiac arrests and ventricular fibrillation was documented in 63 per cent of these patients. If only patients with ventricular fibrillation are considered, similar relationships between outcome and time to definitive care are found although showing higher percentages for both admission and discharge (e.g., of 52 patients in ventricular fibrillation who received definitive care in less than six minutes, 73 per cent were admitted and 57 per cent were discharged).

Table 1 displays the results of the multivariate analysis (logistic regression). Because several variables are related, multiple specifications of a logistic model were considered. The most significant logistic model occurred with the inclusion of time to initiation of CPR, time to definitive care, and age. Other variables studied (type of service, bystander initiated CPR, sex, response time, collapse witnessed directly, patient's weight) when added to the model singly or in

*Stratification at less than four minutes and four minutes or more was chosen because it resulted in the greatest difference in outcome. Accurate times could not be determined in 106 (22 per cent) episodes.

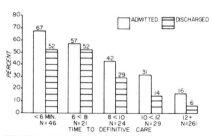

FIGURE 3—Time to Definitive Care for Cardiac Arrests Due to Primary Heart Disease, April 1976–August 1977, King County, Washington

TABLE 1—Results of Logistic Regression Analysis

Variable	Admission	Discharge
1. Time to Initiation of CPR	$p < .01 (-.13 \pm .04)^*$	$p < .01 (-.14 \pm .05)$
2. Time to Definitive Care	$p < .02 (-.054 \pm .01)$	$p < .01 (-.10 \pm .01)$
3. Age	NS	$p < .05 (-.04 \pm .01)$
4. Sex	NS	NS
5. Weight	NS	NS

Constant coefficient for model: .57 (admission); 2.84 (discharge).
*Regression coefficient; ± one standard deviation are in parentheses
NS = Not significant

groups did not significantly improve the predictive value. The variables "time to initiation of CPR," "response time," "bystander initiated CPR," "collapse witnessed directly" are related and substituting any of the latter three variables for time to initiation of CPR provided a predictive model. The model with any of these related variables was not as predictive as with time to initiation of CPR. Similarly, type of service resulted in a predictive model although not as predictive as with time to definitive care. In sum, knowledge of time to initiation of CPR and time to definitive care provided the best predictive model; knowledge of the related variables did not improve the ability to predict the outcome.

Discussion

We have demonstrated several factors which were significantly associated with a successful outcome from out-of-hospital cardiac arrest. Considered separately, the variables of type of service, time to initiation of CPR, time to definitive care, and bystander initiated CPR were significantly associated with outcomes of admission and discharge. Using multivariate analysis (logistic regression) the best predictive model included time to initiation of CPR and time to definitive care. Age was weakly associated with discharge in this model. The fact that the variables of type of service and bystander initiated CPR did not significantly improve the model should not be surprising. Bystander initiated CPR is invariably synonymous with early initiation of CPR. Since bystanders, as we have employed the term, are by definition at the scene of cardiac arrests, it is logical that CPR will be initiated rapidly (assuming the bystander attempts CPR). Hence when considered alone, bystander initiated CPR seems significant but actually is reflecting the significance of early initiation of CPR.

Similarly the type of service reflects the time to definitive care. The treatment ulitmately is the same in both EMT and paramedic areas since patients in EMT areas receive definitive care at the hospital rather than at the scene. However, paramedics bring definitive care (defibrillation, intubation, medication) to the scene of a cardiac arrest while EMTs can only perform CPR and must transport the patient to the hospital for definitive care. Consequently the time to definitive care in EMT areas is much longer (28 minutes) than in paramedic areas (9 minutes). Hence the type of service is largely a reflection of the time to definitive care.

The factors of time to initiation of CPR and time to definitive care are most important in determining successful outcome. A short time to initiation of CPR without a relatively rapid time to definitive care is little better than if the initiation of CPR is delayed. Similarly, a relatively rapid time to definitive care without a rapid time to initiation of CPR also will produce a poor outcome. CPR, no matter how well performed, cannot approximate normal cardiac contraction. Until definitive care can be provided anoxic damage may occur in the vital organs. The sooner definitive care can be provided, the less damage is likely to occur. This is borne out by the linear relationship seen in Figure 3.

The findings of such strongly predictive variables have obvious implications for public policy by confirming that the relatively short time to definitive care provided by paramedics is associated with a higher rate of admission and discharge compared to the longer times and poorer outcomes in EMT areas. This suggests that there may be an intermediate programmatic approach, namely EMTs trained in defibrillation but not certified to perform other definitive procedures.** It also points out that a new paramedic service without CPR being initiated within four minutes is not likely to be successful. One alternative to accomplish early initiation of CPR is with citizen training. Another alternative is to have multiple aid units staffed with EMTs such that a four minute response time is feasible. The latter characterizes the tiered response system which is the foundation of the successful Seattle Fire Department Medic I program. The former alternative is probably the most feasible where population densities are lower and travel times greater. It is interesting to note that the city of Seattle has added wide scale citizen training in CPR to its program and King County has embarked on a similar course of action in 1978. As long as CPR can be initiated within four minutes, it is possible to "buy time" until definitive care can be provided.

The data presented are from the initial period of a before and after outcome evaluation of paramedic services. Since data are from the before period, it is only possible to draw cross-community comparisons. After the initiation of paramedic services in EMT areas, it will be possible to draw before and after comparisons within the same community. Data will continue to be collected in the area that had para-

---

**This approach will be implemented on an experimental basis in King County.

medic services in the before period and in one portion of the study area that will continue with EMT level service thus providing a quasi-experimental situation[13] and reducing the possibility of bias due to intervening variables.

ACKNOWLEDGMENTS

The authors are indebted to the pioneering efforts and high standards of care established by the Seattle Medic I Program and to Dr. Leonard Cobb, Medical Director, Dr. Michael Copass, Director of Training, and Margorie Swain, Research Analyst. This study could not have been possible without the cooperation of the paramedic programs, fire departments and districts, the ambulance companies, police departments, hospitals, and the hundreds of EMTs and paramedics in suburban King County. To these people and organizations we are very grateful. Special thanks also to the research staff: Linda Becker, Deborah Berger, Sheri Schaeffer, Kate Kuhlman, Randy Erickson and Bill dePender.

This project was supported in part by Grant Number HS 02456 from the National Center for Health Services Research, Health Resources Administration, DHEW.

The opinions expressed are those of the authors and do not necessarily reflect those of the Robert Wood Johnson Foundation.

REFERENCES

1. Waller JA: Urban oriented methods, failure to solve rural emergency care problems. JAMA 226:1441-1446, 1973.
2. Pace NA: Emergency cardiac care in a metropolitan office building. Heart Lung 3:775-778, 1974.
3. Carveth SW: Eight-year experience with stadium based mobile coronary care unit. Heart Lung 3:770-774, 1974.
4. Gibson G: Emergency medical services: The research gaps. Health Serv Res Spring:6-21, 1974.
5. Baum RS, Alvarez H, and Cobb LA: Survival after resuscitation from out-of-hospital ventricular fibrillation. Circulation 50:1231-1235, 1974.
6. Cobb LA, Baum RS, Alvarez H, et al: Resuscitation from out-of-hospital ventricular fibrillation: Four years follow-up. Circulation Supp III 51 and 52:223-228, 1975.
7. Liberthson RR, Nagel EL, Hirschman JC, et al: Prehospital ventricular defibrillation: Prognosis and follow-up course, N Engl J Med 291:317-321, 1974.
8. Graf WS, Polin SS, and Paegel BL: A community program for emergency cardiac care: A three year coronary ambulance/ paramedic evaluation. JAMA 226:156-160, 1972.
9. Crampton RS, Miles JR, Gascho JA, et al: Amelioration of prehospital and ambulance death rates from coronary artery disease by prehospital emergency cardiac care. J Am Coll Emer Phys Jan/Feb:19-23, 1975.
10. Crampton RS, Michaelson SP, Wynbeek A, et al: Reduction of prehospital, ambulance, and hospital coronary death by the prehospital emergency cardiac system: A rationale for training emergency medical technicians, nurses and physicians. Heart Lung 3:742-747, 1974.
11. National Center for Health Services Research, Research Management Series: Emergency Medical Services Systems Research Projects, 1977 DHEW Publication No. (HRA) 77-3194, 98-101.
12. Gibson G: Indices of severity for emergency medical evaluative studies: reliability, validity, and data requirements. International Journal of Health Services, In press, 1978.
13. Campbell DT, and Stanley JC: Experimental and Quasi-experimental Designs for Research. Chicago: Rand McNally, 1963.

Medical researchers have recently begun to question the value of certain common medical procedures. The following chapter by Roos et al. presents an excellent quasi-experimental evaluation of one of these procedures: tonsillectomy operations. Several methodological features of this study are of particular interest: (1) the researchers use a large, high-quality archival data set; (2) the entire population is not employed. Only those subjects who meet specified criteria are included in the control and treatment groups; (3) the researchers evidence considerable creativity in the construction of multiple control groups to rule out a wider range of alternative hypotheses; (4) a 23-month follow-up of the subjects permits some assessment of the short-term versus long-term benefits of the operation; and (5) the researchers also examine possible changes in the frequency of non-respiratory medical claims following the operation.

Although this study represents an excellent example of how to exploit fully a good set of data, readers might consider how their confidence in the results might change if the quality of the data were different. It is important to remember that no matter how sophisticated the analyses, the conclusions are no better than the quality of the original data. If possible, multiple sources of data should be employed to minimize the influence of systematic biases in a particular set of data.

12

Assessing the Impact of Tonsillectomies

Leslie L. Roos, Jr., Noralou P. Roos, and Paul D. Henteleff

This paper explores outcomes associated with the tonsillectomy operation using multiple control groups and a large claims-based data bank from the Canadian province of Manitoba. Given the difficulty of conducting large-scale clinical trials of common surgical procedures, the use of multiple methods for evaluating such interventions is both advocated and implemented in this study. When the data are restricted to respiratory diagnoses, the findings suggest that, on the average, tonsil surgery saves between one half and one and a half episodes of illness per patient over the two years after surgery. Such savings are much more pronounced among individuals having several tonsillitis episodes in the preoperative year. However, when all medical claims are considered, the estimated savings from the tonsillectomy operation are somewhat reduced. Individual variation in predisposition to "see the doctor" appears to account for such results; visits about conditions other than respiratory take up much of the "savings" produced by tonsil surgery. The findings are discussed in terms of the costs and benefits of the tonsillectomy operation, and future research needs are outlined.

THIS PAPER is directed toward a better understanding of the impact of a frequent surgical procedure—that of tonsillectomy. Evidence is presented as to the effectiveness of this operation in reducing episodes of respiratory illness and overall use of ambulatory care in the Canadian province of Manitoba. In conjunction with the substantive discussion, the possibilities for improving research designs by using multiple control groups and large data banks are explored.

Tonsillectomy

Questions of the risks and benefits of surgery are receiving increasing attention, particularly since wide variations in surgical rates have been well documented.[23, 27, 30, 31] However, as Bunker has emphasized:[6]

. . . very little outcome data are available from which to predict the benefits for individual operations or for surgery as a whole. What is needed, of course, is detailed information on the natural history of each operation-diagnostic category, including how it is modified by surgery. Such data must be based on the experience of large populations. . . .

The operations being studied—those for tonsillectomy (abbreviated as T) and ton-

A preliminary version of this paper was presented at the 1977 American Institute for Decision Sciences Conference in Chicago, October 19-21, 1977. This research was supported by Grant Number 607-1075-43 Research Programs Directorate, Health and Welfare, Canada, by a Research Scholar Award 606-1114-48 to the senior author, and by a Career Scientist Award 607-1001-22 to the second author.

Please address reprint requests to: Professor Noralou P. Roos, Department of Social and Preventive Medicine, Faculty of Medicine, University of Manitoba, Winnipeg, Canada.

* Faculty of Administrative Studies, University of Manitoba, Winnipeg, Canada.

† Faculties of Medicine and Administrative Studies, University of Manitoba, Winnipeg, Canada.

‡ Faculty of Medicine, University of Manitoba, Winnipeg, Canada.

sillectomy/adenoidectomy (T&A) — are among the most frequent surgical procedures performed in North America.* These procedures are also controversial and have been the subject of considerable study without definitive evidence on their effectiveness. An ongoing randomized clinical trial in Pittsburgh now purports to resolve many of the shortcomings of earlier research, primarily by imposing stringent requirements for patient selection for the operations.[19, 20]

The assumptions of the ongoing clinical trial do not, however, square with the reality of clinical practice. Research in Canada and the United States documents that somewhere between 75 and 95 per cent of the cases routinely selected for tonsillectomies and adenoidectomies do not meet even the minimal criteria being used in the randomized trials. In the Pittsburgh study patients are only considered for surgery if they meet stringent standards, having "recurrent tonsillitis, defined as a history of at least seven episodes in the preceding year, or five episodes in each of the last two years, or three episodes in each of the last three years" or one of several rare conditions.[†]

Given the gross discrepancy between clinical practice and standards recommended by acknowledged experts in the field, it is worthwhile to ask: are the recommended standards appropriate? With the growing emphasis on peer review, both expert opinion and "common practice" should be validated against outcome measures. Results will be presented on the impact of tonsillectomy on cases which do—and do not—meet the standard of at least four episodes of tonsillitis or one episode of

peritonsillar abscess in the previous year.[‡] The impact of the operation is discussed, first in terms of episodes of respiratory disease, and then in terms of overall use of ambulatory care.

Method

The data are from the hospital, medical, and registration files of the Manitoba Health Services Commission. The whole population of Manitoba· is covered by provincially administered health insurance. Hospital and medical care are documented in considerable detail because of the fee-for-service payment system. The data base has been fully described elsewhere.[21, 22] This information has been shown to be an accurate, reliable, and valid representation of the physician's assessment of the patients. This is in accord with research on Saskatchewan physician's recording of claims diagnoses[26] and on the San Joaquin Peer Review Experience using claims data.[14]

Because of the difficulties associated with standard statistical efforts to adjust treatment-control group differences, Campbell has proposed a rather different statistical approach to measuring treatment effects.[8, 10] His basic philosophy is that pretreatment differences (between treatment and control groups) should be accepted; a treatment which significantly alters these differences is judged to have had an effect.[§]

According to Kenny,[16] choosing the appropriate statistical approach depends upon one's model of the process of selection of individuals into treatment groups. None of the "ideal type" models discussed by Kenny fits the tonsillectomy case precisely, but the operated and nonoperated groups are chosen for treatment at least partially ac-

---

* In 1971 tonsillectomy, with or without adenoidectomy, was the most frequent operation performed in the United States.[4]

† These conditions are "confirmed peritonsillar abscess, chronic tonsillitis persisting for at least six months despite intensive antibiotic therapy, chronic anterior cervical lymphadenitis persisting for at least six months despite intensive antibiotic therapy, and tonsillar hypertrophy causing a markedly muffled voice in children above the age of six years."[19, 20]

‡ This recommended standard is somewhat less strict than that suggested by Paradise and Bluestone and represents an intermediate "consensus" position.

§ Pretreatment-posttreatment changes in reliability or treatment-control group differences in reliability can pose methodological problems.[9] Fortunately, a detailed reliability analysis showed no difficulties along these lines.

cording to variables other than their own medical status. The operated group is disproportionately made up of patients of doctors who believe in tonsillectomies, while the opposite is true for the nonoperated group.[23]

Campbell and Kenny have suggested using the following methods for the analysis of quasi-experimental designs where selection is based on group differences:

1. Pretreatment t between experimental and control groups. These are compared with posttreatment t between these two groups. An experimental effect is then taken as significant difference in t's.
2. Point biserial correlations between receiving a treatment (yes or no) and the dependent variable (measured pretreatment and posttreatment) are also calculated; these correlations are called treatment-effect correlations. A significant change in the biserial correlation between pretreatment and posttreatment is taken as evidence of an effect.‖

Control Groups

Control groups are used in research designs to help deal with threats to internal validity, that is, threats to the interpretation of differences in the dependent variable before and after administration of the experimental treatment. When random assignment of individuals to treatment and control groups is not possible, control groups need to be constructed in statistically sound ways which make them appropriately similar to treatment groups.

The desirability of multiple control groups in quasi-experimental designs has been stressed by Webb and Ellsworth:[29]

‖ This approach takes into account fan-spread growth; treatment and control groups may grow at different rates, such that the gap between groups and the variability of within-group performance increases.[16]

Quasi-experimental designs require particular attention to the achievement of appropriate control groups, since the absence of random assignment raises serious dangers of noncomparability of groups and consequent uninterpretability of results. Many studies could be improved by the use of multiple control groups; the more different kinds of control groups (or control observations), the greater the number of rival hypotheses that can be rendered implausible, and the stronger the case for the causal relationship the experimenter has in mind.

Moreover, systematic comparisons of the results obtained from applying various control group selection strategies to the same data set may be valuable.¶ Because different research designs are characterized by different assumptions, using multiple control groups to help understand possible biases associated with each design is important.

Two different ways of producing nonrandomized control groups are used in this paper. The first method depends upon standard techniques for constructing control groups—the treatment and control groups are similar along one or more variables of importance. The second method generates a sibling control group which also meets the criterion (or criteria) of similarity with a sibling treatment group. Because siblings tend to be similar in terms of family environment and, to a lesser extent, genetic endowments, the use of sibling control groups presumably leads to more accurate estimates of treatment effects.

These two methods of developing control groups are explored both to clarify the logic involved and to illustrate the potential of data banks. Questions of convergent validity are involved; the more consistent the results across several different sorts of

¶ One study comparing an experimental design (true randomization to treatment and control groups) with two quasi-experimental designs suggested that systematic, slight differences between treatment and control groups were likely to be missed with quasi-experimental designs.[13]

control groups, the more confidence in the conclusions drawn.

The very large number of potential matches available for control group construction is an important feature of many data banks. Data banks often include information on entire populations, of which the treatment individuals are likely to constitute a very small subgroup. In Manitoba approximately 5,000 individuals out of a population of one million underwent tonsillectomy in 1973. Almost any characteristic of the treatment group was easy to find in the larger pool of potential controls.

Constructing Control Groups

Constructing a control group(s) similar to the treatment group is hindered by a lack of clear, widely accepted decision rules for choosing the control group from the larger pool of available individuals. How close should the treatment and control group be? What variables are important? One suggestion has been to use basic social background variables, such as age and sex, which often bear some relationship to the dependent variable under study. Such variables should, as far as is possible, be uncorrelated with whether or not an individual receives the treatment.** These easily measured background variables help handle an important threat to the internal validity of research results—that of maturation. Having a control group similar in age and sex to the treatment group permits a partial evaluation of the argument that "the changes would have occurred anyway, even without the treatment."

Controlling for several variables is likely to reduce, but not eliminate, differences between nonrandomly achieved treatment and control groups. Morever, efforts to equate these groups may capitalize upon pretreatment measurement error. Matching on pretest scores has been widely used, but efforts to adjust away differences in pre-

---

** Donald T. Campbell, personal communication.

treatment scores inevitably underadjust and are likely to produce results with systematic biases.[9]

Pretreatment scores which deviate substantially from the group mean do so partly because of fortuitous measurement error. Posttreatment (or any other) scores for these individuals will tend to regress toward their group mean; at the posttreatment, measurement selection will not be operating to take advantage of chance. If treatment and potential control groups have different group means, the posttreatment scores will regress toward the respective (different) means, producing spurious effects.

Campbell and Erlebacher mention two paramenters relevant for deciding the extent of problems with matching.[8] Here the term "operation" has been substituted for "treatment" to emphasize that the tonsillectomy operation is the intervention under study, even though other medical treatment is involved. Campbell and Erlebacher note that:

1. The higher the correlation between preoperation and postoperation score, the less the regression toward different means.
2. The larger the difference between group population means, the more the regression toward different means.

These parameters will be discussed in the data analysis section, applying them to the tonsillectomy research.

Basic Comparisons

The selection of an appropriate control group presents the problem of making the treatment and controls as equivalent as possible. In this study, a subpopulation was first selected to control for particular independent variables; operated and nonoperated groups were then identified and compared in the subsequent data analysis. One criterion for selection of the subpopulation was the presence of a respiratory diagnosis specifying the existence of tonsillar tissue (as in tonsillitis, peritonsillar abscess, and hypertrophy) in 1972 (for the nonoperated group) or in the year before the month of 1973 tonsillectomy (for the operated group). Thus, the control group members both had at least some degree of illness and had not had their tonsils removed in the pre 1972 period. Individuals in the control group had to satisfy an additional criterion of not having a T or T&A operation in the 1972-1974 period. A further criterion was patient age of 13 years or less in 1973; this criterion included 72 per cent of the Manitoba tonsillectomy patients in 1973 and roughly equated the age distribution of operated and nonoperated groups. (The means for the two groups were, respectively, 6.83 and 6.33 years of age. Variances were similar, but few operations were done on two year olds.)

Finally, all individuals considered had to be covered in Manitoba over the entire 1972-1974 period; about 88 per cent of the individuals under 14 noted as in Manitoba during this period were so covered. Coverage was slightly higher in the operated group than in their nonoperated counterparts. In this age group, the main reason for lack of coverage over the whole three year period was mobility of patients' families into or out of Manitoba.

Using the criterion of one 1972 diagnosis of a particular type (tonsillitis, peritonsillar abscess, or hypertrophy) for inclusion in the sample makes counts of the mean number of 1973 episodes tend to be lower than 1972 averages, since at least one 1972 episode is guaranteed by the selection criterion. No statistical difficulties seem to result from this procedure; standardizing 1972 and 1973 scores shows no tendency for regression towards the mean. Moreover, control and operations groups constructed without this criterion of a particular 1972 diagnosis showed results similar to those presented in the tables which follow.

The "all 1973 operations" group used in this paper was made up of 1,950 patients from a total of 4,598 tonsillectomies and tonsillectomies-adenoidectomies identified in Manitoba in 1973. The pool of patients eligible for the operated group was reduced because of the three criteria of coverage, age, and diagnosis. Tonsillectomy and tonsillectomy-adenoidectomy operations were not differentiated here. The fees are the same, while the actual hospital records showed some differences as to whether or not adenoidectomies were noted on the computerized records of the Health Services Commission.

The pool of individuals meeting the three basic criteria (coverage, age, and diagnosis) for the nonoperated group was quite large —almost twelve thousand. An 18 per cent sample ($N = 2,089$) of this pool was used as the nonoperated control group. January, 1973, was taken for the nonoperated group as the monthly equivalent to the "operation" month for the operated sample; as noted below, this makes maximum use of the data.

Two operated groups facilitated comparisons with the nonoperated group. One group is made up of tonsillectomy patients operated upon in January, 1973; using this group has several advantages. First of all, the 12 months before a January, 1973, operation all fall in 1972; thus, this group has the same time span for preoperation comparison as does the nonoperated control group. Moreover, using this January, 1973, group permits comparing posttreatment medical histories for almost two years after the operation. But this January, 1973, group contains only 143 patients. The second operated group is made up of all those individuals receiving T and T&A operations in 1973 ($N = 1,950$); this group includes the January, 1973, operations group. Data from both the 12 months preceding the operation month and the 12 months after the operation were available for all patients in this 1973 group.

Data Analysis

Tables 1 and 2 compare the preoperation and postoperation histories of tonsillectomy cases and controls.†† The number of episodes of tonsil/adenoid related illness is the dependent variable.‡‡ Episodes during the month of operation were not counted since preoperative visits were likely to have inflated that figure; this is discussed later in the paper.

Table 1 suggests that tonsillectomy does help reduce the frequency of respiratory episodes. The drop in the operations groups following surgery (from 1.77 to .27 and from 1.75 to .29) is considerably larger than the drop in the control group (from .95 to .38) over the same time period. The t tests (Table 1) indicate significant differences between operated and nonoperated patients at each time period. However, the direction of the differences between means changes only once—during the six months prior to surgery the operated group had more episodes of illness than did the controls. During every other period, the control group reported significantly more respiratory episodes. In similar fashion, the sign of the biserial correlation coefficient (Table 2) differs from the others only for this pre-

†† The design is discussed by Cook and Campbell as the "no treatment control group design."[12]

‡‡ An episode of respiratory illness was counted when a claim for one (or more) of the following diagnoses was filed in a given month: acute otitis media, otitis media, acute tonsillitis, hypertrophy of tonsils and adenoids, peritonsillar abscess, streptococcal sore throat, acute nasopharyngitis (common cold) acute pharyngitis, acute respiratory infection. Thus, a month either had or did not have an episode; no more than one episode/month was possible. Several checks on this definition of episode were made; redefining an "episode" to include all claims made not more than a given number (14, 21, or 28) of days apart made little difference in the results. Other investigators have made roughly similar operationalizations of the episode concept.[18, 24] Our definition of episode is computationally similar to that of "patient initiated" visit in that the initial physician-patient encounter in a given month (for appropriate range of diagnoses) is flagged as indicating an episode.[15]

TABLE 1. Preoperation-Postoperation Histories for Tonsillectomy Patients and Controls

Six-Month Period	Mean Number of Episodes (Relevant Respiratory Diagnoses) in Each Period		
	January, 1973, Operations (N = 143)	All 1973 Operations (N = 1950)	Controls (N = 2089)
Preoperation year			
12 to 7 months before	.47	.59	.75
6 to 1 months before	1.77	1.75	.95
Postoperation years			
1 to 6 months after	.27	.29	.38
7 to 12 months after	.29	.28	.38
13 to 18 months after	.27	–	.36
19 to 23 months after	.19	–	.30

NOTE: T-tests for the comparisons between "January, 1973, operations" patients and control patients were significant at the .05 level for all time periods except the 7 to 12 months after and 13 to 18 months after periods. All T-tests for comparisons between the "all 1973 operations" patients and control patients were significant at the .01 level. Postoperation t-tests differed significantly from the preoperation t-test for the 6 to 1 months before period.

operative period. The results from the two experimental groups—the January, 1973, operations and the all 1973 operations—are convergent. When compared with the control group, both operations groups point in the same direction.

Significant differences between operations and control groups in the mean number of episodes before and after surgery argue for a causal impact of the operation. But the possibilities of statistical artifacts—particularly of "regression toward the mean"—remain. The preoperation-postoperation (1972-1973) correlations for number of episodes were between 0.3 and 0.4 for all three groups (2 operated and 1 control). These correlations are low enough to suggest further analysis. Comparing preoperation and postoperation scores should show whether patients are regressing toward markedly different means. Controlling for pretest (1972) scores, the "regression towards the mean" hypothesis suggests that

TABLE 2. Treatment-Effect Correlations for Tonsillectomy Operations

| Six-Month Period | Biserial Correlation of Number of Episodes/ Period with Having/ Not Having a Tonsillectomy Operation | |
	January 1973 Operations	All 1973 Operations
Preoperation year		
12 to 7 months before	−.09	−.10
6 to 1 months before	.22	.39
Postoperation years		
1 to 6 months after	−.04	−.07
7 to 12 months after	−.03	−.07
13 to 18 months after	−.03	−
19 to 23 months after	−.04	−

For the "January, 1973, operations," the N was 143 individuals with tonsillectomies and 2,089 controls. For the "all 1973 operations," the N was 1,950 individuals with tonsillectomies and the same 2,089 controls.

Biserial correlation coefficients for the "January, 1973, operations" column were significant at the .05 level for all time periods except the 7 to 12 months after and 13 to 18 months after periods. All biserial correlation coefficients for the "all 1973 operations" column were significant at the .001 level.

For both columns, the preoperation-postoperation correlations were significantly different from each other, thus providing evidence of an effect of the operation.

The biserial correlation coefficients were calculated with the controls assigned a 0 and the operated individuals a 1.

differences between control and treatment groups should be greatest at the extremes of the distribution. When there is considerable measurement error, low "before" scores should tend to be higher "after" scores, and high scores, lower. The operated and nonoperated groups are equated on preoperation scores (number of respiratory episodes) in Table 3. In each case, those individuals receiving tonsillectomies had significantly fewer postoperation respiratory episodes than did the candidates. The higher-scoring group before the operation (the T&A patients) became the lower-scoring group after operation. Such an outcome makes the alternative explanation of statistical "regression toward the mean" less likely. A higher-scoring group would be expected to regress toward a lower grand mean upon retesting, but such a mean would not be lower than that of the initially lower-scoring control group on the basis of regression alone.

Maturation can be rejected as an alternative explanation for the tonsillectomy data. As individuals get older, they do have fewer respiratory episodes, but operated and nonoperated groups were very similar in age. Finally, although older subsamples (from both operated and control groups) tended to have fewer respiratory episodes than did the younger, the overall findings were unchanged.

Additional Controls

The relative insensitivity of the findings to changes in the composition of the control and operation groups should be stressed. Results were similar when tonsillectomy-adenoidectomy and tonsillectomy-only patients were compared with the controls. Modifying the definitions of appropriate diagnoses produced few changes.

Other criteria for selection of operated and nonoperated groups were experimented with. Initially the operations group was taken as all tonsillectomy patients in a given time period (January, 1973), rather than using the same "preoperation" diagnoses to select both the operated and nonoperated group. This approach depends upon finding an "appropriate" algorithm for generating the control group. We selected individuals having an episode in January, 1973, for the control group, with no major differences in the findings presented above.

Preexisting differences between control and "experimental" groups often cannot be adjusted in any convenient statistical fashion. Such differences are highlighted here by considering those patients with a relatively large number of respiratory episodes. In the year before their operations, the tonsillectomy patients with four respiratory episodes had significantly more diagnoses of tonsillitis and hypertrophy—with fewer diagnoses of colds, pharyngitis, and upper respiratory infection—than did their counterparts with four episodes and no operations.

Controlling for diagnosis helps deal with the possibility that the surgery patients were more seriously ill than their counterparts who were not operated upon. The most serious of the usual diagnoses indicating possible need for a tonsillectomy is peritonsillar abscess; a single episode may justify the operation. However, the peritonsillar abscess diagnosis was so infrequent that outcome analysis was not feasible. Two other types of diagnoses—tonsillitis and hypertrophy of the tonsils and adenoids—were examined separately, controlling for number of preoperation episodes as in Table 3. The findings for these separate examinations were similar to the overall results. The group receiving an operation had more respiratory episodes immediately preceding surgery and fewer thereafter.

Additional inferences about the severity distribution within and between diagnostic categories can be made from using the basic claims data on physician-patient contact as is, in addition to aggregating it into respiratory episodes. Individuals with a greater number of respiratory episodes had similar number of claims for respiratory illness, regardless of whether they were in the operated or nonoperated groups. Controlling for diagnosis made no difference here. Finally, the analysis presented in Tables 1 through 3 can be repeated counting claims rather than respiratory episodes; the inferences are essentially unchanged.

An analysis of the "before" and "after" data for each 1973 operation month showed few differences according to which operation month was selected. Choosing December, 1973, as the operation month and adjusting the control group appropriately made it possible to compare operated and nonoperated groups for almost two years "before" surgery. The two groups were quite similar up to the six months preceding surgery; the results corresponded with those shown in Table 1.

Sibling Analysis

Sibling data help deal with the hypothesis that operated and nonoperated groups differ along some important dimension not being accounted for in the analysis. For example, operated and nonoperated groups may differ because some families may strongly want the operation. Would such families then tend to take their children to the doctor more frequently before the operation and less frequently afterwards? In similar fashion, the opposite argument could be made for families strongly against the operation. But when one child in a family is operated on and the other is not, the data can be examined to see if the differences between operated and nonoperated groups found in the larger sample remain in the sibling sample. If so, the rival hypotheses become less plausible.

Criteria for the use of sibling and nonsibling control groups are compared in Table 4. Using nonsibling control groups allows many more individuals to become available for inclusion in both the treatment and control groups. Subdividing the sample to better control for additional variables is facilitated greatly. On the other hand, a sibling control group has the important advantage of being more similar to the sibling treatment group than a nonsibling group, since both individual heredity and family environment are partially controlled for. Moreover, such variables as region are completely controlled. Siblings are, of course, not as representative of the general population as the regular treatment and control groups. Indeed, having tonsil/adenoid surgery on two siblings in the same year is popular; over 10 per cent of the 1973 tonsillectomies were on sibling pairs.

Eight hundred ninety-six pairs of siblings satisfying the following criteria were found:

1. one sibling was in the T&A experimental group, and the other in the control group.
2. the siblings were within 5 years of each other in age.

TABLE 3. Postoperation Histories for Tonsillectomy Patients
and Controls Matched on Number of Preoperation Episodes

	Mean Number of Episodes in Each Year				
	All 1973 Operations (N = 632)	Controls (1210)	All 1973 Operations (624)	Controls (534)	All 1973 Operations (352)
Preoperation year	1.0	1.0	2.0	2.0	3.0
Postoperation year	.32	.50	.49	.84	.64

The two righthand columns provide information on the operated and nonoperated groups with 6 or more episodes in 1973.

Differences between operated and control groups were significant at the .001 level for the postoperation year for each level of preoperation episodes.

Analysis using the January 1973 operations indicated similar differences between the operated and control patients in the second year after surgery.

3. the siblings were both fully covered for the 1972-1974 period.

Introducing additional criteria parallel to those for the nonsibling sample reduced the sibling sample considerably—to 148 pairs. These criteria were:

1. have a respiratory diagnosis specifying the presence of tonsillar tissue in 1972.
2. be 14 years of age or younger.

The sibling data in Table 5 show results in line with those presented earlier. Sibling operated and nonoperated groups were

TABLE 4. Sibling and Nonsibling Control Groups

Sibling Control Group	Nonsibling Control Group
Internal Validity Partial control for heredity and environment	Larger numbers in both treatment and control groups permits checking on seasonal effects—do those receiving an operation in January differ from those receiving an operation in July?

External Validity
Group drawn for sibling control is, by definition, somewhat unrepresentative: (a) from families with at least two children reasonably close together in age and (b) of whom one had an operation and one did not.

Statistical controls for age and sex possible in both samples, but the N is larger for the nonsibling group.

roughly similar in age. The mean number of episodes for the six months before the tonsillectomy was considerably higher for the operated group; after the operation, this group was significantly lower than the nonoperated group. Analysis according to treatment-effect correlations was also similar for both sibling and nonsibling samples. Differences between the preoperation and postoperation correlations were significant for the siblings, as for the larger nonsibling sample. Finally, the results were insensitive as to whether the larger sibling sample with 896 pairs or the smaller one with 148 pairs was used.

Overall, these sibling data are remarkably similar to those from the total sample. In this study, individual heredity and family environment do not seem plausible explanations for the findings. Comparing Tables 1 and 5 indicates that episode means for the two sibling groups are not closer than the means for the nonsibling groups. As might be expected, the sibling groups show slightly higher preoperation (and postoperation) episode counts than the regular sample. Doctors who operate on one sibling, but not the other, are probably somewhat more discriminating than the average. In summary, the overall findings receive additional support, but relatively little can be said about specific biases involved in using

TABLE 3.   Continued

Mean Number of Episodes in Each Year						
Controls (200)	All 1973 Operations (177)	Controls (82)	All 1973 Operations (101)	Controls (45)	All 1973 Operations (64)	Controls (18)
3.0	4.0	4.0	5.0	5.0	6.72	6.61
1.35	.85	1.33	1.11	2.40	1.80	2.78

one type of control group rather than an-other.

Claims and the Operation Month

The decision to perform surgery is likely to result in one or more ambulatory visits to the doctor which are linked to the operation itself, rather than to the episode of illness. Separating out those episodes which result from a preoperative visit or consultation is desirable. Unfortunately, our indicators can only give an idea of the general direction of bias in the calculations:

1. Possible overestimation of the number of preoperation episodes for the tonsillectomy group.

a) The diagnosis of hypertrophy is sometimes used to designate a preoperative checkup; this diagnosis is seldom found for the control group (less than 1 per cent of the diagnoses in January, 1973). On the other hand, hypertrophy is noted fairly often (11 per cent of respiratory diagnoses) as the last diagnosis preceding the month of operation. Thirty-eight per cent of the respiratory diagnoses recorded during the operation month were for hypertrophy.

b) The decision to undertake a tonsillectomy sometimes involves consultations. Such consultations are almost always found in the operations group (21 per cent of the January, 1973, operations group, N = 143) rather than in the control group (4 per cent). Such consultations generally occur in the three months before the operation,

but appear to only slightly increase the number of preoperation episodes. Twenty two of the 39 consultations for the January, 1973, group occurred in months with two or more claims. Thus, the number of tonsillectomy patients with an additional episode due to a consultation might be about 6 per cent of the total.

c) As noted earlier, doctors' visits occurring during the operation month were not counted in either the preoperation or the postoperation episode counts. This was a convenient oversimplification, undertaken because more exact data were lacking. A number of the visits in the operation month un-

TABLE 5.   Preoperation-Postoperation Histories for Tonsillectomy Patients and Controls (Sibling Sample)

	Mean Number of Episodes (Relevant Respiratory Diagnoses) in Each Period	
Six-Month Period	All 1973 Operations (N=148)	Controls (N=148)
Preoperation year		
12 to 7 months before	.88	.86
6 to 1 months before	1.81	1.07
Postoperation year		
1 to 6 months after	.29	.57
7 to 12 months after	.32	.44

T-tests for comparisons between the "all 1973 operations" patients and control patients were significant at the .01 level for the 6 to 1 months before and 1 to 6 months after periods.

Postoperation t-tests differed significantly from the preoperation t-test for the 6 to 1 months after periods.

doubtedly represented respiratory problems, rather than preoperative checks. Table 6 provides some information relevant to these episode counts. Thirty-three per cent of the operations group had a one-claim episode in the operation month. Fifteen per cent of the group had episodes with two or more claims; presumably many of these "2+ claims" episodes involved a legitimate episode, rather than a preoperative visit. On the other hand, 41 per cent of the operations group had one-claim episodes in the month before surgery; some of these were probably preoperative visits.

2. Possible underestimation of the number of postoperation episodes for the tonsillectomy group.

  a) Medical care for a throat ailment in the six weeks after tonsillectomy is considered by the Manitoba Health Services Commission as part of the surgical care; there should be no payment for the physician performing surgery. However, claims may be submitted and a record would appear, even though the payment might subsequently be denied. Other physicians may, of course, submit claims during this period. Of the tonsillectomy patients, 7 and 5 per cent, respectively, recorded episodes in the first and second months after surgery; baseline figures for the control group were 6 per cent for both months.

Pharmacare

Because Manitoba has a government-run program reimbursing families for 80 per cent of prescription drug expenses over $50 annually, the use of antibiotics among a subsample of individuals in the 1973 treatment and control groups was also analyzed. Data were available for only 1975, between a year and two years after the tonsillectomy operation. Pharmacare files were searched for individuals receiving tonsillectomies in January, February, or June, 1973; a sample of controls was also used.

Of course, many families would have less than $50 prescription drug bills in any given year. Other families might be eligible, but neglect to file for the reimbursement. Some idea as to the relative illness of operated and nonoperated groups might be obtained by looking at the difficulty in finding individuals for whom Pharmacare claims were submitted. Families suffering from a great deal of illness would be more likely to submit for reimbursement than their healthier counterparts. Because families, rather than individuals, file claims, the evidence is necessarily weak. Using this measure, families where at least one child had a 1973 tonsillectomy appear to be somewhat healthier—only 19 per cent of the operated group families as compared with 24 per cent of the families from the nonoperated group filed for reimbursement.

The drug data obtained from the Pharmacare records provide a valuable check on the findings from the claims data. Findings obtained using two independent data sources

TABLE 6. Distribution of Claims by Month in Period before Tonsillectomy Operation

Number of Claims	4 Months Before, %	3 Months Before, %	2 Months Before, %	1 Month Before, %	Operation Month, %
No claims	78	72	57	31	52
1 claim	16	18	27	41	33
2+ claims	6	10	15	28	15

NOTE: The N was 1,950 individuals with tonsillectomies in 1973.

are clearly more trustworthy than those generated from a single source. The data in Table 7 are not completely compatible with those presented in earlier tables, since they included both some respondents over 14 years of age and some who did not have a 1972 (or year before surgery) diagnosis specifying the presence of tonsillectomy tissue were included. Nonetheless, the information in Table 7 is mutually supportive: in 1975, during the period between two and three years after the operation, the operated group both had fewer episodes of respiratory disease and purchased fewer drugs relevant for the treatment of such disease.

All Medical Claims

Additional information based on *all* medical claims filed over a four-year period (1972-1975) was available for a subsample of the patients used in the preceding analysis. Individuals in the subsample had to satisfy the basic criteria of being fully covered in the 1972-1974 period and having a relevant diagnosis in the year before the operation (in 1972 for the control group). Within this subsample, the operated group was made up of 446 individuals having tonsillectomies in January, February, and June of 1973 while the nonoperated group consisted of 664 individuals randomly drawn from the larger nonoperated group. Data on this subsample were drawn from MHSC records well after the research was underway.§§ As will become clear, the design of the study should have included obtaining such extensive information from the beginning.

The basic data are organized in terms of respiratory episodes and claims and shown in Table 8. Claims, rather than episodes, are emphasized because of the difficulty of using the episode concept for the great

§§ There are very slight differences in the inclusion of particular individuals in Table 8, as compared with Tables 1 to 3.

TABLE 7. Multi-Method Checks—
Pharmacare and Medical Claims

	Pharmacare Claims Submitted in 1975		Pharmacare Claims Not Submitted in 1975	
	1973 Opera-tions (N=87)	Con-trols (96)	1973 Opera-tions (369)	Con-trols (297)
Mean number 1975 respiratory episodes (from medical claims)				
Possibly tonsil related	0.78	1.53	0.58	1.01
Probably not tonsil related	0.87	1.17	0.40	0.43
Mean number 1975 months with relevant antibiotic prescription (from Pharmacare claims)	1.29	2.06	N/A	N/A

NOTE: The list of diagnoses relevant for the two types of respiratory episodes is presentetd in Roos, Henteleff, and Roos.[22] The "possibly tonsil-related" episodes were those used for the episode counts presented in the earlier tables. Those episodes which were "probably not tonsil-related" were counted only for months where there were no "possibly tonsil-related" episodes. The antibiotics designated as relevant for respiratory problems are available on request. Coverage checks only extend through 1974, so a few individuals not submitting Pharmacare claims will have left the province.

variety of other diagnoses used. The findings are both unusual and straightforward. Although the tonsillectomy operation resulted in a reduction of claims (and episodes) for respiratory diagnoses, there was a relative increase in other claims for each of the two years after the 1973 operation. Similar results were obtained when data were analyzed for the almost three-year period after the January, 1973, surgery.

Table 8 shows that the control group initially had more claims than the operated group. Even though the number of respiratory claims drops markedly after tonsillec-

TABLE 8.   Preoperation-Postoperation Histories for Tonsillectomy Patients
and Controls (Respiratory Episodes and All Medical Claims)

	Preoperation Year		Postoperation Year		Two Years Postoperation	
	1973 Operations (N=446)	Controls (N=664)	1973 Operations	Controls	1973 Operations	Controls
Respiratory episodes	2.37	2.34	0.63	1.43	0.58	1.23
Claims						
Respiratory system	5.63	5.43	2.39	3.79	2.02	3.32
All other claims	3.86	4.98	3.66	4.47	3.43	3.81
Total number of claims	9.49	10.41	6.05	8.26	5.45	7.13

NOTE: January, February, and June operations and a random sample of controls were used for this table. For the respiratory episode counts, only claims pertaining to doctor's visits were counted in the algorithm for computing episodes. The calculation is the same as that made for the earlier tables. For the claim counts, all medical claims were used. Postoperation differences between operated and control groups were all significant at the .001 level except for "all other claims, two years postoperation"; none of the preoperation differences were significant at the .05 level.

tomy, this advantage vis-á-vis the controls is substantially reduced by other claims upon the health care system. Accounting for preoperative differences, for the postoperative year, the advantage is somewhat over one claim/year; for the second year after surgery, the advantage is less than one claim/year. Attempts to pinpoint specific diagnoses responsible for these changes were not particularly successful. Relative to the operated group, the controls tended to show a much sharper drop in counts for such miscellaneous procedures as medical examinations.

What sort of overall interpretation can be provided? Obviously, the larger drop in respiratory episodes recorded by the T&A patients, as compared with the control group, might result from factors other than improved health status. First of all, a "placebo effect" is possible. Because having the operation is expected to help, it does help; an operation which left tonsils and adenoids untouched might produce a similar effect. Such effects have been documented across a wide range of medical situations.[3] On the other hand, a drop in illness episodes extending several years after surgery

renders a substantial placebo effect improbable. The "placebo effect" has been found to be comparatively short-lived, lasting only a few months.[17]

Secondly, T&A patients and their families might be less likely to visit the doctor for respiratory complaints because the medical profession has already done what it can to solve these sorts of problems. Instead, such patients seem to visit with other types of complaints. Families may be seeking a particular level of ambulatory care, as expressed in visits to a physician. Because most medical complaints never reach the health care system,|| || operated and non-operated patients might differ in the proportion of particular types of complaints resulting in visits. Without "subjective" data from individual patients and/or their families, this possibility cannot be evaluated.

Another possibility is that, after a tonsillectomy, physicians tend to change their definition as to what is (and what is not) a respiratory problem. If a patient came in

---

|| || This has been documented in Britain and the United States.[1, 2]

with several conditions or a difficult-to-diagnose condition, the physician might enter something other than a respiratory diagnosis on the claims form. Such a possibility is difficult to eliminate; this kind of resolution of ambiguous diagnostic problems might well be noted in medical records, as well as on claims forms. On the other hand, the magnitude of the shift from respiratory claims to other claims would seem difficult to explain by a physician-initiated change of diagnosis.

When all claims are analyzed controlling for preoperative respiratory episodes, as was done in Table 3 for respiratory diagnoses alone, the savings seeming to result from a tonsillectomy are reduced for each degree of preoperative illness. Only when operated and non-operated groups having five or more episodes in the preoperative year are compared does the surgery result in a saving of three claims in the postoperative year. This benefit diminishes considerably by the second postoperative year.¶¶

Although enough controls (in this case, siblings who did not receive tonsillectomies) were not available to permit extensive sibling research, a limited analysis using siblings and all medical claims was performed. Two groups of operated patients were compared: those whose sibling (within 5 years in age, 14 years old or less, and with a relevant preoperative respiratory diagnosis) had also had a tonsillectomy within a one month period, and those whose sibling with similar characteristics did not. Since the number of individuals in each group is small (N=30 and 26, respectively), the findings must be taken very tentatively. Table 9 suggests that individuals in single-tonsillectomy families go to doctors who apply stricter criteria before operating than do those providing the care for multi-ton-

sillectomy families. Year-to-year correlations for medical claims were similar for both groups. They were in the 0.45 to 0.65 range for the postsurgery years, but lower when pre and postoperation years were correlated.°°°

Costs and Benefits of Surgery

Any extended discussion of the costs and benefits of surgery should deal with both 1) generating reasonable assumptions concerning costs of the operation, convalescence, and episodes of respiratory illness and 2) the paradoxical findings reported here. The costs and risks of a tonsillectomy operation plus the associated convalescence should be considered equivalent to at least one episode. There is some difficulty in estimating the longer term benefits of tonsil surgery, but they are diminishing by the second year after surgery. Available data indicate that relatively few benefits in terms of reduced episodes and claims accrue in the third postoperative year.* Finally, any regression toward the mean which does occur is likely to exaggerate the benefits associated with the surgery.

When respiratory episodes alone are considered, children with three or four episodes in a year and subsequent tonsil surgery have between one and one and a half fewer episodes than their nonoperated counterparts in the two years after surgery. Given the costs of the operation and convalescence, surgery in such cases seems generally unwarranted. When two or fewer episodes are involved, the benefits are small enough that justifying surgery would seem difficult in any case.

Moreover, the data on total use of the health care system suggest fewer benefits than those implied by working just with respiratory diagnoses. An underlying ten-

---

¶¶ Measurement error has not been accounted for in these calculations. Savings in episodes assuming various amounts of measurement error are being considered in ongoing research.

°°° This sample is made up of individuals with at least a moderate degree of illness. If a less sick population were included, the correlations would probably be lower.

---

*New evidence from our data bank suggests that this respiratory-related benefit of tonsil surgery drops somewhat more slowly over the four years after the operation.

TABLE 9.   Preoperation-Postoperation Histories for Tonsillectomy Patients
with Ill Siblings (Respiratory Episodes and All Medical Claims)

	Preoperation Year		Postoperation Year		Two Years Postoperation	
	One 1973 Operation in Family (N=30)	Two or More 1973 Operations in Family (N=26)	One 1973 Operation in Family	Two or More 1973 Operations in Family	One 1973 Operation in Family	Two or More 1973 Operations in Family
Respiratory episodes	2.60	1.92°	0.87	0.65	0.57	0.69
Claims						
Respiratory system	5.53	4.77	3.83	2.62	1.50	2.04
All other claims	6.10	2.74°	5.23	3.15	4.47	2.04
Total number of claims	11.63	7.50°	9.07	5.77	5.97	4.08

NOTE: Individuals used in this table were drawn from the same sample as Table 8.
° The asterisked preoperation differences were significant at the .05 level; none of the postoperative differences were significant.

dency to see the doctor a certain number of times a year, regardless of specific complaints, complicates any precise assessment of costs and benefits. The year-to-year correlations for total numbers of claims are more highly correlated than those for claims based on one system of the body (respiratory, nervous, etc.).

The implications for tonsil/adenoid surgery are clear. If the benefits are as low as indicated by an analysis of the total number of claims, a conservative approach is clearly justified. The strict criteria advocated in the Pittsburgh study do not seem inappropriate. Having five or more episodes in the year prior to surgery might be a reasonable criterion for tonsil surgery. Any concern about "under-doctoring" for patients who do not receive tonsillectomies should be confined to this group with many episodes.[5]

Our confidence in such recommendations is buttressed by several factors. First of all, the overall tonsillectomy and adenoidectomy rates in Manitoba do not differ greatly from those elsewhere in North America. In 1973 the rate in Manitoba was 107.2 procedures per 10,000 population in the 14 and under age group; in 1971 the U.S. rate was

128.3 procedures per 10,000 in this age group. Secondly, preliminary analysis of Saskatchewan tonsillectomy data suggests similar trends among the operated patients in that province. Thus, the findings appear generalizable well beyond Manitoba.[†††]

Discussion

Medical treatments such as tonsillectomies vary markedly in their frequency from one physician to another within a particular geographical area. Data from one region in Manitoba show that a few physicians operate (or have operations done) on over twenty percent of their patients diagnosed as having tonsillitis, peritonsillar abscess, or hypertrophy in the previous year; others operate on fewer than five per cent of their patients with such diagnoses.[‡‡‡]

The sibling data on respiratory episodes pointed up few differences between families with only one operated child out of two

––––––
††† Personal communication, Glenn Beck.

‡‡‡ Surgical rates vary greatly among small geographic areas both in the U.S. and Manitoba.[23, 30] Wennberg's research in Vermont has shown that health status, as measured by individually based survey data, is similar across the small areas in his study.[31]

with relevant respiratory diagnoses and those families included in the overall sample. On the other hand, preoperation-postoperation correlations for total numbers of claims indicate a substantial relationship (correlations between .45 and .65) between use of the health care system from one year to another. Although further study is clearly needed, having or not having the operation may be more determined by the doctor, while physician visits may be more determined by the patient.

Ideally, new data collection would support a stronger research design. Rather than relying on data from just a portion of those patients having operations in 1973, continuing information both on all 1973 T&A patients and on a large sample of controls would be most useful. Such material on all contacts with the health care system would permit more extensive analysis of sibling and family data, making it much easier to untangle the complex relationships involved. Finally, if the time period covered by the research were lengthened, the long-term effects of the operation could be better estimated.§§§

Other approaches to analysis and research design do not require new data from the Health Services Commission. Several other statistical models might be applied to the data to provide further checks on the findings.[7, 11, 16] These models may help understand research situations for which such a wide choice of control groups is not available. More advanced data analysis is also relevant for the sibling research. Taubman has developed some regression-based approaches for estimating the effects of family environment by comparing sibling and regular data sets.[25]

The research design might also be reformulated. Rather than taking the characteristics of the operated group as given, situations might be found where the possibilities for selection differences between groups are minimized. When the probability of receiving a treatment is largely outside an individual's control, possible selection bias should be reduced. This design could be implemented by linking information on a surgeon's propensity to perform tonsil/adenoid surgery with patient medical histories. Then the outcomes of patients under the care of physicans with high and low propensities to operate could be compared.

Additional sorts of analysis should be undertaken. The Pharmacare data should be analyzed to look at the effects of drug therapy, both as a subsitute for and in addition to tonsil surgery.[6, 28] Secondly, the data can be further disaggregated—into one month intervals, if necessary—to produce additional time points. A more detailed look at what goes on in the months before and after surgery would be valuable. Preliminary analysis indicates that differences between operated and nonoperated groups in pretreatment episodes become marked only in the three months immediately preceding surgery. Preoperation differences between operated and nonoperated groups may well be because an episode almost always occurs in the three months before an operation; in practice, such an episode is a necessary, but not sufficient, condition for a tonsillectomy. An ongoing computer simulation should shed some light on possible mechanisms underlying differences between operated and nonoperated groups. The research possibilities are many.

Acknowledgments

The authors would like to gratefully acknowledge the help of Fred Toll, Steve Kavanagh, Hazel MacLeod, and Henry Shukier of the Manitoba Health Services Commission with this research. We would like to thank Pat Nicol and Cindy Johnson for their invaluable assistance with programming and data processing and Jerome N. Deverman of the Dikewood Corporation for his suggestions with regard to selection of operated and nonoperated groups.

§§§ Paradise emphasizes the importance of extended patient follow up; it would be desirable to follow a number of patients through adolescence.[19, 20]

References

1. Alpert, J. J., Kosa, J., and Haggerty, R. J.: A month of illness and health care among low income families. Public Health Rep. 82:705, 1967.

2. Banks, M. H., et al.: Factors influencing demand for primary medical care in women aged 20-44 years—a preliminary report. Int. J. Epidemiol. 4:189, 1975.

3. Beecher, H. K.: Surgery as placebo. JAMA 176:1102, 1961.

4. Braun, P., Weinstein, M., and Farber, M.: An inventory for health care research. Center for the Analysis of Health Practices, School of Public Health, Harvard University, 1975.

5. Bunker, J. P., et al.: Elective hysterectomy—pro and con. N. Engl. J. Med. 295:264, 1976.

6. ————: Risks and benefits of surgery. In: Benefits and Risks in Medical Care, D. Taylor, Ed. London, Office of Health Economics, 1974.

7. Cain, G. G.: Regression and selection models to improve non-experimental comparisons. In Evaluation and Experiment. C. A. Bennett and A. A. Lumsdaine, Eds. New York, Academic Press, 1975.

8. Campbell, D. T., and Erlebacher, A.: How regression artifacts in quasi-experimental evaluations can mistakenly make compensatory education look harmful. In: Compensatory Education—a National Debate. In: The Disadvantaged Child, J. Helmuth, Ed. New York, Brunner/Mazel, 1970.

9. Campbell, D. T., and Boruch, R. F.: Making the case for randomized assignment to treatments by considering the alternatives—six ways in which quasi-experimental evaluations in compensatory education tend to underestimate effects. In: Evaluation and Experiment. C. A. Bennett and A. A. Lumsdaine, Eds. New York, Academic Press, 1975.

10. Campbell, D. T.: Temporal changes in treatment — effect correlations: A quasi-experimental model for institutional records and longitudinal studies. In: Proceedings of the 1970 Invitational Conference on Testing Problems. G. V. Glass, Ed., Princeton: Educational Testing Service, 1971.

11. Cook, T. D., and Reichardt, C. S.: Statistical analysis of non-equivalent control group designs—a guide to some current literature. Evaluation 3:136, 1976.

12. Cook, T. D., and Campbell, D. T.: The design and conduct of quasi-experiments and true experiments in field settings. In: Handbook of Industrial and Organizational Psychology, M. D. Dunnette, Ed. Chicago, Rand McNally, 1976.

13. Denniston, O. L., and I. M. Rosenstock: The validity of non-experimental designs for evaluating health services. Health Serv. Rep. 88:153, 1973.

14. Harrington, D. C.: The San Joaquin Foundation peer review system. Med. Care 11:185, 1973.

15. Hershey, J. C., Luft, H. S., and Gianaris, J. M.: Making sense out of utilization data. Med. Care 13:838, 1975.

16. Kenny, D. A.: A quasi-experimental approach to assessing treatment effects in the nonequivalent control groups design. Psychol. Bull. 82:345, 1975.

17. Kolata, G. B.: Coronary bypass surgery — debate over its benefits. Science 194:1263, 1976.

18. Moscovice, I.: Development of a method for the analysis of the utilization of resources in an ambulatory care setting. School of Organization and Management, Yale University, 1976.

19. Paradise, J. C.: Pittsburgh tonsillectomy and adenoidectomy study—differences from earlier studies and problems of execution. Ann. Otol. Rhinol. Laryngol. 84:15, 1975.

20. Paradise, J. L., and Bluestone, C. D.: Toward rational indications for tonsil and adenoid surgery. Hosp. Surg. 11:79, 1976.

21. Roos, L. L., Roos, N. P., Nicol, P., and Johnson, C.: Using administrative data banks. Faculty of Administrative Studies, University of Manitoba, 1977.

22. Roos, N. P., Henteleff, P. D., and Roos, L. L.: A new audit procedure applied to an old question—is the frequency of T&A justified? Med. Care 15:1, 1977.

23. Roos, N. P., Roos, L. L., and Henteleff, P. D.: Elective surgical rates—do high rates mean lower surgical standards? N. Engl. J. Med. 297: 360, 1977.

24. Scitovsky, A. A. and McCall, N.: Changes in the costs of treatment of selected illnesses 1951-1964-1971. Health Policy Program, School of Medicine, University of California, San Francisco, 1975.

25. Taubman, P.: Earnings, education, genetics and environment. J. Hum. Res. 11:447, 1976.

26. Tenny, J. B.: Diagnostic precision for insurance records—a physician's survey. Inquiry 5:14, 1968.

27. Vayda, E.: A comparison of surgical rates in Canada and in England and Wales. N. Engl. J. Med. 289:1224, 1973.

28. Wardell, W. M.: Assessment of the benefits, risks and costs of medical progress. In: Benefits and Risks in Medical Care; D. Taylor, Ed. London, Office of Health Economics, 1974.

29. Webb, E. J., and Ellsworth, P. C.: On nature and knowing. In: Perspectives on Attitude Measurement—Surveys and Their Alternatives. H. W. Sinaiko and L. A. Broedling, Eds. Washington, Smithsonian Institute, 1975.

30. Wennberg, J. E. and Gittelson, A.: Small area variations in health care delivery. Science 182:1102, 1973.

31. Wennberg, J. E. and Fowler, F. J., Jr.: A test of consumer contribution to small area variations in health care delivery. J. Maine Med. Assoc. 68:275, 1977.

The cross-lagged panel correlation design has been proposed as an alternative to the true experiment for some areas in which it seems unlikely that experiments could be successfully implemented. Hart shows both skill and imagination in exploiting archival data to complete a set of cross-lagged panel correlations that appear to converge on a conclusion fraught with consequences. Thomas D. Cook and Donald T. Campbell, who have been proponents of the cross-lag design—indeed Campbell was one of its inventors—are recanting, or at least tempering, their enthusiasm (Cook and Campbell, forthcoming). Readers will want to examine Hart's work carefully to determine for themselves if it makes a persuasive case and may want to read it again when Cook and Campbell's new book* becomes available.

In our estimation, Hart is to be commended for recognizing that it is companies of soldiers, not individual soldiers that are the appropriate unit of analysis. That commendation may not seem extraordinary, but in view of the great frequency with which inappropriate analyses are carried out and published, it is well earned.

*COOK, T. D., and D. T. CAMPBELL (forthcoming) Quasi Experimentation: Design and Analysis Issues for Field Settings. Chicago, Illinois: Rand McNally.

13

Crime and Punishment in the Army

Roland J. Hart

The relationship between crime and punishment is examined and a dilemma in this relationship is identified. Labeling theory suggests that leaders responsible for enforcing the law respond to the crime they see by increasing punishment, under the assumption that punishment will deter crime, whereas recipients often respond to this punishment with a feeling of injustice, which then incites them to break the law more frequently, resulting in more serious problems on a delayed basis. The operation of this sort of dilemma in a U.S. Army population was tested with cross-lagged panel correlation, using companies (groups of about 200 soldiers) as the unit of analysis. In 50 companies, company leaders punished their subordinates, particularly blacks, as a response to the lawlessness they attributed to these subordinates, while subordinates responded to this punishment in the ensuing months with a sense of injustice and increased lawlessness. Observations are offered about the usefulness of the methodology, and about the implications of the dilemma that has been identified, for law-abidingness.

The purpose of this article is to suggest that a dilemma can exist in the relationship between crime and punishment and that this dilemma can have important practical consequences. An example of a methodology that can test hypotheses of the type proposed is provided, along with data that support the hypotheses.

Theoretical Positions

Logically, four possible causal relationships can exist between crime and punishment: (a) Punishment is caused by increases in crime, (b) punishment reduces crime, (c) punishment increases crime, and (d) increases in crime produce a reduction in punishment. The first two alternatives are consistent with a "law and order" interpretation of the crime and punishment relationship and are consistent with what is proposed by deterrence theory. The latter two alternatives are not consistent with law and order or deterrence theory explanations but are generally consistent with predictions of labeling theory.

The major difference between deterrence theory and labeling theory is in their theoretical predictions about the effects of punishment (Tittle, 1975). Labeling theorists maintain that punishment is less a consequence of objective rule breaking than it is of the labels that agents of social control apply to persons who are recipients of punishment. Agents of social control attribute lawbreaking to someone and then act in a manner consistent with this label to see that the person is punished, even though this attribution may not always correspond with "objective" lawbreaking. Thus, labeling theory can encompass Alternative d, in which high rule breaking produces low punishment. The social control agent may not be aware of high levels of offenses that are well hidden but may be well aware of low levels of offenses that are in the open. Since the agent's labels, rather than actual offense rates, produce punishment, a result consistent with Alternative d could be obtained.

The views of the author expressed here are his own and do not purport to reflect the position of the Department of the Army.

Requests for reprints should be sent to Roland J. Hart, U.S. Army Research Institute for the Behavioral and Social Sciences, P.O. Box 5787, Presidio of Monterey, California 93940.

The major premise of labeling theory is that punishment causes the offender to be labeled a deviant by others and motivates those who are punished to fulfill this label through increased rule breaking, as a kind of self-fulfilling prophecy (Payne, 1973). The self-image of the labeled person is transformed, and this person increasingly seeks support from those who have already adopted a deviant career. This prediction is consistent with Alternative c—that punishment increases crime.

Deterrence theory, by contrast, operates from a traditional perspective that people seek to obtain pleasure and avoid pain. The application of punishment should operate to reduce future rule breaking on the part of the offenders, because of operant learning in which the offender seeks to avoid further punishment and obtain positive reinforcement through conformity. In this way, deterrence theory expects punishment to reduce crime—Alternative b. Deterrence theory also assumes the first alternative as a given—that punishment is primarily a response to objective rule breaking rather than a response to such subjective factors as labels.

In terms of time sequences, then, deterrence theory assumes that the offense precedes the punishment. By contrast, however, labeling theory presumes that punishment can often precede the offense. This would occur when the social control agents's attribution of lawlessness is inconsistent with offense rates (see McAllister, 1975). When the inconsistency exists, the attributions, rather than the offense rates, produce punishment, and punishment then increases offenses, resulting in a paradoxical situation in which punishment could precede offenses. If the labeling perspective is correct, at least under specified conditions, then this would create an acute dilemma for contemporary society, since the commonly applied solution to the problem of crime would then tend to exacerbate it.

Current Evidence

The data that would allow us to choose between the labeling and deterrence positions are scant, in spite of the fact that the assumptions made underlie entire legal systems and divide theoretical camps. There is some evidence to support either position. High recidivism and rearrest rates among released prisoners seem consistent with the labeling position. Rearrest rates shortly after release are often as high as 75%, with reconviction rates around 35% (Tittle & Logan, 1973). Comparison between released prisoners, who have presumably been labeled, and offenders not incarcerated but placed on probation have shown that prisoners have higher recidivism rates (Levin, 1971). Gold (1970) compared labeled and nonlabeled delinquents and found more deviance among those who were labeled. Nagel (Note 1) reported that states in the U.S. that built the most prisons over a 20-year period had a slightly higher average increase in crime rates than states that built fewer prisons. Longer time served in prison has often been positively associated with parole failure (Myers, Note 2). Labeling soldiers as potential disciplinary risks, by providing commanders with background and personality data designed to predict disciplinary failure, increased rather than decreased subsequent disciplinary failure among those labeled as risks (Bell, Bolin, Houston, & Kristiansen, 1973). Rosenthal and Jacobson (1968) have shown that teachers' labeling of students' intelligence can affect subsequent performance by those students. In the child development literature, physical punishment by parents is often associated with increased aggressiveness among their children (Becker, 1964, pp. 177–182). On the other hand, consistent with deterrence theory, a variety of studies describe a weak negative association between certainty of punishment and crime rates (Chambliss, 1966; Chiricos & Waldo, 1970; Jensen, 1969; Silberman, 1976; Tittle, 1975; Tittle & Rowe, 1974; Waldo & Chiricos, 1972). Increased certainty of punishment was associated with lower crime.

Much of the relevant data suffers from serious methodological defects. Recidivism data are often of poor quality, and studies in the area lack appropriate control or comparison groups. Much of the data relevant to deterrence theory are correlational data that do not establish direction of causation.

Direction of causation in many cases might be the opposite of what has been supposed, with high offense rates producing less certain punishment.

Conditions for Labeling

In spite of inadequate data, the available evidence suggests that both labeling and deterrence effects can be operative under specified conditions, and the task for the researcher is to specify these conditions (Tittle, 1975). It is proposed that deterrence relationships are most likely to occur when there is agreement between social control agents and offenders about the extent of law violations. This agreement would be higher (a) when social control agents were aware of offenses through surveillance, (b) when they were unbiased in their observations, and (c) when offenders agreed with control agents that the offenders' acts constituted real violations of law. Relatively certain punishment does reflect an awareness of offenses through surveillance. When there is consensus about offense rates, offenders agree that they have broken rules and wish to eliminate the stigma of the offender label by obeying the rules in the future. They are less likely to feel that the punishment was arbitrary and unjustified and would feel no need to defy authorities. The causal sequence expected by deterrence theory is maintained: Agreed-upon offenses cause punishment and punishment reduces offenses.

Control agents and offenders could disagree over offenses (a) because the control agent is aware of only a selected sample of offenses, often the less serious ones, since there is good reason to hide serious offenses; (b) because of racial or other biases in the observations of control agents; or (c) because of differences in values between agents and offenders about what constitutes a real violation of law. Under these conditions, people who are punished are likely to feel a sense of injustice and feel that they have been labeled, since they do not see themselves as offenders, at least relative to their own values or to what else is going on. Those who are punished may then defy control agents by increasing offenses. The causal sequence expected by labeling theory would result: The attributions of the control agents about offenses would produce punishment, and this punishment would increase subsequent offenses, creating the dilemma mentioned previously.

As applied to race relations, in cases of acute disagreement between police and blacks, arrests by police have frequently precipitated riots and increased lawlessness (Lieberson & Silverman, 1970; Toch, 1970). Control agents may label blacks as lawbreakers more readily than whites, regardless of offense, producing discrimination in punishment (see Green, 1972). In the U.S., some 43% of prison inmates are nonwhite. Nagel (Note 1) has found that the percentage of blacks in a state is unrelated to crime rates but highly related to incarceration rates. Deterrence theory, however, suggests that disproportionate minority punishment is likely due to high offense rates by minorities rather than to discrimination.

Available evidence indicates that deterrence relations can occur. The purpose of the present research is to demonstrate with appropriate methodology that labeling relations can occur under conditions that have been specified.

Method

Overview

The crime and punishment relationship was studied using cross-lagged panel correlation, an approach that allows us to distinguish between the four possible causal alternatives indicated previously, given the assumptions of the model (Kenny, 1975). The relationship was studied in a military environment, the Army, using companies rather than individuals as the unit of analysis. In the Army, soldiers are organized by companies, which consist of approximately 200 soldiers who work together. Social control agents in this case are primarily the company commander (CO) and the first sergeant (1SG). The company commander directs the company, and the first sergeant implements the commander's policies. Punishment consisted of the frequencies of "Article 15s" received by enlisted soldiers in 50 companies during the 6-month period of the study. Article 15 (ART-15) punishments consist of fines (often in the range of several hundred dollars), reduced rank (and also reduced pay), restriction, extra duty, and so forth, given separately or in combination. Article 15s are punishments imposed by the company commander in informal nonjudicial proceedings, often upon the recommendation of the first sergeant, for violations of military or civilian laws that are not serious enough in the commander's judgment to warrant courts-martial. ART-15s are by far the most common form of punishment in the Army. The 1,418 ART-15s in the present sample outnumbered courts-martial 20 to 1. ART-15s are usually given to the bottom four pay grades (97% in the present sample).

Frequencies of administrative discharges were also collected. Discharges consisted of actions taken to separate soldiers from the service prior to the end of their regular term of enlistment. Medical and hardship discharges were not included. Offense rates (crime) among the bottom four pay grades (E1-E4) were measured by two surveys that were administered to the 50 companies 3 months apart. Offenses as seen by both enlisted soldiers (E1-E4) and the leaders (CO, 1SG) were measured.

Measuring Offense Rates

Survey procedures. Two surveys were given 3 months apart to (a) company commanders, (b) first sergeants, and (c) enlisted soldiers (E1-E4). Random sampling of enlisted soldiers was stratified by company and race or ethnic background, and the sampling at the two times was done without replacement (different enlisted soldiers at Times 1 and 2). Fourteen soldiers from each company (5 black, 6 white, and 3 with Spanish ethnic background) were randomly sampled each time, producing a sample of approximately 1,400 soldiers. At Time 1, 86%, and at Time 2, 83% of the enlisted sample was actually surveyed, as well as 100% of the leaders at both times. Reasons for not taking the survey were tallied at both time periods and were nearly evenly distributed both times among the following: (a) sickness, hospitalization, (b) school attendance, (c) leave (vacation), (d) absent without leave or in jail, (e) conflicting duties, (f) no show. Virtually 100% of the numbers requested within each company (14 soldiers—5 black, 6 white, and 3 Spanish-ethnic) were obtained, since sampling continued until the appropriate numbers were reached.

The companies sampled consisted of all companies in major commands (brigade-size units) that were fully staffed or nearly so at the time of data collection (August 1975–January 1976) at one infantry division, plus four companies from a second small installation. Population figures showed approximately 6,600 soldiers in the 50 companies, 27% of whom were black and 4% of whom had a Spanish ethnic background (Chicano, Puerto Rican). A majority of the companies were combat companies, which exclude women by law, so it was not possible to include women in the study.

Survey scales. Anonymity of survey responses was assured by not requesting names or identification numbers and by administering the survey in large groups. Survey scales are listed below along with the groups that responded (in parentheses). With one exception, responses were made on 8-point scales.

1. *Fairness scale* (enlisted soldiers). (a) Are punishment and discipline handled unfairly in your company by the company commander and first sergeant? (b) Does your company commander emphasize to everyone in your unit a policy of treating each individual equally and fairly? (c) Does your first sergeant emphasize to everyone in your unit a policy of treating each individual equally and fairly?

2. *Insubordinate label* (enlisted soldiers). How often do your unit leaders consider you to be insubordinate?

3. *Self-reported lawbreaking* (enlisted soldiers). (a) Do you try to break as many rules and regulations as you can without getting caught? (b) How often do you seriously violate the law? (c) Overall do you show respect for the law? (d) How often do you break rules you could reasonably be punished for? (e) How often do you break Army regulations and company rules behind your unit leaders' backs?

4. *Percentage breaking law* (enlisted soldiers and leaders). Within the last 8 weeks how many of the enlisted men (E1-E4) in your company broke laws that they could reasonably be punished for? (Respondents were asked to circle a percentage that varied in increments of 5% from 0% to 100%. In this question, laws were defined as Army regulations, civilian laws, and company rules. Respondents were asked to indicate how many broke laws regardless of whether they were caught or punished.)

5. *Company discipline* (enlisted soldiers and leaders). The discipline scale was based on the concept of discipline as found in interviews with 300 soldiers (Bauer, Stout, & Holz, Note 3). This concept was more closely related to compliance or noncompliance with military standards and norms than to delinquency. Factor analysis indicated that the 12 items used were essentially undimensional (Hart, Note 4). Items are paraphrased as follows: (a) Do members process paper work efficiently? (b) Do they show up on time? (c) Do they cooperate and (d) work as a team? (e) Are they disorderly off post? (f) Do they sit around and do nothing or (g) do just enough to get by? (h) Do they do high quality work or (i) need direct supervision to get the job done right? (j) Are they combat ready? (k) Do they keep things clean and (l) wear their uniforms properly?

6. *Combined three scales* (enlisted soldiers). The enlisted soldiers' responses to the self-reported lawbreaking, percentage lawbreaking, and discipline scales were combined into a single composite scale measuring company offense rates. The three scales were initially standardized, across enlisted respondents, separately within each time period. These individual scores were aggregated, and reliabilities were computed in the same manner, described later, that was used with other scales, except that in this case, the three standardized scales were treated as if they were individual items.

7. *Leader-estimated lawbreaking* (leaders only). (a) How often does the typical enlisted man (E1-E4) in your company seriously violate the law? (b) Does the typical enlisted man (E1-E4) in your company

show respect for the law? (c) How often do enlisted men (E1–E4) in your company break Army regulations and company rules behind their unit leaders' backs?

Aggregation of survey responses. Initially, soldiers' responses were averaged across items to produce scales. With companies as the unit of analysis, enlisted soldiers' responses were averaged across soldiers of the same race or ethnic background (black, white, Spanish) to produce company means for each. To obtain estimates of the company average, disregarding race and ethnic background, a weighted average was calculated, as is appropriate for stratified sampling (Konijn, 1973, p. 138), in which the means for each racial or ethnic group were weighted by the proportion of each group within a given company population. The overall company average was estimated in this way.

Measuring Punishment Rates

Frequencies of ART-15s (and administrative discharges as well) were aggregated for a 2-month period prior to the administration of each survey, for the entire company and for the three racial or ethnic groups. While frequencies may violate assumptions of normality and equal interval scales, Havlicek and Peterson (1977) have found that the Pearson product-moment correlation is robust to violations of these assumptions.

Punishment rates were computed by partialing enlisted (E1–E4) company size at each time period, from the ART-15 frequencies, and survey measures for the same time periods, using regression analysis. Black and white enlisted (E1–E4) size was removed when computing black and white punishment rates. "Synchronicity" was maintained by removing the effects of size separately at each time period (see Kenny, 1975, p. 896). Standardized residuals, with company size removed, were correlated in the customary manner. If company size did not change, the result would equal partial correlation. Company size was stable ($r = .95$). Variables were not divided by company size, since rates computed in this way leave artifacts due to index correlation (McNemar, 1969, pp. 180–182).

Company size (E1–E4) was correlated .27 and .24 at Times 1 and 2 with the total frequency of company ART-15s. The correlations ranged between .29 and .39 when correlating company size for blacks with black ART-15s and company size for whites with white ART-15s. The correlation between company size and survey measures was most frequently not significant.

Cross-Lagged Correlation Model

Hypothesis testing. Analyses were based on the crossed-lagged correlation model as formalized by Kenny (1973, 1975). Inferences about causation are made possible by (a) determining time precedence between variables and (b) eliminating spuriousness,

or a common third variable, as an explanation for the relationship between two variables. Statistical tests are made to distinguish between two models: one model due to spuriousness alone and the other due to spuriousness plus a time-lagged causal variable. Three tests are provided to distinguish between the two models: (a) the cross-lagged difference; (b) the extent to which one or both of the cross-lagged correlations are greater than the synchronous correlations; and (c) the size of the autocorrelation due to the third, or spurious, variable (Kenny, 1973, pp. 155–156). This autocorrelation can be estimated, and if it is greater than 1.0 or less than −1.0 (the bounds for a correlation coefficient) the third or spurious variable model can be rejected.

Assumptions. The validity of the previous tests is dependent upon several assumptions being satisfied.

1. *Synchronicity.* It must be assumed that the two variables are measured at the same point in time. Since the punishment variable was aggregated over a 2-month period prior to each survey, soldiers should have answered survey questions retrospectively, covering the previous 2 months, for the assumption of synchronicity to be satisfied. The item, percentage breaking law, specified a 2-month interval.

2. *"Stationarity."* The causal coefficients of the variables involved are assumed to remain constant over time. Evidence consistent with stationarity is equality or near equality in the size of both synchronous correlations. Furthermore, the reliability with which both variables are measured should (a) not change over time or (b) if a change does occur, the reliability of both variables should shift by the same proportional constant. Other reliability shifts can greatly bias results. Stationarity does *not* need to be assumed to reject the spurious-variables model, using the spurious-variable autocorrelation test.

3. *Homogeneous stability.* The test to see whether one or both of the cross-lagged correlations are greater than the synchronous correlations is based on the assumption of homogeneous stability. All nonerroneous causes of the two variables are assumed to have the same autocorrelation. Evidence consistent with this assumption is equality or near equality of the autocorrelations for both the offense and punishment variables.

Choosing between rival hypotheses. Rozelle and Campbell (1969) have shown that the cross-lagged difference tests competing confounded pairs of hypotheses: A significant cross-lagged difference affirms that either X produced an increase in Y or Y a decrease in X. In this study, the cross-lagged comparison is useful, since the confounded hypotheses pit the two deterrence alternatives against the two labeling alternatives.

The confounded hypotheses can be distinguished if one of the cross-lagged correlations is greater than the synchronous correlations (e.g., $r_{X_1Y_2} >$ synchronous indicates X produced an increase in Y). If the sign of the synchronous correlations is different from the cross-lagged correlations, a "no-cause baseline" is needed to distinguish between confounded hypotheses. Rozelle and Campbell (1969) assume that the no-cause baseline should be smaller than the synchronous correlations, since synchronous correlations are customarily inflated artificially with the correlated errors (response sets, etc.) that usually occur when the same subjects rate both variables at one time. In the present study, the unadjusted synchronous correlations were expected to be an accurate reflection of the no-cause baseline, since artificially inflated synchronous correlations were not expected when (a) variables were measured from different populations at the same time and (b) different types of variables (survey and record) were compared. If the synchronous correlations in this case serve as a no-cause baseline, then cross-lagged correlations can be compared to synchronous correlations of different sign to choose between confounded hypotheses.

Reliability Estimation

Record data. The frequencies of ART-15s, as well as discharges, were aggregated over the appropriate 2-month period within each company, for actions taking place on both odd and even days, like an odd-even split on an intelligence test. ART-15s were tallied by race and ethnic background, within each company, for both odd and even days, when reliability was computed for each racial or ethnic group. Cronbach's alpha was then computed on these odd-even splits.

Survey data. Reliability coefficients for leaders (CO, 1SG) were estimated using Cronbach's alpha on standardized variables, which is equivalent to using analysis of variance to estimate the reliability of the scale mean (Winer, 1962, p. 131).

The scores for enlisted respondents were averaged across scales and across individuals within racial or ethnic groups, and a weighted average was computed across these groups. These company means, then, contain components not found with individual-level data, which necessitated derivation of a reliability model appropriate to these data. The reliability model used analysis of variance (by analogy to Winer, 1962, pp. 124–132) to isolate three relevant components of these aggregated scores (see Appendix A for derivation of model and computational formulas). The relevant components were labeled (a) measurement error, (b) individual differences, and (c) group consensus within companies.

The first reliability reported in Table 2 for enlisted soldiers reflects measurement error $(1 - r_{ss})$. This reliability assumes that individual differences are not error and indicates the extent to which the averaged company scores would be expected to correlate with the aggregated scores from another random sample of soldiers from comparable companies responding to comparable items. The second reliability (in parentheses) in Table 2 assumes that individual differences are error. This coefficient reflects the extent to which there is consensus within the company, or at least within a racial or ethnic group within the company. The difference between the two coefficients reflects the extent of the individual differences.

Individual differences should not be considered to be measurement error, when real individual differences

within the companies exist on such variables as the degree of labeling and lawbreaking, predisposing background characteristics, and so on. When a scale has no zero point, according to Winer (1962, p. 131), individual differences in frames of reference should not be considered measurement error either. The second, consensus reliability is an appropriate reliability for one item (percentage breaking law), since this item has a zero point, whereas the other scales do not. Other legitimate individual differences in frames of reference exist, as when soldiers observe their company from separate subordinate organizations (i.e., different platoons and squads). The first reliability assumes that these nonerroneous individual differences would be replicated in another random sample.

The purpose of these reliabilities is to provide evidence that the variables based on company means are stationary; I need to demonstrate that there are not inappropriate shifts in the measurement error and individual difference components over time. Since the individual difference component may affect correlation coefficients in ways that are not completely clear it is important to show that this component is stationary.

Results

Offense Rate Consensus

Deterrence relationships were expected when leaders and subordinates agreed with each other on offense rates, and labeling relationships were expected when they did not. The extent of this agreement is shown in Table 1. The only agreement between leaders and subordinates, using correlations between offense rates as a measure of agreement, was between the commanders and Spanish-ethnic enlisted respondents. There was no correlation between the estimates of offense rates by first sergeants and enlisted soldiers. In fact, there was little relationship between the estimates of offense rates by the commander and the first sergeant. There was, however, some modest agreement between black and white and between white and Spanish-ethnic enlisted respondents.

Labeling relationships were expected when leaders were not clearly aware of the extent of lawbreaking. Leader awareness is reflected in the percentages of enlisted soldiers that were estimated to be breaking the law. The offense rates on the percentage breaking law item were averaged across time periods and within groups. The black, white, and Spanish-

Table 1

Identification of Intergroup Agreement on Offense Rates

Comparison	Time 1 correlations			Time 2 correlations		
	Computed	Positive	Negative	Computed	Positive	Negative
Correlations between leader and enlisted soldiers						
1SG with BEM, WEM, SEM	27	0	10	27	0	14
CO with BEM, WEM	18	3	7[a]	18	0	5[a]
CO with SEM	9	4	1	9	2	3
CO, 1SG with combined EM	6	0	1	6	0	2
Correlations between enlisted racial or ethnic groups						
BEM with WEM	9	4[b]	2	9	4[b]	1
SEM with WEM	9	3[b]	0	9	1[b]	2
SEM with BEM	9	0	2	9	1	5
Correlations between commander and first sergeant						
CO with 1SG	9	2	4	9	1	2

Note. Computed = number of synchronous correlations computed between all possible pairs of offense rate measures for compared subgroups. Positive = number of *significant* positive correlations ($p < .05$, one-tailed test). Negative = number of negative correlations. CO = company commander; 1SG = first sergeant; BEM, WEM, and SEM = black, white, and Spanish-ethnic enlisted men, respectively; combined EM = weighted enlisted men's averages on the combined three scales.

[a] Included one significant negative correlation at Time 1 and two significant negative correlations at Time 2 ($p < .05$, two-tailed tests).

[b] The corresponding correlations, indicated below, were significant at both time periods: (a) discipline scale for WEM and discipline scale for BEM, $p < .05$; (b) self-reported lawbreaking for WEM and percentage breaking law for BEM, $p < .05$; for SEM, $p < .01$; (and for WEM, $p < .01$).

ethnic enlisted soldiers estimated that 44%, 52%, and 46%, respectively, of the enlisted soldiers were breaking rules, within 8 weeks, for which they could reasonably be punished. Commanders and first sergeants estimated 26% and 21%, respectively—about half of the enlisted men's estimates. The treatment effect from a one-way repeated measures design, with companies serving as cases, showed these differences to be statistically significant, $F(4, 196) = 48.4$, $p < .001$. A similar difference between leaders and subordinates was found on the discipline scale.

Less than 10% of the enlisted soldiers were actually punished with ART-15s during the 8-week periods in question. In this case, enlisted soldiers likely felt that a few soldiers were punished for offenses that a near-majority committed. Enlisted soldiers may have felt that punishment was applied to offenses that the commander happened to find out about that were not nearly so serious as others that were common knowledge among enlisted

soldiers. Soldiers who were caught doing something could have easily felt innocent on a relative basis compared to what else was going on.

Labeling by Leaders

The relationship between the leaders' estimates of the offense rates and the actual punishment given is shown in Table 2. Effects significant at the $p < .10$ level are reported in Table 2 because the tests are low-power (Kenny, 1975, p. 894) and the sample size was small. Comparisons 2, 4, 6, 8, and 9 in Table 2 all indicate that the estimates of offense rates by both leaders (CO & 1SG) resulted in the punishment of black enlisted soldiers. Offense rates estimated by the commander led to the punishment of white enlisted soldiers in Comparisons 1 and 3, but evidence for estimated offenses causing the punishment of whites is restricted to these comparisons. The comparisons between the offense rates as seen by the first sergeant and the punishment rates for whites were not significant (see Comparison 7) and, with the previous exception, were not listed in Table 2. The comparisons not listed in Table 2 for the commander were not stationary, with significant differences in synchronous correlations. None of the relationships with the Spanish-ethnic punishment rates were significant, probably because of the low reliabilities of the Spanish-ethnic ART-15 rates (see Comparison 19).

Racial discrimination. In spite of the fact that there was almost no correlation between the offense rates as perceived by commanders and first sergeants, these offense rates were related in a similar way to the black punishment rates. There was no relationship between offenses seen by the first sergeant and the punishment of whites, and only a tenuous relationship for commanders, which created the suspicion of racial discrimination in punishments. Overall, the ratio of black punishments to black soldiers was .30, while the same ratio for whites was .20, $\chi^2(1) = 76.2$, $p < .001$. In spite of the fact that the punishment rate was higher for black than for whites, the offense rates, based on the self-reported lawbreaking scale, did not differ. Whites reported slightly higher offense rates, but the means were not significantly different, $F(1, 49) = 1.0$. Black and white means were compared in a one-way repeated measures analysis of variance design with companies as cases—after having averaged across time. There was a slight increase in the white self-reported lawbreaking rate from Time 1 to Time 2, so that the offense rate for whites at Time 2 was actually slightly *higher* than that for blacks ($p < .002$), using individuals as the unit of analysis in a factorial design (Hart, Note 5). Together, these data suggest that there was some racial discrimination in punishments because of the leaders' labeling black enlisted soldiers as lawbreakers. While blacks often have had higher apprehension rates than whites by military police, apprehensions may be subject to labeling biases, as found above.

Administrative discharges. A secondary effect of the leaders' labeling and punishment is shown in Comparison 10 of Table 2. This secondary consequence is included because it has important practical implications for the military. As might be expected, Article 15 punishment produced a delayed increase in the subsequent administrative discharge rate. Some 72% of these discharges were under less-than-honorable conditions. Punished soldiers may later be discharged from the service.

Enlisted Soldiers' Responses to Punishment

Punishing nonoffenders. Since there was virtually no agreement between leaders and black and white subordinates, labeling reactions to punishment were expected from the soldiers. Comparisons 15 and 18 (Table 2) illustrate a paradoxical labeling effect reported by white enlisted soldiers: High offenses produced little punishment; or stated in the reverse, low offenses increased punishment. Of course, a relationship of this nature could readily create a sense of injustice and a defiant reaction to punishment. The relationship was not strong and was restricted to the white enlisted soldiers. The identification of this effect was dependent upon the assumption that the synchronous correlations used here provide an accurate no-cause baseline.

Increased offense rates. Comparisons 11 through 18 all illustrate a labeling reaction to punishment by black and white enlisted soldiers. The punishment produced an increase rather than a decrease in subsequent offense rates, as predicted by labeling theory. This effect was consistent and quite strong.

Spanish-ethnic response. Since there was modest agreement between offense rates estimated by commanders and Spanish-ethnic enlisted soldiers, a deterrence rather than a labeling response might be expected from this group. Comparison 19 provided no evidence for a labeling reaction from the Spanish-ethnic enlisted soldiers. The comparison was clearly nonsignificant, as might be expected with such low reliabilities for the ART-15 measure.

Enlisted soldiers' response to offenses seen by leaders. There has been some theoretical confusion about whether a label constitutes actual punishment or the attribution of lawbreaking to someone (Tittle, 1975, pp.

Table 2
Cross-Lagged Analyses Relating the Offenses Reported by Superiors and Subordinates to Punishment

Comparison		Sample size (n)	Synchronous correlations		Cross-lagged correlations		Synchronous difference ($z_{S_1 - S_2}$)	Cross-lagged difference (z_{C-L})
Variable X	Variable Y		Time 1 (S_1) ($r_{X_1Y_1}$)	Time 2 (S_2) ($r_{X_2Y_2}$)	Crossed (C) ($r_{X_1Y_2}$)	Lagged (L) ($r_{Y_1X_2}$)		
			Initiation of punishment by leaders					
1. % break law (CO)	ART-15 (EM)	48	.08	.06	.36***	.09	.14	1.40*
2. % break law (CO)	ART-15 (BEM)	48	.15	.19*	.37***	.13	−.23	1.28*
3. % break law (CO)	ART-15 (WEM)	48	.02	−.08	.25**	.06	.48	.95
4. Discipline (CO)	ART-15 (BEM)	50	.27**	.05	.39***	−.05	1.16	2.46***
			(.24)	(.06)	(.45)	(−.04)		
5. % break law (1SG)	ART-15 (EM)	47	.06	.12	.27**	−.04	−.31	1.71**
6. % break law (1SG)	ART-15 (BEM)	47	.03	.17	.44***	−.02	−.70	2.61***
7. % breaklaw (1SG)	ART-15 (WEM)	47	.07	−.06	−.01	−.08	.68	.37
8. Discipline (1SG)	ART-15 (BEM)	48	.08	−.06	.23	−.32**	.69	2.94***
			(.07)	(−.07)	(.27)	(−.27)		
9. Leader estimate lawbreaking (1SG)	ART-15 (BEM)	49	−.11	−.07	.29**	−.30**	−.24	3.27***
10. ART-15 (EM)	Admin. discharge (EM)	50	.26**	.03	.56***	.02	1.15	3.04***
			(.18)	(.04)	(.67)	(.01)		
			Enlisted soldiers response to punishment					
11. % break law(EM)	ART-15 (EM)	50	.36***	.18	.08	.45***	.99	−2.10**
12. Break law self-report (EM)	ART-15 (EM)	50	−.01	.12	−.02	.38***	−.68	−2.25**
13. Discipline (EM)	ART-15 (EM)	50	.12	.12	−.17	.49***	.01	−3.86***
14. Discipline (BEM)	ART-15 (BEM)	49	−.07	.03	−.09	.23*	−.49	−1.63*
15. Discipline (WEM)	ART-15 (WEM)	50	.14	.12	−.16	.45***	.06	−3.40***
16. Combined 3 scales (EM)	ART-15 (EM)	50	.21*	.19*	−.03	.58***	.11	−3.70***
17. Combined 3 scales (BEM)	ART-15 (BEM)	49	.02	.13	.15	.35***	−.52	−1.04
18. Combined 3 scales (WEM)	ART-15 (WEM)	50	.29**	.12	−.17	.51***	.88	−4.00***
19. Combined 3 scales (SEM)	ART-15 (SEM)	48	.06	−.10	.13	.02	.78	.75
20. Discipline (CO)	Combined 3 scales (EM)	50	−.03	−.01	.23	.04	−.08	1.06
			Factors mediating enlisted soldiers response					
21. Fairness (EM)	ART-15 (EM)	50	.13	.17	.12	.38***	−.22	−1.46*
22. Insubordinate (EM)	ART-15 (EM)	50	.09	.13	.04	.39***	−.18	−1.85**
23. Fairness (EM)	Combined 3 scales (EM)	50	.43***	.61***	.33***	.09	−1.63*	1.48*
			(.41)	(.64)	(.30)	(.10)		
24. Insubordinate (EM)	Combined 3 scales (EM)	50	.24**	.57***	.24**	.13	−2.16**	.58

Note. CO, 1SG, EM, BEM, WEM, SEM = company commander, first sergeant, enlisted men, and black, white, and Spanish-ethnic enlisted men, respectively. The variables were scored so that larger numbers reflected (a) more frequent ART-15s and discharges; (b) higher offense rates on all survey scales; (c) greater feelings of unfairness (injustice); and (d) feelings of being labeled insubordinate more frequently. Significance tests: (a) The z is the Pearson-Filon test (Kenny, 1975, p. 896), and the t is the test with one array shared among three variables (McNemar, 1969, p. 158). Sample size varies slightly because of missing data. Statistics are based on same sample size within comparisons (rows). The same autocorrelation may vary slightly in different comparisons because of sample size and partialing out a control variable. ART-15 rates were aggregated over a 3-month period prior to the

Crossed synchronous difference		Lagged synchronous difference		Spurious common factor (Z) auto-correlation	Autocorrelations		Reliabilities for X		Reliabilities for Y	
Time 1 (t_{C-S_1})	Time 2 (t_{C-S_2})	Time 1 (t_{L-S_1})	Time 2 (t_{L-S_2})	($r_{Z_1Z_2}$)	Variable X ($r_{X_1X_2}$)	Variable Y ($r_{Y_1Y_2}$)	Time 1	Time 2	Time 1	Time 2
Initiation of punishment by leaders										
1.65*	1.50*	.00	.16	6.33	−.01	.32**	—	—	.78	.68
1.44*	.93	−.08	−.39	1.70	−.01	.19	—	—	.71	.61
1.19	1.58*	.19	.70	9.54	−.01	.13	—	—	.73	.68
.73	2.34**	−2.12**	−.55	−1.73	.40***	.19*	.84	.85	.66	.51
1.22	1.05	−.72	−.94	−1.56	.55***	.35***	—	—	.78	.68
2.38**	2.07**	−.35	−1.00	−1.94	.52***	.19	—	—	.71	.61
−.39	.40	−1.06	−.08	−.10	.55***	.16	—	—	.73	.68
.78	1.91**	−2.74***	−1.38*	15.08	.45***	.15	.77	.83	.66	.51
2.23**	2.11**	−1.10	−1.28	−11.35	.29**	.18	.74	.67	.66	.51
1.84**	3.73***	−1.41*	−.04	1.55	.29**	.00	.78	.68	.52	.31
Enlisted soldiers response to punishment										
−1.70**	−.54	.61	1.76**	.59	.26**	.32**	— (.64)	— (.54)	.78	.68
−.06	−.85	2.56***	1.63*	7.89	.36***	.32**	.88 (.52)	.84 (.39)	.78	.68
−1.73**	−1.57*	2.26**	2.47***	−6.01	.19*	.32**	.83 (.51)	.81 (.43)	.78	.68
−.11	−.60	1.53*	1.08	10.55	.09	.19	.77 (.13)	.75 (.17)	.71	.61
−1.56*	−1.44*	1.77**	1.90**	−4.21	.09	.15	.83 (.24)	.81 (.24)	.73	.68
−1.44*	−1.32*	2.60***	2.72***	−.35	.33***	.32**	.66 (.46)	.70 (.48)	.78	.68
.70	.12	1.66*	1.26	18.95	.00	.19	.52 (.02)	.48 (.01)	.71	.61
−2.53***	−1.64*	1.48*	2.38**	−2.43	.26**	.15	.63 (.30)	.69 (.27)	.73	.68
.41	1.06	−.36	.45	.46	−.09	.28**	.56 (.17)	.61 (.13)	.36	.38
1.62*	1.62*	.47	.34	17.14	.40***	.33***	.84	.85	.66 (.46)	.70 (.48)
Factors mediating enlisted soldiers response										
−.08	−.33	1.51*	1.29	1.92	.29**	.32**	.70 (.49)	.60 (.34)	.78	.68
−.29	−.41	1.54*	1.65*	1.36	−.02	.32**	— (.49)	— (.29)	.78	.68
—	—	—	—	.11	.29**	.33***	.70 (.49)	.60 (.34)	.66 (.46)	.70 (.48)
—	—	—	—	.24	−.02	.33***	— (.49)	— (.29)	.66 (.46)	.70 (.48)

survey dates for leaders in Comparisons 4, 8, and 9. The reliability in parentheses reflects consensus in enlisted survey responses (see *Reliability Estimation* in Method section and Appendix). Correlations in parentheses have been corrected for reliability shifts (Kenny, 1975, p. 898), using reliabilities without parentheses.

* $p < .10$, one-tailed test.
** $p < .05$, one-tailed test.
*** $p < .01$, one-tailed test.

401–402), although the label has generally been accepted as actual punishment. Comparison 20 shows that enlisted soldiers reacted negatively primarily to the actual punishment, although a slight negative reaction to the commanders' estimates of discipline was found in this comparison. A similar weak relationship was found between the first sergeants' estimates of discipline and the enlisted offense rate. Other comparisons between leaders' estimates of offense rates and the enlisted combined scale were not significant.

Factors mediating increased offense rates. With disagreement between superiors and subordinates over offense rates, punishment was expected to (a) increase the enlisted soldiers' perception that they had been labeled by their leaders and (b) create a feeling that punishment had been handled unfairly. The feeling of having been labeled, and the sense of injustice, should then lead soldiers to defy their leaders through increased offenses. Comparisons 21 and 22 show that the ART-15 punishment increased both the sense of injustice among enlisted soldiers and the feeling that their leaders considered them to be insubordinate.

Next, Comparisons 23 and 24 show that there was a high degree of synchronous correlation between both the offense rate and the feeling of injustice and of having been labeled insubordinate, particularly at Time 2. Since this relationship occurred entirely within the minds of a single group, the causal time lag was probably much shorter than the 3-month interval used, which would then produce high synchronous correlations. The synchronous correlations at Time 2 were artificially inflated by a common cause—the ART-15 rate at Time 1. The partial correlations of offenses with unfairness and insubordination at Time 2 were .52 and .46, respectively, $p < .001$, removing the effects of the ART-15 rate at Time 1. A long-term causal effect between the feeling of unfairness and the offense rate was also found in Comparison 23, with the sense of injustice producing increased offenses or high offenses reducing the sense of injustice, or both. In Comparison 23, the synchronous correlations were more stationary after correcting for the

artificial inflation of the Time 2 synchronous correlation. In summary, the enlisted soldiers' negative reaction to punishment seemed to be mediated, in part, by a sense of injustice and a feeling of having been labeled insubordinate by leaders.

Limitations of the Data

1. *Synchronicity.* In Comparisons 4, 8, and 9, the ART-15 rates were aggregated over a 3-month period. These effects were stronger than those found with a 2-month aggregation period. For this reason, the leaders appeared to be using a 3-month period of retrospection on these scales. However, if no retrospection is assumed at the other extreme, the first estimate of offenses lies exactly between the punishments. In this case, the comparison of the crossed and synchronous correlations is really a cross-lagged comparison (Kenny, 1975, p. 889). With this latter assumption about retrospection, the interpretation of Comparisons 4, 8, and 9 remains essentially unchanged.

An alternate explantion of the enlisted men's data might be that soldiers estimated offenses simply by referring to the frequency of ART-15s given in their company. If this were the case, then soldiers should have rated offenses by reference to recent punishments (over the past 2 months), since these punishments are immediately posted on the bulletin board for all to see, instead of by reference to punishments imposed 3 to 5 months previously, which must be inferred to maintain this hypothesis. It is more plausible to assume that enlisted soldiers were referring to current events in their company rather than ART-15s, when estimating offenses, just as the questions asked them to do.

2. *Reliability shifts.* Reliability estimates were not available for the leaders' responses to the percentage breaking law scale. This scale was correlated .48 and .53 with the leader estimated lawbreaking scale at Time 1, and .24 and .23 at Time 2, for commanders and first sergeants, respectively. Percentage breaking law was not correlated with company discipline. This evidence suggests reduced reliability for the percentage item at Time 2. However, if corrections were made

for reliability shifts (Kenny, 1975, p. 898), assuming the reliability to be lower at Time 2, the cross-lagged differences in Table 2 would only be accentuated, while reasonable stationarity likely would be maintained. Correlations corrected for slight reliability shifts are shown in parentheses for several comparisons in Table 2. Even in the presence of reliability shifts, the spurious-variable autocorrelation test can be used to rule out the spurious or third variable model, for the comparisons with the percentage item as well as for most other comparisons. The importance of this test resides in the fact that stationarity does *not* need to be assumed for this test to rule out the spurious-variable model.

3. *Homogeneous stability.* Significantly different autocorrelations ($p < .10$) were found in each comparison with the first sergeant except Comparison 9 and in the comparisons with the insubordinate and discharge variables. The tests to distinguish between confounded hypotheses in these comparisons therefore may be biased. The autocorrelations were also significantly different in Comparison 1. In this case, the cross-lagged comparison may be biased, since an *instable* variable at Time 1 may correlate with a stable variable at Time 2 more readily than a *stable* variable at Time 1 can correlate with an instable variable at Time 2. However, this bias probably would occur only in the presence of significant synchronous correlation, which did not exist in Comparison 1.

4. *Confounded hypotheses.* The synchronous correlations in Comparisons 23 and 24 were probably inflated by correlated errors, since both variables were rated at one time by the same group. Confounded hypotheses could not be distinguished in these comparisons, since the synchronous correlations did not constitute a no-cause baseline.

5. *Discharges.* The crossed correlation in Comparison 10 may be artificially high, or the discharge reliability at Time 2 artificially low, since the crossed correlation is higher than is theoretically possible with a reliability this low (McNemar, 1969, p. 171).

6. *Deterrence hypothesis.* It was not possible to test the hypothesis that deterrence relations would occur with leader–subordinate agreement over offense rates, since little agreement was found in this sample. What agreement existed occurred with Spanish-ethnic enlisted soldiers, where low reliability of the measures precluded an adequate test of the deterrence hypothesis.

Discussion

Usefulness of the Methodology

What psychologists really wish to study in many instances is the dynamics of interaction over time in a natural setting. The cross-lagged methodology allows us to look at relationships over time in a natural setting. This approach is more expensive but also much more informative than traditional single-time-slice surveys. Information from a single time may not only be less informative but often may be actually misleading. For example, with one time-slice in the present study it would have been concluded that no relationships existed (see Boyd & Griesemer, Note 6, for a related single-time study that reached different conclusions). Much of the survey data in social psychology is based on sampling single time periods, and for this reason much of these data could be misleading.

The use of groups that are associated together as the unit of analysis, instead of isolated individuals, allows us to study the dynamics of interaction, as has been illustrated, rather than simply the relationships between individual perceptions, personality traits, or background characteristics. Using groups as units provided other advantages including synchronous correlations that did not appear to be inflated by correlated errors, which then produced (a) an adequate no-cause baseline for distinguishing confounded hypotheses and (b) frequently significant tests with the spurious-variable autocorrelation. This test, which does not require the assumption of stationarity, has not been used in the past because it has rarely been significant (Kenny, 1973, p. 156), largely because of inflated synchronous correlations. The group reliability model that provides measures of consensus and individual differences, together with the cross-lagged model, will allow us to examine interactions between individual characteristics and group influences in a natural setting as well.

Practical Consequences

With the advent of the all-volunteer Army, the recruitment and maintenance of adequate numbers of personnel is a high priority issue, particularly since the Army is now faced with recruiting sufficient numbers from a dwindling population of young people who are eligible for military service. The problem of maintaining adequate personnel levels is largely exacerbated by the fact that, according to Assistant Secretary of Defense White (cited in Weinraub, 1977), fully 40% of first-term military personnel receive administrative discharges, often under less-than-honorable conditions, without ever making it through their first term of enlistment. This is an extremely expensive solution to disciplinary problems, not only in terms of people lost after training and of lowered personnel levels, but perhaps more importantly in terms of the large number of people returned to civilian society carrying with them a stigma, and perhaps also a sense of injustice and lowered respect for the law. In the present sample, ART-15s produced an increase in both offenses and administrative discharge rates. As outlined in this article, a solution to these problems might involve attempts to reduce the labeling of enlisted soldiers, particularly black soldiers, by their leaders and efforts to increase consensus between superiors and subordinates about offenses. These issues could be addressed in race-relations and organizational-effectiveness education and training sessions, designed for leaders as well as subordinates, that are already in existence on an Army-wide basis (see Hart, Note 4).

Crime and Punishment Dilemma

At a philosophical level, it is clear that the direction we take to achieve our destination determines whether we will ever arrive. If we head the wrong way because appropriate directions are lacking, the harder we try to get to the appropriate destination, the farther away from the goal we get. We may often be in these circumstances when attempting to solve difficult social problems, in this case

the problems related to crime and punishment. In this study, commanders and first sergeants were clearly operating under the assumptions of deterrence theory, as they have been counseled to do ("Explaining Nonjudicial Punishment," 1978), while enlisted soldiers responded with increased offenses as predicted by labeling theory. Feeling that punishment was effective, the harder the company leaders attempted to achieve the goal of good discipline by applying nonjudicial punishment, the farther from their goal they got, resulting in a serious dilemma.

Generality of Results

The extent to which the results of the present study can be generalized to other military units in the future, and to civilian crime and punishment, is an important empirical question requiring further research using methodologies that can address the issues of causation in natural settings. The present sample was limited to men, because of legal restrictions in the distribution of women in the Army. Beyond this, enlisted ranks can be more representative of the racial, cultural, and intellectual diversity of civilian society than is often realized. Civilian and military survey data often show parallel trends with regard to social issues (see Brown, Nordlie, & Thomas, Note 7).

Punishment, in the present article, however, was limited to nonjudicial punishment of less serious offenses. One of the purposes of the judicial process is to increase consensus about the extent of more serious violations, so that punishment through a judicial process may be more likely to follow a deterrence pattern, although this is an important issue for study.

If the relationships proposed are applicable in the larger society, then trends in the relationships over time may become an object of study. The past 15 years seem to have shown an increase in moral relativity—a situation in which different groups disagree over the morality and legality of a wide variety of actions (e.g., Vietnam war, drug usage, homosexuality, discrimination/reverse discrimination on the basis of race or sex, women's rights, human rights, environmental protection, and many others). Many senior noncommissioned officers volunteer the observation that todays' soldiers do not accept the values and standards of the old Army of 20 years ago. If moral relativity has grown, then a corresponding increase in the labeling response to punishment would be expected. If there has been movement away from traditional values, then punishment of a nontraditional person for violations of traditional laws may provoke a sense of injustice and increased rule breaking. Conversely, punishment of a traditional person for violations of "nontraditional" laws (e.g., regulations related'to racial discrimination) may likewise provoke opposition. By contrast to democratic societies, totalitarian societies appear to maintain the deterrence relation to punishment by increasing agreement about offenses through control of the media, propanganda about the morality of issues and events, and high surveillance of the populations—alternatives that are unacceptable in a democratic society.

Conclusions

The relationship between crime and punishment was examined and a dilemma in this relationship was identified. Deterrence theory clearly predicts that punishment should be effective in reducing future offenses, whereas labeling theory expects increased lawbreaking as a result of punishment. The suggestion was offered that persons punished would respond to punishments with a sense of injustice, a feeling of having been labeled, when there was little consensus over offense rates. This in turn would lead to increased offense rates, creating a more serious problem on a delayed basis. The operation of this sort of dilemma in a U.S. Army population was tested with cross-lagged panel correlation, using organizational units rather than individuals as the unit of analysis. An examination of the interaction within the company organizations revealed (a) that little consensus existed between superiors and subordinates over offense rates; (b) that leaders punished enlisted soldiers, particularly blacks, as a response to lawbreaking labels they applied to these soldiers; and (c) that leaders (first sergeants) felt punishments were effective in improving discipline.

The labeling of blacks resulted in a racially discriminatory pattern of punishments. Enlisted soldiers responded to the punishments by feeling that (a) punishment was applied frequently within companies that had good discipline (white enlisted soldiers), (b) punishment was handled unfairly, and (c) labels of insubordination had been applied to them by their leaders. Under these conditions, rather than conform, enlisted soldiers responded defiantly by increasing subsequent offenses, contrary to what the leaders (first sergeants) thought. The punishments also increased the premature discharge of soldiers from the Army, often under less-than-honorable conditions. Observations were offered about the usefulness of the methodology, and about the implications of the dilemma that was identified, for future law-abidingness.

Reference Notes

1. Nagel, J. H. *Crime and incarceration: A reanalysis* (Fels Discussion Paper 112). Philadelphia: University of Pennsylvania, School of Public Urban Policy, September 1977.

2. Myers, S. L., Jr. *Racism and sexism in prisons: The post-release behavior of parolees.* Paper presented at the meeting of the UCLA Symposium on Institutional Racism–Sexism, Los Angeles, April 1977.

3. Bauer, R. G., Stout, R. L., & Holz, R. F. *Developing a conceptual and predictive model of discipline in the U.S. Army* (Research Problem Review 76-5). Washington, D.C.: U.S. Army Research Institute for the Behavioral and Social Sciences, September 1976.

4. Hart, R. J. *Evaluating racial harmony training for Army leaders* (Technical Paper). Washington, D.C.: U.S. Army Research Institute for the Behavioral and Social Sciences, in press.

5. Hart, R. J. *The relationship between perceived offenses and actual disciplinary rates in the military* (Research Memorandum 77-30). Washington, D.C.: U.S. Army Research Institute for the Behavioral and Social Sciences, February 1978.

6. Boyd, N. K., & Griesemer, H. A. *Racial crises in the Army: Prediction, prevention and intervention* (Report prepared under contract DAHC 19-74-C-0035 for U.S. Army Research Institute for the Behavioral and Social Sciences). Washington, D.C.: Lawrence Johnson and Associates, March 1975.

7. Brown, D. K., Nordlie, P. G., & Thomas, J. A. *Changes in black and white perceptions of the Army's race relations/equal opportunity programs —1972 to 1974* (Tech. Rep. TR-77-B3). Washington, D.C.: U.S. Army Research Institute for the Behavioral and Social Sciences, December 1977.

References

Becker, W. C. Consequences of different kinds of parental discipline. In M. L. Hoffman & L. W. Hoffman (Eds.), *Review of child development research* (Vol. 1). New York: Russell Sage Foundation, 1964.

Bell, D. B., Bolin, S. F., Houston, T. J., & Kristiansen, D. M. Predictions and self-fulfilling prophecies of Army discipline. *Proceedings of the 81st Annual Convention of the American Psychological Association, 1973, 8,* 743–744. (Summary)

Chambliss, W. J. The deterrent influence of punishment. *Crime and Delinquency,* 1966, *12,* 70–75.

Chiricos, T. G., & Waldo, G. P. Punishment and crime: An examination of some empirical evidence. *Social Problems,* 1970, *18,* 200–217.

Explaining nonjudicial punishment. *Commander's Call,* July–August, 1978, pp. 6–7.

Gold, M. *Delinquent behavior in an American city.* Belmont, Calif.: Brooks/Cole, 1970.

Green, E. Inter- and intra-racial crime relative to sentencing. In C. Reasons & J. Kuykendall (Eds.), *Race, crime and justice.* Pacific Palisades, Calif.: Goodyear, 1972.

Havlicek, L. L., & Peterson, N. L. Effects of the violation of assumptions upon significance levels of the Pearson *r. Psychological Bulletin,* 1977, *84,* 373–377.

Jensen, G. F. "Crime doesn't pay": Correlates of a shared misunderstanding. *Social Problems,* 1969, *17,* 189–201.

Kenny, D. A. Cross-lagged and synchronous common factors in panel data. In A. S. Goldberger & O. D. Duncan (Eds.), *Structural equation models in the social sciences.* New York: Seminar Press, 1973.

Kenny, D. A. Cross-lagged panel correlation: A test for spuriousness. *Psychological Bulletin,* 1975, *82,* 887–903.

Konijn, H. S. *Statistical theory of sample survey design and analysis.* New York: American Elsevier, 1973.

Levin, M. A. Policy evaluation and recidivism. *Law and Society Review,* 1971, *6,* 17–46.

Lieberson, S., & Silverman, A. R. The precipitants and underlying conditions of race riots. In E. I. Megaree & J. E. Hokanson (Eds.), *The Dynamics of aggression.* New York: Harper & Row, 1970.

McAllister, V. L. Labeling theory as related to juvenile justice system penetration (Doctoral dissertation, University of Colorado, 1974). *Dissertation Abstracts International,* 1975, *35,* 8041A. (University Microfilms No. 75-13, 448)

McNemar, Q. *Psychological statistics* (4th ed.). New York: Wiley, 1969.

Nie, N. H., Hull, C. H., Jenkins, J. G., Steinbrenner, K., & Bent, D. H. *SPSS: Statistical package for the social sciences* (2nd ed.). New York: McGraw-Hill, 1975.

Payne, W. Negative labels: Passageways and prisons. *Crime and Delinquency,* 1973, *19,* 33–40.

Rosenthal, R., & Jacobson, L. Self-fulfilling prophecies in the classroom: Teachers' expectations as unintended determinants of pupils' intellectual competence. In M. Deutsch, I. Katz, & A. R. Jensen (Eds.), *Social class, race, and psychological development.* New York: Holt, Rinehart & Winston, 1968.

Rozelle, R. M., & Campbell, D. T. More plausible rival hypotheses in the cross-lagged panel correlation technique. *Psychological Bulletin,* 1969, *71,* 74–80.

Silberman, M. Toward a theory of criminal deterrence. *American Sociological Review,* 1976, *41,* 442–461.

Tittle, C. R. Deterrents or labeling? *Social Forces,* 1975, *53,* 399–410.

Tittle, C. R., & Logan, C. H. Sanctions and deviance: Evidence and remaining questions. *Law and Society Review,* 1973, *7,* 372–392.

Tittle, C. R., & Rowe, A. R. Certainty of arrest and crime rates: A further test of the deterrent hypothesis. *Social Forces,* 1974, *52,* 455–462.

• Toch, H. The social psychology of violence. In E. I. Megaree & J. E. Hokanson (Eds.), *The dynamics of aggression.* New York: Harper & Row, 1970.

Waldo, G. P., & Chiricos, T. G. Perceived penal sanction and self-reported criminality: A neglected approach to deterrence research. *Social Problems,* 1972, *19,* 522–540.

Weinraub, B. Dropout rate rises to 40 percent for military. *New York Times,* November 16, 1977, pp. A1; A7.

Winer, B. J. *Statistical principles in experimental design.* New York: McGraw-Hill, 1962.

Appendix

The linear model had the following form:

$$X_{ijklm} = \mu + C_i + R_j + CR_{ij} + S_{(ij)k} + Q_l + CQ_{il} + RQ_{jl} + CRQ_{ijl} + SQ_{(ij)kl} + E_{(ijkl)m}, \quad (1A)$$

where

$C_i = 1, d$ companies, random, between-subjects variable;

$R_j = 1, e$ race, fixed, between-subjects variable;

$S_{(ij)k} = 1, f$ subjects (soldiers), random, between-subjects, variable;

$Q_l = 1, g$ questionnaire items, random, within-subjects (repeated measures) variable.

With a single race, R and the interactions with R were deleted, and with a single questionnaire item, Q and the interactions with Q were deleted.

Assuming a balanced model, the reliability of the *mean* of efg measures was defined by dividing the components of $E(MS_C)$ by efg (Winer, 1962, p. 126). The computational formulas were derived from the $E(MS)$s. The definition of the *measurement error* reliability, which assumes that individual differences are not error, is given in Equation 2A along with the computational formula:

$$\frac{\sigma_C^2 + (\sigma_S^2/ef)}{\sigma_C^2 + (\sigma_S^2/ef) + (\sigma_{CQ}^2/g) + [(\sigma_{SQ}^2 + \sigma_E^2)/efg]} = \frac{MS_C - MS_{CQ}}{MS_C}. \quad (2A)$$

The definition of the *consensus* reliability, which assumes that individual differences are error, is given in Equation 3A along with the formula:

$$\frac{\sigma_C^2}{\sigma_C^2 + (\sigma_S^2/ef) + (\sigma_{CQ}^2/g) + [(\sigma_{SQ}^2 + \sigma_E^2)/efg]}$$
$$= \frac{MS_C - MS_S - MS_{CQ} + MS_{SQ}}{MS_C}. \quad (3A)$$

MS_{SQ} is the within-subjects error term. With one questionnaire item, $MS_{CQ} = MS_{SQ} = 0$.

Since the model was not in fact balanced, $E(MS_C)$ was confounded with variance components from R, CR, RQ, and CRQ, while $E(MS_{CQ})$ was confounded with RQ and CRQ. RQ and CRQ were allocated to measurement error, since with aggregated data they reduce the intercorrelation between questionnaire items. R and CR were allocated to the consensus reliability, since they reflect agreement within a racial group. There was a natural confounding of R and CR in the company populations that were estimated, so R and CR confounding were not error. With this allocation, the reliability definitions can be adjusted to include these terms. The computational formulas do not change, except in this unbalanced case MS_C and MS_{CQ} are estimated without reordering of terms (i.e., without removing the variance of any confounded terms).

With stratified random sampling, company averages were weighted by race and ethnic background (Konijn, 1973, p. 138) to estimate total company means. In order to use analysis of variance to estimate the reliability of the *weighted* means, the following formula was used to weight individual cases, using an SPSS weighting procedure (Nie, Hull, Jenkins, Steinbrunner, & Bent, 1975, p. 143):

$$(1/X_i) + (1/X_i)[(N_{B_i}/N_{S_i})/(n_{B_i}/n_{S_i})]$$
$$+ (1/X_i)[(N_{B_i}/N_{S_i})/(n_{B_i}/n_{S_i})][(N_{W_i}/N_{B_i})/(n_{W_i}/n_{B_i})] = 3, \quad (4A)$$

where X_i is a constant needed to maintain the original sample size; N_{S_i}, N_{B_i}, and N_{W_i} were Spanish-ethnic, black, and white population totals for Company i; and n_{S_i}, n_{B_i}, and n_{W_i} were Spanish-ethnic, black, and white survey sample sizes for Company i. In actuality, the above weights were doubled, and the resultant sums of squares were divided by two in order to minimize the influence of the random component in the weighting procedure used. Weights were not applied to reliabilities for individual racial groups.

In recent years there has been considerable interest in the use of causal (path, structural equation) analysis for testing hypotheses using nonexperimental data sets. If the investigator can assume that the variables under consideration are causally ordered in a specified manner, path analysis permits a test of the hypothesized relationships with nonexperimental data. Both direct effects of a variable on the criteron variable of interest and indirect effects that are mediated through other specified variables can be examined.

The following articles and rejoinders illustrate some of the difficulties of using path analysis in evaluation research. The first article by Brooks, using primarily economic assumptions about the distribution of medical resources, develops a causal model for infant mortality in standard metropolitan statistical areas (SMSAs) in the United States. Given his assumptions, Brooks finds that the number of nonfederal physicians per 1000 residents is the only index of medical resource availability that has an effect on infant mortality. By using a different set of assumptions, Anderson finds that the number of hospital beds per 1000 residents also has important indirect effects on infant mortality. The contrasting results of the two analyses clearly indicate the importance of the underlying causal assumptions in determining the results of the path analysis.

The two articles also point out a number of other important issues in using path analysis (or other regression-based models) to analyse large scale data sets: (a) Regression coefficients are profoundly affected by any unreliability of the measures. Brooks uses highly aggregated data (SMSAs) as his unit of analysis to increase the reliability of his measures, but as Anderson points out, there is a trade-off involved, since the use of highly aggregated data can sometimes obscure relationships that can clearly be seen at a lower level of aggregation. (b) The results of regression analyses depend on the specific set of variables that is included in the model. Deleting variables will tend to alter the coefficients of the remaining variables. (c) Typically, only linear relationships between variables are examined. In some cases, it may be reasonable also to look for curvilinear relationships, yet this possibility is rarely considered.

The disparate results of the Anderson and Brooks papers indicate that extreme caution should be used in accepting the results of causal analyses. At a minimum, these results strongly argue for encouraging multiple investigators who have different but reasonable assumptions about the causal ordering of the variables to do separate analyses of the data set. Such a procedure would provide more information about the range of effects that are possible with the data set. Further, these results also indicate the importance of replicating causal models using independent data sets, particularly when the a priori model is revised on the basis of the first data set.

14

Infant Mortality in SMSAs Before Medicaid
Test of a Causal Model

Charles H. Brooks

Path analysis is applied to data on infant mortality, supplies of physicians and hospital beds, and population percentages of blacks and low-income families in 201 standard metropolitan statistical areas (SMSAs) to test the hypothesis that medical resources mediate the effects of racial composition and low income on infant mortality rates. The hypothesis is not supported for the SMSA data: direct effects of racial composition and low income on infant mortality are stronger than indirect effects. The use of SMSA data for analysis is contrasted with the use of county data in a discussion of a study by Anderson, from which the hypothesis was drawn.

In a study of 32 counties in New Mexico, Anderson [1] developed a structural-equation model in which urbanization, racial and ethnic composition, age, education, and income were shown to relate indirectly to infant mortality rates through the effects of population ratios of physicians and hospital beds. Although the model systematically described complex interrelationships between these variables, Anderson's findings can be challenged on two empirical grounds.

First, he selected counties as his units of observation. For ratios of physicians and hospital beds to population to be valid measures of the relative availability of medical resources in an area, it is necessary that the geographic unit represent a medical service area. Research has shown that counties frequently are not good approximations of medical service areas because a substantial proportion of a population crosses county boundaries to seek medical treatment [2,3].

This is no doubt the situation for many counties in New Mexico. In 1970 there were 943 nonfederal physicians providing patient care and 39 hospitals with 3,437 beds in the state [4]. However, more than half of the physicians (509) and one-third of the hospital beds (1,148) were located in Bernalillo County, which is the only metropolitan county in New Mexico and which contains the only medical school in the state. In marked contrast, nine counties had fewer than three doctors and six counties had no hospital. This amount of skewness must cause residents to cross county lines to obtain medical care.

Second, the stability of the estimated parameters in Anderson's model may be questioned. It is generally recognized that annual rates

An abridged version of this article was presented before the epidemiology section at the 105th annual meeting of the American Public Health Association in Washington, DC, Oct. 31, 1977.

Address communications and requests for reprints to Charles H. Brooks, Assistant Professor, Department of Community Health, School of Medicine, Case Western Reserve University, Cleveland, OH 44106.

of infant mortality based on relatively few births tend to be unstable, and therefore unreliable, measures. Among the 32 counties in New Mexico, nine recorded fewer than 100 live births in 1968, the year Anderson studied, while 11 counties recorded between 100 and 500 infant births. When 1968 and 1969 county infant mortality rates are compared, the zero-order correlation is −0.20, which is not statistically significant ($t = -1.12$; $p > 0.05$). Thus for many counties in New Mexico there is little similarity from one year to the next in infant mortality.

The 32 counties represent too few observations to allow reliable estimation of model parameters when the frequency distributions of the variables are highly skewed: one or two aberrant cases can have a major effect on zero-order correlations between variables. The following illustration underscores this point. In 1968 Harding and DeBaca counties had the highest infant mortality rates in New Mexico, with 90.9 and 55.6 infant deaths per 1,000 live births, respectively. However, these counties together had only 58 of the 20,346 live births recorded in the state. The zero-order correlation between the urban percentage of county population and infant mortality is −0.22 when all counties are analyzed, but it becomes 0.09 when Harding and DeBaca counties are excluded. Thus not only the magnitude but also the sign of the correlation changes when these two counties are excluded. The implication of this change is evident when it is recalled that path coefficients are estimated by solving simultaneous equations in which zero-order correlations are the known values.

The purpose of the study reported here was to reexamine Anderson's proposition that the availability of medical resources is a significant mediating factor in associations between socioeconomic and demographic population characteristics and area infant mortality.

Methods

Path analysis was applied to a structural-equation model with socioeconomic and demographic factors as predetermined background variables, measures of medical resource availability as mediating variables, and rates of infant mortality as consequent variables. Indirect effects indicated the intervening role played by medical resource availability in the total associations.

Standard metropolitan statistical areas (SMSAs) were analyzed instead of counties because SMSAs are better approximations of medical service areas [5–7]. As defined by the Bureau of the Budget [8], an SMSA is a county or an aggregate of counties with boundaries circumscribing an integrated system of economic and social activities. Each SMSA may be assumed to function as a self-contained social, economic, and medical trade area, which is not true of most counties.

The years from 1961 to 1965 were selected for analysis because they preceded implementation of titles XVIII (Medicare) and XIX (Medicaid) of the Social Security Act, OEO-DHEW neighborhood health centers, and maternal and infant care projects. These programs no doubt had a favorable impact on the medical care utilization patterns of medically underserved populations [9–12] and may have affected medical resource availability as a mediating variable. A study of the period 1969–1973, when infant mortality rates had decreased, is planned for the future to determine whether the mediating effect of medical resources has increased.

The Variables

Infant mortality responds to social and economic factors [1,13,14]. Because risk of death varies inversely with the age of an infant and socioeconomic factors predominate as correlates of death for older infants [14–16], infant mortality was partitioned into two variables: neonatal rate (NEO), the number of deaths of infants under 28 days of age per 1,000 live births; and postneonatal rate (PNEO), the number of deaths of infants between four weeks and one year of age per 1,000 live births. To obtain a sufficiently large data base, these two variables were averaged over the five-year period 1961–65. As a consequence, 7,402 is the smallest number of births appearing in a denominator of an infant mortality rate.

Three indicators of medical resource availability were analyzed: the number of nonfederal short-term hospital beds per 1,000 SMSA residents in 1966 (BEDS); the number of nonfederal physicians per 1,000 SMSA residents in 1966 (MDS); and the number of obstetricians, gynecologists, and pediatricians in 1966 per 1,000 live births averaged for the years 1961 to 1965 (OGP). The first two measures are similar to those employed in other research [5,17–19]. The last ratio was included to determine whether the supply of obstetricians, gynecologists, and pediatricians in an SMSA has a greater influence on neonatal and postneonatal mortality than does the general supply of physicians. One might assume that the relative availability of these highly trained specialists is an indication of qualitative differences in the care offered to women and infants. Live births were used in the denominator of OGP because obstetricians, gynecologists, and pediatricians provide services mostly to women and to infants and small children; live births indicate better than general population the number eligible to receive such services.

Low family income (LINC), as measured by the percentage of families in an SMSA with incomes below $3,000 in 1959, and the percentage of blacks (PBLK) in an SMSA in 1960 were the two variables in the socioeconomic/demographic area that were selected for analysis. Previous studies have shown that income is strongly related to infant mortality rates [14–16,20,21] and is a meaningful predictor of medical resource utilization [22] and availability [18,19,23]. Other research has demonstrated that the percentage of blacks in a population is an influential determinant, independent of low family income, of infant mortality [24–26].

Two other variables were initially considered for analysis—the percentage of persons at least 25 years of age with less than five years of school completed in 1960 and the percentage of housing units in 1960 considered "sound, with all plumbing." However, stepwise multiple-regression analysis [27] eliminated this pair from the study with minimal loss in explanatory power: the coefficients of determination of *NEO* and *PNEO* were reduced by only 0.002 and 0.006, respectively.

The data analyzed are from 201 SMSAs as they existed in 1960, when they contained 64 percent of the resident population, 64 percent of the registered live births, 83 percent of the obstetricians, gynecologists, and pediatricians, 79 percent of the nonfederal physicians providing patient care, and 60 percent of the nonfederal short-term general hospital beds in the United States [28]. Hence these 201 observations of the study variables reflect a substantial proportion of the nation's population and medical resources.

The source of the infant mortality data was a collaborative report by the U.S. Children's Bureau and the Operational and Demographic Analysis for Maternal and Child Health Project [29]. Information on physicians and hospital beds was taken from a publication of the American Medical Association [30], and SMSA population characteristics were from the Bureau of the Census [31].

The Structural Equation Model

Figure 1 is a graphic representation of the postulated structural equation (path) model, in which associations between the predetermined background variables, *LINC* and *PBLK*, and the consequent variables, *NEO* and *PNEO*, are accounted for primarily by the mediating effects of medical resource availability, as reflected by *OGP*, *MDS*, and *BEDS*. The direct effects of *LINC* and *PBLK* on *NEO* and *PNEO* are represented by dashed lines and were hypothesized to be weak; the solid lines denote effects of *LINC* and *PBLK* on *OGP*, *MDS*, and *BEDS* and the consequent effects of these three on *NEO* and *PNEO*, all of which were hypothesized to be strong.

The rationale for these hypotheses requires some explanation. In a predominately fee-for-service medical system the relative supply of private physicians and hospital beds may be partly determined by an area's ability to support medical resources financially. A premise underlying this expectation is that private physicians seek locations that will maximize income and charge patients what the traffic will bear [18,32]. Accordingly, it is assumed that SMSAs with larger percentages of families with incomes under $3,000 are less able to support the fee structure of private practitioners than are SMSAs with fewer low-income families. It is hypothesized therefore that relatively fewer physicians practice medicine in SMSAs with higher percentages of low-income families.

Another premise is that hospitals are extremely costly to build and operate and require a stable financial base to remain viable. SMSAs with higher percentages of low-income families are assumed to be economically weaker than others. For this reason the ratios of hospital beds to population among SMSAs are expected to vary inversely with the percentages of families with incomes under $3,000.

The direct effects of *PBLK* on *OGP*, *MDS*, and *BEDS* are also hypothesized to be negative. This hypothesis is based on two arguments offered by Marden [6]. The first is that blacks are a medically underserved population, which is due primarily to the scarcity of black physicians and the fact that many white physicians choose not to practice in predominately black areas [32]. The second argument is that blacks tend to use fewer medical services than whites in the same age and income groups [33], with the result that black neighborhoods are not as economically attractive as white or mixed neighborhoods to private practitioners.

A major proposition of the path model in Fig. 1, that the relative supply of medical resources is inversely related to *NEO* and *PNEO*, is based on the premise that availability of medical resources is a determinant of their use. Accordingly, more high-risk pregnancies and sick infants are assumed to receive appropriate medical attention in SMSAs with larger ratios of physicians and hospital beds than in SMSAs with smaller ratios.

No direct effects are postulated in Fig. 1 among the three measures of medical resource availability, despite the fact that other researchers have reported significant interrelations [1,5,6,32]. There are three reasons for this omission: first, the thesis that the supply of physicians and the supply of hospital beds in a medical service area are

Fig. 1. Hypothesized structural model of mediation by three resource-availability variables between measures of population characteristics and infant mortality. Direct effects (dashed lines) of population variables *LINC* and *PBLK* on mortality variables were hypothesized to be weaker than indirect effects (solid lines) through resource variables.

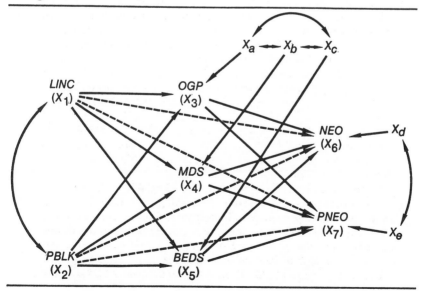

mutually causative variables is an expression of a *dynamic* relationship [7] that cannot be tested adequately by the *static*, cross-sectional data examined here. Second, such reciprocal effects are not central to the objective of this study; and, third, postulating reciprocal effects among the three measures of medical resource supply would result in underidentified structural equations having no unique solution.

Instead, associations among *OGP*, *MDS*, and *BEDS* are indicated in Fig. 1 by their joint dependence on *LINC* and *PBLK* and by postulated correlations among X_a, X_b, and X_c, their respective disturbance terms; these correlations, however, as well as those between disturbance terms X_d and X_e, are not analyzed since they are not relevant to the study objective.

Indirect Effects

The basic theorem of path analysis states that the zero-order correlation, or total association, between two variables in a causal model may be expressed in the general form

$$r_{ij} = \sum_k p_{ik} r_{kj}$$

where p_{ik} are the standardized partial (path) coefficients, i and j denote two variables in the system, and the index k runs over all variables from which paths lead directly to variable i [34]. This theorem can be used to partition zero-order correlations into constituent parts, including direct and indirect effects, spurious correlations, and unanalyzed correlations among predetermined variables [35–37]. The indirect effects are primarily relevant to the objective of this study, because they represent causal effects of the independent variable on specified mediating variables that, in turn, change the dependent variable. By relating the indirect effects to the zero-order correlation between variables, one can ascertain the degree to which medical resource availability accounts for the total association between population characteristics and infant mortality rates in SMSAs.

The structural equations for the path model in Fig. 1, written in standard unit form, are:

$$OGP = p_{32}\,PBLK + p_{31}\,LINC + p_{3a}\,X_a \tag{1}$$
$$MDS = p_{42}\,PBLK + p_{41}\,LINC + p_{4b}\,X_b \tag{2}$$
$$BEDS = p_{52}\,PBLK + p_{51}\,LINC + p_{5c}\,X_c \tag{3}$$
$$NEO = p_{65}\,BEDS + p_{64}\,MDS + p_{63}\,OGP$$
$$+ p_{62}\,PBLK + p_{61}\,LINC + p_{6d}\,X_d \tag{4}$$
$$PNEO = p_{75}\,BEDS + p_{74}\,MDS + p_{73}\,OGP$$
$$+ p_{72}\,PBLK + p_{71}\,LINC + p_{7e}\,X_e \tag{5}$$

where the subscripts of the path coefficients p_{ik} refer to the numbered Xs associated with each variable in Fig. 1.

Results

The intercorrelation matrix for the variables is shown in Table 1. The zero-order correlations between the three indicators of medical

Table 1.   Matrix of Intercorrelations among Variables
(N = 201)

	LINC	PBLK	OGP	MDS	BEDS	NEO	PNEO
LINC	1.000	0.522*	−0.143‡	−0.156‡	0.004	0.352*	0.616*
PBLK		1.000	0.198†	0.121‡	−0.063	0.592*	0.607*
OGP			1.000	0.619*	0.117‡	0.128‡	−0.045
MDS				1.000	0.398*	0.014	−0.170†
BEDS					1.000	−0.024	−0.152‡
NEO						1.000	0.500*
PNEO							1.000
Mean	18.809	10.004	1.246	1.410	4.149	18.064	6.359
Std. devi-ation ...	7.545	10.047	0.404	0.604	1.284	2.135	1.686

* Significant: $p < 0.001$.
† Significant: $p < 0.01$.
‡ Significant: $p < 0.05$.

resource availability and NEO and PNEO are much smaller than the correlations between these two rates of infant loss and LINC and PBLK. This situation is a preliminary indication that OGP, MDS, and BEDS may not be strong determinants of infant mortality rates of SMSAs and therefore may not be influential intervening variables in the model. The estimated coefficients for Eqs. 1–5, shown in Table 2 (p. 10), provide clearer indications.

The coefficients for Eqs. 1 and 2 indicate that LINC and PBLK have significant direct effects on OGP and MDS, as predicted. The positive coefficient of PBLK, however, was unexpected and is not consistent with the findings of other researchers [6,7,32]. One factor not initially considered in this study, but which may account for this surprise finding, is the presence of a medical school in an SMSA; its potential influence will be discussed shortly.

The coefficients for Eq. 3 show that LINC and PBLK have no substantial direct effects on BEDS; together these variables account for less than 1 percent of the variance of the number of beds per 1,000 population.

Two significant findings appear among the coefficients obtained in Eqs. 4 and 5. The first is that MDS is the only measure of medical resource availability analyzed that has an appreciable direct effect on infant mortality. None of the path coefficients for OGP and BEDS is statistically significant at the 0.05 level. Thus the relative supply of maternal and infant care specialists in an SMSA is not a more influential determinant of rates of infant mortality than the general supply of physicians, as was hypothesized. The second finding is that the direct effects of PBLK on NEO and PNEO and the direct effect of LINC on PNEO are substantially larger than the direct effects of the three measures of medical resource availability. This suggests that the zero-order correlations of LINC and PBLK with NEO and PNEO are not primarily accounted for by indirect effects through OGP, MDS, and BEDS.

Table 2. Partial Regression Coefficients for
Path Model 1, Eqs. 1–5

Independent variable	Coefficient		t-value
	Standardized*	Unstandardized†	
EQ. 1: OGP (X_3) $(R^2 = 0.122)$			
$PBLK$ (X_2)	0.374	0.015(0.003)	5.000‡
$LINC$ (X_1)	−0.338	−0.018(0.004)	−4.500‡
Constant	...	1.436	...
EQ. 2: MDS (X_4) $(R^2 = 0.080)$			
$LINC$ (X_1)	−0.301	−0.024(0.006)	−4.000‡
$PBLK$ (X_2)	0.278	0.017(0.005)	3.400‡
Constant	...	1.697	...
EQ. 3: $BEDS$ (X_5) $(R^2 = 0.006)$			
$PBLK$ (X_2)	−0.089	−0.011(0.011)	−1.000
$LINC$ (X_1)	0.051	0.009(0.014)	0.643
Constant	...	4.101	...
EQ. 4: NEO (X_6) $(R^2 = 0.362)$			
$PBLK$ (X_2)	0.565	0.120(0.015)	8.000‡
MDS (X_4)	−0.125	−0.442(0.287)	−1.540
OGP (X_3)	0.095	0.502(0.399)	1.258
$BEDS$ (X_5)	0.050	0.083(0.107)	0.776
$LINC$ (X_1)	0.051	0.014(0.020)	0.700
Constant	...	16.229	...
EQ. 5: $PNEO$ (X_7) $(R^2 = 0.522)$			
$PBLK$ (X_2)	0.418	0.070(0.010)	7.000‡
$LINC$ (X_1)	0.379	0.085(0.014)	6.071‡
MDS (X_4)	−0.149	−0.417(0.196)	−2.128§
$BEDS$ (X_5)	−0.071	−0.093(0.073)	−1.274
OGP (X_3)	0.027	0.112(0.273)	0.410
Constant	...	4.900	...

* Path coefficient.
† Standard errors are shown in parentheses.
‡ Significant: $p < 0.001$.
§ Significant: $p < 0.05$.

Table 3 shows that the combined indirect effects of $LINC$ and
$PBLK$ through the three medical resource variables determine no
more than 5 percent of their total associations with NEO and $PNEO$.
As can be seen, it is the direct effects of $LINC$ and $PBLK$ and the
unanalyzed correlation between them that are the major components
of their total associations with rates of infant mortality.

The Revised Model
The model initially hypothesized for study was revised by applying the backward-elimination approach of stepwise multiple regression [27] to the five structural equations and retaining only direct
effects that were statistically significant. The results of this procedure
are incorporated in the estimated path model shown in Fig. 2.

$BEDS$ is deleted entirely from the path diagram, MDS is the only
medical resource measure that directly affects $PNEO$, and NEO is
determined solely by $PBLK$. This revised model has four overidenti-

Table 3.   Components of Total Correlation of
LINC and *PBLK* with *NEO* and *PNEO*

Component	NEO		PNEO	
	Corre-lation	% of total	Corre-lation	% of total
LINC: total*	0.352	100	0.616	100
Direct†	0.051	14	0.379	62
Indirect, total	0.009	3	0.032	5
Via *OGP*	-0.032	-9	-0.009	-1
Via *MDS*	0.038	11	0.045	7
Via *BEDS*	0.003	1	-0.004	-1
Unanalyzed correlation with *PBLK*	0.292	83	0.205	33
PBLK: total*	0.592	99‡	0.607	100
Direct†	0.565	95	0.418	69
Indirect, total	-0.003	-1	-0.025	-4
Via *OGP*	0.036	6	0.010	2
Via *MDS*	-0.035	-6	-0.041	-7
Via *BEDS*	-0.004	-1	0.006	1
Unanalyzed correlation with *LINC*	0.030	5	0.214	35

* Zero-order coefficient (Table 1).
† Path (standardized) coefficient (Table 2).
‡ Does not add to 100 percent because of rounding error.

Fig. 2.   Revised structural model (see Fig. 1): resource variable
BEDS is not significant, and direct effects of population variables
LINC and *PBLK* on mortality variables are stronger than their
indirect effects through *OGP* and *MDS*.

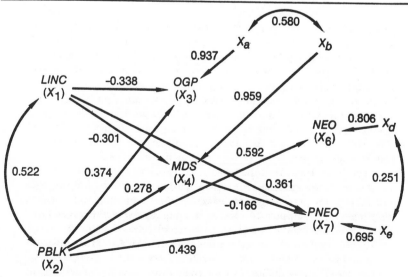

Table 4. **Means of Three Variables in SMSAs With and Without Medical Schools**
(All differences significant by t-test at the 0.001 level)

Variable	With medical school (N = 50)	Without medical school (N = 151)
PBLK	14.3	8.6
Std. deviation	10.8	9.4
Std. error	1.53	0.76
OGP	1.50	1.16
Std. deviation	0.36	0.38
Std. error	0.05	0.03
MDS	2.04	1.20
Std. deviation	0.80	0.33
Std. error	0.11	0.03

fying restrictions, namely, $p_{64} = p_{63} = p_{61} = p_{73} = 0$. These restrictions were tested by a procedure recommended by Duncan [38] and were found to hold for the sample data.

This path model is preferable to that in Fig. 1 because it predicts NEO and PNEO just as well but uses fewer parameters. The proportions of variance explained in NEO and PNEO are 0.351 and 0.517, respectively, compared to 0.362 and 0.522 with the original model. Moreover, the revised model reproduced the total associations among the variables quite well: among the statistically reliable zero-order correlations in Table 1, the more parsimonious path model reproduced 88 percent of the total association of LINC with NEO, and this was the worst case—most of the remaining correlations were reproduced exactly. As with the more complex model, neither MDS nor OGP is a significant mediating factor.

To return to a finding mentioned earlier, the data for 201 SMSAs unmistakably show that PBLK has positive direct effects on OGP and MDS, and not negative effects as originally predicted. This result may be influenced by the presence or absence of a medical school in an SMSA. In a study of 299 metropolitan areas, Joroff and Navarro [5] indicated that the presence of a medical school was an important determinant of ratios of physicians to population in a community: metropolitan areas with medical schools had significantly higher average physician/population ratios than those without medical schools. This difference applied to total private physicians as well as to various specialties, including pediatrics and obstetrics-gynecology.

It may be, then, that the positive correlations between PBLK and OGP and MDS are due to medical schools located in SMSAs with relatively high percentages of blacks. Table 4 provides information that lends some support to this argument: the average percentage of blacks in SMSAs with a medical school, as of 1964–65 [39], was significantly higher than the average percentage in SMSAs having no medical school; also, SMSAs with a medical school, on the average, had higher physician/population ratios than those without. Further, the correlation between *PBLK* and *MDS* in SMSAs without a medical school is –0.165; in SMSAs with a medical school the correlation is 0.101. The difference is significant with $p < 0.05$, which suggests that the presence of a medical school in an SMSA does bear on the positive correlation between *PBLK* and *MDS* for all SMSAs. However, the presence of a medical school does not appear to influence the positive relation between *PBLK* and *OGP*: the zero-order correlation of these variables in SMSAs without medical schools is 0.121, compared to 0.114 in SMSAs with medical schools. Perhaps demand for obstetric and pediatric care is relatively inelastic, so that supply of these medical specialists did not respond to the percentage of blacks in the population, as inferred by Reskin and Campbell [7].

Discussion

The results of this study indicate that the availability of medical resources to residents of SMSAs was not a strong mediating factor in correlations between population characteristics and infant mortality rates in the pre-Medicaid period 1961–65. This conclusion is based on two principal observations: (1) the direct effects of *PBLK* on *NEO* and *PNEO* and the direct effect of *LINC* on *PNEO* were substantially larger than the corresponding direct effects of *OGP*, *MDS*, and *BEDS*; and (2) the indirect effects of *LINC* and *PBLK* that occurred through the three measures of resource availability accounted for a minimal percentage of their total associations with *NEO* and *PNEO*.

This conclusion requires some clarification. First, regarding Anderson's study [1], it is not appropriate to compare results from 201 SMSAs with those obtained from 32 counties in New Mexico. One reason is that Anderson's analysis had the problems previously discussed, and therefore his findings are questionable. More important, however, is that SMSAs are relatively large, urban medical service areas, whereas most counties in New Mexico are small, rural geopolitical units. As a consequence, a model constructed for SMSAs does not necessarily characterize rural phenomena. For the study of medical resource availability in rural areas, medical service areas should be defined in terms of the flow of medical trade [3,40].

Second, although measures of medical resource supply do not account for very many of the observed correlations between socioeconomic and demographic characteristics and area infant mortality rates, it cannot be concluded that medical care plays no important role in these associations. Ratios of physicians and hospital beds to population are relatively crude indicators of the availability of medical resources, tapping only one dimension of medical care. They do not establish the proportion of women and infants that received medical care in an area, the stages of pregnancy at which initial contacts were made, the frequency of care, or the professional status of physicians administering care. Nor do these measures indicate the types of teaching activities in area hospitals, the size of obstetric services, or the categories of personnel performing deliveries. All of these aspects of care have been shown to relate to perinatal loss [41,42];

unfortunately, such information is seldom available for populations of SMSAs.

REFERENCES

1. Anderson, J.G. Causal models and social indicators: Toward the development of social systems models. *Am Sociol Rev* 38:285 June 1973.
2. Ciocco, A. and I. Altman. *Medical Service Areas and Distances Traveled for Physician Care in Western Pennsylvania.* U.S. Public Health Service Monograph No. 19. Washington, DC: U.S. Government Printing Office, 1954.
3. Dickinson, F.G. *Distribution of Physicians by Medical Service Areas.* Chicago: American Medical Association, 1954.
4. Center for Health Services Research and Development. *Distribution of Physicians in the United States, 1970.* Chicago: American Medical Association, 1971.
5. Joroff, S. and V. Navarro. Medical manpower: A multivariate analysis of the distribution of physicians in urban United States. *Med Care* 9:428 Sept.–Oct. 1971.
6. Marden, P.G. A demographic and ecological analysis of the distribution of physicians in metropolitan America, 1960. *Am J Sociol* 72:290 Nov. 1966.
7. Reskin, B. and F.L. Campbell. Physician distribution across metropolitan areas. *Am J Sociol* 79:981 Jan. 1974.
8. Bureau of the Budget. *Standard Metropolitan Statistical Areas.* Washington, DC: U.S. Government Printing Office, 1964.
9. Bice, T.W., D.L. Rabin, B.H. Starfield, and K.L. White. Economic class and use of physician services. *Med Care* 11:287 July–Aug.·1973.
10. Monteiro, L.A. Expense is no object . . . : Income and physician visits reconsidered. *J Health Soc Behav* 14:99 June 1973.
11. Donabedian, A. Effects of Medicare and Medicaid on access to and quality of health care. *Public Health Rep* 91:322 July–Aug. 1976.
12. Wilson, R.W. and E.L. White. Changes in morbidity, disability, and utilization differentials between the poor and the nonpoor: Data from the Health Interview Survey: 1964 and 1973. *Med Care* 15:636 Aug. 1977.
13. Anderson, O.W. Infant Mortality and Social Cultural Factors: Historical Trends and Current Patterns. In E.G. Jaco (ed.), *Patients, Physicians and Illness*, pp. 10–24. New York: Free Press, 1958.
14. Stockwell, E.G. Infant mortality and socioeconomic status: A changing relationship. *Milbank Mem Fund Q* 40:101 Jan. 1962.
15. Donabedian, A., L.S. Rosenfeld, and E.M. Southern. Infant mortality and socioeconomic status in a metropolitan community. *Public Health Rep* 80:1083 Dec. 1965.
16. Hammoud, E.I. Studies in fetal and infant mortality I. A methodological approach to the definition of perinatal mortality. *Am J Public Health* 55:1012 July 1965.
17. Durbin, R.L. and G. Antelman. A study of the effects of selected variables on hospital utilization. *Hosp Manage* 98:57 Aug. 1964.
18. Rimlinger, G.V. and H.B. Steele. An economic interpretation of the spatial distribution of physicians in the U.S. *South Econ J* 30:1 July 1963.
19. Rushing, W.A. and G.T. Wade. Community-structure constraints on distribution of physicians. *Health Serv Res* 8:283 Winter 1973.
20. Altenderfer, M.E. and B. Crowther. Relationship between infant mortality and socioeconomic factors in urban areas. *Public Health Rep* 64:331 Mar. 18, 1949.
21. Willie, C.V. A research note on the changing relationship between infant mortality and socioeconomic status. *Soc Forces* 37:221 Mar. 1959.
22. Feldstein, P.J. and J.J. German. Predicting hospital utilization: An evaluation of three approaches. *Inquiry* 2:13 June 1965.
23. Bentham, L., A. Maurizi, and M.W. Reder. Migration, location and remuneration of medical personnel: Physicians and dentists. *Rev Econ Stat* 50:332 Aug. 1968.
24. Struening, E.L., J.G. Rabkin, P. Cohen, G. Raabe, G.L. Muhlin, and J. Cohen. Family, ethnic and economic indicators of low birth weight and infant mortality: A social area analysis. *Ann NY Acad Sci* 218:87 June 1973.
25. Brooks, C.H. Path analysis of socioeconomic correlates of county infant mortality rates. *Int J Health Serv* 5(3):499, 1975.
26. Brooks, C.H. The changing relationship between socioeconomic status and

infant mortality: An analysis of state characteristics. *J Health Soc Behav* 16: 291 Sept. 1975.

27. Nie, N.H., C.H. Hull, J.G. Jenkins, K. Steinbrenner, and D.H. Bent. *Statistical Package for the Social Sciences*, 2nd ed., pp. 345–47. New York: McGraw-Hill, 1975.

28. National Center for Health Statistics. *Hospitals, A County and Metropolitan Area Data Book*. PHS Pub. No. 2043. Washington, DC: U.S. Government Printing Office, 1970.

29. U.S. Children's Bureau and the Operational and Demographic Analysis for Maternal and Child Health Project of George Washington University. *Infant and Perinatal Mortality Rates by Age and Color: United States, Each State and County, 1956–1960, 1961–1965*. Washington, DC: Department of Health, Education, and Welfare, 1968.

30. Department of Survey Research. *Distribution of Physicians, Hospitals, and Hospital Beds in the United States*. Chicago: American Medical Association, 1966.

31. U.S. Bureau of the Census. *County and City Data Book, 1967*. Washington, DC: U.S. Government Printing Office, 1967.

32. Elesh, D. and P.T. Schollaert. Race and urban medicine: Factors affecting the distribution of physicians in Chicago. *J Health Soc Behav* 13:236 Sept. 1972.

33. National Center for Health Statistics. *Differentials in Health Characeristics by Color, United States—July 1965–June 1967*. Vital and Health Statistics Series 10, No. 56. Washington, DC: U.S. Government Printing Office, 1969.

34. Duncan, O.D. Path analysis: Sociological examples. *Am J Sociol* 72:1 July 1966.

35. Alwin, D.F. and R.M. Hauser. The decomposition of effects in path analysis. *Am Sociol Rev* 40:37 Feb. 1975.

36. Lewis-Beck, M.S. Determining the importance of an independent variable: A path analytic solution. *Soc Sci Res* 3:95 June 1974.

37. Finny, J.M. Indirect effects in path analysis. *Sociol Methods Res* 1:175 Nov. 1972.

38. Duncan, O.D. *Introduction to Structural Equation Models*, pp. 45–50. New York: Academic Press, 1975.

39. National Center for Health Statistics. *Health Resources Statistics, Health Manpower, 1965*. PHS Pub. No. 1509. Washington, DC: U.S. Government Printing Office, 1965.

40. Kane, R.L. Determination of health care priorities and expectations among rural consumers. *Health Serv Res* 4:142 Summer 1969.

41. Institute of Medicine. *Infant Death: An Analysis by Maternal Risk and Health Care*. Washington, DC: National Academy of Sciences, 1973.

42. Committee on Maternal Health. *National Study of Maternity Care, Survey of Obstetric Practice and Associated Services in the United States*. Chicago: American College of Obstetricians and Gynecologists, 1970.

Constructing Causal Models
Problems of Units of Analysis, Aggregation, and Specification

James G. Anderson

In an earlier article [1], I developed a social systems model of the health services system serving the state of New Mexico. The model was based on county data and demonstrated that the availability of physicians and short-term general hospital beds largely accounted for the association between socioeconomic and demographic characteristics of New Mexico counties and their infant mortality rates.

Brooks examines this proposition in an article that appears in this issue of *Health Services Research* [2], fitting a similar model to standard metropolitan statistical area (SMSA) data for the United States. On the basis of his model he reaches quite different conclusions regarding the mediating effect of medical resources. His paper and the results of his analysis raise important issues concerning the appropriate unit of analysis (e.g., counties versus SMSAs) for such studies, the effects of aggregating data, and the importance of properly specifying such models. I intend to address these issues in some detail.

Units of Analysis

Brooks asserts that SMSAs are better approximations of medical service areas than counties, contending that a substantial proportion of a population crosses county boundaries in order to secure medical services. By implication, he seems to view the SMSA as the *only* appropriate unit of analysis for such demographic research on health services. I categorically reject this assertion. Although a variety of units have been used in health services research (e.g., states, SMSAs, counties, urban places, census tracts), it is unusual for the selection of one unit rather than another to be justified within a theoretical framework; this point is discussed in greater detail by Anderson and Marshall [3]. The unit chosen for analysis in a particular study must represent a distinctive system or subsystem with clearly specified boundaries. Whether or not a unit such as a census tract, county, or SMSA is a system depends on the problem under investigation.

Address communications and requests for reprints to Professor James G. Anderson, Department of Sociology and Anthropology, Winthrop E. Stone Hall, Purdue University, Lafayette, IN 47907.

In New Mexico, a sparsely populated state comprising mostly rural counties, there is only one SMSA, and no cities cut across county boundaries. In such states the county is an ecologically coherent unit: the county seat almost always provides the bulk of services to the local population. Medical facilities, including the county hospital (which caters almost exclusively to county residents), physicians, nurses, etc. tend to be concentrated in the county seats, which are typically the largest towns in their counties. My original model [1] hypothesized that rural counties with large concentrations of low-income Spanish-speaking families would experience higher infant mortality rates primarily because of the limited number of physicians and hospital beds available in these counties. The empirical results largely substantiated this hypothesis.

It is possible to assess the appropriateness of counties as units of analysis for states like New Mexico by examining other studies. For example, Marden [4] cited a study by Ciocco and Altman [5] that determined the percentage of Pennsylvania county residents who received their medical care within the county. Four SMSAs and two small metropolitan areas (cities with populations between 25,000 and 50,000 including residents of the counties in which they are located) were common to Ciocco and Altman's study and Marden's study. Marden [4, p. 293] stated that "only two of the eleven counties that are contiguous to a metropolitan area had more than 12 percent of their population receiving medical care within a metropolitan area." It would appear that in states that are largely rural, county boundaries do indeed contain the medical services available to the vast majority of the population.

Brooks fails to justify adequately his choice of SMSAs as his units of analysis. Although it is indeed true that an SMSA can be regarded as a unified labor market, at least for whites, it is not clear that this is true for medical services. I particularly question the assertion that patients, especially expectant mothers, range freely over a metropolitan area seeking medical care. Rather, there is considerable evidence that they seek local care—if not within the same town, very likely within the same county. In fact, the county is the most common unit of organization for physicians and consequently for hospital referral patterns.

Brooks' use of SMSA data is especially problematic in view of the inclusion of percent black and percent low income as major variables in his model. These groups are not distributed randomly within metropolitan areas. Moreover, their distribution depends partly on the size and regional location of the SMSA. SMSAs differ markedly by region and size in their structural characteristics, and these differences have consequences for studies of the relation between variables such as the supply of physicians and infant mortality rates: because of such differences, it is customary to perform separate analyses by region and by size when analyzing data aggregated by SMSA. For example, Marden [4] performed separate analyses for six size categories in his study of the factors that affect physician distribution among SMSAs and small metropolitan areas. His results revealed marked differences in the relative importance of the demographic and medical environment characteristics that account for differences in physician supply. For example, in small communities hospital bed supply was far more important than population characteristics in explaining the supply of both general practitioners and specialists. In larger communities, although population characteristics were most important in accounting for the supply of general practitioners, bed supply and population characteristics had more nearly equal importance in explaining the supply of specialists.

A more serious problem with Brooks' use of SMSAs is the spatial distribution of blacks, and low-income people generally, within metropolitan areas. Less than 5 percent of the people living in suburbs in 1960 were black [6]. At the same time, physicians were increasingly concentrated in suburban counties that ring the central cities: studies by Lieberson [7], Elesh and Schollaert [8], and Kaplan and Leinhardt [9] suggested that an increase in the central-city black population results in a movement of physicians to the suburbs; Navarro [10] cited De Hoff's study of the Baltimore SMSA [11] that found an increasing movement of all types of physicians to the suburbs at the expense of the city during the period from 1930 to 1970, and especially during the period from 1959 to 1965.

Weiss and Greenlick [12] have shown that those with high incomes are willing and able to travel longer distances to obtain medical care than are those with low incomes. This was borne out by studies of Baltimore [10] and Cleveland [13], where most of the patients of physicians who had offices in the central business district lived in the suburban zone surrounding the city. Navarro [10] concluded that the teaching hospital in Baltimore, especially its emergency services, had at the same time become the major source of primary care for the black, low-income population that surrounded the hospital. In short, the availability of medical resources and their utilization differ markedly between black and low-income central-city residents and higher-income, predominantly white, suburban residents.

These facts indicate that Brooks' finding that percent black is positively correlated with both physician supply measures (see Brooks' Table 1, p. 9) is spurious, as he suggests himself. Since he lumps physicians who serve the affluent suburban population together with physicians who serve black central-city residents, it is quite possible to have a significant positive correlation between percent black and physician supply when one is dealing with SMSA data, even though the black central-city population may experience a severe shortage of physicians. This is because metropolitan areas with substantial black populations tend to be large. Given Marden's [4] finding that total size and numbers of physicians are clearly related, and given the tendency for physicians to avoid concentrations of blacks, one would expect a positive correlation between percent black and numbers of physicians in metropolitan areas—but the physicians would be concentrated in the suburbs, not the inner city.

Brooks recognizes the problem in interpretation that this positive correlation presents, since to argue that physicians are attracted to SMSAs with large black populations is contrary to the findings of many other studies [4,8,14]. He suggests that the finding can be accounted for by the presence of medical schools in SMSAs with large percentages of blacks, citing Joroff and Navarro's [15] finding that physician-to-population ratios are generally higher in SMSAs with medical schools. Curiously, however, he does not include this variable in his model and thereby fails to examine this implied hypothesis. Even if he had done so, I doubt that the problem would have been solved. The concentration of physicians in the suburbs surrounding the largely black inner cities in large SMSAs would most likely produce a positive correlation between percent black and physician-to-population ratios even if the presence of a medical school in the SMSA were taken into account.

Level of Aggregation

The highly aggregate nature of the data that Brooks uses to fit his model also poses serious problems. The definition of an SMSA, namely, a central city with a population of 50,000 or more and the surrounding, economically integrated counties, allows for a great deal of variability within SMSAs: for example, some include significant proportions of rural populations. Also, in many southwestern SMSAs Spanish-Americans make up a sizeable proportion of the population whereas blacks are a very small proportion. Medical resources are unevenly distributed within SMSAs as well. For example, Navarro [10] found that although the overall physician-to-population ratio for the Baltimore SMSA was about 1.9 per 1,000 population in 1968, this ratio varied from 11 to 0.21 physicians per 1,000 population as one moved from the central business district to the suburban zone; the number of acute hospital beds per 1,000 population in the same districts varied from 167 to 2.0. Consequently, data aggregated by SMSA do not reflect the vast *within*-SMSA differences in population characteristics, availability of medical resources, and infant mortality rates.

An additional consequence of aggregating data by SMSA is a significant reduction in the variability of jointly-dependent variables. For example, *BEDS*, an important intervening variable, had a mean of 4.149 and a standard deviation of only 1.284 in Brooks' SMSA data, as compared to a mean of 3.09 and a standard deviation of 2.67 among New Mexico counties. Postneonatal mortality rates for SMSAs had a mean of 6.359 and a standard deviation of only 1.686, whereas for New Mexico counties these values were 9.81 and 9.77, respectively. In the SMSA data there is simply not much variation in these variables to explain. This may in part account for Brooks' failure to demonstrate, with data from SMSAs, that availability of hospital beds and availability of primary care physicians are significant intervening variables.

Specification of the Model

Further, Brooks' selection of variables and his specification of their causal sequence are problematic. In any causal model variables should be selected and introduced on the basis of their theoretical relevance. In Brooks' study, variables appear to have been selected largely by omission, with little consideration of their theoretical significance. For example, he eliminates several variables (e.g., education, sound housing, and short-term general hospital beds per 1,000 population) from the model merely on the basis of the results of a stepwise regression analysis. No justification is given for their initial inclusion in the model; nor is the effect of their exclusion on the underlying theoretical model discussed. The problem with this approach, of course, is that variables with significant *indirect* effects are excluded. For example, as I shall show presently, supply of hospital beds has substantial indirect effects on both infant mortality measures, even though its direct effect on the postneonatal mortality rate is small. Additional variables excluded by the stepwise procedure may have important indirect effects as well.

Other variables included in my original model, such as percent Spanish-American, percent urban, percent aged, and percent births in hospital, are omitted, as are lagged measures of physician supply. These omissions make it extremely difficult to compare results of the two studies and may even explain the differences between them in the relative importance of direct and indirect effects of socioeconomic and demographic variables on infant mortality rates.

Certainly it is not absolutely necessary that all of these variables be included in a model of the health services system, but it is most important for any researcher to be aware that the particular selection of variables used to construct a model substantially determines the nature of the underlying theoretical model. Moreover, exclusion of certain variables from a model may seriously affect the statistical properties of parameter estimates and may render findings largely meaningless.

In general, misspecification is inherent in the technique—namely, stepwise regression—that Brooks uses to construct his model. In the construction of my model for New Mexico, variables were retained in the structural equations when the underlying theory dictated their inclusion and their signs and magnitudes were reasonable in light of theory and empirical findings from previous studies. I even reported some regression coefficients and standard errors that fell below the 0.05 level of significance, because omitting relevant variables from the structural equations results in specification errors that bias the coefficient estimates for the variables that are retained. (A second type of specification error, inclusion of a variable that may not belong, increases the variance of parameter estimates without biasing them [16].)

Additional evidence of serious misspecification is the positive sign of the path coefficients defining the effect of percent black on the two physician variables, *OGP* and *MDS*. These findings are nonsensical. Does Brooks really want to say that he has shown that, other things being equal, physicians are attracted to areas with substantial black (or nonwhite) populations? Not only is such a finding difficult to place in any theoretical framework, it is inconsistent with the results of numerous other studies noted above. Such a result should have alerted

Brooks to the obvious—his model is grossly misspecified, and he should have dealt with the problem before he published the results.

Brooks' definition of his two physician-supply variables is also problematic. One measure (MDS) is defined as the number of non-federal physicians providing patient care per 1,000 SMSA residents in 1966; the other (OGP) is defined as the number of obstetricians, gynecologists, and pediatricians in 1966 per 1,000 live births averaged for the years 1961 to 1965. Since obstetricians, gynecologists, and pediatricians are presumably also included in the former variable, the two measures should be highly correlated, since the numerators of the two variables include, in part, the same physicians, even though their denominators differ. In fact, Brooks reports a zero-order correlation between the two measures of 0.619.

This high correlation between the two variables, a problem generally termed multicollinearity [17], leads to specification problems when both measures appear as explanatory variables in the same equation. It becomes almost impossible to separate their effects on the dependent variables. The problem is apparent if one examines Table 2 in Brooks' article (p. 10). In the equation predicting neonatal mortality rates, the sign of the coefficient for MDS is negative and the sign of that for OGP is positive, even though both variables have positive zero-order correlations with NEO in Brooks' Table 1. Similarly, in the equation for postneonatal mortality rates, the sign of the coefficient for MDS is negative and the sign of the coefficient for OGP is positive, even though both have significant negative zero-order correlations with PNEO. Consequently Brooks is forced into deleting one or both of these variables from each equation, or he runs the risk of reporting nonsensical findings (e.g., that an increase in the supply of obstetricians, gynecologists, and pediatricians causes an increase in neonatal and postneonatal mortality rates).

Brooks deals with the nonsense results here by simply deleting the obstreperous variable from the NEO and the PNEO equations, but in the case of the effect of percent black on physician supply, he allows percent black to remain in the equations for OGP and MDS even though its regression coefficient has the "wrong sign." In neither instance does he deal with the underlying problem, namely, gross misspecification.

There is even more evidence of serious misspecification in Brooks' model. He postulates that there are no direct effects among the three measures of medical resource availability, even though he admits that most other major studies [1,4,8,15] have reported such interrelations. Since he finds only weak direct effects of hospital beds on infant mortality rates, he drops this variable completely out of his model. The implied assumption that the supply of short-term general hospital beds has no effect on physician supply and in turn is not affected by the relative numbers of physicians practicing in an SMSA is clearly contrary to the bulk of theoretical and empirical evidence. Physicians are highly dependent on the specially-trained manpower and the highly sophisticated diagnostic and therapeutic facilities in short-term general hospitals [18]; what is more, certain specialists (e.g., pathologists and anesthesiologists) practice almost entirely in hospital settings. Specialization also creates interdependence among physicians. Such interdependence is evident in certain functional relationships (e.g., surgeons and anesthesiologists), referral patterns, and group practice arrangements [3]. Moreover, physicians are usually instrumental in the expansion of existing facilities and the creation of new services. In addition, I have found [19] that changes in the supply of short-term general hospital beds have highly significant effects on physician supply.

Consequently it makes no sense to delete hospital beds from a model that attempts to examine the mediating role of health services on infant mortality rates. Moreover, omission of the hospital-bed-supply variable from the model and the assumption that no relationship exists between the two physician-supply variables has a number of serious consequences.

In the accompanying figure the model is respecified and its parameters are reestimated using ordinary least squares. It is a simple matter to calculate the standardized partial regression coefficients for a hypothetical recursive causal model from the intercorrelation matrix that Brooks includes in his article. Since means and standard deviations of the variables are also provided, it is possible to calculate unstandardized partial regression coefficients and their standard errors [20].

The respecified model reflects the interdependence of the three medical resource variables and hypothesizes that *BEDS* has a direct effect on both physician-supply variables. There is much empirical evidence to support this assertion [18,19]. Moreover, the supply of

---

A respecification of Brooks' model.

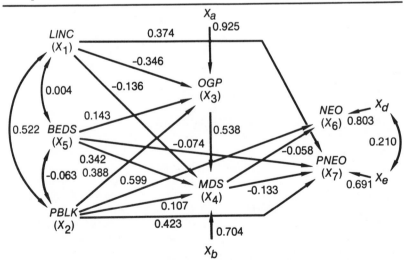

obstetricians, gynecologists, and pediatricians (*OGP*) is also hypothesized to have a direct positive effect on the supply of other physicians (*MDS*). This hypothesis is based on the fact that the first three types of physicians increasingly provide a great deal of the first-contact primary care in a community. Physicians in other specialties are attracted to communities in which obstetricians, gynecologists, and pediatricians practice because of the opportunities for referrals, multispecialty group practices, and the like [21].

Since Brooks omits other characteristics of SMSAs and their populations, such as percent urban and education levels, I treat the hospital-beds variable as exogenous in the respecified model. Without the original raw data Brooks used to fit his model, it is impossible to estimate the coefficients of a nonrecursive model that would include reciprocal links between bed-supply and physician-supply variables.

Parameter estimates for the respecified model and their standard errors are presented in the accompanying table. As hypothesized, the supply of short-term general hospital beds is an important determinant of the supply of both types of physicians. Furthermore, overall supply of nonfederal physicians providing patient care is strongly dependent on supply of obstetricians, gynecologists, and pediatricians.

The consequences of misspecifying the model as Brooks has done

Partial Regression Coefficients for Respecified Path Model
(See accompanying figure)

Independent variable	Coefficient		F-value	Significance level
	Standardized	Unstandardized*		
EQ. 1: OGP (x_3) ($R^2 = 0.143$)				
LINC (X_1)	−0.346	−0.018 (0.004)	19.965	0.000
PBLK (X_2)	0.388	0.016 (0.003)	24.967	0.000
BEDS (X_5)	0.143	0.045 (0.020)	4.659	0.032
Constant	...	1.252	...	...
EQ. 2: MDS (x_4) ($R^2 = 0.504$)				
LINC (X_1)	−0.136	−0.011 (0.005)	4.840	0.029
PBLK (X_2)	0.107	0.006 (0.004)	2.911	0.090
BEDS (X_5)	0.342	0.161 (0.024)	44.941	0.000
OGP (X_3)	0.538	0.805 (0.081)	98.047	0.000
Constant	...	−0.120	...	...
EQ. 3: NEO (x_6) ($R^2 = 0.354$)				
PBLK (X_2)	0.599	0.127 (0.012)	108.363	0.000
MDS (X_4)	−0.058	−0.207 (0.203)	1.033	0.311
Constant	...	17.082	...	...
EQ. 4: PNEO (x_7) ($R^2 = 0.521$)				
LINC (X_1)	0.374	0.084 (0.014)	37.921	0.000
PBLK (X_2)	0.423	0.071 (0.010)	48.289	0.000
BEDS (X_5)	−0.074	−0.097 (0.072)	1.796	0.182
MDS (X_4)	−0.133	−0.372 (0.160)	5.422	0.021
Constant	...	5.001	...	...

* Standard errors in parentheses.

are quite serious. Although he concludes that the supply of hospital beds has no effect on infant mortality rates, the respecified model indicates that, although this variable has a small direct effect on post-neonatal mortality rates, it has important indirect effects on both infant mortality measures through its impact on the supply of both types of physicians. Omission of the hospital-beds variable from Brooks' model omits its important indirect effects on infant mortality.

In addition, misspecification of the medical resource equations leads to seriously biased parameter estimates [16]. The magnitude of this bias can be seen rather dramatically by comparing Brooks' parameter estimates for his *MDS* equation with those contained in the accompanying table. His coefficients for *LINC* and *PBLK* are −0.301 and 0.278, respectively, whereas the estimates from the respecified model are −0.136 and 0.107, respectively: Brooks' omission of *BEDS* and *OGP* from this equation results in a very significant upward bias in his parameter estimates. In fact, percent black is no longer a significant predictor of *MDS* when the supply of hospital beds and other physicians is taken into account. This partially explains a rather anomalous finding of Brooks' study, namely, the large positive direct effect of percent black on the supply of physicians.

The omission of any direct measures of medical resource utilization from Brooks' model (e.g., percent births, in hospital, as in my New Mexico model) also leads to serious specification problems. Brooks finds a large positive direct effect of percent black on both infant mortality measures, but he does not interpret this effect; that is, he does not demonstrate what it is about SMSAs with large concentrations of blacks that yields high infant mortality rates. If he asserts that this finding is due to the high infant mortality rates among blacks, he commits a serious ecological fallacy—not only because his mortality measure includes deaths of all infants and not just black infants, but also because his measures are aggregates, and one cannot make inferences about behavior of individuals on the basis of aggregate data [22].

One is left with the rather strange conclusion that the infant mortality rate in areas with large black and/or low-income populations is high *regardless* of the availability of medical resources. An "ecological" correlation between a variable such as percent black and infant mortality that is based on aggregate data can *only* be interpreted in terms of structural characteristics such as, for example, availability of medical resources or utilization of health services.

Stability of Parameter Estimates

One final issue that Brooks raises has to do with the stability of the estimated parameters of my New Mexico model. Brooks raises this question on the basis of the skewed distribution of medical resources among New Mexico counties and because of the relatively small number of births in some New Mexico counties. Although he does not explicitly say so, I presume that in raising the issue of skewness Brooks assumes that the disturbances of the regression equations are not normally distributed. However, even if the disturbance terms in the structural equation are not normally distributed, the least-squares estimators of the regression coefficients are still the best linear unbiased estimators, since this property is independent of the form of the population. In other words, even without an assumption of normality, the least-squares estimators would be unbiased and would have the smallest variance of all possible linear unbiased estimators of these parameters, although they could not be assumed to be efficient. Nonetheless, if the distribution of the disturbances is not radically different from normal, the confidence limits and tests of significance are not affected to any great extent [23].

A related point is that the estimated regression coefficients are descriptively accurate regardless of the form of the distribution, since no assumptions involving probability distributions were made in the computation of the estimates. It is only when confidence intervals must be constructed or hypotheses concerning the parameters must be tested that assumptions concerning probability distributions are needed.

The second stability problem, the effect of the small number of births on the stability of parameter estimates, cannot be addressed by changing the unit of analysis and the structural form of the model as Brooks attempts to do. Rather, the same model needs to be reestimated with new county data to ascertain whether or to what extent the parameter estimates are invariate. I have, in fact, done this, re-estimating essentially the same model with pooled longitudinal and cross-sectional data from New Mexico counties for the period from 1969 to 1972 [24,25]. The results of this analysis are remarkably similar to the original findings. Moreover, Begun [26] has estimated parameters of the same model using data from North Carolina counties. Although there is no a priori reason that the structural model for North Carolina should be the same as the one for New Mexico, he concludes that "parameter estimates are in general similar to those found by Anderson with data for New Mexico."

In general, human ecology "provides a valuable framework that can be used to generate hypotheses, guide research efforts and interpret the findings of such research" [3, p. 205]. However, successful application of the ecological approach to health services research requires a careful selection of a unit of analysis that is appropriate within the theoretical framework the investigator adopts. Variables need to be selected and introduced on the basis of their theoretical relevance. In particular, relationships between socioeconomic/demographic variables, medical-resource variables, and measures of a population's health status need to be carefully elaborated through selective introduction of additional variables into the analysis. Finally, when such models result in anomalous, nonsensical, or uninterpretable findings, it is important that the investigator respecify his model in order to avoid drawing misleading or even erroneous conclusions.

Acknowledgments. I wish to acknowledge the invaluable assistance of Harvey H. Marshall and John M. Stahura in the preparation of these comments.

REFERENCES

1. Anderson, J.G. Causal models and social indicators: Toward the development of social systems models. *Am Sociol Rev* 38:285 June 1973.
2. Brooks, C.H. Infant mortality in SMSAs before Medicaid: Test of a causal model. *Health Serv Res* 13:3 Spring 1978.
3. Anderson, J.G. and H.H. Marshall. The structural approach to physician distribution: A critical evaluation. *Health Serv Res* 9:195 Fall 1974.
4. Marden, P.G. A demographic and ecological analysis of the distribution of physicians in metropolitan America, 1960. *Am J Sociol* 72:290 Nov. 1966.
5. Ciocco, A. and I. Altman. *Medical Service Areas and Distances Traveled for Physician Care in Western Pennsylvania.* U.S. Public Health Service Monograph No. 19. Washington, DC: U.S. Government Printing Office, 1954.
6. Farley, R. The changing distribution of Negroes within metropolitan areas: The emergence of Black suburbs. *Am J Sociol* 75:512 Jan. 1970.
7. Lieberson, S. Ethnic groups and the practice of medicine. *Am Sociol Rev* 23:542 Oct. 1958.
8. Elesh, D. and P.T. Schollaert. Race and urban medicine: Factors affecting the distribution of physicians in Chicago. *J Health Soc Behav* 13:236 Sept. 1972.
9. Kaplan, R.S. and S. Leinhardt. Determinants of physician office location. *Med Care* 11:406 Sept.–Oct. 1973.
10. Navarro, V. The city and the region: A critical relationship in the distribution of health resources. *Am Behav Sci* 14:856 July–Aug. 1971.
11. De Hoff, J.B. The vanishing diffuse outpatient department. Working paper, Baltimore City Health Department, 1970.
12. Weiss, J.E. and M.R. Greenlick. Determinants of medical care utilization: The effect of social class and distance on contacts with the medical care system. *Med Care* 8:456 Nov.–Dec. 1970.
13. Bashshur, R.L., G.W. Shannon, and C.A. Metzner. The application of three-dimensional analogue models to the distribution of medical care facilities. *Med Care* 8:395 Sept.–Oct. 1970.
14. Reskin, B. and F.L. Campbell. Physician distribution across metropolitan areas. *Am J Sociol* 79:981 Jan. 1974.
15. Joroff, S. and V. Navarro. Medical manpower: A multivariate analysis of the distribution of physicians in urban United States. *Med Care* 9:428 Sept.–Oct. 1971.
16. Rao, P. and R.L. Miller. *Applied Econometrics*, pp. 29–35. Belmont, CA: Wadsworth, 1971.
17. Farrar, D.E. and R.R. Glauber. Multicollinearity in regression analysis: The problem revisited. *Rev Econ Stat* 49:92 Feb. 1967.
18. Williams, R.C. and W.E. Uzzell. Hospitals are the magnets for attracting physicians to smaller communities. *Hospitals* 34:49 July 16, 1960.
19. Anderson, J.G. A social systems model of hospital utilization. *Health Serv Res* 11:271 Fall 1976.
20. Van de Geer, J.P. *Introduction to Multivariate Analysis for the Social Sciences.* San Francisco: Freeman, 1971.
21. Robertson, L.S. On the intraurban ecology of primary care physicians. *Soc Sci Med* 4:227 Aug. 1970.
22. Robinson, W.S. Ecological correlations and the behavior of individuals. *Am Sociol Rev* 15:351 June 1950.
23. Kmenta, J. *Elements of Econometrics*, pp. 247–248. New York: Macmillan, 1971.
24. Anderson, J.G. A social indicator model of a health services system. *Soc Forces* 55:661 Dec. 1977.
25. Anderson, J.G. *Structural Equation Models: Their Structural, Reduced and Final Forms.* Working Paper No. 98. Institute for the Study of Social Change, Department of Sociology and Anthropology, Purdue University, West Lafayette, IN, 1977.
26. Begun, J.W. A causal model of the health care system: A replication. *J Health Soc Behav* 18:2 Mar. 1977.

Reply to "Constructing Causal Models"

Charles H. Brooks

In his comments on my article, "Infant Mortality in SMSAs Before Medicaid: Test of a Causal Model" [1], Anderson [2] asserts that I fail to justify the choice of SMSAs as units of analysis and that their highly aggregate nature caused serious analytical problems. He also states that my selection of variables and specification of their causal sequence led to "anomalous," "nonsensical," or "uninterpretable" findings. I intend to show that Anderson's interpretations are either incorrect or open to debate.

SMSAs as Units of Analysis

If the physician/population and hospital bed/population ratios of a county are to be meaningful, its boundaries must circumscribe the population being served by the physicians and hospitals within it. With respect to this criterion, however, two behavioral phenomena are likely. First, a high proportion of the residents of a county may receive medical care in nearby counties. In this situation, computation of a ratio with population as denominator underrepresents the relative supply of a medical resource. Second, a county may not only provide medical services to its own residents but also to a significant number of residents of adjacent counties. In this instance a ratio overrepresents the relative supply of a medical resource to the extent that the size of the resident population of a county is smaller than the one actually served by the medical care resources within it.

Although the phenomenon is well known, few studies show the extent to which patients cross county boundaries to receive medical care. The one major study, Ciocco and Altman's 1950 investigation of 29 counties in western Pennsylvania [3], showed that neither the population served nor the physicians and hospitals serving it were necessarily circumscribed by a county's boundaries. In more than half of the 29 counties, at least one-fourth of the residents received either physician or hospital care in a county other than the one of residence (Table 1, p. 306).

Address communications and requests for reprints to Charles H. Brooks, Assistant Professor, Department of Community Health, School of Medicine, Case Western Reserve University, Cleveland, OH 44106.

From Charles H. Brooks, "Reply to 'Constructing Causal Models: Problems of Units of Analysis, Aggregation, and Specification,'" 13(3) *Health Services Research* 305-318 (Fall 1978). Copyright 1978 by the Hospital Research and Educational Trust.

Table 1. Percent of Residents Receiving Physician and Hospital Care in County of Residence: 29 Counties in Western Pennsylvania, 1950

(Source: Ciocco and Altman [3])

County of residence	Physician seen in county of residence	Hospital attended in county of residence
Allegheny	98.2	96.7
Armstrong	69.4	33.7
Beaver	86.6	66.4
Bedford	64.1	46.8
Blair	96.6	92.4
Butler	82.7	59.0
Cambria	93.9	86.4
Cameron*†	...	...
Center	86.6	75.0
Clarion†	75.5	...
Clearfield	81.6	61.0
Clinton	89.8	89.9
Crawford	88:4	88.7
Elk	87.1	84.5
Erie	98.0	96.2
Fayette	90.8	76.4
Forest*†	...	...
Greene	81.4	89.3
Indiana	86.6	61.0
Jefferson	88.2	51.1
Lawrence	93.9	93.4
McLean	84.1	85.1
Mercer	93.3	90.0
Potter‡	60.8	...
Somerset	82.9	73.7
Vernango	93.9	88.5
Warren	84.1	79.6
Washington	86.1	68.6
Westmoreland	82.1	68.3

* No physicians in this county replied to the questionnaire.
† County has no general hospital.
‡ The county's one hospital did not reply to the questionnaire.

Ciocco and Altman suggest that counties should be grouped into "medical service areas," an idea proposed earlier by Mountin, Pennell, and Hoge [4]. A medical service area is defined as one that is self-contained with respect to the medical care demands of its population. As outlined by Ciocco and Altman [3,p.12],

> This definition implies that the movement into and out of a given area should be very small relative to the amount of movement among the counties within the area, and the amount of movement in the two opposite directions in the given area should tend to cancel out.

Another investigator, Dickinson, categorically states that the county is not a realistic unit for describing the medical trading habits of the American population, because county boundaries are no barrier to such trade [5,pp.12–13].

Although the "medical service area" concept has not been precisely operationalized, there appears to be a reasonable approximation of it that has both practical and theoretical merit. It is the standard metropolitan statistical area (SMSA), initially developed by the Bureau of the Budget [6]. The fundamental assumption behind the SMSA is that the economic and social activities circumscribed by its boundaries form an integrated system. Its operational definition includes two considerations. First, a city or cities with a minimum population of 50,000 constitute the central city of an SMSA and the county in which the central city is located is the central county. Second, the periphery of an SMSA is determined by the extent to which metropolitan counties contiguous to a central county are economically and socially dependent on it. The major consideration in determining the periphery is the degree to which workers resident in a central county are employed in adjacent counties and vice versa. If this information is not conclusive, then other criteria, such as telephone calls, newspaper circulation, charge accounts, and delivery service practices, are used to make a judgment.

To use an SMSA as an approximation of a medical service area is to assume that the resident population circumscribed by its boundaries is served by the physicians and hospitals in the area. The extent to which this assumption is reasonable may be shown by data collected by Ciocco and Altman. Of the 29 counties in their study, eight counties belong to four SMSAs. Comparing the percentages of births and of residents receiving medical services in county of residence with corresponding SMSA percentages, it is clear that for contiguous counties of an SMSA (e.g., Somerset, Beaver, Washington, and Westmoreland Counties in the Pittsburgh SMSA) the boundaries of a standard metropolitan statistical area are crossed less frequently than those of a county (Table 2). The minimum percentage of residents who receive physician care within an SMSA of residence is 93.3 percent (Westmoreland County), more than 10 points higher than the minimum percentage of residents who receive physician care within the county of residence (82.1 percent). Furthermore, the minimum percentage of residents who receive hospital care (86.2 percent) and the minimum percentage of infants born within the SMSA of mother's residence (89.7 percent) are higher than the corresponding percentages associated with county of residence (66.4 percent and 64.9 percent, respectively). An SMSA, therefore, more closely approximates a self-contained area with respect to the medical care demands of its population than does a county.

I did not intend to imply, as Anderson contends, that the SMSA is the *only* appropriate unit of analysis for demographic research on health services, and I agree that the unit of analysis chosen for a particular study should depend on the problem under investigation [2, p.50]. I would submit that since medical resource availability, as measured by supply ratios of physicians and hospital beds, is the problem under study in both of our articles, SMSAs are more appropriate than counties.

Table 2. Percent of Persons Receiving Physician and Hospital Care and Percent of Births Within SMSA and County of Residence: Eight Counties in Western Pennsylvania, 1950
(Source: Ciocco and Altman [3])

SMSA and county of residence	Percent occurrence within SMSA			Percent occurrence within county		
	Physician care	Hospital care	Births*	Physician care	Hospital care	Births†
Altoona						
(Blair)	96.6	92.4	96.1	96.6	92.4	96.1
Erie						
(Erie)	98.0	96.2	97.7	98.0	96.2	97.7
Johnstown						
Cambria‡	95.5	90.9	92.9	93.9	86.4	90.0
Somerset	95.1	95.4	97.6	82.9	73.7	81.2
Pittsburgh						
Allegheny‡	98.5	98.9	99.1	98.2	96.7	97.3
Beaver	93.9	91.6	90.3	86.6	66.4	64.9
Washington	96.2	86.2	89.7	86.1	68.6	83.1
Westmoreland ..	93.3	95.4	96.0	82.1	68.3	75.5

* Within SMSA of mother's residence.
† Within county of mother's residence.
‡ Central county of SMSA.

The Highly Aggregate Nature of SMSAs

Anderson is quite right when he says that an analysis of differences in population characteristics, availability of medical resources, and infant mortality rates between SMSAs does not reflect the vast differences in these variables within SMSAs [2,p.53]. I also agree that counties, on the average, are more homogeneous geographic units than SMSAs. It should be noted, nonetheless, that populations within counties may also be enormously heterogeneous [7,p.424] and that the variations in health and health services within rural counties are greater than those between counties [8,p.219].

More importantly, Anderson's concern about the highly aggregate nature of SMSAs is not necessarily relevant since we both measure the availability of medical resources to a defined population by using physician/population and hospital bed/population ratios. These indicators require the use of geographic units that approximate medical service areas. For the reasons stated above, I believe SMSAs to be better approximations of medical service areas than counties.

Misspecification of the Model

Anderson claims that the causal model tested in my article is misspecified, as evidenced largely by the "nonsensical" finding that *PBLK* has positive direct effects on *OGP* and *MDS*, the two physician variables, and by my not postulating direct effects among the three measures of medical resource availability. He also states that the analytical variables in the model appear to have been selected by omission, that stepwise regression inherently leads to misspecification, and that there is evidence of multicollinearity problems in my analysis. I shall deal with these criticisms seriatim.

It is understandable that Anderson is upset with the positive sign of the path coefficients defining the effect of *PBLK* on *OGP* and *MDS*. I agree with him; these findings appear to contradict the results of other studies, most notably those reported by Marden [9]. The findings were particularly surprising since my research hypothesis, which predicted negative effects, was based on two arguments offered by Marden, who examined data for 204 SMSAs and 165 "small metropolitan areas." I disagree with Anderson, however, that these findings are "nonsensical," for there is no question that *PBLK* is positively correlated with *OGP* (r =0.198) and *MDS* (r = 0.121). Further, even in Anderson's respecified path model, in which *PBLK*, *LINC*, and *BEDS* are treated as explanatory variables of *OGP* and *MDS*, the path coefficients for *PBLK* remain positive [2,p.56].

Obviously, as Anderson states, the explanation for this finding is not that physicians are attracted to areas because they have substantially black populations. Anderson suggests that the concentration of physicians in the suburbs surrounding the largely black inner cities produces the positive correlation between percent black and the ratio of physicians to population [2,p.53] and that my findings are spurious, but in my opinion the positive correlation between *PBLK* and the total supply of physicians is due to the presence of medical schools in SMSAs with large percentages of blacks. In other words, the association of *PBLK* with *MDS* interacts with the presence of a medical school.

I question Anderson's *PBLK-MDS* thesis on the basis of studies that he cites in his commentary. Although it is recognized that many private practitioners are moving their offices from the central cities to the suburbs of SMSAs (for whatever reasons), the fact remains that the bulk of physicians and hospital beds are still heavily concentrated in the central cities. For example, in Boston, the number of physicians per 100,000 population was 387.0 in 1940, 421.5 in 1950, and 501.9 in 1961, whereas the corresponding ratios for the 70 towns and cities surrounding Boston were 232.0, 232.4, and 145.6 [10]. Navarro's study of the Baltimore SMSA [11] also shows that the relative supply of physicians and hospital beds is higher in the city of Baltimore than in the suburban zone.

It should also be pointed out that I do show zero-order correlations between *PBLK* and *MDS* for SMSAs with medical schools and for SMSAs without medical schools. The correlation coefficient was 0.101 for SMSAs with medical schools and –0.165 for those without medical schools [1,p.13]. These coefficients support my thesis that the positive correlation between *PBLK* and *MDS* reported for 201 SMSAs (r = 0.121) was probably due to the presence of medical schools in SMSAs with relatively large percentages of blacks.

Table 3. Zero-Order Correlations Between
Relative Availability of Nonfederal Physicians
and Two Measures of Racial Composition,
for Five Size Categories of SMSAs, 1960

Size category	N	Percent black*	Percent nonwhite†	Absolute difference‡
All SMSAs	201	0.121	0.118	0.003
1 000 000 or more ..	24	−0.002	0.042	0.044
500 000–999 999	33	−0.080	−0.152	0.072
250 000–499 999	45	0.206	0.222	0.016
100 000–249 999	83	0.175	0.180	0.005
50 000–99 999	16	−0.218	−0.202	0.016

* Source: U.S. Bureau of the Census. *County and City Data Book, 1967* [12].
† Source: U.S. Bureau of the Census. *County and City Data Book, 1962* [13].
‡ None of the six differences is statistically significant, as determined by the t-test for correlated data.

I cannot account for the discrepancy between Marden's findings and my own regarding the sign of the association between racial composition and the total supply of physicians. I suspect that it occurs in part because Marden analyzed data for 165 small metropolitan areas. Since few of these areas had medical schools in 1960, the correlation between racial composition and total physician supply for these areas could not have been influenced by the presence of medical schools.

Another consideration, however, is that Marden and I use different measures of racial composition, which may respond differently to the total supply of physicians. Marden uses percent nonwhite, whereas I use percent black. To investigate this possibility, I compared the zero-order correlations between the relative availability of nonfederal physicians in 1966 (i.e., the *MDS* variable) and these two measures of racial composition, for five size categories of metropolitan areas analyzed by Marden. The results are shown in Table 3. As can be seen, both the percent-black variable and the percent-nonwhite variable relate similarly to the ratio of physicians to population. Thus the fact that Marden and I use different operational measures to indicate racial composition does not appear to be the explanation for our discordant findings.

A third possibility is the presence of multicollinearity in Marden's regressions. (The presence of multicollinearity in my analysis will be addressed shortly.) He shows that, for each category of metropolitan area studied, the percent-nonwhite variable, when considered simultaneously with age, education, and the supply of hospital beds, has a negative direct effect on the total supply of physicians. However, Table 3 shows that for SMSAs with 1,000,000 or more inhabitants and for SMSAs with 250,000 to 499,999 people, percent nonwhite correlates positively with the physician variable. Since the numbers of cases in Marden's analysis for these two categories (24 and 47, respectively) are almost the same as the numbers in Table 3, this apparent discrepancy cannot be accounted for by the effects of SMSA size.

Anderson states that the causal model presented in my article is also seriously misspecified because it does not postulate direct effects among the three measures of medical resource availability, even though other studies have reported such interrelations [2,p.55]. Although it cannot be denied that researchers in other contexts have postulated causal relationships between the supply of hospital beds and the supply of physicians, or at least have specified that hospitals are a determinant of physician supply, the assumptions that underlie such causal postulates are an expression of a dynamic relationship that cannot be validly tested by static cross-sectional data. Instead, longitudinal studies of community structure are needed to provide a more meaningful test of such ecological principles [14, p.996].

Further, Anderson cites Williams and Uzzell's study of 42 hospitals built in rural communities in Georgia [15] as evidence that "physicians are highly dependent on the specially-trained manpower and the highly sophisticated diagnostic and therapeutic facilities in short-term general hospitals" [2,p.55–6]. It should be pointed out, however, that Williams and Uzzell specifically omitted all communities located within metropolitan areas from their analysis because they recognized the difficulty in determining how many physicians were attracted, by the opening of a single hospital, to an area already maintaining several hospitals [15,p.49]. Consequently Anderson is off target when he cites a study of rural communities initially having no hospital as evidence that a constructed hospital attracts physicians. In addition, the evidence in support of the hypothesis that hospital facilities draw physicians to rural areas is contradictory [16,p.457], whereas the evidence for SMSAs is indirect and inconclusive [9,14,17].

On the contrary, it is Anderson's respecified causal model that is problematic. He shows that the supply of obstetricians, gynecologists, and pediatricians has a substantial, positive direct effect (0.538) on the total supply of physicians [2,p.56]. However, this effect cannot be interpreted because, as Anderson himself realizes [2,p.55], the high correlation between OGP and MDS ($r = 0.619$) may not be the result of a causal association but may rather be simply a statistical artifact due to both variables having some of the same physicians included in their numerators. Accordingly, it is inappropriate to directly relate OGP and MDS because it is impossible to separate causal effects from spurious ones.

Additionally, it will be recalled that one purpose of my study was to determine whether the supply of obstetricians, gynecologists, and pediatricians in an SMSA had a greater influence on neonatal and postneonatal mortality than did the general supply of physicians [1, p.5]; it was not to determine whether the OGP variable caused MDS. If the objective of the study had been the latter, the two variables would have been constructed with mutually exclusive numerators.

The implications of Anderson's respecified causal model also de-

Table 4. Components of Correlation of *LINC*, *PBLK*, and *BEDS* with *NEO* and *PNEO*

Component	NEO		PNEO	
	Corre-lation	% of total	Corre-lation	% of total
LINC				
Zero-order coefficient	0.352	100	0.616	100
Implied correlation*	0.322	91	0.616	100
Direct effect†	0.000	0	0.374	61
Indirect effect via *MDS* ..	0.019	5	0.043	7
Unanalyzed correlation with *PBLK*	0.303	86	0.199	32
Unanalyzed correlation with *BEDS*	–0.000	–0	–0.000	–0
PBLK				
Zero-order coefficient	0.592	100	0.607	100
Implied correlation*	0.593	100	0.607	100
Direct effect†	0.599	101	0.423	70
Indirect effect via *MDS* ..	–0.018	–3	–0.042	–7
Unanalyzed correlation with *LINC*	0.010	2	0.218	36
Unanalyzed correlation with *BEDS*	0.002	0	0.008	1
BEDS				
Zero-order coefficient	–0.024	100	–0.152	100
Implied correlation*	–0.061	254	–0.152	101‡
Direct effect†	0.000	0	–0.074	49
Indirect effect via *MDS* ..	–0.024	100	–0.056	37
Unanalyzed correlation with *LINC*	0.000	0	0.002	–1
Unanalyzed correlation with *PBLK*	–0.037	154	–0.024	16

* An implied correlation is one that would be observed if the overidentifying restrictions in an estimated causal model held exactly in the sample [18, p. 47].

† Path (standardized) coefficient.

‡ Does not add to 100 percent because of rounding error.

serve comment. Suppose that the structure of his model is accepted as a valid representation of the causal associations among the variables. Does the analysis of his model substantially change the major conclusion of my article? I submit that it does not.

Table 4 summarizes the components of total correlation of *LINC*, *PBLK*, and *BEDS* with *NEO* and *PNEO*, which are implied in Anderson's causal model. As can be seen, the indirect effects of *LINC* and *PBLK* on *NEO* and *PNEO* through *MDS* account for no more than 7 percent of the total correlations. It will be recalled that in my analysis the combined indirect effects of *LINC* and *PBLK* through the three medical resource variables determined 5 percent or less of their zero-order correlations with the two measures of infant mortality [1, p.11]. Thus the conclusion of my article, that the availability of medical resources before Medicaid did not account for very much of the association between low family income and percent black and SMSA infant mortality rates, is supported unequivocally by Anderson's re-specified causal model. I take issue with Anderson, therefore, when he asserts that the analysis of the causal model postulated in my article leads me to draw misleading or even erroneous conclusions [2,p. 59].

Furthermore, the decomposition of the zero-order correlations between *BEDS* and *NEO* and *PNEO* shown in Table 4 refutes Anderson's claim that the supply of hospital beds has important indirect effects on both infant mortality measures [2,p.58]. Indirect effects of –0.024 and –0.056 can hardly be considered substantial or important. Since Anderson considers –0.074, the direct effect of *BEDS* on *PNEO*, to be small, I fail to understand the basis on which he makes his assertion.

Anderson's suggestion that the analytical variables in my article appear to have been selected largely by omission [2,p.54] is also open to question. Of 10 variables included for study, only those relating to education and housing were eliminated without first justifying their initial consideration. Eight of the 10 variables were justified on the basis of results reported in previous studies and the study hypotheses presented *before* the model was tested. The theoretical relevance of the education and housing variables was not discussed in order to conserve space.

Anderson disapproves of the decision to eliminate the education and housing variables from study "merely on the basis of the results of a stepwise regression analysis" [2,p.54]. Although it is true that stepwise regression, like many other statistical techniques, has its pitfalls, regression solutions performed in steps can be useful when one wishes to check for multicollinearity among the independent variables in an equation and to isolate a subset of available explanatory variables that will yield an optimal equation with as few terms as possible [19,pp.344–5].

Education and housing were dropped from the analysis because they were highly correlated with *LINC*, as indicated by zero-order correlations of 0.789 and –0.807, respectively. This extreme collinearity accounts for the fact that, when in the presence of *LINC*, the education and housing variables did not contribute significantly to the variances of *NEO* and *PNEO*. There is nothing unsound about this practice. As Kim and Kohout suggest, when extreme collinearity exists (i.e., intercorrelations in the 0.8 to 1.0 range), there are two possible solutions: (1) use a new composite scale of the highly correlated variables and substitute the scale variable in the regression equation in place of its components; or (2) use only one of the variables in the highly correlated set to represent the common underlying dimension [19,pp.340–1]. I chose the latter strategy.

Anderson asserts, however, that the high correlation between *OGP* and *MDS* (r = 0.619) creates a multicollinearity problem since both measures appear as explanatory variables in the same equation [2, p.55]. As evidence of multicollinearity he offers the following two observations. In the equation predicting *NEO*, the sign of the coefficient for *MDS* is negative and the sign of that for *OGP* is positive, even though both of these measures of physician supply are positively correlated with *NEO*. Similarly, in the equation for *PNEO*, the sign of the coefficient for *MDS* is negative and the sign of that for *OGP* is positive, even though both of these measures have "significant" negative correlations with *PNEO*.

Anderson is mistaken. The zero-order correlation between *MDS* and *NEO* is 0.014, and that between *OGP* and *PNEO* is –0.045. Neither of these associations is significantly different from the value of zero. Consequently there is no discordance between the negative regression coefficient for *MDS* and its correlation with *NEO*, and there is no discordance between the positive regression coefficient for *OGP* and its correlation with *PNEO*. Moreover, the presence of multicollinearity can be determined better by examining what happens to the signs of regression coefficients and to the sizes of their corresponding standard error terms as collinear explanatory variables are entered into an equation. If the signs of the coefficients change and if the standard errors become extremely large, then multicollinearity is most certainly present [20,p.234]. The stepwise regressions for *NEO* and *PNEO* shown in Table 5 indicate that there is no multicollinearity problem in my analysis. As can be readily seen, the signs of the regression coefficients do not change when *OGP* and *MDS* are entered simultaneously into the equations and the standard error terms do not become extremely large.

I also dispute Anderson's statement that to deal with "nonsense" results I simply delete the "obstreperous" variable, *OGP*, from the *NEO* and *PNEO* equations [2,p.55]. As indicated by the changes in the R^2 terms presented in Table 5, the reason for deleting *OGP* from both equations was that this variable did not contribute significantly to the explained variances of *NEO* and *PNEO* when in the presence of *MDS*.

Anderson also criticizes the causal model tested in my article on the grounds that it does not include à direct measure of medical resource use, such as the percentage of births in hospital [2,p.58]. The problem with this measure is that virtually all babies in the United States, particularly those in metropolitan areas, are hospital-born. For example, in 1961, 98.8 percent of 2.7 million live births in metropolitan counties occurred in the hospital [21,§3,p.59]. Even in Anderson's study of New Mexico counties, the mean percentage of births in the hospital was 97.4 percent [22,p.290], which no doubt was a principal reason why it was not shown as a determinant of infant mortality. Although there is much to be said in favor of including medical resource use as a study variable, I am not aware of an acceptable measure of it that is readily available for counties and SMSAs.

Anderson suggests further that my analysis of SMSAs is ecologically fallacious because certain structural characteristics are not considered. His logic is as follows: (1) Brooks finds a large positive direct effect of percent black on neonatal and postneonatal mortality, even when the availability of medical resources in SMSAs is considered as

Table 5. Unstandardized Regression Coefficients for Neonatal and Postnatal Mortality (Standard Errors are Shown in Parentheses)
(See Brooks [1, Fig. 2])

Regression step	R^2	C	Independent variables*				
			PBLK (X_2)	MDS (X_4)	OGP (X_3)	BEDS (X_5)	LINC (X_1)
1	0.351	16.787	0.126 (0.012)				
2	0.354	17.063	0.127 (0.012)	−0.206 (0.203)			
3	0.358	16.812	0.125 (0.012)	−0.368 (0.257)	0.401 (0.389)		
4	0.360	16.489	0.126 (0.012)	−0.473 (0.283)	0.458 (0.394)	0.094 (0.106)	
5	0.362	16.229	0.120 (0.015)	−0.442 (0.287)	0.502 (0.399)	0.083 (0.107)	0.014 (0.020)

			Independent variables†				
			LINC (X_1)	PBLK (X_2)	MDS (X_4)	BEDS (X_5)	OGP (X_3)
1	0.379	3.770	0.138 (0.012)				
2	0.492	3.972	0.092 (0.013)	0.066 (0.010)			
3	0.517	4.759	0.081 (0.013)	0.074 (0.010)	−0.464 (0.144)		
4	0.522	4.999	0.084 (0.014)	0.071 (0.010)	−0.371 (0.160)	−0.097 (0.072)	
5	0.522	4.900	0.085 (0.014)	0.070 (0.010)	−0.417 (0.196)	−0.983 (0.073)	0.112 (0.273)

* Dependent variable: NEO (X_6).
† Dependent variable: PNEO (X_7).

an intervening variable. (2) Since Brooks does not interpret this effect in terms of structural characteristics, such as medical resource availability or use of health services, he implies that it is due to the infant mortality rates among blacks. (3) However, this implication is fallacious because other groups besides blacks contribute to an SMSA's infant mortality rate and inferences about the behavior of individuals cannot be made on the basis of aggregate data [2,p.58].

I respectfully refute Anderson's suggestion. Nowhere in my article do I make inferences about the behavior of individuals on the basis of characteristics of SMSAs; nor do I cite studies of individuals as theoretical or empirical support for the structure of the causal model proposed for analysis. Other groups besides blacks do contribute to an SMSA's infant mortality rate, but this observation is secondary because my analysis deals with the variations in the percentage of blacks in a population and variations in neonatal and postneonatal mortality rates among 201 SMSAs. Shapiro, Schlesinger, and Nesbitt have shown that when infant mortality rates of whites and nonwhites are compared state by state, nonwhites have consistently higher rates than whites [23,pp.30–41]. Further, the variation in total infant mortality among states is due primarily to the variation in nonwhite rates; the variation in white infant mortality rates is relatively small among states [23,pp.36–40]. These findings provide support for the hypothesis that infant mortality increases as the percentage of nonwhites or blacks increases.

In addition, it may not be all that strange to conclude that the infant mortality rate in areas with large black or low-income populations is high regardless of the availability of medical resources [2,p.58]. The distinction between medical resource availability and accessibility of care is most critical. Before Medicaid, the presence of medical resources in SMSAs with large impoverished populations, including many blacks, was probably unimportant as a determinant of infant mortality, because many of these resources were economically inaccessible to persons most in need of care. As a result, although present in the community, a substantial number of medical resources were underused by these population groups. This explanation is implied in my article, as suggested by the plan to study the mediating effects of medical resources after Medicaid [1,pp.4–5].

Stability of Parameter Estimates

My comments on the stability of the parameters estimated in Anderson's New Mexico model still stand. Although Anderson addresses this issue in his commentary [2,pp.58–9], the fact remains that death rates based on small numbers tend to be unstable, having relatively large standard error terms due to random fluctuation. This problem of data analysis is well known to those who study area characteristics [7,24,25]. It is also illustrated by data assembled for counties in New Mexico, which show nonsignificant zero-order correlation (r = –0.20) between 1968 and 1969 county infant mortality rates. These data also show a change in the magnitude and sign of the correlation between the urban percentage of county population and infant mortality when only two cases are dropped from the analysis [1,p.4].

Furthermore, contrary to Anderson's contention, the effect of the small number of live births on the stability of parameter estimates can be addressed by changing to a larger unit of analysis, as well as by aggregating data over time [7,p.424].

Summary and Conclusion

To summarize, Anderson asserts that my article suffers from major deficiencies, e.g., the choice of SMSAs as units of analysis is not justified, the highly aggregate nature of SMSAs poses serious problems of analysis, the causal model is grossly misspecified because it does not postulate direct effects among the three measures of medical resource availability, the study variables appear to be selected largely by omission, multicollinearity is present in the regressions, and the analysis is ecologically fallacious. I have responded to these criticisms at length, showing that most of Anderson's interpretations are incorrect and others are open to debate.

In conclusion, I maintain that the causal model that I test is specified correctly because the hypothesized relationships are plausible and the structure of the model is consistent with the limitations of the data. Further, SMSAs are appropriate units of analysis because they are reasonable approximations of medical service areas. Finally, the conclusion of the study is supported by the analysis.

REFERENCES '

1. Brooks, C.H. Infant mortality in SMSAs before Medicaid: Test of a causal model. *Health Serv Res* 13:3 Spring 1978.
2. Anderson, J.G. Constructing causal models: Problems of units of analysis, aggregation, and specification. *Health Serv Res* 13:50 Spring 1978.
3. Ciocco, A. and I. Altman. *Medical Service Areas and Distances Traveled for Physician Care in Western Pennsylvania.* U.S. Public Health Service Monograph No. 19. Washington, DC: U.S. Government Printing Office, 1954.
4. Mountin, J.W., E.H. Pennell, and V.M.Hoge. *Health Service Areas: Requirements for General Hospitals and Health Centers.* U.S. Public Health Service Bulletin No. 292. Washington, DC: U.S. Government Printing Office, 1945.
5. Dickinson, F.G. *Distribution of Physicians by Medical Service Areas.* Chicago: American Medical Association, 1954.
6. U.S. Bureau of the Budget. *Standard Metropolitan Statistical Areas.* Washington, DC: U.S. Government Printing Office, 1964.
7. Kleinman, J.C., J.J. Feldman, and R.H. Mugge. Geographic variations in infant mortality. *Public Health Rep* 91:423 Sept.–Oct. 1976.
8. Hamilton, C.H. Health and Health Services. In T.R. Ford (ed.), *The Southern Appalachian Region: A Survey,* pp. 219–44. Lexington: University of Kentucky Press, 1962.
9. Marden, P.G. A demographic and ecological analysis of the distribution of physicians in metropolitan America, 1960. *Am J Sociol* 72:290 Nov. 1966.
10. Robertson, L.S. On the intraurban ecology of primary care physicians. *Soc Sci Med* 4:227 Aug. 1970.
11. Navarro, V. The city and the region: A critical relationship in the distribution of health resources. *Am Behav Sci* 14:865 July–Aug. 1971.
12. U.S. Bureau of the Census. *County and City Data Book, 1967.* Washington, DC: U.S. Government Printing Office, 1967.
13. U.S. Bureau of the Census. *County and City Data Book, 1962.* Washington, DC: U.S. Government Printing Office, 1962.
14. Reskin, B. and F.L. Campbell. Physicial distribution across metropolitan areas. *Am J Sociol* 79:981 Jan. 1974.
15. Williams, R.C. and W.E. Uzzell. Hospitals are the magnets for attracting physicians to smaller communities. *Hospitals* 34:49 July 16, 1960.
16. Eisenberg, B.S. and J.R. Cantwell. Policies to influence the spatial distribution of physicians: A conceptual review of selected programs and empirical evidence. *Med Care* 14:455 June 1976.
17. Joroff, S. and V. Navarro. Medical manpower: A multivariate analysis of the distribution of physicians in urban United States. *Med Care* 9:428 Sept.–Oct. 1971.
18. Duncan, O.D. *Introduction to Structural Equation Models.* New York: Academic Press, 1975.
19. Kim, J. and F.J. Kohout. Multiple Regression Analysis: Subprogram Regression. In N.H. Nie, C.H. Hull, J.G. Jenkins, K. Steinbrenner, and D.H. Bent (eds.), *Statistical Package for the Social Sciences,* 2nd ed., pp. 320–67. New York: McGraw-Hill, 1975.
20. Blalock, H.M. Correlated independent variables: The problem of multicollinearity. *Soc Forces* 42:233 Dec. 1963.
21. U.S. Public Health Service. *Vital Statistics of the United States, 1961.* Volume I—Natality. Washington, DC: U.S. Government Printing Office, 1963.
22. Anderson, J.G. Causal models and social indicators: Toward the development of social systems models. *Am Sociol Rev* 38:285 June 1973.
23. Shapiro, S., E.R. Schlesinger, and R.E.L. Nesbitt Jr. *Infant, Perinatal, Maternal,*

and Childhood Mortality in the United States. Cambridge, MA: Harvard University Press, 1968.

24. Sauer, H.I. Risk of Illness and Death in Metropolitan and Nonmetropolitan Areas. In E.W. Hassinger and L.R. Whiting (eds.), *Rural Health Services: Organization, Delivery, and Use,* pp. 38–55. Ames: Iowa State University Press, 1976.

25. Ventura, S.J., S.M. Taffel, and E. Spratley. *Selected Vital and Health Statistics in Poverty and Nonpoverty Areas of 19 Large Cities, United States, 1969–71.* Vital and Health Statistics Publications Series 21, No. 26. DHEW Pub. No. (HRA) 76-1904. Washington, DC: U.S. Government Printing Office, 1975.

Constructing Causal Models
Critical Issues

James G. Anderson

In a previous article in this journal, Brooks [1] examined my social systems model [2] of the health services system of New Mexico. He questioned my proposition that the availability of physicians and short-term general hospital beds accounted for the association between socioeconomic and demographic characteristics of New Mexico counties and their infant mortality rates.

Brooks' analysis raised important issues concerning appropriate units of analysis (e.g., counties vs. SMSAs) for such studies, the effects of aggregating data, and the importance of properly specifying such models. In my reply [3] to Brooks' article I discussed these considerations, but his response in this issue of *Health Services Research* [4] does not address many of the major issues that I raised. Furthermore, several of the issues that he does address are badly clouded. Consequently, I have attempted to clarify a number of important issues raised in this series of articles.

Units of Analysis

In the earlier paper [3] I pointed out that the choice of an appropriate unit of analysis for health services research depends on the problem under investigation. For example, Elesh and Schollaert [5] investigated the effect of the race of the potential client population on the spatial distribution of physicians. They chose census tracts as the basic unit of analysis for their study; that choice was based on the premise that the spatial distribution of physicians may be seen as a result of attempts by physicians to establish practices consistent with their status performance for white clients with high income and education.

In justifying the choice of a census tract as the appropriate unit of analysis, Elesh and Schollaert [5, p. 240] assumed that tracts are good approximations of physicians' market areas. In order to test this assumption, they developed a population potential measure to characterize tracts in terms of proximity to populations with high demands for physician services. On the basis of their analysis, Elesh and Schollaert concluded that general practitioners largely serve the clients residing in the same census tract. In contrast, specialists can be divided into two groups: those who are located in the central business district near inner-city hospitals and who serve a citywide market and

Address communications and requests for reprints to Professor James G. Anderson, Department of Sociology and Anthropology, Winthrop E. Stone Hall, Purdue University, Lafayette, IN 47907.

From James G. Anderson, "Constructing Causal Models: Critical Issues," 13(4) *Health Services Research* 319-326 (Fall 1978). Copyright 1978 by the Hospital Research and Educational Trust.

those who are located in outlying tracts and who serve local populations much as general practitioners do.

In another study, Benham, Maurizi and Reder [6] chose the state as the unit of analysis for their study of physician and dentist location. One of the questions that they raised concerned the effect that state licensure standards have on physician population ratios. Since licensure is a state function and applies uniformly to all physicians who wish to establish a practice within the state, the appropriate unit of analysis for such a study is the state. In still another study of factors that affect physician location decisions, Yett and Sloan [7] examined the effect of previous attachments to the state, such as birthplace and locations of medical school, internship, and residency on the physicians' choice of a first practice location. Thus, in that study, use of the individual physician as the unit of analysis was appropriate.

The point is that the appropriateness of the unit of analysis depends on the problem under investigation. In a rural state such as New Mexico, which contains only one SMSA, the county is clearly the appropriate unit of analysis for a study of the effects of the supply of medical resources on the health status of the population. Over 90 percent of the population of two New Mexico counties lives in urban areas whereas nine counties are completely rural. In an analysis such as the one in my initial study [2], counties as disparate as those of New Mexico must be differentiated and not aggregated as Brooks proposes. In addition, the counties are ecologically coherent units in such states. Medical services and manpower tend to be concentrated in the county seats and not only are physicians organized in county units, but hospital privileges and referral patterns also tend to be within counties.

Moreover, there is much evidence that county residents overwhelmingly seek medical services within their county of residence, especially in rural states, and, in fact, the data presented by Brooks [4, p. 306] from the Ciocco and Altman study [8] substantiate my argument. Brooks' Table 1 shows that for counties of western Pennsylvania in 1950 the median percentage of residents who sought care from a physician in the county of residence was 87 percent, and the median percentage of residents who attended a hospital in the county of residence was 80 percent. These data indicate that the county is the area within which most people obtain their medical care, which is quite the reverse of what Brooks presumably wants to show.

SMSAs are composed of counties. People do indeed seek care within their own SMSA, but they do so primarily because they seek care within the county in which they reside. This can be seen from an examination of the table that Brooks [4, p. 308] presents, which compares SMSAs and counties. There is very little difference between the percentages of residents seeking medical care within the SMSA and of those seeking care in their county of residence. Even in the case of the four counties that compose the Pittsburgh SMSA, almost 9 out of 10 persons seek physician care within their county of residence.

Moreover, the problem that Brooks raises concerning patients crossing county boundaries in order to seek medical care is not solved by aggregating smaller units such as counties into larger ones like SMSAs. For example, there are a number of contiguous SMSAs along the eastern seaboard that compose the New York standard consolidated area. Movement of individuals across SMSA boundaries in such a situation is likely to be as great as movement across county boundaries.

However, there is a much more serious problem involved in using SMSAs as the unit of analysis for a study such as the one that Brooks has undertaken. SMSAs are internally differentiated in a way that Brooks fails to recognize. In general, SMSAs are comprised of a central city with a population of 50,000 or more and the contiguous surrounding counties that are economically integrated with the central city but which in many instances have a substantial rural component.

Rural towns as well as suburbs of varying sizes and functions are included in a single SMSA. Each of these units (i.e., central city, suburbs, etc.) has a specific ecological role in the metropolitan territorial division of labor. Associated with the different roles of these various areas are populations with characteristics that match the needs of the area's function. Thus, central cities are clearly differentiated from suburban rings in a wide variety of population characteristics, given that the central city and the suburban fringe play different roles in the metropolitan framework. The suburban fringe is also differentiated in terms of population characteristics, given the increasing diversity of function that is now apparent in American SMSAs. The major implication of the internal differentiation of SMSAs for physician distribution is that physicians not only consider central city versus suburban fringe characteristics in locating their practices, but also consider the varying characteristics of suburban locations. Additionally, in locating their practices, physicians react primarily to the characteristics of subareas of SMSAs and secondarily to the SMSAs themselves.

Population groups are differentially distributed across these metropolitan components. Blacks and low-income people were almost entirely concentrated in the central cities of SMSAs in 1960 since less than 5 percent of the people living in suburbs at that time were black. Whites with higher income and better education were largely concentrated in the suburban counties. Furthermore, medical resources are differentially distributed among the components, and this distribution is affected by the racial composition of the population. Elesh and Schollaert [5] found that there were, on the average, two and one-half times as many general practitioners and five times as many specialists in white census tracts as there were in black census tracts in Chicago. Moreover, when they considered the availability of hospitals, they found on the average 0.09 hospitals per white census tract but only 0.03 hospitals per black census tract. This amounts to one hospital for every 51,000 whites as compared to one hospital for every 125,000 blacks. They concluded, rather cogently, that "blacks would appear to lack access to the major alternatives to private physicians—hospital clinics and emergency rooms—as well as to the physicians themselves" [5, p. 24].

Does Brooks really want to contend that blacks and low-income people cross county boundaries freely and are as likely to seek care in the suburbs as in the central-city area? Whereas for some purposes and for some groups SMSAs may be regarded as coherent units, I question whether this is the case for low-income people, especially blacks.

Brooks' argument that SMSAs are more appropriate than counties in studying the effect of medical resource availability on the health status of a population is simply not tenable. His argument that SMSAs approximate medical service areas better because patients are more inclined to cross county boundaries to seek medical care is simply not borne out by the data that he presents from western Pennsylvania.

Moreover, the ecological structure of the SMSA accounts for Brooks' uninterpretable finding that the supply of physicians in an SMSA is positively affected by the percentage of the population that is black. There is no way that this finding can be interpreted except as evidence that Brooks has chosen a poor unit of analysis for his study and has badly specified his analytical model.

Misspecification of the Model

The misspecification of Brooks' model that I elaborated on in some detail previously [3] leads to two major problems that he fails to deal with adequately in his reply. First, his finding that percent black has positive path coefficients with his two physician supply variables, OGP and MDS, is simply uninterpretable. A path coefficient is, *by definition*, the amount of net causal impact that one variable has on another. I again ask, does Brooks *really* want to say that a large percentage of blacks in an area caused the supply of physicians to rise and that physicians, after weighing all the advantages and disadvantages of their location decisions, prefer areas with large black populations? His response to my original criticism is largely ad hominem. Brooks first asserts that "there is no question but that $PBLK$ is positively correlated with OGP (r = 0.198) and MDS (r = 0.121)" [4, p. 309]. What Brooks fails to realize is that such a correlation must be spurious and/or must contain a suppressor component if it is to be interpretable. Brooks tries to explain this discrepancy with other major studies [9,10], especially Marden's [9], by suggesting that it may be due to the fact that Marden included 165 small metropolitan areas with the 204 SMSAs that he analyzed or that Marden's independent variables (i.e., percent nonwhite, age, education, and hospital bed supply) were highly intercorrelated (multicollinearity).

Brooks finally does admit that "Obviously, as Anderson states, the explanation for this finding is not that physicians are attracted to areas because they have substantially black populations." Instead, he suggests that "the positive correlation between $PBLK$ and the total supply of physicians is due to the presence of medical schools in SMSAs with large percentages of blacks" [4, p. 309]. However, he never tests this hypothesis by including the presence of a medical school in his model. If he is correct, then the inclusion of such a variable would account for this anomalous finding, and the path coefficient would either be zero or negative.

Brooks dismisses my argument that the positive correlation of percent black with physician supply can be accounted for by the ecological structure of SMSAs. Briefly, I maintain that blacks are concentrated in the central city whereas physicians are increasingly concentrated in the suburbs. Consequently, a positive correlation exists between percent black and physician supply when data are aggregated by SMSA even though these physician services are largely unavailable to blacks (see ref. 5).

What Brooks fails to discern is that different ecological units are involved as one moves from one level of aggregation to another. For example, it is important to look at one set of structural factors to explain physician distribution across census tracts and still another set of factors to examine variations in physician supply across counties. SMSAs are entirely different ecological units and, consequently, factors that affect physician location in SMSAs are different from those for counties and census tracts. It is highly unlikely that blacks in an SMSA draw physicians to that SMSA unless one can show that physicians are attracted to such areas for economic or other reasons such as welfare-supported medicine (e.g., Medicaid).

The point is that the model is misspecified, whether it is due to Brooks' failure to include medical schools explicitly in his model or whether it is due to the ecological structure of the SMSA. As a result, Brooks is left with a finding that makes no sense (i.e., that physicians are attracted to SMSAs with large numbers of blacks) and that does not agree with the findings of other major studies.

The second major problem that results from misspecification is that some of Brooks' parameter estimates are seriously biased. As a result, conclusions that he draws about the effects of certain variables are misleading. For example, the effect of low income on the supply of physicians in the *OGP* and *MDS* equations is highly biased because percent black is in the equation but has the wrong (i.e., positive) sign. As a result, the magnitude of the low-income regression coefficients is approximately twice the magnitude of the zero-order correlations of low income with *OGP* and *MDS*. This finding is clearly absurd. Since percent black and low income are highly positively correlated (0.522), one would expect the effect of either alone to be reduced when both variables are entered into the equation because of the common variance that the two variables share. Consequently, any conclusions concerning the magnitude of the effect of low income and percent black on other variables in the model are clearly erroneous. This includes calculations of the indirect effects of these two variables on neonatal and postneonatal mortality rates, since these biased coefficients are used in making these calculations. Moreover, Brooks' arguments about the relative importance of direct and indirect effects [4, pp. 311–12] are seriously biased since his calculations are in part based on the obviously biased positive direct "effects" of percent black on the two measures of physician supply.

Misspecification also arises because Brooks does not include any direct relationships among his medical resource variables (i.e., physician supply (*OGP* and *MDS*) and hospital bed supply (*BEDS*)). He excludes hospital bed supply entirely from his model on the basis of a stepwise regression analysis and shows both *OGP* and *MDS* as being independently determined by low income and percent black. As a result, there is a very large correlation (0.58) between the two residuals.

Again, the consequences of Brooks' specification for certain parameter estimates are important. When the model is respecified to include the effect of primary-care physicians and hospital beds on total physician supply [3, p. 56], the magnitude of the effects of low income and percent black on total physician supply are reduced to about one-third of the values reported by Brooks. Clearly, any conclusions about the magnitude of the direct effects of·low income and percent black on physician supply and any conclusions about the relative magnitude of the direct and indirect effects of these variables on infant mortality rates depend markedly on the specification of the model.

Another important issue that Brooks fails to deal with adequately concerns the effect of multicollinearity on the specification of the model. I pointed out that the high correlation between the two physician supply variables (0.619), which is partly due to the way that Brooks defines these variables, leads to specification problems when he enters both variables as predictors in the neonatal and postneonatal mortality equations. Brooks asserts that I am mistaken and that "stepwise regressions for *NEO* and *PNEO* . . . indicate that there is no multicollinearity problem in my [Brooks] analysis" [4, p. 314]. An examination of Tables 1 and 2 in Brooks' article [1], however, confirms my point. Both *OGP* and *MDS* have positive zero-order correlations with *NEO*, but when both variables are entered into the *NEO* equation, *MDS* has a negative regression coefficient whereas *OGP* has a positive coefficient. Brooks subsequently drops both physician supply variables from his *NEO* equation. In the case of postneonatal mortality rates, both *OGP* and *MDS* have negative zero-order correlations with this variable. When both variables are entered into the *PNEO* equation, *OGP* has a positive coefficient whereas *MDS* has a negative coefficient. In this case, Brooks drops the *OGP* variable from his equation. Clearly, there is a serious problem of multicollinearity. The specification of Brooks' model depends on whether or not he chooses to enter one or both of the physician-supply variables in his infant mortality equations.

Stability of Parameter Estimates

Brooks again questions the stability of the parameter estimates in my initial article [2]. But I pointed out in my earlier reply [3] that essentially the same model has been reestimated with pooled longitudinal and cross-sectional data from New Mexico for the period 1969–1972 [11]. The results of that analysis confirm the stability of the original parameter estimates. Moreover, as I reported before, Begun replicated my study of New Mexico with data from North Carolina counties. He concluded [12, p. 2] that his "parameter estimates are in general similar to those found by Anderson with data for New Mexico." Consequently, it would appear that Brooks is raising an academic issue in questioning the stability of my parameter estimates.

Discussion

Brooks' assertions that his causal model is specified correctly, that SMSAs are the appropriate units of analysis for this study, and that the conclusion of the study is supported by the analysis are clearly unwarranted. The evidence suggests that most of the major conclusions that he draws from his study are either uninterpretable or misleading because of his poor choice of a unit of analysis and serious misspecification of the model.

Acknowledgment. I wish to acknowledge the invaluable assistance of Harvey H. Marshall and John W. Stahura in the preparation of these comments.

REFERENCES
1. Brooks, C.H. Infant mortality in SMSAs before Medicaid: Test of a causal model. *Health Serv Res* 13:3 Spring 1978.
2. Anderson, J.G. Causal models and social indicators: Toward the development of social systems models. *Am Sociol Rev* 38:285 June 1973.
3. Anderson, J.G. Constructing causal models: Problems of units of analysis, aggregation, and specification. *Health Serv Res* 13:50 Spring 1978.
4. Brooks, C.H. Reply to "Constructing Causal Models: Problems of Units of Analysis, Aggregation, and Specification." *Health Serv Res* 13:305 Fall 1978.
5. Elesh, D. and P.T. Schollaert. Race and urban medicine: Factors affecting the distribution of physicians in Chicago. *J Health Soc Behav* 13:236 Sept. 1972.
6. Benham, L., A. Maurizi, and M.W. Reder. Migration, location, and remuneration of medical personnel: Physicians and dentists. *Rev Econ Stat* 50:332 Aug. 1968.
7. Yett, D.E. and F.A. Sloan. Migration patterns of recent medical school graduates. *Inquiry* 11:125 June 1974.
8. Ciocco, A. and I. Altman. *Medical Service Areas and Distances Traveled for Physician Care in Western Pennsylvania*. U.S. Public Health Service Monograph No. 19. Washington, DC: U.S. Government Printing Office, 1954.
9. Marden, P.G. A demographic and ecological analysis of the distribution of physicians in metropolitan America, 1960. *Am J Sociol* 72:290 Nov. 1966.
10. Navarro, V. The city and the region: A critical relationship in the distribution of health resources. *Am Behav Sci* 14:865 July–Aug 1971.
11. Anderson, J.G. Structural equation models: Their structural, reduced, and final forms. Paper presented at the 73rd annual meeting of the American Sociological Association, San Francisco, CA, Sept. 1978.
12. Begun, J.W. A causal model of the health care system: A replication. *J Health Soc Behav* 18:2 Mar. 1977.

Evaluations are typically conducted by employing randomized experimental or quasi-experimental designs. Inherent in this strategy is the selection or creation of an appropriate control group to compare with the group receiving the treatment. In the following, Larkey argues forcibly that an excellent control series can be constructed by developing process models or simulations of the organization under consideration. The obtained results can then be compared with forecasts of the model to assess the effects of the program. Larkey illustrates this approach by developing models of municipal revenues and expenditures.

Process models have advantages over simple experimental designs in that they have the potential for providing an extremely accurate estimate of what the effect would have been if the treatment had not occurred. However, caution should be exercised in employing these models—and for three reasons. First, many situations will not be as stable from year to year as the municipal budgets studied by Larkey. Many budget expenditures are mandated by law or are based heavily on historical precedent so that process models would be expected to be especially accurate in this case. Second, as with any time-series data, major historical events (e.g., wars, municipal bankruptcies) could covary with the beginning of the program being evaluated. If these events are not included in the model, serious errors in prediction could result, and the spurious effects would be attributed to the program. Finally, simulations provide only weak plausibility tests of the predictions of the model unless the model can be compared with a wide range of different kinds of data or with data collected over a very long series of trials (see Abelson, 1968*).

Perhaps one of the best potential uses for process models would be in conjunction with experimental or interrupted time-series designs. The process model could be used to make very accurate predictions for the future outcomes of the treatment series and the control series which could then be compared with the actual outcome. Such a design would have the advantage of the accuracy and reduced variance of a good process model, yet would be able more adequately to rule out historically co-occurring factors as plausible alternative explanations of the results.

*ABELSON, R. P. (1968) Simulation of Social Behavior, pp. 274-356 in G. Lindzey and E. Aronson (eds.) *Handbook of Social Psychology*, 2nd ed. (Vol. 2). Reading, MA: Addison-Wesley.

284

15

Process Models of Governmental Resource Allocation and Program Evaluation

Patrick D. Larkey

ABSTRACT

The General Revenue Sharing program poses problems for systematic evaluation that are similar to the problems posed by many public programs. Evaluation is very difficult when programs are not planned experiments and when program effects depend upon the discretionary responses of many individuals or organizations. The main difficulty is in knowing what would have happened without the program. Models of behavioral processes have an indispensable role in evaluating such programs. This paper considers the role of "process models" in program evaluation. It summarizes research on the impact of General Revenue Sharing on municipal fiscal behavior that used models of municipal resource allocation processes. Quasi-experimental research designs have been characterized as inherently inferior to experimental designs for program evaluation. There is no inherent inferiority. When we have good descriptive models of behavior, it is possible to evaluate programs rigorously without classic experimental research designs.

Introduction

The paucity of descriptive theories of behavioral processes, theories of how individuals and organizations *do* behave that are both plausible and accurate in prediction, is an important source of difficulty for the social scientist *qua* policy analyst. The effects of an increasing number of government programs (e.g., tax, regulatory, and transfer programs) are determined largely by the responses of individuals and organizations beyond the direct control of agencies initiating and operating the programs. For the analysis of such programs, models based on descriptive (as opposed to normative) theories of behavioral processes have an indispensable role. Descriptive or "process"

* Revised version of a paper presented at the annual meeting of the Public Choice Society, Roanoke, Virginia, April 1976. The empirical work was supported by the National Science Foundation, Research Applied to National Needs. I am indebted to John P. Crecine, William T. Stanbury, and others for assistance with this paper. All errors, unsupported assertions, value judgments, and labored explications of the obvious are my responsibility.

models are essential to forecast the consequences of alternative program designs *ex ante*. And where programs are not implemented as controlled experiments, process models are essential to generate the counterfactual hypotheses on "what would have happened without the program" that are essential to understand program effects *ex post*.

The primary purpose of this paper is to examine the role of descriptive models of behavioral processes in program evaluation. The first part of the paper discusses more general conceptual and methodological issues on the use of process models in evaluation. Experimental and nonexperimental approaches to evaluation are compared briefly.

The second part of the paper summarizes my research on the impact of the General Revenue Sharing (GRS) program[1] on the fiscal behavior of municipal governments. This research used models based on existing descriptive theory of municipal resource allocation processes to analyze the effects of the GRS program, and illustrates many of the general points from the first part of the paper. Given the focus of this paper on conceptual and methodological issues in program evaluation, my summary of the GRS research is limited to problem formulation, the models used in the research, and model appraisal. The substantive results on the effects of GRS from this research have been reported elsewhere (see Anton et al., 1975 and Larkey, 1975).

It is useful to view program evaluation as consisting of two main conceptual tasks. The first task is to determine program effects, to attribute "changes in the world" causally to the program. The second task is to relate identified program effects to normative criteria. Although much effort and attention have been lavished on the problems of devising normative criteria for evaluation, the description of program effects is the crux of evaluation research. Without an accurate description of program effects, effort on the normative task is, at best, a waste of time.

This paper is concerned primarily with the role of descriptive models in determining program effects. While this evaluative task is not value-free, as the analyst often makes implicit value judgments, its normative content is or should be small relative to its analytic content.[2]

This subject, process models in program evaluation, is important for two reasons. First, experimental designs are the vogue in evaluation research. The "experimental approach" to program evaluation is viewed universally as inherently more rigorous than alternative approaches, and hence superior to them. Alternative approaches are labelled "quasi-experimental". I will argue here that the potential for using models of behavioral processes in program evaluation has been underexploited and that such an approach is not inherently inferior to experimentation. The preferred approach can only be determined in the context of a particular evaluation research problem. Research designs must be problem-directed.

Second, models that are essentially normative have been and continue to be used extensively for research purposes that require descriptive models. The best examples

---

[1] The state and Local Fiscal Assistance Act of 1972.

[2] March (1972) and Nelson (1974) provide excellent discussions of the role of values in policy analysis.

are uses of models derived from neoclassical microeconomic theory for such tasks as predicting business firms' responses to tax and regulatory policies or predicting the responses of municipal governments to grant-in-aid programs. If these versions of *homo economicus* are reasonable approximations of the individuals and organizations they purport to describe and yield accurate predictions of observable behavior, then they are appropriate policy research tools. Although these models are widely used, I suspect that they are rarely appropriate and that the results from using them are frequently misleading.

This paper is not concerned with criticizing any particular misuses of normative models,[3] but I do suggest criteria and procedures for appraising models. These (or similar) criteria and procedures should be used to appraise models that purport, explicitly or implicitly, to be descriptive. Models are always imperfect approximations of behavioral processes, but it is only through successive explicit appraisals and conscious revisions that they can be improved.

Trends in Policy Analysis

Before turning to program evaluation, I want to examine briefly some trends in the "policy analysis tradition". These trends consist of periodic changes in the activities (and methods) that analysts of government programs and policies have perceived as feasible and useful. These changes can be interpreted, albeit narrowly, as adaptations to the experience of confronting a difficult task environment with inadequate tools, particularly descriptive theories.

Richard R. Nelson (1974: 386) has observed that "the scriptures of the policy analysis tradition have been marked by a shifting of emphasis from before the fact analysis, to evaluation of programs *ex post*, to deliberate experimental development of policy." Each shift has been taken in response to experential feedback, often negative, and reflects: (a) a heightened appreciation of the formidable complexity of "real" policy problems vis-à-vis existing tools for policy analysis; (b) a reduction in the level of policy analysts' aspirations for impact on policy formulation processes where timing and magnitude of impact are key attributes of the aspiration level; and (c) a new focus of analytic attention (or "analytic strategy") in a continuing quest by policy analysts for a substantive role in policy formulation. These shifts in "scripture" have taken us from the euphoric pursuit of Planning, Programming, and Budgeting Systems (PPBS) in the 1960s to the carefully qualified program "experiments" of the 1970s.

It is important to note that each shift in emphasis has resulted in an analytic strategy that relies less than its predecessor on the existence of "usable" theories of behavioral processes—theories on how individuals and organizations do behave that can be used to systematically forecast responses to alternative program designs.

The extreme difficulty of providing accurate forecasts, particularly when the variables of interest are the outputs of behavioral systems, is a persuasive explanation for the shift from "before the fact analysis" to "evaluation of programs *ex post*". PPBS is an ambitious and conceptually seductive scheme for institutionalized, comprehensive

---

[3] For one such criticism, see Larkey (1975).

policy analysis. It is voracious in its forecasting and hence, descriptive theoretical, demands. Our ability to satisfy these demands today is only slightly better than it was in 1960 at the advent of PPBS.

The analytic task of predicting observables can have unpleasant characteristics: predictions which are sufficiently specific to be of interest to policymakers are often demonstrably wrong. Even nonexperts, not fully appreciative of forecasting difficulties, can often see prediction errors.[4] *Ex post* explanation is a much safer haven for analysts than *ex ante* prediction, and *ex post* explanation is the object of more recent strategies for policy analysts.

"Evaluation of programs *ex post*" and "deliberate experimental development of policy" are closely related. The distinction between the two is not always sharp, but rests on the degree to which the program experience is preplanned to facilitate understanding of the experience *ex post*. Experimentation, which Kaplan (1964: 147) describes as "only experience carefully planned in advance," is an approach to program evaluation. It is an approach that, through careful planning of the program experience, permits some substitution of the logic of classical experimentation for theory of behavioural processes in analyzing experience. To the extent that two groups can be made equivalent in all respects, except program participation, we can determine program effects without understanding the behaviour of either group.

The ethical, political, and technical difficulties in pursuing a social experimentation strategy have received extensive comment (Rivlin and Timpane, 1975; Taylor and Vertinsky, 1975; and Rivlin 1971), but there is an even more fundamental limitation to the strategy, a limitation to the extent to which the logic of experimentation can substitute for theories of behavioral processes in policy analysis. All evaluation, experimental or nonexperimental, is directed at *understanding* a program experience *ex post*. It is important to recognize that such *understanding*, even if it is absolutely conclusive about the past, is a necessary, but not sufficient, basis for policy choices because such choices require forecasts. *Prediction based on existing descriptive theory is a burden which policy analysts advising on program choices with future consequences cannot evade by altering strategic philosophy or research methods.*

Social experimentation, an evaluative strategy and the latest "scripture" in the policy analysis tradition, should be viewed as an opportunity to garner the knowledge of behavioral processes and data required to develop and estimate models for forecasting. Experiments should not be viewed as necessary and sufficient means for testing programs to support "go/no-go" decisions on large scale versions of the experimental program forms. It is absurd to extrapolate naively the results from a rigorous program experiment into an uncontrolled, dimly understood future. Such

---

[4] When forecasts are complex and include many years, such as the forecasts often made by cost-benefit analysts, the accuracy of the forecasts is usually never appraised. The appraisal can be technically difficult; and the persons best qualified to do the appraisal, those who made the forecasts, have no incentive to do the appraisal. Also, the benefits from appraising forecasts *ex post* are largely improved forecasting capabilities. There are no "direct policy payoffs" from appraising stale forecasts and therefore, no funding for the work. One excellent appraisal of cost-benefit forecasts in the area of water resource projects (Haveman, 1972) indicates very significant, and systematically biased, forecasting errors. These errors in forecasts working with physical systems with known technologies do not augur accuracy for forecasts working with "black box," behavioral systems.

extrapolations are particularly absurd if time and variables that are dependent on it were critical controls in arguing for the validity of the experimental trial.

In the next section I discuss in more detail the experimental and nonexperimental approaches for assessing program effects. The principal difference between the two approaches is in the type of analogy used to make the required counterfactual arguments.

Counterfactual Arguments and Analogies

In his *The Principles of Mathematics*, Bertrand Russell noted the importance of counterfactual thinking

> Rational choice depends upon the construction of two causal series, only one of which can be made to exist . . . thus all statesmanship, and all rational conduct of life, is based upon the frivolous historical game, in which we discuss what the world would be if Cleopatra's nose had been half an inch longer.[5]

Success in program evaluation depends on our ability to construct a causal series that is counterfactual. We must compare "what would have happened" with "what did happen" to determine what the effects of a program have been. Since we can never know a counterfactual state with certainty, we must argue through analogies to attribute effects causally to programs.

One form of analogy for evaluation is the "control group analogy" of classical experimental design. In a perfect experiment, the "control group" is identical to the "treatment group" in every respect save one, program participation (treatment). The control group is a physical analogue of the treatment group. By observing and comparing the behavior of both groups over the same time period in the same context we infer that behavioral differences are attributable to the program (treatment). *Ceteris paribus* conditions are ensured through controls in the perfect experimental design (i.e., the analogy is perfect); and the evaluative inferences on programmatic effects are incontrovertible because no plausible alternative causal explanations exist.

Because perfect experimental design is unattainable in any applied setting, even when we are working with the best understood physical systems, we use approximate methods such as the random selection of participants from the population of interest and random assignment of those participants to control and treatment groups. These methods are intended to strengthen the analogy, and hence, the inferences from comparisons of the groups. For evaluation research, the behaviour of the control group is the counterfactual causal series: "How the treatment group would have behaved without the program."

The control group analogy is an extremely useful, if not essential, analytic tool for determining program effects *ex post* when the "process physics" of the program participants' behavior are poorly understood. This is, of course, the usual circumstance in the social sciences. The control group analogy, when feasible, enables the researcher to focus on behavioral outcomes and to ignore underlying structure and parameters of behavior; the participants can be treated as "black boxes."

---

[5] Quoted in H. A. Simon, *Models of Man* (New York: John Wiley, 1957), p. 4.

The principal advantage of the control group analogy is evaluation research that can determine program effects in spite of ignorance about behavioral processes. This is an advantage only as long as experiments are viewed as means of furthering our understanding of what is inside the "black boxes" (Campbell, 1970; Quade, 1975). Information on program effects of an absolute sort (e.g., the program achieved X, Y, and Z) is inherently less useful in improving future programs than information on why programs produce particular effects or information on program performance relative to other program designs (Quade, 1975: 225–226).

The principal disadvantage of the control group analogy for analyzing government programs is the infrequency with which it can be used effectively. The analogy is totally infeasible for evaluating many government programs because the programs are implemented in ways (e.g., universally or nonrandomly) that make it impossible to identify a plausible control group. The counterfactual arguments for evaluation, when the control group analogy is not feasible to make them, impose the same theoretical demands as *ex ante* prediction with the added twist that the events being described never occur. *Ex ante* forecasts of factual events can be checked through observation, but we can never know if counterfactual hypotheses are correct.

The alternative analogy for making the counterfactual arguments required to understand program effects is a model or symbolic analogue of the behavior of program participants. The past behavior of participants is crucial in developing and estimating such models, and so I will refer to them as "historical analogies".

An ideal form of the historical analogy is conceivable just as it was for the control group analogy. In this form we would possess a "perfect" model of a behavioral process developed from past behaviour. This model would be capable of replicating exactly the behavior of the real system under all conditions, including the conditions (e.g., no treatment) required for counterfactual arguments in evaluation research. The analogy would be perfect because the model would incorporate all factors, internal and external to the process, that might affect behavior, thus precluding plausible alternative causal explanations for observed behavioral differences (program effects).

Like the perfect form of the control group analogy, the perfect behavioral model (historical analogy) is unattainable, and we must use approximate methods. These are the methods for iteratively building and testing symbolic models of behavioral processes. To the extent that a model captures important elements of the processes it purports to represent and is able to replicate observed outcomes of the "real" process in the period prior to the treatment (program) under a variety of conditions, including conditions which approximate those the treatment (program) brings about, we can have confidence in its use as an historical analogy for making counterfactual arguments.

The most common application of the historical analogy has been a static comparison using a single group, of behavior at one point in time prior to a program with behavior at a point in time after the program is in effect. These are pretest–posttest or before–after research designs that are the social sciences' equivalents of the Charles Atlas body-building advertisements. The literature on quasi-experimental research designs (Campbell and Stanley, 1966; Caporaso and Roos, 1973) is generally (and correctly) critical of the weak research designs (e.g., pretest-posttest, one-shot case studies) that have been the dominant instruments for program evaluation in the past. This literature describes several more sophisticated forms of the historical analogy (e.g., the "cross lag panel design" and the "interrupted time-series design") and research designs that attempt to merge the historical and control group analogies (e.g., the "control-series design"). The literature's prescription for the malady of weak research designs in program evaluation is stronger research design, particularly designs which use the control group analogy.

There are two problems with this literature and its prescription. First, the literature is heavily and unnecessarily biased in favor of the control group analogy. Applications of the historical analogy are characterized as inherently inferior and their use is recommended only when use of the control group analogy is impossible. Yet, there is no *inherent* inferiority. The choice of the form of analogy for the evaluation of any particular program must rest on which analogy can be operationalized in the strongest fashion and on coarser considerations such as cooperation of policymakers, data availability, costs, and time. There are numerous threats to the internal and external validity of experimental trials just as there are numerous threats to the validity of models as approximations of behavioral processes. The validity of an analogy is, in either case, a matter for judgment and a matter of degree.

Second, the literature's treatment of research design over-emphasizes methodological mechanics, particularly the use of classical statistics to approximate the logic of experimentation. It under-emphasizes problem formulation (i.e., the purpose of the research design). Specifically, there is little or no explicit recognition of the fact that the statistical models employed in the various time-series designs are being used to construct the counterfactual argument, i.e., "what the individuals or organizations would have done without the program."

The statistical models that are the basis of quasi-experimental designs are being utilized as analogues of the processes generating pre-treatment, post-treatment data. But the models are not evaluated as analogues of process because they are not recognized as such. The only test of a model's correspondence with process in procedures such as the "Double-Mood Test" or the "Walker-Lev Test" [Caporaso and Roos, 1973: 28–29] is implicit in the standard procedures (e.g., t-test and F-test) used for testing hypotheses on differences in the pre-treatment and post-treatment periods. To the extent that goodness-of-fit is poor (i.e., the linear regression line(s) in each period is a poor analogue of process and standard errors are large), the tests are less able to show statistically significant treatment effects (i.e., differences in the level and slope of the lines in each period).

When historical analogies are used to make counterfactual arguments for evaluation, they are theories of process regardless of the form they take (e.g., static, pretest–posttest comparisons, simple extrapolations of trends, or detailed models of behavior). They should be appraised as theories of process. There are real benefits which can accrue from explicit recognition of the theoretical requirements in making counterfactual arguments for evaluation. One important benefit is more and better theory. And further, theory of processes that is developed in an evaluation context can be used predictively for the *ex ante* exploration of the consequences of alternative program forms. At the present time, more effort is being devoted in evaluation research to methods that evade theoretical requirements than to using the theory we have and to improving our theoretical base.

The rest of this paper summarizes research that provided empirical evidence on the effects of General Revenue Sharing on municipal fiscal behavior. The research exemplifies most of the important, albeit abstract, points made in the foregoing discussion. GRS is an excellent illustrative program because most of the more difficult conceptual and methodological problems that it poses for systematic analysis are not idiosyncratic to the program, but generic. The same problems are posed ·by a large number of government programs, particularly programs whose effects depend critically upon the discretionary responses of individuals or organizations.

The General Revenue Sharing Program

In providing financial assistance to "subordinate" units of government (e.g., states and cities), the U.S. Federal Government has traditionally relied on programs designed to retain a significant measure of federal control over the expenditure. These have been programs that: (1) require extensive planning and application efforts on the part of governments seeking to participate; (2) require periodic, often annual, reporting and reapplication for continued participation; (3) limit participation to a subset of all units applying, with the selection of participants nominally based on such factors as "need" and "quality of local, plans;" (4) require a matching "cash" or "in-kind" contribution from participating units; (5) specify limited functional areas for expenditure reflecting *national* (as opposed to *local*) priorities; and (6) are subject to annual review by Congress and the Federal Executive.

The General Revenue Sharing program is significantly different from traditional program forms. It provided U.S. $30.2 billion in general financial assistance to all units of "general purpose" government (e.g., states, counties, municipalities, townships, and Indian Tribal Councils), over the five-year period, 1972–76. Participation in GRS is universal and automatic for units designated as "General Purpose." The amount of money that participants receive is determined on the basis of fixed formulae. The planning and reporting requirements associated with GRS are minimal. Recipient governments are not required to "match" from their own funds the amount of GRS support that they receive. Although the GRS legislation does specify "priority expenditure categories," these are broad and leave substantial, if not total, discretion in the disposition of GRS funds to state and local officials.

The differences between GRS and traditional forms of assistance point to a fundamental conflict in the design of federal assistance programs:

> Loose guidelines or controls may allow state and local governments to waste the money or spend it according to their own, rather than national priorities. Tight guidelines, on the other hand, might stifle local initiative, impose high administrative costs, and lower the effectiveness of services.[6]

GRS can be viewed as a federal experiment with loose guidelines and controls that

---

[6] Edward R. Fried et al., *Setting National Priorities: The 1974 Budget* (Washington, D.C.: The Brookings Institution, 1973), p. 35.

shifts much of the discretion on the expenditure of federal funds from federal officials to state and local officials. Much of the controversy on GRS has been centered on whether state and local governments have "spent" the money "responsibly." Of course, what constitutes a "responsible" expenditure is largely a matter of taste.[7]

Problem Formulation

The central empirical problem for evaluation research on GRS is to determine what impact GRS has had on the revenue and expenditure patterns of recipient units of government. Before we can even begin to address the many interesting normative questions about GRS (e.g., are outcomes (expenditures) resulting from GRS responsible? desirable? preferable to alternative uses?), we must first describe GRS outcomes (fiscal effects) empirically.

Although normative issues of "second-order" empirical issues with obvious normative implications such as redistributive effects are often the dominant concerns of policy analysts and policymakers, there is often, as in the case of GRS, a large amount of descriptive work required before these concerns can be addressed effectively. For example, the redistributive implications of GRS are the object of great interest. The usual mode of analysis in this area is to compare the distribution of GRS funds with the tax contributions and socioeconomic characteristics of recipients. If "poor" jurisdictions receive relatively larger GRS allocations than "rich" jurisdictions, the inference might be that GRS is "progressive" in its distributional impact. The problem with this analysis is that grants to governments are not the same as grants to people, and "poor" governments may find highly regressive uses for their GRS funds while "rich" governments may find very progressive uses for theirs. Until the changes in revenue and expenditure patterns causally attributable to GRS and the redistributive implications of these changes are specified, research on the redistributive implications of GRS will be inconclusive.

Problem formulation is a major issue in appraising research on GRS. One source of difficulty for many concerned with evaluating GRS, researchers and policymakers alike, was a fixation on the question, "how did they (viz., state and local officials) spend the money?" The question suggests an accounting approach to the research in which we trace federal dollars from receipt to disbursement. This approach that was taken in the official reporting associated with the program, and only slightly refined by some survey research projects on GRS, is not useful because of the "displacement phenomenon."

It is important to distinguish between "nominal effects" (e.g., how funds are accounted for) and "net effects" (e.g., substantive changes in allocation patterns). Revenue-sharing dollars are similar to funds from local sources (e.g., revenues from a general property tax) in most important respects; they can be spent for many of the same things by the same people at the same time in the same way. The pie to be sliced is simply larger. Recipients can account for the expenditure of GRS Funds in

---

[7] Some GRS expenditures, particularly those for recreation facilities (e.g., golf courses and tennis courts) have been criticized as "frivolous." There are more extreme examples including the use of GRS funds by the city fathers of Heidelberg, Mississippi, to relocate a confederate war memorial more centrally (see *Ann Arbor News*, May 4, 1975).

one category of expenditure, say Police Protection, without increasing their expenditures on that category at all. The GRS Funds simply displace funds from local sources that would have otherwise gone to Police Protection. The displaced funds may then be used for any other local expenditure purpose or tax reductions.

Given the ease with which funds can be moved from account to account, counterfactual arguments are the only persuasive means of attributing changes in municipal revenue and expenditure patterns to GRS. We must generate counterfactual hypotheses on what revenue and expenditure patterns would have been without GRS for comparison with patterns that actually occur with GRS.

Several factors other than the displacement phenomena complicate the analysis of the program's effects. The program's universal application (in terms of governmental units) precludes the use of a control group analogy. Some form of historical analogy must be used. The program's effects depend critically upon the discretionary responses of recipient units of government. The recipients are many (approximately 38,000 units) and heterogeneous (i.e., New York City and Portales, New Mexico would seem to have little in common). The behavioral units are nominally complex. There are many individuals and organizational sub-units with a hand in fiscal decision-making. And there are many revenue and expenditure variables that make up the "pattern" for each recipient (i.e., thirty to seventy-five expenditure variables for each city). And finally, GRS is a small proportion of state and local expenditures, however defined. This makes it difficult to attribute effects causally to GRS because there are usually more plausible competing explanations for small changes than for large, dramatic changes.

Fortunately, the analysis is facilitated by several other factors. Crucial variables that indicate effects are routinely and consistently measured; and they are expressed numerically. There are public archives (e.g., budget and audit documents) that contain extensive histories on crucial variables and most important, there is good (viz., plausible in its narrative and accurate in its predictions) descriptive theory on governmental behavior in resource allocation decision-making, particularly for one important class of recipients—municipal governments.[8]

In the next section I present descriptive models of municipal resource allocation that have been developed and used as tools for the analysis of GRS. These models are analogies based on a theory of municipal resource allocation behavior, and estimated from historical data. They are used to estimate what municipal governments would have done without GRS. After presenting the models, my discussion will focus on their adequacy for the research purpose.

Expenditure and Revenue Models

For analysis of the impact of GRS on municipal revenue and expenditure patterns, four models of municipal resource allocation processes[9] were developed, estimated

---

[8] John P. Crecine (1967, 1968, 1969) and others.
[9] The models exist as FORTRAN programs and the verbal description that follows is simplified. The flowchart for one of the models, CPRI, in Appendix A is a better description.

for five municipalities,[10] and tested in several ways. Although distinct in their specifications, the models are very similar in their theoretical underpinnings; they incorporate a "bureaucratic process" view of municipal resource allocation. Each model consists of a set of linear equations embodying a change rule (a "basic predictive assertion") and a "balancing routine." The basic predictive assertion is used to make an initial prediction of what the change in expenditures will be for any particular functional account (e.g., Police/Personnel) from one year to the next. The balance routine compares the sum of initial predictions for all functional accounts in each year with a constraint on total expenditures (available revenue) for that year and revises the predicted changes to achieve a balance. Within models as applied to all cities, the basic predictive assertion is identical in variable(s) and mathematical form for all functional accounts. For application to cities, the number of equations in each model varies according to the number of functional accounts by city. The basic predictive assertions vary by account within cities and between cities in the empirically estimated parameter values.

Constant-Proportion-of-Base (CPB)

This model predicts that this year's expenditure for any functional account will be equal to a constant times last year's expenditure for the same functional account. For example, if the Police Department spent U.S.$1,000,000 last year on personnel and the constant growth increment, empirically estimated, is 5.321 %, CPB's initial prediction of this year's expenditure level would be U.S.$1,053,210. The "balance routine" would revise this prediction in accordance with the comparison between the sum of initial predictions for all functional accounts and available revenue.[11]

The basic predictive equation is:

$$EXP^*_{ijk} = b_{ij} EXP_{ijk-1}$$

where

EXP^*_{ijk} = Predicted expenditure for function "i," account "j" in year "k,"

EXP_{ijk-1} = Actual expenditure for function "i," account "j" in year "k—1,"

b_{ij} = Empirically estimated parameter for function "i," account "j." (Estimated in basic predictive equation.)[12]

Constant-Proportion-of-the-Revenue Increment (CPRI)

This model predicts that this year's expenditure for any functional account will be equal to last year's expenditure plus a constant proportion of the revenue increment

---

[10] The cities studied are: (1) Albuquerque, New Mexico; (2) Ann Arbor, Michigan; (3) Cincinnati, Ohio; (4) Detroit, Michigan; and (5) Worcester, Massachusetts.

[11] Each of the models uses the same balance routine in revising initial predictions although this will not be noted in the description of the next three models. For cities in which the analysis indicated no change in local revenue collection efforts with GRS, actual (observed) revenue levels were used. For cities in which revenue collection efforts were affected by GRS, separate models were used to forecast what local revenues would have been without GRS.

[12] All parameters were estimated using ordinary least squares techniques with the line (plane) constrained to pass through the origin. These procedures are described in K. A. Brownlee, *Statistical Theory in Science and Engineering* (New York: John Wiley 1960), pp. 298–302.

(decrement). For example, if the Police Department spent U.S. $1,000,000 on personnel last year, total available revenue for the city government increased by U.S. $1,000,000 from last year, and the empirically estimated proportion of the revenue increment for Police/Personnel is 17.321%, the initial predicted expenditure would be U.S. $1,173,210. The basic predictive equation is:

$$\text{EXP}_{ijk}^* = \text{EXP}_{ijk-1} + b_{ij}(\text{REV}_k - \text{REV}_{k-1})$$

where

EXP_{ijk}^* and EXP_{ijk-1} are defined as above,

REV_k = Total revenue available in year "k,"

b_{ij} = Empirically estimated parameter for function "i," account "j." (Estimated in $\text{EXP}_{ijk}^j - \text{EXP}_{ijk-1} = b_{ij}(\text{REV}_k - \text{REV}_{k-1})$).

Constant-Growth — Revenue-Increment (CGRI)

This model predicts that this year's expenditure for any functional account will be equal to a constant times last year's expenditure plus a constant proportion of the revenue increment (decrement). For example, if last year's expenditure for Police/Personnel was U.S. $1,000,000, total revenue increased by U.S. $1,000,000, and the parameters for growth on base—last year's expenditure—and proportion of the revenue increment are 5 and 15%, respectively, the initial predicted expenditure for Police/Personnel would be U.S. $1,200,000. The basic predictive equation is:

$$\text{EXP}_{ijk}^* = b_{ij} \text{EXP}_{ijk-1} + c_{ij}(\text{REV}_k - \text{REV}_{k-1}^{\square})$$

where

EXP_{ijk}^*, EXP_{ijk-1}, and REV_k are defined as above, b_{ij} and c_{ij} are empirically estimated parameters (estimated in the basic predictive equation).

Dollar-Change—Fiscal Pressure (DCFP)

This model predicts that this year's expenditure for any functional account will be equal to last year's expenditure plus a constant times the product of the proportional change in revenue (i.e., the difference between this year's revenue level and last year's level divided by last year's level) and last year's expenditure for the same functional account. For example, if the city's revenue increased by 10%, last year's expenditure for Police/Personnel was U.S. $1,000,000, and the empirically estimated parameter is 1.5, the initial predicted expenditure would be U.S. $1,150,000.

The basic predictive equation is:

$$\text{EXP}_{ijk}^* = \text{EXP}_{ijk-1} + b_{ij}[(\text{REV}_k - \text{REV}_{k-1})/\text{REV}_{k-1}] \text{EXP}_{ijk-1}$$

where

EXP_{ijk}^*, EXP_{ijk-1}, and REV_k are defined as above,

b_{ij} = Empirically estimated parameter. Estimated in:

$$\text{EXP}_{ijk} - \text{EXP}_{ijk-1} = b_{ij}[(\text{REV}_k - \text{REV}_{k-1})/\text{REV}_{k-1}] \text{EXP}_{ijk-1}$$

Revenue Models

For analyzing GRS fiscal effects, local revenue[13] can be viewed simply as another "expenditure category." By using GRS funds to support functions normally supported by local general revenues and by then using the "freed" local general revenues to reduce collections from local revenue sources (e.g., property tax), local officials can substitute GRS for local revenues. This "displacement effect" may be direct in the form of reduced tax levies or reduced collection on other revenue sources (e.g., fines and fees, service charges to other funds, etc.) that results in an absolute decrease in revenue receipts from local sources. Or the displacement effect may be more subtle, taking the form of averted increases in local revenue collection efforts (e.g., increased tax levies) that would have been required, or at least attempted, if GRS funds had not been available.

Because the expenditure models specified above take the levels of local revenue as an exogenous variable, the first step in the analysis was to determine what the levels of local revenue would have been in GRS years without GRS. It was determined that for three of the five cities, GRS had no impact on levels of local revenue because either they were at statutory limits on collection and there was no reduction (e.g., in millage rates) or they had had a recent large tax rate increase and there was no reduction in local collection effort. For two of the five cities, Albuquerque and Worcester, it was determined that GRS had affected levels of local revenues, and revenue models were developed and used to project what local revenues would have been. Unlike the expenditure models, the revenue models were specified uniquely for cities because there are important differences among cities in sources of revenue used and in decision-making on revenue levels.

The regression model used for estimating the year-to-year changes in Albuquerque revenue is:

$$\Delta REV_k = b(INF_{k-1} \cdot REV_{k-1})$$

where

ΔREV_k = Estimated change in revenues from year "$k-1$" to year "k" ($\Delta REV_k = REV_k - REV_{k-1}$),

REV_k = Total general fund revenue in year "k,"

INF_{k-1} = Inflation factor calculated from the U.S. Department of Commerce's State and Local Government Price Deflator.

The statistical results from estimating b are:

Coefficient	Equation ($n = 10$)
$b = 2.2682$	$F = 231.4$
$SE_b = 0.14911$	$SE = 420380$
$t_b = 15.21$	$R^2 = 0.86442$

The equation and coefficient are significant at the 0.0001 level. The actual revenue

[13]."Local revenue" is defined as the sum of General Fund expenditures from all but federal sources. This definition includes as "revenue" for any particular year: (1) all receipts from local revenue sources except those held as unappropriated surplus; (2) all realized deficits; (3) revenues from state and other local governments; and (4) surpluses carried forward from prior years.

levels (e.g., the solid time-series line) and one-period forecasts using the model (e.g., the dashed time-series line) are shown graphically in Fig. 1. The effect of GRS on local revenues, the gap between the two time-series lines to the right of the vertical dashed line, is obvious.

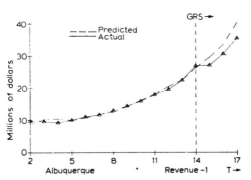

Fig. 1. Albuquerque.

The model used to estimate Worcester revenues is

$$REV_k = a(INF_{k-1} \cdot REV_{k-1}) + b(CERTREV_{k-1}) + c(DIFFAV_k) + d(MUNREV_{k-1})$$

where

REV_k = Estimated general revenue in year "k,"

REV_{k-1} = Actual revenue in year "$k-1$,"

INF_{k-1} = Lagged inflation factor calculated from the Department of U.S. Commerce's State and Local Government Price Deflator,

$CERTREV_{k-1}$ = Certified state shared revenues from year "$k-1$,"

$DIFFAV_k$ = Change in state certified assessed valuation from year "$k-1$" to year "k,"

$MUNREV_{k-1}$ = Municipal receipts (other than property taxes) from local sources in year "$k-1$,"

"a," "b," "c," and "d" are the empirically estimated coefficients.

The statistical results from estimating this equation are:

Coefficients		Equation ($n = 18$)
$a = 0.88581$	$c = 0.26710$	$F = 12525$
$SE_a = 0.0494$	$SE_c = 0.116$	$SE = 1,025,400$
$t_a = 17.94$	$t_c = 2.30$	$R^2 = 0.99798$
$b = 0.40412$	$d = 0.21305$	
$SE_b = 0.12044$	$SE_d = 0.115$	
$t_b = 03.3552$	$t_d = 1.85$	

The equation and "a" are significant at the 0.0001 level. "b," "c," and "d" are significant at the 0.0047, 0.0373, and 0.0862 levels, respectively. The results from using the model are shown graphically in Fig. 2 and again the effect of GRS on local revenues is obvious, if not as dramatic as in Albuquerque.[14]

The next three sections of this paper are concerned with appraising the expenditure models given above. The revenue models will not be considered further here because their role in the research is much more limited than that of the expenditure models. In the next section I present criteria for model development and testing. Subsequent sections discuss one of these criteria, plausibility, more fully.

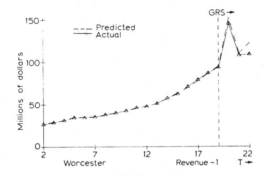

Fig. 2. Worcester.

Criteria for Model Development and Testing

Given the general purpose for the models of generating the complex, counterfactual hypotheses on revenue and expenditure patterns for the analysis of GRS, three criteria guided model development: Explicitness, Feasibility, and Plausibility.

Explicitness

Explicitness is an important virtue for models, particularly models used to make counterfactual arguments, because our ability to appraise them is a function of their explicitness. Where implict models yield explicit predictions, we can infer model quality from appraising the predictions. But where the model outputs are counterfactual arguments that can never be checked against experience, implicit models make appraisal an impossible task. Explicit models such as the computer-based "simulations" presented above are accessible to other researchers and permit direct appraisal, regardless of their inadequacies deriving from the conceptual and methodological limitations of those who build and use them.

James G. March (1972: 413) emphasized the importance of model appraisal, and hence the explicitness criterion, when he stated that "the major claim to legitimacy by a social scientist is the claim that his procedures systematically evaluate the quality of his models and, thus, that his speculations are good ones." The models used by

---

[14] The "blip" in the first GRS year for Worcester is due to a state-ordained change in fiscal year timing that resulted in an eighteen-month budget period during the transition.

various researchers to understand the fiscal impact of GRS varied considerably on the explicitness criterion, and therefore, in the extent to which they are appraisable and "legitimate." The topic is sufficiently important to warrant a brief digression.

Surveys are the best example of the use of implicit models in GRS research. The model of what would have happened without GRS is presumed to exist in the minds of respondents, usually city officials or others in a position to "know." By providing stimuli in the form of questions (e.g., if GRS funds had not been available in FY 1974, would expenditures for function X have been more, the same, or less? If less, how much less (in dollars)?), survey methods evoke responses from model(s) that the respondents hold implicit. The burden of analysis is shifted almost entirely onto the respondents.

It is very difficult, if not impossible, in a survey format, whether personal interview, mailed questionnaire, or some combination of the two, to evaluate the quality (meaning?) of responses because there is no comparative benchmark independent of the technique. Questions are sometimes included to gather data on characteristics of respondents (e.g., the respondent is a thirty-two year old, male, Jewish (orthodox) finance director who has been on the job for five years, holds a masters degree in accounting, belongs to the Municipal Finance Officers Association, votes Democratic most of the time, and believes that GRS is a good, eight on a scale of ten, program), that may be correlated with the types of models the respondent holds and the way he applies them in an interview or questionnaire setting and may bias responses. There are, however, no "unobtrusive" benchmarks[15],against which responses can be checked and no methods, particularly in extensive survey efforts, for exploring sensibly the model(s) the respondent holds and the way that they are applied.

Where the opinion or attitudes of human subjects are the object of research, surveys, in some form at some level of intensity, are the appropriate, perhaps only, research approach. Where the behavior of individuals or collectivities is the object of research, there are some fundamental problems associated with the use of survey techniques. The correspondence between opinions and behavior, whether it is the behavior (past, present, or future) of the respondent or the behavior of some "chunk" of the world that we are asking the respondent to describe, is an empirical question. Human perceptions are notoriously affective in orientation and constrained by individual cognitive abilities. The fiscal effects of GRS in most cities of any size and organizational complexity is a rather complex puzzle that requires a longitudinal perspective and a model of what might have been. In a survey for ascertaining GRS fiscal effects, local officials, who vary greatly in their affective attachments and cognitive skills and who tend to be immersed in the day-to-day details of an often complex environment, are asked on the spur of the moment to speculate on a complex and hypothetical problem. Relying on the models that are apt to be evoked and applied in such a setting for the measurement of GRS fiscal effects is, at best, a risky research strategy.

A great deal of effort is devoted in the application of survey methods to ensure a "representative sample." The logical and statistical apparatus for these efforts is

---

15 See Eugene J. Webb et al. (1966) for an interesting and entertaining discussion of these issues.

impressive, if not conclusive, and discussions of "validity" tend to be dominated by sampling considerations (e.g., the extent to which randomization holds in sample selection and response) from which our ability to generalize on the survey results purportedly flows. Users of survey results, particularly those not privy to the mystiques and totems of the profession, should occasionally be reminded that there is little comfort in the ability to generalize on results with many interpretations. Sampling considerations are necessary, but not sufficient, to the "validity" of survey results.

The strength of survey research for a problem such as the analysis of GRS fiscal effects is that when a question is asked, generally some answer is given. The weakness of the approach is in the reliance on implicit models that are apt to be uneven in quality and are not accessible to the researcher (or others) for appraisal.

Feasibility

A second criterion for model development is feasibility. For a model to be feasible for this research, we had to be able to specify and estimate it with limited research resources for a number of city governments. These governments were heterogeneous. In asserting that such a modeling activity was even possible, we were contending that much of the diversity among cities can either be modeled or safely ignored in the determination of short-run changes in revenue and expenditure patterns. This contention stemmed directly from our conceptualization of municipal resource allocation processes; and, as we shall see in the next section, this contention was largely supported by the results from testing the models.

The diversity among these city governments, particularly diversity in the structure and content of their financial decision processes, did force some compromises in model construction. Specifically, the models developed and employed were much more abstract than they would have been if our task had been to model a single city or a set of cities with striking similarities in their financial decision processes. While city governments face many of the same problems in financial decision-making and there are a great many similarities in the methods they employ to solve these problems and in the solutions they reach, there is also a great deal of diversity in the specifics of financial decision-making among the five cities studied (Larkey, 1975: 114–120).

The decision not to specify different functional forms for different cities and for particular functional accounts within cities, except through the estimation of "free parameters," was an important one. In retaining the simple, general models, a lot of detailed knowledge acquired about the resource allocation processes in particular cities was essentially discarded. Given the research task, however, the judgment was that the gains in model performance (i.e., form and accuracy of the counterfactual arguments) from more detailed models would be marginal and would not justify the increased costs and added model complexity. The trade-off between the *feasibility* criterion and our third criterion, *plausibility*, was real.

Plausibility

The plausibility of the expenditure models specified above is a function of the responses to two questions (Crecine, 1969: 111): "(1) Does the model yield outcomes similar to the real-world phenomena it purports to describe?; and (2) Does the model reach these decisions using the same mechanisms as the corresponding real-world decision system?" For model testing, the first question "implies a comparison between time-series data (decisions) generated by the model (computer program) and data generated by the real decision system (municipal government)." And the second question requires a comparison between the structure—content and sequence of decision points—of the model (computer program) and the structure of the real decision system (municipal government).

Although there is no one-to-one (isomorphic) correspondence between the decision mechanisms in the expenditure models and the decision mechanisms in municipal resource allocation processes, the models do capture key characteristics (i.e., the models are homomorphic representations) of the "real" decision processes. The models are more "reflective" than "simulative" of the underlying processes in that they are simplistic, summarizing extensive, complex processes in a very parsimonious fashion; Occam's razor was well honed. There was no attempt to follow Crecine's lead in establishing detailed correspondence between models and decision processes[16] because the primary objective of the research was not to expound and test a positive theory of municipal resource allocation processes, but to use extant theory to analyze the fiscal effects of GRS. The specifics of the interactions among sub-units within a municipal government are important for theoretical statement, but they are not important for research on GRS except as they alter collective outcomes; for the analysis of GRS, we are not very interested in how departmental budget requests changed *per se*, except as a step in determining expenditure outcomes. As specified, the models are consistent with several underlying causal structures. For precise theoretical exposition this is not desirable.[17] In developing models as practical tools for the analysis of GRS, however, it is essential.

These qualifications on the nature of the correspondence between the models and real municipal resource allocation processes do not, however, excuse the models from appraisal as analogues of process because statistical goodness-of-fit is a necessary, but insufficient, basis for appraising models. As Herbert Simon (1968) has noted:

> It is well known—at least among mathematical statisticians—that the theory of statistical tests gives us no real help in choosing between an approximate generalization and an invalid one. By imbedding our generalization in a probability model, we can ask: If this model describes the real "facts" what is the probability that data would have occurred at least as deviant from the generalization as those actually observed? If this probability is very low—below the magic one percent level, say—we are still left with two alternatives: the generalization has been disconfirmed, and is invalid; or the generalization represents only a first approximation to the true, or "exact" state of affairs . . . Just as statistically significant deviations of data from a generalization should not always, or usually, lead us to abandon the generalization, so we should not be unduly impressed by excellent fits of data to theory. *More important than whether* the data fit is why they fit—i.e., what components in the theory are critical to the goodness to fit. To answer this question, we must analyse the internal structure of the theory.

---

[16] Crecine decomposed the budgetary decision process into three parts: (1) Departments; (2) the Mayor's Office; and (3) the Council. See Crecine (1969).

[17] See Lee W. Gregg and Herbert A. Simon (1972) for a superb discussion and illustration of this fundamental point.

Description and prediction are complementary, reciprocally informing intellectual activities in the context of constructing and using models for analysis. Research purpose determines the appropriate degree of emphasis on description or prediction in model specification and in analyzing and reporting results. But the two activities are inextricably linked. Models are simultaneously the means of predicting process outcomes and descriptions of process at some level of detail and some degree of correspondence to the "real" processes. The level of detail and "correctness" of the process description in a model directly influences the types of predictions that are possible and their accuracy. Predictions comment, in turn, on the quality of the process description that generated them.

Model Appraisal

The purpose of model appraisal for the research summarized here is to test the strength of our historical analogies. We want to know how much confidence can be placed in using them to generate complex, counterfactual hypotheses on what patterns of municipal expenditures would have been without GRS.

The next two sections of this paper consider, in turn, the descriptive and predictive adequacy of the four expenditure models specified above. The first section discusses the qualitative correspondence between the models and real municipal resource allocation processes. The second section presents some results from testing statistically the models' ability to replicate historical time series.

Models and Processes

Models that purport to explain and aspire to predict the behavior of decision-making units must make assertions, explicitly or implicitly, about the structure and motivation of the behavioral units. These assertions are essentially simplifications used to map complex processes, such as municipal resource allocation processes, onto intellectually manageable forms, such as the expenditure models presented above.

The central assertions about "behavioral structure" in the expenditure models are found in the aggregation choices made in specifying them. All models, with the possible exception of physical analogues and those systematically aggregating from the behavior of sub-atomic particles, are subject to the criticism that the level of aggregation obscures underlying causal relationships (structures). The expenditure models are at the level of a city government and, therefore, are aggregate in that they summarize in events (i.e., annual revenue and expenditure patterns) the complex behavior of organizational sub-units and human actors without describing that underlying behavior in detail. The "correctness" or "appropriateness" of such aggregation choices is always a function of the problem context (i.e., the types of predictions desired and the characteristics of the behavioral units).

The expenditure models make two important and strong assertions about behavioral structure. First, they assert that municipal resource allocation processes, when expenditure levels are taken as the relevant behavioral outcomes, can be viewed as "nearly decomposable" sub-systems imbedded in larger socioeconomic environments (Crecine, 1969: 115–146). The models imply that the decision-making systems are relatively autonomous and that their primary link with the larger environment is a constraint that the environment places on aggregate levels of spending; total expenditures must approximately equal total revenues in each year, and the level of potential revenue is constrained. The level of revenues is not wholly under the control of decision-makers for reasons that are either "real" (tax increases require voter approval of a referendum) or perceptual ("the taxpayers will revolt if we raise taxes"). And further, the models assert that environmental forces, such as changes in social, political, and economic characteristics of the environment, are not often important in directly adjusting expenditure levels from year-to-year; but rather, these forces are "filtered through the revenue constraint" (Crecine, 1968).[18]

The assertion that municipal resource allocation processes can be viewed as "nearly decomposable sub-systems" in the short-run is extremely important because of all that it enables us to ignore in modeling the processes. The assertion permits us to focus largely on determinants of change internal to the decision-making unit and to avoid working with many state variables (e.g., population, income, etc.) that would necessitate either extrapolation or modeling larger social systems. As they are specified, the models require only a single exogenous input, total revenue available.

The second important structural assertion that the models make is that the constituent components—sub-units and humans—of the behavioral unit are not behaviorally autonomous with respect to the outcomes we are interested in predicting, but are behaving in a somewhat coordinated fashion toward resolving a common problem—the budget problem. And further, there are characteristics of individual and collective problem-solving behavior, particularly when the problem is as repetitive as balancing a budget, that result in enormous stability in solutions (e.g., revenue and expenditure patterns).

Allocation (expenditure level) decisions are being made by human beings with finite cognitive and information-processing skills. The press of time and the type of information available (e.g., historical data on expenditures by functional account) to support decisions that have to be made constrain and channel problem-solving behavior. In spite of great diversity in cognitive skills, value preferences, and information resources of local officials, there are important similarities among cities and through time in how the repetitive, "potentially complex" problem of balancing the budget is simplified and solved. For example, in determining this year's expenditure levels, the expenditures required to maintain last year's level of service inputs (e.g., personnel) are treated as givens. Attention is focused on marginal changes to achieve and maintain a balance between expenditures and revenues. Also, there are characteristics of the budget problem such as "potential complexity," the need for defensible decisions, and severe time pressure that often necessitate the use of extremely simple decision rules to obtain solutions (e.g., cut 5% across-the-board or "no expenditures

[18] Because we are estimating "free" parameters from data which reflect direct environmental influences on expenditure levels to the extent such influences exist, we cannot argue that the models are totally inconsistent with such influences. However, in using parameters that are not estimated with reference to environmental forces other than change in aggregate level of spending, we would expect that if the structural assumption is "wrong"—environmental changes are a direct, routine basis for year-to-year changes in expenditure levels for functional accounts—serious predictive errors would result.

without historical precedent"). Such decision rules are easily administered and "fair" through even, albeit arbitrary, application. The use of such rules reinforces the stability of outcomes, particularly the relative proportions of the amounts expended for particular functions over time.

The key motivational assertion in the models, already introduced in the foregoing discussion of structural assertions, is that local officials are engaged in solving a large, repetitive, potentially complex[19] problem that is highly constrained and operational. Although specific conditions such as the relative scarcity of dollar resources, legally permitted revenue sources, and functional responsibilities vary by city and over time, there are important similarities such as the "balanced budget requirement," accounting structures, and potential complexity in the budget problem which municipal officials must solve each year. The dominant operational goal in setting allocation levels in any particular year is not to maximize community welfare or the like, but to solve the budget problem in that particular year.[20]

Figure 3 illustrates one full cycle for a typical municipal (General Fund) resource allocation process. Details such as sequence, forecasting procedures and assumptions used, and the relative importance of the steps vary from government to government. However, this illustration captures the key elements of the allocation processes in each of the five cities studied here.

The specific budget problem faced by any municipality in any particular year is perhaps best understood as the difference between estimated revenue receipts (at constant rates) and existing expenditure levels adjusted for "uncontrollable" increases in factor prices and the balance (positive or negative) carried forward from prior years. This difference may take the form of a surplus where estimated receipts exceed estimated "fixed" expenditure requirements or a deficit. The attention and effort of many local officials is directed largely at eliminating this difference, at achieving a balanced budget.

There are several versions of the budget problem in any year as estimates become "actuals" and actions are taken to strike an initial balance or restore a previous balance. The most important version in the budget cycle, however, is usually the first (i.e., First Trial Balance, Fig. 3), because it channels subsequent behavior. The direction and magnitude of the budget problem delimits the set of admissible solutions and focuses attention on an operational problem.

From the First Trial Balance calculation, instructions are given to sub-units for the preparation of budget detail. If the problem is a projected deficit, the instructions are apt to be stringent (e.g., no new expenditures), and a search for new revenue may be evoked. Also, there are apt to be checks of the original calculation for computational errors and evaluation of the assumptions and forecasts used. In extreme deficit

---

[19] My use of "complexity," is taken from Crecine (1968: 45): "The presence of a large number of interdependent real variables, a high degree of uncertainty attached to key variables, and non-linear relationships between real variables."

[20] On the "operationality" of goals, March and Simon (1959: 155) say that "The goals that are included in the definition of the situation influence choice only if there are some means, valid or illusory, for determining the connection between alternative actions and goal satisfaction—only if it can somehow be determined whether and to what extent these goals will be realized if particular courses of action are chosen."

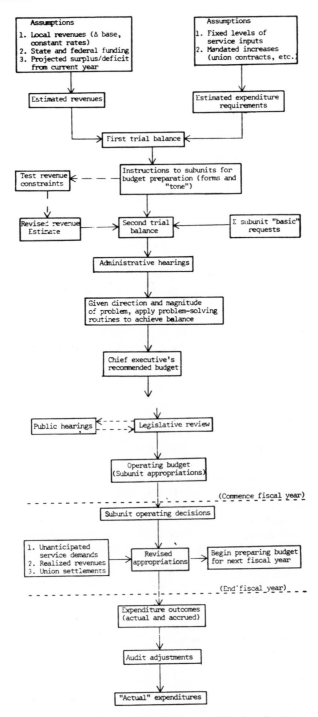

Fig. 3. Typical "General Fund" Resource Allocation Process.

situations, instructions to sub-units can include orders to cut back from the prior year's level of service inputs (e.g., no conference and travel requests, do not fill positions which are vacated, no capital outlay requests, cut 5% across the board, etc.). Such instructions (or actions on the part of the central budget authority) are more likely to occur after calculating the Second Trial Balance and after the administrative hearings have been held.

The operational goal, resolution of this year's "budget problem," is an organizational goal stemming from a mandated decision situation (i.e., city governments are legally required to prepare, consider, and approve a balanced budget in each year at a certain time). Organizations are collections of individuals; and these individuals vary greatly in their orientation (and the intensity with which they hold it) to the operational goal of solving the budget problem. Some individuals (e.g., chief financial officers) have a precise fix on the problem and an enormous commitment to solving it. Other individuals such as heads of operating agencies seeking more money may be working at cross-purposes with those attempting to solve the problem (i.e., when the problem is a projected deficit).

In order to ensure the resolution of such an important and potentially complex problem in a specified time frame, however, the organization must simplify the problem drastically and either manage (or avoid) most of the potential sub-unit conflict on the decision. This is accomplished in several ways. The decision processes are highly structured and routinized. Formal, largely hierarchical, roles are defined for participants. Final responsibility for preparing a balanced budget often rests with one individual (e.g., the mayor or administrator). Statutory provisions to ensure a decision or, at least, fiscal continuity often exist. If the legislative body does not approve a budget by a certain date, the chief executive's budget as proposed is law. Most of the substantive issues implicit in resource allocation decisions (e.g., the relative merits of the various functions) are either ignored or considered in a non-operational public dialogue that does not change allocation levels.

The role of the legislature in budgeting is apt to be limited, particularly if the proposed budget is very similar to the prior year's budget (i.e., there is no large anticipated surplus to appropriate). Crecine (1969: 99) observed that:

> A primary reason for ... [the limited role of city council] is more one of cognitive and informational constraints than lack of interest. The city budget is a complex document when it reaches the council. The level of detail makes considering all or even a majority of the items impossible.

The fact that the budget is usually balanced when presented is also a hindrance to legislative initiative. This balance means that to add money to accounts, they must take money from other accounts or increase revenues. These are often difficult actions to take (Crecine, 1969: 101).

The expenditure models take explicit advantage of key characteristics of municipal budgetary processes. Each of the models states that the amounts expended for a functional account last year is a key determinant of the amount expended this year. Each of the models recognizes the importance of the balance requirement with the use of a balance routine. Three of the models, CPRI, CGRI, and DCFP, recognize the importance of changes in available local revenue in determining expenditures by incorporating such changes as an explanatory variable.

My contention in this section is that there is substantial correspondence, albeit homomorphic, between the models and real municipal resource allocation processes. If this contention is unfounded (e.g., municipal officials are really maximizing community welfare by adapting expenditure patterns to shifting environmental demands), then we would expect the expenditure models as specified to have difficulty in replicating observed process outcomes—to fit badly when exposed to data. The results from the statistical tests reported in the next section should be viewed as evidence of the degree of correspondence between the models and the real processes.

Model Testing

Answering the appraisal question, What is the correspondence between model generated time-series and observed time-series? is a complicated and difficult task.[21] Cohen and Cyert (1965: 331) have remarked that

> Testing the conformity of generated time series to actual data is a problem because of the many possible dimensions which could meaningfully be used ... Any of the following measures might be appropriate: (1) number of turning points; (2) timing of turning points; (3) direction of turning points; (4) amplitude of the fluctuations for corresponding time segments; (5) average amplitude over the whole series; (6) simultaneity of turning points for different variables; (7) average values of variables; and (8) exact matching of values of variables ... There is no single test which will consider all the relevant time-series dimensions at once ... A great deal of judgment must enter into the evaluation of computer models.

The problem is further complicated in that even if we had information on all meaningful dimensions of the comparisons, the information is meaningless in absolute terms. It is only possible to judge the performance of a model relative to the performance of other models. And further, because there are so many potentially meaningful dimensions, it is quite probable that no single model will be preferred on all dimensions.

Given the inherent difficulties with model validation efforts, a multifarious strategy for model testing was adopted. First, four models were retained through full testing even though only one model was required for analyzing the fiscal effects of GRS. One of these models, CPB, was never intended as a serious candidate for use in the GRS analysis, but was used as an "autoregressive rabbit" against which the other models were run. Second, all four expenditure models were operated as both one-period-change models and simulation models for each city. Third, four different goodness-of-fit statistics (viz., R^2, root mean squared error, percentage root mean squared error, and Theil's U-Statistic) were computed for each model run in a variety of ways (e.g., on both levels of expenditure and change in expenditure by year across functional accounts and by functional account across years). And fourth, actual and predicted expenditures were plotted over time for all functional accounts in each city.

---

[21] The literature on "model validation" is lengthy, disputatious, and inconclusive. The philosophic issues are important but secondary here. Therefore, the discussion of general issues that follows is assertive and brief. Three excellent references for discussion of the larger issues are: Kaplan (1964); Popper (1959); and Simon (1968).

Essentially, each model was a competing hypothesis with each of the other models; and the statistics from the various tests were viewed as devices for ordinal comparisons of models. This procedure is more meaningful than using the statistics, extremely blunt instruments, to compare each model with the extreme null hypothesis implicit in the statistic.[22] For example, the competing hypothesis implicit in R^2 is that the mean of the observed series is the best predictor. Clearly, this is a weak competitor when working with nonstationary time-series, series with an important trend component, such as municipal nominal dollar expenditures.

Much of the goodness-of-fit information was redundant for the ordinal comparison of models. The statistics were wholly consistent in their ordinal preference for models on any particular test in spite of the differences in the way they are calculated. And when a model was preferred by all statistics for fit on level of expenditure, the same model was preferred by all statistics for fit on changes in expenditure (Larkey, 1975: 140). I will only report here on the results from one type of test that was the most demanding of the models: RSQR ($\bar{R}^2$) by year across all functional accounts in each city from simulation tests.

The procedures for operating computer models as one-period-change and simulation models are described in several places.[23] One-period-change model runs treat lagged values of endogenous variables as exogenous variables by using actual values rather than model-determined values for forecasting in successive periods. In other words, this type of run is a collection of one-period (annual) forecasts. With corrections through reference to actual data in each period, cumulative model error is avoided. This is the most widely used and reported procedure for operating statistical models and, to a lesser extent, computer models. It is not, however, a particularly rigorous test.

For simulation runs, models are initialized (endogenous variables are given values from actual data) once and model-determined values are used from that point forward. This is a much more demanding test of model performance since without periodic re-initialization, there is a great potential for cumulative model error. The most demanding form of this test is a run in which all variables in the model are endogenous and the data with which model outputs are compared have not been used in estimating model parameters. The simulation runs used for model testing here take values for revenues variables, actual or forecast, exogenously and use parameters that were estimated from the data with which model outputs are compared.

Both one-period-change and simulation tests are important for evaluating the models. In GRS years, the "actual data" are contaminated by the presence of GRS. It cannot be used to re-initialize the models or to estimate model parameters. GRS years are our forecast or simulation period. The one-period change tests give us evidence on the reliability of model predictions for the first GRS year by testing the models' ability to forecast single year changes in pre-GRS years. The "simulation" tests provide evidence on the reliability of model predictions in the second and succeeding GRS years. If cumulative model error is important and performance of the models

---

22 See Simon (1968) for a critical view of the use of extreme null hypotheses in the social sciences.
23 See Crecine, (1969: 114–116) and Cohen and Cyert, (1963: 312–325).

deteriorates rapidly in each succeeding year, it will be difficult to have much confidence in the counterfactual hypotheses and the analysis of fiscal effects beyond the first GRS year.

Charles C. Holt (1965) commented on the severity of "simulation" tests of the type used here

> The first question to explore is how well the model fits known data. Usually the model is estimated from historical data and the use of the same set of data to test the model would appear somewhat questionable. However, two important points can be explored. First, if the model was estimated as a set of individual equations or alternatively as subsets of equations, then it may be a significant test to solve the equations as a simultaneous system. It is quite possible for the individual equations or subsystems of equations, to fit reasonably well, but when all of the equations are solved jointly the errors may accumulate and a bad fit be obtained. Second, the parameter estimates usually are made on the basis of "forecasting" one time period ahead. Since many applications of the model will require forecasts for a time horizon of several or even many time periods, it is important to test whether the model is capable of giving reasonably good forecasts over longer forecast spans. After the unknown endogenous variables for one time have been solved, time is advanced one time period and then the unknown endogenous variables for the following period are solved, and so on. As this process is repeated we would anticipate that the calculated values would gradually worsen. This is a severe test even when the model has the advantage of being tested against the data which was used in its estimation. Should the model fall down badly on either of these two tests, there is clear indication that further work is needed before any great confidence can be placed in the model.

Although the expenditure models are taking one variable, revenue level, exogenously either as observed or as a one-period-change forecast, this test is still demanding. It is a test that checks the models' internal consistency and sensitivity to cumulative error.

Figures 4–8 show RSQR by year across functional accounts for all models in each city from the simulation tests.[24] On the whole, the results from the simulation tests are reasonably good. The stability and goodness-of-fit of most models in the simulation runs over an extensive number of years is strong evidence that the models are capturing important elements of the processes. It is particularly interesting that fit as measured by RSQR is as good or better at the end of the extensive simulation periods as it was at the start for some models in some cities (e.g., CPRI in every city except Ann Arbor).

---

[24] For these plots, RSQR was calculated as:

$$1 - \left[\frac{\sum\limits_{i}^{L} \sum\limits_{j}^{M} (EXP^{*}_{ijk} - EXP_{ijk})^2}{\sum\limits_{i}^{L} \sum\limits_{j}^{M} (EXP^{*}_{ijk} - \overline{EXP})^2} \right]$$

where

EXP_{ijk} = Actual expenditure for function "i," account "j," in year "k"

EXP^{*}_{ijk} = Model predicted expenditures for function "i," account "j," in year "k"

L = Number of functions (e.g., Police, Fire, etc.)

M = Number of accounts (e.g., personnel, nonpersonnel, total only)

$\overline{EXP_{k}} = \sum\limits_{i}^{L} \sum\limits_{j}^{M} EXP_{ijk}/LM$

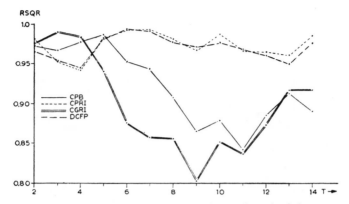

Fig. 4. Albuquerque   RSQR—level of expenditure simulation.

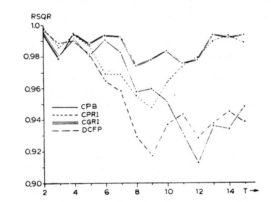

Fig. 5. Ann Arbor   RSQR—level of expenditure simulation.

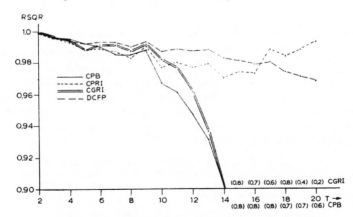

Fig. 6. Cincinnati   RSQR—level of expenditure simulation.

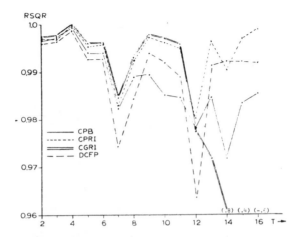

Fig. 7. Detroit   RSQR—level of expenditure simulation.

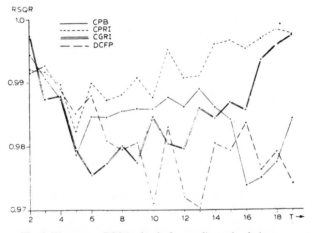

Fig. 8. Worcester   RSQR—level of expenditure simulation.

However, some models in some cities "blow-up." Cumulative model error results in a complete divergence between model behavior and process behavior. CGRI blows up after a period of years for both Cincinnati and Detroit (see Figs 6 and 7). In other cities, Albuquerque (see Fig. 4) and Worcester (see Fig. 8), CGRI performs less well than other models. CPB, our "auto-regressive rabbit," also does not perform well as a simulation. The model blows up for Cincinnati (see Fig. 6) and performs less well than CPRI and DCFP in most cities.[25]

---

[25] The reader should note that the period before CPB or CGRI experience problems in any city is considerably longer than the GRS periods, two years, for which the models are used. In the analysis of GRS, the models are initialized with data from the last year prior to GRS and operate as simulations in only the second and third years of GRS.

CPB and CGRI, the models that perform very poorly on some tests, are different from CPRI and DCFP in that they both use the level of expenditures in the prior year as an explanatory variable in their basic predictive equations. Including this variable with an associated growth parameter in the basic equation results in model instability under certain conditions. Specifically, when functional accounts exist that experience very little or no growth over the early years in the estimation period and then very rapid growth in the later years, CPB and CGRI are instable. This is because the parameters for such functional accounts are heavily influenced in estimation by the high growth in the later years. When such parameters are used in a simulation test, the associated functional accounts capture an increasing proportion of total expenditures, leaving very little for allocation to other functional accounts.[26] These problems exist only in Cincinnati and Detroit, and the problems exist there for only one or two, usually small, functional accounts. These problems do, however, suggest that it is not very hard to go wrong in such simulation tests and lend some credence to the performance of CPRI and DCFP.

The results from these statistical tests support my contention from the previous section that there is a degree of correspondence between the expenditure models and the resource allocation processes in the cities studied. Although abstract as theoretical statements, the models are consistent with an existing, detailed theory of municipal resource allocation (Crecine, 1969), appropriate to the GRS research problem, and adequate in predictive performance. We can have some faith in the use of the models, particularly CPRI and DFCP, as historical analogies for making the counterfactual arguments to analyze the effects of GRS.

Success for a piece of policy analysis is not, however, determined by the size of the R^2 in the fifteenth year of a simulation test, but in terms of contributions to better program decisions. Five city governments in a limited size range is an extremely narrow empirical basis for drawing any general conclusions about the impact of GRS and prescribing changes in the program. However, the "micro," process-oriented view in this research provides insights into the behavior of local governments in response to GRS that were not possible for research attaining more extensive coverage, but using less intensive methods. These insights from directly addressing *why* questions were translated into conclusions and prescriptions for policymakers (Larkey, 1975: 244–250; Anton et al., 1975).

The research that I have described briefly was developmental. It was an attempt to develop an approach to the evaluation of GRS that was not fraught with the conceptual and methodological problems of conventional approaches, notably survey research. The research was also an explicit attempt to use historical analogies for program evaluation in a more rigorous fashion than it is possible to do with the better known quasi-experimental designs. The rigor attainable in any particular application of an historical analogy is strictly proportional to the quality of existing descriptive theory. Existing theory of municipal resource allocation processes is

---

[26] For example, in Cincinnati, the CGRI prediction for nonpersonnel expenditures by the Health Department grew to U.S.$25,231,004 in year 20 when the observed expenditure for the same year was U.S.$1,214, 650. Large error here means large errors in an opposite direction in other functional accounts because of the balancing routine.

excellent. The paucity of usable theory in other research areas is an obvious practical obstacle to immediate, widespread application of rigorous historical analogies.

A Final Comment

My prescription for future evaluation research is easier to give than to follow, but recognizing the difficulty of the evaluation task explicitly is an important part of the prescription. Evaluation researchers should accept and act upon the point of view that methods should be adapted to problems and not problems to methods. Clarity in problem formulation, including recognition of the counterfactual questions that need to be answered and of the theoretical requirements they impose, is extremely important. Donald T. Campbell's (1969) distinction between "trapped" and "experimental" administrators is useful by analogy here. The experimental researcher is committed to solving problems while the trapped researcher is committed to particular methods. Strong commitments to particular methods (e.g., classic experimental design, survey research, linear regression analysis, etc.) that are nothing more than the "tools of analysis," often result in inappropriate and ineffective research applications. Research designs must be problem-directed.

Constant Proportion of Revenue Increment

Estimation Period ($K = 1$ to NN)

1. The initial predicted expenditure for function "i," account "j," in year "k" is the prior year's expenditure for the same function and account.

$$\overline{\overline{EXP}}_{ijk} \leftarrow EXP_{ijk-1}$$

2. The prediction is revised to include a constant proportion of the revenue increment (decrement).

$$\overline{\overline{EXP}}_{ijk} \leftarrow \overline{\overline{EXP}}_{ijk} + \hat{\beta}_{ij}(REV_k - REV_{k-1})$$

3. Check the balance in year "k."

$$\sum_{i}^{L}\sum_{j}^{M} \overline{\overline{EXP}}_{ijk} = REV_k?$$

$\downarrow$ no $\downarrow$ yes

(6)

4. Calculate imbalance.

$$DIFF_k \leftarrow REV_k - \sum_{i}^{L}\sum_{j}^{M} \overline{\overline{EXP}}_{ijk}$$

5. Spread the imbalance proportionately.

$$\overline{\overline{\overline{EXP}}}_{ijk} \leftarrow \overline{\overline{EXP}}_{ijk} + ((\overline{\overline{EXP}}_{ijk}/\sum_{i}^{L}\sum_{j}^{M}\overline{\overline{EXP}}_{ijk})(DIFF_k))$$

$\downarrow$

⑥

Forecast Period (K = NN+1 to N)

6. Set initial prediction for expenditures in function "i," account "j," in year "k" equal to the predicted expenditures for the same function and account in the prior year.

$$\overline{EXP}_{ijk} \leftarrow \overline{EXP}_{ijk-1}$$

$\downarrow$

7. Revise the prediction to include a constant proportion of the revenue increment (decrement).

$$\overline{\overline{EXP}}_{ijk} \leftarrow \overline{EXP}_{ijk} + \hat{\beta}_{ij}(REV_k - REV_{k-1})$$

$\downarrow$

8. Check the balance between the sum of all predictions and revenue available in year "k."

$$\sum_{i}\sum_{j}\overline{\overline{EXP}}_{ijk} = REV_k?$$

$\downarrow$ no $\downarrow$ yes

⑪

9. Calculate the imbalance.

$$DIFF_k \leftarrow (REV_k - \sum_{i}\sum_{j}\overline{\overline{EXP}}_{ijk})$$

$\downarrow$

10. Spread the imbalance proportionately.

$$\overline{\overline{\overline{EXP}}}_{ijk} \leftarrow \overline{\overline{EXP}}_{ijk} + (\overline{\overline{EXP}}_{ijk}/\sum_{i}\sum_{j}\overline{\overline{EXP}}_{ijk})(DIFF_k)$$

$\downarrow$

⑪

11. Produce model output.

> 1. Goodness-of-fit statistics
> 2. Predictions, actuals, and residuals by function, account, and year
> 3. Plots of predicted on actuals, and residuals

Estimation

$\hat{\beta}_{ij}$ is estimated in:

$$\text{EXP}_{ijk} - \text{EXP}_{ijk-1} = \hat{\beta}_{ij}(\text{REV}_k - \text{REV}_{k-1})$$

For:

$$K = 2 - NN$$

Appendix: Variable Dictionary

REV_k = Total general fund revenue from nonfederal sources in year "k".

EXP_{ijk} = Actual expenditures for function "i", account "j", in year "k".

$\overline{\text{EXP}}_{ijk}$ = Initial prediction of expenditures for function "i", account "j", in year "k". ($\overline{\overline{\text{EXP}}}_{ijk}$ and $\overline{\overline{\overline{\text{EXP}}}}_{ijk}$ are successive revisions of this prediction.)

$\hat{\beta}_{ij}$ = Empirically estimated parameter for function "i", account "j", (For models which use two parameters per function and account, $\hat{\beta}_{ij}$ and $\hat{\delta}_{ij}$ are used.)

N = Number of years in sample.

NN = Number of non-GRS years.

REFERENCES

Anton, T. J., et al. (1975) *Understanding the Fiscal Impact of General Revenue-Sharing.* Ann Arbor: Institute of Public Policy Studies, University of Michigan. A report prepared under contract for Research Applied to National Needs, National Science Foundation, Washington, D.C.

Ayres, R. U. (1969). *Technological Forecasting.* New York: McGraw-Hill.

Brownlee, K. A. (1960). *Statistical Theory in Science and Engineering.* New York: John Wiley and Sons, Inc.

Campbell, D. T. (1969). "Reforms as Experiments." *The American Psychologist,* **24**: 4 (April), 409–249.

Campbell, D. T. (1970). "Considering The Case Against Experimental Evaluations of Social Innovations." *Administrative Science Quarterly,* **15**: 110–113.

Campbell, D. T. and J. C. Stanley (1966). *Experimental and Quasi-Experimental Designs for Research.* Chicago: Rand McNally.

Caporaso, J. A. and L. L. Roos, Jr. (eds.) (1973). *Quasi-Experimental Approaches: Testing Theory and Evaluating Policy.* Evanston: Northwestern University Press.

Cohen, K. J. and R. M. Cyert (1963). "Computer Models in Dynamic Economics," in *A Behavioral Theory of the Firm* by James G. March and R. M. Cyert (eds.) Englewood Cliffs, New Jersey: Prentice-Hall, Inc.

Crecine, John P. (1967). "A Computer Simulation Model of Municipal Budgeting." *Management Science*, **13** (July), 786–815.

Crecine, John P. (1968). "A Simulation of Municipal Budgeting: The Impact of Problem Environment." *Simulation in the Study of Politics*. W. D. Coplin (ed.) Chicago: Markham Publishing Co.

Crecine, John P. (1969). *Governmental Problem Solving*. Chicago: Rand McNally.

Gregg, Lee W. and Herbert A. Simon (1967). "Process Models and Stochastic Theories of Simple Concept Formation." *Journal of Mathematical Psychology*, **4**: 2, 246–276.

Haveman, Robert H. (1972). *The Economic Performance of Public Investments*. Baltimore: Johns Hopkins Press.

Holt, Charles C. (1965). "Validation and Application of Macroeconomic Models Using Computer Simulation," in J. S. Duesenberry, Gary Fromm, L. R. Klein, and Edwin Kuh, eds., *The Brookings Quarterly Econometric Model of the United States*. Chicago: Rand McNally and Company.

Kaplan, A. (1964). *The Conduct of Inquiry; Methodology for Behavioral Science*. Scranton, Pa.: Chandler Publishing Company.

Larkey, Patrick D. (1975). *Process Models and Program Evaluation: The Impact of General Revenue Sharing on Municipal Fiscal Behavior*, Ph.D. Dissertation, The University of Michigan.

March, James G. (1972). "Model Bias in Social Action." *Review of Educational Research*, **42**: 4 (February), 413–429.

Nelson, Richard R. (1974). "Intellectualizing About The Moon-Ghetto Mataphor: A Study of the Current Malaise of Rational Analysis of Social Problems." *Policy Sciences*, **5**.

Popper, Karl A. (1959). *The Logic of Scientific Discovery*. New York: Basic Books.

Quade, E. S. (1975). *Analysis for Public Decisions*. New York: American Elsevier.

Rivlin, Alice M. (1971). *Systematic Thinking for Social Action*. Washington, D.C.: The Brookings Institution.

Rivlin, Alice M. and P. Michael Timpane (eds.) (1975). *Ethical and Legal Issues of Social Experimentation*. Washington, D.C.: The Brookings Institution.

Schultze, Charles L. (1968). *The Politics and Economics of Public Spending*. Washington, D.C.: The Brookings Institution.

Schultze, Charles L. (1970). "The Role of Incentives, Penalties, and Rewards in Attaining Effective Policy." *Public Expenditures and Policy Analysis*. Robert H. Haveman and Julius Margolis (eds.) Chicago: Markham.

Simon, Herbert A. (1968). "On Judging the Plausibility of Theories." *Logic, Methodology and Philosophy of Sciences III*, J. van Rootselaar and H. Stall, (eds.) Amsterdam: North-Holland.

Taylor, Ronald N. and Ilan Vertinsky (1977). "Experimentation in Organizational Behavior and Strategy," in W. Starbuck (ed.) *Handbook of Organizational Design*, New York: Elsevier/North Holland (in press).

Webb, Eugene J. et al. (1966). *Unobtrusive Measures: Non-Reactive Measurement in the Social Sciences*. New York: Random House.

One of the recurrent themes in this volume is the need for more attention to integrity of treatment and, especially, the need to assess that integrity. In the following, Patton begins with a striking example of a program that, although never successfully implemented, was evaluated, found ineffective, and had its funding terminated. Patton goes on to discuss the problems involved in evaluating program implementation, which we call treatment integrity, and to make some very useful and practical suggestions on how that evaluation might be done. He anticipates several of the suggestions made in our introductory chapter, written after Patton's but without full benefit of the insights it affords.

16

Evaluation of Program Implementation

Michael Quinn Patton

A Setting

In conducting interviews for our study of the utilization of federal health evaluations, we were told of one quite dramatic instance of research utilization. It concerned an evaluation of a program established by a state legislature as a demonstration program to teach welfare recipients the basic rudiments of parenting and household management. The state welfare department was charged with the responsibility for conducting workshops, distributing brochures, showing films, and training case workers on how low income people could better manage their meager resources and how they could become better parents. A single major city was selected for pilot testing the program, and a highly respected independent research institute was contracted to evaluate the program. Both the state legislature and the state welfare department were publicly committed to using the evaluation findings for decisionmaking.

The evaluators selected a sample of welfare recipients to interview before the program began. They collected considerable data about parenting, household management, and budgetary practices. Eighteen months

Publisher's Note: Complete citations for the works referred to in this chapter may be found in the bibliography of *Utilization-Focused Evaluation,* published by Sage Publications.

From Michael Quinn Patton, "Evaluation of Program Implementation," pp. 149-177 in Michael Quinn Patton (ed.) *Utilization-Focused Evaluation.* Beverly Hills, CA: Sage. Copyright 1978 by Sage Publications.

later, the same welfare recipients were interviewed a second time. The results showed no measureable change in parenting or household management behavior. In brief, the program was found to be ineffective. These results were reported to the state legislators, some of whom found it appropriate to make sure the public learned about their accountability efforts through the newspapers. As a result of this adverse publicity, the legislature terminated funding for the program—a clear instance of utilization of evaluation findings for decisionmaking.

Now, suppose we wanted to know why the program was ineffective. That question could not be answered by the evaluation as conducted because it focused entirely upon measuring the attainment of intended program outcomes, i.e., the extent to which the program was effective in changing the parenting and household management behaviors of welfare recipients. As it turned out, there is a very good reason why the program was ineffective. When the funds were initially allocated from the state to the city, the program became immediately embroiled in the politics of urban welfare. Welfare rights organizations questioned the right of government to tell poor people how to spend their money or rear their children: "you have no right to tell us to manage our households according to white, middle class values. And who is this Frenchman named Piaget who's going to tell us how to raise our American kids?"

As a result of these and other political battles the program was delayed and further delayed. Procrastination being the better part of valor, the first parenting brochure was never printed, no household management films were ever shown, no workshops were held, and no case workers were ever trained. In short, *the program was never implemented—but it was evaluated!* It was then found to be ineffective and was killed.

The Importance of Implementation Analysis

It is important to know whether or not a program is effective after it is properly implemented, but to answer that question it is first necessary to know whether or not the program was indeed properly implemented. This chapter considers the meaning and purpose of implementation evaluation from a utilization perspective.

In the spring of 1974, the entire issue of the periodical *Evaluation* was devoted to a consideration of "the human services shortfall." Lynn and Salasin (1974: 4) defined this shortfall as "a large and growing gap between what we expect from government-supported human service systems, and what these systems in fact deliver." The human services shortfall is made up of two parts: (1) failure of implemented programs to attain desired outcomes and (2) failure to actually implement policy in the form of operating programs. Evaluators have directed most of their attention to the first problem by conducting outcomes evaluations, but there is growing evidence that the second problem is equally, if not even more critical. In a recent book on social program implementation, editor Walter Williams concludes: "the underlying theme of this book is that the lack of concern for implementation is currently *the* crucial impediment to improving complex operating programs, policy analysis, and experimentation in social policy areas" (Williams and Elmore, 1976: 267; italics in original). The preface to the book states the problem quite succinctly.

> The fundamental implementation question remains whether or not what has been decided actually can be carried out in a manner consonant with that underlying decision. More and more, we are finding, the answer is no. So it is crucial that we attend to implementation (Williams and Elmore, 1976: xi).

The problem of making policy operative is fundamental in all realms of government intervention. At the international level, studies collected and edited by John C. de Wilde (1967) demonstrate that program implementation and administration are the critical problems in Third World development plans. Organizational sociologists have documented the particular problem of implementing programs that are new and innovative alongside or into existing programs (e.g., Corwin, 1973; Hage and Aiken, 1970). Diffusion of innovation theorists have thoroughly documented the problems of implementing new ideas in new settings (e.g., Guba, 1968; Rogers et al., 1969, 1971; Havelock, 1973). Provus (1971) pointed to the importance of evaluating implementation of educational programs before outcomes could be usefully evaluated. Yet, Williams and Elmore (1976: xii) find that implementation analysis has seldom been taken seriously, much to the detriment of research utilization:

> The failure to focus on implementation has blighted not only program administration but also policy research and analysis. In the former case, policy ideas that seemed reasonable and compelling when decisions were made often have become badly flawed and ineffective programs as they drifted down the bureaucratic process. It is not just that the programs fall short of the early rhetoric that described them; they often barely work at all. Ignoring implementation has been equally disastrous for research

and analysis. *Indeed, it is possible that past analysis and research that ignored implementation issues may have asked the wrong questions, thereby producing information of little or no use to policy-making* (italics in original).

The notion that asking the wrong questions leads to useless information is fundamental to everything we have discussed. To avoid gathering useless information *it is important to frame evaluation questions in the context of program implementation.* Framing evaluation questions in the context of program implementation is a major approach in identifying and focusing relevant evaluation questions. Implementation evaluation is one of the options available to active-reactive-adaptive evaluators in conducting utilization-focused research.

Both an implementation framework and a goals framework are important; the one that is clarified first in a given evaluation process varies. Implementation evaluation is distinguished as a separate element in order to call attention to its importance and to deal with the unique considerations that affect the conceptualization of an implementation analysis. A utilization-focused approach to evaluation is not, however, a linear process easily represented by a series of logical steps. Both implementation evaluation and outcomes evaluation are important elements in a comprehensive evaluation. The inclusion of both elements can be critical; their ordering is situational.

Outcomes Evaluation Versus Implementation Evaluation

It is perhaps easiest to understand implementation evaluation in contrast to outcomes evaluation. While the ideal evaluation includes both, few evaluations have made this ideal operational. Evaluation research has been dominated by an emphasis on measuring outcomes. Outcomes evaluation is the comparison of actual program outcomes with desired outcomes (goals). One of the major reasons goals clarification has received so much attention from evaluators is because applied social science research has been preoccupied with outcomes evaluation. This has been especially true in education. Provus (1971: 10-11) has cogently described the predominance of outcomes evaluation in the field of educational assessment:

Evaluation of program outcomes establishes performance criteria for program recipients. This approach is represented by all that is most current and "scientific" in educational evaluation. Starting with the work of Tyler and the perfection of standardized instruments with norms for various populations, and continuing with the present interest in group criterion referenced tests, individual situational testing, and unobtrusive measures of performance, the preoccupation of the present generation of evaluators has been and continues to be with microanalysis of a learner's behavior at various times before and after exposure to a lesson, program, treatment, or institution.

In educational research, outcomes evaluation is represented by pretest versus posttest performance on standardized achievement tests; in criminal justice programs, outcomes evaluation measures comparative recidivism rates; in health programs, the outcomes are changes in incidence and prevalence rates; in manpower programs, the outcomes are employment rates; in drug abuse treatment programs, the outcomes are rates of repeated addiction; and so it goes for each area in the human service delivery system. The problem with pure outcomes evaluation is that the results give decisionmakers very little information upon which to act. Simply knowing that outcomes are high, low or different does not tell decisionmakers very much about what to do. What is missing is information about the actual nature of the program being evaluated. In the example which provided the setting for this chapter, the decisionmakers knew only that the welfare parent training program had no measureable effects; they did not even known whether or not a program actually existed that could be expected to have effects. Based only on erroneous outcomes information they terminated a policy approach that had never actually been tried. Unfortunately, such inappropriate decisions based only on outcomes evaluations are not uncommon.

A serious look at the actual substance of the program being evaluated can prevent some of the obvious but oft repeated evaluation failures of the past.

For example, although it seems obvious to mention, it is important to know whether a program actually exists. Federal agencies are often inclined to assume that, once a cash transfer has taken place from a government agency to a program in the field, a program exists and can be evaluated. Experienced evaluation researchers know that the very existence of a program cannot be taken for granted even after large cash transfers have taken place. Early evaluation of Title I programs in New York City provide an illustration of this problem. . . . Obvious though it may seem, evaluations continue without either raising or answering the primary quesion: "Does the program exist?" This error could not arise if evaluation researchers looked carefully and seriously at program content before decisions about evaluation research methods were made (Guttentag and Struening, 1975b: 3-4).

While terminating a policy inappropriately is one possible error when only outcomes data are used, enlarging a program inappropriately is also possible when decisionmakers have no real information about program operations and implementation. In one instance a number of drug addiction treatment programs in a county were evaluated, collecting nothing but outcomes data on rates of readdiction for treated patients. All programs had relatively mediocre success rates, except one program which had had 100 percent success for two years. The county board immediately voted to triple the budget of that program. Within a year, the readdiction rates for that program had fallen to the same mediocre level as other programs. By enlarging the program based on outcomes data the county board had eliminated the key elements in the program's success—its small size and dedicated staff. The highly successful program had been a six patient halfway house with one primary staff counselor who ate, slept, and lived that program. He established such a close relationship with each addict that he knew exactly how to keep each one straight. When the program was enlarged, he became administrator of three houses and lost personal contact with the clients. The successful program became only mediocre. Thus, a highly effective program was lost because the county board acted without any information about actual program operations and without an assessment of the basis for the program's success.

If one had to choose between implementation information and outcomes information because of limited evaluation resources, there are many instances in which implementation information would be of greater value. A decisionmaker can use implementation information to make sure that a policy is being put into operation according to design—or to test the very feasibility of the policy. Unless one knows that a program is operating according to design, there may be little reason to expect it to produce the desired outcomes. Furthermore, until the program is implemented and a "treatment" is believed to be in operation, there is little reason to evaluate outcomes. The decisionmaker on the Hill-Burton evaluation from our utilization of federal health studies made this point quite emphatically:

When we called the committee together and began to discuss the question of evaluating state agency performance there was no decision at that point that there was going to actually be interviews with the state agencies. That's something that grew naturally out of the discussion of the committee members. They concluded fairly early in their discussions that they were groping in the dark to try and evaluate agencies when they weren't really sure what the agencies were doing. And so the idea to interview them and gather all this information relative to what's going on in the state agencies grew out of the committee's feeling that they needed to know what was going on before they could even attempt an evaluation of whether what was going on was good, bad, or indifferent (DM159: 6).

Where outcomes are evaluated without knowledge of implementation, the results seldom provide a direction for action because the decisionmaker lacks information about what produced the observed outcomes (or lack of outcomes). This is the "black box" approach to evaluation: clients are tested before entering the program and after completing the program, while what happens inbetween is a black box. Carol Weiss (1972b: 43) describes this approach and its dangers.

> Why should the evaluator be concerned with program input? Haven't we noted earlier that his job is to find out whether the program (whatever it is) is achieving its goals? Does it make any difference to his work whether the program is using rote drill, psychoanalysis, or black magic? There are evaluators who are sympathetic to such an approach. They see the program as a "black box," the contents of which do not concern them; they are charged with discovering effects. But if the evaluator has no idea of what the program really is, he may fail to ask the right questions.

Most black box evaluations that study outcomes alone do so because of tradition and routine; no thoughtful decision has been made about what kind of evaluative information would be most useful. Nowhere is this better illustrated than in the use of standardized achievement tests in educational evaluation.

The Black Box Approach to Evaluation:
The Case of Standardized Tests

The most widespread example of the routine collection of outcomes data with no corresponding program implementation information is the yearly administration of standardized, norm-referenced achievement tests in public schools. Testing is a multimillion dollar business. Thousands of school districts routinely administer tests. Vito Perrone, in a review of the abuses of standardized tests as instruments for school evaluation, notes that since the Depression testing has become "a part of the conventional wisdom of schools." He goes on to explain that since the educational crisis following the Soviet launch of Sputnik I, there has been increased demand for school evaluations: "evaluation in most instances became synonymous, unfortunately, with outcome data produced by standardized tests" (Perrone, 1977: 18). Yet as evaluation instruments, such tests provide minimal useful information: the results are of little use to teachers or parents and the tests cannot be reliably used for evaluating individual students (cf. Perrone, 1977; Perrone et al., 1976; Patton, 1975b). They may tell the public and school board members how schools rank on achievement, but these rankings do not tell school officials what to do to improve the educational experience for students. To improve schools, officials need information about what actually happens in classrooms— and that they do not have. Standardized tests have little relationship to the actual objectives of instruction at any given time and place (Skager, 1971; Sax, 1974: 258-259), and are likely to have even less relationship to actual educational practice in a particular district. Furthermore, the ranking of schools by achievement is relatively stable from year to year for most school systems. Knowledgeable people in a district already know which schools will rank high and which will rank low; they also know that rankings have more to do with student and community characteristics than with curriculum and actual teaching practices.

Why, then, do communities spend thousands of dollars year after year to collect information that is not used and only tells people what they already know? The school board says it is for parents, parents hope teachers use the tests, teachers just file them with the principal, and principals suppose that school board members want the tests. Clearly no relevant decisionmakers and information users have been identified. On the whole, it is a useless system and a gigantic accountability hoax.

A utilization-focused approach to evaluation carries no simple, ready-made instruments or standardized approaches, but does frame the evaluation question in the context of program implementation, not just program outcomes.

> Unless there is some reasonably accurate and coherent definition of the program, the evaluator does not know to what to attribute the outcomes he observes. Let's remember that evaluation is designed to help with decision making. Decision makers need to know what it was that worked or didn't work, what it was that should be adopted throughout the system or modified. Unless the evaluation can provide evidence on the nature of the program as it existed . . . there is little basis for decision (Weiss, 1972b: 44).

Evaluations that collect only data on student achievement with standardized tests cannot provide evidence on the nature of the educational program as it actually exists; thus, such evaluations have low utilization potential and high potential for abuse and misinterpretation. Educational evaluations that rely entirely on outcomes from standardized achievement tests represent the epitomy of the black box approach. Hidden inside that black box can be quite important information that makes a world of difference in understanding a program.

Unlocking the Black Box of Program Implementation

The first step in unlocking the black box of program implementation is finding out whether or not the program actually moved from an idea to initial implementation. The evaluator asks: "Does the program exist?" According to Williams, the number of programs that fail to ever become operational may be quite high because "the major problem for policy analysis is not in developing relatively sound policy alternatives but in failing to consider the feasibility of implementing these alternatives" (Williams and Elmore, 1976: 268). The crucial implementation stage for Williams occurs between the decision and operation stages, when new programs are being tried for the first time. The weaknesses of the planning process suddenly become quite glaring:

> Surely policymakers at the time of choice ought to have reasonable estimates of the organizational capacity to carry out alternative proposals. But however obvious that may be, few people have ever thought in terms of analyzing implementation during the decision-making stages! (Williams, 1976: 270).

This makes the evaluator's job all the more difficult because it means there are seldom clear criteria for even conceptualizing implementation processes, much less evaluating them.

The further one delves into implementation analysis, the more complex the alternatives become. The black box in pure outcomes evaluations quickly becomes a Pandora's box in more comprehensive evaluation designs with an implementation analysis component. Consider, for example, the Pandorian question of how close an actual program has to be in comparison to its initial proposal or plan before it can be said to be implemented. One decisionmaker interviewed in our utilization of federal health evaluations study felt that policymakers had been misled into thinking that the evaluation report on his program concerned the ideal program as planned, when in fact only partial implementation had occurred. The report was thus discredited in this decisionmaker's eyes because he felt its use in congressional hearings had done the program a disservice.

When you start reading your hearings, for instance, and find them using it as a resource in some ways, frankly, it concerns me a little bit, because I felt like portions of this did not have substantive enough data to be making determinations. That is, how can you judge the effect of the cancellation provision when it wasn't fully implemented at the point in time that the study was using? How could you put any reliance upon a study when the repayment provision wasn't fully implemented? Do you see what I Mean? So I didn't put credence in the thing (DM145: 25).

But just how close to the ideal must the program be before it can be said to be fully implemented? The next section discusses this and related issues within the black box of program implementation.

Ideal Program Plans and Actual Implementation

Once the evaluator has determined that at least some activity actually exists, i.e., that there is indeed a program to be evaluated, the next question is: what should the program look like before it can be said to be fully implemented and operational? This question is difficult to answer because programs are not implemented in the classical, rational fashion of single-mindedly adopting a set of means to achieve a predetermined end. From an incrementalist, satisficing perspective (see Chapter 7) organizations and decisionmakers do not methodically implement a program as if they had found the best means to achieve top priority goals. Programs take shape slowly as decisionmakers react to multiple uncertainties and emerging complexities. Jerome Murphy makes this point quite emphatically in his study of the implementation of Title V of the Elementary and Secondary Education Act. He found great variation in implementation in the various states. He describes evaluations of those programs as exercises in blaming and scapegoating instead of attempts to understand educational change in the context of organizational dynamics, concluding that the widespread assumption that competently led bureaucracies operate like goal-directed, unitary decision-makers may well be a major barrier to dealing with problems of bureaucratic change. Both program evaluations and reform efforts must come to grips explicitly with the enduring attributes of organizations (Murphy, 1976: 96).

Sociologists who study formal organizations, social change, and diffusion of innovations have carefully documented the substantial slippage in organizations between plans and actual operations. For Rogers (1962) it is the difference between trial and adoption; for Smelser (1959) it is the difference between specification, implementation, and routinization; for Mann and Neff (1961) it is the slippage between planning change, taking steps to make change, and stabilizing change; and for Hage and Aiken (1970) it is the difference between initiation, implementation, and routinization of change. In each case, regardless of how these sociologists conceptualize the stages of organizational change and innovations adoption, they emphasize two points: (1) *routinization or final acceptance is never certain at the beginning; and (2) the implementation process always contains unknowns that change the ideal so that it looks different when and if it actually becomes operational.*

Hage and Aiken (1970: 100) found that organizational conflict and disequilibrium are greatest during the implementation stage of organizational change. No matter how much planning takes place,

> the human element is seldom adequately considered in the implementation of a new product or service. There will be mistakes that will have to be corrected. Alteration of the existing structure will also create conflicts and tensions among members of the organization.

As programs take shape power struggles develop:

> The stage of implementation is thus the stage of conflict, especially over power. It is the time when the new program results in the greatest disequilibrium in the organization because it is the stage when the program becomes a reality and the members of the organization must actually live with it . . . tempers flare, interpersonal animosities develop, and the power structure is shaken (Hage and Aiken, 1970: 104).

The difference between the ideal, rational model of program implementation and the day-to-day, incrementalist, and conflict-laden realities of program implementation is explained with a minimum of jargon in the following notice found by Jerome Murphy (1976: 92) in the office of a state education agency:

Notice

The objective of all dedicated department employees should be to thoroughly analyze all situations, anticipate all problems prior to their occurrence, have answers for these problems, and move swiftly to solve these problems when called upon. . . .

However . . .

When you are up to your ass in alligators, it is difficult to remind yourself that your initial objective was to drain the swamp.

Programs are implemented incrementally by adapting to local conditions, organizational dynamics, and programmatic uncertainties. In reporting the findings of RAND's large-scale Change Agent Study, Milbrey McLaughlin (1976: 169) wrote:

> Specifically, the Change Agent Study concluded that *successful implementation is characterized by a process of mutual adaptation.* . . . Implementation did not involve merely the direct and straighforward application of an educational technology or plan. Implementation was a dynamic organizational process that was shaped over time by interactions between project goals and methods and the institutional setting. As such, it was neither automatic nor certain (italics in the original).

Evaluation disasters can result from failing to recognize that implementation of program ideals is neither automatic nor certain. The national evaluation of Follow Through is a prime example of such a disaster. Follow Through was introduced as an extension of Head Start for primary-age children. It was a planned variation "experiment" in compensatory education featuring 22 different models of education to be tested in 158 school districts on 70,000 children throughout the nation. The evaluation alone employed 3,000 people to collect data on program effectiveness. However, as Alkin (1970: 2) has observed, the evaluation lacked focus from the beginning:

> The greatest deficiency of the evaluation project is its failure to provide adequate specification of the kind of study it is intended to be and the functions which it proposes to serve. . . . If they [the evaluators] accepted four million dollars in evaluation funds, it should be expected that they would have been more aggressive in demanding clarification of the objectives and the decision-making purposes.

It was assumed in the evaluation plan that models could and would be implemented in some systematic, uniform fashion. Elmore, however, has rightly pointed out the folly of this assumption.

Each sponsor developed a large organization, in some instances larger than the entire federal program staff, to deal with problems of model implementation. Each local school system developed a program organization consisting of a local director, a team of teachers and specialists, and a parent advisory group. The more the scale and complexity of the program increased, the less plausible it became for Follow Through administrators to control the details of program variations, and the more difficult it became to determine whether the array of districts and sponsors represented "systematic" variations in program content (Williams and Elmore, 1976: 108).

The Follow Through data analysis showed greater variation within groups than between them, i.e., the 22 models did not show systematic treatment effects as such. Most effects were null, some were negative, but "of all our findings, the most pervasive, consistent, and suggestive is probably this: *The effectiveness of each Follow Through model depended more on local circumstances than on the nature of the model*" (Anderson, 1977: 13; italics in original). In reviewing these findings, Eugene Tucker of the U.S. Office of Education suggests that, in retrospect, the Follow Through evaluation should have begun as a formative effort with greater focus on implementation strategies:

It is safe to say that evaluators did not know what was implemented in the various sites. Without knowing what was implemented it is virtually impossible to select valid effectiveness measures. . . . Hindsight is a marvelous teacher and in large scale experimentations an expensive one (Tucker, 1977: 11-12).

Yet the importance of framing evaluation questions in the context of program implementation appears to be a hard lesson to learn. Provus (1971: 27-29) clearly warned against precisely the kind of design used in the Follow Through evaluation at a 1966 conference on educational evaluation of national programs, a conference which included U.S. Office of Education officials. By 1971, he had fully developed and published his "discrepancy evaluation" model, which places heavy emphasis on implementation evaluation:

An evaluation that begins with an experimental design denies to program staff what it needs most: information that can be used to make judgments about the program while it is in its dynamic stages of growth. . . . Evaluation must provide administrators and program staff with the information they need and the freedom to act on that information. . . .

We will not use the antiseptic assumptions of the research laboratory to compare children receiving new program assistance with those not receiving such aid. We recognize that the comparisons have never been productive, nor have they facilitated corrective action. The overwhelming number of evaluations conducted in this way show no significant differences between "experimental" and "control" groups (Provus, 1971: 11-12).

Provus argued that evaluations had to begin by establishing the degree to which programs were actually operating as desired. Discrepancy evaluation is a comparison of the actual program with the ideal program. These ideals "may arise from any source, but under the Discrepancy Evaluation Model they are derived from the values of the program staff and the client population it serves" (Provus, 1971: 12). Evaluation of programs, even national programs, must begin at the local level because

it follows that if there are types of programs with different developmental characteristics, the development standards for these program types will vary also. . . . This local work is usually of the process assessment type in which evaluators systematically collect and weigh data descriptive of ongoing program activity (Provus, 1971: 13).

Provus essentially argued that the nature of the evaluation should be adapted to fit the organizational realities of program development and implementation. *The reality is that actual programs look different from ideal program plans. The evaluation challenge is to assist identified decisionmakers in determining how far from the ideal plan the program can deviate, and in what ways it can deviate, while still meeting fundamental criteria.* How different can an actual program be from its ideal and still be said to have been implemented? The answer must be clarified between decisionmakers and evaluators as they conceptualize the evaluation and focus the evaluation question. It depends on decisionmaker needs and the particular organizational dynamics of the program being evaluated. Williams outlines the issues for negotiation and clarification as follows:

At some point there should be a determination of the degree to which an innovation has been implemented successfully. What should the implemented activity be expected to look like in terms of the underlying decision? For a complex treatment package put in different local settings, decisionmakers usually will not expect—or more importantly, *not want*—a precise reproduction of every detail of the package. The objective is performance, not conformance. To enhance the probability of achieving the basic program or policy objectives, the implementation should consist of a realistic development of the underlying decision in terms of the local setting. In the ideal situation, those responsible for implementation would take the basic idea and modify it to meet special local conditions. There should be a reasonable resemblance to the basic idea, as measured by inputs and expected outputs, incorporating the best of the decision and the best of the local ideas (Williams and Elmore, 1976: 277-278).

I would not belabor these points if it were not so painfully clear that implementation processes are so frequently ignored in evaluation research. Edwards et al., (1975: 142) note in their introduction to the decision-theoretic approach to evaluation that "we have frequently encountered the idea that a [national] program is a fixed, unchanging object, observable at various times and places." Because this idea seems so firmly lodged in so many minds and continues to spawn so many evaluation disasters, I feel compelled to prolong this section with one more piece of evidence to the contrary.

RAND Corporation, under contract to the U.S. Office of Education, studied 293 federal programs supporting educational change. It is one of the largest and most comprehensive studies of educational change ever conducted. RAND's Change Agency Study concluded that implementation "dominates the innovative process and its outcomes:"

> In short, where implementation was successful, and where significant change in participant attitudes, skills, and behavior occurred, implementation was characterized by a process of mutual adaptation in which project goals and methods were modified to suit the needs and interests of the local staff and in which the staff changed to meet the requirements of the project. This finding was true even for highly technological and initially well-specified projects; unless adaptations were made in the original plans or technologies, implementation tended to be superficial or symbolic, and significant change in participants did not occur (McLaughlin, 1976: 169).

The Change Agent Study found that the usual emphasis in federal programs on the *delivery system* is inappropriate. McLaughlin recommended

> a shift in change agent policies from a primary focus on the *delivery system* to an emphasis on the *deliverer*. An important lesson that can be derived from the Change Agent Study is that unless the developmental needs of the users are addressed, and unless projects are modified to suit the needs of the user and the institutional setting, the promise of new technologies is likely to be unfulfilled (McLaughlin, 1976: 180).

In the context of the examples of evaluation absurdities cited in this chapter, and combined with the works of Provus, Williams, Murphy and others, the Rand Change Agent Study has enormous implications for the utilization of evaluation. The conclusion of the RAND study means that *implementation evaluation is critical because program implementation is neither automatic nor certain. It means that implementation evaluation must also be adaptive and focused on users if the evaluation is to be relevant, meaningful, and useful. It means that judging program implementation according to some written-in-stone blueprint is inappropriate and dysfunctional. It means that criteria for evaluating implementation must be developed through a process of interaction with identified and organized decisionmakers and information users in order to determine how they view implementation. It means that evaluators will have to be active-reactive-adaptive in framing evaluation questions in the context of program implementation.*

Types of Implementation Evaluation

In order to be active-reactive-adaptive in framing evaluation questions, evaluators need to understand implementation evaluation alternatives. There are three evaluation options with respect to studying implementation: (1) the effort approach, (2) the process approach, and (3) the treatment specification approach. These are not mutually exclusive approaches; a comprehensive evaluation may include all three types of implementation evaluations.

EFFORT EVALUATION

Effort evaluations focus on documenting "the quantity and quality of activity that takes place. This represents an assessment of input or energy regardless of output. It is intended to answer the questions 'What did you do' and 'How well did you do it?' " (Suchman, 1967: 61). Effort evaluation moves up a step from asking if the program exists to asking how active the program is. If relatively inactive, it is unlikely to be very effective.

> Evaluation of program effort refers to an assessment of the amounts and kinds of program activities considered necessary for the accomplishment of program goals within a particular stage of development. It refers not only to staff time, activity, and commitment, but also to the allocation and use of material resources—funds, space, equipment, etc.... information

such as the following might be obtained about program effort: what techniques for recruiting potential clientele have been employed; how much staff time, effort, funds, etc., have been expended; what ancillary resources have been used, e.g., outside consultation, media, public relations, etc.? (Tripodi et al., 1971: 45).

An effort evaluation establishes the level of program activity by observing the degree to which inputs are available and operational at desired levels. Have sufficient staff been hired with the proper qualifications? Are staff-client ratios at desired levels? How many clients with what characteristics are being served by the program? Are necessary materials available? An effort evaluation involves making an inventory of program operations.

PROCESS EVALUATION

The second option in implementation analysis is process evaluation. This approach focuses on the internal dynamics and actual operations of a program in an attempt to understand its strengths and weaknesses. Process evaluations focus on why certain things are happening, how the parts of the program fit together, and how people perceive the program. This approach takes its name from an emphasis on looking at how a product or outcome is produced rather than looking at the product itself, i.e., it is an analysis of the processes whereby a program produces the results it does. Process evaluation is developmental, descriptive, continuous, flexible, and inductive.

Process evaluations search for explanations of the successes, failures, and changes in a program. Under field conditions in the real world, people and unforeseen circumstances shape programs and modify initial plans in ways that are rarely trivial. The process evaluator sets out to understand and document the day-to-day reality of the setting or settings under study. He tries to unravel what is actually happening in a program by searching for the major patterns and important nuances that give the program its character. A process evaluation requires sensitivity to both qualitiative and quantitative changes in programs throughout their development; it means becoming intimately acquainted with the details of the program. Process evaluations look not only at formal activities and anticipated outcomes, but also investigate informal patterns and unanticipated consequences in the full context of program implementation and development.

Finally, process evaluations usually include perceptions of people close to the program about how things are going. A variety of perspectives may be sought from people inside and outside the program. For example, Hayman and Napier (1975: 84) describe a variety of ways process data can be collected at the classroom level in educational evaluations: "it is now possible to gather reliable process data in numerous ways—from peers, outside resource people, students, and, of course, the teacher's own observations." These differing perspectives can provide unique insights into program processes as experienced by different people.

A process evaluation can provide useful feedback during the developmental phase of a program. It can also be used to collect implementation data for use in diffusion and dissemination processes. One evaluator in our utilization of federal health evaluations reported that process information had been particularly useful to federal officials in expanding a program nationwide.

> We used as our sample those centers which had been in existence for a year. This was to allow for the start-up problems and, you know, gearing up and getting under speed and all that stuff. The reason they wanted it done when it was done was so that it would be able to affect subsequent centers. . . .
>
> I like to think in terms of programmatic issues, in terms of making a difference in the next center that opened, or in the whole series of things that were required in order for a center to get on the way. . . . *The process evaluations that we did for the centers one by one, one at a time, each of those were affected by the results.* And so, the timing was very critical for that, and I think it was the appropriate time (EV51: 22).

Suchman (1967: 67) suggests that

> the analysis of process may be made according to four main dimensions dealing with: (1) the attributes of the program itself; (2) the population exposed to the program: (3) the situational context within which the program takes place; and (4) the different kinds of effects produced by the program.

However, he considers process evaluation an ancillary component in that

> this analysis of the process whereby a program produces the results it does, is not an inherent part of evaluative research. An evaluation study may limit its data collection and analysis to determining whether or not a program is successful . . . without examining the why's and wherefor's (sic) of this success or failure (Suchman, 1967: 66).

Scriven (1967: 49-50) concurs that process analysis has only a limited role to play in evaluation:

It is not inappropriate to regard some kinds of process investigation as evaluation. But the range of process research only overlaps with and is never subsumed by nor equivalent to that of evolution.

Other evaluators, however, think that process evaluation ought to be taken more seriously. Process evaluation is one of the four major components of the CIPP (context, input, process, product) model of evaluation developed by Stufflebeam et al. (1970, 1971). They consider process evaluation to be an integral part of "a total evaluation model." They see process evaluation in a broad sense, as (1) gathering data to detect or predict defects in the procedural design or its implementation during the implementation stages, (2) providing information for program decision, and (3) establishing a record of program development as it occurs.

In a utilization-focused approach to evaluation research process analysis is neither inherently ancillary nor inherently integral to evaluation research. Process evaluation is one of the optional approaches available to decisionmakers, information users, and evaluators as they attempt to frame evaluation research questions in the context of program implementation.

TREATMENT SPECIFICATION

The treatment specification approach to implementation evaluation involves identifying and measuring precisely what it is about a program that is supposed to have an effect. What is going to happen in the program that is expected to make a difference? How are program goals supposed to be attained? What theory do program staff hold about what they have to do in order to accomplish the results they want? In technical terms, this means identifying independent variables that are expected to affect outcomes (the dependent variables). Treatment specification reveals the causal assumptions undergirding program activity. The treatment specification approach to implementation evaluation means measuring the degree to which specified treatments actually occur. This can be a tricky and difficult task laden with methodological and conceptual pitfalls.

Social programs are complex undertakings. Social program evaluators look with something akin to jealously at evaluators in agriculture who evaluate a new strain of wheat or evaluators in medicine who evaluate the effects of a new drug. . . . The same stimulus can be produced again, and other researchers can study its consequences—under the same or different conditions, with similar or different subjects, but with some assurance that they are looking at the effects of the same *thing.*

Social programs are not nearly so specific. They incorporate a range of components, styles, people, and procedures . . . the content of the program, what actually goes on, is much harder to describe. There are often marked internal variations in operation from day to day and from staff member to staff member. When you consider a program as large and amorphous as the poverty program or the model cities program, it takes a major effort to just describe and analyze the program input (Weiss, 1972b: 43).

Yet unless there is basic information about program intervention activities, the evaluator does not know to what to attribute the outcomes observed. This is the classic problem of treatment specification in social science research and, of course, takes us into the arena of trying to establish causality.

Any new program or project may be though of as representing a theory or hypothesis in that—to use experimental terminology—the decision-maker wants to put in place a treatment expected to *cause* certain predicted effects or outcomes (Williams and Elmore, 1976: 274; italics in original).

From this perspective, one task of implementation evaluation is to identify and operationalize the program treatment.

Many evaluations, especially experimental design evaluations, equate program treatment specification with comparing programs bearing different labels. Because this practice is so prevalent—and so distorting— the next section is a critique of the labeling approach to treatment specifications, followed by a more extensive explanation of how treatments ought to be specified when this approach is used in utilization-focused evaluation.

Program Implementation and Treatment Identification: The Problem of Labeling the Black Box

This section is a simple sermon on the Pandorian folly attendant upon those who would unlock the black box of program implementation through the reification of program labels. There may be no more widespread contravention of basic research principles in evaluation than the practice of using program labels as a substitute for actual data on program implementation. Labels are not treatments. Program labels give no clues about causal relationships. Attaching the same label to a set of projects in programs like Head Start, Community Corrections, Community Mental Health Centers, or Job Corps neither makes the projects that bear those labels comparable nor tells you anything about what a given project actually does.

My own suspicion is that the reification of program labels is a major source of null findings in evaluation research. Labels lead to the aggregation of effective with ineffective programs that have nothing in common except their label. A 1976 evaluation of Residential Community Corrections Programs in Minnesota is a case in point. The report was prepared by the Evaluation Unit of the Governor's Commission on Crime Prevention and Control. The evaluation report compares recidivism rates for three types of programs: (1) halfway houses, (2) PORT (Probationed Offenders Rehabilitation and Training) projects, and (3) juvenile residences.

> The term "halfway house" refers to a "residential facility designed to facilitate the transition of paroled adult exoffenders who are returning to society from institutional confinement." The limitation to adults serves to distinquish halfway houses from juvenile residence which serve juveniles. The identification of paroled ex-offenders as the target population of halfway houses distinguishes the *primary* intervention stage of these projects from the PORT projects in which the primary intervention stage is probation (GCCPC, 1976: 8).

The report presents aggregated outcome data for each type of community corrections program. The evaluators take pride in not analyzing differences among individual projects: "efforts have been made to avoid leading the reader to the conclusion that any given residential community corrections program is 'better' or 'worse' than another" (GCCPC, 1976: 4). The evaluators recognize the design problems of attributing causality to individual project outcomes, but they have no problem aggregating projects about which they have no systematic implementation data. In effect they are comparing the outcomes of three labels: halfway houses, PORT projects, and juvenile residences. The evaluators' idea of dealing with the implementation issue is contained in one sentence: "the projects included in this study are in various stages of implementation, but all are at least in their second or third year of funding from the Commission" (GCCPC, 1976: 6). Nowhere in the several hundred pages of the report is there any systematic data presented about the actual nature of the treatment experiences provided in these programs. People go in and people come out; what happens in between is a black box of no interest to the evaluators.

The evaluation concludes that "the evidence presented in this report indicates that residential community corrections programs have had little, if any, impact on the recidivism of program clients" (GCCPC, 1976: 289). These preliminary findings resulted in a moratorium on funding of new residential community corrections, and the final report recommended maintaining that moratorium. With no attention to the meaningfulness of their analytical labels and with no treatment specifications, the evaluators passed judgment on the effectiveness of an $11 million program.

The irony of this travesty is that the Evaluation Unit of the Minnesota Crime Commission prides itself on the scientific rigor of its work because it requires experimental designs in all program evaluations. In the name of Science, the black box lives on—and prospers. Treatments are never specified beyond amorphous program labels. Just what is it about a halfway house that leads one to expect reduced recidividism? The evaluators never tell us; nor do they document the presence of the supposed treatment.

The problem with the aggregated comparisons was that they were meaningless. In talking with staff in a few of these community corrections projects it rapidly became clear that the separate efforts vary tremendously in treatment modality, clientele, and stage of implementation. The comparisons were based on averages, but the averages disguise important differences. There was no such thing as the average project among those settings; yet they were combined for comparative purposes. The report obscured both individual sites that are doing excellent work and those of dubious quality. It included no careful descriptions of individual residences and no data from clients, staff, or others about the actual nature of these programs. The evaluation revealed nothing about what these facilities do; it only stated that, in the aggregate, the facilities were not effective.[1]

Unfortunately, this example is not an exceptional case. One has only to read the journals in any of the disciplines to find comparisons based on aggregations of programs with similar labels, but lacking any implementation or treatment specification data. There are comparisons between "open" schools and "traditional" schools which present no data on relative openness. There are comparisons of individual therapy with group therapy where no attention is paid to the homogeneity of either category of treatment. The list could be expanded ad infinitum. Edwards et al. (1976: 142) confirm the widespread nature of the labeling approach to treatment specification:

A common administrative fiction, especially in Washington, is that because some money associated with an administrative label (e.g., Head Start) has been spent at several places and over a period of time, that the entities spending the money are comparable from time to time and from place to place. Such assumptions can easily lead to evaluation-research disasters.

Treatment Specification: An Alternative to Labeling

A recent newspaper cartoon showed several federal bureaucrats assembled around a table in a conference room. The chair of the group was saying, "of course the welfare program has a few obvious flaws . . . but if we can just think of a catchy enough name for it, it just might work!" (Dunagin, 1977). In black box evaluations the program labels, catchy or not, are the only thing that can be given credit for program success or blame for program failure. In cases like the Minnesota Community Corrections evaluation, simply knowing the project label was of little help in figuring out what the program actually did.

Treatment specification for implementation evaluation purposes means being able to state what is going to happen in the program that is expected to make a difference. How are program goals supposed to be attained? What theory do program staff hold about what they have to do in order to accomplish the results they want? In technical terms, this means identifying independent variables that are expected to affect outcomes. It is what Provus (1971: 50) called "a program design. The design tells us what we're evaluating, what we can expect to find out in the field. Our first task is to gather information on the design."

Treatment specification reveals the causal assumptions undergirding program activity. For example, one theory undergirding community corrections is that integration of criminal offenders into local communities is the best way to rehabilitate those offenders and thereby reduce recidivism. It is therefore important to gather information about the degree to which each project actually integrates offenders into the community. Halfway houses and juvenile residences can be run like small-scale prisons, completely isolated from the environment. Treatment specification tells us what to look for in each project to find out if the program's causal theory is actually being put to the test. At this point we are not dealing with the question of how to measure the relevant independent variables in a program theory, but only attempting to specify the intended treatment in nominal terms.

In 1976, the Ramsey County Community Corrections Department in Minnesota wanted to evaluate their foster group home program for juvenile offenders. In discussions with the identified and organized decisionmakers and information users, it became clear that there was no systematic data about what Ramsey County foster group homes were actually like. The theory undergirding the program was that juvenile offenders would be more likely to be rehabilitated if they were placed in warm, supportive, and nonauthoritarian environments where they were valued by others and could therefore learn to value themselves. The goals of the program were to make juveniles happy and capable of exercising independent judgment, and to reduce recidivism.

The evaluation question was framed in the context of both program goals and program implementation. A major priority of the evaluation effort was to describe and analyze the Ramsey County Group Home "treatment environment." This priority derived from the fact that at the beginning of the study there was no systematic knowledge about what the homes were actually like. What happens in a group home? What does a juvenile experience? What kind of "treatment" is a youth exposed to in a group home? What are the variations in group homes? Are there certain types that seem to be more successful in terms of the outcomes of (1) providing positive experiences for youth and (2) reducing recidivism?

The data analysis showed that group homes in Ramsey County could be placed along a continuum where one end represented homes that were highly supportive and participatory and the other represented homes that were nonsupportive and authoritarian. Homes were about evenly distributed along the continua of support versus nonsupport and participatory versus authoritarian patterns, i.e., about half the juveniles experienced homes that tended to be more supportive-participatory and about half tended to be more nonsupportive-authoritarian. Juveniles from supportive-participatory group homes showed significantly lower recidivism rates than juveniles from nonsupportive-authoritarian ones ($r = .33$, $p < .01$). Variations in type of group home environment were also found to be significantly related to other outcome variables (Patton et al., 1977b).

In terms of treatment specification, these data demonstrated two things: (1) in about half of the county's 55 group homes, juveniles were not experiencing the kind of treatment that the program design called for; and (2) outcomes varied directly with nature and degree of program implementation. Clearly it would make no sense to conceptualize these 55 group homes as a homogenous treatment. We found homes that were run like prisons, homes where juveniles were physically abused. We also found homes where young offenders were loved and treated as though they were members of the family. Aggregation of recidivism data from all of these homes into a single average rate would produce null findings in most comparisons with other aggregated programs. But when the treatment is specified and degrees of implementation are measured, it is possible to evaluate quite reasonably the program theory both in terms of feasibility and effectiveness.

Evaluating Treatment Environments: A Social Ecological Approach

Thus far, most evaluation research has been purely outcomes-oriented, with little or no treatment specification. An important exception is Rudolf Moos, who has drawn upon a large body of social science research on business organizations, prisons, families, schools, hospitals, factories, and a broad range of bureaucratic settings, gradually conceptualizing certain key dimensions of the environment in organizations, families, and treatment programs. The work of Moos is a model for treatment specifications; the group home evaluation just discussed drew heavily on it. Moos (1975: 4) explains his approach as follows:

> The social climate perspective assumes that environments have unique "personalities," just like people. Personality tests assess personality traits or needs and provide information about the characteristic ways in which people behave. Social environments can be similarly portrayed with a great deal of accuracy and detail. Some people are more supportive than others. Likewise, some social environments are more supportive than others. Some people feel a strong need to control others. Similarly, some social environments are extremely rigid, autocratic, and controlling. Order, clarity, and structure are important to many people. Correspondingly, many social environments strongly emphasize order, clarity and control.

Different social scientists use different terms to describe these dimensions of the environment, but there are many similarities in what they are describing (e.g., Hage and Aiken, 1970; Burns and Stalker, 1961; Anderson and Walberg, 1968). Below are some of the terms that are used to specify and distinguish different treatment environments:

Formal	Informal
Centralized	Decentralized
Authoritarian	Participatory (Democratic)
Divisive	Cohesive
Standardized	Individualized
Hierarchical	Egalitarian

Controlled	Expressive
Partitioned	Integrated
Independent Parts	Interdependent Parts
Routinized	Individualized
Isolated	Community-Oriented
Low Communications	High Communications
Interactions	Interactions

It is important to understand that *these terms are meant to be descriptive* rather than pejorative, prejudicial, or prescriptive. These terms or dimensions are ways of thinking about the differences among organizations, families, and treatment programs. Under certain conditions one type of organization or program environment may be desirable, while under other circumstances a different type may be desirable.

Rudolf Moos (1974, 1975) has done the most comprehensive work in conceptualizing and operationalizing the treatment environment for purposes of program evaluation. Moos calls his work "a social ecological approach" to evaluation research. He has developed concepts and scales to describe and measure variations in treatment environments for mental health institutions, correctional institutions, family environments, military units, and classrooms. He is working toward a taxonomy of social environments and has already developed nine "social climate scales" in his work at the Social Ecology Laboratory and Psychiatry Research Training Program at Stanford University.

Moos has related his treatment environment variables to a variety of program outcome variables in criminal justice, education, and health settings, with statistically significant and meaningful results. His work takes on added significance because deinstitutionalization is currently the dominant theoretical direction in social intervention. He has developed a set of variables in a well-constructed theoretical framework to evaluate the implementation and effects of deinstitutionalization.

Moos' work constitutes an exemplary model of the contribution evaluation research can make to social science theory. However, from a utilization-focused perspective any theoretical model, including the sophisticated and comprehensive social ecological approach, must be adapted to the specific evaluation needs of identified decisionmakers and information users. Moos' variables ought not be adopted wholesale; careful consideration must be given to their relevance in representing the nascent theoretical notions of relevant decisionmakers and information users. In the Ramsey County foster group home evaluation described in the previous section, we did just that. Once evaluation task force members identified the relevant treatment dimensions as "warmth, support, involvement, and participatory family decisionmaking," we showed them some of Moos' factors to see if they were representative and descriptive of the program's intervention theory. With additions, deletions, and adaptations, the Moos conceptual and operational scheme proved very helpful. *But the theoretical formulation process began with identified evaluation task force decisionmakers—not with a scholarly search of the literature.* The theory tested was the theory held by relevant decisionmakers and information users.

Evaluators may want to test their own particular theories based on what their disciplinary literature specifies as important independent variables. Where resources are adequate and the design can be managed, the evaluators may prevail upon decisionmakers to include tests of those theories the evaluators hold dear. But first priority goes to providing identified decisionmakers with information about the degree to which their own implementation ideals and treatment specifications have actually been realized in program operations. Causal models are often forced on program staff when they bear no similarity to the models on which that staff bases its program activities. The evaluators' research interests are secondary to the information needs of identified decisionmakers and information users in utilization-focused evaluation.

Implementation Overview: Framing the Evaluation Question In the Context of Program Implementation

There is considerable evidence that failure at the implementation stage is a major reason for the human services shortfall and ineffective social programs. Evaluations that have ignored implementation issues (and such evaluations are abundant) may have asked the wrong questions. Thus, to avoid gathering useless or erroneous information *it is important to understand the option of framing evaluation questions in the context of program implementation.* This can be a major element in utilization-focused evaluation, particularly in comprehensive evaluations that also include framing the evaluation question in the context of program goals.

Evaluatiion research has been dominated by outcomes evaluation. Evaluating outcomes without knowledge of implementation is the "black box" approach to evaluation. Unlocking the black box means studying program implementation. The difference between the ideal, rational model of program implementation and the day-to-day, incrementalist, and conflict-laden realities of program implementation has enormous implications for a utilization-focused approach to evaluation. Successful implementation is characterized as a process of adaptation of the ideal to local conditions, organizational dynamics, and programmatic uncertainties. Active-reactive-adaptive evaluators will work with identified decisionmakers and information users to determine how far from and in what ways the program can deviate from the ideal plan while still meeting fundamental implementation criteria.

Once the evaluator has determined that the program in question actually exists (the first implementation issue in an evaluation), there are three evaluation options with respect to studying implementation: (1) effort evaluation, (2) process evaluation, and (3) the treatment specification approach. Effort evaluations focus on documenting the quantity and quality of program activity; if the program is relatively inactive, it is unlikely to be very effective. Process evaluation focuses on the internal dynamics of a program in an attempt to understand its strengths and weaknesses; this approach takes its name from looking at how a product or outcome is produced, i.e., it is an analysis of the processes whereby a program produces the results it does. The treatment specification approach involves identifying and measuring precisely what it is about a program that is supposed to have an effect; in technical terms, this means identifying independent variables that are expected to affect outcomes (the dependent variables).

Depending on the nature of the issues involved and the information needed, any one, two, or all three of the approaches to implementation evaluation might be employed. The point is that without information about actual program operations, decisionmakers are extremely limited in their ability to interpret performance data or to improve program functioning. *Effort evaluations, the treatment specification approach, and process evaluations answer different questions and focus on different aspects of program implementation. The key is to match the type(s) of evaluation to the information needs of relevant decisionmakers and information users.* One of the decisionmakers we interviewed in our utilization study was emphatic on this point:

> Different types of evaluations are appropriate and useful at different times. . . . HEW tends to talk about evaluation as if it's a single thing. Whereas the important thing is a better understanding within HEW that there are different types of evaluation. That it should not be used as EVALUATION! Using the word generically, as a generic word, is harmful. . . . We ought to stop using evaluation as if it's a single homogenous thing (DM111: 29).

Implementation evaluation is one of the options from which decision-makers and information users can choose as the evaluator works with them to frame the evaluation question. Not all final evaluation designs will include implementation data. Variations in implementation may already be known to decisionmakers, or information other than implementation may be more important, relevant, and useful to them given the uncertainties they face. Thus, whether implementation evaluation is part of the final design depends on the particular evaluation question that emerges as the focus of study. *What is crucial is that during the process of framing the evaluation question the issue of implementation analysis is raised.* Evaluators have a responsibility in their active-reactive-adaptive interactions with decisionmakers and information users to explore evaluation options. Decisionmakers and evaluators both need to know what can be learned through implementation analysis, effort studies, process evaluations, and treatment specification so that they can decide what information is most useful in the particular circumstances at hand.

NOTE

1. I am indebted to two colleagues for their critiques of this evaluation: Malcolm Bush, Urban Affairs and Education, Northwestern University; and Thomas Dewar, School of Public Affairs, University of Minnesota.

III

TECHNOLOGY OF EVALUATION

There are many problems encountered by evaluation researchers—problems not properly conceived as design problems, but which must nonetheless be successfully resolved if quality evaluation is to be accomplished. We use the term *technology* here to refer to those aspects of evaluation research. There are many possible technological problems, so many and so varied, in fact, that we could not anticipate and enumerate all of them here. However, the papers which follow present issues having to do with training, selection, and supervision of evaluation research personnel; with measurement and monitoring problems; with the limitations of surveys and other social indicators. The paper by Hedrick, Boruch, and Ross calls attention to the necessity for making data sets systematically available for secondary analysis, and presents some principles which should be adhered to. The paper by Rhoads is addressed to the particularly troublesome problem of how a monetary value may be placed on human life—not an especially attractive prospect—but one not always avoidable. Evaluation research, like any other enterprise, depends on its tools and its knowledge of how to use them.

How should evaluation researchers be trained? What should they be expected to know? In a field as nearly in its infancy as evaluation research there is a host of questions that need to be pondered as training programs are born and grow. Anderson and Ball's work ponders some of the questions and presents interesting empirical survey data from evaluation researchers who were asked to ponder also. The results are provocative and point to a heterodoxy that may for the immediate future be most healthy.

17

Training Evaluators and Evaluating their Competencies

Scarvia B. Anderson and Samuel Ball

Training program evaluators is an educational enterprise of rather recent vintage. Until recently, evaluators were drawn into the profession by the work to be done—or by the lack of work in related fields. Psychologists, educators, operations researchers, sociologists, economists, medical and health professionals, anthropologists, and MBAs have all done stints in the field. Some have written a critical note here or a how-to-do-it chapter there and then returned to the haven of

Note: We are indebted to William I. Sauser, Jr., for assistance on the survey described in this chapter. A preliminary report was presented at the twenty-second annual meeting of the Southeastern Psychological Association, 1976.

Publisher's Note: Complete citations for the works referred to in this chapter may be found in the bibliography of *The Profession and Practice of Program Evaluation,* published by Jossey-Bass, Inc.

From Scarvia B. Anderson and Samuel Ball, "Training Evaluators and Evaluating their Competencies," *The Profession and Practice of Program Evaluation* 165-190. San Francisco: Jossey-Bass, 1978. Copyright 1978 by Jossey-Bass, Inc., Publishers.

their basic discipline. Others have stayed, some to try to invent new programs to train evaluators.

The nature of these inventions varies from those designed to train program evaluators directly to those designed to train them inductively or by osmosis; from those emphasizing the area in which evaluation is to be conducted (for example, mental health) to those emphasizing methodologies that might be applied to the evaluation of programs in a variety of areas (for example, social, medical, or educational programs); from those that require a major in a specific discipline (such as social psychology) to deliberately multidisciplinary approaches.

Growing out of psychology, for example, are several new kinds of Ph.D. programs that specifically recognize the requirement for some of their graduates to engage in program evaluation. The Wright Institute in Berkeley, California, offers a program in social-clinical psychology that includes training for students with "an interest in working in social agencies or community programs or in social action or evaluation positions" (Freedman, 1976, p. 183). The experience of the Michigan State "Ph.D. Program Aimed at Survival Issues" has been that "the majority of . . . students have gone to nonacademic positions, often as program evaluators at the state or local agency level," even though the authors of the program are not optimistic that the world is ready for the broader ecological psychology they would prefer to foster (Tornatzky, 1976, p. 191). At Pennsylvania State a graduate program designed to prepare students for public-affairs careers includes substantial work in "research methods and quantitative skills"; one of the outcome objectives is "ability to design studies that will empirically reflect the probable concurrent and long-term consequences of putting policy-oriented programs into effect" (Vallance, 1976, p. 197). The doctoral program at Northwestern is cited as one which is "helping to shape the emerging multidiscipline of program evaluation"; Northwestern also has a postdoctoral program in program evaluation (Perloff and others, 1976, p. 573). The environmental-psychology program at City University of New York (Proshansky, 1976) and the public-affairs program at Claremont (Brayfield, 1976) represent other reactions to such contentions as those made by M. Brewster Smith, George Fairweather, and Albee and Loeffler: "Our graduate training, heavily focused on the methodology of laboratory experimentation and its accompanying statistics, is seriously out of date in equipping the coming generations of psychologists for new roles in evaluation and policy research" (Smith, 1973, p. 465). "Most psychologists were, and are, largely inept in field methodology and had virtually no skills to bring to bear on policy-related research" (Fairweather cited in Tornatzky, 1976, p. 189). "Separate professional training schools for psychology must be established, following the historically evolving model provided by other professions, to eliminate role conflicts and make clear the essential division of labor between the psychologist as a scientist and the psychologist as a professional" (Albee and Loeffler cited in Perloff and others, 1976, p. 589).

Phi Delta Kappa has prepared a list of seventy-seven training programs in educational evaluation, including information on degrees offered, number of required credits and semesters, admission requirements, faculty members in the speciality, and costs. The list is available through the Evaluation Network (see Chapter Eleven). The National Institute of Mental Health also has a list of about thirty training programs for evaluators in health or other areas leading to undergraduate, master's, or doctoral degrees, some of them mentioned at the beginning of this chapter. (See Scriven and Ward, 1977, pp. 19–21.)

It should also be noted that there is a growing trend toward continuing education and self-study in program evaluation for concerned lay persons and for those who may have received their Ph.D.s long before program evaluation became popular. For example, there is hardly a meeting of the American Educational Research Association that does not include a training "presession" in program evaluation; the University of Massachusetts holds an annual summer institute in evaluation research (Wright, 1977); Sechrest and Campbell (1975) developed a summer training program in health-care research methodology, and the ETS Programs of Continuing Education regularly include components on evaluation. Instructional materials intended to be largely self-explanatory include Scriven's (1971) cassette, which makes introductory evaluation skills as available to the automobile commuter as foreign phrases are; *A Procedure for Assessing the Performance of a Particular School,* also by Scriven (1976b); *The Evaluation Improvement Program,* developed by the California Department of Education (1977) and distributed by Educational Testing Service to "lead" school district personnel "through the steps required to develop and carry out a comprehensive plan of evaluation"; *Citizen Evaluation of Mental Health Services* (MacMurray and others, 1976) aimed at helping citizens assure themselves of adequate community health care; *Program Evaluation in the State Mental Health Agency,* a manual prepared by the Southern Regional Education Board (1975) and designed to assist administrators in evaluating mental-health programs; and *Resource Materials for Community Mental Health Program Evaluation,* a five-volume set of educational materials produced by the Langley Porter Institute (1974).

The variety of modes of training in evaluation reflects some of the controversies in the field:

- Should evaluation be perceived as a discipline or profession, as opposed to a job? (The latter perception seems to be associated with some bias against formal training and with advocacy of "internship" or "in-service" experiences.)
- Does training in social or educational research per se qualify a program evaluator? (After apparently enormous success in World War II, experimental psychologists were inclined to proclaim that their brand of training was sufficient preparation for work on any problem involving human performance.)
- Do some of the popular terms in the field represent real substance rather than jargon, and thus do future evaluators need to become acquainted with them? (Some of the "models" of evaluation are cited as examples: "CIPP," "Discrepancy," "Goal-free"—see Stufflebeam and others, 1971; Provus, 1971; and Scriven, 1974.)

As other sections of this book suggest, we are inclined to view program evaluation as a profession. We do not hold that training in social or educational research alone is sufficient to prepare people for all of the exigencies associated with evaluation of real-world programs. We favor highlighting the conceptual underpinnings of evaluation rather than the favorite terms of particular people.

However, regardless of the merits of our positions, the first task in a rational approach to specifying a productive training program for evaluators is to define what the important evaluation competencies are, no matter how they are obtained or whether they are applied full- or part-time.

Evaluation Competencies

A panel meeting held in Princeton, New Jersey, in late 1974 (see the Preface) served as the stimulus for an initial listing of important knowledge and skills we might expect of the competent evaluator. We modified that list somewhat in an Office of Naval Research report the following fall (Ball and Anderson, 1975b, Table 6). Then in the spring of 1976 we submitted the list to a larger group of experts for reaction. Since the knowledge and skills evaluators need are a matter of opinion, *whose* opinion takes on considerable importance. We sought counsel from our colleagues, searched the indexes of books in the field, and relied heavily on Stake's unpublished "Partial List of Persons Who Can Give Valuable Counsel on Curriculum Evaluation." The result was a list of sixty-four people whose opinions we would value and which would seem to carry weight in the field: Marvin Alkin, Gilbert Austin, Bernard Bass, Thomas Bice, Urie Bronfenbrenner, Donald Campbell, John Campbell, Hugh Cline, William Coffman, Jacob Cohen, Thomas Cook, William Cooley, Richard Cox, Lee Cronbach, Joel Davitz, Henry Dyer, Robert Ebel, Albert Erlebacher, John Feldhusen, James Gallagher, Eric Gardner, William Gephart, Robert Glaser, Gene Glass, Irwin Goldstein, Egon Guba, Marcia Guttentag, Robert Heath, Gerald Helmstadter, Wells Hiveley, Ernest House, Paul Kelley, Nadine Lambert, Henry Levin, Edward Loveland, Daniel Lyons, George Madaus, Thomas Maguire, Jack Merwin, Jason Millman, Jum Nunnally, Ellis Page, David Payne, Robert Perloff, Robert Rippey, Seymour Sarason, Michael

Scriven, Marvin Sontag, Charles Spielberger, Robert Stake, William Stallings, Julian Stanley, Howard Stoker, James Stone, Elmer Struening, Daniel Stufflebeam, Robert Thorndike, Melvin Tumin, Herbert Walberg, Henry Walbesser, Carol Weiss, Frank Womer, Blaine Worthen, and Albert Yee.*

Since we have been accused in the past of taking too behavioristic a view of program evaluation (behavioristic = objective, psychometric, experimental, mechanistic, rigid, or hard, depending on who makes the charge), we made a deliberate effort to include some people whose positions might be characterized as more phenomenological (phenomenological = subjective, case-study, nonexperimental, comprehensive, responsive, or soft, again depending on the labeler). We also tried to include some professionals who were identified more with evaluation of health and social-action programs than with evaluation of education and training programs (with which we are more familiar).

Although we are less concerned with the etiology of evaluation competencies than with whether those competencies exist, we thought that it would be informative for purposes of this exposition also to ask the experts for their opinions about the best ways to obtain initial levels of competence and information about programs and prospects for training evaluators in their institutions. Opinions and information were sought through a questionnaire. The first part consisted of a list of thirty-two "content areas" and "special skills and sensitivities." Responders were asked to rate the importance of each (essential, desirable, not very important) and suggest the best source of initial competency in each area (formal instruction, independent study or application, supervised field experience, other). Comments and additional listings were invited. The second part of the questionnaire contained questions about training in evaluation for graduate students in the responder's institution. Replies were received from forty-eight, or three fourths, of the group on the mailing list—a fair

---

*We hope that it is not a violation of professional ethics to list these names here. The listing is the only way we can adequately describe the expert sample whose views we sought. The names will not be identified with responses or nonresponses.

record for an undertaking of this kind. But then social scientists—
and especially those who get mixed up in program evaluation—
probably have a peculiar appreciation of the difficulties posed by
nonresponse.

However, of the forty-eight who replied, four did not complete
the questionnaire. Three said they could not cope with it for one reason or another:

> I found the questionnaire impossible to answer. All
> items are essential for some applications. Some are very essen-
> tial but require no training—just smarts and/or effort. Others
> may not generally be essential but require training.

> I am sorry to have to return your questionnaire this
> way because I believe professionals should try to be helpful.
> However, . . . I can't possibly make a decision between instruc-
> tion, independent study, and field experience. We believe that
> all three go together and that is the way we train our students.
> . . . Also, for the importance issue, they are all important. If
> one is more important than others, it can only be determined
> by the particular problem.

> The questionnaire presupposes an orientation to
> evaluation, and therefore the training of evaluators, which I
> do not fully subscribe to. Therefore, I'm afraid my answers
> would be misleading.

One person who did not fill out the questionnaire returned a
comprehensive paper he had written in the general area. And one
responder who completed parts of the questionnaire still had some
pretty scathing things to say about it—but expressed an important,
and not entirely idiosyncratic, view about evaluation: "That was ter-
rible. Such a mindless approach to talking about professional competence. I am ashamed of you for being associated with it. What I mean
is that skills are important to situations. There is no standard evaluation situation and hopefully there will not be one. We should be
encouraging educators and others to think of how *they* can increase
their understanding of the value of a program rather than suggesting
that specialists can find out and tell them. There should not be an edu-

cational specialty, only educators who can observe, think, judge, and so on."

Somewhat chastened, we present Table 6 showing the numbers of responders assigning each of the importance ratings to the "content areas" and "special skills and sensitivities" listed on the questionnaire. The content areas that seemed to appeal to the greatest number as "basics" were in the category of statistics, analysis, and design. Even a couple of people who usually avoid formal designs and analyses in their own evaluation work nevertheless labeled knowledge in these areas as at least a desirable part of the armamentarium of the competent evaluator. Perhaps they also think it is important for abstract painters to know how to draw.

Less than one fourth of the respondents thought that expertise in case-study methodology or job analysis was essential for the pro-

Table 6. Importance of Content Areas and Skills
(Rated by Number of Persons Responding to Each; N = 44)

	Essential	Desirable	Not Very Important	No Response
		Importance		
Content Area				
Descriptive statistics	38	6	0	0
Inferential statistics	38	6	0	0
Statistical analysis	35	9	0	0
Quasi-experimental design	35	9	0	0
Experimental design	34	10	0	0
Data preparation and reduction	33	11	0	0
Correlation and regression methods	33	10	1	0
Survey methods	32	12	0	0
Major literature and reference sources useful for evaluators	32	11	0	1
Method of controlling quality of data collection and analysis	32	10	1	1
Sampling	31	11	2	0
Application of interviews, questionnaires, ratings	31	11	1	1

Table 6 (continued)

	Importance			
	Essential	*Desirable*	*Not Very Important*	*No Response*
Alternative models for program evaluation	31	9	4	0
Psychometrics (reliability, validity, scaling, equating, and so on)	30	12	1	1
Applications of tests (paper-and-pencil, situational, performance, and so on)	27	14	2	1
Application of observation techniques, unobtrusive measures	23	20	0	1
Techniques of setting goals and performance standards	23	16	4	1
Reactive concerns in measurement and evaluation	21	16	3	4
Field operations	21	15	1	7
Major constructs in education and the social sciences	20	16	3	5
Cost-benefits analysis	19	20	4	1
Contracts and proposals	17	20	5	2
Legal and professional standards for empirical studies	15	24	4	1
Content analysis	14	24	3	3
Case-study methodology	11	29	4	0
Job analysis	7	22	15	0
Skills				
Professional and ethical sensitivity	37	4	1	2
Expository skills (speaking and writing)	32	10	0	2
Sensitivity to concerns of all interested parties	31	5	0	8
Interpersonal skills	28	12	3	1
Public-relations skills	17	20	6	1
Management skills	14	26	3	1

gram evaluator, and fifteen relegated job analysis to the "not very important" column. Some of the "no responses" tabulated in Table 6 were asterisked by a responder to indicate "areas which might be of greater or lesser importance, depending upon the nature of the evaluation task. In some situations these items may be of *no* importance." Such comments reinforce the situational nature of evaluation, which is a continuing theme in this book.

In terms of the number of endorsements, professional and ethical sensitivity is as important for evaluators as knowledge of statistics, analysis, and design. Public-relations and management skills were judged less important than the other skills areas listed, but one responder noted that the "need for managerial skills would vary with the size of the project." However, the whole skills area met with enthusiasm or was singled out for special comment by several of the responders. For example:

> The importance of such sensitivities cannot be underestimated! Your "skills areas"—and cost analysis—are very important but often neglected areas of training.

> We do a relatively good job of teaching the evaluator-to-be what he needs to know in the technical role (statistics, measurement, and research design). BUT we are failing in the interpersonal-skills area, in the recognition that research and evaluation serve different purposes, in the ability to identify the decisions on which an evaluation is to focus, in recognition that decision makers, our clients, process information in different ways than we as evaluators do, and in the role and importance of the affective domain in evaluation.

> All essential skills will not generally be found in any one person. Consequently, an evaluation team with complementary skills will generally be required for program evaluation.

Other competency areas listed by respondents as important are given in Table 7. Some of the suggestions overlap somewhat with the tabulated categories, but they are repeated here because some expert

Table 7. Other Suggested Competency Areas
(Numbers in Parentheses Indicate Number of Responders Choosing Each Area)

Preparing reports, papers, and articles (5)

Decision theory and the decision-making process (4)

Knowledge of evaluation politics and political acumen (4)

Substantive knowledge of the content of the program to be evaluated (3)

Bayesian statistics, residual analysis and transformations, trend analysis, etc. (2)

History of evaluation, with special attention to the impact or absence of impact (2)

Philosophy of science, including limitations of the scientific method (1)

Similarities and differences between research and evaluation (1)

Group planning of evaluation (1)

Negotiating the scope and focus of evaluations (1)

Evaluation of evaluability—determining which evaluations are worth doing (1)

Budgeting of evaluations (1)

Identifying goals to be investigated (1)

Cost-benefits judgment regarding trade-offs in design (1)

Cost-benefits judgments in choice of instruments, techniques, and indicators for data collection (1)

Phenomenological procedures: historiography, diaries, logs, etc. (1)

Matrix sampling (1)

Theories of change (1)

Problem solving (1)

Relations with subject individuals and communities (1)

Specifying and delineating values of groups (1)

Interpreting technical results to lay audiences (1)

Listening skills (1)

Social psychology (1)

Organizational psychology (1)

Planning skills (1)

Grantsmanship: how to get money (1)

Wisdom (1)

Judgment, insight, and originality (1)

Understanding of role conflicts and latent objectives (1)

Needs assessment (1)

Systems-analysis skills (1)

Computer skills—included under data preparation and reduction (1)

Picking up side effects—included in design (1)

or experts called specific attention to them. They range from the theoretical (for example, philosophy of science, including limitations on the scientific method) to the very practical (how to get money) and from the very general (wisdom) to the specific (preparing an evaluation budget).

While this chapter focuses on a list of evaluation competencies stimulated by a particular panel discussion, modified by the authors, and supplemented by the responses of the distinguished group we surveyed, it is important to add that other lists of evaluation competencies have been produced by other groups, notably a task force of the American Educational Research Association (Glass and Worthen, 1970; Worthen and Gagné, 1969; Worthen, 1975). The Worthen synthesis of the AERA work, based on a logical analysis of research and evaluation tasks, groups competencies under the twenty-five headings paraphrased below:

1. Obtaining information about phenomenon to be evaluated
2. Drawing implications from prior research and practice
3. Defining object of evaluation
4. Selecting appropriate inquiry strategy
5. Formulating hypotheses or questions to be answered
6. Specifying data or evidence necessary for rigorous tests of hypotheses and unequivocal answers to questions
7. Selecting appropriate designs to collect data to test hypotheses or answer questions
8. Identifying population to which results should be generalized and selecting sample
9. Applying design and recognizing or controlling threats to validity
10. Identifying program goals at appropriate levels of generality
11. Assessing value and feasibility of program goals
12. Identifying standards and norms for judging worth of phenomenon to be evaluated
13. Translating broad objectives into measurable ones
14. Identifying classes of variables for measurement
15. Selecting and developing measurement techniques

16. Assessing validity of measurement techniques
17. Using appropriate data-collection methods
18. Monitoring program to detect deviations from specified procedures
19. Choosing and using appropriate statistical analyses
20. Using electronic computers and computer-related equipment
21. Interpreting and drawing appropriate conclusions from data analyses
22. Reporting findings and implications
23. Making recommendations based on results
24. Providing immediate feedback for decisions on program modification
25. Obtaining and managing resources necessary to conduct the study

A comprehensive review of the AERA and related efforts is provided by Millman (1975). Ricks (1976) offers one of the most succinct and distinctive lists of "training needs for effective evaluators": demystified research techniques (to avoid "isolating research evaluators from clinicians and administrators"), effective communication (to avoid the "Yes, but what does this mean?" reaction from program directors), flexibility and creativity (becoming "unbound by our research or evaluation prejudices"), involvement in decision making ("the researcher should be willing to put his or her money on one or two alternatives"), consideration of ethics (including "the why of particular projects"), and systems theory and practice (to enable "a dynamic conceptualization of evaluation").

Acquiring Evaluation Competencies

Returning to our questionnaire, the items about the best way for future evaluators to obtain initial levels of competence in the various content areas and skills evoked as wide a range of comments and "qualified" responses as the importance ratings. These comments reflected two major points of view: getting beyond the initial levels of competency, and combining training methods, perhaps by adding

Table 8. Best Methods of Obtaining Initial Competence in Content Areas and Skills (Given by Number of Persons Recommending Each Method; N = 44)

Content Areas	Formal Instruction	Independent Study or Application	Supervised Field Experience	Some Combination	No Response and Other Unscorable Responses
Experimental design	39	0	1	1	3
Quasi-experimental design	37	0	3	1	3
Correlation and regression methods	37	0	1	3	3
Sampling	36	0	4	0	4
Survey methods	35	1	4	2	3
Descriptive statistics	35	1	1	4	3
Inferential statistics	35	1	1	4	3
Psychometrics (reliability, validity, scaling, equating, and so on)	33	1	2	2	6
Statistical analysis	31	3	3	4	3
Alternative models for program evaluation	27	8	1	2	6
Cost-benefit analysis	23	9	3	2	7
Major literature and reference sources useful for evaluators	22	14	2	2	4
Major constructs in education and the social sciences	22	9	3	1	9
Reactive concerns in measurement and evaluation	20	9	5	1	9

Data preparation and reduction	20	3	15	3	3
Legal and professional standards for empirical studies	19	10	7	0	8
Applications of tests (paper-and-pencil, situational, performance, and so on)	19	1	15	2	7
Content analysis	14	12	10	1	7
Case-study methodology	14	10	13	1	6
Applications of interviews, questionnaires, ratings	14	2	21	1	6
Techniques of setting goals and performance standards	13	11	12	2	6
Methods of controlling quality of data collection and analysis	13	4	20	3	4
Applications of observation techniques, unobtrusive measures	10	5	20	4	5
Job analysis	9	11	11	1	12
Contracts and proposals	8	9	17	2	8
Field operations	5	0	31	0	8

Skills

Expository skills (speaking and writing)	7	11	17	3	6
Professional and ethical sensitivity	7	7	20	4	6
Sensitivity to concerns of all interested parties	6	4	23	0	11
Interpersonal skills	4	6	24	1	9
Management skills	4	5	26	3	6
Public-relations skills	3	7	24	2	8

case studies. One expert summarized: "What sets off the top-flight evaluator is whether he gets past the *initial* level of competency. I suggest a combination of formal instruction and supervised field experience for attaining that." However, even one of the respondents who was willing to express preferences for the best ways to obtain most of the knowledge and skills listed was frustrated: "Most institutions offer courses in measurement and statistics and call this evaluation training. IT ISN'T! Those are tools used by evaluators, researchers, developers, administrators. But there are a lot more tools needed by the evaluator. I guess this argues that our best training source is field experience. BUT we have so few really competent with whom to apprentice!"

We tabulated the straightforward responses to the training items with the results shown in Table 8. Formal instruction wins out as the preferred source of initial competency in the content areas, and supervised field experience in the skills areas. Initial competency in the art of contracts and proposals and in field operations is evidently viewed as closer to initial competency in the skills areas. It is interesting to note that experts place confidence in independent study as a source of initial competence in many of the areas. However, several comments were of the "born-not-made" variety. For example, "personality," "unteachable," or "What I find most frequently lacking in evaluations is common sense, which I'm afraid is not obtained—you either have it or you don't!"

The liberal reporting of comments here betrays our attitude toward the summaries in Tables 6 and 8. The tabulations certainly do not tell the whole story. They may not even tell a true story. For example, the patterns of importance ratings and preferred training methods marked by professionals reputed to be of somewhat different persuasions appear to be somewhat different. However, our number of respondents is so small and the classification basis so subjective that formal analyses along these lines do not seem to be warranted.

Before moving on to a report on the data obtained about local training, we cannot resist one more quotation, this one summarizing reactions to the competency and training items by one of our favorite respondents: "Pretty funny this. It adds up to a well-trained, mature, discreet, experienced, diplomatic, literate, ethically concerned behavioral scientist. And, of course, formal instruction is *initially* most important and efficient—but then field experience and application also become indispensable."

The thirty-nine persons completing at least part of the last section of the questionnaire came from thirty-three well-known universities in eighteen states. Three of them noted explicitly that their institutions did not offer a degree program specifically oriented toward a "profession" of evaluation, observing that "such a graduate program would be too narrow and too lacking in substantive content" or "methodology divorced from content is a dangerous thing" or "evaluators will come into their roles fortuitously." Indeed, as the summaries in Parts B and C of Table 9 suggest, this state of affairs seems more typical than not. The numbers of students being trained in evaluation (Part D) do not suggest that competition for jobs in program evaluation will increase greatly in the future. Furthermore, it is estimated that only a little more than half of the graduate students who might reasonably conduct evaluations ever will. (We might note here that the numbers of students enrolled in the kinds of ecological-psychology programs described earlier are generally quite small; for example, the Michigan State program graduated only ten people during its first six years.) However, one respondent to our questionnaire noted that the number of students pursuing relevant study in his institution was "increasing rapidly," and another called program evaluation "one of the most promising fields for our graduates at this time."

Other Training Issues

In our report of the survey, we have just barely touched on three issues in the training of evaluators. First, the knowledge and skills that evaluators will need depend to a great extent on the kinds of programs they will be called upon to evaluate and the purposes of their evaluation efforts. The requirements would be very different, say, for a counselor given the added responsibility of providing feedback for program improvement to instructors using new remedial-

Table 9. Responses to "Current Practices" Questions

A. Do graduate students in your institution receive specific training designed to equip them . . . to evaluate?

   Yes: 35[a]   No: 4

B. If so, in what school(s) or department(s)?

Education: 24	Administration: 1
Psychology: 13	Business: 1
Sociology: 5	Communication: 1
Statistics: 3	Community Medicine: 1
Human Development and Family Studies: 2	Social Services Administration: 1

C. What graduate degree(s) do students who receive such training typically obtain?

Ph.D.	29	M.A.	4
Ed.D.	4	M.S.	22
		M.Ed.	2

D. (1) At the present time, about how many graduate students . . . in your institution . . . are pursuing study . . . which will equip them to become program evaluators?
   (2) What percentage of these . . . will ever become practicing evaluators?

Size of Graduate Student Population Receiving Evaluation Training	Number of Institutions in Size Category	*(1)* Total Number of Students Being Trained	*(2)* Estimated Total Number of Students Who Will Become Evaluators
0-5	8	25	15
6-10	4	36	16
11-15	2	28	13
16-20	8	165	102
21-30	2	55	21
31-40	3	115	87
41-50	1	50	1
Total	28[b]	474	255

[a]The 35 persons responding "yes" represent 29 institutions. Four institutions were doubly represented; one was triply represented.

[b]For each of the multiply represented institutions (see note a), a single representative set of figures was estimated, based on the other information provided. Student estimates were not provided for one institution.

reading materials, for an industrial manager charged with designing a program to train a large number of operators at the lowest possible cost, or for a clinician asked to make recommendations to a federal agency about continuing or discontinuing an ambitious parent-child health program; for an experimental psychologist drawn into the business of evaluating the effectiveness of television programs; for an officer of a state licensing board attempting to determine the influence of licensing requirements on the quality of service provided in the occupation of interest; or for a sociologist studying the impact of voter registration drives on election results.

If potential evaluators knew that their primary work would be in the area of needs assessment (estimating the frequency or intensity of student, societal, or other needs in order to plan appropriate action programs), they might "major" in survey methods, sampling, and descriptive statistics. Those planning to evaluate personnel-training efforts might take large doses of job analysis, quasi-experimental design, techniques of setting goals and performance standards, statistical analysis, and cost-benefit analysis. Unfortunately—or fortunately—this is not the way the world works. Evaluators, whatever their primary interest or basic discipline, are usually expected to behave like applied researchers and contribute their talents to a variety of information needs. If they are successful in conducting needs analyses, formative and summative evaluation requirements will probably not be far behind. If they limit themselves to conducting needs analyses, boredom will almost certainly ensue—and possibly unemployment. More fundamental, one of the evaluator's major challenges is to define problems, as well as approaches to their solutions, and definition frequently requires a broad range of experience and a kit with many tools.

A second issue revolves around the degree to which an evaluator needs to be expert in the field in which he or she performs evaluation services. Does the designer of a national evaluation of Head Start have to be a specialist in child development and early education? Does the evaluator of a Suzuki-method program need to know how to play the violin? Can anyone other than a cosmetologist evaluate the effectiveness of a licensing program in that area? Does the evaluator of a bilingual program have to be bilingual? Three responders in the questionnaire study added "substantive knowledge of the content of the program" as essential for the competent evaluator, but they did not specify how much knowledge. Certainly, the evaluator should have some understanding of the content of the program under study. But it is probably asking too much for evaluators to be expert in every substantive area where their evaluation skills might be applied— just as it is probably asking too much for chemists, psychiatrists, or Russian scholars to acquire a full range of evaluation skills just because they are involved in a program with an evaluation component. A team approach such as that advocated by one of the responders to the questionnaire on training and competencies is probably best in many instances, with the members of the team drawn from both evaluation and subject-matter specialties. However, a team approach does not relieve the evaluator from the responsibility of acquiring as much familiarity as possible with the content of the program or "a lively recognition . . . of the formal and informal context within which the program occurs" (Guttentag and Struening, 1975, p. 3). Further, the acceptability of evaluators on such teams may depend on their honest show of interest in the substance and workings of the program. The situation is not unlike that of the foreign visitor whose attempts at the language, however bad his pronunciation, meet with obvious pleasure from the natives.

Our attitude, then, is that the more the evaluator can grasp the content of the program, the better—within reasonable limits of time and effort. However, evaluators can be helpful even when their understanding of the subject matter is limited. We know of evaluators who have participated in evaluation efforts in fields that were initially completely strange to them, yet they were able to make substantial contributions. They also developed strong appreciation for the work of the practitioners in those fields before they had finished.

This discussion of the breadth of expertise of evaluators is closely related to a third issue. Perhaps a distinction needs to be drawn between the skills and knowledge a program evaluator needs to have personally and those he or she might obtain for particular projects by calling in technical consultants. Of course, this means that evaluators would have to have sufficient self-awareness to recognize where they were deficient and needed help. We might add "realistic appraisal of own abilities and limitations" to the skills lists in Tables 6 and 7. The corresponding content area, already listed in Table 6, is "major literature and reference sources useful for evaluators."

Evaluating Evaluators

Three approaches to evaluating the competencies of evaluators are analogous to those practiced or discussed in teacher evaluation and certification (Rosner, 1972): program approval, estimations of competency, and product evaluation. We might assume that if an evaluator was trained in a "good" program, he or she is competent. Definitions of "good" programs vary, of course, and are usually more global-subjective than analytical-objective. But personnel in agencies that let or work on many evaluation contracts seem to be able to agree at least among themselves about the strengths of various graduate departments in turning out people able to perform the evaluation functions they need. As Millman (1975) notes: "One should keep in mind that completion of course work is no guarantee that the individual will have the enablers needed to carry out R and E [research and evaluation] tasks. Nevertheless, training and experience do have some merit, since they are certain to have had some influence on the apprentice" (p. 8). There is little denying that, at present, hiring people for their first jobs in evaluation is predicated far more on where and with whom they studied than on direct assessment of their competencies.

Direct assessment is a possibility, of course. From time to time, there have been calls for certification mechanisms for program evaluators or those working in educational research and development (Gagné, 1975; Worthen, 1972), mechanisms which would provide that individuals have appropriate requirements to enter the "profession." However, none of the proposals has yet been implemented, nor have they received significant national backing, although the emergence of standards for program evaluation (see Chapter Eleven) may provide an impetus for individual certification. Furthermore, it is doubtful that the number of program-evaluation jobs in any single organization will be sufficient to justify that organization's setting up the kinds of elaborate assessment centers that have been used by

Table 10. Checklist for Rating Evaluator Competence

Knowledge and Content Areas

Experimental design
Quasi-experimental design
Survey methods
Sampling
Case-study methodology
Field operations
Legal and professional standards for empirical studies
Techniques of setting goals and performance standards
Job analysis
Alternative models for program evaluation
Major literature and reference sources useful for evaluators
Methods of controlling quality of data collection and analysis
Data preparation and reduction
Applications of observation techniques, unobtrusive measures
Applications of interviews, questionnaires, ratings
Applications of tests (paper-and-pencil, performance, and so on)
Content analysis
Psychometrics (reliability, validity, scaling, equating, and so on)
Reactive concerns in measurement and evaluation
Descriptive statistics
Inferential statistics
Statistical analysis
Correlation and regression methods
Cost-benefit analysis
Contracts and proposals
Major constructs in education and the social sciences

Skills Areas

Management skills
Public-relations skills
Interpersonal skills
Expository speaking skills
Expository writing skills
Professional and ethical sensitivity
Sensitivity to concerns of all interested parties

industry and government agencies to identify potential managers (see, for example, Bray and others, 1974). Therefore, in the immediate future, any direct assessment will probably be limited to self-report measures (Bunda, 1973; Worthen and Brzezinski, 1971), locally developed tests (Worthen and Associates, 1971), or rating procedures—the latter being the most common. As the medical profession seems to be increasingly aware (see, for example, Barro, 1973), systematic rating procedures, relying chiefly on observation and background information, can be useful—in the present case to those concerned with hiring evaluators and commissioning evaluation efforts or to those who train evaluators and want to check up on their training programs through a common look at all of their candidates. At a minimum, a rating procedure requires its authors to specify some of their own values. Such rating systems might also be used for self-evaluation by those of us concerned with whether our ranges and degrees of competency are up to date.

A sample checklist of evaluation competencies derived from the questionnaire and survey results reported in this chapter is provided in Table 10. We suggest that the would-be evaluator of evaluators who wants to try the list go through it first and eliminate the items judged "not very important" with respect to the job requirements or program goals of interest (very much as the questionnaire respondents did). Then additional items specific to the situation can be added (reference to Table 7 might be helpful here). Finally, a rating of 4 to 1 might be assigned to evaluators for each item on the checklist, according to the following scheme:

Knowledge or Skill Sufficient to Select
Appropriate Approaches and Techniques and
to Design and Implement Evaluation

	With technical consultation	*With minimal technical consulation*
No or minimal field experience	1—Lowest competence	2 or 3
Relevant successful field experience	2 or 3	4—Highest competence

The horizontal dimension of the chart relates to an issue discussed earlier: An evaluator may have the necessary skills and knowledge personally, or he may have sufficient sense to obtain technical consultation in areas where he is deficient. Either way is acceptable, although we would feel more comfortable if a person with major evaluation responsibilities had to obtain technical consultations only occasionally. (Consider, as an analogy, the level of skill you would prefer in your medical doctor.) Of course, it is possible to have necessary skills for evaluation without much practical experience (the vertical dimension). Again, however, we would feel more comfortable entrusting major responsibility for an evaluation to someone who has had some practice. (Return again to the medical analogy and consider your selection of the surgeon who is to operate on you.)

Clearly the highest rating (see the cell marked 4) would be earned by an experienced evaluator who needs only minimal technical consultation. The least competent level is represented by the cell marked 1 and defines an inexperienced evaluator with considerable need for technical consultation. Somewhere between these extremes lie the other two cells. Their ordering must depend on the judgment of the rater and must be based on situational factors. In practice, of course, it would be rare for an evaluator to obtain a rating of 4 on every item in the checklist.

What kinds of evidence would raters use in evaluating the competencies of evaluation candidates or students?* For senior candidates, they would probably employ many of the kinds of indicators used in determining faculty promotions and derived from vitae: relevant research and evaluation productivity, publications, fellowships and grants, invitations to participate in important seminars and conferences, estimates of reputation in professional circles, degrees and special study (Dressel, 1976, p. 333). In the case of students, consideration would be given to courses taken, grades, instructors' recommendations, assistantships, and special projects. In all instances, of course, the more specific the evidence with respect to a given item, the more confident the judge can be about assigning a rating. The reliability and validity of background data are not generally held in high

---

*Merrill (1976) would distinguish here between *competencies* and *attainments*, perhaps permitting us to rate the competencies of career evaluators, but allowing assessment of little more than the attainments of graduate students. "The concept of competency," he declares, "although much in vogue in education, is a concept inappropriate to the educational process. Competency is essentially a lifelong issue" (p. 3).

esteem. If feedback to a program designed to train evaluators is the object of running several students through such a rating procedure, the training institution will be particularly interested in the items considered essential but on which students tend to receive low ratings. Maybe a new course or an improved component of an existing course or practicum is needed.

Table 10 represents only one of many possible approaches to rating the competencies of evaluators. We suggest it as a starting point because it is short, relatively simple, and includes items endorsed by a large number of informed people. However, developers of rating forms might prefer to begin with the "universe" of evaluation competencies containing about 250 items (see Bunda, 1973; Stufflebeam, 1973), Coller's (1970) classification of evaluation tasks into sixteen general groups, or some of the AERA-related efforts referred to earlier.

A third approach to evaluating evaluators is through detailed examination of their products. Returning to the teacher-evaluation analogy, we find that one school maintains that "teaching effectiveness must be defined by the effect on students (that is, by changes in student behavior)" (Ragosta in Anderson and others, 1975, p. 269; see also McDonald, 1972). Unfortunately, up to the present time, many evaluators have received rather poor marks on their evaluation studies and reports (Gamel and others, 1975; Horst and others, 1975; Wargo and others, 1972). Some of these marks are no doubt deserved. For example, Tallmadge and Horst (1976) report "outrageous incoherencies" as "just a few of the 'horror stories' uncovered in the course of routinely examining real-world evaluation studies [in the area of compensatory education]. The sad part was that . . . irrationalities were so pervasive that not a single evaluation report was found which could be accepted at face value! Even more disheartening, many of these evaluations followed procedures officially sanctioned by one or more presumably authoritative groups of experts" (p. 2).

Tallmadge and Horst performed one kind of secondary evaluation: a critical review of primary evaluations. Another kind of secondary evaluation involves reanalysis of the data from the primary evaluation (Anderson and others, 1975, p. 363; Stufflebeam, 1974). Some of these secondary evaluations have produced new insights (for example, those by Mayeske and others, 1972; Elashoff and Snow, 1971). Others have produced equivocal results for the simple reason that the main purpose of the reanalysis was not checking the original results for accuracy or testing the reasonableness of the conclusions by using different methods. Rather, answers were sought to questions not asked in the primary evaluation, questions that were not directly answerable in terms of the original measures and design. If the evaluators' products are to be used as the basis for evaluating their competencies, direct critical review is probably in order. Specific instruments for appraising program evaluations (Cummings, 1975) and guidelines commissioned by such agencies as the U.S. Office of Education (Horst and others, 1975; Tallmadge and Horst, 1976) and the National Institute of Mental Health (Little, 1976) may be useful.

Of course, in some cases evaluators cannot be held strictly accountable for their products. They may not have complete freedom in selecting a compatible area of work; they may be pushed into compromises; they may have to work under frustrating organizational constraints (Weiss, 1973); they may have to collaborate with so many others that it is hard to disentangle their contributions (Millman, 1975, p. 9). Certainly, given that the real world offers different opportunities, it is very difficult to compare the competencies of two evaluators in terms of products alone. As Humphrey Bogart said of the Academy Awards, the only way they could be fairly awarded was to have everyone in a given category play the same part in front of the same judges.

On rare occasions, young seers and wise old sages will share their simple truths with lesser mortals. For example, in Julius Caesar, *Shakespeare announced his famous dictum that leaders should avoid the young Cassius, for he "has a lean and hungry look. He thinks too much. Such men are dangerous" (Julius Caesar, Act I, Scene II, 1. 194-195).*

In the following article, George Kelling shares a number of simple truths about evaluation staffs gleaned from his several years as an evaluator for the Police Foundation, some of which may have aged him doubly. He notes what consultants are good (and not good) for, the characteristics of good evaluation staff members, the symptoms of staff cooperation by the agency being evaluated, and the importance of recognizing and publishing one's mistakes. In sharp contrast to Shakespeare, Kelling points out that it is precisely the young Cassiuses who are most likely to make the greatest contribution to an evaluation project. They are the ones who have the methodological skill, the energy, the intelligence, and the curiosity to complete a first rate evaluation.

While Kelling is less explicit about the characteristics of good evaluation directors, the careful reader can gain insight by carefully considering the qualities of a leader who would choose to surround himself with young Cassiuses.

Note: The "Mr. Lewis" referred to in the following article is Joseph H. Lewis, former Director of Evaluation for the Police Foundation, Washington, DC.

18

Development of Staff for Evaluation (A Retrospective View)

George L. Kelling

George Kelling is on the staff of the Police Foundation and has been working as an evaluator in Kansas City and Dallas over the past several years. In particular, Kelling was the Director of Research for the major study of police patrol practices carried out in Kansas City. In gearing up for that project he had to put together from scratch and manage a large and complex research team. This paper presents his views on the problems that are likely to be encountered in putting together an evaluation research staff and on approaches to solving those problems.

When in confirmation class as an early adolescent, I, as many other young Lutherans, was forced to memorize Luther's explanation of the three sections of the Apostle's Creed. While no longer able to pull the explanations back into consciousness, I can clearly recall the last sentence of each explanation. The phrase, identical in each, was "This is most certainly true." The matters Luther was dealing with were, of course, eternal verities. While they may or may not be "most certainly true" for others, they were for Luther and he emphasized their importance to himself and his followers with his declaration.

As a result of administering many evaluations, I have been asked to talk to you about developing personnel for work in evaluative research. While the positions I take in the following pages certainly do not approach, for me at least, the state of eternal verities, they do achieve the level of pragmatic and survival verities in the conduct of evaluations. Part of this feeling comes from a set of values and assumptions which I have and which perhaps is worthwhile for me to identify. These include:

1. It is good to complete evaluations—few really are.
2. It is good to maintain "experienced leadership" in an evaluation staff—read that: "I want to survive."
3. It is good to maintain "experienced leadership" in the organizations in which evaluations are conducted—need I explain the worth of that to you?
4. It is not that the *best* predictor of an individual's or organization's performance is his/her/its past performance—it is the only predictor.
5. And finally, conflict in the activities of organizations and personnel need not be deleterious to achievement but rather, if the rules of conflict are established, can contribute to creative and original work.

With those values, assumptions, confessions out of the way, I will continue with one final venture into the rarified air of theology with a paraphrase of a statement by Paul Tillich.

I shall proceed to lecture now, and continue to perform in evaluations on the assumption that I am absolutely correct in what I am about to say. I am aware that I may be wrong, but I will not let that awareness interfere with this discussion of my future performance as an administrator of evaluations.

If any of you, as you read or hear this, feel like standing, applauding, and cheering, I, of course, invite you to. If on the other hand you feel like booing and hissing, there is nothing I can do to stop you, so feel free.

Verity #1. Where one's tenure is, is where one's heart is—or—the use of consultants.

The use of consultants is standard in evaluations and evaluation proposals. Generally consultants are luminaries from academia who have a superb record of research and thinking about methodology and/or service delivery in a particular endeavor. They are generally competent, leaders in the field, and involved in a myriad of enterprises. Generally they are capable of, and have executed, good research and/or evaluations. They are experts. Basically, they can serve two functions in an evaluation:

1. They can help "young comers" get grants, contracts and exposure. If done responsibly, this is legitimate and ought not to be sneered at. The function of a mentor or sponsor is an important one in academia. "Young comers" present a high risk to both program and evaluation administrators and grantors, but at the same time they have the energy, and are enough "on the make" to complete an evaluation. The "baptism" of "young comers" by luminaries must be un-

From George L. Kelling, "Development of Staff for Evaluation (A Retrospective View)," DHEW Publication No. (PHS) 78-3195 105-114.

derstood for what it is however. Do not expect the "heavies" to conduct the evaluation or write the results. They cannot and will not.

2. They can provide technical consultation on critical points of an evaluation. Three critical points stand out:

   a. "Now that I have all this data, why did I collect it in the first place and what should I do with it." In other words, it is possible that the evaluator will get so immersed in details that he/she will forget what the original goals of the project were and how the data deals with those goals. Further, after being removed from the world of academia during the year or two of the evaluation, the evaluator may need some assistance in updating his/her statistical skills. The consultant or consultants can help the field staff of an evaluation to review their work and update skills.

   b. Review the outline for the presentation of the findings. This is related to "a" and is part of "a" yet is so important that I separate it out. Getting a good outline of the final report is *the* critical issue in getting the evaluator to put his/her pen to paper. It nicely makes a completely unmanageable task (completing the report) into a manageable one.

   c. Finally—reading the preliminary drafts of the evaluation and providing constructive, non-threatening advice. Generally upon completing the first draft, the evaluator thinks (hopes) that he/she is finished writing. In fact, he/she has just begun. Remember, *any* first draft, regardless of its weaknesses, is good. If an evaluator is reasonably good and has good consultation, *any* first draft almost assures completion.

So much for the positive contributions of consultants. They can make real and substantial contributions, but for all parties involved in the conduct of an evaluation, it is certainly best to underestimate their contributions rather than to overestimate them.

They *cannot:*

1. Supervise staff. Young, energetic staff need constant and ongoing stroking, direction, love and supervision. Consultants cannot provide that. They do not have the time, nor do they control the means and rewards necessary to manage staff.

2. Develop evaluation instruments (questionnaires, etc.). Instruments must be developed by resident evaluation staff in close collaboration with agency program staff. Consultants don't have the time, energy and, generally, the patience to collaborate as closely as necessary.

3. Write-up results. The writing of the final report is a consuming full-time task. Consultants are involved in too many things to be expected to write-up a final report.

The key thing to remember in dealing with consultants (and I do not mean this critically) is that they are *un* responsible. They are bright, knowledgeable, clever, but they have no responsibility for the final product and rarely, if ever, will be cornered into accepting such responsibility. They have different responsibilities and will meet those first—and—that is to be expected. Neither the program evaluator or administration should be surprised by this as likely they, too, are consultants some place. *This is most certainly true.*

Verity #2. The children shall lead you (or at least they will do most of the necessary "grunt work"). *Staff Structure*

I will divide this section into two parts: first, the characteristics of evaluation staff, and, second, the characteristics of the evaluation director.

Perhaps it will be easiest if I begin with the characteristics of the staff who are "on site," and who do the daily work of evaluation. (Be clear that I did not always know these verities, and not even when I knew them did I always follow them. One result is that in the early projects I have administered the casualty rate of project staff was very high. In the early days, I often took those persons for staff who were available at the time. Some were less than satisfactory. Applicants were few. I had no track record as an evaluator. Evaluation was considered inappropriate—read "inappropriate" as "sinful"—by major professors for their good students. But, I am getting ahead of myself.) The people who actually "do the daily work" of an evaluation have to have certain characteristics. These include: high levels of energy, methodological sophistication, skill at handling data, keen intelligence and curiosity, being professionally "on the make," the capability of using creatively the great freedom that evaluators have, and the ego strength to move with some comfort into an alien environment. The staff need not have, and, if you recruit the proper persons, probably will not have, organizational "smarts," familiarity with the field of service delivery, or experience in completing a project. (I will discuss these points somewhat later.)

Where are these kinds of people found? (The people who do the daily work.) The answer is quite clear. In the doctoral programs of universities. And *as* important, in the doctoral programs of *good* universities. Their characteristics are as follows:

—They have been born, bred, and expect to die in universities.
—They have never held a job (except maybe Vista or a summer camp).

—They have managed to make avoiding deadlines a fine art and skill.

—They are arrogant. (Often they *are* right—they are more methodologically skillful than their professors and, later, than you as project director.)

—They know how to develop sophisticated questionnaires but they do not know how to talk to people (read "talk" as interview without a pretested questionnaire). They will have to be driven, almost with whips, to work closely with agency program staff and to really talk to them (but once they do, another problem—that of cooptation—rears its head, which we shall discuss in detail later).

—They view all researchers and grantsmen who operate outside of universities as whores and "operators" interested only in the "bucks" (they really believe that their professors live on their salaries alone) and that all truth is to be discovered in the world by conducting methodologically "pure" experiments on freshmen.

And finally, they're marvelous. They believe the world can and will change, they work night and day, they're damned smart, and they have that marvelous characteristic of youth—energy. (Oh, I know its unbounded and undisciplined, but evaluation directors have to do something after all.)

But now in a somewhat more serious vein, I wish to talk about each of the characteristics that I find necessary in staff.

High Levels of Energy

Evaluations are difficult and time consuming. They combine all the intellectual and methodological rigors of laboratory experiments with the messiness and complications of the real world. The real world presents a myriad of problems for which a great deal of energy is necessary to solve. The following are examples.

Agency records were not devised for research. Often when computerized, they contain errors and omissions which, while not a problem for agency administrative purposes, are in such a condition that it is necessary to return to the original documents when they are used for research or evaluation.* (I don't mean to offend agency officials at this point, and maybe it is different in the medical field, but for the most part all agency data have to be verified for research purposes and every evaluation which is based upon agency data which have not been verified in great detail is a terribly suspect evaluation.)

---

* Not only is a high level of energy necessary but also dealing with these sorts of problems requires a gift for great attention to detail and a toleration for the tedious—characteristics sometimes different from and in conflict with high energy levels.

As Mr. Lewis points out in his paper, oftentimes agency program managers who are responsible for the administration of an experiment care less about maintaining the controls of the experiment than they do about "starts" or exporting the program to other areas or jurisdictions. I would underline Mr. Lewis' point about "starts" and recommend that each of you re-read it. The dynamics and consequences of it are substantial. Given the media's interest in "starts" and the fact that *everyone* gets bored with continuing programs, the evaluator must attempt to carefully deal with and exploit both the initial publicity from "starts" and the subsequent obscurity when the experiment or program is ongoing. The management of the momentum of an experiment is critical and a balance has to be developed between the extremes of the publicity and momentum of the "start" and later obscurity of slowdown. Obscurity both has its benefits and problems. Generally, the momentum gained from the initial thrust will not provide enough energy to complete the task. Occasionally "boosters" from agency program and evaluation staff are absolutely necessary to obtain the goal of a completed program. Alertness of the maintenance of the ongoing program is essential for evaluation staff.

A variation of the problem is "restarts." That is when an agency administrator decides that the indicator of his/her wisdom and skill is his/her ability to replicate the program in other departments, divisions, etc., before the evaluation is completed. This not only consumes a great deal of staff energy (both of agency staff who are pushing to do it and of evaluation staff who are trying to stop it) but also potentially destroys the experiment or evaluation by contaminating control areas.

Personnel involved in program efforts may have more of a vested interest in the success or failure of a program than in the conduct of the experiment and as a result inadvertently (or purposely) attempt to bias the outcome. Evaluators must constantly monitor, in as discreet a manner as possible (as monitoring itself may develop resistances) all planned stimuli, controls, and data collection.

Dealing with these and a myriad of the problems simply requires a high level of alertness and effort for a prolonged period of time. There is much "dirty work" which has to be done and on-site personnel have to have the endurance to do it. (In one city the "dirty work" meant night work for at least six weeks in a record division. That was in addition to the regular day activities.)

Methodological Sophistication

Often the exigencies of real world agency existence are such that program evaluation can be quite complicated. Finding the right design—that is an evaluation design which is as powerful as the program allows and warrants—requires considerable methodological sophistication. The "matching" of program and evaluation design is not to be accomplished by returning one more time to the bible of Campbell and Stanley but rather comes through the careful "wedding" of research techniques and operating programs. There is nothing mysterious about this. The evaluator simply must "muck around" in the program, data, and funds and find a design which is appropriate to the program operation, the funds available, the importance of the program, and the available data. That means that the staff must *know* design and scientific method and not just have a shopping basket of designs, one of which she/he pulls out for this program.

Skill at Handling Data

Two important things have to be said about this.

One staff member has to approach the psychological state of being an obsessive compulsive. If someone does not keep careful record of *every* decision made regarding design and data storage, the disaster of having to reconstruct those decisions will result in the waste of spending the time re-doing things and also of not meeting deadlines. Not that things cannot be reconstructed, and generally they can, but to have no way of identifying which questions were related to what indicators means a period of reconstruction beyond that normally required to re-familiarize oneself with the material. Two examples. In the Kansas City Preventive Patrol Experiment, the details and records of the sampling procedures for the community survey were never gathered together in one file or written up when the sample was drawn. When, 18 months later, we had to discuss the sampling procedures, at least three people in three different organizations had to search their files for the various memos, instructions, etc. It was possible, but that which was easy to do at one time, became complicated at another. On the other hand, in Dallas we did two departmentwide surveys. The T_1 survey was completed in 1973, the T_2 survey in 1976. Because we had carefully documented the source of every question, all coding decisions, and every other decision, the time necessary for review was spent relating the theories under which we operated to the forms of analyses we were to use. Thus, an axiom emerges. Never, never, never rely on memory. Rely on it only to fail, and, even worse, to deceive.

The second area of the importance of data handling has to do with the assessment of agency records. This is no simple matter, especially in police agencies, but I suspect in other agencies as well. Again I want to emphasize that I imply no criticism of agency records. I simply have no way of knowing whether they are adequate for administrative purposes. I assume they are. You are in a

better position to know that than I. I do know, however, that almost all records will need considerable work to be suitable for research purposes. If the records are computerized, considerable work will have to be done to insure its accuracy and reliability. (Even at that evaluators must approach them cautiously since much of it is self-reported information, i.e., crime and activity analyses, which are subject to manipulation, whether conscious or unconscious, to show desired or self-serving results.) If records are kept in manual files, other problems, such as coding, or agency policies which allow for several file systems, emerge. (In one police department complaints against police officers are kept in three different places—depending on where the citizen first filed his complaint—and may or may not be stored with the other units. Notice the phrase "may or may not" since that complicates things considerably. If any officer has complaints filed against him in more than one location, and many do, the evaluator has to carefully read each one to determine if they are separate or the same complaint. Thus, even establishing the "n" of complaints is not a counting task but an analytical task.)

The evaluation staff has to know what they know, both in terms of recalling decisions and assessing data. Both tasks are far more complicated than generally thought.

Keen Intelligence and Curiosity

In some respects this is self-explanatory. But while keen intelligence and curiosity are necessary, they are not sufficient. They have to be combined with many of the other characteristics described in this section. Without energy, discipline, and creativity, intelligence simply is not enough.

Let me add one thing about curiosity as I think it to be quite important. The characteristic of asking "why" is absolutely essential. In the first place it helps to keep the intelligent person from seeing the emperor's clothes. The "emperor" can be the agency, the evaluation director, or colleagues. Secondly, it helps the evaluator pursue unanticipated findings. And, if properly pursued, these unanticipated findings can be quite important to an evaluation. It might mean the evaluation is on to something new (I call your attention to Mr. Bieck's study of police response time. The surprise finding of the length of time it takes citizens to report even serious crimes is not only of great research and program interest, but is also an indicator of just how poorly thought through the whole business of the importance of police response time has been by police, researchers, and evaluators.) or reflects an artifact of improperly stored or analyzed data. The evaluator, who, out of his/her curiosity, continues to pursue those leads, either enriches the evaluation immensely or saves it from spurious findings.

Professionally "On the Make"

Perhaps it is purely a personal matter on my part, but I simply have an easier time dealing with people who know what they want. I find it difficult to deal with people, on a project level at least, who are indecisive about their own goals. (By that I do not mean that everyone who comes onto an evaluation staff has to know that he wants to do evaluation research in a particular service delivery system for the rest of his life.) She/he may want to gain research experience, get publications, examine a service system, or do a variety of other things, but they have some sense of their own goals. If that "purposefulness" is not presented in staff members, I have been unable to develop it. (And I don't mean that an individual's goals can't change, but purposefulness remains.) The casualty rate of those who have not been purposeful has been very high.

Those people who are beginning their careers and are purposeful clearly do not yet know the prices of long hours and crash production schedules which they will have to pay to obtain what they want. But they will learn that, and most people "on the make" are willing to pay those prices. People who are not aggressively purposeful simply aren't motivated enough to "pay the price." (That makes sense. If you don't know what you want, why should you "pay the price"?)

A side comment here. People who do evaluations live on grants. Try to think of evaluation bureaucracies that do not live on grants. Few come to mind. While medical, social, police, and other service systems have ongoing existences independent of most specific projects, evaluation people either live from grant to grant, or work full-time in a university or consulting firm and do evaluations part-time. The result is that for an evaluation capacity to survive not only must it do the evaluations at hand but it must also use resources (primarily time) to generate new proposals. The alternative is constant "gearing up" or "dismantling" a staff, either one of which destroys established organizational skills and working relationships. Thus, in my judgment, evaluators must be prepared to "pay the price" of constant pressure to both complete and generate activities simultaneously. ("Workaholics" make good evaluators.)

One final comment about being "on the make." I believe that most good evaluators are from universities and will and ought to return to universities for rest and recreation (in the finest sense of recreation, that is re-creation of knowledge and skills). In order to do that, publishing is an absolute necessity. Thus, from the beginning, I have tried to insure that the data collected will be not only necessary for evaluation, but also, whenever possible, be useful as sociology, political science, or psychology and thus result in publications independent of the evaluation. I must also confess

that I have not always been completely candid about this to agencies or the Police Foundation. We have called these interests the "oh by the ways." To insure the protection of agencies, I have always assured them, and *meant* it, that *nothing* will be published without their review and permission. The resultant problems are different than one would expect. First, the agencies encourage publications—administrators have found that agency reputation is enhanced by such activities. Second, and this gets to be a problem, oftentimes agency administrators get to be more interested in the "oh by the ways" than in the evaluations. (The consequence of this is that staff time can be diverted away from evaluation-specific activities to less critical issues at the *wrong* time.)

But the point is that the data, if properly collected, can be available for publication independent of whether the program succeeds, fails, never gets off the ground, or collapses in the middle (that does happen, unfortunately much, much too often) and young staff can get the publications necessary for their own careers. And, I would add, data is just too expensive to collect to be used for only one purpose. If, at no or relatively little expense, data can be collected which is multipurpose, it seems to me only prudent to do so.

Capable of Using Freedom

For some young researchers, the freedom provided in evaluation is such a burden that they just can't handle it. They search for day to day direction, are terrified of making mistakes, withdraw into obsession about codes or analyses, can't start to write a report because all they can think about is the final product rather than just the page they are on, get preoccupied with the administrative issues of evaluation rather than evaluation itself, etc., etc. At worst they begin to "rip-off" freedom, using their time for activities other than their evaluation work. (Not that I feel that staff should not be involved in other consulting, lecturing, etc., activities. I think they should. It gives them wider exposure at somebody else's expense, they enhance the reputation of the entire capacity, and it keeps them from being too narrowly focused on particular projects. But they must do so at their own expense, not at the expense of the evaluation.) Finally, they may become so cynical that termination is inevitable. They are not necessarily "bad" people; it's just that the available freedom simply leaves them unable to function.

For others, freedom is an opportunity to respond flexibly to the myriad of complexities that occur during the process of an evaluation. They (and I think I am covering somewhat similar ground as I did when I talked of purposefulness) feel comfortable making decisions and making mistakes. They are far more comfortable communicating to the project director what they have done, why they have done it, and—at first I found this surprising—what mistakes they have made. It turns out that, while they obsess less, they are far more thorough in recording their decisions. And finally, when in a jam, they look for help. Those who can really handle freedom are open and communicative. Those who cannot, turn secretive. And once the vicious cycle of secretiveness begins, I have not yet found a way to interfere with it.

One final comment; there are good people who, at times, seem to go into a work moratorium. Generally, those periods occur during the quiet periods of an evaluation. It seems that they go through periods when they can't get anything done, and just can't get started. They, different from those who can't handle freedom, will often feel quite guilty, some even going so far as to suggest a reduction in paid time during this period. They are in need of support and assurances that the moratorium will pass and that when "the work crunch" comes they will more than make up for lost time.

Move Into an Alien Environment

I will begin this section by paraphrasing William Goode who, in one of his books on occupations and professions, says something like the following:

Men at work and forests appear peaceful but upon close examination one finds that in both [work and forests], struggle is both swift and deadly.

It would be nice to believe that evaluators and agency personnel could work together happily and productively with little or no conflict, but that seems rarely to be the case. And it isn't that lined up on one side are the "good guys" and on the other "the bad guys," or that one set of activities are reasonable and another unreasonable, or that which one group is doing is more important than that which the other is doing. In fact, "good guys" are on both sides, both sets of activities are reasonable, and both important. The problem is that agency personnel, whether knowing it or not, turn power over to evaluators when they contract for an evaluation. While it is unfortunate that this is rarely made explicit when the contract is made, and even more unfortunate that it is only barely understood when it is made explicit, this transfer of power is a powerful determinant of evaluation-service agency relationship. Let me give an example. If an agency decides to do an experiment, the administration will impose restraints on the discretion of administrators to transfer personnel, start new programs, reallocate equipment, adjust schedules, etc., etc., etc. It is immediately apparent what this does to the formal power structure of an organization. Just contemplate for a moment on what it does to the *informal* power structure. And, the evaluator becomes, at times, the "tattler" and depending upon circumstances, at other times, the "enforcer." (It should not be surprising that in the

eleventh month of a year's experiment even the chief, or top administrator, will want to give in to his subordinates. Often then only the threat of loss of external funds can assure completion.)

This conflict is compounded by the fact that often evaluators have different norms, goals, and lifestyles than agency personnel (this is especially the case for evaluators who deal with police) and it is possible for mutual "culture shock" to develop. The evaluator is often not used to the 9:00 to 5:00 day of many agencies. As a student he/she found that the computer was less expensive and more accessible *after* 11:00 p.m. His/her work patterns were made more tuned to his/her own personal rhythms than those of an organization. Bureaucratic niceties seem irrelevant. Adjusting to political realities seems dishonest. And so it goes. Both evaluation group and service agency find the work and lifestyles of the other alien. And little can be done to change that. Both staffs can learn to respect and tolerate each other, but only if they understand that conflict is not to be avoided, but rather managed.

So far I have talked exclusively about the necessary characteristics of field members of an evaluation. I would like to talk briefly about key characteristics of project directors. (Just as in the previous discussion, I shall be talking about the ideal. I am certain that just as perfect field staff do not exist in nature, so neither do perfect project directors. The extent to which I, as an evaluator, approach the following characteristics is unclear. I will not burden you with my own assessment of how I rate in striving for the ideal.)

Although I think other characteristics are important, I will identify three key ones: organizational "smarts," familiarity with the service delivery system, and experience in completing a project. I will keep comments about these to an absolute minimum.

Organizational "Smarts"

To me, administration and intra-organizational work is, to a large extent, the effective use of power to get particular tasks done excellently and then distribute fairly the benefits which accrue from getting the job done. Lined up against the struggle to get work done excellently are the work patterns, procedures, and organizational rules of grantors, sponsoring agencies, review groups, evaluation agencies, etc. Think of many of those for a moment.

Planning periods are not allowed. Generally a program is funded and started and then the evaluators are called in. False starts are not allowed. If, as in Kansas City, a false start occurs, most often the response is to "make do" rather than start over. (Read "make do" as "waste all the money, not just part of it.")

Failures are not allowed to be published. Rather than publish a failure so that other people can learn, the tendency is to squelch a failure (so that other people can also fail).*

Decisions are not allowed. Often the administrator asks the question, "What does the rule book, organizational manual, etc., say?" The obvious conclusion is if the rule book says it can't be done then it can't be done. (What marvelous freedom for the administrator! All the prerequisites and none of the decision making.)

(Let me apologize to those of you who consider me outrageously irreverent in my attitude towards organizational rules and procedures. I have become convinced that the purpose of most rules is twofold:

1. They are to protect against "rip-offs"—although I suspect that more often than not, they serve to stop the very minor expense account "rip-offs" rather than the really gross ones.

2. They protect administrators from having to make decisions.

But let me add, it would be an over-simplification to say that procedures and work patterns ought to be removed. They ought not to be. They serve an important function. When properly administered they can protect agencies, grantors, etc., from gross rip-offs and absolute incompetence. Unfortunately, the rules, etc., do little to encourage excellence and can interfere with such achievement. The key is that an effective administrator has to learn how to wend his way through such rules, using them, if possible, to his advantage in getting the tasks done. There are various strategies to do this. I have known and seen "creative bureaucrats" who work 9:00 to 5:00 hours, take breaks and lunch at precise times, and who, because they know the rules and play the rules better than anyone else in the organization, use those rules to get jobs done. They are beautiful to watch because they have really mastered the skills of bureaucracy and remember that, ideally, the function of rules is to get a job done. [I have also seen accountants who understand that money is to spend to get a job done. Not spending money is no merit. It can be irresponsible *not* to spend money.] There are strategies other than being a "creative bureaucrat," but the skillful administrator learns how to use rules to *his/her* benefit. These skills are developed, honed, tested, in the *world*. They are not taught in universities and rarely talked about in bureaucracies. Learning them is accompanied by the acquisition of bruises, welts, scars, burns and *age*. Age alone doesn't do it, but it is only through the attainment of experiences to be reflected upon that these skills can be acquired. There are mentors and tutors to be had, but they rarely formally

teach. *Most often they put you through it.* At early stages of your career you know only after you've been through a particular lesson and you sit bruised and smarting that you have been taught. Later, you know as it happens, and while you may not particularly enjoy it at that time, you can admire the skill with which it is accomplished. [But if you have concentrated during your early lessons, there really aren't all the accompanying pains, just generally the reminder that when doing complex work it is necessary always to be very alert.])

The coupling of energetic, bright, relatively undisciplined young researchers with a seasoned organizational veteran who can provide a certain amount of structure (or the appearance of structure) seems to me a likely guarantee of a reasonable success in completing an evaluation.

Familiarity with the Field of Service Delivery

While I am not sure the following assertion will be absolutely clear, I nevertheless want to begin with it. I am *not* interested in evaluating particular programs. I am interested, and I think my clients are best served, *if I evaluate methods and strategies, not programs.* Let me explain that. The important principle here is generalizability. A program is only of general interest when it exemplifies methods, skills and strategies which are relevant to a wide variety of settings. Programs may or may not be that generalizable. If a program is so dependent upon local circumstances that it cannot be exported to other settings, I, as an evaluator, am simply not interested in it. It may be that it is of legitimate interest to the agency program officer. But I am interested in developing the knowledge base about the effectiveness of methods and strategies which are transferable in a broad field of service delivery. In order to see the broad application of a project, an evaluation director must *know* that service delivery system, must be aware of the intellectual traditions that have given rise to the present knowledge and skill base of that profession. And, it seems to me, she/he must be able to help the client context her/his program in those traditions. If the evaluator can't do that, outcomes are meaningless.

I did not include this in the characteristics of evaluation staff. If they would have such knowledge of the field when they started, that clearly would be desirable. But it is not essential that the evaluation director makes certain that staff acquire it during their work. Staff will, if highly motivated (one clue to the curiosity, skill and interest of an evaluation group is the extent to which they quickly start immersing themselves in the literature to acquire familiarity), acquire familiarity with service theory in relatively brief periods of time. (Methodological sophistication cannot. That has to be learned by doing, as well as studying.) But since the project director is the person who will be set-

---

* This is really a very complex issue and one that can only be referred to here. The publication of failures is dangerous to agency administrators because it simply provides another weapon to those who are always lurking in the wings, waiting to exploit any mistakes made by competent people who make mistakes and are willing to admit them. As a result the publication of mistakes has to be carefully orchestrated.

ting the general directions of the evaluation group and providing the overall guidance, it is essential that he/she know the substance and theories of the field.

Experience in Completing a Project

Evaluations don't complete themselves. A staff can be skilled in data collection, analysis, theory building and grantsmanship and still not be able to complete an evaluation. The best of people can block in completing an evaluation. It's almost a stage in research or evaluation. The person who has been through completing a project knows the project can be completed. The fact that at least one person knows it can be completed is critical. Outlines circulated widely to colleagues and consultants can help disperse the feeling of hopelessness which develops when people sit down to write after five years of work and $600,000 of funds. And, if they have kept their records, exploited the resident obsessive compulsive, and if they can narrowly concentrate on the questions the program addresses rather than the "oh by the ways," the first rough draft is half written by the time they sit down to write. (In other words, if the project has been well run, the writing of the final report began with the development of the original grant. Report writing implements include scissors, scotch tape, xerox machines; as well as pencil and paper.)

These then are the characteristics that I find essential in good evaluators, both staff and director. No doubt there are other characteristics which should be addressed here, but, at least for me, the mentioned ones are most critical. *This is most certainly true.*

Other miscellaneous Verities:

Verity #3. **In order to understand one (police officer, physician, nurse, social worker) you must *not* be one (the other side of—"In order to understand one, you must be one")—or—*cooptation.***

Much police, social and medical work is perceived of, and often is, exciting and important. For young persons who have hardly seen the outside of a university, such real world work will be attractive and interesting. For many it will be a welcome relief from the years of thinking and reading rather than doing. Their high degree of interest in such activities makes them especially vulnerable to cooptation.

My own experiences have led me to the following points of view regarding cooptation.

1. It is to be expected. It is a stage that all researchers must go through if they are properly sensitive to their subjects.
2. Cooptation is a trade-off. Whether agencies and evaluators do it consciously or unconsciously, both try to seduce the other to their respective points of view. In so doing, both allow an unusual amount of access to

the "secrets" of their organizations. When remission from cooptation occurs, the researcher (or professional) is generally much wiser about the other organization and him/herself.

3. Although there are counter-strategies, i.e., supervision, and creation of a staff culture, most often remission is spontaneous and occurs when a terribly biased initial report is reread with horror and shock several months later. (Here, good supervision points out the universality of the ailment, is supportive, and recognizes it as an important learning opportunity.)
4. There is no subsequent immunity to it. It happens over and over, even to crotchity old project directors.
5. If remission does not occur, more likely than not it is terminal and career counseling is in order. Unreconstructed co-optees are a disaster to evaluations. They are divisive, secretive, and generally have all the zeal of religious converts. Truth is theirs alone.
6. Symptoms include: (for police evaluations—people doing evaluations in other agencies will have to fill in their own specifics)
   a. Wanting to carry a gun.
   b. Feeling that nobody really understands the police as well as you do.
   c. Becoming a police "buff."
   d. Overemphasizing confidentiality. (When cooptation has occurred, the principle of confidentiality includes and more often than not is specifically targeted at the project director. The researcher feels that he must "protect the poor police department and police officer" from the rapacious project director.)
   e. Developing the police "swagger."
   f. Using police jargon.
   g. Wanting to get involved in the action, i.e., help with arrests, etc.
   h. Ignoring findings or "twisting the text to meet the message."

And finally, I would argue that the staff member who is never cooptable simply is too disinterested or too far removed from the issues. Cooptation is like sex and love relationships. You might not want it all the time, but without it there's boredom and disinterest. *This is most certainly true.*

Verity #4. **The only truly unforgivable sin is covering mistakes a second time—or—*mistakes at work.***

Mistakes are common for people at work. My own feeling is that I make a minor mistake a day, a middle range mistake every week, and a truly major goof-up once a month. Such is the nature of work. But mistakes are not to be confused with incompetence. People have rights to mistakes, but not to incompetence. And the nature of the world of work is such that, given proper colleagueship, supervision, and direction, most mistakes can be handled and compensated for—most often by extra work. (That is to be expected.) And while it might sound Pollyannaish, I really believe that mistakes and the handling of mistakes provide some of the most critical opportunities for learning and growth to capable reflective people.

Further, it is to be expected that some persons who make mistakes will try to cover them up (not by redoing the task but by hiding what they know or lying). As a result, a project director has to be careful to remain familiar enough with what is going on to be able to spot the covering of a mistake, especially a major one. When "covering" does occur dramatic action is necessary. All must be made to know that that is the one unforgivable sin and, if "covering" ever occurs again, that's it. Termination, firing, is the only alternative.

But, for the most part, mistakes simply have to be lived with as a fact of life. Often one can only shrug off the minor mistakes knowing that it would be more of a mistake to try to undo it than just to forget it. The middle range mistakes often have to be made up for by extra work (not that anyone tells you you have to, it's simply work that has to be corrected). Regarding the major mistakes, they not only require effort to undo (some may be so serious that they cannot be redone) but they also provide rich learning experiences in living with the consequences of life. Be clear, major mistakes generally do have consequences, but most often the consequences are not calamities if faced up to.

For me, my primary goal regarding my own mistakes is to discover them myself and report them. (This can be read as honesty or practical realism.) Such reporting does not free one from the consequences however. It simply is the development of trust in work relationships. I hope that my boss can trust me completely. That is— that he can trust that I will make my mistakes, but that he will never be surprised by them. I have found few mistakes that cannot be handled in civil ways. Covering a mistake, on the other hand, may mean that the opportunity to redo it is lost and potentially is disastrous to a project. (If I sound "preachy" at this point, it is because I feel quite strongly about this. Much of the work we do in evaluation is new and exploratory. If staff runs scared because they are fearful of making mistakes or taking appropriate risks, then the whole enterprise is lost. Evaluations are simply risky business. Bright competent people have the right to mistakes. Evaluations and evaluators can fail. If failures are seen as legitimate, then we can continue to develop our field, both through the successes and failures of ourselves and our colleagues. But

failures, too, should be published so we don't have to go on and on making the same major mistakes in evaluations.) *This is most certainly true.*

Verity #5. "Identifying the laborer who is to be in the vineyard"—or—selecting a subcontractor.

Although I do not have a great deal of empirical evidence about this, I nevertheless am convinced that every evaluative organization has a genius of design working someplace in the inner sanctums of the organization. That person is not only a genius but often too has E.S.P., in that she/he seems to be uncannily aware of exactly the design the contractor has in mind. But the grantor will never meet this design genius and once she/he has completed the design, she/he will be irrelevant to the evaluation. The point I am making is that the key persons to assess in selecting evaluators are the people who will actually do the work. They will make or break the evaluation. Even the project director is not enough. You must see and make judgments about the key on-site evaluation staff member(s). *This is most certainly true.*

Verity #6. The truth shall make them free—or—passing by the crotchity old evaluation director.

And finally, if young researchers are bright and capable, and if an evaluation director has given them the opportunity to really use their magnificent selves and skills, and if he/she believes that knowledge and skills are really crescive, the evaluation director will see young evaluators fly slightly higher and slightly faster than the crotchity old evaluation director. And that's what it's all about and *is most certainly true.*

Conclusion

Those of you familiar with hermeneutical principles will recognize that I have used the classic three point Lutheran sermon style: Introduction, three points in the body with the central part being both the longest and most important, and the third part a miscellaneous section where things are put that don't fit into the outline. The conclusion is generally an exhortation. I have presented my verities. I shall spare you further exhortation. *And that is most certainly true.*

One final point. My evaluation colleagues, the Kansas City Police Department and I have completed an experiment which has been considered to be fairly well done. We were very, very lucky. We worked very, very hard. Most of the things I am telling you are in hindsight. I may be wrong. I think I am right. That is most certainly true. Selah. Amen.

Additional comments on putting together a good evaluation research team.

Lee Sechrest

The skills involved in carrying out good program evaluations are special and not widely available. There are sufficient special characteristics of program evaluation research to make it unlikely that researchers without specific experiments and/or training for evaluation will be able to resolve all the problems that are sure to arise. Therefore, an administrator wanting to become involved in program evaluation research will not maximize chances of successful completion of the evaluation by relying on the usual sources of research expertise in his community, e.g., a local university faculty. Unfortunately, many university faculty members have no notion that their capabilities may be in any way limited.

In fact, most administrators will need some help in locating and recruiting evaluation researchers. There are several sources for such help. First, the potential funding agency for the research will often know a good bit about the local research community and will be able to make recommendations based on their experience of researchers who have the needed expertise and interest. A second source of information often available is the directors of other similar evaluation research projects. If an administrator knows of evaluations which he or she considers to have been well-done, a good move would be to contact the evaluators of those projects for advice. Even though the evaluators are at a considerable distance, evaluation researchers will often know the resources available in the community. Finally, the administrator may inquire locally to determine whether there are evaluators with experience of the type needed. The administrator should not be reticent about asking to examine credentials and samples of previous evaluation reports. If necessary outside help, e.g., from funding agencies, should be sought in assessing the credentials and previous work samples. No competent and honest evaluator will balk at having his or her work examined carefully.

A good evaluation research team begins with a highly competent evaluation researcher. That person will then, ordinarily, be able to put together the staff to the evaluation if it is funded. In the meantime that researcher should be quite willing to participate in planning the evaluation study and in preparation of the proposal to be sent to the funding agency. The greater the input from the potential research director, the stronger the proposal is likely to be and the greater the chances of the ultimate success of the evaluation.

A tradition for secondary analysis is developing such that this type of analysis is becoming entrenched in program evaluation (see Cook and Gruder, this volume), an entrenchment we encourage. Secondary analysis may consist of reanalyses or new analyses and may involve one or several sets of data. Unfortunately, as our own experience attests, secondary analysis is often frustrated substantially or even completely by poor-quality data sets, lack of documentation, tardiness of original investigators in replying to requests, and even, sad to say, unavailability of data altogether. Hedrick, Boruch, and Ross set forth a reasonable and authoritative set of requirements for governing the availability of data sets for secondary analyses. We believe that both researchers and program administrators should make the commitment to make their data available under the conditions specified here.

19

On Ensuring the Availability of Evaluative Data for Secondary Analysis

Terry E. Hedrick, Robert F. Boruch, and Jerry Ross

ABSTRACT

This paper is based on a programmatic effort to elicit and reanalyze data stemming from the evaluation of social programs. The stress is on identifying problems and negotiating for data and analyzing it. This includes: researchers' reluctance to disclose data for documentation and data control systems; vague or nonexistent policy for assuring access. The possible solutions presented here are based on governmental regulation and policy for publicly supported evaluation.

In 1975 an economist at a prominent university published an article which claimed that between 1935 and 1969 each execution in this country may have deterred between seven and eight murders (Ehrlich, 1975). The claim of a deterrence effect for capital punishment was itself noteworthy in diverging from earlier investigators' findings. The research was even more remarkable for its rapid introduction into the policy making process. At the time the results were published, the Supreme Court was reconsidering its 1972 decision declaring capital punishment unconstitutional. In an amicus curiae brief filed by the Justice Department in *Fowler v North Carolina*, Solicitor General Bork used the economist's results to argue for reinstitution of capital punishment. During this period, the data underlying the original article were not manifestly available to other interested researchers. Consequently, it was impossible for outside analysts to determine how well (or how poorly) the deterrence claim was justified based on reanalysis of *identical* data.

* Development of this paper has been supported by NIE Contract C–74–0115. All unpublished documentation discussed here is on file at the Methodology and Evaluation Research Division (Lucina Gallagher, Librarian).

Individuals who kindly provided their reactions to earlier drafts of this paper and/or advice and information in other ways include: Ole Engberg, John Evans, Harold B. King, Sheldon Laube, William Madow, Richard Marciano, Margaret E. Martin, Keith Marvin, Marjorie Powell, Alice Robbin, Peter Rossi, Lee Sechrest, Ernst W. Stromsdorfer, and Frederick Mosteller. Not all their reactions and criticisms have been accommodated, and we alone bear responsibility for the opinions registered here.

The preceding example, along with other cases, illustrates the need for an open access policy to evaluative data. Outside analysts should have access to any data which feeds into the policy making process so that the initial findings can be reexamined, and in particular, verified or refuted as quickly as possible. This paper focuses on that need and on mechanisms for assuring that competing analyses of policy relevant data are possible.

Our general proposal is that data, documentation, and logs from Federally supported research used in policy be made available to the community of analysts as quickly as possible. Our special interest lies in assuring access to data from Federally supported program evaluations, but parallel arguments can be made for open access to any data collected with private or other public funds (e.g., state or local) and which play a notable role in public policy formation. In the following remarks, we discuss the difficulty of accessing data for secondary analysis, the issue of proprietary rights to data, and the problems of confidentiality of information on identified respondents. The illustrations are taken primarily from efforts to reanalyze data from evaluations of social programs. The concluding remarks provide our recommendations and a discussion of implementation mechanisms.

I. Brief Justification for Secondary Analysis

Though routine reanalysis of data from contemporary program evaluations is a relatively new phenomenon, the general idea of secondary reanalysis is not. In the U.S., it dates back to Madison's arguments with Congress about the quality and utility of information collected in the first U.S. censuses. It continued prior to and during the Civil War with the American Statistical Association's secondary analyses of data which, until the ASA reanalysis, were interpreted by some public representatives as showing the genetic inferiority of the Negro race. Its most recent and visible context is evaluation research, exemplified in education by the numerous reanalyses (e.g., Mosteller and Moynihan, 1972) of the Coleman Report data, by the Cook et al. (1975) reanalysis of the evaluation on the effects of Sesame Street, and by Magidson's (1977) reassessment of Headstart evaluations.

Why is secondary analysis justified? The substantive reasons are most obvious. To better understand whether a policy or program works and how well it works, we need good estimates of its effect. Some conventional analytic methods, applied to survey data, can yield results which are seriously biased. Newer and competing methods which avoid or minimize biases implicit in the older techniques are being developed, tested, and used. The more durable reasons for secondary analysis then are scientific: to identify those evaluation designs and analytic methods which yield the least equivocal and least biased estimates of program effect and to build a store of reliable information about program effects. There are also institutional reasons: the political and fiscal importance of a program often demands that analysts with different perspectives examine the data for the sake of assuring that conclusions are robust under different assumptions. The sheer size and complexity of major programs suggest multiple analyses are justified to obtain maximum information for the research and development dollar. The usual pedagogical reasons for secondary analysis also obtain: the data are invaluable for college level courses and for in-service training programs at various government agencies. These justifications have been elaborated by Campbell et al.(1975), Cook (1974), Hyman (1971), and others.

Before we proceed much further, some examples may help to illustrate what we mean by secondary analysis (from Boruch, 1974). It is almost certainly true that the original analyses of some social programs have been wrong at worst and one-sided at best. The Borus–Hardin (1971) analysis of the impact of Manpower Training programs on over 3,000 trainees showed, using ordinary covariance analysis, that the programs reduced rather than increased salaries of job trainees. The competing analysis of analogous data by Steven Director (1974), which has been encouraged by Borus and Hardin, argued persuasively that the original analysis was incorrect and that the job training programs did not have negative effects. Secondary analysis of the Michigan Arthritis Program evaluation by Deniston and Rosenstock (1972) suggests that previous analyses of similar programs, based on time-series and quasi-experimental data, have often been incorrect and that estimates of the effects in these studies were biased upward or downward depending on the particular analystic method. Both the Campbell–Erlebacher (1970) review of Headstart and Magidson's (1977) sophisticated reanalysis of the original Westinghouse–Ohio study strongly suggest that conclusions of the original study were misleading. That is, it is reasonable to argue that the conclusions that Headstart's effects were *negative* are erroneous. The effects found could be due entirely to systematic biases produced by random errors of measurement or to misspecification in the model underlying the analysis.

The utilization of results of secondary analysis is a complex problem. They may generate more heat than light (as in the race–genetics issue). They may generate professional jealousies and vituperation, as in the reanalyses of the impact of prison reform programs (Rezmovic, 1977). They may confuse the public and its representatives. Nonetheless, secondary analyses are likely to be essential, despite occasional confusion, if we are to avoid episodes like the Thalidomide debacle, the use of ineffective or harmful but novel surgery (e.g., frozen stomach operations for ulcers, described in Bunker et al. 1977), and other nominally attractive but otherwise useless programs in the social, medical, and physical sciences. How such reanalyses will affect our social institutions is a question of concern to us, but the topic is much too broad to consider here. Rather, we focus on the more fundamental problem of assuring that the data for the reanalyses will be available.

Though our main interest lies in data stemming from program evaluations, we hasten to recognize the existence of a fine tradition of secondary analysis of some multipurpose governmental surveys. For the past 10 years, for example, the U.S. Census Bureau has maintained a system of public use sample tapes for the benefit of researchers. The Social Security Administration and other agencies have similar programs. Efforts to make data available from these and other general purpose surveys are described in Schoenfeldt (1970). Exemplary uses in testing new hypotheses about social phenomena and building theory are given in Hyman (1971) based on U.S. surveys and in Flaherty and Ennis (1977) for major government surveys in Canada, Sweden, the U.S., and elsewhere. That some problems which we discuss here for evaluation data on social programs, such as aggregation and confidentiality, are identical to those encountered in attempts to make census microdata useful to researchers is clear (Flaherty, 1978).

II. Problems in Accessing Data

Many of the examples in the following pages are drawn from the experiences of members and associates of Northwestern University's Project on Secondary Analysis. The Project is committed to reanalyzing existing evaluation data in order to assure that estimates of program effects are as unbiased and unequivocal as possible, and to test and develop new methods of evaluating educational and social programs (Boruch and Wortman, 1976). Members of the project have encountered a variety of obstacles when requesting evaluative data. The difficulties can be divided into four categories:

A. Locating the data and authority for its release.
B. Insufficient documentation.
C. Inappropriate aggregation.
D. Delays and refusals to data requests.

A. Locating the Data and Authority for its Release

The process of identifying the appropriate person or group to contact for data and its release can be time consuming and confusing. The problem is twofold: (1) locating the data set itself, and (2) locating the appropriate person with authority to release the data.

To obtain a particular data set, a reasonable starting point would appear to be the project director. Yet persons listed as project directors often change employment so frequently that they are difficult to locate. Once located they may no longer possess copies of data or final reports. Two examples help illustrate the problem.

Rindskopf (1976) sought to locate 20 evaluation studies listed as completed in the U.S. Office of Education's FY 1974 Report to Congress. Attempts were made by phone to contact persons listed as primary investigators. Only 13 of the 20 project final reports were available through ERIC (Educational Resources Information Center) and attempts to secure reports from the original researchers yielded only six reports out of nine promised. We expect the success rate for acquiring the actual data, rather than merely reports, would be lower.

A note in *Report on Education Research* (Research Notes, 1976) described the experiences of a researcher who sought to obtain a copy of the Coleman study tapes from the federal government. Fifteen hours and 30 phone calls later, he learned the tapes had been irretrievably filed with some 2,000 other unlabelled tapes. Fortunately, the tapes were available from the research underground.

Upon completion of a project, the responsibility for a data set's maintenance and dissemination is rarely delegated formally to any specific member of the research team. Requests for data by secondary investigators may be shuffled from one person to another for a period of weeks or months. Data from federally supported education program evaluations may reside in a wide variety of locations: in the possession of the original researcher, with the school system as in the Alum Rock

Educational Voucher Demonstration, with a private agency contracted to collect and clean the data as in Follow–Through, or in the possession of a funding agency such as the Office of Education.

The need to locate someone with *authority* to release data to outside researchers compounds the difficulty. For many projects, the raw data and the authority for the data's release do not reside with the same person or group. Federal contracts for evaluation contain a standard phrase to the effect that any materials or methods developed, including raw data, are assumed to be the property of the federal government. Yet agencies may be unable to follow through on this clause and acquire the data set. In the past, the National Institute of Education has not made it a regular practice to acquire copies of raw data along with final reports, and it has been assumed that the contractor might eventually destroy such data. Thus, even if a secondary analyst obtains permission from NIE to acquire a data set, there is no assurance that it exists. Only when projects are assumed a priori to be of wide interest to other professionals are arrangements made to retain the data. Recently NIE has considered drawing up a set of *voluntary* recommendations for contractors, requesting that all data collected be appropriately documented and made available to outside parties (Roistad, 1974). The recommendations were never disseminated, but the agency is again said to be considering such a policy partly because of support accorded by NIE's Work and Experience and Teaching and Education divisions for investigation of the topic.

The Office of Education routinely has required contractors to provide documented copies of all data upon completion of each study (Evans, 1977). This practice is commendable, although its benefits are reduced by the lack of a central storage facility for maintaining data. OE has reported very few requests for data by secondary analysts, a fact which highlights another issue with regard to data access. Before a secondary analyst can request a data set, he or she must know it exists. The expenditures necessary to document and maintain data are likely to be wasted if the data set is overlooked by individuals concerned with research and policy in that area. Guidelines are currently being drawn up for the cataloging of machine-readable data files by such groups as the American Library Association and IASSIST (International Association for Social Science Information Service and Technology). The goal of these efforts is to make it possible for researchers to search for machine-readable data files in the same manner in which other published sources are searched, e.g., Social Science Citation Index.

Cecil's (1975) attempt to secure the data collected by Howard Earle for his book *Police Recruit Training: Stress v Nonstress* (1973), dealing with alternative training programs for policemen, illustrates another aspect of the authority problem. Earle was sympathetic and encouraging regarding the performance of a secondary analysis, but no longer possessed the original data. The study was conducted under the auspices of the Los Angeles County Sheriff's Office and that office had retained the data. The Sheriff's Office's response to the possibility of a secondary analysis was that they were "very satisfied with the original report" and denied the request. In this case, the data and authority for its release resided together, but the original investigator no longer had any control over whether the data could be released.

The preceding examples demonstrate the importance of establishing guidelines for the maintenance and dissemination of evaluative data. Some of these problems will again be addressed in this paper when we discuss the topic of data ownership. If a data set is not to be retained by the primary investigator or submitted to the funding agency with the final report, one alternative is to deposit it with one of the many social science data archives. Copies of final reports or published articles stemming from the project could then contain directions as to data location and availability. We take special pains to applaud several efforts to avoid these problems. Carlyle Maw of the National Institute of Education has been conscientious and effective in making sure that data from evaluation of the Emergency School Assistance Act, archived at NIE, are routinely accessible to educational researchers. Lois-Ellin Datta of NIE encouraged routine access to data on Career Education programs. Kudos should also be given the Riverside School Study Executive Committee on the issue of data access. This committee of lay and professional members regulates access by outside researchers to the data collected on desegregation in Riverside, California (Gerard and Miller, 1975).

B. Insufficient Documentation

Obtaining evaluative data in no way guarantees a fruitful secondary analysis. Among other problems, insufficient documentation greatly limits and may preclude any analysis. "Documentation" is used here in its most comprehensive sense. It refers not only to final reports on the project itself, and to physical characteristics of the data set (e.g., type of magnetic tape, recording method, format of variables, etc.), but also to the purpose of the datum, method of collection and source, and any suspected corruption of data items. The simpler test of comprehensiveness for documentation is whether it "anticipates all of the normal questions a user is going to have about the data file. That includes concepts both analyst-oriented and programmer-oriented" (Zeisset, 1974, p. 3).

Insufficient documentation is a chronic problem in social science data sets lying outside the program evaluation sector. Alice Robbin (1974) surveyed 536 data files maintained by the Data and Program Library Services at the University of Wisconsin and found only a small percentage had documentation of even minimal adequacy. Documentation efforts were broken down into four operations: problem definition and research design, file development, information on quality of data, and successful output. The percentage of data sets with adequate documentation was under 30% for each of the four categories.

The reasons for poor or incomplete documentation are diverse. Social scientists are not rewarded professionally for documentation activities, and they may not reward their students or team colleagues for taking much care in the matter either. Personnel who are given the responsiblity for documentation, especially programmers, may not recognize the need to document files in detail for later researchers and often settle for merely composing lists of locations of variables in the data file. Unless the secondary analyst is already intimately acquainted with the project, this skeletal information is necessary but insufficient. Often the bulk of necessary information about the data set is known only to the primary investigators. If they have left the original research team, it is necessary to track them down to obtain information on the idiosyncracies of the data and its access. Consulting fees may be necessary or long delays incurred if researchers are currently employed full time on other projects. The poorer the original documentation, the more likely primary investigators will be besieged with information requests by secondary analysts attempting to use the data file.

Harold Watts (1972) has recommended that social scientists working with large data sets employ a data technician to serve as a "communicator and ambulating documentation file." Such a person should have a "taste for detail that facilitates acquiring and retaining all of the 'unwritten documentation.'" The danger of over-reliance on a data technician is that the unwritten documentation never moves to a written form and the information becomes lost when the research team disbands. Paul Zeisset of the Bureau of the Census has stressed the importance of documentation activities being handled by a qualified professional who can anticipate possible uses of the data file by future users (Zeisset, 1974).

> To the manager who would say that he can't afford the time and the prospective boredom of his highly qualified professional for the mundane work of producing documentation, I have two things to say: (1) he is not giving that professional the kind of clerical and para-professional assistance needed to get the job done with due attention to the sanity of all; and (2) he is helping to foster an attitude which has resulted in the lousy documentation efforts we are seeking to avoid in the future by setting the standards we are discussing today (p. 2).

One of the greatest losses of valuable information occurs with process data: description and astute impressions of what goes on in an evaluation and in a program. This type of information can be crucial for an analyst who needs to know what a piece of data really means. Anecdotes from data collectors concerning their confidence in the validity of specific data items or impressions of the direction of distortion for an item are not usually transcribed to written form. The secondary analyst working with such items may be wasting his or her time by treating such items as if they reflect high-validity responses.

To illustrate these issues, consider the problems which Hedrick (1976) encountered in attempting to obtain documentation for data on a vocationally oriented high-school program. One of several career education programs being tested with federal funds, the program was designed as an alternative high-school experience for youth deemed high risk for graduation from a traditional public school. The ultimate goal was to increase the employability of participants. The individual appointed to document that data set had never attempted such an activity before. The original documentation effort neglected to include the entering status of enrollees and control group members, i.e., whether the person was currently enrolled in school, or if enrolled, was attending classes regularly. This was a crucial variable since the interim report had indicated that the random assignment of applicants to experimental and control groups might have been destroyed by a differential drop out from the experimental group of individuals originally not attending high-school classes. If individuals not attending classes were less likely to profit by the alternative school education than regular attenders, the differential drop-out rate could bias the estimate of program impact in a positive direction. Further inquiries to the data technician revealed that the interview protocol from which this information was collected had gone through seven editions and there was no longer any way to determine which edition had been used with which participants. Anthropological reports indicated that entering status was a very unreliable variable. At least some applicants for the vocational program appear to have reported their entering status according to whatever they thought would ensure or deny their entry into the program. Furthermore, many of the students and their school counselors no longer knew whether they were officially enrolled in school, and if enrolled, how far they were from graduation. Consequently, a secondary analyst attempting to adjust for differences between the experimental and control groups would have been unjustified in using entering status as a covariate.

In most cases, it's unlikely that an original investigator will have the time, the inclination, or perhaps even the information necessary to answer questions bearing on data files or the data collection process. This constraint argues for far more comprehensive documentation, especially the inclusion of administrative logs and other material which can enhance the outsider's understanding of the data. For larger, more complex files, the identification of a data manager and development of an incentive system to assure their availability seems to us to be essential.

Standards for Documentation

A contributing factor to insufficient documentation is the lack of adequate standards upon which documentation staff can rely. The Federal Information Processing Standards (FIPS) publications are much too technical and narrow to be of use to social scientists undertaking the documentation of data on a sizeable social program. Only FIPS-20, Guidelines for Describing Information Interchange Formats, seems minimally useful, primarily in providing a checklist and glossary to introduce data processing terminology.

Some of the deficiencies in documentation references may be alleviated in the near future. The National Bureau of Economic Research (NBER) sponsored a workshop in April, 1974, which produced several working papers addressing the problem (Grasso, 1974; Zeisset, 1974), as well as a standard magnetic tape physical specification form which should soon be adopted by FIPS (King and Krasny, 1975). A second source of standards may develop from ongoing committees under the auspices of the International Association for Social Science Information Service and Technology, IASSIST (1976). The social science data archives and their relevant professional organizations, such as IASSIST, have strong interests in standardizing documentation and reporting, and they will probably play a major role in shaping new standards. Roistacher's work (1976, 1977) on machine-readable source documentation and on designing a standard data interchange file for the L.E.A.A. Research Support Center also offers hope for future efforts. For the researcher currently faced with the problem of drawing up documentation, several good examples of "in-house" methods are available. The Inter-University Consortium for Political and Social Research provides excellent treatment of national election data (Center for Political Studies, 1972), and NORC's (National Opinion Research

Center's) General Social Survey Codebooks (NORC, 1976) provide good models for codebook construction.

Aside from the standards being developed, and aside from models which might be copied in building documentation, one standard is of fundamental importance. That is, the technician with responsibility for archiving and documentation must keep the product simple. Exploiting practices that are idiosyncratic and complex can only make it more difficult for the outsider user to interpret and use magnetic tapes or other medium, and the documentation which goes with it. The approach should stress human engineering of files and file documentation for scientific use rather than exploiting the file to demonstrate one's sophistication in file architecture and construction.

Requiring comprehensive documentation for evaluation data sets is not without costs. Professional staff must allocate part of their time to the activity, and contracts for evaluations must recognize the increased costs involved. The Office of Education provided $50,000 to the Stanford Research Institute to maintain the Follow Through data in a manner conducive to secondary analysis. The National Institute of Education has targeted funds specifically for documentation to contractors. One mechanism for minimizing the effort involved is for both sponsors and the research team to view documentation as one of the several end products tied to any evaluation. If documentation is planned from the initiation of a program, the process can be much easier and the end product more accurate than a posteriori attempts to recall events and decisions.

C. Inappropriate Aggregation

The usefulness of evaluative data for answering specific research questions can be reduced notably by aggregating procedures. For example, an individual's total achievement test scores, total inventory scores, and the like may be archived, but not the individual's response to each item within a test or inventory. At worst, totals or averages for entire schools are maintained, but information at the student level is destroyed. "Different analyses are likely to apply to different units or even different versions of what is the same unit" (Watts, 1972, p. 184). Particularly in educational research, there is a notable controversy over the appropriate level of analysis—the individual, the classroom, the school, the district, or some combination of two or more levels (Cronbach, 1976; Burstein, 1976). Attempts to compare the effectiveness of programs which have been evaluated at different aggregation levels become problematic.

Under this argument, it becomes essential to build summary data files which contain the lowest (individual or item) level of data possible. If such data is not initially included, secondary analysis can be subject to long delays while files containing individual responses are reconstructed. So, for example, a reanalysis by Wortman et al., (1976) of the Alum Rock Educational Voucher Demonstration project, originally evaluated by Rand, required that the school system be contacted for individual student scores. The Rand analyses had utilized data aggregated at the school level and led to conclusions that the voucher program had either no effect or negative effects on student achievement scores. The reanalysis by Wortman et al. at the individual level allowed a finer distinction to be made. Mini-school programs within schools could be differentiated on a traditional vs. nontraditional dimension, with the resultant finding that any negative effects of the voucher program were confined to nontraditional innovative programs.

The Census Bureau's Economic Series was originally designed to release data in aggregated form to researchers, partially because many economic theories are based on aggregated data. More recently, it has been recognized that individual level data could be used very productively to explore economic changes in business firms. Because use of the data at the individual level was not foreseen initially, and because disclosure at that level might unintentionally allow identification of specific firms, the Bureau has formed an economic research unit that will carry out micro data analysis for outside researchers on a cost-reimbursable basis (Kallek, 1975).

Availability of item-level test responses is also important in evaluation activities. A standard research design involves identical pretests and posttests for experimental and control groups with the pretest used to adjust for any initial group differences. The possession of item responses can allow an analyst to check for factorial similarity of the test over time for both groups (Campbell, 1977) and so appraise the quality of adjustment. It can also allow an analyst to look for changes in factor scores as well as summary test scores. For example, the Internal-External Locus of Control Scale is often used to measure personality change for disadvantaged groups in education programs. The I-E Scale presumably measures an individual's perception of control over his or her world (Rotter, 1966), with the remedial program's goal often being to increase a person's sense of control. Recent research has proposed that two to four factors underlie observations on the scale (Collins, 1974; Gurin et al. 1969; Mirels, 1970). Although an analysis of total scores may not disclose significant change on the I-E Scale, utilizing item responses can allow an evaluator to look for differential changes in the scale's components.

Again, securing data at the item level can produce delays when the original documentation was done for summary scores. Attempts to secure item level data for questionnaire instruments used to assess the effectiveness of the previously mentioned career education program contributed to delays in this data set's acquisition (Hedrick, 1976). The item level responses were contained piecemeal on three different computer storage systems and some of the data were no longer retrievable without going back to the original questionnaire protocols.

The federal government has recognized the concerns of outside researchers with its methods of data tabulation. Section 2 of the Federal Reports Act of 1942 reads:

> It is hereby declared to be the policy of Congress . . . that information collected and tabulated by any federal agency as far as is expedient be tabulated in a manner to maximize the usefulness of the information to other federal agencies and to the public.

The question becomes one of assessing the needs of future research and finding a mechanism to translate these needs into decisions regarding forms of aggregation and summarization. The use of standardized reporting schemes by social science data archives for commonly collected variables such as age, religion, income, etc.

should be encouraged to increase comparability of categories across different research projects.

Archiving microlevel data will be expensive when the amount of computer storage space necessary for retention of data and documentation at this level is large (Rogson, 1976). The time interval from data collection to dissemination can also be lengthened by inclusion of micro-level data. Harold Watts (1972) traced the problems in analyzing and merging individual level data from the Survey of Economic Opportunity (SEO) in 1966, problems which kept the data from routine use by outside researchers for four years. OEO originally commissioned the Census Bureau to provide microdata on the Survey. Watts claims the Census Bureau's high standards for data transcription and documentation greatly delayed the release of data. When the Bureau's stance was relaxed, Brookings Institute, along with Assist Corporation, obtained the data set for further editing. OEO then contracted with the Data and Computation Center at the University of Wisconsin to be the repository, distributor, and service agency for the SEO file. At this point, delays in access shifted to potential user problems. In its original format, access to the data set was much too costly for researchers to make optimum use of the information. It was 1970 before the data were finally available in a form allowing routine exploitation. Similar problems, this time leading to a lag of two years or so, occurred in archiving data from the Graduated Work Incentive Experiment in New Jersey (Watts, 1972).

The decision to require microlevel reporting for evaluative data sets is a trade-off of costs and benefits. Including item level responses may lead to increased expenditures and even longer delays than for summary data files. Exclusion may prevent analyses which would produce valuable additional information and may also prevent the researcher from comparing the results to those of other studies. Attempts to obtain microlevel data after the fact may delay a secondary analysis so long that it becomes useless in the policy-making process. The decisions regarding level of data reporting and coding strategies should be made early in a program's lifetime, preferably before implementation, and they should be made on the basis of costs and benefits from the standpoints of both primary and secondary investigators.

D. Delays and Refusals to Data Requests

Access to data may be delayed or refused for a number of reasons. Although the issues involved often overlap, it is easiest to present some of the more common problems separately.

1. Ownership of the Data

Determining who owns the data and who has authority for its disclosure is not a particularly simple problem. "Historically it has been the privilege of the individual researcher to disseminate his data as narrowly or as widely as it suited him and this is generally still the case" (Campbell, 1970, p. 47). Yet if research is supported by public money or is used to shape public policy, it does seem important to us that competing analysts be given access to the data.

Consider, for example, the arguments about whether capital punishment does in fact deter murder. The Ehrlich article claiming a deterrence effect was immediately used by the Justice Department to argue in favor of the reinstitution of capital punishment. Capital punishment is an issue on which almost every citizen has an opinion, often an emotional one. The controversial nature of this issue makes it particularly important that any research data on the problem are available for careful scrutiny by all interested parties. Shortly after Ehrlich published his findings, an associate of Northwestern's Project on Secondary Analysis sought to obtain the data for secondary analysis (Ross, 1976). The economist replied to the request for data with a statement that the data were no longer available: The disk used for its original storage was dedicated to another project. A subsequent request for the correlation matrix on which the original analysis was based was unsuccessful; the matrix was said to be not readily available. The request eventually yielded a 23-page list of sources from which the original data set had been compiled, including citation of an unpublished memorandum for some of the figures. The reconstruction of the data set from this source list cost the secondary analyst a couple of month's work, as well as leaving him in the dark as to whether the reconstructed data matched the original.

As we mentioned earlier, the federal government owns all data collected under contract, but often no systematic effort is made to collect and maintain such data. To facilitate secondary analysis, the development of clear proprietorship guidelines for evaluative data should be encouraged for all government-funded programs, and the guidelines should specify *more* than voluntary cooperation.

2. Professional Capitalization and Reasonable Time Period for Release of Data

The researcher's interest in making a *unique* contribution to science and the professional prestige which accrues to making such a contribution are major obstacles to the disclosure of data. Researchers who invest time and effort in data collection feel some right to capitalize on their work before others request the data for alternative analyses. The problem is one of balancing the researcher's need for and right to recognition with the benefits derived from a policy of open access to the data he or she collects.

The Steinmetz Social Science Archive in the Netherlands takes the professional interests of its donors into account. Researchers using Steinmetz's facilities can store data under category E (not yet generally available) while completing primary analysis and for a reasonable time period thereafter. "Generally within one year after finishing primary analysis, the data are to be made available to third parties under one of the categories A–D. The archive encourages storage under category A (no restrictions) within at most five years after data collection, but exceptions can be made" (Royal Netherlands Academy of Arts and Sciences, 1974, p. 17).

The definition of a "reasonable time period" for professional capitalization depends on a number of factors. For basic researchers, immediate release of data upon publication may be warranted. Basic research data is less likely than evaluative data to be immediately policy relevant, and retention of data until publication ensures protection of the original researcher's investment. For evaluation research, we believe the data should be made available as soon as the primary analyses are completed. Evaluations of programs which involve long-term follow-ups of several years may require that data be released in waves, rather than waiting until the program's final follow-up. Finally, when a program evaluation is designed to feed rapidly into the policy formation process, it is sometimes feasible for the funding agency to organize simultaneous "secondary" analyses at the beginning of the project (Cook, 1974).

One strategy for ameliorating the threat to professional advancement is for secondary analysts to offer coauthorship to investigators whose data they request. If conclusions of the investigators seem to be irreconcilable, the primary analyst can be offered the option of writing a rejoinder to any publications stemming from the new analysis. The procedure has been adopted as standard practice for members of the Project on Secondary Analysis at Northwestern when unconditional access to data is inappropriate. As a rule, however, such offers are made only for substantive publications rather than methodological articles which only incidentally use a particular data set.

3. Confidentiality Problems

Confidentiality problems can also delay or prevent access to data. Evaluative data on social programs sometimes contain personal information about individuals or staff participating in such programs. The information will usually have been collected with assurances that it would remain confidential. There are numerous techniques to meet confidentiality requirements without unnecessary restrictions on access to data (Campbell, et al., 1977; Boruch and Cecil, 1978). The secondary analyst's use of evaluative data for example, usually requires only statistical records, identifying information being deliberately excluded. When identifying information is needed for merging different data files, safeguards can be implemented to prevent access by unauthorized persons and the identifying information can be purged from the final file after linkage. The Privacy Protection Study Commission (1977) has drawn up useful guidelines bearing on access to research data containing identifying information.

It is also reasonable to argue that confidentiality principles can be and are invoked unnecessarily. For instance, the California Commission for Teacher Preparation and Licensing recently mounted a study, with NIE funding, of the relations between teacher behavior and pupil achievement. The Educational Testing Service (ETS) was given the preliminary task of collecting information on teacher behavior and student achievement variables. One purpose of the research was to make the data available to outside researchers since the volume of information collected was enormous and could fruitfully be explored by many parties. When the California group asked ETS to release the data that began the study, ETS refused, citing problems of confidentiality. ETS felt that even with names, birthdates, etc. removed, deductive disclosure could occur with the information remaining such that release of the tapes would jeopardize the teachers and principals who had participated. To ensure confidentiality, ETS wanted to delete over 50% of the data collected, a procedure which significantly reduces the value of the data set to outside researchers. Outside consultants (Robert F. Boruch and Leigh Burstein) believe the ETS proposal far too conservative a posture (Rezmovic, 1977) and the issue is still being examined.

In the California Commission–ETS controversy, the issue of proprietary rights again enters in. ETS is being paid by the California Commission with NIE funds. It is attempting to balance its responsibility for confidentiality assurance to research participants with its responsibility to the party paying for data collection.

4. Controversiality and Indifference

New social programs and their evaluations are by nature controversial. To begin with, they involve the allocation of tax dollars and disagreements often exist as to the most fruitful way to allocate such money, as well as appropriate goals for social programs to pursue. Professionals may have vested interests in the success of specific programs and the possibility of a negative evaluation by a secondary analyst can contribute to reluctance to release data. In general, the more controversial the program, the more difficult it may be to acquire data for secondary analysis.

For example, Wortman (1976) sought to obtain the data used by the Federal Reserve Bank of Philadelphia in an evaluation of the Philadelphia school system (Summers and Wolfe, 1975). The initial evaluation generated a good deal of publicity because of the disputatious findings that black junior-high children performed best in schools with large black enrollments and that teachers' level of education had no effect on pupil achievement. Negotiations for the data were pursued with the Federal Reserve Bank and the school system officials over a 14-month period. Eventually the data set was judged to be not as valuable as was originally thought and its pursuit was dropped. But the point is that controversiality of the original evaluation contributed to the problems of obtaining access: The data *should* have been made available.

Besides controversiality, secondary analysis can be blocked by simple indifference. The Los Angeles County Sheriff's Office reply to the request for Earle's data on police training is an example (Cecil, 1976). The original evaluation had been completed and the Sheriff's Office announced that it was uninterested in any further information a secondary analysis might yield. In a sense, this reaction is the opposite side of the same coin. Either too much or too little interest can impede data release.

5. The Access Problem in Other Sectors

By describing such problems for educational and social research, we do not mean to imply that the issues are confined to these areas. Indeed, because the investment in physical and natural science is typically much larger and because projects in these areas may also be politicized, the problems can be considerably more severe.

During the controversy over the safety of cooling systems in nuclear reactors, for instance, it was difficult for analysts to verify that adequate data existed at all, much less to obtain copies of Atomic Energy Commission advisory committee reports on safety and the experimental data on which tests were based (see Primack and von Hippel, 1974, and the references therein). Similar difficulties in obtaining research reports have been cited by U.S. Representative Henry Reuss (1969) in investigations of the development of the Supersonic Transport. The refusal by the Department of Defense to disclose actual sites of herbicide spray in Vietnam hampered attempts by the American Association for the Advancement of Science to assess the impact of the herbicide program and the quality of laboratory data on negative program effects (Primack and von Hippel, 1974).

James D. Watson's book *The Double Helix* (1968) illustrates in detail the intrigues and withholding of information that occurred during the race to uncover the structure of DNA. Investigator A's reluctance to disclose raw data from the research to colleagues appears to have been based on the simple fear of being beaten to a solution. Concern that premature disclosure of research results and data will cost one later credit has long restricted the exchange of information in science (Merton, 1966). In an article on the behavior patterns of scientists, Merton claims that Watson's tale of self-interested secrecy would have been seen as a model of restraint in the seventeenth-century scientific community. In general, the hard sciences seem no more immune to data access problems than the soft.

6. Professional Standards and Precedents

One might assume that the problems outlined above could be remedied at the level of professional group action. After all, the spirit of the scientific tradition calls for open scrutiny of results by a researcher's colleagues. However, professional level action has not been particularly successful in fostering access to data even for the small-scale laboratory studies typically reported in professional journals. In 1962, Leroy Wolins and Steve Zyzanski sought to obtain data from studies appearing in two experimental psychology journals. Of the 37 data sets sought, only 11 were eventually obtained, and the requests sometimes yielded hostile and suspicious replies (Wolins, 1962; Zyzanski, 1962). A more recent attempt by Page (1975) to secure detailed procedures and scripts from 70 published laboratory studies, again psychology, did not fare much better. Nineteen authors did not reply at all, and only 34 gave sufficient information to allow replication of the original study.

Partly in response to the problem, one of the leading psychology journals recently instituted an editorial policy requiring that authors sign an agreement to make data and documentation available to requestors for a period of five years after the date of publication (Greenwald, 1976). No information is yet available on the success of this policy, as articles accepted under it are only now appearing in print. Incidentally, the policy has no interdictive features. If authors do not provide requestors with data there is little that can be done except remind them of their original agreement (Greenwald, 1977).

Professional journals do not see themselves as having the resources to provide a regular archival service for data sets. Yet most data sets underlying articles in professional journals are quite small, and would therefore take up little storage space. In a recent paper on fraud and access problems in science, Fred Bryant and Paul Wortman (1978) have proposed that journals require submission of copies of data along with research manuscripts, so that if all else fails and the author refuses data requests, the data can be retrieved from the relevant journal.

The proposals for regulation we outline in the next section are not without precedent. In 1976, the Danish Data Archive (DDA) was established to serve as a repository for research data and as a vehicle for the secondary analysis of data. The institution was set up as a demonstration project in 1973, and was sufficiently successful to establish as a permanent institution in 1977. Any researcher who, in capitalizing on the archival data, also obtains additional data with DDA support, must provide a copy of the new data to the DDA to permit its future secondary analysis. The Belgian Archives for the Social Sciences (Université Catholique de Louvain, 1976) and the Steinmetz Archive, mentioned earlier, have similar policies. The deposit procedure of the DDA immediately makes it clear that researcher claims of permanent ownership of the data set are unwarranted. Moreover, the data submitted must be documented under a uniform set of standards. This strategy assures that the problems which are chronic among social researchers, e.g., sloppy documentation of data files, are not severe for the DDA.

As a result of their own frustrated attempts to secure data for secondary analysis, the Panel on Deterrent and Incapacitative Effects (1976) is considering recommending the establishment of a central depository within the Law Enforcement Assistance Administration for all research data collected by persons studying the criminal justice system. It is further proposed that federal research support be contingent on submission of data to the repository within a reasonable period following project completion.

III. Summary Recommendations: Regulation and Policy

Principle: All data, documentation, and logs stemming from Federally supported research used in policy, especially program evaluations, must be made available to the community of analysts.

Obtaining access to evaluative data on social programs engenders problems beyond the scope of those attending laboratory data. Most data sets underlying articles in professional journals are small, evaluative data sets are often massive, and as the size of the data set expands so does the effort and cost required for documentation and data maintenance. Moreover, most journal articles concern relatively innocuous topics, and, unlike evaluative data, they are often not politically controversial. The principle of open access to evaluative data is warranted on scientific grounds: Data must be subjected to cross-examination to advance the state of the art in public program development. The principle is warranted on public interest grounds: Data collected under government support must remain publicly available. It is warranted on economic grounds, since the cost of repeated competing analyses of data is low, and the collection costs generally very high. It is justified on grounds of protecting the public and scientific community from fraud, for the expense, controversy, and pressures on the original evaluator may corrupt the process of evaluation, and the access to data assures better oversight. For these reasons, regulations governing access to evaluative data are sorely needed. The actions taken by professions within their own boundaries can be viewed as precursors to the regulatory action here proposed.

We suggest that the following provisions be incorporated into any agency regulation governing access to evaluative data on social programs.

1. Ownership of data. Proprietary rights to data ought to be made clear prior to funding a project. Ownership of evaluative data and authority for its release should be clearly established as the right of the funding agency.

2. "Reasonable time period" for release. For evaluative data, release should be feasible upon completion of the preliminary analysis. At the very least, copies of data should be available to others upon completion of the final report; at best, if alternative analyses are desired immediately, simultaneous "secondary" analyses can begin when data collection is complete.

Our experience and the experience of others suggests that after the secondary analyst receives a data file, it takes six to nine months to set it up for reanalysis, i.e., to understand the data's structure, content, scope, and documentation. This time lag makes early release desirable. In the ideal case, data would be released in time to permit the exploitation of both primary and secondary analysis in a policy debate.

3. Disclosure of statistical data. Release of data after preliminary analyses should include all statistical records. Disclosures of records here includes disclosures of individual level data and item level responses (e.g., test items). Identifiers should be deleted from individual records to preserve the privacy of respondents, except in those instances in which secondary analysis justifiably requires identifiers. Guidelines and strategies for preserving confidentiality of the data should be drawn up before project implementation.

We believe that in most instances, release of statistical records involves no problem of deductive disclosure. That is, the secondary analyst will normally be unable to deduce identified responses. For the extraordinary case in which deductive disclosure may be possible, provision should be made for routinizing the process of checking for deductive disclosure and for minimizing its likelihood.

4. Disclosure of identified records. In some instances it is important that the secondary analysts have access to identifiable records rather than records containing only statistical information. In those rare instances, rules governing disclosure should follow the pattern laid down by the Privacy Protection Study Commission (1977). That is, disclosure must be well justified, data must be solely for statistical research, data must not be redisclosed, and adequate safeguards on the data must be employed by the secondary analyst to assure confidentiality.

5. Documentation and data management. Plans for documentation of the data should be submitted as part of the research design plan in any evaluation. Those plans must include estimates of the costs of such documentation and identification of specific standards used. Where possible, uniform standards of quality and of design should be incorporated into documentation. Documentation refers not only to identification of the measures used and copies of instruments not commonly known, but also to information on the purpose of the datum, situational influences that may have corrupted such measures, and the probable direction and degree of the distortion involved. Finally, documentation here includes research logs: description of salient problems, development of solutions, and correspondence bearing on solutions. Microfilm is generally underexploited in the social sciences and is a convenient vehicle for recording this sort of information.

A data management officer should be designated to take responsibility for:

A. Initial documentation of records.
B. Update and correction of individual records.
C. Production of data files for outside users, e.g., secondary analysts.
D. Consultation on and interpretations of file documentation for outside users.
E. Destruction of identifiers and of statistical data which can lead to identification.

The research sponsor's responsibility in this sector is clear. Contractors must be reminded emphatically and consistently to document data collection and archiving *during* the project. For without periodic monitoring, documentation is unlikely to be as comprehensive as it should be, and performance checks at project termination are simply too late to do much good.

6. *Data maintenance for secondary analysis: custodians*

Option A: Individual maintenance and dissemination

In some cases, it will be reasonable to expect the original principal investigator to archive the evaluation at his or her host agency, to maintain and correct errors in the file, and to perform secondary analyses on demand by outside analysts.

The main argument for this option is that the process of secondary analysis can be simplified greatly. The secondary analyst need not rely on his own computer capability and staff; rather the archive provides the service. Although comprehensive documentation of the data set will still be necessary for outside researchers to learn what information is available, the complicated process of eliciting, transmitting, and interpreting data tapes and tape documentation is eliminated entirely. Further arguments for the option concern professional issues. Assuring confidentiality, where privacy is an issue for example, is easier when only summary analyses rather than anonymous statistical records are provided to the outsider. This is a weak argument, however, since in most cases release of anonymous records poses no grave threat to confidentiality.

The arguments against this option concern its flexibility and utility. First, many large research institutes have the capability to archive large data sets, but do not have the capability to do sophisticated reanalyses. The Project on Secondary Analysis, for example, regularly employs special purpose programs for analyzing data which are not generally in the program package offered by research institutes. Second, more importantly, secondary analysis often demands close interaction between analyst and programmer and often cannot be planned entirely in advance. The physical distance separating the analyst and archive under this option is likely to inhibit interaction, and is likely to truncate adaptive analyses. Third, the option does not lend itself well to adversary secondary analyses. That is, it is easy for the institute to make reanalysis difficult since it exercises complete control over data, analysis, and time allocated to each. Moreover, if clean data tapes are routinely generated for outside analyses, the imperfections are too easily submerged. Finally, the economics of this option need to be addressed. Most research institutes have considerably higher overhead and operating costs than academic institutions and the need for secondary analyses is sporadic rather than uniform. These two facts together suggest that options other than routine maintenance and analysis of files by research institutes may be most cost-beneficial.

Option B: Centralized archive or set of archives

A centralized archive, or set of such archives, could serve as the main vehicle for data dissemination and maintenance. A strong argument for this option is the ease with which evaluative data could be located and accessed. Staff experts could handle the maintenance and dissemination activities, and data documentation could be made more consistent, reducing problems that a secondary analyst would ordinarily have in analyzing multiple independent data sets. Provided that financial support was reasonable, the interest of existing archives could probably be assured, and the problems inherent in adversary analyses under Option A would be avoided.

Arguments against this option center on a loss of expertise about the original research. The archive staff would clearly not know as much about the research as the primary investigators. This problem could be minimized by initial comprehensive documentation efforts and by making the archive a custodian for the journal articles, research reports, logs, and records of the original project staff.

Organizational mechanisms for this option include the possibility of adjoining archives to *existing* institutions to minimize costs. An archive might be folded into the normal responsibilities of relevant agencies, e.g., in education—ERIC, Regional Laboratories, and the Center for Education Statistics. Especially for very large-scale evaluations, expanding the role of the National Archives or a similar agency with pertinent experience seems worth considering. In fact, National Archives' Charles Dollar has begun to store some files generated from NIE supported program evaluations, and is developing a regular archive program for all such files. The creation of new institutions solely to maintain data is possible, but rather unlikely unless other activities are also planned. For example, the DUALAB System, which disseminates census data, does special analyses under contract and charges for their services.

While the optimal single form of data maintenance for secondary analysis remains unresolved, the pressing need for such maintenance is clear. The current haphazard responses to the need for ensuring data availability are not conducive to maintaining the integrity of the scientific process. The policy and regulations advanced here are designed to move the scientific community toward a consensus on several aspects of this problem, a consensus that will hopefully lead to the problem's ultimate resolution.

REFERENCES

Boruch, R. F. (1974), "On common contentions about randomized field experiments." In R. F. Boruch and H. W. Riecken (eds.), *Experimental Testing of Public Policy*. Boulder, Colo.: Westview Press.

Boruch, R. F., and Wortman, P. M. (1976). Project on Secondary Analysis: Progress Report. Unpublished manuscript. Evanston, Il.: Northwestern University, Psychology Department.

Boruch, R. F. and Cecil, J. S. (1978). *Assuring privacy and confidentiality in social research.* Philadelphia: University of Pennsylvania (in press).

Borus, M. E. and Hardin, E. (1971). *The Economic Benefits and Costs of Retraining. Lexington, Mass.: Heath Lexington Books.*

Bryant, F. B., and Wortman, P. M. (1978). Secondary analysis: The case for data archives. *American Psychologist,* 33: 381–387.

Bunker, J. P., Barnes, B. A., and Mosteller, F. (eds.). (1977). *Costs, Risks, and Benefits of Surgery.* New York: Oxford University Press.

Burstein, L. (1976). "The choice of unit of analysis in the investigation of school effects: IEA in New Zealand," *New Zealand Journal of Educational Studies,* 11, 11–24.

Campbell, A. (1970). "Some questions about the New Jerusalem." In R. L. Bisco (ed.), *Data Bases, Computers, and the Social Sciences.* New York: Wiley and Sons.

Campbell, D. T. (1977). One perspective on Cronbach day (October 28, 1976) at Northwestern. Unpublished memo. Evanston, Il.: Northwestern University, Psychology Department.

Campbell, D. T., and Erlebacher, A. (1970). "How regression artifacts in quasi-experimental evaluations can mistakenly make compensatory education look harmful." In J. Hellmuth (ed.), *Compensatory Education: A National Debate,* Vol. 3 of *Disadvantaged Child.* New York: Brunner-Mazel.

Campbell, D. T., Boruch, R. F., Schwartz, R. D. and Steinberg, J. (1977). "Confidentiality preserving modes of access to files and to interfile exchange for useful statistical analysis," *Evaluation Quarterly,* 1, 269–299.

Cecil, J. (1976). Memo on attempts to secure data from Howard Earle's police training evaluation. Unpublished memo. Evanston, Il.: Northwestern University, Psychology Department.

Center for Political Studies, University of Michigan. (1972). *The CPS 1972 national election study.* Ann Arbor, Michigan: ICPR.

Collins, B. E. (1974). "Four components of the Rotter Internal–External Scale: Belief in a difficult world, a just world, a predictable world, and a politically responsive world." *Journal of Personality and Social Pyschology,* 29, 381–391.

Cook, T. D. (1974). "The potential and limitations of secondary analysis." In M. W. Apple, M. J. S. Subkoviak, and H. S. Lufler, Jr. (eds.), *Educational Evaluation: Analysis and Responsibility.* Berkeley, Calif.: McCutchan.

Cook, T. D., Appleton, H., Conner, R. F., Sheffer, A., Tomkin, G., and Weber, S. J.(1975). *"Sesame Street " Revisited.* New York: Russell Sage Foundation.

Cronbach, L. J. (1976). *Research on classrooms and schools: Formulation of questions, design, and analyses.* Stanford Evaluation Consortium, August.

Dansk Data Kriv (Danish Data Archive), (1976). *Information on the Danish Data Archive.* Copenhagen: DDA (H. C. Andersens Blvd., 38 mezz).

Deniston, O. L., and Rosenstock, I. M. (1972). *The Validity of Designs for Evaluating Health Services.* Research report. Ann Arbor, Michigan: University of Michigan, School of Public Health, March.

Director, S. (1974). *Evaluating the Impact of Manpower Training Programs.* Ph.D. dissertation, Northwestern University, Evanston, Il.

Earle, H. H. (1973). *Police Recruit Training: Stress vs. Nonstress.* Springfield, Il.: Charles C. Thomas.

Ehrlich, I. (1975). "The deterrent effect of capital punishment: A question of life or death," *American Economic Review,* 65, 397–417.

Evans, J. W. (1977). Correspondence, October 21.

Flaherty, D. L. (1978). "Final report of the Bellagio conference on privacy, confidentiality, and the use of government microdata for research and statistical purposes," *Statistical Reporter,* 8, 274–278.

Flaherty, D. L., and Ennis, J. (1977). Report of the Project on Privacy and Access to Government Microdata. Unpublished. London, Ontario, Canada: University of Western Ontario.

Gerard, H. B., and Miller, N. (1975). *School Desegregation: A Long Term Study.* New York: Plenum Press.

Grasso, J. T. (1974). *Documentation of statistical data sets: The case of the National Longi-*

tudinal Surveys. Paper presented at the NBER Workshop on Documentation of Large Machine-Readable Statistical Data Sets, April.

Greenwald, A. G. (1976). "An editorial," *Journal of Personality and Social Psychology,* **33,** 1–7.

Greenwald, A. G. (1977). Personal communication, January.

Gurin, P., Gurin, G., Lao, R., and Beattie, M. (1969). "Internal-external control in the motivational dynamics of Negro youth," *Journal of Social Issues,* **25,** 29–53.

Hedrick, T. E. (1976). Memo on attempts to secure data on a Career Education Program. Unpublished memo. Evanston, Il.: Northwestern University, Psychology Department.

Hyman, H. H. (1971). *Secondary Analysis of Sample Surveys: Principles, Procedures, and Potentialities.* New York: Wiley.

IASSIST: International Association for Social Science Information Service and Technology. (1976). *Newsletter,* **1.**

Kallek, S. (1975). "Potential applications of Census Bureau Economic Series in microdate analysis," *American Economic Review,* **65** (Suppl.), 257–262.

King, H., and Krasny, M. (1975). "A standard description for magnetic tape files," *Annals of Economic and Social Measurement,* **4,** 449–454.

Magidson, J. (1977). "Toward a causal model approach to adjusting for pre-existing differences in the nonequivalent control group situation," *Evaluation Quarterly,* **1,** (3), 1977.

Merton, R. K. (1969). "Behavior patterns of scientists," *American Scholar,* **38,** 197–225.

Mirels, H. L. (1970). "Dimensions of internal versus external control," *Journal of Counseling and Clinical Psychology,* **34,** 226–228.

Mosteller, F., and Moynihan, D. P. (1972). *On Equality of Educational Opportunity.* New York: Random House.

National Opinion Research Center (1976). *National data program for the social sciences: Codebook for the Spring 1976 General Social Survey.* Chicago, Il.: University of Chicago, NORC, 1976.

Page, M. (1971). Deceiving the deceivers: Compliance, reference group identification, and reactions to deception among social pyschological researchers. Unpublished manuscript. University of Nebraska, Psychology Department.

Panel on Deterrent and Incapacitative Effects (1976). (Committee on Research on Law Enforcement and Criminal Justice, National Research Council). *Third draft of the panel summary report.* December.

Primack, J., and von Hippel, F. (1974). *Advice and dissent.* New York: Basic Books.

Privacy Protection Study Commission. (1977). *Draft recommendations for social research and statistics.* Washington, D.C.: The Commission, December.

Research Notes. (1976). *Report on Educational Research,* June 16, p. 8.

Reuss, H. (1964). Interview with Henry Reuss. *Congressional Record,* **115,** 34743.

Rezmovic, E. L. (1977). *Some design, measurement, and treatment issues in correctional evaluation.* Paper presented to the National Academy of Sciences Panel on Rehabilitation of Criminal Offenders, Woods Hole, Mass., July.

Rezmovic, V. (1977). Memo on attempt to acquire data from the Beginning Teaching Study. Unpublished memo. Evanston, Il.: Northwestern University, Psychology Department.

Rindskopf, D. (1976). Memo on acquisition of evaluation data from 20 studies supported by the U.S. Office of Education in 1974. Unpublished memo. Evanston, Il.: Northwestern University, Psychology Department.

Robbin, A. (1974). "Managing information access through documentation of the data base," *SIGSOC Bulletin,* **6,** 74–75; 56–68.

Rogson, M. M. (1976). *Documentation in social science experiments.* The Rand Paper Series, January.

Roistacher, R. C. (1976). *The Data Interchange File: A first report* (Document No. 207). Urbana-Champaign, Il.: University of Illinois, Center for Advanced Computation, June 21.

Roistacher, R. C. (1977). *L.E.A.A. Research Support Center machine readable source documentation system user's guide* (draft 1). Urbana-Champaign, Il.: University of Illinois, Center for Advanced Computation, July 29.

Roistad, M., (1974). *NIE's proposed voluntary data sharing policy.* Presented at NBER Workshop on Documentation of Large Machine-Readable Statistical Data Sets, April.

Ross, J. (1976). Memo on acquisition of I. Ehrlich's data on deterrent effects of capital punishment. Unpublished memo. Evanston, Il.: Northwestern University, Psychology Department.

Rotter, J. B. (1966). "Generalized expectancies for internal versus external control of reinforcement." *Psychological Monographs,* **80,** 1 (Whole No. 609).

Royal Netherlands Academy of Arts and Sciences: Social Science Information and Documentation (1974). *Steinmetz Archives.* Amsterdam: North-Holland Publishing Company.

Schoenfeldt, L. F. (1970). "Data archives as resources for instruction, research, and policy planning," *American Psychologist,* **25,** 609–616.

Summers, A. A., and Wolfe, B. L. (1975). "Which school resources help learning? Efficiency and equity in Philadelphia public schools." *Federal Reserve Bank of Philadelphia Review,* February 1975.

Taeuber, R. C. (1973) "Problems of access: Some comments," *Annals of Economic and Social Measurement,* **2,** 215–220.

Université Catholique de Louvain. (1976). *B.A.S.S.: Belgian Archives for the Social Sciences.* Louvain-La-Neuve.

Watson, J. D. (1968). *The Double Helix.* New York: Atheneum Publishers.

Watts, H. W. (1972). "Microdata: Lessons from the SEO and Graduated Work Incentive Experiment," *Annals of Economic and Social Measurement,* **1,** 183–191.

Wolins, L. (1962). "Responsibility for raw data," *American Psychologist,* **17,** 657–658.

Wortman, P. M. (1976). Memo on attempt to acquire data from the Federal Reserve Bank of Philadelphia. Unpublished memo. Evanston, Il.: Northwestern University, Psychology Department.

Wortman, P. M., Reichardt, C. S., and St. Pierre, R. (1977). The first year of the Educational Voucher Demonstration: A secondary analysis of student achievement test scores. Technical report, unpublished. Evanston, Il.: Northwestern University, Psychology Department.

Zeisset, P. T. (1974). *Some views on good documentation.* Paper presented at the NBER Workshop on Documentation of Large Machine-Readable Statistical Data Sets, April.

Zyzanski, S. J. (1962). Analysis of variance applied to factors which do not have comparable scales. Ph.D. dissertation, Iowa State University.

In the following, Scheirer points out that program participants, including both providers and recipients of services, often view the outcomes of the program favorably despite the lack of any objective evidence of program effectiveness. This discrepancy in conclusions about program outcome has been viewed from different perspectives as suggestive of the inadequacy of objective outcome measures and of the biased reporting of persons with vested interests. Scheirer attempts to show that the generally positive views of program participants about program outcomes are quite understandable in terms of basic psychological processes, some of which may not operate at a level of complete awareness. Scheirer also suggests that policy decisions may well be affected by commitments to belief in program effectiveness. In conclusion, however, the author indicates that objective, behavioral criteria for change should be accorded the greatest weight.

20

Program Participants' Positive Perceptions
Psychological Conflict of Interest in Social Program Evaluation

Mary Ann Scheirer

A common dilemma of evaluation researchers, that outcome findings do not confirm program administrators' and recipients' perceptions of benefits occurring, is related to a general proposition that participants will have positive perceptions of program effects, regardless of behavioral changes toward program goals. This phenomenon is shown to occur widely, and to be predictable from both behavioral and cognitive social psychological theory, but has not been previously recognized explicitly. Implications are drawn for the policy planning process and for the methodology of program evaluation.

*I*n 1962, a new medical procedure for treating gastric ulcers was introduced which required "freezing" the ulcerated stomach. Placing a special coolant in a "balloon" in the patient's stomach for about one hour was believed to permanently decrease the flow of stomach acid, and thus alleviate ulcers. Laboratory work with animals and observation of test patients had indicated favorable results; the procedure was rapidly adopted by American doctors. By 1964, an estimated 10,000 patients per year received this gastric freezing treatment (Gilbert et al., 1975).

AUTHOR'S NOTE: *Appreciation is extended to Henry Alker, Jay Millmon, Robin M. Williams, Jr., and C. James Scheirer for their helpful comments on earlier drafts of this paper.*

A number of observational studies found high rates of success for the treatment, with as many as 70% of the patients reporting complete remission (unpublished review by L. Miao, summarized in Gilbert et al., 1975). Several experimental comparisons were also done, but all had fewer than 30 patients in each group. Of five such experimental studies found by Miao, three reported no differences in symptom relief between the experimental and control groups, while two studies found favorable results for the gastric freezing procedure. By late in the sixties, some medical complications from the procedure began to be reported. Then, in 1969, a large study was done involving several hospitals, a placebo treatment not using freezing, double-blind administrative procedure, and random assignment of patients to treatments (Ruffin et al., 1969). The results showed no advantage for gastric freezing over the placebo. Soon after, the medical community abandoned the procedure.

While evidence arising from the evaluation of social innovations has seldom been as clear cut as this experimental evidence on gastric freezing, the scenario has often been the same. A new program is hailed by its developers as the solution to a deepseated social problem, initial administrators report substantial success with the program, and it is rapidly disseminated across the country. Evaluators, however, are often not able to produce unequivocal data showing positive behavioral changes resulting from the program while staff and clients strongly believe it is beneficial. Alternatively, evaluation research findings about affective variables, such as reduced anxiety or increased self-esteem, may be unaccompanied by findings concerning expected changes in behavioral variables, such as reduced unemployment or higher academic achievement. Are the measuring instruments or research methods used by evaluators inadequate to capture real, beneficial changes taking place, or are the program benefits mainly in the perceptions of the staff and clients? An example of the dilemma facing evaluators is provided by a critic of evaluation research methodology:

> For decades the evidence produced by the application of conventional evaluation procedures has contradicted the experiential evidence of the practitioner. . . .A recent dramatic example is afforded by the Higher Horizons program [where] test data failed to affirm what supervisors, teachers and clients insisted was true—that the program was making a difference so great that it simply could not be abandoned. . . . Evaluation as we know it has failed and the world of evaluation does indeed require reshaping. [Guba, 1972: 250-251]

The evaluator's dilemma thus involves which kind of evidence should be believed when outsiders' quantitative assessments and insiders' intuitive perceptions yield totally different pictures of the same situation. For Guba, participants' assessments are taken as the standard of accuracy·that evaluation research techniques should validate. In contrast, this paper addresses the dilemma by developing a general proposition about participation in new activities, which, it will be argued, explains the origin of such contradictory assessments of social programs.

The proposition refers to situations in which an innovation—new materials, changes in organizational structure, or new methods of "treatment" for clients—has been introduced in an effort to change behaviors considered undesirable; that is, where "social programs" are in effect. The proposition states:

> Participants like social programs, evaluate them favorably, and think they are beneficial, irrespective of whether measureable behavioral changes take place toward stated program goals.

"Participants" here refers both to the *recipients* or intended beneficiaries of the program and to the *staff* responsible for planning and implementing it. Innovative "social programs" are to be distinguished from ongoing governmental policies, in which a rule or law is routinely applied to the whole population, or a specified subsegment of it. The proposition is intended to apply only to participants in "social programs." "Program goals" are the outcomes that the innovation was explicitly intended to produce, such as increased educational achievement, employment of previously unemployed people, decreased criminal recidivism, and so forth. Thus, this paper excludes from consideration the unacknowledged, often political, goals which may provide important motivation for program supporters, but which are usually not included in program evaluations. Factors such as political support from urban constituencies or intra-agency advancement for program administrators are, of course, intrinsic to the political processes by which governmental programs are adopted and continued, but have no necessary connection to alleviating the problem situation to which the program's resources are ostensibly addressed. The substance of the proposition is that when personal evidence about programs is collected in the form of attitude questionnaires, opinion polls, or interviews concerning satisfaction or dissatisfaction with a program, the results are generally positive, in spite of a frequent lack of evidence for any movement toward the intended program goals.

I shall argue (a) that evidence for the proposition is diverse and extensive; (b) that it could have been predicted from and is supported by several branches of social psychological theory; (c) that the proposition has not in fact been recognized by many program planners and evaluators, nor in the political theory of democratic processes; and (d) that it has important implications for program planning and evaluation. If recognized as a general human tendency, the proposition's predictions may alleviate some of the controversy pervading the current evaluation research literature and lessen some misunderstandings presently dividing program managers and evaluators into opposing groups.

EVIDENCE FOR THE PROPOSITION

Examples of this proposition in action can be found in almost any report of evaluation research which includes participants' opinions about the program. The Westinghouse-Ohio University national evaluation of the Head Start Program (Cicirelli et al., 1969) found no overall effects of Head Start attendance on children's later academic achievement, self-concept, attitudes toward school, or classroom behaviors, but nevertheless found strong support for the program in parent interviews. Similar results occur for the Follow Through program, for both parents (Emrick, 1973; Weikart and Banet, 1975) and for teachers, whose willingness to continue teaching a particular Follow Through model did not differ strongly across the vastly different educational strategies embodied in seven models, from highly structured behaviorism to freely creative open classroom approaches (Stallings and Kaskowitz, 1974). A juvenile delinquency prevention experiment (Reckless and Dinitz, 1972) using special school classes found that both teachers and participating boys liked being in the program and thought it helped the boys, even though later objective data showed no differences between randomly selected experimental and control boys in school achievement or in frequency of contact with the police. Studies of encounter groups and other laboratory training methods typically find high rates of self-assessed change but much less behavioral change when examined by outside observers (Campbell and Dunnette, 1968; Cooper and Mangham, 1971; Lieberman et al., 1973). The effects of "placebo" treatments and medicines in biomedical research, as in the gastric "freezing" example, as well as experimenter biases in psychological research (Rosenthal, 1966), are likely to be manifestations of this proposition.

The general tendency for participants' opinions to be positive has, of course, been noted previously. For example, in his now classic paper, "Reforms as Experiments," Campbell (1969) states this idea as advice for "trapped administrators" who cannot risk more objective evaluative data:

> Human courtesy and gratitude being what it is, the most dependable means of assuring a favorable evaluation is to use voluntary testimonials from those who have had the treatment. [p. 426]

But in contrast to Campbell's apparent assumption that such positive perceptions result from the conscious social motives of courtesy and gratitude, this paper will argue that the phenomenon arises from much more basic, and usually unconscious, social psychological processes.

Recent reviewers of evaluation research reports have found that creating a successful social change program is much more difficult than optimistic program managers would predict. An intensive analysis of 28 methodologically rigorous evaluation studies of both social and medical innovations concluded that only about 20% of the programs produced any measurable positive changes toward often multiple program goals (Gilbert et al., 1975). Yet included in this review were some of the most intensively planned, theoretically workable projects that experts on the problem area could devise; in most cases even these did not produce measurable change toward program goals. Gilbert and his colleagues further warn that the 20% success rate is probably higher than the actual success rate of all programs attempted, since their analysis was restricted to published studies using experimental designs. Another review of evaluation research sampled 93 published evaluations appearing in *Sociological Abstracts* between 1969 and 1973, with examination of both methodological quality and degree of program success or failure reported in the original sources (Gordon and Morse, 1975). They found that as research quality improved, programs were less likely to be reported by the original evaluator as successful in meeting program goals: only 22% of studies judged to have adequate or better methodology reported successful outcomes, but 52% of evaluations with poor methodology reported success. Further, evaluators who were organizationally affiliated with the program being evaluated were much more likely to report program success (58%) than were non-affiliated researchers (14%). Thus, researchers who are also participants appear to be susceptible to the proposition's prediction.

SOCIAL PSYCHOLOGICAL EXPLANATIONS

Not only has the proposition that program participants have positive perceptions received empirical support from a variety of program evaluations and review analyses, but several lines of both methodological and substantive social psychological work would predict the effect to occur. Methodologically, several artifacts of measurement would tend to produce favorable participant response. Questions asking recipients to state their feelings concerning a program are subject to both social desirability response bias (Edwards, 1957), and ingratiation attempts to please program sponsors (Jones, 1964). The "Hawthorne" effect of reactivity to the extra attention generated by being in a special program is likely to generate favorable attitudes toward the program as well as the increased productivity originally found by Roethlisberger and Dickson (1939). As the Gordon and Morse findings reported above indicate, experimenter bias (Rosenthal, 1966) is likely to unconsciously color the results of many less-than-rigorously designed studies.

The fact that such positive reports are likely to occur within subjective data is predicted by some principles of cognitive bias derived from general perception theory some years ago by Campbell (1958). Three of his types of perceptual distortion are relevant here: (a) bias toward cognitive conceptions that oversimplify the environment, thus containing too little information about it; (b) the principle of perceptual set, that when a generalization has been formed, additional information is likely to be perceived in a way that supports, rather than disconfirms, the generalization; and (c) the contrast bias of noticing an unusual stimulus more than the central tendency of a large numer of stimuli. The first two sources of perceptual distortions would encourage participants to extend any initial feelings of satisfaction about a program to their later overall assessments of its effects. The third source, contrast bias, would apply particularly to noticing the outstandingly successful cases among recipients, while overlooking equally numerous cases of declines in performance level or neglecting to collect and analyze appropriate data from all recipients of a program. As Campbell (1958) emphasizes, such biases in perception are probably evolutionary adaptations that characterize all human beings. As such, they are not likely to be overcome simply by a researcher's or participant's attempts to be an "unbiased observer."

Several other social psychological theories provide explanations for the occurrence of program participants' positive perceptions. From a behavioral perspective, most social action programs provide a variety of rewards to both staff and clients simply by their participation in the program. Such rewards may include an addition of resources—money, materials, help, and so forth—to the participants' controllable supplies, thus giving them both material help and social power, which is believed to be rewarding (Blau, 1964). From programs whose aim is treatment of individuals, such as education, job training, or mental health, those treated receive rewards of extra attention from agency officials, sometimes material benefits, the possibility of real political power if the program is guided by "representatives of the community," and/or at least renewed *hope* for solutions to their very real and pressing problems. Both staff and recipients are likely to feel the stimulation of new activities, the exhilaration of increasing their competence (White, 1959), the "feeling that we could really turn things around" (quotation from a senior program official, in Pressman and Wildavsky, 1973: 21). Further, most local agencies are in competition with others in seeking funds from a federal program; the few that receive the scarce resources gain prestige as "effective agencies," as well as personal esteem for their top officials whose "leadership skills" or "brilliant ideas for an innovative program" are thereby reinforced.

Thus, a great variety of potential rewards are likely to become available to program participants regardless of any measurable progress toward any of the official program goals. The prediction that program participants will report positively about their experiences under these conditions can be derived straightforwardly from the economic view that individuals seek to maximize their self-interest. Further, social exchange theory (Homans, 1974), emphasizing that individual behavior is governed by an exchange of activities and reinforcers with one's social environment, would predict the same result, if the program participants believe that reporting positive outcomes will contribute to the continuation of the personally rewarding program. And if staff members' optimistic predictions of program success is a behavior leading to the rewarding new program resources, operant conditioning theory would predict their continued optimistic postdictions as the repetition of a behavior previously rewarded.

But cognitive consistency theories would predict the same results. Festinger's theory of cognitive dissonance states that once people have engaged in an activity, they are likely to report positive feelings about it, presumably to justify having done it, even when the activity involves tasks assumed to be aversive (Festinger and Carlsmith, 1959). A particularly relevant experimental finding is that persons who undergo substantial discomfort, such as "hazing" in order to become members of a desirable group, are likely to report stronger liking for the group than are randomly chosen others permitted to become members without participating in the initiation "program" (Aronson and Mills, 1959; Gerard and Mathewson, 1966). In application to social programs, then, whatever discomfort or effort the participants experience in carrying out the program can be cognitively justified by perceptions of positive changes occurring.

The principle of cognitive balance would also predict that a participant will attempt to maintain consistency between his initially positive feelings derived from participating in the program and his later judgments about the overall success of the program. To do otherwise would be to admit that one's initial impressions were not "perceptive." Such an acknowledgement of "naivete" about the effects of his own program might be political suicide to the career of a program manager in competitive interagency rivalry.

Program staff and planners have investments of time, skills, and professional reputations which must be validated by perceiving positive outcomes for the program. Following from a cognitive consistency theoretical framework, a recent role-playing study found that a "decision maker's" commitment of resources to a course of action was increased, not decreased, when the consequences of the initial action were negative (Staw, 1976). This escalation of commitment was greatest when the decision maker was personally responsible for the negative consequences. While alternate interpretations of this experiment are possible, particularly viewing increased commitment of resources as an attempt to preserve a social position rather than cognitive consistency, both interpretations are compatible with the proposition being developed here. If self-justification processes occur, to maintain either a social position or cognitive consistency, they are likely to induce positive evaluations from participants—both staff members and beneficiaries—who are involved in and committed to the continuation of the program.

CONSCIOUS MANIPULATION OR UNCONSCIOUS BIAS?

The question may still arise whether the tendencies for participants to perceive programs in positive terms stems from conscious or unconscious motivational processes. That is, do they report positive affect because they know it is in their self-interest to do so? Or do the mechanisms discussed operate out of the conscious awareness of the participant? The position being advanced here is that the processes creating positive perceptions are to a great extent not conscious; that the perceptions stem not from an attempt to deceive or manipulate an evaluation, but from the social role position the participant is in (for further explanation of the influence of social roles on perceptions, see Katz and Kahn, 1966, Chapter 7). Thus, the extent of positive subjective evaluations would go much beyond the attempts to show gratitude or to be courteous that Campbell (1969) mentions as sources for positive testimonials, and are likely to occur even when a participant is making a great effort to provide "honest feedback."

The role of program administrator or manager is particularly likely to produce positive perceptions because it is usually focused on action to create a successful program. Such a creation is frequently a political operation more than a scientific one (Katz, 1975), for the successful manager must assemble authorizations, resources, personnel, and participants from their previous locations in the ongoing social system and stimulate their cooperative activity in a new social entity called a "program." The manager's legitimate aim is to gather support to keep the program going; thus, positive program evaluations are likely to be seen as a tool to enable the manager to do his job. Incoming information is likely to be selectively filtered toward positive data which is useful to the manager, rather than scientifically assessed for validity. In this sense, the motivation encouraging positive perceptions may well be conscious within the manager, but the orientation toward the use of information is managerial rather than scientific and the manager is unlikely to realize that his perceptions may be biased.

A TRIVIAL PROPOSITION?

After this extensive recitation of empirical evidence and theoretical explanations for what is basically a simple proposition, a reader might be tempted to feel that it is really a common-sense observation that "everybody knows." This is hardly the case, for the opposite assumption is built into political theory underlying democratic government. In colloquial form, this is the idea that the recipient of a government policy "knows where the shoe pinches"; i.e., can evaluate best the effects of a policy on him. The evidence presented here indicates that often this is not true; instead, the recipient is likely to report positive feelings irespective of whether the program helps alleviate even *his* self-defined underlying problems. Fashionable or otherwise desirable shoes may often be chosen and worn even though ill-fitting and possibly damaging in the long run. A problem with both ill-fitting shoes and social programs is that individual positive reactions are likely to occur in the short run while the longer-term effects—e.g., foot problems or high school graduates who are unable to read—may not be apparent until much later. Hence, evaluation research utilizing social science methods for overcoming the limitations of individual observation is needed to reveal causal connections between behaviors widely separated in time and space, or conversely to reveal an absence of intended behavioral changes from social programs which do provide personal rewards to their participants.

Among evaluation researchers, the recent controversy concerning qualitative versus quantitative approaches (Campbell, 1974; Guttentag, 1976) includes the question of the extent to which participants' assessments of program outcomes are important indicators of effects. One advocate of a new approach to evaluation research (Bayesian decision-making model), Marcia Guttentag, states that since the perspectives of various program participants differ, evaluation research ought to be based on a complex combination of information bearing on all participants' *values* rather than on assessment of behavioral changes by experimental or quasi-experimental methods (Edwards and Guttentag, 1975; Edwards et al., 1975; Guttentag, 1976). By including information from all participants' perspectives in an evaluation study, Guttentag believes that the resulting package will be more useful to decision makers, who often have numerous constituencies to consider. But in neglecting to consider probable sources of bias in the various participants' views, Guttentag and her colleagues fail to incorporate the expectation that participants' perceptions will be positive, and thus fail to provide methods for separating information based on participation benefits from longer-term behavioral changes.

Another example of influential evaluators' failure to consider the effects of the proposition is shown by the alternate approach advocated by the Stanford Evaluation Consortium (1976: 212) as an advancement over the mainstream, experimental view of evaluation research:

> The model that dominates the field as a whole . . . views evaluation as an event that begins runs alongside a program for a time as the evaluator makes observations

and collects data, and ends rather abruptly . . . in a report to an all-powerful decision-maker. . . . [In the alternate model] the evaluator, instead of running alongside the train making notes through the windows, can board the train and influence the engineer, the conductor, and the passengers.

But, as shown by the Gordon and Morse (1975) findings described above, and as argued by this paper, if the evaluator becomes a participant, influence is likely to be reciprocal, and the pressures generating participants' positive perceptions are likely to overwhelm objective research methods.

Even as staunch an advocate of rigorous experimentation as Campbell has conceded that the "qualitative knowing" from reports of program staff, clients, and families can add important information to more rigorous methods (1974), though Campbell is referring more to information about implementation than about outcomes. In sum, although the favorable bias of participants in new programs has often been noted, it has not been recognized as a systematic phenomenon arising from the basic processes of both behavioral and cognitive social psychology.

LIMITATIONS ON THE PROPOSITION

Further questions to consider about this proposition are whether it is potentially refutable, and whether disconfirming evidence now exists. Certainly it is refutable by indications that program participants are not in general positive toward them, but are just as likely to have negative as positive feelings, or that their perceptions are closely aligned with objective measurements of change toward program goals. Some evidence against the proposition may be available from the fact that attrition rates of program recipients are sometimes found to be high, as Rossi (1975) reports for the New Jersey Negative Income Tax experiment. Similarly, high attrition rates greatly hampered a four-year evaluation of the Follow Through program (Stallings and Kaskowitz, 1974). However, in both the Negative Income Tax and the Follow Through studies, attrition was higher from control groups that did not have the benefit of participation (Emrick, 1973; Lyall, 1976); in other programs, high attrition simply may reflect changes in the family or employment status of the participant rather than dissatisfaction with the program.

Qualifications on the applicability of the proposition may also be necessary. For example, it may hold true only for those programs involving obtaining new resources rather than for an innovative re-organization of existing resources. It is probably not applicable to cases in which recipients are overtly forced to participate, such as by legal requirements or among prisoners. The proposition's generality may be limited to programs in which people have voluntarily chosen to participate, which would be supported by the extensive literature on participation in decision-making as leading to higher satisfaction, and usually to compliance with the decision. Yet a counter example to this suggested limitation is provided by the teachers in the Follow Through study, who had no individual choice about which educational model their school would be using, but whose generally high satisfaction did not differ strongly among the seven models examined (Stallings and Kaskowitz, 1974). Further, the proposition probably does not apply to situations in which the program promised is not implemented: if the expected material benefits are not available, if the person is not participating in a stimulating new experience but instead is enmeshed in controversy or chaos, if one's prior ocnceptions of what the program should be are too far from one's experiences within it, then positive evaluations should not be expected from those participants, whether staff or recipients.

Clearly, the proposition's cautionary connotations do not apply if the explicit goals of the program are to change recipients' self-percep-tions, such that participants' reports of increased satisfaction, reduced anxiety, or improved self-concept are the major outcomes desired, as might be the case in a mental health program. But the advocates of such programs should not assume that changes in personal affective states are necessarily related to later behavioral changes. In spite of some studies providing evidence for phenomena such as "self-fulfillment prophecies" (e.g., Rosenthal and Jacobson, 1968), methodology of these studies is controversial (Barber and Silver, 1968; Wilkins, 1977), and too little is known about the linking processes involved for either evaluators or program managers to assume that cognitive or affective changes will automatically lead to desired behavioral consequences. Scheirer and Kraut's (1976) review of educational intervention pro-grams which attempted to increase academic achievement by enhancing children's self-concepts, a commonly believed link between an affective and a behavioral variable, shows the caution necessary when assessing outcome effects of programs. Among the 26 intervention programs reviewed, no program obtained changes in *both* self-concept and academic achievement, although several programs found changes on one or the other variable. Thus, the belief that obtaining positive participant ratings is in itself a significant accomplishment is likely to be premature optimism. Though probably a necessary first step reflecting some degree of program implementation, positive participant ratings are not sufficient indicators of behavioral change toward substantive program goals.

IMPLICATIONS FOR THE PROGRAM PLANNING PROCESS

A final question to be asked about this proposition is, Is it important? Even if it is true, is based on fundamental social psychological principles, but has not been heretofore widely recognized, does it make a difference for the practical problems of program planning and operation?

For the methodology of program evaluation, some important implications have already been raised. The proposition reemphasizes the inappropriateness of attitude and other subjective measures as primary indicators of program effects if the program is intended to influence actual behaviors. As discussed above, the recently renewed advocacy of qualitative evaluation methods as a means for capturing program nuances and effects the participants "know" to be true is likely to be a misdirected effort if it is proposed as a substitute for behaviorally based measures of change, although such qualitative methods are likely to be useful for examining the degree of program implementation or for exploring processes underlying a successful program.

Further, the frequently noted difficulty that evaluators experience when attempting to obtain agreement about specific program goals from various staff members and participants (Weiss, 1972; Williams, 1975) may derive from the proposition's prediction that participants will detach their evaluation of the program from *any* objective outcome effects. If staff members or recipients feel satisfaction merely from participating in a stimulating new experience, as is likely to be the case with any reasonably well implemented innovative program, the specific level of changes in outcome effects is not likely to weigh heavily in their assessment of program success. As a group of evaluators at the Urban Institute has put it, "If you don't care where you get to, then it doesn't matter which way you go!" (Wholey et al., 1975). As a result, program staff members who have influential roles in decisions concerning the continuation of their programs inevitably have psychological conflicts of interest when assessing their own programs: their interest in continuation and their participants' positive perceptions may preclude adequate assessment of other types of evidence.

But more important than the implications for evaluation research methodology are the profound implications for the policy planning process itself. As a general proposition, it means that once government resources for attacking a particular problem are committed to a specific direction, this program is highly likely to be continued, regardless of whether it has any effect toward solving the problem. The orientation of program administrators toward successful management of their program, as well as the political pressure of recipients participating in *that* program, demand that resources continue to flow in the initial direction.

A very instructive example of this outcome is Pressman and Wildavsky's analysis (1973) of the federal Economic Development Administration's plan to promote employment of minority group members in Oakland, California, by subsidizing construction of major sea-terminal and airport facilities, in exchange for which the operators of these facilities were to train and hire minority group employees. Even when all possibility of implementing the necessary training program dissolved and initial results from other EDA projects showed little progress toward employment goals, a major focus of both Washington and local officials was still to continue implementation of the construction project in the face of numerous other delaying obstacles. When this situation occurs, even though the problem remains unsolved, the resources supposed to be directed toward its solution are being spent in the continuation of the original, ineffective program. Each program has its constituency in both administrators and recipients, whose stake in the program is expressed by vocal support, with little opposition from those not directly involved in it (Williams, 1975). This results in the well-known difficulty of phasing out any government programs, which has led to the recent attempts to enact "sunset" laws.

A further implication for policy planning is that adequate data and distance to assess the theory underlying a particular program policy (e.g., that minority employment can be stimulated by public works projects, as in Oakland) is not likely to be generated by those responsible for initiating it. As discussed above, decision makers most responsible for creating a program are likely to see themselves as managers rather than as scientists; managers' orientations are political: "to manage, to control, to maneuver, to outwit, and to outpower the opposition" (Katz, 1975: 488-489), and, therefore, to use information to support their position rather than to assess the substantive adequacy of the theory assumed by the intervention. Thus, committed program administrators are unlikely to seek the fundamental knowledge of educational, economic, and social processes which might lead to real advances in the number of successful programs. This consequence means that the need is critical for evaluation research and program review independent of the agency undertaking the program, yet the potential conflict and noncooperation among program and evaluation staff with such differing perspectives is likely to preclude good, independent research.

The pessimistic end to this dismal scenario of consequences from this proposition for the program planning process is that unless this gap can be bridged between scientifically oriented evaluators not personally involved in the continuation of the program and program administrators whose position creates bias toward perceiving success, little knowledge will be gained about causal processes that might in fact alleviate social problems, while resources will continue to be committed to "programs" that have little impact on the problem. Yet this proposition predicting participants' positive perceptions does suggest some aphorisms of advice for both evaluation researchers and program administrators:

(1) Recognize that the legitimate roles of evaluation researchers and program managers differ, or as a prominent analyst of decision-making states, "Where you stand depends on where you sit" (Allison, 1971).[1]

(2) When looking for evidence of behavioral change toward program goals, don't believe anyone's subjective impressions, including your own. Behavioral changes require behavioral evidence.

(3) If participants have mainly negative assessments about a new program, look for indications of organizational or implementation problems.

(4) The alternative to an ineffective program need not be program cancellation, but can be a search for new theories, new strategies toward the same end. Since political realities may demand commitment of resources benefiting particular groups, appropriate response to a negative or no-difference evaluation report is likely to be program change, not program termination.

(5) Search for the approximately 20% of programs that yield measurable behavioral changes; then build on them.

NOTE

1. Allison attributes the aphorism to Don K. Price, but does not cite a written source.

REFERENCES

ALLISON, G. T. (1971) The Essence of Decision. Boston: Little, Brown.
ARONSON, E. and J. MILLS (1959) "The effects of severity of initiation on liking for a group." J. of Abnormal and Social Psychology 59: 177-181.
BARBER, T. X. and M. J. SILVER (1968) "Fact, fiction and the experimenter bias effect." Psych. Bull. Monograph 70, Part 2.
BLAU, P. (1964) Exchange and Power in Social Life. New York: John Wiley.
CAMPBELL, D. T. (1974) "Qualitative knowing in action research." Address to the Society for the Psychological Study of Social Issues, annual meeting of the American Psychological Association, New Orleans.
——— (1969) "Reforms as experiments." American Psychologist 24; 409-428.
——— (1958) "Systematic errors on the part of human links in communication systems." Information and Control 1: 334-369.
CAMPBELL, J. and M. DUNNETTE (1968) "Effectiveness of T-group experiences in managerial training and development." Psych. Bull. 70: 73-104.
CICIRELLI, V. G. et al. (1969) The Impact of Head Start: an Evaluation of the Effects of Head Start on Children's Cognitive and Affective Development. Athens, OH: Westinghouse Learning Corporation—Ohio University.
COOPER, C. L. and I. I. MANGHAM (1971) T-groups: a Survey of Research. London: Wiley-Interscience.
EDWARDS, A. L. (1957) The Social Desirability Variable in Personality Assessment and Research. New York: Dryden.
EDWARDS, W. and M. GUTTENTAG (1975) "Experiments and evaluations: a re-examination," pp. 409-463 in C. A. Bennett and A. Lumsdaine (eds.) Evaluation and Experiment. New York: Academic Press.
EDWARDS, W., M. GUTTENTAG, and K. SNAPPER (1975) "A decision-theoretic approach to evaluation research," pp. 139-181 in E. L. Struening and M. Guttentag (eds.) Handbook of Evaluation Research, Vol. 1. Beverly Hills, CA: Sage.
EMRICK, A. (1973) Interim Evaluation of the National Follow Through Program, 1969-1971: a Technical Report. Menlo Park, CA: Stanford Research Institute.
FESTINGER, L. and J. M. CARLSMITH (1959) "Cognitive consequences of forced compliance." J. of Abnormal and Social Psychology 58: 203-210.
GERARD, H. B. and G. C. MATHEWSON (1966) "The effect of severity of initiation on liking for a group: a replication." J. of Experimental Social Psychology 2: 278-287.
GILBERT, J. P., R. J. LIGHT, and F. MOSTELLER (1975) "Assessing social innovations: an empirical base for policy," pp. 39-193 in C. A. Bennett and A. A. Lumsdaine (eds.) Evaluation and Experiment. New York: Academic Press.
GORDON, G. and E. V. MORSE (1975) "Evaluation research," pp. 339-361 in A. Inkeles (ed.) Annual Review of Sociology I. Palo Alto, CA: Annual Reviews, Inc.

GUBA, E. (1972) "The failure of educational evaluation," pp. 250-266 in C. Weiss (ed.) Evaluating Action Programs. Boston: Allyn & Bacon.

GUTTENTAG, M. (1976) "Evaluation and society." Presidential address delivered to the Division of Personality and Social Psychology, annual meeting of the American Psychological Association.

HOMANS, G. C. (1974) Social Behavior: Its Elementary Forms. New York: Harcourt Brace Jovanovich.

JONES, E. (1964) Ingratiation: a Social Psychological Analysis. New York: Appleton-Century-Crofts.

KATZ, D. (1975) "Feedback in social systems: operational and systematic research on production, maintenance, control and adaptive functions," pp. 465-523 in C. A. Bennett and A. A. Lumsdaine (eds.) Evaluation and Experiment. New York: Academic Press.

KATZ, D. and R. L. KAHN (1966) The Social Psychology of Organizations. New York: John Wiley.

LIEBERMAN, M. A., D. YALOM, and M. B. MILES (1973) Encounter Groups: First Facts. New York: Basic Books.

LYALL, K. (1976) "Some observations on design issues in large scale social experiments," pp. 59-81 in I. Bernstein (ed.) Validity Issues in Evaluative Research. Beverly Hills, CA: Sage.

PRESSMAN, J. L. and A. WILDAVSKY (1973) Implementation. Berkeley: Univ. of California Press.

RECKLESS, W. C. and S. DINITZ (1972) The Prevention of Juvenile Delinquency: an Experiment. Columbus: Ohio State Univ. Press.

ROETHLISBERGER, F. J. and W. J. DICKSON (1939) Management and the Worker. Cambridge: Harvard Univ. Press.

ROSENTHAL, R. (1966) Experimenter Effects in Behavioral Research. New York: Appleton Century Crofts.

ROSENTHAL, R. and I. JACOBSON (1968) Pygmalion in the Classroom: Teacher Expectation and Pupils' Intellectual Development. New York: Holt, Rinehart & Winston.

ROSSI, P. H. (1975) "Field experiments in social programs: problems and prospects," in G. M. Lyons (ed.) Social Research and Public Policies. Hanover, NH: Public Affairs Center, Dartmouth College.

RUFFIN, J. M. et al. (1969) "A co-operative double-blind evaluation of gastric 'freezing' in the treatment of duodenal ulcer." New England J. of Medicine 281: 16-19.

SCHEIRER, M. A. and R. E. KRAUT (1976) "Increasing educational achievement via self concept change: a review." Cornell University. (unpublished)

STALLINGS, J. A. and D. H. KASKOWITZ (1974) Follow Through Classroom Observation Evaluation: 1972-73. Menlo Park, CA: Stanford Research Institute.

Stanford Evaluation Consortium [L. Ross and L. J. Cronbach, eds.] (1976) "Review essay: evaluating the Handbook of Evaluation Research" pp. 195-215 in G. V. Glass (ed.) Evaluation Studies Review Annual, Vol. 1. Beverly Hills, CA: Sage.

STAW, B. M. (1976) "Knee-deep in the Big Muddy: a study of escalating commitment to a chosen course of action." Organizational Behavior and Human Performance 16: 27-44.

WEIKART, D. P. and B. BANET (1975) "Model design problems in Follow Through," pp. 61-77 in A. Rivlin and P. M. Timpane (eds.) Planned Variation in Education: Should We Give Up or Try Harder? Washington, DC: The Brookings Institution.

WEISS, C. (1972) Evaluation Research. Englewood Cliffs, NJ: Prentice-Hall.
WHITE, R. W. (1959) "Motivation reconsidered: the concept of competence." Psych. Rev. 66: 297-333.
WHOLEY, J. S., J. N. NAY, J. W. SCANLON, and R. E. SCHMIDT (1975) "If you don't care where you get to, then it doesn't matter which way you go," pp. 175-197 in G. Lyons (ed.) Social Research and Public Policies. Hanover, NH: Public Affairs Center, Dartmouth College.
WILKINS, W. (1977) "Self-fulfilling prophecy: is there a phenomenon to explain?" Psych. Bull. 84: 55-56.
WILLIAMS, W. (1975) "Implementation analysis and assessment." Policy Analysis 1: 531-566.

Mary Ann Scheirer is a doctoral candidate in Social Psychology at Cornell University, with primary interests in evaluation and public policy research. Her current research centers on predictors of policy implementation in several mental health organizations.

There have been many claims of benefits accruing from the 1974 law establishing 55 mph as the national speed limit. Chief among the claims has been the reduction in fuel consumption and the decrease in deaths and injuries on the nation's highways. Clotfelter and Hahn attempt to establish reasonable dollar values for these and other benefits of the 55 mph speed limit and to estimate relevant costs resulting from this change in policy. Though the figures obtained represent only reasonable estimates of the order of magnitude of benefits and costs, the chapter illustrates many of the facets of consideration in the economist's benefit-cost analysis of a nationwide policy change of obvious importance.

21

Assessing the National 55 m.p.h. Speed Limit

Charles T. Clotfelter and John C. Hahn

ABSTRACT

This paper evaluates the desirability of the new national speed limit using tools of normative and positive economic analysis. The theoretical case for a speed limit is analyzed, and it is concluded that externalities in driving may justify the use of a speed limit, among other policies. The principal costs and benefits of the present speed limit are then discussed, and available data are used in order to suggest the reasonable orders of magnitude of costs and benefits. A number of conceptual and empirical limitations of the analysis are emphasized. Finally, several alternatives to the national speed limit are noted.

I. Introduction

One of the U.S.A.'s most tangible responses to the Arab oil embargo and subsequent higher oil prices was the 55 m.p.h. speed limit passed by Congress on January 2, 1974. Although compliance has been by no means universal, the law resulted in a dramatic decrease in average driving speeds on highways. Between 1973 and 1974, the proportion of vehicles exceeding 65 m.p.h. fell from 50 to 9% on rural interstates and from 16 to 2% on urban interstates. The average speeds on those highways dropped from 65.0 to 57.6 and from 57.0 to 53.1 m.p.h., respectively. Spurred by the increasing use of citizen band radios and an apparent decline in the law's popularity, speeds have begun to inch back up, but not to any large degree. In 1975, average speeds held steady on rural interstates and increased to 54.7 m.p.h. on urban interstates.[1] The extent to which this decrease in average speed is a result of the new speed limit is unclear, but there is every reason to believe that most of it is due to the speed limit and not due to higher gasoline prices. While higher prices have probably been responsible for a decrease in the number and length of trips taken, they have made little difference in the personal costs of driving at different speeds. In the absence of evidence to the contrary, we therefore assume in this paper that the reduction in speeds between 1973 and 1974 is due wholly to the adoption and partial

---

[1] U.S. Department of Transportation, Office of Public Affairs, *Fact Sheet,* May 14, 1976, p. 7.

From Charles T. Clotfelter and John C. Hahn, "Assessing the National 55 m.p.h. Speed Limit," 9 *Policy Sciences* 281-294 (1978). Copyright 1978 Elsevier Scientific Publishing Co. Reprinted by permission.

enforcement of the new speed limit. However, alternative assumptions as to the extent of speed reductions due to the speed limit would make little qualitative difference in the conclusions.[2]

The reduced highway speeds resulting from the speed limit produce clear benefits for the nation. Supporters of the law emphasize the fuel savings possible from reduced driving speeds as a major benefit of the law. More recently, advocates have pointed to declines in highway fatalities as another important benefit. On the other hand, the reduced speeds may also impose sizeable costs by increasing the time which must be spent on the road for a given trip. The loud protests by independent truckers indicate only a part of this time cost. In terms of additional productive or otherwise valuable time spent on highways, this could represent a substantial economic cost. Given the social importance of the twin goals of saving fuel and reducing highway fatalities as well as the potential importance of the economic cost of increased travel time, it is useful to address the question of whether the new speed limit can be justified in terms of broad concepts of economic efficiency. To answer this question requires consideration of the general case for government regulation of driving speeds as well as an empirical evaluation of the costs and benefits of this particular speed limit.

The second section of this paper analyzes the decision-making of the individual driver and evaluates in normative terms the justification for government intervention. The third section presents a rough calculation of the costs and benefits of the 55 m.p.h. speed limit, using available data concerning driver behavior and the law's effectiveness. The final section concludes the analysis with a brief consideration of alternative policies.

II. Driving Decisions and the Speed Limit

Since a change in the speed limit is a policy directed at changing the behavior of individual motorists, it is essential to begin by considering a model of individual driving choices. The major choices facing an individual motorist involve the frequency and length of trips, the route to take, the time of day or week to travel, the occupancy rate of the vehicle, and the driving speed. A national speed limit is likely to affect primarily two of these choices: how much to drive and how fast to drive. A decrease in the speed limit can be expected to result in substitution to other modes of transportation for some trips and in the complete elimination of other trips. This substitution creates problems in measuring both the costs and benefits of the new speed limit, a point to which we will return in the next section.

The second and more crucial choice for motorists concerns the decision about how fast to travel, given that a trip will be made. Drivers may be seen as having a demand for travel speed while driving, as indicated by a representative motorist's demand curve D in Fig. 1. The curve slopes down to the right because the marginal benefit in terms of value of time saved decreases with each increment in speed. The

---

[2] As is discussed below, effects of the change in average driving speeds dominate the empirical measures of costs and benefits. Only the relatively unimportant compliance and enforcement costs are not a function of speed. If only three-fourths of the reduction were due to the speed limit, both costs and benefits would therefore be reduced by virtually the same proportions.

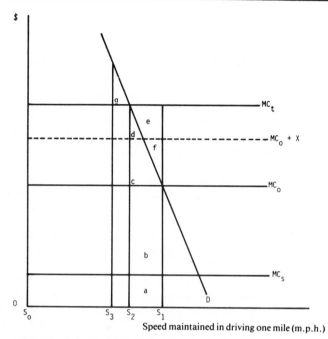

D   = motorist's demand for travel speed

MC_s = expected external marginal costs, in terms of probability of death, or injury to others

MC_o = operator's own marginal cost, in terms of operating costs and probability of death or injury to driver and passengers

X   = excess of social marginal cost of fuel over market price of fuel

$MC_t = MC_s + MC_o + X$

Fig. 1. Determination of Average Driving Speeds.

area under any segment of the demand curve gives a rough approximation of the driver's gross willingness to pay for an increase in his rate of travel speed.

The private costs borne by drivers are represented by the marginal cost curve MC_o. Included in MC_o are the costs of gasoline, other operating costs, and the certainty equivalent value of possible death or injury to driver and passengers.[3] Since engine efficiency decreases at higher speeds, the total cost of fuel consumption per mile rises with speed. Whether the marginal cost of increments in speed rises or falls is uncertain, however. For simplicity, the marginal cost curves in Fig. 1 have been drawn approximately horizontal, although the essential points of the analysis would be the same in the other cases as well. The probability of death or injury also tends to increase with speed.[4] If left to decide his own speed, the motorist will drive

---

[3] As distinct from the expected cost of death or injury, the certainty equivalent is the sure cost such that the motorist would be indifferent between that cost and the unlikely but uncertain prospect of death or injury on the road.

[4] For the individual driver, the probability of death or injury also tends to increase at speeds which diverge from the average speed on the highway, as does the probability of inflicting harm on other motorists. For this reason, the individual's driving speed is partly a function of the speed of others, and vice versa.

at an average speed S_1, the point at which marginal benefit just equals private marginal cost.

Because there are costs that drivers do not take into account, however, S_1 is not the socially optimal speed. The driver's individual calculus ignores two components of social cost. First, one motorist's presence on the road increases the probability of death or injury for other motorists as well as the probability of property damage. The marginal social cost of the increased probability of such deaths, injuries, and damage is represented by MS_s. By ignoring these costs, the individual drives at a faster speed than is socially optimal. This external cost alone may be sufficient justification for public establishment of a speed limit.[5]

A second component of social cost is ignored by the individual motorist if for some reason the market price of gasoline differs from the social marginal cost (or shadow price) of gasoline. In the case of the United States, the social marginal cost of fuel has recently been considerably higher than prevailing market prices owing to a government policy of controlling the price of domestic oil. Whether or not there is any social cost in being dependent on foreign oil per se, the social marginal cost should at least be reckoned on the basis of this more costly foreign oil.

The socially optimal speed is that at which the social marginal cost of increasing the speed of travel is equal to social marginal benefit. If private benefits equals social benefit, that is, if the social value of a traveler's time equals the private value, the efficient speed is S_2, a speed that is lower than that which would be chosen by individuals acting alone. The social cost of allowing motorists to increase their speeds from S_2 to S_1 would be the extra social cost not compensated by additional benefit, or the triangle formed by areas e and f. By the same token, this would be the social benefit of reducing travel speed from S_1 to S_2. This reasoning constitutes the justification for, first, imposing a speed limit and, second, decreasing the speed limit in response to an increase in the social cost of driving. However, it is quite possible that the new speed limit may not be set at the optimal speed. If the speed were reduced from S_1 to S_3, for example, net benefits would be represented by areas e and f less area g, the latter area being the net social cost of reducing the speed from S_2 to S_3. If the speed were initially S_2 and then were reduced to S_3, there would be a clear social loss, represented by area g. Clearly, a given reduction in the speed limit may or may not be desirable.

While it is impossible to relate, a priori, actual driving speeds to speeds shown in the figure—because to do so would require knowledge of the "true" optimal driving speed—this graphical analysis is useful in identifying the components of any cost-benefit analysis of the new national speed limit. For example, assuming that the reduction implied by a national speed limit is from S_1 to S_2, what would be the costs and benefits? For one individual travelling one mile, the cost would clearly be the reduction in the area under the demand curve, areas a, b, c, and d. This is essentially the value of the increased travel time necessitated by the slower travel speed.

---

[5] Government intervention is justified provided that the costs associated with administering such intervention do not outweigh the inefficiency costs caused by the externality. The analysis might also justify a tax which varied with driving speed, although the administrative costs of levying such a tax would certainly be prohibitive.

There would be three major benefits of the new speed limit. The probability of death or injury to pedestrians and to other motorists and the probability of property damage would be reduced, thus reducing the expected external cost of driving. The area under MS_s (a) represents this benefit. Second, the probability of death or injury to driver and drivers would likewise decline, as would the private operating cost per mile. This benefit is represented by the area under the private MC_0 curve (a plus b). Finally, since the social cost of fuel exceeds the private cost, the fuel savings yields an additional social benefit of c plus f. The sum of these various benefits—or reduced social costs—is the entire area under the social marginal cost curve: areas a through f. If this area exceeds the corresponding area under the demand curve, as it does in the example of moving from speeds S_1 to S_2, the change results in a net social benefit.

In sum, because the social cost of driving exceeds the private cost, motorists acting individually will drive too fast. It is therefore possible to justify in principle a number of corrective policies on efficiency grounds. One such policy is a speed limit. Whether the actual reduction to 55 m.p.h. is in fact justified, however, is a question which invites empirical investigation in the form of cost-benefit analysis. In the following section we turn to the issues that would be involved in such an investigation. The question of alternative policies which might also be justified is taken up in the final section.

III. Measuring the Costs and Benefits: Some Rough Estimates

In this section we present a suggestive outline for an economic analysis of the 55 m.p.h. speed limit. While it is by no means intended as a full cost-benefit analysis of the law, the analysis below attempts to provide rough estimates for the major costs and benefits using readily available data. Specifically, we attempt to estimate actual costs and benefits resulting from the implementation of the national 55 m.p.h. speed limit between 1973 and 1974. This contrasts with an evaluation of the *potential* costs and benefits that could be obtained if drivers were to obey the new speed limit universally. The latter approach, taken by Castle, is of limited practical importance and is furthermore incorrect to the extent that it ignores any additional enforcement costs necessary to insure compliance.[6]

Evaluating actual rather than hypothetical changes raises at least three problems. First, as noted above, the increase in the cost of gasoline which did in fact accompany the imposition of the speed limit leaves open the possibility that some of the decrease in driving speeds may be the result of the higher prices rather than the speed limit. As noted above, this is unlikely and in this paper it is assumed that all of the decrease is due to the speed limit. Second, the changes in the speed limit and in the price of fuel were accompanied by a reduction in traffic. This reduction calls for a modification in the valuation of lost time that would not be considered in the evaluation of a hypothetical slow-down of all trips. This problems is discussed below in the section on costs. A third difficulty produced by evaluating actual changes in

---

[6] Gilbert H. Castle, "The 55 MPH Speed Limit: A Cost/Benefit Analysis," *Traffic Engineering* (January 1976), 11–14.

behavior lies in allocating that portion of reduced fatalities, injuries and incidents of property damage actually due to the decreased speed. Fortunately, independent estimates are available for this purpose in the important case of fatalities.

A. Costs

1. Time Cost

The major cost of this national speed limit is clearly the value of the additional time spent in driving at new, slower speeds. For simplicity, if the law affected only the speed at which motorists drive—and not their decisions to drive stay at home, or take other forms of transportation—the time cost of the law would be simply the number of additional hours spent driving multiplied by the average value of time. Indeed, this assumption of no change in driving behavior underlies Castle's hypothetical valuation of time cost due to a decrease in driving speed form 70 to 55 m.p.h. In fact, motorists did cut back their driving from 1973 to 1974, and it is reasonable to believe that this was due not only to the increased price of gasoline but also to the increased time cost of driving. Consumers in effect avoided part of the impact of the increased driving times by substituting other modes of travel and even other activities (including staying at home more often) for driving. Since individuals made them voluntarily, such substitutions would be expected to involve not more, and probably less, cost than the driving which would have been done. To calculate increased driving time using the beginning year mileage would therefore overstate the social cost of the speed limit. On the other hand, to calculate the increased driving time using the second year mileage would clearly understate the cost because the fact that motorists were forced into previously undesirable behavior would be ignored.

This problem of valuation is an example of the venerable index number problem, and occurs because households have changed their behavior over time in response to changes in relative costs and benefits, thus avoiding some of the costs.[7] In such a case, no unambiguous calcualation can be made. It is possible only to suggest bounds for the correct value. For the present application, an upper bound estimate of the time lost due to the new speed limit in 1974 takes the number of vehicle-miles traveled in 1973 as a basis for calculation. Where VM represents vehicle-miles, s is average speed, and R is the average occupancy rate per vehicle, the number of hours lost on a given class of highways is:

$$H = ((VM_{73}/S_{74} - (VM_{73}/S_{73}))R. \tag{1}$$

Where this expression is applied to each of three major highway classifications, shown in the Appendix, the number of hours lost is some 1.87 billion. Replacing the 1973 occupancy rate and number of vehicle-miles by the 1974 values yields the lower bound estimate of 1.72 billion hours. It is useful to note that even these two estimates do not necessarily establish the boundaries for the "true" number of

---

[7] Zeckhauser and Fisher present a general discussion of such "averting behavior," the valuation problems which are implied by such behavior. See Richard Zeckhauser and Anthony Fisher, "Averting Behavior and External Diseconomies," Kennedy School of Government Discussion Paper 41D, April 1976.

hours lost. Each estimate is itself subject to error, due to any errors in measurement or to the possible existence of other factors affecting speeds or miles traveled.

The average value of commuting time has been the subject of considerable study, but estimates of the value of travel time of long-distance motorists or commercial drivers are more difficult to obtain. In order to obtain a reasonable average value to travel time for all motorists, we use two alternative values for the ratio of the value of travel time to the wage rate for those in the labor force: 42% from Lave's empirical analysis, and 33% from Dewees' evaluation of the literature on this question.[8] In 1974, the average wage was approximately $5.05 an hour for all members of the labor force.[9] We assume the same value for other adults not in the labor force in order to take account of the value of their non-market production.[10] Given the alternative estimates of the ratio of the value of travel time to the wage, the implied average values of time are $1.68 and $2.12 per hour. For convenience, other drivers and riders are also assumed to have the same value of time as members of the labor force; however this is probably an overstatement for this relatively small group. Applying this first figure to the lower bound estimate of hours lost yields a lower bound estimate of increased time of $2.89 billion. Applying the higher value of time to the alternative estimate of time yields an upper bound figure of $3.96 billion. Since the time cost is by far the most important cost of the new speed limit, it is important to emphasize the caveats that apply to these figures. First, the estimates of the value of travel time employed above are based on studies of commuters. To the extent that vacation and other long-distance travelers may have lower values of time, the values used may provide overestimates. Second, the opportunity cost of increased transport time for commercial vehicles is not adequately reflected in these values of time. The costs of additional travel time for these vehicles is likely to be more, rather than less, than the values used in the calculations. These considerations imply that a complete analysis of the time costs of the speed limit should involve separate calculations by class of motorist and vehicle.

2. Compliance and Enforcement Costs

Motorists have hardly welcomed the new speed limit with open arms. In order to attain even the levels of compliance that have been reached, certain costs have had to be incurred. New signs had to be made, information on the law had to be disseminated, and some additional enforcement measures had to be undertaken.

---

[8] Charles A. Lave, "The Demand for Urban Mass Transportation," *Review of Economics and Statistics* 52 (August 1970), 320–323; Donald N. Dewees, "Travel Cost, Transit, and Control of Urban Motoring," *Public Policy* 24 (Winter 1976), 61.

[9] Total wages and salaries, other labor income and proprietors' income in 1974 was $895.6 billion. The labor force was about 93.2 million, and the average weekly working week in non-agricultural private establishments was 36.6 hours. U.S. Department of Commerce, Bureau of Economic Analysis, *Survey of Current Business*, July 1975, p. 13; U.S. Bureau of the Census, *Statistical Abstract of the United States 1975*, pp. 343, 353.

[10] The difficulties of measuring the value of time, and leisure time in particular, are well known. For example, it is possible to argue that the use of the average wage understates the value of time of adults not in the labor market simply because they have chosen to remain out of the labor force at that wage. On the other hand, those not in the labor force may well be less productive on average and thus have a lower social opportunity cost.

The measurement of enforcement costs is problematical. On the one hand, casual observation suggests that patrol activity has increased in order to enforce the lower speeds. However, it has apparently been impossible or undesirable in general to hire new personnel to enforce the new speed limits. The increased patrol activity can thus come only at the expense of other police functions. Another cost that is potentially easier to measure is the modification of speed limit signs. One indication of this cost is the amount that states requested from federal highways funds for this purpose. Twenty-five states filed reports on these expenditures, amounting to a total of $707,302. This is surely an underestimate in that only half the states reported. Apparently states would be reimbursed for these expenses under general highway financing if they did not apply under this specific category.[11] Nevertheless, if all states spent on per capita basis what these states reported, the total would be about $1.23 million. If these modifications had, say, three year lives, then the yearly cost of modification would be $0.41 million. Given the weak incentives for state reporting, this must be considered a low estimate. Finally, the federal government has engaged in an advertising campaign to encourage compliance with the speed limit. The Transportation Department has spent some part of its total of $2.0 million advertising and public information budget on this project, and there have no doubt been further costs due to time and space donated by media for related public service messages.[12] There are, however, no data on these costs. We therefore make the modest assumption that the yearly cost of this campaign is 10 percent of this budget, or $200,000, plus an equal amount for donated media time and space. This gives a total for compliance costs of $0.8 million, with police enforcement costs left unmeasured.

B. Benefits

1. Gasoline Saved

Because the gasoline economy of engines generally improves as speeds are decreased over the range from 70 to 55 m.p.h., the reduction in average speeds produced by the new speed limit has resulted in a sizeable gasoline savings. For the average automobile, the miles per gallon ratio rises from 13.3 m.p.g. at 70 m.p.h. to 14.9 at 60 m.p.h. to 16.9 at 50 m.p.h.[13] Given this technical information and the data given in the Appendix for vehicle-miles traveled and average speeds, it is possible to estimate the number of gallons saved due to the decrease in average driving speeds. As in the calculation of time costs, it is possible only to give upper and lower bound estimates for the amount of gasoline saved, one estimate based on each year's vehicle-miles traveled. Using vehicle-miles for 1973 yields the upper bound estimate of the number of gallons saved (G):

$$G = (VM_{73}/MPG_{73}) - (VM_{73}/MPG_{74}), \qquad (2)$$

---

[11] U.S. Department of Transportation, Federal Highway Administration, "Federal-Aid Highway Funds Obligated for Speed Limit Sign Modifications, January 2, 1974 to Date," May 1976.

[12] Charles T. Clotfelter, "The Scope of Public Advertising," in David G. Tuerck (ed.), *The Political Economy of Advertising* (Washington: American Enterprise Institute for Public Policy Research, 1978), Table 2.

[13] U.S. Department of Transportation, Federal Highway Administration, "Highway and the Petroleum Problem—4 Reports," FHWA Bulletin, October 2, 1975, p. 24.

where MPG is the average miles per gallon for vehicles on a given class of highways.[14] The actual calculations shown in the Appendix yield an upper bound estimate of 3.50 billion gallons and a lower bound of 3.39 billion gallons saved in 1974. Again, possible measurement errors, imply that neither estimate should be taken as precise bounds on the "true" value.

Determining the proper valuation of this fuel saving is a more difficult task. In 1974, the average retail price of gasoline was 52.8c per gallon, implying a savings of about $1.8 billion.[15] However, this market price failed to reflect the social cost of gasoline due to the government's price control of "old" domestic oil and to the entitlements program. Intended to equalize the cost of crude oil to refiners after the escalation of the price of foreign oil, the entitlements program effectively guaranteed that the proportion of cheap "old" oil would be the same for all refiners.[16] Thus, the average cost of oil going into refineries was a weighted average of expensive foreign and new oil on the one hand, and cheaper old oil on the other. Because increases in national oil consumption would have to come from the expensive foreign sources, however, the social marginal cost of crude oil was the foreign price, not this weighted average. Likewise, the social marginal cost for gasoline would be, in effect, the market price that would prevail if all gasoline were refined entirely from imported oil or, equivalently, the market price that would prevail in the absence of price controls and entitlements. In other words, the value of resources used up when a gallon of gasoline was consumed was not the artificially low price paid by consumers, but rather the value of goods and services foregone in this country as a result of using one gallon of gasoline made from foreign oil.

In order to arrive at a rough approximation of this price, we assumed that the actual wholesale price of gasoline is a weighted average of two hypothetical wholesale prices: that of gasoline refined from domestic oil (pd^*) and that of gasoline refined from foreign oil (pf^*). Where h is the ratio of the domestic price of oil to the average foreign price and j is the proportion of the nation's oil supply that is foreign, the wholesale market price per gallon (P) is assumed to be:

$$P = jP_f^* + (1 - j)P_d^*. \tag{3}$$

If the ratio of hypothetical gasoline prices (P_d^*/P_f^*) is the same as the ratio of crude oil prices (h), then the market price is

$$P = jP_f^* + (1-j)hP_f^*. \tag{3'}$$

The hypothetical wholesale price of foreign gasoline is then

$$P_f^* = P/(j + (1-j)h). \tag{4}$$

Adding the actual 1974 retail markup per gallon yields the hypothetical retail price of foreign gasoline, which, as we argue above, is a better measure of the social marginal cost of gasoline than is the actual retail price.

---

[14] Average fuel economy rates are interpolated, using average vehicle speed and average fuel economy at each speed interval. However, since the rate of improvement in fuel economy is not constant over all speeds, the actual rate of consumption depends on the distribution of speeds and thus this estimate is at best an approximation.

[15] Federal Energy Administration, *Monthly Energy Review*, May 1976, p. 54.

[16] Federal Energy Administration, *Annual Report 1975/1976* Washington: Government Printing Office, 1977), pp. 44—45.

In 1974 imported crude oil constituted 28.4% of the crude oil going to refineries in the U.S., not counting stock used. Thus j was equal to 0.284. The average price at which regular gasoline was purchased by full-service retail outlets (P) was 43.1¢ and the average selling price was 52.8¢, for an average markup of 9.7¢.[17] The ratio of average domestic crude oil prices at the wellhead to average imported oil prices in 1974 was 0.573.[18] Substituting these values into equation (4) yields an estimate of the wholesale price of gasoline refined from foreign crude oil of 62.1¢ per gallon. Adding the actual markup of 9.7¢ per gallon yields a retail price of 71.8¢, and adjusted fuel savings figures for 1974 of $2.43 billion as a lower bound and $2.52 billion as an upper bound, some 36% higher than the figures based on actual selling prices. It is worth noting that another form of substitution—the increasing use of self-service stations—probably makes this estimate, with its assumption of a constant mark-up, a slight overstatement. But given the time costs to purchasers and the slight savings obtainable in most locations, this does not seem to be an important source of error.

2. Fatalities Averted

A second major benefit of the 55 m.p.h. speed limit—one that seems to have been almost an afterthought by policymakers—is the reduction in highway fatalities that has resulted. Fatalities fell from 55,087 in 1973 to 46,049 in 1974, a decrease of 16.4%.[19] Besides the change in the speed limit, several other factors are responsible for this decrease, including the overall reduction in travel, the reduction in average occupancy, increased use of seat belts, and a shift toward daytime driving. Clearly, it is necessary to separate the effect of the speed limit from these other, largely unrelated, effects. Examining changes in fatalities in two separate 4-month periods between 1973 and 1974, the National Safety Council estimated that the reduction in travel speed accounted for 46 to 59% of the total reduction in fatalities.[20] Applying these proportions to the total reduction in fatalities yields estimates of 4,157 and 5,332 as the number of fatalities averted due to the new speed limit.

The social cost of a fatality includes the loss of earnings, the pain and suffering caused, and the loss of home and family duties performed. Despite the metaphysical nature of the problem, economists have devised ways of arriving at empirical estimates of the value of life. A study by the Transportation Department estimated the total social cost of a traffic fatality at about $200,000 in 1972, or about $240,000 in 1974 dollars.[21] This figure agrees quite closely with an estimate by Thaler and Rosen of about $200,000 in 1967 dollars, using quite different methodology.[22] In the

[17] Federal Energy Administration, *Monthly Energy Review*, May 1976, pp. 6, 54.

[18] Federal Energy Administration, *Monthly Energy Review*, February 1976, p. 57.

[19] U.S. Department of Transportation, Federal Highway Administration, *Fatal and Injury Accident Rates*, 1974, p. 26.

[20] National Safety Council, Statistics Division, "Factors Contributing to the Reduction of Motor Vehicle Traffic Fatalities," October 1974 and March 1975, Chicago, Illinois. Reduction in speed accounted for 11 of the 24% decrease between the January–April periods and 10 of the 17% decrease in the May–August periods.

[21] U.S. Department of Transportation, National Highway Traffic Safety Administration, *Societal Costs of Motor Vehicle Accidents*, Preliminary Report, April 1972, p. 4.

[22] Richard Thaler and Sherwin Rosen, "The Value of Saving a Life; Evidence from the Labor Market," University of Rochester Discussion Paper, 1973.

present context, it is probably more appropriate to interpret such estimates as implying a value of about $240,000 for a 1% increase in the probability of death for one hundred drivers than to take this money figure to summarize "the value" of a life. In the aggregate, however, both interpretations imply multiplying $240,000 by the number of fatalities averted by the new speed limit, yielding alternative estimates for this benefit of $997.7 million and $1,279.7 million.

3. Injuries Averted

Nonfatal injuries-also declined between 1973 and 1974, from 2,835,683 to 2,653,057.[23] There has however been no analysis of the portion of that decline which is attributable to the new speed limit. In the absence of such information, we assume as two estimates the proportions used in connection with fatalities above, 46 and 59%. These estimates yield injury reductions of 84,008 and 107,749 between 1973 and 1974. Among injuries, three levels of severity can be distinguished: permanent total disability, permanent partial disability and permanent disfigurement, and no permanent injury. In 1971 the proportions of traffic injuries accounted for by each was 0.2, 6.5 and 93.3%, respectively; the average cost in 1971 of each was estimated by the National Highway Traffic Safety Administration to be $260,300, $67,100, and $2,465, respectively.[24] This distribution yields an average cost of $8,745 in 1974 dollars, per injury. Applying this figure to the two estimates of injuries averted yields estimates of the social benefit of injury reduction of $734.6 million and $942.3 million.

4. Reduced Property Damage

The reduction in speeds was accompanied by a reduction in property damage as well as injuries and fatalities. Between 1973 and 1974 the number of incidents involving property damage fell from 25.8 million to 23.1 million.[25] There is, however, no data to indicate the effect of the new speed limit on this reduction. Lacking such data, we made the alternative assumptions that 50% and that 25% of this reduction was the result of the new speed limit. These rough calculations yield estimates of 1.30 and 0.65 million as the number of incidents of property damage averted due to the implementation of the 55 m.p.h. speed limit. Applying an estimate of $300 average cost per incident of property damage in 1972—$363 in 1974—yields an upper bound estimate of cost savings due to the lower speeds of $471.9 million and a lower bound estimate of $236.0 million.[26]

C. Summing Up

Table 1 summarizes the estimates of benefits and costs. Separate totals of all upper bound and lower bound estimates are presented in order to suggest limits on the reasonable values of each. Total costs range from $2.89 billion to $3.96 billion.

---

[23] U.S. Department of Transportation, Federal Highway Administration, *Fatal and Injury Accident Rates*, 1974, p. 38.

[24] U.S. Department of Transportation, National Highway Traffic Safety Administration, *Societal Costs of Motor Vehicle Accidents*, Preliminary Report, April 1972, p. 4.

[25] National Safety Council, *Accident Facts*, 1974 and 1975.

[26] *Societal Costs of Motor Vehicle Accidents*, p. 12.

Total benefits are uniformly higher, at \$4.40 billion and \$5.21 billion. On the basis of these total figures, even modest estimates of the benefits of the 55 m.p.h. speed limit exceed the upper bound estimate of costs. Given these rough figures, therefore, the law can be judged to have results which are on balance beneficial.

TABLE I

Total Costs and Benefits of the 55 m.p.h. Speed Limit, 1974 (\$ millions)

	Upper bound estimates	Lower bound estimates
Costs		
Time cost	3,969.0	2,892.1
Compliance and enforcement	0.8	0.8
	3,969.8	2,892.9
Benefits		
Gasoline saved	2,515.1	2,434.8
Fatalities averted	1,279.7	997.7
Injuries averted	942.3	734.6
Reduced property damage	471.9	236.0
	5,208.4	4,403.1

Source: See text.

Several qualifications are very much in order, however. In general, the quantitative estimates of costs and benefits are subject to error of an uncertain magnitude. To some extent we have attempted to allow for this error by presenting alternative estimates of most magnitudes. However, there remains little available empirical basis for some of the calculations. Two specific assumptions for which there is empirical support are also worth noting. First, the most important single number in the analysis is probably the value of traveler's time. Derivation of the average wage for members of the labor force is straightforward, but there is disagreement concerning the ratio of the value of travel time to the wage. Thus two alternative estimates are used. One difficulty lies in determining the opportunity cost for the time of adults not in the labor force and children. The procedure used in the present study assumes that the value of time is the same for all drivers and riders, that is, the same for members of the labor force. This of course overstates the average value of time and thus tends to put the cost estimates on the high side. That problem aside, it is clear that the assumed ratio of the value of travel time to the wage rate is a most important parameter in the analysis. Both the values of 42% and 33% yield cost estimates less than the calculated benefits. In order for costs to equal benefits, that ratio would have to reach 51% in the lower bound case and 55% in the upper bound case. Both of these values lie outside the range of values usually found.

A second important set of assumptions involve the relationship between speed and average gasoline consumption. The figures used, which are published by the Federal Highway Administration, relate to actual average consumption rates by automobiles at different speeds. The Environmental Protection Agency publishes a different set of consumption rates based on steady cruise speed which seem to be less realistic. The use of the latter figures would yield considerably less fuel savings, although the reduction would not be sufficient to cause either estimate of total benefits to be exceeded by the corresponding value of costs.[27]

IV. Conclusion

The two most important goals of the 55 m.p.h. speed limit appear to fuel savings and increased highway safety. The present paper presents, first, a theoretical justification for the establishment of a speed limit in order to meet these goals and, second, an empirical analysis of the specific speed limit instituted in the United States in 1974. While based on rough calculations, the empirical analysis indicates that the benefits of the program outweigh the economic costs. This is certainty not to say, however, that his speed limit is the only or the best policy for achieving the goals of conservation and highway safety. Indeed, a speed limit appears to be a second—or third—best policy for achieving both safety and conservation goals. It is quite possible that other policies, aimed directly at these goals, would be more effective. Alternative policies could also eliminate the present inequity of penalizing, in terms of time costs, drivers of efficient compacts and gas guzzlers alike.

Several possible policies could be used to replace or, more likely, complement a national speed limit. For example, gasoline prices—and thus the cost of driving—could be raised by taxing gasoline or by the elimination of the entitlements program. Both have been proposed by the Carter administration, the latter through an end to entitlements and a crude oil equalization tax. Income effects would be offset by comparable reductions in personal taxes. Similar effects could be achieved by the taxation of automobiles on the basis of rated fuel consumption. This also has been proposed in the Carter energy package.[28] The effectiveness of this policy would depend on the increased inducement to keep old big cars and on the effect of increased efficiency on total driving. Policies aimed directly at reducing highway fatalities would include requiring seat belts to be worn by all occupants of automobiles or requiring air bags to be installed in new cars.[29] Mandatory seat belt

---

[27] These fuel efficiency rates are 22.5 m.p.g. at 40 m.p.h., 21.5 at 50, 19.5 at 60, and 17.3 at 70. U.S. Environmental Protection Agency, *A Report on Automotive Fuel Economy*, 1974, p. 10. These yield the alternative table:

	Average m.p.g.		Gasoline saved (million gallons)	
	1973	1974	Lower bound	Upper bound
Rural main	19.4	20.4	1127.5	1169.9
Rural secondary	21.0	21.6	136.5	139.7
Urban interstate	20.1	20.9	243.1	244.3
Total			1507.1	1563.9
Dollar value at 71.8¢ per gallon ($millions)			1082.1	1122.9

Total benefits would then be $3.1 billion to $3.8 billion.

[28] U.S. Executive Office of the President, *The National Energy Plan* (Washington: Government Printing Office, 1977), pp. 36, 51.'

[29] Another possibility would be simply to make drivers strictly liable for injuries caused by their driving.

laws have been used in Australia, France and Canada, and there is evidence to suggest that fatalities have been reduced as a result.[30] Both policies would entail economic costs, but these costs may be well below the present time costs involved in the speed limit. A gasoline tax would also tend to reduce accidents and fatalities by reducing average driving speeds, although the amount of such reduction would be quite small. In terms of the analysis in section II, the optimal tax is one which would make the driver's private marginal cost of traveling at a higher speed equal to the social marginal cost of driving faster. Each of the policies discussed here will course have distributional consequences which to some extent could be modified, if necessary, through the income tax and related transfers.

APPENDIX

Calculation of Time Costs and Energy Savings

A. Increased travel time			1973	1974
Vehicle miles (VM) (millions)				
Rural main[a]			462,979[b]	446,212[c]
Rural secondary			105,639[b]	103,147[c]
Urban interstate			128,342[b]	127,673[c]
Average speed (S)[d]				
Rural main			60.3	55.3
Rural secondary			52.6	49.5
Urban interstate			57.0	53.1
Average occupancy rate (R)			1.9	1.8
			Lower bound	Upper bound
Number of hours lost[e] (thousands)			(Using 1974 VM,R)	(Using 1973 VM,R)
Rural main			1,204,318	1,318,993
Rural secondary			221,055	238,973
Urban interstate			296,119	314,216
Total			1,721,492	1,872,182

B. Fuel economy and gasoline saved	Average m.p.g.[f]		Gasoline saved (millions of gallons)[g]	
	1973	1974	Lower Bound	Upper bound
Rural main	14.4	15.8	2,774.0	2,878.3
Rural secondary	16.4	17.0	222.5	227.9
Urban interstate	15.5	16.3	394.6	396.7
Total			3,391.1	3,502.9
Dollar value at 71.8c per gallon ($millions)			2,434.8	2,515.1

[a] Includes rural interstate and rural primary.

[b] U.S. Department of Transportation, Federal Highway Adminstration, *Highway Statistics 1973*, pp. 75–76.

[c] U.S. Department of Transportation, Fed. Highway Administration, *News*, Dec. 30, 1975.

[d] U.S. Department of Transportation, Office of Public Affairs, *Fact Sheet*, "The National 55 m.p.h. Speed Limit," May 14, 1976, p. 7.

[e] From equation (1).

[f] Derived from Alexander French, "Highway Planning and the Energy Crisis," U.S. Department of Transportation, Federal Highway Administration, May 1973, figure 24.

[g] From equation (2).

[30] National Safety Council, *Accident Facts*, 1975, p. 52.

In another work in this volume, Scheirer argues that opinions of recipients of services that are discrepant from objective program outcomes may be understood as the normal products of basic social-psychological processes. In the following, Stipak deals with problems in interpreting citizen satisfaction measures which are obtained on an areawide or population basis. In such a case, citizens may be only indirect recipients of services and may not even be aware of that status. Stipak presents evidence that citizen satisfaction may not be very sensitive to levels of service provided, but notes that some of the apparent insensitivity may arise from combining data from groups or areas with different mean tendencies. Stipak then presents a simple regression model to illustrate how citizen satisfaction measures might be improved by regressing out group or area differences.

22

Citizen Satisfaction with Urban Services
Potential Misuse as a Performance Indicator

Brian Stipak

Sample surveys of citizens provide a potentially important method of collecting data for local policy analysis. Several Urban Institute publications have recommended that local governments annually conduct citizen surveys to aid in evaluating city services.[1] Local officials will probably collect information on citizen satisfaction with city services as part of such surveys. A danger arises that policy makers may misinterpret such information, especially if they use citizen satisfaction to measure service performance. This danger stems from two problems: 1) citizen responses to satisfaction and evaluation questions may not reflect actual service performance, and 2) difficult statistical and conceptual problems complicate the use of subjective data to evaluate service performance.

Before examining these two problems, picture how local officials might use information about citizen satisfaction with a particular local service. Policy makers might compare satisfaction levels in different geographic areas, conclude that areas reporting lower overall satisfaction receive poorer quality service, and perhaps even reallocate expenditures accordingly.[2] Similarly, policy makers might compare satisfaction expressed by different types of citizens, such as citizens from different demographic groups, to investigate whether one type receives better service than another. Although such procedures may seem sensible, in general they are invalid and potentially misleading.

Problem #1: Expressed Satisfaction May Not Reflect Service Performance

Policy makers can use subjective indicators constructed from survey items as indicators of service performance only if the responses citizens make to those items are linked to the actual services government provides. In particular, whether expressed citizen satisfaction with a service is a valid performance measure depends on whether it reflects service characteristics or quality. If the characteristics or quality of the service actually provided do not affect citizen satisfaction or evaluations, policy makers cannot logically use such indicators to measure service performance.

In a study within the Los Angeles metropolitan area, I tested whether differences in the services local governments provide do affect citizen evaluations of those services.[3] That study used a data base of merged individual,

■ Policy analysts should exercise caution in using survey data on citizen satisfaction with local services to measure governmental performance. Responses to survey items asking citizens how·satisfied they are with specific local services, or asking them to evaluate service performance, may not reflect the actual service government provides. Also, difficult statistical and conceptual problems often invalidate using such data to evaluate local services. Nevertheless, subjective data like citizen satisfaction may yet have some use in policy-making.

census, administrative, and other data to estimate models of citizen evaluations as a function of 1) service characteristics, 2) governmental characteristics, 3) neighborhood characteristics, and 4) individual characteristics. Subjective evaluation scales were created from survey items asking citizens to evaluate police, parks and recreation, refuse collection, and other basic services. A number of indicators for each service were used to measure different types of objective service characteristics—service outputs, service inputs, administrative workloads, and related community conditions. For example, the indicators examined for the police included clearance rate, property recovery rate, per capita expenditures, per capita employees, and crime rate. The statistical results showed little evidence that service characteristics affect citizen evaluations of local services. Most coefficient estimates for the objective service indicators were not statistically significant, and were too small to be substantively important. Also, the predictive power of the objective service indicators was usually small compared to some of the other predictors.

Tables 1 and 2 display some of the results for police and parks and recreation. The numbers are the estimated change in the subjective evaluation scale for that service, measured in standard deviations, resulting from a particular change in a predictor variable.[4] For example, increasing the clearance rate 10 per cent for the seven major felonies

Brian Stipak is assistant professor of public administration, Institute of Public Administration, Pennsylvania State University. He has been a postdoctoral fellow at the Institute of Public Policy Studies, University of Michigan, and was formerly employed by System Development Corporation, where he was involved in evaluation research.

(e.g. from 20 per cent to 30 per cent) raises the evaluations citizens express an estimated one-third of a standard deviation. Increasing the number of full-time police personnel per 10,000 population by five yields an estimated improvement of less than one-tenth of a standard deviation. For parks (Table 2) the estimated effect of five additional employees per 10,000 population is a .27 standard deviation improvement, and an estimated .18 standard deviation improvement results from an expenditure increase of $10 per capita. The results for the other objective service indicators are not even statistically significant. Interestingly enough, the distance a respondent lives from the nearest park, a rough index of accessibility of park facilities, shows no effect on the respondent's evaluation of park services. Also, differences in the crime rate show no effect on evaluations of the police service.

Even the statistically significant results for the objective service indicators are not substantially impressive. For example, the clearance rate variable shows one of the strongest affects of all the objective indicators in the entire study. Nevertheless, even half a standard deviation improvement in citizen evaluations would require a 15 per cent improvement in the clearance rate—an exceptionally difficult improvement to realize, given that clearance rates for the Los Angeles sample have a mean of 24 per cent and a standard deviation of 6 per cent. Such a huge improvement in objective performance affects citizen evaluations of police only about as much as a respondent's being in the oldest age category, compared to the youngest, or as living in an area served by the Los Angeles County Sheriff's Department (unincorporated areas or contract cities), compared to small cities with their own police departments. A clearance rate improvement equivalent to its standard deviation for the Los Angeles sample, a more reasonable municipal goal, would effect an estimated improvement of less than a fifth of a standard deviation on the evaluation scale. The efficacy of potentially achievable changes in any of the other objective service indicators to improve expressed citizen evaluations is even less, and is surpassed by effects attributable to demographics and to governmental jurisdiction. In short, large improvements in objective performance—large in the sense of what public officials could realistically hope to achieve—generally appear to have negligible effects on citizens' subjective evaluations.

The Kansas City Preventive Patrol Experiment provides experimental evidence that complements the findings of the Los Angeles study. In that experiment, the intensity of routine preventive police patrol was varied widely across areas within the city. The results showed little effect of differences in patrolling on citizen satisfaction with the police service, citizen fear of crime, or a variety of attitudes toward the police.[5] No effect was found even on citizens' perceptions of the time police spent on patrol,[6] despite some experimental areas receiving three times the normal intensity of patrol, and other areas receiving no routine patrol. Although some other existing studies do purport to provide some weak evidence of a correspondence between citizen satisfaction and service conditions,[7] those studies typically rely on bivariate analysis of city-levels data. The Kansas City experiment and the Los Angeles findings

Table 1

Estimated Independent Effects of Selected Variables on Citizen Evaluations of Police Services in Los Angeles County

Change in Predictor	Estimated Effect in Standard Deviations on Evaluation Scale[a]
Objective Service Indicators:	
Clearance rate, 7 major felonies: increase 10%	.33[b](.14)
Recovery rate for stolen property, except automobiles: increase 10%	.05 (.20)
Operating expenditures per capita for police services: increase $10	.049 (.046)
Number of full-time police personnel per 10,000 population: Increase 5	.075[b](.045)
Number of 7 major felonies committed per 1,000 population: increase 20	.032 (.050)
Demographic Characteristics of Respondent:	
Education: increase 4 years	-.016 (.048)
Income level, standardized by poverty level for family type: double	.006 (.037)
Sex: Male compared to female	.023 (.065)
Race: black compared to white	-.15 (.17)
Spanish-surname compared to white	-.02 (.11)
Age: 30-39 compared to 18-29	.11 (.09)
40-49 compared to 18-29	.33[c](.10)
50-59 compared to 18-29	.33[c](.11)
60+ compared to 18-29	.45[c](.10)
Governmental Jurisdiction:	
Unincorporated areas, compared to small cities (16-138 thou. pop.) with own police department	-.53[c](.11)
Los Angeles City, compared to small cities (16-138 thou. pop.) with own police department	-.33[c](.08)
Long Beach City, compared to small cities (16-138 thou. pop.) with own police department	-.15 (.15)
Cities which contract with L.A. County for police services, compared to small cities (16-138 thou. pop.) with own police department	-.48[c](.11)

[a]Standard errors are in parentheses.
[b]statistically significant at .05 level, 1-tail test
[c]statistically significant at .05 level, 2-tail test

clearly warn local officials not to assume automatically that citizens respond to satisfaction or evaluation questions on the basis of objective service performance.

One possible explanation why citizens may not respond to such questions based on service performance is that citizens pay little attention to those services, as long as service quality is within some adequate range. Public opinion research has generally found that citizens know little about government and public affairs, but nonetheless will express political opinions.[1] Similarly, citizens may quite willingly provide evaluations of specific local services, despite a lack

of knowledge or perceptions of service quality.[1] Figure 1 illustrates the plausible hypothesis that within the range of service quality typically found in U.S. metropolitan areas, citizens pay little attention to services and fail to perceive differences in service quality; therefore, their evaluations fail to reflect differences in service quality.

Figure 1

ONE POSSIBLE FUNCTIONAL FORM OF THE RELATIONSHIP BETWEEN EXPRESSED CITIZEN SATISFACTION AND SERVICE QUALITY

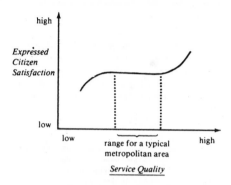

Table 2

Estimated Independent Effects of Selected Variables on Citizen Evaluations of Park and Recreation Services in Los Angeles County

Change in Predictor	Estimated Effect in Standard Deviation on Evaluation Scale[a]
Objective Service Indicators:	
Distance to nearest park: increase .3 mile	-.024 (.030)
Operating expenditures per capita for park and recreation services: increase $10	.18[b](.09)
Number of full-time park and recreation personnel per 10,000 population: increase 5	.27[b](.10)
Demographic Characteristics of Respondent:	
Education: increase 4 years	-.076 (.044)
Income level, standardized for poverty level of family type: double	.001 (.036)
Sex: male compared to female	-.072 (.062)
Race: black compared to white	-.25 (.16)
Spanish-surname compared to white	-.20[b](.11)
Age: 30-39 compared to 18-29	.28[c](.10)
40-49 compared to 18-29	.14 (.10)
50-59 compared to 18-29	.29[c](.10)
60 + compared to 18-29	.35[c](.10)
Governmental Jurisdiction:	
Unincorporated areas, compared to small cities (16-138 thou. pop.)	-.22[c](.10)
Los Angeles City, compared to small cities (16-138 thou. pop.)	-.37[c](.07)
Long Beach City, compared to small cities (16-138 thou. pop.)	.51[c](.15)

[a]Standard errors are in parentheses.
[b]statistically significant at .05 level, 1-tail test
[c]statistically significant at .05 level, 2-tail test

Figure 1 presents an interpretation which can account for the findings of the Los Angeles study mentioned above without arguing that under no conditions do citizen evaluations reflect service quality. If service becomes excessively bad or remarkably good—i.e., sufficiently divergent from citizens' expectations—service quality may become salient enough to affect evaluations. For example, citizens may have little interest in a service like street repair, paying little attention to service performance if quality is above minimum level. However, if large potholes in the streets make driving difficult and unpleasant, the low quality of streets may become conspicuous enough to affect evaluations of street repair obtained by citizen surveys.

Problem #2: Complications in Analyzing Subjective Indicators

Even if we assume there is a strong link between the actual service government provides and citizen responses to evaluation and satisfaction questions, analyzing those responses for performance evaluation faces complex conceptual and statistical problems. It is not valid simply to compare overall levels of satisfaction in different geographic areas and attribute those differences to differences in service performance. For example, a policy maker might find that a higher percentage of citizens in one service area say they are dissatisfied with refuse collection than in another service area. The policy maker cannot validly infer that this difference in overall satisfaction reflects a difference in actual performance, because of both conceptual and statistical complications.

The conceptual complications arise from the unknown form of the relationship between the subject measure and the dimension(s) of service quality upon which citizens base their expressed satisfaction or evaluations. Ideally, from the analyst's point of view, there would always be an increasing monotonic relationship between the subjective indicator and the quality dimension. That is, the subjective indicator would always increase with increases in actual quality. In that case, the analyst could use the subjective indicator to rank the quality of service individuals or groups receive.

. . . large improvements in objective performance—large in the sense of what public officials could realistically hope to achieve—generally appear to have negligible effects on citizens' subjective evaluations.

However, monotonicity may not exist, even if the individual citizens are knowledgeable about the services the researcher asks about and respond according to their knowledge and perceptions. Different respondents may base their subjective assessments on different aspects of the service, depending on what aspects of performance they perceive as most salient or important. Different respondents may have different expectations of what service quality should be, and apply different standards in evaluating performance. Some respondents may respond by comparing perceived performance to a specific desired level of service, perhaps because of their assessments of the marginal costs and benefits of improving performance. Such respondents will express lower satisfaction beyond a certain performance level, whereas other respondents may express greater and greater satisfaction the higher the perceived performance. In short, overall satisfaction levels, such as the percentage from an area which expresses high satisfaction or low satisfaction, result from some unknown mixture of different perceptions, expectations, and types of evaluation processes. Because of these complications, high levels of subjective performance do not necessarily imply that in any other sense service performance is higher.[10]

In order to deal with these conceptual difficulties, analysts using subjective data to evaluate service performance must make a number of strong assumptions, often of questionable validity. The necessary assumptions will depend on the particular type of analysis, as well as the standards of rigor the analysts apply, since some analysts may undertake an analysis not defensible according to strict standards of rigor and logic if that is the only analysis possible. However, almost all reasonable analyses

require assuming at least 1) that most respondents base their responses on the same aspects of service performance, which they perceive fairly accurately, and 2) that most respondents respond monotonically, i.e., that most respondents will express greater satisfaction the higher the perceived performance. Comparing average satisfaction levels requires the additional assumption that the subjective data approximate interval measurement. Also, in comparing group averages for respondents from different areas or demographic categories, any effort to rank-order the groups makes sense only if the groups have comparable intra-group variation. An assumption is thus required that the distributions (about the group means) of quality of service received by members of different groups are similar, or alternatively, that members within each group receive approximately the same quality of service.

The statistical complications which plague analyses of satisfaction data for performance evaluation basically result from the nonexperimental nature of the research. Samples of citizens are not equivalent to experimental groups in the laboratory. Citizens are not randomly assigned to different "treatments" consisting of different service levels in different areas of the city. Rather, citizens from different areas often vary on a number of individual characteristics, such as race and income, which may affect satisfaction independent of the level of service. Also, the different "treatments" (different service levels) found in different areas are not "administered" with all other factors held constant, because areas vary on other neighborhood characteristics besides the quality of governmental services.

Because of these nonexperimental conditions, variations in citizen satisfaction can result from factors other than service performance. For example, the type of citizens living in one area may tend to have especially high expectations for service performance, and therefore tend to express lower satisfaction at a given level of actual performance than do citizens in other areas. To take another example, citizens living in neighborhoods with dilapidated housing may tend to generalize their dissatisfaction with housing conditions to all aspects of the neighborhood, including local governmental services. Comparisons of satisfaction levels in different areas within a city may therefore reveal differences that are merely artifacts of these types of factors, and that cannot validly be interpreted as differences due to the quality of service government provides.

The policy analyst can try to avoid such artifactual findings by employing more sophisticated statistical techniques than simple comparisons of overall satisfaction levels across areas. One approach is to estimate an individual-level multiple regression equation which regresses respondent satisfaction on individual-level variables and a set of dummy variables corresponding to the service areas being examined. The purpose of that type of multivariate statistical procedure is to remove the effects of factors other than service performance, so that the analyst can examine the independent effect of differences in service performance.

To illustrate how policy analysts could use such procedures, I will take a very simple case. Assume that the analyst has an approximately interval-level scale, Y, of citizen satisfaction with a local service, created from a number of survey items. Also assume:

1) Expressed satisfaction, Y, with a particular service increases linearly with some continuous, unmeasured dimension, Q, of the quality of that service.
2) Y is also influenced by some characteristic of the respondent, X, which has an additive effect. For example, X might be a dummy variable corresponding to the respondent's race (e.g. black vs. white), if one racial group is known to have a negative or positive evaluative bias relative to the other.
3) Y has a stochastic component, ε, which is unrelated to Q, X, or the service area in which the respondent resides.

The basic model therefore can be written:

$$Y = \alpha + \beta Q + \gamma X + \varepsilon \qquad (1)$$

For simplicity of presentation assume that Q is approximately the same for all respondents from the same service areas within a city:

$$Q = \begin{cases} q_1 \text{ if respondent is from service area 1} \\ q_2 \text{ if respondent is from service area 2} \\ q_3 \text{ if respondent is from service area 3} \end{cases}$$

Equation (1) can now be rewritten by replacing Q with dummy variables, allowing area 3 to be the reference:

$$S_1 = \begin{cases} 1 \text{ if respondent is from service area 1} \\ 0 \text{ other wise} \end{cases}$$

$$S_2 = \begin{cases} 1 \text{ if respondent is from service area 2} \\ 0 \text{ other wise} \end{cases}$$

Equation (1) therefore becomes:

$$Y = \alpha + \beta q_3 + (\beta q_1 - \beta q_3)S_1 + (\beta q_2 - \beta q_3)S_2 + \gamma X + \varepsilon$$

Finally, let $\alpha^* = \alpha + \beta q_3$, $\lambda_1 = \beta q_1 - \beta q_3$, and $\lambda_2 = \beta q_2 - \beta q_3$, yielding:

$$Y = \alpha^* + \lambda_1 S_1 + \lambda_2 S_2 + \gamma X + \varepsilon \qquad (2)$$

The analyst can now estimate equation (2), requiring only data for X and Y, and knowledge of which respondents live in which service areas. Even though Q remains unobserved, the estimates for λ_1 and λ_2 allow comparison of the relative service quality in the service areas. Since area 3 is the reference, $\hat{\lambda}_1$ and $\hat{\lambda}_2$ are the estimated differences in Y attributable to living in area 1 and area 2, respectively, compared to area 3. Thus, to compare area 1 or area 2 to area 3, we compare $\hat{\lambda}_1$ to $\hat{\lambda}_2$. These comparisons rank the service areas, as well as show the relative magnitude of the differences. Stated more formally, $\hat{\lambda}_1$ and $\hat{\lambda}_2$ allow construction of estimates of a linear transformation of the Q values for the areas. Because these estimates were obtained by estimating equation (2), the possible confounding effects of X have been removed, and the estimates correctly reveal (subject to sampling fluctuation) the areas' ranking and relative differences in service quality.

In contrast, the means for Y within each area may yield misleading information about the ranking and relative differences in service quality. This potential to mislead results from the possible confounding effects of X, which can formally be seen by taking the expectations of the subsample means:

$$E(\overline{Y}_1) = E(Y|S_1 = 1) = \alpha + \beta q_1 + \gamma E(X|S_1 = 1) + E(\varepsilon)$$
$$E(\overline{Y}_2) = E(Y|S_2 = 1) = \alpha + \beta q_2 + \gamma E(X|S_2 = 1) + E(\varepsilon)$$
$$E(\overline{Y}_3) = E(Y|S_1 = S_2 = 0) = \alpha + \beta q_3 + \gamma E(X|S_1 = S_2 = 0) + E(\varepsilon)$$

Whenever X is related to the area a respondent is from, then $E(X|S_1 = 1)$, $E(X|S_2 = 1)$, and $E(X|S_1 = S_2 = 0)$ are not all equal. Therefore, the differences in the X values will affect the sub-sample means and be confounded with the effects of the q_j. Attributing differences in $\overline{Y}_i$ solely to differences in Q can consequently lead to erroneous interpretations.

As the above example illustrates, average expressed satisfaction levels can mislead whenever factors (besides service performance) that affect satisfaction are related to the areas being compared. Only under specific conditions do these statistical problems disappear:

1) Service performance is the only determinant of satisfaction.
2) No determinants of satisfaction, other than service performance, are related to the geographic areas being compared.
3) The determinants of satisfaction, other than service performance, cancel each other and have no net effect on satisfaction within each area.

If any one of these conditions applies, the analyst can forgo more complex multivariate statistics, and simply compare marginal distributions or averages for the different areas. However, these assumptions are probably unrealistic in most situations. In general a preferable approach is to apply multivariate statistical procedures, using the respondent as the case for analysis and including all important respondent-level variables, as in equation (2).[11]

The same statistical issues arise when comparing groups of citizens defined in ways other than geographic area of residence. For example, say a policy analyst compares expressed satisfaction with a particular service for black and white sub-samples. Imputing overall differences in satisfaction to differences in service performance different racial groups receive can mislead whenever other factors affecting satisfaction are related to race. To illustrate, assume that level of education and income strongly affect expressed satisfaction, and that blacks in the city tend to be less educated and of lower income; thus, the effects of education and income would be confounded with the effects of service performance in the satisfaction the groups express. Only when one of the three conditions listed above (for groups from geographic areas) applies to the non-geographic groups do these statistical problems disappear. Otherwise, the analyst must use multivariate statistical procedures to remove the effects of the confounding variables.

. . . within the range of service quality typically found in U.S. metropolitan areas, citizens pay little attention to services and fail to perceive differences in service quality . . .

Unfortunately, multivariate statistics cannot always solve the difficulties of nonexperimental inference. Important respondent-level variables, such as differences in individuals' expectations for service performance, may go unmeasured. The analyst can then proceed only by assuming that other individual-level variables for which data are available, such as demographic variables, correlate highly with the unmeasured variables and can therefore serve as proxy variables in the analysis. Even more seriously, differences in service performance may be confounded with other differences in the service areas, such as neighborhood characteristics, that affect expressed satisfaction. Whenever important individual-level or other (e.g., neighborhood-level) variables go unmeasured and cannot be accounted for in the statistical analysis, multivariate procedures cannot remove these threats to the validity of using subjective data for performance evaluation.

Similar analytical problems can arise when time-series data are used to assess changes in service quality. For example, a policy analyst might compare expressed citizen satisfaction with a service at two different time points to assess the impact of program changes implemented in the interim.[12] The validity of this over-time comparison rests on the assumption that no important changes have occurred in other factors affecting satisfaction. This assumption is analogous to the assumption, when analyzing cross-sectional data for one time point, that no determinants other than service quality are related to the areas being compared. Over long time-periods this assumption will usually be untenable, but over short periods typically of interest to decision makers it may often be reasonable.

Recommendations

To measure the quality of service performance, policy makers should not rely heavily on survey items asking citizens how satisfied they are with particular local services, or asking citizens to evaluate particular local services. The meaning of such indicators is not clear, and some prior research suggests that responses to satisfaction or evaluation items may not accurately reflect the actual service government provides. Also, the potential analytical difficulties are great, and are not always soluble. Using satisfaction data to assess service performance may therefore mislead more than enlighten.

Whenever analysts do use subjective data to evaluate service performance, they should remain aware of the conceptual and statistical complications. Assumptions which underlie the analysis should be stated explicitly in reports to decision-makers. For example, what assumptions about how citizens responded to the survey items are necessary to support the inferences made about service performance? Also, overall satisfaction measures—such as average satisfaction or the percentage satisfied or dissatisfied—should be compared only under special conditions, as described earlier. Otherwise, the analyst should if possible employ multivariate statistical procedures to avoid artifactual conclusions.

More specific subjective indicators than general satisfaction with a service may offer greater potential for evaluating service performance. Even if data from general satisfaction or evaluation questions are 1) closely linked to actual performance, and 2) subjected to sophisticated statistical analysis, they still may confound different aspects of performance in one indicator. Responses to vague satisfaction or evaluation questions probably reflect at best some unknown mixture of different aspects of service provision. Whenever some of these aspects can be measured by more objective questions, perhaps the role of attitude or opinion items should be restricted to measuring more specific performance characteristics too intangible to measure in other ways.

. . . citizens living in neighborhoods with dilapidated housing may tend to generalize their dissatisfaction with housing conditions to all aspects of the neighborhood, including local governmental services.

For example, a vague survey item asking citizens how satisfied they are with police services may reflect a wide variety of factors, such as whether the respondent was 1) a victim of a crime recently, 2) stopped by local police recently, and 3) if he was stopped, how the police treated him. Information concerning the first two factors could be obtained directly by factual questions. An evaluation item which specifically asks the respondent how politely he was treated might be used to measure the third factor. Measuring these different factors separately, rather than confounding them in one general subjective indicator, probably would provide more useful information for evaluating service performance.

Policy makers might profitably use data from general satisfaction and evaluation items for purposes other than performance evaluation. Community attitudes themselves may affect service provision: for example, widespread feelings of dissatisfaction with police may lower citizen cooperation with law enforcement personnel. Variations in satisfaction across time, geographic areas, or demographic groups may consequently affect performance of the police functions, and affect the choice of the best standard operating procedures for law enforcement personnel to use. The sophisticated policy maker, in short, may find some use for general satisfaction or evaluation data, but will exercise caution in making inferences about the quality of service performance.

Notes

1. See Kenneth Webb and Harry P. Hatry, *Obtaining Citizen Feedback: The Application of Citizen Surveys to Local Governments* (Washington, D.C.: Urban Institute, 1973), and Louis H. Blair and Alfred I. Schwartz, *How Clean is our City?* (Washington, D.C.: Urban Institute, 1972).
2. Webb and Hatry, *op. cit.*, pp. 20-22, suggest such a procedure. Similarly, Shin infers from aggregate satisfaction data for different localities the relative service quality the localities receive, and goes on to recommend redistributing service resources. See Doh C. Shin, "The Quality of Municipal Service: Concept, Measure and Results," *Social Indicators Research*, Vol. 4 (May 1977), pp. 218-220, 225.
3. Brian Stipak, *Citizen Evaluations of Urban Services as Performance Indicators in Local Policy Analysis*, Ph.D. dissertation, University of California, Los Angeles (1976).
4. The statistics given in Tables 1 and 2 are estimated partial regression coefficients and their standard errors, appropriately transformed to show the estimated impact of the changes listed in Tables 1 and 2 in standard deviation units of the evaluation scale. The results in each table are based on more than one regression equation, because of data availability for the policy variables and other reasons. For a complete description of model specification and estimation results the technical reader should consult Stipak, *op. cit.*

The statistics in Tables 1 and 2 were calculated based on Stipak, *op. cit.*, Tables 5.1, G.1, G.2, and G.10.
5. George L. Kelling, Tony Pate, Duane Dieckman, and Charles E. Brown, "The Kansas City Preventive Patrol Experiment: A Summary Report," in Gene V. Glass, ed., *Evaluation Studies Review Annual* (Beverly Hills: Sage, 1976), pp.631-637.
6. *ibid.*, p. 637.
7. E.g. Howard Schuman and Barry Gruenberg, "Dissatisfaction with City Services: Is Race an Important Factor?" in Harlan Hahn, ed., *People and Politics in Urban Society* (Beverly Hills: Sage, 1972).
8. For a discussion of information levels and opinion formation in the general public see Philip E. Converse, "Public Opinion and Voting Behavior," in Fred I. Greenstein and Nelson W. Polsby, eds., *Handbook of Political Science* (Reading, Mass.: Addison-Wesley, 1975), pp. 79-83. For a discussion of meaningless responses to attitude questions see Philip E. Converse, "Attitudes and Non-Attitudes: Continuation of a Dialogue," in Edward R. Tufte, ed., *The Quantitative Analysis of Social Problems* (Reading, Mass.: Addison-Wesley, 1970).
9. See Brian Stipak, "Attitudes and Belief Systems Concerning Urban Services," *Public Opinion Quarterly*, Vol. 41 (Spring 1977), pp. 50-51, for a discussion of processes of local political attitude formation in the absence of strong perceptions.
10. For a more detailed discussion of these complications see Brian Stipak, "Are There Sensible Ways to Analyze and Use Subjective Indicators of Urban Service Quality?", *Social Indicators Research* (forthcoming). Also available as Discussion Paper No. 121, Institute of Public Policy Studies, University of Michigan (1978).
11. Stipak, *ibid.*, presents simulation examples which contrast interpretations based on multivariate statistics, as opposed to interpretations based on sub-sample means. The underlying statistical issues are essentially problems of specification error and resulting statistical bias, a topic which is discussed in the econometrics literature.
12. E.g., see Harry P. Hatry, Richard E. Winnie, and Donald M. Fisk, *Practical Program Evaluation for State and Local Government Officials* (Washington, D.C.: Urban Institute, 1973), p. 102.

Some types of social interventions, e.g., in health care, safety, policing, have as their ultimate aim the saving of human lives. There is no question that there are many social interventions that might save lives, at widely varying, but often great cost. It has recently been estimated that automobile safety inspections save lives at a cost of over $2,000,000 per life. If society is to get its value for its money, it may sometimes become necessary, at least for speculative planning purposes, to be able to put some value on the life saved. Economists have discussed several ways in which it might be possible in theory to place a value on a human life, and Rhoads provides a very cogent and readable discussion of that valuing and its implications. It is difficult even to contemplate the matter without discomfort. However, no matter if we do or do not contemplate it; the decision will be made.

23

How Much Should We Spend To Save a Life?

Steven E. Rhoads

In the last decade or so, Uncle Sam has become increasingly interested in keeping us alive. Separate agencies have been established to deal with traffic, consumer, environmental, and occupational safety. Medicare and Medicaid have come into being. And there have been substantial increases in appropriations to reduce maladies such as kidney failure, cancer, and sickle-cell anemia.

Yet as the Federal government has become more involved with lifesaving programs, both academics and interest groups have been quick to point out many areas where still more money could save still more lives. If the government has an obligation to provide dialysis to kidney patients, why does it not have a similar obligation to hemophiliacs who need a continuous supply of costly blood, or to heart patients who need arterial shunts? Moreover, why should the government spend almost $30,000 per year to keep a kidney patient alive at a dialysis center and yet not pay for mobile cardiac units that can provide an additional life-year for as little as $1,765? And what about the old standbys—the F.B.I., the interstate highway system, the Defense Department, and local police and fire departments? If additional money were spent for them, additional lives could surely be saved.

Reprinted with permission of the author from: *The Public Interest,* No. 51 (Spring 1978), pp. 74-92. Copyright 1978 by National Affairs, Inc.

But many wonder if we are not already spending too much. Last year, Dr. Robert Grossman, acting director of the dialysis program at the Hospital of the University of Pennsylvania, took note of the costs of the program ($500 million in 1976 and more than $1.9 billion by 1982):

> I can see us in the next few years having programs for people with heart disease, people with cancer, and it's something we can't afford. I don't even know if we can afford this. The question is, how much is a life worth? We're seeing a resurgence of polio (and other diseases) because children are not getting their shots. Can we afford this at a time when we could be spending the money on basic health care to keep the general population healthy?

In 1974, President Nixon urged a reevaluation of the "trade-off" between economic growth and increasing safety, and President Ford later called for an assessment of safety regulations "in terms of the cost added and benefits gained."

Just as the anti-quantifiers always warned, the cost-benefit analysts have tired of valuing dams and are now valuing lives. Their work is not often publicized, but it is affecting government decisions. It is also causing quite a stir. Senator Harrison Williams thought President Nixon's call for trade-offs "unconscionable." A United Steelworkers representative thought it "despicable" when the Council on Wage and Price Stability questioned coke-fume standards costing at least $4.5 million per worker saved. And when the report of the Artificial Heart Assessment Panel made some vague statements about the need to seek "information on the value weights that would be assigned to various advantages and disadvantages by the individuals to whom they accrue," vigorous dissents were filed by the "ethicist," sociologist, and psychiatrist on the panel—all of whom thought it "neither possible nor useful to attempt to quantify advantages and disadvantages in a manner that will contribute meaningfully and properly to public-policy decision making in a democratic society." From the other direction, the economist on the panel and a supporter expressed regret that they had not had more time to explain the analytic framework that some panel members had found offensive, and they criticized the report itself for failing to make sufficient use of the economic calculus for gains and losses.

Can't we think sensibly about lifesaving programs without trying to put a dollar value on human life? One possibility would be to do cost-effectiveness analyses. We could estimate how many lives could be saved at various levels of expenditure and then leave it up to the responsible political officials to determine how much we could afford, given the other demands on the budget. Most economists, however, think we should try to go further. After all, if we have a successful cost-effectiveness analysis in hand, we know that if we had spent additional dollars, we could have saved additional lives. By not spending the money, we are saying that saving those lives is not worth that amount. We are implicitly putting a value on lives—so why not determine whether our implicit value is reasonable? Furthermore, if the inevitable valuing process is done implicitly by each agency, there are likely to be indefensible differences in the values used throughout the government. The central budget staff could prevent this by sending out a memorandum announcing that "X is as high as the government will go to save a life in 1978." But in a sense "X" then becomes society's value for life. Besides, it is not clear that all differences in life valuations are indefensible. Differences depending on age and lingering disabilities might be relevant. As Richard Zeckhauser and Donald Shepard have suggested, these could be compensated for by comparing the costs of a program with the number of additional "quality-adjusted life-years" it produces. But perhaps there are other relevant differences. For example, should the government spend more per "quality-adjusted life-year" on defense or air travel, where the individual has less control over his safety, than it spends on highway safety or lung cancer, where by wearing seat belts or abstaining from smoking individuals could do much to reduce their risks without government spending? A persuasive way of valuing lifesaving programs could be of real assistance.[1]

Though there is considerable agreement among economists about the need to calculate a value for life, there is no consensus as to how it should be done. There are two fundamentally different general approaches: One focuses on the "discounted future earnings" of potential decedents, while the other tries to determine the willingness of individuals to pay for risk reduction. The advocates of the "willingness-to-pay" (WTP) approach argue, with considerable justification, that only their methodology can correctly be traced to the normative branch of economics. There have, however, been few attempts to apply this methodology, and all the dozens of

---

[1] Although the economic approaches to be discussed are far and away the most often used, occasionally one sees a value of life based on court awards to next of kin in the wake of accidents. All such awards compensate the victim's family for their losses, but include no compensation for the loss to the victim himself. A similar problem exists in using the face value of life insurance as a value for life.

government studies that place a value on life use a variant of the discounted-future-earnings (DFE) approach.

Discounted future earnings

The basic DFE approach takes the average age at which death of people killed by a certain type of disease or accident occurs and computes what their expected future income would have been if they had lived a normal term. This future income is discounted, since a dollar received today can be invested, and is thus worth more than a dollar received in future years. The "present-value" figure that results is taken as the value of life for the average member of the group in question. Though the procedure is simple enough, the actual figures can range from under $100,000 to over $400,000. Significant differences result from the use of different discount rates, or from studying different groups. (Air travelers make more money than motorists, and the value of their lives is consequently higher.) However, the highest values are explained mainly by a decision of many economists to use the DFE amount only as a base figure to which other values are added. And there are also economists who use DFE as a base from which individual consumption is subtracted.

The most widely used value-of-life approach is still the straight DFE method, adopted in Department of Health, Education. and Welfare studies in the 1960's, and used in Federal Aviation Administration and Office of Science and Technology studies within the last few years. When I interviewed at the F.A.A., I found that many analysts were routinely plugging a DFE figure into their studies. One said, "I just followed what X did in the Y study. Presumably the figure is all right. Others seem to be using it." Analysts who had given the matter more thought defended DFE as an indicator of "output loss" from early death: "The individual's marginal product is measured by his earnings. That's his contribution to G.N.P., his contribution to the market place."

But of what interest is "contribution to G.N.P." or "output loss" if one wants to determine an appropriate value of life? Does society's welfare increase whenever more people earn more money? Those who support Zero Population Growth and limitations on immigration do not think so. Moreover, if the rest of society is concerned about economic output, it is concerned only with what the potential decedent would earn *less* what he would consume.

Proponents of the basic DFE approach respond by arguing that the potential decedent is himself a part of society, and his consumption should be seen as an end in itself. However, if a DFE figure is also meant to reflect the utility loss to the individual, it is too small to use as a societal value for life. An economist must presume that an individual experiences pleasure from *all* uses of his income, whether he spends it on himself, his wife, or his alma mater. But if the whole of DFE is needed to represent the decedent's utility loss, how can it also incorporate the losses of wife, family, and alma mater?

This seems to be the objection of the school that adds other values such as family-income loss and employer restaffing costs to a DFE base. Gary Fromm started this approach, and it is still being used by the National Highway Traffic Safety Administration in recent analyses. It does about as well as can be done if one begins with DFE. There is, however, no economic justification for beginning in that way.

In his work on F.A.A. problems, Fromm indicates his belief in the fundamental importance of consumer sovereignty and in the resulting obligation of the F.A.A. to base its activities on an estimate of consumers' willingness to pay for F.A.A. services. Yet by using a modified version of DFE, Fromm has left himself open to the charge that he has ignored those crucial principles of welfare economics. By his own admission, Fromm's modified DFE approach ignores all costs of fear of the risk of death, as well as the non-monetary suffering that death causes. More importantly, DFE does not in fact reflect the individual's utility loss from death. We cannot assume that a man who will earn 10 times more than another values his life 10 times more. Very rich men can be near suicide, and there are life-loving hobos.

DFE figures often yield bizarre guideposts for policy. For example, since men on the average earn more than women, DFE figures show men's lives to be of far more value than women's. Critics of the DFE approach have had great fun asking if there really are husbands and wives in their 30's who would want to pay twice as much to reduce the risk of death for the husband as for the wife, or if families would pay $60,000 to save a baby boy but only $35,000 to save a baby girl.[2]

---

[2] Matters might be even worse had not Dorothy Rice, an early friend of women's liberation, tried to ameliorate this problem by placing a value on a housewife's labor. Rice decided to value such labor at the weekly wage level of domestic servants, though she realized that this was still not altogether fair since "it makes no allowance for the housewife's longer work week." However, women bounce back in later life: Those over 65 are still valued at a good housekeeper's wages, while retired men's lives are worth nothing at all!

From the point of view of discounted earnings, the most valuable people in society are young adult white males. All that feeding and education for no return is at last completed, and society can look forward to 40 to 50 years of good productive output. This view of societal preferences was dramatically illustrated when HEW conducted cost-benefit analyses on a number of programs in the mid-1960's. Studies suggested that a media campaign encouraging the wearing of motorcycle helmets might save a life for $3,000. A cervix-cancer program could do almost as well—$3,520 per life saved. Yet DFE figures prevented the programs from being close competitors. The benefit-cost ratio for the motorcycle program was 55.6, while for the cervix-cancer program it was only 8.9.

Of course, DFE proponents never claimed that they were capturing a person's full worth with their figures. The earnings numbers were a "floor" value, and costs such as pain and grief were not taken into account. Still, these brief disclaimers did not affect the benefit-cost ratios, and were quickly forgotten. Indeed, they almost had to be because the whole point of valuing life was to go beyond cost-effectiveness analysis—which by itself could tell only which programs would save lives at least cost—to use cost-benefit analysis to indicate society's preferences for saving lives in different population groups and to determine how much might justifiably be spent to save people in each of these groups. Ironically, within a year of two of the time the analysts responsible for the HEW studies were arguing that it was "likely" that the "additional (intangible) considerations argue in the same direction" as the sex-and-age-discriminating earnings benefits, Congress was passing Medicare for the elderly, and the Johnson Administration was making a child-and-maternal-health program its highest health-care priority.

The DFE method for valuing lives has probably done as much as anything to convince others that cost-benefit economists are presumptuous and wedded to a crude materialism. Many believe that DFE represents the sole method that economists recommend to deal with the value-of-life question. It is easy to see why: The victory of the DFE approach within the government has been so complete that a 1974 study by the General Accounting Office was content to note somberly the differences in the DFE figures used by the National Highway Traffic Safety Administration, the Office of Science and Technology, and the National Safety Council, suggesting only that the Senate Committee on Commerce have the Safety Administration recheck its data base, assumptions, and discount rate. Outside the government, benefit-cost studies principally concerned with other matters often latch onto a DFE figure for the value of life. And, perhaps most important of all, in her influential *Systematic Thinking for Social Action,* Alice Rivlin, who should know better, mentions only DFE approaches to buttress her argument that cost-benefit analysis is not likely to be of much use in social-policy areas.

Willingness to pay

Almost all economists would agree with Ezra Mishan's view that in normative economics "the worth or value of a thing is determined simply by what a person is willing to pay for it." Unlike their DFE counterparts, those who subscribe to the "willingness-to-pay" approach take this precept very seriously. The WTP school does not focus on how much people would pay to avoid certain death, for in such a situation most would pay almost all they could get their hands on, and thus the WTP figure would reveal more about absolute wealth than about the relative preference for a particular good or service.

WTP proponents point out, however, that most safety and health programs lower the risk of death, but we do not know *who* would have died without the program. In the typical case, the government must decide if it should spend money to make a small probability of death even smaller for a large number of individuals. In such cases, the sum of the willingness to pay for reduced risk of all those affected is seen as reflecting their preferences. This aggregate WTP is divided by the number of deaths prevented to determine what government might justifiably spend to save a life in the program under consideration.

Though all proponents of WTP agree that the preferences of consumers are the best guide for public policy, they disagree about the best means of determining WTP. Some favor consumer polls, while others look to decisions that individuals make when their lives are actually at risk. Although many have advocated one method or the other, there have been only three serious published attempts to apply either approach: One used polling, while the other two made deductions from decisions in the job market.

Jan Acton polled 100 people in Boston about heart attacks and risk reduction. He thought his most "basic" question was the following:

> Let's suppose that your doctor tells you that the odds are 99:1 against your having a heart attack. If you have the attack, the odds are 3:2 that you will live. The heart-attack program would mean that the

odds are 4:1 that you live after a heart attack. How much are you willing to pay in taxes per year to have this heart-attack program which would cut your probability of dying from a heart attack in half (i.e., the chances are two per 1,000 you will have a heart attack and be saved by the program this year)?

In the community sample Acton thought most typical of the general citizenry, the average response to this question was $56. This implies a value of life of $28,000 (1,000 x $56).

$$2$$

There are two standard criticisms of using polling to determine WTP. The first is the possibility that respondents may engage in strategic behavior: Taking account of their likely tax burden and other respondents' likely responses, they may understate or overstate their real WTP in order to shift the average WTP and the resulting tax burden in ways helpful to them. Like Acton, I do not think such behavior is likely to be a serious problem in preliminary efforts to assess people's preferences. The second problem is more fundamental: Many wonder if poll respondents will be able to understand and give consistent answers to questions such as those Acton asked. In other areas, economists have found that people's stated preferences and actual behavior often differ widely.

Acton acknowledges these potential problems. He also notes that the order in which his questions were asked seemed to affect responses, and that respondents frequently gave identical WTP answers for different changes in the probability of death. Still, he believes that most people "thought rather carefully" about his "basic" question, and he thinks the polling approach to WTP "a better guide to true preferences than any of the alternatives."

It is unclear why Acton thought the question above more "basic" than another he asked:

They are thinking about putting ambulances and other devices in communities around the country, but only if people are willing to pay enough for them. This program would be for you and 10,000 people living around you. In your area, there are about 100 heart attacks per year. About 40 of these persons die. With the heart-attack program, only 20 of these people would die. How much would you be willing to pay in taxes per year for the ambulance so that 20 lives could be saved in your community?

This question focuses on community-wide benefits, while the earlier one emphasizes benefits to the individual. Both questions, however, describe the same program—one where the respondent and others in the community are .002 less likely to die the year after implementation than before. Yet in the community sample most representative of the public—in which Acton had the most confidence—the average response was $56 to the first question, and $33 to the second. This means that small changes in the way the same program was described led to WTP values varying from $28,000 to $16,500.

Risky business

Applications of the alternative WTP methodology have also run into serious problems. The two studies of this type, by Robert Smith and by Richard Thaler and Sherwin Rosen, have examined decisions made in the job market. Since people spend much of their lives on the job, the authors believe that workers have an incentive to acquire decent information about their work-related risks. And since risky jobs will be less attractive, the expectation is that after controlling for education, race, experience, unionization, region, etc., wage rates will be higher in high-risk occupations.

Both studies have found this to be the case. Smith used data on injury rates among hourly workers in manufacturing industries and found that where the yearly death rate is 16 per 100,000 workers, employees receive approximately 1.5 percent more in annual wages than do employees of comparable skills in industries with an average rate of eight deaths per 100,000 workers. Smith's estimates imply that workers are collectively willing to forego $1.5 million in pay if employers undertake steps that will save one life. Thaler and Rosen's study used actuarial data to compare the expected number of deaths for those of a certain age with actual deaths in 37 hazardous occupations. The authors found that 1,000 workers in an occupation associated with an extra death risk of .001 per year will each sacrifice $200 per year if the extra death probability is reduced to zero. This implies a value for life of $200,000.

Because of inadequate data neither Smith nor Thaler and Rosen have great confidence in the WTP figures they have come up with.[3] But even if the data were as good as one could wish, information from the job market may never produce a decent WTP estimate for programs that reduce the risk of death. The figures that result will omit the WTP of most white-collar employees and all nonworkers. Moreover, the society's WTP for lifesaving programs may depend

---

[3] Smith's data lump together all hourly workers within an industry. This introduces a large measurement error for individuals, because job risks in each industry are not uniform across occupations. Thaler and Rosen do have data showing death rates by occupations, but only for very risky occupations, and there is reason to believe that those attracted to such jobs are more tolerant of risks than are most Americans. For this reason, the Thaler and Rosen figures will underestimate most people's willingness to pay for risk reduction. Moreover,

on how painful the predeath stages of a disease are, or whether the program is preventive or curative. (We would pay more for a program that would prevent kidney or heart failure than for one that allowed some sort of life after such failures.) But it would be hard to know how the job-market figures should be adjusted to take account of these factors. Even more important is the question whether workers are aware of the real risks of occupations, and thus whether wage differentials really tell us ·what we want to know about workers' attitudes toward their job-related risks.

In any case, WTP proponents do not yet have an alternative figure to substitute for the DFE numbers in various government studies. The work of both Smith and Thaler and Rosen suggests that DFE is too low to use as a value for life. But the Acton study suggests that most DFE figures are too high.

Still, one could make too much of the disagreements among WTP figures at this early state. Acton had a very small sample, and his WTP results were for a program that might allow one to live a possibly crippled life *after* a heart attack. One would expect people to be willing to pay less for such a program than for death-preventing job-related programs. Moreover, two informal applications of the polling approach to WTP—by Thomas Schelling and by H. C. Joksch—both yielded value-of-life figures of $1 million or more. Since other more theoretical work by J. Hirshleifer, T. Bergstrom, and E. Rappaport also suggests that WTP should be much greater than DFE, a WTP proponent could argue that our current knowledge is sufficient to support a WTP figure two or three times DFE. And the government should be doing more polling and collecting information on occupational death rates and cause of death, so that statistical studies of risk premiums in the job market could make more accurate estimates.

If the normative principles of welfare economics and its applied branch, benefit-cost economics, are sufficient for determining the value of lifesaving programs, this reasoning is persuasive. One of the weakest yet most prevalent arguments against benefit-cost analysis accepts its principles but denies their relevance because of difficulties in application. If the principles hold, the sensible course

---

Thaler and Rosen have no information on cause of death, and they simply assume that unusually high death rates in the occupations studied are caused by real work-related dangers. For most of the listed occupations where death rates are high (such as lumbermen or boilermakers) this assumption seems plausible, but for others (like cooks, waiters, and bartenders) it seems much less so. Perhaps cooks, waiters, and bartenders die sooner than most not because they are engaged in risky occupations, but because they are more likely to be transients, alcoholics, or whatever.

is to use the best possible estimate of WTP. But are the principles sufficient guides for public policy on lifesaving programs?

Who should benefit?

Students of philosophy and theologians have not directly addressed the broader questions of resource allocation that concern economists, but they have asked a related question: Who should get exotic lifesaving therapy when there is not enough for all? There are essentially two lines of thought on this problem: that those most deserving should be given preference, and that all should be treated equally. In the first approach, some interpret "deserving" quite broadly, excluding only those over a certain age, the critically ill, or those with a serious criminal record. But many in this school are more demanding. In the 1960's when kidney-dialysis machines were scarce, a group of hospitals made allocation decisions on the basis of factors such as age, marital status, number of dependents, occupation, past performance, and future potential.

Nicholas Rescher has set forth criteria of this sort, together with a justification for them. Rescher would have decisions made on the basis of biomedical factors (likelihood of success and life expectancy), family role (number and age of dependents, etc.), and social factors (prospective and retrospective service). He does not try to put weights on each of the factors, and he acknowledges that a lottery may still be needed to choose among those whom his criteria cannot discriminate. He nevertheless opposes random selection because it blindly ignores considerations that "*deserve* to be given weight." For example, with respect to the social factors, he notes:

> Despite disagreement on many fundamental issues, moral philosophers of the present day are pretty well in consensus that the justification of human actions is to be sought largely and primarily—if not exclusively—in the principles of utility and of justice. But utility requires reference of services to be rendered and justice calls for a recognition of services that have been rendered.

Paul Ramsey supports the alternative position—that all should be treated equally. When kidney-dialysis machines were scarce in the 1960's many hospitals used this criterion; most decided on a first-come, first-served basis, although at least one held a lottery. Ramsey supports these and only these decision procedures. Though he thinks a rule that excludes all those over a certain age preferable to Rescher's social-merit criterion, he ultimately opposes even age-based criteria. He approvingly quotes Paul Freund: "The more nearly total is the estimate to be made of an individual, and the more nearly the consequence determines life and death, the more unfit the judgment becomes for human reckoning. . . ." Ramsey continues, "Here we see the important and informative distinction between a practice that 'plays God' and a practice that is for the reckoning of men to imitate rather God's care (before the Judgment Day!) alike for the good and the bad, the profitable and the unprofitable, the deserving and the undeserving, and seeks to serve those who are only needy no less than those who are needed."

Though the Rescher/Ramsey question is not the one economists (or policy makers) usually ask, some economists would not see the need to give other than their usual answer: Let the scarce dialysis machine, kidney transplant, or whatever go to the person with the highest WTP. If the rich bid up prices dramatically, all to the good: Dialysis-machine manufacturers will then want to get more machines to the market more quickly, and others, concerned about their heirs, will be more eager to arrange to sell their organs in the event of their accidental death. As for Rescher's views, the hard-nosed market economist is likely to see wealth and current salary as at least rough proxies of retrospective and prospective contributions to society. The best pianists and businessmen were and will be paid more than those less talented, and if the businessmen are generally paid more than the pianists, it is only because ordinary consumers value their services more at the margin. Though the poor man who needs the kidney machine will not have the equal chance that Ramsey requires, the poor as a whole would be better off if some of the high sums the rich pay for the machines were used to save more lives of the poor in other less expensive ways. Moreover, the unusually risk-averse among the poor can insure themselves against many exotic diseases at a tolerable price.

Many, probably most, economists would not find these arguments persuasive. In those few cases when supply cannot respond and life-saving expenditures by the rich necessarily doom the poor, economists are as likely to join Rescher or Ramsey as the pure free-market advocates. But in the more usual case, when we are dealing with small changes in small risks of death, most economists would support a WTP criterion. In such cases, the heart of the Rescher argument is not usually applicable, since there are few ways to reduce the risks of dangers like cancer or auto accidents for the deserving without doing it for the undeserving as well.

But what of the Ramsey argument? It surely remains relevant

for many Americans who believe that in something as fundamental as life, the government should ensure that the rich and the poor are given equal protection. The usual response of economists is as follows: If you are solely concerned with the welfare of the poor, it is better to give them money, perhaps by way of a negative income tax, than to give them a specific lifesaving service that they do not value enough to be willing to pay for its costs. If the poor would rather have $100 in cash than $100 spent to make their car or job safer, by giving them the cash we respect their sovereignty as consumers and increase their subjective sense of satisfaction.

Welfare strategies

Given an unequal distribution of income, there are only two ways of equalizing lifesaving expenditures of the rich and poor: Place restrictions on the rich or give tremendous subsidies in kind to the poor. But neither alternative has much to recommend it. Is there any reason to tell a rich businessman who wants to pay higher user charges for increased air safety that he may not do so because the government is already spending more to save the marginal life in air transport than in modes frequented by lower-income people? Why should the rich be allowed to buy as many yachts or minks as they like, but be told that we draw the line on lifesaving equipment and medical care? Yet if we are not to restrict the rich, we will need an enormous subsidy in kind to make every citizen as safe as a Rockefeller. And given the multiplicity of needs of the poor, there are surely better ways to help them.

One can grant this and still argue that the poor should be assured of a certain minimum standard of safety and medical care, even if their income is so low that they would not willingly use their money to purchase such services. Some economists become impatient with such arguments and the policies that flow from them. Thus Richard Zeckhauser, who apparently favors redistributing income to help the poor, has suggested that these arguments and policies are a means of "salving the conscience of the middle class at the expense of the welfare of the poor." But other economists are more sympathetic, believing that if the general public is upset because the poor are deprived of a minimum level of lifesaving expenditures, then government programs that spend more than the poor would be willing to pay are indeed justified—not by any principle beyond welfare economics, but simply because of the external or spillover benefits to the non-poor of lifesaving expenditures for the poor.

Though most early discussions of WTP approaches neglected the importance of externalities for the value-of-life question, Ezra Mishan's *Cost-Benefit Analysis* presents a methodology that adds the preferences of all concerned to determine a composite value for a lifesaving program. Thus, if some of the non-poor are willing to pay to help the poor achieve a minimum standard of safety and medical care, their WTP should be added to that of the poor when deciding if a lifesaving program is justified.

According to the welfare-economic approach the only justification for a special public program to achieve higher safety or medical standards for the poor would be the feelings of *non*-poor consumers. Since the non-poor have little contact with the poor, those feelings are likely to depend on idiosyncratic decisions by television executives and newspaper editors. Citizens will know about, and may be willing to pay to reduce the risks for, threatened groups whose situation is most interestingly presented on film or babies whose strange life-preserving needs make the best "human-interest" story. Instead of correcting for the inadvertent injustice to those whose plight is not made known to benefactors, a public policy based on WTP would accentuate it. As Mishan says, all the data in a benefit-cost study accept "as final only the individual's estimate of what a thing is worth to him at the time the decision is to be made." Thus public money would tend to follow private donations, and those similarly situated would be treated even more unequally than if government had done nothing at all.

A closer look at Ezra Mishan's recommended method for determining the value of lifesaving expenditure will illustrate the extent to which many economists would base public policy solely on individuals' preferences—whatever they might be. Mishan properly applies the consumer-sovereignty principle of welfare economics by allowing for the WTP of direct beneficiaries to be augmented by the external benefits to others. But quite consistently, Mishan's scheme also takes account of the preferences of those who might feel *worse* as more lives were saved. For example, an analysis of a health program especially effective in reducing the risk of death for the elderly would add the WTP of the elderly, their friends, family, and the public at large—but then subtract from this total the amount necessary to compensate any greedy heirs for the decrease in their welfare resulting from the possible lengthening of the lives of their eventual benefactors. Similarly, Mishan's formula would ask analysts to take account of the costs to white racists of a sickle-cell-anemia program. Even if the number and intensity of feeling of those who benefited from such programs far outweighed those who lose, these examples could have practical application. Such programs would undoubtedly involve substantial costs beyond the psychic ones to the greedy heirs and racists, and the decision to count their preferences could make costs exceed benefits. Should we really conclude that lifesaving programs that are in the public interest from the point of view of all but certain heirs and racists might cease to be in the public interest if those heirs and racists were sufficiently greedy or prejudiced?[4]

Mishan argues that in order to accept his methodology for valuing lifesaving expenditures, "all the reader has to accept is the proposition that people's subjective preferences of the worth of a thing is [sic] to count." It would be more accurate to say that one must agree that *only* such preferences are to count. But in fact we have additional standards of societal welfare. Most of us believe, for example, that those similarly situated should be treated equally and that malevolent preferences should not be publicly recognized.

The need for political judgment

A thoughtful political representative should use economic analysis. He should, for example, encourage economists to continue to ask if there are good reasons for the differing implicit values for life that current government policies produce. Programs of the Occupational Safety and Health Administration should not go unquestioned when they require the steel industry to spend at least $4.5 million to save a life. Even in the more controversial area of benefit-cost analysis, economists should be supported in their efforts to determine the public's WTP for lifesaving programs. When given information about the effectiveness of such a program, the average American can envision what is at issue far more easily than he can, for example, in issues concerning defense policy, and his views and decisions will thus be of relatively more importance to representatives trying to make thoughtful choices in this area. But public lifesaving decisions are not like decisions to build a bridge or pick up the garbage more often, cases where WTP might be *all* a representative needs to know. There will be many occasions for political judgment even if econo-

---

[4] It is particularly disconcerting that an economist as willing and able to make judgments about the quality of tastes as Mishan is should have adopted the methodology described. Elsewhere in his *Cost-Benefit Analysis* he recommends that the preferences of people whose subjective sense of satisfaction decreases because of envy of others' success should be excluded from the economic calculus on ethical grounds.

mists some day determine a reliable WTP figure for lifesaving programs.

Some reasons for 'this have already been suggested. Malevolent preferences should be denied public recognition, and those whose plight has been publicized for idiosyncratic reasons should not be given an unfair advantage. The WTP figures may not adequately reflect the greater public responsibility for safety where a collective decision is necessary (Defense Department and F.A.A. regulations and equipment) as compared to areas where individuals are better able to control risks themselves (advertising campaigns to encourage people to wear seat belts). Moreover, since people in their early 60's are generally wealthier than those in their early 30's, WTP calculations may put relatively too much general tax money into programs that prolong the lives of people past middle age, while de-emphasizing lifesaving programs for young adults with low incomes, large family responsibilities, and thus low average WTP.

Our desire to emphasize adequately both individual freedom and society's interests in the well-being of all citizens will also pose difficult issues. In an age when most experts think future lifesaving can best be achieved by changing individual diets and safety-related actions, what is the government responsibility? Should it go beyond publicizing information to mandating action? One can always find financial externalities resulting from another's death (higher life-insurance premiums), and there are often psychic ones as well. But if such externalities justify government regulation, we will soon be regulating the diets of the obese and of many others. WTP figures are not likely to take adequate account of these larger issues.

Without more information on people's WTP it is not clear how significant any of these problems will be. One cannot even be certain whether thoughtful representatives will be more likely to raise or to lower WTP figures when deciding how much to spend on a lifesaving program. Ivan Illich's *Medical Nemesis* has, in effect, popularized the view that our WTP will be too high, that we freely turn too many of our resources over to doctors and let them decide when and how we will die. We will be happier, Illich argues, when we learn to accept pain, decline, and death as parts of life. There is something ugly about a people more interested in frantically scrambling and spending for a few more months and years of life than in the quality of their lives.

But on the other hand, there is also something ugly about callousness and indifference to the situation of others. In his work on the value of life, Mishan calmly predicts an increase in indifference if not callousness: "The gradual loosening of family ties and the decline of emotional interdependence should cause the magnitude of the bereavement-risk compensation . . . to decline." But should a political representative merely adjust his value for life downward as the people's preferences change in this way? Believing that a reverence for life and a concern for others are political goods in a democracy, he may instead want to help extend the people's feelings and make them more public by, among other means, expanding and highlighting lifesaving programs. Analysts in the habit of looking to welfare economics and benefit-cost economics for policy guidance are unlikely to consider such matters. Certainly the economist's assumption that all desires are equal—and his consequent unwillingness even to consider possible distinctions between things that some people desire and things that are truly important—makes him peculiarly likely to suggest that others are ignobly "salving" their consciences if they are more interested in transferring needed medical care to the poor than in transferring cash or the other modern goods the poor may prefer.

Tragic choices

Though representatives will want to consider other criteria as well, economic analysis can help improve choices concerning lifesaving programs and the value-of-life issue. But there is a further issue of how widely such analysis should be publicized and how open the debate and decisions should be. On the value-of-life issue in particular, the results of analysis are not now spotlighted, debate is not encouraged, and if any explicit decisions on values to be used are made, they are not publicized. In a recent speech, Judge David Bazelon noted that his court rarely if ever encounters candid justifications for *not* improving health and safety standards. No one says that a program will save lives but is not worth the cost. Instead there is a tendency to hide behind scientific uncertainties ("There is no *credible* evidence *at this time.* . . .") or to use some other subterfuge. In his discussion of the government's involvement with kidney dialysis, analyst Richard Rettig notes a similar phenomenon: "A basic asymmetry was manifested throughout this complicated policy debate. The proponents of an expanded Federal government role were able to carry their case to the public in a variety of ways, while the opponents made their case in sotto voce fashion." Rettig and probably most other analysts hope that we are "entering a period in which policy-making officials are more willing to debate both sides of value-of-life issues in full view of the public." Bazelon agrees and notes that without such candor we miss a critical opportunity "to inform and thereby raise the level of public understanding."

For my own part I am quite sure that we will never see the day when value-of-life issues are debated as freely and openly as other public-policy issues. Moreover, I do not think we ever should see such a day. Imagine how the perfectly "rational" Congressman might greet his grieving constituent: "Mrs. Jones, I share your grief about the plight of your husband, but we simply cannot afford to spend $30,000 per year to keep him alive when people are dying elsewhere who could be saved for much less. Moreover, your husband would have to be hooked up to a kidney-dialysis machine for eight hours a couple of times a week, and you must admit that the quality of the lives saved by building safer roads would be much higher. Perhaps it would help if you and Mrs. Smith got together and tried to comfort one another. She lost her husband in the recent air crash, and seemed indignant because the F.A.A. for many years has had a radar system that can prevent such crashes. I tried to explain the high cost of putting those systems in every two-bit airport around the country, and I pointed out that without them if it hadn't been her husband's life it would have been someone else's. I'm not sure that I persuaded her. But just because we *can* save lives doesn't mean we *should* save lives. We've got some pretty complete WTP surveys now, and it is clear that the public thinks we are spending enough on lifesaving programs."

It is demoralizing when society collectively and publicly places a value on life. It is especially so when a decision is made not to save an identifiable individual. Thus we spend far more per life on rescue missions and kidney dialysis patients than on life-preserving preventive programs. Charles Fried speaks for many others when he asks why we think we "symbolize our concern for human life by actually doing less than we might to save life." But in fact it does seem more threatening to the life-preserving norm that decent societies should respect when our representatives look a man in the eyes and tell him that it is not worth the cost of saving his life than when those same representatives decide against widening a road shoulder. For one thing, the government's responsibility for the highway death will seem less direct, and thus people will not feel as callous and cynical about themselves and their government. For another, failing to save an identifiable person will mean that we must choose among the WTP, Rescher, or Ramsey criteria for allocating the scarce resources, and thus ignore desert, equality, or some other principle we value. Finally, as Guido Calabresi notes in his thoughtful *Tragic Choices*, "pricelessness, or at least the very high price of human life, is reaffirmed" by saving a whole category of people, such as those who suffer from kidney failure. Many important values depend on society's belief in the sanctity of life. Precisely because "these values are constantly being eroded by decisions which, in fact, place a low value on human life, substantial benefits accrue from any demonstration of societal devotion to 'pricelessness' and to the values it represents."

Public policy on lifesaving programs can never expect to achieve wholly satisfactory solutions. Nevertheless, I would like to see the preference for saving identifiable individuals continue when it is possible for them to live with their reason intact and without excruciating pain. But at the research stage, the cost of delivering therapeutic services if the research is successful should be considered.

As for candor, I would tolerate a little dissembling in this area. Much of the public is unable to reconcile removal of Karen Quinlan's life-support system or other forms of euthanasia with their moral sense, which should be respected whenever possible. Imagine how people would react to explicit, publicized decisions to let a kidney patient die so that we could widen a road shoulder, or to set forth publicly sanctioned limits on how much the public should spend to save a healthy man or woman. Let analysts and political administrators argue that the WTP figures and other explicit values are just one factor in the decision-making process. Let interested Congressmen have the analyses so that they can better appreciate the policy dilemmas, but let them also sympathize with their constituents' anger and pledge to look into the matter. If Congressional hearings are held, one can be sure that they will not lead to a legislated value for life—and that is all to the good. Admittedly, the absence of total candor leaves the way open for the periodic appearance of ambitious reporters and politicians who expose the Dr. Strangelove-like analysts at the heart of the bureaucracy. But this cost seems tolerable in an area where simple enlightenment is not to be expected or wished for.

IV

EVALUATION STUDIES

As was indicated in the Preface, we made no attempt in this volume to cover all the possible content areas or types of social interventions. Rather we sought to include articles which were of good quality generally but which could be used to illustrate some point of general interest and importance about problems in evaluation. The articles in this section, although varied, do not begin to cover the range of social interventions. We believe that they do, however, vary enough to illustrate the range of problems relevant to careful evaluation research. At the same time, each of the papers should be thought provoking in some way pertaining to problems and prospects in evaluation research. Some present problem-solutions, some provide models, and some can simply serve to show the opportunities which are available for carrying out good evaluation. There is growing recognition of the opportunity to exert leverage on some evaluation problems by combining results across studies—the process referred to as metaevaluation. Another important trend may be toward secondary analysis of data previously reported. Other papers show the opportunities for more circumscribed, local evaluations which stand in contrast to evaluations of national scope. The methods illustrated range from time series to experiment to benefit cost analysis, and the data sets from naturally occurring archives to specially generated data. All in all, we believe these articles make a strong case for the idea that at least some form of evaluation is possible and useful in almost any circumstance, and for the corollary that careful thought and planning can produce an improved evaluation in almost any circumstance.

In what may seem like the beginning of an infinite regression, Cook and Gruder have written a detailed and highly useful article on metaevaluations, or evaluations of evaluations. In fact, however, it is a series of recommendations for broadening and improving the "goodness of fit" between evaluations and metaevaluations, primary evaluators and secondary evaluators, decision makers and evaluators, and multiple evaluations. Presented are seven models of possible metaevaluations that are based on three factors of importance for metaevaluations: simultaneous or subsequent analysis of the metaevaluation with the primary evaluation, manipulation or no manipulation of the available data, and use of single or multiple data sets. In addition, each model presented is assessed with regard to its possible weaknesses and strengths and appropriate examples are given.

Although the theme, organization, and recommendations of the chapter are straightforward, there is a recurrent note that is not so simple, rather it seems to call for a restructuring of the review process and reward system of the evaluator's world. The authors themselves note that:

> We have not outlined organizational frameworks to facilitate increased academic participation; nor have we outlined a reward system that ties into the one currently operating in academia (publications, disciplinary visibility, and the like).

Some of the changes that Cook and Gruder recommend are: interim reports and first drafts of final reports be reviewed before the field work is completed, data should be placed in archives with appropriate documentation, consultant metaevaluation should occur more regularly, data be analyzed by primary analyst and secondary analyst simultaneously, and multiple independent replications occur. There can be little question that the above suggestions are worthy of being implemented—in fact, some do occur in an irregular fashion—but how and where does one begin to implement these changes on a regular, widespread scale? What is needed next is an article that details specific mechanisms for the implementation of the suggestions in Cook and Gruder's chapter, or, perhaps, a funding agency with the coverage to begin implementation on its own, by making Cook and Gruder's suggestions mandatory for grantees.

We would like also to point out that the studies discussed by Cook and Gruder and the issues raised about them afford some good instances of problems related to the integrity of treatment as well as to the sizes of effects produced by interventions. Cook and Gruder note that it is critical for evaluations that implementation of treatment be assessed and that the nature of the treatment be adequately documented. They also indicate that it is important to establish ways of determining the social, as opposed to the statistical, significance of evaluation findings.

24

Metaevaluation Research

Thomas D. Cook and Charles Gruder

This paper reviews four projects aimed at evaluating the technical quality of recent summative evaluations. It also helps identify some technical problems that frequently occur in evaluation research, and it outlines practical methods for solving these problems within the limits imposed by the current state of the art. The methods involve evaluating evaluations during or after their completion, with a stress on the former. The limitations of each method are outlined, together with ways of overcoming them.

This paper deals with what Orata (1940) called the "evaluation of evaluations" and what Scriven (1969) termed "metaevaluation." Our purpose is to describe and comment upon some recent systematic attempts to evaluate evaluations and to describe some ways in which metaevaluation can currently be used to improve the technical quality of evaluation research.

AUTHORS' NOTE: *The work was funded by contracts with the National Institute of Education (C-74-0115) and the National Science Foundation (C-1066). The authors would like to thank Alphonse Buccino, Howard P. Levine, and R. Timothy Stein for their insightful comments on previous drafts of this paper. Requests for reprints should be sent to: Dr. Thomas D. Cook, Department of Psychology, Northwestern University, Evanston, IL, 60201.*

We shall use the term "metaevaluation" to refer only to the evaluation of empirical summative evaluations—studies where the data are collected directly from program participants within a systematic design framework. The focus is narrower than Stufflebeam's (1975), whose discussion of metaevaluation includes the evaluation of formative research and nonempirical evaluations (e.g., advocacy evaluations). Our reason for this narrower focus is that summative evaluations play a crucial role in helping meet the highest evaluation goals, which are to pose relevant questions about program impact and to have these questions credibly and validly answered and the results communicated in timely and comprehensible fashion to decision makers and other constituencies that have an interest in how the evaluation results might be used. The purpose of metaevaluation is simply to help evaluators meet their goals by providing diagnostic feedback and helpful advice about what to do.

Three research traditions are of greatest relevance to metaevaluation. One is where an investigator acquires another's evaluation data and reanalyzes them to answer either the same questions as the primary analyst or new ones. Here, the feedback diagnosing strengths and weaknesses and offering fresh probes of a program's impact comes late, perhaps too late to influence policy. A second tradition is exemplified by the work of Bernstein and Freeman (1975) and McTavish et al. (Minnesota Systems Research, Inc., 1976), who rated evaluations from different federal agencies to see how technically competent they were *in general.* The focus of this work is not on evaluating particular evaluations, and so the results are more relevant to persons who make decisions about evaluation research rather than to those who make decisions about individual social programs. A third tradition can be loosely called "research on research," and it is exemplified by questions such as, What are the consequences of writing requests for proposals (RFPs) in highly structured or unstructured ways? Which ways of monitoring evaluations produce the quickest feedback about unexpected problems of design or measurement that emerge only after the planned design and measurement frameworks have been implemented?

In this paper we shall use studies from all three traditions to develop seven models of how metaevaluation research can be profitably carried out in order to improve the technical quality of empirical summative evaluations. But before developing these models we have to make the case that the technical quality of current evaluations needs improving. To do this we shall review four projects.

REVIEW OF THE CURRENT STATE OF EMPIRICAL SUMMATIVE EVALUATION RESEARCH

BERNSTEIN AND FREEMAN

Bernstein and Freeman (1975: 21) wanted "to identify, using generally accepted criteria of social science research quality, the conditions under which high- and low-quality evaluation investigations occur." Hence, they retrieved information about 1,000 federally funded evaluations for fiscal year 1970 that were ongoing, had budgets in excess of $10,000, and were targeted at problems in health, education, welfare, manpower, income security, housing, or public safety. Two judges read abstracts of the studies or the original research proposals, and from these it was determined that 416 of the studies met preordained criteria of "evaluation research." Questionnaires were then mailed to the project directors of each evaluation, and 318 were returned. Of these, 82 were omitted from further consideration because the project directors did not characterize their studies as evaluations. This meant that Bernstein and Freeman's basic data came from 236 evaluations, each of which was rated by personnel doing the evaluation while the study was still under way.

Bernstein and Freeman used the questionnaire returns to determine how well each evaluation met their criteria for a "comprehensive" evaluation. The latter was defined as a study in which appropriate techniques were used to assess whether an intervention had been implemented as planned (the process component), and had produced its intended outcomes (the impact component). Process was defined and rated in terms of sampling, the nature of the data, and statistical procedures. Impact was defined and rated with reference to design, sampling, and measurement. Indexes were constructed for each of these six dimensions, and each was given equal weight in computing a global index of overall quality. Bernstein and Freeman concluded that about two-thirds of the evaluations were "comprehensive" in that they assessed both "process" and "impact," but only about 13% of the total sample of 236 evaluations were "adequate" in that they had "high" ratings on each of the six scales.

Several points must be borne in mind about this last conclusion. First, it might have been even more pessimistic if experts had independently rated completed evaluations instead of having each project director rate his own evaluation while it was still in the field. Second,

Bernstein and Freeman gave low ratings to evaluations that dealt only with process or impact questions, even though such studies may well have met the limited goals set for them. Third, the authors themselves point out that they had to make somewhat arbitrary decisions about how to measure research quality, and the reader of their report may well wonder why only six methodological ratings were made. On what basis were the six criteria chosen? Why were the indexes equally weighted in creating the composite index of quality? How relevant to decision-making are the ratings of "high" on any of the six indexes? Modifying Bernstein and Freeman's assumptions might have significantly altered the pessimistic conclusion that the authors drew from their low ratings.

MINNESOTA SYSTEMS RESEARCH, INC., STUDY (MSRI)

The study by McTavish et al. (Minnesota Systems Research, Inc., 1976) differed from Bernstein and Freeman's in that *final* reports were rated on *more* attributes by *independent, trained* raters, about half of whom held social science doctorates and the remainder of whom were social science graduate students at a respected state university. The first stage in the study was to use the files of seven Health, Education, and Welfare (HEW) agencies to extract all the pertinent information about 110 well-documented projects that had been completed in 1973 and 1974. Since the focus of the study was on HEW research in general —rather than on evaluations in particular—not all of the studies were evaluations. Indeed, at a later date raters classified only about 45% of the projects as evaluations and the remainder as basic research, or as applied research with no specific evaluation component. The 110 projects were not randomly chosen in that the agencies volunteered studies for examination. The authors asserted, however, that this did not result in a sample biased toward projects of higher quality.

The next stage after sampling was to rate each proposal and final report on nearly 200 attributes, including 18 threats to internal and external validity developed from Campbell and Stanley (1966). The ratings of the Campbell and Stanley items suggest that less than 10% of the projects were free of "competing explanations likely to account for or 'explain away' significant parts of the research findings" (MSRI, 1976: 24). The problem with this estimate is that *we do not know what the raters mean by "significant."* Nonetheless, even if the 10% figure is an understatement of the "true" figure by a very large amount, it is still disconcerting. It is all the more so when we consider, first, that some tables in the report indicate that methodological quality was lower for evaluations than for other types of research; and, second, that some agencies may have volunteered their methodologically superior studies for review.

RUSSELL SAGE FOUNDATION SERIES, "CONTINUITIES IN EVALUATION RESEARCH"

In 1971, the Russell Sage Foundation began a project aimed at evaluating important evaluations. The general purpose was to assess, in part by means of data reanalysis, the quality of three primary evaluations, each of which had been conducted by a well-known organization and had been relatively well funded. The three works that the foundation commissioned deviated from the original plan to varying degrees, though each permits some assessment of the quality of the primary evaluations.

In the first study, Cook et al. (1975) took the original "Sesame Street" evaluations (Ball and Bogatz, 1970; Bogatz and Ball, 1971) and tried to use them as a major part of the data base for evaluating "Sesame Street" from scratch. The major question addressed by the original research and reanalyzed by Cook et al. was: How were children affected when they and their parents were visited each week or month in their homes by members of the research staff who encouraged the children to view the show, and left behind promotional games, books, and toys? Both the primary and secondary analysts concluded that encouragement from paid professionals increased both viewing and learning. Cook et al. also suggested that it was important to learn how viewing "Sesame Street" influenced learning when there was no explicit encouragement. Hence, they tried to dissociate viewing from encouragement effects, and found that viewing had a smaller and less generalized impact than did the combined impact of encouragement and viewing. Finally, Cook et al. examined whether "Sesame Street" affected the gap that separates the achievement levels of children from educationally more and less advantaged homes. Although the original evaluators had concluded that the show was narrowing achievement gaps, the metaevaluators' analyses suggested that "Sesame Street" may be widening gaps to a small extent in the cognitive areas where it enhances achievement. Thus, the metaevaluators concluded that the original evaluations were technically adequate for answering the evaluators' major research question, but were less exemplary for answering questions about gaps or how viewing affects learning in the absence of encouragement.

In the second study, Rossi and Lyall (1976) examined the published reports on the New Jersey Negative Income Tax Experiment and, though they found the reports to be adequate given the state of the art when the project began, they were nonetheless critical of the final report. Their major criticisms included: (a) A guaranteed income would be implemented as *national* policy and would affect all the eligible persons in a particular neighborhood. The experiment, though, was restricted to New Jersey and neighboring Scranton, Pennsylvania, and so does not permit extrapolating either to the nation at large or to communities where it is widely known that everyone has a guaranteed income. (b) A "regression" strategy was used in the primary analyses, and this required extrapolating from experimental groups with large samples and lower payment guarantees to groups with smaller samples and higher financial guarantees. Unfortunately, the groups with the smaller samples, and hence the least precise estimates of treatment effect, were the groups of greatest policy relevance. (c) Policy weights were assigned to the cells in the design by James Tobin, who adjudicated between parties with differing viewpoints. Rossi and Lyall wondered whether other individuals, or the representatives of interested constituencies, would have assigned the same weights as Tobin, or would even have asked the same research questions. Indeed, when she checked with member of the House Ways and Means Committee and the Senate Finance Committee, Boeckmann (1976) found that the members were at least as interested in how the money was spent (Did the poor buy Cadillacs?) as in the major research question of whether the guaranteed income decreases work motivation. (d) The New Jersey welfare eligibility requirements changed during the experiment so that few of the experimental treatments remained more generous than the regular welfare. This led Rossi and Lyall to wonder to what extent the original study was "experimental" in the sense of exploring alternatives that might one day enter "policy space," as opposed to being overly cautious and restricted to a narrow conception of "policy space."

The third study reviewed, the Performance Contracting Experiment (Ray, 1972), had been designed to see if student achievement would increase when profit-oriented contractors took over teaching and were paid according to the learning gains made by the classes they taught.

The metaevaluators, Levin and Snow (1976), were highly critical of the way that performance contracting was evaluated, particularly because the original evaluators had assessed effects for each grade level within each school and then had counted the number of positive and negative findings. Because the number of each was similar, the primary evaluators concluded that performance contracting made no noticeable difference. Levin and Snow wondered whether this procedure might have obscured real treatment effects that would have emerged in more detailed analyses of each of the 18 performance contractors' work in particular grade levels at particular schools. The metaevaluators also questioned whether the simple regression analyses computed by the original evaluators adequately controlled for all the pretest differences in achievement between the nonequivalent experimental and control groups. Consequently, they reanalyzed the data adjusting for unreliability in the pretest measurement. Also, Levin and Snow questioned the absence of analyses of achievement in the no-treatment control classes, since the control teachers knew of the experiment and may have believed that their jobs, or at least their profession, would be at risk if the "traditional" classes were outperformed by experimental classes in which regular teachers played little or no role. Levin and Snow were also concerned by the low quality with which the experimental treatments were documented. Because the treatments were introduced in great haste into the day-to-day hurly-burly of low-achieving schools, it seems reasonable to ask in which ways the treatments that were actually delivered differed from what was planned. Finally, Levin and Snow asked whether the evaluation had been directed at the most important policy questions about performance contracting. They suggested that the evaluators should have elicited definitions of the most pressing research questions from a wider range of interested constituencies, i.e., from local educational agencies, parents, teachers, and students, as well as from federal and state officials.

The Russell Sage series is not concerned with evaluating a representative sample of evaluations, and so any conclusions that emerge from it are restricted in generality. Moreover, there is room for honest disagreement about the importance of individual criticisms, and it is unrealistic to expect a single field experiment to provide adequate answers to *all* the relevant evaluation questions. But when all is said and done, two conclusions emerge from the Russell Sage series. First, both Cook et al. (1975) and Rossi and Lyall (1976) were impressed with the technical quality of the research in the (relatively well-funded) projects they reanalyzed, though their enthusiasm was limited to the quality of attempts to answer only the leading research question posed by the original evaluators. And second, in all three cases doubts were expressed about whether sufficient effort had been put into assessing the importance of the guiding evaluation questions. Indeed, each report suggested that the original evaluation would have been improved if wider checks had been made initially with interested constituencies to see what they would have posed as the major operational research questions. Howard and Krause (1976) and Messick (1975) have also suggested the advisability of eliciting evaluation questions from a number of interested constituencies.

BROOKINGS INSTITUTION STUDIES IN SOCIAL EXPERIMENTATION

One imperfect sign that metaevaluation might be needed is when the quality of primary evaluations is felt, *by independent sources,* to warrant reassessment. Of the three studies to date in the Brookings Institution's series on social experimentation, two deal with the same programs reassessed in the Russell Sage series—the New Jersey Income Tax Experiment (Pechman and Timpane, 1975) and the Performance Contracting Experiment (Gramlich and Koshel, 1975). The third study deals with the Head Start Planned Variation and Follow-Through experiments in compensatory education (Rivlin and Timpane, 1975). Despite interesting differences between the Brookings and Russell Sage reevaluations, there is considerable overlap in the less-than-comforting conclusions, and so we shall not explore the Brookings studies any further.

It is worth noting, though, that the Brookings Institution *Bulletin* of 1975 contains some general conclusions about the future of social experimentation that were drawn from the metaevaluation efforts conducted by the institution. The *Bulletin* article clearly indicated the authors' belief that recent social experiments have not fulfilled the goal of providing valid, credible, and timely information that has helped in decision-making. In the *Bulletin's* words, these experiments have "conveyed important messages to experimenters if not always to policymakers." However, this pessimism about current results is mitigated by optimism about potential, for the authors "find the long-term prospects for social experimentation undimmed."

SOME PERSPECTIVES ON THE TECHNICAL
QUALITY OF CURRENT EVALUATIONS

Pessimistic conclusions about the general methodological adequacy of evaluations can be derived from sources less systematic than the four metaevaluation projects we have just reviewed. Indeed, Bernstein and Freeman (1975) cite a variety of such sources (Rossi and Williams, 1972; Stromsdorfer, 1972; Wholey et al., 1970; and Wilkins, 1969). In addition, pessimistic talk can regularly be heard at discussions where practicing evaluators or evaluation methodologists are present. This pessimism has to be seen in perspective. Most persons knowledgeable about empirical summative evaluations can cite some exceptional studies in which the guiding research questions were well posed and the technicalities well handled. They can also cite some studies that were technically adequate and where honest dispute is possible about the appropriateness of the guiding research questions. And they can probably also cite studies where some questions were not dealt with so well but others were handled adequately and provide payoff about at least a subset of the questions originally asked.

We should also not forget that the quality criteria set up by past metaevaluators were rigorous, and that it is legitimate to wonder how many evaluations could realistically be expected to live up to the strict standards set. More importantly, we should ask how many of the evaluations needed to live up to such standards in order to meet their research goals, for some studies may support causal inferences that most judges would rate as "plausible" even though not "definitive." Unfortunately, we are not in a good position to decide whether the standards of past metaevalutors were too high and academic.

Most of the reanalyzed evaluations were conducted prior to 1974, and technical quality may have improved since then. But irrespective of whether it has or has not, we should not forget that systematic evaluation research is new and is only now learning its mistakes and limitations. Given this, some persons might believe that evaluating evaluations by the strictest technical standards is tantamount to treating a *developing* science as though it were already a *developed* science with a large stock of accumulated wisdom. Since evaluation researchers caution each other not to evaluate new projects as though they were stable, it would hardly be logical to evaluate the developing art of evaluation in a summative fashion which implied that it was highly developed.

Another point about the pessimistic conclusions of past meta-evaluators needs making. Most metaevaluators experience pressures that predispose them *not* to corroborate the conclusions of individual primary evaluators and *not* to comment favorably on the general state of evaluation research. These pressures result because metaevaluators have little to gain professionally by confirming the conventional wisdom or by agreeing with others, and they stand to gain much more by reaching surprising or critical conclusions. Indeed, if we can be somewhat psychological about this, surprising or critical conclusions may be the only ones that help metaevaluators justify to themselves the time they have spent on their project. But even if a need to stand out or gain professional visibility may have made past metaevaluations excessively critical, this still would not justify disregarding all the criticisms of the metaevaluators. It does not follow that because a criticism is exaggerated, it is inappropriate.

It should not be forgotten that the evidence which suggests the low technical quality of evaluations is itself far from technically adequate. By their very nature and timing, series like those of the Russell Sage Foundation and the Brookings Institution deal with a restricted universe of evaluations. While the ratings studies of Bernstein and Freeman and MSRI have broader sampling frames, they are totally dependent on rating scales whose numerical values have some obvious social significance, whose items are manifestly relevant to the study being evaluated, and which can be reliably used by persons with experience in evaluation research and social science methods. Their dependence holds in varying degrees for all rating scales, including those used by Bourque and Freeman (1977) for evaluating evaluations pertinent to children and the schemes developed by Robert Boruch for the General Accounting Office, by Kappa Systems, Inc. for the National Science Foundation, and by Leonard Rutman for the Bureau of the Auditor General in Canada. Given the intrinsic limitations to meta-evaluations that use either an intensive case study or a numerical rating approach, it would be naive to claim with any certainty from the present evidence that most evaluations fall short of what the state of the art permits. Yet it would be unwise to overlook the strong suggestion to this effect in the available data. This is because better and better means of evaluating evaluations are now being developed and should it later become clear that most evaluations are indeed below standard, then we may not learn this until the means no longer exist to improve the average quality of empirical summative evaluations. We believe, therefore, that the metaevaluation studies we have just reviewed, while not definitive, do at least justify the suspicion that the technical quality of most evaluations leaves something to be desired and that this suspicion by itself warrants attempts to improve the quality of evaluation research efforts.

REASONS FOR APPARENT LOW QUALITY OF EVALUATIONS

Having documented the apparent low quality of many past evaluations and the perspective in which this might be viewed, we want now to use past metaevaluation research to ask why the quality of past empirical summative evaluations appears to be low. The question is important, for diagnosing the major weaknesses of current evaluations should help identify some of the obstacles to high-quality work that can be overcome with means already at our disposal—including the metaevaluation strategies we shall outline shortly. The major reasons for low quality follow:

(1) In deciding on research questions, evaluators and their sponsors rarely consult formal decision makers, let alone a wide range of interested constituencies. Instead, general program goals are outlined that are either operationally vague or of limited importance to many potential users.

(2) It is still the case today that empirical summative evaluations are conducted by the research staff of the program being evaluated, while other evaluations are monitored by the same office that provided funds for the program development. Neither of these arrangements is satisfactory, because the evaluation sponsors have a vested interest in the results (Scriven, 1975).

(3) Most evaluation research is conducted by profit-making, or not-for-profit, contract research agencies that are supposed to be more efficient than the available alternatives and to have fewer hidden agendas (i.e., publishing in disciplinary journals, teaching, or serving in professional organizations). According to Bernstein and Freeman (1975), contract research agencies are rewarded for writing and winning contracts, and not for doing work that is at the level of the state of the art. Also, few mechanisms exist for punishing firms when the quality of their work falls below that of the state of the art.

(4) Many program and project administrators know that evaluations usually reach negative conclusions about impact. But whether they do or do not know this, they all seem to resent the additional tasks

and complexities that can arise in cooperating with an evaluation. It is not surprising, therefore, that many administrators do not want to provide the level of cooperation that is necessary for a high-quality evaluation.

(5) Inadequate reviews of evaluation research proposals mean that much research goes into the field with less than adequate sampling, design, and measurement. For instance, MSRI (Minnesota Systems Research, Inc., 1976) found that 90% of the funded projects had at least one "significant" validity threat *at the proposal stage*. Moreover, it is questionable whether enough initial thought is put into anticipating problems that might arise in the field and into developing practical means whereby these problems can be detected at a date early enough so that realistic fallback positions can be adopted.

(6) Whatever the level of initial planning, unforeseen problems will arise and threaten the methodological integrity of the research. Therefore, a monitoring system is required to detect problems early so that constructive responses can be made promptly.

(7) Deadline pressures, which are endemic to evaluation research, hinder careful planning and checking at all stages of the research. Proposals are often required just weeks after an RFP is published, and sometimes only a few weeks intervene between awarding a contract and collecting the first wave of data. Things rarely improve after a start like this!

(8) It is difficult to maintain the planned experimental contrasts. This can be because the program changes during the evaluation, because clients are free to choose how much of the treatment they want to receive, and because control group members often receive some of the treatment that they were not supposed to get.

MODELS OF METAEVALUATION RESEARCH

What can be done to improve the technical quality and relevance of evaluation research, particularly with respect to the eight problems outlined above? In answering this question we must acknowledge that little can be done to overcome state-of-the-art problems other than to urge evaluators to keep abreast of latest developments in research methodology and substantive theory. The seven metaevaluation models we shall discuss should help alleviate some of the problems, but they are not by any means universal palliatives.

TABLE 1
Models of Metaevaluation

Subsequent to primary evaluation	Data not manipulated	Single data set	1. Essay review of an evaluation report.
		Multiple data sets	2. Review of the literature about a specific program
	Data manipulated	Single data set	3. Empirical reevaluation of an evaluation or program
		Multiple data sets	4. Empirical reevaluation of multiple data sets about the same program
Simultaneous with primary evaluation	Data not manipulated	Single or Multiple data sets	5. Consultant metaevaluation
	Data manipulated	Single data set	6. Simultaneous secondary analysis of raw data
		Multiple data sets	7. Multiple independent replications

Table 1 illustrates the metaevaluation models that we generated from an analogy with a three-factor analysis of variance. One factor is whether the metaevaluation takes place simultaneously with the primary evaluation or after it; the second describes whether the primary evaluation data are or are not manipulated by the metaevaluator; and the third refers to the number of independent data sets that can be used to evaluate a particular program. (For convenience only, we have illustrated this last factor as having only two levels, but many others are obviously possible.)

This three-factor framework stresses some of the more important attributes of useful evaluation. For instance, the distinction between simultaneous and consecutive metaevaluations highlights timeliness, with simultaneous studies being preferable to consecutive ones. The distinction between metaevaluation with and without data manipulation stresses the enhanced validity and credibility that can result from the sophisticated manipulation of raw data by independent analysts. And the distinction between one and many data sets stresses the gains in credibility, validity, and range of questions that can be answered if there is a convergence of results across multiple (and, we would hope, independent) data sets that evaluate the same program.

Table 1 provides labels for characterizing the metaevaluation models. The *essay review of an evaluation report* refers to after-the-fact commentary on a single set of evaluation data that are not re-analyzed. The *review of the literature about a specific program* refers to after-the-fact commentary on more than one set of data about a program. *Empirical reevaluation* refers to the manipulation of raw data about a program to assess the validity of the conclusions from a primary evaluation. When more than one evaluation data set about a program is manipulated for this same purpose, we have the *empirical reevaluation of multiple data sets about the same program.* Turning to simultaneous metaevaluation models, *consultant metaevaluation* refers to attempts to judge and improve an evaluation while it is under way by means of feedback from one or more consultants who continuously monitor the primary evaluation but do not themselves manipulate data. This label will also be used to refer to the monitoring of multiple evaluations of the same program, e.g., the Educational Testing Service's (ETS) community college and grade school evaluations of the computer-assisted instruction project called PLATO. A *simultaneous secondary analysis of raw data* refers to analysis of the evaluation data by persons other than the primary evaluators who do their work while the primary evaluators are still analyzing their data. Finally, *multiple independent replications* refers to the commissioning of more than one evaluator independently to design and implement a study of a particular program's impact.

These models are not necessarily independent. For instance, if multiple independent replications of a program produced disparate findings, an integrative literature review would be required to try to make sense of them. Likewise, it is easy to imagine a consultant meta-evaluator obtaining copies of raw data and reanalyzing them while the primary evaluator is also analyzing them. Like all typologies, ours is justified by convenience rather than necessity.

MODEL 1: ESSAY REVIEW OF AN EVALUATION REPORT

Though some essay reviews of evaluation appear in press, most are unpublished documents written by in-house staff members or outside consultants at interim stages before a final report is published. We shall deal first with published reviews of final documents, and then discuss unpublished reviews of proposals, interim reports, and preliminary drafts of final reports.

Published Reviews

In assessing an evaluation, reviewers usually concentrate on the utility of research questions and on technical issues of sampling, measurement, data analysis, and the like. Published agreement with the original evaluator's conclusion presumably adds credibility to the original findings, while disagreement presumably detracts from credibility. Given this, reviews are most useful when they break down the major conclusions one by one, and then separately focus on the totality of support for each conclusion. When such a procedure is followed, a review will rarely be uniformly positive or negative, for some conclusions of the primary evaluator will be endorsed, others questioned, and others ignored. However, it must be stressed that such a review will be useful to readers only if it deals with *all* the evidence for or against a proposed conclusion and not with a (possibly biased) subset of the evidence.

Reviews are also useful if, *without questioning the data,* they bring a fresh interpretation to bear. Pettigrew et al. (1973) did this, in part, when they noted that Armor (1972) was declaring busing a "failure" because his criterion for success was that integration should reduce racial gaps in achievement. Their own preference was to demonstrate that the absolute achievement levels of blacks had increased, irrespective of what happened to whites. Such "perspective-conferring" critiques are useful because they do not have to bewilder readers with complicated methodological criticisms, or immerse them in contentious disagreements between protagonists. Instead, the data and analyses are accepted as valid, and the issue is one of interpreting the findings.

Reviews are also helpful if they point out how specific weaknesses in the primary evaluation can be overcome with the data on hand. For instance, Thorndike (1968) claimed that the data that Rosenthal and Jacobson (1968) used to evaluate the impact of teacher expectancies were inadequately normed for first- and second-grade children, and these were the only children who showed statistically reliable teacher expectancy effects in parametric analyses. Thorndike then suggested that an analysis of raw scores would circumvent the problem, and Elashoff and Snow (1971) later performed such an analysis. However, the validity and credibility of Rosenthal and Jacobson's conclusions would have been enhanced if Thorndike's recommendation had been forwarded to the authors before their book appeared, thereby converting a consecutive metaevaluation into a simultaneous one. The widespread circulation of prepublication drafts of evaluations is obviously useful, and drafts should be sent both to persons with acknowledged technical and substantive skills, and to persons who are likely to be strongly opposed to a report's major conclusions. The feedback from these sources can help the evaluator modify a final report so that when it is published any public discussion will be focused on the implications of "results," and not dissipated on disagreements about trivia that could have been corrected before publication.

Essay reviews have sometimes been incorporated into final evaluation reports, presumably for the credibility they confer when they corroborate major conclusions and for the timeliness they have in contrast to post-hoc critiques. For instance, a cross-lagged panel correlational analysis (Lefkowitz et al., 1972) played a crucial role in the U.S. Surgeon General's report on television and violence, because it was the only field study with more than one wave of data and because its conclusions were consonant with the "suggestive" evidence from cross-sectional surveys and laboratory experiments. Kenny (1972) and Neale (1972) were asked to critique the cross-lagged study. Each corroborated its major conclusions and their comments were included in the final report. Consider what might have happened, though, if the external reviewers had disagreed with each other or with the conclusion of the longitudinal field study. Would such unfavorable reviews have been published? Would they have held up the final report? Would they have led to modifications of the executive summary? Were the reviewers told that their work would appear in the final report, regardless of their conclusions? Such questions are important, and evaluation reports that contain published reviews of the report should take pains to detail the procedures whereby reviewers were chosen as well as the guidelines they were given.

Either politeness or belief in the adversary model of evaluation has prompted some researchers to publish their evaluation findings together with commentary by parties who might disapprove of the findings. Campbell and Erlebacher (1970) did this by inviting Cicirelli (1970) and Evans and Schiller (1970) to comment on their criticism of the Office of Economic Opportunity's (OEO) evaluation of Head Start; and it was once planned to have the ETS evaluation of PLATO published together with commentary by the developers, for the developer's beliefs about educational effectiveness may be stronger than the evaluation findings would seem to warrant. In such cases, the work and the review form a single package, and if the analysts disagree, readers can judge for themselves which to believe.

The fear has sometimes been expressed that commentators with a vested interest in program outcomes might use the opportunity for rebuttal to discredit the evaluation in the eyes of less methodologically sophisticated readers, including journalists. The commentators presumably hope that if minor weaknesses are exposed, or if contrary appearing evidence is cited, then the whole of the evaluation and its findings will be called into question. In one case of which we are aware, a two-stage process is being followed to prevent such a strategy from being implemented. First, a draft of the final report will be submitted to the program developer, who will be told that his comments may be used by the evaluator to improve the final report. Second, the developer will be informed that his comments on the evaluator's *revised* draft will be incorporated into the final report if they are received within a month, and that his commentary will be followed by brief remarks from the original evaluators. The rationale behind these procedures is: (1) to bring to light objections by the program developers at an early date so that, in the normal course of modifying their final report, the evaluators can take account of the developer's reasonable objections; and (2) to give the developer time to generate a final response that would be all the more likely to be oriented toward validity rather than credibility because the developer would not have the last word. Whether or not this strategy is effective remains to be seen. In any case, it illustrates one method of trying to be fair to all parties without unduly delaying a final report.

Other advantages to published reviews could be discussed, such as putting the results into a policy or theoretical context. But when all is said and done, published reviews suffer from the fundamental weakness that the metaevaluator cannot reanalyze the data other than by rearranging values in published tables. Consequently, specific validity threats that escaped the attention of primary evaluators cannot be empirically examined in order to estimate their impact or to conduct analyses free of their impact. At most, reviewers can give their own estimates of how plausible particular threats are. These estimates will sometimes confuse readers about a program's impact, since their validity is unclear. Though such confusion is preferable to the mistaken feelings of enlightenment that evaluators and policy makers may have when the clear conclusions they have drawn from the research are wrong, it is nonetheless exasperating if one realizes that the confusion could have been avoided by conducting the review *before the field research was completed.* This means that reviews of proposals, interim reports, and first drafts of final reports are ultimately more important than reviews of published or otherwise completed work.

Pre-Publication Reviews

Though reviews of proposals, interim reports, and first drafts of final reports are all useful, our impression is that the first interim report is the most important. This is because the report is based on the design and measurement procedures that were actually implemented, as opposed to the procedures that were planned in the proposal. Many of the forces that limit the evaluator's range of operations in the field cannot be known at the proposal stage but become evident by the first interim report, which comes at a time when more corrective actions can be taken than with the first draft of a final report. We would like to see the first interim report play a markedly greater role than it does at present, both for diagnosing problems and for suggesting practical solutions to these problems.

To this end, the evaluation field staff should be encouraged to use a first preliminary report for giving a detailed and honest outline of all the problems they are meeting, particularly with respect to maintaining experimental contrasts, eliciting cooperation from project personnel, and implementing the sampling and measurement plans. Often, a first cut of the pretest data can be presented to assess the reliability of measures and the comparability of different experimental groups. And, depending on timing, preliminary unsystematic information about drop-out rates might be presented together with speculations about the reasons for attrition.

Detecting weaknesses and suggesting remedies require a high level of tact, methodological sophistication, interdisciplinary social science knowledge, and experience in conducting large-scale research in politicized contexts. Few agencies currently have monitoring staffs with backgrounds appropriate to these tasks, and academic consultants are needed to supplement in-house staffs. We suspect that the quality of reviews by academic consultants would be higher if reviewers were paid for a written product, if their involvement with the project were long-term, if they knew their reviews were to be shown to the primary evaluators, if their names were attached to reports, if they had to defend their position with literature citations or perhaps even in face-to-face meetings with evaluation and agency personnel, and if they knew that another reviewer with a different perspective was looking at the same materials. Agencies may not like some of the procedures above, especially identifying reviewers, and they may find only a subset of the procedures acceptable. This is fine, for we suspect that any of these procedures will separately contribute to making consultants more accountable than is currently the case.

Diagnostic reviews of the winning proposal will also help detect problems and suggest solutions. It does not seem, however, that reviews are currently being used for these purposes in all agencies because MSRI (1976) found that about 90% of the HEW projects that they rated in terms of Campbell and Stanley's (1966) list of validity threats were already inadequate at the proposal stage and there were no indications that the evaluations had improved as a result of being reviewed. Even if the 90% estimate is inaccurate by a wide margin, the implication is still that many agencies need to review their *funded* proposals more carefully. In this light, we wonder who the current reviewers are and what their mandate is. Do they seek merely to evaluate submitted proposals, or do they provide diagnostic feedback? If it is considered too costly for them to give diagnostic feedback on all proposals, is there any evidence that the winning proposal is subjected to an intensive external review before any data are collected? Such reviews could do more than provide contractors with advice and technical assistance concerning particular field problems which they should anticipate. It would also alert formal technical monitors to the questions they need to ask of the evaluation to see whether it is progressing smoothly. In this last respect, reviewers would be especially useful if they listed the anticipated problems, some solutions to each problem, and the criteria that would have to be met by a specific date in order to infer that a particular problem was not going to emerge or was solved. This is akin to setting short-term behavioral goals, and it is irrelevant whether reviewers or project monitors set the goals. It happens, however, that a reviewer-metaevaluator will be more likely to have the experience and expertise required for setting realistic goals focused around key moments in the evaluation.

MODEL 2: REVIEW OF THE LITERATURE ABOUT A SPECIFIC PROGRAM

Examples already exist of programs that have been multiply evaluated (e.g., the seven studies of "Sesame Street" or "Plaza Sésamo" in Cook and Conner, 1976; or the multiple studies of school desegregation in Armor, 1972; Pettigrew et al., 1973; or St. John, 1975). Examples also exist of multiply evaluated local projects with similar goals (e.g., Lipton et al., 1975, on prison rehabilitation; Fisher, 1973, on the effects of social case work; or the many separate evaluations of individual Head Start centers and community mental health centers). Examples also exist of reviews of studies designed to assess possible *future* policies (e.g., Zeisel and Diamond, 1974, reviewed the studies that compared six and twelve-person juries that the U.S. Supreme Court cited as providing "conclusive" evidence that jury size does not affect verdicts; and it will soon be possible to review at least six experiments on various forms of negative income tax). It seems, therefore, that in the future we shall see more inferences about program impact made on the basis of multiple evaluations.

Multiple evaluations permit more valid and credible research conclusions than does a single evaluation, especially when clear patterns of convergence are found between independent studies that used different versions of a treatment, different kinds of respondents, and different research settings. Such consistency of results has most significance when all of the important validity threats are ruled out in one or more of the studies, and it has least significance when biasing forces are presumed to operate in the same direction in all of the studies.

Though some instances of impressive consistency can be cited (e.g., the prison rehabilitation evaluations), it is our impression that inconsistency is more common. There are four major reasons for this. First, the evaluations available for review may constitute a biased sample. This is especially likely in evaluation research, where many final reports are never published and are only available from agency files to which access is not always easy (e.g., MSRI, 1976, found that about 10% of the final reports could not be found in the project file or only part of the report was present). Obtaining a comprehensive data base will not be possible until archiving is more widespread or is even made mandatory for some kinds of evaluation materials.

A second problem concerns which studies to exclude from the review on grounds of inadequate documentation or methodology. Here, tastes differ. For instance, Lipton et al. (1975) restricted their review to studies with no-treatment control groups, and we suspect many persons would not be so strict. Fisher (1973) went even further and restricted his review to studies with control groups where experimental contrasts were formed—either by random assignment or by matching. Few would be as selective as Fisher, we feel.

A third problem concerns the absence of explicit decision rules for pooling the results of relevant studies. Light and Smith (1971) have scathingly pointed to the most frequently used rule: the metaevaluator counts the positive, negative, and null findings and declares the modal category the winner. Jencks et al. (1972) advocated and used a different procedure, in which each reviewed study is weighted by its sample size. Other standards might also be invoked, such as weighting randomized experiments more than quasi-experiments, or longitudinal studies more than cross-sectional ones. Though it is easy to claim that the studies in a review should not have equal weighting, it is difficult to devise an acceptable decision rule for weighting each study differently. Our own position is that the reviewer should consider all studies meeting basic methodological standards as valid and should look for *a posteriori* hypotheses that fit the pattern of positive, negative, and null findings. This detective-like task will be all the easier if the reviewers ask: "What different kinds of effect do different kinds of projects have on different kinds of people?" and if they do not expect every single study to fit neatly into the interpretive framework they develop from the data.

A fourth problem concerns the difficulty of reconciling different findings across evaluations that appear to be similar. The key word here is "appears," for no evaluation is identical to another. Unless the unique features of each evaluation are documented and, in many cases, numerically estimated, no viable way exists for judging how much each source of uniqueness may have contributed to differences in outcome. However, when reasonable judgments can be made about sources of differences between studies, metaevaluators have the potential for assessing the contingency variables that moderate a treatment's impact. One can ask, for example, whether the treatment effect differs by socioeconomic status, by place of residence, by length of treatment implementation, or by a host of other variables that help specify the nature and range of an evaluation effect.

Let us make the above difficulties concrete by examining evaluations of the educational impact of "Sesame Street" on economically dis-advantaged children. The studies quickly sort themselves into two camps: those reporting large and generalized cognitive gains over six months in the United States (Ball and Bogatz, 1970; Bogatz and Ball, 1971), in Mexico (Diaz-Guerrero and Holtzman, 1974), and in Israel (Salomon, 1974) versus those reporting considerably smaller gains of restricted generality in the United States (Cook et al., 1975; Kenny, 1975; Minton, 1973, 1975) and in Mexico (Diaz-Guerrero et al., 1976). Examining the U.S. studies led Cook and Conner (1976) to conclude that the larger and more generalized gains were obtained in studies or analyses that confounded effects of viewing "Sesame Street" with effects of viewing the show in a context where paid professionals encouraged viewing. This same tentative conclusion was also reached by Diaz-Guerrero et al. (1976) when they tried to explain the dis-crepancy between the optimistic results of their first, small-scale evalu-ation and the more pessimistic results of their second, large-scale study.

This conclusion does not easily account for Salomon's (1974) finding that large cognitive gains seem to have been obtained in a context that may have been devoid of obvious adult encouragement. Salomon's study was different from the others in that: (a) it was not experimental, and (b) it used a more socially heterogeneous group of children. His analysis involved correlating viewing of "Sesame Street" with learning gains after the contribution of pretest scores and some background characteristics had been partialed out. Lord (1960) has shown how such partialing strategies depend on the reliability of the variable used as the covariate, and it is not clear whether all the preexisting differences between viewers were adjusted away by Salomon's analysis. Note, in this regard, that his sample of children was socially heterogeneous, a fact that could easily have exacerbated the correlation between pretest scores and spontaneous viewing. This, in turn, could have created larger pretest differences and a lower likelihood of partialing out all of the pretest bias. The pertinent problem is whether Salomon's sample should be included in the sample to be reviewed. If so, should it be mentioned, criticized, and then discussed? Or what else could be done with it?

The Salomon study notwithstanding, a review of "Sesame Street" evaluations clearly suggests (but does not "prove") that six months' viewing has little effect on the learning gains of economically disadvantaged preschoolers, except when the viewing is supplemented by some form of loosely specified encouragement by adults. Such a contingent conclusion is extremely useful and, though it could have been drawn from the data in the tables in the very first evaluation, it was only the discrepancy between the findings of different evaluations that made salient the need for a contingency explanation. Fortunately, in the "Sesame Street" case it was possible to test contingency explanations *within* individual data sets (Ball and Bogatz, 1970) and also by comparing related studies by the same investigators (the Mexican studies). Such close comparisons are not always possible, and less confident conclusions about contingency relationships inevitably emerge when unrelated studies are used for developing hypotheses about contingency variables.

A review of multiple evaluations often comes only after a program has become politically impacted or has lost its support, thereby restricting its usefulness. Such lateness does not mean that all reviews are without influence, for Lipton et al.'s (1975) review of the prison rehabilitation evaluations seems to have influenced policy in the corrections field. However, lateness does reduce influence, and for this reason we shall later discuss models that permit the advantages of replication without the disadvantages of tardiness.

"Reviewing the literature" is a task at which academics are well experienced, and it does not require the managerial expertise that many academics are said to lack. Moreover, reviews are more theory-relevant than most other aspects of evaluation research, with formal theory guiding both the way review questions are asked and how patterns of positive, negative, and null results are interpreted. Reviews can also probe and extend theories, which is why reviewing evaluation studies may be attractive to some discipline-oriented social scientists. Consider the literature on how school integration does or does not affect academic achievement and racial prejudice. After reading this, no social psychologist can sanguinely accept a simple version of the contact hypothesis (Amir, 1969). Similarly, after reading about the negative income tax experiments, no organizational psychologist or labor economist can sanguinely believe that financial incentives play a simple role in seeking work. This is not to say that reviews of evaluations provide strong tests of theoretical propositions. Rather, they are more likely to shed light on the real-world importance of particular propositions and to point to blind alleys that are not worth further exploration. But note that reviews can also be used at an earlier date to identify blind alleys. For instance, we knew before school integration began that putting persons of different backgrounds into daily social contact sometimes reduces prejudice and sometimes escalates it. Moreover, we knew some of the contingency conditions that lead to each consequence. Yet, little heed seems to have been paid at the policy formulation stage to the voluminous evidence on the contact hypothesis which Allport (1954) had already reviewed. To be sure, not all of the studies he reviewed involved children, busing, or even school settings. Nonetheless, enough multiply replicated findings were available to suggest that school integration would not inevitably lead to reduced prejudice and increased academic learning. This point argues even more forcibly for reviews, since one generation's retrospective review may be another's prospective guide.

MODEL 3: EMPIRICAL REEVALUATION OF A PROGRAM EVALUATION

The best-known metaevaluation model is the reanalysis of another's data to test the published conclusions or to examine new questions. Examples of this include Elashoff and Snow (1971) on teacher expectancies; Mosteller and Moynihan (1972) on the Coleman Report (Coleman et al., 1966); Pettigrew et al. (1973) on Armor's (1972) work on busing; and Wortman and St. Pierre (forthcoming) on the Alum Rock Educational Voucher Experiment.

This model can have all the previously noted strengths of the review of an evaluation report. In addition, validity and credibility can be further enhanced because the raw data are available. For instance: (a) flaws in the original analysis can be corrected, as when Smith (1972) used the index of home socioeconomic status that Coleman et al. (1966) had intended to use but had inadvertently not used; (b) assumptions can be checked, as when Elashoff and Snow (1971) examined Rosenthal and Jacobson's (1968) distributions, found high tails, and so truncated them for some analyses; (c) tests of the social (as opposed to statistical) significance can be conducted, as when effect sizes are estimated and related to needs; (d) the data can be broken down for finer subgroup analyses, as when Smith and Bissell (1970) analyzed full-year Head

Start centers, omitting data from summer centers where less of an impact would be expected; and (e) more appropriate statistical tests can be conducted, as when Wortman and St. Pierre (forthcoming) used reliability-adjusted covariance analysis and standardized change score analysis to equate nonequivalent groups, thereby not relying on simple covariance analysis.

Many empirical metaevaluations do not seek to answer only the questions posed by the primary evaluators. For instance, Jencks et al. (1972) used secondary sources to answer questions of their own choosing that were of little interest to some of the primary analysts, and Cook et al. (1975) asked whether viewing "Sesame Street" without encouragement caused learning gains, though the original evaluators had asked about effects of encouragement. We strongly suspect that answers to new questions will be less definitive than are answers to the questions posed by primary evaluators. The reason for this are obvious, and they imply that a metaevalutor who seeks to answer novel questions has a special need of multiple data sets evaluating a program. It is also desirable with novel questions to have the data analyzed by persons with different perspectives on substance and methodology. This may have been why Mosteller and Moynihan (1972) invited analysts from sociology, social psychology, economics, and education to rework the data in the Coleman Report (Coleman et al., 1966).

The drawbacks of empirical reanalysis have to be noted. First—and perhaps most important of all—though reanalysis of the kind we are discussing can enhance both validity and credibility, this is inevitably at the expense of timeliness. Second, reanalysis can sometimes lead to misleading results, especially if subgroup analyses are conducted on special samples. For instance, Hanushek and Kain (1972) took the Coleman Report data on Negro twelfth-graders in the North and established that the school input factor was associated with more achievement variance than was the peer factor. This result was at odds both with the major Coleman Report finding and with the finding of the other secondary analysts. One possible reason for this is that Hanushek and Kain may have capitalized upon chance by selecting a particularly dramatic sample. (A footnote points out that indeed the sample was chosen because the findings were startling.) And a second reason may be definitional, for unlike the other investigators, Hanushek and Kain defined school inputs as school resources *plus* teacher variables.

A third difficulty with empirical reanalysis arises if the secondary evaluator can identify threats to valid inference but is not able to estimate their impact without additional data. Sometimes, the data can be located in an archive, as happened when Cook et al. (1975) looked to viewing surveys to establish the size and social composition of the "Sesame Street" audience. But at other times the data will not be available or will not come in a form that the secondary analyst would choose if he were designing the evaluation from scratch. This means that some questions cannot be answered without the costly collection of additional data.

A prior problem may exist in obtaining a copy of the raw data. Primary analysts differ considerably in their willingness to release raw data. Many are reluctant to do so because they cannot retrieve their data; they want to avoid "misuses"; they are concerned that flaws in their work will be publicized; they anticipate that making a data tape and providing documentation will be unduly time-consuming; and they believe that they have special rights to the data they have gathered. Obtaining data requires openness, tact, perseverance, a knowledge of legal rights, and acquaintance with the codes of ethics of various professional bodies. Sometimes, only a formal contract will give primary evaluators the security they seek (Freeman, 1975), though a contract could turn out to be restrictive if analysis of the data opens up issues that were not considered when the contract was designed. In this area, evaluation research has much to learn from survey research, where survey tapes and supporting documentation are routinely archived at the Roper Center at Williams College or at the Inter-University Consortium for Political and Social Research. Think how much easier it would be if the demand for reanalysis justified research contracts which require that tapes and documents be deposited in user-oriented archives when a final report is handed in.[1]

MODEL 4: EMPIRICAL REEVALUATION OF MULTIPLE DATA SETS ABOUT THE SAME PROGRAM

There are now multiple independent evaluations of some programs, e.g., school integration, "Sesame Street," and Job Corps. And there will soon be multiple evaluations of other important innovations, such as a guaranteed income. We would expect the multiple reevaluation model to have all the strengths of the model where a single data set is manipulated. These include detecting errors, conducting new statistical tests, asking new questions, and the like. Multiple reanalysis can have other advantages as well. First, if each exemplar of the program takes place at a different time, or at a different set of sites, or reflects different initial value assumptions, then important information about replicability can be gained. Second, hypotheses can be generated and tested about the conditions that mediate effects—tests that are especially required if the various evaluations produce different outcomes. Third, tests of a program's impact may be possible in which core constructs are operationalized in somewhat different ways by different investigators. And finally, multiple evaluations will usually entail measurement of more outcome constructs than a single evaluation would permit, thereby giving a more comprehensive picture of a program's planned and unplanned impact. All these advantages affect validity. Yet if the results replicate across most of the evaluations, or if the pattern of differences is clear and simple, credibility will probably be enhanced too.

The empirical reanalysis of multiple data sets shares some of the weaknesses associated with the empirical reevaluation of a single data set. Lack of timeliness is one; the inability to collect new data to answer new questions is another; and a third is possible uncertainty about outcomes if there are no obvious explanations for different cause-effect relationships observed in different studies. However, the multiple data set model has unique weaknesses. Because a biased sample of evaluations might prejudice the metaevaluation before reanalysis has begun, we need to know whether the metaevaluator has access to all the relevant evaluations. To help assure such access, the metaevaluator can check with knowledgeable others, particularly parties who are strongly in favor of, or opposed to, the program being evaluated. Also, the analyst must be explicit about the methodological criteria used for excluding some studies—criteria that need to be checked with others. Finally, the metaevaluator has to request all the available documentation from primary evaluators and program personnel because it may prove vital in solving any puzzle that arises if different evaluations of the same program produce different results.

When there is no obvious way of reconciling different-appearing results, further research is obviously called for. The issue is, how should this research be conducted? One inexpensive alternative is to conduct small-scale, short-term, controlled experiments that have more of a formative than summative character. The aim of these is to test a variety of interactive conditions that might mediate the different effects found in different evaluations. While it would not be logical to use the results of such experiments to "explain" the difference in results of past evaluations, the explanatory leap would be smaller after such studies than if they had not been conducted. And, as previously mentioned, the search for contingency-specifying interactions moves the empirical reanalysis of multiple evaluations into an area that is close to the building and testing of middle-level theories about differential impact.

Let us expand upon this last point, for many academicians would find the reanalysis of multiple data sets more congenial if they saw its relevance to social science theory. Consider the many negative income tax experiments that we shall soon have. The first was designed to test the work-leisure trade-off problem of classical economics, but subsequent studies were designed to test how supplementary factors or different populations might affect the relationship between income, work, leisure, and consumption patterns. Thus, the evaluation findings may suggest new directions in which the theory of work-leisure trade-offs could be extended to account for contingencies that specify different forms of the basic relationship. It must be pointed out that the income guarantee experiments differ from each other in many ways, and theoretical propositions will usually be indirectly probed rather than directly tested at the most crucial point. Nonetheless, such probing is important and may indicate theoretical avenues that are worth further exploring, particularly those associated with large effects. Consider, for example, what it would mean for the contact hypothesis if there were large effects on prejudice of school desegregation in a small subset of schools (perhaps those with different racial groups *that had similar social statuses),* but there were no effects, or opposite effects, in a larger subset of schools (where the groups had different statuses).

Because of the practical and theoretical gains promised by reanalyzing multiple data sets about a single program, we are surprised that there are not more seminars set up to examine the relevant data. For instance, we know of no efforts to gather and reanalyze the data from all the negative income tax experiments, even though the experiments are likely to produce a considerable yield for anyone interested in the social, psychological, and economic determinants of labor force participation and consumption patterns. To be sure, there have been seminars to reanalyze evaluations. One need only think of the interdisciplinary Harvard group that reexamined the Coleman Report (Mosteller and Moynihan, 1972), or Glass's (1976) work on the effects of different forms of psychotherapy. But neither of these projects seems to have been characterized both by interdisciplinary involvement *and* by relevant multiple data sets, and neither was set up to take the most timely advantage of the original data sources. (The gap between publication of the Coleman Report and its reanalysis was about five years; the gap between publication of the psychotherapy evaluations and Glass's work was up to 20 years for some studies.) The need is to foresee where reanalysis of multiple data sets will be useful, and to begin the task as soon as the first data sets are available.

MODEL 5: CONSULTANT METAEVALUATION

None of the previous models involves metaevaluation that occurs simultaneously with a primary evaluation, though procedures were sometimes specified for turning after-the-fact metaevaluations into simultaneous ones. The remaining models all deal with metaevaluation efforts during a primary evaluation. We shall pay more attention to these simultaneous efforts because they promise a more timely final product.

One model of simultaneous metaevaluation can be characterized as consultant metaevaluation. This model needs to be distinguished from both consulting and technical project monitoring. Consultants are often used when their expertise is needed, and since different kinds of expertise are needed at different times, there is usually a restricted continuity over time in who evaluates an evaluation. Another characteristic of consultants is that they are rarely accountable for the advice they give, whether correct or incorrect, inasfar as their names are seldom linked to particular research decisions. Also, consultants are most used either after a serious problem has emerged or when a periodic review is scheduled, neither of which is particularly conducive to detecting problems *as they occur* or to suggesting specific corrective actions while a problem is still of manageable proportions. In distinction to the modal consulting relationship described above, consultant metaevaluation is characterized by a continuous involvement with an evaluation, by a willingness to accept public responsibility for decisions, and by a mandate to detect problems as soon as they occur and to suggest practical ways of solving them. Also, consultant metaevaluators typically have greater authority than do individual consultants.

There is little difference, in principle, between the activities of consultant metaevaluators and the activities that technical project monitors are supposed to carry out. However, there is a practical difference because metaevaluators almost invariably have greater technical expertise than do monitors. In addition, metaevaluators have more time to devote to a single evaluation, and they experience less difficulty in having their advice considered and accepted by principal investigators. This is because few monitors currently have a professional status or a fund of technical knowledge that inspires respect from principal investigators, while consultant metaevaluators do. Finally, most monitors will want—deliberately or inadvertently—to further their agency's operating interest. Although consultant metaevaluators are mindful of this interest, they should want to assess program impact irrespective of whether the results favor the agency's short-term interest.

The foregoing considerations suggest that many consultant evaluators will be from academe. We suspect that metaevaluation offers few incentives to persons who need to publish fast for career purposes, or to persons whose major reference groups are in traditional social science disciplines. However, the incentives are greater for persons in professional schools or applied research programs because their colleagues value relationships with agencies that permit applying professional skills. Thus, educators, health science personnel, social scientists in law schools, and empirically oriented social workers would probably be most interested in acting as consultant metaevaluators.

Consultant metaevaluations have already occurred. For instance, Glass, Scriven, and Stake once began playing this role for a Systems Development Corporation evaluation of the ESAA Title VII evaluation, and one of the present authors (Cook) has played it as a member of a team that was asked by the National Center for Health Services Research to monitor its evaluation of day-care centers and homemaker services for the elderly. He also has played it on a formal contractual basis with respect to the ETS evaluations of the computer-assisted instruction projects called PLATO and TICCIT, and he was asked by the Peace Corps to monitor and assist a contract research company in developing a system for evaluating the Peace Corps. In each case, the simultaneous metaevaluation has been conducted by small interdisciplinary teams of persons whose primary affiliation is with academic institutions. The presumption is that universities have the high-level technical skill and experience that are required, and that consultant metaevaluation does not strain the resources or violate the purpose of a university (as conducting the entire evaluation might).

To stay on top of an evaluation as it shifts from phase to phase requires both a considerable expenditure of time and also the availability of a range of different technical talents. This suggests that consultant metaevaluation is best done by small teams of persons with different expertises and different perspectives on evaluation, rather than by individuals. Having a small heterogeneous team means that the evaluators know to which member of the team they should turn when they face a particular problem. Moreover, the differences among the team members means that more telling questions can be asked by the metaevaluators as they try to detect difficulties that the primary evaluators may not even have seen. The early detection of problems often requires on-site presence. When a small team is operating, visits can be assigned to team members on a rotating basis, thereby alleviating the burden on any one person. Large groups offer a greater range of skills, but present increased problems of coordination. We know of one effort where a group of 11 persons from diverse academic backgrounds formed a metaevaluation team that conducted multiple site visits in order to detect evaluation problems and to propose solutions. It took time, though, for the members to get to know one another and the points of view they represented. Then, it had to be decided which of the 11 persons should visit which sites. After the visits were arranged, the feedback from each member had to be coordinated. When this was finally done and the recommendations for improvement were spelled out, it was too late to modify the evaluation research project that the metaevaluators were supposed to help! Clearly there are efficient and inefficient ways of coordinating larger groups, and the example we have cited does not embody one of the more efficient ways. But, in general, it is fair to say that the larger the metaevaluation team and the more heterogeneous its members, the more time will be spent on coordination and the greater will be the risk of an untimely product.

Major problems with consultant metaevaluation can result from ambiguities of role and authority relationships between the sponsors of the evaluation, the evaluators, the metaevaluators, the personnel whose program is being evaluated, and the program clients. One issue is: What should be the scope of the metaevaluators' role? Should they be able to insist on modifications of the work, or should they be able to suggest changes? Most agencies will strongly prefer the latter, because it does not imply a formal shift in the locus of authority. However, the issue will often be moot, because many agencies cannot evaluate technical advice when modifications have to be made quickly to an evaluation. Consequently, the metaevaluators' recommendations will often function as prescriptions, though they are formally only recommendations. The evaluators will be loath to lose formal authority, and in most instances of which we are aware the primary evaluators have insisted on being held accountable for technical decisions and actions. Once again, though, we may have a moot point because most contractors will comply with strong agency directives—whether or not they are legally required to do so. And if the agency insists that the metaevaluators' advice be followed, it usually will be. The issue of authority is crucial, because agencies and primary evaluators need to protect themselves against bad advice from metaevaluators for which they will be held responsible. This is easily done when decisions are not pressing, for the sponsoring agency can arrange any adjudication procedures it wants, should the evaluators and metaevaluators disagree about a course of action. In one case we know of, the agency has set up a formal adjudication procedure for this contingency. It has also specified that, when decisions have to made quickly and the original evaluators are forced to take actions that they would not otherwise have taken because the agency sides with the metaevaluator, then this will be noted in the final report and the metaevaluator will be seen to be partly responsible for the particular action even though the evaluators are technically responsible. Though neither of the above procedures has yet had to be used in the project in question, means are available for regulating conflicts, for making the metaevaluator publicly accountable, and for protecting the primary evaluators.

The formal specification of ways to regulate conflicts should not be taken to imply that most conflicts will, or should be, formally regulated. A sine qua non of consultant metaevaluation is tact—the ability to push the task ahead, ever-mindful that evaluators and agency personnel are primarily responsible for the evaluation and identify with it. This leads them to feel a sense of pride and competence as professionals that must be respected. Consequently, collaborative relationships are preferred in which metaevaluators (a) genuinely seek the advice of evaluators and agency personnel; (b) evaluate this advice on its own merits; (c) publicly acknowledge useful help when they receive it; and (d) never publicly discuss mistakes or claim credit for activities that have been well done. Such a relationship is vital, for consultant metaevaluators can do little without the active cooperation of evaluators. For instance, one of the present authors (Cook) was the consultant metaevaluator to a project that, at the midterm, seemed headed for disaster. There were large differences between experimental and control groups at the pretest, the samples were very small and some evaluation personnel felt that the relevant office in the sponsoring agency had little interest in a high-quality evaluation. When this situation became clear to the governing agency, monitoring of the evaluation was assigned to a different office, consultant metaevaluators were hired, and a new design was evolved with much larger samples and appropriate pretest assignment. After great effort by the evaluators, the new design was implemented and the study successfully completed. The metaevaluators played at times a daily role in the modified evaluation, setting short-term practical goals on a regular basis and checking that the subgoals were being met, both at the end of each subgoal sequence and during the time the evaluators were seeking to meet the subgoals. It is important to note that none of the subgoals would have been met had not the original evaluators been willing to go to almost extraordinary lengths to improve the quality of the work, and had they not been prepared to listen openly, yet critically, to the metaevaluators' advice.

Perennial metaevaluation issues concern the access that metaevaluators should have to clients, data, and drafts of reports, and the freedom they should have to disseminate information about an ongoing evaluation. Metaevaluation tasks clearly demand access to all the relevant persons and documents, provided that confidentiality agreements are not broken or field operations unreasonably impeded. We know of one instance in which the metaevaluators were conscientiously trying to help the primary evaluators, but they made such time-consuming demands that the quality of the primary evaluations was threatened and so the consultant metaevaluators were withdrawn. Metaevaluators must be very sensitive to the trade-offs between the needs of busy evaluation staffs for helpful and supportive feedback, and the metaevaluators' own requirement to monitor quality and discover problems before they become salient. Metaevaluators have to realize that being available need not mean being obtrusive.

Why should agencies hire consultant metaevaluators? The advantages for the validity and credibility of evaluation results are obvious. However, the advantages have to be weighed against the possibility that third parties may consider metaevaluation as tantamount to an agency admitting that its in-house technical monitors cannot perform their role and that one of the agency's major responsibilities has slipped into the hands of outsiders. But consultant metaevaluation need not imply any loss of responsibility, for the agency can insist that all decisions arrived at jointly by evaluators and metaevaluators have to be reviewed before being acted upon, even if only by telephone conference. Scriven (1975) has noted that agencies may be cautious lest metaevaluation add to the total cost of the evaluation. It is clearly advisable that metaevaluation add little or nothing, but this may not always be possible. The marginal cost of metaevaluation may well be minimal, though, when the most important programs are being evaluated. Nonetheless, we agree with the concern of agencies and of Scriven, and in this respect it is crucial to note that the functional overlap between consultant metaevaluators and traditional consultants suggests that some or all of the metaevaluation costs can be taken from consultant funds that normally go to primary evaluators.

Agencies should also attend to the possibility that metaevaluation will add indirectly to evaluation costs. For instance, with "cost plus" contracts, the evaluators could claim that the metaevaluators' request led to performing tasks that were not specified in the original contract and so deserve recompense. Metaevaluators have to be sensitive to this possibility and make clear, where new data collection or analyses are involved, how they are to be paid for—preferably out of other budget categories rather than as "add-ons." In this light, it would be useful if agencies made clear to evaluators from the onset that they should expect no new funds to follow from the metaevaluators' interventions, except under unusual circumstances that have to be justified on a time-by-time basis and before the cost-incurring action is taken. Often, such actions can be paid for out of contract funds, for in most of the metaevaluation efforts of which we know, the metaevaluators have helped agency personnel to recognize that some of the activities specified in the contract have little or no relevance to the major evaluation questions, and can be dropped without much loss.

Agencies face yet another problem in working with consultant metaevaluators: they are consultants, and a federal priority is to decrease the use of consultants. It is sometimes the case, though, that metaevaluators can replace consultants to the primary evaluator, thereby decreasing the total number of consultants associated with a program or project. Alternatively, the cost of metaevaluation might legitimately be included in budget categories other then consultation; for example, a consultant metaevaluation team might well qualify as, and be included in, the original contract as a subcontractual or personnel expense.

From a functionalist perspective, it is important that evaluations be closely monitored, and it is largely irrelevant how this is done so long as it is done competently. Consultant metaevaluators are merely one means of (a) checking whether the major research questions are appropriately phrased; (b) overseeing the implementation of treatments; (c) evaluating interim reports and suggesting specific goals that need to be reached by the next report; (d) continuous monitoring, sometimes on a daily basis, which may result in shifting the evaluation priorities; (e) evaluating first drafts of final reports; (f) helping to decide upon dissemination and utilization strategies; and (g) putting the results into wider theoretical and practical contexts. The recommendations of consultant metaevaluators should be heeded at all these junctures, especially those that are technical or rely on disciplinary expertise. However, theirs should not be the only voice heard, and we can confidently predict that it will not be. Agency personnel will also want a major voice, particularly at the stages of formulating and integrating the major research questions, approving any shifts in evaluation priorities, revising the first draft of the final report, and deciding on a dissemination strategy. And they may also want to consult other persons to check on the metaevaluators. It is interesting to note that at present the different kinds of expertise and the disparate interests of the metaevaluators and agency personnel are often complementary rather than overlapping, which suggests where the discrepancies are today between what a technical monitor is supposed to do and what he or she can actually accomplish.

Research advisory boards are sometimes set up to fulfill functions described in the preceding paragraph. A major problem with such boards is that they are composed of busy luminaries who do not have the time to devote to a single project. Also, advisory boards are typically larger than metaevaluation teams, and this can lead to problems of coordination when boards are used actively and decisions have to be made in haste. However, most boards are not used actively and seem to function more as agents of legitimization than of feedback. This is not to say that they do not give feedback. It is merely to note that the feedback often concerns marginal factors and is given without the benefit of extensive firsthand knowledge, either of the program being evaluated or the evaluation as it is actually progressing. This is not to suggest that boards inevitably serve only to legitimize and give sporadic feedback on particular points. We know of several cases in which boards signaled an imminent evaluation disaster. It is nonetheless our general impression that most board members are too busy to play the kind of active and continous role that is required and that might be more useful.

MODEL 6: SIMULTANEOUS SECONDARY ANALYSIS OF RAW DATA

This model requires making primary evaluation data available to someone who can reanalyze them before the primary analyst has completed his own analysis. This model is therefore particularly useful if the analytic capability of the primary evaluators is in doubt, if time pressures indicate that the primary evaluators might not be able to answer all the relevant questions, or if there are no generally accepted ways of analyzing the data and it is useful to have them analyzed from different methodological perspectives. The last will be especially needed if the original design has broken down and the data are not collected within the planned design framework.

The model is not likely to be useful if consultant metaevaluators are on hand to give advice, including advice about the latest methodological innovations. It is also not likely to be useful if the guiding evaluation questions were checked with interested constituencies, or if the strongest design and measurement features were implemented and maintained over time (e.g., randomization). Thus, interim report are crucial for providing clues as to whether a simultaneous secondary data analysis is needed.

Such analyses need not be expensive, for the labor-intensive processes of implementing treatments and collecting and reducing data have been conducted by primary evaluators. The only remaining costs of any significance are salary for a few individuals and computer time. These individuals could easily be academicians, for secondary analysis capitalizes upon the strengths of persons who have reputations as flexible data analysts, or who want to develop new methodological techniques, or who appreciate the challenge of complex data sets, or who consider reanalysis as a means to accomplish other, academically more rewarded, goals.

Simultaneous secondary analysis can enhance validity and credibility without sacrificing timeliness. This is because a secondary analyst is less likely to make the same assumptions or perhaps commit the same errors as a primary analyst, which increases the chances of at least one valid test of certain relationships. But if the analysts disagree, how is one to determine whose test is more valid? Fortunately, reconsideration of the steps in each analysis will often indicate where one analyst has used idiosyncratic or incorrect procedures. When this happens, greater stress should obviously be placed on the other analysis.

Validity is especially enhanced if the different analysts use different operationalizations and analysis models, but still arrive at the same conclusions. This is probably also optimal for credibility. Credibility would presumably be at its lowest when the analysts reach different conclusions and disagree about basic assumptions or about the validity of various procedures. The sponsoring agency then has the choice to call in "expert testimony" to resolve the problem, and it also has the choice —fraught with political dangers—of releasing only what is believed to be the more valid report. However, it is our guess, based on a review of empirical reevaluations (Cook, 1974), that when secondary analysts ask the same questions of the same body of data as primary analysts, they usually come to the same answers. Most of the discrepancies in the past have arisen because secondary analysts have phrased the major research questions differently from primary analysts.

Secondary analysis also provides an opportunity for non-data tasks to be performed. It is our impression that evaluation results are rarely fitted into discussions of the past research on a particular program, or into research on the assumptions behind classes of programs. Nor are the implications of the data for the future of a program spelled out. Secondary analysts can obviously reflect on these issues without prejudicing the integrity of the data, and their reflections need not be untimely because the outline of findings often appears months before a final report. Moreover, the reflections can be particularly well informed if advantage is taken of substantive experts who could give a variety of different perspectives on the results. Of course, these non-data tasks are not necessary for secondary analysis; they are merely possible adjuncts.

We have already mentioned the disadvantages that can arise from irreconcilable discrepancies between the results of various analysts. We have to add that special disadvantages are involved if an empirical and simultaneous secondary analysis is commissioned because the planned design has been compromised, for in such a case no conclusions about a program may be warranted and good money may be poured after bad. It is often impossible, however, to predict whether the data are too poor to allow any reasonable causal inference. Therefore, a suitable strategy for anyone commissioning a simultaneous secondary analysis is to seek out persons with a demonstrated competence and flexibility in handling nonexperimental data or in developing quasi-experimental designs. In any case, the possibility that no conclusion is possible from the data at hand is certainly one that secondary analysts should be prepared to reach.

MODEL 7: MULTIPLE INDEPENDENT REPLICATIONS

There are already instances of multiple data-based evaluations of a single program, and the differences between some of them are worth highlighting. For instance, "Sesame Street" was evaluated for two consecutive seasons by Ball and Bogatz using highly similar (but not identical) manipulations and measures. Thus, the replications were neither simultaneous, independent, nor heterogeneous. However, Minton (1972, 1975) independently evaluated the first season of "Sesame Street" using different measures of cognitive achievement than the ETS team and different samples of children. Consequently, in the context of first-year studies, hers was an independent and simultaneous replication that increased heterogeneity in the outcomes measured and the respondents studied. The negative income tax experiments have taken place in urban and rural environments, in all major regions of the United States, in contexts where the treatment is linked to different mixes of social services, and in contexts where the range of measurement extends to variables beyond labor force response alone. Thus, from a narrow time perspective, the negative tax experiments can be viewed as consecutive, independent, and heterogeneous, though from a broader perspective they are so closely limited in time as to be almost simultaneous.

Nearly all individual empirical evaluations permit testing how a treatment affects different samples of persons, which is one form of replication. However, such replications are less independent than those that result when different contractors set up their own evaluation, for each contractor would not be likely to implement the treatment in the same way, or to follow the same measurement strategy, or to have the same managerial reactions to field difficulties, etc. But, while heterogeneity is important, it is just as important to establish the desired limitations to heterogeneity, because little is gained from irrelevant differences between studies. Sponsors of evaluations have to ask themselves what would be gained from the novel features of each program evaluation if more than one were conducted to assess a program's impact. In particular, sponsors would do well to ask, How will the treatment and outcome be defined, operationalized, and described in each study? Unless there is some knowledge about these matters it will be difficult to reconcile conflicting results should each evaluation appear to produce different findings.

The advantages of simultaneous, independent, and heterogeneous replications are considerable. If the results replicate, validity and credibility are maximal, and if the guiding research questions are relevant when decisions have to be made, it would be difficult to ignore the results in the policy debate. Moreover, if two (or more) evaluations are yoked together as a single package, then neither has to carry the burden of providing all the information, as would be the case if only one study were carried out. Also, if evaluations are yoked, each can have a lower profile than if it stood alone. This would reduce the extent to which the evaluator finds himself alone, center stage, with the eyes of employers, program personnel, research sponsors, and fellow professionals riveted on him as the sole source of eagerly awaited and expensively purchased information. Such a situation may not be conducive to good evaluation. A final set of advantages follows because budget constraints will usually require each of the replications to be smaller than any single evaluation would be. We shall discuss the disadvantages of smallness later, but for the moment it should be noted that with small-scale evaluations (a) evaluators may have greater control over how the treatments are implemented; (b) they may be able to respond more quickly and more flexibly to field problems; and (c) they may be in a better position to measure and describe the treatment and processes that may have mediated any observed effects. Smallness does not guarantee control and its attendant benefits, but it certainly seems to facilitate them.

Multiple simultaneous evaluations have problems. First, they may appear so expensive that they can only be justified for the most important national programs. But this impression is based on assuming that each separate evaluation needs to be as large as a single evaluation would have to be. As we have mentioned, this does not necessarily have to be the case, and in some circumstances several independent evaluations might require a total number of respondents and sites that is not larger than a single evaluation would require. But even when it is advisable to have one large evaluation, it may still be useful on some occasions to yoke this to a smaller evaluation that is more explicitly focused. Perhaps the smaller evaluation could be restricted to a particularly important target group of respondents, or to the single most important question addressed by the larger evaluation, or to refining the construct validity of the casual treatment.

It may be argued that reducing the size of evaluations loses precision in estimation and reduces statistical power. This is true, though it should be noted that concern about these issues is hardly warranted if the "smaller" samples are statistically "large" (i.e., 30 or more in each cell of the design that figures in particular statistical comparisons). But it would definitely not be desirable to conduct multiple independent evaluations if cell sizes fell below about 30, as would be likely if the major research question calls for thorough examination of differences in reaction to a treatment among several subgroups.

A special difficulty arises if independent contractors reach different major conclusions about a program's impact. When this happens, the first step is to see whether or not the disagreement is real. The evaluations can therefore be reviewed for methodological adequacy with a particular focus on whether the evaluators are using common cause-and-effect labels for very different treatments and outcome measures. It is important to realize that disagreement between the evaluators about major conclusions does not preclude agreement on minor issues that are not trivial. Such agreements should be clearly laid out, though an effort will be required to do this since most people's attention is likely to be directed to disagreements rather than to agreements. In this respect, it is worth noting that Minton (1972, 1975) generally disagreed with Ball and Bogatz (1970) concerning the impact of "Sesame Street," but each analysis strongly suggested that the show taught letter-recognition skills. It would have been a shame if this one correspondence had been lost among the more numerous differences between evaluators.

Peter Rossi has pointed out to us that contractors may collude if they know they are evaluating the same program. The incentives for collusion include cutting costs through sharing information, and avoiding the tarnished corporate reputation that could result if different evaluations produce different conclusions and one evaluation is found to be both absolutely and relatively inadequate. Opportunities also exist for more inadvertent kinds of collusion, as might happen when the specialists in one research organization exchange information with others at professional meetings, or when one consultant advises each of the organizations evaluating a program. We do not want to suggest that all collusion (as we have broadly defined it) is harmful. However, there is a trade-off between gaining vicarious experience by consulting others and preserving one's independence of perspective by not consulting others. Of course, there are restraints against collusion, perhaps the major one being that the evaluation research industry is competitive.

Hence, it is not clear whether contractors would collude to a degree where the loss from homogenized perspectives would be greater than the gain from vicariously acquired relevant information.

Another problem with simultaneous evaluations is that their absolute quality might be lower than that of a single evaluation. Quality might drop, for example, if the better-known contractors did not bid for smaller contracts, or if they successfully bid and then assigned their less experienced staff to work on the project. We do not know if this would be the response to lower costs contracts, or even if the better-known companies do better work. However, if this quality problem exists at all, we suspect that it will be reduced by better RFPs, better reviews, and better monitoring.

Having multiple replications occur simultaneously makes it impossible for one contractor to learn from the experiences of another. Much can be said, therefore, in favor of *consecutive* instead of simultaneous replications. Indeed, close examination of the two "Sesame Street" evaluations by Ball and Bogatz (1970; Bogatz and Ball, 1971) led Cook et al. (1975) to conclude that the second was markedly better than the first and that the difference was due to the learning that took place in the first evaluation. The negative income tax experiments, while overlapping in time, were begun at different times, and it is to be hoped that the later investigators learned from the problems and mistakes associated with the pioneering efforts of the New Jersey evaluators. Clearly, a prerequisite for such learning is frank and nondefensive discussion, as well as a reading of whatever earlier evaluators might have written about their field experiences.

A consecutive replication strategy also makes it possible to build upon the substantive findings of earlier evaluations. For example, it is sometimes possible to select particular aspects of a treatment that were demonstrated to have had impact and to build upon these in the later work to increase impact or specify why there was impact. Such follow-up experiments need not be as large scale as the preliminary evaluation, may even take place in less representative settings, and may have as much the appearance of a test of theory as an evaluation study. After all, one of the aims of theory is to suggest programs, while one of the inadvertent consequences of program evaluation is to suggest new areas for theory and new modifications to existing theories.

It is rare today to hear talk of planning for multiple simultaneous or consecutive evaluations that build upon each other and confer greater validity and credibility than any single study could afford. Yet we have seen in this paper that multiple evaluations of some present or possibly future national programs have already been conducted, from school busing to guaranteed incomes. We can expect even more multiple evaluations in the future because we can reasonably surmise that no single program evaluation will answer its major impact questions to the satisfaction of most commentators. Multiple evaluations now occur haphazardly. Would it not be better to explicate when multiple evaluations are worthwhile, and then to plan how each of them can capitalize upon the preceding ones and how the series of studies—however long— can be packaged so as to base inferences about impact on a firmer footing? Just think of the gain that would have accrued had the Coleman Report been presented initially as the first of several studies of school integration. Would the results then have been used so prominently as the social science justification for integration? Subsequent research has shown that this justification was mostly wrong with respect to the causal connection that was claimed between interracial classrooms and achievement, and that the research may perhaps have been misleading because of the failure to consider unplanned side-effects, such as "white flight." Multiple simultaneous replications will usually lead to greater validity and credibility. Multiple consecutive replications will in addition decrease the likelihood that social science evidence will be prematurely used to justify policy decisions that may have unintended consequences both for the persons affected by the decisions and for the future use of social science evidence for informing policy debates.

SUMMARY AND CONCLUSION

The purposes of this paper were to define metaevaluation, to describe seven models of conducting it, and to suggest how each model might be used to improve the quality of empirical summative evaluations. The models we discussed differ considerably in power. The most humble is the review of an evaluation report, and the most ambitious is a seldom-used model based on multiple independent evaluations of a single program. Each of the seven models is appropriate to different kinds of real or anticipated problems that might occur in evaluating a program, and while each has obvious weaknesses, many of these weaknesses can be circumvented with enough foresight. However, metaevaluation is not the only way of improving the quality of evaluations, and it should in no way be considered a substitute for longer-term approaches to improving evaluation (e.g., research on research methodology).

The contribution of the social sciences through their hypothesis-testing methodologies could ultimately be as significant as the contribution they have made through their individual testing and survey sampling methodologies. It is unfortunate that evaluation research (i.e., empirical hypothesis-testing for policy purposes) has not yet achieved the same standards of practical excellence as the research traditions mentioned above. It would be a shame, we feel, if the considerable first-generation problems of evaluation research were to lead to the conclusion that "evaluation research has been tried and has failed," when in fact it has not been tried yet under favorable circumstances. Metaevaluation research should be seen as one means of improving the quality of evaluations and of indirectly testing whether evaluation research can deliver what has been promised, namely, strong tests of causal propositions about policy-relevant relationships.

Metaevaluation research might have another consequence. The applied nature of evaluation work, plus the low standards achieved to date, have probably contributed to the low academic respectability of the field. So, too, has the fact that few academicians have the managerial experience to evaluate national programs of high visibility, as opposed to local projects of less visibility and little theoretical interest. Hence, both respectability and "glamorous" opportunity are lacking for academic evaluation researchers. Most of the metaevaluation models we specified involve tasks that could be easily accomplished by academicians—tasks that would use both their substantive expertise to critique the (all too often implicit) theory behind a social intervention and to put evaluation findings into new and perhaps broader perspectives, and their technical skills as discriminating and flexible methodologists "at the frontier." We have not outlined organizational frameworks to facilitate increased academic participation; nor have we outlined a reward system that ties into the one currently operating in academe (publications, disciplinary visibility, and the like). But, when all is said and done, it is specific evaluation and metaevaluation tasks that have to be done—and done well—and it is of little consequence who does them. Academicians could do many of them, but the tasks may not wait for academicians to make up their minds whether or not they should do them.

Ultimately, the future of metaevaluation rests on whether agency staff want to improve the technical quality of most of the evaluations they are funding, and are prepared to experiment in responsible fashion with ways of trying to improve quality. If they see the need, then the models of metaevaluation we have suggested may be of value to them, particularly the models that describe activities that occur simultaneously with a primary evaluation. It must be stressed that nobody has had extensive experience with metaevaluation, so the promise of past work is just that—a promise, and not a guarantee.

NOTE

1. For a more extended discussion of this and other archiving issues, see Cook (1976) and Cook and Rezmovic (unpublished).

REFERENCES

ALLPORT, G. W. (1954) The Nature of Prejudice. Cambridge, MA: Addison-Wesley.

AMIR, Y. (1969) "Contact hypothesis in ethnic relations." Psych. Bull. 71: 319-342.

ARMOR, D. J. (1972) "The evidence on busing." The Public Interest 28 (Summer): 90-126.

BALL, S. and G. A. BOGATZ (1970) The First Year of "Sesame Street." Princeton, NJ: Educational Testing Service.

BERNSTEIN, I. and H. E. FREEMAN (1975) Academic and Entrepreneurial Research. New York: Russell Sage Foundation.

BOECKMANN, M. E. (1976) "Policy impacts of the New Jersey income maintenance experiment." Policy Sciences 7: 53-76.

BOGATZ, G. A. and S. BALL (1971) The Second Year of "Sesame Street": a Continuing Evaluation. Princeton, NJ: Educational Testing Service.

BOURQUE, L. B. and FREEMAN, H. E. Evaluating evaluation studies: a review and appraisal of current research on the impact of federal programs on children. Paper presented at the Biennial Meeting of the Society for Research on Child Development, New Orleans, February 1977.

The Brookings Bulletin (1975). Washington, DC: The Brookings Institution.

CAMPBELL, D. T. and A. ERLEBACHER (1970) "How regression artifacts in quasi-experimental evaluations can mistakenly make compensatory education look harmful," in J. Hellmuth (ed.) Compensatory Education: a National Debate, Vol. 3: The Disadvantaged Child. New York: Brunner/Mazel.

CAMPBELL, D. T. and J. C. STANLEY (1966) Experimental and Quasi-Experimental Designs for Research. Chicago: Rand McNally.

CICIRELLI, V. (1970) "The relevance of the regression artifact problem to the Westinghouse-Ohio University evaluation of Head Start: a reply to Campbell and Erlebacher," in J. Hellmuth (ed.) Compensatory Education: a National Debate, Vol. 3: The Disadvantaged Child. New York: Brunner/Mazel.

COLEMAN, J. S., E. Q. CAMPBELL, C. J. HOBSON, J. MCPARTLAND, A. M. MOOD, F. D. WEINFELD, and R. L. YORK (1966) Equality of Educational Opportunity. Washington, DC: U.S. Government Printing Office.

COOK, T. D. (1976) Should the archiving of evaluation data be required? Evaluation Magazine 3: 26 ff.

———(1974) "The potential and limitations of secondary evaluations," M. W. Apple, M. J. Subkoviak, and J. R. Lufler (eds.) Educational Evaluation: Analysis and Responsibility. Berkeley, CA: McCutchan.

———and R. CONNER, (1976) "The educational impact." J. of Communication 26: 155-164.

COOK, T. D. and V. REZMOVIC (1977) "Archiving evaluation data: an empirical study of the perceived need and payoff." Available from Department of Psychology, Northwestern University, Evanston, IL 60201. (unpublished)

COOK, T. D., H. APPLETON, R. F. CONNER, A. SHAFFER, G. TAMKIN, and S. J. WEBER (1975) "Sesame Street" Revisited. New York: Russell Sage Foundation.

DIAZ-GUERRERO, R. and W. H. HOLTZMAN (1974) "Learning by televised 'Plaza Sésamo' in Mexico," J. of Educational Psychology: 632-643.

DIAZ-GUERRERO, R., I. REYES-LAGUNES, D. B. WITZKE, and W. H. HOLTZMAN (1976) "'Plaza Sésamo' in Mexico: an evaluation." J. of Communication 26: 145-154.

ELASHOFF, J. D. and R. E. SNOW [eds.] (1971) Pygmalion Reconsidered. Worthington, OH: Charles A. Jones.

EVANS, J. W. and J. SCHILLER (1970) "How preoccupation with possible regression artifacts can lead to a faulty strategy for the evaluation of social action programs: a reply to Campbell and Erlebacher," in J. Hellmuth (ed.) Compensatory Education: a National Debate, Vol. 3: The Disadvantaged Child. New York: Brunner/Mazel.

FISHER, J. (1973) "Is casework effective? a review." Social Work 18: 5-20.

FREEMAN, H. (1975) "Foreword," in T. D. Cook, H. Appleton, R. F. Conner, A. Shaffer, G. Tamkin, and S. J. Weber, "Sesame Street" Revisited. New York: Russell Sage Foundation.

GLASS, G. V. (1976) "Primary, secondary, and meta-analysis of research." Presidential address to the meeting of the American Educational Research Association, San Francisco, April.

GRAMLICH, E. M. and P. D. KOSHEL (1975) Educational Performance Contracting: an Evaluation of an Experiment. Washington, DC: The Brookings Institution.

HANUSHEK, E. A. and J. F. KAIN (1972) "On the value of Equality of Educational Opportunity as a guide to public policy," in F. Mosteller and D. P. Moynihan (eds.) On Equality of Educational Opportunity. New York: Vintage.

HOWARD, K. I. and M. J. KRAUSE (1976) "Program evaluation in public interest: a new research methodology." J. of Community Mental Health 12: 291-300.

JENCKS, C. S. et al. (1972) Inequality: a Reassessment of the Effects of Family and Schooling in America. New York: Basic Books.

KENNY, D. A. (1975) "A quasi-experimental approach to assessing treatment effects in the nonequivalent control group design." Psych. Bull. 82: 345-362.

———(1972) "Threats to the validity of cross-lagged panel inference as related to 'Television violence and child aggression: a follow-up study,'" in G. A. Comstock and E. A. Rubinstein (eds.) Television and Social Behavior (Vol. 3). Washington, DC: U.S. Government Printing Office.

LEFKOWITZ, M. M., L. ERON, L. WALDER, and L. R. HUESMANN, (1972) "Television violence and child aggression: a follow-up study," in G. A. Comstock and E. A.

Rubinstein (eds.) Television and Social Behavior (Vol. 3). Washington, DC: U.S. Government Printing Office.

LEVIN, H. M. and R. E. SNOW (1976) Personal Communication.

LIGHT, R. J. and P. V. SMITH (1971) "Accumulating evidence: procedures for resolving contradictions among different research studies." Harvard Educational Rev. 41: 429-471.

LIPTON, D., R. MARTINSON, and J. WILKS (1975) The Effectiveness of Correctional Treatment—a Survey of Treatment Evaluation Studies. New York: Praeger.

LORD, F. M. (1960) "Large-scale covariance analysis when the control variable is fallible." J. of the Amer. Statistical Assoc. 55: 307-321.

MESSICK, S. (1975) "The standard problem: meaning and values in measurement and evaluation." Amer. Psychologist 30: 955-966.

Minnesota Systems Research, Inc. [MSRI] (1976) Final Report: Evaluation and Prediction of Methodological Adequacy of Research and Evaluation Studies. Minneapolis, MI: MSRI.

MINTON, J. H. (1975) "The impact of 'Sesame Street' on readiness." Sociology of Education 48: 141-151.

———(1973) "The impact of 'Sesame Street' on reading readiness of kindergarten children." Dissertation Abstracts International 33: 3396A. (University Microfilms No. 73-1516)

MOSTELLER, F., and D. P. MOYNIHAN [eds.] (1972) On Equality of Educational Opportunity. New York: Vintage.

NEALE, J. M. (1972) "Comment on 'Television violence and child aggression: A follow-up study,'" in G. A. Comstock and E. A. Rubinstein (eds.) Television and Social Behavior (Vol. 3). Washington, DC: U.S. Government Printing Office.

ORATA, P. T. (1940) "Evaluating evaluation." J. of Educational Research 33: 641.

PECHMAN, J. A. and P. M. TIMPANE [eds.] (1975) Work Incentives and Income Guarantees: The New Jersey Negative Income Tax Experiment. Washington, DC: The Brookings Institution.

PETTIGREW, T. F., E. L. USEEM, C. NORMAND, and M. S. SMITH (1973) "Busing: a review of the evidence." The Public Interest 30 (Winter): 88-118.

RAY, H. W. (1972) Final Report on the Office of Economic Opportunity Experiment in Educational Contracting. Columbus, OH: Battelle Columbus Laboratories.

RIVLIN, A. M . and P. M. TIMPANE [eds.] (1975) Planned Variation in Education: Should We Give Up or Try Harder? Washington, DC: The Brookings Institution.

ROSENTHAL, R. and L. JACOBSON (1968) Pygmalion in the Classroom: Teacher Expectation and Pupil's Intellectual Development. New York: Holt, Rinehart & Winston.

ROSSI, P. H. and K. LYALL (1976) Reforming Public Welare: a Critique of the Negative Income Tax Experiment. New York: Russell Sage Foundation.

ROSSI, P. H. and W. WILLIAMS [eds.] (1972) Evaluating Social Programs. New York: Seminar Press.

SALOMON, G. (1974) "'Sesame Street' in Israel: its instructional and psychological effects on children." Available from Hebrew University of Jerusalem, Israel and Children's Television Workshop (unpublished)

SCRIVEN, M. (1975) "Evaluation bias and its control." Occasional Paper #4, Evaluation Center. Western Michigan University (unpublished)

————(1969) "An introduction to meta-evaluation." Educational Product Report 2: 36-38.

SMITH, M. S. (1972) "Equality of Educational Opportunity: the basic findings reconsidered," in F. Mosteller and D. P. Moynihan (eds.) On Equality of Educational Opportunity. New York: Vintage.

————and J. S. BISSELL (1970) "Report analysis: the impact of Head Start." Harvard Educ. Rev. 40: 51-104.

ST. JOHN, N. (1975) School Desegregation. New York: John Wiley.

STROMSDORFER, E. W. (1972) "Review and synthesis of cost-effectiveness studies of vocational and technical education." Columbus: Ohio State University. (mimeo)

STUFFLEBEAM, D. L. (1975) "Meta-evaluation." Occasional Paper #3, Western Michigan University Evaluation Center. (unpublished)

THORNDIKE, R. L. (1968) "Review of Pygmalion in the Classroom." Amer.Educational Research J. 5: 708-711.

WHOLEY, J. et al. (1970) Federal Evaluation Policy. Washington, DC: The Urban Institute.

WILKINS. L. T. (1969) Evaluation of Penal Measures. New York: Random House.

WORTMAN, P. M. and R. G. ST. PIERRE (1977) "The educational voucher demonstration: secondary analysis." Education and Urban Society 9: 471-492.

ZEISEL, H. and S. S. DIAMOND (1974) "'Convincing empirical evidence' on the six member jury." Univ. of Chicago Law. Rev. 41: 281-195.

Thomas D. Cook is Professor of Psychology at Northwestern University, Evanston, Illinois. He is senior author of "Sesame Street" Revisited *and of a chapter with Donald T. Campbell in the* Handbook of Industrial and Organizational Psychology *on quasi-experiments and true experiments in field settings. He will edit Volume 3 of* Evaluation Studies: Review Annual. *He has extensive experience in evaluation and metaevaluation research.*

Charles Gruder is Associate Professor of Psychology at the University of Illinois at Chicago Circle, where he is also Director of the Organizational Psychology program, which offers doctoral training in applied social and developmental psychology. A current training project involves the design and evaluation of a local smoking-withdrawal treatment clinic.

The Alum Rock experiment on the effects of a school voucher program was an early but very important step toward determining the potential value of this signal educational innovation. Consequently, it is critical that analyses of the early data be correct and maximally informative. One distinct hazard in major experiments—landmark studies—is that early findings can prove so disappointing that further experimentation and study is abandoned. In the following, an excellent example of the value of secondary analysis, Wortman et al. show that some initial discouraging results from the Alum Rock study may have been misleading and that the actual results provide ample basis for continuing investigation.

25

The First Year of the
Education Voucher Demonstration
A Secondary Analysis of Student Achievement Test Scores

Paul M. Wortman, Charles S. Riechert, and
Robert G. St. Pierre

The Education Voucher Demonstration began in the Alum Rock Union Elementary School District during the 1972-1973 school year. Under the voucher concept, parents freely select a school for their child and receive a credit or voucher equal to the cost of the child's education that is paid directly to the school upon enrollment. It was presumed that this form of school finance would foster competition among the schools and improve the quality of education by making schools more responsive to students' needs. An initial external evaluation at the conclusion of the first year found, however, a relative loss in reading achievement for students in the six public schools that participated in the voucher demonstration. The present report reexamines some of these data using a quasi-experimental design involving multiple pretests and individual students' test scores (rather than school means) as the unit of analysis. The results appear to indicate that the deleterious reading effect of the voucher demonstration was confined to a few within-school programs featuring nontraditional, innovative curricula.

*I*n the fall of 1972, the Alum Rock Union Elementary School District in San Jose, California became the site of the first Education Voucher Demonstration. The voucher concept was designed to introduce free enterprise concepts into the educational process. This

AUTHORS' NOTE: *The work on this manuscript was supported by Contract No. C-74-0115 from the National Institute of Education and a National Science Foundation Graduate Fellowship. The authors thank Robert F. Boruch, Donald T. Campbell, and David A. Kenny for their helpful comments on an earlier version of this paper. We are also indebted to Superintendent William J. Jefferds and Lloyd Binen for their assistance in obtaining the data used in the analyses. Requests for reprints should be sent to Paul M. Wortman, Associate Director, Division of Methodology and Evaluation Research, Department of Psychology, Northwestern University, Evanston, Illinois 60201.*

From Paul M. Wortman, Charles S. Riechert, and Robert G. St. Pierre, "The First Year of the Education Voucher Demonstration: A Secondary Analysis of Student Achievement Test Scores," 2(2) *Evaluation Quarterly* 193-214 (May 1978). Copyright 1978 by Sage Publications, Inc.

is accomplished by allowing parents and children complete freedom in selecting their schools, by encouraging the schools to develop a variety of educational alternatives to make this choice meaningful, and, most importantly, by tying school finances to student enrollment. The program is implemented through a fiscal reorganization of the school system whereby each student receives a credit or a voucher, equivalent to the cost of his or her education, that is paid directly to the chosen school upon enrollment. With schools dependent upon these funds for their survival, they should become more responsive to student needs and, presumably, improve the quality of education these students receive. Moreover, by allocating additional compensatory funds to the vouchers of students who were eligible for the free lunch program, the schools were encouraged to be particularly receptive to the special needs of disadvantaged students.

The Alum Rock Voucher Demonstration was initially funded for a period of five years.[1] Attention, however, has been focused almost entirely on the first year. During that time only six of the district's 24 schools agreed to participate in the demonstration. In order to increase the number and breadth of choices available to parents and children, each voucher school agreed to diversify into at least two minischools which would offer varying curricular orientations, instructional strategies, and educational goals. The 22 minischools that resulted from this decision could be divided into two broad categories—those offering a traditional academic orientation ("general and specific basic academic skills") and those offering a nontraditional, innovative approach to education (i.e., "fine arts," "multi-cultural," or "activity-centered" programs). According to the teachers' own estimates, while these different curricula provided a wide range of approaches to learning, there was little difference between the programs in the amount of instructional time allocated to reading and language arts (approximately 45%) in grades 3 through 6 (Weiler, 1974a: 89-90). Other differences, however, did become apparent. For example, in general, there was more individualized instruction in the traditional minischool programs than in the innovative, nontraditional ones (Weiler, 1974a: 89-91).

The Rand Corporation was awarded a contract to monitor the progress of the demonstration, and in its reports on the first year (Weiler, 1976; 1974a; 1974b) examined a wide range of public policy issues including student achievement. On this latter issue, the Rand reports only examined the effects of the voucher project on reading achievement, using nonvoucher schools within the district for comparison. School means were used as the unit of analysis in statistical procedures because more disaggregated data (e.g., student scores) were thought to be unavailable.

The results from Rand's two separate analyses were contradictory. One Rand researcher (Klitgaard, 1974) mainly examined the scores from the Cooperative Primary Reading Tests (CPRT) which were administered by the state each spring. Using a gain-score analysis (see below), Klitgaard found that the performance in voucher schools dropped in the first year of the demonstration compared to both performance in prior years and performance in nonvoucher schools. The drop amounted to one-sixth of an "inter-student" standard deviation, and the same effect was found after using various measures as a control for SES differences. Another Rand analyst (Barker, 1974b) examined performance on the Metropolitan Achievement Tests, which were administered to Title I nonvoucher schools by the state and to voucher schools by Rand. Using both a correlational analysis and an analysis of gain scores, Barker found no significant differences between the performance of voucher and nonvoucher schools with and without using information on Aid to Families with Dependent Children as a control for SES differences. In interpreting these results, the Rand report (Barker, 1974a) cites a number of weaknesses in the analyses and concludes that because of these difficulties and the contradictory nature of the results, "it does not seem prudent to try to draw more than very tentative conclusions from first-year data" (p. 104).

The purpose of this paper is to reexamine these findings from the first year of the voucher demonstration. One reason for doing so is that secondary analyses, conducted from a new perspective with different assumptions, can often shed new light on the original findings and thus provide a firmer basis for decision-making. The present reanalysis, while not solving all of the problems that confronted the Rand analyses, does provide a more fine-grained look at the consequences of the voucher demonstration by focusing on the individual student's reading achievement. By examining these test scores and, in particular, those of a cohort of students who remained in Alum Rock for several years, it is possible to avoid some of the problems arising from student mobility (estimated at 30% per year). Furthermore, the use of individual scores also allows one to determine the effects of smaller and more specific components of the treatment such as the mini- (or within) school programs.

Another reason for this reanalysis was to investigate and comment on the various analytic approaches to data resulting from nonequivalent control group designs such as the voucher demonstration. This general category of designs describes a common research setting where there are pretreatment and posttreatment observations, but the individuals (or other units of analysis) under study have not been randomly assigned to treatment and control groups (Campbell and Stanley, 1966). In general, nonrandom assignment to conditions means that the treatment groups will systematically differ in both predictable and unpredictable ways. In order to reach firm conclusions concerning the effectiveness of the treatment, these selection differences must be taken into account— a situation somewhat more complicated than that encountered in the analysis of a "true" experiment.

Because the nonequivalent control group design is often employed in applied and field research settings, much has been written about the difficulties in analyzing the resulting data (Cook and Reichardt, 1976, provide an annotated guide to some of the current literature). The conclusion reached by many respected methodologists is that no completely satisfactory solution to the problems of analysis exists:

> With the data usually available for such studies, there simply is no logical or statistical procedure that can be counted on to make proper allowances for uncontrolled preexisting differences between groups [Lord, 1967: 305].

> If randomization is absent, it is virtually impossible in many practical circumstances to be convinced that the estimates of the effects of treatments are in fact unbiased [Cochran and Rubin, 1973: 417].

In brief, the difficulty is that in a particular research setting one specific statistical model may be appropriate for the analysis, while for other data a different statistical procedure (or a different adjustment to the same one) is required (cf. Kenny, 1975; Cronbach et al., 1977). So unless the analyst knows what model is appropriate for the specific data at hand, there is a possibility that the results from an arbitrary model will be biased. With the present lack of understanding concerning the processes that govern behavior, this knowledge will rarely be available.

Under these conditions, caution is obviously necessary in interpreting the results of such analyses. But, in spite of this caveat, it is common for prudence to yield to the pressure for hard and fast conclusions and for the shortcomings of the analysis to be ignored. For example, in subsequent reports on the voucher demonstration in more policy-relevant publications (Report on Education Research, 1974; Shanker, 1974; Warren, 1976) the "tentative conclusions" of the Rand analyses were replaced by firm statements concerning the program's failure. It is the purpose of this paper to illustrate the problems in analyzing such data and thereby to demonstrate the need for caution in reaching conclusions based on the results from the nonequivalent control group design.

METHOD

UNITS OF ANALYSIS

Students' test scores were obtained directly from the school district instead of from Rand or the State of California which had school means only. In order to track individual students (rather than schools) over time, the scores from consecutive grade levels in consecutive years were required. The only consecutive grades tested at Alum Rock were grades 1-3. Each spring (May) these grade levels were tested with the CPRT (the test on which Klitgaard's analyses found a harmful effect for the vouchers). Thus is was possible to obtain yearly test scores on a cohort of students who were in the first grade in 1970-1971, second grade in 1971-1972, and third grade during the first year of the voucher demonstration, 1972-1973. Such a sample, it should be noted, represents a trade-off between the requirements of a strong design methodology and the potential generalizability of the findings. This subsample of voucher students allows the analysis to detect the effects of smaller units than the entire school (e.g., student growth and minischool curricula), but, in doing so, the scope of the findings are restricted to the third-grade pupils (whereas Klitgaard's analysis included first, second, and sixth-graders as well).

Five elementary-grade level schools (the sixth was a middle school) joined the voucher demonstration the first year. For a nonvoucher comparison, Rand had relied primarily on the five Title I elementary schools in the Alum Rock District. For the present analysis, student data from only three of these schools were considered because the other two were racially imbalanced (as compared to the characteristics of the district) according to the California Administrative Code (Weiler, 1974a). The eight voucher and nonvoucher schools included in this sample were racially balanced. Further, voucher and nonvoucher schools appeared to be similar in other ways. The three nonvoucher schools, for example, chose to become voucher schools in the second year of the demonstration. Nonetheless, there were some obvious differences between the two groups. Specifically, Title I schools generally had more students from families on welfare than did voucher schools—51% versus 34% (Weiler, 1974a: 169).

The cohort of students who were present during grades 1 through 3 was created by matching student records across the three consecutive years. This was based on reported names, and it is likely that some spelling errors and name changes occurred in the class lists. Nevertheless, slight differences in opinion over the proper matches in a few cases did not substantially alter the results of the analyses.

Given the continuing discussion of freedom of information and rights of privacy, a brief description of the data acquisition is warranted. The recommended procedure for data release usually includes the deletion of all names and personal identifiers. In fact, legal restriction to this effect have been proposed. Such a sanction, however, would have made it impossible to construct the cohort used in the present study. Fortunately, permission for the release of the necessary information was obtained from the school district and did not require the consent of students or parents. (The names of the students, of course, were used only to create the cohort and were not used in the subsequent analyses.) Certainly the data file creation could be done by the organization that has the primary information. In this way, ethical questions concerning secondary analyses can be avoided without loss of valuable policy-relevant information.

DESIGN

With the students' actual test scores, more fine-grained comparisons were allowed in this study than in the Rand evaluation. Although the sample size of the cohort was too small to conduct a meaningful analysis of the impact of individual minischools, it was possible to examine separately the impact of the two previously described categories of mini-school curricula—traditional and nontraditional—that form two non-equivalent voucher groups. In the *complete* cohort, where performance was tracked over three years, there were 354 students—150 in traditional curriculum voucher programs (from 11 mini-schools), 84 in non-traditional curriculum voucher programs (from 5 minischools), and 120 from nonvoucher programs. In analyses based on data from only the last two years, the sample size could be increased by including the scores of those students who were tested in these two years but not in the first year, 1970-1971. This adds 109 more students, for a total of 463, of which 196 were in traditional voucher programs, 103 in nontraditional, and 164 in nonvoucher. Results from this *augmented* cohort are reported only when they differ substantially from the smaller complete cohort.

Using the notation of Campbell and Stanley (1966), the basic design of this secondary analysis is described in Figure 1 where Os represent observations, Xs refer to the imposition of a treatment, and the dashed lines indicate nonrandom assignment. This design is a slight extension of the basic nonequivalent control group design since it includes an additional wave of data (grade 1 scores). Following both Director (1974) and Campbell (1974), the first two waves of data are referred to as a "dry run" quasi-experiment since the voucher program was not in effect during this time. Data from the last two years are referred to as a pre-test-posttest quasi-experiment since if there is any voucher effect it might be discernible from these data.

ANALYSES

A number of statistical strategies have been suggested (and many are widely used) for analyzing data from a pretest-posttest design (Grades 2 and 3 above). One of the most common is the analysis of variance of gain scores (gain-score analysis). In this procedure, the differences between performance in grades 3 and 2 are examined to see if one treatment group gained more than another. Any significant difference in average gain is then attributed to the effect of the treatment. Another popular strategy is the analysis of covariance (ANCOVA)

SCHOOL GROUP	PROGRAM	DRY RUN	PRETEST-POSTTEST		
Voucher	Traditional	O	O	X	O
	Non-Traditional	O	O	X	O
Non-Voucher	Traditional	O	O		O
		1970–71 (Grade 1)	1971–72 (Grade 2)		1972–73 (Grade 3)

O = Observation (pretest or posttest)

X = Treatment (voucher programs)

Figure 1: Design of the Educational Voucher Demonstration Secondary Analysis

where the posttest (grade 3) scores are regressed on the pretest (grade 2) scores within each treatment group separately. Significant differences between the intercepts of these regression lines are attributed to the treatment effect.

Still other analysis strategies have been devised because of the well-known fact that measurement error in the pretest biases the treatment effect estimate in the ANCOVA (cf. Campbell and Erlebacher, 1970; Cochran, 1968). Under the assumption that the ANCOVA would provide the proper results only if the pretest were measured without error, a number of corrections for the effects of using a fallible pretest in the ANCOVA have been suggested (e.g., Keesling and Wiley, 1977; Lord, 1960; Porter, 1967). The adjustment that is most convenient computationally is provided by Porter (1967). Essentially, this procedure uses an estimate of the within-group pretest reliability to regress the pretest scores toward the group means, and these adjusted pretest scores are then entered in the ANCOVA just as the unadjusted pretest scores would be.[2] Porter and Chibucos (1974) have suggested that this strategy is the most appropriate in general for data from the nonequivalent control group design. Campbell and Boruch (1975) agree with Porter and Chibucos that an adjustment to the ANCOVA is to be recommended, but disagree as to the nature of the adjustment. Under some circumstances, Campbell and Boruch argue that the proper adjustment takes account of the (within-group) pretest-posttest correlation rather than the (within-group) pretest reliability so that, computationally, one regresses the pretest scores toward the group means in proportion to this correlation rather than in proportion to the pretest reliability (also see Kenny, 1975).[3]

A more detailed discussion of these strategies is presented by Reichardt (1977), and the interested reader should also examine

Cronbach et al. (1977). Suffice it to say here that: (1) each strategy imposes its own unique and specific assumptions about the state of nature, (2) under certain conditions each strategy will provide an unbiased estimate of the treatment effect, (3) under innumerable other conditions each strategy will be biased, and (4) in general one will not know which state of affairs is encountered in a specific quasi-experimental data set.

In addition to applying these strategies to the pretest-posttest data, the first wave of data (grade 1) could be used to add two other bits of information. First, each of the preceding statistical models could be applied to the dry run data, and since there was no voucher treatment at that point in time, they should, if appropriate, support the null hypothesis. Those models satisfying this criterion on the dry run data could be deemed appropriate for the analysis of the pretest-posttest data, assuming that differences between the test scores in grades 1-2 and 2-3 were due only to the introduction of the voucher programs during the latter period. Second, the data from the grades 1 and 2 can be used directly to predict the patterns of growth in the grade 3 data under the null hypothesis of no treatment effect (Boruch and Gomez, 1976). Again, it must be assumed that the same pattern of change that occurs between the first and second grades would continue on into the third grade in the absence of any voucher effect. Under this assumption, any discrepancy between the observed data in grade 3 and the prediction from grades 1 and 2 would be attributed to the effect of the voucher program. This analysis was labeled the prediction based on grades 1 and 2.

As is typical in this type of research, there was no elaborate and well-tested theory of the behavior that was under investigation nor extensive knowledge of the nature of the selection process, so it was not possible to specify which analysis strategy would be most appropriate for the cohort of students at hand. Rather than arbitrarily choosing just one method of analysis, all of them were used. Since each statistical strategy is based on a different set of assumptions about the nature of the data, if the results of all the analyses agreed, it would indicate that the conclusions were at least robust under a range of conditions. One might also hope that this strategy of multiple tests would bracket the size of the true treatment effect. In other words, while each model might be biased, the direction of the bias might be different, so that one analysis would underestimate the effect while another would overestimate it. Again, agreement among the results of these multiple analyses would lend confidence to their credibility. However, it is possible that the results of the multiple methods could all be biased in the same direction so that agreement would be misleading.

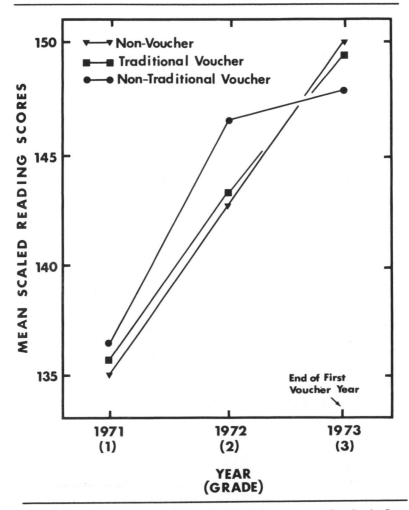

Figure 2: Mean Scaled Scores on the Cooperative Primary Reading Test for the Complete Cohort of Students Enrolled in Traditional and Nontraditional Voucher
Programs and Nonvoucher Schools

RESULTS

The first, second, and third grades had been administered a different
form of the CPRT, namely, Forms 12A, 23A, and 23B, respectively. In
order to make comparisons across grade levels, the raw scores were
scaled according to the published norms (Educational Testing Service,
1967). The means for the three groups tracked over the three years are
graphically presented in Figure 2. In Table 1 the same means appear
along wih the standard deviations and F tests of the group differences

TABLE 1
Summary Description of Scaled Reading Scores for the Complete
Cohort of Students in the Alum Rock Union School District

Group	Statistic	Grade 1 1970-1971	Grade 2 1971-1972	Grade 3 1972-1973
Traditional	Mean	135.86	143.57	149.47
N $\doteq$ 150	SD	4.43	9.33	9.07
Nontraditional	Mean	136.39	146.64	148.19
N = 84	SD	4.72	9.66	9.03
Nonvoucher	Mean	134.93	142.87	149.81
N = 120	SD	4.03	7.01	8.50
	$F_{(2,351)}$	2.75	5.07	<1
	p	.065	<.01	

at each time period. The large increase in standard deviation from the
first to the second grade appears to be largely a result of the norming
process. It is clear from the F tests in the table that, at least prior to the
start of the voucher demonstration, the groups were (statistically)
significantly nonequivalent in terms of reading ability.

A cursory look at Figure 2 reveals that there was little difference
between the mean performance of the nonvoucher and the traditional
voucher students over the three-year period, including the first year
of the voucher demonstration. If anything, the traditional group lost
ground in reading achievement compared to the nonvoucher group
during the voucher demonstration's first year. In contrast, large
differences are evident in comparing the mean performance of the nontraditional voucher group to the other two groups. In particular, it
appears that the nontraditional group started out somewhat superior to
the other two groups but lost that superiority during the first year
of the demonstration. As will be seen below, the various statistical
models generally agree that this latter shift should be attributed to
the effect of the voucher demonstration.

PRETEST-POSTTEST

The results of the numerous tests are presented in Table 2.[4] Looking
first at the pretest-posttest analyses, it is of interest to note that the
results of the different models all tend to agree. Within any one row
(which contains the results of a specific comparison between treatment
groups), the treatment effect estimates are all in the same direction
and, with a few exceptions, roughly comparable. Further, if one test
reaches conventional levels of significance, the others generally do also.
More specifically, the first row of the table compares the voucher programs (traditional and nontraditional combined) to the nonvoucher

TABLE 2
Analyses of the Education Voucher Quasi-Experiments

Comparison	Statistic	Gain Score Analysis[a]	ANCOVA[b]	ANCOVA with Correction for Pretest Unreliability[b]	ANCOVA with Pretest-Posttest Correlation Correction[b]	Prediction Based on Grades 1 and 2[a]
			Pretest-Posttest			
Voucher-Nonvoucher	β	-2.61	-1.88	-2.07	-2.64	-3.29
	F	8.46**	5.38*	6.52*	10.44**	13.48**
Traditional-Nonvoucher	β	-1.05	-.76	-.84	-1.06	-.82
	F	1.14	<1	<1	1.44	<1
Traditional-Nontraditional	β	4.35	3.11	3.44	4.41	6.88
	F	15.96**	9.92**	12.00**	19.16**	40.02**
Nontraditional-Nonvoucher	β	-5.39	-3.88	-4.28	-5.47	-7.70
	F	22.56**	14.00**	16.88**	26.54**	45.99**

Table 2 (Continued)

Comparison	Statistic	Gain Score Analysis[a]	ANCOVA[b]	ANCOVA with Correction for Pretest Unreliability[b]	ANCOVA with Pretest-Posttest Correlation Correction[b]	Prediction Based on Grades 1 and 2[a]
			Dry Run			
Voucher-Nonvoucher	β	.68	.66	.45	-.33	
	F	<1	<1	<1	<1	
Traditional-Nonvoucher	β	-.23	-.25	-.42	-1.07	
	F	<1	<1	<1	1.38	
Traditional-Nontraditional	β	-2.54	-2.52	-2.43	-2.06	
	F	6.44*	6.34*	5.88*	4.22*	
Nontraditional-Nonvoucher	β	2.31	2.28	2.01	.99	
	F	4.90*	4.68*	3.64†	<	

a. The degrees of freedom for the F tests in this column are (1,351).
b. The degrees of freedom for the F tests in these columns are (1,350).

* p < .05
** p < .01
† p < .1

programs. The results reveal a significant superiority of the nonvoucher program, and are consistent with Klitgaard's original analysis based on school means which showed a decline associated with the voucher programs as a whole.

Upon disaggregating the voucher group into the traditional and nontraditional programs, a different picture emerges. There is only a small treatment effect estimate in the comparison of the traditional and nonvoucher programs (row 2) although the small difference does favor the nonvoucher group. The F values are uniformly small and non-significant.[5] On the other hand, it appears that the nontraditional program had a significantly harmful effect when compared to either the traditional or nonvoucher programs (rows 3 and 4). All of these analyses produce consistently large negative treatment estimates and large F ratios.

DRY RUN

The evidence that a harmful effect is associated with the non-traditional voucher program, but not with the traditional program, is reinforced by the results in the dry run analyses. Again, the results of the models, as applied in the dry run, show general consistency within each comparison. The first two comparisons (rows 5 and 6) yield null results. Under the condition that a model must demonstrate its acceptability for a specific comparison in the dry run data (i.e., by revealing null results) before it is deemed appropriate for the pretest-posttest data, the observed null findings in the dry run strengthen the results of the corresponding comparisons in the pretest-postest. The last two comparisons in the dry run (rows 7 and 8) reveal generally large, in absolute value, treatment effect estimates (even when they appear only marginally significant), but they are in the *opposite* direction to the corresponding estimates in the pretest-postest data. This suggests, given the above assumption, that the treatment effects in the pretest-posttest data have countervailed against a natural trend in the opposite direction, and, therefore, that the results of the analyses of the former probably underestimate the size of the true effects.

Overall the results appear to be very consistent. Compared to the nonvoucher program, the traditional voucher group had no effect or at worst a slight negative effect. On the other hand, compared to either the nonvoucher or traditional voucher programs, the nontraditional voucher curricula had a reliable negative effect. The size of this estimated effect, however, is not overwhelming—roughly 5 items on a 50-item test.

More fine-grained analysis probably could provide further insight if more data were available. For example, the mean performance in both the traditional and nontraditional programs in one of the voucher schools exhibited an absolute decline from grade 2 to grade 3 and it was the only school to do so. This is somewhat surprising (assuming that the norms used to scale the test scores are reasonably appropriate) because one expects children of this age to be gradually increasing their reading ability over time. This suggests that perhaps only a few schools or minischool programs are producing the negative effects observed in the data. With this in mind, the Rand data were reexamined (Klitgaard, 1974: 108). The mean loss or decline in reaching achievement for each of the five elementary voucher schools across the first three grades was calculated by simply subtracting the mean raw-reading score for 1971-1972 from the score for 1972-1973. When this was done, this same school accounted for 42% of the total decline but only about 20% of the voucher students.

DISCUSSION

As has been noted above, conducting an appropriate analysis of the data and producing credible results is one of the major problems facing the researcher who employs a nonequivalent control group design. Two approaches have been taken to deal with this problem: (1) multiple analyses have been performed each of which have somewhat different assumptions about the nature of the data, and (2) a dry run (no treatment), double pretest has been used both directly to predict the third-grade test scores and to assess the credibility of the various statistical models. Thus for this design a strategy that employs multiple statistical models (including additional waves of data in the analysis where possible) is superior to the standard, single analysis procedure. Nevertheless, even with these safeguards, the interpretation of the results must proceed with some caution since alternative explanations for the outcomes will always be possible. Such caution usually reflects a realistic assessment of the state of the art in analyzing this quasi-experimental data and not any shortcomings on the part of the analyst.

VALIDITY OF RESULTS

For these reasons, the researcher should carefully consider the assumptions underlying the analyses and examine them in detail for plausible rival hypotheses that could produce the same results. One alternative explanation often found in educational research is that the actual pattern of growth which the individuals followed differed from the pattern that was assumed by the models. In addition to the possibility of differential growth rates, testing effects or problems of attrition also may have produced the observed results.

There is some evidence that the patterns of growth by the models were inappropriate. In particular, our use of the dry run analyses and the prediction based on grades 1 and 2 explicitly assumes similar growth patterns from grades 1 to 2 and from grades 2 to 3 (save for a treatment effect). However, children typically undergo rapid growth in academic skills during this time and it certainly would be plausible for the growth rate to vary from one grade to the next. The empirical evidence supports the contention that conditions did not remain constant over time. The within-group regression slopes of grade 2 scores on grade 1 scores were all roughly equal to 1.0, while the within-group regression slopes of grade 3 on grade 2 scores were all approximately 0.6. Moreover, the distributions of test scores became more negatively skewed over time. The coefficients of skewness within the groups were approximately equal to 1.0, 0.3, and 0.4 in grades 1, 2, and 3, respectively.

Further doubt surrounds the appropriateness of the assumed growth patterns in the other analyses applied to the pretest-posttest quasi-experiment. It was hoped that the results of these multiple analyses would bracket the "true" estimate of the treatment effect. Or in other words, by using analyses with different assumptions about the pattern of outcomes, some models might underestimate the effect while others would overestimate it—forming a sort of "confidence interval." It appears plausible, however, that for these data the models are all biased in the same direction. If these models really do bracket the true effect, then within each dry run comparison the estimates should fall on both sides of the zero value since there was *no* treatment effect during this time. Unfortunately, the range of estimates encompasses the zero point in only one comparison (row 5) out of four. In addition, it is clear that the estimates in one comparison (row 7) are all substantially different from zero. Of course, this does not necessarily imply that the direction of the estimates in the pretest-posttest data are incorrect; it only suggests that they might not bracket the true value. Some of the comparisons could be underestimated, as suggested above, or some could be overestimated.

Other rival hypotheses exist as well. It is possible that a testing effect produced a spurious decline in performance in the nontraditional voucher group. The changes in the skewness of the distributions and the regression slopes of the scatterplots (noted above) indicate that a ceiling effect might have been operating at grade 3. Such an effect could artificially reduce the size of the observed differences between the groups and invalidate the results. A closer examination of the distribution of these test scores suggests, instead, that a ceiling effect probably did not account for the entire decline in the test performance of the nontraditional program relative to the other two groups. The size of the decline is simply too large to attribute it completely to an apparently slight ceiling effect.

Finally, it is necessary to consider whether differential attrition produced the observed effects. Since the performance of an intact cohort was tracked over the entire three-year period, differential attrition appears to be ruled out as a direct explanation of any change in performance. However, students learn from one another perhaps as much as from the teacher. It thus is important to determine the quality of their school environments and therefore to consider the effects of attrition among the classmates of the students in the cohort. Some trends in the data lend support to the hypothesis of differential attrition but the differences were neither large nor statistically significant.

CONCLUSIONS

What then can one reasonably conclude from this study? Despite the various threats to the credibility of the analyses and to the validity of the findings, the above interpretation of the results appears, on the whole, to be the most accurate and reasonable (although still tentative) conclusion. If the data had turned out differently, more caution would be warranted. From the present perspective, however, the trends in the data are more parsimoniously explained as a legitimate treatment effect than by a combination of rival hypotheses. Specifically, the mean performance in the nonvoucher and traditional voucher programs remain so similar over time that it is more plausible to conclude that there was only a small treatment effect (if any) than to conclude that a large effect was almost perfectly counterbalanced by some other factors. Similarly, the relative decline in performance in the nontraditional group is most plausibly attributed to a treatment effect. In educational research it is typically expected that students who are performing better than their peers will retain and even increase that superiority over time. Thus it seems more plausible to infer that the voucher demonstration was responsible for closing the gap in performance between the initially superior nontraditional voucher students and the two other comparison groups than to assume that such a pattern of growth occurred under null conditions.[6] It is unclear whether the size of this presumed effect is of educational significance.

A critical question is whether this reading loss is due to the effects of the voucher demonstration per se or to implementation of the new, innovative, nontraditional curricula. It should be remembered that the voucher concept primarily involved a fiscal and administrative reorganization in the operation of the schools and not curriculum innovation. In fact there is strong evidence (Wortman and St. Pierre, 1977) that these aspects of the voucher concept were not well implemented during the first year! Moreover, it would not be surprising if the nontraditional curricula were responsible. It is quite plausible that the loss of teacher time due to planning, developing, and modifying a new curricula produced a loss in achievement.

In light of these results it is appropriate to consider the proper role of evaluation in such an innovative program. Given the above discussion, it is clear that firm outcome assessments concerning the overall performance of the voucher demonstration are being made where none are warranted. At best this information might have been of value to administrators and teachers in developing and improving minischools. Was the voucher program entirely reponsible for the curricular choices of the bright students? Were teachers in the innovative minischools not allocating enough time to basic reading skills? These would have been relevant questions during the early stages of curiculum design and innovation that comprised a major component of the voucher demonstration. After all, the voucher program had support for at least five years. In general, the first year, or perhaps two, of a major new program should be reserved for such formative evaluation almost exclusively. It is simply too early to form any other judgment.

There is also an important issue involving the choice of instruments or observations that form the basis of the evaluation. It is likely that standard achievement tests will be employed in most educational innovations, simply because they are available and often (as in the present case) because they are mandated. The primary goal of the new voucher programs was not to increase reading or other kinds of achievement as in a compensatory program, but to increase parental choice and satisfaction with the schools. Although measures of these goals were collected and analyzed by Rand, these issues have been largely ignored in the debate over vouchers (though Levin, 1974, provides a counterexample). It is apparent that tests tailored to specific treatments and sensitive to their effects are essential to evaluation. Moreover, such measures will reduce the often encountered hostility to evaluation that results from the insensitivity of the evaluators to the goals of the program staff. Thus multiple measures, as well as multiple analyses, must be employed. Only with a diversity of dependent measures can a less distorted estimate of a program's effects be obtained.

NOTES

1. The Education Voucher Demonstration was initially funded by the Office of Economic Opportunity and subsequently continued under the auspices of the National Institute of Education.

2. There was no way to estimate the within-group reliability of the pretest scores from the data in our sample so we used the lower bound of the test publisher's (Educational Testing Service, 1967) alternate form estimate of reliability, which was .85. Unfortunately we can only speculate on how appropriate this value is for the sample at hand.

3. In our sample the within-group pretest-posttest correlations were all approximately .6.

4. Fitting curvilinear or interaction terms in the relevant analyses does not substantially alter the interpretation. Nor does the interpretation change when different units or analysis are employed. Virtually the same results were obtained in analyses based on classroom means or school means. A copy of these results is available from the author upon request. Finally, the interpretation of the results in Table 2 does not substantially change if one uses a multiple comparison technique (e.g., Scheffe, 1959) that takes into account the number of comparisons involved. The Scheffe contrasts can be generated from the tabled data by halving the F values and changing the degrees of freedom in the numerator from 1 to 2. In this way, one can insure that in examining the results from any one statistical model (but not across models), within either the dry run or pretest-posttest data, the probability of finding one *or more* statistically significant results at the .05 level is .05 (assuming the model and null hypothesis are correct).

5. Both the ANCOVA with pretest-posttest correlation correction and the gain-score analysis reach the .05 level of statistical significance in the augmented cohort ($\beta = -1.75$, $F(1,459) = 4.90$ and $\beta = -1.70$, $F(1,460) = 3.85$, respectively).

6. On inspecting Figure 2, one is tempted to say that the initial gap between the nontraditional voucher students and the others were *reversed* in grade 3. The results of the F tests in Table 1, however, do not support the conclusion that the nontraditional voucher program became inferior in the third grade—only that it became equivalent to the other groups.

REFERENCES

BARKER, P. (1974a) "Methodological issues in measuring student achievement," pp. 96-104 in D. Weiler (ed.) A Public School Voucher Demonstration: The First Year at Alum Rock, Technical Appendix. Santa Monica, CA: Rand Corporation, Technical Report R-1495/2-NIE (June).

――― (1974b) "Preliminary analysis of Metropolitan Achievement Test scores, voucher and Title I schools, 1972-73," pp. 120-130 in D. Weiler (ed.) A Public School Voucher Demonstration: The First Year at Alum Rock, Technical Appendix. Santa Monica, CA: Rand Corporation, Technical Report R-1495/2-NIE (June).

BORUCH, R. F. and H. GOMEZ (1976) "Double pretests for checking certain threats to the validity of some conventional evaluation designs or stalking the null hypothesis." Evanston, IL: Northwestern University, Psychology Department Technical Report.

CAMPBELL, D. T. (1974) "Measurement and experimentation in social settings." Evanston, IL: Northwestern University, Psychology Department Technical Report 627b (May).

――― and R. F. BORUCH (1975) "Making the case for randomized assignment to treatments by considering the alternatives: six ways in which quasi-experimental evaluations in compensatory education tend to underestimate effects," pp. 195-285 in C. A. Bennett and A. A. Lumsdaine (eds.) Evaluation and Experiment: Some Critical Issues in Assessing Social Programs. New York: Academic Press.

CAMPBELL, D. T. and A. ERLEBACHER (1970) "How regression artifacts in quasi-experimental evaluations can mistakenly make compensatory education look harmful," pp. 185-210 in J. Hellmuth (ed.) The Disadvantaged Child, Vol. 3. New York: Brunner/Mazel.

CAMPBELL, D. T. and J. STANLEY (1966) Experimental and Quasi-Experimental Designs for Research. Chicago: Rand McNally.

COCHRAN, W. G. (1968) "Errors of measurement in statistics." Technometrics 10: 637-666.

――― and D. B. RUBIN (1973) "Controlling bias in observational studies: a review." Sankhyā (Series A) 35: 417-446.

COOK, T. D. and C. S. REICHARDT (1976) "Guidelines—statistical analysis of non-equivalent control group designs: a guide to some current literature." Evaluation 3: 136-138.

CRONBACH, L. J., D. R. ROGOSA, R. E. FLODEN, and G. G. PRICE (1977) "Analysis of covariance in nonrandomized experiments: parameters affecting bias." Occasional Paper, Stanford Evaluation Consortium, Stanford University (August).

DIRECTOR, S. M. (1974) "Underadjustment bias in the quasi-experimental evaluation of manpower training." Ph.D. dissertation, Northwestern University.

Educational Testing Service (1967) Handbook: Cooperative Primary Tests. Princeton, NJ: Educational Testing Service.

KEESLING, J. W. and D. E. WILEY (1977) "Measurement error and the analysis of quasi-experimental data." Mehr Licht: Studies of Educative Processes, Technical Report. Chicago: CEMREL (July).

KENNY, D. A. (1975) "A quasi-experimental approach to assessing treatment effects in the nonequivalent control group design." Psych. Bull. 82: 345-362.

KLITGAARD, R. (1974) "Preliminary analysis of achievement test scores in Alum Rock voucher and nonvoucher schools, 1972-73," pp. 105-119 in D. Weiler (ed.) A Public School Voucher Demonstration: The First Year at Alum Rock, Technical Appendix. Santa Monica, CA: Rand Corporation, Technical Report R-1495/2-NIE (June).

LEVIN, J. M. (1974) "Alum Rock, after two years: you, dear reader, have a choice." Phi Delta Kappan (November): 201-204.

LORD, F. M. (1967) "A paradox in the interpretation of group comparisons." Psych. Bull. 68: 304-305.

——— (1960) "Large-sample covariance analysis when the control variable is fallible." J. of the Amer. Statistical Association 55: 307-321.

PORTER, A. C. (1967) "The effects of using fallible variables in the analysis of co-variance." Ph.D. dissertation, University of Wisconsin. (Ann Arbor, MI: University Microfilms, 1968)

——— and T. R. CHIBUCOS (1974) "Selecting analysis strategies," pp. 415-464 in G. D. Borich (ed.) Evaluating Educational Programs and Products. Englewood Cliffs, NJ: Educational Technology Publications.

REICHARDT, C. S. (1977) "The statistical analysis of data from the non-equivalent control group design," in T. D. Cook and D. T. Campbell (eds.) The Design and Conduct of Quasi-Experiments. Chicago: Rand-McNally.

Report of Education Research (1974) "What really hapened to student achievement in Alum Rock?" (September 11): 8-10.

SCHEFFE, H. (1959) The Analysis of Variance. New York: John Wiley.

SHANKER, A. (1974) "Two panaceas take it on the chin." The New York Times (December 1): E9.

WARREN, J. (1976) "Alum Rock Voucher Project." Educational Researcher (March): 13-15.

WEILER, D. (1976) "A public school voucher demonstration: the first year of Alum Rock—summary and conclusions," pp. 279-304 in G. V. Glass (ed.) Evaluation Studies Review Annual, Vol. I. Beverly Hills: Sage.

——— (1974a) A Public School Voucher Demonstration: The First Year at Alum Rock. Santa Monica, CA: Rand Corporation, Technical Report R-1495-NIE (June).

——— (1974b) A Public School Voucher Demonstration: The First Year at Alum Rock, Technical Appendix. Santa Monica, CA: Rand Corporation, Technical Report, R.-1945/2-NIE (June).

WORTMAN, P. M. and R. G. St. PIERRE (1977) "The Educational Voucher Demonstration: a secondary analysis." Educ. Urban Society 9 (August): 471-492.

Paul M. Wortman is Associate Director of Northwestern University's Division of Methodology and Evaluation Research, and he is a Senior Research Associate in the Department of Psychology. He and his colleagues are interested in developing new techniques of analysis, testing them by performing secondary analyses of educational and health data, and enhancing the policy relevance of evaluation methods.

Charles S. Reichardt is currently completing his graduate studies in the Department of Psychology's Division of Methodology and Evaluation Research at Northwestern University. His interests focus on both developing theoretical extensions and overcoming practical difficulties in the design and analysis of applied social research.

Robert G. St. Pierre is a Social Scientist in Education at Abt Associates Inc. of Cambridge, Massachusetts. His primary interest is in evaluation research with an emphasis on the evaluation of compensatory educational programs. He has a Ph.D. in Educational Research, Measurement and Evaluation from Boston College and spent a postdoctoral year in the Division of Methodology and Evaluation Research at Northwestern University.

In this chapter Elesh and Lefcowitz argue that economic and sociological theory would predict that an income supplement should increase the use of health services but that a review of the literature on health care utilization research would suggest that there would be no change. The analysis performed by the authors did, in fact, suggest that the income supplement had no effect on the use of health services. Two questions with respect to the external validity of the study may be raised. First, one can question whether the treatment was actually strong enough to produce a detectable effect since the maximum guaranteed-income value was only 125% above the poverty level with a 50% tax on earnings above that point. At the income levels achieved there may still have been demands on family resources stronger than health care. Even the 50% tax on extra earnings might not be sufficient to cause people near the poverty level to declare themselves sick and unable to work. The second question about external validity arises from the fact that 45% of the families originally enrolled had to be excluded from the analysis of health care utilization. No information is given on variability in health care utilization, and it is at least possible that families for which effects might have been observed were lost from this analysis.

26

The Effects of the New Jersey-Pennsylvania Negative Income Tax Experiment on Health and Health Care Utilization

David Elesh and M. Jack Lefcowitz

This paper examines the effects of the recently completed New Jersey-Pennsylvania Negative Income Tax Experiment on health and health care utilization. Both economic and sociological theory suggest that the negative tax benefits may, in the short run, increase the proportions reporting themselves in ill health and utilizing care, and, in the long run, reduce these figures. However, the empirical literature suggests the effects may be modest, vary by family members, and be swamped by other variables. Data are presented for two or three points in time (depending on the family member) over the three year duration of the experiments and no effects of any kind are observed. The results give credence to suggestions that health and health care utilization may be more a function of life style or preferences than income. While neither economic nor sociological theory asserts the effects of income are simple, these data suggest its theoretical role is still not well understood.

This paper examines the effects of the recently completed New Jersey-Pennsylvania Negative Income Tax Experiment on health and health care utilization.[1] The issue is an important one for two reasons. First, for those family members who are potential or active labor-force participants, the experimental benefits, by lowering the costs of not working and increasing the funds available for health care, may lead individuals to acknowledge health conditions that their need to earn had previously caused them to ignore. Second, the experimental payments may make possible expenditures for health which improve the ability to work or to engage in other, nonwork activities. Thus, the experiment's effects on health and the utilization of health care may have an important bearing on the assessment of the costs and benefits of a negative income tax program.

The conditions under which these possibilities arise can be phrased in terms of both economic and sociological theory. Both types of theory begin by drawing a distinction between the theory appropriate to predictions regarding experimental effects on health itself and the theory appropriate to predictions regarding the effects of the experiment on the utilization of health care. Economic theory stresses the effects of income, while sociological theory, which generally accepts the economic model, elaborates the role of a number of factors recognized but little investigated by economists.

ECONOMIC AND SOCIOLOGICAL THEORY

Economic Theory of Experimental Effects on Health

Predictions as to the effects of the experimental payments on health follow from a simple model of the allocation of time based on the general theory of choice. The unit of analysis is defined as the household, made up of individuals whose preference functions are combined to form the aggregate household preferences and whose activities determine its resource base. For those household members who are actual or potential suppliers

* Names of authors are listed alphabetically. This paper has benefited from the comments of the *Journal's* referees; they are, of course, not responsible for any errors that may remain. The research reported here was supported in part by funds granted to the Institution for Research on Poverty at the University of Wisconsin by the Office of Economic Opportunity pursuant to the Economic Opportunity Act of 1964.

From David Elesh and M. Jack Lefcowitz, "The Effects of the New Jersey-Pennsylvania Negative Income Tax Experiment on Health and Health Care Utilization," 18(4) *Journal of Health and Social Behavior* 391-405 (December 1977). Copyright 1977 by American Sociological Association.

of labor, the fundamental time allocation problem lies in the decision as to the amount of time spent working by each family member. The factors affecting this decision are fourfold: (1) the family's views or preferences; (2) the expected market earning rates of its members; (3) the nonmarket earning rates of its members; and (4) the household's total budget constraint. This last factor is a function of the total number of hours available, the set of prospective market and nonmarket earning rates, any other income the family expects to receive, and the monetary value of its saleable assets. The experimental payments could affect the health of the labor suppliers through all four of these factors.

If the family treats the benefits as additions to what Friedman (1957) has termed their "permanent" or long-run average income—the income on which they base their allocation decisions—then, in the short run, the payments increase the nonmarketing earning rates of the family members relative to their market rates and increase the household's total budget constraint. By thus reducing the costs of not working, the payments may lead some family members not previously willing to acknowledge a health condition to do so, thereby increasing the proportion of persons reporting themselves as in ill health. In addition, other family members, who dislike work and who now find the cost of not working reduced, may become "ill" in order to have a legitimate reason for diminishing their labor supply (Cole and LeJeune, 1972). More generally, the payments may affect the health of all family members (including those who do not supply labor) by increasing the funds available for the utilization of health care, perhaps promoting some individuals (previously inhibited from doing so by their financial inability to afford care) to acknowledge health conditions.

In the long run, however, the proportion of those who were encouraged to declare themselves ill by their greater ability to afford care and the proportion who had otherwise declared themselves ill should decrease in relation to the efficacy of the care received.[2]

Economic Theory of Experimental Effects on Utilization of Care

As is implicit in the above discussion, the effects of the experimental payments on the utilization of health care follow from the theory of consumption. Within this theory, consumption, other things being equal, is considered a function of the household's preferences which are, themselves, typically taken to be a function of the household's permanent income. In other words, at different levels of permanent income, families become accustomed to different expenditure levels for different kinds of goods and services and their preferences change accordingly. The implication of these propositions for utilization of care is that if health care is a normal good—that is, if consumption of it increases with income—then the additional income represented by the payments should increase its utilization—this increased utilization being, in the short run, primarily attributable to the accumulation of health problems that the family could not previously afford to have treated. In the long run, however, the experiment's effects on utilization depend upon whether the families perceive the payments as additions to permanent or to transitory income. If they see the benefits as additions to permanent income, then they can be expected to adopt the higher levels of consumption typical of these higher income levels. On the other hand, if they see the payments as additions to transitory income, then utilization should decline as the backlog of untreated health conditions is reduced.

Sociological Theory of Experimental Effects on Health and Health Care Utilization

Given the *ceteris paribus* assumptions made in the above economic theories, sociological theory would predict the same effects, but would be chiefly directed to analyzing effects when those assumptions are not made. Sociological analysis of the relationship between health and utilization of care begins with the recognition that health is socially defined: that is, individuals and groups differ in their ability to recognize objective symptoms, in terms both of what they define as symptoms of illness and of the interpretations they place upon them. Depending upon their situation and personal characteristics, individuals may or may not be aware of their symptoms, may or may not define these symptoms as being indicative of illness, may or may not consider themselves sufficiently ill to require medical attention, and may or may not obtain that attention. And, again, depending on their situation and personal characteristics, they may be selective in where they seek that attention. Thus, the process may be seen as a series of decision points leading to use of the medical care system with a variety of factors affecting each successive step (Andersen, 1968, Mechanic, 1968).

Among the most important of the factors that have been shown to affect the elements of this process are the individual's values, ethnicity, education, income, age, sex, and family size (Aday and Eichorn, 1972, Andersen et al., 1975). Within the context of the array of these variables, the effects of income are necessarily limited by the extent to which income is correlated with or, more importantly, a function of the other variables. In particular, an individual's income is clearly a function of his age, sex, ethnicity, education, and, perhaps, values. Thus, the effects of income on health attitudes or behaviors can be expected to diminish commensurate with the extent to which these causally prior variables are held constant.

The available evidence suggests that, given such controls, income has little or no net effect on most health variables. For example, Feldman (1966) and Samora et al. (1962) found that when education is controlled, most of the differences in health knowledge due to income disappear; but when income is controlled, the differences by education remain. The findings with respect to illness are more difficult to assess because of inadequate controls in the available data and because of some ambiguity as to how much of the

association between health measures and income is to be attributed to the lower earnings of the unhealthy rather than to an increase in feelings of health, better diet, better housing, or to the higher use of medical care attributable to income. However, Lefcowitz (1973a) has pointed out that with suitable controls for age, or age and sex, the differentials by income for a larger variety of illness conditions become highly attenuated or disappear altogether. Similarly, Luft (1972), in his review of the literature, finds a frequent absence of any income effect on illness; and where the literature does support an income effect—as is the case for injury rates, number of chronic conditions, number of restricted activity and work days lost—one must ask whether the observed effects are due to the occupational hazards faced by and greater physical demands placed upon low-income workers rather than to income itself. Unfortunately, there has been little research on this question. More generally, there has been little research on the relative effects of health on income and income on health, although recent assessments of the existing evidence suggests that the effects of health on income are by far the more important of the two (Harkey et al., 1976; Lefcowitz, 1973a; Luft, 1972; Andersen and Benham, 1970).

A more persuasive argument can be made for the effects of income on utilization because, whatever effects other variables may have on the propensity to seek care, its actual consumption would seem to depend on the family's ability to pay for it. Yet, here again, the effects of income are unclear and are contingent upon the measure of utilization one employs. The National Health Survey (National Center for Health Statistics, 1972a) has found differentials by income for the average length of hospital stays, the rate of hospital discharges, and the rate of surgically related discharges, but for persons above the age of sixteen has found no differences in the number of physician visits per person per year. (For children below the age of 17, income has a substantial effect; children in families with annual incomes under $3,000 average 2.7 physician visits per person per year while children in families with incomes of at least $10,000 average 4.3.) We must note, however, that income effects disappear when head's education or education and age is taken into account (Benham and Benham, 1975; Lefcowitz, 1973b). Similarly, Shortell (1975), analyzing the total number of ambulatory care visits for major illness episodes, found income to have no measurable net effect after controlling for other patient, provider, and source of payment variables.

While it would seem from the above review that the effects of income are uncertain and probably small, it can be argued that the literature has inadequately examined them. First, a serious methodological problem arises from the fact that most of the predicted income effects are predicated on a family's permanent income, but the existing estimates are based on measures that include transitory income. Measured income—because of episodes of unemployment, illness, or on the other hand, temporary good luck—is typically different from permanent income, so the literature has (to some degree) misestimated the real underlying influence of income. The second argument—that studies frequently fail to control for the possession of health insurance—leads to the conclusion that the effects of income are underestimated only if it is presumed that insurance reduces the differentials to be expected by income. However, because income and possession of health insurance are highly correlated (National Center for Health Statistics, 1972b), this presumption may be unwarranted. For example, Richardson, in his study of the use of physicians by a low-income population, found that whether considered separately or together, family income and health insurance had no effect on their use of physicians' services (Richardson, 1971).[3]

In summary, expectations as to the effects of the experimental benefits on health and health care utilization are by no means clear. While the predictions of economic theory may hold if the families treat the payments as additions to their permanent income, the magnitude of these effects relative to those of education, age,

ethnicity, values, and other factors may be so small as to be unobservable.

Apart from the general question as to whether the experiment is likely to affect health and the utilization of care, we may also ask whether effects are more probable for some family members than for others. With regard to medical care, Koos (1954) and Richardson (1971) have suggested that use should be related to the instrumentality of a family member's position in the household because the cost of illness should increase with instrumentality. Since the husband is typically the main earner, this would imply that experimental effects would be most probable for him. Wives would be the next most likely to be affected, since they are the next most instrumental, and the children would be least affected. One may make a similar argument with respect to the effects of the experiment on health of the family members: those who are most instrumental should be least likely to become unhealthy because the costs of doing so are greatest.

On the other hand, there is another line of argument which suggests that the experimental payments may have their primary effect on the use of care by children—particularly children under five or six years old. According to this view, children are most likely to benefit from the payments for two reasons. First, the high socioemotional investment their parents have in them ordinarily leads the parents to seek care at the first signs of illness, and the payments should reinforce that tendency. Second, children, especially young children, in addition to being confronted with many of the diseases of their elders, are subject to a variety of diseases such as measles, chicken pox, and mumps which generally involve the use of medical care; thus, their greater need for care may interact with the presence of the payments to produce greater use of care for children and may, under certain definitions of ill health, produce more ill health among them. For example, parents, who (given the payments) are better able to afford the costs of unhealthy children, may be more willing to accept certain symptoms as indicative of illness and more willing to seek care than they had been previously.

Since there are no a priori grounds on which to decide between these two lines of argument, we must turn to the literature for assistance. Unfortunately, there are almost no pertinent studies. Indeed, perhaps the only systematic research in this area is Richardson's (1971) study of the use of physicians by a low-income population, which showed that the relationship between family status and delay in seeking care or amount of care received was contingent on the seriousness of the illness episode. When an illness was not serious—which is to say, most of the time—children and particularly children under six received care more quickly and had more of it than either of their parents; however, when the illness was serious, the male head of the household was the quickest to receive it and consumed more of it. Wives occupied a somewhat intermediate position: regardless of the seriousness of their illness, they delayed the longest in seeking care; and the amount of care they received was about the same as that of their husbands when their illness was nonserious, and intermediate between the amounts received by their husbands and children when it was serious. Thus, from this evidence, it would appear that instrumentality determines the use of care when an illness is serious; otherwise, what appears to be a generalized parental concern for young children does.

Finally, we may ask whether, aside from the possible general effects of the payments on health and utilization or differential effects according to status in the family, there are effects on the pattern of care. For example, there is some literature to suggest that people prefer private physicians but use "public" physicians when they cannot afford the former (Elesh and Schollaert, 1972). Thus, it is possible that with or without an increase in utilization, the experimental payments may cause a shift toward greater use of private physicians.

THE EXPERIMENTAL DESIGN[4]

The primary purpose of the experiment was to assess the labor supply response of the urban poor in intact families, and con-sequently, the sample was restricted to families (1) with at least one dependent person and an able-bodied male who was between 18 and 58 years of age and not in the armed forces, a student, or institutionalized and (2) with total family income no more than 150 percent of the poverty line for each family size. The sample was drawn from poverty tracts in Trenton, Paterson, Passaic, and Jersey City, New Jersey; and Scranton, Pennsylvania.

Once eligibility was determined from a special screening interview, families were assigned to one of eight negative tax plans, which together defined the experimental group, or to the control group. The eight tax plans were combinations of guarantee levels and tax rates which, in our judgment, encompass the area of greatest policy interest. Guarantee levels are the annual values of the experimental benefits paid when family income is zero.[5] Tax rates are the rates at which the benefits are reduced as family income rises. Four guarantee levels (50, 75, 100, and 125 percent of the poverty line for each family size) and three tax rates (30, 50, and 70 percent) were tested. The eight tax plans involved the following combinations of guarantee levels and tax rates: 50–30, 50–50, 75–30, 75–50, 75–70, 100–50, 100–70, 125–50. Assignment of the experimental and control groups utilized an optimal design model developed by Conlisk and Watts (1969), which minimized, subject to certain budgetary constraints, the error variance of the estimates of changes in family earnings (adjusted for family size) induced by the experimental payments. To have attained comparable precise estimates with a purely random assignment would have required a substantially larger sample at much greater cost. However, use of the model meant that all of the experimental plans differed in average family income and required special analytic controls which are discussed below. Seven hundred twenty-five families were assigned to the experimental group and 632 to the control group, and the sample was stratified by the three major ethnic groups in the experimental sites—whites, blacks, and Spanish-speakers—and by three income strata, where income was weighted by family size.

After the families were assigned, all (experimental and control) received a pre-enrollment interview to obtain baseline data in a variety of areas uncontaminated by knowledge of the experiment or the inception of the negative tax transfers. Subsequently, the three year program was explained to the experimental families and those who agreed to participate (less than seven percent refused) began receiving payments every two weeks. Their obligation was to report their income and family composition each month. Both the experimental and control groups were interviewed quarterly.

METHODOLOGICAL ISSUES

In an earlier section, we commented that the effects of the experiment on health and the utilization of health care may be contingent on the particular measures of these factors employed. In this section, we address this question in greater detail, discussing in turn the kinds and quality of the data on health and utilization of care, the timing of their measurement, the parameterization of the experimental plans, and the operationalization of the sociological model for the estimation of experimental effects. Following this, we describe the sample analyzed here.

Data

Because of the presumed importance of health on labor-supply response and as a response itself to the experiment, a substantial amount of health data were gathered for the head, spouse, and children of the household. The available data include, for the year prior to the interview, measures of the number and type of chronic illnesses, the number of days spent in a hospital, the number of hospital stays, the number of days spent in bed because of illness, the number of days of work (including housework for wives, school for children) lost due to illness, and the number of visits to physicians of various types. The range of these data is sufficiently broad for one to feel confident that any reasonable definition of health or ill health and the most important types of health care utilization will be captured within it, and the information is similar to that collected in many other health surveys (indeed, most of the questions on health were taken from the National Health Survey). It may be, however, of somewhat better quality, in that the head and spouse were each asked to report on his or her health and utilization of care (one parent reported on their children's health), whereas the more common practice is to ask a single informant to report on the health and health care utilization of the entire household.

From these data, we shall examine the effects of the experiment on the head's and spouse's number of chronic conditions, number of work days lost, number of days spent in a hospital, and number of physician visits both in total and decomposed into private and "other" visits; for the children, we shall examine the experiment's effects on the per capita number of chronic conditions, the per capita number of days spent in bed, whether any child has spent at least one night in a hospital in the year previous to the interview, and the per capita number of visits to a physician similarly categorized. For present purposes, we shall ignore possible experimental effects on the adults' types of chronic conditions, number of days spent in bed, and number of hospital stays, and on the children's types of chronic conditions, number of days lost from school, and number of days spent in a hospital. The reason for the exclusion of types of chronic conditions is that our primary interest is in whether any chronic condition appears or disappears as a result of the experiment, not in specific types of conditions. Days in bed is excluded from the adults' analyses because it is highly correlated with days lost from work (average r at a given time point $= .85$),[6] and the latter is more likely to capture something of the family's loss in welfare due to lost income. The number of adult hospital stays is not analyzed simply because there is little variance in the variable and it is highly correlated with the number of days spent in a hospital (average r at a given time point $= .94$). The number of days lost from school was dropped because it does not sufficiently indicate the ill health of the preschoolers and because, in any event, it is highly correlated with per capita days in bed. Finally, the reason that we did not analyze children's per capita hospitals days is that, because so few children are hospitalized, the variable is extremely skewed. Consequently, a simple dichotomous measure of hospitalization was employed. Skewness is, in fact, a general problem in these data, and we attempted to correct for it by applying the transformation, $\log_e (x + 1)$, to all of the nondichotomous variables.

Timing of Measurement

The data for these measures of health and health-care utilization were obtained during the second, sixth, and tenth quarterly interviews for the head and spouse and during the second, eighth, and twelfth quarterly interviews for the children. An additional problem is presented by the children's twelfth quarterly interview which is not comparable to the earlier two because constraints of space limited the data collection to only the youngest and oldest children under 16. Consequently, we have excluded the twelfth quarter data from the analysis presented here. This timing presents a small problem for the analysis of the experiment's effects in that the second quarterly interview, in summarizing health data for the year prior to the interview, includes a period of six months prior to the start of the experiment during which the experiment obviously could have no effects. Thus, other things equal, the possibility of observing experimental effects is only half as likely at the second quarter.

Parameterization of Experimental Plans

Given that there are eight experimental plans combining the four guarantee levels and three tax rates, the problem arises as to how to best estimate the effects of these plans on our dependent variables.[7] Two different approaches were employed here. In the first, the eight plans were represented by a set of linear splines which progressively consider and exhaust the variation in the guarantee and tax rate through the introduction of terms that permit nonlinear and interactive effects.[8] However, as no nonlinear or interactive effects were found in our preliminary analyses, we shall report here only the effects of the three simplest spline variables that describe, respectively, the effects of membership in the experimental group (spline one), the effects of the guarantee level (spline two), and the effects of the tax rate (spline three). Spline one is simply a dummy variable scored one if the family is in the experimental group; zero otherwise. Spline two is defined as G-75, where G is the guarantee level for a particular family; spline three is defined as T-50, where T is a family's tax rate. Spline two tests for variation in the effect of the guarantee levels around a guarantee of 75 percent of the poverty line, while spline three tests for variation in the effect of the tax rates around the middle or 50 percent tax rate. Thus, when the three splines are present together in the same equation, spline one measures the effect of the plan with the 75 percent guarantee and 50 percent tax rate, and the other two splines estimate the effects of deviations from that plan in terms of guarantee and tax rate. The assumption underlying this parameterization is that the families have some genuine understanding of their guarantee level and tax rate and react to the experiment accordingly.

However, whether they actually have such an understanding can be questioned on both empirical and theoretical grounds. On the empirical side, Shore (1971) has found that knowledge of the experimental design was rudimentary in the sense that few families he surveyed could name their guarantee or tax rate; typically families knew little more than that their payments decreased as their earnings increased. On the theoretical side, these findings lend support to our suspicion that families may more readily respond to the actual payments they receive than to the payments they might potentially receive under their particular experimental plan. In suggesting this, we do not wish to imply any support for the notions of some culture of poverty theorists that the poor are distinguished by a strong present time orientation or an inability to delay gratification, for the evidence on this question is highly moot (Miller, et al., 1968). Rather, we suggest that people generally prefer to act in terms of the concrete present—the payments—rather than the abstract future—the potential payments. Thus, our second parameterization is based on the actual payments received. To assess the possibility that the impact of the payments may occur only after a threshold amount is reached, the payments are expressed as a quadratic in the analysis.

We should note, however, that the most generous plans will, in general, make the largest payments.[9] Thus, although families may be explicitly making decisions regarding their health and utilization of care in terms of the size of the benefit check they receive, they will be implicitly reacting to a high guarantee and moderate to low tax rate—these being definitionally true of the most generous plans.

Control Variables

Because the design of the experiment did not randomly assign families to the various experimental plans and because the design was modified during the year-long period of screening and enrollment, several variables must be held constant in order to obtain unbiased estimates of the experimental effects. The most important of these is the income stratum of the family. The income stratum of a family is a gross estimate of its permanent income (the estimate was divided into three categories) conditioned by family size. Use of this model means that the various experimental plans differed in average family income at the beginning of the experiment, and consequently, the estimation of unbiased effects require that this variable be controlled for.

Ethnicity and experimental site must also be held constant because a decision was made to attempt to balance the sample ethnically during the period of screening and enrollment. As the four experimental sites were brought into the experiment sequentially over a year, this decision meant that certain ethnic groups were more heavily sampled in some cities than

in others. For example, the Scranton sample is almost entirely white. Because ethnicity and site are, thus, necessarily confounded, the implication of this decision is that both must be held constant in any analysis. However, ethnicity, in any event, would have been held constant because of its importance in the literature on health and health care utilization (Mechanic, 1968).

In addition, the welfare status of the family must be controlled for because we are dealing with an experiment rather than a national program, and the experiment exists in a natural setting that includes a welfare program as an alternative to the experiment's benefits. The welfare problem exists in both states where there are experimental sites.[10] Moreover, in both states only those on welfare are eligible for Medicaid.

Several other factors, unrelated to design considerations, have been controlled in order to clarify the effects of the experimental plans. The age and education of the appropriate adult and family size, all measured at pre-enrollment, are held constant because of their aforementioned relationships with our dependent variables. The possession of health insurance, measured at the second or sixth quarter as appropriate, is also held constant for reasons given above. Average family earnings for the year (or six months in the case of the second quarterly interview) prior to the interview is also controlled for.

The estimates of effects for the spouse and the children each require one additional variable held constant that is inappropriate for the estimation of effects for the male head. With the exception of the equations for chronic conditions, a measure of whether the wife was pregnant in the year prior to the interview was included in the equations for the spouse, because for women of child-bearing age it is a potentially confounding factor in estimating the experiment's effects on the other dependent variables. In all the equations for the children a measure of the number of children below the age of six is included because of the greater use of medical care by children of that age (National Center for Health Statistics, 1968) and the aforementioned socioemotional involvement of the parents with young children, which may lead to the discovery of chronic conditions. Also the mother's age and education are used for age and education in the children's equations.

Operational Models for Estimating Experimental Effects

In this section we shall describe the operational models, based on the sociological theory of a process leading from illness to the utilization of care, used to estimate the effects of the experiment on our dependent variables. We begin by noting that, although there are three points in time to be analyzed for the adults and two for the children, the first time point is to be distinguished from the others because there are no prior measures of health or utilization to be taken into account in the models. Consequently, in spite of the existence of three timepoints for the adults, there are, except for time differences, only two kinds of models: those that contain measures of health and utilization of care at an earlier point in time and those that do not. The latter, which occur at the second quarter, may be written as

$$C_2 = f(E, X_2, e_f)$$
$$H_2 = g(C_2, E, S_2, e_g)$$
$$W_2 = h(H_2, C_2, E, X_2, e_h)$$
$$TD_2 = i(W_2, H_2, C_2, E, X_2, e_i)$$
$$PD_2 = j(W_2, H_2, C_2, E, X, e_j)$$
$$OD_2 = k(W_2, H_2, C_2, E, X_2, e_k)$$

where the subscript to the upper case letters refers to time and C = number of chronic illnesses; E = the experimental parameterization; X = the array of control variables; H = the number of days spent in a hospital (or at least one hospital stay for the children); W = the number of days lost from work (or the per capita number of days in bed for the children); TD = the total number of physician visits; PD = the total number of private physician visits; OD = the total number of other physician visits; and the e's are the appropriate disturbance terms.

The model asserts that, at the second quarter, a person's number of chronic illnesses is a function of only the control variables and his experimental status.

This is consistent with the notion that a chronic condition is largely unaffected by the use of medical care. Second, the number of days in a hospital is taken as a function of the number of chronic illnesses, since many chronic conditions may require occasional hospitalization. Third, since hospitalization obviously implies that work days will be lost and since a chronic condition may be either occasionally or completely incapacitating, both these variables are assumed to affect work days lost. Finally, all three variables are stated as influences on physician visits; hospitalization implies physician visits; chronic illness and work days lost, if the underlying health condition is recognized as sufficiently serious, will also lead to physician visits.

Given the above model for the second quarter, we may write the following model for the later quarters:

$$C_{t+1} = f'(C_t, E, X_{t+1}, e_{f'})$$
$$H_{t+1} = g'(H_t, C_{t+1}, E, X_{t+1}, e_{g'})$$
$$W_{t+1} = h'(W_t, H_{t+1}, C_{t+1}, E, X_{t+1}, e_h)$$
$$TD_{t+1} = i'(TD_t, W_{t+1}, H_{t+1}, C_{t+1}, E, X_{t+1}, e_{i'})$$
$$PD_{t+1} = j'(PD_t, W_{t+1}, H_{t+1}, C_{t+1}, E, X_{t+1}, e_{j'})$$
$$OD_{t+1} = k'(OD_t, W_{t+1}, H_{t+1}, C_{t+1}, E, X_{t+1}, e_{k'})$$

Since the prior values of the dependent variables are represented on the right, the equations estimate the effects of the experiment on changes in the dependent variables over time.

Because there are two different experimental parameterizations, six equations for each point in time, three points in time for each adult and two for the children, a total of 96 equations must be estimated in order to determine the effects of the experiment on the dependent variables. We cannot present, much less discuss, the coefficients for all 96 equations within the present limitations of space; consequently, we shall present here only the estimates for the experimental effects.[11]

The Sample

Our analysis focuses on the 732 husband-wife families which were in the experiment "continuously." A continuous, husband-wife family was defined as family with husband and wife present that completed an interview at preenrollment, at the twelfth quarter, and at six of the remaining eleven quarters. In addition, the families had to be husband-wife and present at the second, sixth, and tenth quarters—the quarters at which health data were collected for the head and spouse—and they could have missed no more than two quarters in succession. Thus, families that split up for a period longer than two quarters or that attrited in terms of the above definition are not represented in the results reported here. The first exclusion is consistent with our desire to estimate effects for both the head and spouse, but the second is prompted simply by the fact that techniques for estimating the possible biases resulting from attrition have not yet been fully developed. The present sample represents 55 percent of all families originally enrolled.

RESULTS

We shall present the results for the husband, wife and children separately and, as previously noted, only the estimates for the two parameterizations of the experimental plans will be given. Recall that in the design parameterization we would expect the effects of the guarantee level to be positive and the effects of the tax rate to be negative, since an increasing guarantee and a decreasing tax rate both produce an increase in the size of the benefit paid to the family and hence increases their disposable income. However, expectations as to the signs of the coefficients in the payments parameterization are somewhat more complex. If there is no threshold effect—that is, the effect of the payments is linear—then the linear term should be positive and the quadratic term should be insignificantly different from zero. On the other hand, if there is a threshold effect, the linear term may have either a negative or a small positive sign while the quadratic term has a larger positive effect.

Experimental Effects on Family Members

Male head. Table 1 gives the results for male heads of households and they are easily summarized: regardless of the perspective from which they are viewed, there are no apparent experimental effects. First, if we search for coefficients with an appropriate sign and statistically significant at the five percent level, we find only four out of a possible 90 tests, a number which differs trivially from that which would be expected simply on the grounds of chance. Second, if we recall that the coefficients for guarantee and tax rate represent deviations from the 75–50 plan, we can see from the small size of the coefficients for the former two variables that the deviations are trivial. Third, inspection of the signs of the coefficients fails to reveal any pattern, let alone one consistent with our expectations.

Female head. Turning now to the data for the female heads of households displayed in Table 2, we see again that the experiment has had no effects. As in the case of the husbands, the number of statistically significant coefficients does not differ from chance, there is no pattern to the coefficients' signs, and the deviations from the 75–50 plan for either guarantee or tax rate are inconsequential.

Children. The data for the children who, it should be remembered, are the family members for whom effects are most likely, are given in Table 3. In general, there is once again almost no evidence that the experiment has had any effect. But a possible exceptional may exist for per capita total visits to the doctor at the second quarter. Here an apparently statistically significant negative tax-rate effect receives some support from the finding of significance for the payments parameterization. The finding suggests that a 25 percent increase in the rate means a reduction of almost one physician visit.

Aside from this "finding," the results are similar to those for the adults. The effects of the guarantee and tax rate differ trivially from the effects of the 75–50 plan; the coefficients show no particular pattern as to sign; and only ten of the 60 coefficients are statistically significant.

Since some researchers have argued that experimental effects might be slow to develop, it is worth noting that in none of these tables is there any more evidence of significant effects at the sixth, eighth, or tenth quarters than at the second.

TABLE 1. NET EXPERIMENTAL EFFECTS ON HEALTH VARIABLES AT THE SECOND, SIXTH, AND TENTH QUARTERS FOR MALE HEADS OF CONTINUOUS HUSBAND-WIFE FAMILIES

Health Variables	Effects of				
	· 75–50 Plan	Guarantee	Tax Rate	Payments	Payments Squared
A. Second Quarter					
Number of chronic illnesses	.002 (.08)	.001 (1.62)	.001 (.50)	−.049 (−1.08)	.005 (1.18)
Number of hospital days	−.152 (−2.22)	.003 (1.57)	.000 (.06)	−.033 (−.31)	.001 (.10)
Number of work days lost	.146 (1.28)	−.003 (−.99)	−.000 (−.04)	−.001 (−.00)	−.011 (−.67)
Total physician visits	.052 (.74)	−.001 (−.49)	.006 (1.96)	.115 (1.05)	−.013 (−1.28)
Private physician visits	.016 (.22)	−.000 (−.18)	.003 (.87)	.182 (1.68)	−.020 (−2.00)
Other physician visits	.029 (.56)	−.001 (−1.04)	.006 (2.70)	−.031 (−.38)	.002 (.24)
B. Sixth Quarter					
Number of chronic illnesses	.015 (.59)	−.000 (−.69)	.001 (.92)	−.007 (−.27)	.001 (.35)
Number of hospital days	−.940 (−1.36)	.009 (.54)	−.030 (−.98)	.278 (.39)	−.037 (−.84)
Number of work days lost	.037 (.31)	.003 (.93)	−.002 (−.29)	.054 (.44)	−.006 (−.83)
Total physician visits	−.291 (−.43)	.003 (.19)	−.019 (−.64)	.087 (.12)	−.034 (−.80)
Private physician visits	.625 (1.01)	−.002 (−.15)	−.100 (−.37)	.143 (.22)	−.037 (−.95)
Other physician visits	−.826 (−2.58)	.005 (.69)	−.011 (−.77)	−.177 (−.53)	.012 (.58)
C. Tenth Quarter					
Number of chronic illnesses	.002 (−.40)	.001 (.80)	.001 (1.40)	−.049 (−.01)	.005 (.38)
Number of hospital days	−.609 (−.51)	−.018 (−.61)	.049 (.93)	.600 (.51)	−.030 (−.43)
Number of work days lost	.177 (1.45)	.001 (.43)	.002 (.33)	−.386 (−3.23)	.020 (2.83)
Total physician visits	.969 (1.45)	−.006 (−.39)	.032 (1.08)	−.301 (−.45)	.020 (.49)
Private physician visits	.542 (.92)	−.010 (−.68)	.024 (.93)	−.364 (−.63)	.021 (.60)
Other physician visits	.200 (.78)	.005 (.73)	.007 (.63)	.032 (.13)	.002 (.12)

Note: These are unstandardized regression coefficients with t-values in parentheses. See text for variables held constant in making estimates. The effects of the guarantee and tax rate are relative to the 75–50 plan. Payments are expressed in thousands of dollars per quarter.

CONCLUSIONS

In summary, we may say that the experiment had no effects on either our measures of health or on our measures of the utilization of health care. That this is the case should not be surprising, given that review of the literature found that the effects of income on these variables were generally small or nonexistent. The ex-

TABLE 2. NET EXPERIMENTAL EFFECTS ON HEALTH VARIABLES AT THE SECOND, SIXTH AND TENTH QUARTERS FOR FEMALE HEADS OF CONTINUOUS HUSBAND-WIFE FAMILIES

Health Variables	Effects of				
	75–50 Plan	Guarantee	Tax Rate	Payments	Payments Squared
A. Second Quarter					
Number of chronic	−.015	−.000	.002	.065	−.004
illnesses	(−.50)	(−.03)	(1.75)	(1.38)	(−1.04)
Number of hospital	−.210	.003	.001	−.019	.005
days	(−2.54)	(1.47)	(.36)	(−.15)	(.45)
Number of work	.033	.003	.007	−.008	−.005
days lost *	(.30)	(1.25)	(1.44)	(−.05)	(−.29)
Total physician	.018	.002	−.001	.073	−.005
visits	(.22)	(.76)	(−.28)	(.59)	(−.44)
Private physician	−.029	.001	−.003	.218	−.018
visits	(−.33)	(.39)	(−.80)	(1.63)	(−1.45)
Other physician	.071	.000	−.001	−.078	.006
visits	(1.22)	(.25)	(.55)	(−.88)	(.78)
B. Sixth Quarter					
Number of chronic	.051	−.000	−.000	.047	−.003
illnesses	(1.89)	(−.42)	(−.03)	(1.67)	(−1.84)
Number of hospital	.060	.007	−.012	.716	−.047
days	(.12)	(.57)	(−.56)	(1.38)	(−1.49)
Number of work	.109	−.001	−.005	−.018	.004
days lost	(1.10)	(−.53)	(−1.17)	(−.18)	(.65)
Total physician	−.101	−.003	.073	−.437	−.032
visits	(−.15)	(−.16)	(2.53)	(−.63)	(−.76)
Private physician	−.289	−.011	.054	−.458	.027
visits	(−.46)	(−.72)	(1.94)	(−.69)	(.69)
Other physician	.253	.009	.020	−.088	.010
visits	(.89)	(1.28)	(1.60)	(−.29)	(.57)
C. Tenth Quarter					
Number of chronic	−.036	.001	.001	−.019	.001
illnesses	(−1.34)	(1.03)	(.95)	(−.70)	(.70)
Number of hospital	−.216	.013	−.017	1.36	−.061
days	(−.29)	(.74)	(−.50)	(1.83)	(−1.38)
Number of work	−.025	.003	−.001	−.195	.009
days lost	(−.23)	(1.13)	(−.23)	(−1.83)	(1.41)
Total physician	−.757	−.008	−.035	−1.54	.095
visits	(−1.05)	(−.42)	(−1.10)	(−2.16)	(2.23)
Private physician	−.333	.003	−.033	−.901	.067
visits	(.49)	(.20)	(−1.12)	(−1.34)	(1.66)
Other physician	−.354	−.009	.001	−.669	.031
visits	(−1.28)	(−1.30)	(.09)	(−2.46)	(1.91)

See *Note* for Table 1.
* Includes housework.

perimental payments are, after all, only addition to the income of our families, and we should not be surprised if they use this added income in ways similar to those in which they use their other income.

It can, of course, be argued that our failure to find any experimental effects is due to the experiment's limited duration, or to our sample's lack of access to care, or to meagerness of the experimental payments. However, we do not find any of these arguments, individually or taken

TABLE 3. NET EXPERIMENTAL EFFECTS ON HEALTH VARIABLES AT THE SECOND AND EIGHTH QUARTERS FOR CHILDREN OF CONTINUOUS HUSBAND-WIFE FAMILIES

Health Variables	Effects of				
	75–50 Plan	Guarantee	Tax Rate	Payments	Payments Squared
A. Second Quarter					
Per capita chronic illnesses	.038	−.001	.000	.054	−.005
	(1.24)	(−1.49)	(.13)	(1.14)	(−1.11)
Hospital stay	−.091	.002	−.001	.082	−.007
	(−2.70)	(2.33)	(−.55)	(1.57)	(−1.55)
Per capita bed days	.028	−.000	.001	.042	−.004
	(.30)	(−.13)	(.26)	(.29)	(−.31)
Per capita total physician visits	−.054	.002	−.004	−.141	.016
	(−1.21)	(1.45)	(−2.23)	(−2.08)	(2.54)
Per capita private physician visits	−.029	.002	−.004	−.089	.010
	(−.62)	(1.48)	(−2.23)	(−1.26)	(1.58)
Per capita other physician visits	−.053	.000	.001	−.061	.007
	(−1.77)	(.18)	(.53)	(−1.32)	(1.72)
B. Eighth Quarter					
Per capita chronic illnesses	.014	.000	.001	−.012	.000
	(.65)	(.59)	(.74)	(−.49)	(.02)
Hospital stay	.050	.001	−.001	.099	−.005
	(1.51)	(.92)	(−.64)	(1.09)	(−.86)
Per capita bed days	.097	−.002	−.005	−.003	.000
	(1.10)	(−.90)	(−1.25)	(−.09)	(.19)
Per capita total physician visits	.023	−.001	.002	−.049	.002
	(.46)	(−.78)	(.78)	(−.95)	(.76)
Per capita private physician visits	.044	−.001	.000	−.032	.001
	(.88)	(−.76)	(.16)	(−.63)	(.38)
Per capita other physician visits	.009	−.000	.004	−.058	.004
	(.22)	(−.25)	(2.13)	(−1.43)	(1.46)

See *Note* for **Table 1.**

together, at all compelling. While the experiment was limited to only three years, the fact that people generally put an extremely high priority on their health leads us to suspect that the effects—if they were to be observed at all—should have occurred quite rapidly. Moreover, the utter lack of any sign of an increase in illness or utilization over time makes it unlikely that a longer experiment would produce different results. As far as the question of access to care is concerned, we have no evidence that our sample is seriously disadvantaged in this respect. The vast majority of the families report that they have a regular physician within a reasonable distance from their homes. Finally, the argument that the experimental payments are too small to have any effect can be dismissed with the simple observation that the average payment per family per year was about $1,000; since average family earnings for the whole sample were approximately $5,500, this amounts to 18 percent of their earnings—a nontrivial amount.

In conclusion, we would like to point out once again that despite the lack of experimental effects, these findings are consistent with previous research on income and health which indicates that health and medical care are more a function of life style (preferences) than income—at least beyond the level of mere subsistence (Lefcowitz, 1973a; 1973b). Since the experiment was not designed to change life styles, the outcomes reported here were to be expected. Yet it is worth noting that the results were not expected in terms of economic theory and, while sociological research provided some basis for anticipating them, it nonetheless also contained no model that permitted their prediction.

NOTES

1. Introduced by Milton Friedman, the negative income tax has been held to be superior to existing welfare schemes because its tax on earnings is less than 100 percent—thus ostensibly providing an incentive to work absent in existing welfare; its benefits would be paid as a simple function of income rather than in terms of eligibility, in terms of a set of categorical rules, and payments would not be subject to the discretion of caseworkers.
2. Perhaps it should be said that improvement in the ill depends upon both the efficacy of care and the belief of the ill in its efficacy. The efficacy of care on the level of health is increasingly being questioned: see, for example, Benham and Benham, 1975).
3. This statement should be qualified by the fact that Richardson found that persons on Medicare used physicians significantly *less* than those on voluntary insurance; however, this exception is not really germane to the present discussion as our sample is almost entirely ineligible for Medicare. It should also be noted that there was an insurance effect when the condition was not serious.
4. For reasons of space, this discussion is necessarily brief. For greater details, see Part C of the *Final Report of the Graduated Work Incentive Experiment* in New Jersey and Pennsylvania available from the Institute for Research on Poverty, University of Wisconsin, Madison, Wisconsin 53706. The *Report* will also be published by Academic Press during the coming year.
5. Guarantee levels were annually adjusted for changes in the cost of living.
6. This and the following correlation were computed from logarithmitically transformed variables, as described below.
7. Recall that the eight plans represent the subset of the 12 possible combinations of guarantee and tax rate of primary policy interest.
8. We shall not attempt to introduce here the theory of splines to those unfamiliar with the technique as we are making only modest use of it. Readers desiring further background should consult Poirier (1973).
9. The potential generosity of a plan can be expressed in terms of its breakeven point (the point at which payments cease), which can be found by dividing its guarantee level by its tax rate.
10. For an analysis of the impact of welfare, see Garfinkel (1974).
11. A full set of tables is available upon request from the authors.

REFERENCES

Aday, Lu Ann and Robert Eichorn
1972   The Utilization of Health Services: Indices and Correlates. Washington, D.C.: National Center for Health Services Research and Development, Department of Health, Education, and Welfare.

Andersen, Ronald
1968   A Behavioral Model of Families' Use of Health Services. Research Series No. 25. Chicago: Center for Health Administration Studies, University of Chicago.

Andersen, Ronald and Lee Benham
1970   "Factors affecting the relationship between family income and medical care consumption." Pp. 73-95 in Herbert E. Klarman (ed.), Empirical Studies in Health Economics. Baltimore: The Johns Hopkins Press.

Andersen, Ronald, Joanna Kravits, and Odin W. Anderson (eds.)
1975   Equity in Health Services. Cambridge: Ballinger.

Burham, Lee and Alexandra Benham
1975   "The impact of incremental medical services on health status, 1963–1970," Pp. 217–28 in R. Andersen, J. Kravits and O. W. Anderson, (eds.), Equity in Health Services. Cambridge: Ballinger.

Cole, S. and R. LeJeune
1972   "Illness and the legitimation of failure." American Sociological Review 37:347–56.

Conlisk, John and Harold W. Watts
1969   "A model of optimizing experimental designs for estimating response surfaces." Proceedings of the Social Statistics Section. Washington, D.C.: American Statistical Association.

Elesh, D. and Schollaert, P.T.
1972   "Race and urban medicine: Factors affecting the distribution on physicians in Chicago." Journal of Health and Social Behavior 13:236–50.

Feldman, Jacob J.
1966   The Dissemination of Health Information. Chicago: Aldine.

Friedman, Milton
1957   A Theory of the Consumption Function. National Bureau of Economic Research. Princeton, N.J.: Princeton University Press.

Garfinkel, Irwin
1974   "The effects of welfare programs on experimental responses." Journal of Human Resources 18:504–29.

Harkey, J., D. L. Miles and W. A. Rushing
1976   "The relation between social class and functional status: A new look at the drift hypothesis." Journal of Health and Social Behavior 17:194–204.

Koos, Earl
1954   The Health of Regionville. New York: Columbia University Press.

Lefcowitz, M.J.
1973a   "Poverty and health: A re-examination." Inquiry X:3–13.
1973b   "Poverty and Health: Children's Medical

Care.'' Discussion Paper No. 159–73. Madison, Wisconsin: Institute for Research on Poverty, University of Wisconsin.

Luft, Harold S.
  1972 ''Poverty and health: An empirical investigation of the economic interactions.'' PhD. dissertation. Boston: Harvard Center for Community Health.

Mechanic, David
  1968 Medical Sociology: A Selective View. New York: Free Press.

Miller, S.M., Frank Riessman and Arthur A. Seagull
  1968 ''Poverty and self-indulgence: A critique of the non-deferred gratification pattern.'' Pp. 416–32 in Louis A. Ferman, Joyce L. Kornbluh and Alan Haber (eds.), Poverty in America. Ann Arbor: University of Michigan Press.

National Center for Health Statistics
  1968 ''Volume of Physician Visits by Place of Visit and Type of Service.'' Vital and Health Statistics, Series 10, No. 49. Washington, D.C.: U.S. Department of Health. Education and Welfare.
  1972a ''Age Patterns in Medical Care, Illness, and Disability.'' Washington, D.C.: Vital and Health Statistics, Series 10, No. 70. U.S. Department of Health, Education, and Welfare.
  1972b ''Hospital and Surgical Insurance Coverage.'' Vital and Health Statistics, Series 10, No. 66. Washington, D.C.: U.S. Department of Health, Education, and Welfare.

Poirier, Dale J.
  1973 ''Multiple Regression Using Bilinear Splines.'' Social Systems Research Institute Workshop Paper No. 7230. University of Wisconsin Social Systems Research Institute, Madison, Wis.: University of Wisconsin.

Richardson, William C.
  1971 Ambulatory Use of Physicians' Services in Response to Illness Episodes in a Low Income Neighborhood. Chicago: Center for Health Administration Studies, University of Chicago.

Samora, J., L. Saunders and R.F. Larson
  1962 ''Medical vocabulary knowledge among hospital patients.'' Journal of Health and Social Behavior 2:83–92.

Shore, Arnold
  1971 ''Institutional Assistance: A study of the negative income tax experiment.'' Ph.D. dissertation. Princeton, N.J. Princeton University.

Shortell, Stephen M.
  1975 ''The effects of patterns of medical care on utilization and continuity of services,'' Pp. 191–216 in R. Andersen. J. Kravits and O.W. Anderson (eds.), Equity in Health Services. Cambridge: Ballinger.

Whereas Rhoades (p. 448) tried to place a price on life for the purpose of social planning, Bloom and Singer make a start toward placing a monetary value on rehabilitation. They develop a model for assessing the cost of rehabilitating a criminal based on costs to incarcerate and rehabilitate and costs lost due to foregone inmate earnings. As the cost-effectiveness of various alternatives is determined, money allocation decisions can be made so as to maximize efficiency. For example, the criminal justice system has to choose between allocating money to law enforcement, job placement and training for inner city youth, prisons, parole programs, and so forth.

In this evaluation report, Bloom and Singer compare the treatment effect and cost-effectiveness of a controversial program for mentally defective delinquents with a traditional prison setting. A multitude of difficult design problems, including inability to randomly assign subjects, unknown accuracy of outcome measures, and difficulty of follow-up plagued the study, but an effect favoring the treatment was found. However, these putative benefits are at a whopping $38,000 per delinquent per year. Bloom and Singer report the impact of their evaluation on state policy makers, which is a commendable idea.

The Bloom and Singer study also highlights an unfortunate weakness inherent in using a single cost-effectiveness measure for an outcome measure—that is, lack of knowledge about what part of the treatment is responsible for the treatment effects. In a large, multifaceted program such as the one in the present study, the answer to that problem may be very complicated. Here, the impact of the evaluation was to limit the number of days each criminal was incarcerated in the controversial program, thereby decreasing costs. However, if the length of incarceration per se was responsible for the beneficial effects, then the cost-effectiveness of the program would actually decrease, indicating the importance of program evaluation following program change.

27

Determining the Cost-Effectiveness of Correctional Programs
The Case of Patuxent Institution

Howard S. Bloom and Neil M. Singer

This article has two related purposes. One is to extend the methodology for evaluating correctional programs. Two aspects of this methodology are considered: (1) the measurement of a program's ability both to prevent and to postpone criminal behavior; and (2) the use of cost-effectiveness analysis. The second purpose of this article is to present an evaluation of Patuxent Institution, a unique, widely publicized correctional facility located in Jessup, Maryland. Our analysis indicates that Patuxent both prevents and postpones recidivism but at a considerable cost.

The large and growing number of evaluations of correctional programs published in this volume and elsewhere reflect their importance to policy makers,

Authors' Note: This study is based on data obtained through a contract with the Maryland Department of Public Safety and Correctional Services. The views expressed herein represent those of the authors and do not necessarily reflect those of the Department of Public Safety and Correctional Services. We wish to thank Susan E. Philipson Bloom, Helen F. Ladd and John Yinger, for their invaluable assistance.

From Howard S. Bloom and Neil M. Singer, "Determining the Cost-Effectiveness of Correctional Programs: The Case of Patuxent Institution." Unpublished manuscript, 1978.

evaluators, and social scientists. The purpose of our paper is to contribute to this area of research by extending and refining existing evaluation methodologies and presenting substantive findings from a recent evaluation of a particularly important correctional institution.

With respect to methodological issues, we focus on two that have been discussed recently. One is the use of cost-effectiveness analysis for evaluating correctional programs (Gray et al., 1978). The other involves modeling the timing of recidivism (Maltz and McCleary, 1977, 1978; Miley, 1978; Lloyd and Joe, 1978; Stollmack, 1978)[1] for the purpose of estimating correctional program impact.

With respect to substantive findings, we present our evaluation of Patuxent Institution, a unique, high security, intensive treatment facility in Jessup, Maryland.

We proceed by: (1) describing the nature and history of Patuxent; (2) outlining our analytical framework; (3) describing our analysis; and (4) presenting our results and conclusions.

PATUXENT INSTITUTION

The Patuxent Institution opened in 1955 to provide an intensive regime of medical, psychiatric, and therapeutic services for adult male offenders termed "defective delinquents," who, by "persistent aggravated anti-social or criminal behavior, evidence a propensity toward criminal activity" and who are "found to have either . . . intellectual deficiency or emotional disorder or both" (Maryland Annotated Code, Article 31-B, Sec. 5.). Such offenders were to be committed to Patuxent for indeterminate sentences, retained in the institution under maximum-security conditions while undergoing treatment, and released when the institution's staff decided they were "cured."

Patuxent quickly expanded to its designed capacity of approximately 500 inmates and has remained at that level for 20 years. Reflecting its treatment-intensive orientation, the institution was staffed with more psychiatrists, psychologists, and social workers than are found (on a per inmate basis) in any other prison in the United States (Goldfarb and Singer, 1973).

Prior to the Maryland legislature's reconsideration of Article 31-B in 1977, Patuxent's treatment program and its procedures for admission and release differed from other correctional institutions. For example, any convicted felon could be referred to Patuxent for diagnosis. If the institution's staff considered him to be a "defective delinquent," a formal court commitment hearing was held with full legal and medical counsel (including a state-appointed psychiatrist, if necessary) for the offender.

If the offender were committed to Patuxent, he would be encouraged to participate in treatment programs such as counseling, individual or group psychotherapy, and medical treatment (usually tranquilization), plus the standard prison mix of academic or vocational education, recreation, and work assignments. His participation in, and response to, these programs determined his progress through a unique "graded tier" system, consisting of incremental privileges such as unlocked doors, color television in day rooms, and the freedom to decorate one's cell. Inmate progress was reviewed periodically by the institution's staff, and on the staff's recommendation he would be admitted to work release or family furlough programs.

Complete release from Patuxent proceeded in stages: first to the Pre-Release Center on the institution's grounds; then, in most cases, to its Halfway House in Baltimore; and finally to its Outpatient Clinic, which combined the functions of a counseling group and parole authority. Throughout this process the indeterminate sentence clause of Article 31-B insured that offenders who were commited to Patuxent would remain under the institution's purview until its staff felt they were ready to be released.

Both the classification of offenders as "defective delinquents" and Patuxent's indeterminate sentence have been targets of civil libertarians' attack since the institution was established. Defenders of the institution have argued, however, that both provisions were essential. But Patuxent's rising costs gradually tipped the legislative debate in favor of its critics, prompting the 1976 legislature to authorize the Maryland Department of Public Safety and Correctional Services to commission an independent third-party evaluation.

The results presented in this paper are a reanalysis of data we obtained through our participation in that evaluation (Singer and Bloom, 1977). Subsequent to the evaluation, the legislature's 1977 revision of Article 31-B deleted the classification of "defective delinquent" and modified Patuxent's procedures for releasing inmates. In the concluding section of this paper we offer speculation about the effects of these changes.

ANALYSIS

Determining the Relevant Comparison

To be useful, a cost-effectiveness evaluation must compare the costs and effectiveness of the program under review with those of alternatives that are available. Simply analyzing the consequences of a single program option is inappropriate since it does not consider what would happen if that option were not chosen. Likewise, comparison of a serious option with irrelevant alternatives (those that are not feasible due to moral, legal, technological, or political constraints) is equally inappropriate.

Our evaluation was based on a comparison of commitment to Patuxent with the alternative of confinement in a conventional prison. In practice, these are the alternatives available to the Maryland courts. Therefore, we did not consider other alternatives, such as simple release, which is not morally or politically feasible, or commitment to a mental institution, which is precluded by the legal requirement that Patuxent inmates be convicted offenders (rather than those who are not guilty by reason of insanity).

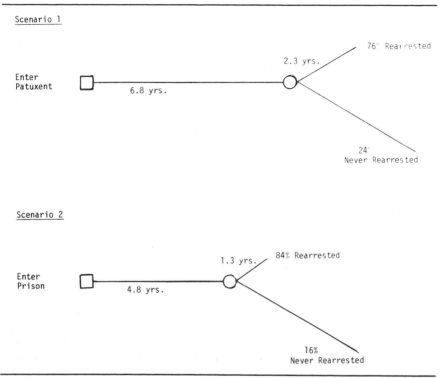

Figure 1: The Typical Patuxent Offender Scenarios

We anticipated that offenders sent to Patuxent would have quite different experiences from those sent to conventional prisons. Differences that we felt were relevant to policy makers, and therefore examined, included the average length of imprisonment, the probability of rearrest following release, and the mean time from release to rearrest. These three factors are summarized in Figure 1. For example, on average, offenders sent to Patuxent spent 6.8 years at the institution before parole. About 76% of those released were eventually rearrested, with a mean rearrest time of 2.3 years after release. If comparable offenders had been sent to prison instead of Patuxent, their average incarceration would have been 4.8 years, 84% eventually would have been arrested following release, and the mean time to rearrest would have been 1.3 years.

The following section explains how these estimates were obtained and how they were used for our analysis.

Defining Program Output

Measuring correctional program output is a difficult task which, in practice, involves many compromises. Difficulties arise at both the conceptual stage of defining program output and the operational stage of obtaining appropriate data.

The principal source of conceptual programs is the fact that not all crimes are the same. To address this issue, criminologists and sociologists have constructed indices which combine different crimes into a common metric. One of the best known was developed by Sellin and Wolfgang (1964). More recently, Gray et al. (1978) presented a seriousness index based on the subjective ratings of 48 parole and probation officers and a severity index based on the maximum sentence of each crime. Such indices suffer, however, from a variety of problems noted by the authors. And perhaps even more important for evaluation purposes, they are very difficult to interpret in terms meaningful to policy makers.

Economists have approached this problem by attempting to measure the monetary cost of crimes. Tabasz (1975) attained limited success with this approach for property crimes such as burglary, embezzlement, and fraud. Crimes such as rape, murder and assault, however, present currently insurmountable difficulties due to problems in valuing human life and suffering.

In the absence of a clearly superior alternative we simply measured program output in terms of crime reduced. To put this measure into effect required data on crimes committed by offenders in our study. Since direct observation of these offenses was not possible we had to rely on reported arrests or convictions. These data contain errors due both to mistakes made by the criminal justice system and to inaccurate reporting. The first error arises when guilty offenders are not arrested or convicted for crimes they commit and when innocent persons are arrested or convicted for crimes they did not commit. The second error depends on the data source used. We used FBI "RAP" sheets to develop the multijurisdictional criminal histories necessary for our study. Since, in the judgement of the evaluation team, arrests were reported to the FBI more accurately and in a more timely fashion than were convictions, we based our analysis on arrest data.[2]

Designing the Study

Our study was designed to determine Patuxent's impact on postrelease criminal behavior. Conceptually, this impact is the difference between the behavior of inmates released from Patuxent and what would have occurred had they been sent to prison instead. Operationally, this difference was estimated by comparing the experience of a sample of Patuxent offenders with that of a comparable group of prison inmates.

The best way to obtain such a comparison group is through random assignment of eligible offenders to Patuxent or prison. Unfortunately, time constraints on our evaluation precluded this approach. But even if we had the ten years necessary to assign offenders, treat them, release them, and observe their postrelease behavior, such social experimentation would have been impossible due to the controversial nature of Patuxent's program. Thus, we were constrained to a retrospective study based on samples of offenders assigned to Patuxent and prison through the medical-legal process described earlier.

Our Patuxent, or "treatment" sample was defined to include all inmates paroled from the institution for the first time in 1971 or 1972 to provide a mini-

TABLE 1
Profiles of the Treatment and Comparison Groups

Characteristic	Treatment Group, Patuxent (n = 106)	Comparison Group, Prison (n = 41)
Mean number of prior arrests	4.4	3.1
Mean number of prior convictions	3.1	2.0
Mean number of prior incarcerations	2.6	1.5
Mean age at current incarceration	27.3	23.8
Mean maximum sentence	12.0	9.8

mum four-year follow-up for each of the 106 offenders involved. The comparison group was defined to include all offenders who from 1964 to 1972 were diagnosed by Patuxent's staff to be a "defective delinquent," but were not so adjudged by the courts and therefore sent to prison. Complete records were available for 54 of the 62 offenders in this group, 13 of whom were still in prison at the time of our study.

Table 1 compares the resulting treatment and comparison groups. They differ according to characteristics such as age and prior criminal record which consistently have been found to influence criminal behavior.[3] These factors were controlled for statistically as described in the following section.

Estimating Program Impact

Correctional programs can both prevent and postpone crime. Maltz and McCleary (1977) recently presented a statistical model capable of distinguishing between these two program effects. In response to certain conceptual problems with their approach, Bloom (1978) developed the following alternative model.

$$P(t) = 1 - e^{-(b/c)}e^{(b/c)e-ct}$$ [1]

where:

$P(t)$ = the probability of recidivism by time t at risk, and
b,c = parameters to be estimated.

To understand this model, consider its application to the comparison of hypothetical Programs A and B in Figure 2. If one simply compared their re-

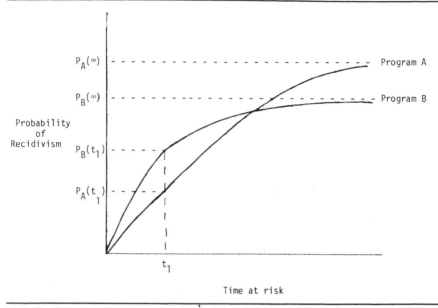

Figure 2: Comparing the Impact Over Time of Two Hypothetical Programs

cidivism probabilities, $P_A(t_1)$ and $P_B(t_1)$, at time t_1 at risk, Program A would appear to be more effective. But if one compared their ultimate recidivism probabilities, $P_A(\infty)$ and $P_B(\infty)$, Program B would be preferred.

Equation 1 specifies a cumulative recidivism probability function shaped like those in Figure 2. Its parameters, b and c, can be estimated using a maximum likelihood procedure (Bloom, 1978). Given b and c, each program's ultimate recidivism probability is simply

$$P(\infty) = 1 - e^{-(b/c)} \qquad [2]$$

For example, if $P_A(\infty)$ were 0.6 then six out of ten Program A recipients would ultimately recidivate. If $P_B(\infty)$ were 0.4 only four out of ten Program B recipients would recidivate. Thus the direct prevention effect of Program B would be greater.

In addition to this prevention effect each program's postponement effect can be measured by using b and c to estimate its mean recidivism time, t_{mean}, as follows (Bloom, 1978):

$$t_{mean} = \frac{e^{-(b/c)}}{c(1 - e^{-(b/c)})} \sum_{n=1}^{\infty} \frac{(b/c)^n}{n \cdot n!} \qquad [3]$$

t_{mean} is the mean time at which offenders who ultimately recidivate do so. Thus if t_{mean}^{A} were 18 months and t_{mean}^{B} were 8 months, Program A would postpone recidivism 10 months longer than Program B. This might occur if, for example, Program A involved a lengthy, closely supervised parole.

To apply the preceding model to Patuxent required several extra steps since our treatment and comparison groups (the counterparts to Programs A and B) were not entirely comparable.

We first estimated recidivism probabilities for the Patuxent sample at six-month intervals for a follow-up period of four years (the longest period for which all members of the sample had been observed). These probabilities equalled the cumulative proportion of the sample rearrested by each point in time. We then applied a nonlinear curve fitting program to this data to estimate b and c for the Patuxent sample. These parameters in turn yielded values of $P(\infty)$ equal to 0.76 and t_{mean} equal to 2.3 years. This implies that 76% of the Patuxent group ultimately will be rearrested and that these arrests will occur 2.3 years after release, on average.

To calculate appropriate prison recidivism probabilities we adjusted for differences between the ages at release and prior criminal records of the treatment and comparison groups using the following LOGIT model.

$$\ln(P(t)/(1-P(t))) = a + b_1 \cdot AGE + b_2 \cdot RECORD + b_3 \cdot PRISON \quad [4]$$

where:

$P(t) =$	the probability of arrest by time t at risk,
$AGE =$	age at release (in years),
$RECORD =$	the number of prior arrests for property crimes (burglary, arson, robbery, larceny, etc.),[4]
$PRISON =$	1 if the offender went to prison and 0 if he went to Patuxent.

This model was estimated from the pooled Patuxent and prison samples at six-month intervals for a period of four years. Table 2 presents some of the results we obtained. As expected, at all times the odds of rearrest increased significantly (at the .10 level) with the length of offenders' prior criminal records. Furthermore, as expected, the odds of rearrest decreased significantly with the age of offenders (after the first year at risk). This is the familiar "burnout" phenomenon. Of most importance, however, is the fact that the odds of rearrest were always significantly greater for prison inmates, controlling for their ages and prior criminal records.

To estimate probabilities of rearrest (at six-month intervals for four years) for the typical Patuxent offender had he been sent to prison instead of Patuxent, we substituted into each LOGIT equation: (1) a value of one for PRISON: (2) the Patuxent sample mean of 33.1 for AGE; and (3) the Patuxent sample mean of 2.1

TABLE 2
Recidivism LOGITS[a]

Years At Risk	Coefficient For:			
	Intercept	Age At Release	Prior Property Convictions	Sent To Prison (1=yes, 0=no)
1	1.192	0.009	.157	1.063
	(1.4)[b]	(.3)	(1.7)	(2.5)
2	1.106	-0.044	.201	.753
	(1.4)	(1.8)	(2.1)	(1.7)
3	1.416	-0.043	.221	.882
	(1.7)	(1.7)	(2.1)	(1.8)
4	1.416	-0.043	.221	.882
	(1.7)	(1.7)	(2.1)	(1.8)

a. Inmates not arrested and not observed for four years were deleted from this analysis, n = 142.
b. Figures in parentheses are estimated asymptotic t statistics.

for RECORD. We then solved for the corresponding probability. Then, as in the case of the Patuxent sample, we applied a nonlinear curve fitting program to these probabilities to estimate b and c, which in turn yielded values for $P(\infty)$ and t_{mean}.

One further complication arose from the fact that unlike the Patuxent sample, not all members of the prison sample had been followed up for four years. To use the data to the fullest extent possible, we employed the following procedure. First we obtained an upper bound for the prison recidivism probabilities by deleting from our analysis all offenders who: (1) were not observed for four years at risk; and (2) were not rearrested while under observation. Results in Table 2 were based on this subsample. We then obtained a lower bound by repeating the analysis using the full prison sample and assuming for each period that all offenders not yet observed to be rearrested were in fact not arrested. This included both offenders who were observed not to be rearrested and those who were not observed for the full period, but had not been arrested while under observation.

Based on this procedure, we estimate that if the typical Patuxent inmate had been sent to prison he would have had a 78-79% chance of subsequent rearrest. Our best single estimate of this figure is 84%, or six percentage points more than if he had been sent to Patuxent. Furthermore, if the offender had been sent to prison his mean time of rearrest would have been 1.3 years or one year sooner than if he had been sent to Patuxent.

Thus, Patuxent offers both prevention and postponement benefits when compared to prison. The next issue to consider is whether or not these benefits are justifiable in light of their costs.

Determining Program Costs

Our cost calculation focused on the two major quantifiable costs of a correctional institution: the cost to the state of constructing, maintaining and operating it, and the foregone earnings of offenders confined there.

Table 3 summarizes our estimates of cost to the state. All figures *not* in parentheses represent annually recurring expenses. They include custody expenditures such as security, food, plant maintenance, housekeeping, and administration, plus expenditures for therapy, education, and recreation. Figures in parentheses represent infrequently recurring expenditures. Of particular importance are costs related to Patuxent's unique commitment and release procedures.

Custody and treatment costs were obtained for Patuxent through the use of a 1975 program crosswalk document and 1976 budgetary data. Capital cost was obtained by annualizing on a per-bed basis the 1976 dollar equivalent of total capital outlays over the lifetime of the institution. Corresponding information for the prison alternative was obtained from the Maryland Division of Correction's budgets for the state's three existing high security prisons, and from recent experience in the construction of conventional high security prisons in other states (National Institute of Law Enforcement and Criminal Justice, 1976). A complication arose during our calculation of prison costs due to the fact that Maryland prisons are currently occupied at 133-200% of their capacity. We consequently calculated capital costs and relevant operating costs both in terms of actual occupancy and designed capacity (Table 3).[5]

The second major cost we considered was inmate forgone earnings. This calculation was particularly difficult since the degree to which one individual's earnings displace those of others is unknown. Thus the opportunity cost of an offender's confinement is somewhere between what he would have earned if he had been free (and no displacement occurred) and zero (if total displacement occurred). Since little is known about the earning power of prison inmates, we attempted to establish a probable upper limit for this parameter.

Earnings data were not available for our sample, so we turned to the 1974 National Prisoners Survey (U.S. Department of Justice, 1974) for this information. Data from this survey for 2081 inmates of Southern prisons (only the

TABLE 3
Components of Costs to the State Per Inmate

Cost Component	Patuxent	Prison At Designed Capacity Utilization	At Actual Utilization
		Cost in 1976 Dollars For:	
CAPITAL	5300	5300	3370
Custody			
Security	6250	3750	2310
Food	850	600	600
Plant Maintenance	1120	1070	670
Housekeeping (e.g. laundry)	360	290	290
Administration	830	460	280
TREATMENT			
During entrance			
Diagnosis	(5520)[1]	(2440)	(2440)
Commitment	(2990)	(0)	(0)
During incarceration			
Therapy	1130	200	200
Ancillary (e.g. education, vocation and recreation programs)	700	590	590
Redetermination	(2460)[2]	(0)	(0)
During exit			
Pre-release center	(170)	(0)	(0)
Halfway house	(1970)	(0)	(0)
Parole	(2900)	(190)	(190)
TOTAL			
Annual	16540	12660	8310
Other	(16010)	(2630)	(2630)

1. Figures in parentheses are infrequently recurring costs.
2. This figure is the mean total cost per inmate for redetermination hearings. It is based on (1) a cost of $2989 per hearing, and (2) the fact that 29% of the Patuxent group had one hearing, 11% had two and 11% had three.

Federal Region was coded for each inmate) updated to 1976 price levels were used to estimate the following regression:

$$
\begin{aligned}
\text{INCOME} \quad = \quad & 3874 + \underset{(7.1)}{371} \cdot \text{EDUCATION} + \underset{(6.4)}{1854} \cdot \text{MARRIED} \\
& + \underset{(6.0)}{1635} \cdot \text{WHITE} - \underset{(3.7)}{1427} \cdot \text{DRUG OFFENSE} \qquad [5] \\
& - \underset{(10.2)}{4074} \cdot \text{TEENAGER} - \underset{(5.7)}{1959} \cdot \text{YOUNGADULT} \\
& - \underset{(0.6)}{489} \cdot \text{OLDADULT}
\end{aligned}
$$

$R^2 = 0.12$

where:

INCOME =	wages, salaries, and fees in 1976 dollars received during the 12 months prior to current incarceration,
EDUCATION =	highest grade attended (in years) prior to current incarceration,
MARRIED =	1 if married, 0 otherwise,
WHITE =	1 if white, 0 otherwise.
DRUG OFFENSE =	1 if ever convicted of drug offense, 0 otherwise,
TEENAGER =	1 if 20 years of age or less, 0 otherwise,
YOUNGADULT =	1 if older than 20 and 30 or less, 0 otherwise, and
OLDADULT =	1 if older than 50, 0 otherwise,
Figures in Parentheses =	t statistics.

Substituting the characteristics of the typical Patuxent offender into this regression equation yielded an estiamte of $8,900 in potential annual earnings.

It should be noted that the earnings data we used were based on the reported legal earned income of prison survey respondents during the twelve months prior to their most recent incarceration. Despite the obvious questions of accuracy of this data source, evidence of its validity is the fact that all coefficients in the regression had the expected signs. Further encouragement is provided by the large t statistics for all but one of the coefficients.

To estimate total cost to the state and inmate earnings forgone required knowledge of the incarceration periods of each alternative. As previously indicated, we estimated these to be 6.8 years for Patuxent and 4.8 years for prison. The Patuxent figure was obtained from the mean incarceration period of the Patuxent sample. The prison figure was obtained using the following regression estimated from the pooled Patuxent and prison sample of 140 offenders.[6]

$$STAY = 7.40 - 5.10 \cdot PRISON + 0.14 \cdot SENTENCE/PRISON$$
$$\quad\quad (6.6) \quad (6.6) \quad\quad\quad\quad (1.8)$$
$$\quad\quad - 0.06 \cdot SENTENCE/PATUXENT \quad\quad\quad\quad\quad\quad [6]$$
$$\quad\quad\;\; (2.1)$$

$R^2 = 0.3$

STAY = the number of years an offender is incarcerated,

PRISON = 1 if the offender went to prison and 0 if he went to Patuxent,

SENTENCE/PRISON = the offender's maximum sentence (in years) if he went to prison and 0 if he went to Patuxent,

SENTENCE/PATUXENT = the offender's maximum sentence (in years) if he went to Patuxent and 0 if he went to prison, and

Figures in Parentheses = t statistics.

Equation 6 specifies that the period for which an offender is incarcerated is a function of his maximum sentence and whether he went to prison or Patuxent. Furthermore, it allows the effect of sentence length to differ between the two alternatives, since the institutional process which determines release from prison is based in part on offender's sentences; but Patuxent's indeterminate sentence breaks this linkage. Thus we expected and obtained a sizable and signficant (at the 0.10 level) positive coefficient for prison sentences. We expected a negligible coefficient for Patuxent sentences, and obtained a small but significant negative one.

Substituting into Equation 6 the Patuxent sample mean maximum sentence and a value of PRISON equal to one, we obtained an estimated prison incarceration period of 4.0 years. To compensate for possible bias due to exclusion of the 13 prison inmates in our sample who had not yet been paroled at the time of our study, we took a weighted mean of the 4.0 year figure for the 39 prison inmates used to estimate Equation 6 and 50% of the maximum sentence for the 13 excluded prison inmates.[7] The 50% figure yielded a probable upper bound since the mean prison term for our comparison group was 35%. This biased our cost analysis in favor of Patuxent.

We next computed the present value of total costs for each scenario. To do so required selection of a discount rate to account for differences in the timing of the two cost streams. Given the lack of agreement on a single most appropriate discount rate, we computed costs for rates of 5%, 7.5%, and 15%. Our resulting cost estimates are presented in Table 4. As can be seen, regardless of the discount rate, Patuxent is substantially more expensive than prison, especially its cost to the state. A Patuxent term costs the state from 2.7 to 2.9 times what a prison term would cost, due to the higher cost of Patuxent's commitment, release, and operating procedures and its longer term.

TABLE 4
The Present Value of Total Costs for Each Scenario

	Patuxent	Prison	
		At Designed Capacity Utilization	At Current Utilization
5% Discount Rate			
Cost to State	112,000	57,000	39,000
Forgone inmate earnings [a]	53,000	40,000	40,000
7.5% Discount Rate			
Cost to State	104,000	54,000	37,000
Forgone inmate earnings	49,000	37,000	37,000
15% Discount Rate			
Cost to State	85,000	47,000	32,000
Forgone inmate earnings	40,000	32,000	32,000

a. Assumes zero displacement and thus represents an upper bound.

CONCLUSIONS

Having computed institutional costs and effectiveness, how does one use the information to make a policy decision? Ideally one should project inmates' full post Patuxent and postprison lifetimes and compare them. This comparison would account for crimes both directly prevented by rehabilitation and confinement, and indirectly prevented by postponing criminal careers. It would also account for costs due to future incarcerations. Such an analysis, however, would have required at least a 30 to 40 year period of observation. We were forced, therefore, to limit our conclusions to those implied by findings presented in the preceding sections.

For example we find that offenders spend two years more in Patuxent than they would have in prison and thus are unavailable for criminal activity for two years longer. Therefore, within the limited time frame of our analysis, Patuxent yields benefits in terms of incapacitation, but only at a substantial cost to the state. If incapacitation were the principal objective of the institution, its expensive and controversial treatment program would not be warranted, since the same benefits could be provided at a much lower cost through longer confinement in conventional prisons.

Instead, Patuxent must be justified in terms of its rehabilitation benefits as reflected by the prevention or postponement of crimes. Our best estimate of these effects is a 6% reduction in the ultimate probability of rearrest and a one-year postponement of rearrests. These benefits are purchased at a cost to the state of at least $38,000 per inmate.

Assuming (as we do) that our estimates of Patuxent's benefits really correspond to a reduction in crime, we nonetheless feel that the Patuxent program was not an efficient allocation of society's resources. It is not difficult to imagine, for example, that the additional $38,000 spent for Patuxent could yield far greater benefits if used instead to increase the number of law enforcement personnel (e.g. policemen, prosecutors, and judges) or to provide job placement and training programs for inner city youth.

This argument is complicated, however, by the many different components of the Patuxent program. For example does Patuxent's differential impact stem from its more selective admission procedures? From its extensive and varied treatment programs? From its careful supervision of released offenders? We have no basis for separating the institution's effect into portions attributable to these elements of its program. But it is plausible to us that some of its activities (such as the elaborate supervision of releasees) are cost effective and should provide models for conventional correctional programs.

When our results were presented to the Maryland state legislature, perhaps its members had similar mixed feelings about Patuxent. That the institution was found to have a differential effect clearly spoke for the continuance of its program. That it was not cost effective in some sense, spoke for change. Seeking change, but reluctant to terminate the Patuxent program, the legislature made three fundamental modifications to the institution. It altered the commitment criteria to stress the ability and desire of offenders to benefit from Patuxent's treatment program and to that end stipulated that any inmate could transfer from Patuxent to a conventional prison. Moreover, the legislature introduced a requirement that each inmate have a treatment program designed specifically for him, and that his progress through the institution be measured in terms of his achievement of the goals set in his program. Finally, the legislature repealed the indeterminate sentence provision in favor of a stipulation that no inmate could be confined in Patuxent beyond the end of his original sentence. The Patuxent staff, however, retained its authority to release offenders when it felt such release was justified.

Since these changes were introduced in July, 1977, there has been no shortage of offenders seeking admission to Patuxent. Many of those seeking admission face long conventional prison terms, and see Patuxent as their one avenue of early release. If, as seems likely, voluntary participants progress more rapidly through the institution's programs than unwilling "defective delinquents," and if the Patuxent staff is able to judge readiness for release by criteria other than length of stay, then this move toward voluntary participation should produce benefits at least as great as those we observed, but at a lower cost due to shorter confinements.

The renewed life given to Patuxent by the 1977 legislative action, coupled with the prospect that the institution's overall cost-effectiveness will improve, underlines the importance of evaluating the separate effects of Patuxent's component programs. To conduct such an evaluation would require considerable methodological sophistication and necessitate development of a detailed data base. The benefits of such an evaluation would be substantial, however, since it would probably provide insights that apply to a wide range of correctional programs.

NOTES

1. Other work has been done on this topic recently by Witte and Schmidt (1977) and Harris and Moitra (1978).

2. This decision was based on the opinion of Dr. Henry J. Steadman, Director of the Special Projects Research Unit, Division of Research, New York State Department of Mental Hygiene. Dr. Steadman developed the database.

3. Given Patuxent's longer incarceration, its inmates were older at both admission and release.

4. Property crimes were used rather than personal crimes since property crimes are more repetitive (Glaser and O'Leary, 1971) and were better predictors of recidivism for our sample.

5. Relevant operating costs are those which vary (on a per-bed basis) directly with the occupancy rate.

6. Offenders with life sentences were not included.

7. Nine of these 13 offenders were in the two most recent cohorts (1971 and 1972) and thus had served five years or less at the time of our study.

REFERENCES

BLOOM, H. S. (1978) "Evaluating human service and criminal justice programs by modeling the probability and timing of recidivism." Department of City and Regional Planning, Harvard University.

GLASER, D. and V. O'LEARY (1971) "The results of parole," pp. 245-260 in L. Radzinowicz and M. E. Wolfgang (eds.) Crime and Justice, Vol. 3: The Criminal In Confinement. New York: Basic Books.

GOLDFARB, R. L. and L. R. SINGER (1973) After Conviction. New York: Simon & Schuster.

GRAY, C. M., C. J. CONOVER, and T. M. HENNESSEY (1978) "Cost-effectiveness of residential community corrections: an analytical prototype." Evaluation Q. 2, 3: 375-400.

HARRIS, C. M. and S. D. MOITRA (1978) "Improved statistical techniques for the measurement of recidivism." J. of Research in Crime and Delinquency 15: 2 (July): 194-213.

MALTZ, M. D. and R. McCLEARY (1977) "The mathematics of behavioral change: recidivism and construct validity." Evaluation Q. 1, 3: 421-438.

——— (1978) "Comments on 'stability of parameters in the split population exponential distribution.'" Evaluation Q.

——— and S. M. POLLOCK (1978) "Recidivism and likelihood functions: a reply to Stollmack." Evaluation Q.

Maryland Annotated Code, Article 31-B.

National Institute of Law Enforcement and Criminal Justice, U.S. Law Enforcement Assistance Administration (1976) Cost Analysis of Correctional Standards: Institutional Based Programs and Parole, Vol. 2. Washington, DC: Government Printing Office, Appendix A.

SELLIN, T., and M. E. WOLFGANG (1964) The Measurement of Delinquency. New York: John Wiley.

SINGER, N. M. and H. S. BLOOM (1977) "A cost-effectiveness analysis of Patuxent Institution." Bull. of Amer. Academy of Psychiatry and Law, Vol. V, No. 2: 161-170.

STOLLMACK, S. (1978) "Comments on 'the mathematics of behavioral change.'" Evaluation Q.

TABASZ, T. F. (1975) Toward An Economics of Prisons. New York: Praeger.

U.S. Department of Justice, Law Enforcement Assistance Administration (1974) Survey of Inmates of State Correctional Facilities.

WITTE, A. D. and P. SCHMIDT (1977) "An analysis of recidivism, using the Truncated Lognormal Distribution." J. of Royal Statistical Society, Series C, Vol. 26, No. 3: 302-311.

The following by Knatterud et al. presents an excellent example of a randomized clinical trial in medicine. Using a well-defined sample of adult-onset diabetics who should have been able to remain ketosis-free on diet alone, they randomly assigned subjects to one of three conditions: (a) a diet-alone condition in which the subject was only given placebo pills; (b) a standard insulin condition in which the dosage was based on the subject's body area; and (c) a variable insulin condition in which the dosage was periodically adjusted based on blood-glucose levels. Notable features of the study include the use of a double-blind design, a long-term (8.75 year) follow-up with quarterly examinations, and the use of a wide variety of outcome measures including morbidity and several indices of cardio-vascular functioning. Thus the study represents an excellent example of well-conducted evaluation research.

The study also illustrates some of the difficulties of comparing different methods of optimizing treatment. The standard-insulin treatment group represents a normative approach, whereas the variable-insulin treatment group represents an attempt to optimize treatment based on the theoreti-cally mediating process (i.e., blood-glucose levels).

Much of the controversy surrounding the UGDP studies (see, for example, Seltzer, 1972*) has specifically concerned this point—were the adjustments in the variable group of the appropriate magnitude and frequency? Further complications are introduced by differences between the treat-ments in the number of hypoglycemic episodes, differential compliance with the drug therapy, and the possibility that subjects were able to infer the condition to which they were assigned. These problems illustrate some of the difficulties in interpretation that may be encountered by evaluation researchers even when the best designs and procedures are employed.

*SELTZER, H. S. (1972) "A summary of criticisms of the findings and conclusions of the University Group Diabetes Program (UGDP)." Diabetes 21, 976-979.

28

Effects of Hypoglycemic Agents on Vascular Complications in Patients with Adult-Onset Diabetes
VII. Mortality and Selected Nonfatal Events with Insulin Treatments

Genell L. Knatterud, Christian R. Klimpt, Marvin E. Levin, Maynard E. Jacobson, and Martin G. Goldner

● The University Group Diabetes Program is a long-term prospective clinical trial designed to evaluate the effects of various hypoglycemic agents on vascular complications in patients with asymptomatic adult-onset diabetes. Mortality and blood glucose levels were determined as well as certain nonfatal events for patients assigned to diet alone or to either of two insulin treatment regimens. Lower levels of blood glucose with mean values close to normoglycemia were achieved in the treatment group in which the

From Genell L. Knatterud, Christian R. Klimpt, Marvin E. Levin, Maynard E. Jacobson, and Martin G. Goldner, "Effects of Hypoglycemic Agents on Vascular Complications in Patients with Adult-Onset Diabetes: VII. Mortality and Selected Nonfatal Events with Insulin Treatments," 240 *Journal of the American Medical Association* 37-42 (July 7, 1978). Copyright 1978, American Medical Association.

insulin dosage was adjusted to achieve normoglycemia compared with the levels achieved in patients treated with diet alone or with a fixed dose of insulin. In spite of differences in blood glucose levels among the treatment groups, there were only minor differences in the occurrence of fatal or nonfatal events.
(JAMA 240:37-42, 1978)

THE University Group Diabetes Program (UGDP) was initiated to study the effects of various hypoglycemic treatments on the development of vascular complications in patients with adult-onset diabetes as well as to obtain information on the natural history of the non-insulin-dependent diabetic. The purpose of this report is to present the findings for degree of blood glucose control as well as findings for mortality and for certain nonfatal events for the patients in the UGDP assigned to diet alone (placebo) or to either of two insulin treatment regimens. In one insulin group (insulin variable) patients were given the amount of insulin required to lower their blood glucose values to defined levels. In the second insulin group (insulin standard) each patient was given a prescription based solely on an estimate of the patient's body surface, which is a function of height and weight. A detailed report on all available information for nonfatal events in these three groups is in preparation.

Patient recruitment for these treatment groups started in 1961 and was completed in December 1965. All patients were asked to return for scheduled follow-up examinations through August 1975. Only the events that occurred on or before Dec 31, 1974, have been included in the analyses presented in this report. After the meeting of all UGDP investigators in October 1974, some clinic physicians modified the assigned study treatment for patients assigned to placebo or insulin standard treatment in preparation for the termination of patient follow-up in 1975. Consequently, some patients in these treatment groups were followed-up according to the study protocol only through the last follow-up examination performed on or before Dec 31, 1974. As of that date, all of the 619 patients in the three treatment groups considered in this report (205 in placebo, 210 in insulin standard, 204 in insulin variable) had been available for a minimum of nine years of follow-up and 460 patients (74%) for 11 or more years of follow-up.

The major design features[1] of this prospective clinical trial were (1) random allocation to treatment, (2) double-blind evaluation of oral agents, (3) common study protocol, (4) long-term observation of patients, and (5) quality control procedures. The principal criteria for patient eligibility included (1) diabetes diagnosis within 12 months, (2) diagnosis confirmed by glucose tolerance test (GTT), (3) ketosis free on diet alone, (4) life expectancy of at least five years, and (5) willingness to participate in the study. Twelve clinical centers, two lipid laboratories, and a coordinating center participated in this study. Special consultants were responsible for reading ECGs, fundus photographs, and soft-tissue x-ray films.

Previous UGDP reports[2-6] have presented the findings for the two oral hypoglycemic agents, tolbutamide and phenformin hydrochloride, studied in the UGDP; these results

Reprint requests to UGDP Coordinating Center, University of Maryland School of Medicine, 600 Wyndhurst Ave., Baltimore, MD 21210 (Dr. Knatterud).

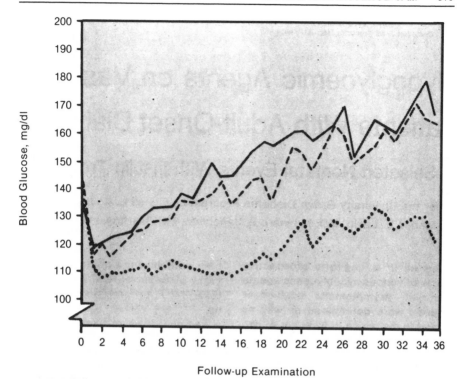

Fig 1.—Mean fasting blood glucose levels at baseline and each follow-up examination for patients observed through 35th follow-up examination. Solid line represents placebo treatment group (n=85); broken line, insulin standard treatment group (n=100); and dotted line, insulin variable treatment group (n=103).

will not be discussed in this report. Both of these treatment groups were discontinued prior to the scheduled termination of the study because of no evidence of beneficial effects and some evidence of adverse effects.

BLOOD GLUCOSE LEVELS

Dosage adjustments because of elevated blood glucose levels without symptoms were permitted only for patients assigned to the insulin variable treatment group, although treatment of patients in all groups was modified or discontinued if the patient's medical condition warranted a treatment alteration.[1] An increase of at least 2 units of insulin per day was to be made for patients assigned to insulin variable treatment if a patient

Table 1.—Percentage Distribution of Patients by Level of Blood Glucose Control*			
Level of Control	Placebo (n=204)	Insulin Standard (n=205)	Insulin Variable (n=198)
Good	23.0	28.8	38.9
Fair	33.8	38.0	46.5
Poor	43.1	33.2	14.6

*Based on a patient's fasting blood glucose values of short glucose tolerance test using definitions derived from Joslin Clinic criteria[7]: good, 70% or more of all of the patient's fasting blood glucose values <110 mg/dl; fair, patient classified as having neither good nor poor blood glucose control; poor, 70% or more of all of the patient's fasting blood glucose values ≥130 mg/dl.

had a fasting value ≥110 mg/dl and a one-hour value ≥210 mg/dl from a GTT. This test, which will be referred to as the short GTT, was performed at each quarterly examination except those performed at annual intervals after entry (eg, quarters 4, 8, 12). A three-hour GTT (long GTT) was performed prior to the initiation of treatment (ie, at a baseline examination) and at each annual follow-up examination.[1]

The short GTT consisted of a fasting blood sample and a blood sample obtained 1½ hours after the patient took the assigned medication and one hour after drinking 50 g of dextrose dissolved in 300 ml of water. The only preparation for this test was an overnight fast. Glucose determinations were performed on whole blood.[1]

The changes in fasting blood glucose levels from the short GTT observed during the course of follow-up for each treatment group are presented in Fig 1 for the cohort of patients observed through the 35th follow-up examination (or 8¾ years of follow-up). Only patients who had a fasting blood glucose value at baseline and the short GTT performed at the 35th quarterly follow-up examination and who had not missed two consecutive examinations were included in this analysis. The mean fasting blood glucose value observed at baseline in the cohort of patients studied was 136 mg/dl for patients in the placebo treatment group, 142 mg/dl for patients in the insulin standard treatment group, and 141 mg/dl for patients in the insulin variable treatment group.

There was a large drop in blood glucose levels in all treatment groups after the initiation of treatment. At the end of the first follow-up period, patients in the placebo group showed a 13.6% reduction in the fasting blood glucose levels from baseline compared with a 19.7% reduction in the insulin standard treatment group and a

20.7% reduction in the insulin variable treatment group. During the 8¾ years of follow-up covered by this analysis, the fasting blood glucose levels for patients in this cohort in the placebo and insulin standard treatment groups gradually returned to the baseline values and then exceeded them. The fasting blood glucose levels for patients treated with variable dosages of insulin, however, did not exceed the baseline levels, and at the 35th quarterly follow-up examination a reduction of 13.5% from the baseline mean was noted. Corresponding values for the other treatment groups were 22.8% increase over baseline levels for the placebo-treated group and a 15.9% increase over baseline levels in the insulin standard treatment group.

The lower fasting blood glucose levels in the insulin variable treatment group were maintained during the course of the study by increasing the number of units of insulin. For the cohort of patients observed for 35 quarters, the mean number of units of insulin was 12 units at the first quarterly follow-up examination and 47 units at the 35th quarterly follow-up examination. The range in daily dosage at the first quarter for this cohort of patients was 5 to 40 units; the range at the 35th quarter was 5 to 240 units.

One measure of glucose control derived from criteria employed by the Joslin Clinic[7] was defined on the basis of the fasting values from the short GTT. These results are presented in Table 1. The highest level of control was achieved in the insulin variable treatment group; 38.9% of these patients had good control, and 14.6% had poor control, compared with 23.0% with good control and 43.1% with poor control in the placebo treatment group. The results for patients in the insulin standard treatment group were intermediate to those for patients in the insulin variable and the placebo treatment groups.

Patients in the insulin variable and insulin standard treatment groups had better levels of control than patients treated with diet alone, as noted previously, but perhaps at some price. A total of 102 patients in the two insulin groups had their prescriptions altered one or more times during the course of follow-up because of reported (suspect or definite) hypoglycemic episodes (80 in insulin variable and 22 in insulin standard). No patients in the placebo treatment group had prescription changes because of reported hypoglycemia.

MORTALITY FINDINGS

In contrast to the findings for glucose, only small differences were observed in mortality. The number of deaths in each group by cause of death is given in Table 2. The final judgment concerning the principal cause of death for each deceased patient was made without knowledge of the treatment group to which the patient had been assigned. As of Dec 31, 1974, a total of 151 deaths had been reported: 54 deaths in the placebo treatment group, 48 in the

Table 2.—Number and Percentage Dead by Cause of Death			
	Placebo	Insulin Standard	Insulin Variable
No. at risk of death	205	210	204
Cardiovascular causes			
Myocardial infarction	1	6	4
Sudden death	11	8	11
Other heart disease	4	4	5
Extracardiac vascular disease	13	9	9
All cardiovascular causes	29	27	29
Other causes			
Cancer	16	10	7
Cause other than above	8	9	11
Unknown	1	2	2
All causes	54	48	49
Percentage dead from			
Cardiovascular cause	14.1	12.9	14.2
Cancer	7.8	4.8	3.4
All causes	26.3	22.9	24.0

Table 3.—P Values Comparing the Observed Distribution of Deaths[*]		
	Insulin Standard vs Placebo	Insulin Variable vs Placebo
All causes		
Difference in % dead	−3.4	−2.3
P value	0.48	0.67
Cardiovascular Causes		
Difference in % dead	−1.2	0.1
P value	0.81	1.00
Cancer		
Difference in % dead	−3.0	−4.4
P value	0.28	0.09

*Evaluated with the Fisher exact test.[6]

insulin standard treatment group, and 49 in the insulin variable treatment group. Almost the same number of cardiovascular deaths was observed in each group. More deaths were attributed to cancer in the placebo treatment group than in either of the two insulin groups (16 in placebo, 10 in insulin standard, and 7 in insulin variable).

The drug-placebo differences in the number of patients who had died were evaluated with the Fisher exact test,[8] and the results of this analysis are given in Table 3. These tests provided no evidence of statistically significant differences among the three groups. P values obtained from the application of this test represent the probability of obtaining the · observed distribution or a more extreme distribution of events in the treatment groups being compared under the null hypothesis of no difference between these groups. P values quoted in this communication should be considered nominal P values since no attempt was made to adjust for the fact that several response variables have been evaluated for multiple treatment comparisons at frequent intervals during the course of the trial. Any adjustment would make the P values larger, or less statistically significant.

Cumulative annual death rates per 100 population at risk have been calculated with life table procedures.[2] These results are given for all causes of death in Fig 2. The death rates for the placebo treatment group, based on all causes of death, are higher than

Fig 2.—Cumulative death rates for all causes per 100 population at risk by year of follow-up. Solid line represents placebo treatment group; broken line, insulin standard treatment group; and dotted line, insulin variable treatment group.

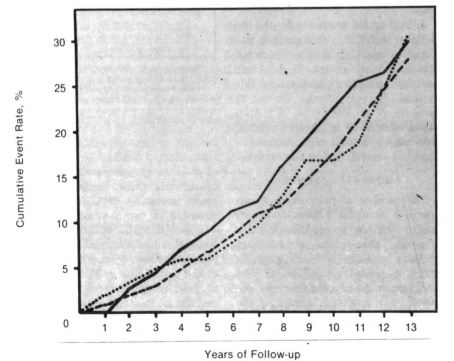

Years of Follow-up

the death rates for either of the two insulin groups beginning with three years of follow-up through the 12th year, but all the differences are small.

Follow-up for mortality for the 619 patients included in this analysis was almost complete; ie, the life-death status for all except 21 of these patients was known at the time this report was prepared. These 21 patients (7 in placebo, 3 in insulin standard, and 11 in insulin variable) were assumed to be alive for all the analyses summarized in this report.

NONFATAL EVENTS

The number of patients in whom specified nonfatal events developed during the course of follow-up are given in Table 4. The percentage of patients experiencing each event is given in parentheses. Patients who were shown to have experienced the event prior to the completion of the baseline examination and those for whom information for that event was not available at the baseline examination were not included in the analysis for that event. Therefore, the number of patients at risk of having a specified event was different for each of the indicated events. The percentages of patients with nonfatal events were remarkably similar in all three treatment groups except for the occurrence of serum creatinine levels ≥1.5 mg/dl and hospitalizations for heart disease. More patients in the placebo-treated group than in either of the two insulin groups were found to have elevated levels of serum creatinine at least once during the course of follow-up, and a few more patients in the placebo group were hospitalized for heart disease.

Comparisons of the occurrence of each of the nonfatal events in each of the two insulin groups with the

occurrence of these events in the placebo-treated group were evaluated with the Fisher exact test. Only one of the comparisons of nonfatal events for insulin standard vs placebo or insulin variable vs placebo yielded $P<.05$, and that was obtained for the comparison of elevated serum creatinine levels for placebo vs insulin standard (Table 4).

ADHERENCE TO TREATMENT

An assessment of the level of adherence based on the percentage of follow-up periods in which patients took all or some of the prescribed medication is summarized in Table 5. A patient was regarded as having taken all of the study medication in a given follow-up period if he took that medication in the dosage specified by protocol for at least 75 days of the three-month follow-up period and if he was not taking any hypoglycemic agent other than the assigned study medication during that follow-up period. A patient was regarded as taking some of the assigned medication if the patient took a dosage different from that specified by protocol (below or above) for at least 75 days of the 90 days in the follow-up period or if he took the exact dosage specified for at least 15 days but fewer than 75 days and if the patient had not taken any other hypoglycemic medication during this period. The percentage of patients who took all or some of the prescribed medication for 75% or more of all follow-up periods was 59.5% in the placebo treatment group, 63.3% in the insulin standard treatment group, and 72.5% for insulin variable treatment group.

The percentage of patients who took little or none of the assigned study medication during the entire time period that they were under observation corresponds to the group

Table 4.—Patients With First Occurrence of Specified Nonfatal Event

	Placebo		Insulin Standard		Insulin Variable		P Value	
	No. (%)	Denominator	No. (%)	Denominator	No. (%)	Denominator	Insulin Standard vs Placebo	Insulin Variable vs Placebo
Heart examination								
Significant ECG abnormality*	38(20.0)	190	32(16.7)	192	33(17.6)	188	0.48	0.63
Use of digitalis	23(12.1)	190	24(12.6)	190	23(12.5)	184	1.00	1.00
Hospitalization for heart disease†	23(11.9)	194	13(6.8)	190	13(7.0)	187	0.13	0.14
Hypertension‡	64(50.0)	128	76(54.7)	139	79(55.6)	142	0.52	0.42
Angina pectoris	37(19.6)	189	29(15.5)	187	31(16.6)	187	0.37	0.54
Eye examination								
Visual acuity ≤20/200 (either eye)	20(11.2)	179	21(11.7)	179	20(11.4)	175	1.00	1.00
Opacity (vitreous, lenticular, or corneal, either eye)	16(9.2)	173	19(10.6)	179	20(11.6)	173	0.80	0.60
Fundus abnormalities excluding exudates§	55(43.3)	127	53(45.3)	117	51(43.2)	118	0.85	1.00
Kidney examination								
Urine protein ≥1 g/liter	8(4.2)	189	4(2.1)	195	11(5.8)	190	0.35	0.65
Serum creatinine ≥1.5 mg/dl	30(16.3)	184	16(8.3)	193	17(9.1)	186	0.03	0.06
Peripheral vascular examination								
Amputation of all or part of either low limb	3(1.5)	194	1(0.5)	198	3(1.6)	190	0.61	1.00
Arterial calcification‖	50(29.6)	169	47(28.8)	163	44(28.4)	155	0.98	0.91
Intermittent claudication	32(17.6)	182	37(19.4)	191	29(16.0)	181	0.76	0.80

*Major or moderate Q waves (codes 1-1-1 through 1-2-7), ST depression (code 4-1), T wave inversion (code 5-1), complete heart block (code 6-1), left bundle-branch block (code 7-1), or ventricular tachycardia (code 8-2). All ECGs evaluated using the Minnesota code.[12,13]

†As reported at Annual Heart Examinations.

‡World Health Organization definition: systolic blood pressure ≥160 mm Hg or diastolic blood pressure ≥95 mm Hg based on a single examination.[14]

§Readings of right central fundus photographs for one or more of the following abnormalities: retinal hemorrhages and microaneurysms, preretinal and vitreous hemorrhages, venous pathology, arterial pathology, or proliferative changes and neovascularization.

‖Evidence of arterial calcification noted in both of two independent readings of the same set of soft-tissue x-ray films of the right lower limb.

Table 5.—Distribution of Patients by Adherence
to Prescribed Study Medication

	Placebo (n=205)	Insulin Standard (n=210)	Insulin Variable (n=204)
Percentage of patients who took all* of prescribed medication			
For ≥75% of follow-up.	51.2	50.5	34.3
For 25%-74% of follow-up	34.6	29.5	50.0
For <25% of follow-up	14.1	20.0	15.7
Percentage of patients who took all* or some† of prescribed medication			
For ≥75% of follow-up	59.5	63.3	72.5
For 25%-74% of follow-up	27.3	24.3	14.7
For <25% of follow-up	13.2	12.4	12.7

*Patient took prescribed study medication in the dosage specified by protocol for at least 75 days during the follow-up period and took no other hypoglycemic agent.

†Patient took prescribed study medication in the dosage specified for at least 25 days and no more than 74 days during the follow-up period or took prescribed study medication in reduced or increased dosage for 75 or more days during the follow-up period and took no other hypoglycemic agent.

who took all or some for less than 25% of all follow-up periods. This was 13.2% for placebo, 12.4% for insulin standard, and 12.7% for insulin variable.

COMMENT

Different blood glucose levels during the course of the study were noted for the three treatment groups as demonstrated by the differences in the fasting blood glucose levels from the short GTT. Only 14.6% of patients treated with variable dosages of insulin had 70% or more of fasting blood glucose values ≥130 mg/dl, or poor control, compared with 43.1% in the group treated with diet alone (placebo) and 33.2% in the insulin standard treatment group (Table 1). However, to achieve these lower levels in the insulin variable treatment group, the daily dosage of insulin was increased during the course of follow-up (the mean number of units per day was 12 at the first quarter and 47 at the 35th quarter), and the risk of hypoglycemic episodes increased (80 patients or 39.2% in the insulin variable group with at least one reported episode of hypoglycemia).

The gradient in observed blood glucose levels among the treatment groups did not result in differences in mortality. The mortality results for the placebo, insulin standard, and insulin variable treatment groups remained comparable through December 1974. Also, there were only small differences in the occurrence of nonfatal vascular complications among the patients in these three treatment groups.

Thus, over the time period studied with an average follow-up of 12 years, insulin used in a fixed dosage or used in a variable dosage to normalize glucose levels was no better than diet alone (plus placebo tablets or capsules) in prolonging life or in preventing the vascular complications considered in this report in the adult-onset, non-ketosis-prone diabetic.

Certainly no one would assert that ideal or perfect control had been achieved for UGDP patients treated with variable dosages of insulin. Better control would have required more monitoring of the levels of blood glucose and urine glucose by both the patient and physician than was specified in the UGDP protocol, which was designed to simulate general clinical practice. However, even if one postulates that the development and progression of vascular disease are affected only if blood glucose levels are maintained within a certain range, one would expect to observe some differences in the occurrence of fatal and nonfatal events corresponding to the differences observed for blood glucose levels. It should also be recognized that more stringent monitoring and resultant dosage adjustments would increase the risk of, and perhaps the severity of, hypoglycemic episodes.

Several explanations have been suggested to account for the lack of correlation between blood glucose levels and the occurrence of vascular events in the UGDP.[9] However, the possibility that control of blood glucose levels will not alter the course of vascular disease in the adult-onset diabetic should not be overlooked as one possible explanation.

The UGDP definition of diabetes has been questioned by some. In view of the lack of general agreement on a standard definition of diabetes, it is perhaps not surprising that all UGDP patients would not satisfy all of the diagnostic criteria that have been proposed; however, blood glucose levels increased in all patients during the period of follow-up in the UGDP. These trends were observed particularly for patients in the placebo and insulin standard treatment groups. Evidence of this trend for patients in the insulin-variable group is provided by the increase in the number of units of insulin required to keep fasting values below 110 mg/dl and one-hour values below 210 mg/dl, thus providing additional evidence that the patients enrolled in the UGDP were adult-onset diabetics. In addition, the few patients who did not meet certain diagnostic criteria are distributed evenly among the treatment groups, and excluding these patients does not alter the overall results.

Another question is whether the number of patients studied was large enough or the period of follow-up long enough to detect differences. To answer that question requires making several assumptions. If one is willing to assume that after eight years of follow-up the event rate in the diet alone group would be 16%, then there is an 80% chance (type II error=0.20) of detecting an 8.8% difference between the placebo group and the drug group (eg, an eight-year rate of 7.2% in the insulin variable treatment group) with a sample size of 200 in each group and a type I error of 0.05. If the eight-year event rate in the placebo-treated group is 25%, a drug-placebo difference of 11% (eg, eight-year rate of 14% in the insulin variable group) has an 80% chance of being observed with this sample size. Some events such as proliferative diabetic retinopathy and renal abnormalities were rarely observed among the UGDP patients, and thus, no detectable differences were observed. It is possible that longer periods of follow-up would yield differences for these events when the rate of occurrence is higher.

SUMMARY

The conclusions of the UGDP are applicable only to the type of patients studied, ie, the adult-onset, non-insulin-dependent diabetic, but this group represents the largest segment in the population that is diabetic, and the patients in the UGDP are representative of this large group.[10] The problems associated with treatment of the insulin-dependent, particularly juvenile-onset, diabetic are different, and whether the UGDP results can be extrapolated to this group cannot be answered on the basis of available evidence. In any case, the use of insulin is essential for this form of the disease.

The UGDP findings provide no evidence that insulin or any other drug lowering blood glucose levels will alter the course of vascular complications in the type of diabetes that is most common, adult-onset diabetes. Weight reduction has been shown to be feasible and effective in lowering blood glucose levels[11]; thus, dietary management deserves greater emphasis in this type of diabetes than it has received to date, as others have also suggested. In any case, the UGDP results suggest that the use of any additional therapeutic agent must be justified on grounds other than the prevention of macrovascular complications.

This study was supported beginning in 1960 by a series of 14 grants from the National Institute of Arthritis, Metabolism, and Digestive Diseases of the Public Health Service.

Nonproprietary Name and Trademarks of Drug

Phenformin hydrochloride—*DBI, Meltrol.*

University Group Diabetes Program

Past and present participating investigators as of January 1977 were as follows:

Aguilo, Francisco, MD
San Juan, Puerto Rico

Albrink, Margaret J., MD
Morgantown, WVa

Barrett, James C., MD
Birmingham, Ala (until 1972)

Becker, Frank O., MD
Chicago

Biern, Samuel, MD
Williamson, WVa

Boshell, Buris R., MD
Birmingham, Ala

Bowen, Angela J., MD
Seattle (until 1970)

Cammarn, Maxine R., MD
Cleveland (until 1965)

Crampton, Joseph H., MD
Seattle (died 1966)

Daughaday, William H., MD
St Louis

Davidson, Paul C., MD
Williamson, WVa

Field, Richard A., MD
Boston (until 1966)

Goetz, Frederick C, MD
Minneapolis

Goldner, Martin G., MD
Brooklyn, NY

Haddock, Lillian, MD
San Juan, Puerto Rico

Jacobs, William H., MD
Williamson, WVa (died 1971)

Jacobson, Maynard E., MD
Minneapolis

Jones, Charles A., MD
Williamson, WVa (died 1974)

Kansal, P. C., MD
Birmingham, Ala

Kilo, Charles, MD
St Louis

Klimt, Christian R., MD, DPH
Baltimore

Knatterud, Genell L., PhD
Baltimore

Knowles, Harvey C., Jr, MD
Cincinnati

Kreines, Kenneth, MD
Cincinnati

Leon, Eloina, MD
San Juan, Puerto Rico (1971-1975)

Levin, Marvin E., MD
St Louis

Mackenzie, Malcolm S., MD
Cleveland (until 1969)

Martin, Donald B., MD
Boston

Maslansky, Robert A., MD
Minneapolis (until 1973)

Meinert, Curtis L., PhD
Baltimore

Metz, Robert J., MD
Seattle

Miller, David I., MD
Baltimore

Miller, Max, MD
Cleveland

Newberry, William B., Jr, MD
Cleveland

Nibbe, Albert F., MD
Chicago (1966-1969)

Nielsen, Robert L., MD
Seattle

Osborne, Robert K., MD
Boston

Prout, Thaddeus E., MD
Baltimore

Recant, Lillian, MD
St Louis (until 1967)

Reeves, Robert L., MD
Seattle (until 1970)

Rovira, Gabriel Martinez, MD
San Juan, Puerto Rico (until 1971)

Schwartz, Theodore B., MD
Chicago

Spergel, Gabriel, MD
Brooklyn, NY

Steenrod, William J., MD
Seattle

Tucker, Randolph, MD
Chicago (until 1966)

Vega, Luis A., MD
San Juan, Puerto Rico (until 1970)

Villavicencio, Elena, MD
San Juan, Puerto Rico (until 1967)

Weisenfeld, Shirley, MD
Brooklyn, NY

Participating consultants included the following:

Jacob E. Bearman, PhD, statistics
University of Minnesota, Minneapolis

Henry Blackburn, MD, electrocardiography
University of Minnesota, Minneapolis

Byron W. Brown, Jr, PhD, statistics
Stanford University, Palo Alto, Calif

Jerome Cornfield, statistics
George Washington University, Washington, DC

Matthew Davis, MD, ophthalmology
University of Wisconsin, Madison

Alan Freemond, MD, ophthalmology
University of Cincinnati, Cincinnati (until 1968)

Philip M. LeCompte, MD, pathology
Faulkner Hospital, Boston

Alexander Lewitan, MD, radiology
Kingsbrook Jewish Medical Center, Brooklyn, NY

Irving M. Liebow, MD, electrocardiography
University Hospitals of Cleveland, Cleveland (until 1966)

J. Wallace McMeel, MD, ophthalmology
Retina Associates, Boston

Frederick A. Rose, MD, radiology
University Hospitals of Cleveland, Cleveland

References

1. A study of the effects of hypoglycemic agents on vascular complications in patients with adult-onset diabetes: I. Design, methods and baseline results, University Group Diabetes Program. *Diabetes* 19(suppl 2):747-783, 1970.

2. A study of the effects of hypoglycemic agents on vascular complications in patients with adult-onset diabetes: II. Mortality results, University Group Diabetes Program. *Diabetes* 19(suppl 2):785-830, 1970.

3. Effects of hypoglycemic agents on vascular complications in patients with adult-onset diabetes: III. Clinical implications of UGDP results, University Group Diabetes Program. *JAMA* 218:1400-1410, 1971.

4. Effects of hypoglycemic agents on vascular complications in patients with adult-onset diabetes: IV. A preliminary report on phenformin results, University Group Diabetes Program. *JAMA* 217:777-784, 1971.

5. A study of the effects of hypoglycemic agents on vascular complications in patients with adult-onset diabetes: V. Evaluation of phenformin therapy, University Group Diabetes Program. *Diabetes* 24(suppl 1):65-184, 1975.

6. A study of the effects of hypoglycemic agents on vascular complications in patients with adult-onset diabetes: VI. Supplementary report on nonfatal events in patients treated with tolbutamide, University Group Diabetes Program. *Diabetes* 25:1129-1153, 1976.

7. Marble A: Oral hypoglycemic agents in the management of diabetes. *Med Clin North Am* 42:1163-1177, 1958.

8. Siegel S: *Nonparametric Statistics.* New York, McGraw Hill Book Co, Inc, 1956, pp 96-111.

9. Cahill GF, Etzwiler DD, Freinkel N: Control and diabetes. *N Engl J Med* 294:1004-1005, 1976.

10. Shen S-W, Bressler R: Clinical pharmacology of oral antidiabetic agents. *N Engl J Med* 296:493-497, 787-793, 1977.

11. Davidson JK: Plasma glucose lowering effect of caloric restriction in obesity-induced insulin-treated diabetes mellitus. *Diabetes* 26:355, 1977.

12. Blackburn H, Keys A, Simonson E, et al: The electrocardiogram in population studies. *Circulation* 21:1160-1175, 1960.

13. Rose GA, Blackburn H: *Cardiovascular Survey Methods*, World Health Organization monograph series No. 56. Geneva, World Health Organization, 1968, pp 137-154.

14. *Arterial Hypertension and Ischemic Heart Disease: Preventive Aspects*, Report of an Expert Committee, World Health Organization technical report series No. 231. Geneva, World Health Organization, 1962.

Health practitioners often eschew experiment designs for the evaluation of new therapies or techniques. This is not surprising: When a patient's life, health, or mental health are seemingly at risk, it is difficult for the practitioner to deliver less than what he or she considers the best treatment required by the experimental design. As a result, decisions to implement new treatments are often based on advocacy by influential professionals and favorable early clinical experiences with the new treatment.

The following randomized clinical trial of a mechanical device for delivering external cardiac compressions illustrates that experimental evaluations of promising new techniques are possible, even when life-threatening conditions are involved. In addition, the investigator's careful examination of possible complications illustrates that possible defects in new treatments can be uncovered and possibly corrected. Finally, readers may want to consider carefully whether they agree with the researchers' optimistic conclusion that mechanical compressions may be superior to manual compressions under less ideal field conditions. The frequency of misuse of sophisticated medical equipment by untrained personnel in the field is quite high.

The work by Taylor et al. is a good example of a fairly small scale and local evaluation that can be of widespread interest and importance.

29

External Cardiac Compression
A Randomized Comparison of Mechanical and Manual Techniques

George J. Taylor, Richard Rubin, Michael Tucker,
H. Leon Greene, Michael D. Rudikoff, and
Myron L. Weisfeldt

● To compare the effectiveness of manual and mechanical chest compression during cardiopulmonary resuscitation, 50 patients who suffered cardiac arrest were randomly allocated to receive manual or mechanical chest compression. Randomization was performed after failure of initial resuscitative measures but within ten minutes after the onset of cardiac arrest (mean, 6.4 ± 1.2 min). Ten patients from each group survived longer than one hour following resuscitation. Three from the mechanical group and two from the manual group were eventually able to leave the hospital. Thus mechanical compression appears comparable with manual compression when manual compression is performed under ideal conditions. Mechanical chest compression may be employed when trained personnel are not readily available or where manual compression is technically difficult to perform.
(*JAMA* 240:644-646, 1978)

REQUIRING only hands, energy, and proper training, external cardiac compression (ECC) is the simple and readily available technique central to cardiopulmonary resuscitation (CPR).[1-3] Despite its proved efficacy,

From George J. Taylor et al., "External Cardiac Compression: A Randomized Comparison of Mechanical and Manual Techniques," 240(4) *Journal of the American Medical Association* pp. 644-646, 18 August 1978. Copyright 1978, American Medical Association.

manual ECC has inherent disadvantages. Proper ECC requires extensive and frequent training and experience to be optimal. It is difficult for one person to deliver vigorous manual ECC for long periods; it is difficult to perform manual ECC under some circumstances, eg, in a moving vehicle or while transporting a patient by other means.

A mechanical ECC device might have none of these disadvantages and thus result in improved CPR under many conditions. However, some have suggested such devices may be less effective than manual ECC and have advised against the use of mechanical compressors.[3] Although the hemodynamic effect of a number of mechanical devices has been reported,[4-12] none was proved effective in the clinical setting. To most directly compare the results of manual and mechanical ECC, we conducted a prospective randomized study of mechanical and manual ECC in a hospital population of patients undergoing prolonged CPR.

METHODS

Eighty patients were randomized to manual or mechanical ECC at The Johns Hopkins Hospital for a ten-month period. Manual ECC, artificial respiration, cardioversion, and drug therapy were begun in the standard fashion by the medical house staff.[2,13] On arrival of the research team, the patient was randomly assigned to manual or mechanical ECC by drawing a card after the mechanical device was made entirely operational. Of these 80 patients, 50 were randomized within ten minutes of starting CPR (6.4 ± 1.2 min, mean ± SD), with 24 assigned to manual and 26 to mechanical ECC. Those randomized after ten minutes of the onset of CPR were not included in this study since these patients had prolonged manual CPR before randomization. These 50 patients comprise the clinical study group.

Those drawing mechanical ECC were immediately placed on the pneumatic piston device, which delivered ECC at a rate of 60 beats per minute and compression duration of 50% of the cardiac cycle.[14] The piston was set to depress the sternum approximately 7 cm, and the time constant for depression was 100 msec. Manual ECC was delivered by the medical house staff in accordance with current recommendations[2] except that it is the general practice in this institution to briefly interrupt compression for ventilation. Physician concern was frequently encountered when compression was not interrupted briefly for ventilation during mechanical ECC. Therefore, a pause was introduced at every fifth compression for respiration.[14] Except for the method of chest compression, conduct of CPR was at the discretion of the house staff in attendance. All patients were intubated as rapidly as possible and ventilated using a positive-pressure bag.

The manual and mechanical study groups had similar ages (54.8 ± 6.6 years vs 57.6 ± 5.2 years) and sex distribution (59% men vs 55% women). Because of

Table 1.—Distribution of 50 Patients Randomized to Mechanical and Manual External Cardiac Compression (ECC)

	Manual ECC	Mechanical ECC
Underlying disease		
Primary arrhythmias or ventricular failure	6	9
Severe systemic illness	19	12
Unmonitored—arrested longer than 5 min before cardiopulmonary resuscitation	1	3
Cardiac monitoring		
Monitored	17	16
Not monitored	9	8

Table 2.—Response of Patients to Mechanical and Manual External Cardiac Compression		
	Manual	Mechanical
No rhythmic electrical or mechanical cardiac activity	5	6
Rhythmic electrical or mechanical cardiac activity but dead at 1 hr	11	8
Alive at 1 hr, dead at 24 hr	6	6
Alive at 24 hr	4	4
Total	**26**	**24**

variability in medical history and presentation of cardiac arrest, a classification of CPR candidates was devised (Table 1). This classification separates those with primary heart disease from those with severe systemic disease and those in whom there was likely a five-minute or longer delay between the onset of cardiac arrest and the beginning of CPR. The groups were also divided according to whether or not the patient had continuous ECG monitoring in an intensive care unit before cardiac arrest.

Thirty of the initial 80 patients had autopsies, and these records were examined for complications of ECC.

RESULTS

Mechanical ECC was as effective as optimal manual ECC in terms of short- and long-term survival (Table 2). Approximately 40% of patients receiving either form of ECC were alive (with a spontaneous pulse) one hour after ECC was stopped, and 40% of these patients survived another day. Of these eight patients alive 24 hours after CPR, five (10%) survived to be discharged from the hospital (three with mechanical and two with manual ECC).

Our results in this relatively small group of patients agree with those of larger studies that identify primary cardiac disease, continuous monitoring, and early restoration of spontaneous cardiac activity as predictors of a favorable outcome of CPR.[15] Since no patient was randomized less than four minutes after the onset of cardiac arrest, this study excluded patients with ventricular fibrillation who were resuscitated promptly with DC cardioversion. However, nine

Table 3.—Complications Evident at Postmortem Examination in 30 Patients		
	External Cardiac Compression*	
Complication	Manual (n=17)	Mechanical (n=13)
Liver laceration	1	0
Cardiac rupture	1	0
Rib fracture	8	7
Bone marrow embolus	1	0
Sternal fracture	0	3

*Manual massage preceded mechanical compression.

(69%) of 13 patients with primary cardiac disease and 15 (45%) of 33 monitored were alive for at least one hour after CPR. All of the patients who experienced cardiac arrest for more than five minutes before CPR ultimately died.

The duration of CPR was inversely related to long-term survival,[16] although a few patients did survive after long periods of CPR. The average duration of CPR was 28.3 ± 20.1 (SD) minutes and the difference between the manual and mechanical ECC groups was not statistically significant. Eleven of 20 patients with cardiac arrest for less than a 20-minute duration were alive for one hour, and four were alive for 24 hours.

Only one of 11 patients receiving CPR for 30 to 50 minutes was alive for one hour, and this patient did not survive a day. All five patients resuscitated for longer than 50 minutes were alive one hour after CPR (three with mechanical and two with manual ECC), and one survived to hospital discharge.

There was no difference in the overall incidence of complications between manual and mechanical ECC. All patients did receive initial manual ECC. Sternal fracture occurred only in the mechanical ECC group (Table 3). One liver laceration occurred in the manual ECC group. Sternal fracture may be related to the small diameter of the piston head (5.2 cm).

COMMENT

While there are theoretical advantages of mechanical over manual ECC, the efficacy of the mechanical devices has not been demonstrated in clinical studies. Pearson et al,[4] comparing mechanical ECC with that performed by ambulance personnel on manikins, reported that mechanical resuscitation equipment produced lower mean cardiac pressures than did trained technicians. These investigators advised against the use of mechanical resuscitators because of the needed setup time, unreliability, and the lower pressure. The present results show that mechanical ECC is comparable with manual ECC in a randomized and prospective study of 50 patients with cardiac arrest undergoing prolonged CPR in our hospital.

Mechanical ECC was compared with the best possible manual ECC. These results were obtained in an institution with considerable interest in CPR and the hemodynamic effects of ECC.[1,14] During CPR our patients routinely have intraarterial pressure monitoring,[14] which enables house officers to alter technique to maximize effectiveness. Consistent with local custom but not with official recommendations,[2] compression was briefly interrupted for ventilation in manual and mechanical groups. A compression duration of 50% of cycle time was used with mechanical ECC, despite the recent suggestion that 60% would provide better flow,[14] because these data were obtained after the present study had been largely completed.

The 40% immediate success rate with manual CPR is a good result considering that patients immediately resuscitated by defibrillation or a brief period of CPR were excluded from the study groups. The 10% leaving the hospital is comparable with other study results where (again) immediate resuscitations were included.[15,16] In the present study group, 62% had severe systemic illness, which likely contributed to mortality.

While Lemire and Johnson[15] reported a 19% long-term survival after CPR, their studies involved a selected population with resuscitation attempted in only 20% of patients with cardiac arrest; this compares with our medical service where CPR is attempted in 55% of dying or patients with cardiac arrest (data obtained for a three-month period). The former study group includes patients with ventricular fibrillation who responded to DC cardioversion. Messert and Quaglieri[16] reported 6% long-term survival after cardiac arrest, again including patients who promptly responded to CPR.

We have confirmed that patients with severe systemic illness fare poorly compared with those with primary cardiac arrest, and that continuous monitoring, which results in more prompt response, similarly improves prognosis.[15,16] We have not, however, identified conditions in which CPR is of no benefit to the patient, for there were unmonitored patients in this study who survived.

Sternal fracture appears to be a complication of mechanical ECC with the device employed (Table 3) and might be overcome by enlarging the area of compression. One patient with cardiac rupture and one with liver laceration were in the group receiving only manual ECC.

Mechanical ECC appears comparable with manual ECC in an optimal hospital setting. Admittedly this is a limited series of patients and a group of patients that had failed to respond to initial resuscitative measures. Nevertheless, similar short-term as well as long-term results were obtained with either mechanical or manual chest compression. With less favorable circumstances for manual compression or when personnel are limited or are not optimally trained, mechanical ECC may have advantages over manual ECC.

This investigation was supported by grant P50-HL 17655-02 from the National Institutes of Health, Public Health Service, US Department of Health, Education, and Welfare.

The pneumatic piston device used in this study was supplied by Michigan Instruments, Grand Rapids, Mich, in the form of the Thumper.

References

1. Kouwenhoven WB, Jude JR, Knickerbocker GG: Closed chest cardiac massage. *JAMA* 173:1064-1067, 1960.

2. Standards for cardiopulmonary resuscitation (CPR) and emergency cardiac care. *JAMA* 227(suppl):833-867, 1974.

3. Del Guercio CRM, Goomaraswamy RP, State D: Cardiac output and other hemodynamic variables during external cardiac massage in man. *N Engl J Med* 269:1398-1404, 1963.

4. Pearson JW, Navarro RN, Redding JS: Evaluation of mechanical devices for closed chest cardiac massage. *Anesth Analg* 45:590-598, 1966.

5. Harkins GA, Bramson ML: Mechanical external cardiac massage for cardiac arrest and for support of the failing heart. *J Sci Res* 1:197-200, 1961.

6. Dotter CT, Straube KR, Strain DC: Circulatory arrest: Manual and mechanical means for emergency management. *Radiology* 77:426-433, 1961.

7. Nachlas MM, Siedband MP: A simple portable pneumatic pump for external cardiac massage. *Am J Cardiol* 10:107-190, 1962.

8. Birch LH, Kenney LJ, Doovules F, et al: A study of external cardiac compression. *J Mich Med Soc* 61:1346-1352, 1962.

9. Beck CS, Leighninger DS: Reversal of deaths in good hearts. *J Cardiovasc Surg* 3:31, 1962.

10. Knight ICS: New apparatus for intermittent cardiac compression. *Br Med J* 1:894, 1964.

11. Nachlas MM, Siedband MP: Clinical experiences with mechanical cardiac massage. *Am J Cardiol* 15:310-319, 1965.

12. Nachlas MM, Miller DI, Siedband MP: Determination of cardiorespiratory variables in experimental cardiac resuscitation using a mechanized pump for external cardiac massage. *Ann Surg* 158:295-308, 1963.

13. Goldberg AH: Current concepts: Cardiopulmonary arrest. *N Engl J Med* 290:381-384, 1974.

14. Taylor GJ, Tucker WM, Greene HL, et al: Importance of prolonged compression duration during cardiopulmonary resuscitation in man. *N Engl J Med* 296:1515-1517, 1977.

15. Lemire JG, Johnson AL: Is cardiac resuscitation worthwhile?: A decade of experience. *N Engl J Med* 286:970-972, 1972.

16. Messert B, Quaglieri CE: Cardiopulmonary resuscitation: Perspectives and problems. *Lancet* 2:410-411, 1976.

Changes in law are often made in response to popular sentiment; yet such changes are sometimes enacted with little understanding of their actual effects. A case in point is the recent change from traditional divorce laws which emphasize fault and adversarial proceedings, to no fault divorce laws with an emphasis on reaching an amicable settlement. Does this change increase the divorce rate as many opponents of the no fault law contend? Or does it merely make divorces less painful as its supporters contend?

Mazur-Hart and Berman present an excellent quasi-experimental evaluation of this question. Using high-quality archival data and an interrupted time series design, they show that changes in the divorce laws have not led to a significant increase in the number of divorces in the general population. However, the authors do not stop with such a simple conclusion. Rather, they identify those subgroups that should be most affected by a change in the divorce law, and conduct separate time series analyses for each of these groups. Interestingly, the divorce rate did increase following the change in the law for certain groups, notably blacks and older couples, although the effect for the latter group was short-lived. Finally, the authors were careful to try to rule out the major threats to the validity of the time series design noted by Campbell and Stanley. Again the authors cleverly used theory and research from the marriage and divorce area to identify the most likely alternative hypotheses. Thus, the work nicely illustrates the interplay between theoretical and methodological concerns in evaluation research.

Although the article is an excellent example of the use of an interrupted time series design, readers should not overlook one easily achieved improvement in the design: a control series in which the same event does not take place. In the present case, the authors could have used time series data from a comparable state (or states) which has not yet adopted the no fault divorce law. An excellent illustration of this latter design may be found in Ross and Campbell (1968*).

*ROSS, H. L. and D. T. CAMPBELL (1968) "The Connecticut speed crackdown: a study of the effects of legal change," pp. 30-35 in H. L. Ross (ed.) Perspectives on the Social Order (2nd ed.). New York: McGraw-Hill.

30

Changing from Fault to No-Fault Divorce
An Interrupted Time Series Analysis

Stanley F. Mazur-Hart and John J. Berman

The removal of fault as a criterion for the distribution of justice in domestic relations represents a major innovation in jurisprudence. Such innovations provide opportunities to evaluate the effects of legal changes on behavior. This research investigated the effects of no-fault divorce on divorce behavior in Nebraska. An interrupted time series quasiexperimental design was employed to test the hypothesis that no-fault divorce leads to an increase in the number of divorces granted. Results showed that the new law had no reliable effect on the overall divorce rate. Separate analyses were performed for urban and rural counties, black and white couples, marriages of various lengths, and people of various ages. No effects of the law were found in most of these analyses. However, no-fault divorce did appear to have significantly increased the number of divorces among blacks, among people over 50 years old, and among couples married longer than 25 years, although in the latter two cases the effect seemed short-lived. The implications of this study for the current debate surrounding no-fault divorce are discussed.

The difficulties that state legislatures face in reformulating divorce laws have been complicated by the central position of the concept of fault in the legal system. Traditionally, divorce has been viewed as one party accusing the other of failure to meet the obligations of the marital contract. Only the innocent party can bring the divorce action; and final settlements are usually made at the expense of the guilty party. Although fault may be a useful principle when applied to other legal areas (e.g., criminal proceedings), it has been attacked as unrealistic when applied to domestic relations. First, it is argued that there is no clear-cut behavioral manifestation of fault in many divorce cases. Second, even if fault does exist, it is generally unfair to blame

[1] Requests for reprints should be sent to Stanley F. Mazur-Hart, Department of Psychology, Saginaw Valley State College, University Center, Michigan 48710.

only one partner in a dyad where few behaviors on the part of either spouse are independent of the other. In response to these arguments, several states have initiated reforms of their domestic relations laws. The State of Nebraska Unicameral passed no-fault divorce legislation in 1972. This legal change represents a naturally occurring manipulation whereby the effects of no-fault versus fault divorce laws can be evaluated.

Despite the radical change to no-fault divorce in Nebraska and elsewhere, systematic assessments of this change are noticeably lacking. Mace (1950) has reported on England's sharp upturn in divorce rates following that country's liberalization of divorce laws. Doroghi (1955) found that the number of divorces in Russia increased once marital dissolution was made a matter of mutual consent. Similarly, critics of no-fault divorce in the United States maintain that divorce rates are increasing rapidly in those jurisdictions which have adopted no-fault divorce laws. For example, one California judge has noted that in the 5 years since the introduction of no-fault divorce in that state, dissolutions of marriage jumped 25% ("5 Years of 'No-Fault Divorce'," 1975). However, it remains to be determined whether this phenomenon should be attributed to the inception of the no-fault divorce law.

The lack of research on this topic may be due to the difficulty in applying a design which would allow adequate manipulation of the data so that meaningful interpretations could be offered. Campbell (1969) pointed out that when a political unit initiates a reform which is put into effect across the entire unit, no group is available as a control and the only base of comparison is the record of observations taken in previous months or years. In those situations, Campbell and Stanley (1966) have recommended using the inter-rupted time series quasiexperimental design. Such a design was employed in the present research to test the effects of Nebraska's no-fault divorce law on the frequency of divorces. Specifically, the main goal of this study was to evaluate the primary criticism voiced against the introduction of no-fault divorce laws, namely, no-fault divorce will increase overall divorce rates (Brody, 1970). In addition, separate analyses were conducted on subgroups of Nebraska's population because there was reason to suspect that certain subgroups might be affected more than others by this change in the divorce law. In general, the people who ought to be affected most by the new law are those who are interested in a divorce but are reluctant to go through with it because of anticipated negative consequences of the traditional legal pro-cedure.

In an investigation of the relationship between divorce rate and various demographic variables, Cannon (1947) found that the strongest correlate of the divorce rate was the urban–rural differential. Later, Cannon and Gingles (1956) attributed this higher divorce rate in urban areas to a reduction of the importance of traditional values—a reduction which they felt was directly related to urbanization. These authors can be interpreted as concluding that rural people believe in the indissolubility of marriage to a greater extent than urban people. If this is so, then rural people should be less affected by changes in divorce procedures than urban people, simply because rural people are less approving of divorce in any form.

Schmitt (1969) identified a U-shaped distribution relating age of marrieds to incidence of divorce, with the lowest divorce rates among couples between the ages of 30 and 50. A reason for the low divorce rate in this group is their responsibility for minor children. Since the introduction of no-fault divorce does not affect the source of this group's reluctance to seek divorces, the new laws should not increase the frequency of divorces among members of this age category.

One reason for adopting no-fault divorce was to reduce the number of divorces by desertion, sometimes termed poor man's divorce. Lawmakers expected that the no-fault law would make divorces not only easier to obtain but perhaps less expensive. If the change to no-fault divorce had this effect, then the new law should produce a greater increase in divorces among the poor than among the rich. The available records in Nebraska did not contain an index of socioeconomic status. They did, however, indicate race which is highly correlated with socioeconomic status. Thus, in order to test any differential effects of the no-fault divorce law on rich and poor, the divorce rates for minority and majority couples were analyzed separately.

METHOD

The observations in these time series were the number of divorces per month over a 6-year period form January 1969 through December 1974. A shorter time period (e.g., divorces per week) was not used as the unit of analysis because Nebraska records divorces by the month in which they occur, not by the week or day. A longer time period (e.g., divorces per 3 months) was not used because it would have produced too few observations on each side of the interruption for analyses to be interpretable. The interruption in the time series was the enactment of Nebraska's no-fault divorce law on July 6, 1972. Because the law was enacted during the month of July, it was impossible to classify that month as either before or after the interruption; consequently, July 1972 was dropped from the series. In addition, an extremely high number of divorces was granted during June 1972. Because such outliers lead to incorrect identification of statistical models, Glass, Willson, and Gottman (1975) recommend excluding them from analyses. Thus, June 1972 was also dropped from the series. The analyses in this study were composed of 41 observations (months) before the interruption and 29 after it. The number of observations pre- and post-intervention were, therefore, well beyond the minimum of 25 suggested by Glass et al.

The data for these timé series were collected from official records, which are maintained by the state's Department of Health as mandated by Nebraska statutes. At the time of final divorce decree, the lawyer(s) involved in the proceeding must complete a Report of Divorce Form, which is filed with the district court where the divorce has taken place and then sent to the Bureau of Vital Statistics. The data used in this research were obtained from this source.

Past work on divorce has sometimes used a ratio of divorces to population size rather than raw frequencies of divorce (e.g., Rheinstein, 1972). Such a ratio index is particularly useful in studies encompassing many years during which the marriageable and, hence, divorceable population may fluctuate greatly. But this study encompasses a 6-year span, and the population size of Nebraska has been relatively stable since peaking in the mid-1950s (Eastman, 1973). Furthermore, there is no completely accurate means of calculating movement in and out of Nebraska's divorceable population. In light of these factors, raw frequencies of divorce were·used here.

Webb, Campbell, Schwartz, and Sechrest (1966) have been justifiably concerned with the limitations ˙of archival research. One serious limitation involves the use of sampled data. In order to avoid such a problem, this study analyzed all the Nebraska divorce decrees granted between 1969 and 1974, inclusive. The total number of divorces for that 6-year period was 25,520. Since all cases were used rather than only a subset of them, statements about the effects of no-fault divorce throughout the state could be made more accurately. Webb et al. (1966) also warn researchers that a change in record-keeping procedures can pose a threat to the internal validity of a study. It is important to note, therefore, that a check on the record-keeping techniques at Nebraska's Bureau of Vital Statistics showed that there were no significant changes during the years studied here.

After the monthly frequencies for divorces in Nebraska were tabulated, the data were separated into divorces occurring in urban and rural counties. An urban county was one which contained either a city greater than 50,000 in population or the immediate suburbs of such a city. By these criteria 3 counties were classified as urban, and the remaining 90 counties were classified as rural. Next, males and females were separately grouped into three categories on the basis of age on last birthday prior to the divorce decree. The three age categories were: 29 years and younger, 30 through 50 years of age, and 51 years and older. The frequencies of divorces per month were then tabulated for each of these six groups and arranged into time series. A similar way of looking at this aspect of the data is to analyze divorces by length of marriage at the time of divorce. Thus, the length of each marriage at the time of divorce was calculated, and each case was put into one of the following six groups: married 1-5 years, married 6-10 years, married 11-15 years, married 16-20 years, married 21-25 years, and married 26 years or longer. The divorce records were also divided on the basis of the race of the couple. Initially several minority groups were to be separately analyzed. But the number of minorities other than blacks is very small in Nebraska, and the frequencies of divorces per month in those groups were too few for meaningful statistical analyses. As a result, only cases where both spouses were either black or white were used for this particular study.

Time Series Analyses

The data were analyzed according to procedures outlined by Glass et al. (1975) and Kepka (1972). Special statistical procedures are required in order to analyze time series data because the observations are frequently correlated with each other. This dependency among observations violates the assumption of independence of errors, which is a necessary condition for making accurate probability statements about the effects of interest. The goal of these statistical procedures is to identify the nature of the dependency and to correct for it. The procedures can be divided into three parts: model identification, parameter estimation, and the testing of intervention effects.

In model identification, one attempts to determine whether there is any dependency among the observations and, if so, which of several statistical models best describes that dependency. To accomplish this, the pattern of autocorrelations and partial autocorrelations are inspected. It has been demonstrated that certain patterns indicate that certain models will best describe the observations in the series. Once the autocorrelations and partial autocorrelations have been inspected and a model chosen, that model is fitted to the data; and the residuals from the fit are tested to determine if any dependency remains. If the test shows that there is dependency, the wrong model has been used and another must be tried. If the test shows no dependence among the residuals, the correct model has been used and one can proceed to parameter estimation and the testing of intervention effects. These last two steps involve transforming the model which was chosen into a form of the general linear model so that standard techniques of parameter estimation and significance testing can be used.

Despite the complexities, the statistical models for testing the intervention effects in the interrupted time series quasiexperimental design have been developed (see Glass et al., 1975, for the most readable presentation); and the necessary computer programs for these analyses are available (Bower, Padia, & Glass, 1974). The method is useful for investigating the effects of new social programs, modifications in old programs, behavioral interventions, or legal changes, where the dependent variables of interest have been collected in a consistent manner for a period of time before and after the innovation.

RESULTS

The first step in analyzing the data was to inspect the autocorrelations and partial autocorrelations of each series. No dependencies in the observations were found and the classical multiple regression model was chosen as the best fit to the data. This model was used for each series, and the residuals were then tested for dependencies. The tests showed no dependencies, indicating that the classical multiple regression model was appropriate. If the tests on the residuals of any of the series had indicated dependence, the data from those series would have had to be fitted to one of the autoregressive integrated moving average (ARIMA) models discussed by Glass et al. as a means to remove the dependency among observations.

The most common types of effects investigated in the interrupted time series quasiexperimental design are changes in the level of the series (i.e., the series shifts up or down by a constant) and/or in the slope (i.e., the series changes direction) at the point of the interruption. Thus, the multiple regression equation fitted to each series was:

$$Y = a + b_1 X_1 + b_2 X_2 + b_3 X_3 + \epsilon$$

where Y = number of divorces per month, a = overall level of the series, b_1 = a coefficient representing change in the level of the series, X_1 = a dummy variable coded to discriminate between months which were pre- and post-intervention, b_2 = a coefficient representing the overall slope the the series, X_2 = a dummy variable coded to discriminate each month of the series, b_3 = a coefficient representing change in slope of the series, X_3 = a dummy variable coded to discriminate post-intervention months from each other and from pre-intervention months, and ϵ = error.

Figure 1 shows a plot of the total number of divorces in Nebraska per month over the 6 years studied here. The partial regression coefficients showed that the overall slope of this series increased significantly, $F(1,66) = 30.9$, $p < .001$; but there was no significant change in level or in slope after the intervention, $F(1,66) = .1$ and .4, respectively. This indicated that during the period of time studied divorces did systematically increase but that the intervention of no-fault divorce had no discernable effects on that increase.

Separate analyses were performed on the data from urban and rural counties. In each case a significant overall slope was found: for urban counties, $F1,66) = 11.71$, $p < .001$; for rural counties, $F(1,66) = 34.47$; $p < .001$. But in neither case was there a significant change in level: for urban counties, $F(1,66) = 1.2$;

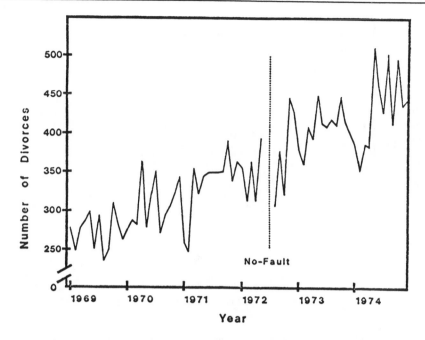

FIG. 1. Number of divorces per month in Nebraska, 1969–1974.

for rural counties, F (1,66) = .8. Nor was there a significant change in slope: for urban counties, F (1,66) = .7; for rural counties, F (1,66) = .1. Thus, divorces systematically increased for both types of county, but no effects of the new law were apparent.

Separate analyses were performed for three age groups of husbands and wives. The pattern of results found above was also found for both husbands and wives who were under 30 years old and between 30 and 50 years old. That is, for all four of these groups there was a significant overall increase in divorces ($p < .001$), but no evidence of any changes in level or changes in slope at the time of the interruption. However, the pattern of results was different for husbands and wives over 50 years of age. Each of these groups showed a significant overall slope: for husbands over 50, F (1,66) = 4.4, $p < .05$; for wives over 50, F (1,66) = 4.8, $p < .05$. Each group also showed a lack of significance for change in slope: for husbands over 50, F (1,66) = .5; for wives over 50, F (1,66) = 2.7. However, both of these groups showed a significant increase in the level of the series after the inception of no-fault divorce: for husbands over 50, F (1,66) = 4.3, $p < .05$; for wives over 50, F

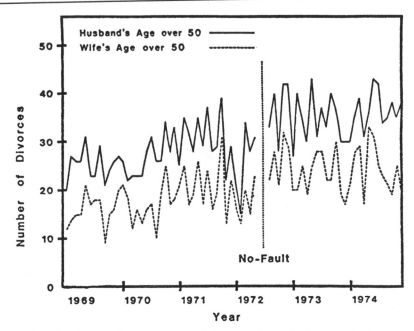

FIG. 2. Number of divorces per month in Nebraska for husbands and wives over 50 years of age, 1969–1974.

$(1,66) = 4.4$, $p < .05$. Figure 2 presents the number of divorces per month for husbands and wives over 50 years of age at the time of divorce.

Another way these data were grouped was by length of the marriage at the time of the divorce. Separate analyses were performed on marriages lasting 1–5 years, 6–10 years, 11–15 years, 16–20 years, 21–25 years, and 26 years or longer. Analyses for the first five of these six groups (i.e., up through 20–25 years of marriage) resulted in the typical pattern found in this research, namely, a significant overall increasing slope ($p < .001$) but no significant change in level or change in slope at the point of interruption.[2] The analysis for those married 26 years or longer, however, showed a significant overall slope: $F(1,66) = 10.4$, $p < .005$; a near significant increase in level: $F(1,66) = 3.8$, $p < .06$; and a significant change in slope: $F(1,66) = 4.5$, $p < .05$. The sign of the partial regression coefficient for change in slope was negative, indicating that the direction of the post-intervention series was downward.

[2] The one exception to this pattern was the lack of significance for the overall slope among those couples married 16–20 years at the time of divorce.

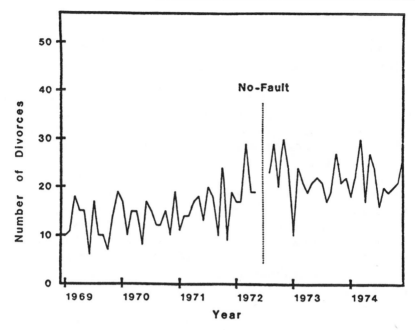

FIG. 3. Number of divorces per month in Nebraska for couples married 26 years or longer at time of divorce, 1969–1974.

The number of divorces per month for couples married 26 years or longer are shown in Figure 3.

Divorces among white couples and black couples were analyzed separately. Among white couples there was the significant overall slope, F (1,66) = 32.4, $p < .001$, but no significant change in level or slope, F (1,66) = .1 and .2, respectively. Divorces among black couples showed somewhat similar results in that the overall slope approached significance, F (1,66) = 2.9, $p < .1$; and the change in slope was not significant, F (1,66) = 1.3. However, the data from black couples did show a significant change in level of the series, F (1,66) = 4.7, $p < .05$. It appears, therefore, that the change in the law did not affect white couples but did affect black couples. Figure 4 shows the data from black couples.

DISCUSSION

Contrary to opinions of some opponents of no-fault divorce, the results of this study showed that the inception of the law was not associated with any increase in the overall number of divorces granted in the state of Nebraska. The data showed that divorce is indeed increasing systematically in the state, but the increase seems totally unrelated to the no-fault divorce law.

There had been reason to expect that the law would affect couples in urban counties more than couples in rural counties. Contrary to expectation, the no-fault divorce law did not differentially affect divorce rates in either urban or rural counties. An overall increase in divorces did occur in both types of counties across the time period studied here, but that increase was not related to the inception of no-fault divorce law.

Analyses of the data for age groups of husbands and wives at the time of divorce also produced results contrary to expectation. It had been predicted that the change in the law would increase the number of divorces among spouses under 30 and over 50 years of age, but not among spouses between 30 and 50. In fact, only the husbands and wives over 50 years of age showed a statistically significant increase in divorces with the inception of no-fault divorce. In addition, the analyses by length of marriage at the time of divorce showed that marriages lasting longer than 25 years demonstrated a significant increase in divorce with the enactment of the new law.

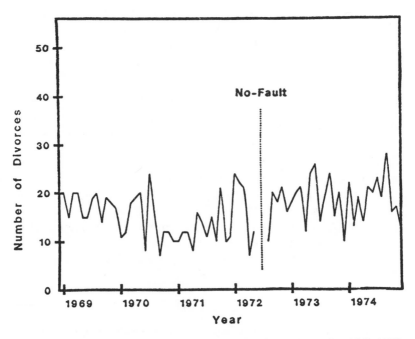

FIG. 4. Number of divorces per month in Nebraska for black couples, 1969–1974.

The most reasonable explanation for this pattern of results seems to be that the longer a marriage lasts the greater are the costs involved in getting a divorce and a significant portion of those costs has been reduced by the no-fault divorce law. Actually there are at least two types of costs that may have been reduced by the change in the law. The first is the emotional cost of establishing fault. In other words, it could be that for older couples the emotional cost of having to establish fault under the former law was too high a price to pay for getting a divorce. Once this price was lessened, however, the balance was tipped for these older people in the direction of proceeding with divorce. A second cost that may have been present under the former law and that may have been reduced by no-fault divorce was the financial one which many husbands in long-term marriages had to pay in order to get a divorce. In the past, the wife was generally favored in the financial distribution after a final divorce decree. Some jurisdictions even specified that the following criteria had to be considered in dividing property and deciding issues of alimony: length of marriage, employability of the wife, and marriageability of the wife (Brody, 1970). Women with no career and a long marriage gained the most whenever involved in divorce proceedings under these fault concepts. Many believe that under no-fault divorce the favors extended to the wife have been removed ("Axing Alimony," 1974). Thus, the new law may equalize the burden by removing benefits previously given the wife. Husbands who previously could not afford the costs of divorce may now more readily file and obtain decrees.

The results of this study showed the effects of no-fault divorce among older and longer married couples to be short-lived. Evidence for this is the statistically significant change in slope of the number of divorces for couples married 26 years or longer. In other words, Figure 3 shows that the introduction of no-fault divorce did actually lead to an increase in the number of divorces among couples married 26 years or longer. However, that change in level was accompanied by a change in slope from positive to negative. Thus, although no-fault divorce did temporarily increase the number of divorces among older and longer married individuals, this increase has reversed; and the number of divorces seems to be returning to its preintervention level. This can be interpreted as indicating that there was a backlog of older and longer married people for whom the inception of no-fault divorce changed the cost-benefit ratio sufficiently for them to seek divorces. It should be noted that this effect of no-fault divorce is similar among older and longer married individuals because of the necessary connection between age and length of marriage.

The separate analyses for white and black couples showed that among white couples divorces have increased over time, but no statistically significant changes in the level or slope as a function of the no-fault divorce intervention were found. On the other hand, among black couples the level of divorces did significantly increase as a function of the new law; and this increase shows no signs of disappearing. It had been expected that black couples would be more affected by the change in the law than white couples. The reason for this was that one intended effect of no-fault divorce was to make divorce less expensive and, therefore, more available to people of low socioeconomic status. If race is highly correlated with socioeconomic status in Nebraska—and there is good reason to believe that it is ("Statistical Abstract of the United States," 1975)—then these data suggest that this objective of the law has been met.

Campbell and Stanley (1966) pointed out that the most serious threat to the internal validity of the interrupted time series quasiexperiment is history, i.e., the possibility that not the intervention but some simultaneous event produced an obtained shift in the series. A review of the divorce literature revealed that two major factors are most likely to account for sudden and dramatic shifts in divorce rates: a sudden economic change and the termination of a major war (Davis, 1950). Various economic indicators for Nebraska were inspected, and none of them showed any dramatic changes around the time of the inception of no-fault divorce. Troops were returning from Vietnam about the time of the change in the divorce law; but the Vietnam withdrawal was a gradual process conducted over several years, rather than an abrupt one. Moreover, when the end of a war affects divorce rates, the youngest age groups show an effect, not the older groups as was found in this study. In short, a consideration of possible alternatives produced no rival hypotheses which could better account for the changes that occurred in some of the interrupted time series of divorces in Nebraska. Thus, the enactment of no-fault divorce apparently provides the best explanation for the changes which did occur.

An analysis of divorce rates in one state certainly does not make a definitive case for or against no-fault divorce. Future studies should compare divorce rates in jurisdictions similar to Nebraska during the same time period examined in this study. Other states which have introduced no-fault divorce would provide interesting comparisons.

Another avenue for future research is a consideration of alimony˙ and property settlements as a function of no-fault divorce. Feminist groups maintain that the financial segment of divorce proceedings is the single most important phase of a divorce. They note that no-fault divorce frequently calls for a 50–50 distribution of wealth between two people who are not socially or economically equal, before or after the decree. Feminists argue that women's work is usually not rewarded appropriately and that no-fault divorce completely strips women of all economic security ("NOW Votes for Changed Family Law," 1976). This so-called unilateral aspect of no-fault divorce law clearly needs further research that includes an analysis of male and female roles vis-a-vis earning power.

REFERENCES

Axing alimony: Some courts, citing women's liberation, go easy on husbands. *Wall Street Journal*, May 29, 1974, p. 1.

Bower, C. P., Padia, W. L., & Glass, G. V. *TMS = Two Fortran programs for analysis of time series experiments.* Boulder, Colorado: Laboratory of Educational Research, University of Colorado, 1974.

Brody, S. A. California's divorce reform: Its sociological implications. *Pacific Law Journal*, 1970, 1, 223–232.

Campbell, D. T. Reforms as experiments. *American Psychologist*, 1969, 24, 409–429.

Campbell, D. T., & Stanley, J. C. *Experimental and quasi-experimental designs for research.* Chicago: Rand McNally, 1966.

Cannon, K. L. Marriage and divorce in Iowa 1940–1947. *Marriage and Family Living*, 1947, 9, 81–83; 98.

Cannon, K. L., & Gingles, R. Social factors related to divorce rates for urban counties in Nebraska. *Rural Sociology*, 1956, 21, 34–40.

Davis, K. Statistical perspective on marriage and divorce. *Annals of the American Academy of Political and Social Sciences*, 1950, 272, 9–21.

Doroghi, E. *Grounds for divorce in European countries.* New York: Research Division of the New School for Social Research, 1955.

Eastman, M. L. *Statistical report of the Bureau of Vital Statistics.* Lincoln, Nebraska: State Department of Health, 1973.

5 years of "no fault divorce" hike California breakups 25%. *The Lincoln Star*, March 12, 1975, p. 11.

Glass, G. V., Willson, V. L., & Gottman, J. M. *Design and analysis of time-series experiments.* Boulder, Colorado: Colorado Associated University Press, 1975.

Kepka, E. J. *Model representation and the threat of instability in the interrupted time series quasi-experiment.* Unpublished doctoral disseration, Northwestern University, 1972.

Mace, D. R. Family life in Britain since the first World War. *Annals of the American Academy of Political and Social Sciences*, 1950, 272, 179–180.

NOW votes for changed family law. *Sunday Journal and Star*, January 11, 1976, p. 4D.

Rheinstein, M. *Marriage stability, divorce, and the law.* Chicago: University of Chicago Press, 1972.

Schmitt, R. C. Age and race differences in divorce in Hawaii. *Journal of Marriage and the Family*, 1969, 31, 48–50.

Statistical Abstract of the United States (House Document No. 94-267) Washington, D.C.: U.S. Government Printing Office, 1975.

Webb, E. J., Campbell, D. T., Schwartz, R. D., & Sechrest, L. *Unobtrusive measures: Nonreactive research in the social sciences.* Chicago: Rand McNally, 1966.

In an evaluation of social policy change, A. John McSweeny found that response-cost procedures were effective in controlling the "real world" behavior of making presumably unnecessary use of directory assistance services. Using an example of a time-series design with nonequivalent dependent variables, the author makes excellent use of time-series analysis and unobtrusive measures (archival data) and shows ingenuity in finding a control variable. Thus, despite the retrospective, nonexperimental nature of the design, McSweeny was able to make reasonable causal inferences.

31

Effects of Response Cost on the Behavior of a Million Persons

Charging for Directory Assistance in Cincinnati

A. John McSweeny

An interrupted time-series analysis of local directory-assistance calls in the Cincinnati area from 1962 to 1976 revealed a significant reduction in the daily frequency of calls after charges were introduced in 1974. No reductions occurred in the daily frequency of long-distance directory-assistance calls, which remained free. The results attest to the efficacy of response-cost procedures with large subject populations in the natural environment. The applicability of response-cost procedures to social and business problems is discussed.

DESCRIPTORS: response cost, social problems, business problems, applications of behavioral principles, quasi-experimental design, time-series design, large populations, humans

Response cost is used extensively in token economies and other behavior-modification programs as a method of reducing the frequency of undesirable behaviors (Kazdin, 1972; Kazdin and Bootzin, 1972). Response-cost procedures involve the withdrawal of reinforcers, and are usually implemented in the form of fines, penalties, or loss of privileges (Bootzin, 1975; Kazdin, 1972). In his reviews of the response-cost literature, Kazdin (1972, 1975) concluded that response-cost procedures were generally very effective in suppressing behavior and rarely resulted in any serious behavioral or emotional side effects.

Although response-cost procedures have been employed most frequently in educational, psychiatric, and correctional settings, a few investigators have evaluated their use in the "natural environment". An interesting example of the use of response-cost procedures in a small-business setting was provided by Marholin and Gray (1976). These authors found that when cash shortages were subtracted from employees' salaries, the size of the shortage was sharply reduced. This result suggests that response-cost procedures are as effective in "real world" set-

[1] Portions of this article were presented at the meeting of the Midwestern Psychological Association, Chicago, May 1977. The research described in this paper was conducted during the author's tenure as a postdoctoral fellow in the evaluation research program at Northwestern University. Preparation of this article was supported by grant number MH 00180 from the National Institute of Mental Health. The author wishes especially to thank Ray Weitzel of the Cincinnati Bell Telephone Company for providing the data and Leslie McCain of Northwestern University for her assistance in data analysis. Thanks are also due Richard Bootzin, Paul Wortman, Robert Boruch, Thomas Cook, and Chip Reichardt for their helpful comments on an earlier draft of this article. Reprints may be obtained from A. John McSweeny, Department of Psychology, Northwestern University, Evanston, Illinois 60201.

tings as in controlled environments and might be used successfully in dealing with large scale business and social problems.

The present study evaluated an attempt to use response cost with a large population in the natural environment, that is, all telephone subscribers in Cincinnati, Ohio. Telephone company personnel have long suspected that subscribers make unnecessary use of directory-assistance services. Despite exhortations in company advertisements to use published directories for information whenever possible, directory-assistance users typically request telephone numbers that have been published in standard directories for several years (Kleinfeld, 1976). The frequent use of directory assistance for published numbers, a service for which the telephone company typically does not levy a direct charge, means that the cost of providing directory assistance must be subsidized by increasing charges for other telephone services. Thus, any procedure that reduces the use of directory-assistance services without restricting their availability would be received favorably by telephone company officials and cost-conscious telephone subscribers.

In March 1974, officials at Cincinnati Bell Telephone company initiated charges for local directory-assistance calls in an attempt to reduce the frequency of those calls. Under this plan, telephone subscribers are allowed three local directory-assistance calls per telephone line per month. Subscribers are then charged 20¢ for each additional call. The use of the 20¢ charge fits the descriptions of a response-cost procedure provided by Bootzin (1975, p. 161) and Kazdin (1972, p. 533). That is, the charge is contingent on the response of making a directory-assistance call.

Cincinnati Bell has been recording each directory-assistance call made within its service area since 1962. Records of the number of calls made on an average business day[2] in any given month exist for the 146 months before and the 34 months after directory-assistance charges were introduced. Thus, the data permit analysis of the intervention effects within an interrupted time-series design (Campbell and Stanley, 1966;

Glass, Willson, and Gottman, 1975; McCain, McCleary, and Cook, *in press*), and it was expected that the effect of the 20¢ charge would be to reduce the number of calls.

Campbell and Stanley (1966) pointed out that the single interrupted time series is a quasi-experimental design that is subject to several threats to validity. Historical events, changes in recording procedures, regression artifacts, and general instability or "noise" represent some of the more serious threats. (See Campbell and Stanley, 1966, or Cook and Campbell, 1976, for more complete discussion of these threats to validity.) Riecken and Boruch (1974) noted that a comparison series can be used to rule out certain threats to validity and strengthen the analysis of the experimental series. Fortunately, in the present study a comparison series was readily available, because Cincinnati Bell has also kept regular records of long-distance directory-assistance calls it receives. Because no charges were introduced for long-distance directory-assistance calls, no changes in the rate of calls made were expected.

Recapitulating, if response cost is an effective method of reducing the frequency of directory-assistance calls, postintervention reductions in number of calls should occur in the experimental series but not in the control series.

METHOD

Subjects and Setting

The subject population for the experimental series consisted of users of local directory assistance in the Cincinnati Bell Telephone Company service area during the years 1962 to 1976. This population was not stable and precise estimates of its size are not available. The 1970 Cincinnati metropolitan area census of 1,385,000 may be used as a crude estimate of the population of potential users during that year.

The subject population for the control series consisted of users of directory assistance from outside the Cincinnati Bell service area. This population is even more difficult to define because the origins of long-distance directory-assistance calls were not recorded.

Data Collection Procedures

The data were obtained from copies of Cincinnati Bell administrative records. Each di-

[2]Number of calls per average business day is defined as the average number of calls received during all weekdays (Monday through Saturday) in any given time period.

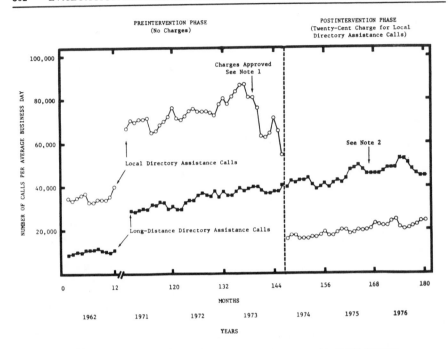

Note 1. Charges for local directory-assistance charges were approved by the Ohio Utilities Commission on August 19, 1973.

Note 2. Long-distance directory-assistance calls from another city were added to Cincinnati Bell's area. This city averaged 3,000 calls per day.

Fig. 1. Number of local and long-distance directory-assistance calls placed per average business day before and after charges were introduced.

rectory-assistance call was recorded automatically as one event on magnetic tape by a computerized electronic recording system. Continuous monitoring of the system assured virtually perfect reliability of the data recorded (Weitzel, Note 1). At the end of each month, the volume of calls per average business day was computed and transferred to a paper record used for administrative purposes.

RESULTS[3]

The volume of local and long-distance directory-assistance calls is depicted in Figure 1, which reveals that the frequency of calls dropped by approximately 60,000 calls per day

in the experimental series after the charge was introduced. In contrast, the daily frequency of calls in the control series did not change significantly at the point of intervention.

Although the introduction of the 20¢ charge markedly reduced the frequency of local directory-assistance calls, the frequency of calls gradually increased in the months following this initial reduction. The rate of increase in calls after the intervention is approximately equal to the rate of increase before the intervention.

---

[3]The results reported in this paper are from a visual analysis of the data. The visual analysis was corroborated by statistical analysis of the time-series data (cf. Glass et al., 1975; Jones, Vaught, and Weinrott, 1977; McCain et al., in press). A report on the results of the statistical analysis is available from the author.

This general upward trend, which is also observable in the control series, is probably due to general growth in population, as well as the number of telephones in the Cincinnati area. Indeed, for the years 1962 through 1973, the number of local directory calls per day was highly correlated with the number of telephone mainstations[4] in service, r (10) = 0.97, $p < 0.001$.

Close inspection of Figure 1 also reveals a drop in the frequency of local calls of approximately 15,000 calls per day during the months of August and September 1973, which is followed by a partial recovery in December and a second drop during January and February 1974. This pattern followed an announcement on August 25, 1973, that the planned directory-assistance charges had been approved by the Ohio Public Utilities Commission.

DISCUSSION

The result of primary interest is the significant change in level in the experimental series. This finding clearly indicates that number of directory-assistance calls made on an average business day decreased markedly after the 20¢ charge was introduced. The fact that the change in level did not occur in the control series strongly suggests that the change observed in the experimental series was not due to historical events, undefined changes in instrumentation, or other factors that threaten the validity of time-series designs.

Studies by Cincinnati Bell indicate that introduction of directory-assistance charges has resulted in savings to the company, which have been passed on to consumers. Telephone company officials estimate that residential consumers were saved an average of $0.65 and business consumers an average of $1.25 on their monthly bills. Because most customers made no more than the three free directory-assistance calls allowed each month, only about 6% of Cincinnati

Bell's customers actually have been billed for extra directory-assistance calls (Weitzel, Note 2). Thus, most customers experienced a decrease rather than an increase in their bills. The primary change appears to be in customer behavior. Apparently, customers now are using alternate sources of information (e.g., telephone directories) to obtain the telephone numbers they need.

Effects of Information

The significant decrease in the frequency of calls following the announcement that charges were approved suggests that the announcement per se may have some effect on the use of directory assistance. Perhaps people began to change their habits in anticipation of the charges. Some individuals may also have had the impression that the charges had already taken effect because they had faulty information or they misunderstood news reports. The hypothesized effect of information is subject to two validity threats: (a) general instability of the series and (b) regression artifacts. Regression artifacts are particularly tenable, since the decrease in calls also followed a period of peak use of directory-assistance services. Thus, this temporary decrease could be due to a secular trend in which rates were returning to normal.

Conclusions

The results attest to the power of response-cost procedures when they are used with large populations within the natural environment. The fact that a relatively small charge resulted in a substantial reduction in responding is consistent with the findings in Kazdin's (1972) review of response-cost procedures. Response-cost procedures are appealing not only because of their efficacy but also because they fit our notions about "justice"; those who use (or abuse), pay. In the present study, much of the cost of directory assistance is now provided directly by the persons who use that service. Previously, the cost of directory assistance had to be financed entirely from general revenues.

---

[4]Mainstations include all phones except extensions.

The present findings suggest that response-cost procedures may have other useful social and business applications. The most relevant situations would seem to be those in which a costly or precious service or commodity is being consumed unnecessarily. For example, restaurants and hotels in drought-ridden northern California might add a small charge to their customers' bills according to the amount of water the customers consume. The charge would not restrict access to water, but would probably reduce the amount wasted. No doubt many social and business applications of response cost exist and should be investigated by government planners and business managers.

REFERENCE NOTES

1. Weitzel, R. L.   Personal communication, September 14, 1977.
2. Weitzel, R. L.   Testimony before the Ohio House Insurance, Utilities and Financial Institutions Committee, May 4, 1977.

REFERENCES

Bootzin, R. R.   *Behavior modification and therapy: An introduction.* Cambridge, Massachusetts: Winthrop, 1975.
Campbell, D. T. and Stanley, J. C.   *Experimental and quasi-experimental designs for research.* Chicago: Rand-McNally, 1966.
Cook, T. D. and Campbell, D. T.   The design and conduct of quasi-experiments and true experiments in field settings. In M. C. Dunnette (Ed), *Handbook of industrial and organizational psychology.* Chicago: Rand-McNally, 1976. Pp. 223-325.
Glass, G. V., Willson, V. L., and Gottman, J. M.   *Design and analysis of time-series experiments.* Boulder: Colorado Associated University Press, 1975.
Jones, R. R., Vaught, R. S., and Weinrott, M.   Time-series analysis in operant research. *Journal of Applied Behavior Analysis,* 1977, **10**, 151-166.
Kazdin, A. E.   Response cost: The removal of conditioned reinforcers for therapeutic change. *Behavior Therapy,* 1972, **3**, 533-546.
Kazdin, A. E.   Recent advances in token economy research. In M. Hersen, R. M. Eisler, and P. M. Miller (Eds), *Progress in behavior modification,* Vol. 1. New York: Academic Press, 1975. Pp. 233-274.
Kazdin, A. E. and Bootzin, R. R.   The token economy: an evaluative review. *Journal of Applied Behavior Analysis,* 1972, **5**, 343-372.
Kleinfeld, N. R.   A big-time operator finds that fast talk helps to get ahead: Sally Bess gives information in New York but don't ask the color of her stockings. *Wall Street Journal,* January 21, 1976, pp. 1, 22.
Marholin, D. and Gray, D.   Effects of group response-cost procedures on cash shortages in a small business. *Journal of Applied Behavior Analysis,* 1976, **9**, 25-30.
McCain, L. J., McCleary, R., and Cook, T. D.   The statistical analysis of interrupted time-series quasi-experiments. In T. D. Cook and D. T. Campbell (Eds), *The design and analysis of quasi-experiments in field settings.* Chicago: Rand-McNally, (in press).
Riecken, H. W. and Boruch, R. F.   *Social experimentation: A method for planning and evaluating social intervention.* New York: Academic Press, 1974.

Received 3 June 1977.
(Final Acceptance 3 October 1977.)

Important questions occasionally arise that can be answered only under very special circumstances. The following presents one such example, namely, the effect on a community of introducing television. Because television is virtually omnipresent in the Western world, its introduction de novo is rarely observable. The chapter that follows is of interest because it exploits an unusual opportunity to observe what happens when a community gains access to television for the first time, and because it illustrates the fact that evaluation studies need not be of large magnitude to produce meaningful and interpretable results.

32

Cable Television in an Eskimo Village

R. J. Madigan and W. Jack Peterson

When color television was introduced to a remote Eskimo village in 1973, twenty-six households viewed for the first time what most of us take for granted. In Wales, Alaska, nineteen-inch sets were installed and a variety of taped programs made available to nearly every household from March through August. The consequent experiment provided an unusual opportunity for the authors to assess the effect of this powerful medium.

The installation of cable television in the village was the project of an Alaska state public utilities commissioner who wished to test cable TV as an alternative to satellite TV as a means of delivering both commercial and educational television programming to remote villages. He saw that should cable TV work at the community level, shipments of week-long video-taped programs could be packaged at some relatively central location, and then cycled through a system of villages. Each schedule of programs would be played and then sent on the mail plane to the next village. The same plane would also deliver the next week's package.

The commissioner asked the authors to measure the effect of the medium on the social structure of the community. Five irregular visits ranging between three and five days were made to Wales between September 1972 and November 1973. While the introduction of television has many implications related to the modernization of traditional villages, the present paper concentrates on its effect on children who are of school age.

Wales is located on the western tip of the Seward Peninsula. It claims the distinction of being the western-most settlement in the Western Hemisphere, lying some 110 air miles north and west of Nome and sixty-five miles south of the Arctic Circle (see Figure 1). To the west of Wales, separated by twenty-six miles of the Bering Strait, are the Diomede Islands and on a clear day the moun-

Authors' Note: This study was supported in part by a grant from the Bering Strait Native Association. The authors wish to thank James Hendershot (who conceived and directed the project), Professor Michael Baring-Gould and Helen Pope, who assisted in data collection. For a more complete description of the material described herein, see Madigan and Peterson (1964).

From R. J. Madigan and W. Jack Peterson, "Cable Television in an Eskimo Village." Unpublished manuscript, 1978.

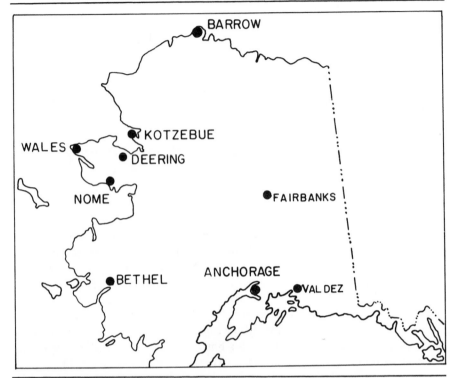

Figure 1: The central and northern portions of the State of Alaska showing the locations of Wales and Deering along with other major population centers.

tains of Siberia, another thirty miles west, can be seen from the low hills running directly behind the village. About thirty wooden frame buildings, not all occupied, currently make up the village. The present population is about 130 permanent residents.

Because of its unique location close to Siberia and the rest of Asia, Wales may be the oldest Eskimo village in Alaska (Oswalt, 1967) and the residents of the village claim it is the oldest village on the North American continent. For centuries the Eskimo has travelled across the narrow Bering Strait by skin boat in the summer and early fall hunting seal and walrus. Fall is also the season for gathering the winter supply of berries from areas around Wales. In the winter and spring, hunters roam the ice pack which begins to build in January and February. Until recently the dog sled and skin boat were used for transportation. Now the dog sled has been replaced by the snow machine, and the skin boat is powered by a gasoline motor, although these technological innovations have not changed many of the traditional subsistence activities other than to increase the pace and introduce new elements of danger.

To accurately measure the effect of television on the village of Wales, and especially its effect on children of school age, a control village was needed which would be as much like Wales as possible with a school population roughly the same in size and make up. We selected the small village of Deering (Figure 1). The schools in the two villages were much the same size and in general the two communities shared a common arctic environment. Deering is located on the southern shore of Kotzebue Sound approximately thirty-five miles south of the village of Kotzebue, and 130 air miles east of Wales. The village proper lies on a narrow spit facing Kotzebue Sound while the Kugruk River forms a small slough at the rear. The Sound is a rich source of seal and fish and the river has a heavy and predictable run of salmon and dolly varden. Caribou has been and continues to be an important source of meat for the village.

The television system installed in Wales consisted of two portable color video tape players located in the village school which were connected to color television receivers in each household by a buried cable. The year before, each of the households in Wales was visited and the television project described to the head of the household: the television test would run for six months, each participating household would have the use of a television set, and at the end of the project all sets would be removed. All but one household agreed to participate. The plan was also presented to the Village Council and, more importantly for the authors, to the local school board which subsequently approved a testing program for the village school children.

After many delays caused by technical and transportation problems, television was installed in twenty households and successfully broadcast to the people of Wales for the first time on March 2, 1973. The television system was operated Monday through Friday by one of the village men who was paid for his services. Video tapes arrived on the twice-weekly mail plane. Two channels were broadcast with their operation staggered so that each channel operated by itself for two hours and in competition with the other channel for two hours. One channel began operation at 2:00 p.m. and continued until 6:00 p.m., broadcasting material taken from the Anchorage Borough School System, which included a wide range of educational offerings ranging in level from pre-school through junior college. Both *Sesame Street* and *Electric Company* were broadcast daily. The second channel showed prime time commercial television recorded in Nome. This channel began operation at 4:00 p.m. and signed off at 8:00 p.m.

VIEWING PATTERNS

Each television set in the village was equipped with a sensor which detected whether the set was off or on and to which channel it was tuned. The video tape operator recorded this information at half-hour intervals, which allowed viewing patterns and program preferences to be determined. Between March and August of 1973 there were 118 broadcast days of which 18 were not analyzed because

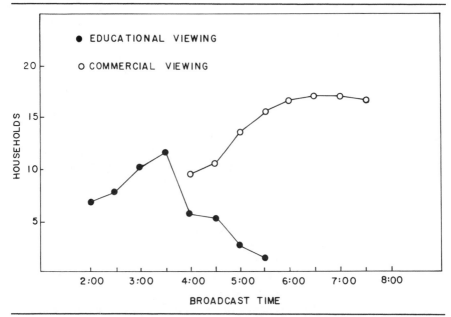

Figure 2: Amount of television viewing by time of day for commercial and educational television. Commercial TV was shown alone between 6 and 8 p.m. while educational TV was shown alone between 2 and 4 p.m. Between 4 and 6 p.m., both channels were broadcast.

of technical problems or the nonarrival of new video tapes. Figure 2 shows the number of television sets tuned to each channel by time of day. The figure shows that a large number of households tuned to the educational channel when it operated without competition. However, at 4:00 p.m. when the commercial channel began operation, educational viewing plummets and the average number of sets in operation increases.

The effects of commercial competition on the viewing of educational programs is dramatically illustrated by Figure 3. Here the viewing of two popular educational programs is examined as a function of whether commercial competition existed on the other channel. *Sesame Street* and the *Electric Company* were shown almost daily over the television period. One was shown early without competition and the other was shown late when the commercial station was operating. The choice of which was shown early was fairly random. The data show that the two programs lost about 80% of their audience when they were shown against commercial competition.

The preference for commercial over educational television programs is also reflected in the average amount of each type of television viewed per day: 1.01 hours of educational television and 2.35 hours of commercial television.

The average daily viewing in Wales (3.36 hours) was slightly more than the average TV viewing (3.05 hours) for a cross sectional sample of Americans (Lo Sciuto, 1972).

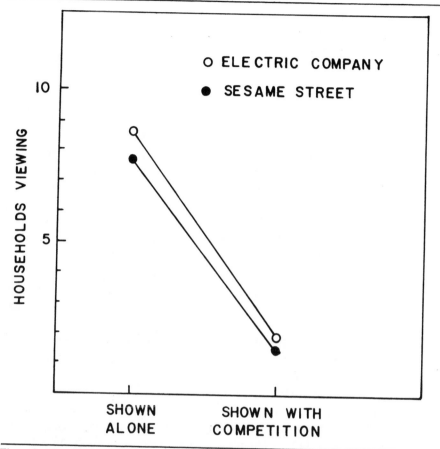

Figure 3: The effects of competition by commercial television on the viewing of Sesame Street and The Electric Company.

THE EFFECTS OF TV ON VILLAGE CHILDREN

The children of Wales were exposed to a maximum of six hours of TV per day for six months. We measured the effects of this exposure on several areas of the children's behavior including communication skills, educational achievement, and verbal intelligence. A set of standardized tests was administered on three occasions—pretelevision (November 1972), midway through the television period (May 1973), and postelevision (November 1973)—to all school aged children in Wales and the control village, Deering. The data to be reported here are from November 1972 and November 1973 and span the television period.

Communication Skills

The Illinois Test of Psycholinguistic Abilities (ITPA) measures a variety of abilities associated with the reception and production of language. The test has twelve subtests which sample both the auditory and visual channels of information processing at several levels: the receptive process, organizational or associative processes, and expressive processes. The test is widely used with children showing poor psycholinguistic development as a diagnostic tool and a prescriptive aid for remediation. The twelve subtests are described briefly below.

(a) *Auditory Reception.* This subtest measures the ability of a child to respond appropriately to verbally presented material. A set of up to fifty questions are asked which can be answered by a simple "yes" or "no" by the child. Examples are "Do dogs eat?" "Do trees fly?"

(b) *Visual Reception.* In this test, the child is shown a stimulus picture and then asked to find one like it from a set of four response pictures. The test measures the child's ability to gain meaning from visual stimuli.

(c) *Auditory Association.* Here the child's ability to relate verbal analogies is examined. The person administering the test reads an incomplete sentence and the child supplies the missing word. An example is "I cut with a saw, I pound with a_____."

(d) *Visual Association.* This is a picture association test. The examiner points to a stimulus picture and asks "What goes with this?" The child selects one of four response pictures as the most appropriate visual analogy.

(e) *Verbal Expression.* The child is given four objects in succession: a ball, an envelope, a block, and a button. He describes each of these to the examiner and is scored on the number of concepts he expresses, such as shape, color, size, and so forth.

(f) *Manual Expression.* In this part of the test, the child is scored on his or her ability to demonstrate concepts manually. Pictures of fifteen common objects are presented one at a time, and the child is asked, "Show me what we do with this," and is required to pantomime the various actions involved, say, in dialing a telephone or playing a guitar.

(g) *Grammatic Closure.* Here the child's ability to correctly use English syntax and grammar is examined. The examiner presents the child with a visual stimuli and an incomplete sentence which the child completes. Examples are "Here is a dog; here are two_____." and "Here is a foot; here are two_____."

(h) *Visual Closure.* This is essentially an embedded figures test. The child is presented with line drawings of cluttered scenes; for example, a living room with many objects in it. The child's task is to find as many of one type of object as possible; for example, shoes in the living room.

(i) *Auditory Sequential Memory.* The child must reproduce from memory sequences of digits which increase in length from 2 to 8 digits.

(j) *Visual Sequential Memory.* The child is presented with a sequence of from 2 to 8 visual figures for 5 seconds. After the figures are removed, the child must reproduce the sequence.

(k) *Auditory Closure.* This subtest measures a child's ability to organize incomplete auditory stimuli into meaningful units. The examiner reads a word with a missing syllable or syllables and the child attempts to guess the word. For example, the examiner might read "airpl ___" or "tele/one" and the child should respond with "airplane" or "telephone."

(l) *Sound Blending.* Here a word or nonsense word is pronounced slowly and discontinuously, phoneme by phoneme, and the child must pronounce the word correctly.

The ITPA test samples a variety of behaviors important in communication, and it is most appropriate for children under ten years old. It was administered to all children who were in grades 1 through 4 in both Wales and Deering.

Table 1 shows the median raw score changes between November 1972 and November 1973 for all ITPA subtests except Visual Closure which is not presented because of an examiner error during the last test administration in Deering. Changes in the Wales scores were compared with changes in the Deering scores using the Mann-Whitney U-Test. Two subtests showed significant differences: Grammatic Closure and Sound Blending. Both differences favored the Wales group; both involve auditory information processing and the mechanics of speech. The Grammatic Closure test requires the child to supply a gramatically correct missing word: "Here is one mouse, and here are two_____." In the Sound Blending subtest, the examiner sounds out a word, phoneme by phoneme, and the child must synthesize the word, such as "sh-i-p."

Educational Achievement

The Peabody Individual Achievement Test (Dunn and Markwardt, 1970) was administered to all school age children in each village. This test contains five subtests: Mathematics, Reading Recognition (the ability to pronounce a written word), Reading Comprehension, Spelling, and General Information. The test is appropriate for children from kindergarten through high school.

Table 2 shows a comparison between Wales and Deering on the subtests of PIAT over the television period. It appears that the Deering children showed more progress in Reading Comprehension, while the Wales group improved most in General Information. Neither of these differences was statistically significant. It is our conclusion that television had no effect on educational achievement in Wales.

Verbal Intelligence

Two tests were used to measure verbal intelligence. Both were administered to all school age children in both villages. In the Peabody Picture Vocabulary Test (Dunn, 1965), the examiner presents a series of pictures and reads a word.

TABLE 1

Changes in Test Scores on the Illinois Test of Psycholinguistic
Abilities over the Television Period

| ITPA Subtest | Median Raw Score Change | | U Value |
	Wales (n=10)	Deering (n=10)	
Auditory reception	11	9.5	44
Visual reception	2	1.5	44.5
Auditory association	2.5	2.5	39
Visual association	4	4	49
Verbal expression	9.5	12.5	33.5
Manual expression	7.5	4.5	31
Grammatic closure	4.5	.5	14[a]
Auditory memory	−1	−3.5	46
Visual memory	−.5	−1	42
Auditory closure	2.5	2.5	43
Sound blending	6	−2	24[a]

a. $p < .05$.

The child must point to the picture associated with the word. The PPVT is administered to children from preschool through high school.

The second measure of verbal intelligence was the vocabulary subtest of the Wechsler Intelligence Scale for Children (Wechsler, 1949), typically used with children from preschool through age fifteen. In this test, the examiner reads a word to the child and the child attempts to define it verbally. Since the WISC vocabulary scale and PPVT measure similar abilities, it is not surprising that their intercorrelation is moderately high ($r = .67$; Dunn, 1965), but there is a significant difference between them. The WISC measures both language reception and language production, while the PPVT, which allows the child to answer by pointing, measures primarily language reception.

There was no significant difference between the improvements each village showed on the WISC; but there was a large difference between change scores on the PPVT. The Wales children registered a median growth in mental ages of 1.58 years over the one-year interval between tests, while in Deering the median growth was 0.58 years in mental age. The difference was statistically significant ($p < .05$).

The measured effects of television on the village children all involve forms of auditory information processing: a better sense of spoken grammar, an improved ability to synthesize a word from its disjointed phonemes, and a large gain on one measure of verbal intelligence. Two of these effects relate to the mechanics of speech. We are puzzled by the fact that verbal intelligence measured by a manual pointing response showed a dramatic increase, while verbal intelligence as measured by a verbal response did not.

TABLE 2

Changes in Test Scores on the Peabody Individual Achievement Test
over the Television Period

| | Median Change Scores | | |
PIAT Subtest	Wales (n=19)	Deering (n=13)	U Value
Mathematics	8	7	100
Reading recognition	9	9	134
Reading comprehension	2	10	123.5
Spelling	7	6	107
General information	12	6	121

Educational achievement did not increase due to the television exposure. Perhaps this was to be expected in that it has generally been difficult to demonstrate the effects of even longer exposures to educational programming. Although carefully produced programs such as *Sesame Street* produce gains in young viewers on some tests relevant to program content (Ball and Bogatz, 1970), generalized effects of less specific programming have not been demonstrated. The PIAT used in this study is a very general measure of educational achievement and is not keyed to the programming presented during the television period. Furthermore, it appears that adult encouragement to watch educational programs is an important determinant to the educational effects that programs like *Sesame Street* produce (Cook and Conner, 1976). In the present study, no systematic effort was made to encourage children to watch any particular type of program or to influence the family's selection of program material.

SUMMARY AND CONCLUSIONS

This study has looked at the effects of a brief period of television viewing on Wales, Alaska. A number of effects were discovered. Village school children showed significant improvement in certain aspects of auditory information processing as compared to children in a control village. These children also showed a significant improvement in one measure of verbal intelligence but not in another. The improvement was noted when the children could point to a picture in response to a question but no improvement was evident when questions required verbal responses. Test of educational achievement did not show a difference between children who were exposed to television and those who were not. Informal observations suggested that preschool children may have increased their psycholinguistic development as a result of television.

The shortness of the television test period makes the data from the children remarkable. It is our opinion that continued exposure to television would enhance the effects we found, and other effects in the same general areas would probably become evident.

Interviews with the village residents and the school teachers revealed several additional effects of television. Although informal social activities such as visiting patterns appeared to have been minimally affected by television, formal social events were affected. The teachers report that attendance at the Mothers Club meetings fell to near zero during the television period. Other meetings such as the school board and the Village Council were similarly affected, suggesting that these activities cannot compete with television programming. One rather innovative solution to this problem was developed when a meeting on the Native Lands' Claim Settlement could not begin because of poor attendance. The television station manager announced the meeting over the air but attendance was still poor. He then announced that the television would be shut off until after the meeting. Attendance at the meeting was high, business was rapidly accomplished, and television resumed at the end of the meeting. This appeared to us as a benefit of a locally controlled television station: Broadcasting can be discontinued to accommodate local events.

Another effect of television will be no surprise to city dwellers: Movies shown at the school during the television period had poor attendance. Sixteen mm movies are shown once a week in many villages in rural Alaska, and they usually draw the entire village. A small fee collected at the door pays for film rental. During the television test period no movies shown in Wales made money.

Television was a powerful and popular medium in Wales; one which, once it returns on a full time basis, will surely hurry the village on its path to the modern world. The greatest single criticism of the project, voiced by people relatively far removed from the village, was concern for the role that television might play in modernizing rural Alaska. That is, television would destroy Eskimo culture and the autonomy of the village. It is interesting that this argument is frequently made against television and yet seldom applied to electricity, education, and public assistance.

We find the arguments of conservationists who feel that we must somehow protect the native from the white man, and from himself, to be patronizing. It is a serious responsibility to presume to say which aspects of the modern world a group of people should be allowed to share and which should be withheld. During the six months of television, the village took the presence of television in stride and made creative use of the medium, fitting it rather nicely into its way of life.

There were two uses of television—especially locally controlled television as was the case in Wales—that had not occurred to us before the study. One was the advantage to the community of being able to play the tapes locally, and the second was the possible use of TV in reinforcing the Eskimo culture. With local control over the scheduling of programs there would be the possibility of playing a particular program over a second or third time much the way disc jockeys play requests over local radio stations. The possibility of producing locally, or elsewhere, material that would reinforce the Eskimo culture is also intriguing. Television is a natural medium for presenting such material as native language programs and land claims information.

Whether the end result of introducing television in rural areas of the state is good or bad is certainly beyond the scope of this study and is in some ways a trivial issue. Television will come to most communities in the state. The decision as to whether (or when) a particular village should have television (or electricity, a water system, sewers, or an airport), it seems to us, should be based on only two considerations. Is it in any way economically feasible, and do the people of the village want it?

At any rate, it is not impossible in these times to feel that television might well make the village—for many people—the best of all worlds. The rural village of the future could share some of the many advantages of an urban life style while maintaining a close tie with a way of living that has its roots in tradition.

REFERENCES

BALL, S. and G. A. BOGATZ (1970) The First Year of Sesame Street. Princeton, NJ: Educational Testing Service.

COOK, T. D. and R. F. CONNER (1976) "Sesame Street around the world: the educational impact." J. of Communication 26, 155-164.

DUNN, L. M. (1965) Expanded Manual for the Peabody Picture Vocabulary Test. Circle Pines, MN: American Guidance Service.

——— and F. C. MARKWARDT (1970) Peabody Individual Achievement Test Manual. Circle Pines, MN: American Guidance Service.

KIRK, S. A. and W. D. KIRK (1971) Psycholinguistic Learning Disabilities: Diagnosis and Remediation. Urbana: Univ. of Illinois Press.

LO SCIUTO, L. (1972) "A national inventory of television viewing behavior." In Television and Social Behavior, Vol. 4, Washington, DC: Government Printing Office.

MADIGAN, R. J. and W. J. PETERSON (1974) "Television and social change on the Bering Strait." University of Alaska. (mimeo).

OSWALT, W. H. (1967) Alaskan Eskimos. Scranton, PA: Chandler.

WECHSLER, D. (1949) Wechsler Intelligence Scale for Children. New York: Psychological Corporation. 1949.

Not all questions of policy will be monumental in their implication. Fortunately, corresponding policy change need not be monumental to effect desired changes in these instances. This work by Goldstein et al. illustrates research evaluating the effects of a rather simple policy change by three newspapers. Considerable concern and effort were given to the proper validation of the primary independent variable, number of found ads placed. The researchers were also sensitive to the perspective of the newspaper staffs in documenting the absence of an undesirable side effect, the loss of revenue from placement of lost ads. Potentially useful advice is offered regarding the means of gaining entry and maintaining support in social-policy settings. And the continuation of the new policy some three years subsequent to the termination of the research attests to the acceptability of the policy change made in this research.

33

Finders, Keepers?
An Analysis and Validation of a Free-Found-Ad Policy

Richard S. Goldstein, Bonnie L. Minkin,
Neil Minkin, and Donald M. Baer

A survey of Lost and Found classified sections in metropolitan and smaller newspapers revealed disparate rates between Lost ads and Found ads: Lost ads greatly outnumbered Found ads, probably because newspapers usually require the finders of lost personal property to pay for Found advertisements. The effect of a Free-Found-Ad policy on the rate of Found advertisements placed in the Lost and Found sections of three community newspapers was investigated using a multiple-baseline design. The results suggested that the Free-Found-Ad policy was effective in increasing the rates of Found ads in all three newspapers. To determine whether increases in Found ads resulted in increases in recovered property, a sample of individuals who placed Found ads were surveyed in both baseline and treatment conditions and asked if the found items had been claimed by their owners. The Free-Found-Ad policy appeared to be effective in increasing the amount of personal property returned. The study concluded that community newspapers can provide incentives to increase such help-giving or altruistic behaviors. The implications of this study for a general policy-research strategy are discussed.

DESCRIPTORS: altruism, newspapers, response cost, policy-research strategy, multiple baseline

People are often placed in situations where behavior that can assist other people is restrained by certain variables. Korte (1974) labelled these environmental situations "altruism dilemmas". Society sometimes has recognized such situations and taken action to remove the restraints. For example, most state legislatures have enacted so-called "Good Samaritan" statutes, which diminish a physician's liability when providing emergency medical care (Fehlberg, 1964). Similarly, several communities have implemented crime-prevention programs that encourage citizens to inform police of the commission of a crime while maintaining their anonymity (Citizens' War on Crime, 1970). The

[1]This research was supported in part by a program project grant to the Bureau of Child Research, University of Kansas, by the National Institute of Child Health and Human Development (HD00870). Reprints may be obtained from R. S. Goldstein, Bureau of Child Research, Department of Human Development, University of Kansas, Lawrence, Kansas 66045. The authors are grateful to Vivian Fueyo, Eugene Ramp, Ruth Morrow, Todd Risley, Carol Davidson, Trevor Stokes, Monte Miller, Doris Miller, David Reece, and Bill Brown.

benefits or disadvantages of these interventions often are difficult to assess at a distance, because they have been implemented without methods to evaluate their effectiveness (cf. Schnelle, Kirchner, McNees, and Lawler, 1975).

However, many researchers have been able to make direct studies of help-giving behavior. For example, Bryan and Test (1967) found that the prior observation by a subject of one motorist helping another change a flat tire increased the likelihood of that subject assisting another motorist in the immediate future. Darley and Latane (1968) reported that subjects are more likely to help when an opportunity to assist is "focused" on an individual, rather than "diffused" within a group. That is, as the number of bystanders to an emergency increases, they become less likely or more hesitant to provide emergency aid. Hackler, Ho, and Urquhart-Ross (1974) found a relationship between community composition and the stated willingness of community members to provide help-giving behavior: individuals in homogeneous neighborhoods with high rates of social interaction are

From Richard S. Goldstein, Bonnie L. Minkin, Neil Minkin, and Donald M. Baer, "Finders, Keepers?: An Analysis and Validation of a Free-Found-Ad Policy," 11(4) *Journal of Applied Behavior analysis* 465-473 (Winter 1978). Copyright 1978 by Society for the Experimental Analysis of Behavior, Inc.

more likely to offer help-giving behavior to others in emergency situations.

Several researchers have investigated some of the contingencies that control help-giving responses. Boren (1966) found that a pair of laboratory monkeys alternately supplied each other with food if reinforcement opportunities were made contingent on this mutual help-giving response. When similar contingencies were placed on institutionalized schizophrenic children, they too cooperated to obtain food. One subject was rewarded with a coin that could be exchanged for snacks when the other subject completed an FR schedule. Often, the children increased the rate of other, slower subjects by slapping, hugging, frowning, smiling, or exhorting them to "Get the coin" (Hingtgen, Sanders, and DeMyer, 1965). This suggests that some help-giving responses are based on the mutual ability to reinforce or punish.

In other situations, altruism may be based simply on the removal of punishment. For example, newspapers usually require finders of lost property to pay for advertisements in Lost and Found classified sections. In effect, they punish the reporting of found property. And indeed, observations of the Lost and Found classified sections of several small-town and metropolitan newspapers show that Lost ads greatly outnumber Found ads. Presumably, the response cost of placing Found ads inhibits large numbers of finders from advertising found property; if so, this constitutes an altruism dilemma.

Another dilemma might exist: analysis of a policy problem does not necessarily guarantee that institutional policy makers will initiate research into improvement of the problem (*cf.* Campbell, 1972). Nevertheless, several behavior analysts have conducted research with public agencies demonstrating that the effects of policy can be measured, and that possible policy changes can be evaluated and subsequently implemented (*e.g.*, Schnelle, Kirchner, Macrae, McNees, Eck, Snodgrass, Casey, and Uselton, 1978; Stokes and Fawcett, 1977). In these studies, the policy problem was apparent and

troublesome to the decision makers, and they (presumably) had strong motivation to attempt policy changes. In the present study, the disparity between Found and Lost ad rates was not of particular concern to the newspapers; consequently, procedures to initiate policy change had to be devised.

Thus, the purpose of this study was to analyze the effects of a policy of free Found ads as a method of solving an altruism dilemma and promoting higher rates of placing Found ads in newspapers. The social value of this policy was analyzed by determining the resultant rates of personal property returned to owners.

METHOD

Newspapers

The *University Daily Kansan* (U.D.K.) is a daily newspaper, published at the University of Kansas, weekdays during the fall, spring, and summer semesters. Although 12,500 daily copies are printed for a student population of 20,000, precise circulation figures are unknown, because the paper is distributed free at various locations throughout the university. The U.D.K. is a nonprofit organization. Funds for the publication come from student fees and university endowment funds.

Kansas State University at Manhattan, Kansas, publishes the *K-State Collegian*. The Collegian prints 13,000 copies daily for a student population of approximately 15,000. Publication schedules for the Collegian are similar to those of the U.D.K. This paper too is distributed free at various places on the university campus. Like the U.D.K., the Collegian is operated on a nonprofit basis.

By contrast, Telegraphics Incorporated (T.I.) has at present a paid circulation of 6,000. It publishes a weekly (Thursday) paper for each of four rural communities in eastern Kansas (*The Baldwin Ledger*, *The Wellsville Globe*, *The Overbrook Citizen*, and *The Eudora Enterprise*). Although the news content of each T.I.

newspaper is varied, the same classified section is prepared for all four publications.

Lost and Found ads are included in the classified sections of all the newspapers. To place these ads in the U.D.K. and Collegian formerly required individuals to write out their ads at the newspapers' business office. Persons placing ads with the U.D.K. had to pay in cash for each Lost or Found ad: each 15 words or less cost $1.50 for one issue, $2.00 for two, and $2.50 for the entire week (five). Advertisers at the Collegian were charged 5¢ a word but a dollar minimum for one day; 10¢ a word but a $2.00 minimum for three days; and 15¢ a word but a $3.00 minimum for five days. In fact, there was no charge for a person advertising a Found item through the Collegian—but this fact was unannounced and largely unknown. T.I. Lost and Found ads could be telephoned to the business office, to be billed at a later date. Classified ads cost 8¢ a word, $1.52 per week up to 19 words.

Procedures

A multiple-baseline design (Risley and Wolf, 1972) across the three newspapers was used to investigate the effects of a Free-Found-Ad policy on the rates of Lost and Found advertisements placed by individuals.

Baseline data were collected on the total number of new Lost and Found ads placed per week in each newspaper. (A week was defined as five successive issues.) A Found or Lost ad was considered new if it had not appeared the previous week. These data were retrieved from the business office of each paper. Information describing each item reported as Lost or Found, as well as the telephone numbers and addresses of all losers and finders, were recorded.

A telephone survey was conducted during baseline and intervention conditions, approximately one week after the final appearance of each person's ad in the newspaper. Observers attempted to survey *all* of the people who had placed Found and Lost ads in the U.D.K. and Found ads in the Collegian, to determine

whether items were recovered by their owners. Those surveyed also were asked to respond to the question, "Should Found ads be free?"

Recovery data for Lost items were not collected for the Collegian, due to the expense of additional long-distance telephone calls. This expense also made it prohibitive to obtain both Found and Lost recovery data for T.I. However, Found-ad recovery data were collected for a 1-yr followup for the U.D.K.

Recovery rates were calculated by dividing the number of items reported returned, by a total including the number of items reported returned plus the number of items reported unreturned.

An observer was successful in contacting and surveying 88% of the U.D.K.'s finders during baseline, 93% during intervention, and 90% during the followup conducted 1 yr later. At the Collegian, 46% of finders were located and surveyed during baseline, and 29% during intervention. Seventy-two percent of U.D.K. losers were surveyed during baseline, and 97% thereafter.

No independent assessment was possible of whether owners actually did recover the property that finders said they had, because finders often did not know or remember the names of those who claimed lost items; thus, losers responding to Found ads typically could not be reached for confirmation of returns.

Intervention

When retroactive rates for the number of Found ads placed in the U.D.K. were obtained, these data were plotted and graphed, and presented to the business manager of the U.D.K. They showed the disparity between the high rate of Lost ads and the very low rate of Found ads. The investigators then proposed that the newspaper change its policy for Found advertisements, on the grounds that there might be a large pool of finders in the community who would advertise their finds if the cost in money and special trips to the business office were eliminated. This suggestion was supported by information obtained from the telephone survey form, in which many individuals stated a preference for a Free-Found-Ad policy.

Subsequently, the U.D.K. directors voted to approve this change in classified advertising. Found ads were then free of charge for their first three days, and the finder needed only to telephone the business office. It was agreed that this change in policy might not last beyond the duration of this investigation. The policy for placing a Lost ad remained the same (cash payment made in person and in advance), for two reasons: (1) there is already strong motivation for losers to advertise their losses, and (2) a policy of free Lost ads could be abused by individuals falsely claiming to have lost vaguely described personal property (*e.g.*, gold watch) in the hope that such an item would be found and "returned" to them.

The readership of the U.D.K. was notified of this change in policy by a 5-cm by 10-cm ad placed directly above the classified section (See Figure 1). Accompanying this ad were smaller notifications within the classified section. One was placed in the masthead, one under the Employment section, and one under the Business Opportunities section. The large ad ran for one issue; the smaller notifications appeared throughout the study.

Baseline data were collected and presented to the business manager of the Collegian, following the same procedures employed with the U.D.K. In addition, the U.D.K. data (baseline and treatment effects) were shown. The Collegian staff then informed the investigators that their paper already had a policy of free Found ads. Although this policy had been in effect 11 yr, it had never been publicized. (Typically, finders discovered the policy only if they went to the business office to place advertisements of Found items.) The business manager decided to publicize the Free-Found policy, exactly as the U.D.K. had done.

To analyze the effect of a Free-Found-Ad policy on a nonuniversity population, the commercial newspapers of Telegraphics Incorporated were contacted. Their business manager was shown the T.I. data as well as the U.D.K. and Collegian data. Although skeptical about having a similar effect in their communities, the T.I. staff decided to implement the Free-Found-Ad policy for the duration of the study.

All three business managers stated that the public relations benefits of free Found ads could

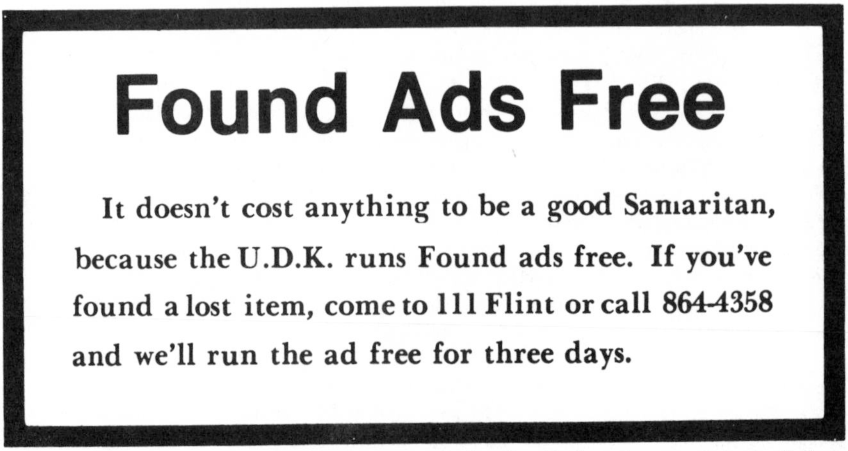

Found Ads Free

It doesn't cost anything to be a good Samaritan, because the U.D.K. runs Found ads free. If you've found a lost item, come to 111 Flint or call 864-4358 and we'll run the ad free for three days.

Fig. 1. Ad notifying U.D.K. readership of Free-Found-Ad policy. Similar ads appeared in the Collegian and T.I.

more than offset the cost in lost Found-ad revenue. For example, the 16 Found ads placed in the U.D.K. during 14 weeks of baseline brought in revenues of only $37.00. In contrast, any one-issue, medium-sized display ad (12.5 cm by 17.5 cm) would earn $38.00 in revenue. If a Free-Found-Ad policy could in fact increase the amount of Found ads placed, the business managers believed that the resultant costs in terms of additional newsprint space could be absorbed by space previously allotted to "house ads". (House ads are not a source of income for a newspaper; they serve to fill space gaps created when setting each issue in print. Typically, these spaces are used to advertise the paper, *e.g.*, "Read Gazette Classifieds".)

RESULTS

Reliability assessments across all three newspapers were conducted by an independent observer who retroactively recorded the number and descriptions of Lost and Found items placed every sixth week for the U.D.K. and Collegian, and every sixth issue for T.I. To determine if the items were unique to that week, the reliability observer had to check the previous week's issues. Reliability was calculated by dividing the number of agreements (occurrence of the specific Lost and Found ads) by the number of agreements plus disagreements, multiplying that ratio by 100. Occurrence reliability was 100% for each sixth-week/issue.

The reliability of the return rate data was assessed by having an independent observer telephone a randomly selected 15% of those surveyed, to check their previous responses. That is, telephone surveys for baseline and treatment conditions at the U.D.K. and Collegian were shuffled separately, and 15% in each condition were checked again. Occurrence agreement was 100% for this measure.

Figure 2 shows the number of new Found and Lost ads placed per week in each newspaper. Each data point represents a total of five successive issues. Sixteen Found ads were placed during the 14-week baseline of the U.D.K., a

rate of 1.14 per week. Ninety-one Lost items were placed during the same period, a rate of 6.50 per week. The Collegian readership placed 26 Found ads and 84 Lost ads during a 2-week baseline, rates of 1.24 and 4.00 respectively. During the six-point baseline at T.I. (30 successive Thursday issues), eight Found ads and 18 Lost ads were placed (rates of 1.33 and 3.00 respectively).

After the Free-Found-Ad policy was instituted at the U.D.K., 136 Found and 72 Lost advertisements were placed during the next 13 weeks, rates of 10.46 and 4.54 respectively. Sixty-four Found ads and 41 Lost ads were placed during the eight weeks of treatment at the Collegian, rates of 8.00 and 5.13 respectively. T.I.'s readers placed 14 Found and 12 Lost ads during three weeks of treatment, rates of 4.67 and 4.00 respectively.

After a three-month period, followup data were collected for all three newspapers. At the U.D.K. the Found rate was 12.50, and the Lost rate was 7.50. The Collegian Found rate was 7.67; its Lost rate was 2.67. T.I.'s readers placed Found ads at the rate of 7.67 and Lost ads at a rate of 5.67.

Institutional finders, such as university departments and local business enterprises, showed increased rates of placing Found ads when Found ads were free. The mean of such institutional ads rose from approximately 6% during baseline to approximately 12% during intervention. Of the total Found ads recorded during treatment, only two individuals placed ads a second time. Several institutional ad-placers, however, advertised repeatedly.

During baseline, 43% of the finders surveyed reported that owners recovered their property through the U.D.K., and 46% through the Collegian. When the Free-Found-Ad policy was in effect, this recovery rate at the U.D.K. was 35% (46% during a 1-yr followup), and 45% at the Collegian. Table 1 categorizes the most frequently placed Found ads and indicates the quantity of those items reported as returned to their owners.

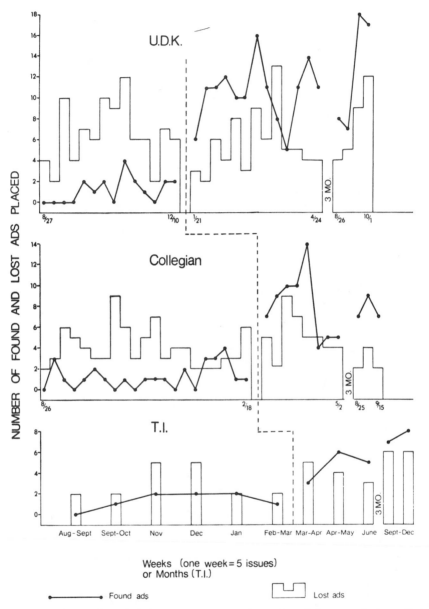

Fig. 2. Rates of Lost and Found ads for the three newspapers. One week equals five consecutive issues. (Each T.I. data point represents five consecutive Thursday issues.)

Table 1

Highest frequency Found items in the U.D.K. and Collegian.*

Item	Baseline Totals	Free Found Ads Total
Glasses	0	24 (14)
Dogs	3 (1)	23 (9)
Clothing	0	16 (5)
Keys	3 (2)	15 (4)
Cats	3 (1)	9 (0)
Books	0	8 (3)
Jewelry	3 (1)	15 (5)
Office Supplies	0	4 (2)

*Numbers in parentheses represent number of items returned to owners.

Recovery rates for Lost items also were calculated for the U.D.K. Thirty-one per cent of all Lost items were recovered during baseline and 35 % during intervention.

In the telephone survey, almost all those who responded stated that Found ads should be free. In addition, when finders were asked (during intervention) to comment on the policy, 35% of those who responded said they advertised the item only because the Found ads were free.

DISCUSSION

Analysis of a publicized Free-Found-Ad policy showed dramatic and durable increases in rates of Found ads placed in three community newspapers. Perhaps the effects were due to the removal of punishment by the newspapers on the altruistic behavior of those who would not otherwise advertise the finding of lost property. Manipulating rate increases in the amount of Found ads placed does not by itself, however, attest to the social value of this intervention.

Since it is possible that increased Found ads could be attributed to an increase in the amount of frivolous ads placed, return rates of lost personal property were considered critical to validate effectiveness of the Free-Found-Ad policy. The absence of substantial differences in recovery rates during baseline and treatment conditions suggests that the greater number of ads

placed increased the amount of lost personal property returned to owners. For example, there were approximately seven instances in which items of personal property were returned as a result of U.D.K. ads during baseline; approximately 48 items were returned during intervention.

Nevertheless, in the absence of an independent assessment of property owners, it is still possible that many of the ads were frivolous; people listing frivolous ads might be likely to give frivolous responses to a telephone survey. The fact that almost all noninstitutional ads were placed by different individuals, however, provides supplementary evidence to support the contention that the Free-Found-Ad policy generated sincere helping responses and was not the result of frivolous listings by pranksters. It is also highly unlikely that such similar recovery percentages across the U.D.K. and Collegian could occur through the efforts of pranksters.

Placement rates of Lost ads remained stable throughout all baseline and treatment conditions, suggesting that newspapers will not suffer a loss of Lost-ad revenue when Found ads are free.

Publicizing the policy in the Collegian, which had a long standing but unpublicized Free-Found-Ad policy, resulted in rate increases comparable to those at the U.D.K. and T.I. However, the importance of daily notification of the policy was not analyzed. Intermittent notification might be shown to be equally effective, but the negligible costs to the newspapers of daily publication suggest its continuation.

The staff of each newspaper indicated that the nominal costs of the procedure were offset by public relations benefits derived from providing community service. For example, the business manager at the U.D.K. reported that many readers stated their approval of this policy change. (This same business manager also found that a local bank could be convinced to pay the full cost of the Free-Found-Ad policy and of the advertisement that it was doing so, as a public-relations technique of its own. Sometimes altruism can be sold.)

Another measure of the feasibility of the Free-Found-Ad policy was the fact that all of the newspapers continued the policy after notification by the experimenters that the study was terminated. Had the policy been impractical or uneconomical, the notification should have served to end the policy. (At last check, the Free-Found-Ad policies were still in effect almost 3 yr later. And T.I., starting a fifth newspaper 3 yr later, extended its Free-Found-Ad policy to it.)

The approach taken to convince newspapers to try this policy change may have implications for a general policy-research strategy. In the present study: (1) data were shown to establish the social problem, (2) close working relationships were developed between newspaper staff and the researchers, (3) formal adoption of the policy change was made contingent on positive results, and (4) the researchers invited the newspaper staff to think through the cost-benefit ratio (whereupon the newspaper staff realized ways to reduce or recover the costs).

An initial presentation of graphed data showing the magnitude of the problem may be an important procedure when recommending social policy change to decision makers. This procedure may be critical in helping investigators initiate public-policy research in a setting where the problem behavior is controlled by institutionalized variables (i.e., formalized policies that are unlikely ever to be scrutinized because they do not seem to be a problem). Presentation of graphically displayed base rates in the present study was thought to have a powerful effect on decision makers, who had only a casual awareness of the large discrepancy between Found- and Lost-ad rates. Conversely, awareness by policy makers of existing problems might help researchers to enter a setting to conduct formal pilot testing of procedures designed to eliminate or minimize the problems (e.g., Stokes and Fawcett, 1977).

Once in the setting, it may be important to establish professional relationships with decision makers in order to develop effective intervention procedures. In the present study, the proposed experimental design was discussed in terms of time and projected costs. The staffs were encouraged to feel that they were part of the experimental endeavor by providing them with intermittent feedback on the status of the data. Staff cooperation may have been enhanced by the straightforward and easy-to-understand logic of a multiple-baseline experimental design. Indeed, staff members of each paper often asked to see the data collected at the other participating newspapers.

Following the study, research findings were discussed with the staff of each newspaper, but no recommendation to retain or discontinue the policy was suggested by the authors. It was left to the decision makers of each of the newspapers to evaluate the cost-benefit characteristics of the intervention.

It is concluded that newspapers, primary sources of public communication, can provide incentives to increase personal help-giving behaviors. Thus, this demonstration may represent an approximation toward the identification of the pertinent contingencies that control help-giving or altruistic behaviors—behaviors critical to the maintenance of any group of interdependent individuals or any society. Future research might well investigate other environmental or institutionalized variables that inhibit, elicit, or maintain help-giving responses.

REFERENCES

Boren, J. J. An experimental social relation between two monkeys. *Journal of the Experimental Analysis of Behavior*, 1966, **9**, 691-700.

Bryan, J. H. and Test, M. Models and helping: Naturalistic studies in aiding behavior. *Journal of Personality and Social Psychology*, 1967, **6**, 400-407.

Campbell, D. T. Reforms as experiments. In C. H. Weis (Ed), *Evaluating action programs: readings in social action and education*. Boston: Allyn and Bacon, 1972. Pp. 187-223.

Citizens' war on crime: Spreading across U.S. *U.S. News & World Report*, March 23, 1970, pp. 55-58.

Darley, J. and Latane, B. Bystander intervention in emergencies: Diffusion of responsibility. *Journal* of *Personality and Social Psychology*, 1968, **8**, 377-383.

Fehlberg, J. H.   Civil liability for treatment rendered at the scene of an emergency. *Wisconsin Law Review*, 1964, 494-501.

Hackler, J. C., Ho, K., and Urquhart-Ross, C.   The willingness to intervene: Differing community characteristics. *Social Problems*, 1974, **21**, 238-344.

Hingtgen, J. J., Sanders, B. J., and DeMyer, M. K.   Shaping cooperative responses in early childhood schizophrenics. In L. P. Ullmann and L. Krasner (Eds), *Case studies in behavior modification*. New York: Holt, Rinehart and Winston, 1965. Pp. 130-138.

Korte, C.   Effects of individual responsibility and group communication on help-giving in an emergency. *Human Relations*, 1974, **24**, 149-159.

Risley, T. R. and Wolf, M. M.   Strategies for analyzing behavioral change over time. In J. Nesselroade and H. Reese (Eds), *Lifespan developmental psychology: Methodological issues*. New York: Academic Press, 1972. Pp. 175-183.

Schnelle, J. F., Kirchner, R. E., McNees, M. P., and Lawler, J. M.   Social evaluation research: the evaluation of two police patrolling strategies. *Journal of Applied Behavior Analysis*, 1975, **8**, 353-365.

Schnelle, J. F., Kirchner, R. E., Macrae, J. W., McNees, M. P., Eck, R. H., Snodgrass, S., Casey, J. D., and Uselton, P. H.   Police evaluation research: an experimental and cost-benefit analysis of a helicopter patrol in a high crime area. *Journal of Applied Behavior Analysis*, 1978, **11**, 11-21.

Stokes, T. F. and Fawcett, S. B.   Evaluating municipal policy: analysis of a refuse-packaging program. *Journal of Applied Behavior Analysis*, 1977, **10**, 391-398.

Received 14 July 1977.
(Final Acceptance 1 August 1978.)

Early in 1978, a report was published indicating that rather sharp but not necessarily drastic interventions with delinquent youngsters could result in the suppression of subsequent delinquencies (Murray et al., 1978*). The youngsters involved were characterized by high rates of delinquency. Moreover, postintervention drop in rate of offenses was impressive. But the very fact that the pretreatment rate was so high (the delinquents had obviously been selected for "treatment" by the courts because of their repeated offenses) immediately suggested that the effect observed might be nothing more than a regression artifact. McCleary et al. make the case for the regression artifact in the following. The case is, in fact, fairly strong but has not proven acceptable to the original authors for reasons they will take up in subsequent papers. For the present, they raise an interesting question: Because a regression artifact could *have occurred, must it* have occurred?

34

How a Regression Artifact Can Make Any Delinquency Intervention Program Look Effective

Richard McCleary, Andrew C. Gordon, David McDowall, and Michael D. Maltz

Figure 1 shows the average monthly rates of arrest for 365 adjudicated delinquents before and after a correctional intervention. These data come from an evaluation of the Unified Delinquency Intervention Services (UDIS) conducted by the American Institutes for Research (AIR). A report of the AIR evaluation (Murray, Thompson, and Israel, 1978) claims that

The recidivism data . . . are surprisingly unambiguous. *Correctional intervention in the life of the chronic juvenile offender . . . had a powerful and apparently long-term inhibiting effect on subsequent delinquent activity.*

Given the data in Figure 1, this claim seems reasonable, and indeed, this finding of the AIR report has been widely publicized and accepted.[1] In our reanalysis of the AIR report (Gordon et al., 1978; McCleary et al., 1978), we have found that these recidivism data are *not* "surprisingly unambiguous." Although some

Authors' Note: Coauthorship is intended. We are indebted to Donald T. Campbell, Louis A. Cox, Carl M. Harris, Charles A. Murray, Stephen M. Pollock, and Douglas Thomson for consultation, critical comments, and suggestions. Our reanalysis of these data was funded in part by Grant #US LEAA 99-0073 from the National Institute of Law Enforcement and Criminal Justice and by a contract from the Illinois Department of Corrections. The points of view we express here are not necessarily those of the funding agencies.

*MURRAY, C. A., D. THOMPSON, and C. B. ISRAEL (1978) UDIS: Deinstitutionalizing the Chronic Juvenile Offender. Washington, DC: American Institutes for Research.

From Richard McCleary et al., "How a Regression Artifact Can Make Any Delinquency Intervention Program Look Effective." Unpublished manuscript, 1978.

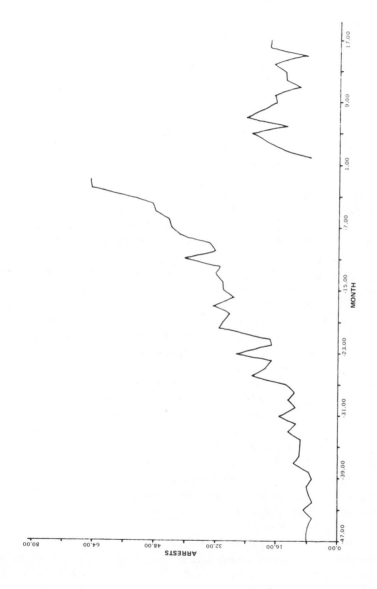

Note: Negative months are preintervention. Positive months are postintervention.

Figure 1: Average Monthly Rates of Arrest for 365 Adjudicated Delinquents (taken from an evaluation of UDIS conducted by AIR)

627

small portion of the effect depicted in Figure 1 may be due to correctional intervention, the largest part of the effect is likely due to a methodological artifact.

The most unusual aspect of the arrest data in Figure 1 is the before/after contrast. The typical delinquency treatment-program evaluation is based on some variation of a Campbell and Stanley (1966) "static group comparison" design. Using the notation of Campbell and Stanley, we diagram this as

Experimental Subjects . X   0
Control Subjects   . .   0

In this design, the experimental and control groups are contrasted by some failure criterion. Of course, delinquency treatment program evaluations seldom have "no treatment" control groups. The status quo treatment is instead used as a control benchmark against which the effectiveness of some novel alternative treatment is contrasted. To contrast the effectiveness of the status quo (control) and novel alternative experimental treatments, the evaluator must assume that both treatments have absolute impacts on the delinquent; that is, for a given delinquent, the treatments are *either* effective *or* ineffective. If after treatment a delinquent does not fail by some criterion (arrest, conviction, and the like), the treatment is deemed effective in that case. To be judged effective, the novel alternative treatment must produce a lower rate (or proportion, or percentage, and so on) of failure than the status quo treatment.

Using a number of highly correlated failure criteria, AIR found that the UDIS treatment was neither more nor less effective than the status quo treatments. In other words, by a static group comparison, the UDIS programs and traditional reformatories produced more or less the same rates of failure. No treatment was significantly more effective than any other treatment. If there is a conventional wisdom of delinquency research, it is that "nothing works" and this aspect of the AIR evaluation is consistent with the conventional wisdom.

One problem with the typical delinquency treatment-program evaluations, and one factor that might easily explain why "nothing works," is that the standard failure criteria may be too sensitive.[2] It may be incorrect to conclude that a treatment has had no impact on a delinquent merely because that delinquent has been arrested once in the posttreatment period. These delinquents after all come from and return to an environment where a single arrest is not necessarily a sign of criminality.

Recognizing this problem, AIR collapsed the experimental (UDIS) and control groups into a single group. Using pre- and postintervention monthly rates of arrest (instead of some failure criterion), AIR generated the before/after data shown in Figure 1. Comparing the last pre- and first postintervention years for these 365 delinquents, AIR reported a 73% reduction in arrests from pre- to postintervention. This effect is calculated by the formula

$$\text{Percent Reduction} = 1 \frac{\text{Postintervention Arrest Rate}}{\text{Preintervention Arrest Rate}}$$

A 73% reduction in arrests from pre- to postintervention is a remarkable effect, of course. But, though the AIR report attributes this effect to a correctional intervention, as we will demonstrate, there is some justification for doubting this interpretation.

However, before we discuss the methodological artifacts in the AIR report we must take note of a provocative point. First, UDIS is not a monolithic treatment program, but rather, is a wide variety of programs ranging from group homes and peer counseling to incarcerative psychiatric residence and wilderness stress camps. Moreover, there is a considerable range of quality among the reformatory institutions that constituted the status quo treatment. Some of the reformatories were "better" (or less incarcerative) than others and most were "better" than the "worst" UDIS program. Without much exaggeration, we might conclude that the operational definition of "correctional intervention" in the AIR report includes almost all delinquency treatments currently used in the United States.

Second, and more important, it appears that whenever a before/after contrast is used to evaluate a delinquency treatment program, the evaluation finds that the treatment is effective. In the Provo experiment (Empey and Erickson, 1972), for example, and in the Silverlake experiment (Empey and Lubeck, 1971), the evaluators reported pre- to postintervention reductions in arrests of approximately 70%. Given the wide range of delinquency treatments judged effective by before/after contrasts, it would seem that a new conventional wisdom of delinquency research is emerging: "anything works." Indeed, many of the UDIS programs (peer counseling and client advocacy, for example) would be described better as "correctional placebos" rather than as "correctional interventions." Yet these UDIS programs too proved remarkably effective by a before/after contrast.

Our interest in the AIR evaluation of UDIS stems from a small research contract to us from the Illinois Department of Corrections, the parent agency of UDIS. (Coincidentally, we were engaged in a larger study of correctional effectiveness measures at that time.) We approached a reanalysis of the AIR data with no preconceived notions, but admittedly with some skepticism. As methodologists, we distrust absolutes whether they be that "anything works" or "nothing works." In our reanalysis (McCleary et al., 1978), we uncovered three threats to internal validity, each of which might account for the before/after effect reported by AIR. We will discuss two of these three briefly here and then will devote the remainder of this essay to the third uncontrolled threat to internal validity.

(1) We found substantial mortality in the AIR data. As a threat to internal validity, *mortality* refers to a before/after difference due only to a selective attrition of cases from the sample. In fact, the AIR evaluation of UDIS began with the sample of 488 delinquents but ended with a sample of 141 delinquents. What happened to the 347 "disappearing" delinquents? Many were simply never released from institutions or programs. Many were released, committed new crimes, and were returned to institutions. Once reincarcerated, of course, these delinquents could not be arrested. We found that, on the average, the least active or "best" delinquents were followed up for longer periods of time than the "worst" delinquents; 35% of the AIR sample, composed largely of the "worst" delinquents, were followed up for less than one postintervention month.

The word "mortality" (or any of its synonyms) appears nowhere in the AIR report. Nowhere in the AIR evaluation of UDIS have we found any attempt to control this rather common threat to internal validity. It is a rather simple matter to track the police records of 488 delinquents back into time. It is much more difficult to track these same records into the future, however. This is especially true when doing research under a deadline—data collection must stop when the contract ends, not when the data are complete. Overall, we found that the uncontrolled mortality threat was so substantial as to render the AIR finding uninterpretable.

(2) We also found substantial maturation in the before/after difference reported by AIR. As a threat to internal validity, *maturation* refers to a before/after difference due only to the natural aging process. It is generally accepted that a delinquent becomes more active up to a certain age and thereafter becomes less active. Unlike the threat of mortality, the AIR report takes explicit note of maturation. There is no credible attempt to control for maturation in the AIR analysis, however. In more than one analysis, the AIR report cites subsample differences without noting that there are substantial age differences among the subsamples.

(3) The third and most important uncontrolled threat to internal validity in the AIR evaluation was *regression*. Due to the threats posed by maturation and (especially) mortality, one might easily dismiss the AIR evaluation of UDIS as a matter of course. There is much to be learned from the AIR report, however. In a general sense, regression is the most important of the three uncontrolled threats to internal validity. Evaluations may be designed to control mortality and (to a lesser extent) maturation. But given the nature of the juvenile justice system, the threat to internal validity posed by regression will be present whenever treatment effectiveness is evaluated by a before/after contrast. *The regression artifact which we describe in the remainder of this essay is fundamentally related to a before/after measure of delinquency treatment effectiveness.*

As a threat to internal validity, *regression* refers to a before/after difference due only to an abnormally high preintervention score. To illustrate this principle, consider the roll of two "honest" dice. On any given roll, the possible numbers that may come up by their combinations are

```
 2 –   (1,1)
 3 –   (1,2) (2,1)
 4 –   (1,3) (2,2) (3,1)
 5 –   (1,4) (2,3) (3,2) (4,1)
 6 –   (1,5) (2,4) (3,3) (4,2) (5,1)
 7 –   (1,6) (2,5) (3,4) (4,3) (5,2) (6,1)
 8 –   (2,6) (3,5) (4,4) (5,3) (6,2)
 9 –   (3,6) (4,5) (5,4) (6,3)
10 –   (4,6) (5,5) (6,4)
11 –   (5,6) (6,5)
12 –   (6,6)
```

From this probability space it is clear that the number seven will come up more often than any other number. The numbers two (snake-eyes) and twelve (box-cars) will come up less often than any other numbers for the same reason.

Now suppose that we roll many pairs of dice and select for "treatment" those pairs of dice which come up as high numbers: say, any number larger than seven. We will "treat" these dice by uttering magic phrases over them. As a second roll of these dice will produce smaller numbers on the average, we might conclude that our "treatment" has "cured" the high-rolling dice. If we draw this conclusion, of course, we will have been victimized by a regression artifact. Our magical "treatment" is effective only because the number seven is the expected value of a dice roll. When a number above seven comes up on the first roll, a smaller number will come up approximately 75% of the time on a second roll.

The same principle holds in the evaluation of a delinquency treatment program. If a delinquent has been arrested 15 times in the year preceding a correctional intervention, we should not be surprised if that delinquent is arrested fewer than 15 times in the year following the correctional intervention. Although delinquent behavior is a more complicated phenomenon than dice rolling, the same laws of probability apply. Delinquents with abnormally high preintervention arrest rates are expected to have lower postintervention arrest rates due only to regression.

The AIR report took explicit note of the possibility of a regression artifact operating in the UDIS evaluation. The authors tried to correct for the possibility of an artifact by excluding from consideration the six months immediately prior to intervention. Even after this correction was made, AIR noted a 70% reduction in arrest activity.

REGRESSION ARTIFACT

At this point it is appropriate to review the characteristics of regression artifacts. The methodological literature in fact describes two distinct types of regression artifacts, each associated with a different quasi-experimental design. The first type of regression artifact is associated with a Campbell and Stanley "nonequivalent control group" design.

Experimental Subjects   0   X   0
Control Subjects   0   ·   0

The reader should note that the data in Figure 1 constitute one half of this design. Campbell and Erlebacher (1970) have demonstrated "how regression artifacts... make compensatory education look harmful" when this design is misused. If either experimental or control subjects are selected due to abnormal pretest scores, a selection-regression interaction is generated. On a posttest, either group will regress to their population means, thus guaranteeing a pretest/posttest difference.

In one sense only, this type of regression artifact is operating in the AIR data: each of these 365 delinquents has been selected for correctional intervention. Each of these delinquents is a "chronic juvenile offender" with, on the average, a half-dozen arrests in the last preintervention year.

The second type of regression artifact is associated with the Campbell and Stanley "time series quasi-experiment."

All subjects   0 0 0 0 X 0 0 0 0

Campbell and Ross (1968; Glass, Willson, and Gottman, 1975) have demonstrated that when an intervention is precipitated by an abnormally high preintervention time series level, a postintervention change in level is guaranteed. In the long run, a stationary stochastic process always returns to its mean level.

This second type of regression artifact may be called a *reactive intervention* threat and it is this type of regression artifact that the AIR report assumes is operating in the data. This assumption is correct in one sense only: each of these 365 delinquents has been selected for correctional intervention at a time when, for some reason, the delinquent has been most active.

The reactive intervention threat refers to time series observations of a naturally constituted group. When the group observation hits an abnormal level, intervention occurs as a reaction. When Campbell and Ross analyzed the Connecticut crackdown on speeding, their time series data were annual traffic fatality rates for the entire state of Connecticut. Because the traffic fatality rate was abnormally high in 1955, in 1956 the governor reacted by instituting a crackdown on speeding. And because the 1955 level was abnormally high, a drop in 1956 would have been expected with or without a crackdown on speeding.

The AIR delinquents did not exist as a group until after the fact, of course; that is, until after each had been selected. A reactive intervention occurs at the case level and the 365 cases have then been aggregated ex post facto into a cohort. Campbell and Ross recommend a crude statistical correction for the reactive intervention threat. As there is no reactive intervention across the group, this correction will not be appropriate for the AIR data.

The misunderstanding in the AIR report is that these two types of regression artifact (as well as the Campbell and Stanley quasi-experimental designs associated with each) are only abstract models. In the real world regression artifacts seldom appear in the ideal model form. There are elements of both regression artifacts operating in the AIR data. First, these 365 delinquents have been selected from a pool of all eligible delinquents. The basis for this selection apparently is that these 365 delinquents have relatively high arrest rates. Second, in each case the time of intervention has been selected also, apparently, as a reaction to a particularly high rate of arrest. When both of these selection factors operate, the resultant artifact is of a hybrid type.

In the next section we will describe arrests over time as a random process. The rate of arrest for a delinquent fluctuates randomly about some mean level, sometimes higher and sometimes lower than the mean. If the individual delinquent is selected for intervention when his rate of arrest is by chance abnormally high (which seems plausible), a postintervention reduction is expected.

After demonstrating this principle at the level of the individual, we present a simulation experiment to demonstrate the implications for the aggregate statistic. By selecting only the "worst" delinquents, and by intervening when the individual delinquent appears to be "worse" than usual, we are able to generate a before/after contrast identical to the one shown in Figure 1.

We point out now that the cohort we generate is an "ersatz" cohort. That is, we have assumed that all members of the cohort have been selected from a larger cohort comprised of individuals *with the same mean arrest rate*. This is unrealistic. However, if we can show that this cohort exhibits the same type of behavior as that in Figure 1, there is no way of distinguishing between the AIR cohort and the "ersatz" cohort.

Finally, we will present some results of our reanalysis of the AIR data which bear on the regression issue. To rule out a regression artifact in these data, AIR should have examined the relationship between pre- and postintervention arrest rates *at the level of the individual delinquent*. By examining only the aggregate statistic, the AIR report misses a great deal of information, and in general, is victimized by an ecological fallacy. In our examination of individual arrest rates, we show that the substantial before/after difference reported by AIR for all 365 delinquents is due largely to a subsample of delinquents with abnormally high preintervention arrest rates. We show a strong and regular relationship between preintervention arrests and the before/after difference which is the signature of a classic regression artifact.

ARRESTS AS A RANDOM PROCESS

An officially recorded arrest is a random variable in time. We are not arguing here that delinquency itself is a random process (that these particular delinquents are the unfortunate losers in a sociological game of chance). Rather, given that these youths are adjudicated delinquents, and given the nature of the delinquent behavior and police-arrest processes, we are arguing that the timing of each officially recorded arrest is random. The AIR data do not contradict this assumption in any substantial manner.

With an assumption of random timing, we can describe the distribution of arrests across the delinquent population and across time as a Poisson process.[3] For a Poisson process, the probability that a delinquent will have exactly k arrests in t months is given by the formula

$$P(\text{exactly k arrests in t months}) = \frac{(\lambda t)^k}{k!} \ e^{-\lambda t}$$

The Poisson rate parameter, λ, is the expected rate of arrest per month during the t-month interval. A maximum likelihood estimate of λ is given by the formula

$$\lambda = \frac{\text{Total Arrests in t Months}}{t} = \lambda \ \text{Arrests/Month}$$

In this section, for the sake of demonstration only, we will use the value of $\lambda = .33$ arrests per month. This value of λ implies that each delinquent is expected to be arrested four times in a given year. By substituting this value of λ into the formula, we can obtain the relative frequencies of k arrests in any given year (t = 12). The expected relative frequencies are

P (*no* arrests in a given year) =	.01831
P (*one* arrest in a given year) =	.07324
P (*two* arrests in a given year) =	.14648
P (*three* arrests in a given year) =	.19537
P (*four* arrests in a given year) =	.19537
P (*five* arrests in a given year) =	.15629
P (*six* arrests in a given year) =	.10420
P (*seven* arrests in a given year) =	.05954
P (*eight* arrests in a given year) =	.02977
P (*nine* arrests in a given year) =	.01323
P (*ten* arrests in a given year) =	.00529

and so forth. What these relative frequencies mean is that, even though a group of delinquents are more or less the same (λ = .33), some will have more arrests than others in any given year. Approximately 1.8% of the delinquents are expected to have *no* arrests, while in the same year, approximately 2.1% are expected to have *nine or more* arrests. This disparity is a short-run phenomenon, randon (Poisson) in nature, and it would be incorrect to conclude that some of the delinquents are "better" or "worse" than others.

Nevertheless, if one were forced to select the "worst" delinquents from a large cohort (as juvenile court judges presumably must do), those delinquents who were arrested most often in the last year would most likely be selected. Moreover, as the number of arrests in one year is independent of the number of arrests in any other year, it can easily be demonstrated that the percentage reduction from the last preintervention year to the first postintervention year is strictly a function of the number of preintervention arrests. The expected reductions are

Preintervention Arrests	Postintervention Arrests	Percentage Reduction
1	4	− 400%
2	4	− 200%
3	4	− 33%
4	4	0%
5	4	20%
6	4	33%
7	4	43%
8	4	50%

and so forth. Delinquents with higher than average preintervention rates of arrest experience higher than average percent reductions. The before/after difference is due only to regression, and in this case, where all delinquents are regressing to the same mean, the size of the regression artifact is determined only by the number of preintervention arrests.

The point of this demonstration is that whenever juvenile court judges select only the "worst" delinquents for correctional intervention, some regression to the mean in postintervention is expected. We will later present pre- and post-intervention arrest rates for the 365 AIR delinquents, demonstrating a strong relationship between preintervention arrests and percentage reductions.

The Poisson distribution formula also describes how arrests are distributed across time for an individual delinquent career. Using λ = .33 again, each month of the individual delinquent's career is viewed as an independent (Bernoulli) trial where as many as k arrests (k = 0, 1, 2, . . .) may occur. Over a period of t months, exactly λt arrests are expected to be recorded. Of course, no single month will have exactly = .33 arrests. That would be impossible. Instead, we expect

$$P \,(no \text{ arrests in any single month}) = \quad .71653$$
$$P \,(one \text{ arrest in any single month}) = \quad .23884$$
$$P \,(two \text{ arrests in any single month}) = \quad .03981$$
$$P \,(three \text{ arrests in any single month}) = .00423$$

and so forth. What these relative frequencies mean is that 71.6% of the months in a delinquent career will have *no* arrests; 23.9% will have *one* arrest; 4% will have *two* arrests; .4% will have three arrests and so forth.

In Figure 2a, we show a hypothetical delinquent career that we have generated with random (Poisson, λ = .33) integers. As we have specified a rate of .33 arrests per month, we expect to derive a distribution of Bernoulli trials within sampling variance of the expected frequencies. The simulated career in Figure 2a has 22 months (of 30: 73.3%), with *no* arrests, six months (20%) with *one* arrest, and two months (6.7%) with *two* arrests. This is quite close to what we would expect.

If we use the entire 30-month career to estimate λ, we find that λ = .33 (10 arrests/30 months), which by chance is the expected rate of arrest. In fact, whenever we use fairly long intervals of time to estimate λ (say 30 months or longer), our estimate will always be close to the expected value. When we use shorter intervals of time, however, our estimate of λ will fluctuate about this expected value.

To illustrate this, consider Figure 2b, where we estimate the rate of arrest for this hypothetical delinquent career using only the preceding six months. The estimate of λ ranges from a high of .5 to a low of .17. When a finite period of time is used to estimate the arrest rate for this hypothetical delinquent, the estimate varies substantially. As a result, it appears that this hypothetical delinquent is sometimes getting "better" and sometimes getting "worse." But this appearance is due to chance alone and to the interval of time over which the rate of arrest is estimated. The month-to-month disparity is a short-run phenomenon, random (Poisson) in nature, and it would be incorrect to conclude that the delinquent is "better" or "worse" at any one point in time than at any other.

Nevertheless, if one were forced to select this delinquent for a correctional intervention, it is likely that selection would occur in the seventh, twelfth, twenty-fourth, or twenty-seventh months. In these months, the delinquent appears to be getting "worse." Viewing only the past record of the delinquent, it is in these months that a juvenile court judge might easily (but incorrectly) infer that the time has come, quoting the AIR report, for "an intervention in the life of the chronic juvenile offender." And if this hypothetical delinquent is selected in any of these months, a postintervention reduction in arrests is guar-

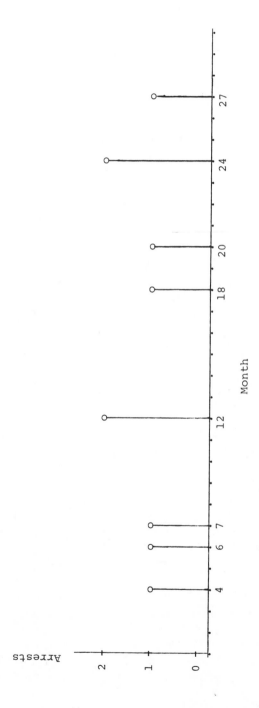

Figure 2a: A hypothetical delinquent career generated with random (Poisson, $\lambda = .33$) integers. There are 22 months with no arrests, six months with one arrest, and two months with two arrests.

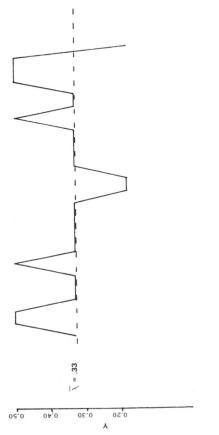

Note: Using a six-month moving average, the arrest rate, λ, fluctuates widely about its mean level, λ = .33.

Figure 2b: Hypothetical delinquent career generated with Random (Poisson, λ = .33) integers

anteed. Using a six-month pre- and six-month postintervention contrast, we see that the percent reductions in this hypothetical delinquent career are

Month	Pre-Intervention Arrests	Post-Intervention Arrests	Reduction
7	3	2	33%
12	3	1	67%
24	3	1	67%
27	3	0	100%

All of these substantial percentage reductions are due to chance alone. If a juvenile court judge selects only those delinquents who have experienced three arrests in the last six months, a regression artifact guarantees the finding of a percentage reduction.

So far, we have demonstrated two principles. First, if a juvenile court judge selects only the "worst" delinquents of a cohort for a correctional intervention, regression to the mean will guarantee a before/after difference. Second, if a juvenile court judge selects delinquents for a correctional intervention at a time when it appears that the delinquents are getting "worse," regression to the mean will guarantee a before/after difference. We will now generalize these principles to the aggregate statistic.

Maltz and Pollock (1978) have demonstrated analytically that a regression artifact operating at the level of the individual delinquent will generalize to the cohort when individual cases are aggregated. We will use Monte Carlo methods here to make a similar demonstration. Monte Carlo methods are more flexible than analytic methods, allowing us to examine basic assumptions about the methods used to select delinquents for a correctional intervention.

MONTE CARLO SIMULATION

As a first step in the simulation experiment, we generated 1,000 hypothetical delinquent careers with random (Poisson, $\lambda = .15$) integers. Except for a lower expected rate of arrest, these careers are similar to the hypothetical career shown in Figure 2a, and all are similar to the careers of the AIR delinquents. Each of the 1,000 careers had a "starting" point and an "ending" point. For the AIR data, the average delinquent experienced his first arrest at the age of eight years. We used this age as the average starting point for our 1,000 simulated careers. Each of our simulated careers ended when the hypothetical delinquent turned 18.

To examine various selection strategies, we programmed a computer to "judge" the 1,000 delinquent careers. Whenever an arrest was recorded (a non-zero integer in the career), the delinquent appeared before a judge. At that time, the judge either selected the delinquent for a correctional intervention or placed the delinquent on probation. When a delinquent was selected, the remainder of his career was used at the postintervention period. After all 1,000 careers had been judged, the data were aggregated.

The first selection strategy we examined has the result shown in Figure 3. Suppose that juvenile court judges do not consider the delinquent's prior arrest record when deciding whether to select the delinquent for intervention. Judges might consider only the absolute seriousness of the incident offense, for example. If an offense is not sufficiently serious, the judge will place the delinquent on probation no matter how many prior arrests (and probations) are reflected in the record. If the offense is serious enough, of course, the delinquent will be denied probation even for a first offense. In Figure 3, approximately 5% of all offenses were made serious enough to warrant an intervention, with seriousness determined randomly. The result of this selection (or sentencing) strategy is a prominent spike, or increase in the rate of arrest, in the last preintervention month.

We note also that arrest rates increase slightly from the first preintervention month up to (approximately) the twenty-fourth preintervention month. This increase is due to the starting points of the 1,000 careers. If a delinquent is selected for intervention after his first offense, then by definition the preceding 47 months will have no arrests. This factor may also be seen in the AIR data (Figure 1) and is due to aggregating a number of delinquent careers with different ages.

The dramatic spike at the last preintervention month is characteristic of all aggregate delinquency data. A delinquent cannot be selected for a correctional intervention unless he has been arrested, so each delinquent has an arrest in this month by definition. Due largely to this spike, the before/after effect in Figure 3, based on the last pre- and first postintervention years, is approximately 32%.

Although the selection strategy depicted in Figure 3 is not realistic, it demonstrates two important principles. First, due to differences in ages across the cohort, a sufficiently long preintervention period will show a slight increase in arrest rates. Second, even when the prior record is ignored, a pre- to postintervention reduction in arrests is expected. This before/after difference is due largely to the dramatic spike in the last preintervention month, however. Given this selection strategy then, the regression artifact could be controlled somewhat by simply deleting the last preintervention month from the before/after contrast. AIR correctly eliminated the month of intervention from consideration and as a check eliminated an additional five months to account for a possible regression artifact. But as we will show, this adjustment is not adequate.

The second strategy we examined has the result shown in Figure 4, and *here we see a striking resemblance to the before/after effect in the AIR data* (Figure 1). To generate the before/after effect in Figure 4, we selected delinquents for intervention on the basis of the absolute seriousness of each offense *and* on the

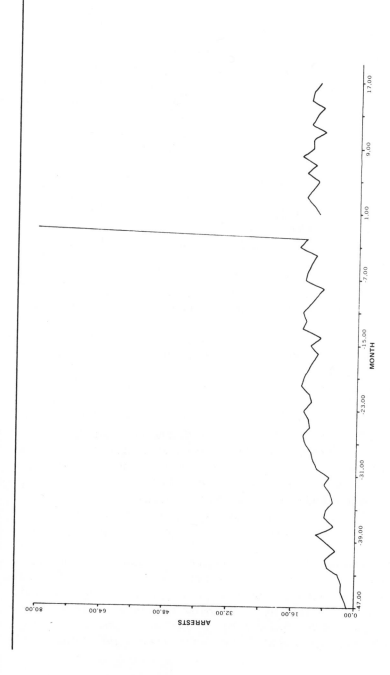

Note: When delinquents are selected for intervention without regard to prior arrest records, a spike is expected at the month of intervention.

Figure 3: Average Monthly Rates of Arrest for Hypothetical Delinquent Careers Simulated with Random (Poisson, λ = .15) Integers

basis of the arrest record of the delinquent. This would seem to be a fairly realistic selection strategy.

For Figure 4, judges first weighed the absolute seriousness of the present offense. Approximately 5% of all offenses were made serious enough to warrant intervention, with seriousness determined randomly. However, if the offense was not serious enough to warrant intervention, the delinquent was not automatically placed on probation. Instead, the judge weighed the delinquent's most recent record of arrest, a period of time ranging randomly from 2 to 20 months. If the number of arrests during that period was "too high," with that criterion determined randomly, the delinquent was selected for intervention. Only those delinquents whose incident offenses were not serious, and whose prior arrest rates were not too high, were placed on probation. By setting both "seriousness" and "too high" as random criteria of selection, we have assumed that some judges are more lenient than others and that a delinquent appears before a lenient or strict judge more or less by chance.

We call this selection (or sentencing) strategy "the straw that breaks the camel's back." The idea underlying this strategy is that each juvenile court judge has a different level of tolerance. So long as the delinquent's offenses are not serious (are not violent, for example), and so long as the delinquent's rate of arrest does not appear to be increasing dramatically, the judge continues to hope that lesser interventions such as probation will be effective. But if the incident offense is serious, or if the incident offense appears to indicate an accelerating pattern of delinquency, the judge abandons all hope. In this sense, the incident offense is the straw that breaks the camel's back.

The before/after effect in Figure 4 represents the aggregate behavior of only 133 (13.3%) of the 1,000 delinquents. The judges in this simulation experiment have selected only the "worst" delinquents of all (that is, those with high rates of arrest and those who have committed serious offenses). In addition, in each case, the time of intervention has been selected. The result is a reduction in arrests from one-year pre- to one-year postintervention of 78%. Unlike the before/after effect of Figure 3, however, the effect here is not due largely to the last preintervention month. Thus, whereas the regression artifact in Figure 3 can be controlled somewhat by deleting the last preintervention month, the regression artifact in Figure 4 cannot be controlled by deleting preintervention observations. The data in Figure 4 increase steadily throughout the preintervention period. Closer to the point of intervention, the data begin to increase exponentially. Then in postintervention, the arrest statistic regresses to the population mean.

We could continue this series of simulation experiments, examining the results of more complicated (and therefore even more realistic) selection strategies. We leave this exercise to the reader, however, because Figure 4 demonstrates the point of interest to us. *Whenever delinquents are selected for a correctional intervention at least in part on the basis of their past record of arrest, a before/after effect of the sort shown in Figures 1 (the AIR data) and 4*

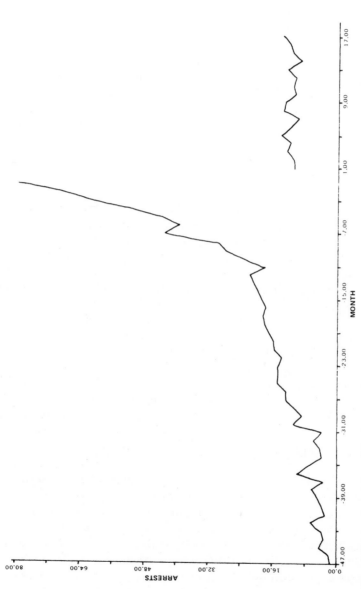

Note: When delinquents are selected for intervention on the basis of prior arrest records, an exponential increase is expected leading up to the month of intervention.

Figure 4: Average Monthly Rates of Arrest for Hypothetical Delinquent Careers Simulated with Random (Poisson, $\lambda = .15$) Integers

643

(simulated data) is expected. We will now examine the AIR data to see if a regression artifact plausibly explains the before/after percentage reduction in arrests.

THE AIR DATA

The before/after effect in Figure 4 is due solely to a regression artifact. We know that this is true because the data are simulated; we built a regression artifact into the data. If we lacked this knowledge, however, we could still make an informed guess by examining the structure of the data. As noted, Figure 4 reflects a 78% reduction in arrests from the last pre- to the first postintervention year. That is

$$\text{Postintervention arrests} = (1 - .78)\,\text{Preintervention arrests}$$
$$= .22\,\text{Preintervention arrests}$$

Given this relationship, *if there is no regression artifact,* we expect *all* delinquents to experience the same percentage reduction on the average. If a delinquent has 10 preintervention arrests, for example, we would expect that delinquent to have 2.2 postintervention arrests; and if some other delinquent has only five preintervention arrests, then we would expect that delinquent to have only 1.1 postintervention arrests. In general, when there is no regression artifact, we expect to find no relationship between preintervention arrest rates and percentage reductions.

We do not find this in the simulated data, however. Instead we find that delinquents with four or fewer preintervention arrests experienced 54% reductions on the average whereas delinquents with more than four preintervention arrests experienced 93% reductions on the average. This relationship between preintervention arrests and percentage reductions is due solely to the regression artifact that we built into the simulated data.

We may now apply this same logic to the AIR data. Table 1 shows the average postintervention arrests and percentage reductions for the 365 AIR delinquents broken down by the number of preintervention arrests. There is a strong and regular relationship between preintervention arrests and percentage reductions for these delinquents. More important, the relationship is in the direction we would expect if a regression artifact were operating in these data.

The smallest percentage reductions (32.3% on the average) were experienced by those delinquents with only two arrests in the last preintervention year. The largest percentage reductions (97.5% on the average) were experienced by those delinquents with 15 arrests in the last preintervention year. Overall there is little difference in the postintervention arrest rates of these delinquents.

But a more interesting picture of the regression artifact can be developed by excluding from our analysis 157 delinquents who had no postintervention

TABLE 1
Arrests in the Last Pre- and First Postintervention Year and Percent Reductions[4]

	For N=365 Delinquents				For N=208 Delinquents		
Pre-I Arrests	Average Post-I Arrests	Average Percentage Reduction	Cases	Pre-I Arrests	Average Post-I Arrests	Average Percentage Reduction	Cases
1	.61	39.5%	11	1	2.22	−122.0%	3
2	1.35	32.4	38	2	2.57	−28.5	20
3	1.62	46.0	56	3	3.49	−16.3	26
4	1.58	60.4	55	4	3.23	19.3	27
5	2.80	43.9	43	5	4.31	13.8	28
6	2.63	56.1	46	6	5.00	16.7	24
7	4.61	34.1	37	7	6.10	12.9	28
8	2.79	65.1	27	8	5.02	37.2	15
9	4.84	46.2	19	9	7.08	21.4	13
10	3.80	62.0	13	10	3.80	62.0	13
11	2.43	77.9	8	11	3.89	64.6	5
12	3.55	70.5	2	12	7.09	40.9	1
13	3.00	76.9	3	13	4.50	65.4	2
14	6.03	57.9	3	14	9.05	35.4	2
15	.38	97.5	4	15	1.53	89.8	1

arrests. There is some justification for this. As we noted elsewhere (Gordon et al., 1978; McCleary et al., 1978; see also, Murray, 1978), the AIR analysis failed to control mortality. In fact, 5 of the 157 delinquents with no postintervention arrests were free for one day. Eighteen percent of these delinquents were followed up for less than one month and an overwhelming majority were followed up for less than the twelve months required for an estimate of the annual arrest rate. By excluding these delinquents from our analysis, we are able to control somewhat the threat of mortality.

Excluding these 157 delinquents gives us the statistics for the 208 delinquents shown in Table 1. All of these delinquents were free for at least one postintervention year. Here we see the other side of the regression artifact coin. The 49 delinquents with three or fewer preintervention arrests experienced negative percentage reductions (or percentage increases). All delinquents were expected to regress to the population mean. If the preintervention arrest rate is below this mean, however, then postintervention increases are expected.

We must emphasize here that we have not "proved" the existence of a regression artifact in the AIR data. Nevertheless, we find a strong relationship between preintervention arrest rates and percentage reductions, and this is exactly the relationship we would expect to find if a regression artifact were operating. Beyond this, we find more evidence to support the regression artifact hypothesis by examining several other variables.

One weakness of the AIR analysis is that only aggregate arrest rates were examined. This raises questions about an ecological fallacy in the AIR finding. To illustrate the principle of an ecological fallacy in this context, suppose four delinquents are each expected to be arrested two times in any given year. By chance, however, let three of the four delinquents have only one arrest in the year preceding a correctional intervention and let the fourth have ten arrests in the same year. In the first year after the intervention, all four delinquents regress to their mean level: two arrests. This gives us the distribution

Preintervention Arrests	Postintervention Arrests	Percentage Change
1	2	-100%
1	2	-100%
1	2	-100%
10	2	80%

Three of the four delinquents are worse off after correctional intervention (although this is due to chance alone), so we might conclude that the intervention was harmful. If we examine only the aggregate statistic, however, we find that the four delinquents have experienced a 38.5% reduction "on the average." This ecological fallacy is set into operation when we attribute characteristics of the group to the individual delinquent.

To avoid ecological fallacy here, we must examine the relationships between preintervention arrest rates and percentage reductions at the individual level. For this, we use the simple model

$$\text{Percentage Reduction} = \text{Constant} \begin{array}{l} + b_1 \text{ (Pre Arrests)} \\ + b_2 \text{ (Age at Release)} \\ + b_3 \text{ (Time Served)} \end{array}$$

We have included Age at Release as an explanatory variable to control (as best as possible) for maturation. Younger than average delinquents are expected to have higher than average postintervention arrest rates and, thus, lower than average percentage reductions. We have included Time Served in programs or institutions as an explanatory variable because, in the AIR report, the major finding is attributed to a specific deterrence mechanism. In effect, correctional intervention has deterred each delinquent from future delinquent acts. If this specific deterrence mechanism is plausible, we expect to find a strong positive relationship between the length of time served and the percentage reduction. Other things equal, those delinquents who were incarcerated longest (or who were in program longest) should experience the largest reductions.

The ordinary least-squares solution of this model is

$$\text{Percentage Reduction} = \begin{array}{l} -269.13 \\ + 8.82 \text{ Preintervention Arrests} \\ + 1.18 \text{ Age at Release} \\ - .15 \text{ Time Served} \end{array}$$

All coefficients are statistically significant at the .05 level except the coefficient for Time Served.[5] The relationship between Age at Release and the percentage reduction is as expected: the older the delinquent, the larger the percentage reduction. We can simplify the model by substituting the mean Age at Release. This gives us

$$\text{Percentage Reduction} = \begin{array}{l} -37.8 \\ + 8.82 \text{ Preintervention Arrests} \\ - .15 \text{ Time Served} \end{array}$$

Here we see a strong relationship between the number of preintervention arrests and the percentage reduction of a delinquent. If a delinquent has only one arrest in the year preceding the correctional intervention, we expect a -29.9% reduction (or a 29.9% increase) on the average. If a delinquent has five preintervention arrests, we expect only a 5.4% reduction and if a delinquent has 15 preintervention arrests, we expect a 93.6% reduction on the average. Of course, older delinquents are expected to have slightly larger reductions whereas younger delinquents are expected to have slightly smaller reductions. Nevertheless, the most important explanatory variable is the number of arrests experienced in the year preceding correctional intervention.

The most surprising result here may be that there is no relationship whatsoever between the length of time served in programs and institutions and subsequent delinquency. This tends not to support the specific deterrence mechanism cited in the AIR report as the basis for the major finding. The AIR finding has a certain common-sense appeal, we suspect, because it can easily be explained in terms of a specific deterrence mechanism. In our reanalysis, however, we have found no unambiguous evidence of an effect nor of any specific deterrence phenomenon.

CONCLUSION: MORE ADVICE
FOR THE TRAPPED ADMINISTRATOR

We have described how a regression artifact can give a delinquency intervention program the appearance of effectiveness. We do not and cannot categorically state that the artifact caused the *entire* suppression effect reported by AIR or even a substantial part of it. However, we *do* state categorically that a regression artifact is a reasonable and viable alternative hypothesis for the effect reported by AIR. Using the AIR data, we have demonstrated that the regression artifact hypothesis cannot be ruled out.

Indirectly, we have demonstrated the practical problems of controlling this threat. In the AIR report, Murray et al. (1978) undoubtedly felt that regression to the mean could be "controlled" adequately by excluding the six months of data nearest the time of intervention. But even this "correction" proves inadequate.

An unintended consequence of the debate on this issue is that the set of programs comprising UDIS has not been evaluated. Because the aggregate suppression effect appeared to be a major finding, the AIR report was relatively unconcerned with the individual UDIS programs. This is entirely understandable given the limited budget for the evaluation and the presumed impact of the aggregate suppression effect. (In fact, had AIR concentrated on an evaluation of the UDIS programs, the regression artifact would likely not have been discovered). But UDIS still remains to be evaluated qua UDIS.

As it turned out, the AIR evaluation of UDIS has more to say about delinquency program evaluation generally than about UDIS specifically. Delinquency intervention programs had traditionally been evaluated on the basis of a contrast between experimental and status quo treatments (by some failure criterion). The consistency among these evaluations has led to a conventional wisdom that "nothing works." Using a before/after contrast, however, the AIR report found a substantial treatment effect for all programs and all treatments. In retrospect, it appears that every delinquency intervention program evaluated with a before/after contrast has reported similar effects. The consistency here leads to a new conventional wisdom: "anything works."

The fact that "anything works" should of itself make one dubious of each specific report. And as we have demonstrated with simulation experiments, a substantial before/after effect is expected whenever delinquents are selected for intervention on the basis of their arrest records. For the AIR data specifically, the reported effect is inflated substantially by the uncontrolled threats of mortality and maturation. Although these factors are important, it appears that the greatest portion of the reported effect is due to a classic regression artifact. In a reanalysis of the data, we have shown that the before/after difference for the entire AIR cohort is due largely to a few delinquents with abnormally high arrest rates in the last preintervention year. A classic regression artifact by itself explains why "anything works" when measured on the basis of a before/after contrast.

This purely methodological problem should not rule out before/after measures of program impact, however. First, as we have demonstrated, there are simple procedures for ruling out or controlling a regression artifact in the evaluation of delinquency intervention programs. But second, and more important, the methodological problems posed by before/after measures of program impact are so obscure that only the most sophisticated audiences will question the validity of a reported effect; and even the most sophisticated audiences will disagree to some extent on questions of validity.

Given this reality, before/after effects such as those shown in Figures 1 and 4 offer new hope to the trapped administrator. By reporting program impacts in terms of before/after, the trapped administrator can finally offer funding agencies and legislatures "hard-headed proof" that a delinquency intervention program is effective. To this end, we offer advice to the trapped administrator. By following these rather simple suggestions, any delinquency intervention program can be made to look effective.

(1) *Insist that your program be evaluated with a before/after design.* Put simply, you must choose between quasi-experimental designs where "nothing works" and quasi-experimental designs where "everything works." The choice is yours and it is a clear-cut choice.

Before we continue, we must note that administrators who feel themselves trapped can rightfully blame social scientists for the predicament. Although we social scientists always hedge our language enough to obey the letter of the laws of scientific logic, we ordinarily run roughshod over the spirit of the law. When we say that "nothing works," of course, what we really mean is that our scientific tools are pitifully simple and inadequate for the task of measuring such complex and complicated phenomena as program impacts. It is not the program that has failed so much as it is our tools that have failed. We try to repair watches using only hammers and saws, and when we fail, we tend to blame the watch, the manufacturer, or the owner. In a technical sense, we blame no one because we have hedged our language. Technicalities aside, however, we do not take the blame on ourselves when it appears that "nothing works." Fortunately, we have now arrived at a point where no one need take the blame. Our advice to the trapped administrator continues.

(2) *Take advantage of mortality.* Before/after contrasts have a built-in advantage in mortality. As a rule, the more incorrigible delinquents in your program will spend less time on the streets during postintervention and, thus, will contribute little to the postintervention arrest rate of their cohort. When one of your incorrigibles commits a new offense, is arrested, and sent to an institution, he cannot easily be arrested again. In the AIR evaluation of UDIS, for example, only 29% of the delinquents were free for one postintervention year. These were by and large the "best" delinquents of the cohort. If all of the delinquents in your program are used in the preintervention measure, but only the "best" are used in the postintervention measure, your before/after contrast will be substantially inflated.

(3) *Take advantage of maturation.* There are a number of ways to do this. If you are able to select the delinquents who enter your program, for example, select only the oldest delinquents. This will enhance the before/after contrast at little cost to you. As a general rule, the older the delinquent, the lower the post-intervention arrest rate. For the same reason, keep your delinquents in-program as long as possible. Finally, follow-up your delinquents for as long as possible after they exit your program. Remember that throughout the postintervention period, these delinquents are growing older and their rates of arrest are growing smaller. A two-year follow-up will ordinarily give you a lower postintervention arrest rate than a one-year follow-up.

There is a related point here. Due to maturation, you will want to use as short a preintervention period as possible when you estimate the before/after effect. Ideally, using only the last preintervention month, you will maximize the before/after difference. Using only the last preintervention month might unfortunately raise eyebrows. Whatever you do, be aware that the preintervention statistic for the group will always be nonstationary. This means that a six-month preinter-vention-rate estimate will be higher than a twelve-month estimate, a twelve-month estimate will be higher than an 18-month estimate, and so forth.

(4) *Take advantage of regression.* The size of the before/after measure of program impact, when a program has no impact whatsoever, will depend on the preintervention arrest rate. The higher this rate, the greater the percentage reduction you can expect. Talk to juvenile court judges. Tell them to send you only the "worst" delinquents of all. The percentage reduction for your program will be highest when you deal with only the "worst" delinquents. Judges will be amazed by the performance of your program, but their amazement will increase sub-stantially when they see that you are dealing only with those delinquents for whom all other interventions have failed.

Related to this point, you should make it your business to know who the "worst" delinquents are. Design a record-keeping system for this. Remember that the "worst" delinquents will deliver the greatest percentage reductions to your program. If you spend more money on these delinquents, your program will appear to be more cost effective than alternative programs. Funding agencies may decide to give you more money because you have demonstrated that you know how to spend money effectively.

Finally, resist the temptation to expand the scope of your program. Stay away from marginal delinquents or from delinquents who, on the basis of their records, appear to be marginal. Turn back to Table 1 and you will see that those delinquents who were arrested only one, two, or three times in the last preintervention year experienced the lowest percentage reductions of all. Due to regression alone, these delinquents who appear to be marginal may destroy the substantial before/after reduction you have worked so hard to establish. *These delinquents are actually expected to have percentage increases in arrest rates from pre- to postintervention.* Of course, if you deal only with these apparently marginal delinquents, a before/after contrast will make it seem that your program is somehow making these delinquents *more* delinquent than they were prior to entering your program.

We offer this advice reluctantly and, we admit, with tongues-in-cheeks. It is sometimes a fact of life that in the areas of delinquency program administration and delinquency research, careers are made and undone on the basis of "hard-headed proof" that a program is effective. But this should not be so. There should be no such thing as a trapped administrator who would need advice from cynical researchers. Although the former advice was offered in a humorous sense only, we can offer this advice in all seriousness. First, when social scientists tell you that your program has no effect whatsoever (or that "nothing works"), be skeptical. Second, when social scientists tell you that your program has a miraculous effect (or that "anything works"), be skeptical. Above all, distrust simple answers to questions that are not simple. Delinquency and delinquency-program impacts are complex and complicated phenomenon that probably cannot be monitored effectively in terms of a single, simple indicator.

NOTES

1. The AIR report is undoubtedly one of the most widely publicized delinquency research projects of the last few years. Summaries of the AIR evaluation of UDIS have been headlined in the Chicago *Tribune* and *Sun-Times,* the *New York Times,* the *Washington Post,* and many other general circulation media; in professional journals such as *Criminal Justice Newsletter* and *Corrections;* the senior author of the AIR report, Dr. Charles A. Murray, has summarized the findings of the UDIS evaluation in testimony before the U.S. Senate Subcommittee on Juvenile Delinquency.

2. We call the statistic in Figure 1 "arrests" only for semantic simplicity. In fact, these data are "police contacts" that appear to be more sensitive than actual arrests. One young man in the AIR sample accumulated over 50 police contacts in a relatively short period of time. It would be unlikely that an adult could accumulate so many arrests in the same period of time.

3. Our discussion here assumes the simplest Poisson process, one that is stationary in time and homogeneous across the population. See Feller (1968) for a lucid introduction to Poisson processes. Although we deal only with the simplest Poisson process, our argument is easily generalized to nonstationary or heterogeneous processes. See Coleman (1964) for a discussion of these more complicated processes.

4. Annual arrest rates here are estimated from the daily arrest rates. Only 141 delinquents were observed for a full preintervention year. Because we use daily rates, our estimate of the before/after effect is lower than the estimate cited in the AIR report: 54% versus 73%. See McCleary et al. (1978) for a discussion of this issue and a critique of the arithmetic in the AIR report.

5. The t-statistics for the four parameters are – 2.34, 3.46, 2.00, and – .10; R^2 = .071. See McCleary et al. (1978) for alternative models. The basic relationship between preintervention arrests and percentage reductions appears in all of the models we have examined.

REFERENCES

CAMPBELL, D. T. and A. ERLEBACHER (1970) "How regression artifacts in quasi-experimental evaluations can mistakenly make compensatory education look harmful," in J. Hellmuth (ed.) The Disadvantaged Child Vol. 3 New York: Brunner-Mazel.

CAMPBELL, D. T. and H. L. ROSS (1968) "The Connecticut crackdown on speeding: time series data in quasi-experimental analysis." Law and Society Review, 3.

CAMPBELL, D. T. and J. C. STANLEY (1966) Experimental and Quasi-experimental Designs for Research. Chicago: Rand-McNally.

COLEMAN, J. S. (1964) Introduction to Mathematical Sociology. New York: Free Press.

EMPEY, L. T. and M. T. ERICKSON (1972) The Provo Experiment. Chicago: Aldine.

EMPEY, L. T. and S. G. LUBECK (1971) The Silverlake Experiment. Chicago: Aldine.

FELLER, W. (1968) An Introduction to Probability Theory and Its Applications, Volume I. New York: John Wiley.

GLASS, G. V., V. L. WILLSON, and J. M. GOTTMAN (1975) Design and Analysis of Time-Series Experiments. Boulder: Colorado Associated University Press.

GORDON, A. C., D. McDOWALL, M. D. MALTZ, and R. McCLEARY (1978) "Evaluating a Delinquency Intervention Program: A Comment." Criminal Justice Newsletter, 9.

McCLEARY, R., A. C. GORDON, D. McDOWALL, and M. D. MALTZ (1978) A Reanalysis of UDIS. Chicago: Center for Research in Criminal Justice, University of Illinois.

MALTZ, M. D. and S. P. POLLOCK (1978) "Artificial inflation of a Poisson rate by a 'selection effect'." Chicago: Center for Research in Criminal Justice, University of Illinois.

MURRAY, C. A. (1978) "Reply from the Principal Author." Criminal Justice Newsletter, 9.

——— D. THOMPSON, and C. B. ISRAEL (1978) UDIS: Deinstitutionalizing the Chronic Juvenile Offender. Washington, DC: American Institutes for Research.

35

The Suppression Effect and the Institutionalization of Children

Charles A. Murray and Louis A. Cox, Jr.

The regression analysis conducted by McCleary *et al.* takes 1-A/B as the dependent variable and uses B as the independent variable for testing the existence of a regression artifact. In doing so—in interpreting the meaning of the regression coefficient and in estimating statistical significance—McCleary *et al.* assume that, given two random variables A and B, the expected correlation of B and A/B is zero. This assumption is incorrect. The expected value of the correlation is negative; the more constrained the range of values permitted A and B, the larger the expected negative correlation. Given the ranges in the present instance, the expected value of the correlation $\rho(A,A/B)$ of a randomly distributed A and B is approximately –.55. Ironically, the observed correlation of B and A/B in our data is only –.15, much less than would be expected if B and A really behaved as independent random variables. Without pursuing that point here, we simply observe that the regression analysis as presented cannot be interpreted at all, let alone interpreted as it is in the McCleary paper.

The second error involves the choice of sample. The analysis uses a reduced sample, "excluding from the analysis 157 delinquents who had no postintervention arrests." This is said to be justifed because it helps "control somewhat the threat of mortality" (p. 28). The 157 represent 43% of the original sample—a rather sizeable proportion to be "selected out of" the analysis. In fact, this drastic surgery on the sample maximizes mortality rather than controlling it. But the main point is the mechanics of what is being done:

- The phenomenon of interest is the relationship between B and 1-A/B.
- The 43% of the sample that have "0" as the value of A are excluded.
- It is then found that (1-A/B) tends to be small when B is small.
- Q.E.D.

Authors' Note: The following is excerpted from the authors' forthcoming book, *Beyond Probation* (Beverly Hills, CA: Sage, 1979). It was written to stand on its own. But because the excerpt is accompanied by a critique of the original UDIS evaluation, we have attempted to ease the task of comparing points by italicizing those paragraphs that bear directly on issues raised by McCleary *et al.*

We are unable to deal in so simple a fashion with the McCleary article's major empirical analysis. It contains two errors that go well beyond the ordinary bounds of scientific license in choice of method. These errors make the analysis uninterpretable.

The passage in question concerns the relationship between prior arrests and the size of the suppression effect (defined as 1 minus the ratio of "after" arrests to "before" arrests, calculated over comparable units of time—or 1-A/B, for short).

From Charles A. Murray and Louis A. Cox, Jr., "The Suppression Effect and the Institutionalization of Children." Unpublished manuscript, 1978.

We hope that the reader anticipates us: having excluded 0 as a permissable value of A, it is guaranteed that A/B can be no smaller than .33 when B = 3, .5 when B = 2, and 1 when B = 1. The procedure hyperbolically inflates the relationship of B to A/B as the values of B become smaller—the very relationship that the analysis is supposed to test.

Predictably, we have an assortment of other bones to pick with the paper by McCleary *et al.* Some are methodological, some are questions of interpretation, some are what we see as distortions of fact. But these are the ordinary, arguable stuff of scientific controversy. The two errors cited above are something less than that.

The analyses presented in the following paper were funded in part by the Illinois Law Enforcement Commission (contract no. 71-NI-9903) and by the National Institute for Juvenile Justice and Delinquency Prevention (Grant 78-JN-AX-0014). The points of view presented here are not necessarily those of the funding agencies.

THE SUPPRESSION EFFECT

What defines "success" when measuring recidivism in a delinquency program? Historically, it has been defined as *cessation:* the extent to which the delinquent's incidence of offensive behavior approached zero after release. The most common measures have been dichotomous ones, asking whether the youth recidivated at all, by whatever measure of recidivism was being employed. This study uses an alternative approach. We compare behavior prior to the correctional program with behavior following the correctional program. The question is not whether delinquency is "cured," but whether things get better. Put bluntly, we are primarily concerned with reductions in the number of crimes inflicted on the community, not with unblemished reclamation of individual delinquents.

The Sample

In this paper we limit the discussion to institutionalization, the archtypical form of juvenile corrections. Other correctional interventions were examined in the full study. A total of 421 Chicago youths were committed directly to the Department of Corrections (DOC) institutions during the period 1 October 1974 through 30 June 1976. Data from at least one of the three principal sources (police, courts, institutions) were incomplete for 43 subjects. Twelve subjects had gone directly from DOC to another program, and thus could not be treated as part of the pure "DOC" sample. This left 366 delinquents for whom complete data were available, and who had DOC as their only correctional intervention. When the observations ceased at the end of February 1978, 49 of the 366 (13.4%) had not yet been released for any period. The sample is thus composed of 317 delinquents.

TABLE 1
Basic Career Variables for the DOC Sample (n = 317)

Variable	Mean	Standard Deviation
	(in years)	
Date of birth	1959.7	.98
Age at onset	12.2	1.86
Total arrests prior to DOC	13.6	6.96
Age at commitment	15.8	.93
Time served before first parole	.9	.47
Follow-up period	1.4	.82

The typical member of this sample was first arrested a few months after reaching age twelve, and then ran up a dozen more arrests before going to DOC. More than 60% of these arrests were for some type of theft or for violence-related offenses (assault, battery, homicide or attempted homicide, rape or other sexual assault). Another 32.4% of the arrests were for damage, trespass, or possession of controlled substances or stolen property. Only 7.4% of the offenses involved status or traffic offenses.

All of these arrests occurred before the delinquent encountered any correctional intervention other than supervision or probation. The typical member of the sample was in a DOC institution shortly before reaching age sixteen, and served an average of 10.8 months before obtaining parole. We observed the subject for an average of almost 17 months following release. The exact figures are given in Table 1.

Estimates of the Suppression Effect

In the year before they were sent to DOC, the 317 DOC subjects were arrested an average of 6.3 times. After they were released, these same 317 boys were arrested an average of 2.9 times during an average follow-up period of 16.8 months on the street. The second figure is much lower than the first—67% lower, when the postrelease figure is converted to an annual rate. And this, in elementary form, is the phenomenon we have called the suppression effect. It can be shown graphically in Figure 1, which plots arrest incidence in the two years preceding and following intervention.

"Suppression effect" refers to the phenomenon of the drop, not to any specific percentage magnitude attached to the drop. For convenience, we do specify a definition. The suppression effect for an individual is obtained from a linear regression of a monthly time series running from 12 months prior to intervention through all months of postrelease street time up to a maximum of two years. In-program months are omitted. Thus, a subject observed for two years after release would have 36 observations; a subject observed for two months, then

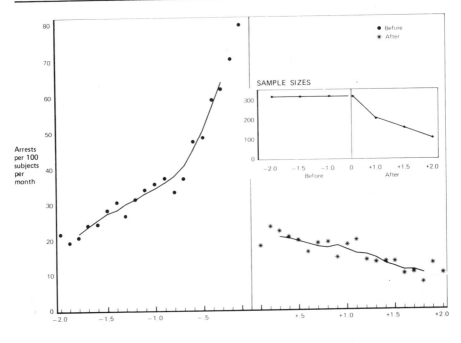

The two years preceding institutionalization   The two years following discharge or parole

Note: Trendline is a half-year moving agerage.

Figure 1: Arrests in the Two Years Before and After Institutionalization

reincarcerated, would have 14 observations. The equation producing the regression coefficient is:

$$\text{ARRESTS} = B_0 + B_1 \text{ INTERVENTION},$$

where

Arrests is the number of arrests in the month in question, B_0 is a constant, B_1 is the regression coefficient, and

INTERVENTION is a dummy variable coded "0" for preintervention months and "1" for postintervention months.

The suppression effect is B_1/B_0. Computed over the whole population, the regression results are

$$\text{ARRESTS} = +.525 \text{ (constant)} -.359 \text{ INTERVENTION}$$

and the aggregate suppression effect is thus

$$-.359/.525 = -.684$$

It is a large drop. But if only the traditional, zero-based measures of recidivism had been used, the reduction would have gone unnoticed, and institutionalization in Illinois would have been pronounced the failure that we all "know" institutionalization to be. If the criterion of failure is one arrest in the year following release, fully 82.3% of the DOC sample would be considered failures. Yet the aggregate number of arrests dropped by about two-thirds.

Are these apparently contradictory results the product of some illusion in the data, or do they indicate that most of our traditional measures have been missing the point? Here we limit the discussion to the three counterarguments emphasized in the critique by McCleary *et al:* mortality in the sample, maturation, and the regression artifact.

MORTALITY

As noted, 49 of the 366 subjects for whom complete data could be obtained had not yet been released when observations ended—13.4% of the sample. To what extent is it plausible that these 49 are the most recidivistic, most intractable youth, and that they would have increased the aggregate postrelease rate had they been given a chance?

The distinctions between the released and unreleased sets are minimal. The unreleased 49 had *fewer* prior offenses than the released 317 (11.9 compared to 13.6). The types of offenses were also indistinguishable, with one predictable exception: The unreleased group had a higher proportion of youth with homicide charges as the instant offense (17 of 49, compared to 9 of 317). Public pressure prompted DOC to hold many of these juveniles until the maximum age of release. Nor were we able to find predictors of high recidivism that might be associated with the unreleased group. The correlation between time in the institution and rate of subsequent arrests was -.016, to take the most obvious example.

The simplest, least ambiguous way to deal with the issue is to break the sample into cohorts with markedly different mortality rates. The two cohorts are subjects who went into DOC during the first year of observation (10/1/74 – 9/30/75), and those who entered during the final nine months of the observation period (10/1/75 – 6/30/76). The first cohort had more time to get out, and there were correspondingly fewer missing delinquents. To be precise:

	Aggregate n	% Not Released	Net n	Aggregate Suppression effect
10/47-9/75 Cohort	248	7.7	229	.686
10/75-6/76 Cohort	118	25.4	88	.673

The difference in mortality is large; the difference in suppression effect is .013, statistically insignificant, and in the wrong direction for a mortality artifact. More to the point, the mortality in the first cohort is so low that even extreme assumptions about the residual incarcerated youth make little difference.

Suppose, for example, that the 7.7% had gotten out and all showed zero sup-pression effect—were arrested at the same rate as before incarceration. Simu-lated data to this effect reduce the estimate of the suppression effect for the first cohort by about one percentage point, and so on through successively worse worst-case assumptions, whether for the first cohort or for the combined sample. Even hypotheses of future mayhem by the unreleased fraction fail to shake the degree of estimated sample suppression by more than a few percentage points.

GROWING OUT OF IT: THE ROLE OF MATURATION

Maturation is widely accepted as an explanation of delinquent behavior. The popular argument is that delinquency is largely a developmental phenomenon, increasing in the early phases of adolescence and falling off thereafter. "The best cure for delinquency is growing up," is one catch-phrase in use. What do the data reveal about maturation and the chronic offender?

The implication of the maturation hypothesis is that *samples of chronic delin-quents of roughly the same age or point in career will behave roughly in the same way, whether or not they have undergone intervention.* And it is this implication that gives us leverage in investigating the degree to which maturation can account for the suppression effect. Some delinquents go into institutions at age 15; some come out at age 15; some are institutionalized after 5 offenses; some after 10 or 20 or 30. Whether maturation is defined by physical age or point in career, the juvenile justice system provides variance in abundance. We take up each defini-tion in turn.

Chronological Maturation

The first maturation model takes chronological age as the agent of matura-tion. The dependent variable in the regression equation is number of arrests. The two independent variables are the subject's age in years at the beginning of the month, and whether the month occurred before intervention (coded as 0) or following release (coded as 1). The results (based on the monthly observations) were as follows:

ARRESTS = +.552 (constant) –.355 INTERVENTION –.002 AGE
std. error: .020   .007

When intervention was taken into account, the relationship of age to arrests was insignificant, statistically and substantively. But a problem of interpretation remains: the correlation between the intervention dummy variable and age was a high .751; a stable interaction term of age and intervention cannot be estimated. Why not ascribe the cause to maturation. For, entered *alone* in the regression equation, age shows the important relationship to arrests that has always been assumed.

The problem is not intractable. We move back from the summary statistics of the regression model to the raw data, and sort the arrests into two piles: arrests occurring prior to institutionalization and arrests occuring after release. We then plot each set against age-at-time-of-arrest as the X-axis. Figure 2 presents the data, and they provide a dramatic plot. Visually, a "maturation effect" does appear to exist, but in a radically different form than the bell-shaped curve implied by the conventional argument. *Arrests with age* throughout *the preintervention period; they decrease slightly with age in the postintervention period. And, most conspicuously, arrest rates for postintervention delinquents are much lower than for preintervention delinquents of the same age. The magnitude of the suppression effect does increase with age, as the conventional wisdom predicts— not for the conventional reason (arrest incidence starts to fall when the delinquent passes an inflection point) but because arrest rates continued to rise at all ages, unless institutionalization occurred.* This unbroken rise remains even when arrests during the last 6 months, or year, or even 18 months prior to institutionalization are ignored.

Maturation as Point-in-Career

Maturation can also be viewed as a career phenomenon. As noted, the average number of preintervention arrests was 13.6. Perhaps the juvenile justice system picked them for institutionalization at just the time that the delinquent disease had run its course.

The unit of observation (month) and the sample (the 317 institutionalized delinquents) remain unchanged. Intervention is one of the independent variables; the other is cumulative number of offenses prior to the month in question. The results are as follows:

	Std. Error
ARRESTS = +.373 (constant)	——
–.311 INTERVENTION	.024
+.022 PRIOR OFFENSES	.002
–.014 INTERACTION TERM	.002

The results again indicate that the "maturation" element—represented by number of prior offenses in this case—exerts no independent downward pull on the arrest rate. But the interaction of intervention and prior offenses does show a negative effect.

To translate the size of this negative effect into more readily interpretable form, we divide the sample into four groups, based on number of arrests in the two years prior to intervention: 0 to 5, 6 to 10, 11 to 15, and 16 to 20. This encompasses all but 7 of the 317 members of the DOC sample. The results are shown in Table 2.

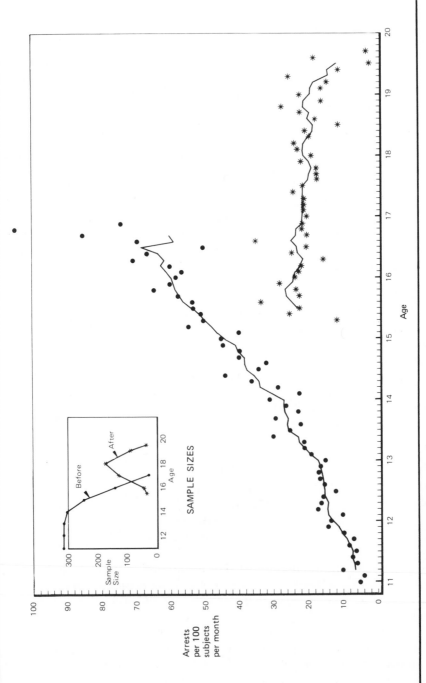

Figure 2: Arrests and Age, Before and After Institutionalization

TABLE 2
Effect of Prior Offenses on the Suppression Effect

Total arrests, 2 years prior to commitment	N	Total arrests, year prior	Total arrests, postrelease	No. of person years of street time, post-release	Reduction
1-5	70	194	135	111.04	−.561
6-10	119	653	303	168.73	−.673
11-15	91	727	303	118.37	−.680
16-20	30	309	126	37.43	−.673
Overall	317*	1,990	906	443.49	−.675

*Seven members of the sample had more than 20 arrests in the two years prior, and are not included in the subgroups.

For youths with five or fewer arrests in the two years before commitment, the reduction was noticeably lower: .561. But, surprisingly, the reductions among the other three groups were nearly identical, even though the range of preintervention offenses went from 6 to 20. This is reflected in the bivariate correlation of arrests in the year prior with percent reduction as computed by individual: .154. The percent reduction is nearly independent of prior arrests, even though "it shouldn't be," given the strong natural relationship between a ratio and its denominator (see introductory note). That arrests dropped 56 percent even among youth with only 5 or fewer arrests in the two years prior is in many respects more startling than the evenness of the reductions among the other groups shown in Table 2.

IT ONLY LOOKS THAT WAY: THE REGRESSION ARTIFACT

The phenomenon known as the regression artifact is essentially a natural drop (or rise) from an abnormally high (or low) state of affairs. This change is caused only by the laws of probability. In the context of the suppression effect, the logic of the regression artifact requires three strong assumptions. These are (1) that delinquents have a certain natural crime rate that remains constant throughout the delinquent career; (2) that short-run fluctuations occur about the long-run natural rate; and (3) that only those delinquents are selected for intervention who have just gone through a fluctuation raising their instantaneous crime rate well above its natural level.

These three assumptions satisfactorily explain a reduction. But they do not fully explain the observed empirical base shown in Figure 1. Operating only under the three assumptions listed above, the regression artifact argument predicts a high constant preintervention aggregate crime rate, followed by a lower, constant postintervention aggregate crime rate (e.g., see the accompanying article by McCleary *et al.* for application to a Poisson process). *But the actual data show rising and falling crime rates instead.*

The regression artifact can explain the rise and fall in the data only if the argument is reinforced by a fourth assumption. In the McCleary *et al.* discussion, the fourth assumption was that *judges estimate individual crime rates from a random amount of past behavior.* Sometimes a judge will base his decision on what the delinquent has done during the past two years; sometimes on his behavior during the past two months; and *this choice of period will be unrelated to any characteristics of the arrest pattern over that period.*

Accept for the sake of argument that the fourth assumption can be sustained by examining judges' behavior (an assumption that is nearly libelous of the juvenile justice system). The problem then becomes how to demonstrate that delinquents have a natural crime rate which remains constant throughout the delinquent career, in the face of the evidence in Figure 2, showing increasing arrests with age throughout the preintervention period.

We run into a classic dilemma. We can at least partly explain away the preintervention curve in Figure 2 if we use only the first three assumptions—we posit that selection acts as a perfect screen, giving the illusion that arrest rates rise with age. Or, we can explain the preintervention curve in Figure 1 if we add the fourth assumption. But by adding the fourth assumption, we can no longer explain away Figure 2. *Both* preintervention curves cannot be explained with an internally consistent set of assumptions. *The delinquents in our sample do not conform to the demand of the regression artifact: their rates of arrests increased over time, rather than fluctuating around a constant mean.*

The foregoing discussion has rested on the technical attributes of a regression artifact. Having followed through that analysis, it is still apparent that some artificiality in arrest rate exists in the few months immediately preceding institutionalization—an instant offense had to occur at about that time, else institutionalization would not have. But there is a simple, very powerful test for dealing with that problem: delete the potentially contaminating observations from the sample. If the deletion of two months is unsatisfactory, delete four. If four is not enough, delete half a year. If half a year is not enough, delete a full year. Whatever, the suppression effect remains large. Taking (absurdly) extreme cases, these are the results when the half year or year prior to intervention are deleted from the monthly data base:

Ignoring the 6 months prior to intervention (Comparison: Postrelease months with the 7th through 12th months prior to intervention):

ARRESTS = +.392 (constant) –.226 INTERVENTION
Suppression effect = –.577

Ignoring a full year prior to intervention (Comparison: Postrelease months with the 13th through 18th months prior to intervention):

ARRESTS = +.313 (constant) –.147 INTERVENTION
Suppression effect = –.470

The reductions are extremely robust, in the face of extreme truncations of the preintervention definition of "career." The characteristic pattern of the delinquent behavior was not a sudden burst of activity out of a low base, but a steadily climbing, multiyear growth in activity.

The implications are intriguing. The analysis persistently indicates that the arrest incidence increases with age, *independently of any bunching effects from selection.* And, if that is so, then *our procedure for computing the suppression effect has significantly understated its magnitude, because it is based on arrest rates considerably lower than the "real" rate that the delinquent took into the institution.* In view of the concern that led us to the analysis (that the suppression effect is some sort of statistical mirage), it is ironic that the outcome points to the possibility that we are underestimating it. But in the absence of any indication that the arrest rate would flatten without intervention, that is where the logic of the problem leads. That logic suggests that the chronic delinquent may not naturally quit being delinquent—that the apt analogy with delinquency is not with the things that adolescents grow out of, but with behaviors that are reinforcing, like making money or winning status.

These speculations take us into topics that are beyond the scope of the study. For our purposes, it is enough to suggest that the data on maturation and their implications are not inexplicable. One may at least entertain the possibility that committing crimes can make sense, and that the chronic delinquent accepts that proposition until the criminal justice system shows him another side of the argument.

V

UNANTICIPATED FINDINGS

Every program or other intervention is planned to have some particular effect or set of effects. These anticipated effects are, quite naturally, the focus of efforts to evaluate the intervention. It is, of course, widely recognized that interventions can have unanticipated consequences, and that these consequences may be either good or bad. There have been regular warnings over the years that evaluators should be alert to unanticipated as well as anticipated outcomes. The warning is appropriate; but the problem is to determine how one can be alert for something unanticipated and for which no provisions for assessment can sensibly be made. The following papers provide no definitive answers, but they are provocative—they stimulate two additional sets of questions worth pondering. First, *could* these unanticipated findings have been anticipated, or might we even ask, *should* they have been anticipated? Is it possible that more systematic prior analysis or more rigorous theory would have suggested the likelihood of what did, in fact, happen? Second, how is it that these unanticipated findings were discovered? Is it largely happenstance, or can investigators develop strategies which will increase substantially their chances of finding things they weren't looking for? One final note that has aroused our curiosity: All these reports of unanticipated findings involve unanticipated, undesirable outcomes. Perhaps we were unwittingly selective in our search. Or is it simply in the nature of things that the good outcomes are more easily anticipated? Many undesirable outcomes seem delayed in their effects, perhaps of necessity, e.g., any undesirable effects of losing weight could not occur until weight was lost.

It is not invariably the case that the interests of researchers, of service delivery personnel, and of clients coincide. To begin with, it must be recognized that the interests of researchers tend very much to lie in the direction of generating research funds and, ultimately, publications, and such interests may be overriding in the making of decisions about program management. When there are conflicts of interest, the results may include outcomes that were neither anticipated nor desired. Fry's work details the developments in a project to do research on a drug abuse program, alleging that the events indicate that the research grant better served the interests of research professionals than those meant to be served by the project. Fry believes that there may be a fundamental and unresolvable conflict between the interests of professionals and clients in self-help programs when large research grants are involved.

36

Research Grants and Self-Help Programs
What Price Knowledge?

Lincoln J. Fry

Based upon 14 months of participant observation in a patient-run drug rehabilitation program located in a mental hospital, this paper is concerned with the impact of certain kinds of funding arrangements upon self-help programs. The findings reported support Cloward and Piven's (1974) contention that large research grants reflect the interests of professionals, not those of the groups that the projects are supposed to serve. Grant-funded activities eventually coopted a self-help program's leadership, and research infringed upon program activity. Funding priorities alienated the institution's treatment staff and contributed to competition between the self-help program and the other drug units located in the institution's treatment complex. The implication of this case study is that self-help programs are not likely to maintain their organizational integrity when implemented by the use of large research grants.

Cloward and Piven (1974) maintain that large scale funding of research connected with social service ventures has resulted in the development of programs which further the careers of various classes of professionals but which provide only meager benefits to the disadvantaged groups the programs purport to serve. From Cloward and Piven's perspective, large scale funding creates bureaucratic structures which become the domain of professionals and their special knowledge, a process the authors define as "the con-

* The comments and suggestions provided by Judith Lorber and Mary E. W. Goss on an earlier version of this paper are gratefully acknowledged.

solidation of expertise.'' Professionals are able to extend and consolidate public sector resources and then distribute them to clients in such a way that the clients, the theoretical beneficiaries, become isolated and left without the collective leverage they should have from the positions they occupy within organizational structures. Benefits accrue primarily to professionals, while rewards are dispersed to individual clients, not to the groups they represent. Elsewhere, Piven (1974) describes this process as one where collaboration between professionals and indigenous non-professionals turns into co-optation. Programs begin to be developed in such a manner that they will lend themselves to research and evaluation. Researchers claim that they are the ones who can best get the money to implement programs, and at the same time, insist that programs be derived from their own theoretical frameworks. Because of this, funding proposals increasingly reflect the concerns and interests of research professionals.

The present report describes a patient-run drug rehabilitation program located in a California mental hospital. The program became fully operational upon receipt of a research grant. Events that occurred before and after receipt of the grant are examined in order to assess the impact of research funds on the self-help program. Did this funding, as Cloward and Piven (1974) maintain, benefit mainly the professional personnel? How did the distribution of rewards to the client population affect this self-help program and its members? How did this funding affect other groups in the hospital environment? Finally, how did involvement with this program affect the research?

Related Approaches and Studies

The extent to which Cloward and Piven's (1974) observations can be generalized to other research settings is problematic. Others have also been concerned about the distribution of rewards to client groups and have conceptualized social research as an exchange process (Hessler and New, 1972; Cromwell et al., 1975). From this perspective, successful project completion is seen as dependent upon mutual cooperation between researchers and influential community groups, while the negotiation of an acceptable balance between the respective interests of researchers and subjects is seen as a crucial task. Commenting upon this problem as it relates to evaluation research, Weiss (1975) indicates that co-optation and phoniness will not suffice. Researchers must engage in sustained dialogue and cooperative planning with target groups; indigenous people may not be used merely to front for the study.

The notion of mutual exchange has evolved primarily from urban (Hessler and New, 1972; Cromwell et al., 1975) and evaluation research (Twain et al., 1970; Weiss, 1975). In urban settings subjects are free not to cooperate with survey ventures which offer respondents few inducements. Social service projects may not comply with evaluation efforts because research and project objectives may not be co-extensive, especially when evaluation may not provide favorable assessments of project effectiveness. By way of contrast, Cloward and Piven's (1974) observations were gleaned at the massive program level where they posit a marriage between research and program interests generated by funding considerations. Furthermore, these programs represent expenditures large enough to affect the structures of communities, especially in terms of substantial impacts upon employment opportunities in disadvantaged areas; these programs offer strong individual inducements for cooperation, regardless of the interests of local community groups.

A standard way that rewards for cooperation have been distributed to indigenous people is through their use as paraprofessionals. The social service field has provided numerous reasons for this practice, including the desire to provide therapeutic experiences based on a self-help rationale (Reissman, 1965), to change social service organizations (Cloward and Epstein, 1967), and to change the image of a disadvantaged group (Coser, 1965). As Katan (1973) notes, few empirical studies have dealt with the relationship between professionals and non-professionals in this context. The available evidence suggests that professionals will tend to channel indigenous workers into conforming roles and relegate them to routine assignments, thus allowing professionals to concentrate on their own tasks. Further, Berman and Haug (1973) identify a major dilemma for paraprofessionals, one which impinges on group versus individual differences. Upward mobility within an agency may weaken the bonds between paraprofessionals and the client community. Clients may resent the indigenous worker's advancement and upwardly mobile paraprofessionals can lose a sense of identification with clients; Bullington et al. (1969), document this phenomenon in a community-based drug abuse treatment program, calling it the "purchase of middle class conformity."

Nevertheless, Weiss (1975) argues that it may be good policy to hire local people in certain communities that are otherwise closed to research access because of militancy. And Moffett et al. (1974) stress that, because professionals lack proper preparation in drug abuse treatment, the use of ex-addict paraprofessionals should be expanded and refined in community treatment programs. Yet in a nationwide study of alternative community treatment programs (mainly drug abuse ventures), Holleb and Abrams (1975) find that a pattern of pre-professionalism rather than paraprofessionalism had developed. Several years after they started operation, these programs began to look more professional and actually to resemble the service organizations they had initially opposed, especially in terms of staffing. One indicator of this change was the replacement of indigenous paraprofessionals by persons who were working in the programs in preparation for return to graduate school.

This discussion suggests that contextual differences may be crucial in determining who benefits more from grant funding of research connected with social service projects and that benefits may be short-lived in any case. Yet in a concrete instance there remains the problem of attempting to sift through a maze of interrelated factors, including the rewards, inducements, and constraints placed upon

the various groups who interact within grant-funded project environments, as well as the problem of how to operationalize, measure, and weigh group versus individual considerations. The approach taken here is to attempt to document historically some effects of funding within a single restricted environment, based on facts gained from participant observation in that environment. Hopefully, this case study will contribute to a better understanding of the way research funding may affect various groups involved in similar arrangements.

BACKGROUND AND SETTING

Known as "The Family," the self-help program had been in existence for two years when the study began. It was founded by professionals who had been connected with a similar program in northern California. Occupying one entire forty bed unit, the Family was an integral part of the drug abuse treatment complex of a large state mental hospital in California. A high percentage of the hospital's drug abuse patients came from a large metropolitan center located in an adjacent county and the bulk of the remainder from the encompassing county. Most entered the hospital involuntarily, as an alternative to criminal justice processing.[1] Addicts fresh off the street entered a detoxification unit and most left the hospital from there, usually in a period of from five to seven days. Those adults who chose to receive further treatment had the option of entering a staff-run 90-day program or the Family. There were two Family programs, one for adults and another for adolescents. Drug abusers under 18 were automatically assigned to the adolescent Family program if they remained in the hospital. Neither Family was designed to accommodate large numbers of patients; the adolescent program averaged 23 members and the adult Family averaged 28 members over the course of the study, while the range in the other adult program for the same period was between 18 and 40 members.

The Family did its own recruitment through paraprofessional work in the hospital's short-term and detoxification units, where recruits were supposedly selected on the basis of their motivation to enter a drug-free life. Recruits were thoroughly screened by Family members, which meant they were subjected to intensive interviews by selected Family members. Once accepted as initiates, men had their heads shaved and women were not allowed to wear makeup or jewelry, while both sexes wore state-provided clothing. Upon acceptance, they entered a program theoretically based upon voluntary membership participation. It contained six phases, including the initiate (candidacy) and five hierarchical membership phases, which collectively constituted a program of about one year in length. Membership phases contained increasing levels of responsibility with two alternatives available at the upper end. Senior members were either chosen as members of the governing body (elders) or routed into a "re-entry into society" phase. All program decisions supposedly emanated from the elder body.

The first member had completed the program after one year, but the total number of Family graduates had only reached six when the research began.[2] The early period had been one of turmoil while the Family attempted to structure itself internally into an effective treatment vehicle. Furthermore, several members had chosen not to graduate even though they had completed the program and were eligible to do so. They had decided to wait until the hospital received the grant funds for which it had applied and from which they expected to benefit.

The Research Grant and the Qualitative Study

The grant funds were intended to provide employment and halfway houses for ex-drug addicts, as well as to support research on drug abuse and its treatment, including the Family as a treatment modality. The proposed participants in the research were a university affiliated group of investigators. Research components initially included a psychophysiological laboratory for the measurement of physiological responses to treatment activity and an extensive survey project designed to provide longitudinal analysis of the effect of treatment. However, a site visit conducted by the funding source prior to receipt of the research funds resulted in recommendations that highlighted the need for some qualitative assessment of the Family program as well. As a result, the study described below was added in order that the project could begin. While the research population theoretically consisted of all the patients in the hospital's drug treatment complex, the Family was in fact the central concern of all the research components funded by the grant.

Qualitative Study

The initial design set up to meet the need for some qualitative assessment of the Family required that two observers, a sociologist and an anthropologist, attach themselves to a cohort of addicts and become socialized into the Family in the same manner as other members. What this participant observation study would require was not clear but became so in the course of forming an agreement with the elder body. The key issue in the negotiation process between the elders and the observers was how much autonomy either party was willing to give up. After the purpose of the study was explained, the elders agreed to allow access to the information the researchers wanted to collect and made assurances that no information would be held sacred. At the same time, they were adament about exercising control over the researchers' conduct within the Family program. The elders demanded the right to socialize the researchers in the same manner as they did other Family members. Thus, in exchange for access, the elders received the following concessions from the observers: (1) the promise of active participation in Family program activity; (2) the acceptance of program discipline; (3) the promise to wear state-provided clothing; and (4) the promise to make a sincere effort to complete the entire program.[3] Whether these were reasonable concessions will be discussed below. The account which follows is primarily concerned with the impact of the grant funds upon the program and the way involvement in this program affected the observational study. The differential effects of the program and institution on patients are described in a separate paper.[4]

IMPACT OF RESEARCH FUNDS AND PROFESSIONAL INVOLVEMENT ON THE PROGRAM

Even before receipt of the grant funds, professionals were of course involved in and with the Family. A professional (an MSW who was also a doctoral candidate in psychology) held the position of elder-advisor and was designated by the institution as the Family program director. The Family also had a full complement of staff, including a physician. Psychiatric technicians were always on duty, as was mandated by law in California. Hospital personnel were required to be physically present in any instance where treatment was delivered regardless of whether they actually delivered treatment. The Family also shared a social worker with the short-term program and the assistant-director of that program periodically held marathons exclusively for Family members. The purpose of those 24-hour events was defined as self-disclosure in depth.

But after the grant was received, the level of professional involvement in the Family became even greater. While the two observers were in the initiate phase, there were three other non-addicts engaged in the socialization process (two psychiatric technicians and the unit social worker). During the same period, the number of addicts in the initiate phase ranged from six to eight. The majority of the Family unit psychiatric technicians were program members, which meant that they had at least completed the initiate phase. They had completed the socialization process prior to the receipt of the grant and none of them were ex-addicts. However, the most significant change in professional involvement was the beginning of negotiation between the Family and the larger research project for research access. While such access had been taken for granted in the grant proposal, Family members resisted being "subjects" until the psychophysiological laboratory study hired the individual who

was considered the charismatic leader of the Family as a research assistant. Then preparation for the extensive laboratory and field research studies began in earnest.

This process was overshadowed by another significant professional eruption which occurred during the several months that the observers were in the initiate phase.[5] In a conflict between treatment and research personnel, a major treatment professional who considered himself to be one of the founders of the Family was discharged from the institution. This event clearly polarized the loyalties of the program members and had lasting effects on the stability of the Family. From that point forward, efforts were continually afoot to move the Family to other locations. During one period, at least four distinct plans were under discussion, each sponsored by a displaced professional who had been attached at one time to the Family program or by someone who remained in the institution but who no longer had official contact with the Family. Eventually these plans became an open issue and one of them became a major source of conflict between the hospital and two county health departments. A major metropolitan newspaper became interested and ran a feature story based upon interviews with Family members, including those still in the program and graduates employed by the grant as paraprofessionals in the hospital, as well as with some graduates who were working in a rival facility sponsored by another neighboring county's health department. The feature story highlighted the views of two groups, namely, those employed to start the rival program, accentuating their claim that they were being used as slave labor, and members still in the Family, emphasizing especially their concern that the hospital program would be closed and the members' treatment disrupted.

The institutional arrangements surrounding the Family were unsettling. Rumors about possible program moves ran rampant among members, while new moving dates to various locations were set month in and month out. The program leadership found it necessary constantly to reassure members that the Family would continue to exist and to try to stop energy from being diverted from program activity. They were worried because the potential program move meant that the funds providing jobs and the halfway houses would be lost. The hospital administration and the university-sponsored research component found it necessary to assure the funding source that the program would remain in the hospital. Eventually a coalition of the Family program, the research component, and the hospital administration began to emerge in order to fight those who sponsored the various program moves—individuals the coalition defined as "pirates." Although these allegiances were shaky and shifted from time to time, in general these factions remained loyal to one another in the face of the threatened program moves.

Historically, the Family's leadership had been resistant to all research activity. While the input of the departed treatment personnel must be seen as contributing to that stance, the nature of the program itself suggested that research activity was not consistent with the Family's approach to treatment. The basic premise of the program was that effective treatment was dependent upon trust, which could best be developed by disclosure in depth of past activities. Mutual disclosure was seen as the first step toward the building of faith among members and, thus, toward the developing of their capacities to help one another. This basic premise was the thrust of the leadership's argument against research, and it resulted in the collection of all "hard" data taking place away from the Family unit once the larger study began operation; subjects were taken to a laboratory to have their psychophysiological responses measured or to be interviewed in a separate research unit by the survey project. The way data collection, per se, might affect the integrity of the program had not been a central concern of the departed treatment personnel. These individuals believed that it was their moral responsibility to protect the Family from the encroachment of the research component, and especially to see that the membership received its fair share of the grant proceeds. From this perspective, research access was something that should be "ex-changed" for a larger share of the grant proceeds. Employment opportunity, including the right to dictate how the job slots included in the grant would be allocated, was crucial here.

Immediately upon the receipt of the grant, the larger research project began to act as if it were the Family's "angel." The components of this project came to hire as research assistants almost exclusively Family members, while the other drug units in the treatment complex complained because of their failure to share equitably in the grant proceeds. Graduating senior Family members (non-elders) tended to be hired as treatment paraprofessionals on the other drug units, which was a major source of irritation to the staff of the 90-day and detoxification units. The staff members of the short-term program were especially annoyed because they could not hire their own graduates. Elders tended to be hired as research assistants and there was also a great deal of external competition for their services; all of the potential program moves included jobs for Family members, especially elders. This can be accounted for by noting that any relocation of the program had to be approved by the elder body. In one meeting that was observed a professional formerly attached to the Family requested that an elder approve the program move to another county. Tied to this proposed move was a high salaried job for the elder which he readily accepted. When asked how this decision would affect the program, the elder's reply was "You offer me a better deal and I'll go with you." Yet the fierce competition to hire elders was of limited tenure. The elder body consisted of five members, usually three still in the Family and two who had most recently graduated. When other elders completed the program, those outside lost their elder status, and more importantly, their vote. Once displaced and no longer able to dictate Family affairs, these elders found their services no longer in demand.

Furthermore, there were other institutional realities to contend with, especially the problems the program periodically experienced with the other drug units in the hospital. Several times during the observational study, the Family was denied the right to recruit new members on these other drug units. For short periods of time, the short-term and detoxification units were closed to the Family, and it received new recruits only directly from probation or parole workers. The Family's recruitment of new members on these other units clearly contributed to this action on the part of treatment personnel. The reason given for denial of access in each instance was that the Family had to learn that these other units served another capacity besides providing it with a recruiting ground. Continual lack of access could have ended the program and, in combination with the limited time their own employment opportunities were viable, elders were presented with valid reasons to acquiesce to the requests of various professional groups.

Eventually the extent to which research personnel had succeeded in co-opting the leadership of the Family became obvious. It was a common occurrance for an elder to defend the program's integrity by resisting increased data collection within the program itself and then to return several days later as a research assistant, calling the new elders stupid because they did not seem to realize that research was there to "help" them. Slowly, more and more data collection began to take place on the Family unit, eventually reaching the point where Synanon Games were videotaped and members wired to measure their psychophysiological responses to program activities. Professional research interests, for instance, requiring members to write extensive autobiographies, began to be introduced into the program as "therapy."

In summary, such events suggest that the research effort coopted the therapeutic activity of the program by coopting its leadership. In this context, we now return to the observational study, with some attention given to the role it played in this process.

THE IMPACT OF THE PROGRAM ON THE OBSERVATIONAL STUDY

The original intent was for both observers to proceed through the program until completion with a single cohort of addicts.

Reacting to the conflict and disruption which surrounded the program, both observers fell behind schedule. One observer completed the initiate phase almost on schedule, nine weeks as compared to the normal six-to-eight-week period, but then made little progress towards completing the other phases. The second observer completed the initiate phase in thirteen weeks, but then dropped out of program activity. There was a lull in the qualitative study which ended when the survey part of the larger research project became operational six months after the observational project had started. Both observers contributed to the development of the basic survey instrument on the basis of their experiences in the Family to that point in time. The research population of this project consisted of all the drug patients in the treatment complex, including those in the adult Family, short-term, and adolescent Family programs. A follow-up instrument was also designed to be administered to a random sample of those who had received treatment and who could be located once they left the institution, regardless of whether they had completed their respective programs. Once the survey project began, the more involved observer was somewhat adrift because the future direction of the observational project was unclear. At that point, the other member of the team decided to cease observation in order to write up his results.

The observational and survey projects were separate entities. In reassessing the future of the observational project, both observers agreed that the collective efforts of the larger project, including both the survey and psychophysiological components, could not adequately assess the impact of program activity on members and that there was still a requirement to provide some qualitative assessment of the Family. One project objective had been to investigate the way peer networks affected the adjustment of members while they were in the program as well as after they left the institution.[6] The observers decided that the observer who had remained in contact with the Family should return to the original design and complete the program, thus providing the opportunity to follow up on program peers in the outside community. The repercussions of this decision will be described below.

During the period the observers had been in the initiate phase of the Family program, they continually received the condolences of other professionals—research, treatment, and administrative. As was previously indicated, most of these other professionals had been exposed to the same process and knew it was not a pleasant experience. Several had left the initiate phase prior to completion because of the type of treatment they received. This was important because Family membership was acquired upon completion of the initiate phase; as a result these professionals were no longer able to work within the Family program structure itself. However, once the more involved researcher began to re-engage in the Family program activity, suspicion about his motives and purposes became apparent on the part of members of the research component, treatment staff, and hospital administration. The decision to re-enter actively and complete the program, therefore, turned out to be a mistake professionally, yet the reasons why were not obvious at the time. The observational team's most obvious concern had been the way participation affected the results. This was a setting where all of the problems inherent in participant observation described by Lofland (1971) were apparent and possibly magnified by the closed nature of the Family. Program responsibility was a part of membership and could not be avoided; the Family leadership was adamant that observation must include active involvement in program activity. The only role successfully avoided by the involved observer was an assumption of leadership. It was impossible for observers to avoid professional contamination of the program, and as we have already stated, the Family was already highly contaminated by professional involvement. The rationale the observational team provided itself to justify the one observer's renewed involvement with the Family was that this would provide alternate sources of data for the field research and psychophysiological components.[7] But reciprocal relationships with

the other research projects did not develop and the observational study did not make a contribution to the larger study.

The reasons for the splintering off of the observational study illuminate the relationships between self-help programs and institutions. Researchers and hospital staff began to make it clear that it was their opinion that the involved observer had "gone native." He became professionally deviant and stigmatized by his relationship with the program. Suspicion had been the first major problem encountered with the *research* population, but it began to subside when Family membership was attained. Suspicion then shifted, now coming from the professionals. Eventually the involved researcher was distrusted by the treatment and the research staff. For example, on one occasion the program social worker had the observer brought to her office. Claiming that the observer was in danger of "becoming a patient," she offered him therapy free of charge. Other professional treatment staff reacted in the same way and requested that the involved observer come to their offices or homes for treatment.

While the reactions of treatment staff were interesting, they did not directly affected the involved researcher or the objectives of the observational study. However, when similar reactions were encountered from other researchers, as well as hospital administrators, it became apparent that the involved researcher's relationship with the larger institution was becoming very strained. This appears to be an almost inevitable result, given the extreme enemy orientation which pervaded the relationships among the Family and these other groups; the Family universally viewed outsiders with suspicion, regardless of their affiliations. Therefore, the best way for an observer to "make out" in this setting was to avoid all possible non-program contacts. This course of action was taken by the involved observer over the length of the study. The less involved observer, on the other hand, did become more integrated into the research and administrative components, especially after he suspended his participation in the program. In sum, one observer stayed in the Family camp and the other went over to those seen as the "enemy" by Family members.

Lofland (1971) makes the point that it is primarily "young and inexperienced" researchers who engage in observational studies; the involved researcher was clearly the most "junior" member of the research component. This researcher's subordinate status provided the impetus for a major confrontation which made clear the state of his relationships with the significant others concerned with the Family. Eligible for a promotion because of the receipt of a degree, this researcher went for an oral before a board consisting of major research and hospital administrators, supposedly as a matter of courtesy. That is, the promotion was automatic but the oral was held in deference to their positions in the hospital administration component. Yet, one hospital administrator indicated that he did not think a promotion was justified. The administrator's reasoning was that this researcher had never met with him in his office, despite the fact that the observational study had been in progress for almost a year. Furthermore, he felt that the researcher had been influenced by the Family's image of him (the Administrator) as a "bad guy." The researcher's response that the observational project was supposed to study the Family only irritated this administrator more. It must also be reported that the researcher's response included a statement of willingness to study the political turmoil that surrounded the Family and the grant, including the question of why certain administrators appeared to be frightened of individuals who began to understand some of the problems associated with the Family.[8] The researcher received the promotion, but it was clear that the relationships between the observational project and the larger research program, as well as the relationships with some hospital administrators, were at a very low level. It was questionable whether cooperation would ever exist.

The conflict the observational project experienced in this setting seems most interpretable in terms of the role it played in the larger research effort as well as in terms of the disruption that surrounded the Family. The observers had begun the study under a major illusion; specifically, both, disregarding the fact that their component had been "tacked on" at the request of the funding source, believed that the observational project had been established to evaluate the Family. Gradually it became clear that the observational study had not been taken seriously by anyone connected with the hospital. This reality became more obvious when no interest was expressed about the findings, or even about the observer's opinions of the program. Furthermore, when the one observer became too integrated into the Family, he represented one more staff member who might attempt to "rip off" the program, and who, thus, might present a threat to the research complex; every faction that had a vested interest in the Family was suspicious of anyone with the potential to create additional problems, an indication that the enemy orientation characteristic of the Family was contagious in this environment.

Even if the observational project had become an integral part of the larger project, the integration of observers into this kind of program is of questionable value to participants. In retrospect, the observational project was a contributing factor in the cooptation of the research population of the goals of the larger research effort. The relationships that both observers had established and that the one researcher had maintained, certainly opened the door for the increased level of research activity within the Family itself. Even if the study had not been a factor in the cooptation of the Family, the concessions given for access to the program were too great. Lasting fourteen months, the study required too great an investment in time and should have been restricted to a much shorter time span.

WHAT PRICE KNOWLEDGE?

Our impressions of the impact of research funds on the program under study support the position advanced by Cloward and Piven (1974). The benefits of this funding did accrue primarily to professionals, especially research personnel, and the distribution of rewards to the client group appeared to be directed mainly toward individuals who had the ability to further research interests. The implications of the exchange system were brought sharply into focus in this mental hospital environment and had some major repercussions.

Treatment personnel were angered, not only about the way these rewards were distributed, but also about the way the grant itself affected institutional arrangements, especially about the way power accrued to research professionals as recipients of the grant. It was their feeling that one treatment program had attracted the funds and researchers reaped the rewards. Once the grant had been received, some treatment personnel began to see the Family as a vehicle to attract funds; others had held that position even before the grant was secured. At a time when other drug abuse programs suffered from a shortage of resources, the Family appeared to them to have an abundance of funds which were grant-generated. As a result, a key consideration in all of the proposed Family moves was whether the grant would move with the Family,[9] thus allowing treatment personnel to administer monies which they saw as primarily treatment funds. Those who had departed the program, but maintained contact, emphasized this point to the Family members with an interesting result.

Periodically the Family elders would attempt to administer the grant, stressing to the administrator that their program was responsible for the receipt of the funds and, therefore, that the grant proceeds were theirs, especially in terms of deciding who would be hired to work on the project. In each instance, this administrator, indicating that he was stunned by the elders' attitudes, refused their request to render a full accounting of the way funds were being dispersed. In his opinion the Family made it a policy to alienate its best friends. Noting their ingratitude, the administrator stressed that the grant provided jobs and halfway houses for the Family, while the other drug units barely received any resources, although theoretically the funds belonged to the entire treatment complex.

The administrative components of the

grant and the hospital did appear to comprehend that there was some "minor" competition for resources among the other drug units in the hospital's treatment complex and the Family. Yet they never demonstrated an understanding of the sources of resentment which caused the hospital treatment staff's attitude toward the Family and its membership. Administrators were of the opinion that the Family unit staff had the easiest job in the hospital, which they described as nothing to do, because the members themselves essentially ran the program. Some of the psychiatric technicians on the Family unit indicated that the assignment was the worst in the hospital, while others liked it. Those who complained emphasized that all they could do was to spend eight hours confined in an office because their major work roles had been usurped by the Family members. Those who did like the assignment said that the Family members were a welcomed change from typical mental hospital patients. At larger staff meetings, technicians on the other drug units said they also felt superfluous because of the Family graduates hired as paraprofessionals on their units.

There were other criticisms, some related to job displacement, of the paraprofessional roles Family graduates began to play. Some technicians simply stated that being an ex-addict was a poor sole criterion on which to base employment. Others stressed the fact that the institution did have an accredited psychiatric technician program, yet the jobs which did open were funded by the research grant and, thus, went primarily to Family graduates. (There was a state freeze on the hiring of psychiatric technicians at that time.) Later in the study, a number of Family graduates did complete the institution's psychiatric technician program, but this training did not appreciably change the hostility of the majority of technicians who still identified them with the Family program. Although research was seen as the perpetrator of that injustice, the paraprofessionals the research grant helped to employ bore the brunt of this antagonism.

The implication that outside funding created competition between lower level hospital personnel, such as psychiatric technicians, and ex-addict paraprofessionals is important. Empey (1970) suggests that the major task facing criminal corrections is to integrate the ex-offender into a larger scheme in which, by being of service, these paraprofessionals might realize lasting career benefits. The literature based upon broad surveys of paraprofessionals and their performance in education, health, and social service programs (Gartner, 1971), and the use of ex-offender paraprofessionals in corrections (Scott, 1975), generally suggests that paraprofessionals have been accepted by coworkers. Scott (1975), in a study of ex-offender paraprofessionals in Ohio, finds no support for the assumption that parole officers would resist accepting exoffenders as colleagues. Furthermore, it was discovered that these paraprofessionals were satisfied with their jobs as well as their fellow workers. However, in a national survey of those states that use ex-offender paraprofessionals, generated for comparative purposes, Scott (1975) reports that professional staff resistance was listed as the major disadvantage in the hiring of ex-offender paraprofessionals.

Perhaps the distribution of resources in this study sheds some light on the factors that affect paraprofessional integration. The hiring practices, resulting from the grant, were interpreted by the psychiatric technicians to mean that eventually they would be in competition with ex-addicts for their very jobs. Also, the short term and adolescent programs competed with the Family for grant resources and the short term program also competed with the Family for patients. The short term and adolescent programs did receive several job slots, but no major support for halfway houses. The failure to fathom the competition which existed among the hospital programs and to determine its effect upon paraprofessionals was a major oversight, one which was self-defeating in terms of development of paraprofessionals as treatment personnel. Possible competition between trained technicians and ex-addict paraprofessionals should be a primary issue in planning programs which intend to recast former patients in a treatment role.

The significance of the failure to comprehend the ultimate impact of the distribution of rewards on paraprofessionals pales by comparison with the effect research had upon the Family. Little by little, research began to impinge upon the actual operation of the program and affected it in ways that were not apparent when the observational project had been started. The observational project did introduce research activity into the Family, contributing to the cooptation of the research population to the goals of the research. When the cooptation process became apparent, the involved observer maintained his role as program participant and did not interfere. Sponsorship, not the usual ethical problems of research with deviant groups such as how others might use the information collected, was a crucial issue here. Rather, research activity began to infringe upon and possibly deflect a rehabilitation program from its programatic objectives. Research thus shook a structure which individuals were dependent upon for their personal rehabilitation, whether real or fancied. What course of action should be taken by other researchers involved in similar projects when such a situation presents itself is unclear. Rainwater and Pittman (1967) have at least indirectly discussed this issue in terms of the ethics involved in relation to sponsorship, but how their conclusions apply here is again unclear. Because their primary concern was the release of information, their focus is upon who should receive research findings, suggesting that various types of sponsorship determine different informational publics. One implication of their discussion does relate directly to the employer-employee relationship and the obligation to communicate directly with those who have contracted for service, as opposed to basic research where all interested parties should share equally in terms of receipt of information. As someone who was an employee of the research grant, it was never clear to the involved observer where his allegiances should lie. Was the funding agency the sponsor or was the administrative component, which wrote the grant, the real sponsor of this project? If peers are the measure of appropriate professional conduct,[10] it was their universal opinion that the involved observer's position was totally mistaken. Their stance was that the observer rather than the research population had been coopted. In short, peers were not receptive to the position advocated here and the research population was the only group which might have been responsive to this stress, and they had been manipulated enough. The decision to attempt to disrupt a major research effort was not considered a realistic alternative by the involved researcher. Did the researcher who opted out take the wiser course?

SUMMARY

This paper has described the effect of certain kinds of funding arrangements on the implementation of self-help programs. The findings describe the ways large research grants appear to affect the relationships among groups that such funding arrangements are likely to bring together in treatment settings. Cloward and Piven's (1974) assertion that research objectives will come to dominate grant-funded programs, thus furthering the careers of professionals, not the disadvantaged, is supported here. The description of the interaction between the Family and the research component specifies the way rewards are likely to be distributed in the instance where research objectives are paramount. In the course of pursuing research goals, the grant-funded effort coopted the leadership of the research population and turned a treatment program into a laboratory. It also managed to alienate the institution's treatment staff and facilitated competition between this self-help program and other drug units in the hospital. Some clients did benefit from the project, especially those ex-addicts who became research assistants, and a few have gone on to work on other projects. These individual instances of the development of new roles and rewards were consistent with the overall grant objectives, but not necessarily with the goals of the self-help program, which was developed to restore addicts to normal life outside of treatment institutions. The major implication forthcoming here is that self-

help programs are likely to be deflected from their original purpose if implemented by the use of grant funds, and will reflect instead, the interests of research personnel.

NOTES

1. A study of drug abuse patient admissions revealed that 86 percent had entered the hospital because of some form of legal pressure. The majority were white (roughly 67 percent), predominantly male (about 67 percent), and primarily between 21 and 25 years old (approximately 50 percent). About half of those admitted (actually 49 percent), had been in treatment programs prior to that admission.

2. By way of contrast, 27 members graduated during the fourteen months the observational project took to complete.

3. It was of interest to learn later that these conditions of research access had been imposed by professional treatment staff. The leaders indicated that they had not been sure at the time that they were either desirable or realistic requirements.

4. See Fry (1977).

5. The relationships between the research component and some treatment personnel who had cooperated to obtain the grant had been severely splintered before the funding was received, resulting in several treatment personnel leaving the Family and the institution. The departing treatment personnel were seen as "victims" of the research component by some Family members who took to heart their parting shot, namely, that "research would attempt to take the program away from its members."

6. One stated goal of the Family was the establishment of a graduate phase in the community, revolving around the halfway houses. However, this phase of the program did not develop as expected. Graduates demonstrated little sense of personal commitment to each other, refusing to attend meetings designed to keep them together in the community.

7. The expected role of the observational project in the larger research project has been described in detail elsewhere (Fry, 1973).

8. For this indiscretion, several days later the promotee received an official communication which indicated that he was not to "research" any unsuspecting, unconsenting subjects in the hospital environment unless he had them sign an "informed consent statement" beforehand.

9. The rival facility sponsored by the neighboring county's health department did open and eventually took over the bulk of the mental hospital's drug abuse patients, forcing closure of the entire hospital drug treatment complex. However, the research grant remained in the hospital until funding expired.

10. Daniels (1973) provides an overview of the problems inherent in attempting to determine how peer review contributes to appropriate profes-

sional conduct. Both Daniels (1973) and Barber (1973) stress the need for more control over powerful professions. Daniels (1973) questions the degree to which professional autonomy is justified, while Barber (1973) stresses the need to recognize that sociology is a powerful profession and necessarily must be open to criticism from outsiders because internal controls will not suffice.

REFERENCES

Barber, B.
1973 "Research on research on human subjects: Problems of access to a powerful profession." Social Problems 21:103–12.

Berman, G.S. and M.R. Haug
1973 "New careers: Bridges or ladders?" Social Work 18:48–58.

Bullington, B., J.G. Munns and G. Geis
1969 "Purchase of conformity: Ex-narcotics addicts among the bourgeoisie." Social Problems 16:456–63.

Coser L.
1965 "The sociology of poverty." Social Problems 13:140–48.

Cloward R. and I. Epstein
1967 "Private social welfare's disengagement from the poor: The case of family adjustment agencies." Pp. 45–63 in G. Brager and F. Purcell (eds.), Community Action Against Poverty. New Haven College University Press: New Haven, Conn.

Cloward R. and F. Piven
1974 "The professional bureaucracies: Benefit systems as influence systems." Pp. 7–27 in R. Cloward and F.F. Piven (eds.), The Politics of Turmoil. New York: Pantheon.

Cromwell, R.E., C.E. Vaughn and C.H. Mindel
1975 "Ethnic minority family research in an urban setting: A process of exchange." American Sociologist 10:141–50.

Daniels, A.K.
1973 "How free should professions be?" Pp. 39–57 in E. Freidson (ed.), The Professions and their Prospects. Beverly Hills: Sage.

Empey, L.
1970 "Offender participation in the correctional process: General theoretical issues." Pp. 5–21 in Offenders as a Correctional Manpower Resource. Washington D.C.: Joint Commission on Correctional Manpower and Training.

Fry, L.J.
1973 "Participant observation and program evaluation." Journal of Health and Social Behavior 14:274–78.
1977 Program content and context: Some neglected considerations in the problem of determining correctional treatment effectiveness. Unpublished paper.

Gartner, A.
1971 Paraprofessionals and their Performance: A Survey of Education, Health and Social Programs. New York: Praeger.

Hessler, R.M. and P.K. New
1972 "Research as a process of exchange." American Sociologist 7:13–15.

Holleb, G. and W. H. Abrams
1975 Alternates in Community Mental Health. Boston: Beacon Press.

Katan, J.
1973 "The attitudes of professionals toward the employment of indigenous non-professionals in human service organizations." Pp. 229–43 in P. Halmos (ed.), Professionalization and Social Change. The Sociological Review Monograph 20.

Lofland, J.
1971 Analyzing Social Settings. Belmont: Wadsworth.

Moffett, A.D., J.D. Bruce and D. Horvitz
1974 "New ways of treating addicts." Social Work 19:389–96.

Piven, F.
1974 "The new urban programs: The strategy of federal intervention." Pp. 284–313 in R. Cloward and F.F. Piven (eds.), The Politics of Turmoil. New York: Pantheon.

Rainwater, L. and D.J. Pittman
1967 "Ethical problems in studying a politically sensitive and deviant community." Social Problems 14:357–66.

Reissman, F.
1965 "The helper therapy principle." Social Work 10:27–32.

Scott, J.E.
1975 Ex-Offenders as Parole Officers. Lexington: Lexington Books.

Twain, D., E. Harlow and D. Merwin
1970 Research and Human Services. New York: Research and Development Center, Jewish Board of Guardians.

Weiss, C.H.
1975 "Evaluation research in the political context." Pp. 13–26 in E. Struening and M. Guttentag (eds.), Handbook of Evaluation Research 1. Beverly Hills: Sage.

The Cambridge-Somerville Youth Study, conducted during the early 1940s, remains today one of the best designed and most ambitious studies of the effects of counseling. In this program, both "delinquency-prone" and "average" boys were randomly assigned either to a treatment or a control group. The boys in the treatment group were to have received regular counseling and other services from a social caseworker. Follow-up studies have been periodically conducted on the boys (now men) in the treatment and control groups to assess the long-term effects, if any, of the program. The three works that follow present different perspectives on a new and rather startling conclusion concerning the long-term effects, namely, that subjects originally in the treatment group have had worse subsequent histories than control subjects.

The first work, by McCord, reports the results of a thirty-year follow-up of the participants and controls. Although the program was initiated in an attempt to reduce delinquency, little effect was observed on the measures of adult crime rates. However, the subjects in the control group have fared significantly better than the treatment group members on several measures related to health and occupational status. These unexpected side effects suggest that caution should be exercised in implementing large-scale treatment or counseling programs for delinquent youth. In the second essay, Sobel questions a number of aspects of the outcome measures, the nature of the comparisons, and the interpretations of the results of McCord's study. Specifically, Sobel notes that McCord failed to include measures of the intrapsychic processes presumably affected by the treatment. Further, Sobel points out that counseling may lead the subjects more readily to admit and seek treatment for their problems (although McCord's results for signs of, and treatment for, alcoholism are not entirely consistent with this hypothesis). Finally, Sobel notes that the "consistently positive subjective reports of the treatment group about their experiences must have some pervading impact on their lives today" (but see the Scheirer chapter in this volume).

The third work by Marquis and Gendreau identifies a number of problems in Sobel's critique, notably its lack of specificity and failure to operationalize several of the variables that are deemed inadequate.

The Cambridge-Somerville Youth Study is an important pioneering example of a large-scale evaluation of treatment effects. It did, however, have several possible problems in implementation that are not addressed in the three works that follow. Of most importance, there were no checks on the quality of the treatment delivered, nor on the participants' expectations of treatment and how well those expectations were met. With the coming of World War II, considerable disruption of treatment occurred as counselors were drafted into or volunteered for military service. Those boys who in fact did receive continuing treatment may have had serious concerns about the possibility of having their counseling disrupted. These subjects may have experienced a loss of feeling of control over their lives, possibly leading to a variety of stress-related medical symptoms in later life (see the Schulz and Hanusa work in this volume).

Another problem in interpreting the results of the thirty-year follow-up is that little attention has been given to the specification of the variables that mediated the negative effects of treatment. It is possible that the treatment may have had a direct effect on a single variable that is linked to many of the other observed effects. For example, the experience of counseling may have led these men to value personal independence more highly than control subjects. Hence, these men may have been more reluctant to get married.

It may be that the lower percentage of married men in the treatment group accounts for the higher rates of stress-related diseases and lower occupational status.

These considerations illustrate the importance in studies of therapeutic or counseling interventions to examine both the direct and indirect effects of the program on the participants and to explore the possible relation among the network of outcome measures.

37

A Thirty-Year Follow-up of Treatment Effects

Joan McCord

ABSTRACT: *Over 500 men, half of whom had been randomly assigned to a treatment program that lasted approximately 5 years, were traced 30 years after termination of the project. Although subjective evaluations of the program by those who received its benefits would suggest that the intervention had been helpful, comparisons between the treatment and control groups indicate that the program had negative side effects as measured by criminal behavior, death, disease, occupational status, and job satisfaction. Several possible processes are suggested in explanation of these findings.*

In 1935, Richard Clark Cabot instigated one of the most imaginative and exciting programs ever designed in hopes of preventing delinquency. A social philosopher as well as physician, Dr. Cabot established a program that both avoided stigmatizing participants and permitted follow-up evaluation.

Several hundred boys from densely populated, factory-dominated areas of eastern Massachusetts were included in the project, known as the Cambridge–Somerville Youth Study. Schools, welfare agencies, churches, and the police recommended both "difficult" and "average" youngsters to the program. These boys and their families were given physical examinations and were interviewed by social workers who then rated each boy in such a way as to allow a selection committee to designate delinquency-prediction scores. In addition to giving delinquency-prediction scores, the selection committee studied each boy's records in order to identify pairs who were similar in age, delinquency-prone histories, family background, and home environments. By the toss of a coin, one member of each pair was assigned to the group that would receive treatment.[1]

The treatment program began in 1939, when the boys were between 5 and 13 years old. Their median age was 10½. Except for those dropped from the program because of a counselor shortage in 1941, treatment continued for an average of 5 years. Counselors assigned to each family visited, on the average, twice a month. They encouraged families to call on the program for assistance. Family problems became the focus of attention for ap-

proximately one third of the treatment group. Over half of the boys were tutored in academic subjects; over 100 received medical or psychiatric attention; one fourth were sent to summer camps; and most were brought into contact with the Boy Scouts, the YMCA, and other community programs. The control group, meanwhile, participated only through providing information about themselves. Both groups, it should be remembered, contained boys referred as "average" and boys considered "difficult."

The present study compares the 253 men who had been in the treatment program after 1942 with the 253 "matched mates" assigned to the control group.

Method

Official records and personal contacts were used to obtain information about the long-term effects of the Cambridge–Somerville Youth Study.[2] In 1975 and 1976, the 506 former members of the program were traced through court records, mental hospital

This study was supported by U.S. Public Health Service Research Grant No. 5 R01 MH26779, National Institute of Mental Health (Center for Studies of Crime and Delinquency). It was conducted jointly with the Department of Probation of the Commonwealth of Massachusetts.

An earlier version of this paper was presented at the 28th annual meeting of the American Association of Psychiatric Services for Children, San Francisco, California, November 10–14, 1976.

The author wishes to express appreciation to the Division of Alcoholism, to the Cambridge & Somerville Program for Alcoholism Rehabilitation, to the National Institute of Law Enforcement (through Grant NI 74–0038 to Ron Geddes), to the Massachusetts Departments of Mental Health, Motor Vehicles, and Correction, and to the many individuals who contributed to this research.

Requests for reprints should be sent to Joan McCord, 1279 Montgomery Avenue, Wynnewood, Pennsylvania 19096.

[1] An exception to assignment by chance was made if brothers were in the program; all brothers were assigned to that group which was the assignment of the first brother matched. See Powers and Witmer (1951) for details of the matching procedure.

[2] A sample of 200 men had been retraced in 1948 (Powers & Witmer, 1951), and official records had been traced in 1956 (McCord & McCord, 1959a, 1959b).

records, records from alcoholic treatment centers, and vital statistics in Massachusetts. Telephone calls, city directories, motor-vehicle registrations, marriage and death records, and lucky hunches were used to find the men themselves.

Four hundred eighty men (95%) were located; among these, 48 (9%) had died and 340 (79%) were living in Massachusetts.[3] Questionnaires were mailed to 208 men from the treatment group and 202 men from the control group. The questionnaire elicited information about marriage, children, occupations, drinking, health, and attitudes. Former members of the treatment group were asked how (if at all) the treatment program had been helpful to them.

Responses to the questionnaire were received from 113 men in the treatment group (54%) and 122 men in the control group (60%). These responses overrepresent men living outside of Massachusetts, $\chi^2(1) = 10.97$, $p < .001$.[4] Official records, on the other hand, provide more complete information about those men living in Massachusetts.

Comparison of Criminal Behavior

The treatment and control groups were compared on a variety of measures for criminal behavior. With the exception of Crime Prevention Bureau records for unofficial crimes committed by juveniles, court convictions serve as the standard by which criminal behavior was assessed. Although official court records may be biased, there is no reason to believe that these biases would affect a comparison between the matched groups of control and treatment subjects.

Almost equal numbers in the treatment and control groups had committed crimes as juveniles— whether measured by official or by unofficial records (see Table 1).

It seemed possible that the program might have benefited those referred as "difficult" while damaging those referred as "average." The evidence,

TABLE 1

Juvenile Records

Record	Treatment group	Control group
No record for delinquency	136	140
Only unofficial crimes	45	46
Official crimes	72	67
Total	253	253

TABLE 2

Juvenile Delinquency and Adult Criminal Records

Record	Treatment group	Control group
Official juvenile record		
No adult record	14	15
Only minor adult record	33	27
Serious crimes as adults	25	25
No official juvenile record		
No adult record	71	70
Only minor adult record	86	99
Serious crimes as adults	24	17
Total	253	253

however, failed to support this hypothesis. Among those referred as "difficult," 34% from the treatment group and 30% from the control group had official juvenile records; an additional 20% from the treatment group and 21% from the control group had unofficial records. Nor were there differences between the groups for those who had been referred as "average."[5]

As adults, equal numbers (168) had been convicted for some crime. Among men who had been in the treatment group, 119 committed only relatively minor crimes (against ordinances or order), but 49 had committed serious crimes against property (including burglary, larceny, and auto theft) or against persons (including assault, rape, and attempted homicide). Among men from the control group, 126 had committed only relatively minor crimes; 42 had committed serious property crimes or crimes against persons. Twenty-nine men from the treatment group and 25 men from the control group committed serious crimes after the age of 25.

Reasoning that the Youth Study project may have been differentially effective for those who did and did not have records as delinquents, it seemed advisable to compare adult criminal records while holding this background information constant.

[3] Two hundred forty-one men from the treatment group and 239 men from the control group were found; 173 from the treatment group and 167 from the control group were living in Massachusetts.

[4] Among those sent the questionnaire, the response rate for men living in Massachusetts was 53%; for men living outside Massachusetts, the response rate was 74%. A similar bias appeared for both groups.

[5] For the treatment group, 18% had official records and an additional 13% had unofficial records. For the control-group "average" referrals, the figures were 19% and 13%, respectively.

Again, there was no evidence that the treatment program had deflected people from committing crimes (see Table 2).

The treatment and control groups were compared to see whether there were differences (a) in the number of serious crimes committed, (b) in age when a first crime was committed, (c) in age when committing a first serious crime, and (d) in age after which no serious crime was committed. None of these measures showed reliable differences.

Benefits from the treatment program did not appear when delinquency-prediction scores were controlled or when seriousness of juvenile record and juvenile incarceration were controlled. Unexpectedly, however, a higher proportion of criminals from the treatment group than of criminals from the control group committed more than one crime, $\chi^2(1) = 5.36$, $p < .05$. Among the 182 men with criminal records from the treatment group, 78% committed at least two crimes; among the 183 men with criminal records from the control group, 67% committed at least two crimes.

Comparison of Health

Signs of alcoholism, mental illness, stress-related diseases, and early death were used to evaluate possible impact of the treatment program on health.

A search through records from alcoholic treatment centers and mental hospitals in Massachusetts showed that almost equal numbers of men from the treatment and the control groups had been treated for alcoholism (7% and 8%, respectively).

The questionnaire asked respondents to note their drinking habits and to respond to four questions about drinking embedded in questions about smoking. The four questions, known as the CAGE test (Ewing & Rouse, Note 1), asked whether the respondent had ever taken a morning eye-opener, felt the need to cut down on drinking, felt annoyed by criticism of his drinking, or felt guilty about drinking.[6] The treatment group mentioned that they were alcoholic or responded *yes* more frequently, as do alcoholics, to at least three of the CAGE questions: 17% compared with 7%, $\chi^2(1) = 4.98$, $p < .05$.

Twenty-one members of each group had received treatment in mental hospitals for disorders other than alcoholism.[7] A majority of those from the treatment group (71%) received diagnoses as manic-depressive or schizophrenic, whereas a majority of those from the control group (67%) received less serious diagnoses such as "personality disorder" or "psychoneurotic," $\chi^2(1) = 4.68$, $p < .05$.

Twenty-four men from each group are known to have died. Although the groups were not distinguishable by causes of death, among those who died, men from the treatment group tended to die at younger ages, $t(94) = 2.19$, $p < .05$.[8]

The questionnaire requested information about nine stress-related diseases: arthritis, gout, emphysema, depression, ulcers, asthma, allergies, high blood pressure, and heart trouble. Men from the treatment group were more likely to report having had at least one of these diseases, $\chi^2(1) = 4.39$, $p < .05$.[9] In particular, symptoms of stress in the circulatory system were more prevalent among men from the treatment group: 21%, as compared with 11% in the control group, reported having had high blood pressure or heart trouble, $\chi^2(1) = 4.95$, $p < .05$.

Comparison of Family, Work, and Leisure Time

A majority of the men who responded to the questionnaire were married: 61% of the treatment group and 68% of the control group. An additional 15% of the treatment group and 10% of the control group noted that they were remarried. Fourteen percent of the treatment-group and 9% of the control-group respondents had never married. The remaining 10% of the treatment group and 13% of the control group were separated, divorced, or widowed. Among those ever married, 93% of each group had children. The median number of children for both sets of respondents was three.

About equal proportions of the treatment- and the control-group respondents were unskilled workers (29% and 27%, respectively). At the upper end of the socioeconomic scale, however, the con-

[6] This test was validated by comparing the responses of 58 acknowledged alcoholics in an alcoholism rehabilitation center with those of 68 nonalcoholic patients in a general hospital: 95% of the former and none of the latter answered *yes* to more than two of the four questions (Ewing & Rouse, Note 1). Additional information related to alcoholism is being gathered through interviews.

[7] An additional five men from the treatment group and three men from the control group had been institutionalized as retarded.

[8] The average age at death for the treatment group was 32 years ($SD = 9.4$) and for the control group, 38 years ($SD = 7.5$).

[9] Thirty-six percent of those in the treatment group and 24% of those in the control group reported having had at least one of these diseases.

trol group had an advantage: 43% from the control group, compared with 29% from the treatment group, were white-collar workers or professionals, $\chi^2(2) = 4.58$, $p < .05$. For those whose occupations could be classified according to National Opinion Research Center (NORC) ranks, comparison indicated that the control-group men were working in positions having higher prestige, $z = 2.07$, $p < .05$ (Mann-Whitney U test).

The questionnaire inquired whether the men found their work, in general, to be satisfying. Almost all of the men who held white-collar or professional positions (97%) reported that their work was satisfying. Among blue-collar workers, those in the treatment group were less likely to report that their work was generally satisfying (80%, compared with 95% among the control group), $\chi^2(1) = 6.60$, $p < .02$.

The men described how they used their spare time. These descriptions were grouped to compare the proportions who reported reading, traveling, doing things with their families, liking sports (as spectators or participants), working around the house, watching television, enjoying music or theater or photography, doing service work, enjoying crafts or tinkering, and participating in organized group activities. The treatment and control groups did not differ in their reported uses of leisure time.

Comparison of Beliefs and Attitudes

The men were asked to evaluate their satisfaction with how their lives were turning out, their chances for living the kinds of lives they'd like to have, and whether they were able to plan ahead.[10] Men from the treatment and the control groups did not differ in their responses to these questions.

A short form of the F scale (Adorno, Frenkel-Brunswik, Levinson, & Sanford, 1950) developed by Sanford and Older (Note 2) was included in the questionnaire. Men were asked whether they agreed or disagreed with the following statements: "Human nature being what it is, there must always be war and conflict. The most important thing a child should learn is obedience to his parents. A few strong leaders could make this country better than all the laws and talk. Most people who don't get ahead just don't have enough willpower. Women should stay out of politics. An insult to your honor should not be forgotten. In general, people can be trusted."

Despite diversity in opinions, neither answers to particular questions nor to the total scale suggested that treatment and control groups differed in authoritarianism. Both groups selected an average of 2.9 authoritarian answers; the standard deviation for each group was 1.7.

Each man was asked to describe his political orientation. About one fifth considered themselves liberals, two fifths considered themselves conservatives, and two fifths considered themselves middle-of-the-road. No one considered himself a radical. Treatment and control groups did not differ reliably.

The men also identified the best periods of their lives, and, again, there was little difference between control and treatment groups.

Subjective Evaluation of the Program

Former members of the treatment group were asked, "In what ways (if any) was the Cambridge–Someville project helpful to you?"

Only 11 men failed to comment about this item. Thirteen noted that they could not remember the project. An additional 13 stated that the project had not been helpful—though several of these men amplified their judgments by mentioning that they had fond memories of their counselors or their activities in the project.

Two thirds of the men stated that the program had been helpful to them. Some wrote that, by providing interesting activities, the project kept them off the streets and out of trouble. Many believed that the project improved their lives through providing guidance or teaching them how to get along with others. The questionnaires were sprinkled with such comments as "helped me to have faith and trust in other people"; "I was put on the right road"; "helped prepare me for manhood"; "to overcome my prejudices"; "provided an initial grasp of our complex society outside of the ghetto"; and "better insight on life in general."

A few men believed that the project was responsible for their becoming law-abiding citizens. Such men wrote that, had it not been for their particular counselors, "I probably would be in jail"; "My life would have gone the other way"; or "I think I would have ended up in a life of crime."

More than a score requested information about their counselors and expressed the intention of communicating with them.

---

[10] This set of questions was developed at the University of Michigan Survey Research Center as a measure of self-competence. It has an index of reproducibility as a Guttman Scale of .94 (see Douvan & Walker, 1956).

Summary and Discussion

This study of long-term effects of the Cambridge–Somerville Youth Study was based on the tracing of over 500 men, half of whom were randomly assigned to a treatment program. Those receiving treatment had (in varying degrees) been tutored, provided with medical assistance, and given friendly counsel for an extended period of time.

Thirty years after termination of the program, many of the men remembered their counselors—sometimes recalling particular acts of kindness and sometimes noting the general support they felt in having someone available with whom to discuss their problems. There seems to be little doubt that many of the men developed emotional ties to their counselors.

Were the Youth Study program to be assessed by the subjective judgment of its value as perceived by those who received its services, it would rate high marks. To the enormous credit of those who dedicated years of work to the project, it is possible to use objective criteria to evaluate the long-term impact of this program, which seems to have been successful in achieving the short-term goals of establishing rapport between social workers and teenage clients.

Despite the large number of comparisons between treatment and control groups, none of the objective measures confirmed hopes that treatment had improved the lives of those in the treatment group. Fifteen comparisons regarding criminal behavior were made: one was significant with alpha less than .05. Fifteen comparisons for health indicated four —from three different record sources—favoring the control group. Thirteen comparisons of family, work, and leisure time yielded two that favored the control group. Fourteen comparisons of beliefs and attitudes failed to indicate reliable differences between the groups.

The objective evidence presents a disturbing picture. The program seems not only to have failed to prevent its clients from committing crimes—thus corroborating studies of other projects (see, e.g., Craig & Furst, 1965; Empey, 1972; Hackler, 1966; Miller, 1962; Robin, 1969)—but also to have produced negative side effects. As compared with the control group,

1. Men who had been in the treatment program were more likely to commit (at least) a second crime.

2. Men who had been in the treatment program were more likely to evidence signs of alcoholism.

3. Men from the treatment group more commonly manifested signs of serious mental illness.

4. Among men who had died, those from the treatment group died younger.

5. Men from the treatment group were more likely to report having had at least one stress-related disease; in particular, they were more likely to have experienced high blood pressure or heart trouble.

6. Men from the treatment group tended to have occupations with lower prestige.

7. Men from the treatment group tended more often to report their work as not satisfying.

It should be noted that the side effects that seem to have resulted from treatment were subtle. There is no reason to believe that treatment increased the probability of committing a first crime, although treatment may have increased the likelihood that those who committed a first crime would commit additional crimes. Although treatment may have increased the likelihood of alcoholism, the treatment group was not more likely to have appeared in clinics or hospitals. There was no difference between the groups in the number of men who had died before the age of 50, although men from the treatment group had been younger at the age of death. Almost equal proportions of the two groups of men had remained at the lowest rungs of the occupational structure, although men from the treatment group were less likely to be satisfied with their jobs and fewer men from the treatment group had become white-collar workers.

The probability of obtaining 7 reliably different comparisons among 57, with an alpha of .05, is less than 2%. The probability that, by chance, 7 of 57 comparisons would favor the control group is less than 1 in 10,000.[11]

At this juncture, it seems appropriate to suggest several possible interpretations of the subtle effects of treatment. Interaction with adults whose values are different from those of the family milieu may produce later internal conflicts that manifest themselves in disease and/or dissatisfaction.[12] Agency intervention may create dependency upon outside

---

[11] This estimate is conservative: The count of 57 comparisons includes comparisons that are not independent (e.g., adult criminal record and crimes after the age of 25), but only 7 independent significant relationships have been counted. If comparisons for any stress-related disease, for NORC ranking of occupation, and for job satisfaction without controlling work status are counted, 10 out of 60 comparisons were significant.

[12] Such conflicts seem to have been aroused by intervention in the lives of hard-core unemployables (Padfield & Williams, 1973).

assistance. When this assistance is no longer available, the individual may experience symptoms of dependency and resentment. The treatment program may have generated such high expectations that subsequent experiences tended to produce symptoms of deprivation. Or finally, through receiving the services of a "welfare project," those in the treatment program may have justified the help they received by perceiving themselves as requiring help.

There were many variations to treatment. Some of these may have been beneficial. Overall, however, the message seems clear: Intervention programs risk damaging the individuals they are designed to assist. These findings may be taken by some as grounds for cessation of social-action programs. I believe that would be a mistake. In my opinion, new programs ought to be developed. We should, however, address the problems of potential damage through the use of pilot projects with mandatory evaluations.

REFERENCE NOTES

1. Ewing, J. A., & Rouse, B. A. *Identifying the "hidden alcoholic."* Paper presented at the 29th International Congress on Alcohol and Drug Dependence, Sydney, New South Wales, Australia, February 3, 1970.
2. Sanford, F. H., & Older, J. J. *A short authoritarian-equalitarian scale* (Progress Report No. 6, Series A).

Philadelphia, Pa.: Institute for Research in Human Relations, 1950.

REFERENCES

Adorno, T. W., Frenkel-Brunswik, E., Levinson, D. J., & Sanford, R. N. *The authoritarian personality.* New York: Harper, 1950.

Craig, M. M., & Furst, P. W. What happens after treatment? A study of potentially delinquent boys. *Social Service Review,* 1965, *39,* 165–171.

Douvan, E., & Walker, A. M. The sense of effectiveness in public affairs. *Psychological Monographs,* 1956, *70*(22, Whole No. 429).

Empey, L. T., & Ericson, M. L. *The provo experiment: Evaluating community control of delinquency.* Lexington, Mass.: Lexington Books, 1972.

Hackler, J. C. Boys, blisters, and behavior: The impact of a work program in an urban central area. *Journal of Research in Crime and Delinquency,* 1966, *12,* 155–164.

McCord, J., & McCord, W. A follow-up report on the Cambridge–Somerville youth study. *Annals of the American Academy of Political and Social Science,* 1959, *322,* 89–96. (a)

McCord, W., & McCord, J. *Origins of crime.* New York: Columbia University Press, 1959. (b)

Miller, W. B. The impact of a "total community" delinquency control project. *Social Problems,* 1962, *10,* 168–191.

Padfield, H., & Williams, R. *Stay where you were: A study of unemployables in industry.* Philadelphia, Pa.: Lippincott, 1973.

Powers, E., & Witmer, H. *An experiment in the prevention of delinquency: The Cambridge–Somerville youth study.* New York: Columbia University Press, 1951.

Robin, G. R. Anti-poverty programs and delinquency. *Journal of Criminal Law, Criminology, and Police Science,* 1969, *60,* 323–331.

Throwing the Baby out with the Bathwater
The Hazards of Follow-up Research

Suzanne B. Sobel

ABSTRACT: *This article is a critique of the foregoing article by McCord (1978). It is suggested that McCord's conclusions are too strong and may lead policy makers astray. Although the idea of a 30-year follow-up is good, McCord's variables are not strong enough to justify the conclusions drawn.*

Follow-up studies of intervention programs with delinquent youths are often greatly lacking. Although the preceding article by McCord (1978) confirms the previously reported negative results of the Cambridge–Somerville Study (McCord & McCord, 1959a, 1959b; Powers & Witmer, 1951), one can only admire McCord's continued pursuit of this type of research and analysis. Today, with the impact of the increased number of intervention programs in all areas of mental health, research documenting that intervention was not sufficient to deter future criminal behavior merits our careful attention. Although the Powers and Witmer (1951) study addressed "treatment," it is important to remember that it did not address the "psychotherapeutic treatment" of today's standards. Knowledge of psychotherapy has come a long way since the social casework model of the late 1930s. However, the techniques of subject selection were quite detailed, and one wonders whether a more productive study could be designed and executed today.

The data presented by McCord (1978) bring to light many important issues involved with the design and evaluation of studies of treatment outcome. The present article focuses on a few issues directly related to McCord's work.

McCord has not investigated whether the data conform to the "deterioration effect" of treatment, a phenomenon documented by Bergin (1967, 1971). The omission in the analysis of a breakdown of the subjects into "improved" and "not-improved" groups may lead to erroneous and misleading conclusions. Such conclusions become potentially dangerous when utilized to justify planning and programming in the delinquency field that effectively excludes the active involvement of mental health professionals. McCord's view is literal and simplistic. It lacks an appreciation of intrapsychic processes that are affected by treatment. One wonders what her preconceived notions regarding this research may have been and whether or not they were borne out.

McCord reports seven measures that significantly discriminate the treatment and control groups. The relevance of some of these measures is questionable, especially the variable of age at death. Whether the 113 men in the treatment group were judged as improved, worse, or unchanged by their counselors is unknown. If the treatment group had been broken down into these categories and then analyzed with their controls, some differences favoring the "improved" treatment subjects might have appeared. Although it is speculative, but highly possible, that the reported negative effects of treatment might not persist or might remain only for those who had shown no improvement or who had seemed to get worse as time went on, the globalness of the data comparisons leads one to speculate that perhaps the differences may have been washed out.

However, there are some interesting results from a psychological point of view that McCord appears to overlook or discount. That the treatment group was more likely to report having had a stress-related disease is an important result. It is highly possible that the study had a positive impact on the treatment group by getting these men, who traditionally may not have consulted medical facilities, to seek assistance in times of stress, whereas the control subjects were not predisposed to do so since they did not have the relevant experiences and familiarity with the agen-

Requests for reprints should be sent to Suzanne B. Sobel, 230 F Street, N.E., Washington, D.C. 20002.

cies that the treatment group did. Another interesting result was that the treatment group seemed to report more negative self-characteristics; perhaps this resulted because of their involvement in intrapsychically oriented counseling. However, the consistently positive subjective reports of the treatment group about their experiences must have some pervading impact on their lives today. Inquiry into how the subjects relate their experiences with their counselors to their current lives would have been revealing.

McCord's speculation that interaction with adults with different value systems and social statuses may have produced internal conflicts that later manifested in disease or dissatisfaction may be inaccurate. Rather, interaction with these professionals may have led those in the treatment group to develop an awareness of differences and thus a consequently more realistic self-image that may have been negative.

If McCord's speculation about internal conflicts is correct, then professionals involved in intervention programs must be careful to resolve this tension and internal conflict before the termination of a study. Does this then bind us to working with patients for their whole life spans or for the life spans of the psychotherapists or intervention researchers? Perhaps the internal conflict that McCord is speculating about may only be the result of the abrupt. termination of the program, thus reflecting only the effects of incomplete treatment.

The wealth of data from the Cambridge–Somerville Youth Study has not yet been put to adequate use by investigators designing prevention programs. With the abundance of funds spent on intervention programs today, and with assessment occurring only at the cessation of programs, it is a highlight that McCord has continued to assess and reassess these results. Few studies exist in this area. Notable exceptions are the 5- and 10-year follow-ups by Shore and Massimo (1969, 1973) of their studies of the use of vocationally oriented psychotherapy to prevent delinquency. Our data banks on the assessment of the effectiveness of such intervention are incomplete. McCord's analysis challenges the increased use of psychotherapy and psychological input in the rehabilitation and treatment of criminal offenders, especially juvenile ones.

How tragic that this study can be interpreted as showing negative results and, therefore, as indicating extreme caution in the design of intervention programs. While McCord seems to be overconcerned about the potential damage of intervention programs of a social-action nature and desires to mandate pilot projects with mandatory evaluation, it is questionable whether one could pilot a longitudinal study that would insure only positive results. Her conclusion lacks realism.

The legacy that the Cambridge–Somerville Youth Study leaves us is one of careful intervention, constant evaluation, and longitudinal follow-up. The importance of this is emphasized by McCord's work, which guides us toward follow-up studies rather than evaluations solely during the implementation phase. Whether or not the Cambridge–Somerville project prevented crime is an academic question. Certainly the data do not indicate success. But were we to analyze the data systematically in order to structure intervention programs based on them, we might then be in a position to prevent crime, at least as a result of some of the variables that Powers and Witmer (1951) have delineated. The Cambridge–Somerville study and McCord's (1978) follow-up 30 years later should be appreciated and used as guideposts for continuing research on the outcome of intervention.

REFERENCES

Bergin, A. E. Further comments on psychotherapy research and therapeutic practice. *International Journal of Psychiatry*, 1967, *3*, 317–323.

Bergin, A. E. The evaluation of therapeutic outcomes. In A. Bergin & S. Garfield (Eds.), *Handbook of psychotherapy and behavior change.* New York: Wiley, 1971.

McCord, J. A thirty-year follow-up of treatment effects. *American Psychologist*, 1978, *33*, 284–289.

McCord, J., & McCord, W. A follow-up report on the Cambridge–Somerville youth study. *Annals of the American Academy of Political and Social Science*, 1959, *322*, 89–96. (a)

McCord, W., & McCord, J. *Origins of crime.* New York: Columbia University Press, 1959. (b)

Powers, E., & Witmer, H. *An experiment in the prevention of delinquency.* New York: Columbia University Press, 1951.

Shore, M. F., & Massimo, J. L. Five years later: A follow-up study of comprehensive vocationally oriented psychotherapy. *American Journal of Orthopsychiatry*, 1969, *39*, 769–773.

Shore, M. F., & Massimo, J. L. After ten years: A follow-up study of comprehensive vocationally oriented psychotherapy. *American Journal of Orthopsychiatry*, 1973, *43*, 128–132.

Letting the Baby Drown in the Bathwater
Fear of Facts

H. A. Marquis and Paul Gendreau

Sobel (March 1978), in a critique of an article by McCord (March 1978), purports to argue that McCord draws conclusions too strong from variables too weak, with the resulting possibility of leading policymakers astray. In fact, Sobel does not specify which conclusions were too strong nor which variables too weak but presents instead a flailing, unstructured attack characterized by innuendo, unsubstantiated assertions, and inappropriate speculations.

Basically, McCord (1978) reported two findings in her 30-year follow-up of the Cambridge–Somerville Youth Study, a 5-year treatment program designed to prevent delinquency in an eastern Massachusetts area: (1) Of the 57 specific comparisons of treatment and control on objective measures of criminal behavior, health, and family variables, none showed any positive treatment effects. (2) Of these 57 comparisons, 7 showed deleterious effects associated with treatment. Sobel (1978) deals with these findings separately and appears to object to the first on the grounds (a) that treatment was unsophisticated by today's standards, (b) that deterioration effects were not examined, (c) that more detailed analysis on the basis of "improved"– "not improved" may have led to different conclusions, and (d) that

McCord's view is literal and simplistic.

Sobel's first argument appears to be that the "psychotherapeutic treatment" of today would have been more effective. However, no attempt to document this is offered. Moreover, the argument is based on the fact that *knowledge* of psychotherapy has come a long way since the 1930s and that this increased knowledge is reflected in later intervention programs. Again, Sobel fails to substantiate this assumption, and it may be argued that many "modern" intervention programs attempt to modify delinquency patterns with essentially the same sort of programs employed in the Youth Study (cf. Martinson, 1974).

Second, Sobel points out that McCord failed to analyze for deterioration effects. However, if deterioration effects were present, they were not strong enough to wipe out the seven deleterious effects cited. Moreover, it should be pointed out that McCord drew *no* conclusions regarding the failure of positive treatment effects and is therefore less compelled to such rigorous data analysis.

A similar argument can be marshaled against Sobel's assertion that McCord should have analyzed the data after a breakdown into "improved" and "not-improved" sub-

From H. A. Marquis and Paul Gendreau, "Letting the Baby Drown in the Bathwater: Fear of Facts," *American Psychologist* 180-181 (February 1979). Copyright 1979 by the American Psychological Association. Reprinted by Permission.

jects. Since McCord's main point was the possible deleterious effects of treatment, a breakdown of this sort could not have mitigated this finding. Although it might have been possible to demonstrate some positive treatment effects for the "improved" group while showing even more harmful effects for the "not-improved" group, this would not have altered McCord's conclusion regarding the possible harmful effects of treatment.

Unfortunately, Sobel does not explain or elaborate on her assertion that McCord's view is literal and simplistic and as it stands is meaningless. Sobel's exhortation for more appreciation of intrapsychic processes (unidentified) suggests she is confusing *literal* and *simplistic* with *objective* and *measurable*. Such criticism would carry weight if those intrapsychic processes were identified and their relevance to behavior suggested. Sobel's snide speculation about McCord's "preconceived notions" does not elucidate or enhance her critique, and can only be considered as inappropriate for a scientific journal as well as in poor taste.

Regarding McCord's major finding of deleterious treatment effects, Sobel has little of substance to say. She doubts the relevance of some of the variables reported. These are unspecified (except age at death), and her use of *relevance* is unexplained. Surely, age of death is relevant, if only to those undergoing treatment. If Sobel means by relevance "connection to treatment," then that is a matter for further experimentation and/or data analysis but does not mitigate against McCord's findings.

Sobel does, however, quibble with McCord's speculation, suggesting that it may be inaccurate, an inherent danger of all speculation including Sobel's. In fact, while failing to see the "relevance" of age of death, Sobel goes on to speculate that apparent treatment-related increases in stress-related diseases could be due to increased contact with medical authorities. Perhaps a more parsimonious explanation would be that the stress-related diseases were more prevalent among the treatment group, and these, at least in part, helped account for earlier age at death.

Sobel continues her critique with a statement on the tragedy of the McCord study. This, according to Sobel, is that the McCord study "can be *interpreted*" (p. 291, italics added) as showing negative results and, therefore, as indicating *extreme* caution in the design of intervention programs. We think little interpretation is needed; the study, justifiably indicates, and it claims no more, that *some* consideration be given to the design of intervention programs. In fact, we would argue that in this instance McCord could have elaborated on her point. That is, evaluation of the usefulness of correctional treatment programs has focused almost entirely on the adequacy of research design and the measurement of outcome. Completely forgotten has been the issue of whether in fact many of the programs implemented in the past could have been expected to have had any positive effect on delinquent behavior whatsoever. Only recently has anyone bothered to address this problem (Quay, 1977). Quay has convincingly demonstrated that the failure to deal with this particular question has been a major flaw in preventive work in corrections.

In fact, there have been a substantial number of studies since Martinson's (1974) review indicating that correctional treatment programs can be successful. One of these reviews (Gendreau & Ross, in press) reported over 80 studies published since 1973 indicating that correctional programs do work. These programs ranged from contingency management, family intervention, and diversion to counseling approaches based on a social-learning-theory format. All of them, it should be noted, employed multimethod approaches, and the intensity and duration of the service provided far surpassed what was employed in intervention studies done a decade ago. Thus, McCord (1978) could have made her conclusions more realistic if she had referred to some

of this literature and contrasted these with the Youth Project when she argued that "new programs ought to be developed" (p. 289).

Finally, Sobel (1978) claims that the efficacy of the Youth Study is an academic question. If Sobel is using the word *academic* as it is often used, to mean without resolution or basis in fact, then she is decidedly mistaken. The efficacy of the Youth Study is an empirical question, one McCord has gone a long way in answering. Moreover, reviews of the recent literature support one of McCord's conclusions— that is, some of the traditional counseling and relationship models (similar to those used in the Youth Study) have been associated with either no significant or significantly negative effects in regard to changing offenders' behavior (Andrews, 1977). This is a fact that Sobel appears reluctant to face.

REFERENCES

Andrews, D. A. *Dimensions of correctional counselling and the supervisory process in prediction and parole: 1. Quality of the relationship.* Ottawa, Canada: Canadian Volunteers in Corrections, 1977.

Gendreau, P., & Ross, R. Effective correctional treatment: Bibliotherapy for cynics. *Crime & Delinquency,* in press.

Martinson, R. What works? Questions and answers about prison re-

form. *Public Interest,* 1974, *35,* 22–54.

McCord, J. A thirty-year follow-up of treatment effects. *American Psychologist,* 1978, *33,* 284–289.

Quay, H. C. The three faces of evaluation: What can be expected to work. *Criminal Justice and Behavior,* 1977, *4,* 341–354.

Sobel, S. B. Throwing the baby out with the bathwater: The hazards of follow-up research. *American Psychologist,* 1978, *33,* 290–291.

Intestinal bypass surgery is a medical procedure that has recently been developed for the treatment of extreme obesity. By reducing the absorptive capacity of the small intestine, significant weight losses can be achieved in many obese patients. However, the weight loss comes at a considerable cost in terms of direct side effects of the operation—including chronic diarrhea, electrolyte imbalance, possible liver impairment, and psychological depression (see Leon, 1976**). Medical researchers have been less careful in tracking down some of the possible secondary effects of weight loss resulting from the changes in the patient's appearance.

The following presents a retrospective study of changes in marital relationships after intestinal bypass surgery. This work reminds us that medical procedures that alter markedly the appearance or the chronic level of mental or physical functioning of a patient may have profound effects on not only the patient, but on those around the patient (see Berscheid and Walster, 1974*). Specifically, Neill and his associates found that increased marital discord and diminished sexual functioning followed the successful bypass operation.

Although this finding is provocative, it must be considered with caution because of the retrospective case study methodology. A number of rival hypotheses are also consistent with the results. For example, perhaps patients who were beginning to have difficulties in their marriages were highly likely to seek treatment. Or, perhaps spouses were quite displeased with the patient's decision to undertake a voluntary operation (with major side effects and a minor risk of death) to achieve primarily cosmetic benefits. Although Neill et al. have performed a service by alerting us to important possible secondary effects of certain medical procedures, only more sophisticated prospective research designs can allow us to determine the importance and magnitude of these effects.

*BERSCHEID, E. and E. WALSTER (1974) Physical Attractiveness, pp. 157-215 in L. Berkowitz (ed.) Advances in Experimental Social Psychology (vol. 7). New York: Academic Press.
**LEON, G. R. (1976) Current Directions in the Treatment of Obesity. Psychological Bulletin 83, 557-578.

38

Marital Changes After Intestinal Bypass Surgery

John R. Neill, John R. Marshall, and Charles E. Yale

● A retrospective interview study was undertaken of 14 spousal pairs in which one member had undergone the intestinal bypass procedure for massive obesity. Much unanticipated marital discord occurred. Sexual problems were particularly troublesome and affected both members in the spousal pairs. The results point to the role of massive obesity as a selective and stabilizing factor in the marriages of this subset of overweight persons.

(*JAMA* 240:447-450, 1978)

From the Departments of Psychiatry, University of Kentucky College of Medicine, Lexington (Dr Neill); and the Departments of Psychiatry (Dr Marshall) and Surgery (Dr Yale), University of Wisconsin Medical School, Madison.

Reprint requests to Department of Psychiatry, University of Kentucky College of Medicine, 800 Rose St, Lexington, KY 40506 (Dr Neill).

ALTHOUGH professional acceptance of intestinal bypass for the treatment of massive obesity is far from universal, many feel that operative risks and medical complications have been sufficiently reduced to justify the procedure for some patients.[1] The majority of patients who have undergone bypass surgery are reported to be pleased and would still elect to undergo the surgery if they had to do it over.[2-4]

Although most postoperative reports speak of increased levels of interpersonal function and satisfaction, Solow et al[4] described several spouses who could not accommodate to changes in the marriage following the weight loss; these workers believed that this eventually led to divorce. Castelnuovo-Tedesco and Schiebel,[3] noting emotional crises related to interpersonal issues among bypass patients, mention three divorces and several sexual affairs. Husbands of patients in the study of Kalucy and Crisp,[5] in addition to gaining weight themselves, felt pressure to change in other ways. Winkelman and co-workers[6] reported a number of patients who became "totally estranged from their family as well as unable to work." Because of these reports, we investigated the effects of the surgery and weight loss on the marital relationship. This was part of a general assessment of postoperative complications in the bypass procedure.

MATERIALS AND METHODS

Volunteers were solicited from a series of 17 bypass patients who were married at the time of their surgery; 14 agreed to take part. The patients and their spouses participated in separate semistructured interviews of 1½ to 2½ hours' duration. Two of the 14 patients had been divorced since surgery and their ex-spouses were unavailable. We focused on the marital relationship before surgery, the decision to have the surgery, and postoperative changes. Information was supplemented with medical records and by staff personnel.

RESULTS

Patient Characteristics.—Of the 14 patients, 12 were women (Table 1). They ranged in age from 29 to 51 years, with an average age of 37 years. All fell within class 3 or 4 on the Hollingshead Index of social position. All were white. The average time lapsed from surgery to interview time was 22 months, with a range of eight to 36 months. Preoperative weight averaged 150 kg, with a range of 96 to 218 kg. The patients averaged 152% over desirable weight, with a range of 110% to 256%. Postoperatively, the average weight loss at the one-year mark was 7 kg per month, with a range of 3 to 10 kg. At last follow-up (at time of interview), the average weight loss was 41% of preoperative weight (94 kg).

Marital Assessment.—Twelve of the 14 patients were moderate to extremely overweight at the time of marriage (Table 2). The majority of the couples spoke of mixed satisfaction with marriage prior to surgery but felt fortunate that they had been able to marry at all. Ten of the 12 female patients described their husbands as inadequate, docile, weak, clinging, and in other ways dependent on them. Spouses of the patients tended to openly confirm their dependence and passivity. They felt shy, introverted, and not eager for adventure. Feeling lucky to be married, they did not voice strong negative feelings about their spouses' weight problem. Six of the 12 male spouses fit the "Jack Sprat and wife syndrome" described by Fink et al,[7] consisting of a very thin man married to an obese woman.

Decision to Undergo Surgery.—Motivations for the surgery were carefully examined, but categorization of such

Table 1.—Patient Characteristics					
Patient/ Sex/Age at Bypass, yr	Preoperative Weight, kg	Over Desirable Weight, %*	Months Postoperative	Weight Lost, kg*	Initial Body Weight Lost, %
1/M/51	171	111	36	9	38
2/F/45	144	138	34	10	22
3/F/33	171	181	30	9	36
4/F/32	112	113	30	6	32
5/F/26	179	178	28	7	59
6/F/29	134	151	26	5	53
7/F/42	127	110	24	3	43
8/M/36	218	217	27	8	52
9/F/38	141	145	26	4	44
10/F/45	181	256	12	5	36
11/F/29	96	114	9	5†	31
12/F/31	147	156	8	5†	28
13/F/46	126	133	12	5	50
14/F/32	122	125	8	6†	43

*Per month, average.
†Less than one-year follow-up period.

motives was not easy. Seven of the patients spoke primarily of psychological reasons, such as the wish to be less self-conscious, to feel more attractive, or to be less critical of themselves. Of these, five specifically mentioned fears that their obesity threatened the continuation of their marriages. Four sought relief primarily from physical distress, and three offered mixtures of these as their rationale. It was apparent during these conversations that though the patients attempted to communicate conscious motivation, most had several, mixed, and less ostensible hopes. This rough categorization of motives was not related to subsequent satisfaction with the procedure or degree of marital distress noted.

These patients actively sought out the procedure. A high level of perseverance and assertiveness was needed, as there was little support from their loved ones; this was puzzling and disappointing to the patients. According to the patients, only three spouses were supportive of the procedure. Eight were character-ized as neutral. Three spouses were strongly opposed to the surgery, ascribing their opposition to concerns over the risks. The original families tended to have the same attitude, leaving the patients with a strong sense of "going it alone."

Postoperative Experiences.—Both patients and spouses found the immediate postoperative phase of untoward postoperative sequelae (nausea, vomiting, diarrhea, and fatigue) extremely stressful. All patients experienced some degree of depression or affective lability. Two reported suicidal ideation but did not seek psychiatric attention. Many recalled that during this period they doubted the wisdom of their decision. However, most physical symptoms, generally self-limiting, abated gradually over the ensuing three to six months, only occasionally lasting up to one year. Following this recuperative period, the patients described positive attitudinal and behavioral changes similar to those reported by subjects in other studies. Most noteworthy and consistent were the changes in self-image; all patients reported these changes were positive. They still experienced some periods of depression, but these were less frequent and less severe than during the early postoperative phase.

Though satisfaction with the amount of weight lost varied at time of interview, all but one married patient who had reached the one-year postbypass anniversary were happy with the results of the surgery. They were coping well with residual effects and were pleased with personal changes that they attributed to their weight loss. All but one patient would have done it over if given a chance to decide again. The one exception was a female patient who had suspected her husband of homosexual tendencies prior to the surgery. Not shared with the physician prior to the procedure, it had been her hope that in becoming more attractive, she could "lure him back." When this did not occur, she asked for the bypass to be taken down.

Changes in Marital Relationship.—Striking changes were noted in the couples' relationships. Only one patient denied any change. The others described varying amounts of turmoil, ranging from brief disruptions to rather severe upheavals threatening the marriage. Two patients were eventually divorced, and one other planned separation at time of interview.

The stresses were numerous. Some emanated from the same personality changes the patients viewed as positive. For example, as confidence grew and fears of rejection diminished, patients became more expressive and assertive. Some spouses greeted these changes with dismay, eg, "I don't know what she wants anymore, I can't please her."

A major area of conflict occurred around the issue of spousal autonomy. Several of the female patients reported that their increased social activity (previously curtailed by their obesity) provoked hostility and withdrawal in their mates. Fears of abandonment were prominent in both. One wife-patient described the changes as follows:

I want to know better-quality people now and to discuss something other than diapers and baby food. I want to improve my mind. The more I get around, the more I see that I was holding myself down.

Her husband responded, "She's gotten it into her head that she's too good for anybody and that includes me. I don't have any interest in that sort of people. She probably is going to have an affair and go on and marry one of them." Spouses also attempted to place restrictions on the patients' time spent outside of the home, but this resulted in more conflict and marital strife. Distribution of family work load also became an issue. Now that the patient was less housebound, who was going to do much of the housework and take care of the children? Nonpatient spouses were angered and reluctant to renegotiate these previously defined and accepted roles.

New educational and vocational enterprises stimulated further conflict. The general movement out into the world resulted in four patients becoming employed. One opened a specialty service shop, and two opened clothing stores specializing in fashions for the overweight. The attitudes of the spouses fluctuated between skepticism and resentment. At no time were they enthusiastic or supportive. This appeared contradic-

				After Bypass		
Patient	Weight Gain During Marriage, kg	Spouse Attitude	Satisfied With Bypass	Marital Relationship	Sexual Relationship	Comment
1	70	N	Yes	NC	NC	None
2	67	N	No	DET	IMP	Spouse had affair; patient not satisfied with weight loss
3	UNK	O	Mixed	NC	DET	Now feels spouse is inadequate
4	74	N	Yes	DIV	DIV	Felt spouse inadequate for needs
5	0	O	Yes	DET	IMP	Spouse has begun bisexual activity
6	67	N	Yes	NC	DET	Spouse spending more time at work
7	51	O	Yes	DIV	DIV	Spouse discovered to be homosexual recently
8	107	S	Mixed	DET	DET	Spouse had affair since operation
9	60	N	Mixed	DET	DET	Spouse is impotent
10	109	S	Yes	NC	NC	Spouse fears patient will leave him
11	50	N	Yes	DET	NC	Separation being considered
12	90	N	Mixed	DET	IMP	Patient feels spouse "not good enough"
13	36	N	Yes	NC	DET	Patient has ceased sexual relations since operation (spouse lost interest)
14	9	S	Yes	DET	IMP	Spouse has increased homosexual activity since bypass

Table 2.—Marital Assessment*

*UNK indicates unknown; N, neutral; S, supportive; O, opposed; NC, no change; IMP, improved; DET, deteriorated; DIV, divorced.

tory, since prior to bypass surgery the wives maintained that these men had been sharply critical of their economic unproductivity.

It appeared that fears of abandonment underlay most of these ostensibly practical disagreements. One husband of a patient was explicit. He said "Before [the operation] she was very dependent on me; now she can help herself. . . . It would bother me if she got too active." In separate interviews, his wife said scornfully, "He treated me like his mother. I felt like he was my child and dependent on me for everything. . . . I have a terrific feeling now. . . . I still feel as if I got to 145 pounds, I'd be up and gone. I can work and support myself, and my husband knows it."

Sexual Effects.—Most unexpected was the noticeable disruption in many couples' sexual relationships following surgery. Nine patients described an increased level of interest in sexual fantasies and intercourse. The patients felt sexually attractive, playful, occasionally flirtatious, and more willing to initiate sexual encounters. Several attributed this change to a diminished fear of rejection. Others felt the change might be due to a more basic physiological change, perhaps hormonal. For three patients, libido severely declined, which was both puzzling and troubling. Most commonly, as their partners began to lose weight, spouses felt threatened; a spouse said, "I suppose you will find someone better now," and another declared, "With legs as attractive as those, I am sure you will find another man." Jealousy, tinged with anxiety, was a common response of the husbands.

During the postoperative period, three of the nonpatient husbands became openly homosexual. Three others became impotent, attributing this directly to the increased demands placed on them by their patient-spouses. At least five other couples reported a "cooling of interest" in the nonpatient partners, though two of these men had engaged in extramarital affairs. One other spouse had an affair prior to the surgery following his wife's decision to undergo the procedure. Only two spouses described themselves as pleased with the sexual interest of their wives. One husband stated, "We could use another man around the house to keep her rejuvenated." He described spending more hours at work, admitting it was to avoid his wife's "sex need." He concluded, "Now I've got the headache in the family." Most noteworthy is the reciprocating pattern of these changes.

COMMENT

From what is known of the three couples who declined to participate in this study, it does not appear that the subject couples represent a biased sample. There was conflict in the majority of these marriages. For a few, it appeared that as the patient's personal satisfaction increased, the marital relationship deteriorated.

There are several possible explanations for our findings. First, this is a highly self-selected group, and how the decision to have the surgery relates to prior interpersonal events is unclear. Perhaps the surgery occurs at a point of crisis in the relationship when other coping mechanisms are failing. Thus, the surgery and subsequent weight loss would be a result of conflict rather than a cause of it. For several of our couples, this explanation appeared plausible.

It has also been suggested that these massively obese patients are neurotic, and that their spouses usually are noticeably psychopathologic.[3] Thus, marital discord may be the natural result of these relationships and surgery only a nonspecific stress. However, this is not compatible with the reports of these couples, who view both the surgery and the weight loss as direct precipitants of their difficulties.

The most heuristic explanation, we believe, comes from viewing the patient as part of a dynamic system in which the obesity plays an important role. Most of the patients were obese when mutual mate selection occurred, and subsequent interactions within the marriage appeared to have reinforced the meaning of the obesity for the couple. The obesity of one partner also has a protective function and exerts a stabilizing influence on both the individuals and the marriage. The surgery, weight loss, and subsequent changes seem to have upset an equilibrium, temporarily for some, and more permanent for others. Perhaps the reservations about surgery by spouses and families reflect their awareness of this delicate balance.

CONCLUSION

We recommend that preoperative screening and preparation include the spouse and perhaps others in the extended family. Couples should be told of the possibility of marital discord following surgery. Ideally, a careful, thoughtful discussion of these issues by the couple would ensue prior to commitment by the patient and the surgical team. This would ensure a broader informed consent.

Further, we recommend that psychiatric follow-up in the form of brief screening interviews be instituted at intervals corresponding with medical examinations. This may forestall breakdown.[3] Including the spouse of the patient in such follow-ups assures a complete review of systems and lays the groundwork for effective intervention when indicated. Such an approach is not only consonant with comprehensive patient care, but will generate information on the important and poorly understood role of family and interpersonal dynamics on physical symptoms.

References

1. Malt RA, Guggenheim F: Surgery for obesity. N Engl J Med 295:43-44, 1976.
2. Abram JS, Meixel SA, Webb WW, et al: Psychological adaptation to jejunoileal bypass for morbid obesity. J Nerv Ment Dis 162:151-157, 1976.
3. Castelnuovo-Tedesco P, Schiebel D: Studies of superobesity: II. Psychiatric appraisal of jejuno-ileal bypass surgery. Am J Psychiatry 133:26-31, 1976.
4. Solow C, Silberfarb PM, Swift K: Psychosocial effects of intestinal bypass surgery for severe obesity. N Engl J Med 290:300-304, 1974.
5. Kalucy RS, Crisp AH: Some psychological and social implications of massive obesity. J Psychosom Res 18:465-473, 1974.
6. Winkelman EI, Schumacher OP, Hermann RE, et al: Result of the jejunoileal shunt in the treatment of morbid obesity. Read at the annual session of the American College of Physicians, New York, April 1, 1974.
7. Fink G, Gottesfeld H, Glickman L: "The superobese" patient. J Hillside Hosp 11:97-119, 1962.
8. Weight distributions. Metropolitan Life Insurance Co Statistical Bull, Nov-Dec 1959, pp 2-3.

It is not uncommon in health care interventions for planners to propose large-scale screening of populations for premorbid conditions in the expectation that when the conditions are properly recognized, they can be dealt with, preventing or postponing morbidity. However, labeling theory from sociology leads to the expectation that identifying and labeling a person as characterized by some pathological condition may exacerbate that condition through a sort of self-fulfilling prophecy. Labeling effects have been claimed for conditions as diverse as delinquency, schizophrenia, and sickle-cell anemia. Now Haynes and his associates have evidence that even more ordinary medical conditions may, if identified and labeled, be associated with undesirable consequences. These results should give pause to program planners and evaluators who, during the course of their activities, intend to engage in case-finding efforts or other efforts with the potential to produce a reactive effect.

39

Increased Absenteeism from Work After Detection and Labeling of Hypertensive Patients

R. Brian Haynes, David L. Sackett, D. Wayne Taylor,
Edward S. Gibson, and Arnold L. Johnson

Abstract A study of hypertension in an industrial setting allowed us to confirm and explore an earlier retrospective finding that the labeling of patients as hypertensive resulted in increased absenteeism from work. After screening and referral, we found that absenteeism rose (mean ±1 S.E.) 5.2±2.3 days per year (P<0.025); this 80 per cent increase greatly exceeded the 9 per cent rise in absenteeism in the general employee population during this period. The main factors associated with increased absenteeism were becoming aware of the condition (P<0.01) and low compliance with treatment (P<0.001). Subsequent absenteeism among patients unaware of their hypertension before screening was not related to the degree of hypertension, whether the worker was started on therapy, the degree of blood-pressure control achieved or exposure to attempts to promote compliance. These results have major implications for hypertension screening programs, especially since absenteeism rose among those previously unaware of their condition, regardless of whether antihypertensive therapy was begun. (N Engl J Med 299:741-744, 1978)

THE rationale for the detection and treatment of hypertension is the expectation that, in the long run, these steps will reduce premature morbidity and untimely death. One comprehensive detection and treatment program has, in fact, documented a reduction in "disability days" (absences from work of five or more days) among hypertensive employees of a department store.[1] On the other hand, a recent United States survey reported twice as many days away from work or usual activities among employees who were aware of their hypertension as among those who either were normotensive or were unaware that they had hypertension,[2] and a retrospective study that we performed several years ago at a Canadian steel mill produced similar results for work absence.[3]

Because of the latter finding, we have gathered data on absenteeism both before and after screening steelworkers for hypertension as part of a series of randomized clinical trials of compliance-improving strategies.[4,5] The following specific questions were addressed: Does the labeling of a worker as hypertensive result in increased illness absenteeism? And, if increased absenteeism does occur, what relation does it bear to the institution of antihypertensive therapy, to compliance with that therapy, to the success of blood-pressure control and to efforts to improve compliance?

METHODS

The patients in this investigation were participants in a series of randomized trials of strategies to improve compliance with antihypertensive therapy that have been described in detail elsewhere.[4,5]

From the Department of Clinical Epidemiology and Biostatistics and the Department of Medicine, McMaster University Faculty of Health Sciences, and Dominion Foundries and Steel Limited, Hamilton ON, Canada (address reprint requests to Dr. Haynes at the Department of Clinical Epidemiology and Biostatistics, McMaster University Health Sciences Centre, 1200 Main St. West, Hamilton, ON, Canada, L8S 4J9).

Supported in part by a grant (MA-5195) from the Medical Research Council of Canada, by the Sun Life Assurance Company of Canada and by the Dominion Foundries and Steel Company of Canada.

In brief, a random two thirds (5400) of the male employees of the Dominion Foundries and Steel Limited of Hamilton, Canada, were asked whether they had ever been told that they had high blood pressure, and were then screened for hypertension. A total of 245 men met the following criteria: average fifth-phase diastolic blood pressure >95 mm Hg (average of the second and third of three readings taken with the patient sitting quietly on each of two separate occasions over a three-month period); no antihypertensive therapy for at least six months before screening; no other daily medications; and no remediable secondary form of hypertension. After explanation of the nature of the study, 94 per cent of these men consented to participate in six-month randomized trials of compliance-improving strategies (mastering facts about hypertension and its treatment,[4] care at the work site on "company time,"[4] and a package of behaviorally oriented strategies, including self blood-pressure measurement at home and increased supervision.[5] A summary of each man's clinical findings was forwarded to his physician, who was free to decide whether and with what regimen to treat the hypertension. At subsequent six-month intervals, we performed standardized measurements of treatment status, blood-pressure control and medication compliance. The last was assessed by pill counts performed unobtrusively at a home visit, the ostensible purpose for which was to determine the patient's blood pressure while at home.[4,5]

Absenteeism was determined directly from routine company time-clock records, gathered by an independent department at the mill. These records classified absences from work into three categories: "illness" (employees calling in "sick"), "compensation" (work-related injury) or "other" (such as leave of absence for bereavement). All absenteeism was included beginning with the first day of any episode. Employees on hourly wages constituted 88 per cent of the study subjects and, by company policy, lost pay for the first three days of any episode of illness absenteeism. Absenteeism records of each study subject were abstracted for "mirror" periods of the same length before and after blood-pressure screening. The exact duration of a subject's participation in the study was used for analysis and for creation of the mirror periods; for most subjects this interval was somewhat longer than one year. To standardize comparisons, absenteeism for the few subjects who joined the mill less than one year before screening was pro-rated to give a yearly rate. Weekends and statutory holidays (for which pay was not lost) were included in an illness episode only if scheduled days were missed both before and afterward.

Statistical analyses were performed on absenteeism rates with paired and unpaired t-tests. One-tailed tests were applied because the direction of the results was apparent from our preliminary study.[3] Nonparametric analyses of the data were also performed because of the positive skew of the absenteeism distribution: the results were similar to those of the parametric tests and therefore will not be reported here.

RESULTS

Complete follow-up observation for one year or more after screening was achieved for 208 (90 per cent) of the participants. Data were missing for 11 men who left employment at the plant and an additional 11 men who either refused or were unavailable for part of their assessments.

Absenteeism for all study subjects is shown in Table 1. As compared with the year before screening, days of absenteeism increased 80 per cent ($P<0.025$), greatly exceeding the 9 per cent rise in absenteeism among the general plant population during the same period.

Most of the increment in absenteeism (79 per cent, $P<0.001$) was due to increased days absent because of self-reported illness, rather than to compensable work-related injury or leaves of absence, for which there were no consistent changes and which will therefore not be considered further. The increased length of illness episodes was due mainly to an increase in the proportion of episodes lasting longer than 10 days ($P<0.005$), with no apparent shift occurring at the four-day time of onset of sickness pay benefits. These observations apply consistently throughout the data set, and the remainder of the report will therefore focus on the most pertinent measurement: days of illness absenteeism per year.

Relation to Prior Awareness and Labeling

One hundred and thirty-eight men denied ever having been told that they had hypertension previously ("unaware" group), and 70 men stated that they had been so told ("aware" group). In a review of company records, however, all the unaware group had documented diastolic blood pressures of at least 90 mm Hg for over a year before screening, although their pressures were somewhat lower (diastolic blood pressure

Table 1. Work Absenteeism in the Year before and after Labeling.

DATUM STUDIED	ALL 208 SUBJECTS	138 PREVIOUSLY UNAWARE SUBJECTS	70 PREVIOUSLY AWARE SUBJECTS
Total days absent/yr:			
Yr before screening	6.7±1.1*	6.6±1.6	7.0±1.4
Yr after screening	11.9±2.1	12.3±2.7	11.1±3.7
Increase	5.2±2.3†	5.7±2.8‡	4.1±3.8
Days absent due to illness/yr:			
Yr before screening	3.6±0.62	2.7±0.61§	5.4±1.4
Yr after screening	7.6±1.2	8.4±1.6	6.1±1.9
Increase	4.1±1.2¶	5.8±1.5§¶	0.7±2.1
No. of illness episodes/yr:			
Yr before screening	1.4±0.12	1.2±0.14	1.6±1.9
Yr after screening	1.6±0.14	1.6±0.18	1.6±1.9
Increase	0.3±0.13†	0.4±0.14‡	None
Days/illness episode:			
Yr before screening	1.4±0.17	1.1±0.17§	1.9±0.38
Yr after screening	3.6±0.69	4.0±1.0	2.7±0.68
Increase	2.2±0.70¶	2.9±1.0‡§	0.8±0.53

*Mean ± SE.
†P<0.025 for 1-tailed paired t-test (within group).
‡P<0.05 for 1-tailed paired t-test (within group).
¶P<0.01 for 1-tailed paired t-test (within group).
§P<0.05 for 1-tailed unpaired t-test comparing aware & unaware subjects.

Table 2. Effect of Treatment on Illness Absenteeism.

GROUP	DAYS ABSENT BECAUSE OF ILLNESS		
	YR BEFORE SCREENING	YR AFTER SCREENING	INCREASE
Previously unaware:			
Treated (85)*	2.3±0.32†	8.6±2.0	6.3±2.0‡¶
Untreated (53)	3.3±1.5	8.1±2.6	4.8±2.4§¶
Previously aware:			
Treated (53)	3.9±1.1	7.1±2.5	3.2±2.2‖**
Untreated (17)	10.1±4.5	2.9±1.1	−7.2±4.5‖

*No. of patients.   †Mean ± SE.
‡P<0.01 within group for increase.   §P<0.05 within group for increase.
¶P not significant between groups for increase.
‖P not significant within group for increase.
**P<0.001 between groups for increase.

averaged 102 mm Hg) than those of the aware group (average of 105 mm Hg; $P<0.05$). Thus, a portion of the unaware may have been informed previously and had merely forgotten that they had been told. In either event, screening resulted in the labeling of these 138 "unaware" hypertensive patients, whereas the "aware" group of 70 men were merely reminded of their hypertension by the screening process.

As shown in Table 1, aware patients exhibited twice as much illness absenteeism as the unaware group in the year before screening. Furthermore, this difference in absenteeism in the year before screening could not be explained by differences in blood pressures at screening, in age or in the occurrence of target-organ damage.

During the year after screening and labeling the unaware group demonstrated a dramatic rise in illness absenteeism, more than trebling it. The previously aware group, on the other hand, showed only a small rise that was not statistically significant, with the net result that their absenteeism rate in the year after screening was surpassed by the newly labeled group, although not to a degree achieving statistical significance.

Relation to Treatment

The decision to start antihypertensive medications was left entirely up to the 83 attending physicians involved in the study, and they elected to prescribe antihypertensive medications for 138, or 66 per cent, of patients. The other 70 either remained untreated or were prescribed regimens that did not include antihypertensive drugs (in this analysis, tranquilizers, weight reduction and exercise were not regarded as antihypertensive regimens).

A striking finding (Table 2) was the observation that illness absenteeism rose substantially after labeling of previously unaware patients as hypertensive even if they were not treated.

Among previously aware patients, on the other hand, there were no statistically significant changes in illness absenteeism for either the treated or the untreated subgroups. However, a rise in absenteeism in the treated patients and a substantial fall in the untreated ones resulted in a statistically significant difference between the two categories. The interpretation of this finding is problematic, however, because the previously aware group which remained untreated was small (17 in number) and had a very high absenteeism rate in the year before screening as compared with the aware group who were treated. Thus, these two subgroups were substantially different before the institution of therapy in the subsequently treated group.

Relation to Compliance with Treatment

Treatment compliance was assessed for the 128 patients for whom antihypertensive drugs were prescribed throughout the entire year after screening, and the relation between compliance and absenteeism is shown in Table 3. Among those previously unaware, compliant patients (those consuming at least 80 per cent of their medication during the 12th month of therapy) experienced no statistically significant rise in absenteeism whereas noncompliant patients did show a significant rise. Noncompliance was not associated with a rise in absenteeism among aware patients, however.

Relation to Blood-Pressure Control

There was no association between achievement of "goal blood presure" (diastolic blood pressure <90 mm Hg at the 12-month assessment) and absenteeism among either previously unaware or aware patients.

Relation to Compliance-Improving Strategies

As reported previously, the instructional program and the work-site treatment strategy both failed to increase compliance or improve blood-pressure control.[4] The behavioral-modification program, however, improved both compliance and blood-pressure response.[5] Rises in absenteeism occurred in each of the three intervention trials, with no statistically significant differences appearing between any group of experimental subjects and their corresponding controls. The increases were again restricted to previously unaware subjects.

Table 3. Relation of Compliance with Medications to Illness Absenteeism.

Group	Days Absent Because of Illness		
	YR BEFORE SCREENING	YR AFTER SCREENING	INCREASE
Previously unaware:			
⩾80% compliance (43)*	2.0±0.49†	3.2±0.70	1.2±0.72‡ } ¶
<80% compliance (35)	2.6±0.47	12.0±3.4	9.4±3.5§
Previously aware:			
⩾80% compliance (31)	3.6±1.2	4.3±1.4	0.7±1.8‡ } ‖
<80% compliance (19)	3.4±2.1	5.1±1.9	1.6±1.3‡

*No. of patients.
†Mean ± SE.
‡P not significant within group for increase.
§P<0.025 within group for increase.
¶P<0.01 between groups for increase.
‖P not significant between groups for increase.

Table 4. Multiple-Regression Coefficients for the Dependent Variable, Increase in Illness Rate.

Independent Variable*	All Patients			Treated Patients		
	TOTAL	AWARE	UNAWARE	TOTAL	AWARE	UNAWARE
	(208)†	(70)	(138)	(128)	(50)	(78)
Awareness	−0.149‡	N/A§	N/A	−0.129	N/A	N/A
Treatment status	+0.101	+0.320¶	+0.025	N/A	N/A	N/A
DBP at 12 mo	−0.033	+0.146	−0.104	−0.062	−0.045	−0.013
Education program	+0.046	−0.081	+0.105	+0.118	−0.074	+0.222‡
Convenient care	−0.011	−0.169	+0.028	−0.035	−0.223	+0.001
Compliance	N/A	N/A	N/A	−0.233¶	−0.037	−0.326¶

*Independent variables in the analysis were coded as follows: awareness, unaware before screening = 0, & aware before screening = 1; treatment status, antihypertensive therapy not prescribed = 0, & prescribed = 1; diastolic blood pressure (DBP) at 12 mo, <90 mm Hg = 0, & >90 mm Hg = 1; education program, not received = 0, & received = 1; convenient care, not received = 0, & received = 1; compliance, compliance at 12 mo, <80% = 0, & ⩾80% = 1. Figures in table are regression coefficients representing the independent contribution of a given variable to the increase in illness rate after screening when all other variables in the analysis are controlled for.
†No. of patients.
‡P<0.05, by 1-tailed test.
§Not applicable.
¶P<0.01, by 1-tailed test.

Multiple-Regression Analyses

To determine whether the above associations persisted when other factors were taken into account, multiple-regression analyses were performed as recorded in Table 4. When the findings of the regression analyses are compared with those reported in Tables 1-3 it can be seen that the associations were confirmed to be independent. An additional finding in the multiple-regression analysis was that among previously unaware patients, the education program was associated with increased absenteeism.

Discussion

We have found dramatically increased absenteeism, particularly that due to illness, when steelworkers are labeled hypertensive. This increase in illness absenteeism bears a striking relation to the employee's awareness of the diagnosis but appears unaffected by the institution of antihypertensive therapy or the degree of success in reducing blood pressure. The application of attempts to promote compliance with therapy did not influence absenteeism, although an instructional program appears to have resulted in increased absenteeism among previously unaware patients. On the other hand, treated workers who were compliant with therapy did not exhibit increased absenteeism.

How can these findings be explained? A tempting interpretation is that the labeling of a person as hypertensive is deleterious, causing many patients with newly labeled hypertension to adopt the "sick role" and treat themselves as more "fragile." Consistent with this labeling hypothesis are the findings that patients previously aware of their hypertension had significantly higher illness absenteeism to begin with, that previously unaware patients experienced a sharp increase in absenteeism, and that the educational program appeared to enhance the effect of labeling among unaware subjects.

Are these findings unique? The Harris Poll community survey of hypertension discovered that respondents who stated they had high blood pressure reported missing twice as many days from work as those who were either normotensive or not aware that they were hypertensive.[2] Furthermore, psychologic well-being and reports of physical health in the United States Health and Nutrition Examination Survey were significantly lower among people who were aware that they had hypertension (regardless of their treatment or control status) than among those who were unaware or those who were normotensive (Monk M: personal communication). Finally, studies of other conditions have documented substantial activity restrictions among children labeled as having cardiac disease mistakenly[6] or sickle-cell trait,[7] even though only highly selected activities were intended to be restricted.

On the other hand, employees participating in a department-store hypertension detection and comprehensive treatment project[1] exhibited reduced "disability days" as compared with other employees and with their experience before treatment. However, disability days in this latter study included only illness episodes in excess of four days (Alderman MH: personal communication), which is not comparable to the collection of absenteeism data from the first day of absence in our study. Thus, the two investigations are not necessarily contradictory. Another study also reported findings that may be at odds with the "sick-role" hypothesis. Mann[8] described decreasing psychiatric morbidity among patients in a clinical trial for mild hypertension in England, in comparison with control subjects with either normal blood pressure at screening or blood pressure that fell to normal without therapy. However, a direct comparison between our investigation and that of Mann is not possible, since the latter study focused on psychiatric symptoms, did not report the prior awareness status of its subjects and was not designed to examine absenteeism. We hope that future investigations of this problem will combine the strategies of both these studies.

Given that absenteeism rises when hypertensives are labeled, can this increase be prevented? Our study was not designed to answer this question, but since high compliance was associated with low absenteeism, our compliance trials could be reanalyzed to determine the effect of these strategies on absenteeism. Such an analysis revealed that the hypertension education program actually increased absenteeism among previously unaware subjects, while leaving compliance unaffected. The other two compliance strategies tested, care at the work site and the behavior-modification program, had no statistically significant effect on absenteeism. Since the former did not improve compliance, its failure to reduce absenteeism

is not unexpected. However, the latter strategy substantially improved compliance, and its failure to reduce absenteeism is disappointing, although the number of subjects upon which this latter conclusion was based is small and the results must be accepted with reservation.

What implications do we derive from this research? First of all, labeling people as hypertensive should be done only with utmost discretion. Patients should not be informed that they are hypertensive until the diagnosis has been firmly established by serial blood-pressure recordings, taken under carefully controlled conditions such as those recommended by the United States Department of Health, Education, and Welfare.[9] Secondly, detection should only be carried out in settings in which adequate therapy and long-term follow-up observation can be ensured. For this reason, and in view of the increased absenteeism of the previously unaware hypertensive patient even if he is not treated, Canadian task forces on hypertension have recommended that the "shopping-plaza" type of hypertension screening program be abandoned in favor of a vigorous push toward case finding in primary care.[10] Finally, it might be considered that perhaps only the patients who will comply with therapy should be labeled. However, in addition to the ethical issues raised by this suggestion there is no way as yet to predict future compliance accurately on an individual basis. Clearly, however, everything feasible should be done to promote compliance so that patients suffering from the short-term disadvantages of being "labeled" hypertensive will receive the long-term benefits of blood-pressure control.

We do not intend that our findings should impede the current drive to achieve community control of hypertension, but we do hope that they will add perspective to the tallying of the costs and benefits of such community programs. The price of efforts to achieve blood-pressure control may be higher than any of us have anticipated.

REFERENCES

1. Alderman MH, Davis TK: Hypertension control at the work site. J Occup Med 18:793-796, 1976
2. Harris L, and Associates, Inc: The Public and High Blood Pressure: A survey (DHEW Publication No. [NIH] 74-356). Washington, DC, Government Printing Office, 1973
3. Gibson ES, Mishkel M, Gent M, et al: Absenteeism from work among hypertensives, Newsletter of The Council on Epidemiology of the American Heart Association, January, 1972
4. Sackett DL, Haynes RB, Gibson ES, et al: Randomised clinical trial of strategies for improving medication compliance in primary hypertension. Lancet 1:1205-1207, 1975
5. Haynes RB, Sackett DL, Gibson ES, et al: Improvement of medication compliance in uncontrolled hypertension. Lancet 1:1265-1268, 1976
6. Bergman AB, Stamm SJ: The morbidity of cardiac nondisease in schoolchildren. N Engl J Med 276:1008-1013, 1967
7. Hampton ML, Anderson J, Lavizzo BS, et al: Sickle cell "non-disease": a potentially serious public health problem. Am J Dis Child 128:58-61, 1974
8. Mann AH: The psychological effect of a screening programme and clinical trial for hypertension upon the participants. Psychol Med 7:431-438, 1977
9. Report of the Joint National Committee on Detection, Evaluation, and Treatment of High Blood Pressure: a cooperative study. JAMA 237:255-261, 1977
10. Hypertension: A report of the Ontario Council of Health. Toronto, Ontario Council of Health, 1977

Considerable attention has recently been focused on the declines in physical and psychological well-being that often accompany aging. One promising approach to this problem was demonstrated recently in a small-scale, field experiment with elderly retirement-home residents. In this experiment, subjects in two treatment groups were provided with a college-age visitor who came either on a completely predictable schedule or on a schedule determined by the subject. Subjects in two control groups were either not provided with a visitor or provided with an equal number of visits on a random schedule. At the conclusion of the experiment, the subjects in the two treatment groups were superior to the subjects in the two control groups on a variety of measures of physical and psychological health.

The following reports a number of sobering findings from a 42-month follow-up of the subjects following the termination of the experiment. Subjects in the two experimental groups showed sharp declines in health status and zest for life relative to the control groups. Indeed, there is also some suggestion of increased mortality in the treatment groups relative to the control groups.

This experiment then raises important ethical and policy issues concerning the impact of the withdrawal of treatment. Typically, in conducting social experiments, little concern is given to the welfare of the participants following the completion of the project. Treatments that enhance the subjects' feelings of predictability and control over their lives or that raise the expectations of subjects may be especially likely to have negative impacts if these positive feelings cannot be maintained.

40

Long-Term Effects of Control
and Predictability-Enhancing Interventions
Findings and Ethical Issues

Richard Schulz and Barbara Hartman Hanusa

The long-term effects of participating in a field experiment on the effects of control and predictability-enhancing interventions are reported. Retirement home residents who had initially benefited from being exposed to a specific positive predictable or controllable event were assessed at three different intervals after the study was terminated. Health and psychological status data collected 24, 30, and 42 months after the study was terminated indicated no positive long-term effects attributable to the interventions. In fact, groups that had initially benefited from the interventions exhibited precipitous declines once the study was terminated, whereas groups that had not benefited remained stable over time. The theoretical and ethical implications of these data are discussed.

In a recent field experiment, Schulz (1976) tested the hypothesis that some of the frequent negative consequences of aging, such as feelings of depression and helplessness, as well as accelerated physical decline, are at least in part attributable to loss of control. Institutionalized aged subjects were randomly assigned to one of four conditions in order to assess the effects of increased control and predictability upon the physical and psychological well-being of the aged. Individuals in three of the four conditions were visited by college undergraduates under varying contingencies, while persons in the fourth condition were not visited and served as a baseline comparison group. Subjects in the control-enhanced condition could determine both the frequency and duration of visits they received. To assess the effects of predictability, a second group of subjects (predict) were informed when they would be visited and how long the visitor would stay, but had no control over

We wish to thank Phil Brickman, Thomas Cook, Liz Holland, Linda Perloff, and Camille Wortman for comments and suggestions on this manuscript. This research was in part supported by National Institute on Aging Grant AG00525, awarded to the first author.

Requests for reprints should be sent to Richard Schulz, Department of Psychology, Carnegie-Mellon University, Pittsburgh, Pennsylvania 15213.

these details. A third group (random condition) was visited on a random schedule.

With the amount of visitation and the quality of interaction held constant across the three groups, the results supported the hypothesis that predictable and controllable positive events have a powerful positive impact on the well-being of the institutionalized aged. Subjects for whom the visits were predictable or controllable were consistently and significantly superior on indicators of physical and psychological status when compared to subjects who were visited on a random schedule or who received no visits. No significant differences were found between the predict and control groups or between the random and no-treatment groups, suggesting that the positive outcome of the predict and control groups is attributable to predictability alone.

In sum, this study demonstrated that the decline in physical and psychological status and level of activity associated with increased age may be inhibited or reversed by making a predictable or controllable significant positive event available to aged individuals. The study further supported the notion that some of the negative consequences of aging may be mediated by increased unpredictability and uncontrollability and that to the extent that aged individuals are able to maintain a predictable and controllable environment, they should experience relatively less physical and psychological deterioration with increasing age (see also Schulz & Brenner, 1977).

While subjects exposed to the predictability and control-enhancing manipulations exhibited large positive effects at the completion of the study, it was deemed important for both ethical and theoretical reasons to investigate the long-term effects of these interventions. To this end, three waves of follow-up data assessing health and psychological status and mortality rates were collected. These data were collected 24, 30, and 42 months after the experiment was terminated.

Method

Subjects

All 40 residents of a retirement home who had originally participated in the study were included in the follow-up.

Procedure

While direct access to the subjects was not permitted, the activities director was willing to provide ratings of each patient using the scales provided. At the time of the initial follow-up, the activities director had worked at the home for approximately 11 years, first as a nurse and for the last 3 years as the activities director, and was as a result personally acquainted with all the participants in the study. Although she was aware that some of the residents of the home had participated in a research project, she was unaware of any details of the study.

For the 24-month follow-up, each patient was rated on two 9-point Likert-type scales assessing health status and zest for life. The endpoints of the health status scale were labeled "in perfect health" and "extremely ill," and the endpoints for the zest for life scale were labeled "extremely enthusiastic about life" and "completely hopeless." Identical scales had been completed by the same activities director at the completion of the original experiment.

The validity of these scales is evident from the high correlations obtained at the completion of the original study between the ratings on these scales and other indicators of physical and psychological status. Ratings on the health status scale correlated with subjects' self-ratings of health ($r = .47$, $p < .005$), the number of different types of medication subjects used ($r = -.33$, $p < .02$), and the number of trips subjects made to the infirmary each week ($r = -.27$, $p < .05$). Ratings on the zest for life scale correlated with level of hope ($r = .63$, $p < .0005$) as assessed by the Wohlford Hope Scale (Wohlford, 1966) and

with subjects' self-assessed level of happiness ($r = .59$, $p < .005$).

In addition to the health status and zest for life scales, the activities director completed four other 9-point scales assessing activity, sociability, awareness, and pleasantness at the 30- and 42-month follow-up intervals.[1]

Results

As reported in Schulz (1976) the comparison of the no-treatment plus random groups against predict plus control-enhanced groups carried out at the conclusion of the experiment yielded a statistically significant effect for both health status, $F(1, 36) = 4.46$, $p < .042$, and zest for life, $F(1, 36) = 8.07$, $p < .007$. For both measures, subjects in the predict and control-enhanced groups were superior to persons assigned to the random and no-treatment groups. These data, along with the three sets of follow-up data on the same variables, were analyzed with a 4 (treatments) × 4 (time measurement) repeated measures analysis of variance.[2] This analysis yielded a significant main effect for time of measurement for both health status, $F(3, 108) = 12.72$, $p < .001$, and zest for life, $F(3, 108) = 3.64$, $p < .02$. The interaction between treatments and time of measurement was also significant for both health status, $F(9, 108) = 2.65$, $p < .008$, and zest for life, $F(9, 108) = 3.81$, $p < .003$. As indicated in Figures 1 and 2, health status and zest for life declined substantially over time among persons in the predict and control-enhanced groups, whereas persons in the random and no-treatment groups exhibited a slight increase on these measures prior to the first follow-up.

Twenty-four months after the study was concluded, 14 of 20 persons (six remained unchanged) in the predict and control-enhanced groups combined exhibited a reduction in zest for life, whereas only 6 of 20 (3 remained unchanged) in the no-treatment and random

---

[1] Interpretation of the 42-month follow-up data must remain clouded. A fire killing several persons occurred shortly before these data were collected, and while none of the study participants were directly injured by the fire, all were inconvenienced by it and all suffered emotionally.

[2] Persons who died were included in the analysis by giving each a score of zero on each measure.

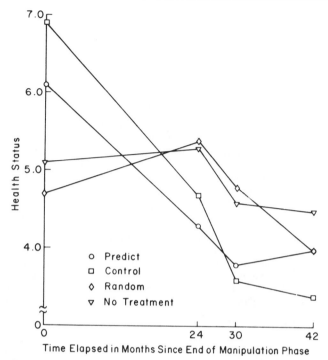

Figure 1. Mean health status ratings by experimental condition presented at four different points in time.

groups combined exhibited declines on this psychological status indicator, $\chi^2(1) = 6.40$, $p < .02$.[3] The data on health status parallel these findings. Fourteen of 20 (3 remained unchanged) persons in the predict and control-enhanced groups exhibited declines in health status, whereas 7 of 20 (4 remained unchanged) in the random and no-treatment groups exhibited declines, $\chi^2(1) = 5.00$, $p < .05$. In sum, both the number of persons exhibiting declines and the magnitude of the declines were significantly greater for predict and control-enhanced groups when compared to the no-treatment and random groups.

The preceding data clearly indicate that the groups that gained most as a result of the interventions (predict and control enhanced) also declined most after the completion of the study. The two groups that showed no gains (random and no treatment) also exhibited no immediate declines when the study was termi-

nated. In addition to examining the magnitude of declines of the four groups, we can also examine the relative standing of each of the four groups on the two dependent measures. The important question to be answered here is whether the predict and control groups fell significantly below the random and no-treatment groups at any of the three follow-up periods. Figures 1 and 2 show that the means for the predict and control-enhanced groups on both dependent measures fall below the random and no-treatment groups at each of the three follow-up periods. To test the signif-

---

[3] This analysis was justified, since there were no statistically significant differences between the predict and control-enhanced groups or between the random and no-treatment groups. For the purposes of this analysis, the combined data for the predict and control-enhanced groups were compared against the combined data of the random and no-treatment groups.

icance of these differences, a 4 (treatments) × 3 (time of measurement) repeated measures analysis of variance was carried out on each dependent measure. This analysis yielded a significant time of measurement effect for both measures: $F(2, 72) = 10.29$, $p < .0001$, for health status, and $F(2, 72) = 4.98$, $p < .001$, for zest for life. As indicated in Figures 1 and 2, all groups generally exhibited declines over time. Neither the main effect for treatments nor the interaction between treatments and time of measurement approached statistical significance.

Individual analyses comparing the predict and control-enhanced groups combined against the random and no-treatment groups combined at each of the three follow-up intervals were also carried out, but only one of these comparisons approached statistical significance. At the 30-month follow-up, the predict and control-enhanced groups were marginally lower in zest for life than the random and no-treatment groups, $F(1, 108) = 2.76$, $p < .10$. However, this difference is almost entirely at-

tributable to the four deceased persons in the predict and control-enhanced groups. The means for the two sets of groups are virtually identical when the deceased persons are removed from the analysis (see Footnote 4). In sum, these analyses indicate that while the predict and control-enhanced groups are consistently below the random and no-treatment groups on both indicators, there is little evidence that these differences are statistically reliable.

In addition to being assessed on health status and zest for life, each subject was evaluated on each of the following four 9-point scales at the 30- and 42-month follow-up: activity, sociability, awareness, and pleasantness. The data for each of these scales were analyzed using a 2 (time of measurement) × 4 (treatments) repeated measures analysis of variance. Significant main effects for time of measurement were found for two variables. All groups were judged to be more pleasant at the 42-month than at the 30-month follow-up, $F(1, 32) = 4.83$, $p < .05$. The no-treatment

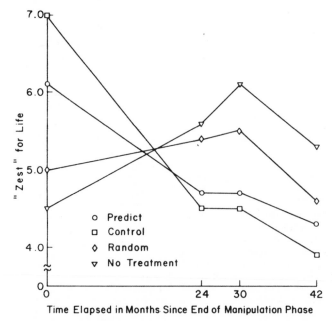

Figure 2. Mean zest for life ratings by experimental condition presented at four different points in time.

and random groups were judged to be less aware of their environment at the 42- than at the 30-month follow-up, $F(1, 32) = 8.05$, $p < .008$.

Mortality Rates

The final data to be considered are mortality rates. Two persons in the predict group and one person in the control-enhanced group died prior to the 24-month follow-up. A fourth person, also in the control-enhanced group, died between the 30- and 42-month follow-up.[4] Fisher's exact probability test was used to analyze these data (Siegel, 1956). Combining the no-treatment with the random group and the predict with the control-enhanced group yields a marginally significant Fisher's exact probability of .053.

Discussion

This study was carried out to determine the long-term effects of control and predictability-enhancing interventions on the institutionalized aged. The results show that the effects of the particular interventions used in this study were temporary. Persons who had previously improved in psychological and health status when an important positive event was made either predictable or controllable for them exhibited significant declines after the study was terminated.

These findings stand in sharp contrast to the follow-up results obtained by Rodin and Langer (1977). In their study, an intervention designed to encourage aged nursing home residents to feel more control and responsibility for day-to-day events was used. One group of residents was exposed to a talk delivered by the hospital administrator emphasizing their responsibility for themselves. A second group heard a communication that stressed the staff's responsibility for them as patients. These communications were bolstered by offering to subjects in the experimental group plants that they could tend, whereas residents in the comparison group were given plants that were watered by the staff. The results of this study indicated that residents in the responsibility-induced group became more active and reported feeling happier than the comparison group of residents who were encouraged to feel that the staff would care for them and try to make them happy. Patients in the responsibility-induced group also showed significant improvements in alertness and increased participation in nursing home activities. Follow-up data on health and psychological status were collected 18 months after the Rodin and Langer study was completed. It was found that subjects in the responsibility-induced condition showed better health and activity patterns, smaller declines in mood and sociability, and somewhat lowered mortality rates (see Rodin and Langer, Erratum, 1978) when compared to the staff-support group.

Theoretical Issues

Viewed from a theoretical perspective, these data are consistent with an attributional analysis of learned helplessness recently proposed by Abramson, Seligman, and Teasdale (1978). According to this analysis, persons generate reasons for their ability to control outcomes, and these reasons can be classified along three orthogonal dimensions. Two of these dimensions (internal–external, stable–unstable) have been frequently used by at-

---

[4] One interpretation of these data is that random assignment of subjects to conditions was not completely effective, causing the more vulnerable persons to be included in the predict and control groups. An analysis of the data with the four deceased persons removed supports this interpretation. First, an analysis of the health status and zest data collected at the end of the study shows that the deceased persons were several points lower on these indicators than the survivors in the predict and control groups. Their scores were, in fact, no different than those of individuals in the random and no-treatment groups. The means for health status were 4.25, 4.99, and 7.44 for the deceased, random plus no-treatment, and predict plus control groups, respectively. Second, there is evidence to suggest that the deceased did not benefit from the interventions. For example, the deceased did not exhibit any change in level of hope as a result of participating in the study. They changed an average of .08 on this measure, whereas the survivors increased an average of .31. Finally, the deceased group was on the average 5 years older (mean age = 86.8 years) when the study was initiated than persons in the predict and control groups (mean age = 81.3 years) or the no-treatment plus random groups (mean age = 80.7 years).

tribution theorists (e.g., Weiner, 1974), while the third (global–specific) is introduced as a new dimension by the authors. Thus, internal causes stem from the individual and external causes from the environment; stable factors are long-lived and recurrent, whereas unstable factors are short-lived and intermittent. Finally, global factors occur across situations, whereas specific factors are unique to a particular context. The authors further suggest that each type of attribution has specific consequences for the individual: Attributions to internal–external factors should affect self-esteem; attributions to stable–unstable factors should determine the long-term consequences of a particular experience; and attributions to global–specific factors should determine the extent to which individuals will generalize a particular experience to other situations.

While there is no direct evidence indicating the types of attributions made by individuals in either the Langer and Rodin (1976) or Schulz (1976) studies, the long-term effects in each study can be understood from an attributional perspective. It is likely that the intervention used by Langer and Rodin altered subjects' self-attributions regarding their ability to control outcomes in an institutional environment. More specifically, the communication delivered to the experimental group emphasizing their responsibility for themselves and their outcomes probably encouraged subjects to make internal, stable, and global attributions (e.g., "I control important outcomes because I am responsible and competent, and this should not change as long as I am here"), and as predicted, the gains evidenced by the experimental group persisted over time.

On the other hand, when increased control is attributed to unstable factors, the long-term impact of such an intervention should be temporary. The results of the present follow-up study are consistent with this analysis. The intervention used by Schulz probably caused subjects to make external, unstable, specific attributions (e.g., "I can control one outcome; I can do this because someone is allowing me to do it; and I can do it only for a specific period of time"). Feelings of control in this situation are dependent upon the presence of

an external agent and should not persist once that agent is removed.

Since the attributional patterns generated in the two studies may be different on all three dimensions, it is difficult to conclude with certainty that the stability dimension alone accounts for the long-term differences between the two studies, although the Abramson et al. (1978) model would suggest that this is the case.

A second possible explanation for the declines exhibited by subjects in the present study is that their expectations for a predictable and/or controllable environment were violated by the termination of the study. Subjects' expectations for controlling or predicting important events in their lives may have been raised by the interventions used and then abruptly violated when the study terminated and experimenters and visitors disappeared. This analysis suggests that the declines might have been avoided had we provided substitute predictable or controllable events.

Ethical Issues

From an ethical perspective, the critical question raised by this research is, Did the termination of the study actually harm the participants? While subjects in the enhanced groups did drop below baseline on both indicators, the analysis showed that these differences were only marginally significant. This is suggestive, but hardly compelling. Nevertheless, we might ask, What factors might account for such negative effects?

The interventions accomplished two things. First, they resulted in strong personal attachments between the subject and visitor. Second, they raised expectations for a predictable and controllable environment. Any harm attributable to the termination of the study could be due to either of these causes.

The fact that the nature of the relationships did not differ across experimental groups (e.g., persons in the random group enjoyed the visits just as much as persons in the predict and control-enhanced groups) and the fact that the random group did not exhibit the same declines found for the predict and control-enhanced groups suggest that the severing of personal attachments was not the primary cause for the decline. Furthermore, it was anticipated when the study was initiated that the termination of the visits might upset the participants. As a result, several precautions were taken. First, subjects were informed that the college visitors would return to their homes for summer vacation. Second, visitors were not suddenly withdrawn at the end of the study. The visits continued after the initial follow-up data were collected and terminated gradually at the end of the semester. Third, visitors were encouraged to keep in touch with subjects whenever strong attachments had developed.

The intent of these precautions was to alleviate the potential stress of severing strong attachments. The fact that the random group suffered no declines when the study was terminated suggests that these precautions served their purpose. Hindsight suggests that had we provided a substitute predictable or controllable positive event, the declines exhibited by the predict and control-enhanced groups might also have been avoided. Whether these results could or should have been anticipated is debatable, but they do contain several important lessons for researchers engaged in methodologically similar approaches to this topic.

Manipulations in field settings. Experimental research necessarily calls for random assignment and the use of manipulations. Most researchers would agree that only manipulations that can be expected to have positive effects on the participants of the study are justified. Although it may be theoretically interesting to use negative manipulations, such procedures are unethical in field settings where experiments sometimes take months to carry out. For example, inducing feelings of incompetence may be justified in the laboratory where the time frame is short and the experimenter is able to monitor subjects and intervene if necessary. Since it is impossible to monitor subjects in field settings, there is the danger that negative manipulations might result in prolonged discomfort and/or self-injurious behavior that would go unnoticed. These considerations limit the researcher to designs in which positive manipulations are

used, with no-treatment groups or treatment-as-usual groups serving as controls.

Assessing long-term effects. The research reported here suggests another precaution necessary in judging the ethicality of manipulations used in field experiments. That is, the manipulations should be evaluated in terms of both their probable short *and* long term impact, and researchers should make plans for assessing long-term effects before the study is initiated. Thus, manipulations must not only be positive but their probable long-term impact should also be positive or at least neutral.

Debriefing in field settings. In the laboratory, the experimenter also has the opportunity to counteract a negative manipulation via the debriefing process. Several researchers have demonstrated that an effective debriefing can neutralize the impact of powerful negative manipulations (Hanusa & Schulz, Note 1). This option is, of course, available to the field researcher engaged in deception research, but its desirability is questionable. Given the necessity of using positive manipulations in field settings, there is some danger that a debriefing will do more harm than good. Informing subjects that their positive outcomes were provided by the experimenter or that positive performance feedback was contrived may result in large self-esteem decrements, leaving subjects worse off than they would have been had they not participated in the research. Further, if the research is carried out in institutional settings, debriefing may foster distrust among subjects who are regularly dependent upon others (e.g., administrators and caretakers) for important outcomes.

Impact on nonparticipants. A final consideration important in carrying out experimental field research concerns the impact of an experiment on those who do not participate in the treatment conditions. Nonparticipants who perceive that their neighbors are receiving special treatment or study participants assigned to no-treatment control conditions who discover that someone else is receiving a better outcome may become resentful or envious or make negative self-attributions (for example, see Miller, Brickman, & Bolen, 1975). A cause and consequence of such perceptions is that subjects may discuss their differential treatment and thereby contaminate the manipulations. Cook and Campbell (1976) further suggest that persons assigned to control groups may be motivated to compete with treatment groups, thereby decreasing between-group differences.

Another potential problem is that awareness of different treatment conditions may result in differential attrition rates and hence invalidate between-group comparisons. Laboratory research examining subjects' reactions to random assignment suggests that both internal and external validity may be jeopardized should subjects accidentally become aware of different experimental conditions (Wortman, Hendricks, & Hillis, 1976). Within institutions these problems can in part be avoided by (a) assigning subjects randomly by floors, assuming that location within an institution does not reflect important differential subject characteristics such as health status, or (b) making sure that subjects are widely dispersed throughout an institution, minimizing the possibility of interaction. In either case, data should be collected assessing the extent of participant interaction.

Conclusion

In sum, while the research described here raises both ethical and practical problems, the benefits of such research can be great. Subjects typically benefit from the increased attention given them as individuals and may receive valuable services that are not available to them otherwise. Manipulations developed may be easily translated into programs that positively affect a large number of persons. A recent example of this comes from a study by Schulz and Hanusa (Note 2). An experimental treatment that alleviated the stress of institutionalization of new admissions to a geriatric hospital was adopted by the admissions department of the hospital. Finally, there is much to be gained from studying the impact of social-psychological variables in complex real-life settings. An experimental field approach may entail some compromise in methodological rigor and may raise a variety of important ethical issues, but these potential problems are often offset by the increment in

external validity achieved by using such methodology.

Reference Notes

1. Hanusa, B. H., & Schulz, R. *Long-term effects of participating in a learned helplessness experiment.* Unpublished manuscript, 1977.

2. Schulz, R., & Hanusa, B. H. *Facilitating institutional adaptation of the aged: Effects of predictability-enhancing intervention.* Paper presented at the meeting of the American Gerontological Society, San Franciso, November 1977.

References

Abramson, L. Y., Seligman, M. E. P., & Teasdale, J. Learned helplessness in humans: Critique and reformulation. *Journal of Abnormal Psychology,* 1978, 87, 49–74.

Cook, T. D., & Campbell, D. T. The design and conduct of quasi-experiments and true experiments. In M. D. Dunnette (Ed.), *Handbook of industrial and organizational psychology.* Chicago: Rand McNally, 1976.

Langer, E. J., & Rodin, J. The effects of choice and enhanced personal responsibility for the aged: A field experiment in an institutional setting. *Journal of Personality and Social Psychology,* 1976, 34, 191–198.

Miller, R. L., Brickman, P., & Bolen, D. Attribution versus persuasion as a means for modifying behavior. *Journal of Personality and Social Psychology,* 1975, 31, 430–441.

Rodin, J., & Langer, E. J. Long-term effects of a control-relevant intervention with the institutionalized aged. *Journal of Personality and Social Psychology,* 1977, 35, 897–903. Erratum to Rodin and Langer. *Journal of Personality and Social Psychology,* 1978, 36, 462.

Schulz, R. The effects of control and predictability on the psychological and physical well-being of the institutionalized aged. *Journal of Personality and Social Psychology,* 1976, 33, 563–573.

Schulz, R., & Brenner, G. F. Relocation of the aged: A review and theoretical analysis. *Journal of Gerontology,* 1977, 32, 323–333.

Siegel, S. *Nonparametric statistics for the behavioral sciences.* New York: McGraw-Hill, 1956.

Wohlford, P. Extension of personal time, affective states, and expectation of personal death. *Journal of Personality and Social Psychology,* 1966, 3, 559–566.

Weiner, B. *Achievement motivation and attribution theory.* Morristown, N.J.: General Learning Press, 1974.

Wortman, C. B., Hendricks, M., & Hillis, J. W. Factors affecting participant reactions to random assignment in ameliorative programs. *Journal of Personality and Social Psychology,* 1976, 33, 256–266.

Received March 3, 1978 ∎

VI

UTILIZATION

The "bottom line" for evaluation research is, after all, the effect it has on decisions and policies. In the long run the best evaluations can be counted no better than disappointing if their findings never affect policy. In truth, however, we still know very little about the relationship between research findings and policy-making, and what we do know is more intuition than hard empirical knowledge. The papers in this section indicate that our understanding of how evaluation research findings are used is improving. There are also some potentially useful hints about how our understanding might be improved and, hence, how evaluations might be conceived, planned, and implemented for maximum utility for those charged with the development of policy.

When an area, such as evaluation research, is developing its expertise, the focus of most work tends to be on techniques and methodology. This is as it should be for that stage; however, once the methods have achieved some degree of stability, the social policy implications begin to assume some importance in the field. The article by Pillemer and Light emphasizes that the social policy implications of studies may be an additional, and perhaps more important, criterion for determining the desirability of large-scale implementations. The authors also touch on some points that are developed in other chapters in this volume. For instance, they note the importance of the longitudinal follow-up of a program as well as variations on that theme (see Schulz and Hanusa), and the problem of "imprecise treatment labels" may also be seen as a problem of adequate description of the treatment. Finally, Pillemer and Light refine both the philosophy and the methodology of evaluation research by emphasizing the importance of treatment by setting interactions.

41

Using the Results of Randomized Experiments To Construct Social Programs
Three Caveats

David B. Pillemer and Richard J. Light

INTRODUCTION

Much of the debate about how experimentation should influence social policy enters on the adequacy of different research designs. A key question is whether or not randomized, controlled field trials are useful or necessary for conducting good policy research. A strong case has been made for the importance of randomization to accurately assess program effects (e.g., Campbell and Boruch, 1975; Gilbert et al., 1975; Riecken and Boruch, 1975). Randomly assigning people to different treatment groups has the advantage that, for reasonably large samples, the groups are likely to have similar distributions on most background variables. Therefore, randomization allows the causal attribution of post-treatment group differences to the differential effects of the treatments.

While randomization is very desirable, it does not by itself insure good social policy inferences. As important is the careful interpretation of research findings to improve our predictions of a program's probable effects in real-life settings. *It is this inferential step, from experiment to implementation, that we focus on in this essay.*

As part of a review of a large number of areas of social policy research, we have analyzed many research studies. For the major studies in each area, we have compared their reported findings and the quality of their research designs. These secondary analyses have helped to identify several methodological caveats that we believe are general and quite separate from the question of randomization. They all pertain to situations in which a well-evaluated experimental treatment may perform unpredictably if implemented more widely.

From David B. Pillemer and Richard J. Light, "Using the Results of Randomized Experiments To Construct Social Programs: Three Caveats." Unpublished manuscript, 1978.

We therefore present here three caveats that apply to a large number of areas of social policy research. They all suggest a central role for secondary analyses of experimental studies in formulating social policy. Comparing the major studies in an area serves two purposes: (1) these comparisons may help to identify situations where the policy implications of experimental studies are unclear; and (2) they may also improve predictions of program success or failure in these situations. These important functions of secondary analysis will be illustrated in discussing each caveat.

1. CONSIDERING RELATIVE GAIN

Suppose a new program is developed to train paramedics. The program is to be evaluated, using the best research design possible. From a pool of 40 applicants, 20 are randomly assigned to the training program and 20 to a control group. One year after the program, a comparison is made. The results are clear: the 20 trainees are all employed, at good salaries, and their supervisors and patients are highly satisfied with their performance. The control group is not nearly as well off. The conclusion concerning program effectiveness seems obvious. The training program is a success, as determined by a well done randomized field trial. The next policy step is to implement this program on a large scale and to give more people the same excellent training.

Next year the program is widely implemented. All 20,000 unemployed but trainable people in a city are given the paramedic training. What happens? The trial is a failure. A year later almost all of the trainees are unemployed. Why? Because while there was demand for the 20 trained paramedics, there was not demand for 20,000 trained paramedics. So the highly successful and well-evaluated experimental program broke down when expanded to a large-scale program.

This example illustrates an important concept. There are some special programs where *the benefit that the program confers to any one recipient is a function of how many other people received the program*. The program value to the individual participant depends on the program size. In this case, the wider the training program is disseminated, the lower the expected benefit to any one trainee. While the program may produce the same *absolute* increase in performance for all participants, the *relative benefit* that this increase confers to any individual decreases as the program size increases (i.e., a relative gain constraint). We have rarely seen this simple point made in evaluations of job training programs, yet this is precisely the sort of caution that evaluators making policy recommendations cannot afford to forget.

A second example also illustrates that program value may depend on program size. Suppose a law school has 1000 applicants for 100 places in its entering class. The school decides to accept the 100 people with the highest scores on an entrance exam.

Professor X alleges that she has developed a curriculum that can uniformly raise scores of applicants by 200 points on the test. An evaluator is incredulous, and she designs a randomized trial to assess the effects of Professor X's curriculum. Forty applicants are randomly assigned to two groups of 20; one group attends Professor X's curriculum, while the other receives no special training. After four months the two groups are given the test and, shortly thereafter, the law school announces its acceptances: from the treatment group, all 20 applicants are accepted, while from the control group only 2 are accepted.

Looking at the test scores, admissions data, and the excellent research design, the evaluator concludes that the new curriculum is indeed effective. Professor X, encouraged by these exciting findings, sets up a chain of "prep schools" for the law school test. But, next year, when the evaluator returns to see what happened to the graduates of Professor X's curriculum, she finds out that the probability of being admitted for any applicant who takes the course has dropped from 100 percent back to 10 percent, the value for the control group in the original evaluation.

What is the explanation for the program's large-scale ineffectiveness? What appears to have happened is that all 100 applicants took the prep course, while the law school continued to accept only 100 students. As promised, the program may still have produced an average *absolute gain* of 200 points for its participants. However, if all 100 applicants took the course, no sub-group of applicants would experience a *relative gain* in test performance. As in the previous example, the benefit that this program confers to any one applicant depends on how many other applicants also participated.

Comments on Relative Gain

In order to accurately assess the relative gain afforded to program participants, it is necessary to consider the availability of *opportunities for success* as well as the ratio of the number of program participants to the total number of competing individuals. If there are many opportunities for success, increasing the number of program participants may have little influence on the program's effectiveness. In the extreme case when there are as many opportunities as competing individuals, the number of people who receive special program services is unimportant. Thus, in the law school admissions example, if there are 1000 applicants and 1000 acceptances, the number of applicants who participate in a special program to improve entry test scores is not related to program success as measured by the acceptance ratio. *All* applicants will be admitted due to the large number of acceptances.

As the number of opportunities for success decreases, increasing the number of program participants diminishes program effectiveness. For instance, with only 100 law school acceptances, increasing the number of people who attend the prep course severely limits the advantages provided to program participants. It should be clear that relative gain depends on two factors—the number of opportunities for success, and the ratio of program participants to the total number of competing individuals. Both pieces of information must be considered to predict whether an experimental program is likely to be successful when implemented on a larger scale.

It is possible using secondary analysis to get a preliminary indication of whether a particular program has a relative gain constraint. This can be done if data on program effectiveness exist at several sites with different sampling fractions, n/N. If so, one can compare each site's sampling fraction with the program's demonstrated effectiveness. When those sites with larger fractions have smaller program effects, one should suspect that a relative gain constraint may be operating for this program.

The examples presented here underscore the importance of considering the *relative gain* experienced by any participant. But often, *absolute gains* produced by large-scale program implementation are important in their own right. For example, if a program that produces uniform gains in children's reading skills is administered to all children, no participants will experience a relative gain. However, *all* of the children may benefit from the program, in terms of increased productivity, happiness and so on. Programs that improve the general quality of life (such as those resulting in better health or increased life span) provide examples of situations where absolute gains are of primary importance.

2. UNPREDICTABLE INTERACTIONS BETWEEN IMMEDIATE AND FOLLOW-UP PROGRAM EFFECTS

Our second caveat concerns the potential hazards of judging the success of a program prior to observing the participants' later performance. In particular, a treatment may result in considerable initial gains for its participants, yet these gains may dissipate when followed by incompatible programs. Or a program that initially appears to be a failure may combine productively with a follow-up program, resulting in an eventual "success."

As with the first caveat, the dangers of prematurely judging a program to be a success or a failure are not eliminated simply by conducting controlled, randomized field trials. In fact, evaluators may place high levels of confidence in the initial outcome of a well-done study, and de-emphasize more "secondary" aspects of the study design such as following participants longitudinally. In situations where a program interacts unpredictably with a follow-up program, this may lead to poor long-term outcomes.

The importance of following program participants longitudinally is widely noted in the abstract. A concrete illustration may be useful. From education, two evaluation studies provide an example of unpredictable interactions between preschool programs and later elementary school. One was conducted by Louise Miller and Jean Dyer (1971), and the other by Edsel Erickson and associates (1969). We emphasize that we have chosen these particular studies because they provide examples of the general *methodological* point that we wish to make. We are not trying here to provide substantive insights into preschool curricula.

Both evaluations were well done according to a number of experimental design criteria. In particular, assignment of subjects to treatments was at least partially randomized in both studies. Two types of programs were evaluated in both: a "regular" Head Start Program, and a highly structured Bereiter-Engelmann curriculum.[1] Erickson's preschoolers subsequently attended either Bereiter-Engelman or regular kindergarten programs. Miller and Dyer's preschoolers moved on to either regular or highly academic Follow-Through kindergarten and first grade programs. We will focus on the long-term effects of the Bereiter-Engelmann (B-E) and regular preschool programs on one outcome measure: Stanford-Binet Intelligence Test performance.

Erickson's results indicate that the B-E preschool program was superior to the regular program. Students in the B-E program demonstrated higher IQs than the traditional students following one year of preschool. In addition, B-E preschoolers remained above average intelligence one year after preschool regardless of the type of kindergarten (B-E or regular) they attended. Traditional preschoolers were close to their age level in intelligence following either kindergarten experience, with those children attending B-E kindergarten scoring slightly higher than those in regular kindergarten.

Miller and Dyer's B-E preschoolers also demonstrated slightly higher IQs than traditional preschoolers immediately following preschool. However, while both the B-E and regular preschool groups experienced an overall decrease in IQ following preschool, B-E preschoolers decreased at a faster rate. This rapid decrease was due primarily to the poor test performance of B-E preschoolers in regular kindergarten and first grade. In contrast, the regular preschoolers' rate of IQ decrease in regular elementary school programs was more gradual. As a result, the overall IQ performance of the regular preschoolers was higher than the B-E preschoolers by the end of the first grade.

Comments on Unpredictable Interactions

This example illustrates several methodological points. First, it demonstrates the critical importance of evaluating a subjects' performance *longitudinally*. Had these studies reported only the immediate effects of preschool on students' IQ scores, the B-E program would have appeared superior in both studies. Since both studies were well designed, a large degree of confidence would have been placed in these convergent findings. However, we have seen that the effectiveness of the programs over time is not stable, but depends strongly on what follows.

Second, the unpredictable interactions of preschool with follow-up programs were identified only by comparing the different preschool evaluations. Had either of these studies been read in isolation, a reader would have drawn different conclusions about the long-term effectiveness of the different preschool curricula. Erickson's study indicates that the B-E curriculum is consistently superior, while Miller and Dyer suggest that the B-E preschool effectiveness dissipates rapidly when followed by regular schooling.

Once conflicting results are identified through secondary analysis, it is important to attempt to account for the discrepancy. A possible explanation is the use of imprecise treatment labels. The B-E and regular preschool programs may not have been identical in the two studies. And even if these two programs were similar, the follow-up programs certainly differed in some important aspects. The fact that Erickson's B-E preschoolers maintained a high IQ performance in regular kindergarten, while the performance of Miller and Dyer's B-E preschoolers dropped so sharply, may be a result of substantive differences between similarly labeled programs. These conflicting results indicate that follow-up programs, as well as the primary treatments, need to be carefully defined and monitored.

3. UNPREDICTABLE CONSEQUENCES OF IMPLEMENTING EXPERIMENTAL TREATMENTS OVER LONG TIME PERIODS

The preceding discussion emphasized that the long-term impact of a program depends, to some extent, on the experiences that follow it. Predicting the long-term impact of social programs becomes even more problematic when the effects may differ depending on the tenure of the treatment. It is possible that the long-term implementation of a particular treatment may exert a qualitatively different influence on participants than is indicated by the short-term experimental effect of the same treatment.

Studies investigating the effects of TV violence on children illustrate this. There appears to be converging agreement among TV researchers that viewing violent TV causes children to act aggressively (Leifer et al., 1974). Several randomized experiments examining the immediate effects of exposing children to aggressive media content support this conclusion (e.g., Hanratty et al., 1969; Drabman and Thomas, 1974).

Conclusions that can be drawn from the few longer-term experimental studies are less clear, but suggest some conflict with short-term findings. For example, Feshbach and Singer (1971) manipulated the TV watching of institutionalized boys over a six-week period. Half the subjects watched violent shows, while the other half viewed nonviolent shows. Surprisingly, certain subgroups of subjects who watched mostly nonviolent shows demonstrated more aggressive tendencies than subjects in the violent viewing group. Critics of this study (e.g., Leifer et al., 1974) have stated that it contains serious methodological weaknesses, and that Feshbach and Singer's unexpected finding of increased aggression in viewers of nonviolent shows may be an artifact. Wells (1973) replicated the study by Feshbach and Singer, but with some modifications. He found that while a violent viewing condition increased physical agression, a nonviolent TV diet increased viewers' verbal aggression.

It is possible that limiting TV violence for different time periods qualitatively changes the treatment. Short-term exposure to certain types of TV shows does not alter children's normal viewing patterns. However, manipulating children's TV viewing over extended periods of time disrupts their normal viewing behaviors. For example, the control boys in Feshbach and Singer's study did not simply watch nonviolent shows; this "treatment" meant they could not watch well-liked violent shows. It is possible that not allowing control subjects to watch their favorite shows resulted in their increased aggressiveness. Further, limiting children's TV violence exposure for even longer time periods could result in another reversal of subject reactions. It is quite possible that over longer periods of time the control subjects' anger and aggressiveness would diminish.

We could continue to speculate about the possible effects of long-term changes in children's TV violence exposure, but that is not the key issue here. The important point is that qualitative differences may emerge in the effects of a treatment, depending on whether it is temporarily superimposed on naturally existing behaviors, or whether it forces the reorganization of those behaviors. However well-done, short-term experiments do not provide conclusive evidence about long-term implementations of similar treatments.

A second area of TV research—investigating the effects of TV advertising on children—also illustrates how the outcomes of long-term treatment implementation are difficult to predict. Like TV violence, TV advertising has recently stimulated public and academic interest. There are a number of studies of the effects of TV advertising on a variety of outcomes, such as children's purchase requests, attitudes, and consumer learning. Two principal findings emerge: (1) that the young child's understanding of commercials increases with age (e.g., Robertson and Rossiter, 1974; Rubin, 1972; Ward and Wackman, 1973); and (2) that short-term exposure to specific commercials may influence children's behaviors and attitudes (e.g., Atkin, 1975, 1975a; Liefeld, n.d.). The experimental studies by Atkin and Liefeld used randomization to some degree. The evidence suggests that although young children may lack the sophistication to accurately evaluate the information presented in commercials, they are often influenced by television advertisements.

Citing this evidence, consumer advocate groups such as Action for Children's Television have called for the elimination of commercials directed toward children (Charren and Sarson, 1973). The Federal Trade Commission is currently studying whether formal regulations are appropriate.[2] As with TV violence, however, it is difficult to predict the effects of severely limiting children's exposure to TV ads over very long time periods. Although much of the present evidence may be interpreted as supporting consumerists' attempts to restrict TV advertising, it is possible that extreme limitations would result in unexpected outcomes.

One such outcome might be an impeded development of adult consumer skills. According to this position, it is necessary to watch commercials to learn to judge their merits more accurately. Thus, children may benefit more from the critical analysis of commercials, guided by parents or teachers, than from their prohibition. A counterargument is that TV commercials directed to children are not a necessary part of consumer socialization, especially since children are often exposed to ads directed to adults. But our point is not to argue here for one side or the other. It is to illustrate how a long-term treatment implementation may have unpredictable consequences. In the TV area, both viewpoints concerning long-term effects of eliminating TV ads directed to children are speculative at this time. Existing studies do not provide conclusive evidence about the results of more permanent changes.

Comments on Unpredictable Long-Term Consequences

While it is often difficult to predict the outcomes of long-term programs from the results of short-term experiments, existing research may still be useful in formulating social policy. We would argue that present policy should be based on the best available data. However, when the long-term impact of policy interventions is uncertain, they should be accompanied by frequent monitoring for unintended long-term consequences.

It is important to emphasize the role of secondary analysis in identifying policy areas where the short- and long-term effects of a specific treatment may differ. Comparing the result of experimental studies that differ in the length of the treatment is instrumental here. Conflicting results would suggest that the tenure of a treatment is a critical determinant of program success.

Comparing the results of experimental studies with those of carefully done descriptive studies may also prove useful in identifying treatments that may potentially result in unintended long-term consequences. Descriptive studies investigate subjects' naturally existing behaviors with observational techniques, interviews, or questionnaires. Their principal advantage is that they avoid the problem of artificially manipulating a subject's exposure to a treatment. These studies can provide valuable information about more stable influences on behavior.

Unfortunately, the validity of cause and effect inferences based on descriptive data is difficult to assess. Despite this limitation, however, descriptive studies provide estimates of the effects of ongoing influences on human behavior. Thus, in using the results of research studies for formulating policy, it may be useful to conduct analyses in which the results of experimental and descriptive studies are compared (Boruch, 1975). When the outcomes of descriptive studies conflict with experimental results, social programs based on the results of controlled experiments should be carefully monitored for unintended long-term consequences.

CONCLUSIONS

Our basic theme is that conducting randomized experiments is not a sufficient condition for determining if a program will be successful when implemented in non-experimental settings. There are a number of caveats that should be kept in mind before widely implementing an experimental program. In this paper we have reviewed the importance of considering relative gain, observing participants' performance in follow-up programs, and monitoring for unintended consequences of long-term program implementations based on short-term experimental findings.

Secondary analyses may often identify policy areas where the results of different research studies conflict. However, these discrepancies are no cause for despair. Real treatment effects may often vary drastically, depending on factors such as the number of participants, the length of time the program is in operation, and the types of experiences that follow it. This information is invaluable for deciding how and where to implement similar programs.

The view that conflicting outcomes among studies may provide us with valuable information is not a unanimously held view. Often it is argued that if a large number of studies are available concerning the effectiveness of a program, we should be able to decide whether the program really "works." But perhaps this is a bit oversimplified view of reality. Take the effects of busing on children's school achievement as an example. Some evaluation studies show substantial positive program effects, some show clear negative program effects, and the majority show no effect at all (Light and Smith, 1971). One way to view all of these studies is to search for "convergence" over time. This implies not only that a true average effect of busing exists, but that it would be useful to know such an average, and that as more and more studies are performed the true effect will be estimated more and more precisely. But what if this is based on a wrong assumption? Suppose that reality has dealt out settings in which busing is highly effective, and other settings where busing is a disaster for children's achievement. Then, as more studies and data accumulate, there is no reason to expect convergence of results. Rather, our job as secondary analysts would be quite different: to accept the variation of results, not as confusion, but rather as offering a good representation of reality. Once this idea is accepted, the next step is to identify setting by treatment interactions, so that policy makers can understand more fully under what precise circumstances a program will work or not work. For example, one might want to see if busing works in small cities but not in large ones, or with young children but not with older ones.

The three caveats we have discussed may serve the same purpose: to identify the particular settings in the real world where a well evaluated experimental program is likely to succeed. Certain programs will be successful only when the number of participants is limited, when follow-up programs are compatible, or when a treatment is implemented for a certain length of time. The ultimate goal is to identify precisely those combinations of setting and program that lead to successful outcomes.

NOTES

1. Miller and Dyer use the label "Traditional." Erickson refers to the "regular" preschool program as the "Enrichment Program," but emphasizes its "traditional" nature. Miller and Dyer also evaluated DARCEE and Montessori programs.

2. *Wall Street Journal*, November 9, 1977, p. 5.

REFERENCES

ATKIN, C. (1975) Effects of Television Advertising on Children, First Year Experimental Evidence. Report 1, in TV Advertising and Children Project, Final Report (OCD), June.

——— (1975a) Effects of Television on Children, Second Year Experimental Evidence. Report 2, in TV Advertising and Children Project, Final Report (OCD), June.

BORUCH, R. F. (1975) "Coupling randomized experiments and approximations to experiments in social program evaluation." Sociological Methods and Research (August): 31-53.

CAMPBELL, D. T. (1975) "Making the case for randomized assignment to treatments by considering the alternatives: six ways in which quasi-experimental evaluations in compensatory education tend to underestimate effects." In Evaluation and Experiment. New York: Academic Press.

CHARREN, P. and E. SARSON (1973) "Children's TV: sugar makes cents." News and Comments (July): 10-12.

DRABMAN, R. S. and M. H. THOMAS (1974) "Does media violence increase children's toleration of real-life aggression? Develop. Psych. 10, 3, 418-421.

ERICKSON, E. et al. (1969) Experiments in Head Start and Early Education: Curriculum Structures and Teacher Attitudes, Final Report (OEO).

FESHBACH, S. and R. D. SINGER (1971) Television and Aggression: An Experimental Field Study. San Francisco: Jossey-Bass.

GILBERT, J. P., R. J. LIGHT, and F. MOSTELLER (1975) "Assessing social innovations: an empirical base for policy," pp. 39-193 in Evaluation and Experiment: Some Critical Issues in Assessing Social Programs, C. A. Bennett and A. A. Lumsdaine (eds.). New York: Academic Press, 1975, pp. 39-193.

HANRATTY, M. A. et al. (1969) Imitation of Film-Mediated Aggression Against Live and Inanimate Victims. Proceedings of the 77th Annual Convention of the APA, pp. 457-458.

LEIFER, A., N. GORDON, and S. GRAVES (1974) "Children's television: more than mere entertainment." Harvard Ed. Rev. 44 (May).

LIEFELD, J. P. (n.d.) Television Advertising and Children: An experimental Study. University of Guelph, Ontario. (unpublished)

LIGHT, R. J. and P. V. SMITH (1971) "Accumulating evidence: procedures for resolving contradictions among different research studies." Harvard Ed. Rev. (November).

MILLER, L. B. and J. DYER (1972) Four Preschool Programs: Their Dimensions and Effects, Progress Report to PHS.

——— (1971) Two Kinds of Kindergarten After Four Types of Head Start. Presented at the Biennial Meeting of the Society for Research in Child Development, Minneapolis, April 1-4, 1971.

——— (1970) Experimental Variation of Head Start Curricula: A Comparison of Current Approaches. Progress Report 5 to OEO, Nov. 1, 1969-Jan. 31.

RIECKEN, H. W. and R. F. BORUCH (1975) Social Experimentation: A Method for Planning and Evaluating Social Intervention. New York: Academic Press.

ROBERTSON, T. S. and J. R. ROSSITER (1974) "Children and commercial persuasion: an attribution theory analysis. J. Consumer Research (June).

RUBIN, R. S. (1972) "An exploratory investigation of children's responses to commercial content of television advertising in relation to their stages of cognitive development." Ph.D. dissertation, University of Massachusetts.

WARD, S. and D. WACKMAN (1973) "Children's information processing of television advertising," pp. 119-146 in P. Clarke (ed.), New Models for Mass Communication Research. Beverly Hills, CA: Sage.

WELLS, W. D. (1973) "Television and aggression: replication of an experimental field study." University of Chicago. (unpublished)

Despite the lack of positive results, Blumstein notes that the criminal justice literature has had an impact on public policy. Although research has not provided much information useful either in rehabilitating criminals or in controlling crime in other ways, the effects of the criminal justice system itself are better understood. This understanding can in itself, Blumstein believes, lead to "more informed trade-offs between social costs associated with crime and social costs associated with crime control." In addition, Blumstein stresses the importance of not using a single study as the basis of a policy action. However, this caveat leaves open the difficult question of when research is in a form usable for policy makers. Blumstein has no answers for this question, but implies that a judgment call is necessary. How difficult this judgment is to make is discussed by Moynihan elsewhere in this volume.

42

The Positive Values of Negative Research

Alfred Blumstein

The last decade has seen a major increase in the national investment in research on crime control and the criminal justice system. Much of that research was naively directed at finding the "silver bullet" that would "solve" our crime problem. It is no great surprise to criminologists that such solutions have been elusive, and most of the research findings have been negative, indicating how little we can do about crime. However, this should not obscure the usefulness of the research.

Much of the research has been directed at evaluating alternative rehabilitative treatments for identified offenders. The most common result of such evaluations has been a "null effect"—no difference between one treatment and another. These results have been disappointing, particularly to the champions of the treatment under test, but also to the many of us who wish we could find some decent way to reform individual behavior. The null effect is not very surprising, however, in light of the complexity of human behavior, the powerful forces that drive it, and the very limited leverage that any acceptable criminal-justice treatment might possibly exert.

However pessimistic these findings might be for the eventual promise of offender rehabilitation, they do illustrate how the accumulation of research can have a major impact on public policy. The fact that the criminal justice system is now looking for approaches other than rehabilitation is a tribute to the accumulated credibility of the rehabilitation research. This development suggests that research can become useful to policy makers only by accumulating a number of separate, independent studies that are individually valid and show consistent results. No single study can or ever should be sufficient to bring

From Alfred Blumstein, "The Positive Values of Negative Research," 3(1) *The Criminologist* 16-17 (July 1978). Copyright 1978 by American Society of Criminology.

about a direct policy action. Social science research is too often plagued by sensitivity to the particular setting, to features of an individual research study, or by the assumptions inherent in a particular analysis, to warrant any such action. But the accumulation of related studies can force an underlying pattern to emerge and this can provide very valuable policy guidance and impact.

The evidence on the other utilitarian modes of crime control available to the criminal justice system—deterrence and incapacitation—have not been studied as intensively. A National Academy of Sciences Panel recently reviewed the current state of the evidence in these two areas. Its report (Alfred Blumstein, Jacqueline Cohen, Daniel Nagin, eds., *Deterrence and Incapacitation: Estimating the Effects of Criminal Sanctions on Crime Rates,* National Academy of Sciences, Washington, DC) was issued in February 1978. That Panel was charged with assessing what we now know about both the deterrent and the incapacitative effects of the sanctions of the criminal justice system.

In reviewing the statistical evidence on deterrence, the Panel found that the hypothesized negative association between crime rates and sanction level did exist. Unfortunately, however, this still leaves open some critical questions of causality. All that we really know is that higher sanctions are associated with lower crime rates. There are many possible explanations for this association, only one of which is the deterrence effect. For example, those jurisdictions which have high crime rates (which could be generated by demographic or socioeconomic factors exogenous to criminal-justice sanctions) are more likely to find their police, prosecutors, courts, and prisons saturated, and so they may lack the resources to punish more. Or, it may be that their high crime rates simply inure them to the less serious offenses.

Thus, unfortunately, the available research cannot yet provide useful information for policy decision. We can, at this time, make no sensible statement about the number of crimes averted by a one percent increase in the risk of imprisonment. This is not to say that the research can be used to disprove the deterrence argument either, however, because the evidence is certainly no better on the other side. It simply means that the contributions of research to this policy issue are not yet ready to be made, and further accumulation of more sharply focused studies is needed.

The research questions on incapacitation are somewhat different. We all can calculate that if we imprison for three years a man who commits five crimes per year, then we would avert 15 crimes. The most critical problem limiting such calculations is the great difficulty in knowing how many crimes a person actually commits. Self-reports and arrest records might yield such information, but there would still be considerable anxiety about their respective sources of error.

The problem is further compounded by the fact that the individual crime rate varies across the offender population, and that the risk of getting arrested may also vary, but probably in an inverse way. That is, the offending population might be viewed as comprising two major groups—a few "pros" with high crime rates and low arrest vulnerability, and many "amateurs" with low crime rates but high arrest vulnerability. If that is the case, then the criminal justice system can expect to see many more "amateurs" than "pros." Locking *them* up would not go very far in reducing crime. Although we would much prefer to populate our prisons with the offenders who will commit more crimes in the future, we have great difficulty in identifying them when they are arrested and convicted.

This picture does not look extremely bright for those who are looking for a panacea for the overburdened criminal justice system. But that is not the fault of the research; it is a tribute to the stability of much of human behavior in the face of our many efforts to manipulate it.

The picture is bright, however, from the perspective of knowing much better the effects of the actions taken by the criminal justice system. The past decade has seen a significant growth in understanding the effects of the criminal justice system. If research can continue to bring such information to the political process, then perhaps we will be able to make more informed tradeoffs between the social costs associated with crime and the social costs associated with crime control. Research can see to it that the debate on crime control policy becomes more informed and less dominated by ideology and rhetoric.

Assessments of the impact of cigarette smoking on the health status of smokers typically receives widespread public scrutiny. The results of the report that follows suggesting that certain levels of cigarette smoking are associated with tolerable risk has also proved to generate considerable controversy. Gori and Lynch's standard of an acceptable rate of smoking where risks are equal to those of a nonsmoker makes clear the importance of the measurement system's sensitivity to impact and comprehensiveness of scope. Since current-day cigarettes have substantially lowered amounts of cigarette smoke constituents as compared to pre-1960 cigarettes, higher rates of smoking could logically be accepted without additional risk. But the benefits of smoking less hazardous cigarettes today can only be validated when these smokers have smoked for a considerable period of time. And this time delay of positive effects assumes that other factors which may tend to exaggerate the harmful effects of smoking (e.g., drinking, taking birth control pills) will remain constant during the delay. However, one cannot make light of the potential benefits to the health of a nation of less hazardous cigarettes.

43

Toward Less Hazardous Cigarettes
Current Advances

Gio B. Gori and Cornelius J. Lynch

● Critical levels of selected cigarette smoke constituents have been expressed in terms of maximum numbers of pre-1960 cigarettes that a smoker may consume daily without increasing his mortality risk substantially above that of a nonsmoker. This could still imply an important risk, although it may be difficult to detect. We relate these levels to the yields of 27 current low tar and nicotine commercial cigarettes, as measured at the Oak Ridge National Laboratory. In addition, the yields of these selected constituents concomitant with the yield of 1 mg of nicotine are provided as a guide for the smoker who titrates or adjusts his smoking pattern to accommodate a fixed daily intake of nicotine.

(*JAMA* 240:1255-1259, 1978)

SINCE the Surgeon General's report on smoking and health,[1] considerable attention has been focused on cigarette smoke constituents implicated in the cause of tobacco-related diseases. Many such components have been considered, the most frequently cited being total particulate matter (tar), nicotine, carbon monoxide (CO), nitrogen oxides (NO_x), hydrogen cyanide (HCN), and acrolein. Several investigations document the contribution of these components to cancer, chronic pulmonary disease, or cardiovascular impairment.[2-13] Many studies also indicate that there is a dose

From the National Cancer Institute, Bethesda, Md (Dr Gori), and Enviro Control, Inc, Rockville, Md (Dr Lynch).

The views expressed herein are those of the authors and do not necessarily reflect the views or policies of the National Cancer Institute, Public Health Service.

Reprint requests to Division of Cancer Cause and Prevention, National Cancer Institute, Bldg 31, Room 11A03, Bethesda, MD 20014 (Dr Gori).

response between the number of cigarettes smoked and disease incidence and morbidity.[1,3,6,9,10] Since publication of the Surgeon General's report, average tar values of commercial cigarettes have decreased by 29%, and nicotine yields have decreased by 21%, indicating a continuing preoccupation toward reduced hazard.[14]

Evaluation of health benefits resulting from these reductions would be premature because of the long latent periods involved. Available data suggest that, for the present, smoking-related diseases have not abated substantially, with the possible exception of cardiovascular diseases. However, factors contributing to the decline in these latter diseases are not yet clear. On the other hand, mortality from tracheal, bronchial, and lung cancer has continued to rise; projections for the immediate future indicate that further increases may be expected. This probably is because smokers now in the age groups in which cancer is most likely to develop have spent a considerable part of their smoking history using high tar and nicotine cigarettes. As younger smokers who are exposed to lower tar and nicotine cigarettes approach cancer-susceptible ages, a reduction in morbidity and mortality rates could be expected. However, considering tar and nicotine alone may give an incomplete and misleading picture of hazard reduction: the full impact of low tar and nicotine cigarettes on health effects should be evaluated in terms of all the major toxic smoke components mentioned previously.

Critical levels of daily smoke inhalation have been discussed recently in terms of the maximum number of pre-1960 cigarettes that may be smoked daily without detectable increase to the average smoker's risk of mortality beyond that of a nonsmok-

Table 1.—Average Critical Levels of Pre-1960 Cigarette Consumption[15]

Disease	No. of Pre-1960 Cigarettes
Cancer of the oral cavity	8.8
Pharyngeal cancer	2.5
Esophageal cancer	7.3
Pancreatic cancer	9.0
Laryngeal cancer	6.8
Lung cancer	5.7
Bladder and kidney cancer	9.5
Coronary artery disease	4.2
Coronary heart disease	3.5
Aortic aneurysm	4.5
Emphysema, bronchitis, or both	10.0
All causes for current smokers	2.0

er.[15] These are by no means safe levels but merely imply that, for a smoker whose daily consumption does not exceed these levels, any attendant tobacco-related mortality risk may be epidemiologically indiscernible from that of a nonsmoker.

This could still imply a substantial although less readily apparent risk. For instance, if the smoker's risk of developing lung cancer could be reduced from the present level of approximately 10:1 to some value less than 2:1, this risk, while considerable, could be difficult to establish epidemiologically. The inability to verify this reduced risk might lead to its being considered socially tolerable.

Average critical levels relative to diseases to which smokers are particularly susceptible are listed in Table 1, expressed as daily numbers of pre-1960 cigarettes. The last entry in Table 1, "All causes for current smokers," is a comprehensive category representing the effect of cigarette consumption on mortality in general. These values are based on typical yields per cigarette of pre-1960 cigarettes: 43 mg of tar, 3.0 mg of nicotine, 23 mg of CO, 270 μg of NO$_x$, 410 μg of HCN, and 130 μg of acrolein.[15]

CURRENT COMMERCIAL CIGARETTES

Most commercial brands today have yields that are below the typical pre-1960 levels, with particular interest in lowered tar and nicotine yields. A recent publication from the Oak Ridge National Laboratory[16] lists the yields of the six constituents referred to previously for 32 brands of commercial low tar and nicotine cigarettes. Twenty-seven of these brands have measured tar yields that do not exceed 10.0 mg by more than two SEs. Results of testing for these 27 brands are summarized in Table 2.

The lowest measured tar yield is 1.2 mg, and the highest is 10.3 mg (SE, 0.40 mg).

Table 3 presents the percentage reductions in yields of these brands compared with yields of typical pre-1960 cigarettes. Reductions range from a high of more than 98% (Stride HCN yield) to a low of 24% (King Sano Menthol NO, yield). On the average, the brands under consideration have had the greatest percentage reduction in tar yield (86%) and the least percentage reduction in CO and NO, yields (69%) compared with pre-1960 cigarettes.

Table 2.—Analytical Data for Selected Low Tar and Nicotine Cigarettes[16]*						
Brand	Tar, mg/cig†	Nicotine, mg/cig	Carbon Monoxide, mg/cig	Nitrogen Oxides,‡ µg/cig	Hydrogen Cyanide, µg/cig	Acrolein, µg/cig
Benson & Hedges Lights	10.1	0.81	12.1	135	116	61
Carlton	1.5	0.15	2.6	34	16	15
Carlton Menthol	1.2	0.14	2.0	12	12	10
Decade	5.5	0.46	4.3	57	49	38
Decade Menthol	6.6	0.69	4.4	61	50	47
Iceberg 100's	3.1	0.32	5.7	44	44	42
Kent Golden Lights	8.9	0.71	9.2	61	51	47
Kent Golden Lights Menthol	8.3	0.66	8.3	71	62	37
King Sano	5.8	0.29	11.6	196	79	35
King Sano Menthol	5.3	0.25	13.6	205	102	44
L&M Flavor Lights (King)	7.2	0.80	4.8	40	65	30
L&M Long Lights (100's)	6.5	0.67	5.5	41	69	47
Lark II	7.5	0.61	7.3	83	84	44
Lucky 100	3.1	0.28	5.3	68	34	28
Merit	8.8	0.60	12.1	168	151	49
Merit Menthol	8.4	0.61	10.2	172	140	52
Newport Lights Menthol	10.3	0.85	12.5	86	133	57
Now	1.9	0.19	2.4	25	16	15
Now Menthol	1.8	0.16	2.1	30	9	13
Pall Mall Extra Mild	5.1	0.47	5.8	76	65	38
Real	10.2	1.01	12.9	99	155	76
Real Menthol	7.9	0.81	10.2	84	105	44
Stride	3.3	0.36	1.8	5	<10	12
Tareyton Lights	7.8	0.72	2.6	85	75	31
Tempo	6.9	0.56	10.1	166	98	31
True	4.8	0.46	5.2	72	34	29
True Menthol	5.2	0.42	5.7	64	43	31

*Data analyzed by Oak Ridge National Laboratory.
†Abbreviation cig indicates cigarette.
‡Total oxides of nitrogen.

Brand	Tar, mg/cig*	Nicotine, mg/cig	Carbon, Monoxide, mg/cig	Nitrogen Oxides, μg/cig	Hydrogen Cyanide, μg/cig	Acrolein, μg/cig
			Table 3.—Reduction in Yields as Percent of Pre-1960 Cigarette Yields			
Benson & Hedges Lights	77	73	47	50	72	53
Carlton	97	95	89	87	96	88
Carlton Menthol	97	95	91	96	97	92
Decade	87	85	81	79	88	71
Decade Menthol	85	77	81	77	88	64
Iceberg 100's	93	89	75	84	89	68
Kent Golden Lights	79	76	60	77	88	64
Kent Golden Lights Menthol	81	78	64	74	85	72
King Sano	87	90	50	27	81	73
King Sano Menthol	88	92	41	24	75	66
L&M Flavor Lights (King)	83	73	79	85	84	77
L&M Long Lights (100's)	85	78	76	85	83	64
Lark II	83	80	68	69	80	66
Lucky 100	93	91	77	75	92	78
Merit	80	80	47	38	63	62
Merit Menthol	80	80	56	36	66	60
Newport Lights Menthol	76	72	46	68	68	56
Now	96	94	90	91	96	88
Now Menthol	96	95	91	89	98	90
Pall Mall Extra Mild	88	84	75	72	84	71
Real	76	66	44	63	62	42
Real Menthol	82	73	56	69	74	66
Stride	92	88	92	98	>98	91
Tareyton Lights	82	76	89	69	82	76
Tempo	84	81	56	39	76	76
True	89	85	77	73	92	78
True Menthol	88	86	75	76	90	76
Average	86	83	69	69	83	71

*Abbreviation cig indicates cigarette.

The numbers of these cigarettes smoked daily without exceeding critical levels have been calculated from the data in Tables 1 and 2, as in the following example: since the critical level for all causes is two pre-1960 cigarettes, each yielding 43 mg of tar, the number of Benson & Hedges Lights (10.1 mg of tar each) with the equivalent tar yield is 8.5. Thus, 8.5 Benson & Hedges Lights have a total tar yield equal to the critical level for the "All causes for current smokers" category.

Similar values for all of the brands and constituents considered in this article are given in Table 4, rounded

off to the nearest integer. Critical levels were calculated under the assumption of a smoking pattern uniformly distributed over a ten-hour period for any given day. Deviations from such a smoking pattern could alter some critical values, such as those associated with CO effects.[15]

The lowest entry in each row of Table 4 represents the maximum number of cigarettes of that brand that if smoked daily would not exceed the critical level for any of the smoke constituents considered. The highest row entry represents the maximum number of cigarettes of that brand that if smoked daily would not exceed

Table 4.—Critical Levels of Selected Smoke Constituents

Brand	Tar	Nicotine	Carbon Monoxide	Nitrogen Oxides	Hydrogen Cyanide	Acrolein	Lowest Row Entry	Highest Row Entry
				No. of Cigarettes Required				
Benson & Hedges Lights	9*	7	4†	4†	7	4†	4	9
Carlton	57*	40	18	16†	51	17	16	57
Carlton Menthol	72*	43	23†	45	68	26	23	72
Decade	16	.13	11	9	17*	7†	7	17
Decade Menthol	13	9	10	9	16*	6†	6	16
Iceberg 100's	28*	19	8	12	19	6†	6	28
Kent Golden Lights	10	8	5†	9	16*	6	5	16
Kent Golden Lights Menthol	10	9	6†	8	13*	7	6	13
King Sano	15	21*	4	3†	10	7	3	21
King Sano Menthol	16	24*	3†	3†	8	6	3	24
L&M Flavor Lights (King)	12	8†	10	14*	13	9	8	14
L&M Long Lights (100's)	13*	9	8	13*	12	6†	6	13
Lark II	11*	10	6†	7	10	6†	6	11
Lucky 100	28*	21	9	8†	24	9	8	28
Merit	10*	10*	4	3†	5	5	3	10
Merit Menthol	10*	10*	5	3†	6	5	3	10
Newport Lights Menthol	8*	7	4†	6	6	5	4	8
Now	45	32	19	22	51*	17†	17	51
Now Menthol	48	38	22	18†	91*	20	18	91
Pall Mall Extra Mild	17*	13	8	7†	13	7†	7	17
Real	8*	6	4	5	5	3†	3	8
Real Menthol	11*	7	5†	6	8	6	5	11
Stride	26	17†	26	108*	>82	22	17	108
Tareyton Lights	11	8	18*	6†	11	8	6	18
Tempo	12*	11	5	3†	8	8	3	12
True	18	13	9	8†	24*	9	8	24
True Menthol	17	14	8†	8†	19*	8†	8	19

*Highest row entry.
†Lowest row entry.

735

Table 5.—Yields of Selected Constituents Concomitant With Yield of 1 mg Nicotine *

Brand	No. of Cigarettes Necessary to Yield 1 mg Nicotine	Tar, mg	Nicotine, mg	Carbon Monoxide, mg	Nitrogen Oxides, µg	Hydrogen Cyanide, µg	Acrolein, µg
Benson & Hedges Lights	1.2	12.1	1.0	14.5	162	139	73
Carlton	6.7	10.1	1.0	17.4	228	107	101
Carlton Menthol	7.1	8.5	1.0	14.2	85	85	71
Decade	2.2	12.1	1.0	9.5	125	108	84
Decade Menthol	1.4	9.2	1.0	6.2	85	70	66
Iceberg 100's	3.1	9.6	1.0	17.7	136	136	130
Kent Golden Lights	1.4	12.5	1.0	12.9	85	71	66
Kent Golden Lights Menthol	1.5	12.5	1.0	12.5	107	93	56
King Sano	3.4	19.7	1.0	39.4	666†	269	119
King Sano Menthol	4.0	21.2	1.0	54.4†	820†	408	176
L&M Flavor Lights (King)	1.3	9.4	1.0	6.2	52	85	39
L&M Long Lights (100's)	1.5	9.8	1.0	8.3	62	104	71
Lark II	1.6	12.0	1.0	11.7	133	134	70
Lucky 100	3.6	11.2	1.0	9.1	245	122	101
Merit	1.7	15.0	1.0	20.6	286	257	83
Merit Menthol	1.6	13.4	1.0	16.3	275	224	83
Newport Lights Menthol	1.2	12.4	1.0	15.0	103	160	68
Now	5.3	10.1	1.0	12.7	133	85	80
Now Menthol	6.3	11.3	1.0	13.2	189	57	82
Pall Mall Extra Mild	2.1	10.7	1.0	12.2	160	137	80
Real	1.0	10.2	1.0	12.9	99	155	76
Real Menthol	1.2	9.5	1.0	12.2	101	126	53
Stride	2.8	9.2	1.0	5.0	14	<28	34
Tareyton Lights	1.4	10.9	1.0	3.6	119	105	43
Tempo	1.8	12.4	1.0	18.2	299	176	56
True	2.2	10.6	1.0	11.4	158	75	64
True Menthol	2.4	12.5	1.0	13.7	154	103	74
Critical Value	Not Applicable	86.0	6.0	46.0	540	820	260

* Each column also gives constituent/nicotine ratio. For example, entries under column headed "Tar" give tar/nicotine ratios.
† Exceeds critical value.

at least one of the smoke constituents considered. The range from highest to lowest row entries provides the smoker with intermediate goals for gradually reducing his smoking habit through progressively less hazardous smoking stages: proceeding in this manner, he would gradually reach the lowest row entry as a daily maximum cigarette consumption level. At this point, the smoker is likely to be more receptive to taking the final step toward total cessation.[17] Similar considerations apply to brands not explicitly addressed in this article. If the majority of smokers proceeded along these lines, it would be reasonable to predict a substantial decrease in tobacco-related morbidity and mortality.

It should be noted from Table 4 that the highest row entries for 14 brands are for tar yields, whereas the lowest row entries for 13 of the brands are for NO_x yields. In addition, lowest row entries for nine brands occur for CO and acrolein. These values suggest that the cigarette manufacturers should concentrate on the further reduction of NO_x yields, while still attempting to reduce further the yields of other constituents, particularly CO and acrolein.

With the introduction of relatively low nicotine yields, it has been suggested that some smokers may compensate by increasing the total number of cigarettes smoked to maintain a fixed daily level of nicotine intake.[18] The daily intake of other constituents for such a person would depend on the nicotine compensation rate. Table 5 lists the yields of selected smoke constituents concomitant with the yield of 1 mg of nicotine for the brands under consideration. For example, for Benson & Hedges Lights, about 1.2 cigarettes yield 1 mg of nicotine. This same number of cigarettes yields 12.1 mg of tar, 14.5 mg of CO, 162 μg of NO_x, 139 μg of HCN, and 73 μg of acrolein. Thus, a smoker compensating to 1 mg of nicotine would be exposed also to these yields of other smoke constituents.

Compensating to other nicotine values would affect associated yields proportionately. Table 5 allows a smoker to estimate his smoke constituent intake, depending on his own nicotine compensation rates. The 1 mg of nicotine yield (one sixth or 17% of the critical value) is accompanied by an NO_x yield that exceeds the critical level for two brands and by a CO yield that exceeds it for one of these brands. For the remaining brands, the nicotine intake can exceed 1 mg before concomitant yields of other constituents exceed critical values.

COMMENT

Pre-1960 cigarettes have contributed most to the current epidemic of tobacco-related diseases, and epidemiologic studies show a relationship between number of cigarettes smoked daily and the risk of the development of disease. From these studies, we can define the critical daily smoke intake that would not appreciably increase the risk of the smoker over that of the nonsmoker.

Because different cigarette brands deliver different amounts of smoke of different compositions, this critical smoke intake can be met by smoking different numbers of cigarettes, depending on brand.

Today, cigarettes having toxic constituent yields considerably below pre-1960 cigarettes are feasible, and forerunners of such cigarettes are commercially available. Twenty-seven brands that fall into this category were tested at the Oak Ridge National Laboratory, and the numbers of these cigarettes smoked daily without exceeding critical values have been estimated for six major toxic smoke constituents. These critical values may serve as intermediate goals for a smoker who is intent on reducing his smoking habit through progressively less hazardous smoking stages. These calculations are based on the assumption that the smoker of the low tar and nicotine cigarettes will not change his smoking habits in terms of depth of inhalation, frequency of puffing, and butt length. Findings of recent studies support this assumption.[19]

Although the yields for the 27 brands are considerably below the yields of the typical pre-1960 cigarettes, additional reductions are warranted, particularly with respect to NO_x, CO, and acrolein. Otherwise, smokers who compensate for fixed levels of nicotine intake, even though these levels do not exceed critical values for nicotine, may be subjecting themselves to daily intakes of other toxic smoke constituents in excess of their estimated critical values.

Methods for further reductions in yields of toxic smoke constituents have been developed through research such as that conducted by the National Cancer Institute's Smoking and Health Program.[20] One of the principal objectives of this program is to identify those characteristics of cigarettes that lead to toxic and other adverse effects and to develop methods for reducing or eliminating such factors. Progress has been made thus far in improving methods for reducing tar yields through the use of reconstituted tobacco sheet and in reducing nicotine yields through tobacco extraction processes and re-blending. Other smoke yields have been adjusted through selected combinations of filters and smoke-dilution devices, the use of high-porosity paper, the use of tobacco blends rich in nitrates, and the adjustment of the cigarette's burning rate. Further incorporation of these and other state-of-the-art advances coupled with flavor acceptability characteristics can improve commercially available cigarettes to the point where they may properly be termed less hazardous.

The rationale for developing less hazardous cigarettes rests on the fact that despite the publicity given to the health risks associated with smoking, more than 50 million Americans still smoke. While programs to discourage smoking should continue, these educational efforts should be coupled with others directed toward reducing the risks to persistent smokers.

Persuading the smoker to wean himself to progressively less hazardous cigarettes may provide an alternative to smoking cessation that is perhaps more effective than the self-denial approaches of current anti-smoking messages. Although this would not eliminate the risks to the smoker, it is an approach that has the potential to reduce the current epidemic of smoking-associated diseases to a considerably less serious public health problem.

References

1. *Smoking and Health Report of the Advisory Committee to the Surgeon General of the Public Health Services.* publication 1103. Public Health Service, 1974.

2. Anderson EW, Andelman EJ, Strauch JM, et al: Effect of low-level carbon monoxide exposure on onset and duration of angina pectoris: A study in ten patients with ischemic heart disease. *Ann Intern Med* 79:46-50, 1973.

3. Auerbach O, Stout AP, Hammond ED, et al: Histologic changes in esophagus in relation to smoking habits. *Arch Environ Health* 11:4-15, 1965.

4. Aronow WS: Smoking, carbon monoxide,

and coronary heart disease. *Circulation* 48:1169-1172, 1973.

5. Aronow WS, Swanson AJ: The effect of low-nicotine cigarettes on angina pectoris. *Ann Intern Med* 71:599-601, 1969.

6. Doll R, Hill AB: Mortality in relation to smoking: Ten years' observations of British doctors. *Br Med J* 1:1460-1467, 1964.

7. Fraumeni JF Jr: Cigarette smoking and cancers of the urinary tract: Geographic variation in the United States. *J Natl Cancer Inst* 41:1205-1211, 1968.

8. Gross P, de Trexille RTP, Babyak MA, et al: Experimental emphysema: Effects of chronic nitrogen dioxide exposure and papain in normal and pneumoconiotic lungs. *Arch Environ Health* 16:51-58, 1968.

9. Hammond EC: Smoking in relation to the death rates on 1 million men and women, in Haenszel W (ed): *Epidemiological Approaches to the Study of Cancer and Other Diseases*, monograph 19. Bethesda, Md, Public Health Service, National Cancer Institute, 1966, pp 127-204.

10. Kahn HA: The Dorn study of smoking and mortality among US veterans: Report on 8½ years of observation, in Haenszel W (ed): *Epidemiological Approaches to the Study of Cancer and Other Diseases*, monograph 19. Bethesda, Md, Public Health Service, National Cancer Institute, 1966.

11. Krain LS: Crossing of the mortality curves for stomach and pancreatic carcinoma. *Int Surg* 57:307-310, 1972.

12. Morrow RC, Suarex G: Mucosal changes and cancer in intraoral smoking. *Laryngoscope* 81:1020-1028, 1971.

13. Wynder EL, Mabuchi K, Maruchi N, et al: Epidemiology of cancer of the pancreas. *Natl Cancer Inst* 50:645:667, 1973.

14. Maxwell JC Jr: The 1976 Maxwell report. *Tobacco Rep* 103:16-17, 1976.

15. Gori GB: Low risk cigarettes: A prescription. *Science* 194:1243-1246, 1976.

16. Griest WH, Quincy RB, Guerin MW: *Selected Constituents in the Smoke of Domestic Low Tar Cigarettes*, Oak Ridge National Laboratory, technical memorandum No. 6144, part 1. Oak Ridge, Tenn, Oak Ridge National Laboratory, 1977.

17. Harris RW: *How To Keep on Smoking and Live*. Lincoln, Mass, Chestnut Publications, 1976.

18. Russell MAH, Wilson C, Patel VA, et al: Comparison of effect on tobacco consumption and carbon monoxide absorption of changing to high and low nicotine cigarettes. *Br Med J* 4:512, 1973.

19. Weber KH: Recent changes in tobacco products and their acceptance by the consumer. Proceedings of the 6th International Tobacco Conference, Coresta, Tokyo, 1976, pp 47-63.

20. Gori GB: *Smoking and Health Program: National Cancer Institute Status Report, December 1977*. Bethesda, Md, Public Health Service, National Cancer Institute, 1977.

Of all the ways in which social science research findings, including program evaluations, might be used, none is quite so interesting nor of such long-term significance as use by the courts. Even more important is the possibility of use of such findings by the Supreme Court. In the work that follows, Senator Moynihan shows how social science findings have, in fact, been employed by the Supreme Court and by various Justices. The article is enlightening in the way it disabuses us of any notions we might have had regarding the belief that the effect of social science findings on court decisions should be clearcut and straightforward. However, as complex as the true state of affairs may be, Senator Moynihan is neither cynical nor discouraged and points to some possible developments which would provide a more dependable link between the findings of social scientists and the courts that might well make use of them.

44

Social Science and the Courts

Daniel Patrick Moynihan

FROM the time, at the beginning of the century, that American legal scholars and jurists began to speak of the "science of law" it was rather to be assumed that the courts would in time find themselves involved with the social sciences. This was perhaps more a matter of probability than of certainty, for it was at least possible that the "legal realists," or "progressive realists," as they are variously denominated, would have found the social science of that and subsequent periods insufficiently rigorous for their standards—a case at least some social scientists, then as now, would have volunteered to make for them. But Pound and Cardozo and Holmes were indeed realists, and seemingly were prepared to make do with what was at hand, especially when there was such a correspondence with the spirit and structure of their own enterprise.

In 1908, Pound in a seminal article, "Mechanical Jurisprudence," in the *Columbia Law Review* declared: "We have ... the same task in jurisprudence that has been achieved in philosophy, in the natural sciences, and in politics. We have to ... attain a pragmatic, a sociological legal science."

This passage suggests, of course, an alternative explanation for the easy acceptance of the social sciences by the lawyers: to wit, that

Reprinted with permission of the author from: THE PUBLIC INTEREST, No. 54 (Winter 1979), pp. 12-31. Copyright 1979 by National Affairs, Inc.

Pound and his associates were not themselves intolerably rigorous. For what else are we to think of the suggestion, even in 1908, that philosophy and politics had been advancing arm and arm with the natural sciences toward some presumed methodological maturity!

Equally we may wonder at the legal realists' seeming perception of "natural law" as pre-scientific. It may have been for them, but it was nothing of the sort to the framers of the Constitution, for whom "natural law," as we think of it, and scientific law were parts of an integrated understanding of the behavior of both physical objects and human beings. As the late Martin Diamond has reminded us, the framers' respect for human rights, which constituted liberty as they understood it, was not an idiosyncratic "value" of a remote culture. Rather, liberty was seen as *the* primary political good, of whose goodness any intelligent man would convince himself if he knew enough history, philosophy, and science. Indeed, it was because our constitutional principles seemed so self-evident, so much at harmony with the results of enquiry in other fields, that the Founders felt such confidence in them.

But this is perhaps to cavil. The point is that as between the legal scholars and jurists of two and three generations ago, who were seeking to establish a "science of law," and those seeking to establish scientific principles and methods in, say, sociology, there was indeed that symmetry of technique and purpose which Paul Horgan has observed in the arts and sciences of most eras.

There was a corresponding bustle of organization and the discovery of likemindedness among persons who may have thought themselves quite alone in their new and sometimes radical purposes. At the same time that a new judicial philosophy was making its appearance, the social sciences were organizing themselves. The Anthropological Association was founded in 1902; the American Political Science Association in 1903; the American Sociological Association in 1905. The innovators in the legal and academic realms were, in the popular saying of the period, made for each other.

Progressive realism

Even so, the process whereby social science argument became more prominent in the proceedings and decisions of American courts was gradual, and followed the equally gradual rise to ascendency of the "progressive realists," to use Alexander M. Bickel's term, from whom, as he wrote, "the Warren Court traced its lineage."

In its most famous decision, *Brown v. Board of Education* (1954), the Warren Court drew upon a spectrum of social science—ranging from discrete psychological experiments to broad-ranging economic and social enquiry—in reversing the Court's earlier ruling in *Plessy v. Ferguson* (1896), which had established the separate-but-equal standard in racial matters. Taking their lead from the Supreme Court, subordinate Federal courts began to resort to social-science findings to guide all manner of decisions, especially in the still troubled field of schooling, but extending to questions of tax policies, of institutional confinement and care, of crime and punishment, and a hitherto forbidding range of ethical issues.

Social science had become familiar to the courts in the course of hearing advocacy before them. From the time that Louis D. Brandeis began to argue facts and figures before various courts—arguing, however, for judicial restraint in the face of legislation establishing minimum labor standards—judges had had to contend with social-science arguments presented *to* them. Brandeis's data consisted in the main of social statistics, the early measurement devices on which most subsequent social research has been based. But it should be emphasized that the "Brandeis brief" did not assert that its view of the facts was totally accurate; its purpose was merely to demonstrate that the legislature, in acting as it did, had a reasonable basis, that the facts *might* be accurate in holding, for example, that minimum standards were necessary to protect workers' health.

The Supreme Court itself soon became accustomed to and comfortable with this kind of brief. The Court's capacity to cope with social-science arguments was much on display, for example, in *Witherspoon v. Illinois* (1968). At issue was the constitutionality of an Illinois statute providing for the exclusion of jurors having scruples against the death penalty. Mr. Justice Stewart, for the Court, took note of the social-science arguments presented by those contending that the statute was illegal:

> To support this view, the petitioner refers to what he describes as 'competent scientific evidence that death-qualified jurors are partial to the prosecution on the issue of guilt or innocence.'

The Justice, in a footnote, took further note of the academic papers —nicely and accurately describing them as "surveys"—which the petitioners had presented. He went on, however, to declare:

> The data adduced by the petitioner . . . are too tentative and fragmentary to establish that jurors not opposed to the death penalty tend to favor the prosecution in the determination of guilt.

In a footnote to this passage, the Justice commented on these studies in language that will be familiar to graduate student and thesis committee alike:

> We can only speculate . . . as to the precise meaning of the terms used in those studies, the accuracy of the techniques employed, and the validity of the generalizations made.

. Having thus acquitted itself in the matter of methodological rigor, and having in effect rejected the social-science data presented by the petitioners, the Court went on to rule *for* them, and to rest its decision on *other* social-science data! Specifically, Justice Stewart found that ours is a nation "less than half of whose people believe in the death penalty." To establish this he cited opinion polls for the year 1966, as compiled in the *International Review on Public Opinion,* and judged that an Illinois jury culled of "all who harbor doubts about the wisdom of capital punishment" would thus speak only "for a distinct and dwindling minority." Accordingly, the statute was deemed to fail under the Sixth Amendment.[1]

Law, social science, and the future

In these changed—or perhaps it were better to say these now-developed—circumstances it would seem useful to suggest, from the point of view of the social sciences, something of the limitations of this kind of information in the judicial process. If it is quite clear that the courts employ social science with considerable deftness on some occasions, then it must be allowed that on other occasions the courts have got themselves into difficult situations by being too casual, even trusting, about the "truths" presented to them by way of research on individual and group behavior. Here it is not necessary to get into the question of where the courts might have erred. If there are those who wish to challenge particular decisions, they are free to do so under the arrangements so ably, indeed wonderfully, presided over by the American judiciary itself. It is enough to state that the social science involved in a great many judicial decisions—including, for that matter, *Brown* itself—has been sharply criticized by social scientists with differing or competing views.

Hence there are two points which a social scientist would ask jurists to consider before deciding how much further to proceed, and in what direction:

---

[1] It may be that few persons will think of public-opinion polls as social science, but they represent one of our largest achievements in the field of direct measurement, having been developed largely by Lazarsfeld and his colleagues at Columbia University in the 1930's and 1940's.

The first point is that social science is basically concerned to pre-dict future events, whereas the purpose of the law is to order them. In this respect both are unavoidably entangled with politics which, as Maurice Cranston has put it, is an argument about the future. But where social science seeks to establish a fixity of *relationships* such that the consequences of behavior can be known in advance —or, rather, narrowed to a manageable range of possibilities—law seeks to dictate future performance on the basis of past *agreements*. It is the business of the law, as it were, to order alimony payments; it is the business of social science to try to estimate the likelihood of their being paid, or their effect on work behavior and remarriage in male and female parties, or similar probabilities.

In the end social science *must* be a quantitative discipline dealing with statistical probabilities. Law, by contrast, enters the realm of the merely probable at some risk. For the law, even when dealing with the most political of issues, must assert that there are the firmest, established grounds in past settlements on which to order future set-tlements. The primary social function of the courts is to preserve the social peace embodied in such past settlements, and to do this by establishing a competent, disinterested forum to which parties in dispute can come, ask, and be told *what it was we agreed to.* Hence Marshall's dictum in *Marbury v. Madison:* "It is emphatically the province and duty of the judicial department to say what the law *is.*"

To restate, for emphasis: The courts are very much involved with the future; indeed to declare the future is what they do, and not infrequently they do so in the largest conceivable terms. (Bickel writes that the Warren Court "like Marshall's, may for a time have been an institution seized of a great vision, that it may have glimpsed the future, and gained it.") But the basis for ordering the future is that which the judges conclude were the standards and agreements reached in the past for the purpose of such future or-dering.

Hence, also, the concern of the courts to be seen to be above politics. If they are to keep the King's peace they had best not be seen to be involved in planning the King's wars. And so long as the courts confine their references to established *past* agreements —constitutions, customs, statutes, contracts—they are protected by the all-important circumstance that among the things we have agreed to is that for these purposes *the past is what the courts say it is.* It is a living past, and clearly enough it changes, but only the courts can make these changes. It is all very well for others to have opinions about what the Sixth Amendment intends with respect to the composition of juries, but it is what Justice Stewart says, in the company of a sufficient number of his colleagues, that decides, *and there is no way to disprove him.* In this sense, what the court decrees to be the past thereupon has the consequence of *being* the past. On the other hand, when the courts get into the business of predicting the *future* by the use of various social-science techniques for doing this, then others, who need not be lawyers even, much less judges, can readily dispute them, and events will tell who is right and who is wrong.

In this circumstance, perhaps the first thing a jurist will wish to know about the social sciences is: How good are they? How well do they predict? Have they attained to any of the stability that Pound observed in the natural sciences in the early years of the century? The answer must be that the social sciences are labile in the extreme. What is thought to be settled in one decade is as often as not unsettled in the very next; and even that "decent interval" is not always observed. Consider, for example, the cycles of professional opinion concerning the desirability of putting persons with various behavior disorders in institutions, as against maintaining them in their communities. True, there are some areas of stability. With a sample of 500 or so persons, a "psephologist" can predict the popular vote in a Presidential election within a few percentage points. But who will foretell the fate of the administration that follows?

It is fair to state that the unsettled condition of the social sciences represents something of a disappointment, even a surprise. It was thought, especially in economics, that matters were much further advanced than they now appear to be. With respect to the slow progress, or nonprogress, of the social sciences a range of explanations is put forward. It is said that the subject matter is more complex than that of the physical sciences. Experimental modes are usually unattainable. The disciplines are relatively new. They probably have not attracted their share of the best talent. Other reasons come readily enough to mind. But the fact of slow progress is clear enough. The judiciary is entitled to know this, for it needs to acquire the habit of caution, the more perhaps when the work presented to it declares itself to be the most rigorous and "scientific."

Consider the venerable, yet always troubled and constantly shifting "advice" which social science has to offer in the matter of crime and punishment, a subject of the greatest relevance to the judiciary. For the longest while, 20th-century criminology, such as it was, tended to hold that capital punishment did not deter capital crimes. This tendency persisted until the 1960's, when a number of empirical analyses appeared which seemed to establish a "negative association between the level of punishment and the crime rate." Concepts borrowed from economics were employed, often with great elegance, and once again (!) it was discovered that as price goes up demand goes down. We began to talk of the "elasticity of the crime rate to changes in the probability of imprisonment." Next, studies appeared which seemed to establish that capital punishment *saved lives,* as it were, by preventing subsequent capital crimes. This was important and responsible research, and bid fair to make a considerable impression on public and even judicial policy, coming as it did at a time when the courts were banning capital punishment and elements in the public began to demand its return.

In 1976, however, the National Academy of Sciences established a panel to study the relation between crime rates and the severity of punishments. Two years later, the panel concluded that "the available studies provide no useful evidence on the deterrent effect of capital punishment." Thus, research lends support to the decision of the Supreme Court in *Gregg v. Georgia* (1976), in which Justice Stewart, for the Court, declared:

> Statistical attempts to evaluate the worth of the death penalty as a deterrent to crimes by potential offenders have occasioned a great deal of debate. The results simply have been inconclusive.

It could perhaps be argued that Justice Stewart was judging just a little ahead of the evidence, *Gregg* having preceded the NAS panel report by two years. But if it is accepted that the Courts ought to be hesitant to the point of reluctance before accepting any social-science finding as final, Justice Stewart's 1976 cautionary decision seems warranted indeed.

For it is a melancholy fact that, recurrently, even the most rigorous efforts in social science come up with devastatingly imprecise stuff. Thus, a few lines after the *Summary* of the National Academy of Sciences study informed us in plain enough language that execution may or may not deter murder, another murkier passage sums up the evidence on the effect of imprisonment on other kinds of crime:

> Since the high-crime jurisdictions that are most likely to be looking to incapacitation to relieve their crime problems also tend to have relatively lower rates of time served per crime, they can expect to have the largest percentage increases in prison populations to achieve a given percentage of reduction in crime.

As English composition, the sentence itself calls for punishment of some sort. To say that high-crime jurisdictions can expect to "have" the largest percentage increases in prison populations, rather than to "require" them or some equivalent term, is to leave the reader with a sense of surpassing fuziness that all manner of mathematical notation does not overcome. Or conceal. Thus, further in the same study, we are told that the lower bound on the probability of arrest for an "index" offense is given by the formula

$$q_\wedge > \frac{\lambda q_\wedge T\left(\dfrac{V}{A}\right)}{\dfrac{C}{A} - \dfrac{V_1}{A}}$$

and we are also told that if prison use is expanded there is a potential for "two to fivefold decreases in crime." Now one need not be much of a mathematician to know that a twofold decrease in anything will likely lead to antimatter, and that a fivefold decrease might well produce a black hole.

The profession, in a word, has a way to go.

Social science and politics

The second point is that social science is rarely dispassionate, and social scientists are frequently caught up in the politics which their work necessarily involves. The social sciences are, and have always been, much involved with problem-solving and, while there is often much effort to disguise this, the assertion that a "problem" exists is usually a political statement that implies a proposition as to who should do what for (or to) whom. (This essay, for example, which suggests that there are limits to the value which social science can have for the courts, will almost certainly be searched for clues as to whether its implications are politically liberal, or conservative, or whatever.) Social scientists are never more revealing of themselves than when challenging the objectivity of one another's work. In some fields almost *any* study is assumed to have a more-or-less-discoverable political purpose.

Moreover, there is a distinct social and political bias among social scientists. In all fairness, it should be said that this is a matter which social scientists are quick to acknowledge, and have studied to some purpose. It all has to do, one suspects, with the orientation of the discipline toward the future: It attracts persons whose interests are in shaping the future rather than preserving the past. In any event, the pronounced "liberal" orientation of sociology, psychology, political science, and similar fields is well established.

This observation, however, leads us to one of the ironies of the present state of the social sciences. The explanatory power of the various disciplines is limited. Few serious permanencies are ever established. In a period of civilization in which the physical sciences are immensely advanced, when the methodology of proof is well established, and when discoveries rush one upon the other, there are not many things social science has to say. To the degree that it strives for the rigor of the physical sciences, its characteristic product is the null hypothesis, i.e., the discovery that two social phenomena are *not* causally related. In some circumstances this can be rather liberating for social policy. There are, for example, few recent works in social science that have had the immediate impact of James Q. Wilson's *Thinking About Crime*. After examining the research concerning the effect of rehabilitation programs on criminals in this country and abroad, Wilson concluded that no consistent effects could be shown one way or the other. Seemingly, all that could be established for certain about the future behavior of criminals is that when they are in jail they do not commit street crimes. Two centuries of hopes collapsed in that proposition, and not a few illusions. But out of the wreckage came the idea that fixed and predictable prison terms are a sensible social policy, and in short order this was being advocated across the spectrum of political opinion. Indeed, if anything, while social scientists tend to be liberal, the tendencies of social-science *findings* must be judged conservative, in that they rarely point to the possibilities of much more than incremental change. In 1959 the Yale political scientist Charles Lindblom set this forth as a necessity, the one *law* of social change, in a celebrated article entitled "The Science of Muddling Through."

The political orientation of the social sciences has been particularly evident (and is, I believe, least objectionable) in the shifting fashions in research topics. One will find a score of books, mostly of the period 1910-1950, about trade unions and strikes for every serious study of a middle-class organization such as the American Bar Association. But it is also to be noted that these preferences change with some regularity. Trade unions, having been judged "conservative," are not much written about any longer. Of late, community organizations, such as those funded by government anti-poverty efforts, have been in vogue. Tomorrow, doubtless, it will be something else again.

This is not to be understood to suggest any deliberate attempt to distort. One has little more than impressions to offer here, but it seems mostly to be a matter of a somewhat-too-ardent searching for evidence that will help sustain a hoped-for conclusion. Sometimes the search succeeds; just as often it does not. Where there is deliberate fudging in the research, success is brief and retaliation can be truly termed draconian. The social sciences are serious professions, seeking to become ever more professional. They are also highly competitive, at times perhaps damagingly so. Edward C. Banfield has described this as the Fastest-Gun-in-the-West-Effect—which is to say, the melancholy knowledge of anyone briefly on top of any particular subject matter that the graduate schools are abrim with young scholars who dream of making their own reputations by bringing him down in a brief, violent encounter. Such efforts may or may not succeed. But *anyone* who brings questionable data or methodology into the various fields can expect to be devastated. And even the most impeccable work will be challenged simply because "it is there."

The prudent jurist will be aware of this, and take it into account. That this can be done was splendidly demonstrated by the Supreme Court in its decision in *San Antonio School District v. Rodriguez* (1973). Here a class action on behalf of certain Texas schoolchildren was instituted against school authorities challenging the constitutionality, under the equal protection clause of the 14th Amendment, of the state's system of financing public education. The system was characterized by a heavy reliance on local property taxes, which is associated with substantial differences in per-pupil expenditure. Now it happens that just a very few years before this issue came to the Court, a series of research findings appeared which were quite devastating to the previous assumption that achievement in education was more or less a direct function of spending. Best understood, this new research seemed to show that, after a point, this just wasn't so.[2]

The *Rodriguez* case was the culmination of an effort, primarily the work of academics, to disestablish the general American pattern of local-school-district financing in favor of statewide, or even nationwide systems, with uniform per-pupil expenditures. (In passing, it may be noted that moving an issue *upwards* in the federal system has been well documented by political scientists to be a technique of

---

[2] In the interest, as lawyers say, of full disclosure, I should state that this is the intrepretation that Frederick Mosteller and I presented in a reanalysis of the Coleman data, in *On Equality of Educational Opportunity* (1972). Mr. Justice Powell cites our work, along with that of others, in a passage in his decision in *Rodriguez*.

effecting social reform.) In briefest summary, these scholars did not anticipate that their research establishing differentials in school expenditure would be vitiated, at least in part, by the enquiries that were simultaneously taking place which cast grave doubt on just what significance was to be attributed to such differences.

In any event, the matter did not escape the attention of Justice Powell, who, writing for the majority, observed:

> On even the most basic questions in this area the scholars and educational experts are divided. Indeed, one of the major sources of controversy concerns the extent to which there is a demonstrable correlation between educational expenditures and the quality of education— an assumed correlation underlying virtually every legal conclusion drawn by the District Courts in this case.

Further on, Justice Powell declared, "We are unwilling to assume for ourselves a level of wisdom superior to that of legislators, scholars, and educational authorities in 50 states," and found that the Texas system of school financing met the constitutional standard of the equal protection clause. It is not necessary to side either with the majority or the dissenting justices in this latter judgment to state with some confidence that, if the District Courts depended overmuch in their decisions on the existence of a "demonstrable correlation between educational expenditures and the quality of education" —which Justice Powell says they did, and no dissenting Justice said they did not—then the District Courts either did not know their social science or, perhaps, did not know their social scientists.

The impact of social science

The attentive reader might well be given pause by the somewhat remonstrative suggestion that "the District Courts . . . did not know their social science." Since when, it might well be asked, has this been required of judges? Is it not sufficiently demanding to expect that they will know the law?

No, alas, it is not. Herewith we encounter what is arguably the major impact of social science on law.

The social sciences may be at an early state of development, but this has not in the least inhibited their assertiveness. It may well have served to abet it. For the moment their ambitions are truly imperial. There is little by way of human behavior which the social sciences do not *in theory* undertake to explain, to account for.

As a result, there are fewer and fewer areas of social behavior for which traditional or "common-sense" explanations will any longer suffice in serious argument. A cursory reading of the District Court decisions which preceded *Rodriguez* suggests that the judges' views on the relation of educational expenditure to educational achievement were based on nothing more than common-sense everyday opinion. And this is the point. Common-sense everyday opinion no longer persuades. Everybody asks: who *knows?* If it is theoretically possible to know something—and there are few relationships about which it is not theoretically possible to know *something*—then until the research is done, no one is in a very good position to speak!

If we may adopt for a moment the lawyers' term "material," then we may say that the range of what is material in lawsuits is now greatly expanded—or will be as the courts submit to the logic, or perhaps it may be better to speak of the spirit, of the social sciences. Some years ago Kenneth Boulding spoke of the advent of the social sciences as an historical event comparable for society to the beginnings of consciousness in human beings. That we are only at the beginning of this era does not at all limit what we expect of it; it may be, and probably is, the case that we greatly exaggerate. But that changes nothing as yet. The Supreme Court in *Rodriguez* found there was *no evidence* to support the charges. Accordingly, the Texas school-financing system was found Not Guilty. (Or was it a Scottish verdict: Not Proven?)

Thus does social science rend the "web of subjectivity," the phrase which Bickel used to describe aspects of the Warren Court. His references were primarily to the Court's reading of the past. On more than a few occasions, he wrote, "the Warren Court has purported to discover in the history of the Fourteenth Amendment, and of the Thirteenth, and of other constitutional provisions, the crutch that wasn't there." Now this can be seen to be a traditional enough critique. Here the Court interprets the past, and it is altogether to be expected that legal scholars should occasionally criticize the Court (however gently, in Bickel's case) for its interpretation of the past. But where the Court essays to predict the *future*, which is the realm of social science, the idiosyncratic and the subjective are even more conspicuous, and more subject to criticism.

As litigation concerning educational matters has illustrated some earlier propositions, it may do so also with respect to this last, most important one. Commencing at least with the *Brown* decision, the Supreme Court has held that "education is perhaps the most important function of state and local governments." But a decade prior to *Brown*, the Court ruled in *Everson v. Board of Education* (1947) that the First Amendment requires that government assistance to

schools that are not in the public sector, strictly defined as not operated by government, must be severely restrained, and as near as
possible nonexistent.

Here was a common enough situation for the courts. They were
asked to determine what it is the Constitution decrees with respect
to matters that clearly were remote from the thoughts of those
who drafted the document, including its various amendments. Anyone who will trouble to read the debates concerning this part of the
First Amendment—and this will not entail a great deal of trouble, for
the question was debated for the equivalent of about a day in the
House and a day in the Senate and the entire record in the *Annals
of Congress* takes up only 119 lines—will find no mention of aid to
education. Hence judges have had to interpret as best they could.

Now in the judgment of some, they have quite misinterpreted this
history. In the manner that Bickel chides the Warren Court for discovering things in the history of the 13th and 14th Amendments
that simply are not there, scholars such as Walter Berns, Michael
Malbin, Antonin Scalia, and Philip Kurland find that, with respect
to aid to nonpublic schools, the Court's interpretation of the establishment clause is non-historical. In his 1962 study, *Religion and
the Law*, Philip Kurland writes: "Anyone suggesting that the answer,
as a matter of constitutional law, is clear one way or the other is
either deluding or deluded."

In the interest, once more, of full disclosure, I must state that I
quite agree with the critics of the Court in this matter. In my view,
the only *truly* comparable situation is that long period when the
Supreme Court repeatedly claimed to find in the 14th Amendment a
whole series of restrictions on the power of legislatures to enact labor
legislation. Thus in *Lochner v. New York* (1905), the Court—striking
down a 60-hour-work-week law—said that it was not at all "a
question of substituting the judgment of the Court for that of the
legislature," but simply that there was "no reasonable ground for in-
terfering with the liberty of person or the right of free contract."
Now there was no real difficulty in 1905 in discovering the purposes
for which the 14th Amendment had been adopted, and establishing
that it was in no wise enacted to prevent the New York State legislature from regulating the hours of bakers. But such nonsense had
been solemnly invoked by the Supreme Court in *Allgeyer v. Louisi-
ana* (1897) in the closing years of the 19th century and was only
overruled in the fourth decade of the 20th century. It is all forgotten now, save by historians, but it was once a burning issue of American politics—as it should have been.

In just this manner, the establishment clause has been held to prevent legislatures from providing various forms of assistance to church-related schools, albeit that the establishment clause has the plain and unambiguous meaning—reflecting the Founders' intention—that Congress will not establish a national religion.

There are those who are not happy with this state of affairs, but few, one would venture, who are actively angry. We go through these things every so often, and have done so for generations. One day a Justice will come along who will make the equivalent point that Holmes made in *Lochner* when he declared, "The 14th Amendment does not enact Mr. Herbert Spencer's *Social Statics.*" It will come to be seen that the Court's rulings on aid to private schools merely reflected a particular religious point of view—i.e., that there is no public interest in the promotion of religion—which reached its peak of intellectual respectability in the 1920's and 1930's, the period in which most of the judges who made the decisions were educated.

Having stressed the shaky reliability of social science, a certain kind of fairness suggests that the infallibility of judges might usefully be questioned also. The establishment-clause decisions are an intellectual scandal. Without intending to do so, the courts in the school-aid cases have been imposing on the country their *own* religious views. This point was well understood in 1841 by John C. Spencer, Tocqueville's first American translator and New York's Secretary of State and Superintendent of Public Schools. To those who feared use of public funds for sectarian purposes, Spencer in an official report replied that all instruction is in some ways sectarian:

> No books can be found, no reading lessons can be selected, which do not contain more or less of some principles of religious faith, either directly avowed, or indirectly assumed.
>
> Even the moderate degree of religious instruction which the Public School Society imparts, must therefore be sectarian; that is, it must favor one set of opinions in opposition to another, or others; and it is believed that this always will be the result, in any course of education that the wit of man can devise.
>
> On the contrary, it would be in itself sectarian; because it would be consonant to the views of a peculiar class, and opposed to the opinions of other classes.

All this will be borne with sufficient good will and even good humor. The greater problem is for the courts, and it is a problem much complicated by social science. For social science affects what the court *can* say. Thus the case of *Tilton v. Richardson* (1971), which is the controlling decision regarding Federal aid to church-related schools. The Higher Education Facilities Act of 1963 provided Federal construction grants for college and university facilities. Tilton *et al.* sued, contending that grants to four church-related colleges and universities in Connecticut had the effect of promoting religion. The Court held that this was not so, even though it would never tolerate a Federal statute that provided construction grants to church-related high schools or suchlike institutions. Colleges and universities, the Court said, are different from elementary and secondary schools where religious matters are concerned, and college students are different from high school students.

An unassailable argument

Before grappling with the decision of the majority, it will help to touch upon the dissent of Mr. Justice Douglas, who thought such aid to church-related colleges to be unconstitutional. It was an impassioned dissent: in his own words, a despairing dissent. The respect, he said, "which through history has been accorded the First Amendment is this day lost." Before coming to this sad conclusion, he presented an argument which some may view as wrong, but which is also logically quite—or almost—unassailable. By contrast, the less idiosyncratic decision of the majority is nonetheless indefensible, and it is a weakness which the advent of social science has brought about.

There is *one* unimpeachable sentence in Justice Douglas's opinion. "The First Amendment," he writes, "bars establishment of a religion." Just so. There was to be no established religion such as the Church of England or the Church of Ireland of that period. The meaning and intent of the amendment was most clear in the version considered by the House of Representatives on August 15, 1789, which read "no national religion shall be established by law." Elbridge Gerry objected, as the word "national" was a matter of contention between Federalists and Anti-Federalists, and the final version emerged, accessible in meaning to anyone who can read English. No established religion. Surely this has nothing to do with construction grants made available to religious institutions of *all* denominations. Hence a judge who is going to contend that it does, had best give considerable thought to what kinds of available evidence will tend to prove or disprove his contention. On this score Douglas was unassailable. He advanced arguments that some will find curious, but which none can refute.

To begin with, he would brook no distinction between levels of "parochial schools." They all looked alike to him. There is, he stated, a "dominant religious character" to all such schools. He then introduced in evidence the work of Loraine Boettner. A passage from Boettner's book, *Roman Catholicism*, is reproduced in a footnote. It should be clear, Boettner writes, "that a Roman Catholic parochial school is an integral part of that church." The title of ownership is vested in the bishop as an individual, a person "who is appointed by, who is under the direct control of, and who reports to the pope in Rome."

Now this "pope in Rome" is a person much on Mr. Boettner's mind. His book was published in Philadelphia in 1962, by the Presbyterian and Reformed Publishing Company, but it could as well have appeared in Edinburgh four centuries earlier. To him, very simply, the pope is an Antichrist; his church is an heretical church; its teachings utterly subversive of true religion. As for the followers of the pope, they are, in Boettner's view, to a greater or lesser degree, agents of papal subversion. On one page of his book, for example, he states that Roman Catholics ought not to be allowed to teach in *public* schools.

Boettner's full view of the matter, with respect to schools, is seen in another passage from this book which Douglas reproduces word for word in his concurring opinion in *Lemon v. Kurtzman* (1971):

> In the parochial schools Roman Catholic indoctrination is included in every subject. History, literature, geography, civics, and science are given a Roman Catholic slant. The whole education of the child is filled with propaganda. That, of course, is the very purpose of such schools, the very reason for going to all of the work and expense of maintaining a dual school system. Their purpose is not so much to educate, but to indoctrinate and train, not to teach scripture truths and Americanism, but to make loyal Roman Catholics. The children are regimented, and are told what to wear, what to do, and what to think.

Now here we are at the crux of the matter: Catholic schools do not "teach scripture truths." In Boettner's view Roman Catholic schools are heretical. In Douglas's view they are unconstitutional, i.e., they are not *Presbyterian.*

Now this is a venerable view, entertained over the years by many more Scotsmen than the Justice. Equally interesting is the passage that Douglas quotes in his dissent in *Tilton* from an article by Dr. Eugene Carson Blake which appeared in *Christianity Today* in 1959, the year after Blake completed his distinguished eight-year tenure as Stated Clerk of the General Assembly of the Presbyterian Church of the United States of America. (Douglas, to be quite fair, identifies him as "Dr. Eugene C. Blake of the Presbyterian Church.") Blake, who had studied in Edinburgh as a youth, had a lively imagination of the sort associated with that city. He had also, more rare, the gift of prophecy. It was his judgment that owing to the tax-exempt state of church properties "it is not unreasonable to prophesy that with reasonably prudent management, the churches ought to be able to control the whole economy of the nation within the predictable future." This alarmed him:

> That the growing wealth and property of the churches was partially responsible for revolutionary expropriations of church property in England in the 16th century, in France in the 18th century, in Italy in the 19th century, and in Mexico, Russia, Czechoslovakia, and Hungary (to name a few examples) in the 20th century, seems self-evident.

Now this is a range of historical reference which Gibbon would have admired, and in our time perhaps only Toynbee might have essayed. It is also of course gibberish, much as Boettner is . . . well, if not harmless, surely not serious. But these arguments are all but irrefutable. Boettner thinks the pope is an Antichrist. Douglas cites Boettner. *Who is to disprove them?* Blake thinks rich monasteries cause peasant revolts. Douglas cites Blake. *Who is to disprove them?* Douglas chose his ground well. He asserted a range of particular values and ultimate truths which he claimed to find in the Constitution; and that was that.

By contrast, the majority of the Court chose the most exposed arguments on which to rest its decision. The Chief Justice, for the majority, stated that "there are generally significant differences between the religious aspects of church-related institutions of higher learning and parochial schools." Two particular differences are cited. First, that religiously-affiliated colleges and universities do not attempt to indoctrinate their students while religiously-affiliated elementary and secondary schools do. Second, that college students are different, that "college students are less impressionable and less susceptible to religious indoctrination," that the "skepticism of the college student is not an inconsiderable barrier to any attempt to subvert the Congressional objectives and limitations."

Enter social science. For these are *researchable* subjects. The facts are *discoverable*, if not easily. It is no longer possible to make such statements and expect to be taken seriously unless one has proof.

The Court in a sense acknowledges this. Proofs are provided. One is tempted to observe that, as in the evocation of the Dreyfus case in *Penguin Island,* this was fatal. For what the Justices offer with respect to the assertion that "there are generally significant differences between the religious aspects of church-related institutions of higher learning and parochial elementary and secondary schools" is a *Harvard Law Review* article by Paul A. Freund. And what does Professor Freund report? He reports that "institutions of higher learning present quite a different question, mainly because church support is less likely to involve indoctrination and conformity at that level of instruction." The argument grows tautological. What is Freund's evidence? What studies? What survey data? *None.* No evidence of any kind. Freund is among the most distinguished legal scholars of the age. But it is not for anyone to describe the pedagogical practices of a group of colleges and universities without having inquired into the matter, preferably in accordance with reasonably well-established methodological rules. "Less likely," will not do. A modern bench requires harder data than that. Social science establishes new standards for what it is that can be taken as "self-evident," what, to use the words of the Court, "common observation would seem to support." This of course is a special problem for the Supreme Court. One cannot imagine that the bloopers of *Tilton* would have survived review—but with the Supreme Court there is no review.

Consider the second assertion, that "there is substance to the contention that college students are less impressionable and less susceptible to religious indoctrination." The Court again offers in evidence a *Harvard Law Review* article, this by Professor Donald A. Giannella. Again the tautology: Church-related colleges, Giannella writes, do not "attempt to form the religious character of the student by maintaining a highly controlled regime . . . to attempt such control of the college students is highly inappropriate, and would probably prove self-defeating." Again, no evidence, no data.

This kind of assertion by the Court is bound to be challenged. Anyone with any experience of a liberal-arts faculty would immediately suspect that psychologists would not have any reliable findings on a subject so vast as "impressionability to religious indoctrination." This almost surely would come under the heading of things researchable but not researched. The methodological problems, especially of definition, are clearly formidable.

And, indeed, in response to an enquiry which I sent, the 1978 President of the American Psychological Association, Professor M. Brewster Smith of the University of California, replied:

> There is no comparable comprehensive treatment of religious change over the high school years that I know of, and while surely a close

search might turn up scattered studies, I think it is fair to say, in answer to your question, that solid evidence regarding the high school vs. college comparison in which you are interested *does not exist* (his italics).

Inasmuch as I have called the *Tilton* case into question in the course of Senate debate, allow me to be particularly explicit as to what I judge the Court to have done in this case. The Court's confidence in what some might call its "secularist" position on the establishment clause has declined steadily since it first pronounced on the matter in *Everson* in 1947. In *Tilton* it was trying to find grounds for allowing a clear intent of Congress to be carried out, and did so by distinguishing between higher-education facilities, which are the only ones affected by the law, and other facilities. But the point I would wish to make, for purposes of this essay, is that the Court, in an effort to base its decision on contemporary modes of argument, was rigorous but not rigorous enough. On examination, there is no evidence with which to support its finding. Justice Douglas, arguing in a prescientific mode, made no such mistake.

A great wisdom

Is this distressing? Not, I think, unless one is distressed by the modern age. Primitive man, presumedly, had an explanation for everything. There is a sense, of course, in which science has made ignoramuses of us all. So much is *not* known. But modern man still does know more than his ancestors, even immediate ones, and we would do well to recall the saying of 19th-century Americans that "it's not ignorance that hurts, it's knowin' all those things that ain't so." Courts will learn to adapt to the changed conditions of evidence which social science imposes on contemporary argument. One would not be surprised, for example, to see the emergence of a group of lawyers trained in both disciplines, much as there are now specialists trained both as lawyers and as medical doctors. Indeed, lawyers with no more than a good undergraduate grounding in social-science methodology could have quite an impact in this area simply by establishing standards of cross-examination which are infrequently attained today.

This would be no small thing. To take yet another, and now concluding example from the field of education: Consider the controversy which broke out in the late 1970's over reinterpretations of the Equal Educational Opportunity Report, commonly known as the Coleman Report after its principal author, Professor James S. Coleman. In the late 1960's Coleman's data on pupil achievement were the basis for a number of major court decisions calling for school busing. Subsequently—in the familiar pattern—his initial interpretations were challenged. Much confusion and some bitterness followed. It is at least arguable that much of this might have been avoided had it been made clear to the courts, in the first place, either through exposition by plaintiffs or cross-examination by defendants, that Coleman had not found any race effect as such in his analysis of student-body characteristics and educational achievement. He had found a social-class effect.

Judges in the future should be able to look for such cross-examination. This will help them protect the special space that we give to the courts, for if there is one thing they don't need, it is another group of critics, claiming to know their tasks better than they.

One hopes it does not transgress any boundaries to suggest that these developments might also encourage in the courts a somewhat more easeful acceptance that, in the end, law is after all only long-established preference, codified opinion. When Pound and Cardozo and Holmes began talking of the "science of law," perhaps they, too, were mostly trying to impose a different set of opinions from those then prevailing. But at least they were doing so in an effort to get the bench back to the business of interpreting opinion as *embodied in legislation,* rather than as embodied in the education and social-class preferences of a particular body of judges. This was great wisdom, and this is precisely the import of Chief Justice Burger's decision in *Tennessee Valley Authority v. Hill* (1978) in which it was held that, inasmuch as the Tellico Dam would endanger the snail darter, it was prohibited by the Endangered Species Act. In civil but firm tones the Congress was informed that it must expect that, when called upon, the Court will enforce such laws as Congress enacts regardless of any individual appraisal of the wisdom or unwisdom of a particular course. Whether that was to be considered a warning or not will depend on one's judgment as to the balance of wisdom against unwisdom in recent Congressional enactments. But that it is the policy of the present Court, none need doubt. We may all take pleasure in the nice touch of the Chief Justice who closed his opinion not with a citation of social science, nor yet of any "science of law," but rather lines ascribed to Sir Thomas More by the contemporary playwright Robert Bolt: "The law, Roper, the law. I know what's legal, not what's right. And I'll stick to what's legal . . . I'm *not* God."

If research findings are to be used, they must come to the attention of the right audience. The scientific research community tends to be oriented toward a rather amorphous audience of peers, fellow scientists, who share a good bit of knowledge about concepts and methods and who begin analysis of information with much the same set of assumptions. Scientists, including social scientists, appear to assume that in some dependable but unspecified manner the information they produce will filter through the layers of government bureaucracy, being correctly translated and interpreted at each level, until it finally reaches the minds of an audience of the ultimate decision makers. It is probably safe to say that most social scientists have only the vaguest notion of who that final set of influentials might be. Consequently it was with some degree of fascination that we encountered in what follows the exact specification of the final audience for a report—the listing of forty-three people whose reading alone would justify the production of the report.

The following is excerpted from the Preface to a report of the National Research Council on The Federal Investment in Knowledge of Social Problems.

45

Preface to The Federal Investment in Knowledge of Social Problems

National Research Council

Since this report lays great stress on the importance of knowing your audience, I will begin by saying who we hope will read it. We would be pleased if it were closely read by 43 people who exercise a critical oversight of federal efforts to create and use knowledge of social problems. Let me name them:

The Director of the Office of Management and Budget

The Science and Technology Adviser to the President

The Director of the National Science Foundation and the Chairman of the National Science Board

The Chairman of the U.S. Civil Service Commission

The Secretaries of Health, Education, and Welfare, of Housing and Urban Development, of Labor, and of Transportation

The Chairmen of the Senate and House Appropriations Committees and of their Subcommittees on Housing and Urban Development—Independent Agencies, on Labor, Health, Education, and Welfare, and on Transportation

The Chairmen of the Senate Committee on Banking, Housing and Urban Affairs, of the Committee on Commerce, Science, and Transportation and its Subcommittee on Science, Technology, and Space, of the Committee on Governmental Affairs, and of the Committee on

Reproduced from *The Federal Investment in Knowledge of Social Problems* (1978), pages vii-xii, with the permission of the National Academy of Sciences, Washington, DC.

Human Resources and its Subcommittees on Health and Scientific Research, on Aging, on Alcoholism and Drug Abuse, on Child and Human Development, on Education, Arts, and Humanities, on Employment, Poverty, and Migratory Labor, on the Handicapped, and on Labor

The Chairmen of the House Committee on Banking, Finance and Urban Affairs, of the Committee on Education and Labor and its Subcommittees on Compensation, Health, and Safety, on Economic Opportunity, on Employment Opportunities, on Elementary, Secondary, and Vocational Education, on Postsecondary Education, on Select Education, on Labor-Management Relations, and on Labor Standards, of the Committee on Government Operations, and of the Committee on Science and Technology and its Subcommittees on Domestic and International Scientific Planning, Analysis, and Cooperation and on Science, Research and Technology

The Comptroller General of the United States

The Assistant Secretary for Planning and Evaluation of the Department of Health, Education, and Welfare, the Assistant Secretary for Policy Development and Research of the Department of Housing and Urban Development, and the Assistant Secretary for Policy, Evaluation, and Research of the Department of Labor.

We would be well satisfied if our analysis reached only this critically important oversight group—but we want and expect to reach a wider audience as well. This report is meant to help those who administer the system of federal support for the production and application of knowledge of social problems. Some of our ideas are directed to those who manage federal programs of support for social research and development (R&D); some to those in the Congress and the executive branch who help to shape federal policy on social R&D; and some to all those in the government, the research community, and the nation at large who want to see knowledge brought effectively to bear on social problems.

The Study Project on Social Research and Development grew out of concerns of federal officials responsible for both science policy and social policy. It was commissioned by the Science and Technology Policy Office, then the staff arm of the director of the National Science Foundation in his role as science adviser to the President. The director and officials in the Science and Technology Policy Office were concerned about the limited information available to the government on the scope of programs of social research and development, the lack of consistency in policies for managing research programs, and the lack of understanding of the impact on the research community of the decisions made by the managers of these programs. These concerns were shared by officials in the Office of Management and Budget and in several other executive departments and agencies. As a result, the National Academy of Sciences was asked to survey the size and location of budgetary support for social research and development throughout the executive branch. Subsequently, the Academy was asked to broaden its study to recommend ways in which the federal government could more effectively develop and apply knowledge about social problems.

The need to develop a comprehensive view of the present system of social research and development was plain from the varied diagnoses of what is wrong with it. We found a remarkable range of ideas as to where the problem lies.

Some of these locate the difficulty within the policy-making arms of government. It is said that the time perspectives of policy makers are excessively short; that they cannot free themselves from urgent matters of the moment to deal with the important longer-term problems facing the country; that they cannot conscientiously seek out available information on social problems; that they rarely understand the process of research or surround themselves with those who do; that they bend research and development to political ends; that they defend the turfs of their particular agencies or committees, with too little regard for the need to coordinate the planning and use of research across units of the government with interdependent functions.

Others locate the difficulty in those officials in the government who are responsible for managing the funding of social research and development. It is said that these managers do not plan effectively; that they use the wrong instruments to support research work; that they pay too little attention to quality; that they have unrealistic ideas of what can be accomplished by research in a given amount of time; that they are preoccupied by new starts and individual projects and fail to accumulate the knowledge that can be gained from a series of projects; that they devote too little attention to disseminating the results of the research they support.

Still other diagnoses locate the difficulty in the research community. It is said that research performers resist being held to account; that to obtain funding they promise results they cannot deliver; that they adapt their results to the sponsor's biases; that the for-profit performers, despite islands of excellence, have flooded the market with shoddy work as they pursue new contracts; that the universities have been unwilling to create the institutions and the faculty incentives that would turn disciplinary knowledge toward social needs.

Although there is a kernel of truth in most of these assertions, their varied content argues the need to see the system whole. The body of this report describes the steps we took to develop a more comprehensive view.

This report is one of a number published over the past decade that deal with specific facets of social research and its use. Each is a product of its time and of the aspirations social scientists then held. It is useful to characterize these earlier efforts, even if selectively, to better appreciate the background and climate in which our study was undertaken.

The Behavioral Sciences in the Federal Government (Young Report) was published by the National Academy of Sciences in 1968. It was primarily concerned with means of improving the use of social research by agencies of the federal government in making federal policy. The deliberations of the Young committee took place before an assessment could be made of the impact of the significant increase in expenditures for social research that accompanied the programs of the Great Society. The committee sought to improve the capacity of the government to commission and use social research by recommending that more trained social scientists be hired by federal agencies and that the representation of the social science community on the President's Science Advisory Committee (PSAC) and in the Office of Science and Technology be enlarged. It also recommended that an independent National Institute for Advanced Research and Public Policy be endowed by the government to conduct interdisciplinary and future-oriented research.

In 1969 the Academy and the Social Science Research Council published *The Behavioral and Social Sciences: Outlook and Needs* (BASS Report). This report was one of a series that assessed the status and needs of various scientific disciplines, and a number of discipline-specific volumes were issued. There was also a central report, which asserted that federal support for the behavioral and social sciences should increase at the rate of 12 to 18 percent per year on the ground that the normal growth of the social and behavioral science community, as well as social need, justified it. Beyond this, the report echoed the Young committee's call for improved representation on PSAC, proposed the development of improved and interlinked data bases, stressed the importance of providing for the training of social and behavioral scientists, and proposed the creation of a system of social indicators. It also suggested that social and behavioral scientists outside the government issue an annual social report to the nation. The report recognized that discipline-centered work frequently was unable to grapple with social problems and proposed that funds be provided to create a number of graduate schools of applied behavioral science.

At about the same time, the Special Commission on the Social Sciences of the National Science Board published *Knowledge into Action: Improving the Nation's Use of the Social Sciences* (Brim Report). This report was concerned with improving the use of social science research and called for better social science training for the professions, employment of individuals with social science training in key government positions, improved data bases, and better understanding of social science by labor, community organizations, and the public. The Brim Report also recommended the continued presence of social scientists on PSAC and the presence of social scientists other than economists on the staff of the Council of Economic Advisers. The report also recognized the limitations of disciplinary approaches to social problems. In view of the pervasive disciplinary organization of universities, it called for the establishment of problem-centered institutes of social research, which might be independent of universities.

Most of these reports were written from a disciplinary perspective. Each included recommendations that could easily appear self-serving to critics of social research even if they were not. None looked deeply into the motives of the government for supporting research or into the limitations of applying the results of social research in the policy process. The discussions of use dealt almost entirely with federal officials, although the Brim Report did consider nonfederal audiences.

Four reports of quite a different nature, which relate to our task, have appeared recently. Each of them was published by the National Academy of Sciences. *Knowledge and Policy in Manpower: A Study of the Manpower Research and Development Program in the Department of Labor* examined the programs of the Office of Manpower Research and Development in the Department of Labor; *Social and Behavioral Science Programs in the National Science Foundation* evaluated the quality of those programs within the National Science Foundation; *Assessing Vocational Education Research and Development* evaluated the programs of vocational education research and development supported by the Office of Education of the Department of Health, Education, and Welfare; *Understanding Crime: An Evaluation of the National Institute of Law Enforcement and Criminal Justice* focused on the research program of the Law Enforcement Assistance Administration of the Department of Justice. Collectively, these reports differed from the earlier ones in that they were based on evaluations of selected federal programs of social knowledge production and application. Each examined the nature of the management processes in the agencies in question. Each was critical of some aspects of the way in which research is commissioned, funds allocated, and research monitored. Each provided some guidance as to the research issues that need attention.

Our study differs from these earlier studies in several respects. Both this report and the supporting studies devote considerable attention to describing the nature of the policy process itself in order to provide a more realistic basis for assessing the contribution that can be made by social knowledge. Concern for the policy process led the Study Project to stress the limitations of social research as a tool for making social policy or for operating social programs. The earlier reports hinted at these limitations, but few addressed directly their implications for the federal role in social R&D.

This study encompasses all government agencies that commission and fund social research and deals with some general problems of the system of federal support. In this sense, it extends across the whole of the government the concerns of the committees that examined the performance of individual agencies. We are therefore able to ask how well the entire complex of agencies funding social knowledge production and application fits together, what problems these agencies seem to share, and whether there are modifications of government policy that would benefit the system as a whole. The scope of the study permitted us to take a portfolio view of the federal investment in social research and development.

This report focuses on several issues that were largely ignored in the earlier reports. We have, for example, traced the implications of the fact that more than half of all federally supported social knowledge production and application is meant to benefit policy makers and others outside the federal government; past studies paid little attention to the needs of these nonfederal users. We also give sustained attention to program activities intended to support the application as opposed to the production of knowledge. This subject has attracted an extensive literature but is often neglected by those concerned with federal science policy.

Donald E. Stokes, *Chairman*
Study Project on
Social Research and Development